A Quarter-Century of Normalization and Social Role Valorization: Evolution and Impact

A Quarter-Century of Normalization and Social Role Valorization: Evolution and Impact

Edited by

ROBERT J. FLYNN
Community Services Research Unit
School of Psychology, University of Ottawa

&

RAYMOND A. LEMAY
Société de l'aide à l'enfance de
Prescott-Russell
Children's Aid Society

University of Ottawa Press

University of Ottawa Press gratefully acknowledges the support extended to its publishing programme by the Canada Council, the Department of Canadian Heritage, and the University of Ottawa.

We acknowledge the financial support of the Government of Canada through the Book Publishing Industry Development Program for this project.

Canadian Cataloguing in Publication Data

Main entry under title:
  A Quarter-Century of Normalization and Social Role Valorization: Evolution and Impact

Revised versions of papers originally presented at a conference held in Ottawa, May 1994
Includes bibliographical references and index.
ISBN 0-7766-0485-6

  1. Sociology of disability—Congresses.   2. Handicapped—Social conditions—Congresses.
3. Social role—Congresses.   I. Flynn, Robert J. (Robert John), 1942-   . II. Lemay,
Raymond A., 1952-   .

HV3004.Q34   1999   362.4'045   C99-900593-6

 UNIVERSITY OF OTTAWA
UNIVERSITÉ D'OTTAWA

Cover design : Danielle Péret

ISBN 0-7766-0485-6 ✓

© University of Ottawa Press, 1999
  542 King Edward, Ottawa (Ont.), Canada K1N 6N5
  press@uottawa.ca   http://www.uopress.uottawa.ca

Printed and bound in Canada

To BENGT NIRJE and WOLF WOLFENSBERGER, pioneers.

Table of contents

The editors gratefully acknowledge the financial support received for the publication of this volume and for the conference at which initial drafts were presented. We wish to thank the Social Sciences and Humanities Research Council of Canada, the Department of the Secretary of State of Canada, the Faculty of Social Sciences and the School of Psychology, University of Ottawa, the Children's Aid Society of Prescott-Russell, and the University of Ottawa Press. We also wish to thank YOLANDE FARRELL for her assistance in organizing the conference, LYNNE LEMAY for her help in the preparation of the manuscript, and GENEVIÈVE DUBOIS-FLYNN for her construction of the subject and author indexes.

CONTRIBUTORS

TIM D. AUBRY, Ph.D., Associate Professor, Community Services Research Unit, School of Psychology, University of Ottawa, Ottawa, ON, Canada

ANDRÉ BLANCHET, M.D., F.R.C.P. (C), Medical Advisor, Shriver Clinical Services Corporation, Watertown, MA, USA

SARA N. BURCHARD, Ph.D., Associate Professor of Psychology, University of Vermont, Burlington, VT, USA

ANDRÉ DIONNE, B.Sc., Agent de recherche et de planification socio-économique, Direction de la Recherche et de l'Évaluation, Ministère de la Santé et des Services sociaux, Québec, QC, Canada

ROBERT J. FLYNN, Ph.D., Professor, Community Services Research Unit, School of Psychology, University of Ottawa, Ottawa, ON, Canada

BETH FRENCH, Executive Director, Brockville and district Association for Community Involvement, Brockville, ON, Canada

LAIRD W. HEAL, Ph.D., Professor Emeritus of Special Education, Psychology, and Social Work, University of Illinois, Urbana-Champaign, IL, USA

ANNA HOLLANDER, Ph.D., Reader, Department of Social Welfare, University of Stockholm, Stockholm, Sweden

MICHAEL KENDRICK, Kendrick Consulting Services, Holyoke, MA, USA

KRISTJANA KRISTIANSEN, Ph.D., Associate Professor, Faculty of Social Sciences, University of Trondheim, Trondheim, Norway

RAYMOND A. LEMAY, M.Sc., Directeur Exécutif, Société de l'aide à l'enfance de Prescott-Russell Children's Aid Society, Plantagenet, ON, Canada

PETER MILLIER, M.A., Senior Trainer, Training and Evaluation for Change (TEC), Adelaide, SA, Australia

BENGT NIRJE, Ph.D. h.c., Uppsala University Center for Disability Research, Uppsala, Sweden

JOHN O'BRIEN, Responsive Systems Associates, Lithonia, GA, USA

MICHAEL J. OLIVER, Ph.D., Professor, Disability Studies, University of Greenwich, London, England

JOE OSBURN, M.S.W., Director, Indiana Safeguards Initiative, Indianapolis, IN, USA

PETER PARK, National Coordinator, People First of Canada, Toronto, ON, Canada

JACQUES PELLETIER, M.P.A., Directeur Général, Réseau de services en déficience intellectuelle de l'Outaouais, Hull, QC, Canada

BURT PERRIN, Independent Consultant, Policy and Program Development and Evaluation, Vissec, France

DEBORAH REIDY, M.Ed., Director, Cornerstone—a center for leadership and community initiatives, Easthampton, MA, USA

CAROLE ST-DENIS, Ph.D. candidate, School of Psychology, University of Ottawa, Ottawa, ON, Canada.

JUDITH SANDYS, Ph.D., Dean, Faculty of Community Services, Ryerson Polytechnic University, Toronto, ON, Canada

MÅRTEN SÖDER, Ph.D., Professor, Department of Sociology, Uppsala University, Uppsala, Sweden

DAVID SCHWARTZ, Ph.D., Harrisburg, PA, USA

SUSAN THOMAS, M.Sc., Training Coordinator, Training Institute, Syracuse University, Syracuse, NY, USA

JAN TØSSEBRO, Ph.D., Professor, Department of Social Work, Norwegian University of Science and Technology, Trondheim, Norway

TONY WAINWRIGHT, D. Phil., Dip. Clin. Psychol., Director of Quality and Clinical Audit, Head of Clinical Psychology Services, Cornwall Healthcare NHS Trust, St. Lawrence's Hospital, Bodmin, Cornwall, UK

WOLF WOLFENSBERGER, Ph.D., Research Professor, School of Education, Syracuse University and Director, Training Institute for Human Service Planning, Leadership, & Change Agentry, Syracuse, NY, USA

JACK YATES, Director of Staff Development, SE Region, Department of Mental Retardation, Carver, MA, USA

Part 1

Introduction

Normalization and Social Role Valorization at a quarter-century: Evolution, impact, and renewal

ROBERT J. FLYNN AND RAYMOND A. LEMAY

There can be little doubt of the central importance of Normalization and Social Role Valorization (SRV) principles in shaping human service policies and practices in several fields over the past quarter-century. This has been very much the case in mental retardation and, to a lesser degree, in mental health and aging, as a few examples will illustrate. Heller, Spooner, Enright, Haney, and Schilit (1991) found that Wolfensberger's (1972) book *The Principle of Normalization in Human Services* was rated by a panel of 178 experts as the most influential work published since 1966 in the field of mental retardation (out of a total of over 11,000 articles and books), in terms of its impact on practice. Moreover, Heller et al. (1991) discovered that Wolfensberger's (1983) article in which he proposed that SRV replace Normalization as a term was rated the 17th most influential work. Sara Burchard, at the outset of chapter 11 in this volume, states that "Normalization has had an *immeasurable* impact on human services, education, and the social fabric of North America since its introduction 25 years ago." Kozleski and Sands (1992) identified Wolfensberger's conceptualization of Normalization and SRV as the philosophical ground within which other major service developments of the past quarter-century took root, including deinstitutionalization, supported employment, community residential options, and increased community participation. Pilling (1995, pp. 56-57) observed that in the UK, Normalization and SRV have brought about an enormous change in services, particularly for people with developmental disabilities, and Felce (1995) expressed the hope that a greater appreciation and application of SRV in the future would lead to better protection and safeguarding of vulnerable people's welfare.

On December 20, 1993, the United Nations General Assembly adopted the *Standard Rules on the Equalization of Opportunities for Persons With Disabilities* (United Nations Department of Public Information, 1994). The UN referred to Normalization as a precursor of its *Standard Rules,* which it introduced at an international conference in 1994 in Reykjavík, Iceland, attended by more than 700 participants from around the world. The title of this UN-sponsored conference was *Beyond Normalization: Towards One Society for All* (Lemay, 1994a). Rather than going "beyond" Normalization, however, the *Standard Rules* are mainly concerned with the *physical* integration of persons with disabilities through changes to the legal frameworks of nation states (Lemay, 1994b). We can also add that the major emphasis placed by Normalization (and later by SRV) on integration as participation in the mainstream of a culture (Wolfensberger, 1972) was probably an important influence on the increased attention given to the participation in society of persons with disabilities by ICIDH-2, the new version of the *International Classification of Impairments, Activities, and Participation* (World Health Organization, 1997). ICIDH-2 incorporates the UN's *Standard Rules.*

Earlier, Lakin and Bruininks (1985) had affirmed that "Of all the terms used. . .to describe the nature of recent changes in the philosophy and substance of contemporary services for handicapped persons, none has been more appropriate or influential than Normalization" (p. 67). Heal (1988) introduced his important book on integration by stating that "Because of its current popularity among professionals interested in the integration of handicapped individuals into the community, Normalization dominates the remaining chapters of this volume" (p. 67). Ellis (1990) noted, in his presidential address to the American Association on Mental Retardation, that "the dominant ideology has become a series of variations on the principle of Normalization" and that "a dominant theme in our work under the banner of Normalization has been working toward the integration of people with disabilities into their home communities" (p. 264). Finally, Trainer and Boydell (1986) suggested that Normalization had been one of the most influential concepts in the development of community mental health services in Canada.

1 ORIGIN AND PURPOSES OF THIS VOLUME: AN APPRAISAL OF THE EVOLUTION AND IMPACT OF NORMALIZATION AND SOCIAL ROLE VALORIZATION AFTER A QUARTER-CENTURY

The chapters in this book are revised versions of papers that were originally presented at the "Ottawa conference," *Twenty-Five Years of Normalization, Social Role Valorization, and Social Integration: A Retrospective and Prospective View,* held in May 1994. We organized the conference to mark, in a special way, the 25th anniversary of the publication of *Changing Patterns in Residential Services for the Mentally Retarded* (Kugel & Wolfensberger, 1969). This landmark monograph included Nirje's celebrated chapter, "The Normalization Principle and Its Human Management Implications," which was the first formal articulation of Normalization in the world literature. The keynote speakers at the Ottawa conference were Bengt Nirje and Wolf Wolfensberger, the pioneers of Normalization and SRV. Papers were also presented by other well-known contributors to Normalization and SRV from North America, Europe, and Australia. The four-day conference attracted more than 400 participants from 15 countries, attesting to the continued interest in Normalization and SRV throughout

the world. It was held under the joint auspices of the School of Psychology of the University of Ottawa and the Children's Aid Society of Prescott-Russell (Plantagenet, Ontario).

In planning the conference, we began by drawing up a tentative list of topics related to the overall theme of the evolution and impact of Normalization and SRV. On several occasions, we sought the views of the North American Social Role Valorization Development, Training and Safeguarding Council (Thomas, 1994), of which we are members. We are grateful for the many useful suggestions made by SRV Council members, many of whom presented papers at the conference and contributed chapters to this book. Our final list of topics, which grew into the table of contents of the present volume, consisted of those that we, the editors, were most interested in and that we thought would be of considerable interest to others. After delivering their papers in Ottawa, the speakers revised and updated them, sometimes very substantially. We believe that this book makes an important contribution to the literature in tracing the history of Normalization and SRV and in describing its international impact as one of the most significant human-service reform movements of the last quarter-century. We also think that the book offers authoritative insights into the role that Normalization and SRV may play in the future.

We organized the Ottawa conference with both personal and substantive purposes in mind. On the personal level, we felt that 1994 was an occasion not to be missed because *Changing Patterns,* published 25 years earlier, had had such a decisive influence, in a number of countries, on the development of community mental retardation services. Although *Changing Patterns* contained a number of new ideas, the most significant, in terms of its eventual impact, was certainly that of Normalization. The conference allowed us to honor Bengt Nirje and Wolf Wolfensberger, the two main initiators and promulgators of Normalization, and, coincidentally, to help Bengt celebrate his 70th birthday and Wolf, his 60th. We also hoped that the conference would provide a vehicle for overcoming the isolation in which many key Normalization and SRV actors were working, in North America, the UK, Scandinavia, Europe, and Australia and New Zealand. Many of these individuals had never met, knowing one another only through their writings or personal correspondence. Increased interaction among people in different countries has been an important legacy of the Ottawa conference.

On the substantive level, we had several objectives in organizing the conference, to which correspond the various sections of this book. First, we thought that it would be illuminating to elicit detailed personal accounts of the origins and evolution of Normalization and SRV from Bengt Nirje and Wolf Wolfensberger. Bengt and Wolf, in chapters 2 and 3, respectively, present their vivid and sometimes humorous accounts, which reveal how each came to the Normalization principle and how they contributed to its evolution. Wolf's chapter includes a description of how Bengt's famous chapter came to be written. (As former students of Wolf at Syracuse University, we were amused, but not surprised, to learn of the effective editorial tactics he used to help Bengt produce his compelling contribution, which quite literally helped to change the world.)

Second, we wanted to stimulate debate. Normalization and SRV have engendered intense debate from the beginning, which has contributed greatly to their prominence as a service innovation, their ongoing renewal, and their staying power as a reform movement. To ensure as clear and fruitful an exchange of ideas as possible, we invited Jack Yates to provide an overview of the "North American" version of Normalization (chapter 4), Susan Thomas and Wolf Wolfensberger to contribute an exposition of SRV (chapter 5), and Burt Perrin to furnish a description of the "Scandinavian" model of Normalization (chapter 8). Perrin also included a defense of the continued relevance of Scandinavian Normalization and a critique of Wolfensberger's version. We invited Michael Oliver, author of the influential *The Politics of Disablement* (1990), to provide a critique of Normalization (chapter 6). From his perspective as a Marxist/materialist sociologist, Oliver criticizes Normalization as at best neutral and at worst a contributor to oppression. He believes that Normalization is based on a discredited functionalist and interactionist sociology and offers neither an explanation for nor a solution to the oppression and social and economic exclusion of persons with disabilities in capitalist society. This oppression and exclusion are, for Oliver, the central realities facing people with disabilities and are at the heart of his social model of disability. The latter conceptualizes disability as a social construction superimposed by capitalist society on disabled people's original impairments. Oliver also sees the community services on which Normalization has had such an impact as merely perpetuating the basic power imbalance between professionals and persons with disabilities that had been characteristic of the institutions that community services have replaced.

In his rejoinder to Oliver, Wolfensberger (chapter 7) characterizes Oliver's position as unavowed religion, not empirical science, and criticizes Marxism/materialism as empirically incapable of ever delivering the liberation and justice that it promises. Wolfensberger locates the fundamental problem of oppression in the human propensity to socially devalue and calls for a radical, personal choice to side with oppressed people, without any illusion that oppression will ever be vanquished.

In his contribution to the debate, Laird Heal (chapter 9) investigates the relationship of individuals' competence to their own and others' assessments of their quality of life (QOL) and, by implication, to their Normalization and SRV outcomes. Heal (who, we regret to say, died in 1998) finds that the dominant dimension underlying informants' assessment of the quality of life of individuals with mental retardation is the latter's competence. This suggests that it will be a challenge to assess QOL, achieve Normalization, or provide access to the SRV desideratum of valued and satisfying social roles in a way that is independent of individuals' abilities.

Third, we wanted to foster closer links between Normalization and SRV and mainstream social science. Raymond Lemay's review of role theory (chapter 10) shows that SRV theory, despite its focus on social roles, has only scratched the surface in terms of appropriating and putting to creative use the sociological and psychological riches to be found in the various versions of role theory. Sara Burchard (chapter 11) provides an impressive example of the sizable payoff to be derived from a sustained program of research on Normalization and social integration. Robert Flynn and Tim Aubry (chapter 12) provide what appears to be the first systematic review of attempts to conceptualize and measure integration among persons with developmental or psychiatric disabilities. It is surprising that the research on integration has not previously been reviewed, given the central importance that integration has assumed throughout the world in all areas of disability—intellectual, psychiatric, and physical. Judith Sandys (chapter 13) presents a summary of her doctoral thesis research, one of the only prospective tests of SRV theory of which we are aware. In her qualitative study, she found some support for the central SRV hypothesis that people in valued roles tend to get the good things of life. Finally, Robert Flynn (chapter 14) provides a comprehensive review of 48 studies carried out with the main instruments used to assess human service quality in light of Normalization and SRV, namely, PASS (Program Analysis of Service Systems; Wolfensberger & Glenn, 1975) and PASSING (Program Analysis of Service Systems' Implementation of Normalization Goals; Wolfensberger & Thomas, 1983). The review is encouraging in its overall assessment of the reliability, factorial validity, and construct validity of PASS and PASSING and should encourage more widespread use of these instruments in applied research and evaluation studies. At the same time, it points out some of the perennial challenges that service agencies face in trying to improve their programs, especially in achieving higher levels of social integration and service quality.

Fourth, we thought it useful to assess the impact of training and community education on the improvement of services. Training and education have been the main Normalization and SRV-related strategies used over the last quarter-century to enhance the quality of service programs. Complementary evaluations of the success of these efforts are provided by several individuals who have been highly involved as Normalization or SRV trainers, researchers, or evaluators: Susan Thomas (chapter 15), Deborah Reidy (chapter 16), and John O'Brien (chapter 17).

Fifth, we thought it was time to take stock of the international impact of Normalization and SRV. Kristjana Kristiansen (chapter 18), Anna Hollander (chapter 19), and Kristjana Kristiansen, Mårten Söder, and Jan Tøssebro (chapter 20) evaluate the effect that Normalization and SRV have had in two Scandinavian countries, Sweden and Norway. Michael Kendrick (chapter 21), André Blanchet (chapter 22), Tony Wainwright (chapter 23), and Peter Millier (chapter 24) assess the impact of the approach in the English-speaking world in general and in Canada, England, Australia, and New Zealand, specifically. Jacques Pelletier (chapter 25) and André Dionne (chapter 26) evaluate the effects of Normalization and SRV in the French-speaking world as a whole and its impact on government policy-making in Quebec in particular.

Sixth, we wanted to assess the impact of Normalization and SRV on a more personal level. Peter Park and Beth French (chapter 27), Joe Osburn (chapter 28), and David Schwartz (chapter 29) describe the considerable influence that Normalization and SRV have had on them as individuals, in their respective roles as service recipients, providers, or administrators.

Seventh, we thought it essential to conclude our appraisal of the evolution and impact of Normalization and SRV with a look toward the future. Wolf Wolfensberger (chapter 30) offers a candid view of the accomplishments of Normalization and SRV to date and of their possible contributions in the future.

Finally, we wanted to provide readers with a comprehensive bibliography of Normalization and SRV-related sources published in English or French, to help them find the relevant literature. In an appendix, Carol St-Denis and Robert Flynn present an 800-item bibliography of writings on Normalization, SRV, PASS, and PASSING. The bibliography covers a 30-year period, beginning in 1969, and is as complete as its authors could make it.

2 THE ONGOING RENEWAL OF NORMALIZATION AND SRV: THE NEED FOR VALIDATING EVIDENCE, PROCEDURAL EVIDENCE, PERSONAL COMMITMENT, AND MULTIPLE PERSPECTIVES

It is a truism that intellectual and reform movements must renew themselves on an ongoing basis to counteract the staleness and entropy that menace them from within and the rapid changes in context that threaten them from without. Normalization and SRV are no exceptions, and, in fact, we planned the Ottawa conference and edited the present book as instruments of renewal. For the future, we see four complementary strategies as needed for the continued vitality of Normalization and SRV: the generation of fresh validating evidence, the production of up-to-date syntheses of procedural evidence, the encouragement of personal commitments, and the development of multiple theoretical perspectives.

2.1 THE GENERATION OF FRESH VALIDATING EVIDENCE IN SUPPORT OF NORMALIZATION AND SRV

Rychlak (1993) made a useful distinction between two broad forms of evidence that can and should be adduced in support of theories. *Procedural evidence,* based on a coherence theory of truth, tests the plausibility of theories by appealing to their congruence with criteria such as reasonableness, internal consistency, tautology, and face validity. *Validating evidence,* based on a correspondence theory of truth, tests the empirical robustness of theories by arranging events according to hypotheses and making predictions to appropriate criteria. While maintaining that both types of evidence are necessary to support a theory, Rychlak insists that any truly scientific theory must involve the control-and-prediction, hypothesis-testing stage of validation. Thus, the production of validating evidence is an essential methodological tie that alone binds a theory to the family of sciences.

Over the last quarter-century, much of the evidence adduced in favor of Normalization and SRV theory has been procedural rather than validating in nature. More of each type is desirable in future, but additional validating evidence is especially needed in order, in Rychlak's (1993) words, to strengthen the ties that bind Normalization and SRV to the family of sciences. Prospective hypothesis-testing research would be especially useful if it addressed what is probably the most central SRV hypothesis of all, namely, that people in valued roles tend to obtain the good things of life and those in devalued roles tend to get the opposite. Thomas and Wolfensberger formulated this key hypothesis in chapter 5 of the present volume, as follows:

> A fifth premise underlying SRV. . .is that a society is apt to extend what it defines as the "good life" to those people whom it values, and whom it perceives in a positive light. This will largely be those people whom that society perceives as filling roles which are valued positively in that society. *The more positively valued the roles that a party fills, the more will that party's society be likely to extend good things to it. In contrast, those people in devalued roles tend to get the bad things.* [italics added.]

To our knowledge, this key SRV hypothesis has not yet been subjected to many prospective validating tests. Fortunately, Sandys has provided one such test, in chapter 13 of the present volume. In her qualitative study, she interviewed 21 employers in 18 work settings who had hired 16 people with intellectual disabilities through supported employment programs. Sandys concluded that her findings were supportive of the key SRV hypothesis in question. She also suggested, however, that a wider

web of often negative roles in which the supported employees remained embedded continued to exercise a countervailing, negative impact:

> Social Role Valorization theory is rich and complex, stressing the interplay between societal values and the devaluation of specific individuals, groups, and classes of people. It recognizes that people invariably fill multiple roles, with each having an impact on how people are perceived and treated within society. Nevertheless, there is perhaps a tendency for service providers to think that finding one particular valued role for an individual will overcome the impact of other, devalued, roles. This study does support the relationship between valued roles and positive life experiences. While outcomes were not entirely positive, as evidenced by work that was most often part-time and poorly paid (or not paid), the role of worker did affect the way that employers perceived the supported employee. While the focus of the study was not on the experiences of the supported employees, the data that were available in this regard did suggest many positive outcomes. However, while the role of worker may have had a positive impact, it did not overcome or erase the impact of the other more characteristic and negative roles into which people with disabilities are so often cast. (Sandys, chapter 13, p. 305)

With regard to Normalization (as distinguished from SRV), Burchard's contribution to the present volume (chapter 11) presents a superb example of the ability of a focused and long-term research program to generate fresh validating evidence. Her work and that of her colleagues is a model of the benefits to be reaped from making clear conceptual and methodological links between key Normalization-related constructs, such as *lifestyle Normalization* and *physical and social integration,* and central social science concepts, such as *social networks, social support, stress and coping,* and *personal satisfaction.* In investigating fundamental Normalization-derived policy and practice questions, Burchard's 15-year program of research produced numerous findings that are supportive of Normalization theory, such as the following:

1. Vermont was successfully accomplishing many of its key social policy objectives, including the implementation of Normalization.

2. Residence managers' possession of Normalization-oriented and person-oriented competencies, rather than narrow technical skills, fostered greater program

Normalization, community integration, and residential satisfaction.

3. The most tightly supervised residential settings (i.e., group homes) were the least desirable environments to live in, for residents, and to work in, for staff.

4. Clients' level of community integration was affected by the composition and stability of their social networks.

5. Clients' inclusion in friendship networks that included ordinary citizens (i.e., persons beyond family members, other residents, or staff members) tended to be minimal, such that residents' level of social integration was generally weak.

6. Normalization was consistently and positively related to clients' well-being and personal satisfaction.

Another prospective validating test of Normalization theory can be found in an evaluation of a set of 28 Normalization-based community-care projects that were carried out in the UK in the latter half of the 1980s. In 1983, the Department of Health and Social Security (DHSS) invited the Personal Social Services Research Unit (PSSRU) at the University of Kent at Canterbury to evaluate the 28 projects composing the Care in the Community Demonstration Programme (CCDP; Knapp, Cambridge, Thomason, Beecham, Allen, & Darton, 1992). DHSS had allocated £15 million to support the CCDP projects, which were intended to help long-term residents of hospitals move to community settings. Of the pilot projects, 11 served people with learning difficulties (the British term for mental retardation). Of the 17 other projects, 1 served young people with multiple disabilities, 1 served people with physical disabilities, 8 served people with mental-health problems, and 7 served elderly persons (3 served physically frail elderly people and 4 served elderly people who had mental-health problems, mainly dementia). Overall, the PSSRU evaluation team followed the progress of more than 900 people over a 9- to 12-month period after they moved from hospital to community settings.

Because of the pervasive influence of Normalization on national policy in the UK (Knapp et al., 1992), all of the projects for people with learning difficulties and most of the other projects had an explicit emphasis upon Normalization as a guiding policy. The evaluation of outcomes and costs for the 356 people with learning difficulties who returned to the community during the evaluation period was inspired by multiple perspectives on Normalization, including those of Wolfensberger

(1972), O'Brien and Tyne (1981), and O'Brien (1986). O'Brien's (1986) perspective was especially influential and consisted of his "five accomplishments," or positive life experiences: *community presence,* in valued settings; *choice* in everyday life, in things large and small; *competence* in being able to perform meaningful activities, with whatever assistance may be required; *respect,* in valued relationships and roles; and *community participation,* as a member of a network of personal relationships.

The evaluation of the CCDP projects indicated that some of the projects were successful in establishing settings that adhered closely to Normalization ideals, in encouraging autonomy and independence. In these projects, the people with learning difficulties who moved to the community (Knapp et al., 1992, pp. 301-302):

- gained new self-care skills related to dressing, preparing meals, shopping, finding their way around, taking care of their clothes and personal possessions, writing and counting;
- had a greater degree of choice concerning their daily activities and participated much more in decision making;
- made greater use of community amenities, although integration into community life was far from complete for the vast majority, particularly in the areas of education and employment;
- had fewer social contacts than in the hospital but were rated as more skilled at initiating and engaging in social interactions;
- expressed a higher level of satisfaction with their social networks and with their overall lives in the community;
- had better outcomes if they were in smaller, more homelike community accommodations, especially group homes and independent living; and
- enjoyed better quality care and better quality of life overall.

Among the more than 200 people with long-term mental health problems served by the CCDP projects, the researchers found similarly positive results. Overall, upon moving to the community, the clients with mental health difficulties (Knapp et al., 1992, p. 324):

- made regular use of shops, churches, or pubs, and participated in many more activities outside of their place of residence;
- were twice as likely to express positive attitudes about activities in the community, compared with those who remained in the hospital;

- had more choice about how they spent their time, even though better social security benefits and greater availability of paid jobs would have provided an even greater improvement;
- reported slightly more social contacts in the community, compared with the hospital;
- reported modest improvements in their satisfaction with their social interactions and environment, as well as in their psychosocial functioning, general morale, and level of depression; and
- were served at lower cost than in hospital, even after adjustment had been made for the tendency of projects to serve less dependent clients than the hospital average.

Finally, the evaluation of costs and outcomes among the elderly people served by the CCDP showed that following a move to the community, the elderly people (Knapp et al., 1992, p. 335):

- experienced a quality of life that was not inferior to, and in some respects was better than, that previously known in hospital;
- experienced no decline in skills, behavior, satisfaction with activities, and social contacts, and experienced an increase in morale;
- enjoyed more pleasant physical surroundings;
- had a greater range of choices and opportunities; and
- were served at lower cost than in hospital (i.e., more cost-effectively).

Overall, Knapp et al. (1992) described the personal and financial outcomes of the 28 CCDP projects as showing that it is possible to organize community care in a way that makes better use of resources than is typical in hospitals and to target services at needs more effectively. In relation to the outcomes in the 11 projects serving people with learning difficulties, and in which Normalization constituted a particularly prominent policy framework, Normalization was judged a success:

> Improvements in quality of life and well-being after leaving hospital were very marked for most of the people with learning difficulties included in the evaluation. Statistically significant improvements were found along numerous dimensions. The cost of community care was higher than the cost of hospital for more than half the sample, but higher costs bought better quality care and better quality of life. Smaller and more domestic community accommodation settings were associated with better client outcomes: *in other words, a policy of normalisation appeared to work* [italics added]. (Knapp et al., 1992, p. 346)

Five years after the people with learning difficulties moved to the community, Cambridge, Hayes, Knapp, Gould, and Fenyo (1994) followed them up to assess the long-term outcomes associated with the move. This follow-up research showed that, in the long term and not only in the short run, "Normalization worked." Cambridge et al. (1994) summarized the five-year outcome findings as follows:

> From our involvement with the twelve services included in the evaluation, we know of no reasonable basis on which to challenge the policy of care in the community for people with learning disabilities who would otherwise be long-term hospital residents. In fact, most people with learning disabilities are demonstrably better off living in the community than in hospital, over both the short and long term. For most people who have lived for long periods in hospital, a number of self-care and life skills can improve significantly after the move to the community and can be maintained in the longer term. This applies similarly to a range of key welfare dimensions. People are happier in the community than in hospital, and integration into the community continues over time, along with the maintenance and development of wider social networks and more meaningful social contacts. Physical aspects of people's homes are "more ordinary" and remain of better quality than those of the hospitals they left behind. There is also evidence of slightly more choice over living environments and support networks in the longer term. (p. 105)

2.2 THE PRODUCTION OF UP-TO-DATE SYNTHESES OF PROCEDURAL EVIDENCE SUPPORTIVE OF NORMALIZATION AND SRV

Procedural evidence relevant to Normalization and SRV is available in numerous social science journals and monographs. Lipsey and Wilson's (1993) landmark quantitative review of 302 meta-analyses of the efficacy of psychological, educational, and behavioral interventions is a particularly rich example. Lipsey and Wilson found that such treatments show a strong and consistent pattern of positive overall effects. The latter cannot be explained away as mere artifacts of meta-analytic techniques or generalized placebo effects, nor can they be dismissed as so small as to be lacking in practical or clinical significance. Among the 302 meta-analyses reviewed by Lipsey and Wilson, many were based on research carried out on interventions that, in general, appear relatively congruent with the *competency-enhancement goal* of Normalization and SRV. For example:

1. Innovative out-patient programs, compared with traditional aftercare for mental health patients released from hospitals, had a mean effect size on all outcomes, across 130 studies, of 0.36 standard deviation (SD) units. (An effect size of 0.20 SD units would be small, one of 0.50 SD units would be moderate, and one of 0.80 SD units would be large.)

2. Deinstitutionalization programs for persons with long-term psychiatric disorders had a mean effect size on all outcomes, across 111 studies, of 0.36.

3. Vocational programs for persons with "mental illness" had a mean effect size on all outcomes, across 18 studies, of 0.54.

4. Social skills training for persons with schizophrenia had a mean effect size, across 27 studies, of 0.65.

5. Subjective well-being interventions among elderly people had a mean effect size on subjective well-being outcomes, across 31 studies, of 0.42.

6. Computer-assisted instruction for special education students, in elementary through high school, had a mean effect size on achievement, across 18 studies, of 0.66.

7. Computer-assisted instruction for learning disabled and educable mentally retarded students had a mean effect size on achievement, across 15 studies, of 0.57.

8. Cooperative versus noncooperative task arrangements for handicapped, nonhandicapped and ethnically different groups had a mean effect size on all outcomes, across 98 studies, of 0.75.

9. Tutoring of special education students by other special education students had a mean effect size on the tutor's achievement, across 19 studies, of 0.65, and a mean effect size on the tutored student's achievement, across 19 studies, of 0.59.

10. Early-intervention programs for handicapped preschoolers had a mean effect size on all outcomes, across 74 studies, of 0.68.

11. Mainstreaming versus segregated special education for disabled K-9 students had a mean effect size on achievement, across 11 studies, of 0.44.

12. Direct instruction in special education had a mean effect size on achievement, intellectual ability, readiness skills, on-task behavior, and affect, across 25 studies, of 0.84.

13. Early-intervention and sensory-stimulation programs for organically impaired developmentally delayed children had a mean effect size on development, motor, cognitive, language, social, and self-help outcomes, across 38 studies, of 0.97.

14. Language therapy/training for language/learning disabled children had a mean effect size on language improvement, across 43 studies, of 1.04.

15. Educational treatment programs for emotionally disturbed students had a mean effect size on achievement and classroom behavior, across 99 studies, of 1.02.

16. Training for mentally retarded persons on memory and learning tasks had a mean effect size on all outcomes, across 96 studies, of 0.70.

Interestingly, only one meta-analysis was related to the *image-enhancement goal* of SRV: Interventions to modify attitudes toward persons with disabilities had a mean effect size on attitudes, across 273 studies, of 0.37.

Another example of procedural evidence from a mainstream social science journal that is supportive of Normalization and SRV is Heller's (1993) call for a conceptual reorientation of psychological services to older adults toward prevention and the maintenance of useful social roles. In what appeared to be an independent "rediscovery" of the core of SRV theory, as applied to the field of aging, Heller suggested ways of promoting more active social engagement on the part of older persons. Citing examples from the areas of housing, part-time employment, and the development of supportive social ties, Heller made a strong case for the role that public education can play in helping the general public understand the social dilemmas faced by older adults and the value of their continued integration as useful citizens. Heller's insights could be used in application of SRV to services in aging, such as those that have emerged in Australia, where strong evaluation and publication links are being forged between SRV and services to older persons.

In sum, as these various examples suggest, many of the findings of mainstream social science are consistent with the assumptions of Normalization and SRV theory and provide procedural evidence supportive of it. Such parallels need to be made explicit and require regular updating and renewal.

2.3   THE ENCOURAGEMENT OF PERSONAL
        COMMITMENTS CONSISTENT WITH
        NORMALIZATION AND SRV

At the Ottawa conference, we were struck by the extent to which Nirje's and Wolfensberger's own personal experiences, especially their involvement and solidarity with marginalized people, had contributed to their positions on Normalization and SRV. In the case of Nirje, first of all, his critique of institutional life for persons with mental retardation stemmed directly from his work in 1956 for the Swedish Red Cross, which he describes in chapter 2 of the present volume. In this early phase of his career, which preceded his work in mental retardation, Nirje assisted Hungarian refugees living in a camp near Vienna after escape from Hungary. Nirje understood that refugees (like people who have been institutionalized) had lost their past, dwelt in an uncertain present, and had an unpromising future. He also saw how difficult it was for refugees confined to camps to live with a large number of other persons. Later, Nirje worked with children with cerebral palsy and their families, understanding the importance of the family setting for the child, the reality of dependency, and the importance of believing in the child's potential.

In the case of Wolfensberger, who was a native of Mannheim, Germany, personal experience of the Nazi terror during his childhood marked him deeply. Coming to the United States in 1950 at the age of 16, he undertook studies in philosophy and psychology. It was in 1956—the same year that Nirje began working with the Hungarian refugees—that Wolfensberger, at the time an intern in clinical psychology at George Peabody College in Nashville, Tennessee, had his first contact with a mental retardation residential institution. He was outraged by the conditions he encountered there, an experience that ignited the "passion for justice" of which he spoke in Ottawa and eventuated in his formulations of Normalization and SRV. In 1961, Wolfensberger spent a year with Jack Tizard, an eminent British psychologist, in England, where he saw excellent community programs for persons with mental retardation. This exposure helped him later, when he and colleagues in Nebraska were establishing the first Normalization-based community-service system in the United States, to combat the very low expectations that were commonly held of such persons in the United States.

The importance of this kind of highly personal experience, in the instance of both Nirje and Wolfensberger, leads us to think that the future of Normalization and SRV will depend, to a considerable extent, on the continuation in others of this same "passion for justice." Such individuals should be prepared for controversy, if another interesting parallel between Nirje's and Wolfensberger's careers is any guide. Their criticism of institutions, advocacy of Normalization, and personal activism led them into conflict with authorities in Sweden and Nebraska, respectively. Partly as a result, Canada had the good fortune to welcome both in the early 1970s when they came to work in Toronto, Nirje for the government of Ontario, Wolfensberger for the Canadian Association for the Mentally Retarded (now the Canadian Association for Community Living) and its National Institute on Mental Retardation (now the Roeher Institute).

2.4   THE DEVELOPMENT OF MULTIPLE
        PERSPECTIVES ON NORMALIZATION AND SRV

At the Ottawa conference, both major perspectives on Normalization and SRV, Nirje's and Wolfensberger's, were much in evidence and are present in various chapters of this volume. For example, "Scandinavian" Normalization, as articulated by Perrin (chapter 8), places an overriding emphasis on the equality of rights that persons with disabilities have vis-à-vis nondisabled people. Wolfensberger, on the other hand, remains unconvinced (see chapter 30) that a strategy consisting mainly of conferring rights upon devalued and powerless people will have much positive effect. He characterizes an emphasis on rights that is not accompanied by an equal emphasis on obligations as one-sided and naive. Aside from the philosophical divergences involved, however, this "rights" debate raises an important empirical issue that would benefit from some impartial evaluative research: How effective is a change strategy that is couched mainly in terms of "rights" and implemented mainly through efforts to effect changes in the law? Such a strategy has undeniable appeal to those oriented to the law and other normative approaches to change, but the empirical efficacy of such an approach is, to our knowledge, largely unknown.

The Ottawa conference also revealed that Normalization and SRV are not without their detractors. Michael Oliver (chapter 6) exemplifies one strand of critique, but Wolfensberger (chapter 3) also provides an overview of other critical positions. These critiques have contributed to the conceptual evolution and renewal of Normalization and SRV.

Overall, we were struck by the loyalty that the Nirjean and Wolfensbergian perspectives on Normalization and SRV continue to command in different individuals and groups, even after a quarter-century. On balance, this pluralism and clash of perspectives strikes us as invigorating rather than as something to be decried. Social science areas of research or practice that are progressing rather than stagnating are almost always marked by theoretical diversity and a degree of conflict. The absence

of such pluralism and tension is likely to be more a sign of conceptual sclerosis and decline than of continued development and vitality. It is thus a distinct advantage for the researcher or practitioner to be able to draw on the particular perspective on Normalization or SRV that seems to him or her to be the most philosophically coherent, the most clearly articulated, or the best supported empirically. A vigorous pluralism and dialogue and debate among different formulations of Normalization or SRV will be as important in the future as they have been in the past.

REFERENCES

CAMBRIDGE, P., HAYES, L., KNAPP, M., GOULD, E., & FENYO, A. (1994). *Care in the community: Five years on. Life in the community for people with learning disabilities.* Aldershot, UK, & Brookfield, VT: Ashgate.

ELLIS, J. W. (1990). Presidential address 1990—Mental retardation at the close of the 20th century: A new realism. *Mental Retardation, 28,* 263-267.

FELCE, D. (1995). Summing up: Safeguarding quality. In D. PILLING & G. WATSON (Eds.), *Evaluating quality in services for disabled and older people* (pp. 213-216). London, UK: Jessica Kingsley.

HEAL, L. W. (1988). The ideological responses of society to its handicapped members. In L.W. HEAL, J. I. HANEY & A. R. NOVAK AMADO (Eds.), *Integration of developmentally disabled individuals into the community* (2nd ed., pp. 59-67). Baltimore: Paul H. Brookes.

HELLER, H. W., SPOONER, F., ENRIGHT, B. E., HANEY, K., & SCHILIT, J. (1991). Classic articles: A reflection into the field of mental retardation. *Education and Training in Mental Retardation, 26,* 202-206.

HELLER, K. (1993). Prevention activities for older adults: Social structures and personal competencies that maintain useful social roles. *Journal of Counseling and Development, 72,* 124-130.

KNAPP, M., CAMBRIDGE, P., THOMASON, C., BEECHAM, J., ALLEN, C., & DARTON, R. (1992). *Care in the community: Challenge and demonstration.* Aldershot, UK, & Brookfield, VT: Ashgate.

KOZLESKI, E. B., & SANDS, D. J. (1992). The yardstick of social validity: Evaluating quality of life as perceived by adults without disabilities. *Education and Training in Mental Retardation, 27,* 119-131.

KUGEL, R., & WOLFENSBERGER, W. (Eds.). (1969). *Changing patterns in residential services for the mentally retarded.* Washington, DC: President's Committee on Mental Retardation.

LAKIN, K. C., & BRUININKS, R. H. (1985). Contemporary services for handicapped children and youth. In R. H. BRUININKS & K. C. LAKIN (Eds.), *Living and learning in the least restrictive environment* (pp. 3-22). Baltimore: Paul H. Brookes.

LEMAY, R. A. (1994a). A Reikjavík Journal. *The International Social Role Valorization Journal/La Revue Internationale de la Valorisation des Rôles Sociaux, 1*(2), 42-44.

LEMAY, R. A. (1994b). A review of the standard rules on the equalization of opportunities for persons with disabilities, 1994, United Nations Department for Policy Coordination and Sustainable Development. *The International Social Role Valorization Journal/La Revue Internationale de la Valorisation des Rôles Sociaux, 1*(2), 47-51.

LIPSEY, M. W., & WILSON, D. B. (1993). The efficacy of psychological, educational, and behavioral treatment: Confirmation from meta-analysis. *American Psychologist, 48,* 1181-1209.

NIRJE, B. (1969). The Normalization principle and

its human management implications. In R. KUGEL & W. WOLFENSBERGER (Eds.), *Changing patterns in residential services for the mentally retarded.* Washington, DC: President's Committee on Mental Retardation.

O'BRIEN, J. (1986). *A guide to personal futures planning.* Atlanta, GA: Responsive Systems Associates.

O'BRIEN, J., & TYNE, A. (1981). *The principle of normalisation: A foundation for effective services.* London, UK: Campaign for Mental Handicap.

OLIVER, M. (1990). *The politics of disablement.* Basingstoke, UK: Macmillan and St. Martin's Press.

PILLING, D. (1995). Do PASS and PASSING pass? A critique of PASS/ING. In D. PILLING & G. WATSON (Eds.), *Evaluating quality in services for disabled and older people* (pp. 50-60). London, UK: Jessica Kingsley.

RYCHLAK, J. F. (1993). A suggested principle of complementarity for psychology: In theory, not method. *American Psychologist, 48,* 933-942.

THOMAS, S. (1994). A brief history of the SRV Development, Training, and Safeguarding Council. *International Social Role Valorization Journal, 1*(2), 15-18.

TRAINER, J., & BOYDELL, K. (1986). The politics of Normalization. *Canada's Mental Health, 34*(1), 19-24.

UNITED NATIONS DEPARTMENT OF PUBLIC INFORMATION (1994). *Standard rules on the equalization of opportunities for persons with disabilities* (DPI/1454-April 1994-20M). New York: United Nations.

WOLFENSBERGER, W. (1972). *The principle of Normalization in human services.* Toronto: National Institute on Mental Retardation.

WOLFENSBERGER, W. (1983). Social Role Valorization: A proposed new term for the principle of Normalization. *Mental Retardation, 21*(6), 234-239.

WOLFENSBERGER, W., & GLENN, L. (1975). *Program analysis of service systems: A method for the quantitative evaluation of human services. Handbook: Vol. 1. Field manual: Vol. 2.* (3rd ed.) Toronto: National Institute on Mental Retardation.

WOLFENSBERGER, W., & THOMAS, S. (1983). *PASSING (Program analysis of service systems' implementation of Normalization goals): Normalization criteria and ratings manual* (2nd ed.). Downsview, ON: National Institute on Mental Retardation.

WORLD HEALTH ORGANIZATION. (1997). *ICIDH-2: International classification of impairments, activities, and participation. A manual of dimensions of disablement and health. Beta-1 draft for field trials.* Geneva, Switzerland: Author.

Part 2

Historical Evolution of Normalization and Social Role Valorization Theory

2

How I came to formulate the Normalization principle

BENGT NIRJE

In this chapter I will talk about the personal, intellectual, educational, and professional experiences that led me to articulate the principle of Normalization. I have previously discussed this topic elsewhere: in the introduction to the book *The Normalization Principle Papers* (Nirje, 1992) and in the papers *The Normalization Principle—25 Years Later* (Nirje, 1993) and *Basis and Logic of the Normalization Principle* (Nirje, 1985). The written version of the Normalization principle consists only partly of the short paper originally published in *Changing Patterns in Residential Services for the Mentally Retarded* (Nirje, 1969b), on January 10, 1969, in the very last days of the Johnson administration. I say partly because the paper had to be short and I still had more material "in the oven," so to speak. In fact, the Normalization principle is expressed not only in the first paper from 1969, but also in additional papers written between 1967 and 1972 (which were expressed in summary form in the 1976 edition of *Changing Patterns* [Nirje, 1976]) and in the "rearview mirror" update of 1993 (Nirje, 1993).

1 THE NORMALIZATION PRINCIPLE

At the outset, I think it useful to present a brief summary of the Normalization principle, borrowing liberally from one of my previous papers (Nirje, 1993):

The Normalization principle means that you act right when you make available to all persons with intellectual or other impairments or disabilities those patterns of life and conditions of everyday living that are as close as possible to, or indeed the same as, the regular circumstances and ways of life of their communities and their culture.

The facets or elements of the normal patterns or conditions of life that the principle refers to and which persons with disabilities have equal rights to experience or share are the following:

1. A normal rhythm of the day.
2. A normal rhythm of the week.
3. A normal rhythm of the year.
4. The normal experiences of the life cycle.
5. Normal respect for the individual and the right to self-determination.
6. The normal sexual patterns of their culture.
7. The normal economic patterns and rights of their society.
8. The normal environment patterns and standards in their community.

The proper use of the Normalization principle rests on an understanding of how the normal rhythms, routines, and patterns of life in any culture relate to the development, maturity, and life of disabled persons. It also rests on an understanding of how these patterns apply as indicators of proper human programs, services, and legislation.

The Normalization principle applies to all persons with (for example) intellectual disabilities, whatever the degree of their impairments and wherever they live. It is useful in every society, for all age groups, and can be adapted to individual developments or social changes. Thus, it should serve as a guide for medical, educational, psychological, social, legislative, and political work in these fields. Decisions and actions taken according to the principle should turn out more often right than wrong. (pp. 1-2)

Often when studying texts where the Normalization principle is mentioned, I wonder whether the authors really have read any of my writings, including the first one. I cannot blame them, really, because the papers have been difficult to obtain and there was a limit to the number of copies I could distribute to those who were interested. Also, I have never published anything unless I was asked to, and not always then. The papers were always too brief or specific to form a book, or too long or general to be published in magazines or congressional records. Except for my chapter in *Changing Patterns*—which, I was recently told, was printed in 200,000 copies—and for two magazines and one book, my papers have been *samisdats*— underground papers for friends, interested colleagues, or students, disseminated to the extent that I had the opportunities or resources to do so. Only two of my papers have been translated into Swedish.

I developed the principle during my work for the Swedish Association for the Developmentally Disturbed (FUB), where, in 1961, I first learned about and experienced the situations of intellectually disabled persons and their families. Thus, I will start with glimpses of the kind of experiences and points of view I brought with me to FUB and that had a bearing on the creation of the principle.

2 STUDIES AND PRELUDES

I will begin with my studies. After my student exam in 1943, I went to Uppsala to study law, perhaps to become a defense lawyer. During those initial years of my studies, which were interrupted in 1944-1945 by my military service, I encountered subjects such as economics and population statistics, the history of law, constitutional and international law, legal philosophy, and ethics. These were the years when the United Nations was founded, the horrors of the war were brought out into the open, and, as a result, we were much concerned with human rights. I also took seminars in philosophy, in which concepts of rights, theories of value, ethics, and the history of philosophy

were discussed. I switched from law to what is called practical philosophy, as a stepping-stone to my main interest, literature, and to cultural anthropology.

These first years of study were a great help to me later, in my work with refugees, in my role as the ombudsman of FUB, and in articulating the Normalization principle. I described this evolution in *Basis and Logic of the Normalization Principle* (Nirje, 1985):

As a former student of law and philosophy, I had once had my own development stimulated by the questions raised by the Uppsala School of Philosophy, by Hägerström and Hedenius [my teacher]. Consequently I knew that concepts of "rights" serve as background for legislation, but also that in some respects, only those conditions which are regulated by specific laws and statutes constitute "rights" in the proper practical legal sense. The rest was called "metaphysical," arbitrary, culture-bound opinions or emotive statements. Human rights consequently involve more than what is actually covered by legislation. Laws can regulate certain conditions for persons with mental handicaps, but they still cannot in a wider sense completely affect the conditions of their existence and their opportunities for personal development. Laws and legislative work cannot provide total answers as to problem solving and proper actions with regard to the realization of human rights. These can only come into existence in the full cultural and human context.

Such problems are not only practical but also ethical, as they relate to what might be right or wrong in making and taking decisions and actions concerning other people. It was apparent that any coherent series of statements on such issues must ultimately be formulated within the demands raised by what in the field of philosophy is called an ethical value theory. Later, that insight was uppermost in my mind in the final work on my first statement of the Normalization principle. (p. 65)

Toward the end of my academic career, I also studied art history, especially architecture (later, I found most institutions to be architectural abominations), and cultural anthropology. I learned about African, Asian, American, and European tribes, their habits, rites, and creations. Ruth Benedict's *Patterns of Culture* (1934), and her analysis of how the modus operandi in different cultures affected the lives of individuals and their values, made a lasting impression.

During my years of studying comparative literature, my main interest was modern literature and theatre. French, English, American, and, of course, Swedish writers, poets, and dramatists of the 1920s and 1930s offered much to a young man trying to find his way and his views on life. I learned about "life," "reality," and what was "meaningful" from those who were good at expressing and forming images of their experiences and views: Lagerkvist, Martinson, Ekelöf, Lindgren, Ahlin, and Dagerman—great writers whose works are still alive and outstanding. Without a close reading of these writers, listening to their minds, in books or in person, I would not have made the choices I made nor would I have come to the insights that enabled me to find a point of view of my own.

I formed a literary club with some friends which quickly became one of the largest student societies and a place where we could listen to and discuss with the writers of our time. I started to write a little criticism and was also able to take a break from my studies to work as the culture editor for a small but famous anarchist newspaper in Stockholm, well known for its anti-Nazi stand during the war. After almost a year, I was able to return to Uppsala for more advanced studies, preparing a thesis about the early poetry of one of the leading Swedish writers, with roots in French modernist art and poetry.

My studies were modestly supported by lectures on modern Swedish literature that I gave at Folk High Schools or adult education organizations. I also led study groups in the literary club, where we talked about the poetry of figures such as T. S. Eliot. Reading in a group, compared to reading alone, can help one attain richer interpretations and deeper understanding.

Thanks to this experience, I was invited, in 1952, by a professor in Stockholm to take part in an experimental two-week session in group dynamics at an isolated Folk High School near the Norwegian border, with about 20 young scholars from other Swedish universities. The procedure was as follows. Groups of four were assigned tasks to solve and present in writing within 24 hours. Group members were allowed to use the telephone for one hour and the library at all hours. Critical analyses of the work then followed within the group. New groups were formed and the same procedure was followed, for a second and then a third time. The tasks assigned had no relation to our fields of study: My groups dealt, respectively, with how to create a new drainage system in a complex environment, how to reorganize the fire brigades in a large city, and how to present a specific finance plan for the Swedish parliamentary standing committee on finance.

It was stunning how much we could accomplish by working together. We found that we had rarely experienced an "intellectual high" like the one we all felt at the end of the course. Part of the background to this experimental course was provided by new findings in adult education. Many years later, Maja Witting, who was a special-school teacher with strong pedagogical and methodological interests, told me about the ideas of professor Luria in Moscow, as they related to adult education. Apparently, adults learn mainly in a "horizontal" way, from peers, other adults, and their own interests, rather than in a "vertical" way from the teacher "up on the rostrum" to them "down there in their ignorance." This also touched a familiar theme, which was later to become another part of the procedures of the many clubs we would set up. I could draw on these experiences later in my work in a refugee camp and in courses I organized for leaders of clubs in local associations of FUB. People with and without disabilities would participate in these clubs.

Some of the pedagogical insights leading to this approach to group dynamics were furnished by prisoners of war. Some Norwegian professors held in a Nazi prison in Oslo had challenged each other to present short lectures when they had occasions to sit together, as lecturing is what professors normally do. These were later published as the famous "Lectures in Grini." Similarly, British airmen in prisoner-of-war camps had insisted on having their normal five o'clock tea ritual—without cups, tea, or scones—in spite of the guards. Doing normal things in groups in adverse circumstances fortifies the individual, such as leaving the mental institution for a fishing expedition, to take a well-known example. These kinds of lessons I could remember when later faced with situations, in camps or institutions, that offered challenging problems created by the abnormal conditions of life involved.

In 1952, I went to Yale University, in the United States, on a Smith-Mundt scholarship for graduate studies in literary criticism and structural analysis, concentrating on Yeats, Pound, Eliot, Joyce, Hemingway, and Faulkner. A visit to Ezra Pound for an interview gave me my first look at a large American mental institution, St. Elizabeth's Hospital, in Washington, DC. St. Elizabeth's was a run-down asylum for about 7,000 persons, a city of old red barracks with gray, dusty-looking corridors.

Finally, after some highly stimulating studies at Yale, I went to Paris for half a year of research. I thus learned about American society and French society, as well as the respective languages.

When I returned to Sweden, I found a position with the Swedish Institute that was related to cultural relations with other countries. The job entailed organizing study-visits by foreign university groups, parliamentary committees, and experts wanting an orientation to and information about Swedish education, architecture, industry, and so forth. It was not the administrative systems involved that were important but rather the aims, processes and results within the areas of interest in question. Administrative systems are highly specialized and cannot be copied in the first place. I found this organizational work highly stimulating, with its frequent problem-solving demands, constant meeting of very different personalities, and exchange of specialized information. I was also active as a freelancer, doing radio programs on political and cultural events in the United States and France, including half a year at the United Nations in New York.

Such was my situation in the autumn of 1956. I had had a good Swedish education and had also acquired some international experiences, including foreign languages and academic training. On the other hand, I had no steady job as yet. Also missing were some real-life experiences and a clear sense of where I should apply my skills. I was soon to get answers—in spades, as the saying goes—and my life changed dramatically and decisively.

3 REFUGEES

In November 1956, the Hungarian revolution was crushed by Soviet tanks and troops. Almost 200,000 refugees crossed the border into Austria. Late one evening, I got a telephone call from the secretary-general of the Swedish Red Cross, just back from Vienna, where he had been put in charge of Red Cross

services in camps that were being opened quickly. The next morning, I had five minutes to decide whether I would accept a position as a social welfare officer in the first Swedish team being set up. Within a week, it would be in Traiskirchen. I accepted within the time limit. My main instruction was that "your responsibility is the morale of the camp," which could not be allowed to get into the depressing rut of the camps for "old refugees." More than 300,000 of the latter had been living in dilapidated wooden huts or stone barracks since the end of the war. Some of the children born there were almost 10 years old. In time, I was going to meet them.

Traiskirchen, a small town near Baden, south of Vienna, was the seat of an old regiment from the last century, where the emperor's cadets had received their training. Earlier in the year, the last Russian soldiers had left what had served as their headquarters. Their physical demands had been far more than the old buildings could take, to put it diplomatically. By the first of December, the camp already had 3,500 new residents, with 100 to 160 persons per dormitory, sleeping in three-tiered wooden beds. The scene was one of wet snow and rain, loaded buses going to new countries, and more buses entering than leaving. Family members were often missing, and few of the refugees had documents to establish their background or to help locate their relatives or acquaintances abroad. They were people marked by the tragedy behind them and uncertainty about when or where the future would bring them a meaningful life. How was I to create "morale" out of this chaos?

The first need was to find and communicate reliable information on the complicated emigration situation. This task was mostly depressing, because the quotas from receiving countries were filled and increases in the quotas were slow in being established. Still, telling the truth was essential to establish trust and stop rumors. And there were many daily problems and dramas to solve. As a matter of principle, I worked with an open door (if it was not too cold—but then it was warmer with many people present!). Thus, I could be heard giving the same information or assistance to all. When people came with problems, complaints, concerns, or requests, I often asked if they could find others with the same interests and suggested, "Why don't you sit down together and come back with a proposal?" I thus put my group dynamics experience to frequent use. Yet the Austrian guards used to ask me: "What are they doing? They should be quiet and grateful, and not hold meetings!" (Later in life, when organizing meetings for persons with intellectual disabilities, I was going to hear the same complaints again. Democratic processes are always a threat to persons in need of complete power.)

But my approach in the camp worked, and that was the main thing. We got a lot of programs going: kindergartens, short dictionaries, language courses, orientation to various countries, sports, watch repairs. People can do many things and have many inner resources, which they need to fight the tedium and the waiting. I learned a lot during those five months in the camp. Then, I was nominated Voluntary Agency Liaison Officer with the Vienna office of the United Nations High Commissioner for Refugees (UNHCR). In this capacity, I also served as a camp inspector, recommending those to be closed first. I also initiated a Scandinavian project, in cooperation with UNHCR and the Austrian authorities, that provided proof of work skills or training opportunities for young people who had no paper credentials attesting to their vocational experience. My cooperation with Swedish labor-market authorities during this project proved beneficial later when we started our sheltered workshops for intellectually disabled people in Sweden.

This period taught me that when you are a refugee, you have a past that is gone and does not count in your new country. No one cares about it, no one believes in it, and nobody trusts you. Your past is really gone, and you really know nothing about the future. Your situation is bleak, uncertain, and anonymous. Such a situation can create a very unhealthy climate and dark moods. I also learned how hard it is to live with so many other persons in close quarters, day and night—100 to 160 per room, week after week after week. It means never having a "private space" for oneself for daily recuperation, satisfying daily activities, or meaningful recreation. There is no place for you, your family, and your few belongings. You have to be strong, even if you are competent and not intellectually disabled. But you can become mentally "wounded" and socially handicapped, of that you can be sure! What keeps you going are your dreams, hopes, and desperate expectations of the future.

4 PEOPLE WITH CEREBRAL PALSY

Back in Sweden, the Red Cross put me in charge of the Folke Bernadotte Action, a fund-raising drive to provide new opportunities for children with cerebral palsy. The aim of the drive was to establish examples of small, homelike conditions instead of hospital settings, improve physiotherapy methods and programs, and to ensure close cooperation with parents, as well as to start a fund encouraging international exchanges and stipends for studies abroad. My work with this fund over a period of several years gave me a good orientation to developments in the field.

A funny thing happened at the first large information meeting held as part of the fund drive. I overheard someone exclaim in a conversation: "And she got so angry that she resigned—the boys wanted to read Hemingway! So now we have no teacher for the evening literature group!" It seems that for years, once a week, a nice elderly lady had held Swedish literature readings for young men with cerebral palsy, 19 to 25 years of age, who were living at home or in one of the two hospitals. So I interfered and offered to take over. And it was, of course, a pleasure. I could lead them in the study of some of Hemingway's Nick Adams stories and *The Old Man and the Sea*, discussing the points of view that Hemingway expressed therein, how he worked, and what he meant. For their part, the young men were able to bring me to an understanding of their views on life and of their social and human situation.

Hemingway is a good writer to encounter when you are confronting tough circumstances. He has a matter-of-fact style of great sensibility. He often insists, in the face of difficulty, on the importance of being truthful to one's own experiences, of being true to oneself, of being able to face oneself with dignity. Hemingway offered fairly strong challenges for young men with cerebral palsy who were trying to come to grips with their lives. And they, in turn, taught me a lot. Talking about literature in a serious way is talking about life.

I started to understand how dependent these young men were and how powerless they felt—much as the refugees had felt. They, too, had a past that did not count, an education that they knew was not as good as their peers', and no solid ground on which to establish a future. Refugees had some hopes and aspirations for the future, but not these young men. They could not be certain of where they were going, their present situation was bleak, and they had very little power. They enjoyed no independence during the week, and their weekends were very different from those of other young people. Their opportunities for dating in regular ways were nonexistent, and their vacation adventures were confined to summer camps. Physically, they could not slam the door and go to a movie, even if their parents said no. They were dependent, and their state of dependence humiliated them. From these experiences, I got my first inkling of the meaning of independence and the right to self-determination and of the difficulty of becoming an adult when one is disabled.

5 MY WORK AS THE FUB OMBUDSMAN

By the time I arrived at FUB in 1961, I had some education in law, an intellectual attitude, and a humanistic approach, experience with adult education and group dynamics, some practice as a journalist and speaker, familiarity with the ongoing process of improving Swedish conditions of life, and a commitment to the United Nations and human rights. I also had the experience of dealing directly with many administrative and practical problems that came about in my position as camp inspector. These personal attributes and experiences helped me to develop and interpret my work at FUB and find the threads and tendencies that allowed me to gradually see and formulate the Normalization principle. The principle grew out of my need to understand what to do, and why, and how best to interpret situations. It also grew out of other needs: a need for new legislation to correct the social situation of intellectually disabled persons and their families; a need for a new approach and a new language, both nationally and internationally; and especially a need for a new approach for young and older adults. I will try to describe these themes one at a time, showing how—especially during the years 1963 to 1966—they influenced the evolving formulation of the Normalization principle.

In the summer of 1961, I began my service as the ombudsman for FUB, the Swedish Association for the Developmentally Disturbed, as it was then called.

When parents formed the first local association in Stockholm, in 1952, they did not like the official term "mentally retarded" but preferred "developmentally disturbed" They thus pioneered the use of this new term, which was accepted by the law of 1968—which I will speak of in the next part of this chapter. It is still in use, but today one generally uses the term "intellectual disability."

The Swedish Association was formed in 1956, and I was the first person they employed. My tasks were the following: to strengthen the development of the association; to assist in forming a foundation, called ALA, with a sheltered workshop, boarding homes, and a research council, in Uppsala; to establish international relations; and to strengthen the position of FUB with regard to national and regional authorities. And all this with a half-time secretary! I chose not to be called "executive director" or "secretary general," but simply "ombudsman," for the obvious reason that I was trying to work and speak in the interests of intellectually disabled persons and their families. It so happened that some months earlier, Karl Grunewald had taken up his position at the Royal Medical Board (later incorporated into the Royal Social Board) as the inspector general of institutions for the mentally retarded. It turned out to be a lucky coincidence, and we soon established good cooperation and friendly relations.

With this new phase of my "career"—some friends called it "another one of your peculiar choices"—I became an explorer, as it were, in a new, complex, and paradoxical world, one with hidden tensions and controversies, great stresses on parents, and pitiful isolation in institutions for children and adults. It was a world that functioned differently from the surrounding, affluent society. I quickly became fully immersed in it, trying to learn and understand, starting more or less from scratch, knowing next to nothing about mental retardation, the developmentally disturbed, or the social conditions of their parents and families.

I was neither a parent nor a professional, with no credentials as a lawyer, psychiatrist, teacher, psychologist, or social worker, although to some degree I had had contact with all these fields. To some extent, I was an information and communications man. As a person, I found satisfaction in organizing, problem solving, and getting things changed and new things going. I had always found that the "make it new" maxim of modernist poets and writers was an attractive proposal. I liked teamwork, but in these contexts, I was certainly an outsider.

During 1961-1970, I visited most of the Swedish boarding schools, county-based central institutions for children and adults, and the 10 or so state special hospitals, plus many smaller homes. And during these many visits, I listened and talked to staff and—most important—to the residents. I also visited, talked, and listened at meetings and weekend conferences of our local and county associations in every county in Sweden, and at the many courses we organized. Various yearly conferences were also very important, including those of the Swedish Board of Education for deans of special schools, those of the Medical (Social) Board for head doctors of county services and special hospitals, directors of county services (toward the end of my career, I became one of them myself), directors of institutions, and social workers in the services, and those for supervisors of sheltered workshops and leisure-time leaders. There were many issues and problems on the agendas of these meetings, but the Normalization principle was not one of them, although I might have referred to it when taking part in discussions during my very last years as the FUB ombudsman.

During the 1960s, my work consisted of learning and of using new contacts and informational opportunities. I got, of course, rare and extensive insights into the many situations facing persons with intellectual disabilities at the time. This was a privileged education into very sheltered and hidden fields, a special world, as it were. The institutions opened my eyes about the loneliness of the residents and their aimless life, monotonous routines, and drab settings, even though the newly built institutions offered improved environments and more pleasant interiors.

During these years, I also assisted in the development of local associations, which increased from 55 to over 100, and in the founding of 23 county associations, which were needed to obtain regular contact with the county Central Boards for the Care of the Mentally Retarded. The FUB associations eventually operated more than 90 services, including preschool day care, training programs for children without schools, over 20 adult workshops, and more than 25 summer camps. Most of these community programs were later taken over by the central boards, after the new law of 1968 went into effect. I also sat on the boards of a summer home serving children with severe cerebral palsy and intellectual disability and of two homes for blind preschoolers with intellectual impairments, operated with the support of the DBF, the Federation of the Blind, the Red Cross, and the Scouts. During this period, both organizations developed a considerable number of leisure and summer programs for children with various disabilities. The work also involved discussions with authorities on different levels and a lot of information and public-relations work. Having started out with a half-time secretary, I ended up with a staff of over 10. These were dynamic years, during which our budget rose from less than 100,000 Swedish crowns a year to over 1,000,000—and at that time a crown was a crown! And in 1966, we could at last start a magazine of our own.

The following sections will describe in more detail the main spheres of experiences and developments that led to the Normalization principle: the need for and content of new Swedish legislation (particularly the law of 1968); the emphasis on legal aspects and rights, in an international context; the need for new attitudes and new language; and the problems and new possibilities for adults with disabilities.

6 LEGISLATIVE DEVELOPMENTS

The legislation dating from 1954 allowed for institutional services only. Thus, the social circumstances for intellectually disabled persons and their parents were very unsatisfactory and taxing. Writing in 1993, and looking back to the 1950s, I described the situation as follows (Nirje, 1993):

> There were no community services for the children, no schools for those who were not considered "educable," no occupation for those who could not work in the open market—sheltered workshops were not intended for them—or on farms for a meagre board and lodging, which was sometimes only a cover for humiliating serfdom. There were no family services to speak of and no leisure-time arrangements, except for a few small summer programs run by the FUB local associations.
>
> If the parents could not cope, the responses were institutions—central boarding schools for children, or central county institutions or care homes for

children or adults, or state special hospitals for those with profound or severe, complicated, or additional disabilities, or work homes for adults, privately or county run, mostly separate for men and women. The institutions very often used large dormitories (for up to 8-12 persons) and had very limited activity programs, giving depressing impressions not only to the parents, who were faced with hard and fateful choices. Sometimes the conditions were horrifying and scandalous. (pp. 2-3)

For Swedish parents, the institutions were bleak residences. But visitors from abroad, including the members of one of President Kennedy's committees in 1962 and others who followed in their and Gunnar Dybwad's footsteps, were shocked for quite different reasons: They thought that the modern Swedish facilities were small and nice, compared to their huge and horrible institutions! They had difficulty in understanding why we were criticizing the new institutions, which looked almost like modern suburban row housing. But the reality was that we did not like their implied segregation and their lack of programs. They were still not homes. Swedish parents wanted other choices and opportunities and more human contact. And there were still very few alternatives to institutions, only a few of which were new, although many more were on the drawing boards. So, the choice for parents was often between the unthinkable and the impossible.

The 1954 Swedish legislation thus did not offer much in terms of services in the community. Various demands and shifting views were discussed within FUB by groups that each had a different focus, although all were cautious, apprehensive and dissatisfied. My job was to coordinate these differing views, which I did by bringing forward all the positive proposals as new legal texts or as new paragraphs in the existing law. This turned out to present an understandable alternative. From then on, we were able to meet regularly with a four-member committee, of which Karl Grunewald and Lennart Wessman, the inspector of special schools in the Royal Board of Education, were significant members. The views of FUB were shared by the committee, and their basic proposal for a new law was presented at the FUB biannual general assembly in 1964. Later on, their final proposal was sent out to all concerned political and administrative bodies—the regular way of handling important legislative matters in Sweden—and was very favorably received. This led to the final bill, which was passed by the Swedish Parliament in December 1967. The law was no longer centered on institutions but rather on the legal right of developmentally disabled persons to services in the community. Education and meaningful occupation now became obligatory, with community services to include education for all children, small pupils' homes, and group homes and occupation centres for adults. Administrative responsibilities still remained with the 23 county parliaments.

The point I want to stress here is that these main legislative demands and efforts, presented by FUB in 1962-1963, were made well before the first conscious expressions of the Normalization principle. These legislative concerns and directions were thus a prerequisite for my formulation of the principle, a process that took place during 1963-1967.

Every fourth year the Nordic professional associations hold a congress, and in 1963 I was asked to present the parents' views on institutions. I was therefore invited to Denmark to see some of their institutions. There, I got to know Niels Erik Bank-Mikkelsen, the dynamic leader of state services for the mentally retarded. In his office, reading the preamble to the Danish Law of 1959, for which he had been the driving force, I found—and later helped to make famous—the words expressing the fact that the aim of the law was "to let the mentally retarded obtain an existence as close to the normal as possible." This law preceded the Swedish law by almost a decade. Still, the Danish institutions were larger and often had much bigger dormitories than those in Sweden. At the Oslo conference in 1963, where we took part in the special session on institutions, I presented the criticism of the institutional conditions in our countries, with some sharp examples, especially from Denmark, where conditions were not "as close to the normal as possible," here using the quote for the first time. The other participants did not altogether share our views, and some parents were upset with mine. Bank-Mikkelsen, however, was very cheered by them and found them helpful. Our presentations were then published by a small Swedish professional magazine. One can see that none of us were ready yet to talk about "Normalization," much less about a "principle." Its time had not yet come.

There was interest at the time in the legal aspect of services, which also had an international aspect. In 1963, the cooperation of parent associations within a European League was widened into an International League, with the chairman of FUB, John Philipson, a parent, as the new president. He was a medical doctor and vice-chairman of the Swedish Red Cross, whom I had met in my refugee work in Austria. He was warm, diplomatically skilled, and internationally experienced. He brought me in to assist in his new tasks. One of the things the International League promoted was exchange of information on legal developments. The Scandinavian experiences were of great interest to many.

This led to the Stockholm Symposium of the International League on Legislative Aspects of Mental Retardation, in 1967. This gathering, of which I was the organizer and one of 30 participants, was masterfully led by Richard Sterner. It included active representatives from Great Britain, Ireland, the United States, France, Switzerland, Spain, and the Nordic countries. Niels Erik Bank-Mikkelsen, Lennart Wessman, and Karl Grunewald acted as experts. The symposium was a landmark for the League. I can still remember the happy atmosphere of accomplishment and satisfaction as we realized that we had put together something quite important and internationally significant.

Students analyzing the statements of the symposium will not only find the words "normal conditions" a few times. They will also recognize the main themes in the statements, including their human rights base. The Stockholm symposium led the International League to adopt the motto "From Charity to Rights" for their Jerusalem Congress in 1968 and to use the work as a basis for the Jerusalem Declaration of the Rights of the Mentally Handicapped. This, in turn, through French efforts, was brought to the United Nations, where it led to the United Nations Declaration on the Rights of the Mentally Handicapped in 1971. This was followed by the United Nations Declaration of the Rights of the Disabled in 1975. In both of these UN documents, the word "normal" can be found.

However, at the Stockholm symposium in 1967, the Normalization principle was not yet written and thus not known to the participants, even though I had presented it in lectures in the United States at the beginning of the year. At the symposium, I used slides to present my views on institutions. In doing so, I was supported by Bank-Mikkelsen, who had just returned from his visit to the United States and, specifically, California. This was the visit that had so upset Governor Reagan and cost Leo Lippman his job. During his visit, Bank-Mikkelsen made his famous comment, "In Denmark, we treat cows better than you treat people in your institutions."

Looking back at the conclusions of the 1967 Stockholm symposium, these specific views of Bank-Mikkelsen and mine are not to be found therein. The written sections, representing an international perspective, express very modest proposals, reflecting the helplessness that many felt in the face of the authoritarian systems that lay behind the austere facades of the large institutions, which were the main societal option at the time. Proposals were made for improved staff education, for stimulating training programs, for placing new smaller institutions nearer the communities, and for providing more day programs in the community, for better contact. Much importance was placed on safeguards such as guardianship and parental participation in decisions. The conclusions reflect a distrustful, cautious, and overprotective approach—from today's vantage point, which says a lot about the changes that have taken place during the last three decades! It was a very representative and competent group of parent association leaders behind the conclusions. In parentheses at the end of some sections—but only in parentheses!—the more advanced experiences from Scandinavian countries were mentioned, describing smaller-sized institutions and dormitories, and forums for parental influence.

7 SOME PROFILES: BANK-MIKKELSEN, GRUNEWALD, AND WESSMAN

The major trends of the time were directed toward the establishment, through legislation, of reliable social services in the community instead of institutions. No parent—whether in Belgium, Spain, France, Ireland, the United States, or Sweden—wanted to place their sons or daughters in these institutions. They were given no other alternative, however. The urgency felt for such alternatives was the driving force behind the Nordic parent associations. Their situation was made easier by the fact that these views were expressed by professional leaders, who, in their administrative capacities, were able to lead developments in the desired directions: Niels Erik Bank-Mikkelsen in Denmark, and Karl Grunewald and Lennart Wessman in Sweden. They all enacted their roles with gusto.

After his work as a journalist in the resistance movement during the war, and imprisonment when caught by the German occupiers, Niels Erik Bank-Mikkelsen became a lawyer. He got his first job as the temporary director of the section for mental retardation in the Ministry of Social Affairs. He never left that job. In Denmark, the institutions were administered by the state. Being densely populated, the country had made them large to accommodate their few regions. In the 1960s, he worked on reorganizing the inner structures of the institutions. The doctors were no longer solely in charge but, rather, had to collaborate with psychologists, social workers, and administrators. Bank-Mikkelsen cooperated with the parent association in establishing sheltered workshops and group homes in the community. He had also established a special institute of higher learning for staff training. He was a strong advocate for the civil rights of the mentally retarded and had the courage and the standing to be the harshest critic of the institutional situation. His main view of Normalization, when that word began to come into use, was that it meant a home to live in, a job to go to, the same leisure time and civil rights as were enjoyed by others, and services that were the responsibility of communities, not the state. I met him in 1963 and heard him at congresses, and we became friends. Especially after *Changing Patterns,* we sometimes made presentations on the same occasions. He was inspirational, a fighter, and a warm humanist.

Karl Grunewald was a child psychiatrist who, in 1961, became the inspector general of the institutions. These were run mainly by the counties, but there were also some special hospitals operated by the state and a large number of smaller institutions or privately operated "homes." As Sweden was sparsely populated, the counties had smaller institutions, with those for children being mostly separate. Two state and two county institutions held more than 500 residents. Grunewald's office often severely criticized the conditions encountered. But he also stimulated new activities and programs in these institutions and fought

against doctors' advising parents to place newborns with Down's syndrome in institutions. He also spoke out against the practice of sterilization. Like Bank-Mikkelsen, he was very active on the architectural side when it came to approving new facilities, working for more homelike and normal environments. He recommended very strongly his "small group principle" when organizing life in institutions or in the community. He enjoyed writing and was also an inspirational and creative programmer of the many annual conferences for the various groups of professionals. Bank-Mikkelsen was in charge of the Danish institutions, and Grunewald was the sharp inspector of county services in Sweden. Although their roles were different, they shared the same approach toward community services. As the FUB ombudsman, I worked very closely and enjoyably with Grunewald. I often knew about his inspection reports in advance and could prepare the FUB people in the county concerned. Thus, when the reports were made public, according to Swedish procedure, we could alert the press. Together, we pressured the counties to improve standards and services.

Lennart Wessman, Karl Grunewald and I were often involved in the same causes, and we were sometimes called the three musketeers by friend and foe. Wessman was the inspector of special schools, fighting boarding schools, which he found detrimental to the work of education, increasing and improving classes for the trainable, and all the while pressing for integration within the regular school system. He strongly promoted work education and work training. With his interpretation of the law of 1967, he could at last make sure that all children had educational rights, including the most profoundly disabled.

I discussed problems with Grunewald and Wessman that I learned about from the local associations or had noted myself. We talked about desirable changes in regulations, future changes, or issues for the conferences, where I always presented current views from FUB and international news. We rarely had time to talk about "philosophy"—there was no need to do so, as we readily found that we shared the same humanistic views. Such talks happened more frequently after I had written the Normalization principle. I no doubt mentioned themes from the principle in talks about conditions with county deans or directors of institutions or homes.

8 ROADS TO "NORMAL"

During the visits mentioned above, I always tried to find time for quiet talks with residents, if they were able to speak. Most of the time, their language had not been developed in stimulating environments, with the silence of the wards a recurring experience—unless the radio or, later, the TV on. They told me about their boredom and tedium, how they understood their parents' earlier problems because of them, and how they realized that they would never get the opportunity to leave the institution. The boarding-school pupils sometimes spoke about the envy they felt toward their siblings, who had so much more exciting leisure times.

In the early 1960s, I had the opportunity to see a series of five documentaries from the British Mental Health Society, where a hidden camera followed the reactions of five small children, all under the age of 3 (6, 12, 18, 24, and 30 months old), who had been separated from their mothers for a longer than usual but still brief period. They were not disabled and were taken care of in the very best way. Still, it was horrifying to follow the children's withdrawal, anxiety, regression, and aggression during and after separation from their mothers. These films informed me of the undoubted impact on children with disabilities, who are placed in institutions soon after birth and never allowed to experience creative relationships with their parents, from the very beginning. They were bereft even of their past. Such an existence was debilitating and abnormal, no matter what the doctors said.

I was struck by the fact that so many families cared for children who were far more impaired than those I found in the wards for multidisabled children. I was also struck that many of the children, young adults, or adults I met in the community were as impaired as those I met in the institutions. It was thus evident that an isolated institution could not be the only option. Growing up in the community offered more stimulating experiences to learn from, provided a better feeling of security, and offered more joy and family connections. As a matter of fact, more persons with intellectual disabilities were living in the community, even though the services there were negligible and cost the counties little or nothing. Nevertheless, the counties were planning new, modern institutions. I found that the developmentally disturbed had their development additionally disturbed by institutional environments that did not allow them to learn and grow from experiences of the so-called "normal" world. Certainly, the institutions and special homes were not "normal." Rather, they were often scary and abnormal, unsuitable for their complicated developmental purposes. The situations were not socially normal in either the institutions or the communities where the families lived.

On the other hand, so much was in the works, including making institutional environments more "normal" and creating new services in the community to diminish the demand for institutional placements and to make possible more "normal" social situations. In the atmosphere of the progressive 1960s, it was in the air to improve the lives of people with disabilities, to allow them at last to share in the increase in the social capacities of their communities and countries. There were sufficient and sometimes appalling reasons to make this a necessity.

In explaining the Swedish approach to architecture or social services, we often used the expression, "It is normal to have a room of one's own." Especially if one is profoundly impaired, a ward for 10 or 20 or 50 or 100 is not an environment that can be understood. With a room of one's own and a normal home environment, on the other hand, it was easier for people with disabilities to understand and to acquire the skills needed to manage personal issues such as using the toilet, dressing, or eating—in a word, the activities of normal daily life, ADL. This was a better way of talking and dealing with the facts of life of disabled persons, rather than merely comparing systems.

I had found that wide variations in national patterns of legislating, implementing laws, delivering services, and establishing regulations were expressions of different administrative cultures. These variations often prevented us from efficiently exchanging experiences, insights, strivings, remedies, aims, or solutions. The reason was that basic meanings and patterns of life, according to which persons with disabilities and their families lived each day, were not communicated in understandable and relevant ways. More and more, I felt it urgent to find a common language. I also felt that the word "normal" was a key to the needed language of mutual understanding. I had often used it in my own talks and presentations to various groups, as well as in discussions.

During the 1963-1966 period, I began to use a pedagogical device in my talks to nurses, social workers, parents, or the general public, including politicians. I described a normal day, week, or vacation for a typical individual or family and then contrasted these with the days, weeks, or vacations experienced by intellectually impaired children, adolescents, or adults and their families. In this way, I was able to show what needed to be done to make the situation of the latter more normal and less handicapped. I found this point of view made it easier to analyze the components of problems and recommend priorities for action. From these contrasting perspectives, it was also easier to analyze the situations of persons with intellectual disabilities living in institutions.

I reached an understanding of the components of my principle during those years through observation and analysis. The Normalization principle is an inductive theory, rather than a deductive one to be imposed from above, as I have often had reason to explain. I gradually saw an underlying coherence in my observations and analyses, such that I started to call this coherence a "principle." This also made it possible to define its logical structure.

The origins of the perspectives underlying the principle of Normalization were not rooted merely in demands for rights that were to be attained through new legislation, nor in tools for describing problems and solutions on an international level. These perspectives also stemmed from the point of view of people with intellectual disabilities themselves.

9 TOWARD INDEPENDENCE

I had become acquainted with the views of people with intellectual disabilities from listening to them in homes, institutions, leisure-time clubs, and sport training sessions. The FUB leisure-time clubs were started to create more meaningful and entertaining leisure opportunities for the "children," who, in fact, were mostly young adults. Since 1962, I had been a member of the advisory committee for sports for people with disabilities and helped to start FUB sport groups. During the summers of 1962 and 1963, I assisted Daniel Melin, a legendary pastor, special school dean, and mentor for FUB developments, as well as my predecessor as the executive member of the FUB board and the "father" of many associations. I helped him run confirmation sessions for those who, because of their intellectual disabilities, had not been accepted for these initiation rites by the officials of the Swedish church. (A protest letter to the Swedish bishops later changed this situation.) During these pleasant summer weeks, my job—being a heathen—was to take care of sporting activities, leisure time, and excursions. It was very educational, especially for me.

My first visit to Denmark in mid-summer 1963 included a planned meeting with staff and workers at a sheltered workshop. For technical reasons, their place of vacation had suddenly been changed, so I had to meet them at the famous Askov Folk High School, started by the legendary theologian Grundtvig in 1844. The first Swedish school of this kind opened in 1868. Since then, several hundred such "People's Colleges" have been founded in the Nordic countries by organizations, churches, parties, and counties. There, adults with limited formal education who wanted to learn new things and improve their lives could do so, thereby preparing themselves for a better and more active community life. In these boarding schools, people could study, for a year or two, what they were highly motivated to learn. They also had opportunities to talk about life and what they wanted from it with new acquaintances who had similar interests. Toward the end of the last century, the Folk High Schools became cradles for democratic movements and processes in the Nordic countries. This Danish group, however, only used the school as a hotel between excursions. But they were intrigued by the new environment, as I found out when, in the evening, I helped them enter and explore some of the new buildings, which contained laboratories, music rooms, and a library, and had geography and history maps on the walls. Afterward, on a little hill below a giant tree, we had a memorable talk about why adults still wanted to go to school. Even if going to school was not always a pleasant experience, it was easy to understand that anyone could profit from learning how to handle money better, or vote, or travel. I was also struck by the need to create teaching methods to make such learning possible.

Later that year, I met Elliot Avedon, who was a professor of recreation—an unheard-of subject in Sweden at that time—at Columbia University in New York City. On the recommendation of his older colleague Ignacy Goldberg, Avedon visited Stockholm, where I described the Swedish "mental retardation" scene. He gave me his book on the social training of persons with intellectual disabilities, which had been used in leisure-time programs in New York since the end of the 1950s. The book was valuable in describing a three-step approach, to which we later added a fourth step, through the experiences and developments of our clubs, the step being a report about having made a decision on one's own and carrying it out. Such reports became more and more frequent, suggesting increased social contacts and participation, independence, and self-determination.

In 1964, I wanted to organize a two-week summer course in social training but was turned down by my board. Later, at a conference for the Swedish deans of special schools in 1963 or 1964, when I pointed out the necessity of developing adult-education methods and opening Folk High Schools for persons with intellectual disabilities, people just shook their heads. One of the leading deans came up to me and said: "You are really funny. I'll bet that next year you'll stand up here and say that they should have an entrance exam and be able to go to Uppsala University, just like yourself!" Happily, I was going to get the last laugh before long.

In 1965, Daniel Melin saw to it that I got funding for my two-week social-training course, under the guise of a reunion for some of his "pupils" who knew me from the previous summers. I had questioned the young people's parents about their children's social skills, special habits, likes, and dislikes. In a setting like a Folk High School, we could also use small cities as venues in which more and more complicated and challenging tasks were presented to groups of two, one girl and one boy, who were accompanied by an assistant teacher. The course taught the participants some new skills and improved others. We also found, however, that they had skills that their parents did not believe they had or had never seen. Friends in this group later that year formed the first club. My assistant in the course was Ann Bakk. She was a young journalist and, later, a psychologist and writer. She also became the driving force in the creation of clubs and courses for club members. Half were "camouflaged" assistants who, in reality, were often friends of ours. These courses took place on weekends. The subject was "how to be a tourist." Later, I called it my "attitude-changing machine." I always achieved the same, predictable result with it, although the result was surprising for some, including a few times in the United States and in an institution in Canada (the director of which was a former Hungarian). There were eight pairs of persons with intellectual disabilities and eight pairs of persons without disabilities, each composed of one man and one woman. Every pair met three pairs from the other groups, persons they had never seen before, much as a tourist meets new people. I had based the three components of the course on my interpretation of "mental retardation" as consisting of, first, the individual cognitive impairment, second, the disability in learning, and third, the awareness of being handicapped. With the help of some funding to cover the costs of practical problem solving, meals, transportation, and amusements, the course consisted of a short introduction where participants found out that they were in a group with an unknown person and were going to meet a lot of new people. They did so while exploring the city, having lunch and dinner, experiencing fun in the evening, and having a Sunday-morning constitutional, followed by lunch. At the end of each session, the "assistants" were debriefed. The persons with intellectual disabilities had their own evaluation discussion at the end of the workshop, after which they presented their findings and views to the others. As the wheels of the attitude-changing machine came to this final turn, the other participants came to realize that the real teachers at the workshop were the people with disabilities.

The clubs and workshops gave rise to some 40 clubs within a few years. This led to courses in parliamentary rules and procedures, to enable the young people to run their own clubs, hold elections, be board members, plan programs, and make their own decisions about leisure-time and other activities (e.g., putting on their own conference with members of other clubs to discuss issues of mutual interest). The first such conference took place in May 1968, with 20 participants. The starting point for us was always the wishes and self-expressed needs of the young adults themselves. Their interests and motivation were the main driving force. Being in groups developed their strengths and abilities, as well as their confidence to do things on their own.

The "fourth step," as we called it, was achieved by members when they called up a friend to go to a movie or went to a museum or event on their own. The loneliness of the young adults was a great concern for their parents and thus these peer-group models, whom participants found in the club, were very important. Our experience taught us over and over again that parents, because of anxiety, often underestimated or were unaware of the skills and competencies that their children possessed. The young adults often mentioned that they were sad because they understood how sad their parents were because of their disability. The young adults also often wanted a life in which they would be on their own, like their older siblings. They wanted to learn how to handle themselves and be as independent as possible, by learning how to vote, cook, speak English, use a bank, and so forth. The clubs made them feel stronger, and the conferences gave them a voice. They began to be heard and respected on their own, for themselves. Their disabilities were not unknown to them, although their future was, despite their having often hidden hopes. It was really important for them to become adult, be respected, be seen and understood, and have the same right to self-determination as everyone else.

The common concerns of the leading organizations for people with disabilities, including those who were blind, deaf, or physically disabled, were for social improvements, such as better labor-market opportunities, transportation, and technical aids for use in the home, on the job, or in the community. In 1963, the perspectives and goals of these organizations were widened due to increased pressure from the parent associations for persons with cerebral palsy or intellectual disabilities. I was much involved in this development. The Handicap Associations Central Committee (HCK) was formed, which led to new strengths. Opportunities for persons with cerebral palsy or intellectual disabilities were also strengthened, because their interests were now articulated from within a wider perspective and were advocated from a larger platform.

In 1965, the Swedish Board of Education asked HCK to appoint a committee of three to prepare ideas and rationales for wider cultural opportunities for persons with disabilities. I was one of the three

committee members. We recommended things such as sign-language dictionaries and expanded interpreter training to serve deaf people, and more and better Folk High School opportunities for persons who were blind, deaf, physically disabled, or intellectually disabled. I was also able to recommend the development of adult-education methods and materials for evening study-circles, such as adult "easy readers" (i.e., shorter versions of classic and modern literature, in language suited to the needs of intellectually disabled persons). Our proposals were accepted the following year by the Riksdag, the Swedish Parliament, to the surprise and consternation of FUB, which at the time did not consider these matters very important. These ideas were all new and untested.

New developments and dynamics started, which rather quickly turned into new centers for activities. Today, more than 4,000 persons with intellectual disabilities have studied at year-long Folk High School courses, and about half of all intellectually disabled adults have taken part in study circles. Also, more than 300 "easy readers" have been published and can be found in public libraries. A weekly magazine and easy-to-read public information are available as well.

I was heavily involved in and often the initiator of these new endeavors (e.g., as a member of the committees for adult-education circles and "easy readers," beginning in 1966), which played a significant role in my later articulation of the Normalization principle. They added to the feeling of urgency regarding the rights of young adults with intellectual disabilities, including the right to have opportunities for "higher education" equivalent to those enjoyed by other adults, to have a voice and social situation appropriate to their status as adult citizens, and to have the right to grow, develop, mature, and attain self-determination. This emphasis on the importance and meaning of adulthood is the most "revolutionary" part of the Normalization principle.

The first conference for persons with intellectual disabilities took place in mid-May 1968, concurrently with the biannual assembly of FUB. At the end of the last assembly session, the young adults presented their report—it must have been the first time in history that such a parent assembly received a report from "their children." The conference for these 20 persons was a great success. By the use of group dynamics and democratic procedures, we had assisted the intellectually disabled to "make it new"—to create something that had not existed before; a new content in an old form, a new form for an old human content. Not everyone was pleased with these developments, as I will recount further on.

Two weeks later, I left for the United States to write a paper on U.S. institutions, at last. It had not been easy to go there, but the pressure and means to do so had presented themselves. How all that happened is the next act in this story.

10 INTERNATIONAL DYNAMICS

Before going on with the actual writing of the Normalization principle, I think it important to set the stage by recounting some of the trends that were present and influential in those years. In the field of mental retardation, the 1960s were characterized by the many endeavors of concerned parents and professionals to find one another within and across borders, to learn, to exchange experiences and, above all, to search for new solutions, new ways, and new approaches. The European League became the International League of Societies for the Mentally Handicapped in 1963, and the International Association for the Scientific Study of Mental Deficiency (IASSMD) was formed in 1964. Previously, President John F. Kennedy had appointed a President's Panel on Mental Retardation, which, in 1962, sent study groups around the world. One group came to Denmark and Sweden, where FUB and Karl Grunewald were much involved in the visit. Harvey Stevens, commissioner of mental retardation for the state of Wisconsin, was one of the participants and in 1964, he became the first president of the IASSMD.

In 1963, Gunnar Dybwad left his position as executive director of the U.S. National Association for Retarded Children (NARC) to work in Geneva, Switzerland, for the international Save the Children organization as an adviser on mental retardation. Gunnar and Rosemary Dybwad formed a remarkable dynamic couple who, for decades as benevolent spiders, built a strong web that connected people and ideas around the world. When they left the US, a scholarship fund was raised in Rosemary's honor, which sent study visitors to places of special interest. Almost all of the first recipients made the Grand Tour to Copenhagen, Stockholm, and Oslo.

One of the reasons FUB hired me was to acquire more international information. In 1961, for the first time, in London and The Hague, we met persons from other national parent associations. FUB was particularly interested in obtaining information on sheltered workshops, which is why the second part of the conference—the Dutch part—was the most interesting. At that time, sheltered workshops were a new idea for Sweden, where up until then such services were not intended for persons with an intellectual disability. The man behind this new approach was Bengt Junker, an industrial economist, who as chairman of the Swedish Boy Scouts had led the Folke Bernadotte Drive for Cerebral Palsy. He had asked me to take on the job as executive director of FUB to, among other things, start the ALA Foundation for a pilot workshop project. His wife, Karin Stensland-Junker, vice-chairman of FUB, was the one who guided me on my first tours to meet some of the children with the most complicated or profound impairments and to see institutional settings that were not always up to par. She invented the "lekotek" (toy library), an ingenious solution that offered mothers advice for the stimulation of their impaired child during their early years, with toys from the library at their disposal. The first lekotek was in the room next to my office, where I did most of my work. Her lekotek later proved to be an idea for export.

Our main concern was to import the sheltered workshop idea from the Netherlands. The president of the European League was Mr. van Daym, the director of the workshops in The Hague. In these years, papers presented by Speijer, Wehrmeier, and Meuzelaar were important events, and I was also sent to visit their workshops, as well as others. My translations of their papers formed a substantial part of the lectures I gave as part of the instructional courses offered by the Swedish Labour Market Board to the foremen of the new workshops for the developmentally disabled. These were mushrooming in the mid-1960s due to the work by FUB, much to the irritation of county authorities. But in our association we had fathers who were competent in a number of trades and who found great satisfaction in these new opportunities for their young adults.

At that time, in London, we heard and saw Jack Tizard's presentation of the Brooklands "experiment," in which multidisabled children were given a special child-stimulation program that was very similar to those that had started in Sweden. Later, we succeeded in showing the program on Swedish TV, and I served as a translator and speaker. In Brussels, in 1963, Ignacy Goldberg, from the US, was one of the main speakers. He continued on to Sweden with his lectures on preschool education and, as his interpreter, I learned a great deal on the subject.

Many other new developments were presented at such conferences, which provided many stimulating exchanges. In 1966, Herbert Gunzburg, a psychologist from England and the editor of the *British Journal of Mental Subnormality,* presented his system for assessing social capacities. At the same congress of the International League in the UNESCO building in Paris, professor Henry Cobb of the US gave a fascinating presentation on *The Attitude of the Retarded Person Towards Himself* (Cobb, 1967). That paper helped me to underline some important statements at the end of my first paper on the Normalization principle. Henry Cobb and Ignacy Goldberg were invited by John Philipson to a memorable lunch at the restaurant in Brussels that had served as an important place for the Belgian resistance movement. This was Ignacy Goldberg's first visit to Europe after he had left Poland at the beginning of World War II, when he joined the Polish troops in the British army and was later severely wounded at El Alamein. Ignacy, Henry, John, and I found each other talking the same language when we discussed the necessity of changing the European League into an International League, to strengthen international cooperation and exchanges of ideas and experiences. Henry Cobb later followed John Philipson as president of the International League. International dynamics were thus very strong in the 1960s, and I would be remiss if I did not mention that Niels Erik Bank-Mikkelsen and Karl Grunewald played leadership roles and were often heard abroad at many of these congresses.

There were also many transatlantic exchanges, with a considerable influx of American visitors to Scandinavia and return invitations for some of us to visit the US to present our views. G. F. Jerry Walsh, the executive director of the Minnesota ARC and the initial Rosemary Dybwad award recipient, was the person who first invited me to visit the US. I had met him when he visited Scandinavia in 1966. As I relate later, he came to play a significant role in my life in the creation not only of the Normalization principle but also of "the right to self-determination" and the setting up of the International Association of Sports for the Mentally Handicapped. He has been a promoter, guide, and friend for more than 30 years. He was also a Marine Corps veteran who served in the war in the Pacific in Guadalcanal, Tarawa, and Saipan. After the war, he received a B.A. and M.S. in business administration from the University of Minnesota. He was the first executive officer of the first state Association for Retarded Children (ARC) in the United States, and was later the first of the Rosemary Dybwad explorers.

In April 1966, around Easter time, Jerry met with experts and visited institutions in and around Stockholm. He stayed in my home, which gave us much time to talk. I was able to show him a brand-new institution for 450 persons, featuring small apartment houses with single and double rooms grouped together in the form of a modern village, with a piazza, restaurant, barbershop, shop, and café. The institution was located in pleasant, hilly terrain that overlooked the rivulet that meandered across the village. It was so new that only the very first residents had moved in. That Good Friday, the institution was deserted. At the end of the visit, when I showed him one of the houses for multidisabled persons, with all the new technical aids, I turned to find that Jerry had disappeared. After a while, I found him in a bathroom, wiping his eyes. He burst out: "Here you are, telling me about all the things that are wrong with this place—that it is far too big, that it should not be here but in a community, and that it should really not exist at all—but I will never in my life be able to see anything as nice and good in my country!" And then he started to tell me about American institutions. Thus began our friendship, which would lead to so many more developments and meetings.

11 THE U.S. INVOLVEMENT

Upon his return, Jerry Walsh presented his European observations to the annual convention of the Minnesota ARC, on June 10, 1966, in Duluth. He quoted us as having the following exchange: "The philosophy I found can best be expressed thus: The key, then, is trying to achieve the same good standards of life for those retarded children as you want for people who live in general society?" I responded: "Yes, our aim is to create such facilities, and we are far from it. Our aim is to make conditions of life as similar or the same as for the rest of the population. You have to do it for human dignity and human decency." And later I added: "We in the Swedish Parents Association want the institutions not to be institutions at all. Rather, the conditions there should be as homelike as possible, not too different from the situation in a private home. In that way you can have a continuum of existence in the family home and in the care home, and you would not be alien in any place."

After commenting on the high quality of staff members compared to those found in American institutions, the efficient inspection services, and the fact that service financing was in addition to pensions for all disabled persons (regardless of whether they lived in institutions or in the community), all of which contributed to the high Swedish standards, Jerry Walsh shared with his audience the impact the study tour had made on him: "It's truly amazing and almost unbelievable that a few thousand miles away, 10 hours by air, the problems we are struggling with are being solved." He ended his presentation with a series of recommendations for changes in the policies of the Minnesota ARC regarding institutions.

In the autumn of 1966, the Minnesota ARC established an extensive policy platform for legislative changes, aimed at broadening services in the community and modifying institutions to serve smaller numbers. I was invited to visit for a few weeks to help "bridge the gap between Europe's advanced methods of care and our outdated practices," according to their newsletter. At the same time, I got to see for the first time the huge, desolate wards of American institutions. The visit, in March 1967, was an intense experience: walks through institutions, views of workshops and community programs, and talks to various groups, from early breakfast meetings, luncheon addresses, and radio and TV interviews, to evening lectures. On the very last days I had 13 "performances" a day, with my form and confidence getting better and better. I learned a little about the meaning of "running for office," and I met some people who had. A magazine reported: "He talked for an hour with governor Harold LeVander, had lunch with Hennepin county legislators, and spoke

at a House subcommittee meeting at the invitation of the chairman."

This first tour brought with it reciprocal shocks: American audiences were shocked by my slides from Swedish programs, and I was shocked by what I saw in the institutions, which opened my eyes and camera. In my presentations I used slides, sometimes as many as 80, forming a narrative about the normal rhythms of the day, week, year, and life cycle in Swedish institutions and communities. Without them, I might not have been believed. These slides provided my words with the impact of realism. Several times I encountered the reaction that Jerry had once displayed, with people in the audience wiping their eyes. I was a decent photographer, capturing scenes that fit the movie in my mind and illustrated my narrative and analysis. My slides were parts of my memory. I never took a picture of persons that showed something that they did not want me to photograph. On the other hand, institutions are public places, with no privacy. If the results were shocking, it was not of the residents' doing. So I sometimes took pictures despite the protests of persons in authority.

The stages offered by the large U.S. institutions felt too large for my simple little camera. The ARC newsletter writes about my visit to Faribault State Hospital:

> where he saw large wards with as many as 104 patients with "little staff and no program." He used words such as "horrible," "inhuman" and "impersonal" to describe the situations he saw, "things I am deeply shocked by, that I did not think existed. . . ." "That's degrading human beings in a way I have never seen before. . . ." "[T]he horror of the situation came to me afterwards, when I realized that I was not able to remember any single person, only abstract beings moving around; as you say, it is a dehumanizing effect. . . ." "It is an utterly costly system, a mismanagement of human resources. Patients who aren't receiving needed services now are doomed to be severe-care cases for the rest of their lives—and in the long run the cost will be much greater. . . ." [H]e expressed many of these thoughts to Minnesota Governor Harold LeVander in a private meeting on March 15 in the Governor's office. (Minnesota ARC, 1967a)

Under the headline "Retarded Need Chance for Normal Life," the newsletter (Minnesota ARC, 1967b) presented quotes such as these:

"Mentally retarded people should be able to attain an existence as close to the normal as possible. . . ." "Normal means the normal rhythms of life, whether it be home life, institutional life or educational life. It means normal standards of housing, the same kinds of schools, the same kinds of hospitals, the same kind of medical care as are provided for the rest of us. . . ." "It means learning how to develop and grow into adulthood, to have responsibility, to play a role. Such a sense of role-playing should be given to the mentally retarded person whether he is in an institution or living at home. It means the normalcy of working, or travelling or having free time—we aim to have integration of the mentally retarded in our social living. . . ." "It means abandoning the concepts that the retarded are always children and planning help for them to live through a complete life cycle."

So there it was, in a nutshell, in black and white, most likely in print for the first time.

Nirje said that the Swedish Association also is working for the Normalization of the parents' situations, of the attitudes of authorities and the general public. . . . [He] told how the principle of normalcy had been applied in the development of Sweden's institutions: in the 1930s, we were planning for units to serve 40 residents, in the 1940s it was down to 30 per unit, in the 1950s to 20, and now we are building small units for six to eight persons, the number of people one might find living together in normal home conditions. . . . [He] showed slides of some of the newer institutions, where patients sleep in single or double bedrooms in which they have their personal belongings. Dining and all living activities are in small groups.

Such were the themes and statements in the presentations, including some in Iowa and Wisconsin. The most memorable for me took place in Lincoln, Nebraska, on March 11, 1967, where I was exposed as a banquet speaker without appetite to a very large audience with hungry eyes. If memory serves me correctly, it was in this presentation that, for the first time, I put in some fresh slides from Minnesota institutions as telling contrasts to further illustrate my analysis. Anyhow, I got my first standing ovation. And in the audience was Wolf Wolfensberger. Afterward, we were introduced to each other but had no opportunity to talk. The occasion was the NARC North Central Region meeting and the scene after the speech and the banquet was very lively.

During my stay in Minnesota, I was introduced to U.S. Vice-President Hubert Humphrey, who invited me to his home in Washington, DC, where I showed my slide presentation to Muriel Humphrey and some guests. She was a very knowledgeable and interested "grandparent."

My stay in the USA was extended, as I had been asked to visit the President's Panel, see a new institution in New Jersey, and give a presentation organized by Elisabeth Boggs. My visit to the Special Olympics office, where I advised them also to take up wheelchair events, resulted in an invitation by Senator Edward Kennedy to go to Boston to give a banquet speech at the Harvard Club. There, to give me a bit of assurance, I asked that the lectern be placed in front of the plaque honoring John Quincy Adams, one of my favorite American statesmen. Before the lecture, I had been invited to the office of Governor Volpe for a conversation, and among the banquet guests was Elliott Richardson. Both of these men came to play significant roles in the next U.S. administration, which took over 10 days after the publication of *Changing Patterns*.

During these intense weeks in the US, I had seen a number of institutions that were 10 times as large as the one I had shown Jerry Walsh, which was one of the five largest in Sweden. I had been in vast, foul-smelling dormitories for over 100 persons, and in dayrooms that had hardly any furniture, with no activities or functions for the half-naked inhabitants, who were anonymous. The inactivity of the residents was made worse through a medicated passivity that assisted the sparse staffing. At the same time, I had had the opportunity to concentrate on and develop my own thinking, analysis, and expressions through my talks, discussions, and lectures. Step by step, as it were, I had conquered a feeling of doubt concerning the validity of my point of view and became confident that it could serve as a tool for constructive analysis and criticism. The services enabling normal conditions of life in the community had to be significantly strengthened to allow for the abolition of these monstrous institutional abominations—and not only in the US.

I finally returned to Sweden in April 1967, where it was work as usual but with a new ingredient: preparing for the Stockholm Symposium on the Legal Aspects of Mental Retardation, held for the International League of Parent Associations. There were also preparations for informing the intellectually disabled about the change from driving on the left side of the road to the right side. After the Stockholm symposium, described earlier, we all met in Montpellier, France, for the 2nd Congress of the International Association for the Scientific Study of Mental Deficiency.

At the congress, one seminar was on "The Adolescent Retardate," chaired by psychologist Emanuel Chigier, of Israel, a specialist in group dynamics. Among the speakers were S. Masovic, from Yugoslavia, my old friend Elliot Avedon, from the US, and I. My subject was "Integrational Know-How: Swedish Programs in Social Training" (Nirje, 1967), which described our efforts to provide adult education programs, activities to increase social competence, and club structures, as well as provided examples of demands made by young adults themselves. As background, I commented on some facts from a study conducted by Lennart Wessman that looked at the need for vocational education:

> A few years ago an investigation was made in Sweden of the conditions of life for the about 1,500 young men and women of IQ 50-70 who now are 25-30 years old and who left Special School during five years in the 1950s. More than 50% were jobless and had to live on pensions, 50% were found to be shy, reticent, insecure, withdrawn, without friends. Only 10% took part in regular leisure time activities. These are not conditions of life that are close to the normal. The loneliness and isolation of the adolescent retarded are crushing conditions of life—far harder than those of the normal youngsters. And they lack the self-defence, the force to rebel.

In the opening of the paper I made these statements:

> In Scandinavia we usually say that the aim is to give the mentally retarded an existence as close to the normal as possible—in their daily life and in the regular community. How does this principle apply to adolescents? For instance, there ought to be a normal daily rhythm—not having to go to bed earlier because you are retarded; a normal rhythm of the year, including summer vacations and not having to go to camps for children when you are 16 or 18, but instead a summer course as other youngsters do; normal routines of life: a home, a place to work, leisure time activities; the normal development of life: growing from childhood through adolescence into adulthood; and being respected as an adult." (Nirje, 1967)

I believe that this was the first time the Normalization principle was mentioned in such an international context. With only 30 people or so in the audience, the impact was discreet. Anyhow, partly hiding behind the authoritative "we" that expressed an attitude shared with some professional friends, I presented a basic summary of the main facets of the principle, still without having completely understood its deeper meaning and significance.

12 THE WRITING

The Stockholm symposium and the Montpellier presentation led to an invitation to go to Israel to advise on legislation, to assist in preparing the upcoming Congress in Jerusalem of the International League of Parent Associations, and to study the group-dynamics approach of Manny Chigier. The Israeli parent association, AKIM, published the Montpellier presentations. I went to Israel in February 1968. The country was still quietly grateful for its youth. After all, 1968 was to be the year of youth but also of violence: the demonstrations in Paris, Chicago, and Prague, and the Martin Luther King and Robert Kennedy assassinations.

Before this travel, I had received a letter with another special request. It came a few days before Christmas 1967, written on behalf of "Dr. Robert Kugel, Chairman of the President's Committee on Mental Retardation," by his assistant, "Wolf Wolfensberger, PhD, Mental Retardation Research Scientist." The letter told about "a project aimed at reviewing residential care programs for the retarded in the US, and in speeding along innovation in this area." The planned publication had as its theme "Toward Innovative Action on Residential Care." Seven sections were foreseen, and I was asked to write for the one called "As Others See Us": "On your visit to Nebraska, we were impressed with your forthright and eloquent evaluation of US residential centers. We are hoping that you would write as you spoke, giving Americans the chance to have their residential services evaluated by someone coming from a nation with more advanced social services. We suggest that you mince no words, but be direct and forceful."

The letter went on to state that "The President's Committee is under intense time pressure." The deadline was February 29, 1968, and the paper should be written so as to be intelligible and appealing to professionals in other areas, as well as to intelligent and educated laymen. . . . Indeed, it might not be a bad idea to pretend that you are trying to inform a busy, intelligent, uninformed but sincere, unbiased and sympathetic legislator. (Wolfensberger, personal communication, 1967)

Thus, my paper was to be short, simple, and soon, with the subject being my views on large U.S. institutions.

The letter was certainly more of a shock than a kind of Christmas present. I answered on January 17 with a hesitant "yes," because

I have no definite notes on my talks in the US. I always speak without a script. However, my impressions were and still are vivid, and I think I can give a fair description of and the motivations for them. . . . I hope you are aware that I only saw very few residential institutions during my stay, and the main experience was Faribault. I then very quickly visited the Central Colony in Madison, Wisconsin, and after that spent a day at Woodbridge, New Jersey. . . . [B]ut my reactions are not mainly to a geographical place or house, but to specific situations and standards within an institution which, when described, will stand for a recognizable type. . . . The main line in my paper will be a description of what we mean here by Normalization, which forms the base for my evaluation of the US facilities. (Nirje, personal communication, January 17, 1968)

I asked that a copy of *Christmas in Purgatory* (Blatt and Kaplan, 1967) be sent by airmail, as the letter of invitation had come to me by boat and had taken three weeks.

The point of interest here is that I was not asked to write on the principle of Normalization, an unknown entity. Instead, I was to write about institutions—and almost a year had gone by since I had seen any, and I had no notes. Time was of the essence, and I had my hands full with other commitments and duties: the visit to Israel; the FUB magazine we had started; the courses in social training; the biannual FUB congress in May; the need for more staff; and, not least, the new law that was coming into effect, with all the information required by and for the local associations. The request from the U.S. President's Committee was not very popular with the FUB executive board. Jerry Walsh, who was now at NARC headquarters in New York, came to my rescue. For my trip to the US, he arranged for me to give a few talks and to see some institutions—for I felt I had to see more and have fresh impressions to write on—and also to discuss the situation in general. The President's Committee offered the services of their office in Washington for the final work. I was allowed to take a few weeks of vacation to get there.

So after the FUB congress at the end of May 1968, a few days after the death of my closest friend and the murder of Robert Kennedy, I flew to the US. I find that the plane is always a good place for relief and concentration, and I remember making notes on the eight facets of the principle and finding their proper order. I must have made other notes as well—or brought them with me—because, while I was writing the present chapter, Wolf Wolfensberger sent me a copy of a memo I signed on June 12, 1968, at the NARC offices, a few days after my arrival in New York. The memo consisted of six concentrated pages, on issues that I must have been grappling with from the time of the December request. I had completely forgotten about this memo, but I certainly recognize my own writing and ideas. The memo had a very heavy heading: "Outline for a plan to attack inhuman conditions in the United States' institutions for the mentally retarded." The plan contained strategy and tactics, targets, and logistical needs. Because it has never been published, I have included it at the end of the present chapter as an appendix. Why did I not include parts of this memo in the paper I subsequently wrote for the President's Committee? I probably looked upon the memo as confidential recommendations and advice to NARC. I would continue to deal, in papers to come in the following years, with the concerns expressed in this outline regarding what came to be called deinstitutionalization. The points expressed concerned the U.S. scene of the time, but the stand and approach were the ones I later brought with me to Canada, and to Ontario institutions, for further development.

With the load of that memo off my chest, I could go on to visit institutions. On June 13, I saw my old professor Norman Holmes Pearson at Yale University. That day, he autographed a book for me. At Yale, I met up with John Belmont who took me to visit Southbury. And then my friend Frank Kelly showed me a large institution south of Boston. There, I remember quite vividly the smells in one building that forced me to go outside and throw up—my nose had always served me well on inspections. Frank comforted me, saying: "Bobby Kennedy puked here too; we will put up a plaque!" After a speech I gave to a large regional conference in New Hampshire, I returned to New York to visit Letchworth, a large institution on the west side of the Hudson River, where, in the 1930s, as a fairly new arrival to the US, Gunnar Dybwad had worked. I was surprised to find that at Letchworth they had different burial grounds for men and women. These were on opposite ends of the small (institutional) city where 5,000 people (not including staff) lived in the drab barracks of the old institution.

I returned to Hyde Park, for a return visit with Jerry and his family, to gather my strength. Then, the moment of truth "soon" arrived when I reached Washington, DC. Installed at the old Willard Hotel, I spent three days "locked in" at the Department of Health, Education and Welfare (HEW). The procedure was simple: With the help of my notes, I dictated to three secretaries, who took turns. I stopped dictating to the second when the first came back with her part for corrections, and so it went. First came the impressions of the institutions, with comments, which took up four pages. Then came the rationale for the criticism, the Normalization principle, which took up eight pages. To the paper was added a seven-page translation of an article I had written on the new Swedish legislation.

When *Changing Patterns* was published, the four pages on institutions were placed in a section with Burton Blatt's *Purgatory*. My contribution was late, and certainly short. The "Normalization Principle" part of my paper—with the appendix on the law—was placed in the section "Toward New Service Models."

I had been asked to write about U.S. institutions, not about what I called the Normalization principle. But I needed to state the principle as a basis for the criticism of the conditions of life for persons with mental retardation in such environments. I should add, however, that the principle described a view of the general situation of disabled people in the community.

But of these editorial considerations and decisions I knew nothing at the time. At the end of the three days of intense concentration, I left HEW. In the beautiful midsummer evening, I walked across the Mall, with a thorough feeling of relief and happiness. I can never see that magnificent Mall without remembering that crossing.

13 AFTERWARD

Thus, it all came together: the involvement in literature and academic education; the orientation toward human rights and international cooperation; a humanistic and multicultural approach; the group-dynamics experiences and the voices of refugees; young adults with cerebral palsy and intellectual or other disabilities; the legislative concerns and the social interests of parents and the disabled; the drive to find a shared language that would provide a common ground for the many specialties and special interests involved; and the international developments and stimulation. All of these factors and experiences had, at different times and in different ways, contributed to and shaped the forming of the Normalization principle.

Opportunity and need also conspired. Without the problems that I and other visitors had seen in American institutions, the invitation of the President's Committee, and the resolute actions of Jerry Walsh, the paper on the Normalization principle might never have been written. Moreover, the invitation and request had asked for my impressions of large institutions, not for the Normalization principle! To offer such a critique required, I felt, a coherent and explicit point of view. This first version had given me a platform, as well as binoculars and a magnifying glass, with which to view and expand on further experiences. But I knew none of this at the time. Then, I was mostly happy the ordeal was over. There certainly were tasks and troubles enough to handle in my job.

Later in 1968, I learned of the editors' decision to divide the paper into two parts and that they were pleased. At the end of the year, I think I was also told that Gunnar Dybwad had highly appreciated my contribution. The positive reception of my work was indeed confirmed when Grunewald and I each received 10 complimentary contributors' copies. We gave most of them to colleagues. In this way, the principle became known in Sweden, and later in 1969 a translation was published both in the FUB magazine and in one of the two professional journals. The FUB, however, was not impressed. Before its publication, I was permitted to read it to the board, but no discussions were allowed. I think the general attitude was that the paper was a nice, commonsensical presentation by a well-meaning amateur who should not travel abroad so much. Board members had not authorized these views, which were probably controversial. But people stopped saying that the views on American institutions were exaggerations. Swedish institutions, on the other hand, were thought to be so good that one did not need to speak about them. So members did not think there was a need for a special principle, other than one based on common sense.

Such issues were, at that moment, only minor concerns. There was much to be done. The new legislation was starting to be implemented in all 23 counties. Many programs—over 50—run by the local associations could at last be handed over to the responsible county financing authority. And the youth clubs were growing like mushrooms. Soon, there were over 40 of them.

Since 1962, I had been a member of the advisory committee for sports for the disabled, including the intellectually disabled. Changes were needed and because I took the initiative, I was given the responsibility for founding the Swedish Handicap Sports Association (SHIF). This took place in May 1969. This new organization meant that the sections devoted to sports of the various handicap organizations became independent sports clubs. These were grouped into districts, and the whole organization immediately became a member of the Swedish Sports Federation. Thus, our committees for the various sports practiced by handicapped athletes, whether paraplegic, amputee, deaf, cerebral palsied, or intellectually disabled, had direct relations with the equivalent Swedish Sports Associations. I had written the constitution and was elected vice-chairman. As I spoke more languages and had more international experience than other board members, I became our first international representative, joined later by other Swedish colleagues.

Between 1971 and 1995, I was elected to a number of positions in international sports federations for disabled persons. In 1986, I could at last finalize the preparations for the founding of the International Association for Sports for the Mentally Handicapped (INAS-FMH). As our clubs tended to be locally based or to become parts of regular sports clubs, sporting activities became one area where intellectually disabled athletes could share and take part in normal adult activities and social relations. INAS-FMH has now become a founding member of the International Para-Olympic Committee (IPC), and since 1992

intellectually disabled athletes, together with other disabled athletes, have been able to compete in summer and winter games and in world championships. The Swedish organizational model was followed by other countries, but only a few included intellectually disabled athletes. In Sweden, they were present from the beginning. Not all members on the FUB board appreciated this, and I was told that there were certainly more important issues to deal with than sports. Until 1995, when I resigned as vice-president of INAS-FMH, the international development of sports for handicapped athletes was an important area of endeavor for me. This involvement in sports has given me great satisfaction.

Back to 1969. While all of this was going on, Wolf Wolfensberger arrived in Stockholm by train with Bank-Mikkelsen from Copenhagen. We had only met casually, but now he was in my home for a week and the next week he stayed with Karl Grunewald. Wolf has told me that when he first heard me at the banquet in Lincoln, Nebraska, he thought the ideas rather good but nothing remarkable. When he read my paper as co-editor of *Changing Patterns,* he found it quite good and interesting. Then Gunnar Dybwad advised him to go to Scandinavia to see for himself how the situation of the intellectually disabled looked in a different cultural environment.

Right from the train station, we walked a few blocks and visited an apartment used by some of our clubs for meetings and activities. While I discussed some business in a meeting with some members, Wolf was introduced as an American visitor and left to form his own impressions. I remember vividly Wolf standing in a corner watching the dancing that had started—a birthday was being celebrated—and then he hesitantly asked me: "That girl, she asked me for a dance, and we did. Is she. . . ?" She spoke some English, and so he did not quite know whether she was a typical Swedish girl who happened to speak English or really an intellectually disabled girl who had learned some English. I assured him she really was the latter.

On the way home, I explained the purpose, functioning, and activities of the club. Half of the members were disabled, and all the positions on the elected board were held by an equal number of disabled and nondisabled persons. The nondisabled were trained to let the disabled make the decisions about the activities. Later, we talked a great deal about his many visits to programs and facilities and with key persons in and around Stockholm. I remember a particular discussion when Wolf was upset by all the nice, new, modern furniture he had seen in a renovated institution. I had to explain that quality was more economical in the long run and that it was quite normal to buy regular furniture from regular firms, as people normally do. Moreover, the counties were likely to get better prices because of the quantities we purchased. Old and recycled furniture of a decent standard would turn out to be far more expensive. "Scandinavian design" did not imply luxury in Sweden. I do not know if it was this experience that led him to his "conservatism corollary" (Wolfensberger, 1972). He spent the following week with Karl Grunewald, learning about the Swedish organization of services and the controls over quality that were used.

In 1969, I wrote a paper entitled "Toward Independence" (Nirje, 1971) for the 11th World Congress of the International Society for Rehabilitation of the Disabled, in Dublin. There, I presented my own interpretation of "mental retardation"—the individual cognitive impairment, the learning deficiencies, and the awareness of the handicap—and applied it to the programs and living conditions on three levels of functioning. I had discussed my model for the definition of intellectual disability with Gunnar Kylén, who encouraged me to write about it. He had been the psychology expert in Grunewald's office and, on my initiative, he was now the research director of the ALA Foundation, which had been started by FUB to stimulate sheltered workshop developments. The programs for the three different levels were a simplified version of the views I had expressed in my recommendations for U.S. institutions. The paper, which started and ended with examples, explained that the aims of social training, adult education programs, and club and conference activities were to support adults who were striving for independence. This theme was later to be developed in greater detail in my paper "The Right to Self-Determination" (Nirje, 1972a).

This paper was written under very special circumstances. At the same time as the Dublin congress, a symposium on institutions was being held in Frankfurt, Germany, organized by the International League. I had been invited to speak at the symposium but it was decided that I should not go to Frankfurt. Instead, a

parent would attend, and I could go to Dublin. At the last minute, the parent chosen got cold feet, so I was ordered to go to Frankfurt and to cancel Dublin. This sudden decision complicated things for me, for, as I usually did, I had made some notes and mulled over my presentation in my mind. Right after I was told of the decision, I biked to my office, angry and upset, and started at 5:00 p.m. to write. At 5:00 a.m. the next morning, I left the manuscript at a hotel near the bus for the airport, where a person headed for the Dublin congress picked it up. She was allowed to read it in my stead. I was happy with the result, but the circumstances of writing were certainly not those one would wish for.

I flew to Frankfurt, for a rather miserable symposium experience. The first session dealt with the Normalization principle. In a surprise move, I was appointed secretary of the session, but after a while I was told that secretaries were not allowed to take part in the discussions. One of the German participants, who was highly agitated, burst out that Nirje's principle meant that the most disabled should live at the bottom of society, *"mit die Dieben und Huren!"*—with the thieves and whores! At this point, Bank-Mikkelsen had had enough and, in no uncertain terms, demanded that I should be allowed to take part in the discussions about my own ideas! Alas, the symposium did not measure up to *Changing Patterns*.

14 CRISIS

The events around the two international conferences were additional indicators that the mood within FUB was changing. There was no longer the same enthusiasm regarding small, local programs, because these had now been handed over to the proper authorities. Instead, there were all these new programs for young people: clubs, adult education organizations, and sports clubs, and the need to find voluntary helpers for all of these endeavors. The new law also brought about changes in residential programs, and not everybody was happy with these. They did not know if the new system would work and guarantee quality care. Could the new types of group homes really be as good as the rather recently built, nice institutions? Voices against these developments were now heard from new board members. Some thought that international relations were now of less importance because they felt that we had less to learn and were spending more and more time assisting with developments in other countries. As we had grown in numbers and responsibilities, I had recommended changes in the operation of our office. Those changes were desired by a majority of the staff but were not popular with a majority of the board.

My job required a lot of travel, to local or county associations or to courses and conferences around the country. On my return, there were often new problems and irritations in the office. All in all, the atmosphere had changed, and too often the mood was negative. Moreover, I was the ombudsman, and I believed that the association was a spokesperson for all intellectually disabled persons, whether their parents were members or not and irrespective of where they lived, be it in institutions or in the community. We should act and speak on behalf of those who were blind, had cerebral palsy, were deaf, were multidisabled or mildly disabled. There were other groups defending the institutions who, in advancing economic reasons that they hoped slow-moving county boards would support, wanted to decrease the pressure for deinstitutionalization. Not everyone appreciated the new attention given to young disabled adults who, more and more frequently, were being interviewed in the newspapers and receiving more space and attention than parents. And, not least, FUB was a parent association; it was the parents who should be heard, and I was not a parent.

Thus, at the 1970 biannual general assembly, in Malmö, the more negative voices elected more representatives to the board and the executive committee. The chairman was made executive director as well, in effect replacing me. Earlier, two staff members had moved to a lawyer's office to concentrate on legal matters, and the chairman took on the responsibility of coordinating what were now two branches. While this was going on, a three-day conference for 50 intellectually disabled young people—one man and one woman for each of the 24 counties, and two Danish guests—worked out the statements that I eventually presented at the end of the chapter "The Right to Self-Determination" (Nirje, 1972a). I was unable to attend this conference, as I was tied up with the general assembly. The youth conference attracted far more newspaper coverage than our routine general assembly.

A few weeks later, the board held a meeting, mainly to discuss a response to the youth conference. It quickly developed into a stormy meeting, where the apparently well-prepared negative voices expressed their dislike and distrust of the program and the proceedings. They did not trust the results, stating that the disabled could not have come to these conclusions by themselves, but that they must have been instructed and directed. They concluded that such programs had to be controlled by the parents—of course, none of the persons speaking were parents of the conference participants. At the end, the two young women who had been in charge of organizing this perfectly arranged conference rushed out of the meeting in tears.

This new backlash was hurting. Afterward, I heard I was a danger to the intellectually disabled: "Nirje teaches them that they can think!" Others repeated that I was not a parent and too radical, "even worse than Karl Grunewald!" Some days later, by misfortune—or good fortune—I happened to overhear the chairman, from the telephone in my office, inform someone that "Nirje's Normalization principle is his private idea and not the line of FUB" and that the youth activities should be controlled by parents. The chairman added that he was not worried that I might leave, "now he knows nothing else." Shocked, I took a long walk and, upon my return, asked for a luncheon appointment with the chairman. When all I got were vague and evasive answers, not in keeping with what I had overheard, I made up my mind. There was no basis for confidence left.

Over the weekend before midsummer in 1970, I cleared out my desk and wrote a letter of resignation to the board members, quoting from the views expressed by the chairman in our conversation but not mentioning the words I had overheard. I then left the office for good. I felt it would only be conflictual if I stayed. My role had become impossible and compromised. It was a traumatic experience, but necessary. Had I stayed, I might have had to contribute to harming disabled persons. Now the association had to face issues without my advice. Now they were free, but so was I. And without a job.

15 A NEW START

It would be a year and a week before I would start a new job. To begin with, I had a lot of unused vacation time, which was needed. As luck would have it, the World Games for the disabled were scheduled to be held in St. Etienne, France, during the second week of my newfound free time, and I had been appointed "chef de mission." Because we were now members of the Swedish Sports Federation, we were allowed, for the first time, to wear the national colors. About 50 of us, paraplegic, amputee, and blind athletes and leaders, were flown down on an air force Hercules. The team was quite successful, which boded well for the future. But we also became aware of all the problems involved with different national approaches to the classification and interpretation of impairments. Without a proper and adhered-to classification system, the basic sporting goal of competition with fair play and on equal conditions is, at best, very difficult. There was much work to be done during the coming years. But we flew back with 13 gold medals and a strong team spirit, which continued through the years.

In August 1970, the 3rd Congress of the International Association for the Scientific Study of Mental Deficiency (IASSMD) was held in Warsaw, Poland, and Karl Grunewald and I drove down together. Poland felt like an occupied country, which was quite appropriate, given my mood. Gunnar Dybwad had advised me to speak to a Dr. Zarfas from Canada, who was interested in hiring people, but I felt too tired and dejected to try to find him. I spent most of the time with the architecture group around Bank-Mikkelsen and Arnold Gangnes, from Seattle. In April, I had been invited to speak at the annual meeting of the British Parents Association and, on the ferry back to Sweden, Herbert Gunzburg, editor of the *British Journal of Mental Subnormality,* engaged me in a long conversation that ended with my promising to write a paper on the Normalization principle and how it applied to profoundly and severely disabled persons.

In order to do a good job on this paper, I went to the special state hospital, Vipeholm, in Lund, where I worked as a ward attendant's assistant with the most disabled and self-injuring residents. Here I met Ingrid Liljeroth, who led a small ADL-training program for persons who had been brought out from the wards and who were living in single rooms, with varied schedules and one-to-one support relationships. This pioneering program opened the way for more positive services in the field. It would also help me explain, later on, how things could be done to assist profoundly disabled persons to have a normal day, a normal week, and a normal year. I was thus able to write my paper, which included part of "Toward Independence." It was called "The Normalization Principle: Implications and Comments" (Nirje, 1970). Thus, the principle became known in the British Commonwealth, and here and there around the world.

Jerry Walsh knew of my predicament and thought that I could be put to some use. He made an agreement with his Wisconsin colleagues, Merlen Kurth and Harvey Stevens, the state commissioner for mental retardation, that Wisconsin could have me for three weeks and Minnesota for one, thus reversing the 1967 arrangement. So, in November 1970, I happily left for the States, with new photos added to my presentation, such that the photos could now be chosen to fit the interests of the various audiences. I also had special presentations for social training, leisure-time activities, parliamentary-technique courses, and conferences for young adults, which could include demonstrations of my "attitude-changing machine." The theme of these different presentations was the importance of the right to self-determination for persons with intellectual disabilities.

In Wisconsin, I spent a few days at each of the three large "colonies"—institutions for more than a thousand persons—visiting wards and programs and lecturing to group after group of staff and administrators. I also visited all 10 Wisconsin regions, to talk to the local parent associations. Then, by automobile, I did a quick tour of Indiana, and then went on to Seattle, Washington, and Arnold Gangnes', for a New Year's celebration. Some parents from Vancouver flew in to one of my lectures and insisted that I come with them, which I did. I very much liked my first taste of Canada.

Then it was on to Nebraska and ENCOR, where I found a worn and tired Wolf Wolfensberger. I returned to Wisconsin and then to Pennsylvania, with one request after another coming in through Jerry Walsh. I now enjoyed my lecturing. I always spoke without a manuscript from a list of points, gradually polishing formulations and angles. I especially liked the question-and-answer periods, in which concerns and problems were expressed. These experiences and lectures became the context and build-up for papers later written in Canada.

I had yet to meet Allan Roeher, but I got an invitation to speak at his National Institute for Mental Retardation (now the G. Allan Roeher Institute) in Toronto and to meet Don Zarfas. I was later given to understand that it was Rosemary Dybwad who had insisted that I go there. After the lectures at the institute, I was invited to stay with Don Zarfas and visit some institutions, to talk about these and to talk with the staff. After a few days, on the way from the showplace institutions—the Children's Psychiatric Research Institute (CPRI) in London, Ontario, and Palmerstone—to the old large institution in Orillia—I was asked if I would consider a position on Don Zarfas's staff. I liked what I had seen so far. I asked to see the worst and the best, which I did. I also spent a few days with his two assistants, one responsible for staff development and the other for community relations. My task would be to coordinate training and program development for Ontario institutions, where about 11,000 persons lived, with the two largest housing over 2,500 residents each. My participation was also wanted in preparing the changes needed so that people could move into the community and in giving lectures in the staff-development programs. I had seen much worse scenes in U.S. institutions, and I liked the positive atmosphere and the desire for change. At the end of the week, I accepted. I phoned home and said I had a job in Canada.

On the way home, I was invited to give a few lectures at Syracuse University and at last had the pleasure of meeting Burton Blatt. It was March 1971, and I had been away for almost four months. On July 1, I started work at the Mental Retardation Services Branch in the Mental Health Division of the Ministry of Health of the Government of Ontario. I, who had tried in many ways to demonstrate how wrong institutions were, was now partly responsible for them! But there were people in them who badly needed training programs, evacuation plans, and preparatory planning for obtaining new kinds of services in the community. Later, I would be shocked by the cold attitude some people took toward the persons left in the institutions, in advocating that all the money go to programs run by nongovernmental agencies in the community.

So, I left Sweden and cannot be blamed for the developments that took place there. In what ways my Normalization principle had anything to do with these is not for me to say, for I do not know. What might I have accomplished had I stayed on as ombudsman and gone on as before? I know for sure that there were four things that I would have attempted to do: (a) provide training, to strengthen the capacity of the county associations to tackle the planning required by the new law; (b) promote coordination between pedagogical developments in adult education in the Folk High Schools with those taking place in adult education organizations, foster the development of easy reading materials, and stimulate pedagogical research at the ALA Foundation, thereby unifying efforts to strengthen the social life opportunities of the adult disabled; (c) clarify that the Normalization principle covered all disabled persons and their right to self-determination and expressed a perspective on rehabilitation; and (d) develop cooperation between the Handicap Sports Association, other relevant sport associations, and handicap organizations, in line with principles that I had included in the constitution of the association.

Be that as it may, I left Sweden—for good, I thought—and the only link left was the Handicap Sports Association. They had nominated me for a position on the board of the International Sports Organization for the Disabled (ISOD). Throughout my years in Canada, they took on the extra cost for my attendance at meetings two or three times a year, mostly in Stoke-Mandeville, England. During the following decade, considerable changes were to take place, most of which were positive, and it was a pleasure to be an instrumental part in the struggles to come. There, at least, I was not alone.

16 IN CANADA

The same week I started work at the Ontario Ministry of Health, Walter B. Williston, a prominent lawyer and a dynamo, began a six-week investigation that resulted in his report *Present Arrangements for the Care and Supervision of Mentally Retarded Persons in Ontario* (Williston, 1971). The previous spring, two young men from a large institution in Smiths Falls,

Ontario, housing 3,000 persons, had escaped from the farms where they had been placed. One had hung himself and the other, who had been lost, was found with severe frostbite. The minister had given Williston the task of carrying out a complete legal analysis of the whole service system and of making recommendations. Williston and his office worked with extraordinary speed and thoroughness. Don Zarfas, Connie Hawley (my colleague responsible for community relations), and I worked closely with Williston. With him, I visited institutions and explained my views of them. I made him familiar with some important new literature, including *Changing Patterns,* the work of Edgerton, Tizard, and Blatt, the symposium reports of the International League, and the new Swedish legislation and ways of operating. It felt good to be in the right place at the right time again.

The Williston (1971) report catalogued institutional failings and demonstrated the lack of coordination among existing community services. It also showed the lack of coherence and efficiency among the responsibilities of the many ministries involved in financing and overseeing the numerous pieces of legislation involved. The report brought about important changes that renewed the Ontario approach. It was followed by two additional government ministry reports, with recommendations for step-by-step changes that led to the transfer of all mental retardation services to the Ministry of Community and Social Services.

These were years filled with rapid changes, new initiatives, and new resources. In the autumn of 1974, under David McCoy, some of us, including John Webster, Burt Perrin, and I, worked on a plan to establish a detailed compendium of social services. It listed types of accommodation, occupational opportunities, family-support options, leisure-time activities, day-care options, and "adult protective service workers" who were each to assist no more than 40 disabled persons in the community. This compendium eventually became known as *The Blue Book,* and in March 1975, it was accepted by the legislature of Ontario.

In September 1971, a few months into my new job, I had the pleasure of personally welcoming Elliot Avedon to Waterloo, Ontario, and Wolf Wolfensberger to Toronto. Wolf told me that he was writing and editing a book and asked me to write about my ideas

on social training and adult education. This became a chapter, "The Right to Self-Determination" (Nirje, 1972a), in Wolfensberger's (1972) book on Normalization. It took some time before I started to realize that my concept—which had been written with many cultures in mind and had been published in an official U.S. publication, in plain English—had been "Americanized" and slightly twisted by Wolf. Over the years, this became somewhat embarrassing, especially when some of his students, who had been unaware that it happened to be in the audience, objected to my correcting their glaring mistakes and misunderstandings!

At the 1972 Montreal Congress of the International League, I presented some of the things I had been stressing in my lectures in the USA and Canada. My presentation was entitled "Application of the Normalization Principle: Comments on Functional Planning and Integration" (Nirje, 1972b). "A funny thing happened," as the saying goes, at the Montreal congress. The rather large room for the session where I presented my paper was overflowing, with people standing along the walls and sitting on the floor. Right in front of me, in the very first row on the floor, sat Niels Erik Bank-Mikkelsen. After the presentation, I saw a beanstalk of a man rise from the floor in the back and, with giant steps, climb over the people in the aisle, including a surprised Niels Erik. A whisper went through the room, a whisper I could not make out. The man put his elbows on the edges of the lectern, his head in his hands, his eyes staring straight into mine: "But, Dr. Nirje, if the world is not normal, what then?" I swallowed and said something like, "wherever we are, a day starts, a week goes by, the years pass," and then, grabbing for Hemingway, I added, "'and the sun also rises'!" "Oh," he said, "now I see: You are a poet too!" Thus I met for the first time the remarkable Jean Vanier. It was indeed a pleasure to talk with him and assist him on a later occasion, even though we came from different directions.

At the Ministry of Health, and later at the Ministry of Community and Social Services, I had my papers distributed to colleagues, personnel in training, institutional staff, and staff in district offices. In 1976, I was asked to contribute to the bicentennial issue of a new version of *Changing Patterns* for the President's Committee on Mental Retardation. They wanted my paper on the Normalization principle brought up to date, so I included parts from the paper published in the *British Journal of Mental Subnormality* (Nirje, 1970), from "Toward Independence" (Nirje, 1971), and from the Montreal presentation (1972b), with some additions, updates, and clarifications. This paper (Nirje, 1976), with some revisions, including a new appendix entitled "On Integration," was reprinted (Nirje, 1980) in Flynn and Nitsch's (1980) book *Normalization, Social Integration and Community Services.* In a way, this closed a circle. The additions to the original papers were done. What came later were perspectives on the principle from various angles and its relation to basic ideas on ethics.

It was stimulating to work with the new people and the new opportunities in the districts around the large province of Ontario. But there were frustrations, as the "higher ups" seemed to have cold feet in the face of the dynamic developments and program demands in the districts, where people did not hesitate to go to the parliamentary representatives to get what they wanted, which was not, however, always related to the proper priorities.

In 1978, for personal reasons, I returned to Sweden. It was possibly a mistake, as Sweden had changed in ways that I did not at first appreciate. I became a Care director in Uppsala county and found myself tied to an already existing five-year plan that I did not feel met the requirements of the law. In 1983, a heart operation forced me to leave this position which, in a sense, took care of these problems. In 1985, I became associated, on a part-time basis, with the development of the Uppsala University Centre for Handicap Research. I returned to Toronto for the 1982 International Association for the Scientific Study of Mental Deficiency (IASSMD) Congress where, with the Uppsala group, I presented "The Basis and Logic of the Normalization Principle" (Nirje, 1985). This paper describes the relationship of the principle to scientific theories in the fields of ethics and anthropology. It also presents my basic criticism of what I have called "the Wolfensberger fallacy." With Burt Perrin, I coauthored the paper "Setting the Record Straight: A Critique of Some Frequent Misconceptions of the Normalization Principle" (Perrin & Nirje, 1985). The first part, of which I was the principal author, deals with eight frequent misunderstandings. The second part, of which Burt Perrin was the main author, consists primarily of criticisms of some of Wolfensberger's statements.

17 CONCLUSION

In the 1980s and 1990s, the Normalization principle has frequently been quoted in scientific studies, almost around the world. I have had the pleasure of invitations to Australia, India, Belgium, Germany, Switzerland, Finland, and Japan, and of return visits to the USA and Canada. In 1992, a collection of my papers and articles entitled *The Normalization Principle Papers* (Nirje, 1992) was published by the Centre for Handicap Research in Uppsala. In 1993, I wrote "The Normalization Principle: 25 years later" (Nirje, 1993) for the University of Jyväskylä, in Finland. It deals mainly with perspectives on services for adults, both the most and least severely impaired. It also takes up ethical issues and the relation of the principle to human rights. It was part of a larger project, aimed at renewing services for intellectually disabled adults in Finland. This year (1998) a five-year comparative study on the application of the Normalization principle in Sweden, Finland, and Japan will be completed. And just a few years ago, Gunnar Dybwad and Hank Bersani (1996) published *New Voices: Self-Advocacy by People with Disabilities,* which provided a forum for the voices of "intellectual" intellectually disabled persons from different parts of the world in the "People First" movement who expressed their right to self-determination.

In this lengthy exposé I have tried to point out the factors that led to the birth of an idea and the gradual construction of an instrument for analysis, which expressed a distinctive point of view. This point of view, I frankly think, tries to delineate in general and understandable terms the point of view of disabled people, wherever they might be. It articulates their demands for a normal day, a normal week, and a normal life in their communities. This concept I called the Normalization principle.

It seems as if this point of view, for more than a quarter-century now, has contributed to changes in views and policy direction. For example, institutions have gone from being seen as the normal and supposedly most efficient solution for dealing with the problems of mental retardation in society to being viewed as abnormal, as failing to improve, and even as worsening the situation of persons with intellectual impairments and disabilities. In the 1960s, did we ever hope that in the 1990s we would take this latter view and concomitant social developments for granted, with institutions even outlawed in some countries? Now, intellectually disabled persons hold international conferences to present their views and fortify their rights!

Obviously, I have reasons to feel cheerful about having been able to contribute to this new understanding, where the development of services for intellectually disabled persons now has less to do with national interests or financial priorities, religious creeds or beliefs, or political ideologies or prejudices. Today, services must be related to the demands for proper human development in the culture of a community where a child with an impairment is born, for now such a child is born with the same right to proper development as all other children in their community, society, and culture. Moreover, the child with an impairment has the right not to be exposed to but, on the contrary, to be protected from neglect and abuse, ignorance and superstition, and segregation and extinction. I hope that the Normalization principle will turn out to be a useful instrument for social development in large parts of the world where the number of children born in the future will be much greater than in Sweden, Europe or North America.

I wish to conclude with a quote from my Jyväskylä paper (Nirje, 1993, pp. 16-17):

The principle as instrument
The Normalization principle with its eight facets or components engenders concerns in several directions or dimensions and is useful in many ways and at many levels, as it may relate to separate individuals, families, staff, professionals, community services or the society at large.

The first level obviously serves the individual with intellectual disability, and can be used by persons responsible in any way for him or her . . . "as an instrument for determining that which is appropriate both for raising questions and for finding answers. It implies, when in doubt how to meet a problem, how to advise, how to plan actions, what to do: compare the situation for any person, for example for yourself, with that of the person with mental or other handicaps, then try to see what is

missing to possibly be able to determine what to do to shorten the gap between the two situations to let the handicapped person obtain the equivalent situation or one as close to it as possible. In that framework, we can use the following derivation: *the Normalization principle means that you act right when you let the handicapped person obtain the same, or as close as possible to the same, conditions of life as you would prefer if you were in his situation*" (Nirje, 1985; italics added).

On the second level, it serves the community as an instrument for the development or refinement of the educational and social services required and for an understanding of the needed training, support and cooperation of the various specialized staff. The principle helps in establishing goals and objectives, competencies and needs—both for the disabled persons and the staff.

The third level where the principle is useful is for the society as a whole, as shown by its use as one of the bases for legislation, for principal structures of services, and as an assist in providing a framework for laws, regulations and standards, even serving as an aid and guide in the work of the courts.

On a fourth level, the principle can also be seen as an instrument for understanding and analyzing—from a legislative, social, sociological, or anthropological point of view—the changes gradually taking place in the patterns of culture or conditions of life affecting not only persons with intellectual or other disabilities or other disabled, but also other groups in the society, such as immigrants, minorities, victims of crime, the elderly, etc. The principle as such is not culture-specific; but, being universal, is useful in any society, at any time, as a tool for description and evaluation. It can serve as a screen for the delineation and analysis of the social conditions of the intellectually disabled in Denmark or India, in Chile or China, in Germany (of the 1930s or today) or the USA, in Tokyo or Timbuktu, or in Outokumpu. (pp. 16-17)

Or, for that matter, it can be used in Ottawa at this conference on "Twenty-Five years of Normalization, Social Role Valorization and Social Integration," in the province where, some years ago, I myself stimulated our regional and district staff of the Ministry of Community and Social Services to properly apply the principle. It has been indeed nice to be back!

REFERENCES

AVEDON, E. M. (1967). Therapeutic recreation service and mentally retarded adolescents. In Israel Association for Rehabilitation of the Mentally Handicapped (AKIM), *The Adolescent Retardate* (pp. 9-11). Symposium conducted at the meeting of the 1st Congress of the International Association for the Scientific Study of Mental Deficiency, Montpellier, France (September 12-20).

BENEDICT, R. (1934). *Patterns of culture*. Boston: Houghton Mifflin.

BLATT, B., & KAPLAN, F. (1967). *Christmas in purgatory*. Boston: Allyn & Bacon.

CHIGIER, E. (1967). The use of group dynamics in the rehabilitation of severely retarded adolescents in an institution in Israel. In Israel Association for Rehabilitation of the Mentally Handicapped (AKIM), *The Adolescent Retardate* (pp. 1-4). Symposium conducted at the meeting of the 1st Congress of the International Association for the Scientific Study of Mental Deficiency, Montpellier, France (September 12-20).

COBB, H. V. (1967). The attitude of the retarded person towards himself. In International League of Societies for the Mentally Handicapped, *Stress on families of the mentally handicapped* (pp 62-74). Brussells: ILSMH.

DYBWAD, G., & BERSANI, H., JR. (1996). *New voices: Self-advocacy by people with disabilities.* Cambridge, MA: Brookline Books.

FLYNN, R. J., & NITSCH, K. E. (Eds.). (1980). *Normalization, social integration, and community services*. Baltimore, MD: University Park Press.

MINNESOTA ARC. (1967a). *Newsletter*.

MINNESOTA ARC. (1967b). *Newsletter*.

NIRJE, B. (1967). Integrational know-how: Swedish programs in social training. In Israel Association for Rehabilitation of the Mentally Handicapped (AKIM), *The Adolescent Retardate* (pp. 5-8). Symposium conducted at the meeting of the 1st Congress of the International Association for the Scientific Study of Mental Deficiency, Montpellier, France (September 12-20).

NIRJE, B. (1969a). A Scandinavian visitor looks at US institutions. In R. B. KUGEL & W. WOLFENSBERGER (Eds.), *Changing patterns in residential services for the mentally retarded* (pp. 51-57). Washington, DC: President's Committee on Mental Retardation.

NIRJE, B. (1969b). The Normalization principle and its human management implications. In R. B. KUGEL & W. WOLFENSBERGER (Eds.), *Changing patterns in residential services for the mentally retarded* (pp. 179-195). Washington, DC: President's Committee on Mental Retardation.

NIRJE, B. (1970). The Normalization principle: Implications and comments. *British Journal of Mental Subnormality, 16,* 62-70.

NIRJE, B. (1971). Toward independence: The Normalization principle in Sweden. *Déficience Mentale/Mental Retardation, 21,* 2-7.

NIRJE, B. (1972a). The right to self-determination. In W. WOLFENSBERGER, *The principle of Normalization in human services.* Toronto: National Institute on Mental Retardation.

NIRJE, B. (1972b). Application of the Normalization principle: Comments on functional planning and integration. Paper presented at the meeting of the 5th International Congress on Mental Retardation, International League of Societies for the Mentally Handicapped, Montreal (October).

NIRJE, B. (1973). The Normalization principle: Implications and comments. In H. C. GUNZBURG (Ed.), *Advances in the care of the mentally handicapped.* London: Bailliere, Tyndall, Cox.

NIRJE, B. (1976). The Normalization principle. In R. KUGEL & A. SHEARER (Eds.), *Changing patterns in residential services for the mentally retarded* (Rev. ed.) (DHEW No. (OHD) 76-21015). Washington, DC: President's Committee on Mental Retardation.

NIRJE, B. (1980). The Normalization principle. In R. J. FLYNN & K. E. NITSCH (Eds.), *Normalization, social integration, and community services* (pp. 31-49). Baltimore, MD: University Park Press.

NIRJE, B. (1985). Basis and logic of the Normalization principle. *Australia and New Zealand Journal of Developmental Disabilities, 11,* 65-68.

NIRJE, B. (1992). *The Normalization principle papers.* Uppsala, Sweden: Centre for Handicap Research, Uppsala University.

NIRJE, B. (1993). The Normalization principle: 25 years later. In U. LEHTINEN & R. PIRTTIMAA (Eds.), *Arjessa tapahtuu. Comments on mental retardation and adult education.* Finland: The Institute for Educational Research, University of Jyväskylä.

PERRIN, B., & NIRJE, B. (1985). Setting the record straight: A critique of some frequent misconceptions of the Normalization principle. *Australia and New Zealand Journal of Developmental Disabilities, 11*(2), 69-74.

WESSMAN, L. (1966). *After Special School.* Swedish Board of Education.

WILLISTON, W. B. (1971). *Present arrangements for the care and supervision of mentally retarded persons in Ontario.* Toronto: Government of Ontario, Queen's Printer.

WOLFENSBERGER, W. (1972). *The principle of Normalization in human services.* Toronto: National Institute on Mental Retardation.

Appendix

OUTLINE FOR A PLAN TO ATTACK INHUMAN CONDITIONS IN THE UNITED STATES' INSTITUTIONS FOR THE MENTALLY RETARDED

The following outline has divided the contents of the plan into four sections, which are inter-dependent. The first part indicates presentations of present conditions, the foundations of a criticism of the negative factors. Section two completes the criticism, stressing the positive factors that can help in making change possible. The third section tries to demonstrate the practical aims of the attack, indicating the direction to move. The fourth section gives the rationale for the aims outlined in section three and the criticism of sections one and two. In each section, only headlines are given and they have to be filled out by special study groups. The angles in the four sections are inter-dependent.

I   To stress the dehumanizing situation in the back wards, the following points are presented:
    A.   Summary survey of all the scientific studies on the damage caused to the individual by institutionalization; the main findings should be presented in an authoritative way.
    B.   The point should be made that the dehumanizing conditions in institutions represent an imposed poverty and cultural deprivation, imposed by society with taxpayers' money.
    C.   The lack of personnel and of trained personnel, and what it means for the individual mentally retarded ought to be dramatized.
    D.   Defeat of the medical profession and the experts must be shown. The work for the mentally retarded must come out from under the authorities on mental health. The main task for the medical profession in this field is as experts in habilitation.
    E.   A condensed version of Mr. Allen's comparative study on US legislation on mental retardation should be made, and the lack of teeth in the laws should be dramatized.
    F.   The general difficulty in presenting the facts of life in the back wards to the general public must be pointed out. The difficulties in taking photos, making films, etc., preserve the general ignorance, assist the lack of concern, keep prejudices alive, and enforce the segregation, fears and anxiety.

II   A critical survey of the factors in the present status that are of promise and can form a basis from which to start a new development.
    A.   The concern of the parents—not only in the US but all over the world. The symposium arranged by the International League of Societies for the Mentally Handicapped in Stockholm, June 1967, on the legal aspects of mental retardation and the human rights of the mentally retarded contains a series of recommendations and statements with a strong bearing on institutional standards and programs.
    B.   Existing good programs in the US, probably most to be found in private institutions, should be selected and presented, possibly also descriptions of programs and principles in some other countries.
    C.   Good staff training programs and their aims should be presented. It should also be stressed that the trained personnel have small chances to implement their education in the back wards, where the sheer numbers and the unsuitable facilities defeat their creative efforts.

D. It should be stressed that professional experience that is modern and of high quality exists in the USA, and that more attention should be given to these experts. From the Allen study should be found that which he states as offering the most promise for an attack that can lead to practical results and give a reasonable hope for change.

E. NARC has to recommend a realistic legislative model that places the responsibility for institutions as close to the people as possible.

F. The mentally retarded's right to a pension or minimum salary should be pushed with all energy. With the help of the retarded's own guaranteed income, the financing and the development of proper and worthwhile institutions gets a firmer basis.

III   The present dehumanizing conditions in the large wards of the big institutions; new facilities and new and more human environments—more conducive to the personal development of each single individual, to efficiency in educational efforts, and to realistic social integration—are created. To create humanizing facilities means to arrange them as close to the patterns and standards of regular home and school life as possible. These aims can be obtained through decentralization, differentiation and specialization. A prerequisite to eradicate the bad conditions in the back wards is a creation of new homes, schools and institutions to move the majority of the retarded to. Thereafter, the facilities in large institutions can be rearranged for a much lesser number than at present, who can profit from the rearranged facilities to better advantage.

A. Children should never be in large institutions or in institutions with retarded adults. For the children are needed: special hospitals for the profoundly retarded and for the severely and moderately retarded with multiple handicaps or complications; care homes—fairly close to a good hospital—with a home-like atmosphere and setting for the severely and moderately retarded, equipped with adequate educational and ADL training facilities. Consequently, the aim is to take small children out of large institutions.

B. School age children: The moderately and mildly retarded must have special schools and live in boarding homes and student hostels. School education has to be given in a regular setting, never in the framework of a large institution. The aim is consequently to take the special school children out from the institutions.

C. Adults who are mildly and moderately retarded and can work in the open market or in workshops shall be given hostels or smaller care homes, with suitable social training programs. They shall live in as normal a setting as possible, never in the framework of a large institution. The aim is consequently to take this large group out of institutions.

D. Some severely and moderately retarded with no important complications, but who cannot work in sheltered workshops, should be given smaller care homes with industrial therapy facilities. Thus, they will be able to live more close to their own homes. Consequently, the aims are to move a large group of this category out of institutions.

E. Adults who are profoundly retarded and severely or moderately retarded with multiple handicaps or complications should be given suitable special hospitals with adequate treatment and training facilities. Existing institutions could be rebuilt to suit the demands of these groups by using the wards for 80 to 100 people at present, for 15 to 20 in the near future. The aims are consequently to rearrange the present institutions to serve mainly for this category.

F. Old age! Some of the old retarded might with advantage be given the opportunity to move to smaller care homes, but some might be more at home in familiar surroundings and can stay in current institutions, which can be rebuilt into smaller home units. Consequently, the aim is to re-create the existing facilities to serve certain parts of this category.

IV   The rationale for the aims and recommendations made in the previous parts.
    A.   All environments and programs have to be created with regard to the psychological requirements of the individual. A survey of the basic demands in this respect from the psychological experts ought to be made. Of special interest is a study by Henry Cobb on the retarded person's attitude towards himself, a paper published in the proceedings of the Congress of the International League in Paris, 1966.
    B.   The specific educational requirements of the mentally retarded should be stressed:
        1) Special school and training school standards.
        2) The additional requirement of ADL, social training and leisure time activities.
        3) Education for mentally retarded takes place not only under 1 and 2 above, but also in the boarding home, which consequently has to have a setting as close to a regular home as possible.
    C.   The social integration aspects must be kept in the foreground:
        1) Homes, hospitals and institutions should be placed as close to the community as possible or preferably within the community and never be larger than the developments of natural inter-relations realistically will permit.
        2) The architecture and facilities within a home or institution should permit good patterns of social life within the institution.
        3) The programs of institutions shall contain many points of contact with life outside the institution.
        4) For some of the retarded the programs should aim at preparing and assisting them for a life outside the institution.
    D.   Mainly irrespective of the degree of the handicap, the programs for the mentally retarded should aim to give them possibilities to achieve more independence, to experience more individual dignity and regard and to obtain more self-confidence. The programs should feed them more of the normal motivations of regular human life and be more attentive to their own wishes and demands.

V   With the points made in sections I and IV above, the following tentative recommendations are made:
    1) Coincidental with the publication of the President's Panel Study on Institutional Conditions, a first class TV documentary ought to be shown, contrasting present conditions with examples of good programs.
    2) The idea of creating a NARC Robert F. Kennedy fund for human rights in institutions for the mentally retarded should be taken into consideration.
    3) A national public conference of experts and parent representatives could be arranged, concentrating on the following issues:
       -   Why has all the scientific research on institutional damage not been a cause for positive action?
       -   Why has the medical profession been defeated in this field?
       -   Why have the voices of the modern experts not been listened to?
    4) The conclusions of the Allen paper should be dramatized with a NARC proposal for model legislation.
    5) The meaning of the lack of personnel for the life and development of a child in a large back ward should be dramatized. The ignorance and lack of concern of society show themselves through the lack of effort to provide personnel, who could give the mentally retarded the personal attention and concern needed.
    6) The positive practical aspects of sections III and IV should be dramatized by presenting the possibilities for individual development of the mentally retarded. A positive appreciation of the mentally retarded is a prerequisite for changing the image of the retarded in the eyes and minds of the general public, which precedes a willingness to positive action.

Bengt Nirje
June 12, 1968

3

A contribution to the history of Normalization, with primary emphasis on the establishment of Normalization in North America between 1967-1975[1]

WOLF WOLFENSBERGER

1 INTRODUCTION

In recent years, there have been many references in the literature to the early days of Normalization where the authors cited references that were not from the founding period, but secondary or retrospective ones from the 1980s. Among the reasons people cite post-1980 literature when discussing events that occurred up to 20 years earlier appear to be four: (a) they were not on the scene at the time; (b) they do not know the primary literature (perhaps the computer bases that were consulted did not go back far enough); (c) if they do know it, they do not have ready access to it; and (d) they prefer recent revisionist ideas to the historical truth, and therefore avoid the original literature.

So I went to my extensive personal archives and drew on these for this presentation. In fact, this was the first time that I methodically mined my relevant archives from the 1960s and 1970s for Normalization material. Historical revisionists may commence quaking in their boots because I can now cite genuine original sources and prove many of the points I will make.

The material will be presented in distinct sections, roughly chronologically, but with some overlap between time periods. In tracing the history of Normalization and Social Role Valorization (SRV), I will try to minimize—as much as is practical—overlap with earlier writings on that topic and emphasize new material instead. Therefore, because this congress observes the 25th anniversary of the appearance of the monograph *Changing Patterns in Residential Services for the Mentally Retarded* (Kugel & Wolfensberger, 1969), I decided to devote a disproportionate amount of material to it and treat several other historical elements in much more condensed fashion.

2 IDEAS AND SCHEMES THAT WERE WIDELY PROMOTED AS MAJOR ANSWERS IN HUMAN SERVICES, AND/OR FOR THE CONDITIONS ADDRESSED BY THESE, PRIOR TO THE ADVENT OF NORMALIZATION AND/OR SHORTLY AFTER IT, AND SOME IN COMPETITION WITH IT

In this section, I want to take a look at what the conceptual landscape in human services was like in the years or decades prior to the advent of Normalization, and to some degree overlapping with it, with selected emphasis on services close to the mental retardation field. More specifically, I will try to reconstruct the conceptual schemes that were viewed by many people as broad in scope, or as high-order foundations for major sectors of human service, or for social change as it related to those human problems that human services addressed, at least somewhat comparable to the way some of us have viewed Normalization and SRV since their advent. Some of these schemes were very much alive around 1970 and were dangerous competitors with Normalization.

Of course, literally billions of people during the last century thought that Marxist arrangements would bring about something close to a paradise on earth, since a huge number of problems were seen to be no more than the fruits of economic and power inequalities, capitalism, and other ills for which Marxism claimed to have remedies. Today, materialistic social theories that assiduously try to avoid the idiom of Marxism but that are otherwise nearly identical to it have taken the place of Marxism in many intellectual and academic circles, and among people who formerly were professed Marxists but are now too embarrassed to admit it because of the recent ignominious downfall of communist regimes and economies worldwide.

For several decades, eugenic measures were seen as the most overarching package of solutions to social problems, and to many clinical and personal ones. This included a massive program of institutionalization, with specialized institutions erected for a large variety of afflicted people—those with leprosy, venereal diseases, TB, blindness, deafness, epilepsy, physical impairments, mental disorder, mental retardation; as well as for the inebriated, juvenile delinquents, orphans, elderly, and paupers—to say nothing of less numerous very esoteric institutions, such as the Home for Jewish Friendless and Working Girls in Chicago in the early 1900s (*Twentieth Biennial Report of the Board of State Commissioners of Public Charities of Illinois*, 1909) or the Home of the New York Society for the Relief of the Ruptured and Crippled.

The poverty of service conceptualization was such that even when the social alarm associated with eugenics had been heavily discredited by about 1930, institutionalism barreled right on for another 30 years in what I characterized in 1969 as "momentum without rationale" (Wolfensberger, 1969a). As I will emphasize repeatedly, there was also very little critique of institutionalism prior to about 1965. Almost everybody was willing to say that this or that could be better about institutions, but one will not be likely to find much in the *professional* literature—at least not

from the human service sector—that said (a) that institutions were awful places, or even (b) that there was anything intrinsically defective about the very idea of large institutions. If there were people who believed these things, they were not afforded a forum to voice such thoughts. What published critique there was of institutions came mostly from a few exposés, and mostly from outside the service system.

In response to both the terrible conditions in institutions of all sorts and to the fact that, nevertheless, waiting lists for them were normatively very large and long, a major reform concept for about 100 years was "more institutions" and "better institutions." After circa 1930, the cry for more institutional space was not so much motivated by eugenic reasons as it had been before, but simply to reduce overcrowding in existing institutions and to service the huge institutional waiting lists. After all, some institutions had more people on their waiting list than they had inmates.

What did people mean by "better institutions"? Above all, they meant less crowding, and reducing it was widely considered to be the single biggest key to improving institutional conditions. They also meant things such as smaller dormitories[2], smaller wards, more cleanliness, less ugliness in the environment, less stench, a better toilet-to-resident ratio, better educated attendants and a few more of them, a few more professional staff members, and fewer who were very deviant themselves, and for most residents, a small cabinet for keeping some personal clothes and perhaps a few other items. An institution that had even some of these was considered a model institution to which observers streamed in envious admiration.

By the 1950s, 1960s, and 1970s, "better institutions" also began to mean two more things: (a) smaller institutions with only a few hundred to a low thousand or so residents; and (b) more equitable distribution of institutions across a state or province, both for humane reasons and reasons of local economy.

One of the "better institution" concepts that captivated many minds and was seen as a major reform idea was the "therapeutic community" concept originated by Maxwell Jones after World War II (e.g., Jones, 1953). This concept spread to many other kinds of institutions and seemed to experience occasional reincarnations through similar schemes, such as so-called "remotivation" schemes in the 1960s and 1970s.

Many people looked to therapeutic community schemes as at least a major foundation of "good institutions." In one of my first published articles on Normalization, namely, the one for a psychiatric audience in 1970 (Wolfensberger, 1970b), I had to explain why and how Normalization was not the same as the "therapeutic community," and that we should quit invoking images of the medical model with "therapy" language and instead think in terms of a "normalizing community" (p. 296). The article was promptly reprinted by the Pennsylvania Association for Retarded Children, together with a statement that "we must begin to practice the *Normalization PRINCIPLE*," and widely disseminated over the state.

One idea that had many similarities to the "therapeutic community" but was inspired by different rationales was Project Re-Ed. Even though it was not of very broad scope or a high order, it is deserving of mention in this context because it had similarities with later Normalization developments. Project Re-Ed was launched in the US in 1961 with a $2 million grant, on the initiative of Nicholas Hobbs, later president of the American Psychological Association. Hobbs and other visitors to Europe had been very impressed by the functioning of a professional identity called, in French, *éducateur*, which was like a combination of the German *Heilpädagoge* (healing pedagogue) and traditional child governors and governesses, and they worked mostly with emotionally troubled children and in small residences. This model of service to such children had been developed in France after World War II in order to address a critical problem of child care created largely by the war. In Project Re-Ed, the equivalent of the *éducateurs* were to be young live-in teacher-counselors with training roughly corresponding to a master's degree. But, unfortunately, the project had more of a personnel identity as its special focus rather than a concept of what was needed for certain children, other than that the approach was to be "ecological." Also, it had a narrow focus on one particular class of children (i.e., those with mental problems) and mostly in a residential context. However, this model had enough parallels to Normalization that it is possible that Normalization would have been embraced as its overall service strategy if it had been available at the launching of the project. (See Hobbs [1966, 1983] and Linton [1969] for relevant literature.)

Even though Hobbs had been one of my professors, his work on Project Re-Ed had very little, if any, influence of which I am aware on the evolution of my thinking. One reason was that I was wrapped up in mental retardation, and, furthermore, I left Nashville, Tennessee—where Project Re-Ed was launched—just as it was being funded because my course work for my doctorate was completed. By the way, the Nashville Project Re-Ed was called Regional Intervention Project, hence RIP, which underlines how little consciousness people then had of image issues.

Vestiges of Project Re-Ed are still alive, but overall, the scheme did not catch on—in part undoubtedly because the mental field in the US is so clinically, ideologically, and morally bankrupt and has been intensely resistive to good things, and to anything resembling Normalization, in part probably because the things that work would delegitimize highly credentialed professional control over services and clients.

The antidehumanization and prodignity measures by David Vail, to be discussed later, were basically also a "better institution" scheme. Even among reformers in mental retardation, the "better institution" concept remained prominent until Normalization afforded an alternative vision, but the "better institution" concept has kept lingering, and still has many adherents. Vestiges of the idea of the "therapeutic community" still spook around in the mental field; and in aging specifically, the notion of "better institutions" (e.g., "better nursing homes") is even one of the dominant ideas today.

One idea pursued ever since the great founding period of American services in the mid-1800s was "more public funding" for all sorts of services, and that was the cry one heard all the time everywhere. But proposals about how more money would be used were always tied to whatever the prevailing program concept was, which often was bigger or better institutions.

During the 1940s and 1950s, many people looked on psychotherapy and personal counseling—and some on psychoanalysis specifically—as a major answer to problems of living. Many people really thought that individual problems of a psychic nature would yield to this service modality if only (a) enough therapists or counselors could be trained, and (b) the people with the problems would come to them. Obviously, some people still cling to this notion, as is evident from the extremely widely syndicated advice column of Ann Landers during recent decades, and to this day. The advent, and relatively sudden dissemination, of Rogerian counseling had much to do with this, because it was widely seen as both more readily learnable by more people than other forms of psychotherapy and as applicable to more situations and needs than the "heavy" psychotherapies, such as psychoanalytic ones.

A strategy that was perhaps the most broadly promoted one since World War II was a very vague construct of "attitude change." It probably had some of its roots in the social psychology developed in response to fascism, especially by refugee psychologists from Nazism. This body of theory and research had much to do with the so-called "authoritarian personality" and the development of mass prejudices. However, the ideas on how to overcome prejudices that we today would call social devaluations were very vague, and often outright naive. For instance, a major idea was that prejudice came out of ignorance, that ignorance gets dispelled by education, and that, therefore, prejudices by one collectivity about another are overcome by education. Out of this reasoning must have come the intense efforts to educate the public about mental disorder and mental retardation by means of tours of institutions, and such tours became very common in the 1950s and 1960s. Apparently totally unrecognized at that time was the fact that education by itself does not combat prejudice, and that contact with devalued persons or classes that is experienced as unpleasant is even apt to have an effect opposite to the desired one.

It was only in the 1970s that attitude change theories became more sophisticated, but we can still perceive vestiges of the old theories. In the public policy arena, one of the most prominent recent examples of false notions about attitude change has been the idea that racial barriers can be broken down by tedious cross-bussing of children in the school system, even though in many schools, the contact itself is largely negatively experienced, and the arrangement requires many children to get up hours earlier (often still in the dark) and spend hours on the bus every day—an imposition for which each group blames the other.

Before the advent of Normalization, and during its early days, behavior modification (which then was usually still known as operant conditioning) presented itself as a quasi-savior for certain groups, including the mentally retarded. Many films were made that tried to show what behavior modification could do, and some of the accomplishments in individual instances were impressive—even amazing. However, so many of these films were made in institutions, and displayed little sense of awareness—or none whatever—either of the badness of the institutional arrangements or that the clinical methods of behavior modification were a very displaced response to institutionalism. For example, the 1967 film "Operation Behavior Modification" failed to bring out the limitations of institutional environments even though these were quite obvious in the film. The 1970 film "Operant Conditioning: Token Economy" brought this point out even more drastically without any apparent awareness of this by the filmmakers (Sandoz Pharmaceutical Co.). Also, almost all these films displayed an appalling unconsciousness of image issues and quite unnecessarily interpreted retarded people in all sorts of negative ways.

One of the most threatening major potential competitors of comprehensive normalized community services was the idea of (hard to believe these days) the "comprehensive community services facility" into which many people in the 1950s and 1960s put much hope. In essence, this was a single building in which, and to a lesser degree from which, it was believed all or most needed services could be rendered to a service region. Such a facility would have components such as a children's day service center, a sheltered workshop, some residential units, soft services (such as assessment and guidance) rendered to people coming in on an "ambulatory" basis, some specialized "ambulatory" medical services, and offices for people who might go out and render limited services in the community, probably mostly consulting other services, plus a very modest amount of home visiting. Obviously, this idea was rooted in the then-prevailing medical model, and the idea of Louis XIV's *hôpital général* and its later offspring, the *Allgemeine Krankenhaus* (Foucault, 1973; Thompson & Goldin, 1975).

Comprehensiveness was thought by some people to require service centers where each center constituted an agency, while other people thought that colocation of different agencies in the same building on the same campus would do the trick.

One version of the comprehensive service center concept was the so-called neighborhood center scheme. It was seen as more of a generic nature than "comprehensive" mental health or mental retardation centers. Many people had the idea that with many services colocated in neighborhood centers, citizens would rarely have to go outside their neighborhoods to be served. This just underlines how naive people were as to what constitutes comprehensiveness.

Unfortunately, it is this idea that ensouled the ill-fated community mental health centers, and the so-called "university-affiliated facilities" in mental retardation all over the US that became (a) financial milch cows for universities, and especially medical schools, (b) major consumers of mental retardation funds, and (c) only relatively minor contributors to the welfare of retarded people. That this idea would win out over community services that were normalized, diversified, dispersed, and citizen-controlled was for years a distinct possibility and a major fear among people like myself.

The single biggest service related to mental retardation that such centers, and other center-based units, rendered was the hugely expensive and stereotyped multidisciplinary assessment of retarded people—mostly children. These assessments tended to have a strong neuropsychiatric slant, and to be rather meaningless dead ends because there was hardly ever any meaningful follow-up and hardly any other or new services which the assessed person would receive as the result of the assessment. Conceptual poverty and program nihilism in mental retardation specifically were such that into the late 1960s, some people used the term "service" (in a community context) when they meant no more than a multidisciplinary assessment of a retarded person. This was perhaps not surprising, considering that in many locales in the US, this kind of assessment was often the first service established for retarded people and remained the only one for years. I wrote an exposé of this scandal (Wolfensberger, 1965a, 1965b) and had the hardest time getting a brief version of it published in the US, and only in something like an opinion column.

Many people argued around 1965-1975 that the biggest problem was not lack of services but lack of coordination, or what came widely to be called "services integration." These were mostly harebrained—but extremely popular—schemes on which vast efforts were expended with hardly any payoff.

Aside from attitude change, all these schemes were either incredibly naive, or low-level, or both. Marxism was extremely high-level but also incredibly naive despite its vast number of adherents.

During the 1960s, one step ahead of Normalization, a movement gathered a great deal of momentum that was high-level and only medium naive, namely, a "rights" orientation. But there was always some fuzziness about whether people intended to invoke legal or transcendent rights, the latter often called "human rights" or "moral rights," and how the two should be linked. I remember promoting the idea in those days that *human* rights should be pursued, as being of a higher order and greater universality than legal rights.

The rights movement reflected at least some European influences, because the idea that certain services were a right rather than a privilege had long been established in the laws of several European countries, with additional such rights being defined in the mid-1960s, as exemplified by the Netherlands, Denmark, and West Germany (the latter in 1961).

In the US, Gunnar Dybwad played a very large role in this development, at least as far as the field of mental retardation was concerned. He promoted a rights orientation and judicial recourse for years, and all this work suddenly erupted into fruition with an avalanche of litigation in the late 1960s and early 1970s, most of it successful. In almost all the early cases, Dybwad was involved behind the scenes, exhorting and/or consulting.

The "rights" thinking first rested on two rationales. One was to finally achieve the old goal of "more money" by having certain services defined as a legal right. The second rationale was the removal of the social stigma that went with selective, arbitrary, or charitable funding. We now know that rightful funding does not necessarily accomplish this.

The early rights movement focused on one big goal, and several smaller ones. The big goal was *rightful* funding of schooling for handicapped children, but the movement might at first have settled for such funding for most rather than all children, and would certainly have settled for segregated education. Smaller goals included less compulsion in institutional settings, less compulsory drugging, and so forth.

In my opinion, the rights orientation would have had different, and less favorable, outcomes than it did if the lawyers had not begun to draw on the Normalization-related writings as soon as these came out. In fact, the lawyers often incorporated material from the Normalization-related literature within weeks or months after it appeared and used this material very well.

Altogether, if one had asked people active in mental retardation specifically during roughly the years of 1965-1968 what it is they wanted, one would generally have found a terrible impoverishment of concepts. For instance, most parents were so worn out battling the school system that they could hardly see around the corner of the next small step forward. Also, many had been brainwashed into holding extremely low expectations for retarded persons. Protection and kindness loomed much larger in their minds than anything else. And most professionals were very bankrupt in their visions, if not outright dehumanizing.

Just how pessimistic and outright nihilistic people tended to be about the mentally retarded in the 1950s, and to a large degree the 1960s, and how modest the aspirations of even most advocates for the retarded were, is difficult to imagine by people who were not there at that time.[3]

Because of the widely prevalent sense of futility about the retarded condition, expectations were low, and the more retarded a person was, the less was expected. The term "incurable" was also closely linked to mental retardation. Even people like Edgar Doll, one of the grand old men of mental retardation, who, as far as I know, was very kindly toward retarded people, insisted to me in 1961 or 1962 that "a mongoloid is a mongoloid is a mongoloid" when I argued on behalf of the 1959 definition of mental retardation of the American Association on Mental Deficiency that left open the possibility that a retarded person might become unretarded.

The attitude of futility was also dominant, and exemplified, at the Plymouth State Home and Training School in Michigan where I assumed the position of director of research and training in 1963. There were only one teacher and one teacher's aide for the whole institution. From the rest of the staff, there was hardly any engagement with residents, even though a very large proportion of them were children and adolescents. The most dramatic incarnation of this nonengagement was the following. Many of the dayrooms (perhaps even all of them) had gigantic picture windows, in my memory about 12 feet long, opening up to other areas, including spacious corridors. And yet it was normative to see as many as seven white-clad attendants sitting on chairs *outside* a dayroom, in front of the picture window, and looking *into* the dayroom in which there might be 50 children or youths milling about aimlessly without staff contact. Every once in a while, a staff member would dash into the dayroom to attend to somebody's toileting, break up a fight, and so forth. Otherwise, it was not considered important that the attendants be with residents and do anything with them.

This attitude of futility prevailed from the lowest to the highest echelons of the institution. In fact, the superintendent (though a pediatrician) once remarked in my hearing that it was a good idea to just wait for the infants to become 5 or 6 years old before doing anything with them, because at that age "programming will be much easier." Overall, the attitude was that the residents needed only custodial, nursing, and medical care. From among maybe 500 staff members, I could only identify at most five who had positive attitudes toward the residents, as well as significant developmental expectations for them. One result was that I constantly got into trouble, was terribly isolated, and only stayed one year.

And yet theoretically, this was the place where one might have expected a breakthrough, for five reasons: (a) the institution was new and therefore might have been unencumbered in many ways from breaking with all sorts of patterns and assumptions of the past; (b) it had one of the highest levels of funding for a public institution for the retarded in the US; (c) it had perhaps the highest ratio of staff to residents in any such institution; (d) it had a wide range of professional workers with solid credentials who, for the most part, were not dropouts from the mainstream of professional practice, as was so often the case in other institutions; and (e) the residents were very disproportionately children, and the superintendent was a pediatrician and a leader in the field.

An interesting hint on what parents envisioned and/or where the rights orientation was headed comes to us from a June 1967 symposium on "Legislative Aspects of Mental Retardation" held in Stockholm by the International League of Societies for the Mentally

Handicapped (the world association of national parent associations), with Bank-Mikkelsen, Nirje, and Grunewald among the 30 participants. It recommended that "accommodations" should "not exceed 15-20 persons" (ILSMH, 1967, p. 10).

As late as at the annual conference of the Canadian Association for the Mentally Retarded in October 1970 in Vancouver, I noted in my diary that the members were just arriving at the stage of what I described as "Isn't it wonderful that the mentally retarded can do anything!"

So the answers from even the most enlightened people to "what is the wildest reform idea you can think of" would generally have been—and at best—(a) rightful funding for segregated special education, and (b) more money for more smaller better institutions, more equitably distributed across one's respective state. And these are exactly the two directions into which post-World War II reform had been moving.

But, ironically, the new institutions that were constructed after World War II were usually vastly worse in design than the old ones, because the old ones actually came much closer to culturally normative features than the new ones. The new ones incorporated culture-alien features that—though interpreted as improvements—turned out to be primarily for management convenience, and very dehumanizing. This included tile walls and floors that were easier to clean or that could even be hosed down, hence more sound-reflective surfaces and noises; cold steel and plastic furniture that could be hosed; toilets and bathrooms that were open to visual inspection; and so on.

So, in my opinion, if Normalization had not come along when it did, and possibly even if it had come along but not been interpreted in a convincing fashion and on a massive scale, we would have seen mental retardation develop in the following directions:

1. There would have been massive investments into building new, smaller, regionalized institutions. This trend was already underway from the late 1950s on. For instance, Tennessee had one large central institution for the retarded, and built two more so that each third of the state would have its own, with the new ones intended for a number in the low thousand—which was low then.

Other states converted old TB sanatoria into mental retardation institutions, usually with several hundred residents.

Some states that had never had a public institution got themselves one in the 1950s, either by new construction or by conversion of other facilities.

Some states were in the process of simply rebuilding their old institutions. In the early 1970s, New York State pulled down every single residential building of its Syracuse institution and rebuilt from the ground up.

2. There would have been many more states pursuing the regional center model. Some states had already begun to make huge investments in it, which took many forms, depending on the respective states. Aside from Connecticut (a very small state), giant California committed itself to a regional center scheme, and many other states might have followed these leads if Normalization ideas of community-dispersed services had not become available as an alternative. The university-affiliated mental retardation centers, with their expensive clinical components that were beginning to bloom then, were playing right into the "center" concept.

Not surprisingly, the models for people from the late 1950s to the early 1970s were the Yakima Valley institution in Washington State, the Arkansas Children's Colony, Seaside Regional Center in Connecticut, and the Rolla Regional Center in Missouri. They were examples of "better institutions" that drew streams of visitors.

3. A third thing that would have happened is that group residences would have developed, but they would have been very large and very abnormal. This is what was happening in Connecticut in the late 1960s and was considered a model. There were group homes with 20 residents, and they looked like institutions on the inside. In other states, facilities with scores of residents did spring up that were institutional in nature but enough tied to the community to be commonly referred to as community residences. Some states still have these to this day.

4. A fourth thing that would have happened would have been vastly more segregated education. Again, some states were well on their way toward segregated schools, and even segregated school districts, that is, school districts only for handicapped children.

In some states, it took decades to halt the above four developments, but others retreated from their previous plans along these lines almost right away, though often only after big local battles.

5. A fifth thing that would have happened is much slower expansion of the education of the more severely handicapped children.

Without Normalization, many of the positive things that have come about would have come about anyway, but many of them anywhere between 10-20 years later, and some of the more subtle corollaries of Normalization would not have come about to this day. In fact, some corollaries of at least the Wolfensberger formulation are still normatively rejected even on the conceptual level, to say nothing of the implementive one.

This brief sketch of selected ideas that constituted people's major "hopes" in regard to human services or major human service sectors, or in regard to social changes that would have a bearing on human problems and human services, reveals the poverty of truly high-order ideas, and especially ideas that were not outright utopian or divorced from practicality, as Marxism has always been.

In a later section, I will have more to say about where some of the early mentions of notions of a "normal life" fit in, because they played a very small role on the North American scene until *Changing Patterns* came out.

3 INFLUENCES ON SERVICE REFORMERS AND WOLFENSBERGER THAT PREPARED THEM FOR THE NORMALIZATION IDEA

In this section, I will review some of the major influences that predisposed me to be receptive to the Normalization principle. This coverage not only sheds light on why I embraced and promoted Normalization, but also why many other persons who had similar experiences became disposed in the same direction.

First of all, a new generation of people might easily forget that, at least in North America, the evolution and acceptance of the Normalization principle was deeply rooted in efforts at reforming institutions—mostly those for retarded people—as my subsequent account will strongly bring out. After all, besides institutions, there was not much else to look at except the relatively few educational programs for children, and when one looked at institutions at the start of the post-World War II reform movement, all one could think of was "better institutions." Had institutions not been so awful, even people with a sense of justice and compassion would probably not have felt a great need for a radical alternative.

However, we also have to call to mind that until the late 1960s, there was only an occasional outcry about an institutional scandal or atrocity here and there, but very little protest about the normativeness of bad institutional conditions, and hardly any opposition at all to institutionalism *per se*. As I will recapitulate later, even if one wanted to cry out, one would probably not have found a forum controlled by the human service professions and structures in which to do so.

My own odyssey toward Normalization started in 1956, when my sense of justice was outraged by the conditions in the so-called "back wards" of a mental institution in which I was then working as a clinical psychology trainee (at the Norfolk State Hospital, Norfolk, Nebraska, 1956-1957). This outrage was fueled in subsequent years by additional tours of, and episodes of work in, several other institutions of different kinds.

Another thing that laid important groundwork for Normalization and SRV in my mind from my earliest days in human services in the 1950s was that I found it easy to evoke positive behavior from devalued people through my positive expectations of them and my expressions of trust in them. As early as 1956, while still working on my master's degree, I conveyed expectations and trust to inmates of the most violent and locked ward of a large state mental institution (the one mentioned above) in such a fashion that I was never attacked, though many other people were. Similarly, despite being present in all sorts of violent situations in human service contexts since, I have never been attacked myself, and have attributed this at least in part to the positive role expectations that I conveyed to potential attackers. (Strangely enough, while I found it relatively easy to convey positive expectations to wounded and devalued people, I have always found it very difficult to do the same to imperial people.)

People with experiences and sentiments similar to mine had their consciousness boosted by several related publications that started coming out after 1955, that drew attention to the process of degradation to which new members of institutions and totalitarian contexts are normatively subjected in order to bring them to conformity and submission (e.g., Garfinkel, 1956; Stone, 1961). Goffman (e.g., 1958, 1961) began to call this process "mortification." This concept helped reformers a great deal in formulating measures that were recognized later as being concordant with Normalization.

In 1958, Goffman had begun to publish on what he called "total institutions," culminating in his 1961 book *Asylums*. Under this construct of total institutions, Goffman subsumed not only human service institutions, but certain other social contexts that were highly separated from their societies, even in those instances where their members were societally valued people, as in the military, or on ships at sea. This analysis was very impactful on reformers, and on many people in North America who eventually ended up embracing Normalization.

In 1963, Goffman published *Stigma*, in which he addressed many issues that became very important in the later thinking on social imagery, social devaluation, Normalization, and Social Role Valorization. For instance, what Goffman called "courtesy stigma" (one of those awful terms without any readily identifiable meaning of which sociology abounds) referred to the fact that those who are closely associated with—or viewed as identified with—a devalued ("stigmatized") person acquire some of the same devaluation ("stigma") in the eyes of observers as the devalued person him/herself. Of course, this is the same as what the Wolfensberger version of Normalization theory and Social Role Valorization has called (in language that is much more descriptive and intelligible) "deviancy image juxtaposition" and "image transfer." However, the image juxtaposition and transfer realities have been dealt with in much broader and higher-level (more universal) fashion in Normalization and SRV theory than Goffman did, though both are indebted to him a great deal. Similarly, what Goffman called "spoiled identity" in 1963 I later subsumed (in my version of Normalization, and in Social Role Valorization) under (severe) image degradation, or incumbency in a distinctly devalued role of great "band-width" (role

band-width is explained in Wolfensberger, 1998). As I only noted consciously in 1994, he even used the terms "Normalization" and "normification" a few times in this book, but like everybody else in those days, in a very limited sense. He used "Normalization" to refer to the process through which nonstigmatized people treat stigmatized ones as if they were not stigmatized, and "normification" as the effort of stigmatized persons to present themselves as ordinary persons. Goffman attributed his idea of "Normalization" to a yet earlier writer (Schwartz, 1957) who, however, did not use that term but the phrases "strain toward a normalcy definition" and "behavior within a normality framework."

Thus, these publications prepared many minds for what was to come, and not only in North America. An example is the scale for measuring the nature and quality of residential care developed by Raynes and King in the mid-1960s, which was heavily based on Goffman, as the authors themselves stated (my diary notes of the September 1967 convention of the International Association for the Scientific Study of Mental Deficiency in Montpellier, France; the proceedings also included their presumedly edited presentation [Raynes & King, 1968], and the book by King, Raynes, and Tizard [1971] reports on a whole series of related pieces of work).

Into a category similar to Goffman fell the work done by, or stimulated by, David J. Vail, who himself had been influenced by Goffman's works. In the early 1960s, Vail was the medical director of the Medical Service Division of the Minnesota Department of Public Welfare. Under his leadership, his division began (apparently in 1963) a drive to improve the living conditions in Minnesota's eight mental, and four mental retardation, institutions, via what he called an "attack on dehumanization" (Karlins, 1971-1972). The evolution of this project was apparently influenced by Vail's visits to services in Britain and Scandinavia on which he reported in 1965 and 1968 respectively (Vail, 1965, 1968).

Vail was one of those people who had been deeply influenced by Goffman's *Asylums*, and so he had a copy of that book distributed to each Minnesota institution as a basis for staff discussion ("Bronze Award," 1967) and scheduled a series of presentations and discussions on it. In 1966, Vail published his ideas and results (with many references to Goffman) in a book entitled *Dehumanization and the Institutional Career* (Vail, 1966), which had a big impact on at least those people who could bring themselves to acknowledge that institutions were bad places. The book systematically brought to consciousness many of the institutional practices that workers in institutions had unconsciously adopted or copied and revealed their demeaning nature and debilitating impact in creating so-called "institutionalism" in inmates.

The book gave major emphasis to two concepts. The first construct was "dehumanization," by which Vail meant something that we would now subsume under the broader construct of social devaluation, and, more specifically, the casting of humans into the role of some kind of subhuman, that is, animal, plant life, or object. In a very systematic fashion, Vail delineated this construct as mostly encountered in institutions, and especially so in mental ones, with many compelling examples. As early as 1963, Vail also noted that when institutional staff dehumanized residents, they lost their own humanity.

While Vail had used the term "dehumanization" since at least 1963, he did not coin it. Dictionaries tell us that "dehumanize" was already used as a verb early in the 19th century and "dehumanization" as a noun was used in the late 19th century. However, Vail gave the term new nuances of meaning that it did not seem to possess previously, and contributed to the term becoming so well known that by the 1980s, educated people generally had begun to use it routinely.

Today we have available to us a much more sophisticated analysis of devalued roles and would no longer agree that all of the practices that Vail pilloried would put people into the roles of objects, insensate plants, or animals. However, this fact does not detract from Vail's insights.

Vail's second concept was "dignity" (which he also called "rehumanization"), and as earthshaking as it then was, it also revealed the poverty of ideas that prevailed then—as late as the mid- and late 1960s—as to what might constitute a desirable practical alternative to the prevailing patterns. In fact, while Vail's "dignity" measures were certainly concordant with the Normalization and SRV concepts yet to come, they suffered from the following deficiencies: (a) These measures consisted of little more than *not* doing the things that he called dehumanizing, though Vail also had much to say about what he called "the round

of life," by which he meant something close to Nirje's later routines and rhythms of a normal day. This section on "remedies" took up less than 13 out of 266 pages in his book. (b) Vail's dignity measures fell far short of what I have called the conservatism corollary implications of Normalization and SRV, because they merely involved abstention from "dehumanization." (c) Much of Vail's analysis and dignity measures were phrased in terms applicable first and foremost to *mental* institutions, though there were some efforts made by others later on to translate the relevance of all this to other settings and client classes—though still mostly in institutions. One reason Vail's dignity measures would have only modest relevance outside of institutional settings is that it would not occur to most people *not* to practice such measures most of the time anywhere else. (d) Finally, Vail was still an adherent of the concept of "better institutions." He made sure to clarify that he was not "against institutions," but trying to "soften" them and make them "more effective" (Vail, 1966, p. 206).

Vail's 1966 book was widely drawn on even by institutional in-service training programs, in part because it contained so many concrete examples and visual aids, which people widely copied. Also, for some years, the term "rehumanization" was a minor craze in intra-institutional improvement efforts. (Apparently, Charles Bernstein, superintendent of the Rome Custodial Asylum in New York State between circa 1902 and 1942, had already campaigned for a program of "humanization" of retarded people ["A Century on Ice," 1995].)

Vail's staff also developed other teaching aids, such as brochures that contrasted dehumanization with dignity. The National Association for Retarded Children (NARC) reprinted one such brochure entitled "Dehumanization vs. Dignity" in the late 1960s, and some local ARC chapters also reprinted Minnesota materials. One other teaching aid was a training film (Karlins, 1966) made in the 1960s in connection with Vail's book, called "Dehumanization and the Total Institution." It used animated cartoons with a Maxwell Smart-type of humor to teach the constructs of dehumanization and dignity, but largely prescribed "better institutions" rather than any alternatives to them. Also, based on the idea that retarded people should not be dehumanized, another film was made about the same time by the Association for Retarded

Children in Minnesota, entitled "In the Name of Humanity," which I first saw in March 1967 (at the North Central regional conference of the National Association for Retarded Children in Lincoln, Nebraska). Soon, in 1967, a better version of this film was made jointly by the Minnesota and the National Associations for Retarded Children, called "To Bridge the Gap." It contrasted Minnesota's programs and services with those in Sweden, Denmark, Norway, the Netherlands, and England, and featured Dr. Spejer from the Netherlands and Bengt Nirje from Sweden. The depiction of the Minnesota institutional snake pits was striking. Some of the scenes of severely deprived and retarded adults dancing and posturing in the back wards were almost incredible vignettes of man's inhumanity to man. One unforgettable scene showed a little child huddled in a corner for contact with the three convergent cold stone surfaces. Also, I heard Miriam Karlins, Vail's colleague, speak at the annual NARC convention in Detroit in October 1968.

Vail might have made other significant contributions to the reform movement had he not died in 1971 at the early age of 45 (Karlins, 1971-1972).

While Vail hardly went beyond "better institutions," his book was very important to Normalization developments because after reading it, I received the inspiration to interpret retarded people as needing to be accorded the three identities of human being, citizen, and developing person.

The most important one of these in the 1960s was the identity of human being, because it would negate all the dehumanizing that had been going on. The identity of "citizen" established the idea that a retarded person possessed rights, and that these rights could only be abridged by due process. This was a rather radical idea then. The image of citizen identity also suggested to people a participatory role in society for previously or otherwise devalued and excluded people.

Finally, the idea that a retarded person—even if profoundly impaired—was to be viewed as having growth potential was intended to counteract the widely prevalent nihilism about the prospects of retarded persons. I used to teach that I had never met a retarded person from whom I could not rather readily elicit a response that revealed unutilized—and usually also unrecognized—capacity for learning or growth. I prided myself in being able to demonstrate such responses rather quickly before students, parents, or service workers, even from profoundly impaired persons whom I had never seen before. The expectations of such observers had normatively been so low that they were often quite astonished at my little demonstrations, which today would probably be considered elementary.

I certainly did not invent the notions that retarded people were human, citizens, and capable of further development. These were ideas whose time had come. For instance, in 1964, Bank-Mikkelsen gave a major presentation to the first international congress of the International Association for the Scientific Study of Mental Deficiency in Copenhagen. He interpreted this talk as an opportunity by the host country to present its work for the mentally retarded (Bank-Mikkelsen, 1964, p. 1). In this speech, he made a big point that the mentally retarded individual was "first of all a fellow-being" and therefore must have "full rights as a fellow-citizen" (p. 3). This led him to state that "the aim is to give the mentally retarded a normal existence, that is to say to assist with treatment of any kind and ensure living-quarters and work in the ordinary community for as many as possible" (p. 3). (By the way, this was the only use of the word root "normal" in his talk.) He also said that the mentally retarded ". . . do not need pity . . . they need to be respected as human-beings—with their particular handicaps" (pp. 6-7).

Thus, I merely collated notions that retarded people were human, citizens, and capable of further development, tied them together, and taught them in a way that caught people's attention—but I did not invent them. However, I cannot recall that anyone else had prepared a systematic presentation that contrasted the dehumanization of retarded people on the one hand with a precise and elaborated exposition of the three alternative interpretations on the other hand. In my speaking, I also heavily interpreted how the view of people as developing organisms implied a "developmental model," as I also briefly sketched in *Changing Patterns* (Kugel & Wolfensberger, 1969, p. 81). Later on, some people proposed that the term "developmental model" should be used in lieu of the term "principle of Normalization."

This, then, was the core of my service-reform teaching for about three years between 1966-1969, and what preceded Normalization in my mind. For instance, I can document from my archives that already in November 1967, I spoke on "Dehumanization and

Total Institutions" to the Greater Omaha Association for Retarded Children at a time when most parents looked with great and emotional favor on institutions. Relatedly, I also taught—as I put it in a 1969 article—"we are already 40 years behind what is known about the retarded" (Wolfensberger, 1969b, p. 53).

However, I rarely invoked the "dignity" notion in my change agentry but instead emphasized the notion of respect, and especially so vis-à-vis people who meant well toward the mentally retarded but who operated on a pity or object-of-charity model. Toward them, I emphasized respect instead of pity, and services and inclusion on the basis of rightfulness rather than charity. However, unlike people who came after me, I never intended to abolish charity—in the sense of *caritas* and voluntary compassionate acts—as a major motive force in human interaction, nor would it have occurred to me then that other people would soon want to do this.

The impact of what I call the Vailish ideas can be noted in vignettes such as the following. When the National Association for Retarded Children (1968) issued a *Policy Statement on Residential Care* document in October 1968, the term "dehumanization" played a major role in it. While it was too early for the term "Normalization" to make an appearance in the document, it did emphasize humanization, rights, and "home-like environments." (By the way, there were only the barest and vaguest hints in that report that "residential care" was thought of as anything but institutional care!)

Also, one visitor in 1968 to mental retardation services in Denmark and Sweden reported being impressed by the "dignity" being accorded to retarded individuals but did not mention Normalization (October 14, 1968, letter of three pages from Irving R. Stone to Rosemary and Gunnar Dybwad). When Grunewald (1971, 1972) translated and published portions of *Changing Patterns* into Swedish and Danish, he also included a long excerpt from Vail's 1966 book. The impact of my teaching the three positive interpretations is exemplified by the Pennsylvania Association for Retarded Children already arguing (PARC flyer of December 8, 1969) that a retarded child was "a child...a human being and a citizen."

One other development helped me understand and teach how those conditions came about against which Normalization measures were needed. This was that when the first publications on Normalization were being crafted, sociology had recently given prominence to the term "deviancy." This construct came in extremely handy to Normalization discourse, although it had two big disadvantages: Most people outside of sociology had never heard of it, and even many people in human services had not. The second drawback was that in spelling and phonetics, the adjective "deviant" was uncomfortably close to the word "deviate," which many people did know, and associated with sexual perversion. The terms "deviant" and "deviate" must have received a big boost when psychologists and others began to speak a lot in terms of normal distributions, and deviations from the mean, which happened mostly in the 1930s through 1950s. It is interesting that the entirely descriptive term "deviancy" would quickly acquire a pejorative meaning, and/or be used pejoratively, even though strictly speaking, both terms—deviant and deviate—are just as applicable to deviations into the positively desired side of a normal distribution as into the devalued side. However, I, for one, could simply not find a suitable alternative at that time for the term "deviancy" that had a sufficiently broad umbrella meaning, particularly since my later phrase "social devaluation" was simply inaccessible in those days.

Finally, more in the line of a relevant experience than an idea was what I learned during a year in Europe in 1962-1963. The doctoral program at George Peabody College in which I was enrolled from 1957 to 1962 had helped send two of its doctoral students (Gershon Berkson and James Moss) for a year to England to study under the illustrious Drs. Jack Tizard and Neil O'Connor at the Maudsley Hospital in London. By obtaining a U.S. Public Health postdoctoral research fellowship shortly after completing my doctoral work, I was able to follow not only in their footsteps, but also in the yet earlier tradition of human service study tours of Europe. I worked under the same two mentors for a year in 1962-1963, during which I undertook several minor and two major tours of human services—mostly to the mentally retarded—in England, Scotland, Northern Ireland, Eire, Germany, Belgium, and Switzerland. Later, I lectured extensively on my findings in the US and

Canada, reported on them in print (Wolfensberger, 1964a, 1964b, 1964c, 1965c), and drew on what I had learned in several other of my publications (e.g., Wolfensberger, 1965a [reprinted in Gunzburg, 1973, and Jones, 1971], 1965b [reprinted in Dempsey, 1975], 1967, 1979).

One of the research projects that Tizard assigned to me was to play an important role in my evolving service conceptualization, and that was to study and document the mental retardation service system of the county of Middlesex that was planned by rationally and systemically evolving a dispersed, centrally coordinated network of moderately diversified community services. This was cutting-edge stuff in those days, and taught me to think in terms of services that were (a) regional, (b) comprehensive, and (c) systemic, such as I was to help design later in Nebraska. Also, on the purely programmatic level, amazing achievements were attained, with even very severely retarded adults being taught to perform work at a very high level of skill and productivity. Their work performance was so impressive that Tizard, a medical officer, and I administered a homemade IQ test to all workers in one of the centers, and confirmed that they were indeed not misclassified as retarded: 32% could not tell their age, 67% could not write their name, and only 13% could combine two basic coins to make a sum of money. In one of my published reports on this, I called the Middlesex services "some of the most remarkable services to the retarded that I had ever seen" (Wolfensberger, 1965a, p. 62).

After my return to the US, I wrote Jack Tizard on November 20, 1963, that I had been speaking, and showing the slides I had taken in Europe, to an average of one parent group a week, and had also been talking to professional groups and showing them Tizard's film on the Brooklands project of more family-like living for retarded children. I reported that I had not been able to convince one single professional of the need for the kind of progressive things I had seen in England, but that the parents went wholeheartedly along with it. Unfortunately, my monograph-length documentation of the Middlesex project (Wolfensberger & Tizard, 1964) could find no publisher, Middlesex County itself was abolished, and soon thereafter the service system in Britain lost not only its frontier status, but also its connection to cutting-edge developments elsewhere and slipped into

mediocrity. However, very relevant to my evolution of Normalization-related ideas was the recognition of what high expectations and adaptive environmental structures could accomplish, and that a community-based comprehensive service system simply had to be dispersed and diversified. Dispersal was concordant with smallness and integration, and diversification was concordant with what—in my version of the Normalization theory—became the construct of model coherency via the intermediate construct of "specialization," that is, that different services would provide different things to different people, according to their needs.

4 THE HISTORY OF INTERCONTINENTAL EXCHANGE IN HUMAN SERVICES THAT WAS THE CONTEXT FOR THE TRANSFER OF NORMALIZATION FROM SCANDINAVIA TO NORTH AMERICA

Next, I want to make a further contribution to an understanding of the sociohistorical context that facilitated the transfer of Normalization ideas from Denmark and Sweden to North America. This has not yet been done to any extent, as far as I know.

What laid the groundwork for this transfer was, first of all, the long tradition of people from North America visiting human services in Europe, and then telling and writing about it back home, and of outright importing new ideas and practices that they had learned abroad. Sometimes, they even recruited European practitioners of new developments and established them in North America.

This tradition goes back a long time. For instance, when a certain Dr. Mason Fitch Cogswell (1761-1830) learned in the early 1800s that his daughter Alice (1805-1830) was deaf, he recruited Thomas Hopkins Gallaudet (1787-1851) to go to Europe to learn ways of educating deaf children and to apply his learnings at the American Asylum for the Deaf, established in 1817 in Hartford, Connecticut. In Europe, Gallaudet also recruited a French teacher of the deaf, Laurent Clerc (1785-1869), to come back to Hartford with him.

In the 1830s and 1840s, Samuel Gridley Howe and other American human service leaders visited human services in Europe and wrote about it after they came back home. Howe had seen the work of Édouard Séguin with the mentally retarded in France, and helped him to become established as a leading mental retardation pedagogue in the US, to which Séguin came in 1848. (There are some disputes about the exact year, but I believe 1848 is correct.)

Of course, the information flow was not all one-way. At a certain point, it became more reciprocal. For instance, many eugenic ideas that had originated in Britain, and then had been taken up and implemented in the US, began to be carried back to Europe as Europeans began to take intense note of these developments and to cite them in support of the promotion of parallels in Europe—and, in the case of the Nazis, surpass them (e.g., Kevles, 1985; Proctor, 1988).

During the 1950s and 1960s, there had been a slow but influential trickle of American visitors (many from the mental health field) to Europe that included—perhaps for the first time—Scandinavia as a major source of noteworthy innovations. Coverage of mental retardation services was often a secondary aspect of their visits because, in those days, mental retardation services were generally administered by mental health services and professionals. However, what did intrigue visitors was that starting around 1960, a good number of institutions were built in Sweden that were not only "better institutions," but came close to being "best institutions." They were small and anticipated later Normalization formulations by having small sleeping spaces (instead of dormitories), small and diversified social spaces (instead of "day rooms"), a culturally normative internal decor (in fact, they were often breathtakingly beautiful), being well-staffed, and increasingly locally administered. (See also Grunewald, 1969a.)

When North Americans planned to go abroad to learn from human services there, some of them at least tried to prepare themselves by first reading English-language accounts about services in the countries they planned to visit. I will now give a sketch of the publications that were available to visitors during the period of about 1960-1975, since this time span included both the years that laid the groundwork for the Normalization transfer and the years that constituted the actual transfer period itself. This review has no pretense to being exhaustive but is probably more extensive than readers are apt to find elsewhere.

Within different categories of publications, I will list the items in sequence of date rather than alphabetically by author.

A number of publications dealt with *services in many countries, or even the world.* Taylor and Taylor (1960) wrote about the evolution and organization of special education for the handicapped in various countries of Western Europe. This would have been very useful to visitors, but the publication was not well known and, hence, not much used.

A British booklet (Robinson, 1961) reviewed "patterns of care for the mentally disordered" in the US, the Netherlands, and the European part of the USSR. Also in 1961, Linn (1961) surveyed the state of general hospital psychiatry in many countries around the world, including Austria, Germany, Switzerland, Italy, and Scotland. In 1965, Furman (1965) wrote a description of community mental health services in Great Britain, the Netherlands, Denmark, and Sweden. Since this was published by the U.S. Government Printing Office, it was easily available and well disseminated. Kiev (1968) and Masserman (1968) reviewed psychiatric services in the Communist countries of Eastern Europe.

Of course, in 1969, *Changing Patterns in Residential Services for the Mentally Retarded* (Kugel & Wolfensberger, 1969) came out, and it had chapters describing model services in Denmark, Sweden, Britain, and the US, but more will be said about this later.

Perin (1970) wrote on the design of environments, with special emphasis on Britain and Scandinavia, but only tangentially concerned with human services or handicapped people.

In 1969, Dybwad (1969) reviewed patterns of organizing services for the mentally retarded in different countries around the world, and in 1970, Dybwad and Dybwad (1970) wrote a chapter on community services for the mentally retarded in selected countries all over the world.

Programs we would call "social security" for the handicapped in the Netherlands, Sweden, Britain, and the Soviet Union were sketched by the (US) Secretary's Committee on Mental Retardation (1971) in 1971.

Lancaster-Gaye (1972) reviewed the services for the handicapped in the same countries as Furman (1965) had (Britain, Netherlands, Denmark, Sweden), but promoted residential services as the bulwark of long-term security for handicapped persons.

On behalf of the Joint Commission on Mental Health of Children in the US, David (1972) wrote a book with a wide range of program vignettes, and descriptions of services and personnel training structures, in Europe. This included much of relevance to mental retardation, although some of this was already outdated when published.

Holowinsky (1973) reviewed the status of special education and defectology research in Communist Eastern Europe, namely, the USSR, Poland, Hungary, Czechoslovakia, Yugoslavia, Bulgaria, and Romania.

Various European human services, especially for the elderly, were reviewed, and to some degree compared to American services, by Kahn and Kamerman (1975), with special emphasis on Denmark and Sweden.

Thursz and Vigilante (1975, 1976) wrote a two-volume work on social services in 19 countries, including Britain and Sweden in the 1975 volume, and Denmark and Finland in the 1976 volume.

One class of publications about multiple countries consisted of reports by visitors from North America who were reporting back home what they had seen and learned abroad.

Among these were two 1961 monographs on European services to the mentally disordered (and to a lesser degree, the retarded) in Belgium, Britain, Denmark, France, and the Netherlands. One was by Barton, Farrell, Lenehan, and McLaughlin (1961) and the other by a team of visitors on behalf of the then influential Southern Regional Education Board (1961)—a southern multistate quasi-public consortium headquartered in Atlanta, Georgia. Bank-Mikkelsen was already mentioned in it as the major Danish contact person. But, strangely enough, while the six visitors were very influential people in the professions and state government, including from Tennessee (my own state at that time), I could never detect any evidence that they tried vigorously or successfully to apply what they had learned. Perhaps they had only seen but not learned.

Among the travel reports of North Americans in the 1960s was a whole series of papers that I produced between 1963 and 1965, pointing out features of services and the professional scene—mostly in mental retardation—that I had observed during my 1962-1963

study tour in England, Scotland, Northern Ireland, Eire, Germany, Belgium, and Switzerland. First, I wrote a long report to the National Association for Retarded Children (NARC) that had given me a small supplemental grant.[4] NARC—mostly Rosemary and Gunnar Dybwad—drew on this report to advise other travelers. I built on this report to produce an entire series of publications (Wolfensberger, 1964a, 1964b, 1964c, 1965c), three of which (Wolfensberger, 1964a, 1964b, 1964c) were reprinted later in Henry David's (1972) book on *Child Mental Health in International Perspective*. Several of my later publications (Wolfensberger, 1965a, 1965b, 1967) also drew on what I had learned on these travels. As mentioned earlier, I also wrote a monograph (Wolfensberger & Tizard, 1964) reporting my extensive study of one of the most significant regional mental retardation service programs in Britain, namely, the one run by the since defunct county of Middlesex. This was never published but was privately widely circulated, and what I learned from this study was very instrumental in paving the way for my being so receptive later to the Normalization concept. Thus, in contrast to the travelers of the Southern Regional Education Board, I was deeply impressed and shaped by my experiences in Europe and vigorously tried to put my learnings into action.

Vail (1965) described the British mental health system. Faber (1968) wrote on services to retarded children in 12 countries around the world, including England and Denmark. Kelley (Staff, 1970a) reported on what he thought were the relative strengths and weaknesses of services to the retarded in six European nations (Denmark, England, France, Germany, the Netherlands, and Sweden). (Kelley was then superintendent of a very bad institution, Mansfield in Connecticut, and his comparison seemed to be rather unrevealing.) The President's Committee on Mental Retardation sent a subcommittee to Britain, Denmark, Sweden, and France in 1967, and it reported on its findings in 1968 (Humphrey, Jones, & Kugel, 1968). Gregor (1972), then president of the Canadian Association for the Mentally Retarded, reported on his 1971 visit to Norway, Sweden, Denmark, Germany, France, and the Netherlands.

Until the mid- to late 1960s, many people thought that the Netherlands was the model country in Europe as far as human services were concerned, and there was much visiting there by North Americans. (In fact, in the late 1950s, the Swedish association of parents of the mentally retarded [the acronym of which was FUB] sent Nirje to the Netherlands to study sheltered workshops [Nirje, 1992b].) In addition to reportage in multicountry publications cited previously, a President's Panel on Mental Retardation (1963b) study mission reported on the Netherlands in 1963, Dolnick (1971) reported on Dutch sheltered workshops for the handicapped, and Jonson (1971-1972) reported on his visits to many Dutch services for the retarded. The Dutch National Association for the Care of the Mentally Retarded, together with the Bishop Bekkers Institute (1973), described the structure of Dutch services for the mentally retarded in a monograph—very like one of those produced in Scandinavia in English to orient the hordes of foreign visitors to Scandinavia. However, this publication seemed a bit late because by then the gaze of North American visitors had shifted heavily to Denmark and Sweden.

Indeed, as Nirje put it in a memorial to Bank-Mikkelsen (see Nirje, 1991, and the Nirje, 1992a version), the President's Panel on Mental Retardation had "discovered" Denmark and Sweden in 1962. By the late 1960s and early 1970s, something like Scandimania broke out, with Denmark and Sweden especially being overrun by North American visitors. Sweden facilitated this process by establishing (ca. 1970, through the Swedish Medical Council) a postdoctoral fellowship for U.S. biomedical scientists.

Most of the material published in English during the 1960s and 1970s on Scandinavian services seems to have been on Sweden, followed by Denmark, with Norway a poor third, and material on Iceland and Greenland (which belongs to Denmark) being next to nonexistent.

This material falls into several broad groups: items written as high-level broad descriptions, reports by visitors to their peers back home, and Scandinavians themselves explaining their services to each other and the anglophone world. The latter included items written at first for domestic consumption in the respective Scandinavian tongue and then translated into English, apparently in large part in order to be used by the many visitors to the Scandinavian countries. These latter items included a category describing specific service agencies or sites.

Publications on two or more Scandinavian countries that were written at least in part (in some cases, entirely) as reports by returning visitors (in all such cases, visitors from the US) included ones by the President's Panel on Mental Retardation (1963a), the Scandinavian Study Group (1966) on health services, Vail (1968) on "mental health systems" but also covering mental retardation, Smith (1968) on mental retardation, Lippman (1969) on the handicapped, Clark and Clark (1970) on the mentally retarded, Graf (1972) on advocacy on behalf of the handicapped, and Scheiner (1975) on mental retardation.

Further, because the demand for information from Denmark and Sweden had become ravenous by circa 1970, in these countries a great many unpublished human service-related documents were developed in English, to be used mostly as handouts to visitors. (I have a fair number of these in my archives.) For instance, in January 1968, Nirje prepared a summary in English of the 1967 Swedish "Law About Provisions and Services for the Mentally Retarded" as an unpublished handout. Some of these documents were very sizable, such as a two-volume Danish curriculum for retarded pupils. Some of these documents were so much in demand by foreigners that they were eventually published.

Other descriptions of only Swedish services, specifically written or coauthored by Swedish writers themselves in English, included Nilsson (1967) on special education, Myrdal (1969) on Swedish society in general, Fors (1969) on Swedish social policy, Tidman, von Sydow, and Thiberg (1969) on the elderly, Sterner (1969) on services for the handicapped, Grunewald (1969b) on the mentally retarded, Lundstrom (1969) on special education, Wester (1970) on children and child services in Sweden, Grunewald (1970) on economic opportunities for the mentally retarded, Montan (1972) on the Swedish Institute for the Handicapped, and Berfenstam and William-Olson (1973) on early child care.

Reports on Sweden exclusively by visitors to it included Engel (1968) on the health system, Perske (1969a) on services to the handicapped (mostly retarded), Woolf (1970) on services to the retarded, Elliot (1971) on the handicapped, and Kimberly (1972) on sheltered workshops.

On Denmark specifically, Rowe (1964), a visitor, reported on attendant training in mental retardation. In

1966, the Minnesota Association for Retarded Children (*Lillemosegard*, 1966) printed a bilingual brochure on the flagship of Danish mental retardation institutions, *Lillemosegard*, obviously intended as a model of what a "better institution" would be. Muriel Humphrey, the U.S. vice-president's wife, had visited Denmark in 1967 and briefly reported on it in 1968 (Humphrey, 1968). Bank-Mikkelsen (1968) wrote on services to retarded children, and Melchior (1968) described the segregated regional day schools ("center-schools") for pupils with all kinds of handicaps. The Danish National Service for the Mentally Retarded (1969) reported on the work of its previous 10 years. (This was a *Festschrift* for Bank-Mikkelsen's 50th birthday.) Perske (1969b) wrote up the observations of his study tour of services to the handicapped and retarded. Moise (1972), mother of a retarded young woman, Barbara, and later author of *As Up We Grew With Barbara* (Moise, 1980), reported on her visit to Denmark (accompanied by Barbara) in a monograph studded with pictures.

We can see that more was written about Sweden than Denmark, both by the natives and by visitors. I never encountered a good explanation of why Norway was either trailing behind Denmark and Sweden, or was so much less popular for study tours than the other two countries, especially considering that knowledge of English may have been even more widely prevalent in Norway than in the other two countries. Perhaps some other writers will be able to give us a good explanation.

Among miscellaneous other single-country reports was the one of the study commission sent by the President's Panel on Mental Retardation (1964a) to the USSR. The panel also sent a mission to England, but it never wrote a report (Gunnar Dybwad, private communication, April 19, 1994).

By the early 1970s, a vast informal guidance and referral network had sprung up, with people who wanted to visit European services asking those who had already been there for advice on where to go, and for names and addresses of contact persons. (I have many such inquiry letters in my archives.)

After 1971, the visits of North Americans to European mental retardation services were mightily facilitated by the *International Directory of Mental Retardation Resources*, edited by Rosemary Dybwad (1971, 1977-1978, 1989). The 1971 edition was followed by 1972 and 1973 supplements, and by revisions in 1978 and 1989. (There had been a forerunner of this work in 1960 [International Bureau of Education, UNESCO, 1960], covering mental retardation services in 71 countries, but, as far as I know, this work was hardly known or used in North America.)

Sterner (1976) wrote a voluminous work on *Social and Economic Conditions of the Mentally Retarded in Selected Countries* around the world, based on an earlier (1973) informally circulated mimeographed draft entitled "Some Data and View-points on the Social and Economic Conditions of the Mentally Retarded in Countries at Various Stages of Economic Development."

After my 1963 return from a year in Europe, I began to receive so many requests for information from other prospective travelers that I began to write, and periodically update, an unpublished guideline for such persons. It did not so much advise where to visit as (a) where to get further information, and (b) *how* to visit.

This concludes my review of the kind of background of publications in English about European and Scandinavian services—based heavily on study tours—that constituted the fertile soil for a transfer of Normalization concepts to North America. Not covered in this sketch are the reverse kinds of visits and reporting by Scandinavians in their own countries and tongues. Of course, only a few of the people going on study tours abroad wrote up or published their observations. For instance, between 1968 and 1972, I mediated extended work-study stays (up to one year) for four students from Nebraska in Denmark, Germany, and Sweden respectively, but they never published about the things they learned.

However, there are four points I want to add before going to the next topic.

1. When I toured services on the European mainland in 1963, one thing that struck me was that the leaders I met were rather smug about what they were doing. They felt that they had a good angle on their field and had little to learn from what was going on elsewhere—even elsewhere in Europe. The United Kingdom and Eire were different, with much orientation to the US. Especially in Eire, many service leaders in the early 1960s had been in the US, or were planning to go, as I discovered on my 1963 study tour

there. The innumerable family ties of the Irish to relatives in the US may also have been a factor.

2. One remarkable thing about so many American visitors to other countries is how little they perceived of what they saw that was good or even exemplary (at least for its time), and how often they interpreted as old hat good things that they had probably never seen. By the time I went to Scandinavia in 1969, I was already on the leading edge of reform thinking in North America and well prepared by my earlier exposure to Normalization and the editing of *Changing Patterns*. Nonetheless, where so many other visitors came away with an "isn't it nice" response or "we are already doing this or that," I came away with my mind blown, as they say these days. But then, we had the same experience with visitors to our Nebraska services between 1969 and the mid-1970s who could look at things they had never seen and go away without a conversion experience, perhaps allowing that "this is nice" or even muttering "this is old hat."

3. There was one kind of reverse visiting that is relevant to the transfer process, and that is the one that consisted of several trips each by Niels Erik Bank-Mikkelsen, Karl Grunewald, and Bengt Nirje to the US between 1967 and 1971. At that time, Bank-Mikkelsen was head of the Danish mental retardation service, Grunewald was his counterpart in Sweden, and Nirje was executive director of the Swedish parents' association in mental retardation. They toured and spoke widely, a lot of what they spoke on reflecting Normalization thinking, and they received a great deal of press when they expressed their disgust at what they saw in U.S. institutions. In Massachusetts, after Dybwad (1969) took him through an institution, Grunewald told him, "Don't you ever do this to me again!" When Grunewald shortly after came to Nebraska, he only wanted to see some of the best wards of Nebraska's only state institution for the retarded (the Beatrice State Home), because he said he could not stand to see any more bad places. Even in some of the least-worst children's units there, Grunewald said that where he saw two staff members, he would see 35 in Sweden. In late 1967, Bank-Mikkelsen made national news in the US when he said that in Denmark, cattle were better kept than retarded people in U.S. institutions such as Sonoma State Hospital in California.

All three visitors got so burned by the negative reactions of institution defenders to their comments that they became very reticent to use strong language (as I can document from my correspondence files). These visits and the press they got also contributed part of the background for the transfer of Normalization to North America. Other people from Europe who were doing remarkable things also were visiting in North America during those years, but none that I know of made the same impact as regards the transfer of Normalization.

4. It is my impression that until the early or mid-1970s, the Americans were indeed primarily the learners in this travel exchange, but that then the balance began to tip the other way, with Europeans beginning to fall all over themselves to visit North America—mainly the US—and transfer developments from there to Europe. This was partly just one element of the Americanization of the developed world, but part of it had to do with the explosion of human service ideas and practices in the US, including those in response to *Changing Patterns*, the Nebraska mental retardation service system model, the Normalization principle, and the legal rights victories. To this day, many European countries eat up as fast as they can every service craze cooked up in the United States, and the less meritorious ones perhaps even more enthusiastically than the meritorious ones.

The next section will address the actual Normalization transfer itself.

5 THE PRODUCTION OF *CHANGING PATTERNS IN RESIDENTIAL SERVICES FOR THE MENTALLY RETARDED*

What follows next is both the story of how I came to understand and embrace Normalization, and at least part of the story of how it achieved massive dissemination in relatively short order. This section of the story is difficult to organize because two parallel developments are involved: the mental retardation service revolution in Nebraska that started in 1967 and the production of the book *Changing Patterns in Residential Services for the Mentally Retarded* (Kugel & Wolfensberger, 1969), which contained the first systematic written exposition of Normalization, namely, in the chapter by Nirje (1969). Because this congress celebrates the 25th anniversary of *Changing Patterns*, and because the Nebraska story has been told in more detail than the *Changing Patterns* story, I will now focus on the latter. However, I want to emphasize that without the experiences of the Nebraska reform group to which I belonged, *Changing Patterns* would neither have become what it did, nor have had the impact that it did.

From fall 1964 to fall 1971, I was a "mental retardation research scientist" at the Nebraska Psychiatric Institute, with an academic appointment (first as assistant, then as associate, professor) in the department of psychiatry at the University of Nebraska College of Medicine in Omaha, and, in the years toward the end of my stay there, with a joint appointment in the department of pediatrics.

Nirje made several speaking trips across the US during the later 1960s and early 1970s. According to my diary, I met him first when on one of these trips, he spoke about Normalization at the North Central Regional Convention of the National Association for Retarded Children in March (10-11) 1967 in Lincoln, Nebraska. What made Nirje's presentations so impactful were two things: (a) While he had stage fright before presentations, once the curtain went up—so to speak—he was a charismatic, electrifying speaker with great rapport with his audience. He later reported that he got his first standing ovation in the US in Nebraska in 1967. (b) He had more and better illustrative slides than anyone else and interpreted them very well. I found a note in my diary that I should recommend to Dr. Kugel, my dean, to spring the expenses to invite him to give a seminar in Omaha sometime.

According to my diary, I met Nirje again at the September 1967 conference of the International Association for the Scientific Study of Mental Deficiency in Montpellier, France. There, he introduced me to Karl Grunewald, head of the Swedish mental retardation services. I also met Bank-Mikkelsen there, Grunewald's counterpart in Denmark, who invited me to Denmark—an offer I was to take up less than two years later.

Dr. Robert Kugel joined the faculty as head of pediatrics soon after I arrived in Omaha, and became dean of the medical school not long after that. He had an established history of involvements and publications in mental retardation, and had been appointed by

President Johnson to the President's Committee on Mental Retardation (PCMR). The PCMR was the successor to President Kennedy's extremely influential President's Panel on Mental Retardation that had produced an epochal report in 1962 (President's Panel on Mental Retardation, 1962, with several subcommittee reports: 1963a, 1963b, 1963c, 1963d, 1963e, 1963f, 1964a, 1964b).[5]

In September 1967, the PCMR sent a subcommittee, including Kugel, to Denmark, Sweden, Britain, and France (Humphrey, Jones, & Kugel, 1968). Later that year, the PCMR commissioned Kugel to compile a resource package on residential services for the mentally retarded in the US so that the committee could draw on it for formulating recommendations, and gave him a grant to cover expenses. In turn, Kugel enlisted me to do the bulk of the hands-on work of the project. Somewhere along the line, the decision was made that the compendium should not merely be an in-house resource, but a book, and about halfway through the project, when it became clear how much editing I had to do, I requested to be a coeditor instead of only the major staff worker on the book.

Our basic plan for the book was to first document compellingly just how awful institutions were, then to sketch some alternatives and positive models, and then come up with an integrative chapter that would point to the necessary action measures.

The significance of that part of the book that documented the bankruptcy of the institution system can hardly be appreciated any more these days, because until then, hardly any criticisms of institutions—or even institutionalism—had appeared in the *professional* literature, in part because it would simply not be permitted by those in power and in part because critics who were professionals figured that they could kiss their careers good-bye. As far as I know, all the other exposés had been by journalists, politicians, lawyers, former institution inmates, and some of the conscientious objectors to military service who had been assigned to alternative service as attendants in 65 public institutions all over the US between 1942 and 1946, including at least 16 mental retardation institutions (Sareyan, 1994). To the best of my knowledge, Blatt's *Christmas in Purgatory* (Blatt & Kaplan, 1966) was the first book-length institutional exposé by a leading professional. I suspect that the publication of this book facilitated the appearance of subsequent critiques of the mental retardation institutions. Prior to Blatt, I barely managed to get away with a few critical comments in my three 1964 and 1965 articles (Wolfensberger, 1964a, 1964b, 1965c; reprinted in David, 1972) that reported on my more noteworthy observations of mental retardation programs in Europe. Even these criticisms were almost unique then.

One issue that became totally clear to us right away—in good part because of my concurrent involvement in the reform of the Nebraska mental retardation services—was that it would be impossible to come up with a meaningful proposal for residential services outside the context of the total service system. But since our mandate was focused on residential services, we did what I have always done: "Give them not what they say they want, but what they really need," and we used the reference to residential services in the book title as a cover for addressing the total service system.

Kugel and I came up with a list of chapters we wanted and their potential authors, which included some authors whose work we already knew to be relevant. One problem was that the PCMR wanted to get the work done in very short order because it had been charged by the President to come up with concrete recommendations within a year. Nonetheless, when we contacted the potential contributors, almost all agreed right away, which was amazing considering how prominent some were and how busy they all were.

Grunewald was the only invitee who at first declined but eventually yielded to some arm-twisting by Nirje and I. Also, once most contributors were aboard, the National Association for Retarded Children chipped in a small but crucial amount of money to help a few of the contributors with their expenses.

Who and why some contributors were solicited is almost self-evident. The reason for others I can only imperfectly reconstruct, but "political" considerations played a part in one or two cases. Because the rationale for inclusion of the British service model may now be less obvious than the others, I will briefly comment on its history in Appendix A.

By the end of January 1968, we not only had all contributors aboard (see Appendix B for a table of contents of *Changing Patterns* as actually published), but one, Michael Klaber, had already sent in a first draft of his description of the mental retardation system in Connecticut, which was then considered a model.

However, what later turned out to be the biggest conceptual contribution of the book—namely, the Normalization principle—was hard and late to come by; in fact, it was a heart-stopping cliff-hanger.

To begin with, we had not even asked Nirje to write on Normalization, but an evaluation of the U.S. institutions for the retarded that he had visited in 1967 (Faribault in Minnesota, Central Colony in Wisconsin, and Woodbridge in New Jersey), and we planned to put this in the section entitled "As Others See Us." Nirje indicated that he would evaluate these institutions in light of "what we mean here by Normalization." As late as January 24, 1968, I wrote to Nirje that "the presentation and elaboration of the concept of Normalization strikes me as particularly appropriate," showing that I perceived it as a good idea to include, but not as yet as the centerpiece of the book, let alone as the cornerstone of the reform movement.

Furthermore, whether we would ever actually get a manuscript from Nirje was very iffy. Believe it or not, our deadline was the end of February 1968. In March, Grunewald wrote us that Nirje was stressed, had not yet begun to write, but had said that he knew very well what to write. In turn, I conveyed to Nirje that I knew he was stressed and hoped he would stay stressed until he was done, since he was legendary for performing best when under stress. By late May, we not only had many final chapter drafts in hand, but preliminary drafts from all the remaining authors—except Nirje. But while he had difficulty writing the paper, he had no difficulty writing us long, literate letters, apparently meant to be reassuring, with messages such as the following:

> I am still alive and aware of the fact that you are
> waiting for my paper. . . I realize that you are
> pressed for time, and I am writing this to confirm
> that I am aware of the lack of time now. . . I am now
> taking out a week vacation to be able mentally to
> concentrate on the paper. To be on the safe side I
> will leave the country for a week.

Nirje may well have been stressed, but my own stress level was astronomical, and I found his reassurances not very reassuring. On June 8, 1968, he wrote, "My paper is still not written, and I feel very bad about it. I can too well imagine your disappointment and irritation."

However, that month, he also came on another trip to the US, and so we arranged for him to be virtually taken prisoner in Washington and locked up with some secretaries at the President's Committee office for three days—and this worked! He dictated to them at a furious pace, and, by June 20, he had his first draft completed there and sent it to us. We recognized quickly that a section of his chapter had something that we had come to realize that the book lacked. Namely, despite the presence of several chapters on services that were exemplary for their time, the monograph did not contain a clearly stated unifying idea for an alternative to the prevailing institutional scene. In fact, until we got Nirje's chapter, we considered the chapters by Tizard and Dunn to be the pivotal ones.

So we divided Nirje's chapter into two: one chapter early in the book on how bad U.S. institutions were, and another one late in the book sketching Normalization as one of the major alternatives. Within days after Nirje got back home to Sweden in late June, he had our proposed revisions in hand, and he was actually quite ecstatic about how well they read.

Amazingly, Nirje's (1969) Normalization chapter consisted of less than eight pages of text, plus an appendix of less than seven pages summarizing the Swedish law on "provisions and services for the mentally retarded" of 1967 that reflected Normalization thinking, though at least the English translation did not actually mention "the Normalization principle," much as the Danish mental retardation "care" law of 1959 reflected the idea without giving it a name.

Anticipating skepticism and resistance from opponents to reform, Nirje made two observations in a July 1968 letter. Namely, even in his few visits to U.S. institutions, he (a) had already seen worse things than those shown in Blatt and Kaplan's (1966) *Christmas in Purgatory*, and (b) he underlined something that Grunewald had said earlier, which was that the services in Sweden "are not dreams in the blue but actual accomplishments of 'hard-headed' and penny-pinching appropriation committees of the county councils."

The last chapter on action implications was to be authored by Gunnar Dybwad, who was given much less time to work on it because he had to see everybody else's work first.

According to my correspondence, I proposed to Dybwad on June 21, 1968, that the

cardinal features of future trends in mental retardation residential services [be] four basic and highly interrelated components:

1. *Integration* of the retarded with the non-retarded, which implies location of services in population centers.

2. *Dispersement*, implying smaller units and achieving closeness to family and community.

3. *Specialization*, which also implies smaller units and individualization, but which calls for reduction in closeness between resident and family in some cases. [As mentioned, this was the seed of the later construct of "model coherency," elaborated in Wolfensberger and Glenn, 1975b.]

4. *Continuity* between residential and other services, resulting in less fragmentation, more individualization, and economy.

Of course, this concept of continuity was not at all the one against which the postNormalizationists these days have been railing.

The reason I suggested to Dybwad to work these concepts into his chapter, which he did, was that they had already been evolved in connection with, and written into, two sets of Nebraska's mental retardation reform plans (a state-level and a local county-level one) that were published in July 1968 by groups of people to which I belonged (Governor's Citizens' Committee on Mental Retardation, 1968a, 1968b, 1968c; Menolascino, Clark, & Wolfensberger, 1968a, 1968b).

However, before this chapter came about, it became clear that Dybwad had a Nirje problem in brimming with insights but having difficulty staying put in front of paper and pen. By late June, we had finals of many chapters and advanced drafts of all the others except Dybwad's, and by early August all the advanced drafts had been finalized and distributed to all the PCMR members for review, but we still had no draft from Dybwad.

Then Dybwad did another Nirje on us. With everyone on pins and needles to get his chapter, and us not even having a draft, Dybwad took off on a world tour, leaving a string of forwarding addresses where he generally could *not* be reached by our mail. And then in early August, Kugel received a sorrowful letter from Dybwad dated August 1: "I am now in my 60th year..., all alone here in my sickroom in Adelaide"

(Australia!), "weak. . .weary. . .with plenty of time to think and worry"—especially about what he called me later in the letter, "an editorial aggressopath." ". . .That's why I am writing to *you*, Bob," expecting Kugel to protect him from me. But Kugel also took off on vacation, so I had to write Dybwad a long letter.

With time running out on us, and having learned a lesson from Nirje, we did to Dybwad as we had done to Nirje, except more so. After his recovery and return, we got him to fly to Omaha on several weekends in a row and locked him up in my office suite with secretaries or myself by his side virtually around the clock for days to write or type everything he thought, said, dictated, or wrote by hand, with mountains of food always close at hand. When he was not in my office, he was in our home sleeping, but he also often slept in my office.[6] This also worked very well, and he produced a great chapter that recapitulated, elaborated, and extrapolated certain Normalization issues, also incorporating some of the ideas already developed in Nebraska at that time, such as elements of the above-mentioned construct of "specialization" of services.

All chapter drafts underwent at least one editing by me, and a critique by Kugel, and some underwent very extensive editing and revising. Also, all chapters were reviewed and commented on (sometimes with implications for yet further revision) by several members of the PCMR, and also by several of the expert consultants of the PCMR (Gerard Bensberg, Curtis Krishef, E. L. Johnstone). On February 16-17, 1968, the PCMR had also held a national conference in the Washington area for 25 or so selected leaders and consultants to take a preview at the direction of the monograph, with Kugel, Gunnar Dybwad, and myself as major presenters.

Actually, the final decision whether the PCMR would officially sponsor the publication of the book was not made until all the members had reviewed the manuscript in its totality later in 1968.

Around early December 1968, the final version of the monograph went to the U.S. Government Printing Office and appeared in print within weeks in January 1969. (Nirje [1992b] recalled January 10 as the publication date. In a 1997 personal communication, he also claimed that the PCMR hurried *Changing Patterns* into print before Richard Nixon was inaugurated in February, lest his administration interdict the printing.) Both in its mode of coming into

being and in the reaction to it, one could characterize the book as having had a caesarean birth. It soon became known as "the blue book," and sometimes as the Kugelberger book, as a lot of people began to refer to either Kugel or myself as Kugelberger, some in jest and some from temporary disorientation.

Of the first printing run of 5,000 copies, 2,160 were immediately distributed, free of charge, with a cover letter, to all state governors, all members of the U.S. Congress, all state mental retardation coordinators, all 450 superintendents of public institutions for the mentally retarded and "mentally ill," 550 directors or operators of private residences for the mentally retarded, all leaders of the National Association for Retarded Children (NARC) and of the American Association on Mental Deficiency, all leading figures of all the state units of the NARC, and miscellaneous others.

There were at least two more printings, for a total of over 20,000 copies, and when these ran out (sometime between 1972 and 1974), the Pennsylvania State Office of Mental Retardation paid to have facsimile reprintings done, again with very wide distribution, especially all over Pennsylvania because it was then in the forefront of reform.[7] One reason for this was that this office had recruited one of the senior staff members of the community service system around Omaha, Mel Knowlton, who was still working in that office as of 1998.

In his 1983 text on the history of mental retardation, Scheerenberger (1983) called *Changing Patterns* "one of the most consequential and successful publications of the reform era" (p. 227) and of a quarter-century. Among the likely reasons for this, we can point to five.

1. Unbeknownst to most people today, the book contained the first published explicit formulation and description, of any length in any language, of the Normalization principle. This is the reason why portions of it got so quickly translated back into Swedish (Grunewald, 1971) and Danish (Grunewald, 1972), and soon after into German (Kugel & Wolfensberger, 1974).

2. However, not only was Normalization presented in its clearest form to date, but it was presented in stark contrast to the devastating institutional realities and their history. It is well known that a change agentry effort is vastly more likely to succeed if the inadequacies of a prevailing pattern are exposed

simultaneously with the presentation of an appealing and plausible alternative.

3. A great many of the recommendations incorporated into *Changing Patterns* had begun to be implemented in Nebraska, even before the book was published, via a virtual service revolution. This implementation took place both on the level of systems organizing, and on the programmatic and clinical level. The principle of specialization was demonstrated by the initiation of a wide variety of services. Also, all this began to be sketched in various publications (e.g., Wolfensberger & Menolascino, 1970a, 1970b), and was otherwise widely disseminated. People came from all over the world to see for themselves, and many experienced a mental paradigm shift. This lent credence and power to *Changing Patterns*.

4. By a fortuitous coincidence, three of the contributors to the book (Cooke, Bank-Mikkelsen, and Tizard) were announced in spring 1968 as winners of the Kennedy Foundation International Award—at that time, the closest thing to a Nobel prize in mental retardation—for achievements prior to their contributions to the book. (Gunnar and Rosemary Dybwad were to receive the award belatedly in 1986.)

5. The strategy of massive distribution of the book by the PCMR must also have played a big role.

Editing *Changing Patterns* was one of the greatest balancing acts of my career, with the 14 contributors having been born in eight different countries, working in four different countries, several being very temperamental, and time being so short. In July 1968, Norris, who wrote up the Essex model, complained that the pace I demanded of him was "ungentlemanly." Often, we talked past each other because people did not understand each other's terminology, even when they spoke or used the same tongue. The terms used by the Scandinavians would often not be understood by Americans, and when I told Norris that we wanted data on client movement, he threw us behind by asking through the mail what that was, perhaps wondering if we were asking about toilet-behavior statistics, which was a common preoccupation then on the American service scene.

In retrospect, I have marveled that as extensive a work as *Changing Patterns* could attract so many senior and competent people as authors on such a rapid schedule of production. The prestige of the President's Committee on Mental Retardation probably had much

to do with it, plus the attraction of being part of an extensive reassessment of the field. One reason that motivated many invited contributors to participate was well expressed in Lloyd Dunn's acceptance letter of December 15, 1967: "All I need is another assignment as I attempt to get my affairs in order for my leave of absence from the United States. However, the business of residential facilities in this country is such an important matter that I cannot refuse your kind invitation. . . ." Another reason was a recognition that the prestige of the PCMR made it very likely that the product would have an impact. Also, it is my impression that people actually had more time in those days prior to the introduction of so many timesaving devices, and to the increasing formalization, bureaucratization, and complexification of everything. People today might also not have the leeway to devote so much time to a project without receiving funding for it. Further, modernistic values have made people more prideful, and I doubt that authors of the same calibre as those in 1968 would today be as accepting of extensive editing by a person much less senior to most of them. All in all, I thus doubt that the same feat could be duplicated today.

By the way, no one received any royalties for working on *Changing Patterns*; however, Kugel, who collected antique pewter artifacts, gave each contributor a reproduction of such an item, in my case a candle sconce. On my part, my wife and I sent the Dybwads a gigantic box of Omaha steaks which arrived just in time to replenish Gunnar's protein for writing a chapter (Dybwad & Dybwad, 1970) for a book by Joseph Wortis that was, as Gunnar put it, "about as overdue as my chapter was for your book, and that is hard on Rosemary's nerves not to mention those of Dr. Wortis" (letter, February 5, 1969).

I do not want to leave readers with the impression that all the contributors to *Changing Patterns* agreed with its major conclusions. Far from it: Some have continued to champion institutions to this day; I believe that some never came to understand systemic diversified community-dispersed services; some never did anything to promote Normalization; even some who liked Normalization understood it incompletely and/or did not embrace some of its implications, as documented later on in Appendix C. Some contributors dropped off the cutting edge of reform into the human service woodwork; some, though they eventually approved of the work, engaged themselves in other pursuits and were for all practical purposes no longer involved in the reform struggle. But then—as I will show later—the PCMR itself never endorsed the book either. The contributors most prominent in continuing the war joined by *Changing Patterns* in North America on an ongoing basis were—in my opinion—Nirje, Blatt, Dybwad, and I, and even we either continued to have differences on some important issues, and/or developed such as time went on. Also, all of us who did embrace Normalization still had incomplete and still-evolving notions of it, as I will also elaborate in a later section.

Interestingly, in 1970, Rothman published *Changing Patterns in Psychiatric Care*. One cannot help but wonder whether it was trying to capitalize on, or compete with, *Changing Patterns in Residential Services for the Mentally Retarded*, but it did not cite the latter, nor any of its authors, nor even carry any term that would suggest "mental retardation" in its index.

In the mid-1970s, and as part of the U.S. bicentennial of the 1776 revolution, Kugel undertook a revision of *Changing Patterns* on behalf of PCMR and invited me to co-edit it again, but I felt that such a revision was—so to speak—overtaken, and I wanted to do things I considered more important for that moment in time. So he recruited Ann Shearer to do the kind of nitty-gritty work I had done on the first edition, and the work was published—again by the PCMR—in 1976 (Kugel & Shearer). However, as I had anticipated, it received relatively little attention.

6   THE ELEMENTS OF NORMALIZATION THAT INITIALLY WERE NOVEL OR HIGHLY CONTROVERTED

A later section of this chapter will be devoted to the impact of Normalization, but in order to lay the groundwork for that topic against the historical background, I will briefly sketch some of the elements that were part of either Nirje's or my Normalization formulation, or of both, that were either new to the service scene of their time or that were intensely controverted. In order to do this, it can be very helpful to contrast some of these Normalization elements or corollaries with the ideas that prevailed previously or

concurrently about what constituted high-order promising concepts of service and/or human relationships, as covered in an earlier section.

Few of the people who came upon the human service scene after circa 1975 can even imagine how bleak things were in many human service domains, and especially in mental retardation. Rather than recapitulating the history of horror stories prior to that era—a lot of which I have done elsewhere (e.g., Wolfensberger, 1969a [reprinted 1974b, 1975a], 1991b; and in our Training Institute workshop entitled *Developments in the Field of Handicap and Mental Retardation From Prior to the Reforms of the 1950s-70s Up to the Present, With Implications for the Future: What Is Better, What Is Still the Same, What Is Getting Worse, and What Lies Ahead*)—I want to list here some of the positive measures that blew people's minds when they encountered them in real life.

For over 100 years, people had never seen a public institution get smaller, and hardly ever a private one that did. In fact, most had never seen a small institution, period. That is why so many people were bowled over by seeing some of the new small institutions that sprang up in the 1950s and 1960s, such as a small number of newly founded private ones, and others interpreted as "regional centers."

In early 1968, most of the 12 leaders of the mental retardation reform movement in Nebraska toured a small Lutheran institution for people with many kinds of handicaps in the small town of Axtell, Nebraska, and could not get over the fact that residents were called "guests," and that those who were bedridden were nonetheless dressed in normative clothes every morning. To this day, ambulatory residents of U.S. Veterans' Administration hospitals still commonly go about in bedclothes and housecoats all day.

On a visit to Germany in 1967, I learned that mentally retarded residents of an institution went integratingly to public swimming pools. This was worth writing home about!

In 1969, people's minds were blown when they saw retarded residents of group homes having free access to telephones, and conducting uncensored telephone conversations with family and friends.

My mind was blown in 1971 by witnessing retarded and nonretarded people living together on a close-to-equal basis in North America's first l'Arche community in Toronto.

People who visited the ENCOR service system in the Greater Omaha area of Nebraska in 1972 were struck by the fact that in its various service settings, there were many pictures displayed of the retarded clients.

The realistic but dignified depiction of retarded people in normative relationships and contexts in high-quality art work by Marthe Perske, starting in 1970, "gob-smacked" many people, and was a profound new kind of mental boost to many parents.

Against the background of the "bad old days" conditions, the poverty of higher-order ideas for proper services, and the little things that blew people's minds as revolutionary, we can now appreciate much better certain concepts or implications that were associated with either Nirje's and/or my Normalization formulation. I will only briefly sketch those that one would not have encountered as popular at the time, either because these things were novel, or because they had not been widely disseminated previously, or because they had been forgotten or outright rejected. It seems to me that 11 things can be put into this category.

1. The idea of applying normative conditions to deviant people. By the way, before people learned to think and talk of normalized residential settings, they sometimes did talk of "homelike" ones, but the term was almost always applied to institutional settings since the vast majority of people had never seen other kinds of residences and could not even conceive of them. Also, "homelike" largely meant "less institutional" rather than normalized. After all, such settings were literally thought of as similar to a home, but not truly like an ordinary home.

2. Striving beyond normativeness toward the societal ideal for vulnerable persons, i.e., what I later called the conservatism corollary. (See Wolfensberger, 1998, for a recent elaboration of this construct.)

3. The notion that a single theory or principle could be applied not only to all retarded people, and not only to all handicapped ones, but to all deviant ones.

4. The delineation of major historic deviancy roles and their impact on "models" of (a) social interactions, and (b) human services.

5. The power of role circularities.

6. The concept of a "developmental model."

7. The concept of (deviancy) image juxtaposition, its components, and its importance.

8. The concept of age-appropriateness, and the distinction between age-appropriate and culture-appropriate phenomena. (From my diary, I could recover that I already spoke about age-appropriateness at the October 1970 conference of the National Association for Retarded Children in Minneapolis, and possibly earlier.) The term "age-appropriate" is now encountered in generic public discourse.

9. The separation of certain service and life functions from each other; "specialization," later "model coherency."

10. The dispersal of services, in order to achieve the five desiderata of (a) avoidance of negative dynamics within larger groupings of deviant people, (b) "specialization," (c) not overloading social assimilation potentials, (d) avoidance of deviant-person and deviant-group juxtapositions, and (e) easier access by users and the public.

11. The distinction between physical and social integration, already greatly elaborated in Wolfensberger and Glenn (1973b).

In regard to numbers 7 and 10(d), the phrase "juxtaposition of deviancies" is already found in my work-related diary as early as October 1970, but its most systematic formulation came in the 1975 edition of PASS (Wolfensberger & Glenn, 1975b). The person who gave me the most decisive help in spelling out this construct was Dr. Bill Bronston, who had been sentenced by the New York State Department of Mental Hygiene to a year of penal servitude under Burton Blatt and me at Syracuse University for his role in bringing about the Willowbrook exposé.

The concept of "service specialization," which eventually became model coherency, evolved from an idea apparently first presented in 1959 by Lloyd M. Dunn, chair of the Department of Special Education at George Peabody College for Teachers (since become part of Vanderbilt University) in Nashville, Tennessee, in an advanced graduate course on social and educational aspects of mental retardation which I attended. He proposed that "omnibus" institutions for the mentally retarded be replaced by smaller, more dispersed specialized institutions for specific subgroups of different identities and needs. He also proposed this concept in a keynote address to the Southeast Region conference of the American Association on Mental Deficiency on November 9, 1961, in Nashville, Tennessee, and then later that month wrote it up into an unpublished manuscript, which he also distributed to his students. Although it was a keynote address, apparently nothing came of it, and no one apparently acted on it until I drew on his ideas to sketch a wide range of different types of residences for the mentally retarded during the 1968 crafting of the Nebraska state plan for reforming mental retardation services (Governor's Citizens' Committee on Mental Retardation, 1968a, 1968b, 1968c). Some elements of the concept of "specialization" have now become so self-evident that one has to tell horror stories in order to get people to appreciate their importance. For instance, when I visited the Elwyn Institute in Media, Pennsylvania, in April 1970, despite the fact that it was considered one of the better publicly supported institutions for the mentally retarded in the US—particularly since it also accepted residents on the basis of private payment—a living unit for females (called "Hope") had in it residents all the way from children of age 8 to adults in their 40s. However, "specialization" was not conceptualized only for residences, but as a way of designing any kind of service for what I—starting in 1974 or 1975—called "model coherency."

Among the reasons that Normalization was so powerful were three interrelated ones. (a) It enabled people to put together, into one unified mental scheme, so many things that they had seen here or there, that had positively impressed them, and that previously they had not known how to connect to each other. (b) It often told them something that they had known "inside," and to which they could now explicitly assent. (c) It gave them an idiom that enabled them to discourse explicitly and effectively on these things.

So, for instance, if they had seen persons with severe behavior problems occupy spaces that contained many breakable items and had ordinary glass windows, and own some personal possessions, who were not being unnecessarily locked up, who had some beauty in the environment, and so forth, people could now subsume all this under the "aha" idea "why, yes, these are normal things, and these are human beings, and if one treats people more normally, that will get them to act more normally."

7 THE PERIOD BETWEEN *CHANGING PATTERNS* AND THE TEXT ON *THE PRINCIPLE OF NORMALIZATION IN HUMAN SERVICES*

We will next look at certain events between 1969 and circa 1973 that had to do with people's response to *Changing Patterns*, the evolution of Normalization thinking, and how it came about that the 1972 book *The Principle of Normalization in Human Services* (Wolfensberger, 1972c) got written. Some of the items that will be covered in this and other sections of this chapter will overlap a bit, but that is unavoidable.

As it turned out, *Changing Patterns* broke the back of the institutional movement. However, it is hard to describe how, in the next few years after *Changing Patterns*, there coexisted both a wave of enthusiastic and epidemic acceptance of Normalization and the idea of community services across the US, as well as the most bitter opposition to these. Whenever I describe either one or the other, I am afraid that an audience will get the wrong impression.

Because of the bitterly divided response to Changing Patterns, the *American Journal of Mental Deficiency* (March 1971, 75[5], 645-649) took the extraordinary step of publishing reviews of it by three different parties. One of these reviews called reading it "an adventure." Another (by Cleland & Shafter, 1971) said that "If the authors . . . intended to employ social-psychological principles to evoke 'in-group' attitudes on the part of their reading audience, they appear to have achieved a breakthrough . . . ," adding that the work outlined "a plethora of scapegoating, vitriolic and stridulous censure . . . ," and "much 'sizzle' and a little 'steak.'. . ." "If these are the attitudes of the future, institutions are in for dark times—and with them, the residents . . ."

In turn, an institution superintendent in Virginia wrote (May 12, 1971) to Cleland and Shafter,

> May I congratulate you both on your restraint and detached review of "Changing Patterns in Residential Services for the Mentally Retarded" which probably has the distinction of being, next to "Christmas in Purgatory," the worst publication in the field of mental retardation. Since I am more straight forward [sic] and call "a spade a spade," I would not have been so benign in my evaluation of this pamphlet. The only disagreement I have is with

your evaluation of Wolfensberger's chapter which although somewhat better than some of the other writing, is too long and probably intended for those who are completely ignorant in this field. It intrigues me to note that the executive leadership of the NARC concurs in the views expressed in that publication. I am not too surprised.

The reason I have a copy of this letter in my files is that copies were sent all over the country by the writer.

Ironically, in 1978, Cleland wrote a textbook on mental retardation which a reviewer (Newberger, 1979) said "consistently (applied) principles of Normalization."

Another reader described the *Changing Patterns* book as "vituperative and sensationalistic."

Strangely enough, not one of these reviews, and only one of the seven others in my files, mentions the Normalization principle or Nirje's chapter (1969) on it. The one reviewer who did (Hallahan, 1970) only mentioned that the editors considered Normalization to be the single most important concept in the book. The most lauded chapter by virtually all reviewers (even those who did not like the book) was the one I wrote on "The Origin and Nature of Our Institutional Models."[8] However, while it indicted the institutional model and called for alternatives, it gave no prescriptions for such. In other words, the reviewers were so gob-smacked by the book's thorough indictment of the institutional model that their minds reeled and could hardly register the prescriptive elements, and least of all the radical nature of the Normalization principle.

Even though the PCMR had sponsored and published *Changing Patterns*, and lavishly disseminated it, the PCMR never formally endorsed it and maintained an ambivalent—sometimes even undermining—stance toward it. To begin with, the PCMR had made clear by a statement on the inside front cover of *Changing Patterns* that "the Committee has taken no position on these works. The Committee's views are presented in two reports made to the President," namely, its 1967 and 1968 annual reports.

In its own newsletter, *PCMR Message*, the PCMR announced *Changing Patterns* only in a brief neutral blurb in the February 1969 issue. It carried a brief laudatory response to it by Elsie Helsel (at that time, a major actor in the Cerebral Palsy Association of America, as well as in mental retardation) in its May

1969 issue—and that was it as far as coverage in its own very widely disseminated periodical was concerned.

Although the PCMR members had seen prepublication drafts of *Changing Patterns*, the PCMR's September 1968 second annual report to the president, *MR 68: The Edge of Change* (PCMR, 1968) did not mention it, and gave very little emphasis to proposals consistent with its reform thrust. However, it did have many proposals for making institutions better institutions!

The PCMR's third annual report (PCMR, 1969) did a bit better. While it did not mention Normalization and referred to *Changing Patterns* only by including it in a list of the PCMR's nine previous publications, it did have a sprinkling of both Vailish and Normalization-type passages.

One passage contained the Vailish formulation of "The retarded as fellow human beings having individuality, dignity and a personal stake in daily life and work" (p. 22). Normalization-inspired passages said that "we must make as great as possible integration of the retarded into normal community living" (p. 26), and "the total integration of the retarded into normal community living, working and service patterns is a long-range objective" (p. 26). A rights orientation was called for (p. 26) and institutional warehousing was condemned, but not institutions themselves (p. 26).

Worst of all, even with *Changing Patterns* in hand, the PCMR authorized a subcommittee, entitled "PCMR Work Group on Residential and Family Living" and chaired by an arch-institutionalist, to work on a separate monograph entitled *Residential Services for the Mentally Retarded: An Action Policy Proposal* (PCMR, 1970). I was given a rough draft of it to critique, and I did. It was plain awful, promoting a thinly disguised pro-regional-center-with-regional-institution model that reflected the concept of "the comprehensive residential facility" "close to the community" for "serving a region or community" that would be "participating in all phases of comprehensive planning." Residents in this center would "be helped to live as normal a life as possible in safety." In the draft of this document, the director of this kind of facility was still referred to as a "superintendent," which was changed to "administrator" in the published version. Parents and citizens were interpreted as volunteer workers "to the mentally retarded and the staff," not in governing board positions. *Changing Patterns* was listed among its references but as authored by the President's Committee, probably in order to avoid the distasteful word "Wolfensberger." Nirje was quoted—but only a 1967 paper of his, not his 1969 Normalization chapter. Two papers by Dybwad were also quoted—but again, vastly less trenchant ones than his 1969 chapter in *Changing Patterns*.

All this underlined what I had said in a previous section on the prevailing bankruptcy of vision.

After getting the prepublication copy of this document, I wrote the following:

> To my surprise I find again and again that even leading professionals in the field have neither fully conceptualized or internalized the notion of the comprehensive service system of the future of which residential components are an integral part, but merely a part. This confusion is often symptomatized by proposals to diffuse institutions, by attempts to place community services under institution administration, by attempts to interpret institutions as regional resource centers, etc. Also, many individuals confuse the concept of local services with the concept of local service centers, and fail to distinguish between local or regional offices and local or regional service systems which may be administered by but usually should not be located in a regional office. This confusion is all the more remarkable because everybody pays lip service to the concept of continuous and comprehensive services.
>
> Confusion is particularly marked in the current standards for residential services by the American Association on Mental Deficiency (AAMD)—a set of standards which only applies to institutions and not at all to the new conceptualization of local, special-purpose, dispersed services which are part of a regional service system. These standards can be cited as an example of lack of commitment to the principles of Normalization. Even the most recent statement of the President's Committee on residential services, as well as that of NARC itself, is primarily relevant to institutions, rather than to residential services in the new sense of the term. This confusion must be overcome! We may have to go back to the President's Panel report of 1963, if need be, and begin all over to explain the concept which we erroneously had assumed was understood.

One of the reasons why I referred to the AAMD standards was that they were favorably mentioned in the PCMR's June 1970 monograph. I gave feedback along the above lines to Fred Krause, a senior staff officer of PCMR (later its executive officer) with whom I was on friendly terms.

When the PCMR published the document in mid-1970, there were only two minor changes from the draft I had critiqued, and the document was published as an official document of the full PCMR, rather than only one of its committees, and without the kind of disclaimer put on *Changing Patterns*. This made it appear that even though the PCMR had published *Changing Patterns*, the PCMR did not agree with it, but did agree with what was in the 1970 document.

The low profile of the PCMR in regard to *Changing Patterns* and Normalization probably had multiple reasons. (a) The committee was divided, having several very strong pro-institution members. (b) Many of its members were oriented to center approaches and medical and/or university dominance of services, and were not very favorable to the idea of community-controlled diversified and dispersed services. (c) Some committee members were probably afraid of appearing too radical, especially with the election of Richard Nixon to the U.S. presidency in late 1968.

We therefore have to conclude that as a committee, the PCMR never realized, or wanted to acknowledge, that it had godfathered *the* crucial service reform document in mental retardation. The closest it came to such an acknowledgment occurred seven safe years later in its 1976 report *MR 76: Mental Retardation: Past and Present* (PCMR, 1977), which was published as a substantial book interpreted in a cover letter as "a concise and accurate history of mental retardation in America." Among other things, it gave considerable coverage to its own past activities and products, and, in this connection, devoted one brief paragraph to *Changing Patterns*, mentioning the principle of Normalization in connection with it and calling *Changing Patterns* one of the committee's "most influential documents"—but in the area of "institutional living" (p. 130). In its otherwise extensive index, Normalization was not even listed.

In early September 1969, the International League of Societies for the Mentally Handicapped (ILSMH), the international confederation of parent-founded national organizations, held a *Symposium on*

Residential Care in Frankfurt, Germany. In connection with this symposium, it published a monograph (*Symposium on Residential Care*; ILSMH, 1969) that contained a mixture of what appear to be background documents for, and in some cases by, participants, mostly focused on the theme of "better institutions." Ironically, this included lengthy excerpts from *Changing Patterns*, namely, from Nirje's Normalization chapter, my history chapter, and Dybwad's action implications chapter. Nirje (1992b, p. 10) also tells us that the idea of normalized residential services received a very divided reaction, despite these inclusions and despite the fact that the symposium was attended by world leaders from among the parent groups, and by Nirje, Bank-Mikkelsen, and Grunewald. Nirje said that the three of them felt frustrated, but I think that Bank-Mikkelsen and Grunewald were a bit at fault for this because their chapters in the publication were on the theme of "better" or "normalized" institutions.

While the parties with institutional investments were in an uproar over *Changing Patterns*, and while the PCMR and ILSMH leaders were equivocal, one party that embraced *Changing Patterns* literally with a vengeance was the civil rights lawyers. By the very early 1970s, material from it had already been incorporated into some of the major litigation cases on behalf of handicapped people. Even where the work was not cited directly in such cases, some of its key ideas were unmistakably used.

One promotion of *Changing Patterns* was that Grunewald, Bank-Mikkelsen, and Nirje made speaking tours across North America during 1969-1971. Grunewald's tour in spring 1969 lasted 6 weeks. At its end, he addressed the PCMR in Washington and included an almost schoolmasterly lecture on Normalization implications, which apparently did not sink in since it did not stop the publication of the PCMR's deplorable 1970 residential monograph.

At the October 1969 annual conference of the National Association for Retarded Children in Miami (where I was on a panel), Bank-Mikkelsen spoke and said that if he came back 10 years later, he would be talking of apartments for retarded adults rather than of them having private bedrooms. (Actually, our Nebraska service system started small apartments [two to three people each] as early as 1970, and three of us [Fritz, Wolfensberger, & Knowlton, 1971] wrote the

first monograph-length treatise on Normalization-based apartments.)

In early 1970, Bank-Mikkelsen and his architect, Jens Pedersen, toured the US and also addressed the PCMR and government officials, telling them that "a new epoch for the mentally retarded is here" (Staff, 1970b). In spring 1971, Bank-Mikkelsen again spoke in the US.

Between November 1970 and March 1971, Nirje spent months in North America lecturing and consulting, and with a brilliant new Normalization presentation that used many compelling slides.

I, too, was invited to speak all over North America, sometimes at the same event as other reformers, and, for this purpose, I very early began to design and use colorful teaching transparencies that were very impactful on audiences, especially since I was one of the first people to use multiple screens simultaneously. (When I saw Nirje during a visit to Sweden in April 1969, he was very interested in this development and requested that I send him copies of the transparencies, which I did.)

Also, beginning with a lecture on Normalization at the University of Minnesota in Minneapolis on July 27, 1970, I started projecting 35 mm slides on two screens simultaneously, usually pairing up a shot of a very bad situation on the left screen with an analagous shot of a similar setting and service of a positive nature on the right screen. I used this method many times during the next few years, and it was very impactful. Of course, one could only do this if one had many slides from among which one could make proper pairings.

On several occasions Bank-Mikkelsen and I spoke to the same audience, as at the May 1971 convention of the California Association for Retarded Children. At many of my presentations related to Normalization and residential services during circa 1967-1972, audiences would leap to their feet in standing ovations, especially at state ARC conventions, despite the fact that Normalization was so new to them that some people had difficulty pronouncing and spelling it.

Several of my friends or allies also began to speak widely. For instance, Robert Perske was beginning to make a national reputation for himself in the very early 1970s, and he, too, began to speak widely on Normalization, especially his novel idea of "the dignity of risk." In June 1972 alone, he spoke on

Normalization to the very influential Pennsylvania Association for Retarded Children, and to the North Dakota one.

As mentioned, key reform ideas contained in *Changing Patterns* had begun to be promoted in print even before *Changing Patterns* was published (in Governor's Citizens' Committee, 1968a, 1968b, 1968c; Menolascino, Clark, & Wolfensberger, 1968a, 1968b). Once it was published, Dybwad heavily promoted it in his many presentations, which were often converted to circulated handouts. (However, strangely enough, in the 1970 chapter by Dybwad and Dybwad [1970] on mental retardation community services around the world, *Changing Patterns* was not mentioned as the blockbuster it was, but only in extremely understated and casual fashion as "a very useful book" [p. 235]. It was not mentioned at all in Lippman's [1970] chapter on "Community Organization: USA" in the same book. Apparently, it required a bit more hindsight to perceive how this document was different from other reform-oriented documents of the era of circa 1965-1975.) I wrote a small avalanche of works that were not on Normalization specifically, but that mentioned it or promoted its corollaries (Wolfensberger, 1969b, 1970a, 1970b, 1971a, 1971b [both reprinted in Rosen, Clark, & Kivitz, 1976], 1972a, 1972b; Wolfensberger & Menolascino, 1970a, 1970b).

For instance, I discovered that the president-elect of the American Association on Mental Deficiency had read some of the same historical documents as I had for my "Origins and Nature" chapter. We agreed to coauthor an article (White & Wolfensberger, 1969) that drew heavily on this chapter. White was probably the first president ever of the American Association on Mental Deficiency to indict the American institution system in mental retardation. His coauthorship lent prestige to the reform ideas.

Another example was a 1969 article in which I made 20 predictions about the future of residential services for the mentally retarded and where I said, "The model implied by Nirje, Dunn, Tizard and Dybwad is the only one on the horizon that is both truly new and consistent with contemporary values" (Wolfensberger, 1969b, pp. 53-54).

In his *Changing Patterns* chapter on Normalization, Nirje (1969) had spelled out eight specific corollaries of Normalization, which he elaborated in his later publications. Soon, someone (I am not sure who) took these eight points and rewrote them in telegraphic and colloquial style. These are reproduced in Appendix D under Nirje's name, though I doubt he ever wrote the points in this fashion. I suspect that they were composed in this format by staff at the National Institute on Mental Retardation in Canada for inclusion in the institute's *Orientation Manual* (e.g., National Institute on Mental Retardation [1977] and perhaps also its earlier first edition which—amazingly—I could not find in my archives). Then some other unknown party reprinted this list on a single sheet of parchment, which was distributed by the zillions and used as a handout, pinup, in manuals, and so forth.

Normalization ideas were also widely disseminated to parents of retarded persons by Perske's very successful 1973 book, *New Directions for Parents of Persons Who Are Retarded* (Perske, 1973; revised 1982).

The first large-scale practical application of Nirje's Normalization ideas in North America of which I know was enabled by the production and use of the first edition of the Program Analysis of Service Systems, or PASS, tool in Nebraska (Wolfensberger & Glenn, 1969). The reform leadership in the state called for a tool that would enable it to channel almost all of the first state fund allocations under the state's new mental retardation reform bill to normalizing community services, and keep some powerful bodies—such as the university and private institutions—from de facto stealing this money. With the help of Linda Glenn, I conceptualized what was to become the first of three editions of PASS (Wolfensberger & Glenn, 1969) in mid-1969, with the final version of the first edition being released to a restricted circulation on November 1, 1969. It was heavily referenced to Nirje's and Dybwad's chapters in *Changing Patterns*, with five of its 31 ratings being called "Normalization-related": Normalization itself, integration, dispersal, specialization (which eventually became model coherency), and deviancy contact. The latter dealt with the amount of client contact with deviant staff and other deviant clients and was probably highly related to the integration rating. A "deinstitutionalization" rating was put under the rubric of ideological state priorities.

Between January and March 1970, PASS was already being administered to service agencies that applied for state funding. It turned out that when the agencies that we were afraid of saw the instrument, they decided not to even apply for funds because they could not hope to compete in terms of the instrument's criteria. Those that did apply and fell short, but not too short, were funded with the requirement that they would bring their practices into closer conformity with the instrument. The same process was repeated the next year, and there were significant improvements in PASS scores.

About 1½ years after *Changing Patterns* appeared, some of the giants started blinking.

Dybwad and I had been involved up to our eyeballs in change agentry activities in or with Pennsylvania. In May 1970, Dr. Donald Jolly of the mental retardation office of Pennsylvania convened a small invitational get-together in Hershey, between several top people in the state's mental retardation system, potential new commercial service providers from all over the US, two key people from the Pennsylvania ARC (Pat Clapp and Hannah Geisel), and I, which was a little like a struggle of the latter three against the devil—and we won. A superintendent of one of the state's worst hellholes made one of the most explicit public confessions of an evil commitment to enmity toward the retarded that I have ever witnessed, and I chastised him grimly for it, after which he had nothing more to say.

Among others, one of the things that happened there was, unbeknownst to most people, the most crucial turning point in mental retardation in Pennsylvania, a key state. Only two days after this meeting, the governor of Pennsylvania announced that he would seek a break with the past and endorsed a community services approach much along the lines pioneered in Nebraska and recommended in *Changing Patterns*. In July 1970, the Pennsylvania Senate approved a bill that included a provision for "normalizing accommodations." After Nebraska, Pennsylvania was one of the first states, and the first large state, to commit itself to normalized community services, which made this event so important. The reason I am not mentioning Connecticut along the same lines is that it remained stuck stubbornly on its regional center model for many years to come—a model that would have been impressive if it had not been overtaken almost as soon as it was being implemented to any extent.

In October 1970, the annual convention of the U.S. National Association for Retarded Children (now called The Arc) passed a resolution endorsing "Normalization of the retarded and their assimilation into society as persons and citizens," and expressing its "appreciation and gratitude to Dr. Wolf Wolfensberger for his untiring commitment of time, energy and thought" on behalf of retarded people and the Normalization principle.

On December 10, 1948, the UN adopted a universal declaration of human rights.[9] In June 1967, a symposium on *Legislative Aspects of Mental Retardation* of the International League of Societies for the Mentally Handicapped, held in Stockholm, spelled out various proposed rights of retarded people. In October 1968, the league adopted a "Declaration of General and Specific Rights of the Mentally Retarded" that was modeled on the UN declaration. (It had been drafted largely by Elizabeth Boggs, one of the parent founders of NARC.) In turn, on December 20, 1971, the UN General Assembly passed a "Declaration on the Rights of Mentally Retarded Persons," which differed only in minor ways from the League's statement. It incorporated two references to "normal life," which probably would not have happened if Nirje's 1969 chapter on Normalization had not been produced. One of these passages referred to "the necessity of assisting mentally retarded persons to develop their abilities in various fields of activities and of promoting their integration as far as possible in normal life . . ." The second one said that "if care in an institution becomes necessary, it should be provided in surroundings and other circumstances as close as possible to those of normal life." Unfortunately, this phrase still resonated with the idea of the "better normalized institution."

Obviously, Normalization, service reform, and community service ideas were gathering an avalanche of momentum. It was largely in response to the threat posed by these ideas that the superintendents of U.S. institutions for the mentally retarded got together in 1971 and formed an organization named the National Association of Superintendents of Public Residential Facilities. It held its first annual meeting in conjunction with the annual convention of the American Association on Mental Deficiency in 1971. Of course, it is very likely that association members and others would have denied then, and may still deny today, that the organization was founded as a defensive measure against the new community services avalanche. However, that this was a real concern is apparent in an editorial article in the fourth issue of the organization's newsletter in March 1972 by its chairman, entitled, "The Need for Accountability in Community Mental Retardation Programs," which preposterously implied that institutions had been and were accountable but community services were not. In order to buttress that idea, and in support of the "better institutions" concept, a major concern of the new organization in its early years was the development of institutional accreditation standards.

The appearance of *Changing Patterns* also gave yet another big spin to European study visits by North Americans, and in fact launched something I earlier called "Scandimania." Among other things, several universities—above all the University of Wisconsin—and some private entrepreneurs organized annual tours of human services in Europe, especially, Scandinavia. Some of the tours specialized in taking parents of retarded children.

In 1971, Sweden held what appears to have been the first European conference on special education, and much of it, and the material about it, was in English. At first flattered by their status as models, services in Denmark and Sweden soon felt overrun by overseas visitors.

8 AN INTERPOLATIVE NOTE ON THE ONGOING EVOLUTION OF NORMALIZATION IDEAS INTO THE EARLY 1970S

Before going on to the description of how the writing of *The Principle of Normalization in Human Services* (Wolfensberger, 1972c) came about, I want to interpolate a section that documents the fact that during the late 1960s and early 1970s, there was still much evolution going on in the thinking about Normalization, including by Nirje himself. I believe that it is failure to parse the history of the idea of Normalization into its proper phases, and to recognize the different steps in the evolution of Normalization, that has led to much confusion about whom to credit for what.

Many people have claimed that this or that speaker or writer had invented Normalization prior to its Scandinavian formulation of the 1959-1972 era. One thing that is true is that the moral treatment scheme had been very concordant with Normalization, though the British version of William Tuke (1732-1822) much more so than the French version of Philippe Pinel (1745-1826). In the US, moral treatment ideas were particularly strongly—but futilely—promoted by Samuel Gridley Howe (1802-1876) over a period of decades during the mid- and late 19th century. The reason this turned out to be futile was that moral treatment was resoundingly rejected between circa 1860-1885 in favor of a new materialized and medicalized way of thinking about human beings and human services, and by the mid-20th century, few people in human services who were not also historians would have known what moral treatment was, or even have heard of it. In fact, the systematized Normalization from 1969 onward can be considered to be almost a reinvention of moral treatment from a different perspective.

However, all the claims that Normalization had been formulated in a recognizable form in the 20th century prior to the 1959-1972 era I have so far found to be false. It is true that the verb "to normalize" had been used in English since at least 1865 to mean making something abnormal normal, and the noun "Normalization" had been used in the same sense since at least 1882. One can even find the verb "to normalize" in an English-German dictionary of 1906, if not earlier. But mere uses of these words outside a more systematic context of explicated meaning cannot be taken to signify the same thing as Normalization did once it was defined by Nirje (1969).

Prior to 1969, there had been a few instances of the term "Normalization" in reference to human service, a rare outcry to let people be normal, and a fair number of calls for specific isolated measures that we can interpret as having been consistent with parts of the Normalization theory yet to come. Beatrice Wright—a prominent leader in the field of physical impairment—even used the term "anormalization" (1960, 1966). However, the only way one could interpret any of these instances to be equivalent to what Normalization became in 1969 is if one did not understand Normalization, or wanted to depreciate the achievement of Nirje's, and later Wolfensberger's, systematization.

According to Ericsson (1986), the "Normalization of life conditions," and even the term "Normalization principle," were used with a limited meaning as early as 1943 by a Swedish government commission, but he does not provide a reference to any such commission document. Ericsson also credits Bank-Mikkelsen with having spoken in the 1950s of the enablement of "a normal existence" for retarded people, but he cites a 1964 statement by Bank-Mikkelsen, rather than a 1950s document. In light of the many erroneous retrospective claims and historical revisionisms that I have been able to identify in regard to Normalization history, with people often being said to have spoken about Normalization when they never actually used Normalization terms, a verbatim citation of original documents is essential in order to buttress a claim.

What I mean by this is illustrated by the fact that Normalization is never mentioned in at least the English translations of the two major pieces of Scandinavian legislation that are often said to be major milestones in the legal encoding of the Normalization principle.

The 1959 Danish "Act Concerning the Care of the Mentally Retarded and Other Exceptionally Retarded Persons" (Bank-Mikkelsen, 1969)[10] certainly does not mention Normalization in its English translation, and even the terms "normal" or "normally" appear only once each in respect to compulsory education being normal, as well as its termination at age 21 (p. 248). However, according to Nirje (1992b), the preamble of the law also contained the phrase "to let the mentally retarded obtain an existence as close to normal as possible" (the phrase is not included in what Bank-Mikkelsen [1969] called a "copy" of the law in English in *Changing Patterns*), but as Nirje said, "none of us were yet ready to talk about 'Normalization' and even less about a 'principle.'"

The English translation of the 1967 Swedish "Law About Provisions and Services for the Mentally Retarded" (e.g., Nirje, 1969) also does not seem to mention "Normalization," nor does it even seem to use the phrases "normal" or "normally." Even to the degree that elements of a Normalization idiom had been used early on, this cannot be automatically assumed to mean that it referred to an idea that came close to Nirje's 1969 formulation. I therefore offer the following proposal.

While Nirje (1992a, 1992b) credits Bank-Mikkelsen with the idea, I would put it differently. I would say that Nirje was the first publicly prominent person who stated, in 1969, a systematized formulation of the Normalization principle, *and* in conjunction with a highly developed Normalization idiom, such as the terms "the principle of Normalization" and "the Normalization principle."

As for Bank-Mikkelsen, I would say that he had the vision of a direction into which things should move and was the person in an executive capacity to be able to actually implement measures in this direction earlier, on a higher level, and more systematically than others, but his thinking was not evolving as rapidly as Nirje's during the late 1960s and early 1970s. Instead, he was more of a "pathbeater," a *Vorgänger*. I also suspect that even on the administrative-implementive plane, he may have been overtaken by Grunewald and Swedish developments around 1970, because Danish developments were by then going too much according to an earlier plan that was already being overtaken by new ideas, much as happened in Connecticut at the same time, while Sweden was still unfreezing its earlier patterns and showing more flexibility with new ideas.

Evidence that Bank-Mikkelsen was still evolving his thinking includes that, in 1969, he praised the use of convicts as ward aides in a Massachusetts facility (Staff, 1970b, p. 7)—something that my own formulation of Normalization interpreted, as early as the same year, as denormalizing (e.g., in Wolfensberger & Glenn, 1969) because of what we later called "deviant staff juxtaposition."

Evidence that Nirje's own Normalization ideas were still very much evolving between 1967 and 1971 includes the fact that his March 1967 presentation on it in Nebraska was not nearly as well developed as one he gave there in January 1971. Also, I have in my archives a six-page memo Nirje wrote, dated June 12, 1968, entitled "Outline for a Plan to Attack Inhuman Conditions in the United States' Institutions for the Mentally Retarded" [see appendix to chapter 2]. From the dating, it is clear that Nirje wrote these recommendations at the headquarters of the National Association for Retarded Children in New York, and probably at least in part in preparation for his trip to the Washington office of the President's Committee, and only about a week before writing the first draft of

83

his contribution to *Changing Patterns*. The document was full of new ideas and proposals, many of which have since been accepted and implemented—but strangely enough, the principle of Normalization was not mentioned once. Instead, the language revolved around combatting "dehumanization," and "dignity" was mentioned—that is, the two key concepts of Vail. Also, better, smaller, and less remote institutions with wards of up to 20 residents continued to be promoted in this document as a major remedy for some types of retarded persons.

When I visited Bank-Mikkelsen in Denmark in April 1969, and *Changing Patterns* had already been out several months, one expression he used, which meant as much as Normalization to him, was that the mentally retarded "need the same living conditions as the population in general." How underdeveloped the concept of image juxtaposition then still was in Bank-Mikkelsen's mind was brought out by the fact that he was rather gleeful about the Danish mental retardation services being funded to a very large extent by a tax on alcohol and tobacco (called a "vice tax" in the United States), which he said was also a practice in Iceland at that time. Further, neither in Denmark nor in Sweden did I hear it stated in 1969 that even the most lavish institutional or segregated educational provisions fell short of full Normalization. In 1964, Bank-Mikkelsen (1964) had spoken of "day institutions" for people living at home (p. 3), of "non-residential institutions" (p. 5), and of "regional centers." Indeed, in Denmark, several large old institutions served in this capacity for some time into the 1970s, at least.

Altogether, it is not surprising that some people who had been to Scandinavia during the late 1960s picked up some Normalization ideas and language, but also the idea that institutions could be normalized. For instance, in October 1967, after coming back from her tour of Denmark and Sweden as part of the PCMR subcommittee mentioned earlier, Muriel Humphrey (1968), the vice-president's wife, a member of PCMR, and a grandmother of a child with Down's syndrome, called for "[creating] in institutions as normal a living pattern . . . as possible," and to "encourage normal living . . ." Her remarks were published in the March 1968 issue of the PCMR newsletter, *PCMR Messenger*. Note that while she had gotten the phrasing "as normal as possible" from her visit to Denmark, she was also still thinking of normalized institutions, just

as continued to be pursued in Scandinavia for years to come.

Also, Nirje saw it apparently as no big problem to work for a branch of the Ontario government between 1971-1978, that was concerned mostly with institutions for the retarded. This is, in fact, when tension between us developed because I also worked in Canada during 1971-1973. (We moved there within two months of each other, both having been extruded from our jobs, as further told in the next section.) My main role there was to dismantle the institution system in favor of community service systems that were run by community bodies rather than the provincial government, and I saw Nirje's boss as being largely on the other side.

I also observed—and got the data to prove it—that in 1969, residential placement outside the home of retarded children in Denmark and Sweden was not strongly discouraged and that for retarded adults, it was actually encouraged. In fact, Nirje's (1969) statement that it is normal for adults to move out of the parental home was often translated to mean that the person should move into a group home or agency apartment. This accounted in good part for the fact that these countries had higher residential placement rates than the US *despite* lower rates of prevalence of mental retardation (e.g., Wolfensberger, 1980).

Now let me say something about the evolution of my own thinking on Normalization. My first exposure to Normalization—namely, to Nirje's 1967 presentation in Lincoln, Nebraska—did impress me, but it did not produce a breakthrough in my mind. I can only hope that this was Nirje's fault and not my own, but I doubt that we will ever know. Four more things had to happen before my "aha" experience was completed.

The first was to—finally—see Nirje's writing for *Changing Patterns*, upon which Kugel and I agreed, and stated so in *Changing Patterns*, that Normalization was "perhaps the single most important concept that emerged in this compendium" (p. 10), as was also reiterated in Dybwad's chapter (p. 385).

The second thing was Grunewald's visit to Nebraska on his spring 1969 tour of the US. We scheduled his visits wall-to-wall, starting with a TV news conference at the airport when he arrived, parties late into the night, early-morning working breakfasts, meetings with the governor, and speeches. At one public presentation in Omaha (March 18, 1969), Grunewald explained the Swedish service situation and elements of the Normalization principle and showed a number of very persuasive slides. He emphasized that we should be using Normalization-relevant terminology, citing as an example the phrase "preschool" for a child center as being normalizing, but not the expressions "prevocational" or "day developmental child center." After Grunewald came down sick from exhaustion and we had evidently used him up, we put him on an airplane to his next host. But then getting sick was partly his own fault because I had written him beforehand to "come well-steeled and well-rested—as we are planning a rich experience for you."

The third contribution to my "aha" experience was touring services in Denmark and Sweden in spring 1969. Because of a providential accident of history, I received a subsidy from the American Baptist Home Mission Societies to visit services in Denmark and Sweden for two weeks in spring 1969. (This organization had recruited me to lead a group study tour, but when the group idea fell through, they gave me the funds to do it on my own.) These two weeks were scheduled so hectically that I hardly got any sleep. In Sweden, the wall-to-wall scheduling by Karl Grunewald and Bengt Nirje was a bit of an act of gleeful revenge for my having done the same thing to them earlier in Nebraska. Soon, I came down with a throat infection, which Karl Grunewald cured with penicillin.

There were days when I visited as many as five different services, but the brevity of visits did not prevent me from prodigious learning. The range of services visited was very wide, from integrated athletic after-school programs to segregated institutions. The area in which I learned the most, and where I felt North America was furthest behind, was what the Scandinavians called "activation," that is, keeping severely handicapped people from becoming, or remaining, nonambulatory and mentally dulled. My notes say that second most important to my learning was Normalization and humanization with respect to even the most profoundly retarded people.

Prior to my trip, I anticipated that I would be taking a great many photos for teaching purposes back home, but I had no idea how many things worth photographing I would encounter. Already on the first

or second day, I had to send someone out to replenish my supply of film and flashbulbs. Those were the days when one had to set one's camera's focus and exposure by hand, and I had no light meter because it was a very expensive item then, but to my great relief several weeks later, virtually all my pictures came out good—a staggering 300 of them, which became the foundation of years of my teaching on Normalization and activation. Surprisingly, many of these pictures are as valid today in what they could teach as they were then.

One of the things that I found aesthetically almost overwhelming was the consistent tasteful beautification of indoor environments in Scandinavia, in people's homes, public places, and service settings, with much use of color, plants, and candles.

When, promptly upon my return, I wrote a letter of gratitude to the Baptist Home Mission Societies, I mentioned naively that I might write one or two papers on what I had learned. To Nirje I wrote—admittedly in an awkward style—that "The single profoundest learning experience I had was in regard to the virtual abolition of the bedfast person and how this is to be abolished." However, I added three criticisms. (a) I said that "I did not see a single institution that I really found to be necessary, not even if it was small." (b) I felt that resources, though lavish, were not efficiently used. (c) People in Scandinavia had very little interchange with each other and were therefore woefully ignorant of what was going on in locales other than their own, and I proposed that something be done about this. I sent almost identical feedback to Grunewald.

The idea that nonambulation could be almost 100% prevented or reversed, and that, at any rate, no one needed to be bedridden, was so unimaginable in North America that people simply did not believe it. For instance, when I lectured with my Scandinavian slides, people would often claim that the Scandinavians were simply hiding their nonambulatory people from visitors. One line of argument was that in Sweden, the profoundly retarded and multiply handicapped were classified as "chronically ill" and put into facilities other than mental retardation institutions. I wrote to Grunewald about this in late 1969, and we discussed in several letters the idea of making comparative surveys of the prevalence of nonambulation among retarded people in Nebraska and Sweden.

In Appendix E, I have noted some of my experiences on this trip on which I have either never reported in print, or which are worth recapitulating.

The fourth event that nailed down my "aha" experience was Nirje's aforementioned return trip to Nebraska in January 1971. He spoke on several occasions, one of these being in Lincoln on January 9, 1971, at a workshop for training the new workers in the new community services in Nebraska. Even at this late date, I learned a great deal and made many notes in my diary. Here are some of his statements that I recorded.

"If need be, education must be brought to the bedside."

"Mentally retarded people are normal persons with a specific handicap."

"The larger the place, the shorter should be a person's stay there," which referred to residences for the retarded.

"When I see faces in the window, I know something is wrong," referring again to residences for the retarded.

"Don't speak of a person as mentally retarded in his presence unless he does it first."

In my diary, I organized my notes of response to Nirje's talk. I told the audience that there were so many new ideas and concepts in the presentation that, like with Nirje's 1967 presentation, it was almost too much to digest. But as we had told all the Scandinavians, I promised that "we will not merely apply Normalization, but outnormalize the Scandinavians," which, at least in many respects, did in fact happen. I said that I had seen the best institutions in Denmark and Sweden, and still believed that these were not needed if only we were to "specialize." I said that, as in Sweden, we must begin to include retarded persons on service-related committees, and that they would often function as "hidden teachers" to other committee members even if their contribution was not of a problem-solving nature. I also issued a warning to the directors of the new community services who were there: "Brace yourselves! We will put our demands into a little red book"—an allusion to Mao's little red book in China—but, as it turned out, my 1972 text on Normalization had a big red circle on its covers.

A few days later, Nirje gave a similar presentation in Omaha, where I also continued my line of remarks that retarded persons must not only be trained for committee work, but must also be oriented to represent others, not just their own person. I pointed out that the apartment-living projects Nirje had helped start in Uppsala, Sweden, were the "parents" of the apartment projects that had just been launched in Nebraska. A retarded man with limited sight and hearing was in the audience, and someone told him, "Because of this man [i.e., Nirje], you can live in your apartment like any of us."

Even as I was still learning Normalization, my own ideas began to diverge with what I consider to be three kinds of contributions to the theory in the early 1970s: (a) teasing out some of the rules implied by specific stated Normalization implications, (b) generalizing them to all (what I then called) deviancies, and (c) relating these rules to the larger body of sociopsychological science.

I saw it as a waste of my time to undertake the writing of the detailed reviews of the relevant research in the sociopsychological literature that people of academia love, and thought that others would gladly jump on the opportunity to do so. In this hope I was somewhat disappointed, but I was satisfied with stating what I considered to be empirically well-established facts that were proof of the validity of Normalization, and later SRV, as a high-level and consistent theory for addressing social devaluation.

There is much else to say about the evolution of Normalization thinking, such as via the three editions of PASS (Wolfensberger & Glenn, 1969, 1973a, 1973b, 1975a, 1975b), the construct of model coherency, the various editions of PASSING (Wolfensberger & Thomas, 1980, 1983, 1988), and the Social Role Valorization monograph (Wolfensberger, 1991a, 1992, 1998), but here, I only wanted to cover the topic enough (a) to convince readers that Normalization was very much an evolving concept all along, and to some degree still is, considering the steady progress being made in SRV theory by the members of the North American SRV Development, Training and Safeguarding Council (Thomas, 1994), and (b) to make clear what the relative roles were of the early key actors in Normalization during the crucial founding era.

One reason that everyone with previous human service involvement had to do a lot of evolving and working through was that we were all caught up by old mental bonds that needed to be broken. Our reorientation to new ideas simply could not occur all at once, but just one step at a time—though many of us took many steps in very rapid succession. The only people around 1969-1971 who took to Normalization like fish to water were lawyers and ordinary citizens of goodwill who were given a good explanation of it. Many of them responded in a way one could summarize as "Of course, why not?"

9 THE PRODUCTION OF THE *NORMALIZATION* TEXT

The next topic I will cover interlaces the story of how the *Normalization* text (Wolfensberger, 1972c; partially reprinted in Blatt, Biklen, & Bogdan, 1977, and Romot, 1979) came about, how I universalized Normalization applicability to deviancy in general,[11] and how my reform work got me into trouble in my job and got me driven out of the country.

Even before *Changing Patterns* was sent to the printer, I had begun to incorporate Normalization into my teaching and speaking. While attending the annual conference of the National Association for Retarded Children in Detroit in October 1968, I noted in my diary that the Normalization coverage contained in *Changing Patterns* would not be enough and that some other "paper" on it would be needed, and soon began to write some position papers and articles on it, the first one being on its applicability to "mental health" services.

One reason for this was that my primary academic appointment at the University of Nebraska was in the Department of Psychiatry, which in turn was located in a building that was both part of the university as well as one of the state's mental institutions, though its smallest one. It was called the Nebraska Psychiatric Institute. It had several clinical service units, of which several were residential units that deeply scandalized me, partly because of their dehumanizing features and partly because of their otherwise low quality and irrational nature.

There never was any interest among the vast majority of the 300-plus staff members at the institute in the mental retardation reform work in which I was a major actor on the national, state, and local levels, not even when the developments in Nebraska became

a world model. In fact, to the director of the institute, who was also the chairperson of the psychiatry department, the more local our successes were, the more threatening they were because they made local psychiatric practices look very bad. He also had the idea that since I was a psychologist, I should be "doing real clinical work," by which he meant testing and psychotherapizing people.

My job started down the skids when, in May 1968, I wrote a memo to the institute director protesting the violation of citizenship rights of our "patients," including their confinement in locked units, and warned that this might lead to lawsuits against the institute. In July 1968, I pointed out the irony of the institute releasing a public relations film about itself that was entitled "Opening Doors" while it put people behind locked doors "for their own good."

In October 1968, I wrote three position papers on what I now call "shrink" services (a term I later began to use in order to avoid the term "mental health," which might convey a legitimizing message) in Nebraska and at the institute, and also sent the director prepublication copies of Nirje's two *Changing Patterns* chapters, spelling out how Normalization could be applied in the field of mental disorder. This development had great significance for Normalization because it established—as far as I know, for the first time—that Normalization was readily generalizable to fields other than mental retardation. I also spelled out the profound conflict of interest created by a university department being paid to run a state institution and other clinical services, and how this was a major obstacle to staff becoming community-oriented.

One of the psychiatrists who was asked to critique one of these position papers wrote an apoplectic response to it, among other things characterizing it as "autistic reductionism," and Normalization was greeted with "what else is new"—and all that in a setting that was just short of being a snake pit for its inpatients.

Undaunted by these onslaughts, I took parts of my in-house position papers and drafted a manuscript, which, in August 1969, I submitted boldly to the *American Journal of Psychiatry*, the flagship publication of American shrinkery. Within weeks, the editor advised me to reduce it by half, throw out a section on the contemporary context of psychiatry in society and on the service-model crisis in psychiatry, and to resubmit it. This I did, with a heavy heart, in

October, and the resultant paper that was very narrowly focused on Normalization was then accepted in January 1970 and—to the fury of my psychiatric colleagues and superiors—published in the September issue (Wolfensberger, 1970b; reprinted in Smrtic, 1979). One of the points the article made was that "obviously, a community mental health center attempting to offer 'comprehensive' services under one roof is likely to violate the Normalization principle" (p. 294), which probably crazified the minds of most readers, because these centers were then widely seen as the best new hope in mental care, as mentioned before.

Soon after the article came out, several people who had been victims of the mental field and/or its institutions wrote to me in gratitude. Also, *Time* magazine got wind of the article and wrote a piece on it in the October 12, 1970, issue, entitled "Is Basket Weaving Harmful?", that just about sealed my doom at the Nebraska Psychiatric Institute.

It also certainly did not help that in 1970, I published a chapter in a major psychiatry text (Wolfensberger, 1970a) that described the tension between the status quo defensiveness in psychiatric agencies and services, and the culture and functions of change and research. Since this description also applied to the service function of the institute, it was yet another nail in my coffin, together with the point I made that most of the functions performed by psychiatrists in mental retardation could be—and commonly were—performed by other professions.

Starting soon after these events, both personnel support and physical space began to be taken away from me, my position was "reorganized," and my situation there became untenable to me in a number of ways. All my other achievements at that time were not of relevance or interest to my psychiatric colleagues and superiors, including my work on *Changing Patterns,* which probably few even knew about. So, mournfully, I began looking for another job. My dean, Kugel, was not pleased to see me leave but apparently thought that protecting me would incur too high a political cost to his position. Unlike other professors who perished when they did not publish, I perished in good part because of *what* I published.

Interestingly, the impact of the offending article on the mental field, for all I can tell, has been nil, as had been the distribution of *Changing Patterns* to all mental institution directors and other mental health leaders. Among other things, the mental field in the US has assimilated relatively few Normalization ideas, including the importance of keeping residential congregations of its clients small.

Before I left the institute, I also rewrote the part of my manuscript that the *American Journal of Psychiatry* had made me throw out, and submitted this in February 1970 as a separate article to the *American Journal of Psychiatry*, by which it was rejected in April with the advice to submit it to a social or community psychiatry journal. So within days, I submitted it to the *Community Mental Health Journal*, by which it was also promptly rejected in June 1970. I then submitted it in September 1970 to *Psychiatry*, after revising it to fit its different manuscript style. In November, I was told that even though the referees were divided in their opinions, it would not be published because it covered nothing "strikingly new to those who are already conversant with the issues." After that, I gave up trying to get shrink journals to publish it, but I mention all this here because the manuscript eventually played a part in bringing about the 1972 *Normalization* text.

Overlapping with these developments, but limping somewhat behind them, was the production of some articles for the mental retardation field. Some of these were not specific to Normalization, but featured it in significant ways. For instance, already in 1970, two colleagues from Omaha (a student under my supervision, and the residential director of the newly created ENCOR service system described by Lensink [1976]) and I wrote a monograph that was the first systematic statement on Normalization-based apartment living. This was published in 1971 (Fritz, Wolfensberger, & Knowlton, 1971) by the Canadian Association for the Mentally Retarded, to whose National Institute on Mental Retardation I was about to move for two years as a visiting scholar.

Also, in the October 1971 issue of *Mental Retardation* (Wolfensberger, 1971a; reprinted in Rosen, Clark, & Kivitz, 1976), I wrote about four phenomena of high concern to Normalization that are major corollaries of deindividualization such as one typically finds in institutions: (a) congregation of clients in numbers larger than one typically finds in the community; (b) an environment that is geared to the least functional member(s) of a grouping; (c) reduction of autonomy and increase in regimentation, including moving people about in groups; and (d) the conflation into a single setting of life functions that ordinary citizens tend to carry out in different settings (i.e., the opposite of "specialization"). In a continuation article in the December 1971 issue of the same journal (Wolfensberger, 1971b; reprinted in Rosen, Clark, & Kivitz, 1976), I sketched the normalizing opposite, namely, residences of family size that were highly specialized in their mission and manpower structure, with "separation of functions such as sleeping . . . working, treatment and playing," physically and socially integrated into the community so they could be "individualized and individualizing," convey "high expectancy for normalized behavior," and afford greater autonomy (Wolfensberger, 1971b, p. 31). However, I also predicted that the need for group homes could be reduced by two measures: individual placements and family subsidy (pp. 32-33), for which I pleaded. This idea had been presented in chapters by Cooke (1969) and me (Wolfensberger, 1969c) in *Changing Patterns*, but had been totally ignored. Spelling out the economic benefits, I characterized such subsidizing as "one of the most efficient service options" and predicted that it "will become an accepted provision that will contribute to the lowered demand for removal of a child from his home" (p. 34). (Today, this is hailed as a postnormalization era invention under various new names, which may include the words "individual," "supported," "planning," "brokerage," or "direct funding.") I even predicted that "the need for any type of group residence will decline, except perhaps for the aged retarded . . ." (p. 37).

However, entirely specific to Normalization was a series of four articles on which Robert Perske and I had begun to collaborate (three by me, one by him, but each critiqued by the other author) that incorporated what we had learned in Scandinavia. In March 1970, we submitted these four articles as a single package to *Mental Retardation*, one of the two major journals of the American Association on Mental Deficiency. Usually, manuscripts got reviewed in about four months, but parts of these manuscripts—believe it or not—got misplaced by the editor, and it took several letters of inquiry and complaint, and a full seven months, to get the reply (in October 1970) that the papers had all been rejected, allegedly because they had nothing new or substantive to say. A reviewer of one of the papers said ". . . so much of this paper has been said elsewhere and—in recent years—has been

said so many times . . . for example, the question of integrated and segregated special class education and the principle of Normalization both have been covered many times in our literature." The claim that Normalization had been covered many times in the literature prior to 1970 was, of course, totally false. After all, even the very term "Normalization" had been almost completely alien to human services before 1969.

All this made me angry, so in late October or early November 1970, I decided to bypass the article review process of my field by taking all four rejected manuscripts, plus the one rejected by the psychiatric journals, plus the psychiatric one that got published, enlarging all these, adding yet other chapters, and working it all into a book, to be entitled *The Principle of Normalization in Human Services*. I asked Nirje to write two chapters, one on "Normalization in Law: An Example from Sweden" and the other on "The Right to Self-Determination," which was to include a description of the beginnings of what is now called self-advocacy, and the integrated social clubs that I had seen in Sweden that formed the training ground for retarded young people to participate in public affairs, but only the latter chapter came to be—and it turned out to be another cliff-hanger.

According to my notes, I had Nirje start writing on his chapter as early as during his January 1971 visit to Nebraska, entailing more sleepless nights on many people's parts. However, once again, the chapter was not finished until late 1972, when the rest of the book was virtually in hand. I had to lure Nirje once more into a trap and lock him up around the clock at the National Institute on Mental Retardation in Toronto, with 24-hour coverage by secretaries and me, which once more worked.

Braving a snowstorm, I attended the 1971 convention of the North Central Association for Retarded Children in Des Moines, Iowa, and there heard Gunnar Dybwad speak (on February 5) on the role of the law. So I asked him to write a chapter on legal aspects of Normalization, drawing on the legal developments in Pennsylvania, and also a chapter on "The Role of the Consumer Movement in the Implementation of Normalization Principles." Because he was too busy (among other things being acting dean at Brandeis University), I asked Perske to write the latter, but he could not do it either, so both chapters remained unwritten. But Dybwad (1973) did produce a chapter similar to the one I wanted on the "consumer" movement for the book on *Citizen Advocacy and Protective Services for the Impaired and Handicapped* (Wolfensberger & Zauha, 1973) on which I was working at about the same time.

At first, I tried to get a major commercial publisher for both the *Normalization* text and for what was to become the 1973 edition of PASS (Wolfensberger & Glenn, 1973a, 1973b). Starting in April 1971, I submitted the manuscript of *Normalization* in turn to Allyn & Bacon, Brunner/Mazel, Basic Books, Harcourt Brace Jovanovich, and Academic Press, but without success. A senior person with one of these publishers even acknowledged that he considered the book "seminal"—but that it did not fit in with their plans. So eventually, after I had moved in September 1971 to the Canadian National Institute on Mental Retardation in Toronto as a visiting scholar, its director, G. Allan Roeher, came to the rescue.[12] The institute was a part of the Canadian Association for the Mentally Retarded (founded by parents of retarded persons and the Canadian equivalent of the National Association for Retarded Children in the US) in Toronto. The institute and its sponsoring body were very much in the publishing business and decided to publish the book, which might never have come about if *Mental Retardation* had not rejected all four of our manuscripts on the topic!

Though copyrighted in 1972, the book did not actually appear until early 1973. By then, almost 4 years had lapsed since *Changing Patterns*, and more than 3 whole years had been lost and wasted in getting to the relevant public something substantial beyond it on Normalization!

Soon after the book's appearance, some people started to call it "the big red dot," because that is what the designer had put on the front and back cover in order to draw attention. Interestingly, the publisher felt so uncertain about how the book would be received that only 3,000 copies were printed. And indeed, there were some people who were very unhappy with it. Some thought that the price of $8.50 in U.S. funds and $9.50 in Canadian for a "paperback" book was exorbitant. Some readers said that the first chapter on "The Role of Ideology in Shaping Human Management Models" was the best in the book, while others said it was the worst.

Roeher sent the book out to several Canadian leaders in human services and asked them for their critique. One of the most prominent figures in the province of Manitoba wrote back a letter dated September 1973, advising that the text not be used with people involved in community college programs for entry-level human service positions, citing a long list of reasons:

1. The writing is wordy and inclined to be repetitious . . .

2. The writing style is too emotionally charged. At times the writer is almost evangelical in his style. This is clearly evident in Chapter 9 (Normalizing Activation for the Profoundly Retarded . . .). Mental retardation has, for too long, been a field in which emotionalism has been used to sway public opinion, often at the expense of veracity.

3. The writing style is too subjective to be acceptable. Dr. Wolfensberger has, I believe, fallen into the trap of 'riding his own hobbyhorse' to such a degree that it would seem he is concerned more with persuading his readers toward his own biases rather than them making their own decisions based upon an objective presentation.

4. This being a Canadian publication, it is regrettable that the writer had done such little research in the field in Canada. It is quite evident that he has been influenced almost entirely by his experiences in the United States, and a brief tour of Scandinavian facilities. This does not for a moment suggest that the principles could not be the same, but there is shown a lack of knowledge, or concern for the field in Canada.

5. Dr. Wolfensberger has frequently made inferences, some of which are untenable, and then later has used his own inference as fact to support an hypothesis.

The above factors lead me to believe that this publication should not be used as a text for NIMR Levels I and II, and only judiciously as reference material. I feel that a much more objective approach should be presented to students in this vitally important area.

However, even with hardly any publicity, 700 copies of the book sold within a month, with the Pennsylvania Office of Mental Retardation alone buying up 300 for mass distribution. By now, close to 100,000 copies must have been sold, and the book qualified for the ranking of a best-seller in the non-fiction category on the Canadian market. Two chapters were reprinted in a book by Blatt, Biklen, and Bogdan

(1977), and portions were reprinted in Israel (Romot, 1979). Also, in 1982, a Japanese translation was published (Wolfensberger, 1982).

In 1991, a Delphi panel of 178 leaders in mental retardation identified this book as the single most impactful one on mental retardation in the last 50 years, including from among over 11,000 publications since 1966 (Heller, Spooner, Enright, Haney, & Schilit, 1991). Ironically, I had never intended the book to be specific to mental retardation, but it was never widely received outside of it.

In connection with the production of the 1972 text on *The Principle of Normalization in Human Services*, it also seems appropriate to say something about the difference between Nirje's Normalization formulation, my own, and for that matter, anybody else's. That there are differences, and what these are, has already been discussed at some length in the literature (e.g., Perrin & Nirje, 1985; Wolfensberger, 1980), though one party's characterization of another party's formulation must not be taken as necessarily correct.

In order to have a rational and productive discussion about the definition of Normalization (and later SRV), it is essential to keep in mind four tenets of the philosophy of science: (a) all definitions are arbitrary, (b) they should have clarity so that people can discourse on a defined entity without projecting conflicting meanings into it because of a definition's lack of clarity, (c) a definition should have utility, and (d) much like classification schemes, a definition that conforms to Occam's razor (i.e., "one should not multiply entities without necessity") and has parsimony is generally to be preferred. It is doubtful whether any definition other than a parsimonious one will earn the accolade of being called elegant, which is a term used for theories that economically and harmoniously have a lot of explanatory power.

We can now see that there could be many definitions of Normalization that meet the first three criteria, in being clear and useful despite their arbitrariness. However, different definitions relating to a topic are extremely unlikely to have the same degree of parsimony, and, most likely, no more than one—if any—will be deemed elegant.

Thus, when it comes to definitions of Normalization, one should ask which—if any—meet the criteria of clarity, utility, and parsimony, and which does it best, and it is these aspirations that led me to depart in some very significant ways from the definitions formulated by Bank-Mikkelsen and Nirje. These departures took a number of incremental steps over 14 years (see the chapter by Yates, and also Wolfensberger, 1986), and I want to point to three ways in which my Normalization formulation, even from its primitive divergence from Nirje's starting in 1968, accumulated parsimony credits.

1. If one combs the writings of Bank-Mikkelsen and Nirje prior to 1973, one will note that they had only or primarily mental retardation applications on their minds. Even Nirje's (1992b) revised 1992 definition of Normalization only expanded it to other handicaps. In contrast, I felt as early as 1968 that Normalization could and should be generalized to all conditions considered to be deviant by society, that is, to people who are rejected and devalued by their societies for other reasons, such as appearance, nationality, race, age, or whatever; or who are in devalued states (such as that of sickness) or devalued roles (including that of hospital patient).

2. In human services, goals and means are very intertwined. My formulation not only speaks to both means and goals, but also has things to say about which of multiple competing means are preferable.

3. The more other meritorious pre-existing or later arriving lower-order concepts, theories, or service means can be subsumed by a theory, the more parsimonious it is, and my Normalization formulation—and SRV even more so—subsumes a zillion ideas and measures on many levels that have been, and will be, promoted in human service and human relationships. For instance, my formulation subsumed actions on all levels of social organization: from the societal all the way to the single individual, and it allowed both for actions on a group or individual, and/or on the environment of such parties, including actions that change the perception and valuation of a person by others so that they no longer view the person in a devaluing fashion.

Parsimony is one of the great attractions of Normalization, as Lakin and Bruininks (1985) noted in reference to Wolfensberger's formulation: "Normalization as a concept has endured primarily because it is elegant in its simplicity, yet it provides both a utilitarian and an equalitarian guide against which to measure the coherence of programs and services for handicapped citizens" (p. 12).

The only other thing that I want to say here on this topic is that a constant bone of contention in Normalization circles, and outside them too, has been whether Normalization ever means making people normal. Nirje has strongly asserted that it should not, and that Normalization should only refer to life conditions, whereas the Wolfensberger formulation of Normalization allowed for that possibility from the first, but with the proviso that one is clear about different meanings of the phrase "making normal."

Of the many meanings of normality, two are particularly relevant to this discussion. One is that something is concordant with its proper nature, for example, cows have four legs, and cows with more or fewer legs are abnormal; humans are meant to see and hear, and therefore, being blind or deaf is abnormal; and so forth. Another meaning is in terms of statistical norms prevailing in a society.

The Wolfensberger formulation does not say that one absolutely must change a person or class, or even make a person or class normal in one of the above meanings, but rather that this is often possible; *nor* does it say that *only* changing the environment, or society, is permissible, but it does delineate means that are known to be relevantly efficacious in modifying societal and personal perceptions and evaluations, and therefore also devaluation. In fact, people could exercise knowledge of these very same lawful rules to achieve the opposite end of making people devalued. If one applies the Wolfensberger formulation pretty much across the board, one *will* end up "making normal" all sorts of people, whether one wanted to or not, as is implied in the last sentence of number 3 above.[13]

However, since I have abandoned a Normalization formulation in favor of a Social Role Valorization construct, the question of "making normal" recedes into the background in favor of the question of whether someone's social roles can be valorized, and of course we know from social science what the overarching strategies are through which this can be accomplished *if* that is what one wants to pursue. However, *whether* one wants to pursue this or not is a value issue above the level of social science.

But, in my opinion, even within Nirje's formulation it is not really possible to interpret Normalization as involving only action on the environment. Waking someone up at six o'clock in the morning so that the person can get to work on time and thereby live in a normal rhythm of day and week, and earn a normative income, certainly acts plentifully upon that person. And are all the things that one does on behalf of a sick or injured person that act directly on that person rather than only on that person's environment to be defined as outside the realm of Nirje's formulation? Would all medical and health measures be excluded that restore a sick person to health, or a bodily impaired person to normative functionality? Where would personal counseling fall? After all, some forms of psychotherapy are aimed very much at what one can call "person Normalization," leaving aside for the moment the question of the validity and effectiveness of such measures. Would Nirje's formulation imply that anything whatever that acts on the person is not Normalization? Then what about environmental actions that are known to be extremely likely to control the person? Where would they fall?

Nirje himself (1969, p. 187) spoke of "a basic requirement for helping [the retarded adult's] life development come as close to the normal as possible," which most people would have read to mean that retarded persons might grow less retarded—hence more normal—via the rearrangement of life conditions.

Therefore, as long as one grants that abnormalization abnormalizes a person, and not just the person's environment, as Vail brought out so powerfully, one cannot say that Normalization only normalizes life conditions. Obviously, we must apply the same interpretive framework both to normalizing and abnormalizing measures and outcomes.

In short, I cannot see how Nirje's formulation allows an exclusion of actions on a person. Even the very distinction of action on persons versus on their environments is a largely artificial and verbal one, since environments exert vast—sometimes total—control over people.

People who state that Normalization *never* means making a person normal are usually not only mentally fixated on applications to mental retardation, but also view mental retardation as a static condition. This was highlighted by some correspondence I had in 1973-1974 with Dr. Richard Sterner from Sweden, whom I had met on my visit there in 1969. Dr. Sterner was a person of international renown who had been president of the Swedish association of parents of the mentally retarded. He questioned my Normalization formulation because it would allow retarded persons to become nonretarded, and I assured him that this was deliberate on my part and not a mistake, in that intellectual functioning was not necessarily fixed for life, and that retarded identity might be reversed especially in younger and less retarded people, and in those of these who receive intensive programming.

Before going to the next topic, I want to mention that the *Normalization* text contained an entire chapter on "direct subsidy" to persons or families as "a powerful adjunct to the armamentarium of tools useful in implementing Normalization" (p. 234), recapitulating an idea already presented in *Changing Patterns*. Again, this was one of the most ignored chapters of the book. The time for this idea was yet to come, and when it finally came, its early presentations had been completely forgotten.

10 WHAT WOULD HAVE HAPPENED IF NORMALIZATION HAD NOT APPEARED ON THE NORTH AMERICAN SCENE WHEN IT DID, OR IF IT HAD NOT FOUND VIGOROUS CHAMPIONS

Other contributors to this book are presenting material on the impact of Normalization, but one thing I want to say on this issue is what would have happened if Normalization had *not* come onto the scene when it did, and even if it had come but had not found vigorous, articulate, and creative interpreters and promoters. There are a lot of people who simply assume that the community service movement *had* to evolve the way it did, but they are very, very wrong.

While the deinstitutionalization of the mentally disordered was a de facto process starting in the mid-1950s, it is important to recall that for a number of years, the reality of this process was hardly recognized, in part because it was not the result of a conscious plan based on a high-order concept. Nor was it given a conscious and explicit direction by national leaders even as it became clear that it was happening, nor was it adequately interpreted for some years to come. One can liken it more to a drift that occurred without much planning, intent, or consciousness, and that was described on a somewhat low level of awareness and

meaningfulness by only a modest number of people. Further, virtually all the early interpreters of this drift pointed to the new psychoactive drugs as its cause, which, as research has since revealed, was at least in part an erroneous assumption. Finally, this deinstitutionalization was not accompanied by a strong, clear, and practical conceptualization of community alternatives. The community mental health centers were promoted as being that, but never were.

Deinstitutionalization in mental retardation was entirely different. Here, explicit, highly ideologized ideas and ideological leadership came first. Largely as a result thereof, there occurred a dramatic increase in community services, both of the residential and non-residential kind. As soon as deinstitutionalization became a statistically ascertainable fact as reflected in national institutional movement statistics (which occurred about 1970), these statistics were interpreted (mostly in oral rather than written forums) for what they were by the leaders of the scene, such as myself.

It was only after the early successes of deinstitutionalization in mental retardation that mental health began its notorious and unconscionable systematic dumping policy, and it was only after mental health began to do this that similar dumping also became normative in mental retardation, roughly in the mid-1970s.

So altogether, I believe that the following things would have happened instead. (This is somewhat along the lines of "predicting the past.")

1. Without the thinking generated by the Normalization culture, the impact of the civil rights thrust would probably have been not only less, but also very different.

2. The major reform emphasis in education would have been (a) on rightful funding, (b) for most but not necessarily all retarded children, and (c) without any major controversy over integration. In other words, rightful segregated education would have been the major thrust for a long time.

3. There would have been a larger number of smaller institutions, more equitably distributed over a state or province.

4. There would have been a very slow rise in mini-institutions for several score to perhaps 200 residents. These might have been interpreted as "community residences," as several small institutions in the 1970s and even into the 1980s were.

93

5. Institutions of all types would have been "better," for example, with less crowding, better staff ratios, less ugliness, and so forth.

6. There would have been a much larger number of "regional centers," that is, multipurpose facilities with both residential and non-residential components.

7. Even more money would have gone to rather worthless university-affiliated service centers than eventually did anyway.

8. Group homes would have developed, but these would have been large, with 12 to 20 residents, and would have developed much, much more slowly than they did.

9. Because the rights movement would have gathered further strength, there might very well have been even more "dumping" of people out of mental retardation institutions in the name of "rights" than took place anyway.

10. Finally, Normalization-related ideas would have penetrated, though not necessarily under that name. By the time they would have gathered sufficient theoretical formulation and social strength, they would have been confronted by such a massive capital investment in smaller regionalized institutions and non-normalized, large community residences, plus yet other economic interests, that a transition to small normalized community residences and integrated education would have been a long, drawn-out process that might have taken at least 10, more likely 20, and possibly even more years longer to get to where we are now.

As mentioned before, among the powerful reasons to project this kind of "alternative present" is that these were the *very* directions into which things were moving already in the late 1960s and early 1970s. It was exemplars of these very things that were held up as models. The regional center concept was then considered the forefront of reform, with different versions thereof being developed in California, Connecticut, and Missouri. Another cutting-edge idea was to move toward a larger number of smaller and presumedly better institutions, either by using already existing facilities—predominantly former TB sanatoria—or by fancy new construction, as in Illinois (i.e., the Ludemann Center).

Of course, these models, and some others as well, were outright atrocious when evaluated from a Normalization perspective. One example of this is that the Rolla Regional Center in Missouri was depicted in the 1967 training film *To Bridge the Gap* (Walsh, 1967) as a model, whereas people versed in Normalization/SRV would see it as an abomination.

Also, these were some of the very directions into which even Denmark and Sweden were moving in 1969. For instance, as mentioned, there was a much greater emphasis there than in North America on agency residences versus independent or family living. Until the Americanized version of Normalization began to find its way back to Denmark, emphasis there had been on lavishly designed, furnished, and staffed new small institutions and schools, the latter not only segregated but—for day schools—also so far outside the population centers that they were even called "green schools,"that is, schools out in the greens.

In Sweden, it was only with a 1986 law that more extensive provision was made for community residential living for severely retarded persons outside of institutions (Pedlar, 1990). Also, Pedlar reported that retarded people in community residences were not very well integrated, for which she was able to identify at least three reasons. One was that these residences had been so lavishly staffed that personnel ended up doing everything for residents, and this became a disincentive for integrative undertakings. Second, a relatively high proportion of the staff had once worked in institutions and had been transferred to community residences as institutions were being downsized. Third, there prevailed such a strong faith in Sweden in the public operation of whatever services were needed that volunteerism suffered from not being encouraged, and from even being discouraged. Even so-called "contact" persons, called for by the 1986 law and supposed to be ordinary citizens who provide some personal involvement with retarded residents, received some payment. (This is one of the perverse fruits of socialist ideology.) Thus, we get a peculiar situation in Sweden where there is much of what one might now call "integration" with paid people and relatively little contact with ordinary citizens. While we have the same problem of poor integration of people in community residences in America, it is largely for different reasons.

It took a superhuman effort to avert a non-Normalization reform concept in Nebraska, and it is quite possible that if Nebraska had also gone to the regional center and smaller institutional model (as most of the reformers even there had initially envisioned), we might have seen very few community residences and apartment projects in North America even decades later. After all, even Burton Blatt continued to exalt the "good small institution" until just a few years prior to his death in 1985 (e.g., Blatt, Ozolins, & McNally, 1979).

11 CONCLUSION

Unfortunately, I have unfinished drafts for several more sections on the history of Normalization and the evolution of Social Role Valorization, a lot of it as yet unpublished, but my writing time simply ran out, and these materials will—I hope—be published later in some other context. Fortunately, the contributions of several other speakers at the Ottawa conference further add to the history of Normalization and SRV, and my concluding presentation also covers a few more historical points.

Somewhat arbitrarily, I decided to end with two reflections.

The first one is on the five different ways people during the late 1960s and early 1970s tended to react to presentations on Normalization.

1. Benevolent and polite rejection, derived from the conviction of the listeners that the speakers simply did not know the relevant realities about the lives of handicapped (mostly retarded) persons, because if they did, they certainly would not be making such outlandish claims and proposals. This kind of response was particularly apt to be forthcoming from parents of retarded persons, who were pleased that someone was well-intentioned toward people such as their children, even though ignorant or misguided.

2. The grossest kind of hostile rejection, which came almost entirely from service professionals. In the early years of teaching Normalization, the teachers would often get into the nastiest arguments with hostile listeners or entire audiences, and sometimes even the smallest and most obvious elements of Normalization were vehemently contested.

3. Noncomprehension, in that what was presented was simply not grasped because it was so remote from what people knew and were able to conceptualize. However, in that case, the response did not tend to be hostile but bland, often of the nature of "What else is new?"

4. An "aha" response, when what we were teaching made profound sense to people but they had never heard it stated before, or never in a way in which they could understand it. This latter response most likely was emitted by ordinary citizens who were neither human service workers nor parents of handicapped persons.

5. Finally, there were people who were open to learning about Normalization but who did not agree with at least portions of it because they held high-order beliefs, perhaps of a religious, political, or socioeconomic nature, that clashed—or seemed to them to clash—with Normalization. Many persons in this group found that the more they understood our Normalization formulation, the less conflict there would be in implementive measures. However, there often was also agreement on many implementive measures—but not for the same reasons. For instance, it was not unusual for services of Christian bodies to get higher scores on the PASS instrument than most other services, but not necessarily for reasons that would have derived from Normalization.

This pattern of five kinds of response continued pretty much the same throughout the 1970s, except that in the early 1970s, several additional ones gained greater ascendancy.

1. One came almost exclusively from human service workers. Some concluded that Normalization was the craze of the moment and they did not want to be left behind or appear outdated, but they really had no commitment to it. They figured that they had better learn the Normalization idiom and its superficial notions lest they be viewed as archaic, or lose prestige or positions, especially if they worked in settings where Normalization had been mandated from the top. Some people went on doing whatever they had been doing or wanted to do and simply called it "Normalization." These people of empty minds and often weak service souls almost all jumped off soon and onto whatever other popular and "safe" crazes came into vogue.

2. There were people who had opposed Normalization from day one but were embarrassed to admit it once so many Normalization corollaries became everyday conventional wisdom. Instead, they continued their opposition by calling for going "beyond Normalization." For instance, Rosen, Clark, and Kivitz (1977) issued a "beyond Normalization"

call as early as 1977, and one has heard that phrase ever since, and often from people who never were "in Normalization" enough to go beyond it.

3. Another group also consisted largely of the same old enemies of Normalization who now began to shift their arguments into the form that Normalization lacked research evidence. These people are still with us, and probably always will be, since they continue to stutter the same argument despite mountainous supportive evidence from both formal research and other forms of empiricism—and this group of largely social science academicians can generally not relate to the latter.

4. As the years passed by, we also had to begin increasingly to combat not merely opposition to Normalization, but also all the misconceptions or wrong teachings about it. That became increasingly a problem until SRV began to be formulated in 1983 (Wolfensberger, 1983). Relatedly, there were the well-intentioned people who either (a) thought they had understood Normalization but had not, and therefore applied the term "Normalization" to non-normalizing practices, or (b) subscribed to one of several competing formulations of Normalization. With the latter group, one might be in very extensive agreement—perhaps on 80% of the relevant measures, but even then not always for the same reason.

It was only around 1980 that a distinct change set in, apparently for four reasons. (a) Many ideas that had been taught in connection with Normalization became more widely known and accepted. (b) Particularly with the evolution of SRV, striking improvements took place in our teaching. (c) Certain ideas arising from other sources, such as the civil-rights movement, were sufficiently concordant or overlapping with Normalization or SRV to make these latter appear reasonable. (d) More and more, people began to actually see instances of implementation of what had been taught, and saw that it either worked or was better than what went before.

After that, new problems set in that I will address in my chapter at the end because they have implications for the future.

My second concluding reflection is that one of the best favors that I could have rendered to Normalization would have been to die after finishing the PASS 3 manuscript in 1975 (Wolfensberger & Glenn, 1975a, 1975b).

During the early 1970s, I began to be widely considered one of the foremost leaders and teachers on issues related to Normalization, residential services, comprehensive service-system planning and implementation, and Citizen Advocacy. But about that time, I also began to speak on several new controversial issues.

One was that dynamics of social decadence were beginning to dominate Western society, which nobody then believed or wanted to hear.

A second was the growing danger of "deathmaking" of devalued people, and, because of that, just about everybody concluded I must be insane.

A third was that before ARC audiences, and during my year (1976-1977) on the NARC board, I began to warn not only that the ARC movement had to get ready to start fighting deathmaking, but also that the parent movement was in the gravest danger of decline. Between 1968 and about 1976, I had been very popular and influential in ARC circles, being invited endlessly to talk at their national, state, regional, and local conventions, and to serve on national committees—but all that changed almost overnight.

Fourth, I began to teach that paid service without life-sharing is bankrupt. For instance, in a speech before a shrink audience in 1974 (later published [Wolfensberger, 1975b] as a chapter in a psychiatric text), I pointed out how people in the mental services were deeply devaluing and socially distantiating of their clients. I believe that this was the last time I was invited to speak to such an audience. For making a similar point at the 1979 national convention of the American Association on Mental Deficiency in Miami—namely, that we were doing very well, financially and socially, off retarded people—a woman in the audience wrote to me that never in her life had she ever disliked anyone so much as me. This was of course very revealing, considering how large is (a) the variety and number of reasons for not liking someone, and (b) the number of people one might dislike.

Fifth, in the field of special education, I was first disfavored for opposing the prevailing practice of low expectations, the watered-down curriculum, exclusion, and segregation. But when the field flip-flopped and converted Normalization into one simpleminded term—namely, "mainstreaming"—I tried what little I could to stem this tide of stupidity and simple-mindedness (e.g., Wolfensberger, 1974a), trying to emphasize the many components and degrees of integration, but to no avail. The mainstream of education in America has always been unintelligent and simpleminded. At any rate, because I did not endorse what went under "mainstreaming," nor even the very term itself, the education field bulldozed right past me and left me isolated once again. By 1994, "inclusion" was just as mindlessly mouthed as only about three years earlier "mainstreaming" had been, with no one who talks inclusion admitting having been a mainstreamer.

Finally, in response to my contact with l'Arche, I began to try to bring my religious faith and my work into closer harmony, which resulted in my being interpreted as having had a conversion to religious fanaticism.

Altogether, these things quickly isolated me, because people no longer wanted to be perceived as having anything to do with whatever my name was associated with. Even while people claimed to be trying to implement Normalization and residential services, they quit coming to my workshops on these topics, and the Normalization-related workshops did not experience a second upswing until less "tainted" people began to teach them. Also, some of my innovations began to be attributed to other people, which sometimes was rather funny.

Although time proved me to be right on deathmaking and the decline in the ARC movement, this changed nothing with most people who had started either shunning me or scaring others away from me. After all, as Burton Blatt had warned me, the one thing people will never forgive one for is having been proven right.

At any rate, if I had done Normalization the favor of dying when I was at the peak of my reputation and effectiveness, it probably would have been more explicitly embraced and more systematically studied. But I certainly have no regrets for God's gift of more years.

REFERENCES

A century on ice. (1995, January/February). *Journal for the Office of Mental Retardation and Developmental Disabilities, 9*(1), 7.

BANK-MIKKELSEN, N. E. (1964). The ideological and legal basis of the national service of the treatment, teaching, training, etc., of the mentally retarded, as well as a description of the structure of the national service. In J. OSTER & H. V. SLETVED (Eds.), *Proceedings of the International Copenhagen Congress on the Scientific Study of Mental Retardation: Vol. 1* (pp. 1-7). Copenhagen, Denmark: Det Berlingske Bogtrykkeri.

BANK-MIKKELSEN, N. E. (1968). Services for mentally retarded children in Denmark. *Children, 15,* 198-200.

BANK-MIKKELSEN, N. E. (1969). A metropolitan area in Denmark: Copenhagen. In R. B. KUGEL & W. WOLFENSBERGER (Eds.), *Changing patterns in residential services for the mentally retarded* (pp. 227-254). Washington, DC: President's Committee on Mental Retardation.

BARTON, W. E., FARRELL, M. J., LENEHAN, F. P., & MCLAUGHLIN, W. (1961). *Impressions of European psychiatry*. Washington: American Psychiatric Association.

BERFENSTAM, R., & WILLIAM-OLSON, I. (1973). *Early child care in Sweden*. New York: Gordon & Breach.

BLATT, B., BIKLEN, D., & BOGDAN, R. (Eds.). (1977). *An alternative textbook in special education*. Denver: Love Publishing.

BLATT, B., & KAPLAN, F. (1966). *Christmas in purgatory: A photographic essay on mental retardation*. Boston: Allyn & Bacon.

BLATT, B., OZOLINS, A., & MCNALLY, J. (1979). *The family papers: A return to purgatory*. New York: Longman.

Bronze Award: The attack on dehumanization. Medical Services Division, Minnesota Department of Public Welfare, St. Paul, Minnesota. (1967). *Hospital & Community Psychiatry, 18*(12), 362-364.

CLARK, M. J., & CLARK, K. (1970). *Scandinavian programs for the mentally retarded: How they work.* Chippewa Falls, WI: Social Service Dept., Northern Wisconsin Colony & Training School.

CLELAND, C. C., & SHAFTER, A. J. (1971). [Review of KUGEL, R. B., & WOLFENSBERGER, W. (Eds.). (1969). *Changing patterns in residential services for the mentally retarded.* Washington, DC: President's Committee on Mental Retardation.] *American Journal of Mental Deficiency, 75*(5), 646-647.

COOKE, R. E. (1969). The free choice principle in the care of the mentally retarded. In R. B. KUGEL & W. WOLFENSBERGER (Eds.), *Changing patterns in residential services for the mentally retarded* (pp. 359-365). Washington, DC: President's Committee on Mental Retardation.

DANISH NATIONAL SERVICE FOR THE MENTALLY RETARDED. (1969). *Ten years of planning and building: 1959-1969.* Copenhagen: Nyt Nordisk Forlag Arnold Busck.

DAVID, H. P. (1972). *Child mental health in international perspective: Report of the Joint Commission on Mental Health of Children.* New York: Harper & Row.

DEMPSEY, J. J. (Ed.). (1975). *Community services for retarded children: The consumer-provider relationship.* Baltimore: University Park Press.

DOLNICK, M. M. (1971). Sheltered workshop programs in the Netherlands. *Rehabilitation Record, 12*(2), 35-38.

DUTCH NATIONAL ASSOCIATION FOR THE CARE OF THE MENTALLY RETARDED & BISHOP BEKKERS INSTITUTE. (1973). *The structure of the Dutch services for the mentally retarded.* Utrecht, Netherlands: Author.

DYBWAD, G. (1969, December). Lest we forget. *Pennsylvania Message, 5*(3), 2, 6.

DYBWAD, G. (1973). The role of the volunteer movement in safeguarding the rights of the impaired. In W. WOLFENSBERGER & H. ZAUHA (Eds.), *Citizen advocacy and protective services for the impaired and handicapped* (pp. 163-173).

Downsview, Ontario: National Institute on Mental Retardation.

DYBWAD, G., & DYBWAD, R. F. (1970). Community organization: Foreign countries. In J. WORTIS (Ed.), *Mental retardation* (pp. 224-238). New York: Grune & Stratton.

DYBWAD, R. F. (Ed.). (1971). *International directory of mental retardation resources.* Washington, DC: President's Committee on Mental Retardation.

DYBWAD, R. F. (1977-1978). *International directory of mental retardation resources* (Rev. ed.). Washington, DC: President's Committee on Mental Retardation; & Brussels, Belgium: International League of Societies for the Mentally Handicapped.

DYBWAD, R. F. (1989). *International directory of mental retardation resources* (3rd ed.). Washington, DC: President's Committee on Mental Retardation; & Brussels, Belgium: International League of Societies for Persons With Mental Handicap.

ELLIOT, J. (1971). That Swedish look. *Parents Voice, 21*(3), 12-13.

ENGEL, A. G. W. (1968). *Planning and spontaneity in the development of the Swedish health system.* Chicago: Center for Health Administration Studies, Graduate School of Business, University of Chicago. (The 1968 Michael M. Davis Lecture, Billings Hospital, University of Chicago.)

ERICSSON, K. (1986). Der Normalisierungsgedanke: Entstehung und Erfahrungen in skandinavischen Ländern. In BUNDESVEREINIGUNG LEBENSHILFE (Ed.), *Normalisierung: Eine Chance für Menschen mit geistiger Behinderung* (pp. 33-44). Marburg/Lahn: Lebenshilfe. (Edited address, in Bericht des Ersten Europäischen Kongresses der Internationalen Liga von Vereinigungen für Menschen mit geistiger Behinderung, Hamburg, October 1985. Vol. 14, Grosse Schriftenreihe of Lebenshilfe.)

FABER, N. W. (1968). *The retarded child: A practical guide to the important recent advances in the care and rehabilitation of the mentally handicapped child.* New York: Crown Publishers.

FORS, A. (1969). *Social policy and how it works* (K.

Bradfield, Trans.). Stockholm: Swedish Institute.

FOUCAULT, M. (1973). *Madness and civilization: A history of insanity in the age of reason.* New York: Vintage Books.

FRITZ, M., WOLFENSBERGER, W., & KNOWLTON, M. (1971). *An apartment living plan to promote integration and Normalization of mentally retarded adults.* Toronto: National Institute on Mental Retardation.

FURMAN, S. S. (1965). *Community mental health services in Northern Europe: Great Britain, Netherlands, Denmark, Sweden.* Washington, DC: National Institute of Mental Health (U.S. Government Printing Office).

GARFINKEL, H. (1956). Conditions of successful degradation ceremonies. *American Journal of Sociology, 61,* 420-424.

GOFFMAN, E. (1958). Characteristics of total institutions. In *Symposium on Preventive and Social Psychiatry* (pp. 43-84). Washington, DC: Walter Reed Army Institute of Research.

GOFFMAN, E. (1961). *Asylums: Essays on the social situation of mental patients and other inmates.* New York: Doubleday.

GOFFMAN, E. (1963). *Stigma: Notes on the management of spoiled identity.* Englewood Cliffs, NJ: Prentice-Hall.

GOVERNOR'S CITIZENS' COMMITTEE ON MENTAL RETARDATION. (1968a). *The report of the Nebraska Citizens' Study Committee on Mental Retardation* (Vol. 1). Lincoln: Nebraska State Department of Public Institutions.

GOVERNOR'S CITIZENS' COMMITTEE ON MENTAL RETARDATION. (1968b). *The report of the Nebraska Citizens' Study Committee on Mental Retardation* (Vol. 2). Lincoln: Nebraska State Department of Public Institutions.

GOVERNOR'S CITIZENS' COMMITTEE ON MENTAL RETARDATION. (1968c). *Into the light.* Lincoln: Nebraska State Department of Public Institutions.

GRAF, T. (1972). Advocacy in Scandinavia. *News and Views 2*(1), 4. (Newsletter of the Atlanta Association for Retarded Children).

GREGOR, T. (1972). *Report: Study trip to Norway, Sweden, Denmark, Germany, France & the Netherlands, Nov.-Dec. 1971.* Ontario, Canada: Ontario Association for the Mentally Retarded.

GRUNEWALD, K. (1969a). A rural county in Sweden: Malmöhus County. In R. B. KUGEL & W. WOLFENSBERGER (Eds.), *Changing patterns in residential services for the mentally retarded* (pp. 255-287). Washington, DC: President's Committee on Mental Retardation.

GRUNEWALD, K. (1969b). *The mentally retarded in Sweden* (K. Bradfield, Trans.). Stockholm: Swedish Institute.

GRUNEWALD, K. (1970). Economic opportunities for the mentally retarded. In V. APGAR (Ed.), *Annals of the New York Academy of Sciences: Down's Syndrome (Mongolism), 171,* 671-678.

GRUNEWALD, K. (Ed.). (1971). *Människohantering på totala vårdinstitutioner: Från dehumanisering till normalisering.* Stockholm: Natur och Kultur.

GRUNEWALD, K. (Ed.). (1972). *Menneskemanipulering på totalinstitutioner: Fra dehumanisering til normalisering.* Copenhagen: Thaning & Appels.

GUNZBURG, H. C. (Ed.). (1973). *Advances in the care of the mentally handicapped.* London: Bailliere, Tindall.

HALLAHAN, D. P. (1970). [Review of KUGEL, R. B., & WOLFENSBERGER, W. (Eds.). (1969). *Changing patterns in residential services for the mentally retarded.* Washington, DC: President's Committee on Mental Retardation.] *Psychological Aspects of Disability, 17*(1), 29-34.

HELLER, H. W., SPOONER, F., ENRIGHT, B. E., HANEY, K., & SCHILIT, J. (1991). Classic articles: A reflection into the field of mental retardation. *Education & Training in Mental Retardation, 26*(2), 202-206.

HOBBS, N. (1966). Helping disturbed children: Psychological and ecological strategies. *American Psychologist, 21,* 1105-1115.

HOBBS, N. (1983). Project Re-Ed: From demonstration project to nationwide program. *Peabody Journal of Education, 60*(3), 8-24.

HOLOWINSKY, I. Z. (1973). Special education in Eastern Europe. In L. MANN & D. A. SABATINO (Eds.), *First review of special education, 2* (pp. 287-302). Philadelphia: Buttonwood Farms. (JSE Press series in special education)

HUMPHREY, MRS. H. H. (1968, March). Better institutional planning. *PCMR Message*

(President's Committee on Mental Retardation), No. 9, 11-14.

HUMPHREY, MRS. H. H., JONES, G., & KUGEL, R. B. (1968, May). Special report: Programs and trends in Europe for the mentally retarded. *PCMR Message* (President's Committee on Mental Retardation), No. 12, 8-12.

INTERNATIONAL BUREAU OF EDUCATION, UNESCO. (1960). *Organization of special education for mentally deficient children: A study in comparative education* (Publication No. 214). Geneva: Author.

INTERNATIONAL LEAGUE OF SOCIETIES FOR THE MENTALLY HANDICAPPED. (1967). *Legislative aspects of mental retardation: Conclusions, Stockholm Symposium, 11-16 June 1967.* Stockholm: Nordisk Bokindustri AB.

INTERNATIONAL LEAGUE OF SOCIETIES FOR THE MENTALLY HANDICAPPED. (1969). *Symposium on residential care, Frankfurt, Germany, September 1969.* Brussels: Author.

Is basket weaving harmful? (1970, October 12), *Time,* 57.

JONES, M. (1953). *The therapeutic community: A new treatment method in psychiatry.* New York: Basic Books.

JONES, R. L. (Ed.). (1971). *Problems and issues in the education of exceptional children.* Boston: Houghton Mifflin.

JONSON, J. (1971-1972). Windmills, wooden shoes, and welfare. *Minnesota Welfare, 23*(4), 6-21.

KAHN, A. J., & KAMERMAN, S. B. (1975). *Not for the poor alone.* Philadelphia, PA: Temple University Press.

KARLINS, M. (Originator). (1966). *Dehumanization and the total institution* [Film]. St. Paul, MN: Minnesota Department of Public Welfare; & Omaha, NE: Nebraska Psychiatric Institute.

KARLINS, M. (1971-1972, Winter). Dr. David J. Vail, a tribute. *Minnesota Welfare* (Minnesota Department of Public Welfare), *23*(4), 24-26.

KEVLES, D. J. (1985). *In the name of eugenics: Genetics and the uses of human heredity.* New York: Alfred A. Knopf.

KIEV, A. (Ed.). (1968). *Psychiatry in the communist world.* New York: Science House.

KIMBERLY, J. R. (1972). Sheltered workshops in Sweden. *Rehabilitation Record, 13*(2), 35-38.

KING, R. D., RAYNES, N. V., & TIZARD, J. (1971).*Patterns of residential care: Sociological studies in institutions for handicapped children.* London: Routledge & Kegan Paul.

KUGEL, R. B., & SHEARER, A. (Eds.). (1976). *Changing patterns in residential services for the mentally retarded* (Rev. ed.). Washington, DC: President's Committee on Mental Retardation.

KUGEL, R. B., & WOLFENSBERGER, W. (Eds.). (1969). *Changing patterns in residential services for the mentally retarded.* Washington, DC: President's Committee on Mental Retardation.

KUGEL, R. B., & WOLFENSBERGER, W. (Eds.). (1974). *Geistig Behinderte—Eingliederung oder Bewahrung? Heutige Vorstellungen über die Betreuung geistig behinderter Menschen* (Translated & abbreviated by W. Borck). Stuttgart, Germany: Georg Thieme.

LAKIN, K. C., & BRUININKS, R. H. (1985). Contemporary services for handicapped children and youth. In R. H. BRUININKS & K. C. LAKIN (Eds.), *Living and learning in the least restrictive environment* (pp. 3-22). Baltimore, MD: Paul H. Brookes.

LAMBERT, F. (1970). Special education for backward children in Denmark: Its development: And current problems. *Forward Trends, 14,* 23-30.

LANCASTER-GAYE, D. (Ed.). (1972). *Personal relationships, the handicapped and the community: Some European thoughts and solutions.* Boston: Routledge & Kegan Paul, and the International Cerebral Palsy Society.

LENSINK, B. (1976). ENCOR, Nebraska. In R. B. KUGEL & A. SHEARER (Eds.), *Changing patterns in residential services for the mentally retarded* (Rev. ed.) (pp. 227-296). Washington, DC: President's Committee on Mental Retardation.

Lillemosegard: Institution for mentally retarded adults. (1966). Gladsaxe, Denmark; & Minneapolis, MN: Minnesota Association for Retarded Children. (Reprinted, with translation of texts, by MARC)

LINN, L. (1961). *Frontiers in general hospital psychiatry.* New York: International University Press.

LINTON, T. E. (1969). The European educateur program for disturbed children. *American Journal of Orthopsychiatry, 39,* 125-133.

LIPPMAN, L. (1969). Sweden remembers—and provides for—the handicapped. *Mental Retardation, 7*(4), 26-27.

LIPPMAN, L. (1970). Community organization: USA. In J. WORTIS (Ed.), *Mental retardation* (pp. 239-249). New York: Grune & Stratton.

LUNDSTROM, K. (1969). Special education in Sweden. *Volta Review, 71*(9), 528-538.

MASSERMAN, J. H. (Ed.). (1968). *Psychiatry: East and West. An account of four international conferences.* New York: Grune & Stratton.

MELCHIOR, J. C. (1968). The Danish center-schools. *Developmental Medicine & Child Neurology, 10,* 671-673.

MENOLASCINO, F., CLARK, R. L., & WOLFENSBERGER, W. (1968a). *The initiation and development of a comprehensive, county-wide system of services for the mentally retarded of Douglas County* (Vol. 1). Omaha: Greater Omaha Association for Retarded Children.

MENOLASCINO, F., CLARK, R. L., & WOLFENSBERGER, W. (1968b). *The initiation and development of a comprehensive, county-wide system of services for the mentally retarded of Douglas County* (Vol. 2). Omaha: Greater Omaha Association for Retarded Children.

MEYERS, R. (1978). *Like normal people.* New York: McGraw-Hill.

MOISE, L. (1972). *See how they grow: Report to the Rosemary F. Dybwad International Awards Committee of the National Association for Retarded Children.* Fort Bragg, CA: Gull Press.

MOISE, L. E. (1980). *As up we grew with Barbara.* Minneapolis, MN: Dillon.

MONTAN, K. (1972). The Swedish Institute for the Handicapped: Its tasks and potentiality. *Rehabilitation Literature, 33*(4), 103-106.

MYRDAL, A. (1969). *Nation and family: The Swedish experiment in democratic family and population policy.* Don Mills, Ontario: Musson Book.

NATIONAL ASSOCIATION FOR RETARDED CHILDREN. (1968). *Policy statement on residential care.* New York, NY: Author.

NATIONAL INSTITUTE ON MENTAL RETARDATION. (1977). *Orientation manual on mental retardation: Part I* (Rev. ed.). Toronto: Author.

NEWBERGER, D. A. (1979). [Review of CLELAND, C. (1978). *Mental retardation: A developmental approach.* Englewood Cliffs, NJ: Prentice-Hall.] *Exceptional Children, 46*(1), 59-60.

NILSSON, I. (1967). Current trends in special education in Sweden. *The Slow Learning Child, 14*(1), 22-28.

NIRJE, B. (1969). The Normalization principle and its human management implications. In R. B. KUGEL & W. WOLFENSBERGER (Eds.), *Changing patterns in residential services for the mentally retarded* (pp. 179-195). Washington, DC: President's Committee on Mental Retardation.

NIRJE, B. (1991). *Niels Erik Bank-Mikkelsen in memoriam.* (E. Berg, Trans). Unpublished manuscript.

NIRJE, B. (1992a). Bank-Mikkelsen: Founder of Normalization principle. *News & Notes* (American Association on Mental Retardation), *5*(2), 4.

NIRJE, B. (1992b). *The Normalization principle papers.* Uppsala, Sweden: Uppsala University, Center for Handicap Research.

PEDLAR, A. (1990). Normalization and integration: A look at the Swedish experience. *Mental Retardation, 28*(5), 275-282.

PERIN, C. (1970). *With man in mind: An interdisciplinary prospectus for environmental design.* Cambridge, MA: MIT Press.

PERRIN, B., & NIRJE, B. (1985). Setting the record straight: A critique of some frequent misconceptions of the Normalization principle. *Australia & New Zealand Journal of Developmental Disabilities, 11*(2), 69-74.

PERSKE, R. (1969a). *Sweden: Part one of two parts.* Topeka, KS: Unpublished.

PERSKE, R. (1969b). *Denmark: Part two of two parts.* Topeka, KS: Unpublished.

PERSKE, R. (1973). *New directions for parents of persons who are retarded.* Nashville, TN: Abingdon Press.

PERSKE, R. (1982). *Hope for the families: New directions for parents of persons with retardation or other disabilities.* Nashville, TN: Abingdon Press.

PRESIDENT'S COMMITTEE ON MENTAL RETARDATION. (1968). *MR 68: The edge of change.* Washington, DC: U.S. Government Printing Office.

PRESIDENT'S COMMITTEE ON MENTAL RETARDATION. (1969). *MR 69: Toward progress: The story of a decade.* Washington, DC: U.S. Government Printing Office.

PRESIDENT'S COMITTEE ON MENTAL RETARDATION. (1970). *Residential services for the mentally retarded: An action policy proposal.* Washington, DC: U.S. Government Printing Office.

PRESIDENT'S COMMITTEE ON MENTAL RETARDATION. (1977). *MR 76: Mental retardation: Past and present.* Washington, DC: U.S. Government Printing Office.

PRESIDENT'S PANEL ON MENTAL RETARDATION (1962). *A proposed program for national action to combat mental retardation.* Washington, DC: U.S. Government Printing Office.

PRESIDENT'S PANEL ON MENTAL RETARDATION (1963a). *Report of the mission to Denmark and Sweden.* Washington, DC: U.S. Government Printing Office.

PRESIDENT'S PANEL ON MENTAL RETARDATION (1963b). *Report of the mission to the Netherlands.* Washington, DC: U.S. Government Printing Office.

PRESIDENT'S PANEL ON MENTAL RETARDATION (1963c). *Report of the task force on coordination.* Washington, DC: U.S. Government Printing Office.

PRESIDENT'S PANEL ON MENTAL RETARDATION (1963d). *Report of the task force on education and rehabilitation.* Washington, DC: U.S. Government Printing Office.

PRESIDENT'S PANEL ON MENTAL RETARDATION (1963e). *Report of the task force on law.* Washington, DC: U.S. Government Printing Office.

PRESIDENT'S PANEL ON MENTAL RETARDATION (1963f). *Report of the task force on prevention, clinical services and residential care.* Washington, DC: U.S. Government Printing Office.

PRESIDENT'S PANEL ON MENTAL RETARDATION (1964a). *Report of the mission to the USSR.* Washington, DC: U.S. Government Printing Office.

PRESIDENT'S PANEL ON MENTAL RETARDATION (1964b). *Report of the task force on behavioral and social research.* Washington, DC: U.S. Government Printing Office.

PROCTOR, R. (1988). *Racial hygiene: Medicine under the Nazis.* Cambridge, MA: Harvard University Press.

RAYNES, N. V., & KING, R. D. (1968). The measurement of child management in residential institutions for the retarded. In B. W. RICHARDS (Ed.), *Proceedings of the First Congress of the International Association for the Scientific Study of Mental Deficiency* (pp. 637-647). Montpellier, France: Michael Jackson Publishing.

ROBINSON, K. (1961). *Patterns of care: A study of provisions for the mentally disordered in two continents.* London, England: National Association for Mental Health.

ROMOT, A. (Ed.). (1979). *A collection of articles on the subject of Normalization, individualization, integration.* Jerusalem: Ministry of Labor & Social Services, Service to the Retarded, Unit for Programs & Information.

ROSEN, M., CLARK, G. R., & KIVITZ, M. S. (1976). *A history of mental retardation* (Vol. 2). Baltimore: University Park Press.

ROSEN, M., CLARK, G. R., & KIVITZ, M. S. (1977). Beyond Normalization. In M. ROSEN, G. R. CLARK, & M. S. KIVITZ (Eds.), *Habilitation of the handicapped: New dimensions in programs for the developmentally disabled* (pp. 115-128). Baltimore, MD: University Park Press.

ROTHMAN, T. (Ed.). (1970). *Changing patterns in psychiatric care: An anthology of evolving scientific psychiatry in medicine.* New York: Crown.

ROWE, F. B. (1964). Attendants' training in Denmark. *Mental Retardation, 2,* 153-157.

SAREYAN, A. (1994). *The turning point: How persons of conscience brought about major change in the care of America's mentally ill.* Scottsdale, PA: Herald Press.

SCANDINAVIAN STUDY GROUP. (1966). Health services research in Scandinavia. *Milbank Memorial Fund Quarterly, 44*(4, Part 2), 227-261.

SCHEINER, A. P. (1975). *Dignified caring.* Unpublished report on a World Health Organization Fellowship. Rochester, NY: Monroe Developmental Services.

SCHEERENBERGER, R. C. (1983). *A history of*

mental retardation. Baltimore, MD: Paul H. Brookes.

SCHWARTZ, C. (1957). Perspectives on deviance—wives' definitions of their husbands' mental illness. *Psychiatry, 20,* 275-291.

SECRETARY'S COMMITTEE ON MENTAL RETARDATION. (1971). *Programs for the handicapped: Selected material on social security programs in the United States of America and abroad affecting the mentally retarded* (Bulletin No. 71-7). Washington, DC: U.S. Department of Health, Education & Welfare.

SMITH, J. P. (1968). Care of the mentally subnormal in Scandinavia. *Nursing Mirror, 127*(2), 27-29.

SMRTIC, J. D. (1979). *Abnormal psychology: A perspectives approach.* Wayne, NJ: Avery Publishing Group. (2nd ed. 1980, 3rd ed. 1982).

SOUTHERN REGIONAL EDUCATION BOARD. (1961). *European mental health programs as viewed by mental health specialists and legislators: A study of the care of the mentally sick and handicapped, Sept. 6-Oct. 4, 1961.* Atlanta, GA: Author.

STAFF. (1970a, March). Kelley: Both US and Europe M. R. programs have excellences, shortcomings. *PCMR Message* (President's Committee on Mental Retardation), No. 24, 1-2.

STAFF. (1970b, March). Visiting Danes hail new M.R. epoch, deplore "old models in modern design." *PCMR Message,* No. 24, 7.

STERNER, R. (1969). *Services for the handicapped.* Stockholm: Swedish Institute.

STERNER, R. (1976). *Social and economic conditions of the mentally retarded in selected countries.* Brussels, Belgium: United Nations & International League of Societies for the Mentally Handicapped. (Printed in Boston, MA, by the Cotting School for Handicapped Children)

STONE, O. (1961). The three worlds of the back ward. *Mental Hygiene, 45,* 18-27.

TAYLOR, W. W., & TAYLOR, I. W. (1960). *Special education of physically handicapped children in Western Europe.* New York: International Society for the Welfare of Cripples.

THOMAS, S. (1994). A brief history of the SRV Development, Training, and Safeguarding Council. *SRV/VRS: The International Social Role Valorization Journal/La revue internationale de la Valorisation des rôles sociaux, 1*(2), 15-18.

THOMPSON, J. D., & GOLDIN, G. (1975). *The hospital: A social and architectural history.* New Haven, CT: Yale University Press.

THURSZ, D., & VIGILANTE, J. L. (1975). *Meeting human needs: An overview of nine countries. Social Service Delivery Systems: An international annual (Vol. 1).* Beverly Hills, CA: Sage.

THURSZ, D., & VIGILANTE, J. L. (1976). *Meeting human needs: Additional perspectives from ten countries. Social Service Delivery Systems: An international annual (Vol. 2).* Beverly Hills, CA: Sage.

TIDMAN, Y., VON SYDOW, T., & THIBERG, S. (1969). *New lives for old* (K. Bradfield, Trans.). Stockholm: Swedish Institute.

Twentieth biennial report of the Board of State Commissioners of Public Charities of Illinois (Vol. 20, 1906-1908). (1909). Springfield, IL: Illinois State Journal Co., State Printers.

VAIL, D. J. (1965). *The British mental hospital system.* Springfield, IL: Charles C. Thomas.

VAIL, D. J. (1966). *Dehumanization and the institutional career.* Springfield, IL: Charles C. Thomas.

VAIL, D. J. (1968). *Mental health systems in Scandinavia.* Springfield, IL: Charles C. Thomas. (With special comment by C. Astrup, Oslo, Norway)

WALSH, G. (Producer). (1967). *To bridge the gap* [Film]. Minneapolis, MN: Minnesota Department of Public Welfare Library, & Minnesota Association for Retarded Children; & Arlington, TX: National Association for Retarded Children.

WESTER, A. (1970). *The Swedish child* (K. Bradfield, Trans.). Stockholm: Swedish Institute.

WHITE, W., & WOLFENSBERGER, W. (1969). The evolution of dehumanization in our institutions. *Mental Retardation, 7*(3), 5-9.

WOLFENSBERGER, W. (1964a). Reminiscences on a British Psychological Society convention [Letter to the editor]. *American Psychologist, 19,* 774-775.

WOLFENSBERGER, W. (1964b). Some observations on European programs for the mentally retarded. *Mental Retardation, 2,* 280-285.

WOLFENSBERGER, W. (1964c). Teaching and training of the retarded in European countries. *Mental Retardation, 2*, 331-337.

WOLFENSBERGER, W. (1965a). Diagnosis diagnosed. *Journal of Mental Subnormality, 11*, 62-70.

WOLFENSBERGER, W. (1965b). Embarrassments in the diagnostic process. *Mental Retardation, 3*(3), 29-31.

WOLFENSBERGER, W. (1965c). General observations on European programs. *Mental Retardation, 3*(1), 8-11.

WOLFENSBERGER, W. (1,967). Vocational preparation and occupation. In A. A. BAUMEISTER (Ed.), *Mental retardation: Appraisal, education, and rehabilitation* (pp. 232-273). Chicago: Aldine.

WOLFENSBERGER, W. (1969a). The origin and nature of our institutional models. In R. B. KUGEL & W. WOLFENSBERGER (Eds.), *Changing patterns in residential services for the mentally retarded* (pp. 59-171). Washington, DC: President's Committee on Mental Retardation.

WOLFENSBERGER, W. (1969b). Twenty predictions about the future of residential services in mental retardation. *Mental Retardation, 7*(6), 51-54.

WOLFENSBERGER, W. (1969c). A new approach to decision-making in human management services. In R. B. KUGEL & W. WOLFENSBERGER (Eds.), *Changing patterns in residential services for the mentally retarded* (pp. 367-381). Washington, DC: President's Committee on Mental Retardation.

WOLFENSBERGER, W. (1970a). Facilitation of psychiatric research in mental retardation. In F. J. MENOLASCINO (Ed.), *Psychiatric approaches to mental retardation* (pp. 663-689). New York: Basic Books.

WOLFENSBERGER, W. (1970b). The principle of Normalization and its implications for psychiatric services. *American Journal of Psychiatry, 127*, 291-297.

WOLFENSBERGER, W. (1971a). Will there always be an institution? I: The impact of epidemiological trends. *Mental Retardation, 9*(5), 14-20.

WOLFENSBERGER, W. (1971b). Will there always be an institution? II: The impact of new service models. *Mental Retardation, 9*(6), 31-38.

WOLFENSBERGER, W. (1972a). Comprehensive community services of the future. In SASKATCHEWAN ASSOCIATION FOR THE MENTALLY RETARDED, & SASKATCHEWAN COORDINATING COUNCIL ON SOCIAL PLANNING, *Comprehensive community services* (pp. 1-22). Regina, Saskatchewan: Authors.

WOLFENSBERGER, W. (1972b). Implementation of comprehensive community service systems. In , SASKATCHEWAN ASSOCIATION FOR THE MENTALLY RETARDED, & SASKATCHEWAN COORDINATING COUNCIL ON SOCIAL PLANNING, *Comprehensive community services* (pp. 45-60). Regina, Saskatchewan: Authors.

WOLFENSBERGER, W. (1972c). *The principle of Normalization in human services.* Toronto: National Institute on Mental Retardation.

WOLFENSBERGER, W. (1974a). Normalization of services for the mentally retarded: A conversation with Wolf Wolfensberger. "The Now Way to Know." *Education & Training of the Mentally Retarded, 9*, 202-208.

WOLFENSBERGER, W. (1974b). *The origin and nature of our institutional models.* Syracuse, NY: Center on Human Policy.

WOLFENSBERGER, W. (1975a). *The origin and nature of our institutional models* (Rev. & ill.). Syracuse, NY: Human Policy Press.

WOLFENSBERGER, W. (1975b). Values in the field of mental health as they bear on policies of research and inhibit adaptive human service strategies. In J. C. SCHOOLAR (Ed.), *Research and the psychiatric patient* (pp. 104-114). New York: Brunner/Mazel.

WOLFENSBERGER, W. (1979). Posibles desajustes en la formulación del diagnóstico. *Siglo Cera* (63), 23-26.

WOLFENSBERGER, W. (1980). The definition of Normalization: Update, problems, disagreements, and misunderstandings. In R. J. FLYNN & K. E. NITSCH (Eds.), *Normalization, social integration, and community services* (pp. 71-115). Baltimore: University Park Press.

WOLFENSBERGER, W. (1982). *The principle of Normalization in human services.* (S. Shimizu & Y. Nakazono, Trans.). Tokyo: Gakuen-Sha/Tuttle-Mori Agency.

WOLFENSBERGER, W. (1983). Social Role

Valorization: A proposed new term for the principle of Normalization. *Mental Retardation, 21*(6), 234-239.

WOLFENSBERGER, W. (1986). Die Entwicklung des Normalisierungsgedankens in den USA und in Kanada. In Bundesvereinigung Lebenshilfe (Ed.), *Normalisierung: Eine Chance fur Menschen mit geistiger Behinderung* (pp. 45-62). Marburg/Lahn: Lebenshilfe.

WOLFENSBERGER, W. (1991a). *A brief introduction to Social Role Valorization as a high-order concept for structuring human services.* Syracuse, NY: Syracuse University, Training Institute for Human Service Planning, Leadership and Change Agentry.

WOLFENSBERGER, W. (1991b). Reflections on a lifetime in human services and mental retardation. *Mental Retardation, 29*(1), 1-15.

WOLFENSBERGER, W. (1992). *A brief introduction to Social Role Valorization as a high-order concept for structuring human services* (2nd ed., rev.). Syracuse, NY: Syracuse University, Training Institute for Human Service Planning, Leadership and Change Agentry.

WOLFENSBERGER, W. (1998). *A brief introduction to Social Role Valorization: A high-order concept for addressing the plight of societally devalued people, and for structuring human services* (3rd ed., Rev.). Syracuse, NY: Syracuse University, Training Institute for Human Service Planning, Leadership and Change Agentry.

WOLFENSBERGER, W., & GLENN, L. (1969). *Program Analysis of Service Systems (PASS): A method for the quantitative evaluation of human services* (1st ed.). Omaha: Nebraska Psychiatric Institute.

WOLFENSBERGER, W., & GLENN, L. (1973a). *Program Analysis of Service Systems (PASS): A method for the quantitative evaluation of human services: Vol. 1. Handbook* (2nd ed.). Toronto: National Institute on Mental Retardation.

WOLFENSBERGER, W., & GLENN, L. (1973b). *Program Analysis of Service Systems (PASS): A method for the quantitative evaluation of human services: Vol. 2. Field Manual.* (2nd ed.). Toronto: National Institute on Mental Retardation.

WOLFENSBERGER, W., & GLENN, L. (1975a, reprinted 1978). *Program Analysis of Service Systems (PASS): A method for the quantitative evaluation of human services: Vol. 1. Handbook* (3rd ed.). Toronto: National Institute on Mental Retardation.

WOLFENSBERGER, W., & GLENN, L. (1975b, reprinted 1978). *Program Analysis of Service Systems (PASS): A method for the quantitative evaluation of human services: Vol. 2. Field manual* (3rd ed.). Toronto: National Institute on Mental Retardation.

WOLFENSBERGER, W., & MENOLASCINO, F. (1970a). Reflections on recent mental retardation developments in Nebraska. I: A new plan. *Mental Retardation, 8*(6), 20-25.

WOLFENSBERGER, W., & MENOLASCINO, F. (1970b). Reflections on recent mental retardation developments in Nebraska. II: Implementation to date. *Mental Retardation, 8*(6), 26-28.

WOLFENSBERGER, W., & THOMAS, S. (1980). *PASSING (Program Analysis of Service Systems' Implementation of Normalization Goals).* (Experimental edition). Syracuse, NY: Syracuse University, Training Institute for Human Service Planning, Leadership and Change Agentry.

WOLFENSBERGER, W., & THOMAS, S. (1983). *PASSING (Program Analysis of Service Systems' Implementation of Normalization Goals): Normalization criteria and ratings manual* (2nd ed.). Toronto: National Institute on Mental Retardation.

WOLFENSBERGER, W., & THOMAS, S. (1988). *PASSING (Programme d'analyse des systèmes de services application des buts de la valorisation des rôles sociaux: Manuel des critères et des mesures de la valorisation des rôles sociaux* (2ième éd.). (M. Roberge, Trans.; J. Pelletier, Adap.). Toronto: l'Institut G. Allan Roeher & Les Communications Opell. (Original work published 1983)

WOLFENSBERGER, W., & TIZARD, J. (1964). *Survey of an area-wide industrial training program for adult retardates in England.* Unpublished manuscript.

WOLFENSBERGER, W., & ZAUHA, H. (Eds.). (1973). *Citizen advocacy and protective services for the impaired and handicapped.* Toronto: National

Institute on Mental Retardation.

WOOLF, P. G. (1970). Subnormality services in Sweden. *Developmental Medicine & Child Neurology, 12,* 525-530.

WRIGHT, B. A. (1960). *Physical disability: A psycho-logical approach.* New York: Harper & Row.

WRIGHT, B. A. (1966). Disability and discrepancy of expectations. In B. J. BIDDLE & E. J. THOMAS (Eds.), *Role theory: Concepts and research* (pp. 159-164). New York: John Wiley & Sons.

NOTES

1. An advanced draft of the material in this chapter had been prepared for the Ottawa congress, but only portions of it were selectively presented.

2. During the 1950s, the Southbury Training School of the State of Connecticut was considered a model because of its so-called "cottage system" with its smaller living units.

3. Gunnar Dybwad (private communication, April 19, 1994) disagrees with this interpretation and believes that the President's Panel on Mental Retardation (1962) report is evidence of a community services vision, and that many parents had a good community services vision. I believe that the more ambitious visions were held by a very small minority of people, though some of them were in leadership positions. I also believe that my assertions are supported by much evidence later in this chapter.

4. By the way, NARC's subsidy of my trip evolved into the NARC's Rosemary Dybwad Award for study travel abroad, which was formally launched in 1964.

5. Some of the President's Panel on Mental Retardation Reports have a different date on their face page than the date given on another page by the U.S. Government Printing Office. The discrepancy was never more than one year, and I have used the U.S. Government Printing Office dates in my references here.

6. It was with a combination of flattery, bribery and threats that I got Dybwad to agree to this arrangement, writing to him as follows:

   > Your participation in this book is of the utmost importance. We do not know anyone who has your stature in the field or who would be capable of writing that chapter the way it should be written. . . . we suggest that you come to Omaha to be waited upon hand and foot by legions of . . . research assistants and secretaries . . . We would set you up in comfort and style, and provide you with dictating machines, secretaries that take dictation, etc. Also, if you so desire, you could do much of your work at a nice quiet sunny swimming pool or any other leisurely setting that facilitates a creative flow of your apperceptive masses. As you create, these creations would be transcribed and edited on the spot and sent back to you for further consideration. This leisurely creative pace would be punctuated by sumptuous meals, including exotic components such as the finest Sauerbraten, Pakistan curry, Beef Bourguignon, etc. You might wish to have your honored spouse by your side (to amuse, assist, or support you), which also can be arranged. The idea is that after a week or two of this, you would have had both an enjoyable rest as well as a productive period, at the end of which your chapter would essentially be done . . . At this point, we have finalized all chapters except yours. If worse came to worst, we would do the chapter ourselves, but we don't want this to happen. Burning incense daily for your recovery, we remain worshipfully but nevertheless editorially yours . . .

7. Thus, for archival reasons, it is important to note that there are three versions of the first edition of *Changing Patterns*: (a) the original printing(s), (b) a reprinting acknowledged on the inside title page as having been made possible by NICHD, and (c) a 1974 reprinting by the Pennsylvania Department of Public Welfare (Harrisburg, PA), acknowledged on the inside cover. The reprints all look like the original in color and size, and are facsimiles in nature.

8. In 1974, the chapter was also published as a separate monograph by the Center on Human Policy at Syracuse University, and again in a more lavish format in 1975, and was long one of its best sellers.

9. The 1948 UN statement had been preceded by a long-forgotten "Declaration of the Rights of Children," written in 1921 by Eglantyne Jebb, which was later adopted by the League of Nations but forgotten upon its collapse in the 1930s (Meyers, 1979). Beginning in 1956, the U.S. Department of Health, Education and Welfare (since reorganized) published a widely-disseminated poster of a "Creed for Exceptional Children." Leonard Mayo had been instrumental in drawing it up in 1954 at a conference he chaired that had been sponsored by the US Office of Education, and while he was director of the Association for the Aid of Crippled Children (since become the Easter Seal Society). While not framed in rights terms, this creed did call for "equality of opportunity" and an "ideal of a full and useful life for every exceptional child." This creed probably helped pave the way for later proclamations of the rights of handicapped people.

10. Even prior to the 1959 law, a law had been passed on June 18, 1958 that governed education and special education. While it mandated access to public education for all handicapped children (Lambert, 1970) 15 years before this happened in the US, a huge number of handicapped children began to be put into special segregated public schools that were called "center-schools," in part because they were regional schools (hence, in a certain sense, "central" even though they were usually not centrally located for the population), but in part probably also because of the then prominent concept of service centers, mentioned earlier.

11. This generalization of Normalization was already evident in my first Normalization publication in early 1970 (Wolfensberger, 1970b), in which I had not only generalized certain specific Normalization implications into general rules, but also had already framed them as applicable to deviant persons in general. For instance, I proposed that services should "employ culturally typical means" generally to

> shape, enhance, and maintain behavior that is as much as possible also culturally typical. . . The use of culturally normative rather than esoteric means is intended to minimize the appearance of separateness of deviant individuals. The attitudes and values of society should be shaped so as to be more accepting and tolerant of harmless types of differentness, such as differentness in appearance, demeanor, intelligence, speech and language, nationality, education, race, skin color, ethnic background, dress, etc. (p. 4).

12. Roeher had approached me to come to Canada at least as early as March 1971, at the Annual Conference of the Canadian Association for the Mentally Retarded in Winnipeg. He said it could be for a "sabbatical." On his invitation, I then visited the National Institute on Mental Retardation in Toronto in late March 1971 but did not decide until later that year to move there for a year or two, upon which we agreed that my appellation would be "visiting scholar."

13. Quite aside from how I did formulate Normalization, the fact is that one could say that the North American Normalization movement had three major thrusts.

    a. A sociopedagogic approach that emphasized what one could do in contact with devalued people to enhance *either* their competencies or their social image, on *either* the individual or group level, and *either* within or outside of formal services. Examples would be addressing people's personal appearance, providing groupings with other people that contributed to devalued persons' competency development and image enhancement, engaging devalued persons in activities that were challenging and age-appropriate, presenting devalued persons to others in physical settings that were image-enhancing, and emphasizing positive interactions of any parties with devalued persons, to name just a few.

    b. Social-systemic measures in support of competency or image enhancement even outside of contexts in which devalued people were present, for example, in the language that one used about them even when they were not present, in the names and logos that one gave to their services, in the funding efforts (such as fund-raising appeals) for services that would benefit devalued people, in the image juxtapositions created about them by and in art, the media and advertising, etc.

    c. A thrust that is perhaps best described as a rights orientation. Within this thrust, one could in turn identify two distinct emphases: a legal orientation (e.g., trying to define all sorts of things as rights in law) and a human/transcendent rights orientation (e.g., emphasizing people's human rights even apart from whatever the law may say).

In respect to the third thrust, it is interesting that the rights orientation that developed both out of, as well as independent from, the Normalization movement first of all increasingly focused on legal rights that were largely decontextualized from the broader context of human rights; and that secondly, it sought to resolve almost all problems of a sociopedagogic and social-systemic nature via the medium of legal rights. I believe that the latter was and is a very unwise strategy, in part because it cannot possibly succeed.

Appendix A

A BRIEF SKETCH OF THE SELECTION
OF THE ESSEX SERVICE SYSTEM AS A SERVICE-MODEL CHAPTER

While at the 1967 International Association for the Scientific Study of Mental Deficiency congress in Montpellier, France, I also met David Norris from Chelmsford in Essex, England, northeast of London. I was so impressed by him and what he told me that I took up his invitation to visit him in Essex on my way home. He toured me through a most impressive community service system there—one that was truly systemic—and a few nonsystemic pubs as well. This service system seemed to have taken up about where Middlesex had left off. It demonstrated how important it was for dispersed and diversified community services to be carefully planned years in advance, and very sequentially implemented, which contributed greatly to my concepts for U.S. services, especially in Nebraska. On returning home, I wrote Norris—an Irishman—with apologies to Swinburne,

Let us praise while we can
The wild Irish man
Though they may honor none
But the tamed one.

When it came time to write *Changing Patterns*, we decided to ask Norris to write up the Essex model, especially since we did want one from Britain. It was not easy to get him to do it, and, among other things, we had to write letters to his bosses to let him do it. When he delivered his first draft, he did it, in his words, "to our mutual surprise and relief." But actually, his chapter was one of the more literate and even poetic ones.

Appendix B

TABLE OF CONTENTS OF KUGEL, R. B., & WOLFENSBERGER, W. (EDS.). (1969). *CHANGING PATTERNS IN RESIDENTIAL SERVICES FOR THE MENTALLY RETARDED*

Appendix C

DOCUMENTATION OF RESERVATIONS ABOUT NORMALIZATION IMPLICATIONS BY CONTRIBUTORS TO *CHANGING PATTERNS*

Although Lloyd Dunn had been the first to conceptualize a diversified range of residential settings for retarded people, he was thinking mostly of facilities for between 10 to 200 people, most of them between 10 to 50 people. As early as March 6, 1968, after seeing his chapter draft, I wrote him the following:

I am not too sure about the continued role of the large institution that you suggest might still be needed even if special-purpose facilities are developed. . . . It may well be timely to call for a planned phasing away of these institutions to go hand in hand with any long-range regionalization and specialization plan, since otherwise we will be confronted with an unplanned but foreseeable catastrophe similar to the one confronting communities where large VA hospitals were closed down overnight. What I am asking myself lately is whether we have been belaboring a rationale for continuation of the traditional institution not because we really see much of a role for it in the future, but because the implications of not seeing a role for it are so drastic or charged that we can't face them, or we are afraid others can't face them.

In regard to the issue of whether to replace the traditional institution with small special-purpose facilities, Tizard once told me he would advocate going ahead even if we still do lack evidence of the type that you call for, because, as he put it, we couldn't possibly do worse than we have in the past.

Even Burton Blatt still held up large facilities, such as the Seaside Regional Center in Connecticut, as models as late as 1979 (Blatt, Ozolins, & McNally, 1979).

As regards educational integration, Dunn asked me in a January 1973 letter what some of us meant by "...normalizing education for the trainable mentally retarded. I assume you do not mean that most mongoloid children can be educated in the educational mainstream . . ." To this I replied (February 7, 1973) as follows:

To me, school does not mean the three R's, but preparation for life. As such, I can see no viable rationale for having separate structures for severely handicapped children.

. . . To me it is merely a question when and how all children will be served, and how fast we can extend the age limit downward. Here, tremendous opportunities for physical and social integration are opened up, and I do firmly believe, and have actually seen it done with great success, that the younger handicapped child is the one that can be socially integrated quite readily. Thus, I mean indeed that mongoloid and epileptic and hydrocephalic children can be educated in the same room with non-handicapped children, and that from such arrangements, no one will suffer, while many will gain.

However, I am strongly opposed to what I have come to call "dumping," which is the mere placement in the mainstream, without the necessary support. Integration is meaningless if it is only physical, and in order to be social, all sorts of supports are needed. Among these might be an intensive program of making the handicapped children physically and socially more attractive prior to physical integration; attitudinal preparation of parents, staff, and children; overstaffing the integrated group; provision of high-level consultancy; the presence of an adequate range of teaching materials, etc.

At present, a transfer of the severely retarded from special MR agencies to public schools usually means a drop in quality. However, I am willing to live with this temporarily in order to establish the clear mandate, and to set up the necessary administrative and service structures. In the long run, I see it as absolutely essential that monitoring and program evaluation mechanisms be instituted as never before.

I have just come back from Pennsylvania where now, since there is no other alternative left, the educational establishment in the state has made a 100% turn-around and has embraced the profoundly retarded, running noses and all. Because all loopholes have been closed, teachers are suddenly totally and for the first time re-orienting themselves, and are developing a willingness to become child developmentalists, change diapers, etc. This was a most heartening experience, because it opens teachers' attitudes now to being trained as to what to do with the more severely, profoundly and multiply handicapped.

Appendix D

NORMALIZATION
Bengt Nirje

Normalization means . . . A normal rhythm of the day.
You get out of bed in the morning, even if you are
Profoundly retarded and physically handicapped;
You get dressed,
And leave the house for school or work,
You don't stay home;
In the morning you anticipate events,
In the evening you think back on what you have accomplished;
The day is not a monotonous 24 hours with every minute endless.

You eat at normal times of the day and in a normal fashion;
Not just with a spoon, unless you are an infant;
Not in bed, but at a table;
Not early in the afternoon for the convenience of the staff.

Normalization means . . . A normal rhythm of the week.
You live in one place,
Go to work in another,
And participate in leisure activities in yet another.
You anticipate leisure activities on weekends,
And look forward to getting back to school
Or work on Monday.

Normalization means . . . A normal rhythm of the year.
A vacation to break routines of the year.
Seasonal changes bring with them a variety
Of types of food, work, cultural events, sports,
Leisure activities.
Just think . . . We thrive on these seasonal changes!

Normalization means . . . Normal developmental experiences
Of the life cycle:
In childhood, children, but not adults, go to summer camps.
In adolescence one is interested in grooming, hairstyles,
Music, boy friends and girl friends.
In adulthood, life is filled with work and responsibilities.
In old age, one has memories to look back on, and can
Enjoy the wisdom of experience.

Normalization means . . . Having a range of choices,
Wishes, and desires respected and considered.
Adults have the freedom to decide
Where they would like to live,
What kind of job they would like to have, and can best perform.
Whether they would prefer to go bowling with a group,
Instead of staying home to watch television.

Normalization means . . . Living in a world made of two sexes.
Children and adults both develop relationships with
Members of the opposite sex.
Teenagers become interested in having
Boy friends and girl friends.
Adults may fall in love, and decide to marry.

Normalization means . . . The right to normal economic standards.
All of us have basic financial privileges, and responsibilities,
Are able to take advantage of
Compensatory economic security means,
Such as child allowances, old age pensions, and
Minimum wage regulations.
We should have money to decide how to spend;
On personal luxuries, or necessities.

Normalization means . . . Living in normal housing
In a normal neighbourhood.
Not in a large facility with 20, 50, or 100 other people
Because you are retarded,
And not isolated from the rest of the community.
Normal locations and normal size homes will give residents
Better opportunities for successful integration
With their communities.

Appendix E

OBSERVATIONS FROM MY STUDY TOUR TO MENTAL RETARDATION SERVICES IN DENMARK AND SWEDEN IN APRIL 1969

The observations reported below are drawn from my travel diary and my correspondence shortly after returning from my trip, and are meant to supplement those reported in the body of the chapter or elsewhere.

One of the things I learned in Scandinavia was the incredible power of attractive and normative environments to elicit normative behavior even from very impaired, disturbed, and self-abusive persons. While people might still be engaging in very stereotypical behavior, they could be seen doing so in the midst of beautifully normative environments without doing harm to them, something which apparently nobody I knew of in North America thought would be possible.

Perhaps one of the most crucial aspects of Normalization in Denmark and Sweden was that handicapped people received either rather large pensions, or good payment for work, or both, and this enabled them to lead a more normalized lifestyle in all sorts of ways, both in institutions and in the community.

Already by 1969, it had become quite common for retarded people in both Denmark and Sweden to spend their vacations all over Europe, particularly its southern parts. This had many normalizing effects and was only possible because of the lavish personal subsidies mentioned above.

About Denmark specifically, one thing that was so remarkable was not only the normalizing features of so many services, but the sheer magnitude of the service system, in that during the 10-year period of 1959-1969, 150 new service settings had been created, all but about 10 of these of a nonresidential nature, and all that in a country that had fewer than 5 million inhabitants.

Bank-Mikkelsen said that reform in Denmark would not have been possible if it had not been for the "new attitude" of parents of retarded people, which, he said, "changed the whole thing." But while Bank-Mikkelsen saw parents as the motive force behind the reforms, I found that people lower down in the mental retardation services almost uniformly saw parents as the enemy. At one place, I was even asked whether the parent group where I was from gave us any trouble, to which I replied that "I am part of such a parents group, and I do."

Visiting the Karens Minde institution for the mentally retarded in Copenhagen, I met a man with Down's syndrome who kept a picture of President Kennedy on his wall. I happened to have an American half-dollar with me with Kennedy's head on one side and tried to make it a present to him, but he rejected it and said, "It won't work."

In one of the workshops of that institution, I wanted to buy a plate hanger that was being made there, but instead my host insisted that I take it free, with the comment, "Remember the Marshall Plan."

Bank-Mikkelsen told me that even though Norway was wealthier than Denmark, its service development was much slower, and parents were sending their retarded children from Norway to Denmark to be served there, with the Norwegian state paying only part of the cost. The net effect was that the Danish taxpayers were thereby subsidizing the rich Norwegians.

After visiting the Danish school for mental retardation workers, I wrote the following comments, which, I believe, I shared with Bank-Mikkelsen.:

June 17, 1969

A. Some observations which impress me.
    1. The large number (1,200) of students in training at any one time, considering the small size of the country.
    2. The length of training (3 years and more).

3. The breadth and depth of training which not merely includes content directly relating to mental retardation, but also aims at self-actualization and general upgrading of the trainee's personality and academic and civic skills.

4. The balance between practical and theoretical training.

5. The great amount of monies the Danish Mental Retardation System is willing to invest in the training program.

6. The industrial and business-like setting of the industrial school.

7. The youth of the trainees.

8. The advanced training for houseparent work.

B. Points which bear further exploration and discussion or which might be definite weaknesses.

    1. The theoretical training has certain unreal qualities as exemplified in the following aspects:

        a. Teachers have little practical experience in general, and even less in mental retardation.

        b. Some content appears to have been decided upon very arbitrarily and by college-oriented academicians.

        c. Some texts appear to be college texts, and some content appears to be somewhat irrelevant, much too advanced, or both.

        d. In some areas, there appears to be little evaluation of either the student's grasp of material or its relevance to them.

        e. There appears to be limited feedback from advanced or graduated students to the training program or its content.

    2. A relatively rigid European status system appears to impose considerable limitations to the rapid advancement of competent young personnel.

    3. I understand that there is a high turnover among graduates, due to a significant degree to low salaries. This sounds like poor economy to me, considering the high cost of training.

    4. I am not sure on this point, but I suspect that personnel statistics and follow-up data are scanty.

Suggestions for possible changes are an inherent part of some of the above comments. An additional point would be to intensify and accelerate the training of training personnel, especially in practical experience, and have students evaluate the performance of the teachers.

During my visit to Sweden, Grunewald enunciated what we have since called the "grouping-up" principle, that is, a small group should not have more than one or two severely impaired members because this way, these can be "pulled up" and do not, what he called, "dominate" the group.

I also learned that for years already, there had been a group home on the very street on which Grunewald lived.

The fact was also amazing that so many retarded people in Sweden—even some very retarded ones—could speak some English, considering the low expectations that American special education teachers generally held of their pupils.

One thing that was almost too good to be believed was that there were over 900 Swedish "circles" for retarded adults that were analogous to similar ones for nonretarded people that had been started long ago by labor unions and political parties in order to promote adult education of workers. These circles were called something that would roughly translate as "study groups."

One peculiar thing about word usage in Sweden was that the term "research" was commonly applied to doing "diagnostic work-ups."

Despite the fact that I saw an enormous amount and variety of impressive things in Denmark and Sweden, at the same time, my diary also recorded many shortcomings, which underlines what had been a red thread in my teaching ever since, namely, that no service will ever practice or bring together everything that is already known as being good.

One weakness in both countries was in the domain of the work ethic, which was weak both on the part of service personnel and handicapped people. Workers had relatively few demands made upon them, and they in turn made relatively light demands on their retarded charges, though surprisingly, the normativeness of the surroundings and the expectations for normative behavior—even if not for productive behavior—worked very well in eliciting normative behavior. In other words, the environment was one in which people acted relatively normally even if they did not necessarily have to work hard.

Also, many other visitors may not have noted how many of the workers below the top level held a great many attitudes inconsistent with Normalization and were quite ignorant about the good things that were going on in the services other than their very own, or in other Scandinavian countries. Relatedly, retarded adults doing rather high-level work in workshops were often still called "patients."

One big obstacle to integration in Denmark was that some services were run by the localities and others by the state, and the latter included special education for retarded children. This observation underlined the importance of the concept of "continuity" among provisions, and the importance of a single administrative or controlling umbrella.

One interesting feature that I elaborated on elsewhere (Wolfensberger, 1971a, 1971b) was that in Sweden, group homes and apartments built specifically for retarded people had an institutional flavor, while such residences in generic buildings did not.

Not included in my feedback to Nirje and Grunewald, but published in one of my articles as early as December 1969 (Wolfensberger, 1969b), was the conclusion that failure to specialize residential service types was one of the main reasons why even progressive countries such as Denmark and Sweden still relied so heavily on traditional institutions. Unfortunately, this is one of the points that I have preached consistently all these years that has been least understood and least implemented, exemplified most clearly today by the near-total failure to provide a highly specialized type of small residential service for people who display very severe social problems but who are not mean of spirit.

Despite these shortcomings in Denmark and Sweden, the overall achievements were so dramatic that I noted in my diary that I experienced a feeling of "acute envy."

4

The North American formulation of the principle of Normalization

JACK YATES

1 INTRODUCTION

Bengt Nirje (chapter 2) and Wolf Wolfensberger (chapter 3) presented the historical and conceptual evolution of the principle of Normalization. My assignment from the editors is more narrow, essentially to offer a systematic presentation of the North American (i.e., Wolfensberger's) formulation of the principle, as it would have been presented circa 1975. Immerse yourselves, then, in the social and human service milieu of 1975, and we will examine this (at the time relatively new) principle to guide our work.

2 DEVALUATION: WHAT IS PEOPLE'S PROBLEM?

How we define a person's problem has clear implications for how we might go about trying to solve it or address it. To oversimplify, let's look at that in two different ways. What happens if we define the problem *within* the person? For instance, we might look upon the inability to walk or the lack of intellectual or verbal quickness as indicating such problems. We might define the problem within the person because of his or her recurrent outbursts of violent behavior. The problem within the person may be an inability to speak.

If the problem is essentially within the person, then the human service response would need to be an attempt to change the person.

That sounds a bit overbearing or condescending to say it that way. But changing a person could take a nicer sounding form: rehabilitation, education—change the person. That's where the problem is.

But suppose we define the problem in a different way. Suppose the essence of the problem is in the *context around* a person and in the interaction of the person *with* that context. If that were the case, then our human service response would need to be an attempt to change the context, in addition to or instead of changing the person.

To take that second way of defining the problem in the context and the person's interaction with the context, to take that into more of the language of sociology, then we might say that in any society, it seems, some people are *cast* into devalued or deviant roles.

"Deviant" was a word that I didn't run into until I went to a Normalization presentation; it's a word from another field, not having necessarily the sexually charged connotation that we might find in popular usage. Many groups in American society might be perceived as deviant, having been cast into devalued roles by others or by the dominant society.

Those groups have different things going on inside; but we are saying that that is *not* the essence of their problem. The essence is that they have been cast into devalued roles. That deviancy might be defined as being different from others in one or more dimensions, with those dimensions perceived as significant by others, and with that difference valued negatively by others.

Such a definition of the problem has its implications for what we will need to do, then, to address or to try and solve the problem. If deviancy is, as in that definition, socially and also subjectively and variably defined, then deviancy or devaluation is relative. That is, a particular characteristic of a person, something that may be true inside, of the person's appearance or behavior, might be perceived negatively in one society but not in another. A characteristic might be perceived negatively, therefore enabling others to cast the person into a deviant role in one era of a certain society and yet not in others. An example of that relative nature of devaluation that is to me the clearest and the most overwhelming is that the idea that there might be such a thing as segregated housing for people because they are elderly had never been conceived in human history until our lifetime. Devaluation, we note, varies over time and varies from place to place, from society to society, depending on what is highly valued and therefore, by implication, what is devalued. Now, if deviancy is subjectively defined, existing subjectively in the eyes of the perceiver, or beholder, then it follows that there could be two major avenues toward attempting to reduce or eliminate deviancy or devaluation. First, we could work with that person who has been cast into deviant roles to minimize the stigmata of deviancy. We might ask, what is it that we could do with or for that person? But then, deviancy being in the eyes of the beholder, it could also be reduced or eliminated by changing the perceptions or the values of the beholder, the perceptions or values of the person who is doing the casting into deviant roles.

3 THE PRINCIPLE OF NORMALIZATION AS A RESPONSE TO DEVALUATION: DEFINITIONS

In 1972, Wolf Wolfensberger took those two ways of responding and expressed them as a principle with a definition. One way in which Wolfensberger defined the principle of Normalization is to say it is the use of culturally normative means (techniques, methods, tools) to enable people's life conditions (income, housing, jobs, recreation) to be at least as good as those of average citizens. Culturally normative is not used here to mean *the* average, *the* normal, *the* mean, but rather, in the sense of a range of what's broadly accepted, a range of what is expectable and ordinary, where people would not raise their eyebrows to encounter. Moreover, culturally

normative means would be called into play to, as much as possible, enhance and support people's behavior, appearance, experiences, status and reputation, in their own eyes and in the eyes of others.

An alternative way in which Wolfensberger defines the principle of Normalization is the utilization of means that are as culturally normative as possible in order to establish, enable, or support behaviors, appearances, and interpretations that themselves are as culturally normative as possible.

4 THE CONSERVATISM COROLLARY

If a person is, or is in danger of being, devalued by others, then we might even work toward the upper end of that range, maybe a little better than "okay." The principle of Normalization implies we work toward what is normative but also toward what is the most highly *valued*, the most enhancing options. Formally, that implication is termed the "conservatism corollary." More informally, one might try to explain the conservatism corollary as the "bend-over-backward" corollary. Let me explain.

Most people have some characteristics that are devalued in some ways. A person may have some little impairment of functioning, or some way in which the person is not at the top of society's expectations. Many or most people are, you might say in sociological language, deviant in few and minor ways. Not necessarily hindered in functioning, not necessarily different in such a way as to be cast into a devalued role that becomes life-defining, no. But as the personal characteristics perceived by others in a significantly, negatively, different way increase in number or severity or variety, they will tend to have a multiplicative effect. Negative perceptions tend to accumulate: that one characteristic that other people devalue about a person will tend to make the next thing have even more weight than it would without the first having been there. Even more than a cumulative impact, adding negatively valued characteristics will have a multiplicative effect on the person who is in danger of being devalued. Therefore, what might for you or me or any valued person in society be an irritation or a minor setback, for a person in danger of being cast into a devalued role in life-defining ways, that same event or occurrence might be devastating to his or her whole life.

For instance, losing a job is no fun and not particularly valuing for anyone; but if you are a person defined by others as incompetent, the impact of losing a job for *you* may be that most of the world is telling you, don't even try it again.

If a person is in danger of being cast in life-defining ways into devalued roles, then unluckily that means that adding one more deviant characteristic, or characteristic others are ready to see as deviant, may send the person down a negative spiral. And yet luckily, if a person is in danger of being cast into a devalued role in a life-defining way, the conservative corollary would also imply that it becomes even more impactful to reduce one of those stigmata; similarly, it becomes even more impactful to balance that negatively perceived characteristic by something that is especially enhancing, the positive end of the continuum of what is expected, what is in the range of predictable and ordinary. The conservatism corollary would advise us to choose the most *enhancing* option.

Usually, we would have a range of what one might be able to provide for a person or present to that person as an option from which to choose: a range of options, a range of possibilities. The conservatism corollary would imply that we try to provide the most enhancing, not just the average or the ordinary. If somebody is in danger of being seen or stereotyped in negative ways, then we must bend over backward to avoid adding one more deviancy, and bend over backward to provide positive compensation.

5 EXPLORING THE IMPLICATIONS OF NORMALIZATION: TWO DIMENSIONS AND THREE LEVELS

So we have two definitions of the principle of Normalization, two slightly different definitions. What would it mean to follow that principle? What would we need to do in practice? Well, we could follow the implications of the principle of Normalization by looking at what might be our practices, looking at what we might do with and for people who are in danger of being cast into deviant roles. We will explore the implications of the principle of Normalization conceptually by looking at our practices through two dimensions and three levels.

The first of the two dimensions of the principle of Normalization would have us ask, what can we do in the way of interaction? What should I do if I have a role to play in somebody's life and that person is in danger of being cast into a deviant role? How should I act with that person, what direct impact can I have on her or him? And then the second dimension of the principle, besides interaction, would be to ask, what can we do in the way of interpretations? What kinds of messages are sent about a person consciously, or even unconsciously, and how can we influence those too? Interaction dimension: How do I act *with* a person? Interpretation dimension: How do I act to *surround* a person with positive interpretations, instead of negative?

Those two dimensions then can be enacted at three levels. What can we do at the level of the person? What can we do at the level of the primary and intermediate social systems that surround that person (family, program, neighborhood), and what can we do at the level of society to make those two kinds of changes?

First, at the level of the person and in the dimension of interaction, what can a person do directly with and for another person? What can we do to help that person in their health and in their health habits? What can we do to help that person to gain very practical skills? What can we do to help that person to learn? What can we do to help that person to learn not only things that you can take a test about, but what can we do to help a person to learn how to act, how to be, how to be with other people? What can we do to help that person to have more richness in his or her life, activity, recreation, work, and job opportunities? What can we do to help that person to see him or herself in a more positive way, enhance his or her self-image and awareness? What can we do to help a person to gain not only the skills but perhaps also the habits and the inclinations that will make him or her a more powerful participant among other people, by self-mastery and discipline and courage? What can we do to try to provide directly with and for that person the kind of security that will make a difference for any of us, as to what kind of life we will live and how we will feel about it as we live it? The dimension of interaction at the level of the person proposes many ways we can enrich and fulfill a person's life directly:

Normalization would also ask us to look at the level of the person in the dimension of interpretation. In other words, we should examine the ways in which we might help a person to be interpreted well to other people, to the eyes of the perceivers. For instance, we might want to look at what we *call* people. What do we say to people, what do we say about people, particularly about people who are in danger of being devalued? How might we help a person to present himself or herself in ways that will make it just that much more likely that someone will accept him or her and will extend a welcome? We will count in that person's life if we can help him or her to come across positively, even in such superficial things as personal appearance. We might be tempted to say that those perceivers, those beholders, should not be judging a person by first impressions. Well, no, they shouldn't, I agree. And yet, sometimes people do. We can lament and complain about that, or we can try to help a person to come across more positively, more enhancingly. Further, what can we do to provide a person with valued work? Not only so that it will enrich and fulfill his or her life, on the interaction dimension, but it will also help that person to come across better to others because he or she will be filling a valued work role and perhaps enabled to fill other valued roles in life. That will change the views of the perceivers too. How can we allow reasonable risk, not only because we learn by it and the person at risk of devaluation learns by it, but also to allow and encourage challenge and risk in a person's life because that, too, will change the way that other people look at that person.

Normalization would ask us not only to work with and on behalf of a person at the level of the person, but it would next have us ask, what can we do in that person's life and in the interpretation of that person, by the changes we might make in the person's primary and intermediate social systems? How might we change the context, not only change the person? What can we do, in other words, that works directly with those primary and intermediate social systems by, for instance, dispersal of groups as opposed to the segregation and congregation of people who (I guess the old idea ran) must belong "with their own kind"? How might we present alternatives in the way that we design programs? How might we especially try to work toward the valued social participation of people who have been for too long excluded from community and society? Full integration at work, integration in one's residence, integration in education? Why would that be important? The principle of Normalization asks us to think about that along the dimension of interaction because it makes a difference to the person we have in mind.

There are some things in our lives that we have learned by formal instruction: people stood up and delivered lectures; our teachers in high school taught us things. Here's an example. Once upon a time I learned, and most of you all learned, what is the capital of Colorado. You learned it, I learned it, you know it. What is the capital

of South Dakota? You probably learned that one too, and you probably got it right on a test. How did you learn that? You learned that by formal instruction, and we learn a lot of things that way. It is a valuable thing in life to be able to learn that way: We read books, we hear lectures, we read blackboards, we read handouts at presentations, we learn by formal instruction. But, there are a lot of other things in our lives that we did not learn by formal instruction. For instance, whether you know the capital of Colorado or not, I can see just by looking at you that you all know how to dress presentably for an evening presentation at a conference. Now, that is something you also had to learn. You weren't born knowing how to dress presentably, and you probably didn't get formal instructions about it. By how to dress, I don't mean how to do buttons or zippers. I mean, what is presentable. What is okay. What is within the range of things that won't get people staring at you and saying you look weird. How did you learn that? Never read it in a book. Never had a course. Never took a class. There are a lot of things in life—just how to act, how to be, how to be more or less presentable most of the time—things in life that we learn just by being around other people. We pick them up from other people. And how would we have learned those things had we been *segregated*, forced to spend all our time with people who didn't know those things? Social integration or valued social participation, then, would have an impact on a person by creating a context around him or her that includes people who know those things already. To be surrounded by ordinary valued people who have those ordinary competencies would make a difference in a person's life.

We could work also at the level of the primary and intermediate social systems in a person's life to use the kinds of settings and services that are used by everyone. We should enable and assist people to use settings that are part of our communities, that are not for a specific group labeled by age, not for a group of people labeled by disability. They are for everyone, generic. We need also to look at the ways in which what we do within programs becomes part of the context around a person: How is that programmatic context supportive to a person by being demanding, challenging? How is the context supportive to a person by being age- and culture-appropriate? How does the context make it likely to help a person learn not only the formal skills you could take a test on, but also to learn how to act, how to be, how to make social acceptance more likely?

The principle of Normalization would also imply that we work at the level of the primary and intermediate social systems along the dimension of interpretation. We need to ask of service settings, for instance, that they be in a place that you would expect them to be, normative locations. We need to ask that service settings look about the way you might expect them to look for you and me, for anyone; in other words, we should arrange and design normative program appearances and facilities. About a residential service, we would ask, indoor, outdoor, what does it look like? Does it look like a home for you or me, for ordinary citizens? That would count for the way that we interpret the people who live there. We need to describe people in enhancing ways, and we also need to refer to the places where people go and are served, and the programs that serve people, in enhancing ways instead of devaluing ways. We should group people in ways that send a positive message about who they are, valued in the eyes of the perceiver. We can get mad at the perceivers for not accepting people, but we can also try to influence how those perceptions occur, the interpretations that are affected at this intermediate level of the context around a person.

The principle of Normalization would ask us to look at another dimension, at another level: How is it that we might work at the level of changing society, through the dimension of interacting with society? So Normalization would ask what might we do to structure not only a program, but that broader context of a social service system into the kinds of patterns and governance that will give people continuity in their experience and breadth of opportunity through their human service experience. How can we affect also the ways that people are hired and then the ways that people are trained to try to offer those supports at the systems and the societal level so that supports will be most enhancing to their competence, richness of life, relationships? How can we influence legislation that will, in turn, have influence on the lives of people that we care about? How can we interact with the key institutions of society to make a difference in people's lives? Then, too, we need to work at the level of society, but through the dimension of interpretation. What kinds of messages can we send about people, perhaps even people in broad groups, to the whole society? How can we shape societal attitudes to accept groups of people who are in danger of being cast into deviant roles? How can we broaden the public's definitions of who is okay, who is acceptable, who is welcome, who is included? How can we interpret people positively by public education? How can we interpret people positively by how programs and systems operate and by what they are called, by program terms, and by nonstigmatized funding? And how can we interpret people positively, too, by setting examples that a whole society might see of how people might be with one another?

6 SOCIAL INTEGRATION

Now we'll go back to the question I asked a few minutes ago about how we learned the capital of Colorado and about what difference it makes to people if they have been segregated. Well, it limits their learning directly, how they will learn how to be among people. But there is another problem with segregation, and therefore another kind of importance to social integration as an implication of the principle of Normalization. That is, what difference does social integration make in the eyes of the perceiver? Maybe not only the eyes; maybe we should ask also, what difference does social integration make in the minds and the hearts and even the souls of the perceivers?

We are taking ourselves back to a presentation of the North American formulation of the principle of Normalization as of 1975, so it seems appropriate to share with you a short story from 1975, in which we visited an early-childhood education program in Syracuse, New York, the First Baptist Church Child Development Center. It was not a typical place to visit for a human service training group like a PASS team, in that where we visited was not set up for people who had a certain label; it was set up generically for anyone who was 3, 4, or 5 years old in Syracuse. Something that we had as a special focus as a visiting training team, however, was that two of those students, out of the 32, were youngsters who were visibly handicapped in some way. I remember meeting Angela and Billy.

Angela was a youngster who could not walk, and people were working with her on that. She had some adaptive equipment she was strengthening her leg muscles. She had had surgery too, and it was hoped that she might soon learn to walk. But at the moment that we went there to visit, Angela could not walk. This is a story about the impact of social integration on Angela: It was a good place for her to be. Why? Because she could learn from the other students. She could learn what it was like to be a 4-year-old, which she probably would not have gotten from a book or from a teacher. She could learn that only by being among a variety of other 4-year-olds. Those were her peers.

This is a story about meeting Billy too. Billy, at least as far as we knew, had no particular impairments. Billy was an ordinary, typical 4-year-old boy. In fact, he was turning 5 the day that we were there, which is one of the reasons that Billy sticks in my mind. When we visited there, Billy was telling anybody he could get his hands on, including us visitors: "Hey, today's my birthday. I'm five years old." So, naturally, to try to be polite and be good guests while we were visiting, we asked Billy, "Five years old, hey, that's great! Are you having a party today for your birthday?" Billy said: "Well, we're having cupcakes here at the day-care center, but the real party is going to be Saturday. My mom said it should be Saturday 'cause then all of my friends can come, not just here from the day-care center." We responded: "Sounds great. Who is coming to your party on Saturday?" Billy replied: "Oh, all my friends are coming. Tommy's coming, Bobby's coming, *Angela's* coming."

I think back to that story as a story about Billy too, even more than as a story about Angela. What difference does social integration make to Angela? Well, I hope that maybe someday, Billy will be a big employer or the mayor, and he'll be able to make some difference to Angela's life; but I think social integration will make a difference to Billy's life whether or not he becomes a powerful person someday. Perhaps by growing up with Angela, Billy will have grown up with a little more variety of people, he will have grown up gentled by the experience of having known Angela, especially if he is able to keep that relationship going as they both grow into their teens, when many of us start to stigmatize each other. Social integration is implied by the interaction dimension of the principle of Normalization, and it is implied also by the interpretation dimension. This, then, has been a story about Angela's life, but it is just as powerfully a story about Billy's life and his mind and, metaphorically speaking, his heart.

The principle of Normalization in summary would ask us to consider how might we help people in danger of being cast into deviant roles, how might we help them to be enabled to be valued instead in their appearance, in their behavior, in their speech, but not only in things about the person. But also how might we help people by changing the context around them, job opportunities that they might have, other opportunities for other kinds of

inclusion, other kinds of valued roles, other kinds of richness? How might we help people to be valued in the relationships that they have? How might we help people to become valued even in the services that they receive, and how those services send messages about those people in enhancing ways instead of deviancy-invoking ways?

Well, we might be able to help people to be valued in all of those six ways that come into that matrix scheme of dimensions and levels. If we attend to each of those two dimensions and we attend to each of those three levels of action, well, that will certainly have its challenging implications for how we might change the insides of human service programs. That looks like a tall order, and it give us plenty of work to do. But of course, from its earliest statements by Wolfensberger, the North American conceptualization of the principle of Normalization has always stressed social integration, compelling us to break out of the insides of human service programs. That demand may not have been sufficiently appreciated by people who have made cosmetic changes in segregated programs. And that demand for social integration may not either have been justly credited by those people who more recently have worked toward inclusive communities. But we have got to break out of just changing the insides of segregated programs; we must provide the needed services and supports so that people who have been cast into devalued roles can become and remain full participants in their families, in their schools, and in their communities. The principle of Normalization, perhaps above all, implies social integration.

7 CONCLUSION

Let me tell you a story.

Also in 1975, I had the opportunity to visit a summer day camp near Albany, New York. It was a typical day camp in many ways. About 300 campers came each day, and they were organized by age group. So the 10-year-old boys were the Tigers, the 8-year-old boys were the Eagles, the 9-year-old girls were the Apaches, and the 12-year-old girls were the Mohawks. Through the day, campers in their groups engaged in activities typical of a day camp: swimming, canoeing, nature groups, horseback riding, and so on.

One thing was not so typical at the camp, however. Its owner and director, Ben Becker, decided that it would be a good learning experience for everyone concerned to have a number of campers be children with physical or mental impairments. So he had an informal quota system to ensure that 5-10% of the campers in any given week were children with handicaps, and he gave out scholarships to assist in this plan. Thus when the Mohawks went horseback riding, not every Mohawk could just jump on a horse and ride; and not every Mohawk could learn as easily or as quickly as every other Mohawk.

For instance, in the group of 30 Mohawks, one was a girl who was blind. So when she went horseback riding with the Mohawks, another girl rode on another horse next to her to call over instructions and encouragement. Another of the Mohawks was a girl with cerebral palsy, and she had limited control, especially on one side of her body. So when she went horseback riding with the Mohawks, another girl would ride alongside for encouragement, and sometimes on curves one of the counselors would run along the other side of the horse, like a spotter in gymnastics. They certainly didn't want Mohawks falling off horses. Another of the Mohawks was a girl who had had polio as an infant, and she had no control over her legs at all. So when she went horseback riding with the Mohawks, one of the bigger girls who was already a good rider would ride behind her in the saddle, holding her shoulders to make sure she stayed on the horse.

We visitors on a PASS team were very impressed with Ben Becker's camp, but it was only looking back a few years later that I realized that his camp operated under a rule, that every Mohawk is a horseback rider. They didn't state it as a rule, but that was the principle that guided the camp every day.

In human services for people with handicaps back in the bad old days, we seemed to operate under a different rule, essentially that some people are horseback riders and some are not. It is a shame, really, since horseback riding is such a fine experience, but some people just don't have it in them to be horseback riders. Now in services in these more progressive days, it seems that we most often operate under a more enlightened rule. We have high expectations for all of our campers, so our rule now is that every Mohawk will be a horseback rider, someday. In the meantime, we will hire the best teachers and the gentlest horses for our special group of future horseback riders, working with them patiently and intensively until, someday—I know it will come—they will be able to become horseback riders and rejoin the Mohawks.

Doesn't sound so bad. But at Ben Becker's camp they had a different rule: Every Mohawk is a horseback rider *now*, today. What varies is not who is a horseback rider and who is not; *every* Mohawk is a horseback rider. And what varies is not *when* someone will attain horseback-riderhood; every Mohawk *is* a horseback rider. What varies is only how much help a person needs to stay in the saddle.

If we can work well in the dimension of interaction with a person and in the dimension of our interpretation of a person to others; and if we can work well at all three levels, directly with the person, with their family and program contexts, and with the broad community and society; then we will be able to make the best possible difference in that person's life. As Samuel Gridley Howe noted in 1866, "Meaning well is only half our duty; *thinking right* is the other, and equally important, half." It may be that meaning well, and caring deeply, about another person cannot be taught, it must be a given. But many of us are grateful that we had the privilege of learning, through the principle of Normalization, a bit of what it might mean to work at thinking right.

REFERENCE

WOLFENSBERGER, W. (1972). *The principle of Normalization in human services*. Toronto: National Institute on Mental Retardation.

5

An overview of
Social Role Valorization[1]

SUSAN THOMAS AND WOLF WOLFENSBERGER

1 INTRODUCTION

In this chapter, we will present an overview of Social Role Valorization (SRV), including its major implications and its rationales. However, readers should note that this paper does not purport to be the kind of scholarly literature review that would support the various points made herein. That kind of review would require a different context—and would probably constitute something like a PhD dissertation, given the number of references in the literature that do support the claims and action implications of S.R.V. For instance, there is a very substantial body of literature on social roles, role expectancies, and role performance that has been and is being developed without any relationship to SRV (as covered by Raymond Lemay in chapter 10), and much of it prior to the formulation of SRV. There are easily over a thousand studies in the social science literature on the power of role expectancies to elicit the expected performance, and role expectancies play a major part in Social Role Valorization theory. Similarly, there must be a thousand or more studies that bear on the power of imitation and modeling to affect behavior. The validity of this literature and research does not depend on the validity of SRV. But what SRV has done is to apply the knowledge generated by this body of study and theory to the plight of societally devalued people, in a unifying fashion apparently not done before.

Readers who are interested in searching the literature for works that support or contradict Social Role Valorization might consult pages 129-130 in Wolfensberger (1998), where he lists the numerous topic areas in which one can find research relevant to Social Role Valorization.

As was explained in an earlier chapter by Wolfensberger in this book, Social Role Valorization (Wolfensberger, 1983, 1984, 1985, 1991a, 1991b, 1991c, 1991d, 1992, 1998) grew out of his formulation of the principle of Normalization (Wolfensberger, 1972), which in turn had been based on the Scandinavian formulations, and especially that of Nirje (1969). Because the phrase Social Role Valorization is a mouthful, people usually abbreviate it to SRV, or, in French, Valorisation des Rôles Sociaux (VRS). In Italian, the term is Valorizzazione del Ruolo Sociale (also VRS). In German, Aufwertung or Bewertung der sozialen Rollen was used briefly, and now it is called Valorisation sozialer Rollen (VSR). The Norwegian term is Verdsetjing av Sosial Rolle (VSR). In Icelandic, Gildisaukandi Félagslegt Hlutverk (GFH) has been used. And in Welsh, the term is Faloreiddio Rôl Gymdeithasol, or FRG.

The definition of SRV between 1995 and 1998 was "the application of what science has to tell us about the enablement, establishment, enhancement, maintenance and/or defence of valued social roles for people."[2] This very parsimonious definition implies a wealth of action strategies, as will be explained further below. Also, readers who are familiar with earlier definitions of Normalization and of SRV will note four important differences between those definitions and this one.

1. The definition makes no reference to devalued people because the measures that can craft valued roles

for people would be the same regardless of who those people are.

2. The definition refers to "the science of" how to enhance people's social roles, which means SRV pulls together what is known from the world of fact, experience, and empirical research that is relevant to role-crafting.

3. The definition no longer includes the phrase "culturally valued means," because the use of culturally valued means is implied in what is known from social science to enhance people's roles. (Roles are less likely to be enhanced if the means employed are not consistent with what is culturally valued.)

4. The definition no longer includes the phrase "as much as possible" for two reasons. (a) In part, the phrase refers to decisions that are value-laden, ideological, and therefore not empirical in nature (e.g., about how much SRV to pursue for any person or group, or how much SRV knowledge to employ). (b) It also refers to the limits that may be imposed by various external constraints, such as insufficient funds, lack of commitment by responsible servers, what the laws mandate or permit, and so forth. These things are real; they do often constrain what would theoretically be possible, but they do not affect what empiricism can tell us is known to work, and to be doable, for people.

SRV proposes that people who hold valued roles in society are more apt than people in devalued roles to be accorded "the good things of life" by their society. Consequently, if people who are devalued by their society, or who are at risk of being devalued, are to be given the good things of life, then they should be helped to as much as possible fill roles that are highly valued in society. Otherwise, they will probably be very badly treated. (All this will be explained in much more detail later.)

2 CLARIFICATION OF ISSUES RELATED TO SOCIAL ROLES

Because the concept of social roles is so central to SRV, it is important to first clarify what social roles are, and, in doing so, we will also clarify what social roles are not—at least, not within SRV. Six such clarifications follow.

2.1 DEFINITION OF SOCIAL ROLES

A first clarification is that the term "social role" means a combination of behaviors, privileges, duties, and responsibilities that is socially defined, is widely understood and recognized within a society, and is characteristic or expected of a person occupying a particular position within a social system. The responsibility or duty elements of a role might be thought of as "you must" or "you should" or "you shall not" types of expectancies. For instance, in our society it is expected that parents should rear and take care of any children they bring into the world, and not mistreat them. Similarly, it is expected that an employee should carry out the duties of a job, obey the dictates of the employer who pays the worker's salary, and not loaf or steal from employers. In contrast, the privileges of a role might be thought of as "you may" or "you are permitted" types of expectancies. For instance, a person in the sick role is permitted to stay home from school or work. A grandparent may (but need not) spoil the grandchildren a bit. And so on.

It thus seems that all elements of a role can be defined as being aspects of expectancies of one type or another held by both perceivers and the person in the role, that is, the person incumbent in the role is expected to do, or not do, this or that. People who violate the expectancies of a role are not apt to be confirmed in that role by others, and people who meet, or fill, the expectancies of a role will tend to be confirmed or even legitimized in that role by others. (And some roles do require the legitimization of others, in order for an aspirant to the role to fill it and to be perceived as filling it.) When a person is perceived—at least in a general way—to live up to the expectancies associated with a particular role, we say that the person is carrying out, playing, or filling that role.

2.2 THE TERM "ROLE" HAS SEVERAL—SOMETIMES CONFUSING—CONNOTATIONS

A second clarification, also addressed in a separate chapter by Raymond Lemay (chapter 10), is that the term "role" has several connotations, and one of the most problematic is the idea of an artificial character, such as one might play on a stage. In SRV, we are most certainly *not* talking about artificial identities that a person consciously and briefly puts on and off, and "plays," but that have no relation to the person's "real" identity. Rather, we can say that for all practical purposes, many of the roles that a person fills in life, especially the major ones and in their aggregate, become that person's identity; or, put another way, people generally become the social roles that they fill. Thus, roles are not something that people simply step in and out of, or shed like their clothes, but they become an integral part of their identity in the eyes of others—and to a very large degree also to themselves. For instance, a woman does not simply "play" the role of wife and mother for 20-plus years; she actually *becomes* a wife and mother, and fulfills the role elements that are part of this. One does not merely play the role of a physician, but one actually becomes a physician. And so on.

This is certainly the case with those social roles that a person assumes voluntarily, and perhaps with great eagerness, such as those of husband and wife. But it can even be the case with those roles that are reluctantly assumed, or that are even forced on a person. For instance, one may not want to be an assembly-line worker, and might prefer some other career, but if one holds this kind of job for long, one's identity probably will eventually become that of a blue-collar assembly-line worker, and will be shaped by the exigencies of that role. Similarly, even if a person does not want to be seen and treated in the role of a menace, the person is nonetheless very apt to become one if enough other people give that person convincing, strong, and consistent role cues and expectations that he or she is, indeed, a social threat.

2.3   SOCIAL ROLES FALL ALONG A CONTINUUM OF PERCEIVED VALUE

A third clarification is that there is a continuum of social valuation of different roles, ranging from extremely devalued to extremely valued. Some roles that are very devalued are those of subhuman, social menace, and garbage picker. Some roles that are very positively valued are those of president, scholar, and champion athlete. Yet other roles probably fall somewhere in between these two extremes, such as those of voter, neighbor, and garage mechanic.

Of course, individuals may attribute a different value to specific social roles than does their society. For instance, a particular individual may devalue the role of president or other national government official, but the majority of that person's society may still value such roles highly. Similarly, a certain individual may place high personal value on the role of idler or atheist, but that individual's society may devalue such roles. However, there tends to be a good deal of concordance between the value that individuals attribute to social roles and the value that their society as a whole attributes to those same roles, in good part because individuals' perceptions and values are shaped by their social context.

In later sections, we will elaborate more on some very devalued roles into which devalued people get cast, and some roles that are positively valued, at least in our contemporary Western societies.

2.4   ROLES FALL INTO DIFFERENT DOMAINS

A fourth clarification is that most roles can be seen to fall into certain broad domains (see Table 5.1).

For instance, there are positive roles in the domain of social relationships, such as husband or wife, mother or father, daughter or son, brother or sister, grandchild, grandparent, acquaintance, friend, best friend, fiancé. Negatively valued roles in the relationship domain include orphan, "old maid," and "black sheep of the family." These are not artificial characters that people "play," but rather, relational identities, commitments, social functions, or positions that people fill, make uniquely their own, and/or have forced upon them. For instance, certain behaviors are expected of grandparents, and certain privileges and responsibilities are accorded to them. By and large, most grandparents will meet these expectations, though they will do so in ways that have a great deal of individual variation to them. Similarly, the "black sheep" of any family is apt to be talked about and treated in much the same way across families, though the individual family members in this role may have different personalities and do different things that merit them this dubious distinction.

TABLE 5.1

SOME MAJOR "ROLE DOMAINS" IN HUMAN EXISTENCE, AND COMMON VALUED AND DEVALUED ROLES IN THEM

DOMAIN	COMMON DEVALUED ROLES	COMMON VALUED ROLES
Relationships	"Old maid"	Wife/husband, parent
	Old fogey, dotard	Grandparent
	Orphan	Son/daughter
	"Black sheep of the family"	Brother/sister
	Harlot, pimp, gigolo	Grandchild
		Aunt/uncle, niece/nephew
		Godchild
		Friend, confidante
		Fiancé
Work	Idler, loafer,	Worker
	Goldbrick	Laborer
		Wage-earner
	Ne'er-do-well	Breadwinner
	"Sponge," freeloader	Artist
		Craftsman
	"Scab"	Union-member
	Union-buster	Expert
	Informer	Apprentice
		Employer, business-owner
		Boss
		Board member
Education	Dunce	Teacher, professor
	Scatterbrain	Scholar
	Slowest member of the class	Student, learner
	"Special class" pupil	Peer tutor
		Outstanding pupil
Sports	Oaf, klutz, lummox	Athlete
		Athletics champion
	Invalid	Competitor
	Loser	Coach
	Sore loser	Fan, booster
	Bad sport	Cheerleader

Community participation

	Public official
Foreigner, stranger	Citizen
Prisoner	Consumer
Welfare recipient	Taxpayer
"Sponge"	Voter
Shoplifter	Customer
Isolate	Community activist
Jury-duty-shirker	Juror
	Club member, board member

Religious

Atheist	Minister, priest, rabbi
Heretic	Pastor
Apostate	Deacon
Sinner, lost soul	Sexton, acolyte
Lukewarm follower	Cantor, choir member
	Parishioner

Residence-related

Homeless street person	Homeowner
Inmate	Tenant
Vagabond, hobo	Landowner
Bad neighbor	Good neighbor
	Building superintendent

There are also positive social roles in the domain of work, such as employee, labor union member, small-business owner, stockholder, chief executive officer, board member. There are also more specific work roles, such as janitor, registered nurse, cancer researcher, film director, telephone repairman, secretary, bank teller, car salesman, plumber, mechanic, letter carrier, and so on. Negatively valued social roles in the domain of work include idler, loafer, ne'er-do-well, beggar, and union-buster or "scab."

There are roles related to the domain of education, such as pupil, peer tutor, teacher, outstanding student in a subject area, and school athletic team star. Devalued roles in this domain include dunce, scatterbrain, and "special class" student.

Positive roles in the domain of recreation and leisure include athlete, jogger, swimmer, bridge-player, chess master, painter, and so on. Some such roles are based on organizational and associational membership, such as member of a card club or member of a sports fan club. Negatively valued roles in this domain include oaf, klutz, sore loser, and bad sport.

There are positive roles related to what one might broadly call the domain of public life, including those of citizen, activist, voter, licensed automobile driver, village clerk, elected official (such as member of a local council), and taxpayer. Negatively valued roles in this domain include foreigner, prisoner, recipient of public welfare, shoplifter.

And there are positive roles related to the domain of higher-order beliefs, worldviews, and religious life, such as philosopher, prophet, pastor, minister, deacon, choir member, secretary to the altar society, cantor, sexton, and so on. Negatively valued roles include atheist, heretic, backslider, and lost soul.

Of course, these role domains may not be so clearly differentiated in a person's life. For instance, to one person, the major work role may be the same as a role related to religion, as in the case of a parish priest. For another person, a recreation-related role may become the major or dominant work role (as in the case of a champion athlete whose entire time is devoted to getting in shape for a major competition, or teaching others to do so), and the person's recreation thus displaces, or becomes, his or her work.

Also, the role domains that we have reviewed are by no means exhaustive, and the specific roles in them are only a small sampling of the many social roles that there are in society and life. In fact, social roles are so much a part of human life that, like fish with water, we take them for granted and do not even recognize that we are filling them. For instance, in the course of a day, one woman may fill the roles of wife, mother, secretary, daughter, leader of a Girl Scout troop, bank customer, coach, good neighbor, and probably yet others. A child may fill the roles of son or daughter, brother or sister, student, athlete, Girl Scout or Boy Scout, acolyte, and perhaps a role related to the upkeep of the family home.

2.5   ROLES MAY RANGE FROM NARROW TO BROAD

A fifth clarification is that different roles are of different widths (Wolfensberger, 1991a, 1992). That is, some roles are narrow and are only apparent at very specific times and places, while others are very broad, perhaps controlling—or at least affecting—much of a person's life (Wolfensberger, 1992). An example of a role that is rarely anything but very narrow is that of bank customer. An example of a role with a broad width is that of husband or wife, or full-time student. However, and interestingly, the width of a role is not necessarily or entirely inherent in the role, and it can change. Two features seem to be the largest determiners—at least in contemporary Western societies—of how broad a particular role is in a person's life.

1. The first determinant is how much of a person's life is occupied in and by a role. The more a person's time is taken up by the role, then the more broad in that person's life (and the more life-defining) that particular social role is apt to be. For example, if one's work role occupies a great deal of one's day, it tends to be broadly determinative of one's life and identity in Western society. Or, contrast the role of being a hospital patient with the role of being a dentist's patient or an optometrist's. The first is apt to be very life-defining, the others are not. This is because the

hospital patient actually resides in a hospital, clinic, or nursing home; is very much surrounded by other patients, and by medical and medically imaged workers, such as doctors, nurses, and therapists; is dressed in hospital garb or lounges around all day in pajamas and bathrobe; gets classified as "chronic" or "acute"; and has to follow hospital schedules and routines. In contrast, the dentist's patient does not reside in the dentist's office; is only treated as a patient for a few hours at a time together with very few other patients, perhaps a few times a year; and does not have his or her appearance, activities, associates, and companions all determined by the act of getting dental care.

2. The second determinant seems to be how many other normative or even valued roles a person has. The fewer valued roles a person fills, the broader—and therefore the more life-defining—will become those roles that the person does hold, including devalued ones. Conversely, the more valued roles a person holds, the narrower—and the less life-defining—is any particular one of them apt to be, including any devalued roles that the person also fills. Another way of saying this is that *the more positive role elements there are in a person's life, the less will devalued roles invade and take over, and the less powerful they will become in that person's life.* This reality means that *the greater the number of positive roles a person holds, and the greater the number of positive functions a person plays, the less overpowering will be any negative roles into which that person is also cast.* People who hold mostly valued roles, and one or a few devalued roles, may still be able to maintain a valued life because the power of the greater number of valued roles outweighs that of the smaller number of negative ones. People who hold mostly devalued roles, but one or a few valued ones, will have their lives defined and shaped by the mixture of both such roles. But a person who holds no valued roles at all is apt to have his or her life defined and shaped for the worse by that fact.

Thus, for instance, a man who fills the valued roles of father, businessman, church deacon, officer in a men's club, and local politician—and who is also cast into the dying role—is apt to continue to be seen in, and to fill most of, his valued roles even as he is also seen to be dying. In other words, for such a person, the dying role will have much less of an identity-defining impact. In contrast, for a person who has few or perhaps no valued roles, and who is also now pronounced to be dying, the dying role is apt to become very broad and identity-defining, and to even control or determine just about everything that happens to that person. These facts have much bearing on the so-called "conservatism corollary" of SRV, to be explained later.

2.6 EVEN PARTIAL FILLING OF THE REQUIREMENTS OF A ROLE MAY BE ENOUGH TO CAST A PERSON INTO THE ROLE

A sixth clarification is that, in at least certain circumstances, a person may be perceived as the incumbent of a role even when that person does not fill all the role requirements or expectations. For instance, an adult woman may be cast into the child role if she has childish speech and childlike gestures and mannerisms, even if she is mature in most other ways. A person may get cast into a role simply for looking menacing, and for using violently aggressive speech, even if the person never hurts, or even tries to hurt, another soul. A person who goes through the marriage ceremony and shares a dwelling with his or her spouse will be cast in the role of husband or wife, even if that person fails miserably at those things expected of a spouse, such as faithfulness, child rearing, financial and other support, and so on.

There seem to be three conditions especially under which a person will be seen as an incumbent of a role even though the person fills that role only partially.

One is when the perceivers are already disposed to view the person in that role and are therefore prepared to interpret all sorts of behavior by the person as confirming their role expectancies. For instance, if an observer believes that "those kind of people" tend to be menaces, then the observer may cast a particular person who is "one of them" into the menace role just on the basis of a furtive glance, a baleful eye, or a forceful gesture.

A second condition is when the person has gone through some public ritual of entry into the role. Examples are marriage ceremonies, public election and swearing-in to office, registration for school or college, job interview, and filling out of new employee forms. The public ceremony casts the person into the role in the eyes of observers, and even if the person subsequently fails to meet the requirements or expectations of the role, having gone through the

ceremony may still be enough to keep the person in that role.

A third condition is when the person actually meets at least some of the expectations attached to a role, even if these are not sufficient to role success. For instance, many youths who attend college hardly go to class, but they are nonetheless seen as college students because they have registered, paid their tuition, live in university dormitories, and are of college age.

This entire point has implications both for preventing people who are devalued or at risk from being cast into devalued roles, as well as for helping them be cast into valued ones, even if they cannot meet all the requirements of a specific valued role.

3 PREMISES UNDERLYING SRV

Having reviewed six clarifications of social roles, we will now present five basic premises that are crucial to understanding issues of role valuation, and hence to SRV theory overall.

3.1 HUMANS REGARD EACH OTHER EVALUATIVELY

One premise is that because human perceptual processes are by their very nature evaluative, humans regard each other in an evaluative fashion. Everything we perceive by any of our senses, on either a conscious or unconscious level, is judged either positively or negatively. Even preverbal infants may howl upon perceiving something that their perceptual/evaluative system has informed them to be unpleasant or potentially threatening. For instance, they may scream when a parent leaves the room, when strangers appear, or when a gruesome face is shown them. In other words, it appears that there is no such thing as sensation that is "pure" and isolated, as psychologists once believed. They once thought that sensory data registered in the brain before they were interconnected with whatever already existed there, including memory, knowledge, meanings, values, interpretation, and so on. However, it is now believed that sensation is really part of a feedback process whereby preexisting content in the brain is intermingled with, and added to, sensory inputs as they come in, thereby instantaneously transforming these inputs and giving them meaning.

Judgments as to whether a stimulus might be good or bad, pleasant or unpleasant, are made so rapidly that inputs deemed negative can even be repressed, so that a person will deny that he or she saw or heard something that was in fact witnessed, and that did enter the brain and its memory.

Thus, sensation cannot be factored out of perception, and perception involves evaluation. Therefore, there is no such thing as "pure" or value-free or neutral perception. However, there is much denial and repression of the reality that such value judgments take place.

What this means to SRV is that because people are perceived by others, they, too, get evaluated positively or negatively by their perceivers as do objects or events. In fact, some scholars (e.g., Freedman, Carlsmith, & Sears, 1970) have concluded that evaluation appears to be the *main* component in perceptions of people. As Freedman et al. (1970) put it: "Once we place someone on this dimension (good-bad), we never add much else to our impression of him. A favorable or unfavorable impression in one context at one meeting extends to all other situations and to other, seemingly related, characteristics" (p. 48).

When perceivers attribute low or negative value to a person or group, we refer to this as social *de*valuation. This means that the people at issue are judged as being of lesser value, lesser worth—either lesser than the perceiver, and/or lesser than certain other persons. However, the terms "valued" and "devalued" must always be understood in relation to a referent person or group that does the valuing or devaluing. In other words, within the boundaries of SRV, one cannot speak of people being intrinsically valued or devalued, but only valued or devalued *by,* and *in reference to,* others. Thus, social devaluation is something that is done *to* another person by a perceiver; it is not something that is inherent in the person perceived.

3.2 SOCIAL DEVALUATION CAN BE OF AND BY INDIVIDUALS AND CLASSES

A second premise underlying SRV is that the above-described process of social valuation can range all the way from the person-to-person level to that of class-to-class. In other words, one individual may devalue one other person, often for such idiosyncratic reasons that the same person would not be devalued by others, or not for the same reason. At the other end, an entire class of people—even a whole nation—may devalue an entire other class, or type, of people, and possibly for just one single reason. And in-between these two ends, there can be devaluation of specific groups or classes by a single individual, and devaluation of specific individuals by an entire group or class. These possibilities are depicted in Table 5.2.

TABLE 5.2

POSSIBLE RELATIONSHIPS BETWEEN DEVALUED AND DEVALUING PARTIES

		DEVALUED PARTY	
		Individual	*Group or class*
DEVALUING PARTY	*Individual*	One specific person is devalued by one other specific person	An entire group or class of people is devalued by one person
	Group or class	One specific person is devalued by all or most of a group or class	One group or class is devalued by all or most of another group or class

---

FIGURE 5.1

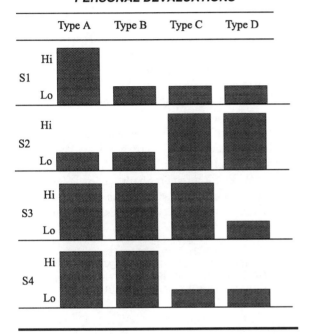

A SAMPLE OF THE INDIVIDUAL VARIATION IN PERSONAL DEVALUATIONS

societal devaluation, meaning that the dominant sectors of society, and perhaps even society pretty much as a whole, hold the same one or more classes of people in very low esteem.

That individuals can harbor their own idiosyncratic devaluations that differ from those of other individuals is illustrated by Figure 5.1. In it, we see that one particular person—S1—may hold people of Type A in high esteem but may devalue people of Types B, C, and D. Another person—S219475

—may devalue people of Types A and B but value very highly those of Types C and D. Yet another person—S3—may value people of Types A, B, and C but not people of Type D. And so on.

However, if one compiles the various positive and negative valuations held by specific individuals, one can begin to see how these can aggregate into a global and consistent pattern of group devaluations, as shown in Figure 5.2.

FIGURE 5.2

HOW INDIVIDUAL VALUATIONS ACCUMULATE TO BECOME COLLECTIVE ONES

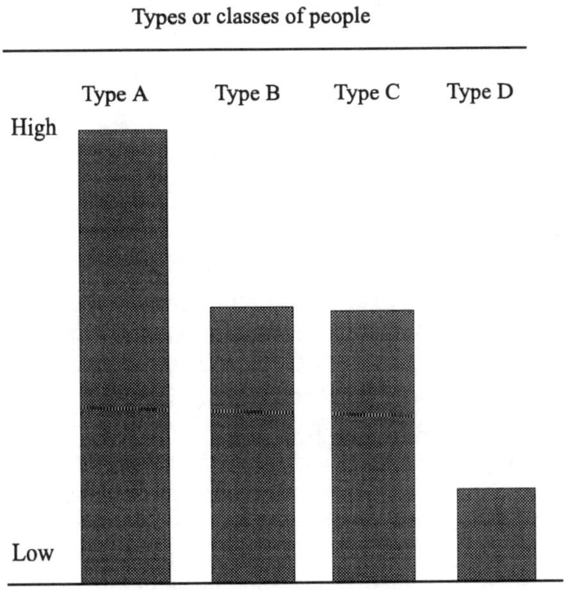

Types or classes of people

	Type A	Type B	Type C	Type D
High				
Low				

On the individual-to-individual level, one family member may devalue another family member, a person may devalue someone who once inflicted a real or imaginary slight to him/her, someone may devalue someone else who habitually smells of garlic, and so on. On the individual-to-group level, one person may despise Catholics, another may feel contempt for those with leftist political views, another may consider vacuous rich people to be of low value, and so on, though these devalued groups may be held in high esteem by other persons. On the group-to-individual level, an entire class of rich people may devalue a particular advocate for the poor, much as the U.S. "robber barons" of the early 20th century devalued the populist William Jennings Bryan. On the group-to-group level, the rich may devalue the poor, one ethnic or racial group may scorn another, and much of an entire society may devalue one of its major subsectors. It is this latter type of devaluation that we refer to as

3.3 THE COLLECTIVE/SOCIETAL TYPE OF DEVALUATION IS THE MOST DESTRUCTIVE ONE

The third premise underlying SRV is that societal devaluation is more devastating than individual devaluation, because it creates whole classes of people who systematically receive bad treatment in and from society. When a person sees his or her whole society or social class devaluing an entire other group or class of people, then for several reasons that person is extremely likely to join that devaluation process. As each separate member of a class or society joins in collective or societal devaluation, eventually almost the whole collectivity and its structures militate against the good of that entire devalued class. In contrast, one specific person's idiosyncratic devaluation is much less likely than collective devaluation to recruit many others into joining it.

Another reason societal devaluation is more destructive than other kinds is that when a party is the object of devaluation by only one or a few persons, that party generally has options to escape the devaluation—options that hardly exist when that party is devalued by an entire society. For instance, the party can avoid the presence of the devaluers and remain in, or enter, other social circles; or the party can take refuge with others who hold it in high esteem. But when the party is devalued by an entire society, then such escape options hardly exist, or at least are very much reduced.

3.4 SOCIAL DEVALUATION IS VASTLY MORE LIKELY TO BE UNCONSCIOUS THAN POSITIVE VALUATION

Another premise underlying SRV theory is that individuals, and especially entire collectivities, are much more likely to be unaware of their devaluations than of their positive valuations of other people. In fact, it is not at all uncommon for people to deny that they do or could hold any such devaluations. Actually, the reason is very simple: People tend to repress things they perceive as unpleasant or unworthy, but not those that they perceive as pleasant or noble. And in the Western world, viewing others in a positive light is seen as something good, but viewing them in a negative light is seen as something bad, sometimes even outright despicable, or at least as something to be ashamed of.

This reality points to certain things that are necessary in attempts to promote SRV and to improve the lives of devalued people by implementing SRV. One is to get the relevant parties to acknowledge the existence of devaluation. For instance, there may be denials that this or that group is societally devalued, or is systematically engaged in devaluation, and, therefore, there are also apt to be denials that there is a problem requiring address. Unconsciousness can go so far that people will even deny the most blatant ongoing collective devaluations by others, not just their own idiosyncratic, personal ones. Also, even when the reality of devaluation is acknowledged in the abstract, it may be denied when it hits close to home. For instance, many parties have no trouble identifying devaluing practices of others but resist any such identification of their own devaluations. One problem is that because SRV requires both acknowledging *and* then addressing an unpleasant social reality—that of devaluation—it is apt to generate resistance and even hostility.

3.5 PEOPLE IN VALUED ROLES TEND TO GET THE GOOD THINGS OF LIFE, AND THOSE IN DEVALUED ROLES THE OPPOSITE

A fifth premise underlying SRV, already mentioned, is that a society is apt to extend what it defines as the "good life" to those people whom it values, and to whom it perceives in a positive light. This will largely be those people whom that society perceives as filling roles which are valued positively in that society. The more positively valued the roles that a party fills, the more will that party's society be likely to extend good things to it. In contrast, those people in devalued roles tend to get the bad things.

3.5.1 THE COMMONLY ACKNOWLEDGED GOOD THINGS OF LIFE

What "the good things of life" are considered to be will vary somewhat from culture to culture, and over time. Still, if one looks across cultures and time, one will find a great deal of convergence on what these "good things of life" are: respect, acceptance (or at least tolerance), positive relationship, integration into the valued activities of society, access to material goods and welfare, housing that is decent according to the standards of that place and time, functions (work-related and other ones) that are considered important and contributive. People who are valued in society are apt either (a) to be given these things—or access to them—by others who have it in their power to do so, or (b) to be able to take or acquire these things for themselves. But people who are cast into devalued status and devalued roles are apt to have these things withheld or taken from them and to instead get such things as rejection; separation, segregation, and exclusion, even to the point of exile; poorer quality food, housing, clothing, education, and health care; work that no one else wants to do if they can help it; and even violence and brutality, all of which we will elaborate in the next section.

Note that it is only in relation to a referent group or individual who is doing the valuing or devaluing that we can say that they will or will not extend "the good things of life" to those whom they value and devalue. Further, it is what *they* consider "the good things of life" that they will extend to those whom they value, and probably withhold from those they devalue. And yet further, they will only be able to extend what they actually have to offer, even if they want to extend more. For example, a society that values warmth and beautiful shelter but is in the middle of war, famine, plague, or other social calamity, may only be able to offer the crudest mud hut even to those people it does value.

3.5.2 COMMON HURTFUL EXPERIENCES THAT BEFALL SOCIETALLY DEVALUED PEOPLE BECAUSE THEY ARE DEVALUED

People who are devalued, and especially who are devalued by their society, have all sorts of hurtful things done to them precisely *because* they are seen as being of low value. Sometimes, these things are done with conscious and explicit intent; sometimes, they are done unconsciously; and sometimes these things are simply the result of life conditions and circumstances that are the way they are for the devalued party because of that party's devalued status and life experiences.

Very briefly, the following are the hurtful things that are apt to characterize the lives of societally devalued people. Many people within the SRV teaching culture refer to these bad things as the common "wounds" of societally devalued people. This

brief summary has been extracted from the more than four hours of presentation on it that is given at introductory SRV courses. A similar summary is found in Wolfensberger (1998) and a much briefer one in Wolfensberger (1992).[3]

1. Many devalued people are, or become, impaired in body, including in brain or sense organs. Some get devalued because they have impairments of body that were either evident at birth or acquired afterward. However, so often, the opposite also happens, in that people who were devalued for other reasons become impaired in body as a result of that devaluation, and this usually makes them even more devalued. For instance, people may become impaired as a result of poverty, poor nutrition, unsafe living conditions, poor health care, or being assaulted—all things that are very likely to happen to them as a result of being devalued.

2. Many devalued people are impaired in functioning. These impairments may have been the reason they were devalued in the first place, or they may be the result of the person having been devalued for some other reason. In either case, the functional impairment may be a result of a physical impairment, though functional impairments can also exist in the absence of physical impairments. Examples of functional impairments include deficiencies in seeing, hearing, speaking, thinking, mobility, or self-care. Because of their devalued state and bad living conditions, children from devalued classes may grow up less intelligent, virtually illiterate, and/or mentally conflicted, even if they are physically whole. Many devalued people are or end up impaired in some area of functioning that most valued people possess and take for granted, such as basic literacy, getting along adaptively with other people, running and maintaining a household, attending to one's personal appearance, and so on.

3. Devalued people get relegated to low social status in society and are looked down upon. They are considered second-class citizens—or even worse—and treated accordingly.

4. One of the hurtful things that happens to devalued people that is of special relevance to SRV is that they get cast into roles that are devalued in society, and their access to valued social roles is severely diminished, or even eliminated. Typically, there is some kind of link between lowered social status and the specific devalued role that gets imposed on a status-

degraded person, or the valued roles that get withheld from such a person. In other words, devalued people are given a role identity that confirms and justifies society's ascription of low value or worth to them. Over and over, societally devalued people get perceived or treated as occupying, and even shaped into becoming, the following common negative social roles.

a. A common devalued role is that of a person as "other," that is, an alien (perhaps like a creature from outer space), as so different that one does not know how to classify the person. In French, the term *les autres* (the others) may be used to refer to what sociologists call "out-groups."

b. Devalued people may be cast into subhuman and nonhuman roles, and sometimes this is done by denying "personhood" to them. For instance, if they are young enough, they may be seen and treated as "prehuman," that is, not yet human (perhaps as creatures who will never attain humanhood). This is apt to be done to the unwanted unborn and handicapped newborns. Or, they may be seen as creatures who once used to be human but are not any longer. This role is apt to be imposed on elderly people, particularly those who are senile or comatose. Devalued people may be cast into the role of a subhuman animal and be perceived as having primitive, animalistic feelings and behaviors. Interestingly, people who are seen as "animal-humans" commonly get treated worse than "animal-animals" get treated. Devalued people may be perceived as vegetables and be called "vegetables" or "vegetative." They may be cast into the role of object, that is, an insensate item, perhaps to be warehoused or used as sources of organs for other people.

One overall fact about the nonhuman roles is that it is generally seen as permissible to kill creatures that are not human, and, therefore, when people are cast into one of these roles, they are usually treated very badly, and often even made dead.

c. Either individually or as a class, devalued people are at risk of being cast into the role of menace or object of dread, in which case they are perceived and interpreted as a threat to others, society, and/or themselves. People cast into this role are usually also very badly treated. For instance, during the height of the social Darwinism era, mentally retarded people were seen as a grave threat to the very survival of civilization and systematically subjected to extremely hurtful "eugenic" measures.

d. When they are put in the object of ridicule role, devalued persons are made the butt of demeaning jokes, laughed at, teased and tormented, and even socialized into behavior patterns that provide amusement and entertainment to others.

e. Devalued people may be viewed as objects of pity, in which case observers feel sorry for them; and perhaps because they want to make life easy for the afflicted, they place few or no demands on them for performance, learning, or growth.

f. Devalued people may be seen as burdens of charity, in which case others may feel a duty to take care of the person, but without gladness or any positive feelings, and perhaps while resenting the obligation. The devalued person may then be provided for at only a bare subsistence level, or may only be given occasional or other benefits whenever the donor or caretaker is moved by guilt.

g. Many devalued people get cast into a child role, which can take two forms. One is the role of the eternal child who never matures into adult status and competence, and whose behaviors, interests, capabilities, and so on, will always remain at a childlike level. Mentally limited people are often cast into this role. A second form is that of having reverted from adulthood back to childhood. Elderly people are commonly cast in this role, as when they are said to be "in their second childhood."

h. Devalued people may be cast into the role of sick or diseased organism, or even into the identity of sickness personified. Typically, the devalued characteristic or condition is said to be a disease, usually one for which the afflicted person is not held culpable. Such a perception may also exonerate any other parties—family, community, even society as a whole—from any responsibility in having brought about the condition. At any rate, the "disease" is said to require "treatment" by various forms of "therapy," which are to be given to the "patient" in settings, and by personnel, that are medical, or at least medically imaged, thus resulting in a medical service model. This may go so far that the person's entire life and identity are medicalized.

i. Death-related and death-imaged roles (e.g., dying, as good as dead, or indeed already dead) may be inappropriately and/or destructively imposed on certain devalued people. For instance, live people may be declared dead, perhaps so that their organs can be taken from them. People who are not dying may be put into the dying role. Elderly or chronically ill people may be cast as dying. They, plus others (such as disliked people, long-term prisoners, or people viewed as having "outlived their usefulness") may be related to as if they had already died.

For further elaboration of the first eight roles, see Wolfensberger, 1972, pp. 12-25; or Wolfensberger, 1977, pp. 135-148; or Wolfensberger, 1978, pp. 1-16. For elaboration of the dying role specifically, see Wolfensberger, 1989, pp. 1-4.

Here, only those negative roles have been identified that have a great deal of historical continuity, and which tend to be nearly universally imposed upon all sorts of societally devalued people. However, there are also other negative roles that may be specific to a particular cultural era or devalued group. One example is the devalued party as a source of income —something like a milch cow—to the valued people in a locale, or to valued people of a particular type, such as those in one occupation. For instance, devalued people have increasingly been serving this function to the human service professions since the 1950s. Similarly, all devalued people who receive services from a formal service agency are in the role of service client, and, as documented in Wolfensberger and Thomas (1994), this is a problematic mix of some positive, some neutral, and mostly negative elements. However, unlike the other devalued roles, these are obviously not roles that could have been found virtually everywhere and at all times.

5. As a result of being relegated to low social status, people who are devalued get systematically rejected, not only by society as a whole, but quite often even by their own family, neighbors, community, and even by the workers in services that are supposed to assist them. Rejection means that other people really do not want these people around.

6. Internal feelings of rejection usually get externalized into behaviors that push the devalued person away. So valued people put distance between themselves and those they devalue and reject. The valued people may do this by removing themselves (i.e., by withdrawing as far as possible from those they devalue) or by moving the devalued people away. For instance, they may segregate devalued people into separate settings, perhaps even ghettos and reservations, or send them into a form of exile. Thus, the distance may be physical, as in segregation; and when people are segregated because they are devalued, they usually also get congregated with other devalued

people, often into huge groups. But the distance may also be social, as in various forms of degradation that make it clear how lowly the devalued party is seen to be even when no physical distance is put between the two parties. For instance, a distinctly different and less honoring form of address may be used for devalued people than for valued ones, even when both are present in the same physical space.

7. Quite naturally, when a party is devalued and rejected, and other people withdraw from contact with that devalued party, this also means that natural relationships—such as family and friends—get withdrawn and severed. When natural relationships are no longer freely and voluntarily given to devalued people, other people are apt to be recruited to do what is needed for them. These other people almost always have to be paid, because that is the only reason they would be involved with the devalued person, and when such payment ceases, so does their presence. So the lives of devalued persons often begin to be filled with artificial and "boughten" relationships that are really substitutes for the "real thing" that valued people enjoy, such as the voluntary and willing relationships of family, friends, loved ones, and acquaintances. Some devalued people do not have one single enduring unpaid relationship.

8. Furthermore, devalued people commonly get moved around a lot and therefore experience a very wounding discontinuity with places and physical objects. Often, these physical moves are interpreted as for a devalued person's own good, or as progress and growth in independence. There can be scores of such discontinuities in a person's lifetime, and many can be quite traumatic.

9. Commonly, the devalued person also suffers a great many social and relationship discontinuities, meaning that people come and go in that person's life endlessly—all this while the natural relationships are not there. Often, relationship discontinuity accompanies, or is the result of, physical discontinuity, but even when a person is stable in one place, there may still be many, many people who walk in and out of the person's life. What makes this even more hurtful is that many of these very people (especially paid ones) make either explicit or implicit promises that they want to be friends, that they are going to help, that they are "not like the others"—and yet all of them may end up leaving, perhaps after only a brief presence. When

such an explicit or implicit promise has been made and then gets broken, the wound of the discontinuity is compounded by the wound of betrayal.

10. Devalued people also experience loss of control over their lives. It is other people who gain power over them and make decisions for them, in both overt and subtle ways, some of them already mentioned above.

11. Devalued people also get deindividualized. They are subjected to regimentation and mass management, and they so often have to accommodate themselves to whatever is available, rather than getting what they need or want when they need or want it, and the way that they need or want it.

12. Devalued people commonly end up poor. In both overt and subtle ways—some so subtle that they may not be recognized for what they are—devalued people end up with very little in the way of material goods. If they need services, they may have to impoverish themselves in order to receive them, or they may end up poor as a result of receiving services. Some devalued people come from families and classes that have been poor for generations.

13. Devalued people also suffer impoverishment in the world of experience, which is often very narrow for them. They are denied participation in valued society and its activities, and there may even be places to which they are forbidden—or otherwise unable—to go. Many experiences that valued people take for granted may be withheld from, and be strange to, devalued people.

14. One particular experience from which devalued people may get cut off is knowledge of, and participation in, the religious or spiritual life of society. There are handicapped people who have never really been given instruction in the religion they may have been born into, nor been permitted to participate in the community life of their fellow believers.

15. One of the major results of all this is that devalued people's lives so often get wasted. Days, weeks, months, years, a lifetime goes by while they are denied opportunities, challenges, experiences, and their earlier potential is wasted or destroyed. When they do receive service, it is often the wrong kind, or, at any rate, of less intensity or quality than they could benefit from, or than valued people would get. Many devalued people spend much of their time just sitting and waiting, wasting away, often even in the service programs in which they are enrolled.

16. Devalued people are at extreme risk of being society's scapegoats. Whatever the problem is, devalued people are apt to be suspected of causing or exacerbating it, and punishing devalued people in some way is widely promoted as the solution to a societal problem. For instance, devalued people are more likely than valued people to be suspected of an offense that has been committed by unknown parties, accused of it, arrested, prosecuted, convicted, and given a harsh sentence. Entire devalued classes may be accused as guilty when a society experiences a natural disaster or social or economic problem.

17. Devalued people get systematically and relentlessly juxtaposed to images that carry very negative messages in the eyes of society. Services to them get put in locations where valued people do not want to be; devalued people get placed with other people whom society also does not want; image-degrading names are given to their services; elements of their personal appearance that attract negative attention are not addressed, or their deviant appearance may even be enlarged by people in charge of their lives; services to them are funded by appeals that are image-tainting. All these (and other) sorts of negative images convey messages such as that these people are worthless, subhuman, menaces, dangerous, and despicable—and this negative-imaging perpetuates the social devaluation and invites other people to do bad things to the devalued people.

18. Devalued people are thus very much at risk of being badly treated, brutalized, violated, even to the point of being made dead. They may get assaulted on the streets, in their families, or by their service workers. Other people will think they are justified in getting rid of them permanently, that is, ending their lives.

19. As a result of all these things, devalued people become very much aware that they are aliens in the valued world, that they do not fit in, that they are not welcome. They are apt to become very insecure and may even begin to dislike themselves and think that they really are despicable, unlovable, worthless, and that it is their own fault.

20. Many devalued people may become embittered and perhaps even full of resentment and hatred toward the privileged world for having done, and continuing to do, these things to them.

21. Some devalued people (especially impaired ones) may be very aware that they are a source of anguish to whatever people may still be around who love them, especially their family members. They realize that they are not what others wish they were, and that others—especially their loved ones—are suffering because of who and what they are.

What we have just sketched is the real way that devalued people tend to experience the world, and this way of seeing their lives is radically different from the typical technical teaching of human service training programs. This real story happens over and over, and can be retold at least in part in virtually any devalued individual's life.

Obviously, the bad things that happen to devalued people are not only hurtful, but can also become life-defining. Examples are having to live in poverty, being perceived for much of one's life as a social menace or as subhuman, being segregated, being excluded from major opportunities in life, having one's life wasted, and so on.

4 THE IMPORTANCE OF SOCIAL ROLES IN DETERMINING HOW A PERSON IS VALUED BY OTHERS AND BY SOCIETY AS A WHOLE

If one wants to help devalued people be seen more positively by others and be accorded more value by them, then one has to recognize how important social roles are in determining how people are valued by others, and whether others will extend and do good or bad things to a person. Therefore, with the foregoing as background, we will now explain the importance of social roles to whether a person is positively or negatively valued by others.

4.1 PEOPLE ARE ALWAYS ENCOUNTERED IN A SOCIAL CONTEXT THAT SUGGESTS SOME ROLES

First, it helps to understand that one never really encounters people "in the abstract" (i.e., stripped of their social roles and role-related functions, or even of role cues). In fact, one always encounters people in contexts that at the very least suggest some roles. The very fact that people are encountered so often in settings where (as we will explain) they have been put because of the roles they are perceived to hold, and with other people with whom they get put because of the roles they are perceived to hold, means in turn that the social context will suggest what a person's roles are. Additionally, things such as bodily appearance, attire, activities, and other language or social cues contribute to at least a tentative social role perception in the eyes of beholders.

For example, aspects of appearance and behavior suggest various degrees of competency, dependence, or age, which in turn affect whether an observer will get the idea that the person holds certain roles. Thus, a person who appears in the uniform of a security or police officer, or of a member of the military, will be assumed by observers to *be* a security officer, policeman, or member of the military. And orders issued by such a person (to disperse, to clear the sidewalk, etc.) are apt to be obeyed, whereas persons lacking such a uniform will not be perceived to have the authority that compels other people to obey their orders.

A person who appears in the clothing of a young child, whose grooming is like that of a young person, whose behavior is immature, and who looks very young would hardly be perceived in such roles as those of college professor, accountant, or homeowner. This can create a problem where the person really does hold a role competently and legitimately but fails to meet certain expectations in regard to role elements such as age, gender, appearance, demeanor, and so forth. For instance, a young adult male who is put in charge of a group of adolescents but who is perceived as very young—perhaps as little more than a child himself because of youthful appearance—is apt to have a lot of trouble controlling the adolescents and getting them to extend to him the authority, respect, and obedience due someone in that role. Similarly, two homosexual men who adopt and rear a child will have great difficulty getting a lot of observers to treat them as the child's "mother and father." A person who is supposed to be a brain surgeon and appears for surgery dressed in a clown costume is not apt to receive cooperation from either the patient or from fellow physicians, the anesthetist, and operating-room nurses.

Furthermore, people are almost always embedded in a context of language and other symbols. More often than not, people are introduced and accompanied by language that interprets them as filling some social roles. For instance, there is language associated with different work-related roles such as secretary, electrician, supervisor, employer. Then there are relationship role interpretations, such as husband, wife, brother, mother, and so on, mentioned earlier. A positive introduction of a newborn would be "Come, see the new addition to our family," "Here is our new baby daughter," or "This is our long-awaited crown prince." A negative role about a newborn could be conveyed by language referring to it as "a monster," "a vegetable," or "preemie trash."

4.2 PEOPLE RELATE TO EACH OTHER LARGELY ON THE BASIS OF SOCIAL ROLES, RATHER THAN ON THE BASIS OF THEIR INHERENT VALUE

In addition to the fact that people always encounter each other in a context that suggests that they hold certain roles, it also seems to be a fact that people relate to each other largely on the basis of the social roles that they fill. Then, much as one might wish they would, people have the greatest difficulty relating to each other as unique divine creations made in the image of God, and therefore of absolute and intrinsic value. Nor do people even relate to each other "soul to soul," as humans might in paradise, or as name to name. We hardly even relate to each other only as child to adult, adult to adult, male to female, and so forth. Instead, either in addition to one or more of the above elements, and sometimes even in lieu of them, we relate to others as friend, best friend, acquaintance, stranger, the boss, the shop steward, a bank teller, a traffic cop, a store clerk, the President, that nasty neighbor, the class clown, my husband, my mom, my "ex," and so on—in other words, largely via social roles just as SRV posits. Even our most intimate personal relationships are shaped and determined by the roles that each party to a relationship fills.

Among other things, one's roles—and especially one's major roles—will largely determine three important things: how one gets treated, where one gets placed or is permitted to be, and who one gets associated with and juxtaposed to.

4.2.1 ROLES STRONGLY DETERMINE HOW A PERSON IS TREATED

In regard to how a person is treated and what gets done to the person, someone in the role of prince or princess is apt to be treated royally. People who are seen as animals may not only be called animals, but may even be given food that is all mixed together like pig slop, and perhaps no utensils to eat with. It is no surprise, then, when people so treated act like animals. Similarly, people who are seen as menaces may be put in fetters or dressed in prison attire. Again, it is no surprise when people so treated end up believing they are a threat to others and behave as if they were.

4.2.2 ROLES STRONGLY DETERMINE WHERE A PERSON GETS PUT

In addition, one's major roles are apt to define where one gets put, so to speak. For example, someone in the valued role of daughter or son is apt to be put in the family home. Someone in the dying role (e.g., a person in the terminal stages of cancer or in a prolonged coma) is apt to be put in a place for those seen to be dying. Someone in the clearly devalued role of animal is apt to be put in an animalistic environment, perhaps in a cage, nest, or the equivalent, and usually into places that are fit for animals but not for people. These places can have all sorts of animal imagery attached to them, such as walls and floors that are easily hosed down. People cast into the menace role will be relegated to places that are considered suitable for such persons, such as places of detention, isolation, or where they can be easily watched and where workers are guards or police-imaged.

However, some devalued roles (such as object of pity or charity, or eternal child) are apt to be less defining of where one gets put than others (such as those of subhuman animal or menace), though they will certainly strongly influence how one is treated.

4.2.3 ROLES STRONGLY DETERMINE WHO A PERSON'S ASSOCIATES ARE

Third, one's major roles will certainly affect, and even determine, who one gets to be associated with and juxtaposed to. For instance, a person in the role of head of government will be associated with other heads of state, politicians, security personnel, and so forth. A person in the role of elementary school student will be juxtaposed to and associated with other students and teachers, school bus drivers, and so on. A person in the eternal child role will get put with children and childish adults, or those who are perceived that way.

4.3 SRV, BEING ON THE EMPIRICAL PLANE, CANNOT SPEAK TO THE QUESTION OF THE VALUE OF PERSONS

People sometimes raise the objection that instead of doing so on the basis of social roles, people ought to relate to—and value—each other "as persons," or "for themselves," regardless of social roles. In examining this issue from the perspective of SRV, it is important first to separate empirical issues from nonempirical ones. And here, it must be recognized that to the degree that one attaches a different meaning to the terms "person" and "personhood" than one does to "human" and "humanhood," the question to what degree someone "is a person" or "has personhood" or is valuable "as a person" is an issue that is above the level of empiricism. Instead, it is an issue on the level of belief, of worldview—in a word, religion.

Second, the question of whether humans or persons have absolute or relative value is also on a level of belief above the empirical realm.

What social science, and SRV as a social science theory, can do is identify what roles are positively and negatively valued in a society; what life conditions get afforded to people who fill devalued roles and to people who fill valued ones; what the relationship is between the social image that a party possesses and the social roles that that party is likely to fill; what the relationship is between a party's degree of competence and the social roles that that party will be able or even allowed to hold; what it takes to secure and maintain valued social roles for oneself or others; and so forth.

But social science (and therefore SRV) cannot address whether any person or human, or all of them, *should* be positively or negatively valued, or whether any human, person or group *should* be more or less highly valued than another. In other words, it cannot give one a premise for deciding to pursue those measures which will result in people being accorded a more or less valued life in their society. It can reveal what it is that individuals and society value; what is

and is not likely to happen when people are subjected to certain measures that make them valued or devalued in other people's eyes; what will or will not secure valued participation for a person in society; what will or will not elicit respect, cooperation, presence, and positive attitudes toward a person by others; and so on.

In light of this, we should also be very clear that at least the modernistic formulation of personhood is strongly linked to—and probably even motivated by—a "religion" that wants to define some people as *not* persons and therefore as legitimate to kill, such as by having essential treatment withheld or withdrawn, or by abortion. Thus, even though this modernistic conceptualization has built elaborate constructs of personhood, it most certainly does *not* value *all* humans "as persons" or "for themselves"; instead, it values them only to the degree that they meet certain criteria—usually utilitarian ones. A prime example of all this is the set of 15 criteria established by the influential bioethicist Joseph Fletcher (1972, 1975), who died in 1991, that a creature has to meet before it can be considered a person, namely: (a) minimal intelligence (IQ below 40 "questionably a person," IQ below 20 "not a person"); (b) self-awareness; (c) self-control; (d) a sense of time; (e) a sense of futurity; (f) a sense of past; (g) capability to relate to others; (h) concern for others; (i) communication; (j) control of one's existence; (k) curiosity; (l) changeability, and not being opposed to change; (m) balance of rationality and feelings; (n) idiosyncrasy; and (o) neocortical functioning. These criteria have been widely accepted and cited in the field of "bioethics."

This being the dominant theme of contemporary discourse around "personhood," it is dangerous to rely on such a slippery construct to protect people who are already seen as having little value.

4.4 SRV IMPLICATIONS ARE IMPORTANT AND POWERFUL IN ENACTING THE POSITIVE VALUATION OF A PERSON "FOR HIM/HERSELF"

Even if one used personhood in a fashion to mean human from conception to death, and as of absolute intrinsic and indivisible value, one would still be up against the reality that humans relate to other humans not in the abstract, but through the medium of their characteristics, and their perceived or actual roles. Thus, even if one grants that it is crucially important for people to be valued "for themselves" (as indeed we do believe), one still has to conclude that the implications of SRV are both very important and very powerful in converting the abstract valuation of a person into meaningful action in the social world. That is, taking society in the aggregate, there is clearly a relationship between the degree to which a person is valued "as a person" or "for him or herself," and the value of the roles extended to the person. The more valued a person is for him or herself, the more likely it is that valued roles will be given to him or her. But at the same time, the more valued roles a person fills, the more likely it is that he or she will *become* valued by others "for him or herself," and/or will not be devalued.

We can turn this insight around and note that when people claim to be valuing others "as persons" or "for themselves," but at the same time cast or keep these others in devalued roles, then there is good reason to distrust their rhetoric and to suspect that there is devaluation at work, even if only unconsciously so. Thus, claims that people should be valued "for themselves" must go beyond rhetoric and *must* be accompanied by efforts to enhance their social roles, so that it will be more likely that they will, in fact, become valued *by others* "as persons." In the words of Peter Maurin, a personalist who was the cofounder of the Catholic Worker movement in the US, one should do things that make it easier for others to be good.

So the evidence appears to be quite strong for the SRV proposition that social roles are the major medium through which people relate to each other. One might put it that social roles are the field, the battleground, on which the question of *whether* to positively value others and how to treat them, is fought out in most people's minds, at least on an unconscious level.

4.5 IMPLICATIONS OF THIS DISCUSSION TO SOCIETALLY DEVALUED PEOPLE

All of this has implications to people who are societally devalued or at risk of such devaluation. Namely, if people relate to each other largely on the basis of social roles, and if "the good things of life" (such as respect, prestige, accommodation to one's wishes, access to material resources, etc.) are extensively accorded based on the value of the social

roles a person fills, then it follows that *if devalued people are to be accorded these good things, then as a general rule they must obtain and hold valued social roles,* and, if necessary, be helped by others to do so. The roles that a party holds must be valued by that society, and/or by those people, from which the good things of life are desired. If the good things of life that are desired can be had from a societal subsector, then the party must hold roles that are valued within and by that subsector. Further, the larger the number of broad valued roles a person fills, the more likely is it that his or her life will be defined and shaped to resemble that of valued people. Also, to the degree that devalued people are mentally capable of doing so, they, too, have to decide whether they are willing to enter and carry out valued social roles, or whether they would rather eschew or forfeit such roles. Of course, they will bear the consequences of doing so, among which will be that they are much less likely to be given what are ordinarily considered the "good things" of life.

These various *probabilistic* assertions about how the number and width of a person's roles affect the way that others treat that person are crucially important. This is underlined here because people constantly fall into simplistic and binary interpretations, and find it difficult to deal with a phenomenon that is multidimensional and complex. Normalization theory and SRV have been relentlessly plagued by such simplistic misunderstandings and misinterpretations of their complexity.

Note that what determines access to specific social roles, and the importance of these roles, is at least to some extent culturally relative. For instance, in the past, much more so than now, gender was a very important determinant in Western societies of which roles a person could fill. It also helped to determine how important a specific role would be in different people's lives, and which roles were assumed to be more important to and for a man than to and for a woman. In other societies, gender may still rule out eligibility for certain social roles and may still dominate the importance of certain social roles.

In contrast to culturally relative determinants of social roles, there are other factors or characteristics that rather universally determine or constrain what roles a person may fill. Age is one of these. Apparently in all societies without exception, a person's age will rule out certain roles and open access to others, will reduce the likelihood of some social roles and increase the likelihood of others, and will also determine how life-defining certain roles will be. A newborn infant may be perceived as filling, and cast into, such social roles as: new son or daughter; sibling; helpless dependent child; little prince or princess; unwanted burden; prehuman nuisance; and so on. But the newborn is extremely unlikely to be perceived or cast into the roles of worker, student, or parent, though he or she might be cast into the role of future student (e.g., when its parents establish a college fund), future spouse (e.g., when it is betrothed to the heir of a neighboring kingdom), and so forth. Some roles may even be "set up" by a child's origins from birth on. For instance, a child of a ruling house may be designated from birth as heir to the throne and treated accordingly. Again, these are some of the realities that call for nuancing and judgment, which are commonly lacking in how people interpret SRV.

5 SOCIAL IMAGE AND PERSONAL COMPETENCY AS TWO MAJOR MEANS FOR ENHANCING PEOPLE'S VALUE IN THE EYES OF OTHERS, AND FOR CONFERRING, PURSUING, OBTAINING, AND HOLDING VALUED ROLES

The more positive is a party's image in the eyes of others, and the more competencies the party possesses, the more will other people be apt to perceive that party positively, value that party highly, accord that party valued roles, and accept that party in valued roles. Specifically regarding social roles, we will now examine how people's social image and/or their competencies affect the conferring, the pursuit, the obtaining, and the securing of valued roles.

5.1 THE IMPORTANCE OF A POSITIVE IMAGE IN THE EYES OF OTHERS

The more a person is seen by others as projecting a positive image, and is esteemed, admired, respected, and positively identified with, the more will positively valued roles be open to him or her. For instance, a handicapped child who is dressed like other children of the same age and carries all the school-related accessories that other children carry—books, book bag, pencils, gym bag, and so on—will be more likely to be accorded the role of a pupil or student and the good things that go with this than one who does not fit the image of a pupil.

In fact, other people will often bend over backward to accord valued roles to people who are positively imaged. Just think of how people who are highly valued in society are always being invited to sit on this or that board, to be an honorary chairperson of this or that, to join something; and how often they are given gifts that range anywhere from small tokens to lavish and expensive items. (For instance, the U.S. President and the President's family are the recipients of literally mountains of gifts, ranging from souvenirs to jewelry to designer clothes to large live animals.) Valued people are given these things in good part because other people want to be somehow positively associated with such persons, and giving a gift is seen as one way of positively associating oneself to a party. In the same way, if devalued people were interpreted and presented more positively in society, others would be more likely to be receptive to their presence or even eager for it, want to give good things to them, and not object to providing—within reasonable limits—what they need.

Because the meanings of images do get associated or transferred to whatever it is they are juxtaposed to, especially if the juxtaposition is a strong and consistent one, this means that devalued people need to be strongly and consistently juxtaposed to all sorts of images that carry positive meanings and messages—or at least less negative ones—if they are to become more valued. This has implications to the settings that they use, the people they are associated to, the activities they carry out, and all the miscellaneous avenues by which images can be associated to people. More on image transfer later.

Because it is people in *positively valued* social roles who are apt to be granted access to those good things of life that others can afford them, it is important that everything associated with the procuring, the maintenance, and the defense of these roles also be positively valued by those who have it in their power to extend good or bad things to the devalued persons. Otherwise, (a) the valued roles may not be obtained or kept, and/or (b) valued roles that are procured or kept may lose some of their perceived value—i.e., be image-tainted—by association with things that are not so positively valued. Thus, SRV emphasizes using, as

TABLE 5.3

SRV IMPLICATIONS THAT HAVE TO DO MOSTLY WITH IMAGE ENHANCEMENT

Related to the places and settings associated with a party

Harmony of the setting used by the party with the appearance of the rest of the neighborhood
Harmony of the activities or program that take place in that setting with the nature of the rest of the neighborhood
Beauty of the exterior of a setting used by a party
Beauty of the interior of a setting used by a party
Congruity of the external appearance of a setting used by a party with the appearance of culturally valued analogous settings for valued people
Congruity of the internal appearance of a setting used by a party with the appearance of culturally valued analogous settings for valued people
External appearance of the setting that positively reflects the age of its users
Internal appearance of the setting that positively reflects the age of its users
Location of a setting next or near to positively imaged other settings
Location of a setting in or on a site that has a positive, or at least neutral, history
Positive messages conveyed by the other imagery of a setting

Related to juxtapositions of a party being served with other parties

Proximity of the activities or program of a party to other programs that are positively imaged
Size of a social grouping that does not overwhelm the assimilation capacity of the surrounding valued community
Grouping a party with others so as to convey a positive image
Grouping a party with others in a way that is congruent with the age mix of culturally valued analogous groupings for valued people
Promotion of image-enhancing social integration of a party with valued people
Positive image of those who serve upon a party
Identity of servers that is congruent with the needs of a party, and the nature of the service being rendered

Related to the activities and uses of time by a party

Maintaining a separation of functions in a party's program or activities that is appropriate to the valued culture
Activities, and timing/scheduling of activities, that are congruent with the practices of valued people in valued society, and consistent with expectations for people of the same age as the party
Promotion of the image-enhancing exercise of autonomy and rights by a party

Related to miscellaneous issues

Address of a party's personal appearance and presentation so that these are as enhancing of its image as possible, and as little image-damaging as possible
Promotion of image-enhancing personal possessions for a party
Language and labeling practices to and about a party that are as enhancing of its image as possible, and as little image-damaging as possible
Names of a party's service and the service setting that are as enhancing of the party's image as possible, and as little image-damaging as possible
Funding support for services to a party that is as image-enhancing as possible
All other image projections that are as image-enhancing of a party as possible

144

much as possible, *culturally valued means or processes* for the crafting, keeping, and carrying out of valued roles; and identifying, capitalizing upon, using, or at the very least emulating, what is done for valued people in society and what they aspire to. When things that are positively valued in society are associated with devalued people, then three good things are likely to happen for them. (a) Observers who might have assumed that negative stereotypic expectations applied to an observed member of a devalued class will be thrown into ambiguity by the positive imagery and have to begin to entertain new possibilities for that party. (b) At least some of the positive value attached to these things will transfer, by association, onto the devalued people themselves. (c) Valued people will see devalued people as more like themselves, will therefore positively identify with them and will want good things to happen for them, because one usually wants goods things to happen to those with whom one identifies. (More on this later.) Table 5.3 lists the major implications of SRV that have to do with image enhancement. In all cases, when a table refers to a "party," this means a person *or* group or class whose social image is at issue.

An entire set of implications has to do with the imagery projected by the places or settings that are associated with a party. For instance, the party's image will be affected by whether the setting looks like it fits in to its neighborhood. Similarly, the attractiveness of a setting, whether it appears like the settings that are used for the same purpose by valued people, and whether it positively reflects the ages of its users, will all influence the image of its users. A setting's history, and its location next to or near other settings, will also contribute to the image of the people with whom the setting is associated.

Images are also conveyed by juxtapositions of people to each other. For instance, if a program for one group of people is juxtaposed to a program for another group of people, then the image of either group may affect that of the other. Also, the size and composition of a congregation of people will influence the capacity of the surrounding valued community and its resources to absorb them. The image of people is also affected by whether the age range of their groupings parallels the age range of similar groupings for valued people, and whether they are integrated with valued people. The image of the servers, too, can influence the image of the people served.

Activities and uses of time can also convey images about people. For instance, the activities, their schedules, and the ways they are carried out will be valued differently, depending on whether they are the same as those for valued people in society, and particularly valued people of the same age. As well, the degree of autonomy accorded and exercised by a party can image it as either incompetent, age-degraded, and unlike valued people, or as competent and like valued people of the same age in society.

Then there are all sorts of other miscellaneous sources of imagery about a party including its personal appearance, its possessions, the language and terminology used to and about it, the names of any services to the party, and any funding that the party receives.

5.2   THE IMPORTANCE OF POSSESSING VALUED COMPETENCIES

The second avenue to valued roles is through competence, at least in the very wide sense in which it has been defined in SRV theory (see Table 5.4).

One broad area of competency is that of bodily integrity, health, and functioning. The more a person's body is whole, the more physical health, strength, stamina, and coordination a person possesses, the more competent the person probably is, or can become.

Then there are various skills that come under the rubric of self-help. These include walking, eating, dressing and grooming oneself, toileting and bathing, and the capacity to project a positive personal appearance.

Communication is another broad area of competence, which would normatively include hearing, speaking, and writing.

A next area of personal competence is mental ability and capacity, including habits of initiative, curiosity, reasonable risk-taking, and engaging oneself in tasks.

Competence also includes the exercise of autonomy and control in one's life, yoked, it is hoped, to responsibility for oneself and one's actions, to self-control and mastery over one's passions and appetites, and to acceptance of the consequences of one's acts.

TABLE 5.4

BROAD AREAS OF PERSONAL COMPETENCY

1. Bodily integrity and health, and the capacity to protect and maintain these
2. Bodily competence: strength, agility, stamina
3. Self-help skills: walking, eating, toileting, dressing and grooming, personal hygiene, capacity to project a positive personal appearance
4. Communication
5. Intellectual ability, skills, habits, and disciplines: knowledge, reasoning, curiosity, mental engagement, prudent risk-taking, foresight
6. Motivation, initiative, drive, stick-to-it-iveness
7. Competent exercise of personal autonomy and control, including responsibility, self-control and self-mastery, anticipation and acceptance of consequences
8. Confidence, self-possession, ability to be decisive
9. Social and relationship competency: social graces, "manners," etiquette, friendliness, considerateness of others; capacity to enter into and maintain adaptive relationships of different types, including intimate ones
10. Unfolding and expression of self, individuality, uniqueness

Another broad area of competency is in social relationships. This includes such skills and habits as social graces, good manners, friendliness, and responsiveness to others and their needs. Deeper elements of relationship competency include a sense of personal security, self-confidence, and the capacity to engage in and sustain various types of relationships with others, including very intimate and demanding ones.

Lastly, there is the domain of self-discovery and self-expression.

The more competent a person is in all these domains, the greater is the number and the wider is the range of socially valued roles the person will be able to fill. For instance, a wider range of potential work roles are open and possible for a person who can read, write, do math, and perform hard manual labor than for one who is illiterate, and incapable of hand labor. Also, certain competencies are needed in order to assume and carry out the functions associated with various valued roles. For instance, if one is to be a member of a choir, one has to have hearing and voice, be able to learn to sing on key, and possibly even to read music, or at least follow the choirmaster. Similarly, if one

wants to fill the valued role of firefighter, then one has to be able to pass the written examinations, be strong enough to fight a fire while carrying and wearing heavy equipment, be level-headed so as not to panic under stress and danger, perhaps be able to get up at a moment's notice from a sound sleep and get ready to go out to a fire right away, and so on.

Also, apart from being needed in order to fill and carry out many social roles, personal competency is highly valued in and of itself in society. This means that people who are more competent will tend to be more valued "for themselves," even aside from any specific valued social roles they may fill.

Table 5.5 lists the major SRV implications that have to do with personal competency enhancement.

Competency can be affected by the place and settings used by a party, for instance: the accessibility of a setting to its users; whether the setting is located near community resources that are relevant to the identities and needs of the users; the comfort of the setting; whether a setting permits individualization by its users, and is neither dangerous nor overprotective of them—all bear on the competencies that users will practice or develop.

People's competencies can also be affected by their associations and juxtapositions to other people. For instance, people's competencies will be affected by the size of any program groupings of which they are members, and by whether the composition of a grouping provides positive intragroup models for imitation, and elevates the expectancies for the group as a whole. Also, people's competencies are more likely to develop if they are treated as individuals, if they are encouraged in and even taught positive interactions with others, and if a valued sociosexual identity is enabled or fostered for them.

As regards activities and uses of time, a party's competencies will be profoundly shaped by whether their most pressing needs are incisively addressed, and whether their time is used efficiently, rather than wasted by others as it is so often in the case of devalued people. The objects that people are encouraged to possess and/or keep in order also influence the competencies they can exercise or will develop.

5.3 THE RELATIONSHIP BETWEEN IMAGE AND COMPETENCY

Social Role Valorization implies that in order for people to fill and maintain valued roles, they will need *both* a positive social image and personal competencies; and the more they are devalued, the more they need these. To the extent that people are deficient in either positive social image or personal competency, then things will have to be done to enhance one or both if they are to be able to fill valued roles and be valued by others. Conversely, SRV also

---

TABLE 5.5

SRV IMPLICATIONS THAT HAVE MOSTLY TO DO WITH COMPETENCY ENHANCEMENT

Related to the places and settings associated with a party
Setting that is accessible to a party and families
Setting that is accessible to the public
Setting location that is near easily accessible community resources that are relevant to the identities and needs of a party
Setting that is physically comfortable
Setting that is neither over- nor underprotective of its users
Setting that permits individualization by users

Related to juxtapositions of a party being served with other parties
Size of a grouping of a party with others that is facilitative of the competency development of its members
Composition of a grouping of a party with others that facilitates the competency development of its members, via positive intra-group modeling and imitation, and positive group expectancies
Promotion of competency-enhancing social integration of a party with valued people
Promotion of positive interactions between and among service recipients, service workers, and others
Individualization of a party
Promotion of a valued sociosexual identity for a party

Related to the activities and uses of time by a party
Address of a party's real and most pressing needs
Intense and efficient use of a party's time for competency development
Promotion of personal possessions that are enhancing of a party's competencies

---

implies that the more a positive social image and personal competencies adhere to people, then the more valued roles will be available to them, and the more value will be accorded to the roles that they do fill.

Obviously, there are relationships and feedbacks between image and competency, as shown in Figure 5.3.[4]

FIGURE 5.3

FEEDBACK LOOP BETWEEN IMAGE AND COMPETENCY

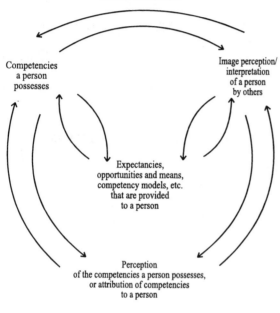

For instance, the more competencies a person is seen to possess, and the more valued these competencies are, the better an image the person will have in the eyes of observers. The power of the mere presumption that competency exists, even if it really does not, is attested by the fact that a person who is only assumed to possess competencies is also more apt to be accepted and integrated into valued society. This is sometimes referred to as a "competency halo." In contrast, people who have, or are believed to have, few competencies are apt to have a poor social image as a result.

Also, once a person is either observed to possess competencies or even is merely believed to possess them, the person will be expected to exercise such competencies, and to acquire new ones. Thus, opportunities to this end will be provided to the person, as well as models of competency for the person to imitate. Once a person demonstrates competence, this will enhance the person's image. If the person fails to live up to the opportunity presented, as by not performing well, allowances will be made and leeway will be given, at least for a while.

However, with certain exceptions, people who have a negative social image are less apt to be given opportunities to develop valued competencies; are apt to be segregated and therefore surrounded by poor models of competence; and are apt to have their failures judged, and be treated, much more harshly. As a result, such people are not only less apt to develop new competencies, but also less likely to exercise those they already possess. The exceptions are illuminating because they show the power of specific social roles. For instance, one exception is the child role. Even if that role is held by adults, others tend to be lenient about their failures and make allowances for them that they would not make for people in the menace role. The same is true with the sick role: People in this role are excused from all sorts of things, and failures may be written off to their "illness," whereas the same accommodations would not be made for people not seen as sick.

Even quite aside from the more intricate and roundabout elements of this feedback loop, it is also an empirical fact that positively imaged people are more likely to be judged as competent, and that people who are seen in a negative light are less likely to be attributed with competencies. In fact, others often seem to deny their real competencies in a way that suggests that this serves the function of meting out what to them seems to be deserved punishment to the devalued person.

Some implications of SRV have more to do with imagery, and others more with competency; but even where one dominates, both are apt to be affected via the feedback mechanism discussed above, and this feedback is extremely strong, regardless of its directionality. Thus, even minor enhancements can have disproportionately dramatic positive impacts, while minor degradations can quickly become disastrous, and especially so for a person of already devalued identity.

Before going to the next section on applying SRV, let us look at the question that might be raised why SRV should so heavily emphasize, and be interpreted in terms of, image and competency. This question might especially arise because in Wolfensberger's (1972) earlier formulation of Normalization, two different dimensions—namely, interaction and interpretation—were used. In response, we can say the following:

First, it is natural and logical to invoke the concepts of image and competency since that is largely what filling a role consists of: fulfilling people's image (i.e., ideas) of what a role entails, and all the expectations associated with it; and exercising the competencies necessary to carry out any functions of the role.

Second, image is a higher-level construct than interpretation; and competency is a more useful construct (to us, at least) than was interaction, because there are some aspects of both image and competency that involve interaction.

Third, it is difficult to think of another way to encompass SRV implications in a parsimonious fashion. (Remember Occam's razor: The more parsimonious a theory is, the better or more elegant it is considered to be.) Other less parsimonious, less elegant ways can be thought of, such as the lower-order constructs of expectancies without reference to roles; authoritarianism and obedience; conditioning; or even "human differences," such as was once commonly done in psychology under the rubric of "individual differences." But some such explanations would be less related, others overlapping, and overall less efficient and elegant in explaining the reality of social devaluation, what happens to societally devalued people, and what can be done about it. Therefore, these lower-level ways of thinking would have formed a less powerful and less elegant version of SRV theory—though not necessarily an invalid one.

6 CONVERSION OF KNOWLEDGE ABOUT SOCIAL ROLES INTO SOCIAL ROLE-VALORIZING ACTION

With all the foregoing as background, we can now begin to apply this knowledge to specific actions that are social role-valorizing. There are three major and distinct ways in which the roles of devalued people can be positively "valorized."[5]

6.1 PROVIDING NEW VALUED, OR AT LEAST LESS DEVALUED, ROLES TO INDIVIDUALS OR CLASSES

The first is enabling a party to assume or enter one or more valued roles that it did not previously possess, or at least new roles that are less devalued than the ones the party currently holds or would have been relegated to. That is, new roles are crafted or obtained for the party.

6.1.1 PROVIDING NEW ROLES TO INDIVIDUALS

With regard to individuals, a child may be enabled to take on the valued role of student. An adult may be enabled to enter and maintain the valued role of worker or employee.

A person may be enabled to enter the role of church choir member, or to assume the role of homeowner, and some or all of its related roles as well, such as taxpayer, customer, renovator, gardener, and so on. The person may be enabled to fill roles that, if not fully valued, are at least less devalued than he or she might have held previously or would have ended up in. For instance, instead of being or becoming an idle consumer of unemployment benefits, an adult may be enabled to take on at least part-time paid work for a few hours or a few days a week, even if not full-time work. A person who holds a job that is not highly valued might be helped to find another job that is less devalued. Instead of being out of school entirely, a child may be enabled to attend school at least part of the day. Being a prisoner and a parolee are both devalued, but parolees are generally less devalued than prisoners, so it would be role-valorizing for a person to move from the role of prisoner to that of parolee. And so on.

6.1.2 PROVIDING NEW ROLES TO CLASSES

New valued roles, or at least less devalued ones, might also be created for members of an entire devalued class, perhaps by systemic action. For instance, the leaders of the French Revolution opened up new roles to the previously lowly and oppressed classes, including roles associated with running the government and the courts. The "Senior Olympics," and similar athletic games that have been created for older people, enable members of this class to fill the valued roles of competent athlete and competitor. Legislation might be passed that gives to members of a disadvantaged class opportunities to enter roles that they had been denied. The U.S. civil rights legislation of the 1960s and 1970s opened up, for many racial minority members, roles related to schooling, jobs, places to live, and "consumership" from which they had previously been excluded.

This first strategy of role valorization is usually the most accessible one and also presents the greatest number of opportunities.

6.2 ENHANCING THE PERCEIVED VALUE OF ROLES ALREADY HELD BY AN INDIVIDUAL PERSON, OR BY MEMBERS OF A DEVALUED CLASS

The second major way of role valorization is to do things that enhance the value attributed to those roles that are already filled by an individual, or by members of a class. This may be done via image and interpretation, or by adding valued functions to the role. All of these things help the incumbent of even less valued roles to be perceived more positively by others.

6.2.1 *ENHANCING THE ROLES HELD BY INDIVIDUALS*

The image of a role that an individual holds can be improved. For instance, valued titles may be given to a person's role such as "office assistant" instead of clerk. (Of course, one should avoid being outright deceptive, or even confusing and misleading.) A handicapped member of a Christian congregation may be interpreted to other members of the congregation in an even more enhancing fashion as the one who is closest to the identity of the so-called "Hidden Christ." A person who is in the devalued sick role may be enabled to put on street clothes during the day, rather than go around in nightclothes or a hospital gown all day. Even though the person may still be in the sick role, he or she will be perceived less negatively as a result. An adult who has been cast in the eternal child role might be dressed in very age-appropriate fashion and served in a highly adult-appearing setting, even if

the person continues to engage in childish activities and to behave childishly.

Roles that a person already fills may also be enhanced by adding to them valued and important functions that require competency. For instance, a person in the role of assistant to an athletic coach may be given some of the valued tasks usually carried out by the coach. A role that is mainly ceremonial may be given additional functions that are actually productive and contributive—more "real," one might say. For instance, an honorary chairman might not only open and close meetings, but also be consulted and cast the decisive vote on split decisions.

6.2.2 *ENHANCING THE ROLES HELD BY DEVALUED CLASSES*

Things can be done to enhance the value attributed to those social roles typically held by many members of an entire *class* of persons at value risk, so that the individual members of that class benefit even when nothing more is done on behalf of any one specific member. For instance, one could give positive interpretation to those laboring roles usually occupied by lowly classes, instead of interpreting such roles as degrading. This is exactly what some of the more radical Marxist nations did, such as Communist China and Vietnam: They exalted laboring roles even over intellectual ones, and therefore also laboring people over intellectuals. This strategy went beyond mere interpretation and included equalization of payment to people such as laborers and physicians.

A good example of the systematic valorizing of roles already occupied by lowly classes have been certain efforts by artists to illuminate the positive elements in such roles. For instance, in his paintings, drawings, and especially sculptures, the Belgian artist Constantin Meunier (1831-1905) depicted the lowly working classes at their labors in a very dignifying fashion. He had much impact because he was a good artist and widely acclaimed. Less skilled or esteemed artists might have had much less impact, but even they can still make a similar contribution, as evidenced by so much of Soviet art in the 1920s and 1930s. Regardless of what one might think of it as art, it did depict laboring people, country folk, and their work in a highly valued, even exalted fashion.

The English writer Charles Dickens (1812-1870) made similar portrayals and interpretations in his writings. The impairments and afflictions of handicapped and poor people were never denied, nor was their lowliness, but he interpreted them in a positive light and even identified some of the positive elements within the less valued roles that they might fill, such as the positive elements (e.g., innocence) in the child role.

Or, take the fact that in North America, it is primarily poor people who live in government-subsidized public housing. Being a tenant of public housing is not a valued role, a situation made worse by the fact that such subsidy is provided only for people to live in specially constructed housing, which is not only segregated but also congregated, located in parts of town where no one else wants to live if they can help it, often poorly constructed, often poorly maintained, and so forth. The perceived value of the role of publicly-supported tenants as a class would be enhanced if some of the following things were done.

1. Instead of constructing special housing into which such people are gathered, subsidies could be provided for poor people to live in ordinary housing that is already available throughout the community.

2. Even if new housing had to be constructed, it could be dispersed throughout a community, for example, by locating small units in many neighborhoods instead of large units in a few.

3. Making public housing more attractive, and keeping it well-maintained.

4. Keeping out the drug dealers and street gangs that in recent decades have so often taken over congregate public housing projects.

5. Giving the tenants greater responsibility for, and authority and control over, the running of the housing.

6. Making other demands for adaptive and responsible behavior by tenants of such housing.

Doing any of these things might not mean that poor tenants of publicly supported housing would escape devalued identity, but they would probably be much less devalued. (Also, doing any of these things probably would not cost any more than public housing already does, though cost is not an SRV issue.)

Representatives of a devalued class could also be shown in valued roles in the news and entertainment media, thus trying to create positive expectancies in viewers' minds about that class as a whole.

6.3 VALUED PARTIES ASSUMING AN OTHERWISE DEVALUED CHARACTERISTIC

A third way to enhance the role perception of a person or class at risk of devaluation is for valued people to take on the characteristic for which the person or class at issue would be devalued. In this way, the negative imagery associated with the characteristic is apt to be diminished, because the characteristic has become associated with valued people, and their positive value rubs off a bit onto the otherwise devalued characteristic. An example with which most readers would be familiar is what happened with the appearance and dress of men in the 1970s and 1980s in most of the Western world. Up until the late 1960s, men who wore their hair any longer than their ears, or who wore sideburns, or who wore scraggly beards, or who wore certain jewelry, were very much at risk of devaluation, especially if they did not fill highly valued roles that could compensate for these aspects of appearance that were then perceived as bizarre and uncouth. However, through the 1970s and 1980s, more and more men began to wear their hair long, to grow mustaches and beards, and to sport jewelry such as earrings. Even highly valued men began to do so, and once this happened, the negative imagery and devaluation that had been associated with these appearance features greatly decreased.

In the same way, if valued people adopt other devalued characteristics, the characteristic itself—and the people who have it—are apt to become less devalued. For instance, a child went bald as a result of chemotherapy he was receiving against cancer. When this happened, all his male classmates, and the male teacher, shaved their own heads so that he would not stand out in a negative way from them, thereby minimizing his image loss and raising the value attributed to baldheadedness. Similarly, a man shaved his own head when his fiancée lost her hair to chemotherapy, so that she would not be embarrassed by it. And in a 1960 Spanish film *El Cochecito* (The Little Coach), a man who does not need a wheelchair to get around nonetheless obtains one, so that he can cavort with his mobility-impaired friends who do have to use such vehicles. If valued people who did not need wheelchairs to get around began to use them, and especially if they began to practically live in them (as some physically handicapped people do), then the use of a wheelchair would certainly become less devalued.

Because SRV addresses (a) the "up-valuing" of the roles already held by people at value-risk (via the second strategy explained above), (b) embedding such people into new roles that are more valued (the first strategy), and (c) improving the social value attached to otherwise devalued characteristics (the third strategy), one should really use the broad term "valorizing" (as in role valorizing or role valorization) when referring to any of these avenues of enhancing people's roles.

It should also be clear by now that these measures will be cumulative, that is, the greater the number of valued roles a party enters, and/or the more valued (or less devalued) any of these roles are, and/or the more that valued people assume devalued characteristics, the more the party is apt to be positively valued (or less devalued) by others, and the more the party is likely to have access to the good things of life—or at least, the likelihood is diminished that bad things will be done to that party.

7 THE TEN THEMES THAT ARE USED TO TEACH SRV

Social Role Valorization is taught in most training workshops by means of so-called "themes," that is, motifs or issues that recur throughout all the implications of SRV. However, most of these themes should not be seen as "being" or constituting SRV. Rather, most of them are simply pedagogic, heuristic devices for helping people to understand SRV, to learn it, tie its various elements together, (very importantly) to organize the content of the theory, and then to figure out how it applies to specific situations. But SRV does not stand or fall as a valid social science theory on the basis of any single one of these themes and how it is taught, and it is certainly possible to use other ways to teach and learn SRV and to interpret the implications.

We will say more about this after reviewing the themes, which are as follows.

7.1 THE ROLE AND REALITY OF UNCONSCIOUSNESS IN DEVALUATION, DEVIANCY MAKING, AND THE PERPETUATION OF DEVALUATION AND DEPENDENCY

This theme teaches the reality and dynamics of unconsciousness on the level of both individual humans and entire collectivities. It explains why there is so much unconsciousness in human functioning, and that certain things are less apt to be available to conscious awareness (e.g., due to repression) than others. As regards social devaluation and SRV specifically, the teaching then explains that identifying certain kinds of people as devalued, and maintaining them in devalued status, plays certain real functions in society that escape the awareness of almost all the affected parties, including devalued people themselves, those who serve them, their advocates, and societal institutions. Stress is placed on the importance of attaining consciousness of the relevant issues (such as of the heightened vulnerability of devalued people, as addressed in the second theme) as a crucial precondition to selecting appropriate role-valorizing measures.

7.2 CONSERVATISM COROLLARY

The "conservatism corollary" of SRV states that the more a person or group is devalued or at risk of devaluation, the more important it is to (a) not further add to the party's vulnerability, (b) reduce those vulnerabilities and devaluations that already exist, and (c) compensate for existing vulnerabilities and devaluations by adding value and competencies wherever possible. The conservatism corollary raises consciousness (as emphasized in the first theme) about the fact that for many reasons, devalued people are much more vulnerable than valued ones to all sorts of bad things happening to them, in good part because they *are* devalued, and they are not uncommonly reduced in important competencies that could protect them. For this reason, those who want to see devalued people become more valued, and who want good rather than bad things to happen to them, need to bend over backward to make sure that vulnerable people do not become yet more vulnerable, and that those vulnerabilities that already exist are reduced and/or compensated for. Among other things, this often means that it is not good enough to settle for what is typical or normative where vulnerable people are concerned; instead, one must aim for what is the more or most highly valued and is apt to bring the most value to them.

7.3 THE IMPORTANCE OF INTERPERSONAL IDENTIFICATION BETWEEN VALUED AND DEVALUED PEOPLE

This theme emphasizes that the more that people identify with each other—that is, the more they see themselves "in" the other, or the more they see the other as similar to themselves—the more they will want good things to happen to each other and the more they will act to bring or give good things to each other. It is then explained that in order for devalued people to become more valued in society, it is important to help valued people identify with devalued people, and to help devalued people identify with people of adaptive identity so that they will be more likely to imitate them (explained later) and be more able to fill valued roles. Ways in which people can be helped to identify with each other are then elucidated, including helping people to be more "approachable," trying to ensure that the contact between people is positively experienced by each party, and helping each party to see the world through the other's eyes, to experience the world the way the other party does, and to empathize and sympathize with each other.

7.4 THE CONCEPTS OF RELEVANCE, POTENCY, AND MODEL COHERENCY

Any service measure should be relevant to real, important needs of the people to whom it is addressed, and more fundamental or more urgent needs of people should be addressed before lesser needs. As well, whatever means are used to address people's needs should be as powerful as possible, that is, capable of effectively and efficiently addressing the need at issue, rather than being wasteful of people's time and growth potential. Model coherency combines these two concepts of relevance and potency, and can be formulated in very simplified form as bringing together valid assumptions, relevant service content, and potent service means, with the means being such that they avoid creating a new need or magnifying a preexisting

one, which could diminish either service relevance or potency, or even do more harm than good. Model coherency also requires that service measures should fit together in a way that both (a) matches the culturally valued analogue (that is, the way in which similar needs are addressed for valued people in society), and (b) is harmonious and makes sense. For instance, it is not harmonious to address nonmedical needs with medical means; doing so is apt to reduce at least potency if not relevance, and may also violate culturally valued analogues.

7.5 REALITY OF SOCIAL IMAGERY AND IMAGE TRANSFER

This theme explains that much human communication uses imagery, that images and symbols convey messages, and that these meanings and messages are received and processed by those who are exposed to them even if the receivers are unaware of it (as explained in the first theme). This theme also explains that when meaning-laden images get juxtaposed or attached to people, then the meanings and messages of the images also get associated, generalized, or transferred to those people, who come to be seen as embodying in their identity the message conveyed by the image. For instance, people who are consistently juxtaposed to images of childishness and triviality are apt to be seen—at least eventually—as childish themselves, as "lightweight" and not to be taken seriously. As regards SRV action, this theme stresses that the ways in which devalued people present themselves and are presented to others affect how others will value them; what others will do to, for, and vis-à-vis them; and what roles they will get cast into or be allowed to enter. Thus, all the imagery associated with societally devalued people—from the direct personal level all the way up to the broad societal level—should convey positively valued messages and meanings.

7.6 THE POWER OF MIND-SETS AND EXPECTANCIES, AND THE DEVELOPMENTAL MODEL

People are very strongly affected—indeed, often controlled—by what has been put into their minds about what certain people are like, and what can and should be expected of them. This theme emphasizes that if what is put into people's minds about devalued people is devaluing (e.g., that they are subhuman, menaces, as good as dead), and/or if it is low-expecting (e.g., that they cannot grow and learn, will "always be like that," are capable of very little or of only a few very specific competencies), then the perceivers will do things that reflect these mind-sets and expectancies so that they become self-fulfilling prophecies. The perceivers will fail to provide challenging environments and opportunities if they do not believe that (devalued) people can benefit from them. On the other hand, if people believe and expect that (devalued) people are capable of learning to fill valued roles, even very demanding ones, and that they are capable of a great deal of growth and performance, then perceivers are more likely to create the conditions that will elicit growth and performance, and that will foster (devalued) people into valued roles.

This theme also emphasizes that all human beings, regardless of their age or degree of impairment, do in fact possess a tremendous capacity for growth, though this is hardly recognized and elicited, especially not where devalued people are concerned. This assumption about the capacity of all human beings to develop is the cornerstone of what is called "the developmental model" or a developmental approach. The developmental model was first made prominent with the publication of *Changing Patterns in Residential Services for the Mentally Retarded* (Kugel & Wolfensberger, 1969).

7.7 THE COMMUNICATORS OF ROLE EXPECTANCIES, AND THE FEEDBACK BETWEEN THEM AND ROLE PERFORMANCE

The social reality covered in this theme can be stated simply as: People will generally live up (or down) to what is expected of them. Role expectancies are communicated via (a) the settings in which a person functions, is served, or is forced to occupy; (b) the other people with whom a person is associated; (c) the activities and behaviors that are permitted, structured for, or required of a person; (d) the language that is used to and about people, their settings, and their activities; and (e) other imagery that is associated

with people. Thus, if devalued people are to be more competent, and/or to fill more valued social roles, then expectancies must be conveyed to them—via the five above communicators of role demands—that they do in fact become more competent and/or enact the competencies they already possess, and that they fill valued rather than devalued social roles.

7.8 THE IMPORTANCE OF PERSONAL COMPETENCY ENHANCEMENT

This theme emphasizes the importance of (a) reducing any obstacles that exist to learning, growth, development, competency enhancement, and its exercise; and (b) enlarging a person's actual functional repertoire of knowledge, skills, habits, and disciplines. This includes, among other things, correctly identifying what a person needs and then enabling, mediating, or conveying what is really needed; individualization of approach and service; grouping people in a way that maximizes the likelihood of positive rather than negative intragroup imitation, of positive rather than negative expectancies for the group as a whole, and of the ability of servers and others to deal positively with the group as a whole; and facilitating growth and development via the power of the physical environment itself.

7.9 THE POWER OF IMITATION AND MODELING

This theme stresses that imitation is a human universal and one of the most powerful ways that people learn. Its SRV relevance is that the models for societally devalued people should be as positively valued and competent as possible, if such persons are to become more competent and assume valued roles. This implies structuring groupings so as to facilitate positive intragroup imitation, increasing positive interpersonal identification between devalued people and those they should imitate (since people will want to imitate those they identify with), providing a surfeit of positive models in the environments of devalued people, encouraging positive modeling, and being a good model oneself.

7.10 THE IMPORTANCE OF VALUED SOCIAL PARTICIPATION AND PERSONAL SOCIAL INTEGRATION

This theme emphasizes that the more people participate in valued society, the more they will learn what is valued by society, the more competent they are apt to become in it and the more they are likely to be able to fill valued roles. Also, social integration of devalued people—if it is experienced as pleasant by the assimilators in valued society—can help to make society more tolerant and accepting. This theme delineates those physical features of a setting and broader "programmatic" features that can facilitate (or conversely, hinder) the social integration of people; how to actually bring about real social integration (not just physical presence); and what some limitations are to full social integration and participation.

Social Role Valorization deals with the issue of valued social participation and personal social integration on an empirical basis, that is, on the basis of rationales that can be—and largely have been—tested by experience. However, people may also hold ideological rationales in support of social integration of societally devalued people and may advance these regardless of issues of evidence.

7.11 CONCLUSION TO THE THEMES

Certain themes are well established, and interesting and extremely useful in their own right, even apart from Normalization/SRV theory. For instance, knowledge of the reality and power of modeling and imitation, and of the dynamics of human unconsciousness, certainly did not derive from Normalization or SRV teaching and thinking. However, some others of the themes have a more intimate theoretical and historical tie to Normalization/SRV. For instance, prior to the advent of Normalization, one would not find much in the social science literature that promoted the integration of devalued people, or spelled out the rationales for it and the "how to" of doing it. Relatedly, at least

Scandinavian Normalization practice was long content—at least in its early years—to develop normalized but *non*integrated settings and arrangements, on the assumption that this met the desideratum of making available to the handicapped "patterns and conditions of everyday life which are as close as possible to the norms and patterns of the mainstream of society" (Nirje, 1969, p. 181).

Also, the conservatism corollary is very closely tied to Normalization/SRV, and even more so to SRV than to Normalization. One may find less on this theme in the social science literature than on other SRV themes, though there is a great deal of support for it in folk wisdom, such as sayings on the difference between what the privileged classes and the lowly classes can get away with. It was largely Wolfensberger's Normalization formulation of the 1980s that increasingly elaborated the reality that people who are valued are much less damaged by association with devalued entities and sites than are people who are already devalued, that devalued people have vastly more to gain by value enhancement than do people who are already valued, and that they often also have more to lose by (continued) value degradation than valued people.

Thus, the themes are a very useful way of capturing the many implications or thrusts of SRV, of analyzing and supporting its implications, and of conveying to learners major action strategies or action spheres. But conceivably, SRV could also be taught without any reference to the themes. For instance, SRV could be taught by just focusing on image and competency, or by sorting its implications into a 2 x 3 schema that identifies image and competency implications on three different levels of social organization (see Wolfensberger, 1992, p. 50)—much as Wolfensberger's Normalization construct used to be taught prior to about 1980 without invoking the themes. In the same way, the common "wounds" of devalued people (discussed above in section 3.5.2 "Common Hurtful Experiences That Befall Societally Devalued People Because They Are Devalued") have proven to be an extremely useful way of capturing the realities of devaluation as it is experienced by devalued people. But again, the realities of devaluation could be taught in different ways, much like they used to be taught under the sociological concept of "deviancy" in Normalization teaching of the 1970s.

However, one advantage of using the themes to *teach* SRV (in contrast to constructing the theory) is that they bring out the complexity of many issues, including that of the recipient grouping, since grouping is examined from the perspective of all the themes, and each one sheds a different light on it. Without the themes, it is difficult to convincingly teach people about the complexity of grouping and the difficulty of making wise grouping decisions. This probably accounts for the fact that grouping issues are still extremely poorly handled in most human services.

The fact that the themes are merely a heuristic device, as mentioned earlier, is underlined by the following. (a) One might have identified more themes, and perhaps this will happen some day, though it is difficult to see how there might be fewer. (b) The theme of imagery is actually only an elaboration and recapitulation of one of the two major avenues (image enhancement and competency enhancement) for achieving valued roles. If the themes were meant to *constitute* SRV rather than to illustrate and teach it, the inclusion of imagery among the themes would be illogical. Competency enhancement is also thoroughly embedded in several of the other themes, for example, the developmental model, role expectancies, imitation, and integration.

Another way of clarifying the difference between SRV itself and the themes that may be used to teach and learn it is to imagine SRV theory as an integral whole, similar to the human body. The human body may be better understood, and important realities about how the body functions can be taught by identifying various of its subsystems, such as the respiratory system, the endocrine system, the circulatory system, the skeletal system, the muscular system, and so on. However, these various systems could only be said to "constitute" the human body in a very narrow sense. And it would certainly be possible for people to learn about the body in different ways, for example, by looking at the head, the neck, the legs and feet, and so on. Which particular way of teaching and learning about the body is employed would depend on such things as who is doing the teaching, who is learning, and what roles vis-à-vis the human body those learners will have to carry out (e.g., are they going to be neurosurgeons or are they going to teach children in the primary grades about the body?).

8 THE "IF-THEN" FORMULATION OF SRV AS A FRAMEWORK FOR MAKING SRV DECISIONS

In about 1992, it was recognized that SRV decisions could all be formulated in terms of an "if this, then that" sequence (Wolfensberger, 1995) and that such a formulation would be very helpful in clarifying the nature and boundaries of SRV as an empirical theory and the decisions that people would have to make based on the knowledge that SRV provides.

There are four ways of formulating the "if this, then that" statements relevant to SRV.

1. If X is done, then one must expect that Y will occur. For instance, *if* devalued adults are consistently presented as childlike, via their settings, appearances, and activities, *then* observers are apt to see them as "eternal children" and respond to them as if they were. *If* devalued people are congregated together in numbers that are greater than the surrounding valued community can easily assimilate, *then* the devalued people are apt to be rejected. *If* the images that are associated with devalued people and services to them convey messages of animality, menace, contagion, death, and decay, *then* valued people will certainly want to distantiate themselves from such devalued people and may endorse bad things being done to them.

2. If Y has already occurred, then X has probably been done earlier. For instance, *if* certain devalued people are now seen as subhuman or nonhuman, and their being put to death is seen as legitimate, *then* it is very likely that devalued people had been interpreted as nonhuman, and had been consistently, systematically, and massively surrounded with subhuman and nonhuman imagery.

3. If one wants Y to occur, then one will probably have to first do X; and, conversely, if one wants to avoid Y, then X will probably have to be done. For example, *if* one wants people to be seen as similar to their age peers, *then* one has to present them to others in ways that are consistent with their age, and that heighten the things they have in common with their age mates. *If* one wants people to be accepted and positively integrated into society, *then* one must do the things that enable them to be present and participative in ways that are not perceived as threatening and that help other people to be receptive and welcoming. *If*

one does not want people in society to view a certain devalued group as a menace, *then* one must not do things that interpret that group or its members as a threat. And so on.

4. If one concludes that doing X in order to obtain Y is too costly to either oneself or the party at issue (i.e., that the price to be paid for Y is too high), then one may have to modify or even sacrifice the goal Y. For example, *if* one is unwilling to use culturally valued means and adopt culturally valued imagery in relation to some party, *then* one has to accept that it is very unlikely that one is going to win acceptance and positive valuation of that party from that culture. *If* one decides to reject the dominant society's values, norms, and good things of life, *then* one cannot expect to be accepted and treated well by and in that society.

The formulation of SRV and its implications as constituting an "if this, then that" series of logical decisions has several benefits. One—unfortunately very belated—benefit is that it may lay to rest a lot of futile controversy that has plagued Normalization and SRV teaching and implementation efforts in the past. This is because the "if this, then that" conceptualization forces people to determine logically three things: first, what it is they want to achieve and avoid (e.g., for themselves, for the devalued people they serve or advocate for); second, what empiricism has shown is and is not likely to attain this goal, or at least is and is not consistent with attaining this goal; and third, what it is that they are willing to do. This illuminates more clearly the boundaries between the empirical theory of SRV, and any supra-empirical values and worldviews that might suggest that a certain outcome or action course, and not another, is preferable, and why. It therefore forces the debate about SRV-related issues into its proper domain: either that of empiricism—that is, what do we know tends to work, what do we know does not work—which is where SRV lies, or that of "religion." In the empirical domain, we can examine evidence for specific assertions, for instance, how does congregating

devalued people together affect the likelihood that the surrounding value society will accept and assimilate them; do childish activities, routines, and appearances for adults improve, harm, or have no effect on how they are perceived by others. On the supra-empirical level of religion are such questions as whether certain people *ought* to be valued or devalued, whether certain creatures are human, whether it is a good or bad thing to interpret certain people as subhuman, whether certain kinds of people deserve bad treatment, whether one should cultivate societal acceptance of a rejected and mistreated group, whether society has an obligation to its weakest members, and so on. Even if people controvert the empiricism, this is a level of controversy that is more amenable to rational resolution than controversy on the level of ideology and religion.

Of course, religious and ideological decisions *must* be made in human services. But such decisions must be made before, so to speak, one undertakes to apply Normalization or SRV. That is, one must decide whether and on what basis to value people who are handicapped, poor, foreign, or different in any negatively valued way, and *that* is a religious or ideological decision (e.g., should one value them because it is morally right, because whatever is my god and religion says so). Only *if* one decides that such people should be positively valued does Normalization/SRV *then* make any sense, because it can tell one what to do that has the best chance of bringing that about.

Thus, *if* one wants societally devalued people, or those who are at risk of societal devaluation, to be more positively valued, *then* one must do those things that will help others and society as a whole to see them in a more positive light, and SRV can tell one on the basis of empirical social science what many of the things are that need to be done to bring about that desired end. But SRV cannot provide one with a reason for wanting devalued people to be valued in the first place. Only "a religion" can do that.

REFERENCES

FLETCHER, J. (1972). Indicators of humanhood: A tentative profile of man. *Hastings Center Report, 2,* 1-4.

FLETCHER, J. (1975). The "right" to live and the "right" to die. In M. KOHL (Ed.), *Beneficent euthanasia* (pp. 44-53). Buffalo, NY: Prometheus Books.

FREEDMAN, J. L., CARLSMITH, J. M., & SEARS, D. O. (1970). *Social psychology.* Englewood Cliffs, NJ: Prentice-Hall.

KUGEL, R. B., & WOLFENSBERGER, W. (Eds.). (1969). *Changing patterns in residential services for the mentally retarded.* Washington, DC: President's Committee on Mental Retardation.

NIRJE, B. (1969). The Normalization principle and its human management implications. In R. B. KUGEL & W. WOLFENSBERGER (Eds.), *Changing patterns in residential services for the mentally retarded* (pp. 179-195). Washington, DC: President's Committee on Mental Retardation.

WOLFENSBERGER, W. (1972). *The principle of Normalization in human services.* Toronto: National Institute on Mental Retardation.

WOLFENSBERGER, W. (1977). The Normalization principle and some major implications to architectural-environmental design. In M. J. BEDNAR (Ed.), *Barriers in the built environment* (pp. 135-169). Stroudsburg, PA: Dowden, Hutchinson & Ross.

WOLFENSBERGER, W. (1978). *The Normalization principle and some major implications to architectural-environmental design.* Atlanta, GA: Georgia Association for Retarded Citizens.

WOLFENSBERGER, W. (1983). Social Role Valorization: A proposed new term for the principle of Normalization. *Mental Retardation, 21* (6), 234-239.

WOLFENSBERGER, W. (1984). A reconceptualization of Normalization as Social Role Valorization. (Canadian) *Mental Retardation, 34*(2), 22-26.

WOLFENSBERGER, W. (1985). Social Role Valorization: A new insight, and a new term, for Normalization. *Australian Association for the Mentally Retarded Journal, 9*(1), 4-11.

WOLFENSBERGER, W. (1989). *The new genocide of handicapped and afflicted people.* Syracuse, NY: Syracuse University, Training Institute for Human Service Planning, Leadership and Change Agentry.

WOLFENSBERGER, W. (1991a). *A brief introduction to Social Role Valorization as a high-order concept for structuring human services.* Syracuse, NY: Syracuse University, Training Institute for Human Service Planning, Leadership and Change Agentry.

WOLFENSBERGER, W. (1991b). *Die Bewertung der sozialen Rollen: Eine kurze Einführung zur Bewertung der sozialen Rollen als Grundbegriff beim Aufbau von Sozialdiensten.* (C. Agad & A. Bianchet, trans.) Genf (Geneva), Schweiz (Switzerland): Éditions des Deux Continents.

WOLFENSBERGER, W. (1991c). *La Valorisation des Rôles Sociaux: Introduction à un concept de référence pour l'organisation des services.* (A. Dupont, V. Keller-Revaz, J.-P. Nicoletti & L. Vaney, trans.) Genève, Switzerland: Éditions des Deux Continents.

WOLFENSBERGER, W. (1991d). *La Valorizzazione del Ruolo Sociale: Una breve introduzione al concetto di valorizzazione del ruolo sociale inteso come concetto prioritario per la strutturazione dei servizi alle persone* (M. Costantino & A. Domina, trans.) Geneva, Switzerland: Éditions des Deux Continents.

WOLFENSBERGER, W. (1992). *A brief introduction to Social Role Valorization as a high-order concept for structuring human services* (2nd ed., rev.). Syracuse, NY: Syracuse University, Training Institute for Human Service Planning, Leadership and Change Agentry.

WOLFENSBERGER, W. (1995). An "if this, then that" formulation of decisions related to Social Role Valorization as a better way of interpreting it to people. *Mental Retardation, 33*(3), 163-169.

WOLFENSBERGER, W. (1998). *A brief introduction to Social Role Valorization as a high-order concept for addressing the plight of socially devalued people, and for structuring human services* (3rd ed., rev.). Syracuse, NY: Syracuse University, Training Institute for Human Service Planning, Leadership and Change Agentry .

WOLFENSBERGER, W., & THOMAS, S. (1994). An analysis of the client role from a Social Role Valorization perspective. *SRV-VRS: The International Social Role Valorization Journal/La Revue Internationale de la Valorisation des Rôles Sociaux, 1*(1), 3-8.

NOTES

1. This chapter has incorporated not only the presentation in Ottawa in May 1994, but also some SRV theory elements that were developed in early 1995.

2. Since this presentation was made in May 1994, there has been further conceptual development in SRV, including further refinements in the definition. As of 1998, the most current definition of SRV is "the application of what science has to tell us about the defense or upgrading of the socially perceived value of people's roles" (see Wolfensberger, 1998, p. 58).

3. In Wolfensberger (1998), a clearer distinction was made between the bad things that commonly happen to devalued people—the typical "wounds"—and the results or expressions of deep woundedness. See Wolfensberger, 1998, pp. 12-24.

4. The 1998 SRV monograph (Wolfensberger, 1998) contains a more elaborate version of this feedback loop (p. 75).

5. Since this presentation was given, there has been further thinking on the ways in which roles can be positively valorized. Six ways have now been identified, namely: (a) valorizing the roles that a party already holds; (b) averting the party's entry into (additional) devalued roles; (c) enabling the party to enter positively valued new roles, or to regain positively valued roles that were once held; (d) extricating a party from its current devalued roles; (e) reducing the negativity of the roles the party currently holds; and (f) substituting less devalued new roles for the more devalued roles a party currently holds. This is elaborated in Wolfensberger, 1998, pp. 84-95.

Part 3

Critical Perspectives on Normalization and Social Role Valorization

6

Capitalism, disability, and ideology: A materialist critique of the Normalization principle

MICHAEL J. OLIVER

1 INTRODUCTION

At the outset, I should say two things. I have no particular interest in the history of Normalization and, therefore, I am not attempting to provide a revisionist history of it. Neither do I think that Normalization, nor Social Role Valorization as it has become in its reincarnation, has much to offer in developing a social theory of disability. I am interested, however, in the oppression of disabled people in capitalist societies and what Normalization does, or rather does not, say about it.

This interest has led me to begin to sketch out what a social theory of disability might look like (Oliver, 1990). For me, all social theory must be judged on three interrelated elements: its adequacy in describing experience; its ability to explain experience; and, finally, its potential to transform experience. My own theorizing on disability is located in Marxist political economy, which, I would argue, offers a much more adequate basis for describing and explaining experience than does Normalization theory, which is based upon interactionist and functionalist sociology.

In fact I would go further and argue that the social theory that underpins Marxist political economy has far greater transformative potential in eradicating the oppression that disabled people face throughout the world than the interactionist and functionalist theories that underpin Normalization ever can have. And I will go even further than that and argue that already this theory has had a far greater influence on the struggles that disabled people are themselves currently engaged in to remove the chains of that oppression than Normalization, which is, at best, a bystander in these struggles and, at worst, part of the process of oppression itself.

In presenting this argument, I will begin by articulating my own theoretical position based upon Marxist political economy and hereinafter referred to as materialist theory. I will then demonstrate the inadequacies of Normalization theory's explanation of the rise of the institution before going on to provide a critique of the ideology that underpins it. Next, I will take issue with the argument that Normalization has been successful because it is based upon "experience." Finally, I will look at what both Normalization and materialist theories say about change, having briefly described the appalling material conditions under which disabled people live throughout the world.

Before proceeding further, it is perhaps necessary to explain the use of terminology in this chapter. Underpinning it is a materialist view of society; to say that the category "disability" is produced by capitalist society in a particular form implies a particular worldview. Within this worldview, the production of the category "disability" is no different from the production of motor cars or hamburgers. Each has an industry, whether it be the car, fast food, or human service. Each industry has a workforce that has a vested interest in producing their product in particular

163

ways and in exerting as much control over the process of production as possible.

2 PRODUCING A MATERIALIST THEORY OF DISABILITY

The production of disability, therefore, is nothing more or less than a set of activities specifically geared toward producing a good—the category "disability"—supported by a range of political actions that create the conditions to allow these productive activities to take place and underpinned by a discourse that gives legitimacy to the whole enterprise. As to the specifics of the terminology used in this discourse, I use the term "disabled people" generically and refuse to divide the group in terms of medical conditions, functional limitation, or severity of impairment. For me, disabled people are defined in terms of three criteria: (a) they have an impairment; (b) they experience oppression as a consequence; and (c) they identify themselves as disabled persons.

Using the generic term does not mean that I do not recognize differences in experience within the group, but that in exploring this we should start from the ways oppression differentially impacts on different groups of people rather than the differences in experience among individuals with different impairments. I agree that my own initial outlining of a materialist theory of disability (Oliver, 1990) did not specifically include an examination of the oppression that people with learning difficulties face (and I use this particular term throughout my paper because it is the one that democratic and accountable organizations of people with learning difficulties insist on).

Nevertheless, I agree that "For a rigorous theory of disability to emerge which begins to examine all disability in a materialist account, an analysis of Normalization must be included" (Chappell, 1992, p. 38).

Attempting to incorporate Normalization in a materialist account, however, does not mean that I believe that beyond the descriptive it is of much use. Based as it is upon functionalist and interactionist sociology, whose defects are well known (Gouldner, 1971), it offers no satisfactory explanation of why disabled people are oppressed in capitalist societies and no strategy for liberating us from the chains of that oppression.

Political economy, on the other hand, suggests that all phenomena (including social categories) are produced by the economic and social forces of capitalism itself. The forms in which they are produced are ultimately dependent upon their relationship to the economy (Marx, 1913). Hence, the category "disability" is produced in the particular form it appears by these very economic and social forces. Further, it is produced as an economic problem because of changes in the nature of work and the needs of the labor market within capitalism.

> The speed of factory work, the enforced discipline, the time-keeping and production norms—all these were a highly unfavorable change from the slower, more self-determined methods of work into which many handicapped people had been integrated. (Ryan & Thomas, 1980, p. 101)

The economy, through both the operation of the labor market and the social organization of work, plays a key role in producing the category "disability" and in determining societal responses to disabled people. In order to explain this further, it is necessary to return to the crucial question of what is meant by political economy. The following is a generally agreed definition of political economy:

> The study of the interrelationships between the polity, economy and society, or more specifically, the reciprocal influences among government . . . the economy, social classes, state, and status groups. The central problem of the political economy perspective is the manner in which the economy and polity interact in a relationship of reciprocal causation affecting the distribution of social goods. (Estes, Swan, & Gerard, 1982)

The central problem with such an agreed definition is that it is an explanation that can be incorporated into pluralist visions of society as a consensus emerging out of the interests of various groups and social forces and, indeed, this explanation has been encapsulated in a recent book on disability:

> A person's position in society affects the type and severity of physical disability one is likely to experience and more importantly the likelihood that he or she is likely to receive rehabilitation services. Indeed, the political economy of a community dictates what debilitating health conditions will be produced, how and under what circumstances they will be defined, and ultimately who will receive the services. (Albrecht, 1992, p. 14)

This quote lays out the way in which Albrecht pursues his argument in three parts. The first part shows how the kind of society people live in influences the kinds of disability that are produced, notably how the mode of production creates particular kinds of impairments. Further, he traces the ways in which the mode of production influences social interpretation and the meanings of disability and he also demonstrates how, in industrial societies, rehabilitation, like all other goods and services, is transformed into a commodity.

The second part of the argument shows how intermediate social institutions in America, such as the legal, political, and welfare systems, contribute to the specific way in which disability is produced, and their role in the transformation of rehabilitation into a commodity.

The final part considers what this may mean in terms of future developments in social policy and what effects it may have on the lives of disabled people.

It is difficult to disagree with this formulation at the descriptive level, but the problem with this pluralist version of political economy is that the structure of capitalist America itself goes unexamined as does the crucial role that the capitalist economy plays in shaping the experience of groups and individuals. Exactly the same criticism can be leveled at Normalization theory. Devaluation according to Normalization theory is a universal cognitive process, and economic and social conditions are only relevant to who gets devalued.

Political economy, as it is used here, takes a particular theoretical view of society, one that sees the economy as the crucial, and ultimately determining, factor in structuring the lives of groups and individuals. Further, while the relationship between various groups and the economy may differ in qualitative ways, the underlying structural relationship remains.

> The convergence and interaction of liberating forces at work in society against racism, sexism, ageism and economic imperialism are all oppressive "isms" and built-in responses of a society that considers certain groups inferior. All are rooted in the social-economic structures of society. All deprive certain groups of status, the right to control their own lives and destinies with the end result of powerlessness. All have resulted in economic and social discrimination. All rob (American) society of the energies and involvement of creative persons who are needed to make our society just and

humane. All have brought on individual alienation, despair, hostility, and anomie. (Walton, 1979, p. 9)

Hence, the oppression that disabled people face is rooted in the economic and social structures of capitalism. And this oppression is structured by racism, sexism, homophobia, ageism, and disablism, which is endemic to all capitalist societies and cannot be explained away as a universal cognitive process. To explain this further it is necessary to go back to the roots of capitalism itself.

3 DISABLED PEOPLE AND THE RISE OF CAPITALISM

Whatever the fate of disabled people before the advent of capitalist society and whatever their fate will be in the brave new world of the 21st century, with its coming we suffered economic and social exclusion. As a consequence of this exclusion, disability was produced in a particular form: as an individual problem requiring medical treatment.

At the heart of this exclusion was the institution—something on which we would all agree. In the 19th and 20th centuries, institutions proliferated in all industrial societies (Rothman, 1971) but to describe this, as Wolfensberger does, as "momentum without rationale" (Wolfensberger, chapter 3, p. 48) is patently absurd. The French Marxist Louis Althusser (1971) suggested that all capitalist societies are faced with the problem of social control, and they resolve this by a combination of repressive and ideological mechanisms.

The reason for the success of the institution is simple: It combines these mechanisms almost perfectly. It is repressive in that all those who either cannot or will not conform to the norms and discipline of capitalist society can be removed from it. It is ideological in that it stands as a visible monument for all those who currently conform but may not continue to do so—if you do not behave, the institution awaits you.

It is for this reason that the institution has been successful. Its presence perfectly meets capitalism's needs for discipline and control (Foucault, 1972). It is also the reason that, despite the fact that the defects of institutions have been known for the 200 years that they have existed, they have remained unaddressed. Indeed, the principle of "less eligibility" was central to the rise of the institution. It is simply not true to say that we have only known of their defects in recent years because, if this were the case, they would then not have been performing their ideological control function. Day trips to institutions, which originated in the 1850s, not the 1950s, were precisely for this purpose; to demonstrate how awful they were for the purposes of social control, not to educate the public about their reform (Wolfensberger, chapter 3, p. 50).

What is also not in dispute between us is that in the second half of the 20th century, the physical and ideological dominance of the institution began to decline (Scull, 1977). What is in dispute, however, is why this should be so. While not claiming that the Normalization principle was the only causal factor in what has become known as deinstitutionalization or decarceration, Wolfensberger (chapter 3) nonetheless claims that it "broke the back of the institutional movement" (p. 72) and without it "there would have been massive investments in building new, smaller, regionalized institutions" (p. 53). I would not wish to dismiss the role of ideas or, more appropriately, ideologies in this process, but there were other more important factors.

Most importantly, the rising costs of institutional care were becoming a major factor in the shift to community-based care. Ideology was turned into political action when this, along with other factors such as rising oil prices, spiraling arms expenditure, and so on, brought about fiscal crises in many capitalist states (O'Connor, 1973; Gough, 1979). This fiscal crisis explanation stands in stark contrast to Wolfensberger's (chapter 3) assertion that while deinstitutionalization may have started in the 1950s, it was a "drift that occurred without much planning, intent or consciousness" (p. 89).

The transition to late capitalism (the postindustrial society, as some writers have called it, or its more recent fashionable manifestation as postmodernity) has seen this process continue apace. The question it raises is what does this process mean. Cohen suggests that it "is thought by some to represent a questioning, even a radical reversal of that earlier transformation, by others merely to signify a continuation and intensification of its patterns" (1985, p. 13).

Those who have promoted the idea of Normalization would, I suspect, place themselves in the first camp. That is to say, the move from the

institution to the community is part of a process of removing some of the apparatus of social control by the state. I would place myself in the latter camp, seeing this move as an extension of the processes of control within the capitalist state.

After all, the balance of power between disabled people and professionals has not changed at all. The situation described by Cohen (1985) remains unchanged:

> much the same groups of experts are doing much the same business as usual. The basic rituals incorporated into the move to the mind—taking case histories, writing social enquiry reports, constructing files, organizing case conferences—are still being enacted (p. 152).

In the world of late capitalism, the same people, albeit with different job titles and perhaps in plusher buildings, are doing the same things to disabled people, although they may now be calling them "doing a needs-led assessment" or "producing a care plan" in Britain. Elsewhere it may be called individual program planning, social brokerage, change agentry, and the like. But the material fact remains, it is still professionals doing it, whatever "it" is called, to disabled peuple.

4 THE IDEOLOGY OF NORMALIZATION

All social changes require an ideology to support the economic rationality underpinning them. So the ideology underpinning the rise of the institution was ultimately a medical and a therapeutic one; accordingly, placing people in institutions was not only good for the health of individuals, it was also good for the health of society. Normalization, it could be argued, is the ideology (or one of the ideologies) that allowed people to be returned to the community in that they can be "normalized" or, in its later variant, be allocated normal (valued) social roles. After all, we do not want the different, the deviant, or even the dangerous returned to our communities.

I fully realize that here I am stepping on dangerous ground and that both Wolfensberger (chapter 3) and Nirje (1993) would probably argue that I am confusing normal with Normalization. There is not the space to demonstrate that I realize that this is not the case nor to draw attention to their own published ambiguities on this issue. Instead, I wish to point out that Normalization is part of a discourse that is predicated on the normal/abnormal distinction, and it is certainly clear that Wolfensberger (chapter 3) thinks this distinction is real rather than socially constructed (p. 88).

A materialist approach to this would suggest, as does the French philosopher Foucault (1973), that the way we talk about the world and the way we experience it are inextricably linked—the names we give to things shape our experience of them and our experience of things in the world influences the names we give to them. Hence, our practices of normalizing people and normalizing services both construct and maintain the normal/abnormal dichotomy.

It is becoming clear that the social structures of late capitalist societies cannot be discussed in a discourse of normality/abnormality because what characterizes them is difference: differences based on gender, ethnic background, sexual orientation, abilities, religious beliefs, wealth, age, access or nonaccess to work, and so on. And in societies founded on oppression, these differences crosscut and intersect each other in ways they we have not even begun to properly understand, let alone try to resolve (Zarb & Oliver, 1993).

The concept of simultaneous oppression (Stuart, 1993) may offer a more adequate way of understanding differences within the generic category of disability. Certainly, people are beginning to talk about their experience in this way.

> As a black disabled woman, I cannot compartmentalise or separate aspects of my identity in this way. The collective experience of my race, disability and gender are what shape and inform my life (Hill, 1994, p. 7).

Kirsten Hearn provides a poignant account of how disabled lesbians and gay men are excluded from all their potential communities. First, "the severely able-bodied community and straight disabled community virtually ignored our campaign" (1991, p. 30) and, "issues of equality are not fashionable for the majority of the severely able-bodied, white, middle-class lesbian and gay communities" (1991, p. 33).

The point that I am making is that the discourse of Normalization (whatever the intent of its major proponents and however badly they feel it has been misused by its disciples) can never adequately describe or explain societies characterized by difference because of its reductionist views of both humanity and society. Individual and group differences cannot be described solely in terms of the normality/abnormality dichotomy, and inegalitarian social structures cannot be explained by reference only to valued and devalued social roles. Normalization can also never serve to transform peoples' lives, a point to which I shall return.

5 THE ROLE OF EXPERIENCE

In explaining why the idea of Normalization was so powerful for many people, Wolfensberger (chapter 3) claims that it connected with their common sense, it gave them a language or discourse in which to talk about the issues, and it gave them a "unified mental scheme" (social theory) connecting a range of issues (p. 72). Of course, in talking about this he is talking about the connection of these ideas to the experience of academics, professionals, and policy makers, not to the experience of people with learning difficulties.

He also claims that "a single theory or principle could be applied to all; not only to all retarded people and not only to all handicapped people but to all deviant ones" (p. 71). I remember attending the first conference on Normalization in Britain in the mid-1970s when such claims were made. A colleague and I vociferously denied the claim that the half-digested mishmash of functionalist and interactionist sociology we were being presented with had anything to do with our experiences as disabled people.

Our claims were, of course, denied, as they often have been in the past, on the grounds that as isolated, elite disabled individuals, our experiences did not accord with those of the majority of disabled people (a basis on which you may wish to deny my claims in this paper). And, of course, the Normalization bandwagon rolled on in Britain, into social service departments, health authorities, and undemocratic voluntary organizations. But not into the newly emerging democratic and accountable organizations that disabled people were setting up at the time. To this day, not a single one of these organizations of disabled people has adopted the Normalization principle as the basis for its operations or as a rationale for its existence.

Our experiences at that conference mirrored our experience in terms of disability politics more generally. We were already being told by groups of able-bodied experts that not only did they know best what our problems were, they also knew best how to solve them. And disabled people were developing our own views both on those experts who wished to define or colonize our experience and to identify what our problems really were. These views were encapsulated in "a little red book" called *Fundamental Principles of Disability* (UPIAS, 1976), which, I would argue, is far more important for disabled people than all the publications on Normalization put together.

This slim volume is not widely available, but the debt that disabled people owe to it is enormous. I, and many other disabled people, openly acknowledge our debt to the document in the way it shaped our own understanding of disability (Oliver, 1995). Because the document has never been widely available, and with the demise of the Union in 1991, it will become increasingly difficult to obtain. I reproduce two passages here, the first of which exposes the role of "experts" in our lives and the second which defines our own problems for us.

> The Union maintains that, far from being too concerned with the cause of disability, the "experts" in the field have never concerned themselves with the real cause at all. The fact that they had delusions that they were looking at the cause, when they were typically concentrating on its effects, on confusing disability with physical impairment, underlines the imperative need for disabled people to become their own experts. It is only when we begin to grasp this expertise that disabled people will be able to see through the "experts'" attempt to disguise as something "entirely different" the traditional, clearly failed, "spontaneous" struggle against aspects of disability, such as poverty.

> Disability is something imposed on top of our impairments by the way we are unnecessarily isolated and excluded from full participation in society. Disabled people are therefore an oppressed group in society. To understand this it is necessary to grasp the distinction between the physical impairment and the social situation, called 'disability,' of people with such impairment. Thus we define impairment as lacking part of or all of a limb, or having a defective limb, organ or mechanism of the body; and disability as the disadvantage or restriction of activity caused by a contemporary social organization which takes no or little account of people who have physical impairments and thus excludes them from participation in the mainstream of social activities. Physical disability is therefore a particular form of social oppression.

It was from this work that I and a number of other disabled people began to write and talk about the social model of disability. For my own part, I originally conceptualized models of disability as the binary distinction between what I chose to call the individual and social models of disability (Oliver, 1983). This was no amazing new insight on my part dreamed up in some ivory tower, but was really an attempt to enable me to make sense of the world for the social work students and other professionals I was teaching at the time. The idea of the individual and the social model was taken quite simply and explicitly from the distinction originally made between impairment and disability by the Union of the Physically Impaired Against Segregation in the *Fundamental Principles* document (1976).

The articulation of this new view of disability did not receive universal acceptance. Originally, it was professionals, policy makers, and staff from organizations for disabled people who, because they had vested interests in maintaining the status quo underpinned by the individual model, questioned the experiential validity and explanatory reliability of the social model. However, we have seen a paradigm shift, and many professional bodies and groups have now come to espouse the social model, in theory at least (DHSS, 1988; Gillespie-Sells & Campbell, 1991). Whether it has had much impact on professional practice is another question altogether and beyond the scope of this paper.

The articulation of the social model was received much more enthusiastically by disabled people because it made an immediate connection to their own experiences. It quickly became the basis for disability awareness and later disability equality training.

It was adopted by democratic disability organizations all over the world, including Disabled Peoples International (DPI) and the British Council of Organizations of Disabled People (BCODP), and remains central to their rationale.

In reading Wolfensberger's (chapter 3) comments about how *Changing Patterns* came to be written, I am struck by just how much in the way of economic resources (plane tickets, hotel bookings, secretarial support, etc.) went in to producing it. Similarly the World Health Organization has spent millions of pounds, dollars, and yen on trying to describe and classify us (Wood, 1980) and has lamentably failed.

Disabled people, whose intellectual labors have produced the social model, have done this without access to the kinds of resources available to international academic superstars, professionals, and policy makers, as well as the usual coterie of hangers-on and freeloaders. Imagine how much farther down the road we might be if disabled people had been given these resources to develop our own social theory, our own quality measures for human services, and our own classification schemes.

6 THE MATERIAL CONDITIONS OF DISABLED PEOPLE THROUGHOUT THE WORLD

Developing materialist theory with respect to disability requires us to understand the material conditions under which disabled people live throughout the world. A recent UN report (Despouy, 1991) has confirmed earlier estimates that there are more than 500 million impaired persons in the world; that is 1 in 10 of the world's population. The report goes on to suggest that at least "25 per cent of the entire population are adversely affected by the presence of disabilities."

There have been very few international studies of the lives of disabled people although the UN report did come to the following conclusion:

these persons frequently live in deplorable conditions, owing to the presence of physical and social barriers which prevent their integration and full participation in the community. As a result, millions of disabled people throughout the world are segregated and deprived of virtually all their rights, and lead a wretched, marginal life. (Despouy, 1991, p. 1)

It is possible to put some descriptive flesh on the bones of these figures, and what follows relies heavily on figures present in a recent special edition of the *New Internationalist* called "Disabled Lives" (1992).

Of the 500 million disabled people in the world, 300 million live in developing countries, and of these 140 million are children and 160 million are women. One in 5, that is 100 million of the total population of disabled people, are disabled by malnutrition. In the developing countries, only 1 in 100 disabled people have access to any form of rehabilitation and 80% of all disabled people live in Asia and the Pacific, but they receive just 2% of the total resources allocated to disabled people. In the Third World, the death rate of people with a spinal injury within 2 years of the injury is as high today as it was in the developed world before the Second World War.

While not being able to put an accurate figure onto it, there is no doubt that all over the world, there is a close link between disability and poverty.

malnutrition, mothers weakened by frequent childbirth, inadequate immunisation programmes, accidents in overcrowded homes, all contribute to an incidence of disability among poor people that is higher than among people living in easier circumstances. Furthermore, disability creates and exacerbates poverty by increasing isolation and economic strain, not just for the individual but for the family: there is little doubt that disabled people are amongst the poorest in poor countries. (Coleridge, 1993, p. 64)

While in an absolute sense, the material conditions of disabled people in the developed world are vastly superior to their Third World counterparts, they still experience conditions of life far inferior to the rest of the population. Thus, for example, more than 60% of disabled people in both Britain and America currently live below the poverty line.

Labor markets in the developed world continue to discriminate to the point where disabled people are three times more likely to be unemployed than their able-bodied counterparts. In education, the majority of disabled children are still educated in segregated special schools and less than 3 in 1,000 disabled students end up in higher education, when, according to prevalence figures, it should be 100. On any indicator, disabled women and black disabled people fare worse than their white, male counterparts.

While the accuracy of some of these figures might be called into question with respect to both the developed and developing world, no one would deny that they paint an authentic picture of the lives of disabled people throughout the world. The point at issue is what can be done about producing the necessary changes. In the next section, I shall discuss the different positions of Normalization and materialist theories with respect to producing changes in the lives of disabled peuple.

7 ECONOMIC, POLITICAL, AND SOCIAL CHANGE—HOW WILL IT BE DELIVERED?

In comparing what Normalization and materialist theory have to offer with respect to these changes, I want to concentrate on three interrelated areas: change in individuals, change in social policy and welfare programs, and change through the political process.

Partly, I suspect, because of the unacknowledged impact that the social model has had, both Nirje and Wolfensberger are anxious to claim that Normalization does not mean making individuals normal. They go further and suggest that it can be applied even more fruitfully to environments. Wolfensberger, however, honestly admits that

> as long as one grants that abnormalization abnormalizes a person, and not just the person's environment, . . . one cannot say that Normalization only normalizes life conditions . . . In short, I cannot see how Nirje's formulation allows an exclusion of actions on a person (chapter 3, p. 88).

It is the final sentence which raises issues of grave concern. The history of oppression is underpinned by allowing "actions on persons," and the crucial questions this raises are who decides, what actions, and which persons? To answer, as Normalization does, that prevailing life conditions, environments, and values are the ones into which to normalize individuals, begs huge questions and may take us down the road to death making, sterilization, physical torture, incarceration, and mind control. This list is part of our collective history as disabled people, as we are discovering as we begin to write this history, and not some emotive or exaggerated imagining to make a political point (Morris, 1991; Coleridge, 1993).

Materialist theory does not have the same problem with changing individuals, although it is their consciousness that it wants to change, not their bodies, their behavior, or their social roles. Transforming

consciousness is a matter of changing personal experiences into political issues. This materialist theory does, and it also links the two: At the collective level, disabled people may "false consciously" believe that the difficulties they face are because of their individual impairments. Hence they "internalize oppression" (Sutherland, 1981; Morris, 1991) by believing that it is their fault that they cannot get a job, use public transport, and so on.

Social and individual transformations are inextricably linked. However, in materialist theory individuals must transform themselves through collective action, not be transformed by others who know what's best for them or what's best for society. Empowerment is a collective process of transformation on which the powerless embark as part of the struggle to resist the oppression of others, as part of their demands to be included, and/or to articulate their own views of the world. Central to this struggle is the recognition by the powerless that they are oppressed—first articulated with respect to disability by the Union of the Physically Impaired Against Segregation in the 1970s and more recently been given a theoretical reformulation within "oppression theory" more generally (Abberley, 1987).

Normalization theory sees improving human services as a major platform for improving the quality of life for disabled people, and, indeed, much time and energy is devoted to precisely this. Wolfensberger's position on this is unequivocal; he is vehemently opposed to services provided by institutions but has spent much of his working life developing and improving community-based services. As I suggested earlier, this is because he views community-based services as radically different from institutional ones in that they are not part of the social control apparatus of the state.

While his position on community-based human services may be unequivocal, it is certainly contradictory. In the paper he gave at the International Disability Conference in Bristol, in 1987, he came very close to taking a materialist position on all human services, not simply institutional ones, when he argued that their real purpose (latent function) was to provide employment for the middle classes, and in order to continue to do that,

> merely enlarging the human service empire is not sufficient to meet all the requirements that a post-

primary production economy poses. In addition, one has to make all the services that do exist as unproductive as possible—indeed one has to make them counterproductive if at all possible, so that they create dependency, and so that they create impaired people rather than habilitate them (Wolfensberger, 1989, p. 34).

The problem with this formulation is that it mistakes the symptom for the problem. If human services under capitalism are part of the state apparatus of social control, as materialist theory would argue, the reason they employ the middle classes is simple: They are not the groups who pose a threat to capitalism and, therefore, they do not need to be controlled, but instead can become agents for the control of others.

It is precisely for this reason that the demands of disabled people all over the world are not, any longer, for improvements in existing services but for control over them. And, further, their struggles around welfare issues are about producing and controlling their own services through centers for independent living, direct payments to enable them to purchase these services for themselves, and peer counseling to enable them to develop the necessary skills and support to meet their own self-defined individual and collective needs. This is not an antiwelfare or antihuman-services position, but one that raises fundamental issues of who is in control and in whose interest.

In looking at the issue of political change, within Normalization theory it is difficult to find anything beyond descriptions of the kinds of things devalued people should be entitled to. How to achieve these entitlements at the political level is not really discussed although Wolfensberger (chapter 3) confidently asserts that if we want to valorize someone's social roles "we know from social science what the overarching strategies are through which this can be accomplished *if* that is what one wants to pursue" (p. 88).

I don't know what social science he is referring to, but I have to say that I know very few social scientists who are, any longer, convinced that the concept of social roles has very much value to the development of social theory let alone for the promotion of political action. Not only are Talcott Parsons and Erving Goffman dead in a material sense but so are their products, the macro and micro versions of role theory. One can only assume from Normalization writings that political change will be a gift from the powerful to

powerless once they have come to a true understanding of disability through exposure to the teachings of Normalization and Social Role Valorization. Nowhere does Normalization acknowledge that

> the conviction that one's group is worth fighting for has to come at least partly from within. The alternative is to wait passively for the advantaged group to confer limited equality which does not essentially alter the status quo, and which it may be motivated to avoid. (Dalley, 1992, p. 128)

Again, materialist theory is much more upfront about political change. It will only be achieved through struggle, and that struggle will be by oppressed groups themselves against the forces that oppress them. In order to do this, it is necessary for oppressed groups to organize collectively to confront this oppression. That inevitably means confrontation and conflict with powerful groups, interests, and structures, for there are few examples in human history of people willingly giving up power to others.

As far as disabled people are concerned, we have seen over the past 15 years disabled people coming together to organize themselves as a movement at local, national, and international levels. In Britain, for example, in order to harness this growing consciousness of disabled people, to provide a platform to articulate the redefinition of the problem of disability, and to give a focus to the campaigns for independent living and against discrimination, the British Council of Organizations of Disabled People (BCODP) was formed in 1981, and its success in the subsequent decade is entirely an achievement of disabled people themselves (Hasler, 1993). Its conception and subsequent development have been achieved without extensive financial support from government or from traditional organizations for disabled people. On the contrary, the BCODP was criticized from the start as being elitist, isolationist, unrepresentative, and Marxist by a collection of unrepresentative people with abilities, right- and left-wing academics, isolated and elitist staff and management of traditional organizations, and many professionals whose very careers were bound up with keeping disabled people dependent.

Yet despite these attacks, BCODP has gone from strength to strength, now representing over 90 organizations of disabled people and 300,000 disabled individuals. These initiatives not only established BCODP as the only representative voice of disabled people in Britain, but by its very success it stimulated an ever growing number of disabled people to adopt a disabled identity. Similar stories of the rise of the disability movement could be told from other parts of both the developing and the developed worlds.

With this growing sense of a collective, political identity has developed the self-confidence not simply to ask for the necessary changes, but to demand them and to use a whole range of tactics, including direct action and civil disobedience. What's more, this movement is democratic and accountable to disabled people themselves (Dreidger, 1988; Oliver, 1990; Davis, 1993) and its collective voice is demanding that we be included in our societies everywhere by ending the oppression that confronts us, not by offering us and our oppressors Normalization or Social Role Valorization programs.

8 CONCLUSION

In this paper I have argued that Normalization as a social theory is inadequate in that it does not describe experience satisfactorily, that its explanation of why disabled people have the kinds of experiences they do is wholly inadequate, and that its potential for transforming those experiences to something better is limited. It is not only those unsympathetic to Normalization who question its future, however.

> What does Normalisation now have to do in order to be a positive force for change in the 1990s? The answer may lie in going back to its roots and realigning itself in relation to other sociological theories (Brown & Smith, 1992, p. 176).

Whether such a realignment, even with materialist theory, is likely to resuscitate Normalization is itself doubtful, because what is at stake is a vision of the kind of society we would like to live in. Normalization theory offers disabled people the opportunity to be given valued social roles in an unequal society that values some roles more than others. Materialist social theory offers disabled people the opportunity to transform their own lives and in so doing to transform the society in which they live into one in which all roles are valued. As a disabled person, I know which of those choices I prefer, and I also know which most of the disabled people I meet prefer.

REFERENCES

ABBERLEY, P. (1987). The concept of oppression and the development of a social theory of disability. *Disability, Handicap And Society*, 2(1), pp. 5-19.

ALBRECHT, G. (1992). *The disability business.* London: Sage.

ALTHUSSER, L. (1971). *Lenin and philosophy and other essays.* London: New Left Books.

BROWN, H., & SMITH, H. (Eds.). (1992). *Normalization: A reader for the nineties.* London: Routledge.

CHAPPELL, A. (1992). Towards a sociological critique of the Normalisation principle. *Disability, Handicap and Society, 7*(1).

COHEN, S. (1985). *Visions of social control.* Oxford: Polity Press.

COLERIDGE, P. (1993). *Disability, liberation and development.* Oxford: Oxfam Publications.

DALLEY, G. (1992). Social welfare ideologies and Normalization: Links and conflicts. In H. BROWN & H. SMITH, (Eds.), *Normalisation: A reader for the nineties.* London: Routledge.

DAVIS, K. (1993). On the movement. In J. SWAIN, V. FINKELSTEIN, S. FRENCH, & M. OLIVER, *Disabling barriers—Enabling environments.* London: Sage.

DESPOUY, L. (1991). *Human rights and disability.* New York: United Nations Economic and Social Council.

DHSS. (1988). *A wider vision.* London: HMSO.

DISABLED LIVES. (1992, July). *New Internationalist, 233.*

DREIDGER, D. (1988). *The last civil rights movement.* London: Hurst and Co.

ESTES, C., SWAN, J. & GERARD, L. (1982). Dominant and competing paradigms in gerontology: Towards a political economy of ageing. *Ageing and Society, 2* (2).

FOUCAULT, M. (1972). *The archaeology of knowledge.* New York: Pantheon.

FOUCAULT, M. (1973). *The birth of the clinic.* London: Tavistock.

GILLESPIE-SELLS, C., & CAMPBELL, J. (1991). *Disability equality training: Trainers guide.* London: CCETSW.

GOUGH, I. (1979). *The political economy of the welfare state.* Basingstoke: MacMillan.

GOULDNER, A. (1971). *The coming crisis in western sociology.* London: Heinemann.

HASLER, F. (1993). Developments in the Disabled People's Movement. In J. SWAIN, V. FINKELSTEIN, S. FRENCH, & M. OLIVER, *Disabling barriers—enabling environments.* London: Sage.

HEARN, K. (1991). Disabled lesbians and gays are here to stay. In T. KAUFMAN, & P. LINCOLN, (Eds.), *High risk lives: Lesbian and gay politics after the clause.* Bridgeport: Prism Press.

HILL, M. (1994, March). Getting things right. *Community Care Inside, 31.*

MARX, K. (1913). *A contribution to the critique of political economy.* Chicago: Chicago Press.

MORRIS, J. (1991). *Pride against prejudice.* London: Women's Press.

NIRJE, B. (1993). *The Normalization Principle—25 years later.* Finland: The Institute for Educational Research.

O'CONNOR, J. (1973). *The fiscal crisis of the state.* New York: St. Martin's Press.

OLIVER, M. (1983). *Social work with disabled people.* Basingstoke: MacMillan.

OLIVER, M. (1990). *The politics of disablement.*

Basingstoke: MacMilla

OLIVER, M. (1995). *Unders theory to practice.* Basi

RYAN, J. & THOMAS, F. *mental handicap.* Harm

ROTHMAN, D. (1971). *The* Boston: Little Brown.

SCULL, A. (1977). *De-ca _____unity treatment and the deviant—A radical view.* New York: Prentice-Hall.

STUART, O. (1993). Double oppression: An appropriate starting-point? In J. SWAIN, V. FINKELSTEIN, S. FRENCH, & M. OLIVER, *Disabling barriers—Enabling environments.* London: Sage.

SUTHERLAND, A. (1981). *Disabled we stand.* London: Souvenir Press.

SWAIN, J., FINKELSTEIN, V., FRENCH, S. & OLIVER, M. (1993). *Disabling barriers—Enabling environments.* London: Sage.

UNION OF THE PHYSICALLY IMPAIRED AGAINST SEGREGATION (UPIAS). (1976). *Fundamental principles of disability.* London: Author.

WALTON, J. (1979). Urban political economy. *Comparative Urban Research.*

WOLFENSBERGER, W. (1989). Human service policies: The rhetoric versus the reality. In L. Barton, (Ed.), *Disability and dependency.* Sussex: Falmer Press.

WOOD, P. (1980). *International classification of impairments, disabilities and handicaps.* Geneva: World Health Organization.

ZARB, G., & OLIVER, M. (1993). *Ageing with a disability: What do they expect after all these years?* London: University of Greenwich.

7

Response to Professor Michael Oliver

WOLF WOLFENSBERGER

(To Professor Oliver:) I have put all my comments about your comments on little red cards. I am well prepared, you see. Would you like to have some? Are they red enough?

There are some comments I want to make first, not because they are the most important ones but because they are relevant to the foregoing discussions. I happen to believe that there are a lot of universals in reality, both in the universe generally and in human experience: enduring laws, regularities, dynamics, and things that happen over and over with universal lawfulness. One such universal consists of certain regularities and patterning in human perception that are not just temporary, ad hoc, or culture-bound constructions. I was particularly struck with that when I studied the history of mental retardation and looked at people's ideas about low intellectuality—in essence, stupidity—over the millennia and across many, many cultures. I found several recurring—and even universal—patterns of perceiving low intellectuality, and of thinking about it. People did not possess terms such as "mental retardation" and "mental deficiency," nor did they have any number of other terms and fine distinctions of classification that we now have, nor did they have our scientific knowledge on this issue. But what all did have was language for stupidity—and it was a very stable kind of language so that in some cultures, the same words were used for long, long periods, perhaps 1,000 years or more. Contrary to what some texts tell us, people were quite capable of identifying—and discoursing on—people of low intelligence.

Furthermore, the images of, and the icons for, low intelligence also seem to have much that is universal to the human mind. For instance, the distinction between an object being sharp (like a knife) or dull is one you will find applied as a simile to intellect in language after language. Other such images found over and over include those of slowness and low viscosity. Apparently, most of these images have a basis in concrete sensory experience and were then made into something like similes or metaphors that were applied symbolically to stupidity. One other universal image of low intellectuality that befell people from childhood on—what we now call mental retardation—was that of slow mental growth, childishness, and the eternal child.

I also happen to believe that there will always be social devaluation and devalued people—in other words, that this is also a universal. *Who* it is that gets devalued, may be different from culture to culture and time to time. But *how* persons get treated once they become devalued, has remarkable universality to it across time and across cultures, and I am afraid that the negative descriptions that Professor Oliver decried—and rightly so—are, however, in good part built into the human perceptual process and cannot be talked away. We have to combat them because they are hurtful and destructive, and we can do better, but I believe that the tendency to engage in this sort of thing is built into the human mind.

So the poor "quality of life" of physically handicapped people that was mentioned does not exist because they are physically impaired, but because they are devalued by others. If one were valued, one could have all sorts of impairments and yet not experience subjectively what is now called "poor quality of life." (By the way, "quality of life" is another of the presently popular terms that I do not use in my own language.)

So I believe that people are quite capable of perceiving all sorts of differences among human beings, though they may differ in how they value or interpret these differences. In fact, the perception of human differences also seems to have a certain hard-wired element to it. One of many reasons, I believe, is that there is something hard-wired in the human mind about ideas of contagion, contagious things, and contagious people that is, in fact, biologically adaptive and protective. There is actually empirical evidence for this belief. This should not be surprising in light of the fact that even many animal species display conspecific preferences—positive or negative—toward features of appearance.

Whenever we deal with universals, these tend to resist attempts to restrict or deny them with language, or to nail them down with one definite or technical term that does not correspond fully or adequately to people's phenomenological experience of them: People perceive and in their minds know about what it is that they are observing. This keeps popping up with such regularity that we can draw an analogy to the phenomenon of "regression to the mean," to pigs rooting the moment you quit beating them for it, and to cats acting like cats the moment the cat trainer relaxes the training routines. So I am a little skeptical of any Rumpelstiltskin-type attempt to control people's minds entirely through language, as powerful as language might be in controlling perception and thought. I am convinced that there are some things that are going to defy attempts at imprisoning or "enjailing," and certain perceptions of human characteristics and phenomena are of a nature that *will* keep breaking out. For instance, anyone who really understands human nature and is reconciled to reality knows that humans will never abandon ideas about what is attractive in other humans, and especially in members of the opposite sex. Yet I thought that such enjailing attempts were

manifested by the way Professor Oliver used the term "disability."

Now we go to another topic. I felt a little bit like Marc Gold, who wrote a book (1980) with the title *Did I Say That?* I did not recognize myself, my writings, and my teachings in a lot of things Professor Oliver said, and a lot of people here who have been to a lot of teachings that I have given probably feel the same way. That puts me at a great disadvantage, as I hardly even know in this context where to start responding. Some things he had quite right, and could have been quoting what I had written; other things were either incorrectly attributed or incorrect interpretations. However, a big, big problem—on which we need to be very clear and which goes far beyond Professor Oliver and myself, and which is a crucial issue for SRV and for a lot of other debates—is which niveau of critique or discourse we apply to an issue.

We need to be clear that Professor Oliver has presented a critique on the religious niveau. He has expressed a worldview that is above the level of social science—a de facto religion based on assumptions of what the universe, the cosmos, human nature, relationships, and so on, are about. He has declared himself to be an adherent of the supra-empirical religion that I consider to be not only invalid, but also utopian and naive. It is, and historically has been, attended by perfectionism ideas and perfectionism cults, all of which have failed so far. But the same is true of many other religions that preach that humans are going to perfect society. Note a peculiar, illogical feedback loop here that is found in Marxism, namely, that all these people who are so imperfect as individuals are somehow going to get together and form a perfect collectivity. That is one of the things that I consider to be not only invalid, but an outright naive circularity. And in many quarters these days—in the political correctness (PC) circles particularly, but even beyond them, in the mind of modernism generally—there has been a tendency to exalt will and want: "What I would like" or "what I feel like" or "what I wish things were like" is almost the way people think that things really are or are really going to be. So in PC ideology, we see many denials of the most fundamental aspects of reality, and, above all, we see a never-ending denial of the most basic realities of human nature.

Now, as part of Professor Oliver's Marxist critique (which more recently has begun to be called materialistic critique), we have been told that human social organization is governed by economics. Again, I consider that a naïveté. What I have taught is that how people relate to each other will be very heavily influenced by what is in their minds. So whatever one can do or does to put things in people's minds, one will get bad things back, as in "garbage in, garbage out." Good things put into the mind, will yield good—or at least less worse—things coming back out. And there are many, many ways other than through economics to put things in people's minds. Why is that hard to see?

Now, more on the level of discourse. Professor Oliver has declared his religion, everybody finds that in order, and once it is on the table, we can talk about it. But not all religions are considered equally acceptable for debate, and that puts me at a disadvantage. If I talked about my religion, many people would be deeply offended, though other people with other religions would be granted the scope to critique the world of theories in terms of their religion. All this becomes even more problematic when a theory that is essentially a social science theory is critiqued from a religious niveau. That would be appropriate if the religious concept had something to say about particular social science theory, such as whether it is valid, or whether it is concordant with the religion at issue even if it is not valid, and so on. But a social science theory is in no position to critique a religion, as I believe all the epistemologists would agree. Even a very high-level social science theory is at a lower level, and you are only to critique one religion with another religion. Now you see, that is one of my dilemmas: How do I respond to Professor Oliver's religion when he invokes it to critique my social-science theory?

Well, let me first say a bit more about his religion. Materialistic religions have a basic dilemma, and that is: From where are they going to get a morality? If there is nothing but a materialistic world, you are going to have either a materialist morality—or no morality. And in my opinion, if one were coherent as a materialist, one would say there is no morality: There is only force, there is violence, and the stronger force prevails. At best, morality consists of a utilitarian set of social conventions for dealing with material reality, including other people. That is the logical ethics of materialism. Admittedly, there have been many attempts to construct higher-level material moralities. They have all failed, and they are actually kind of ridiculous. For instance, attempts to form a morality on the basis of a materialistic biology led to social Darwinism, which led to eugenics, which led to the Nazi killing of the handicapped—a Nietzschean sort of materialistic power morality. There is a lot of logic to that when you are a materialist. Many, many other kinds of material moralities have been attempted, and as I say, I think they are all naive, and they have certainly not been successful; in fact, they have been less successful than moralities derived from any number of other religions, including some that I consider invalid.

Now, to profess my religion: It is that of a Christian personalist anarchist. I feel rather frustrated trying to tell you what that is because it would take a lot of time, and most people would not understand it readily even then. At any rate, from my religious viewpoint, social stratification is assumed to be a universal. It will always be there, at all times and in all places. It makes no difference who is on top: whether the communists or the capitalists, kings or tribal chiefs, there is going to be a stratification of power, of command, of control—yes, in part, of economics too, but even more of power than of economics. Even the smallest new collectivities will stratify very quickly, including collectivities in which economic exchange and control play no part. When you overthrow one tyrannical stratification, what you get is just a new stratification. In any of the stratifications, the people on top are going to oppress and lord it over those on the bottom. This is what my religion informs me—and, by the way, I am relieved to be able to report that this religious belief happens to be totally consistent with a universal historical empiricism, which is not the case for a lot of other religions that are utopian, such as Marxism.

My religion says that in the context of this kind of stratificatory reality, one should ally oneself in empathy with the oppressed, the lowly, and the weakest party. One does not necessarily embrace their values, or what they say, nor necessarily their goals, which might be contrary to one's own religion, such as when they pursue the violent overthrow of the oppressors and the creation of a new and different oppressive stratification. But one does stand against whatever oppression exits at the moment. And should that oppression ever be somehow terminated (which does not happen very frequently), then one must be immediately ready to ally oneself with the new oppressed class, and against the new oppressors. Often, the oppressed under the new system are the same kinds of people as the oppressed under the previous system, but sometimes not. Maybe those who were on top will now be oppressed by those who were once the oppressed, and now one must be standing by those who once were the oppressors because now there is going to be oppressive warfare made against them.

From that perspective, I think it is extremely naive to look to Caesar for relief from oppression. Do not put your trust in princes! Caesar is always the imperial power, or is allied to it, and you will never get genuine relief from it. By definition, there will always be lowly people on the bottom, and Caesar is a major part of the control mechanism from the top. People who very naively look to Caesar for salvation will be betrayed by their idol because all idols will eventually betray their worshippers; and, in between, they will usually demand human sacrifices. So, if one expects that one can go to Caesar and get public funding for the lowly in a way that will do them a lot of good, this does not make any sense. Either Caesar is not going to fund something that is genuinely good for the lowly (maybe we think it is, but there is a catch built in that is bad for the lowly that we have not seen yet, some perversion that will soon surface), or there are strings attached. If you want something that has to do with funds without strings attached, do not ask the state, do not ask Caesar; that you have got to ask your fellow human beings to give freely. You simply cannot expect to be given money from taxes without social policy attached. You are never going to get it, ever. And again, it mystifies me how anybody can think that it can be otherwise. And the social policy that will be attached to public money will ever and always have imperial identity, with minor exceptions that often are there by accident, or for imperial purposes of image-detoxification and deception, comparable to the so-called loss leaders in advertisement, that is, the items advertised that are sold below cost in order to hook in customers. (One would think that the above logic would make anarchists of all thoughtful moral actors.)

In this connection, I want to tell those of you who put so much hope into the new situation in South Africa that I do not think you have pinched yourselves yet, or done so in the right parts of your anatomy. In all likelihood, based on the way human beings are, you are going to see bloodshed—possibly worse than anything that preceded it under the Boer and Caucasian management. You will probably see events comparable to those in Rwanda, and maybe worse, and I would like to have on record all the current utopian exclamations of how wonderful things will be in South Africa, because so often, later on, when reality overtakes wishful thinking, people deny that they believed or said these things.

And that brings me to the issue of violence. As a Christian personalist anarchist, I do not believe in violence and force by anyone, against anyone, for any purpose, or by any means. My anarchism is different from most other anarchists' anarchism in that it is not one that seeks to destroy power with violence and force, but one that calls for taking a nonviolent position against it regardless of what happens to one, fully aware that one will be persecuted, and that in a certain sense of *realpolitik,* one will be defeated. Those with the swords will use their swords, but the victory of the people who embrace nonviolence for moral and religious reasons is in another realm—a moral and spiritual realm, which is much "realer" and more enduring.

Also, there are never going to be armies of handicapped people with planes, guns and cannons, and in control of the food depots in a chaotic world. There are not going to be any large and/or long-lasting coalitions among all sorts of devalued groups with each other—because they devalue each other too much, which is a universal. Hopes or predictions to the contrary are once again fantasies (including Marxist ones), and come with the kinds of false promises that all idolatries make, but that will inevitably end in a betrayal by the idols. Neither what Professor Oliver would like to see will happen, nor what I would like to see.

Decades ago before my worldview had matured, I thought Normalization was going to "win," or something like that, but not for very long. That change in view was, in fact, one of the reasons why I became treated as an alien in my field, as I told you this morning. What I want, and what Normalization/SRV or any number of other things might achieve, or even what my religion would tell me we should want for this earth and its people, is not going to happen. This is a dysfunctional—I would say a fallen—world. It is imperfect, it will remain imperfect, human beings will remain imperfect, violence is laid not only into our bodies but also our souls, incoherency is laid in our minds and identity, and we are going to oppress. As individuals, we can and should strive to minimize and oppose these impulses in ourselves and others, to behave as moral actors, assuming a personal moral responsibility for one's behavior regardless of whether others also do so, and regardless of what happens, usually opposing oppression but sometimes stepping aside when both opposed parties are deeply in the wrong. But there are not going to be utopian solutions, no nirvanas, no problems laid forever to rest, and only the most fleeting occasional abeyance in oppressive social stratification.

REFERENCE

GOLD, M. (1980). *"Did I say that?": Articles and commentary on the "try another way" system.* Champaign, IL: Research Press.

8

The original "Scandinavian" Normalization principle and its continuing relevance for the 1990s

BURT PERRIN

1 INTRODUCTION

The Normalization principle emerged from Scandinavia in the late 1960s. It was first published and circulated in 1969 (Nirje, 1969). Since then, it has had a profound effect around the world. It has greatly advanced opportunities for *all* people, including people with a mental handicap as well as with other forms of disabilities, to be able to live in the community on the same basis as everyone else. It has also served to redirect social policies and the nature of service provision in order to make "normal" living possible.

This paper discusses the nature of the Normalization principle, as it originally emerged from Scandinavia, along with its major characteristics and implications. The principle has been subject to numerous misinterpretations, as well as confusion with the version of Normalization (and its successor, Social Role Valorization) later developed by Wolfensberger (see Perrin and Nirje, 1985, for a more comprehensive discussion of misconceptions of the Normalization principle). Thus where it will help in clarification, it occasionally clarifies what the principle is *not*, as well as identifying essential differences from Wolfensberger's version.

In my view, the principle is every bit as relevant now as when it was first formulated some 25 years ago. To help explain both the meaning of the principle and its implications, I will discuss some current examples of the principle at work, drawing in particular upon my own experiences and other developments within Canada.

2 GENESIS OF THE PRINCIPLE

The Normalization principle gradually emerged over a period of time in Scandinavia.[1] It was first applied with respect to people with mental handicaps, but later broadened to apply to people with any form of disability.

In the 1960s, Bengt Nirje served as executive director and ombudsman of FUB, the Swedish Association for the Developmentally Disturbed. In this capacity, starting in 1962, he was active in the development of a new Swedish law, which eventually came into being in 1968.

Meeting in Copenhagen in 1963 with Niels Erik Bank-Mikkelsen, Nirje reviewed the 1959 Danish law, for which Bank-Mikkelsen had been a driving force. Nirje was struck by the words in the preamble: "to let the mentally retarded obtain an existence as close to normal as possible." Neither the terms "Normalization" nor "principle" emerged until some time later. But this was the starting point for discussions where Nirje and some of his colleagues, most notably Bank-Mikkelsen and Karl Grunewald of Sweden, increasingly used the word "normal" as a means of describing how living conditions should be for people with disabilities.

The roots of the concept of Normalization can be traced to the development of the modern social welfare society in Sweden in the late 1930s and 1940s (e.g., Billimoria, 1993; Pedlar, 1990). Swedish social welfare policy was based upon principles of equality and the right of all people to live in society and to be guaranteed a good standard of living. It also recognized the obligation of the state to provide social services, if necessary, to make this possible. Normalization emerged from this context of egalitarianism. As far back as 1946, a government "Committee for the Partially Able-bodied" said, in the context of employment, that people with mild disabilities "should as far as possible be included in the ordinary system of social services which is under development in our land" and even spoke of "Normalization" (Ericsson, 1992). But the committee did not concern itself with those with a more severe handicap who were relegated to institutional care. The work of this committee, however, was not publicized, and was uncited and unknown when the Normalization principle later came to be developed in the 1960s.

Thus Nirje can be considered responsible for the modern development and statement of the Normalization principle. He gradually developed his ideas through discussions with colleagues and lectures in Scandinavia, and also during a lecture tour in the United States in 1967. In 1968, he presented his landmark paper "The Normalization Principle and Its Human Management Implications" in Washington to the President's Committee on Mental Retardation, which was published by the committee the following year (Nirje, 1969)—the first formal published statement of the Normalization principle, in any language. Only later was the Normalization principle translated back into Swedish and Danish!

Let me take this opportunity, right now, before going any further, to clear up any possible misunderstandings. The principle, in its original version, is *not* a museum piece or obsolete. It was *not* replaced by the later Wolfensberger version of the principle, as Wolfensberger, for example, asserted (e.g., Wolfensberger, 1972), which differs from it in many essential respects (e.g., Billimoria, 1993; Emerson, 1992: Perrin & Nirje, 1985; Wolfensberger, 1980). Nor did "Scandinavian" Normalization stop developing and evolving after 1969. Indeed, Nirje and many others, in Scandinavia but also in other countries

around the world, have continued to refine, explain, and apply the principle, as well as carry out research documenting its impact on quality of life.

I am also uneasy about referring to the original version of Normalization as "Scandinavian." Indeed, the principle emerged from Scandinavia, in particular, from Sweden and Denmark. But, as Nirje has indicated throughout his writings (e.g., Nirje, 1993), it is universal in its implications, relevant in all cultures and societies, and it has been applied in many different countries around the world. And while the original Normalization principle has greatly influenced successively more community-oriented pieces of legislation in Scandinavia (e.g., Billimoria, 1993; Hollander, 1993; Pedlar, 1990), it has never totally dominated policy (e.g., Bank-Mikkelsen, 1976b). In Scandinavia, as elsewhere, the principle has been controversial and there is a divergence of views.

And, as noted above, Normalization, as defined by Nirje, was first published in English, in the United States, by no less an authority than a committee established by the President of the United States. The "Scandinavian" version of the principle was widely publicized by this American committee and played a major role in the redirection of social policy regarding services for people with mental handicaps within the United States and elsewhere. Thus as Dybwad (1982) has said, the Nirje definition should, at the very least, be considered an alternative "North American" orientation. Hence my use of quotes in speaking of "Scandinavian" Normalization.

3 WHAT IS THE NORMALIZATION PRINCIPLE?

The Normalization principle was originally defined by Nirje (1969) as: "Making available to the mentally retarded patterns and conditions of everyday life which are as close as possible to the norms and patterns of the mainstream of society."

Most recently, Nirje (1985) rephrases this as: "Making available to all persons with intellectual disabilities or other handicaps, patterns of life and conditions of everyday living which are as close as possible to or indeed *the same as* the regular circumstances and ways of life of society" (italics in original). This revised definition reflects the applicability of the principle to all persons with disabilities. It gets away from the terms "norms" and "mainstream," which have been misunderstood and misused. And it puts "as close as possible" into context, implying that people with disabilities have a right to live in society on the same basis as anyone else.

As Nirje has indicated throughout his writings (e.g., Nirje, 1993), normal patterns of conditions of life can be viewed in terms of eight different facets or elements:

1. A normal rhythm of the day.
2. A normal rhythm of the week.
3. A normal rhythm of the year.
4. The normal experiences of the life cycle.
5. Normal respect for the individual and the right to self-determination.
6. The normal sexual patterns of one's culture.
7. The normal economic patterns and rights of one's society.
8. The normal environmental patterns and standards in one's community.

Bank-Mikkelsen (1976c) has described Normalization as the "acceptance of the mentally retarded *with* their handicap, and offering them the same conditions as are offered to other citizens" (italics in original). It means making normal housing, working (including training and education), and leisure conditions. Bank-Mikkelsen adds that "the Normalization principle simply means that all citizens shall have equal access to the same benefits," that people with disabilities have the right to the same services and facilities that are open to others. They are "ordinary people with ordinary civil rights who happen to have a handicap" with "the legal and human rights of all other citizens" (1976b). He also indicates that:

> [Normalization] means that mentally retarded people should not be treated in any special way. . . . This, of course, does not mean that mentally retarded and other handicapped people do not have a right to special education or special treatment. But this should be provided according to need and not merely because they are mentally handicapped and the same should apply to other citizens who need special provision for a short period of time or for their whole lives (1976b).

In the UK, they talk about the Ordinary Life movement. This means that people, even with severe disabilities, "can (and should) live their lives in the community like anyone else" (Ward, 1992). The means of achieving this include: "ordinary houses in ordinary streets, ordinary jobs in ordinary workplaces, ordinary friends, neighbours, social and leisure opportunities, with whatever support is needed to enable this to happen" (Ward, 1992).

The essence of "Scandinavian" Normalization is really quite simple. As Nirje and Bank-Mikkelsen have emphasized since the principle was first stated, it means no more—nor less—than the right of people with disabilities to live their lives on the same terms as anyone else in society, along with the necessary supports to make this possible. It means that "disabled people should be part of the community and live together with other people" (Hollander, 1993). It means that *all* people with disabilities have the right to normal community conditions of life and the same rights to equality, to be different, and to be respected as anyone else in society.

As Nirje indicates, the principle with its eight facets serves as an instrument at four different levels:

1. At an *individual level*, providing guidance for persons responsible for people with disabilities about "how to meet a problem, how to advise, how to plan actions, and what to do" (Nirje, 1985).

2. At the *community level*, providing guidance for "the development or refinement of the educational and social services required and for an understanding of the needed training, support and cooperation of the various specialized staff" (Nirje, 1993).

3. At the *societal level*, providing guidance for the development of legislation and policies and the structure of services.

4. At the *cultural level*, serving as an instrument for understanding and analyzing "the changes gradually taking place in the patterns or culture or conditions of life affecting not only persons with intellectual or other disabilities . . . but also other groups in society." Normalization, as it emerged from Scandinavia, was never intended to be an "ism" or a comprehensive theory and set of strategies. It was never intended to be a dogma. Indeed, as Bank-Mikkelsen (1976a, 1976b, 1976c) states, it is an "antidogma," saying that we do not need special theories for people with mental handicaps or with other

disabilities, but rather equality. It was developed as a response to the dogma of protectionism.

Thus Normalization was not intended as an all-encompassing directive with specific do's and don'ts. It is silent, for example, about the appropriateness of specific forms of treatment, provided that they are consistent with advancing the goal of Normalization.

"Scandinavian" Normalization is a general philosophy about how we should view human beings. It is a guiding principle that provides a direction for social policies. It is a general approach that should be straightforward and easy to understand. It has been subject to misinterpretation, partly due to basic disagreements with its assumption that people with disabilities can and should have the right to live in the community, but also partly due to well-intentioned but misguided attempts to overcomplicate it and to be overprescriptive.

The Normalization principle first evolved in the days of institutions. Some of the ideas leading to its development grew out of analyses of living conditions within institutions. As noted above, a major initial reason for the development of the principle was to counter the dogma of protectionism, which was used to support and defend institutions. Normalization is a relative concept and one of its uses, especially in its early days when institutional settings were the norm for people with mental handicaps, has been to improve conditions within institutional and quasi-institutional settings.

For this reason, there has been some misunderstanding that the Scandinavian version of the principle endorsed institutionalization (e.g., Emerson, 1992; Wolfensberger, 1980). But this is just not so. Community living for people with disabilities, on the same basis as others, has always been the goal of Normalization. It has always supported the concept that regular community services should be available to everyone, including to those who happen to have a disability. Nirje and Bank-Mikkelsen, in their writings and public addresses, have always made clear their strong opposition to institutions. The phasing out of institutions in Sweden, Denmark, much of North America, and elsewhere is fully consistent with the principle. Indeed, as Dybwad (1982) points out, the principle played a major role in influencing a number of judicial judgments to close down institutions within the United States.

4 NORMALIZATION AND THE PRIMACY OF RIGHTS AND SELF-DETERMINATION

The Normalization principle, as it originated in Scandinavia, first and foremost, is rooted in a strong sense of equality for *all* people within society, including those who happen to have a disability. A concern for rights is—and always has been—paramount. Indeed, Bank-Mikkelsen (1976c) has said: "The Normalization principle does not by itself stand for anything else than the idea that the handicapped . . . shall have the same rights and obligations as other citizens."

As Nirje has emphasized (for example, in a paper discussing the basis of the Normalization principle), human rights and normal respect for the integrity of the individual "form a basis for all the other facets of the Normalization principle" (Nirje, 1985). In his chapter in this volume, he indicates how his formulation of the principle in 1968 closely followed the 1967 Stockholm conference of the International League of Societies for Persons with Mental Handicaps (ILSMH) which led to the declaration of the rights of people with mentally handicaps at the league's Jerusalem Congress, with the theme "From Charity to Rights," the following year. This, in turn, led to the UN Declaration of the Rights of Persons with Mental Retardation in 1971 and the subsequent UN Declaration of the Rights of Disabled Persons in 1975. All these documents contain the word "normal" in referring to conditions of life for people with disabilities and also incorporate the philosophy of "Scandinavian" Normalization.

Let me repeat this point. Normalization is—and always has been—about rights. As Bank-Mikkelsen (1973) puts it: "The principle of Normalization [means] that all human beings are equal and that all human beings are entitled to the same rights." Everything else follows from this crucial point.

Rights mean self-determination. This means that people have the right to decide for themselves what they want to do with their lives. This means that people with disabilities have the freedom to live a life based on the same values and on the same terms as others in society. This means that they have the freedom to choose among a range of options, life circumstances, patterns of life, and opportunities on the same basis as do others. A focus on rights implies consideration for quality of life, *as people view and define this themselves.*

This has major implications for human services and for the role of professionals. Normalization does *not* mean making people normal. It does *not* mean that the behavior of people with disabilities needs to be normalized or made to conform to any particular standard. It does *not* involve some people deciding, however benevolently, what is best for others. It does *not* include dictating which standards or conditions of living, or which particular roles are or are not appropriate for people with disabilities. This represents a major area of misunderstanding, and of disagreement between the "Scandinavian" and Wolfensberger versions of Normalization.[2]

The Nirje definition of Normalization, presented earlier in this paper, talks about *making available* to people. As Nirje (1985) says: "The principle starts with respect for the integrity of the individual and does not simply mean by manipulation 'to establish, enable, or support behaviors, appearances and interpretations which are as culturally normative as possible' (Wolfensberger, 1972)." "Scandinavian" Normalization emphasizes the primacy of individual preferences. Wolfensberger (1972), in stark contrast, says that "normalizing measures can be *offered* in some circumstances, and *imposed* in others."

Indeed, as Dybwad (1982) says: It is normal to be different. As Bank-Mikkelsen (1976b) puts it: "A mentally retarded person is not normal—who is? What is normality, and does anyone want to be 'normal' at a time when there is so much understanding for people who are trying not to be uniform?" Indeed, the watchword of the 1990s is "diversity"—in North America, Europe, and around the world. Businesses, for example, are spending huge sums of money in training, reflecting an increasingly diverse workforce and a diverse population and a recognition that diversity is not only here to stay, but can have many advantages. Why would human service workers deny people with disabilities the right to be themselves?

Nondisabled people have the right to define which social roles they themselves value and to decide which of these, if any, they would like to emulate. They have the right to alternative lifestyles, including to those which may be rejected by many others. The principles of "Scandinavian" Normalization and of self-determination say that people who happen to have a

disability should have the same right. There are alternative lifestyles and routes to empowerment other than conformity to the most conservative options in society, as implied by the conservative corollary in Wolfensberger's definitions of Normalization and Social Role Valorization. People with disabilities should have the right to choose for themselves how they wish to live and to what extent they wish to emulate the pillars of society. This is in stark contrast to Social Role Valorization, which asserts that "Valued social roles for people need to be attained and preserved in order for them to be or become [more] positively valued socially" (Wolfensberger, 1992).

Everybody, no matter how severe their disability, is capable of expressing preferences in some way. It may, however, require extra effort on the part of others to understand these desires. As Nirje (1976) has said, we need to give "sensitive attention to those who do not speak or have difficulty in expressing themselves." Normalization implies "normal respect and understanding for the silent wishes as well as for expressed self-determination of people with disabilities."

Many people may have difficulty at first in making their own informed choices. This is hardly surprising for those who have been used to a lifetime of others making decisions on their behalf and who have had little exposure to the range of options that are available. The appropriate role of service providers, in these instances, is *not* to act as substitute decision makers. Rather, "individuals should be encouraged and assisted in expressing their *own* preferences and making their *own* choices; Normalization implies that opportunities and training should be provided to assist in this process" (Perrin & Nirje, 1985). For people who have difficulties in actively voicing their own preferences, the role of advocates should be to help them to do so as much as possible and where necessary, to speak on behalf of the choices and desires that people with disabilities have themselves expressed. The success of People First has demonstrated that labeled people, given the opportunity, can be perfectly capable of speaking for themselves.

To tell people what they must do, what is "best" for them, however benevolent one's intentions, without respecting their own feelings, is authoritarian. As Brown and Smith (1992b) say: "Any situation in which an individual or group's subjective experience is discounted in favour of an 'objective' account of what they feel, think or want clearly signals an abuse of power." Perrin and Nirje (1985) describe this as "an unwarranted abuse of the powers of the therapeutic state."

5 THE ENVIRONMENT, NOT NECESSARILY THE INDIVIDUAL, NEEDS TO CHANGE

Consumers—people with disabilities—are demanding the right to live in the community, *with* their disabilities, on the same basis as others. They are demanding a society that allows them to be themselves, like other people, and which accommodates their disabilities and special needs. They are demanding a society in which all public facilities and opportunities are accessible to them and appropriate for their needs and abilities.

"Scandinavian" Normalization, arising as it does from a context of equality and respect for self-determination, has been saying exactly this for 25 years. It calls for Normalization of the conditions of life, *not* of individuals, their behavior or appearance. As Bank-Mikkelsen (1976c) says, Normalization means the acceptance of people in the community *with* their handicap.

Nirje (1985) has defined integration as: "to be yourself—to be able and to be allowed to be yourself—among others." Nirje (1980) has distinguished among six different forms of integration. The mere physical presence in the community does not, by itself, constitute either true integration nor represent Normalization. As we all know by now, dumping people "in the community" without the provision of necessary support does not result in anything other than the appearance of integration. A prerequisite to true integration is a society that accepts people as they are.

It is interesting to note that, as Hutchison (1986) has indicated, when professionals plan programs they tend to identify problems in individuals that keep them from fitting in. In contrast, when people with disabilities are involved in planning, they tend to identify barriers in the ways programs are structured and offered that prevent them from participating. For consumers, barrier removal is key to being able to be part of the community.

As Hollander (1993) says:

A disability is not a characteristic of a person but a relationship between the person and the environment. A disability is relative in this sense. This is important because it places the responsibility on the environment rather than on the person... All activities in the society have to be accessible to everyone, including disabled people, thus preventing a disability from becoming a handicap.

This has profound implications. Specifically, the assumption inherent in Wolfensberger's version of Normalization and Social Role Valorization that individuals must change to blend in or "pass" in society or that they need to conform to someone else's idea of what constitutes acceptable or valued behavior, and at the most conservative end at that, was never part of "Scandinavian" Normalization. Indeed, it is contrary to the precepts of equality and self-determination. As Nirje (1985) says, "Scandinavian" Normalization "deals with realities of life, not with appearances of conformity and passing, hiding what some call deviancy." What needs to be "normalized" are not individuals, but the environment and opportunities, in order to accommodate people *with* their differences and unique needs.

Most societies are full of people with different beliefs and values, with different views of life, with different standards of behavior and of "appropriate" dress, and so on. Almost every society tolerates some downright eccentrics. What are considered "valued social roles" is changing. Former pillars of society, including prominent newspaper publishers (e.g., Conrad Black), leading business people (e.g., the Reichmanns in Canada or Schneider in Germany), highranking politicians (e.g., Canada's former prime minister Brian Mulroney), and royalty (e.g., Prince Charles) have fallen off their pedestals, at least in the eyes of many people.

Ironically, these days, it is often those at the most conservative end whose values have been questioned the most. Today's heroes take a wide variety of forms, from across the full spectrum of society. They, for example, may be female or male, from any social background, and may or may not wear a coat and tie. They can just as easily be a single mother on welfare who has helped her community. (e.g., One such "hero" is discussed in Osborne and Gaebler's [1992] influential book *Reinventing Government*.) Why then, would human service workers tell people with disabilities that they need to conform to any given standard of behavior (or dress), particularly to standards that are increasingly coming into question?

Some people with disabilities may be able to disguise the nature of their disability, at least at times. But as Brown (in press) says: "The reality is that people who are different, particularly if they look different, cannot blend in." And why should they—in order to be entitled to the same rights as others? This is contrary to the original Normalization principle, which means the acceptance of people *with* their differences, *with* their disabilities in a society which accommodates *all* people, including those with special needs. As Nirje (1993) has indicated, "Scandinavian" Normalization has its basis in "the recognition of the right to be different and to have the same right to be respected as anyone else."

As Brown and Smith (1992b) and others have observed, other minority groups have rejected assimilation or mimicking "socially valued roles" as a route to equality. For example, the women's and black power movements now recognize that empowerment comes from asserting, rather than hiding, their differences. Self-assurance, confidence, and power come from taking pride in who they are. They demand the right to full participation in a society that welcomes and accommodates them with their differences. Moreover, saying that people with disabilities have to conform to the roles, culture, and expectations of the dominant group within society serves to reinforce rather than to challenge the inappropriate dominant ideology (Dalley, 1992). As Nirje (1985) has observed, "the concept of deviancy seems to be based on accepting prejudice as a 'normal' social occurrence—a peculiar culture-bound phenomenon."

But what about competence? Do not people with disabilities need to increase their competence? Of course. But the key is, who decides. Ericsson (1992) contrasts what he refers to as the competence and the citizen perspectives. The former, which derives from institutional patterns of service but has been carried over into professional-run community services, focuses on a person's deficiencies as defined by someone else. With the citizen perspective, in contrast, the starting point is what an individual wants to do. The individual's "own views are needed to express in what respect, under what conditions and by which means the

person's competence is to be increased" (Ericsson, 1992).

Furthermore, independence—and competence—comes when people make their *own* decisions about how they wish to live. The way to help people become independent is to assist them in learning how to make their own decisions, rather than to dictate to them standards of behavior that they must follow.

6 EXAMPLES FROM CANADA

Is it pie-in-the-sky, or unrealistic, to assert, in accordance with the "Scandinavian" Normalization principle, that the physical and social environment—indeed society itself—must change to accommodate people with disabilities? To be sure, there is a long way to go. But major strides *are* being made. Indeed, all progressive legislation, social policy, and program development now are concerned with ways of accommodating people with disabilities in the community and in regular community services.

Let me give some examples from Canada. Judge Rosalie Abella, in her highly influential *Equality in Employment: A Royal Commission Report*,[3] states that:

> To treat everyone the same may be to offend the notion of equality. Ignoring differences may mean ignoring legitimate needs. It is not fair to use the difference between people as an excuse to exclude them arbitrarily from equitable participation . . .
> Ignoring differences and refusing to accommodate them is a denial of equal access and opportunity. It is discrimination. (Abella, 1984)

Canada's constitution, since 1985, provides for equal protection and equal benefit of the law without discrimination based upon mental or physical disability as well as other factors such as gender, race, and so on. In a recent decision of the Supreme Court of Canada (1989), the Court affirmed that equality does not mean sameness since "identical treatment may frequently produce serious inequality." The Court further stated that:

> Recognizing that there will always be an infinite variety of personal characteristics, capacities, entitlements and merits among those subject to a law, there must be accorded, as nearly as may be possible, an equality of benefit. . . . A law expressed to bind all should not because of irrelevant personal differences have a more burdensome or less beneficial impact on one than another.

Similarly, human rights legislation, such as Ontario's Human Rights Code, requires all publicly available facilities and services to provide "reasonable accommodation." This means that both public and private services and facilities need to accommodate the special needs of people with disabilities, up to the point where this would involve "undue hardship." Canada has had employment equity legislation with respect to federally regulated businesses for some time. While this legislation has been criticized for being weak, Ontario has just put somewhat stronger legislation into effect. This legislation requires public and private workplaces to carry out "employment systems reviews" to identify systemic barriers to employment and to demonstrate "reasonable progress" toward the achievement of employment equity.

In other words, there is a legal onus in Canada to accommodate people with disabilities to modify the physical and social environment as necessary to provide for full participation.

In Canada, the federal government and all the provinces and territories recently undertook a joint review of services affecting Canadians with disabilities, entitled "Mainstream 1992," with the objective of developing "a collective strategic framework which explores from a social perspective the full integration of Canadians with disabilities in the mainstream of Canadian society." The final report (*Pathway to Integration*) of the review articulates a vision in which Canadians with disabilities could participate fully in society. It identifies the three key principles of equality, empowerment, and full participation. Strategic directions identified include: the provision of disability-related supports that people with disabilities need to participate in the community and provide for their own well-being; mainstream sectors that are fully accessible; social services playing an educative and facilitative role; removal of barriers in the workplace that prevent people with disabilities from being employed; and increased consumer participation, including moving toward individualized funding models in social services.

To give a couple of examples from other jurisdictions, the Americans With Disabilities Act spells out the obligations of all publicly available services and facilities in the United States, including, for example, employment settings, transportation and communications, and leisure settings, to take whatever steps are necessary in order to make them available to people with disabilities. New Swedish legislation places responsibility on the environment rather than on the person (Hollander, 1993).

These and related legislative and policy steps have not ended all discrimination, of course. But they are important forward steps. Physical accessibility is easier and more commonplace than changes required to address more systemic and invisible barriers to participation. For example, curb cuts and building codes that require all facilities intended for the use of the public to be physically accessible are now commonplace.

But, partly as a result of the visibility of more and more people with disabilities in the community (so much for the "advantage" of "blending in") and as a result of the insistence of consumer advocacy groups (so much for the "advantage" of not associating with other "devalued" people), there are many examples where attitudes are changing.

An excellent example of how the public is now willing to accept people with visible disabilities comes from a recent election campaign in Canada. An ad from the then government in power attacked Jean Chrétien, leader of the Liberal Party, not for his policies, but for his visible impairment. It showed a close-up of him speaking with the camera focused on his mouth, which is paralyzed on one side from a childhood illness, and asked if we wanted "this man" to represent Canada. The universal reaction to this ad, for daring to ridicule handicapped people, was one of outrage. It has been credited as being the decisive moment in the election campaign, which ended with Chrétien becoming Prime Minister with a comfortable majority (Smith, 1994).

There are many good examples of community-based services that have examined all their programs, activities, facilities, and ways of operating, often in cooperation with disability organizations, in order to identify and to address both overt as well as invisible or systemic barriers to participation. Let me illustrate this with some examples from the leisure area, although I could just as easily speak of developments concerning housing or employment.

I have recently completed a major research study, examining innovative approaches across Canada and beyond, which culminated in a guide to how community recreation and disability agencies can enable people with disabilities in regular leisure and recreation (Perrin, 1992; Perrin, Wiele, Wilder, & Perrin, 1992). We found many successful approaches. To cite just a couple of examples, one Ontario recreation department has a "Barrier Breakers" program, which does not hesitate to help solve any barrier to participation in recreation, including barriers such as transportation. The departmental staff will provide other forms of assistance, for example in introducing individuals to a range of different activities. Anything goes, from having coffee in the mall to joining in a more structured recreation program. Other recreation departments offer an activity sampling program to young adults. One department will even help form "friendship circles" where lack of a support network is keeping a person from engaging in recreational activities.

Some programs use a variety of strategies to assist people who say they do not feel welcome when participating in integrated recreation. In some places, a coparticipant will meet a new participant with a disability, showing them around and working together if any assistance is required, for example in activity modifications or interpretation of instructions.

We found strong interest among municipal recreation authorities in learning how they can include more people with disabilities in their programs. In general, however, we found stronger resistance to community integration among social service agencies, many of whom were reluctant to "let go" of their segregated services. But we also found positive examples. In southwestern Ontario, a number of different agencies have formed a Community Involvement Council, which jointly discusses how they can support people in using the community, including many people who have spent much of their lives in institutions. Some agencies have undergone reorganization, and now, instead of providing segregated services, use their staff to help individuals take advantage of regular leisure opportunities in the community.

7 ROLE OF SUPPORT SERVICES, INCLUDING "SPECIAL" SERVICES

The "Scandinavian" Normalization principle supports, indeed insists upon, the right to whatever services, training, and support are required to permit regular living conditions in the community. In contrast with Wolfensberger's reformulation, these services may or may not be "normative." Special or "unnormal" services are fully appropriate, as long as they support the objective of "ordinary" living and full participation in the community.

Everyone needs assistance of some kind in order to live in the community. None of us, unless we are total hermits, are truly independent of others. Everyone makes use of a variety of forms of assistance—some personal and informal, others formal and/or purchased. What constitutes "special" services? Generally, these are defined as services that are used by a minority of people. But an accommodating society recognizes that everybody is unique and that everybody needs "special" assistance from time to time.

For example, as Perrin and Nirje (1985) indicated: "A person with heart trouble may consult a cardiologist; in extreme cases, a pacemaker, a decidedly "unnormal" foreign body, may be surgically implanted in the body. The purpose of this abnormal treatment is to permit the continuation of everyday living patterns (i.e., 'normal' living)." Someone who happens to have a disability should have the same right to whatever "special" services are needed to permit "normal" living.

This is consistent with consumers demanding access to services that enable them to participate in the community on the same footing as others. For example, the Council of Canadians with Disabilities (formerly COPOH), the national crossdisability consumer association in Canada, has said, "Equality of opportunity does not mean 'same treatment' but rather the development of programs and services which address the disadvantages most experienced by persons with disabilities."

As discussed earlier, the Canadian constitution, Judge Abella, and human rights and employment equity legislation all recognize the need for special or different treatment in order to result in equality of benefit. Indeed, as Abella has said, to do otherwise is discrimination.

Let me be very clear. People with disabilities *need* disability-related services and assistance in order to live a life with some semblance of normalcy, in order to be able to take advantage of regular community-based opportunities. Some people may require only a minimum amount of support on occasion. Others may require more intensive support on an ongoing basis.

189

It is absurd to say that use of such services, including visible aids, are not appropriate because they are "devaluing." For example, the Wolfensberger version of Normalization and Social Role Valorization says that a person with a hearing impairment should not use a visible hearing aid, that washrooms in residences should not have grab bars. People with disabilities are now demanding the right to make their *own* decisions about whether or not they will use aids and make their disabilities visible. As noted earlier, Jean Chrétien was elected Prime Minister of Canada in spite of, or perhaps partly because of, his facial impairment.

Consumers now are demanding *control* over the services that they need in order to live independently in the community. For example, they are demanding the ability to choose which services and service providers they want to use and control over funds to purchase these directly. They are also demanding the right to direct how these services should be provided, at both the individual and the policy level. Models providing for such consumer control or individualized purchase of services are now being developed. This, incidentally, contrary to Wolfensberger's claim, suggests that paid services, at least under certain circumstances, can work to the benefit of the consumer.

Proponents of "Scandinavian" Normalization have been described as supporting segregated services (e.g., Emerson, 1992; Wolfensberger, 1980). To the extent that they do not reject out of hand any form of service that leads to the goal of Normalization is consistent with the principle, there is some truth to this. But it is important to view this in context. Normalization, as mentioned earlier, is silent about the appropriateness of specific treatment modalities. "Special" services that support the ability of people to participate in society are consistent with the principle. But they are *not* appropriate when they isolate or otherwise separate people from the community.

For example, Bank-Mikkelsen, one of the fathers of Normalization, says: "It is a mistake to adopt any particular strategy for all persons" and "in some cases, segregated, intensive programs may be best suited" for some individuals (Bank-Mikkelsen, 1976a). But he also said, back in 1976: "In the near future, Denmark will show that no special service is needed to take care of the mentally retarded" (Bank-Mikkelsen, 1976b); and "The ordinary authorities of society must serve all citizens: some need more help than others, but nobody should be left out—this also means Normalization" (Bank-Mikkelsen, 1973).

This means, as Bank-Mikkelsen indicated, that regular community (or mainstream) services should be open to everyone, including people with disabilities, and should accommodate any special needs. I just provided some examples of how this can work in the leisure area. The challenge is to address barriers to "normal" living in a way that in turn does not create other barriers. In most cases, the only special services that are now appropriate are those that support the ability of people to use regular community services. Segregated, parallel programs for people with disabilities are rarely necessary. They are harmful in that they not only isolate people from the community; they, in common with institutions, indirectly "teach" skills (e.g., passivity, going along with what others think is best rather than learning how to make one's own decisions) that are the opposite of what are needed to live independently.

Twenty years ago, even 10 years ago in some places, when Normalization was still a controversial concept, the major focus was keeping people with disabilities from going into institutions and enabling people within institutions to enter the community. This battle is now being won. It is now necessary to address less obvious forms of segregation that keep people from true integration and full participation in the community. For example, there is now little need for specialized "separate but equal" programs such as sheltered workshops, congregate living, or segregated recreation. There is ample evidence, including from my own research, illustrating the superiority of alternative models such as supported employment and supportive housing.

One important development involves the increasing use of natural supports. In this model, support workers help people with special needs to develop connections with others. For example, a coparticipant in a recreation program or a coworker in an employment setting may be encouraged to provide assistance when required, sometimes on a completely volunteer basis, sometimes with some form of compensation. Sometimes, arranging for "natural support" is as simple as asking. Consider the following examples from a recent publication of the Community Involvement Council of southwestern Ontario (1993):

Della needed a ride to the pool. I approached Della's neighbour, and they went to the pool together. As I look back now, thank goodness I wasn't given any staffing resources. Della and her neighbour gained a friendship which they still have today.

Isaac kept going over to another table in the restaurant where a woman was sitting alone. She responded warmly. Blaine [the worker] tried to encourage Isaac to come back to their table, but he was pretty insistent. Finally, Blaine approached the woman and asked if Isaac could join her for dinner. She said, "Yes." Blaine was pleased the two were getting to know each other. He went back and had dinner alone!

8 THE NORMALIZATION PRINCIPLE AND THE CONSUMER MOVEMENT

The most important development in the 1990s in the disability area is the growth of the consumer movement. Consumers with disabilities the world over are no longer willing to accept others deciding on their behalf what is best for them. As Mike Oliver makes very clear in his chapter in this volume, people with disabilities are demanding the right to make their *own* decisions about what services they need and on what basis these should be provided. They are demanding the right to what they feel are essential services to enable them to participate fully in the community. For example, this was a theme in the Third International People First Conference held last year in Toronto, which had representatives from 32 different countries. This was the major focus of Independence '92, an international conference in Vancouver organized by and for people with all forms of disabilities that drew thousands of people with disabilities from numerous countries around the world.

Consumers are increasingly getting together with others to assert their rights. For example, the Council of Canadians with Disabilities (formerly COPOH) represents people across Canada with all forms of disabilities. The disability movement is increasingly cooperating with other movements, such as the women's movement and organizations representing Aboriginal people and racial minorities, in its fight for rights.

As Nirje states in his chapter in this volume, "From Charity to Rights" was the theme of the ILSMH Jerusalem Conference in 1968, a key year for rights around the world, as evidenced, for example, by the French student revolt and demonstrations in the United States about its participation in the Vietnam War and its implications for the democratic process. That same year Nirje drafted and first presented the Normalization principle. This is a critical point. In the 1990s, any approach to human service that does not respect the right of consumers to decide for themselves what they want is no longer legitimate.

"Scandinavian" Normalization, given its grounding in rights and on self-determination, has always been strongly supportive of consumer action at all levels. For example, unlike Wolfensberger's definition of Normalization and Social Role Valorization, which views it as devaluing for people with disabilities to associate with other disabled people, it recognizes that it is normal for people to associate with their peers, such as through social bodies whose members share common interests, goals, and life experiences.

Nirje (1972) acknowledges that there can be a danger of segregation with self-directing groups consisting entirely or substantially of people with disabilities. But he says that this danger must be balanced against important functions these groups serve. For example,

> Through these bodies, common feelings and needs can be shared and expressed, and common demands formulated. . . . [They provide] an opportunity for social interaction and self-expression which otherwise may not be available in the same quantity or quality. . . . [They also serve as] an essential media for bringing about greater integration, by providing occasions of sharing in the social life of the community.

And perhaps most importantly, such groups provide opportunities for self-assertion.

People First members have said similar things to me. For example, they say that they feel comfortable participating in People First meetings and enjoy the understanding and support from their peers. They feel that participation is a way to increase their confidence and social skills, which some of them may then be able to use in other settings. And People First provides an opportunity for them to express their own views about the quality of their lives and about services that are offered to them.

As far back as 1965, Sweden has had leisure clubs, consisting mainly of people with mental handicaps. These clubs quickly took on an expanded, advocacy role, enabling members to express their views about the quality of their lives, their aspirations, and what they felt about the services they were using. Regional and national conferences have provided further opportunities for self-expression and advocacy. For some time, programs and services (e.g., special schools, group homes) in Sweden and Denmark have been required to establish councils to provide an opportunity for consumers to play a role in deciding the way in which services are provided.

In conjunction with the "Mainstream 1992" review, I reviewed statements prepared by consumers and consumer organizations across Canada. A very consistent theme emerged from this review. Consumers, irrespective of the nature of their disability, indicate their desire to live and participate in the community. They identify barriers preventing them from doing so. But they say that one of the greatest barriers to independence are disability services themselves, which they describe as "the problem rather than the solution" to them.

Consumers do not appreciate being treated as charity cases. More than anything else, they bitterly resent "professionals" deciding what is best for them. They want to make their *own* decisions. They resent being told what is wrong with *them*, when what they see are barriers, created by others, that turn their disabilities into handicaps and that prevent their full participation in society.

Consumers are demanding the right to determine not just what services they receive at an individual level, but also the right to participate in deciding policies that affect them and how services are to be organized and delivered. They need to be given the opportunity to play a major role in decision making at three levels: a) individual, b) policy, and c) program.

8.1 INDIVIDUAL LEVEL

I have already spoken of the right of individuals who happen to have a disability to make their own decisions and their own choices about how they wish to live, as well as about services they need and how

these should be provided. This carries with it the corresponding obligation for human service workers to support individuals in their own choices, rather than to decide on their behalf what is best for them. It also means that services need to be flexible, adaptable, and portable in order to respond to the needs and interests of individuals, rather than forcing clients to fit into the boundaries—or physical settings—of existing programs. It implies that services need to take more of a customer approach in addressing the interests of the client, as determined by the client rather than the service provider.

8.2 POLICY LEVEL

With respect to the development of policy, it is noteworthy that the major legislative and policy advances I have spoken of, as well as most others, have resulted from the advocacy efforts of persons with disabilities themselves. In Canada, people with disabilities, according to Statistics Canada, now constitute some 15% of the population. This is larger than many other interest groups, especially when one adds in family members, friends, associates, and supporters. The disability community is now a significant political force. But this is so *only* because people with disabilities have asserted their right to be disabled *and* to live and participate in the community, and because they have not hesitated to associate with other disadvantaged or "devalued" people in the pursuit of a common cause.

For example, rights of people with disabilities were not initially protected in the first draft of Canada's new constitution. In particular, there was initial opposition to providing for the equality of people with mental disabilities. They received this protection only after strong representation by the entire disability consumer community. This would not have happened if people with disabilities had tried to be as invisible as possible. It came about because they were willing to assert themselves and demand their right to participate in society on the same basis as others.

The same phenomenon has also happened elsewhere. For example, the Americans With Disabilities Act resulted from political pressure from people with disabilities and their advocates. Legislative advances in Sweden and Denmark have been a result of advocacy efforts of people with disabilities themselves, as well as parent organizations (e.g., Bank-Mikkelsen, 1976b; Billimoria, 1993; Ericsson, 1992; Hollander, 1993). It is also worth noting that the Normalization principle itself was first expressed not by a service professional, but by an advocate, one Bengt Nirje, who at the time was ombudsman for the Swedish Association for the Developmentally Disturbed, which, unlike parent associations on this side of the Atlantic, does not operate services and acts solely in an advocacy capacity. It is also not irrelevant that Nirje's background is not in social services, but in the humanities (poetry and comparative literature) and in humanitarian aid (e.g., working with refugees on behalf of the Red Cross and the United Nations).

Professionals and service agencies have been sometimes supportive, and too often strongly opposed, to the above and related policy changes. But for the most part, they have played, at best, a secondary role. It is the people most affected who have played a leadership role in advocating for change.

There is increasing willingness by governments to include people with disabilities in the policy development process. I will provide just one example.

The "Mainstream 1992" federal/provincial-territorial review of services, mentioned earlier, set up a reference group, with representatives of the major national consumer organizations in Canada to provide for consumer participation in the review. (It also used other media to give others input into the review.) Consumer participants appreciated the openness extended to them by the government representatives, for example, by giving them access to all documents as well as the opportunity to meet with senior government officials. A typical comment was: "They actually listened to our and my input with sincere interest and have shown honesty in their efforts to incorporate our feedback." Reference group members felt that their participation *did* make a difference. As one person stated, the final report reflected an agreement on vision and philosophy that was different from what either government or the community would have come up with on their own but which both parties could accept.

Members of the reference group were also given the support they said they needed in order to participate fully in the review. For example, a deaf participant was supported in bringing along a sign interpreter, a person with a physical disability had an attendant, and the People First representative, at his request, was permitted to have a supporter of his own choice to help in participating fully in the review.

8.3   PROGRAM LEVEL

The greatest resistance to consumer involvement tends to be at the program or service level. I am founding president of the Advocacy Centre for the Handicapped (ARCH), a Toronto-based legal advocacy centre that carries out test case work and engages in legal and consumer advocacy. Since the center was founded, its bylaws have required that a majority of the members of its board of directors must be consumers. In Ontario, an advocacy commission is being established to provide advocacy services for vulnerable adults. A majority of the commission directors must be consumers. How many social service programs and agencies provide for more than token involvement of consumers in establishing their direction?

The importance of the consumer movement—and Normalization in the 1990s—has important implications for future roles for professionals and for social service agencies. I already have spoken of the need to support individuals in making their own decisions, rather than in doing so on their behalf. But even more profound changes are necessary. The organization and the focus of service agencies and the role of professionals need to change.

For example, segregated, parallel services that remove people from the community are no longer appropriate. The role of social service agencies needs to change away from the provision of direct, segregated services to that of advocate, facilitator, enabler, and supporter in order to help make it possible for people to participate *in* the community, using regular community services, as much as possible.

Even more profoundly, social service workers and agencies need to act in a new and different way that involves less control over people. This implies a very real transfer of power from the professional to the consumer. It requires a letting go, for example, supporting consumers and community service providers rather than providing services directly and making all the decisions.

It is difficult for agencies to change their mode of operation. And, ironically, as noted earlier, there tends to be *more* resistance from social service agencies to independent community living than from many mainstream sectors. But it can—and is—being done. There are good examples of organizations that have succeeded in reorienting and restructuring away from a former model of direct delivery of segregated programs to supporting people in the community. A portion of my consulting work involves working with organizations to help them in changing their roles and strategic direction.

And change is necessary. In the 1990s, consumer control or "empowerment" is more important than anything—including Normalization, Social Role Valorization, or any other theory. It is no longer appropriate for anyone to dictate what they feel is best for labeled people. Any professional service, theory, or approach that does not support the right of consumers to decide for themselves what they want is no longer acceptable nor legitimate. This implies using concepts and language that are simple and understandable to consumers and not steeped in jargon or excessive theory. The overall Normalization field has much to answer for in this regard, and I would hope that its next steps will be to bring its concepts down to earth and make them consumer-centered. And I believe this *can* be done.

I will go further still. Within a decade, or even sooner, I predict that services that are not consumer-centered and consistent with the priorities of people with disabilities will cease to exist. The newly developing private-sector focus on service and quality—which is now defined by the consumer rather than by the service provider—has yet to hit the public sector. But it will. And when consumers have the right to choose their own service providers and to dictate how services are to be provided, along with the control over funds to make this possible, agencies will be forced to respond to what consumers want—or go out of business. And this is also coming.

What does this have to do with Normalization? As noted earlier, consumer control, empowerment, and self-determination are, and always have been, central to "Scandinavian" Normalization.

9 CONCLUSION

Consumers with disabilities want the right to full inclusion in society—but *with* their disabilities and their differences. They do not feel that they should have to try to hide their disabilities in order to be accepted and in order to have the same right to participate in the community as anyone else. They want access to power, to determine how they live and the direction of policies and programs that affect them.

The original Normalization principle, as it emerged from Scandinavia is, first and foremost, about rights. It means that society should not turn a disability into a handicap. It means that people—all people—are entitled to whatever support they need in order to participate fully in society.

Normalization means that *all* people, whether or not they happen to have a disability, have the right to make their *own* choices about how they live their own lives. This really is a very simple concept. It does not need to be, indeed it should not be, overcomplicated. It is quite in keeping with the demands of the consumer movement. And it is just as relevant now for the 1990s as when the Normalization principle first emerged a quarter-century ago.

REFERENCES

ABELLA, R. S., Judge. (1984). *Equality in employment: A Royal Commission report.* Ottawa: Supply and Services Canada.

BANK-MIKKELSEN, N. E. (1969). A metropolitan area in Denmark. In R. B. KUGEL & W. WOLFENSBERGER (Eds.), *Changing patterns in residential services for the mentally retarded.* Washington, DC: President's Committee on Mental Retardation.

BANK-MIKKELSEN, N. E. (1973). Implementation of the rights. In B. NIELSEN (Ed.), *Flash on the Danish National Service for the Mentally Retarded.* Copenhagen: Personnel Training School.

BANK-MIKKELSEN, N. E. (1976a). Bank-Mikkelsen talks about Normalization. *National Association of Private Residential Facilities for the Mentally Retarded Newsletter, 6*(10).

BANK-MIKKELSEN, N. E. (1976b). Denmark. In R. B. KUGEL & A. SHEARER (Eds.), *Changing patterns in residential services for the mentally retarded* (Rev. ed.). Washington, DC: President's Committee on Mental Retardation.

BANK-MIKKELSEN, N. E. (1976c). The principle of Normalization. In B. NIELSEN (Ed.), *Flash #2 on the Danish National Service for the Mentally Retarded.* Copenhagen: Personnel Training School.

BILLIMORIA, R. B. (1993). *Principle and practice of Normalization: Experiences from Sweden and application to India.* Uppsala: Centre for Handicap Research, Uppsala University.

BLEASDALE, M. (in press). Deconstructing Social Role Valorization. *Interaction, 7*(4).

BROWN, H. (in press). What price Normalisation if you can't afford the busfare: Normalisation and leisure services for people with learning disabilities. *Health and Social Care in the Community.*

BROWN, H., & SMITH, H. (Eds.). (1992a). *Normalisation: A reader for the nineties.* London and New York: Routledge.

BROWN, H. & SMITH, H. (1992b). Assertion, not assimilation: A feminist perspective on the Normalisation principle. In H. BROWN & H. SMITH (Eds.), *Normalisation: A reader for the nineties.* London and New York: Routledge.

COMMUNITY INVOLVEMENT COUNCIL. (1993). *Jumping the gap: More stories and ideas.* Tillsonburg, ON: Community Involvement Council.

DALLEY, G. (1992). Social welfare ideologies and Normalisation: Links and conflicts. In H. BROWN & H. SMITH (Eds.), *Normalisation: A reader for the nineties.* London and New York: Routledge.

DYBWAD, G. (1982). Normalization and its impact on social and public policy. In *Advancing your citizenship: Normalization re-examined.* Eugene, OR: Rehabilitation Research and Training Institute, University of Oregon.

EMERSON, E. (1985). *The origin and consequences of the Normalization principle.* Paper presented at the IASSMD Conference, New Delhi.

EMERSON, E. (1992). What is Normalisation? In H. BROWN & H. SMITH (Eds.), *Normalisation: A reader for the nineties.* London and New York: Routledge.

ERICSSON, K. (1992). *Housing for the person with intellectual handicap: Consequences of a citizen perspective.* Paper presented at the AAMR Annual Meeting, New Orleans.

HOLLANDER, A. (1993). Rights to special services for people with developmental disabilities in Sweden. *Scandinavian Journal of Social Welfare, 2,* 63-68.

HUTCHISON, P. (1986). Social, recreation and leisure opportunities. In N. J. MARLETT, R. GALL & A. WIGHT-FELSKIE (Eds.), *Dialogue on disability: A Canadian perspective: Vol. 1. The Service System.* Calgary, AB: University of Calgary Press.

NIRJE, B. (1969). The Normalization principle and its human management implications. In R. B. KUGEL & W. WOLFENSBERGER (Eds.), *Changing patterns in residential services for the mentally retarded.* Washington, DC: President's Committee on Mental Retardation.

NIRJE, B. (1972). The right to self-determination. In W. WOLFENSBERGER (Ed.), *The principle of Normalization in human services.* Toronto, ON: National Institute on Mental Retardation.

NIRJE, B. (1976). The Normalization principle. In R. B. KUGEL & A. SHEARER (Eds.), *Changing patterns in residential services for the mentally retarded.* (Rev. ed.). Washington, DC: President's Committee on Mental Retardation.

NIRJE, B. (1980). The Normalization principle. In R. J. FLYNN & K. E. NITSCH (Eds.), *Normalization, social integration, and community services* (pp. 31-49). Baltimore, MD: University Park Press.

NIRJE, B. (1985). The basis and logic of the Normalization principle. *Australia and New Zealand Journal of Developmental Disabilities, 11*(2), 65-68.

NIRJE, B. (1992). Introduction. In B. NIRJE, *The Normalization principle papers.* Uppsala: Centre for Handicap Research, Uppsala University.

NIRJE, B. (1993). The Normalization principle—25 years later. In U. LEHTINEN & R. PIRTTIMAA (Eds.), *Arjessa tapahtuu!: Comments on mental retardation and adult education.* Jyväskylä, Finland: The Institute for Educational Research,

University of Jyväskylä.

OSBORNE, D., & GAEBLER, T. (1992). *Reinventing government: How the entrepreneurial spirit is transforming government.* New York: Penguin Books.

PEDLAR, A. (1990). Normalization and integration: A look at the Swedish experience. *Mental Retardation.* 28(5), 275-282.

PERRIN, B. (1992). Community recreation for all: How to include persons with disabilities in regular leisure and recreation. *Leisurability,* 19(4), 28-36.

PERRIN, B., & NIRJE, B. (1985). Setting the record straight: A critique of some frequent misconceptions of the Normalization principle. *Australia and New Zealand Journal of Developmental Disabilities,* 11(2), 69-74.

PERRIN, B., WIELE, K., WILDER, S., & PERRIN, A. (1992). *Sharing the fun: A guide to including persons with disabilities in leisure and recreation.* Toronto: Canadian Rehabilitation Council for the Disabled.

SMITH, P. (1994, January) A new era of acceptance. *ARCHTYPE,* 11(5/6), 61-62.

SUPREME COURT OF CANADA (1989, February 2). *Andrews v. Law Society of British Columbia.*

WARD, L. (1992). Foreword. In H. BROWN & H. SMITH (Eds.), *Normalisation: A reader for the nineties.* London and New York: Routledge.

WOLFENSBERGER, W. (1972). *The principle of Normalization in human services.* Toronto, ON: National Institute on Mental Retardation.

WOLFENSBERGER, W. (1977). An overview of the principle of Normalization. In S. A. GRAND (Ed.), *Severe disability and rehabilitation counsellor training.* Albany: State University of New York at Albany.

WOLFENSBERGER, W. (1980). The definition of Normalization: Update, problems, disagreements, and misunderstandings. In R. J. FLYNN & K. E. NITSCH (Eds.), *Normalization, social integration, and community services.* Baltimore: University Park Press.

WOLFENSBERGER, W. (1992). *A brief introduction to Social Role Valorization as a high-order concept for structuring human services* (2nd ed., rev.) Syracuse, NY: Syracuse University, Training Institute for Human Service Planning, Leadership and Change Agentry.

WOLFENSBERGER, W., & GLENN, L. (1975). *Program analysis of service systems (PASS 3). Vol. 1: Handbook. Vol 2: Field manual* (3rd ed.). Toronto, ON: National Institute on Mental Retardation.

NOTES

1. See Billimoria (1993) for the most comprehensive review in English of the background in Scandinavia leading up to the formulation of the Normalization principle, as well as a discussion of legislative developments and services in the Scandinavian countries for people with mental handicaps. Also see Nirje (1992) for a personal account of how he came to develop, and later expand upon, the principle.

2. A detailed critique of Wolfensberger's perspective on rights, conformity, and deviancy, and its implications, is beyond the scope of this paper, but see Bleasdale (in press), the various papers in Brown and Smith (1992a), and Perrin and Nirje (1985).

3. "Employment equity," which was coined by Abella, is used in Canada in similar ways to which "equal opportunity" or "affirmative action" is used elsewhere.

9

Are Normalization and Social Role Valorization limited by competence?[1]

LAIRD W. HEAL

1 INTRODUCTION

1.1 NORMALIZATION & SOCIAL ROLE VALORIZATION

We are all familiar with the defining characteristics of Nirje's Normalization. Its superseding principle is attributed by Nirje to Bank-Mikkelsen: "To let the mentally retarded obtain an existence as close to the normal as possible" (Nirje, 1969, p. 181). Corollaries to this principle include normal rhythms of the day, week, month, year, and lifetime; integration of people with disabilities with their age peers into the settings that characterize those used by their age peers; the opportunity to exercise their choices, wishes, and desires; and economic support commensurate with that of any other social security recipient (Nirje, 1992).

While embracing the principle of Normalization, Wolfensberger has been impressed by a construct that might be seen by some to have made Normalization necessary in the first place—valuation. Wolfensberger, through Social Role Valorization (SRV), which he proposes as a social science theory to replace Normalization, urges human service professionals to pursue whatever avenues they might find to increase the valuation of people whose physical or mental deviance might engender devaluation. Especially important in Wolfensberger's view is to associate people who are disabled with positive and valued imagery.

Having common roots, these two constructs have much in common. Both of these approaches are ideologically based and provide guidelines for human service providers. Social Role Valorization, and to some extent Normalization, especially as they have been quantified by PASS (Wolfensberger & Glenn, 1975) and PASSING (Wolfensberger & Thomas, 1983), are prescriptive. Both assume that the best strategy for individuals with disabilities is to pursue cultural norms. Nirje and Wolfensberger distinguish between cultural norms and statistical norms. They would not urge people with disabilities to pursue the normal daily seven hours watching television, normal rates of divorce, or other statistically prominent activities of their age peers. Normalization, and especially Social Role Valorization, reserves for disabled individuals the pursuit of culturally ideal, not culturally probabilistic, roles and expectations.

1.2 QUALITY OF LIFE (QOL)

Most would agree that providing people with disabilities a life as close as possible to cultural norms and further assigning them roles and activities designed to increase their value has been an inestimable benefit to people with disabilities. Unfortunately, very little direct research has been carried out to ascertain the extent to which these constructs can have a positive impact upon the lives of disabled persons. For instance, does the implementation of SRV increase the likelihood that disabled persons will be afforded the "good things in life," which, according to Wolfensberger (1992), is the ultimate goal of SRV? Wolfensberger (1980) suggests that one may find at least indirect evidence and sometimes direct evidence in related research, even though Normalization and SRV might not even be referred to by the authors.

Quality-of-life research is one possible area that one may argue is related to SRV and Normalization and that may hint at some of the effects and limitations of their implementation. Wolfensberger (1994), though highly critical of the quality-of-life construct, nonetheless argues that SRV is its equivalent and even suggests that SRV replaces quality of life.

Quality of life is a simple concept that has generated much discussion although some have suggested that it has turned out to be intractable to investigation, both ideologically and empirically (Goode, 1994; Heal, Borthwick-Duffy & Saunders, 1996; Jamieson, 1993; Parent, 1993; Parmenter, 1992; and Schalock, 1990, 1996). Ideally all approaches to the assessment of quality of life—that is, through cultural norms as embodied by Normalization and Social Role Valorization, through statistical norms, through choices that individual people with disabilities make, through well-being as seen by intimate acquaintances, through subjective well-being as reported by the individual clients themselves, through professional judgment, or through objective indicators of quality of life—should indicate similar levels when they are compared to one another. Unfortunately, the results of assessment using these different approaches have not always been parallel.

The many approaches to the assessment of quality of life were summarized quite nicely in a recent paper by Hughes, Huang, Kim, Eisenman & Killian (1995). A summary of the classification developed inductively by Hughes et al. appears in Table 9.1. Hughes' review is very revealing in the present context. First, one is immediately struck by the variation in the instruments that have been used to assess quality of life. These measurements range from psychological well-being and personal satisfaction to the existence of and extent of support services from family and community. "Well-being" heads Hughes's list in popularity, with 31 references being cited. Unfortunately, this count mixes both interviews of clients themselves and interviews of informants describing their perceptions of clients. We shall see later that clients and informants do not necessarily agree. Second, Social Role Valorization is not mentioned as a category, and Normalization is measured more indirectly than directly. It is surprising that the ideology that has dominated the revolution of human services during the past 25 years would not be seen as a larger component

of quality of life. Two other large categories are conspicuous by their absence. The first is the goodness of fit between one's needs and one's service supports. This conceptualization of quality of life has been offered in two variations by Schalock and Jensen (1986) and Saunders and Spradlin (1991), and is implied by the new definition of mental retardation by the American Association on Mental Retardation (AAMR, 1992), which stresses the supports necessary to minimize the effect of one's disability on one's lifestyle. The second is spiritual fulfillment, which is for many individuals the only QOL pursuit.

The pages that follow report two recent investigations that bear on the dimensionality of quality-of-life assessment. The first considers three conceptually different dimensions of quality of life—*esteem*, which Hughes et al. (1995) would presumably list under Category I, "well-being," of Table 9.1; *competence*, which would be listed under Category IV, "Self-Determination and Supporting Skills," of Table 9.1; and *support*, which would appear under Category VI of Table 9.1. The second investigation compares the self-reports of satisfaction given by clients with mental retardation and the reports regarding quality of life by informants who know the clients well. Both clients' and informants' assessments were classified by Hughes under the first major heading in Table 9.1, "Well-being."

2 QUALITY-OF-LIFE DIMENSIONS

The first investigation was inspired by the existence of a unique data set from the National Longitudinal Transition Study (Valdes, 1989; Wagner et al., 1991), which featured thousands of variables describing a national sample of current and past special-needs high-school students. This dataset offered an opportunity to evaluate the geoeconomic, educational, family, and personal characteristics that might influence the quality of life of the graduates of special education programs.

For this study Wagner et al. (1991) contacted a stratified probability sample of all students with disabilities attending U.S. high schools in 1985 and gathered in-school and out-of-school information about them in 1987 from their school records, school personnel, and parents. Three quality-of-life composites

—esteem, independence, and support—were constructed from 17 of these variables, using conventional item analysis procedures. These were related to 28 geoeconomic, demographic, cognitive, disability, and school program variables using a canonical correlation.

2.1 DATA SOURCES

The National Longitudinal Transition Study had three major sources of data: (a) the *Parent Survey*, (b) *School Records Abstracts*, and (c) the *Survey of Secondary Special Education Programs*. In the *Parent Survey,* parents or de facto guardians of the selected youths were asked by telephone in 1987 to provide information on youths' family background, characteristics, special services, educational attainment (including postsecondary education), employment experiences, social integration, and their expectations for the youths in the future. *School Record Abstracts* consisted of information abstracted from the school records of sampled youths for their most recent year in high school (either the 1985-1986 or the 1986-1987 school year). Information abstracted from school records related to disability description and classification, courses taken, grades achieved (if appropriate), school placement, related services received from the school, status at the end of the year, attendance, and other records.

TABLE 9.1

CLASSIFICATION OF QUALITY OF LIFE [a]

I. Well-being
1. Psychological well-being and personal satisfaction (31 references)[b]
4. Physical and material well-being (22 references)

II. Socialization
2. Social relationships and interaction (27 references)
8. Social acceptance, social status, ecological fit (17 references)
11. Recreation and leisure (14 references)
14. Civic responsibility (5 references)

III. Employment
3. Employment (24 references)

IV. Self-determination and supporting skills
5. Self-determination, autonomy, and personal choice (21 references)
6. Personal competence, community and living skills (19 references)
9. Personal development and fulfillment (16 references)

V. Normalization
7. Community integration (19 references)
10. Residential environment (16 references)
12. Normalization (13 references)
13. Individual and social demographic indicators (11 references)

VI. Support
15. Support services received (5 references)

[a]Adapted from Hughes et al. (1995). [b]The number of references in which Hughes et al. (1995) reported an application.

The *Survey of Secondary Special Education Programs* was completed by school personnel in schools attended by sample youths in the 1986-1987 school year. School personnel provided schoolwide information on student enrollment, staffing, and programs, and related services offered secondary special education students, policies affecting special education programs and students, and community resources (paraphrased from Wagner, 1989, appendix).

2.2   SAMPLING

Sampling was completed in two major stages, school sampling and student sampling. In sampling schools, 712 school districts that served students with disabilities at the seventh grade level or higher were selected to represent as completely as possible the 96 strata of four regions of the country, six size (student enrollment) categories, and four levels of district poverty. Student rosters were provided by 325 (45.6%) of the 712 school districts that were approached. From these rosters, 12,833 students or their families were approached, and 65.5% agreed to participate. The sampling is carefully documented by Javits and Wagner (1987). The present study was limited to 713 (21.2%) of the 3,357 students who were out of school when data were gathered in 1987, and had complete data on all 54 variables chosen for the present analyses

2.3   DEPENDENT VARIABLE: QUALITY OF LIFE

The composite scale of quality of life should ideally assess all of the categories noted by Hughes et al. (1995) and listed in Table 9.1. However, the variables in the National Longitudinal Transition Study data set permitted the construction of composite scales for only three domains of quality of life—self-esteem, independence, and security and support. The variables used in the construction of each of these domains are presented in Table 9.2.

For each individual in the sample, the composite scale for each domain of quality of life was constructed as follows. First, the cumulative percentage of each variable was computed. The response of each individual was then represented by the cumulative percentages of the 713 cases scoring at his (or her) response level or below. For example, suppose that the valid responses of variable x were 1, 2, 3, and 4, and the corresponding cumulative percentages for the study

sample of 713 individuals were 20, 50, 70, and 100 respectively. The responses of individuals were then transformed to their cumulative percentage as follows: 20 for a response of 1; 50 for 2; 70 for 3; and 100 for 4. Thus, if an individual's level was the highest in the sample, it was represented by the cumulative percentage of 100. This transformation provided a simple metric for combining or comparing ordinal variables. The average of the cumulative percentage scores over items was taken as the quality-of-life level of each domain for each individual in the sample. Thus, the individuals in the sample could be differentially valued on their overall quality of life.

2.4   PREDICTOR VARIABLES

The composite scales for self-esteem, independence, and security and support reflect three components of quality of life. In an attempt to uncover the meaningful predictors of each of these domains, the potential predictors were drawn from a list of those that had been used in two previous studies, one predicting home independence (Heal & Rusch, 1994) and the other predicting employment (Heal & Rusch, 1995). Predictors consisted of community characteristics, parent characteristics, student characteristics, and school program characteristics.

2.5   INFERENTIAL STATISTICS

A *multiple regression analysis* was used to identify the significant predictors of each of the three composites: esteem, independence, and security and support. For this, the composite scale for each of the three domains of quality of life was regressed separately onto the predictors in Table 9.3. Parallel to Heal and Rusch (1994, 1995), the 28 potential predictors were entered in eight ordered blocks into each regression analysis. Their order of entry was specified in advance. The strategy used was to enter geoeconomic characteristics first, followed by family characteristics, three blocks of students' personal characteristics, then disability categories, next school philosophy, and finally a block of individual students' school programs. The rationale for such a blockwise regression analysis is that earlier blocks of variables function as the control variables for later blocks (Heal & Rusch, 1994). In most cases, control variables are characteristics of the individual and his or her environment that are relatively permanent, that is, not amenable to intervention. By entering these into a regression equation before one enters programmable features of individuals and/or "their" environment, one can estimate the extent to which one's schooling can improve one's future quality of life through programmatic intervention. A *canonical correlation analysis* was used because the composite scales for the

three dimensions of the quality of life were correlated. (See Table 9.4.) The canonical correlation analysis facilitates the study of the relationship between a set of correlated criterion variables and a set of correlated predictor variables, with the objective of predicting one from the other. This approach identifies a canonical variate (linear combination) for the predictor variables that has the highest correlation with the canonical variate (linear combination) of the criterion variables.

TABLE 9.2

COMPOSITION OF EACH DOMAIN OF THE QUALITY-OF-LIFE SCALE: SELF-ESTEEM, INDEPENDENCE, AND SECURITY AND SUPPORT

Self-esteem indicators

THPYEVER[a]	Respondent's or school's claim of therapeutic counseling for the youth
NOFSVCS[a]	Number of DD services of 12 attributed to the youth
PROSTHCS[a]	Youth used some DD prosthetic device in the past year
PDFORWK	Youth worked for pay in the past year
ANYJOB	Youth worked with or without pay in the past year
EDSTAT	Educational status, dropout to college graduate (9-point scale)

Independence indicators

FUTRIND	Parent's prediction youth's future home independence (4-point ordinal scale)
HOMESKLS	Sum of cook, shop, wash, clean skills up to 16
LVGSKLS	Sum of phone, time, count, read skills up to 16
SELFSKLS	Sum of dress, feed, go out skills up to 12
CANANSR	Youth's ability to respond on follow-up questionnaire

Security-and-support indicators

PUBAID	Number of sources of public aid up to 9
F&FSUPRT	Number of family or friend sources of services for youth up to 6
CLOSEREL[a]	Respondent's relationship to the youth (1 = close, 14 = far)
COMSVCS	Number of community services up to 7
TRANEVER	Youth has used special DD transportation at some time (0 = no, 1 = yes)
VRSVCS	Degree of involvement with State Vocational Rehabilitation (4-point ordinal scale)

[a]Item required reverse scoring to make low values reflect low quality of life and high values reflect high quality of life.

TABLE 9.3

PREDICTORS OF QUALITY OF LIFE GROUPED BY CHARACTERISTICS

Variable	Definition
1. County economic characteristics	
CNTYINCM	Personal income from service industries in the youth's school county
CNTYUNEM	1986 unemployment rate in youth's school county
2. Family characteristics	
FAMINCOM	Household income before taxes in 1986
NOFSIBS	Number of siblings
NDDSIBS	Number of disabled siblings
HHEDUC	Highest school grade of head of the household
3. Noncognitive personal characteristics	
SEX	Sex of the out-of-school youth (0 = F, 1 = M)
AGE	Chronological age, in years
ETHNIC	Ethnicity of out-of-school youth (0 = Minority, 1 = Caucasian)
4. Cognitive competence	
ACADGPA	Grade point average in academic courses
IQEST	IQ, as reported in school records or estimated from regression of IQ on competence measures
5. Maladaptive behaviors	
BADACTOR	Report of incarceration, school dismissal, or both
SUSPENDED	Report of any suspension from school
DAYSABS	Number of days absent in the reference year (1986 or 1987)
6. Primary disability	
MILDDIS	Mild speech, emotional or learning disability
MR	Mild or moderate mental retardation
VISDIS	Vision disability
PHYSDIS	Physical disability
HEARDIS	Deaf or hard of hearing
(SEVDIS)	Severe emotional or mental disability (reference variable; withheld from regression predictor list because of its linear dependency [redundancy] with the other five primary disabilities)
7. School characteristics	
PCTSPED	% of school's student body in special education
COMVISIT	Approximate number of visits into the community per year
JOBPREP	Intensity of school-based job preparation
SCHINTEG	Extent of school integration
8. School programs	
PCTREG	% of hours spent in regular education classes in 1986-1987
VOCAMT	Hours in 1985-1986 or 1986-1987 in vocational education courses
ACAMT	Hours in 1985-1986 or 1986-1987 in academic courses
OCCVAMT	Hours in 1985-1986 or 1986-1987 in occupational training

TABLE 9.4

RAW SCORE MEANS, STANDARD DEVIATIONS, AND TRANSFORMED SCORE ITEM-DOMAIN CORRELATIONS OF THE VARIABLES USED IN EACH DOMAIN OF QUALITY OF LIFE—ESTEEM, INDEPENDENCE, AND SECURITY AND SUPPORT

Domain	M	SD	r [b]
Esteem			
THPYEVER[a]	0.444	0.497	0.060
NOFSVCS[a]	1.430	1.543	0.247
PROSTHCS[a]	0.415	0.493	0.185
PDFORWK	0.620	0.486	0.525
ANYJOB	0.686	0.464	0.440
EDSTAT	3.362	1.407	0.028
Independence			
FUTRIND	2.888	1.085	0.663
HOMESKLS	10.322	3.212	0.560
LVGSKLS	13.315	3.411	0.665
SELFSKLS	11.084	1.924	0.543
CANANSR	0.680	0.467	0.480
Security and support			
PUBAID	1.174	1.297	0.192
F&FSUPRT	0.119	0.387	0.074
CLOSEREL[a]	2.479	5.697	0.046
COMSVCS	6.170	1.586	0.114
TRANEVER	0.409	0.492	0.348
VRSVCS	1.979	1.275	0.218

Intercorrelations among three quality-of-life domains

	ESTEEM	INDEPENDENCE	SUPPORT
ESTEEM	1.0000	0.4740*	-0.3940*
INDEPENDENCE	0.4740*	1.0000	-0.3929*
SUPPORT	-0.3940*	-0.3929*	1.0000

[a]Item required reverse scoring to make low values reflect low quality of life and high values reflect high quality of life.
[b]r is the correlation of the item with the remaining items from its dimension. Scores for this analysis were the cumulative percentages associated with each of the ordered categories for each variable.
*$p < .001$.

2.6 RESULTS

The results are summarized in Tables 9.4 through 9.6. Table 9.4 shows the raw score means and standard deviations of the component variables of the three quality-of-life domains as well as the correlations of each cumulative percentage score with its domains and the intercorrelations among the three. Intercorrelations among the three domains indicate that esteem and independence are positively correlated, and that both

are negatively correlated with support. Cronbach's alphas were 0.494, 0.796, and 0.277, for esteem, independence, and security and support respectively.

Table 9.5 shows the means and standard deviations of the predictor variables as well as their correlations with each of the three quality-of-life domains. Each quality-of-life domain is characterized by a different set of predictor correlates. Esteem is greater for those with mild disabilities (learning disabilities, speech disorders, and emotional disturbance) who have had minimal special education. Independence is greater for younger students with mild disabilities who have had minimal special education. Support is greater for those with more severe disabilities who have had substantial special education.

TABLE 9.5

MEANS AND STANDARD DEVIATIONS OF POTENTIAL PREDICTORS OF QUALITY OF LIFE AND THEIR CORRELATIONS WITH EACH OF THE THREE QUALITY-OF-LIFE DOMAIN VARIABLES

Block	Variable	M	SD	Corr. with Esteem[a]	Corr. with Independence[a]	Corr. with Support[a]
1.	CNTYINCM	18,393.25	3,323.83	-0.041	0.018	0.163
	CNTYUNEM	7.65	2.97	-0.067	-0.080	-0.037
2.	FAMINCOM	2.28	0.77	0.166	0.149	-0.159
	NOFSIBS	2.38	1.40	0.042	0.057	-0.019
	NDDSIBS	0.13	0.34	0.038	0.019	0.066
	HHEDUC	2.55	1.68	0.021	0.093	-0.020
3.	SEX (1 = Male)	0.64	0.48	0.108	0.089	-0.126
	AGE	19.77	1.69	-0.180	-0.345*	0.250
	ETHNIC (1 = Cauc)	0.72	0.45	0.183	0.092	-0.168
4.	ACADGPA	2.13	0.76	-0.069	-0.003	0.110
	IQEST	80.77	16.96	0.194	0.396*	-0.157
5.	BADACTOR	0.14	0.35	0.214	0.137	-0.230
	SUSPENDED	0.05	0.22	0.059	0.052	-0.097
	DAYSABS	11.99	13.38	-0.074	-0.030	0.001
6.	MILDDIS	0.29	0.45	0.378*	0.349*	-0.467*
	MR	0.21	0.41	-0.047	-0.257	0.105
	VISDIS	0.07	0.26	-0.108	0.062	0.105
	PHYSDIS	0.10	0.31	-0.120	-0.027	0.122
	HEARDIS	0.19	0.39	-0.056	0.170	0.128
7.	PCTSPED	36.67	41.89	-0.318*	-0.395*	0.296*
	COMVISIT	3.21	1.88	-0.154	-0.243	0.252
	JOBPREP	18.20	5.71	0.069	0.109	0.093
	SCHINTEG	6.25	4.51	0.321	0.369*	-0.232
8.	PCTREG	41.64	37.25	0.321*	0.477*	-0.346*
	VOCAMT	246.30	258.30	0.015	-0.045	0.121
	ACAMT	326.35	270.37	0.083	0.263	-0.077
	OCCVAMT	143.22	204.83	0.065	0.108	0.002

[a]$p < .001 = \pm0.13$.
*$|r| \geq 0.30$.

FIGURE 9.1

PROPORTION OF VARIANCE (R^2 CHANGE) ATTRIBUTABLE TO SUCCESSIVE BLOCKS OF PREDICTOR VARIABLES FOR EACH OF THE THREE QUALITY-OF-LIFE DOMAINS

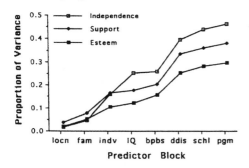

Cumulative Proportion of Variance (RSQ) Predicted by Eight Blocks of Predictor Variables

Predictor block labels are abbreviations of the eight successive numbered sections from Table 9.3

A separate multiple regression analysis was conducted for each of the three quality-of-life domains as its dependent variable and the 28 variables from Table 9.3 as the predictor variables entered in the eight ordered blocks shown in Table 9.3: county economic characteristics, family characteristics, noncognitive personal characteristics, cognitive competence, maladaptive behaviors, primary disability, school characteristics, and school programs. Figure 9.1 presents the cumulative proportion of variance (R^2) for each domain of quality of life for each successive block of variables. The final multiple R^2 was 0.286 for esteem, 0.451 for independence, and 0.368 for support. The sizes of these multiple R^2's were ordered (limited) as one would expect from their alpha reliabilities. The location and family characteristics chosen for this analysis contributed about 0.05 to the total R^2; individual characteristics—demographic, IQ, behavior problems, and especially disability category—accounted for an additional 20% in esteem, 40% in independence, and 24% in support.

School characteristics and individual students' school programs accounted for a final 5% of the variance in each of the three quality-of-life domains. This final increment added to the proportion of variance was 0.046 for independence, $F(8,682) = 10.31$, $p < 0.001$; 0.066 for support, $F(8,682) = 6.23$, $p < 0.001$; and 0.045 for esteem, $F(8,682) = 4.54$, $p < 0.001$.

The canonical loadings (the correlation between each variable in the predictor or criterion set and its respective canonical variate), *proportion of variance* (R^2) in each set of variables (criterion or predictor set) that is explained by the respective canonical variates, and the *canonical correlations* (correlations between the criterion and predictor canonical variates) and *redundancy coefficients* (proportion of variance in a predictor set multiplied by the squared canonical correlation) are presented in Table 9.6. Three canonical variates were identified—the most possible because the smaller set of variables (i.e., the criterion set) had only three domains—each one defined by positive correlations with two of the QOL domains and a negative or negligible correlation with the third. The first might be labeled "competence" because of its association with youth, high IQ, bad behavior record, mild disability classification, and minimal exposure to special education services. The second might be labeled "sensory disability" because of its association with sensory disabilities, IQ, and academic and/or vocational (as opposed to special) school placements. The third might be called "valued support" because of its positive association with the esteem and support quality-of-life domains, with having other disabled siblings, and with attendance in special employment and vocational school programs.

The proportion of criterion set variance accounted for by the canonical variates is inflated by the fact that there are as many quality-of-life variables as canonical variates, assuring that the sum of the proportion of variances accounted for by three canonical variates is 1.0.

The first canonical variate (competence) accounts for 59.2% of the variability in the criterion set. The second (sensory disability) and third (valued support) canonical variates account for 20.2% and 20.6% of the criterion set variability, respectively. The squared canonical correlations indicate that the first canonical

TABLE 9.6

CANONICAL LOADINGS, ASSOCIATED SQUARED MULTIPLE CORRELATIONS, CANONICAL CORRELATIONS, AND REDUNDANCY COEFFICIENTS FOR QUALITY OF LIFE AND ALL 28 PREDICTORS

Canonical Variates (Dimensions)

		Competence	Sensory Disability	Valued Support
Criterion Set				
	ESTEEM	0.659	-0.287	0.695
	INDEPENDENCE	0.889	0.457	0.028
	SUPPORT	-0.742	0.560	0.368
Squared Mult. R^2 with Canonical Variates		0.592	0.202	0.206
Squared Canonical R^2		0.507	0.243	0.096
Product (Redundancy Coefficient)		0.300	0.049	0.020
Predictor Set				
	CNTYINCM	-0.090	0.328+	0.221
	CNTYUNEM	-0.068	-0.154	-0.264
	FAMINCOM	0.271	-0.103	0.114
	NOFSIBS	0.074	0.046	0.065
	NDDSIBS	-0.011	0.107	0.273+
	HHEDUC	0.100	0.133	-0.034
	SEX	0.183	-0.118	0.025
	AGE	-0.503*	-0.127	0.177
	ETHNIC	0.230	-0.246	0.189
	ACADGPA	-0.087	0.228	0.016
	IQEST	0.498*	0.360+	0.053
	BADACTOR	0.315+	-0.282	0.122
	SUSPENDED	0.119	-0.103	-0.054
	DAYSABS	-0.048	0.010	-0.237

MILDDIS	0.687*	-0.379+	0.010
MR	-0.303+	-0.301+	0.246
VISDIS	-0.036	0.383+	-0.174
PHYSDIS	-0.129	0.245	-0.116
HEARDIS	0.061	0.583*	-0.010
PCTSPED	-0.612*	-0.031	-0.163
COMVISIT	-0.406	0.052	0.202
JOBPREP	0.062	0.296+	0.382+
SCHINTEG	0.552*	0.074	0.337+
PCTREG	0.715*	0.110	0.007
VOCAMT	-0.107	0.086	0.360+
ACAMT	0.302+	0.322+	-0.062
OCCVAMT	0.113	0.157	0.161

+Indicates canonical loading > 0.3.
*Indicates canonical loading > 0.5.

variate of the criterion set shares 50.7% of its variability with the first canonical variate of the predictor set. The second and third criterion canonical variates share 24.3% and 9.6% of their variability with the corresponding canonical variates of the predictor set, respectively. These result in the redundancy coefficients of 0.300, 0.049, and 0.020 for the first, second, and third canonical variates of the predictor set. The redundancy coefficient is the variance of one set of variables that can be accounted for by a canonical variate from the other set (Dillon & Goldstein, 1984). In other words, the first canonical variate of the predictor set accounts for 30% of the variability of the criterion set (0.592 x 0.507). The second and third canonical variates of the predictor set account for 4.9% (0.202 x 0.243) and 2.0% (0.206 x 0.096) of the criterion set variability, respectively. These three redundancy coefficients sum to 36.9%, the percentage of the criterion set variability accounted for by the linear combination predictor set of variables.

2.7 DISCUSSION

In summary, the primary dimension along which these former special education students varied was competence (a dimension whose positive pole was characterized by high independence), high esteem (few stigmata and high employment), and minimal dependency on family or government. Correlates of this factor from the predictor set were mild disability, more integrated and less special school programs, and young age. Presumably this last correlate reflected the common finding that more competent individuals disappear from disability service networks soon after high school graduation, leaving only younger, more competent graduates in a follow-up cohort.

The second dimension might be called "sensory disability" because of its high loadings from hearing and visual disabilities. It had moderate positive correlations with independence (adaptive skills and estimated future independence), family and government support, and a moderate negative correlation with esteemed status, including employment. The negative pole of this dimension was also characterized by mild disability and mental retardation. The second canonical variate of the predictor set accounted for only 4.9% (redundancy coefficient = 0.049) of the variability in the criterion set. Finally, the third dimension, which had an almost negligible redundancy coefficient of 0.020, was labeled "valued support" because of its high positive correlation with the esteem criterion domain and moderate positive correlation with the support criterion domain.

The identification and labeling of factors are always subject to interpretations. This problem is compounded in retrospective studies, where the selection of variables is limited to those available. Furthermore, once QOL variables have been identified, their assignment to QOL subscales is subject to the judgment of the investigator. For example, the dimension of esteem reflected evidence of achievement or absence of stigmata, whereas security and support reflected evidence of family or government support. One could challenge the assignment of specialized transportation to government support instead of stigmata. Independence is probably less controversial, being comprised of three adaptive skill variables and two parents' attribution-of-skill variables. Given their composition, it is not surprising that these subscales were factorally multidimensional when they were entered into a canonical analysis.

The most salient implication of these results is that quality of life for young adults with disabilities may be defined primarily by a single dimension, competence, which is positively correlated with esteem and independence and negatively correlated with family and governmental support. Furthermore, to the degree that multidimensionality is indicated in these results, it appears related primarily to type of disability—severity of disability, especially mental disability, defining the first factor, and sensory disability defining the second.

3 DISENTANGLING COMPETENCE AND SATISFACTION

Notwithstanding the seductive parsimony of such a straightforward interpretation, closer scrutiny is probably warranted. While competence and mastery are undoubtedly very satisfying and may be a central

developmental drive (e.g., Harter, 1977, 1978), quality of life is likely to be manifested on several planes, not all of which are variations of competence. Like all analyses, the one just reported is a slave to its data set. The National Longitudinal Transition Study (NLTS) focused on disability and competence, not quality of life, limiting the range of variables that addressed QOL nuances. Table 9.1 shows the large number of QOL topics for which there were insufficient or incomplete NLTS items. Excluded were material comforts, social relationships with family and friends, the social responsibilities that accompany these relationships, spiritual fulfillment, creative expression and active recreation, passive recreation, and Normalization and Social Role Valorization. Other multivariate analyses (Borthwick-Duffy, 1986; Halpern, 1993; Harner & Heal, 1993; Heal & Chadsey-Rusch, 1985; Schalock, Keith, Hoffman, & Karan, 1989) have revealed convincing multidimensional structures for these constructs. Furthermore, recent thinking has accorded personal choice the highest value in calculating quality of life for people with disabilities (Goode, 1994; Heal, Borthwick-Duffy, & Saunders, 1996; Saunders & Spradlin, 1991), a dimension that was precluded by the nature of the NLTS data set. Exercising ones own choices is empirically, logically, and legally correlated with competence, but within each competence level these authors propose or imply that quality of life be indexed by the degree of control that each person with a disability can exercise over his or her environment.

Finally, the NLTS data set has no variables that assess, directly or indirectly, the former students' own claims of lifestyle satisfaction or subjective well-being. It is illogical and arrogant to select and assess quality-of-life components without asking the subject of study whether he or she values them. In terms of the classification of quality of life shown in Table 9.1 (Hughes et al., 1995), this analysis requires a separation of the well-being domain into that inferred from psychological indicators and informants' judgments on the one hand and that claimed by the respondent with disabilities herself on the other. To this end, Harner (1991) gathered parallel data by two methods, a client interview and an informant interview. The second investigation compared clients' and informants' perceptions of clients' well-being, using what appeared to be comparable components of these two subscales.

TABLE 9.7

DESCRIPTIVE STATISTICS FOR THE LIFESTYLE SATISFACTION SCALE (LSS) AND CONSTRUCTED QUALITY-OF-LIFE QUESTIONNAIRE (QOLQ) SUBSCALES (N = 46)

	Items[a]	M	SD	α[b]
QOLQ				
JOBQOL[c]	9, 12, 13, 14, 15, 16, 17, 19	16.85	2.55	0.80
COMQOL	1, 3, 4, 5, 6, 40	12.27	2.03	0.74
PALQOL	7, 8, 33, 34, 35	10.05	2.00	0.62
RECQOL	2, 27, 31, 32, 37	12.00	2.14	0.72
CTLQOL	21, 23, 24, 26, 28, 30	12.34	2.99	0.86
LSS				
JOBSAT	23, 30, 32, 33, 34, 35, 38, 39	5.51	2.78	0.60
COMSAT	1, 2, 4, 5, 6, 7, 8, 9, 28, 29, 63, 64	4.28	4.11	0.58
PALSAT	10, 11, 12, 14, 15, 16, 40	1.13	3.16	0.66
RECSAT	42, 43, 44, 46, 47, 48, 49, 50, 51, 52, 53, 54, 55, 56, 58, 59, 60	-6.85	10.21	0.92
CTLSAT	24, 26, 27, 61, 66, 67, 69	4.34	2.55	0.47

[a]The QOLQ item numbers are taken from Schalock, Keith, & Hoffman, 1990; the LSS item numbers are taken from the 76-item trial LSS (Harner, 1991). Both lists are available from the author. The value of each QOLQ item could range from 1 (low) to 3 (high); the value of each LSS item could range from -2 (very dissatisfied) to +2 (very satisfied). [b]Cronbach's alpha coefficient of internal consistency. LSS coefficients are from a crossvalidation sample. [c]Abbreviations: QOL = quality of life assessed by the newly constructed QOLQ subscales; SAT = satisfaction assessed by the LSS subscales; JOB = job; COM = community, home, and neighborhood; PAL = friends and most social activities; REC = recreation and most leisure activities; CTL = control of one's choices, self-determination.

3.1   METHOD

Forty-six clients from developmental disabilities service agencies were recruited for *Multifaceted Lifestyle Satisfaction* (LSS; Harner, 1991) interviews while their direct care supervisors were recruited for *1990 Quality of Life Questionnaire* (QOLQ; Schalock Keith, & Hoffman, 1990) interviews. Scores from presumably parallel items of the two instruments were correlated to estimate the agreement of caretakers with their clients regarding the quality of their clients' lives.

3.2   SUBJECTS

Subjects were 46 adults (21 males and 25 females) with mental retardation who were drawn from five service provider agencies in west central Indiana and east central Illinois. These adults were drawn unsystematically for assessment with both the LSS and QOLQ questionnaires from a larger sample of 149 adults who were assessed with only the LSS. The mean IQ from agency records was 60.8 ($SD = 13.7$), 4 being classified as severely retarded, 7 as moderately retarded, and 35 as mildly retarded or borderline. Ages ranged from 22 to 65 with a mean of 35.7. Individuals in the sample lived in one of five out-of-home community residential placements: large (16 or more beds) intermediate-care facilities ($n = 9$), small (15 or fewer beds) intermediate-care facilities ($n = 7$), sheltered group homes (eight or fewer beds) ($n = 11$), apartment training programs (three or fewer beds) ($n = 9$), or semi-independent and independent programs ($n = 10$).

3.3   ASSESSMENT INSTRUMENTS—LSS AND QOLQ

The *1990 Quality of Life Questionnaire* (Schalock et al., 1990) contains four subscales, each with 10 items: Satisfaction; Empowerment and Independence; Competence and Productivity; and Social Belonging and Community Integration. Each item requires the informant to decide on behalf of each client among three levels of quality of life.

For instance, Item 1 (Satisfaction subscale) was

Overall, would you say that life:

(3) Brings out the best in you

(2) Treats you like everybody else

(1) Doesn't give you a chance.

Item 26 (Empowerment subscale) was

Do you have a key to your home?

(3) Yes, I have a key and use it as I wish

(2) Yes, I have a key but it only unlocks certain areas

(1) No.

The 1991 LSS is comprised of 53 items in six subscales, five of which were used in the present investigation. Each question requires a response of yes or no. For instance, question 1 is "How do you like living here?"; question 10 is "Do you have enough things to do in your free time?"; and question 23 is "Do you like your job?" (Harner, 1991).

Although both instruments stress quality of life from the client's perspective, the QOLQ prompts informants to evaluate clients' activities and control over personal decisions, whereas the LSS uniformly elicits the clients' self-report of their subjective satisfaction with their conditions of life.

3.4   ITEM SELECTION

For the present analysis, only those QOLQ items that appeared conceptually to measure the same constructs as the LSS subscales were selected, so that a QOLQ subscale was constructed to parallel each of the LSS subscales. The items selected and descriptive statistics appear in Table 9.7. Final selection of items was based on an internal consistency reliability analysis. For each subscale the Cronbach's alpha was calculated with each item included or excluded. Items were retained if they increased the alpha and deleted if they decreased the alpha. The alpha coefficients for the items in the final subscales are presented in Table 9.7. The reliability of selecting the items for the newly constructed QOLQ was also evaluated. The author and two colleagues independently selected items for each of the five subscales to establish agreement with the items that had been nominated for selection by the three as a team several months earlier. The 15 agreement statistics (three colleagues by five subscales) ranged from 72.5% to 97.5% (kappa = 0.290 to 0.925) with a median of 85% (median kappa = 0.490). Agreement with the items selected after item analysis ranged from 77.5% to 97.5% (median = 92.5%); kappa ranged from 0.05 to 0.925 (median = 0.545). For interpretation of the comparison of percentage agreement and kappa, see Johnson and Heal (1987).

The LSS had 1.8% missing scores, 1.7% of which was due to clients having no jobs, and the QOLQ had 4.9% missing scores. In order to avoid losing data from cases with some missing scores, the mean of an item was substituted into the place of the missing data of any subject.

3.5   INTERVIEW PROCEDURES

Each LSS interview took about 20 minutes. A question was repeated and/or rephrased until the interviewer judged that the client understood it. In accordance with the instructions in its manual, the QOLQ was administered to two informants who knew the client well, and their scores were averaged. One informant was always a direct service person (group home manager, behavioral technician, or staff person), and the other was a qualified mental retardation professional who had a direct service relationship with the client.

3.6   RESULTS

The correlations between the LSS subscales and the newly constructed QOLQ subscales are presented in Table 9.8. It is disappointing that the only statistically significant diagonal coefficient, that for RECSAT, was negative in valence, indicating that informants' judgments of recreational satisfaction were at odds with clients' judgments. Three off-diagonal correlations—COMSAT with CTLQOL, CTLSAT with JOBQOL, and PALSAT with RECQOL—were statistically significant; two of the three were negative.

FIGURE 9.2

CORRELATIONS OF THE MLSS AND THE MQOLQ SUBSCALES WITH THE QOL DIMENSIONS OF SATISFACTION (I) AND COMPETENCE (II)

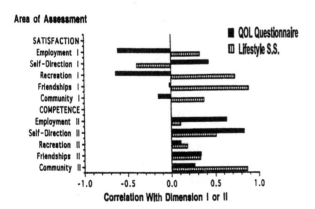

A canonical correlation analysis was performed to evaluate the predictive accuracy of the LSS subscales from the QOLQ subscales. The results are presented in Table 9.9 and Figure 9.2, which show the canonical loadings for the first two canonical variates.

The first canonical variate was associated with PALSAT and RECSAT from the LSS subscales as indicated by their high canonical loadings. On the other hand, RECQOL and JOBQOL from the QOLQ subscales were associated with the first canonical variate. The negative algebraic signs of these canonical loadings imply that PALSAT and RECSAT from the LSS set of subscales are associated negatively with RECQOL and JOBQOL from the QOLQ set of subscales. The second canonical variate was more interpretable than the first. All subscales of both sets of scales were positively correlated with this canonical variate, making it a good candidate for a general competence dimension. The redundancy coefficient of 0.192 in Table 9.9 indicates that only 19.2% of LSS set variability is accounted for by the first canonical variate from the QOLQ when LSS and QOLQ are treated as criterion and predictor sets respectively. This result follows because (a) the first canonical variate of the LSS set of subscales contains only 34.6% of the LSS variability and (b) this canonical variate shares only 55.7% (squared canonical correlation) of its variance with the first canonical variate from QOLQ set. If both the canonical variates are considered, a total of 27.5% of the LSS variability is accounted for by the QOLQ subscales. When the criterion and predictor sets are reversed, only 20.2% of variability of the QOLQ set is predicted by the two LSS canonical variates.

3.7   DISCUSSION

The results of this second investigation are very puzzling. Why would two reasonably reliable scales that were designed to measure the same constructs have such subscale by subscale incongruence? Only 4 of the 25 correlations between the 5 LSS and 5 QOLQ subscales were statistically reliable, 3 in counterintuitive directions.

We suggest that this pattern of results reflects (a) the real differences in the perceptions of clients and managers, (b) the differences in response biases in the two groups of respondents, and (c) imperfect substantive comparability of the two instruments. Looking first to response biases, we would expect greater acquiescence bias (saying "yes" regardless of the question asked) in the clients than in the informants, as it is correlated with intelligence (Heal & Sigelman, 1990, 1995). In this regard, RECSAT consisted entirely of reverse-scored items (e.g., "Would you like to do x more?"), and so an acquiescence bias would lower RECSAT scores and tend to produce a negative correlation with a more objective measure of recreation satisfaction, which RECQOL may have been.

The negative mean score for RECSAT in Table 9.1 implies that many more respondents said "yes" to these reverse-scored "more" items (e.g., "Would you like to play more board games?" "Yes" = dissatisfaction) than said "no." On the other hand, PALSAT had a balance of reverse-scored and normally scored items, which logically removes acquiescence bias. Because RECSAT and PALSAT from the LSS were positively correlated, it is likely that RECSAT scores were driven by true satisfaction as well as acquiescence bias. Nevertheless, the possibility exists that "yes" to these items really means "yes," that they were wrongly reverse-scored, and that satisfaction with friends is, in fact, negatively correlated with the recreation activities because they tend to preclude each other. Turning to respondents' choices, the informants were likely to let their understanding of current best practices influence their responses. For example, the moderate negative loading of CTLSAT and the moderate positive loading of CTLQOL on the first canonical variate could reflect the clients' satisfaction with decision-making support (i.e., relief from the stress of making one's own decisions), whereas the informants could feel obligated to embrace the principle of maximizing clients' freedom of choice and accordingly to attribute higher quality of life to those clients who have the least assistance in making choices.

TABLE 9.8

CORRELATIONS BETWEEN LSS AND CONSTRUCTED QOLQ SUBSCALES (N = 46)

	COMQOL[a]	PALQOL	RECQOL	CTLQOL	JOBQOL
COMSAT	0.090	0.072	-0.179	-0.513*	0.182
PALSAT	-0.024	0.014	-0.379*	0.435	-0.283
RECSAT	-0.112	0.155	-0.480*	0.355	-0.218
CTLSAT	0.131	0.208	0.210	0.149	0.385*
JOBSAT	0.008	-0.249	-0.239	0.053	-0.057

* $p < .01$.

[a]See Table 9.7 for a legend of abbreviations.

TABLE 9.9

CANONICAL LOADINGS CORRESPONDING TO THE FIRST TWO CANONICAL VARIATES, CANONICAL CORRELATIONS, AND REDUNDANCY COEFFICIENTS BETWEEN THE LSS AND QOLQ SUBSCALES

	Loadings on Canonical Variates	
	Canonical Variate 1 (Satisfaction)	*Canonical Variate 2 (Competence)*
LSS set		
COMSAT	0.373	0.865
PALSAT	0.889	0.326
RECSAT	0.731	0.182
CTLSAT	-0.399	0.508
JOBSAT	0.328	0.106
Proportion of variance	0.346	0.232
Redundancy coefficients[a]	0.192	0.083
QOLQ set		
COMQOL	-0.149	0.263
PALQOL	-0.020	0.335
RECQOL	-0.638	0.107
CTLQOL	0.432	0.832
JOBQOL	-0.611	0.633
Proportion of variance	0.198	0.257
Redundancy coefficients[a]	0.110	0.092
Squared canonical correlations	0.556	0.359

[a]The product of the squared canonical correlation multiplied by the proportion of the total variance of the set of subscales explained by the canonical variate.

Other evidence indicated that the discrepancies between clients and informants on these two instruments should not be attributed to the inability of these informants to predict clients' responses. As one of her validity evaluations, Harner (1991) selected two items from each LSS subscale and asked 75 informants to predict their clients' responses. Informants predicted their clients' LSS responses quite well. All 5 of the subscale correlations were positive, 4 significantly so, $p < .01$. Similarly Schalock et al. (1990) reported that the correlations between the 374 clients who provided their own responses on the QOLQ and the responses of their caretakers were high and statistically significant: Correlations were 0.66, 0.73, 0.81, 0.46, and 0.73, respectively, for their four subscales of Satisfaction, Social Belonging and Community Integration, Empowerment and Independence, and Competence and Productivity, and the total QOLQ score. Thus, the ability of caretakers to predict their clients' responses on the LSS and the QOLQ contrasts with the mismatch between their quality-of-life judgments and corresponding clients' LSS claims of lifestyle satisfaction. Given all these considerations, the first canonical variate appears to reflect different values of the clients and their caretakers that are exposed when caretakers are not explicitly instructed to guess their clients' responses, and to greater acquiescence by clients than by informants.

The second canonical variate appears to reflect a general competence factor, with informants' attributions of self-determination and quality of employment dominating the variate and clients' satisfaction with their community and self-determination contributing to their linear combination. The agreement on the competence dimension is reminiscent of Halpern, Irvin, and Landman (1979), who found extraordinarily good agreement between scores on an informant-completed employability scale and self-assessment by employment candidates with mental retardation.

4 GENERAL DISCUSSION

Returning to our theme "Are Normalization and Social Role Valorization limited by competence?", we must accept very tentative conclusions. Normalization and Social Role Valorization are presumably only two of the many constructs that comprise quality of life. This diminution is supported by the Hughes et al. (1995) systematic review of the quality-of-life literature, which was summarized in Table 9.1.

If quality of life looms so large conceptually, can it be operationalized as well as Normalization and Social Role Valorization have been through PASS (Wolfensberger & Glenn, 1975) and PASSING (Wolfensberger & Thomas, 1983)? The present analyses have exposed two problems in this operationalization, both of which may yield to subsequent research. First, it appears that the many conceptually discrete features of quality of life will be difficult to disentangle from competence. This was seen in the first investigation from the high correlation of both the esteem and independence quality-of-life subscales with several competency predictors, accounting for 30% from the 37% total in the redundancy coefficients. Independence, of course, weighs heavily as a Normalization and SRV value as well as being a premier proxy for competence and self-determination in quality-of-life conceptualizations. The rather distasteful implication is that the most highly valued outcome for human service practice, independence, is best predicted by the entry skill of the client and almost trivially by human service practice. "Blaming the victim" for his or her constraints seems justified by this result. Elsewhere in this book, Flynn (chapter 14) interestingly suggests that PASS and PASSING results are correlated with attributes of individuals such as their level of adaptive behavior. The second canonical analysis supported the first in its detection of a competence dimension, but in this analysis it was swamped by another dimension that, while somewhat enigmatic, appeared to reflect in part areas in which the client and caretaker disagreed on what constituted the good life for the client.

Is there Normalization, Social Role Valorization, or quality of life beyond competence? Scholars and practitioners in human services would like to think so. Only more refined assessment of these constructs and more concerted efforts to find valued and satisfying roles that are independent of competence will help us understand and separate one's quality of life from one's ability.

REFERENCES

AAMR (AMERICAN ASSOCIATION ON MENTAL RETARDATION) (1992). *Mental retardation: Definition, classification, and system of supports.* Washington DC: Author.

BORTHWICK-DUFFY, S. A. (1986). *Quality of life of mentally retarded people: Development of a model.* Unpublished doctoral dissertation, University of California, School of Education, Riverside, CA.

DILLON, W. R., & GOLDSTEIN, M. (1984). *Multivariate analysis: Methods and applications.* New York: Wiley.

GOODE, D. (1994). *Quality of life for persons with disabilities.* Cambridge, MA: Brookline Books.

HALPERN, A. S. (1993). Quality of life as a conceptual framework for evaluating transition outcomes. *Exceptional Children, 59,* 486-498.

HALPERN, A. S., IRVIN, L. K., & LANDMAN, J. T. (1979). Alternative approaches to the measurement of adaptive behavior. *American Journal of Mental Deficiency, 84,* 304-310.

HARNER, C. (1991). *Assessing the satisfaction of adults with mental retardation living in the community.* Unpublished doctoral dissertation, University of Illinois, Urbana, IL.

HARNER, C. J., & HEAL, L. W. (1993). The multifaceted lifestyle satisfaction scale (MISS). Psychometric properties of an interview schedule for assessing personal satisfaction of adults with limited intelligence. *Research in Developmental Disabilities, 14,* 221-236.

HARTER, S. (1977). The effects of social reinforcement and task difficulty on the pleasure derived by normal and retarded children from cognitive challenge and mastery. *Journal of Experimental Child Psychology, 24,* 476-494.

HARTER, S. (1978). Effectance motivation reconsidered. *Human Development, 21,* 34-64.

HEAL, L. W., BORTHWICK-DUFFY, S. A., & SAUNDERS, R. R. (1996). Assessment of quality of life. In J. W. JACOBSON & J. A. MULICK (Eds.), *Manual of Diagnosis and Practice in Mental Retardation.* Washington, DC: American Psychological Association.

HEAL, L. W., & CHADSEY-RUSCH, J. (1985). The lifestyle satisfaction scale (LSS): Assessing individuals' satisfaction with residence, community setting, and associated services. *Applied Research in Mental Retardation, 6,* 475-490.

HEAL, L. W., & RUSCH, F. R. (1994). Prediction of residential independence of special education high school students. *Research in Developmental Disabilities, 15*(3), 223-243.

HEAL, L. W., & RUSCH, F. R. (1995). Predicting employment for students who leave special education high school programs. *Exceptional Children, 61,* 472-487.

HEAL, L. W., & SIGELMAN, C. K. (1990). Methodological issues in measuring the quality of life of individuals with mental retardation. In R. L. SCHALOCK (Ed.), *Quality of life: Perspectives and issues* (pp. 161-176). Washington, DC: American Association on Mental Retardation.

HEAL, L. W., & SIGELMAN, C. K. (1995). Response biases in interviews of individuals with limited mental ability. *Journal of Intellectual Disability Research.*

HUGHES, C., HUANG, B., KIM, J., EISENMAN, L. T., & KILLIAN, D. J. (1995). Quality of life in applied research: Conceptual model and analysis of measures. *American Journal of Mental Retardation.*

JAMIESON, J. (1993). *Adults with mental handicap: Their quality of life.* Vancouver, BC: British Columbia Ministry of Social Services.

JAVITZ, H. S., & WAGNER, M. (1987). *The national longitudinal transition study of special education students: Report on sample design and limitations, Wave 1.* Menlo Park, CA: SRI International.

JOHNSON, L. J., & HEAL, L. W. (1987). Inter-observer agreement: How large should kappa be? *Capstone Journal of Education, 7,* 51-73.

NIRJE, B. (1969). The Normalization principle and its human management implications. In R. B. KUGEL AND W. WOLFENSBERGER (Eds.), *Changing patterns in residential services for the mentally retarded.* Washington, DC: President's Committee on Mental Retardation.

NIRJE, B. (1992). The normalization principle—25 years later. In U. LEHTINEN & R. PIRTTIMAA (Eds.), *Arjessa Tapatuu: Comments on mental retardation and adult education* (pp. 1-25). Jyväskylä, Finland: University of Jyväskylä, Institute for Educational Research.

PARENT, W. (1993). Quality of life and consumer choice. In P. WEHMAN (Ed.), *The ADA mandate for social change*. Baltimore: Paul H. Brookes Publishers.

PARMENTER, R. R. (1992). Quality of life for people with developmental disabilities. In N. W. BRAY (Ed.), *International review of research in mental retardation, 18*, 247-287. New York: Academic Press.

SAUNDERS, R. R., & SPRADLIN, J. E. (1991). A supported routines approach to active treatment for enhancing independence, competence, and self-worth. *Behavioral Residential Treatment, 6*, 11-37.

SCHALOCK, R. L. (1990). *Quality of life: Perspectives and issues*. Washington, DC: American Association on Mental Retardation.

SCHALOCK, R. L. (1996). *Quality of life: Perspectives and issues, Vol. 1, Conceptualization and measurement* (2nd ed.). Washington, DC: American Association on Mental Retardation.

SCHALOCK, R. L., & JENSEN, C. M. (1986). Assessing the goodness-of-fit between persons and their environments. *Journal of the Association for Persons with Severe Handicaps, 11*(2), 103-109.

SCHALOCK, R. L., KEITH, K. D., & HOFFMAN, K. (1990). *1990 Quality of Life Questionnaire Standardization Manual*. Hastings, NE: Mid-Nebraska Mental Retardation Services.

SCHALOCK, R. L., KEITH, K. D., HOFFMAN, K., & KARAN, O. C. (1989). Quality of life: Its measurement and use in human services programs. *Mental Retardation, 27*(1), 25-31.

VALDES, K. A. (1989). *The national longitudinal transition study of special education students*. Menlo Park, CA: SRI International.

WAGNER, M. (1989). *Youth with disabilities during transition: An overview of descriptive findings from the national longitudinal transition study*. Menlo Park, CA: SRI International.

WAGNER, M., NEWMAN, L., D'AMICO, R., JAY, E. D., BUTLER-WALIN, P., MARDER, C., & COX, R. (1991). *Youth with disabilities: How are they doing? The first comprehensive report from the national longitudinal transition study of special education students*. Menlo Park, CA: SRI International.

WOLFENSBERGER, W. (1980). "The definition of normalization: Update, problems, disagreements and misunderstandings." In R. J. FLYNN & K. E. NITSCH (Eds.) *Normalization, social integration, and community services*. Baltimore: Pro-ED.

WOLFENSBERGER, W. (1992). *A brief introduction to Social Role Valorization as a high-order concept for structuring human services*. (2nd ed., rev.). Syracuse, NY: Syracuse University, Training Institute for Human Service Planning, Leadership and Change Agentry.

WOLFENSBERGER, W. (1994). "Let's hang up 'Quality of Life' as a hopeless term." In D. GOODE (Ed.), *Quality of life for persons with disabilities*. Cambridge, MA: Brookline Books.

WOLFENSBERGER, W., & GLENN, L. (1975). *PASS 3. Program analysis of service systems handbook*. Toronto, ON: National Institute on Mental Retardation.

WOLFENSBERGER, W., & THOMAS, S. (1983). *PASSING (Program Analysis of Service Systems' Implementation of Normalization Goals*. Toronto, ON: National Institute on Mental Retardation.

NOTE

1. The present report was supported in part by the Office of Special Education and Rehabilitative Services, U.S. Department of Education under a contract (300-85-0160) to the Transition Research Institute at the University of Illinois. I am grateful to Dr. Madhab Raj Khoju for his statistical consultation on the analyses reported herein, to Cathy J. Harner for the use of the data from her dissertation, and to Mary Wagner, Ron D'Amico, and Kathryn Valdes for their assistance in interpreting the data collected in the National Longitudinal Transition Study.

Part 4

Links Between Normalization, Social Role Valorization, Social Science Theory, and Empirical Research

10

Roles, identities, and expectancies: Positive contributions to Normalization and Social Role Valorization

RAYMOND A. LEMAY

1 INTRODUCTION

In 1982, Steve Tullman and Wolf Wolfensberger reformulated the Normalization principle, stating that Normalization hinged upon the attributions of valued social roles to otherwise devalued individuals and classes of people. It was "the insight that the creation of valued social roles for people at risk of social devaluation was the epitome of Normalization" (Wolfensberger, 1983, p. 237). A year later Wolfensberger concluded that this new formulation was such a drastic departure from traditional Normalization theory that he decided, for a variety of reasons, to rename the principle and push even further its relationship to role theory. Thus it is the access to valued roles that will enable individuals to have access to the good things in life (Wolfensberger & Thomas, 1994).

This new direction in theorizing has led to some confusion and also to a great deal of debate. For some this has meant that Social Role Valorization (SRV) is a more reductionist formulation than Wolfensberger's (1972) classic Normalization definition.

From the beginning, North American Normalization and to a lesser extent Scandinavian Normalization have always made some reference to role concepts. But with SRV, roles have become the focal point of the definition as well as the defining term included in its name. Some of the confusion undoubtedly stems from the fact that Wolfensberger calls into play a vast new area of research and theorizing that up until now has remained virtually unknown for SRV and Normalization aficionados.

The following aims to chart Normalization's and SRV's historical relationship with role theory, to selectively review the considerable work that has gone on over the past years in the realms of sociology and social psychology that has been termed "social role theory."

This review will also attempt to answer some very basic questions that will hopefully inform the ongoing debate concerning SRV's new formulation and its research, practice, and training implications.

1. Is SRV's reference to role theory in keeping with the formulations now present in social science literature? Is Wolfensberger's use of the terms "role" and "social roles" in keeping with the current definitions found in the literature of psychology and sociology, or is his use idiosyncratic? At the outset, though, Wolfensberger's own claims to theory building should lead us to believe that he is here, in the new SRV synthesis, speaking of role theory as it is generally accepted in the social sciences literature.

2. Does social science research and theorizing support SRV's contention that social roles are fundamental? Do social roles, for instance, have an effect upon positive or negative valuation and one's access to the good things in life? Does the literature support that the attribution of positive roles is the way

to assuring the valorization of the individual and should therefore be the end and means of human service endeavor? Does role theory and do social roles have the conceptual breadth and power to subsume all that is, on the one hand, the experience of devaluation, and on the other, the possibility and strategy of redressing that which we agree is a great social wrong? Do other researchers and theorists share Wolfensberger's view that social roles can play an important conceptual role in building a theory of psychosocial intervention?

2 EARLY REFERENCES TO SOCIAL ROLES IN THE LITERATURE ON NORMALIZATION

2.1 ROLES IN THE 1969 BOOK CHANGING PATTERNS IN RESIDENTIAL SERVICES FOR THE MENTALLY RETARDED

The term "roles" and the concepts associated with social roles are almost entirely absent from the Scandinavian formulations of Normalization (e.g., Nirje, 1969; Bank-Mikkelsen, 1969). Though these early articles give the impression of individuals and groups having things done to them and for them, from a roles perspective one can reread these articles and see how roles fit between the lines, so to speak. By having access to a normal rhythm of day and normal routine of life, the attribution of certain roles are certainly assumed. Being in one's home assumes that one would be at least a resident or tenant, if not a homeowner. Participating in leisure time activities would make one a player, or at least a participant. Certainly Nirje (1969) proposes that mentally retarded individuals should have sex roles and of course that their roles should be related to their chronological ages, and he also raises the notion of roles in the context of employment or vocational services.

From the beginning, social roles have been highlighted in North American Normalization. The 1969 *Changing Patterns in Residential Services for the Mentally Retarded* (Kugel & Wolfensberger, 1969), which first gave prominence to Normalization, also included Wolfensberger's (1969) "Origin and Nature of Our Institutional Models," which, among other things, surveyed the negative historical roles that

defined the lives of devalued classes of individuals. Wolfensberger gave a far-reaching exposition on how these roles were created and then maintained by complex feedback systems that included stereotypes and expectancies, which were conveyed by language and physical environments. In his 1969 monograph, Wolfensberger had only one specific positive role to propose for mentally retarded individuals, and that was of the role of a "developing individual."

Changing Patterns contained many important contributions by some of the then leading lights in the social sciences and services to persons with mental retardation. Few of the authors make more than a passing reference to "roles" and then usually in relation to work. Seymour Sarason (1969), who later became president of the American Psychological Association, wrote a suggestive article about the problems of creating healthy settings that echoed Wolfensberger's discussion on the "meaning of a building." Sarason tied his discussion on settings to Blatt and Kaplan's (1966) pictorial essay *Christmas in Purgatory,* which graphically described the scandalous failure of contemporary settings by concluding: "if one thinks that defective children are almost beyond help, one acts toward them in ways which confirm one's assumptions" (p. 7). This evocation of expectancy effects is very suggestive of role theory, to which it is intimately tied.

Gunnar Dybwad (1969), in his concluding "overview" chapter, lists the necessary changes that needed to be brought about to renovate the residential service system for mentally retarded adults and children. Echoing Wolfensberger, Sarason, and Blatt, he proposes that one of the great obstacles to change is "the societal role perception of Retardates as deviants" (p. 391).

2.2 ROLES IN THE 1972 BOOK THE PRINCIPLE OF NORMALIZATION IN HUMAN SERVICES

The 1972 book *The Principle of Normalization in Human Services*, which has recently been identified as the most classic work in the field of mental retardation (Heller, Spooner, Enright, Haney, & Schilit, 1991), has had a tremendous influence on human services. It is with this book that Normalization becomes inextricably linked with social roles and role theory.

In his discussions of ideology, Wolfensberger (1972) speaks of combinations of beliefs, attitudes, and interpretations of reality that have derived from one's experiences, one's knowledge of what are presumed to be facts, and, above all, one's values. Interestingly, the whole notion of roles subsumes this notion of ideology in the sense that roles are, by and large, culture-bound and constrained by the very same dynamics that make up ideology. Prior to this definition of ideology, Wolfensberger speaks much of the role of human service manager and how much power and control is wielded, though unconsciously, through this role. Later he suggests that ideology can lead one to view the mentally retarded as menaces to society, thus dramatically altering the relationship betweeen the "managers" and the helpees. The important insight here, upon which the future edifice of SRV will be built, was that roles are one of the important and ubiquitous means for transacting ideology and particularly devaluation.

In chapter 2 of the 1972 Normalization book, Wolfensberger explains deviancy in terms of roles: "When a person is perceived as deviant, he is cast into a role that carries with it powerful expectancies" (p. 15). In this chapter Wolfensberger summarizes the then eight historical roles of deviancy. Here, his discussion of roles and role expectations is classical, explaining it as a feedback mechanism affecting both perceiver and perceived. The first North American formulation of the Normalization principle speaks to the issue of roles, if only in an indirect way, by proposing that culturally normative means be used "to establish and/or maintain personal behaviors and characteristics which are as culturally normative as possible" (p. 28). Certainly roles are about behaviors and characteristics. The missing element in this first formulation is the relationship factor whereby one understands that the behaviors and characteristics of individuals are most often expressed in social (and physical) contexts in relation to other people and settings.

The issue of roles becomes even clearer in chapters 4 and 6 of the Normalization book, where Wolfensberger addresses the issue of programmatic and architectural implications of the Normalization principle. Interestingly, he divided the implications into two dimensions. The interaction dimension and the interpretation dimension, which resemble very closely the feedback loop system in classical definitions of social roles, where interpretations are vehicles for beliefs and stereotypes and as such create expectancies and where interactions provide the opportunities for role attribution and for skill acquisition. In fact, he invokes many of the concepts that are quite close to role theory, such as stereotypes, role perceptions, and role expectancies, as well as making clear that even architecture can convey strong role expectancies. Moreover, he shows that these dimensions are active on three levels: the person level, the intermediate social system level, and, finally, the societal level. Once again, this echoes fairly closely the classical descriptions of role theory that operate on individuals in small groups through societally broad mechanisms (Biddle, 1979; Newcomb, Turner, & Converse, 1975; Thomas & Biddle, 1966).

In his chapter on mental health and Normalization, Wolfensberger (1970) states: "if role expectancy is as powerful as we believe we know it to be then it should be manipulated consciously and/or systematically, rather than unconsciously and/or haphazardly, as is typically the case now" (p. 104). One also finds an early discussion of the client role where it is sketched as inspired by the "developmental-Normalization model" and shown as an alternative to the sick role of the medical model. Wolfensberger also develops the notion of "developmental" role perceptions in his chapter on the profoundly retarded, stating "we must endeavour that, with the aid of our services, the handicapped attain their potential, and we must formulate roles for them that discourage dependency and encourage growth" (Wolfensberger, 1972, p. 132).

Simon Olshansky (1972), in his article on changing vocational behavior through Normalization, states that "industry has little interest in hiring clients; it wants workers who can function as workers. It has little patience or tolerance of workers sliding into the role of clients. And even though some large employers are beginning to offer some clinical services, many workers interpret them as a public relations deception" (p. 156). His discussion of the workshop is one of roles and role expectancies and how one should create the expectancy for work and the worker role. Wolfensberger (1972) also provides an interesting discussion of sociosexual roles of the severely impaired in his chapter on sociosexual needs. In it, one would find a very frank discussion on what these roles are in the culture and the barriers to having them transacted for persons who are severely handicapped.

It is clear that from the outset, at least for the North American formulation, role theory was a pervasive influence. Interestingly, it is almost absent in the discussion on physical and social integration in the Normalization book of 1972. This suggests that up until then, the theorists of the movement had not pushed the connection to its ultimate conclusion. The connections of Normalization to role theory continued to evolve over the years, especially in the various training formats and teaching modules that were developed by Wolfensberger and his colleagues.

3 SRV'S ASSERTIONS CONCERNING SOCIAL ROLE THEORY

"The Social Role may be defined as a socially expected pattern of behaviors, responsibilities, expectations and privileges" (Wolfensberger, 1992, p. 13). People learn the expected responsibilities of a role through a "feedback loop between role expectations and role performances" (p. 13). Persons may enter into social roles through choice, because of their competencies or by imposition. Wolfensberger goes on to propose that different roles have different "bandwidths," which he defines in terms of time (for instance, the work role taking up 35 hours in a week and therefore being relatively important) and of location, occasion, and possibilities of manifestation. As an example, he points to the difference between the role of spouse, which is very broad and allows for many manifestations across many settings, and the role of customer, which is manifested in relatively fewer locations.

In SRV, all of this is tied in parallel to the notions of valuation and devaluation, which are an evaluative comment on things and persons and are a product of the human perceptual process. These social judgments are formed through a complex filtering of the human perceptual process. Thus, an observer is deeply influenced by various factors:

a) The observer's own characteristics and experiences including expectations from previous

contacts with observed persons or group.
b) Characteristics of observer's physical environment, e.g., deprivation, stress.
c) Characteristics of the observer's social environment, e.g., values, expectations, norms and conventions.
d) What is actually observed, i.e., another person/group appearance, e.g., red hair, behavior, etc. (Wolfensberger, 1992, p. 16).

Wolfensberger points out that when the stigmata of impairment is observed, it will have a definite impact upon the evaluative judgment of the observer, especially if there is concordance between the role behavior observed, the impairments observed, and the observer's own stereotypic beliefs and prior experience. Despite this, Wolfensberger proposes that roles may be more powerful than impairments. "Some roles are stronger than impairments in shaping the attitudes of the observers." Early, he had stated that some roles become embedded in one's identity, and then, "roles are so powerful that they largely define who we are, what we do and with whom we act, even what we wear" (p. 20).

In *The Origin and Nature of Institutional Models,* Wolfensberger (1969) made the point that persons with impairments often had historically embedded negative stereotypic deviancy roles attributed to them. But with the SRV monograph (Wolfensberger, 1992), he goes on to propose that valued social roles can neutralize the impact of impairments and afflictions or even capitalize upon them. Thus, "people who are accorded positive roles despite their impairments, can lead almost totally integrated, highly valued, productive and full lives" (1992, p. 29). Valued roles, therefore, will provide persons with positive opportunities that will in turn promote competency enhancement and finally, afford the person "the good things of life" (p. 34). The attribution of valued roles, or as Wolfensberger states it "the enablement, establishment, enhancement, maintenance, and/or defence of valued social roles for people" (p. 32), can be the necessary corrective to social devaluation, and thus the essence of psychosocial intervention.

Two major strategies stand as "avenues to valued social roles" (p. 34). These are competency enhancement, and image enhancement, which, in essence, is the creation of positive attitudes by the enhancement of social image so that they (the impaired persons) will be more positively perceived by others, and others will therefore be more inclined to extend to them valued roles . . . and the enhancement of their competencies, so that they will be better able to fill certain valued roles, and so that valued roles which require certain competencies can be accorded to them (p. 34).

In a sense, SRV, and the last formulation of Normalization, are not such a radical departure, and in hindsight it is only natural that the formulation evolved as it did.

However, Wolfensberger's claims concerning social roles are largely unsubstantiated through the traditional method of referring to the relevant and up-to-date literature. Thus, his theoretical model, though intuitively appealing, is nonetheless open to question. Moreover, his theoretical version of social role theory seems, at first glance, to be largely based on the work of one sociological theorist—Talcott Parsons (1951)—and is now more than 40 years old. Do any of these claims have any empirical support?

4 LIMITATIONS OF ROLE THEORY

4.1 ROLES: METAPHOR OR REALITY

When we refer to roles, we often think of Shakespeare's *As You Like It*, and the famous soliloquy "All the world is a stage." It is, for instance, Wolfensberger's (1969) introductory quote to his exposition on the historical deviancy roles. Rosenthal and Jacobson, in their 1968 book *Pygmalion in the Classroom*, also refer to the theater, and George Bernard Shaw's play *Pygmalion*, where Henry Higgins builds a new role set for Eliza Doolittle, thus making the "guttersnipe" flower girl into a "lady" who will be able to fit and participate in high society. The analogy between the theater and social life goes back at least to Greek antiquity, in which the Stoics saw the world as a stage where each person played a role ordained and scripted by the gods (Rocheblave-Spenlé, 1962). These foremost references to the theater, as well as the theater's use of the terms "role," "scripts," and others means oftentimes that readers conclude that there is something disingenuous, contrived, or metaphorical about roles (Lemay, 1994).

The theater, of course, is the metaphor for life, not the other way around (Riggins, 1993). In the theater,

the concept of role is used to organize the one-dimensional figure played on a stage. A role represents one person, a character, played according to a script and in relationship to other actors also playing scripted roles. Of course, the actor is successful if his rendering of the role is plausible according to what we, the audience, would expect and predict.

But the roles people play in everyday life are incredibly different. We do not play one role but many in any given day, and we must stand on many stages. La Fontaine (Rocheblave-Spenlé, 1962), recognizing this, writes in his *Fables* that life is "une comédie à cent actes divers et dont la scène est l'univers." Real life "scripts" are conveyed by expectations, stereotypes, beliefs, and attitudes (including our own) thus providing an incredibly broad set of possibilities that allows us a great deal of spontaneity and idiosyncracy in our expression of roles (Newcomb, Turner, & Converse, 1975). Of course, we don't think of ourselves as playing roles. We think of ourselves in different situations and of being ourselves, and yet the regularities of behavior that exist from day to day and between persons who are in similar situations has led the common man to express in the vernacular that which is commonly used and understood by all. In this sense, roles are also how the common folk have come to understand the very same regularities and structures that have occurred to social scientists. It should not be surprising that the common folk can come up with parsimonious explanations for social phenomena.

But this use of the common language also means that some will too quickly come to a superficial understanding of role theory without sufficiently studying the great complexity of the concept (Lemay, 1996a). In a sense, role theory suffers from the same confusions that plagued Normalization (e.g., Perrin & Nirje, 1985; Wolfensberger, 1980). The terms "role," "identity," "expectation," and many others commonly used by role theorists, are, like Normalization, imbued with much surplus meaning. For instance, Biddle (1979) found that the term "expectation" had been given to at least a score of very different concepts and that the concept of "a covertly held prescriptive expectation has received at least 15 different names in theoretical studies and more than twice that number in empirical research" (p. 14). But where the confusions about Normalization were not without unfortunate consequences for its purported beneficiaries, the confusions about role theory exist mostly among scientists who have trouble eschewing the rich surplus meanings of its terminology in their search for exact scientific and empirically verifiable definitions. In many ways, it is the "surplus" meanings of role language that make them so relevant and useful to our understanding of the person and his social situation. For SRV, this should not be seen as an impediment. Rather, role theory's use of the vernacular to express scientific concepts is in keeping with SRV's phenomenological parti pris. It is thus a language that is close to experience and readily understandable in a broad sense.

4.2 THEORETICAL CONFUSION OR AN ABUNDANCE OF RICHES

In his 1986 review article on role theory, Bruce Biddle states that there are five main perspectives on role theory.

1) Functional role theory (Parsons, 1951), where roles are conceived as the shared normative expectations that prescribe and explain these behaviors (p. 70).

2) Symbolic interactionist theory (Mead, 1934), which is "the evolution of roles through social interaction in various cognitive concepts through which social actors understand and interpret their own and others' conduct" (Biddle, 1986, p. 71).

3) Structural role theory, which makes much of mathematical models and which focuses more on social structure than on individual behaviors.

4) Organizational role theory, which applies role theory to business and industrial organization and sees most if not all problems as role conflicts.

5) Cognitive role theory, of which Biddle is an ardent exponent, which basically studies the relationship between expectations and behavior.

These theorists argue quite strenuously among themselves about the apparent inconsistencies in their varied approaches (Biddle, 1979; Hilbert, 1981). On the one hand, it is argued that roles and identities account for behavioral regularities and apparent stability of social structure. On the other hand, there seems to be an incredible amount of variability between persons playing the same roles—even in the same settings—having the same identities, and even between the identities and the roles of a single person (Biddle, 1986; Hilbert, 1981; Newcomb, Turner, & Converse, 1975). These confusions, or debates, that are

present in scientific social science literature, are due mostly to important epistemological differences between the various theorists (Biddle, 1979). Some argue that roles are merely "objects of perception" (Morgan & Schwalbe, 1990). For others, role theory is of necessity a narrow reductionistic notion that lends itself very well to empirical research. For others still, role theory is an incredibly broad and inclusive phenomenon that is used in speculative theory building (Morgan & Schwalbe, 1990; Biddle, 1986) but lends itself less well to number crunching (Biddle, 1986).

4.3 ROLE THEORY, SRV, AND FUNCTIONALISM

Though Wolfensberger gives credit to Talcott Parsons (1951) for first formalizing role theory, many other important theorists were at it years earlier. George Herbert Mead (1934) expounded at length on the importance of the subject and Bruce Biddle (1986) gives reference to Ralph Linton (1936), Jacob Moreno (1934), and G. Simmel (1920). In her sweeping review of role theory, Rocheblave-Spenlé (1962) traces role theory back to G. Tarde and his 1888 book *Les lois de l'imitation*, Émile Durkheim's 1893 *De la division du travail social* and Alfred Binet's 1900 work *La suggestibilité*. Moreover, Wolfensberger's own version of role theory has little in common with Parsons's functionalist version, which unsatisfactorily emphasizes the stability of social systems and the conformity of role performance. The functionalist perspective is now by and large discredited, but its early association to role theory continues to debilitate role theory's reputation (Biddle, 1986). Wolfensberger's possibly unfortunate reference to Parsons and role theory's historical association to functionalism might explain why some critics accuse North American Normalization of being authoritarian in that it supposedly proposes conformity (Perrin & Nirje, 1985; Szivos, 1992) or that it is a functionalist theory (Chappell, 1992). In any event, the influences on SRV are much too wide and varied for it to be so easily nutshelled. Certainly Wolfensberger's (see chapter 3) early reliance on Goffman's (1961) social analysis of "total institutions" and description of role theory, and SRV's treatment of imagery (Thomas & Wolfensberger, 1982/1994) would suggest that SRV is at the very least sympathetic to symbolic interactionism.

According to Biddle's (1986) review of the interactionist perspective, this version of role theory stresses

> the evolution of roles through social interaction, and various cognitive concepts, through which social actors understand and interpret their own and others' conduct . . . norms are said to provide merely a set of broad imperatives within which the details of roles can be worked out (p. 71).

According to Morgan and Schwalbe (1990), "the evolving interactionist approach is more cognitive and offers better opportunities to sociology and social psychology for understanding how social structure and social cognition are linked" (p. 148). Thus, this version of role theory provides a dynamic and complex conceptualization that captures the experiential aspects of social interaction from the perspective of the perceiver (Turner, 1978) and the perceived (Thoits, 1983; Stryker, 1987). Role theory from its interactionist perspective accounts for, among other things, beliefs, stereotypes, and attitudes; norms, contextual demands, and expectations; and identity and self-concept.

Biddle's criticism of the symbolic interactionist approach to role theory rests primarily in the broadness of its ambition and its sometimes "fuzzy" language and definitions, which do not lend themselves well to empirical research.

5 STRENGTHS OF ROLE THEORY

5.1 THE BROAD APPLICABILITY OF ROLE THEORY

Bruce Biddle points out in his 1986 review article that social roles are one of the most popular ideas in sociology and one of the most popular ideas in the social sciences. "At least 10% of all articles currently published in sociological journals use the term role in a technical sense" (p. 67). Biddle, taking up a point made by a number of theorists (Rocheblave-Spenlé, 1962), goes on to suggest that role theory is the nexus between anthropology, psychology, and sociology. Other researchers and theorists (Eagly, 1987; Morgan & Schwalbe, 1990; Turner, 1988) also make the case that both sociology and social psychology are improved by their use of role theory. As we have seen, the social role concept seems to be well embedded in social science theorizing. Social role theory has

engendered a great deal of theoretical work and seems to be of prime importance in explaining human behavior from the individual up and the social structure down. Thomas and Biddle (1966) concluded in their review that "Role concepts are not the lingua franca of the behavioral sciences, but perhaps they presently come closer to this universal language than any other vocabulary of behavioral science" (p. 8).

As used by social scientists, roles are a fundamental tool of analysis that helps explain apparent regularities of behavior and the structure of social systems (Biddle, 1979, 1986; Newcomb, Turner, & Converse, 1975). Roles are thus an organizing concept of great usefulness.

> Role theory concerns one of the most important features of social life, characteristic behavior patterns or roles. It explains roles by presuming that persons are members of social position and hold expectations for their own behaviors and those of other persons" (Biddle, 1986, p. 67).

Importantly, Biddle notes that role theory has led to very few derivations or utilizations. This is not to say that role theory has not been used in the past to generate possible practical utilizations. George Kelly (1955/1963) constructed his own social role theory and put it to use both as a diagnostic tool and as a therapeutic technique where people were called upon to script new roles for themselves. Jacob L. Moreno (Moreno, 1989) also developed his own version of role therapy and called it "psychodrama," where the therapy included the acting out rather than reporting of problems by clients and other persons who were in role relationships with them.

5.2 SOCIAL ROLES ARE INTIMATELY TIED TO PHENOMENOLOGICAL REALITY

Urie Bronfenbrenner (1979) in his *Ecology of Human Development* makes the point that the concept of roles and phenomenology are tied together in the work of a number of theorists in both psychology and sociology. Roles are not only about perceived behaviors or position, but just as important, roles are about a person's perception of a given situation and his self-conception within that situation. Roles are perceived by others and experienced by the incumbent.

It is not surprising that the language of roles has a great deal of everydayness about it

Roles occur in everyday life, of course, and are of concern to those who perform them and others. Children are constantly enjoined to act in a more grown up fashion; new recruits into the armed services must learn roles of deference and deportment." (Biddle, 1979, p. 57)

Newcomb, Turner, & Converse (1975) had previously made a similar observation

As we pursue our daily round of activities, we are called on to take a remarkable succession of roles. Within a few hours, we are likely to be called on to switch back and forth between the different role behavior required as students, as roommates, as sons or daughters, as church members, as dates, as discussion group leaders, and the like." (p. 393)

Moreover, as was noted above, many of the terms and concepts that surround role theory are taken from the common language (Biddle, 1979), thus, the experience of roles and the self-realization that one plays roles is such that a repertoire of words are readily available in the vernacular to build a theory. This is of particular importance when one considers SRV's foundation upon a phenomenological view of the life experiences of devalued classes of people. This might explain Wolfensberger's seeming eschewance of empirical support in favor of descriptive vignettes or illustrative stories to support his propositions. This theory-building, based as it is on a terminology embedded in the vernacular, suggests that scientific theorizing can thus be productive and even possibly more meaningful since it relates directly to everyday experience and, as we shall see, also lends itself to empirical review and support.

Just a cursory review of research themes shows an impressive relationship between social role theory and day-to-day life experiences. Thus we find role research on identity and self-conception; personality; the person and role person merger; health and well-being; stress reduction and social support; status, social position, social participation, social structure, and predictability and regularity of behavior; variation in behavior; sex differences, differences in helping behaviors and aggression; leadership, positive, and negative attitudes.

There is a profound consonance also between role and self-conception. From this perspective, roles are an essential component of our regular day-to-day lives. We assume roles, live our lives in a variety of roles,

and make them ours. George Herbert Mead (1934) pointed out that we learn and practice the intricacies of role taking and role play as children when we interact with imaginary companions or play at being mother, father, police officer, soldier, or great athlete. These games are a natural part of development and do not strike us in any way as being contrived in the sense of a theater role. The role-playing game is a more formal rendering of imitation or practice of what has been learned from a model. This capacity to "try" on such roles is not limited to children but occurs also with adults, as has been demonted spectacularly in Zimbardo's prison experiments (Haney, Banks, & Zimbardo, 1973) and Milgram's (1974) obedience experiments. Thus from early on and throughout our lives, roles are inextricably tied to our existence in a natural spontaneity that is altogether unconscious in the sense that we do not conceive of ourselves as playing a role but rather of being a role (e.g., a father, a mother, a nurse, a customer, etc.).

One might speculate that the role play of children predates even the most primitive theater forms; very possibly the first "plays" were adult renderings of child's play, if not nostalgic yearnings for them. In any event there is a conceptual richness about the vernacular version of roles that goes way beyond any scientific theorizing. The fuzzy folk notion is more comprehensive and satisfying than the effort to extract from it a precise and exact, and thus limiting, scientific idea (Lemay, 1994). Role theory's reliance on terms taken from the common language allows for both the expression of the concrete experiences of subjects and the "abstract notions of investigators" (Biddle, 1976, p. 12).

Role theory, concerned as it is with individuals in context, is a positive solution to Seymour Sarason's (1981) criticism that an ambitious psychology, searching as it were to become a "hard" science, arbitrarily separates the individual from society for purposes of research, theory, and intervention, thus leaving it bankrupt. Individuals are inseparable from their relationships, such as when Newcomb, Turner, and Converse (1975) describe the mother-child relationship as "two halves of the same habit" (p. 7). Role theory provides a useful gestalt that allows us to identify, label, and thus understand that with which we perceive and that which we experience: living among and with others.

6 THE DEVALUATION HYPOTHESIS: GROUP ROLES AND STEREOTYPES

Wolfensberger and Thomas (1994) and McKnight (1995), among others, have written about the inescapability of societal devaluation and how these are economic and social phenomena that have little or no bearing on individual differences. For instance, in a postprimary production economy, which is mostly based on human service, if there are to be persons who play professional server roles, then there are bound to be individuals who will play client roles. Thus in this sense, the employment of some requires the dependency of others. This suggests that there are finite numbers of positive roles to go around and thus Social Role Valorization will only work for relatively small groups at any given time and will require that other groups take their place in lower status social positions unless profound societal changes occur that democratize the value of roles.

An interesting source that can be used to provide some empirical support for this view is available in the work of ecological psychologists. Roger Barker and his colleagues (Barker, 1968; Barker & Wright, 1954; see also Wicker, 1979) in their field studies of American midwest life found that in any given context, the number of social positions or roles is finite and in similar types of settings this number is something of a constant. There are only so many roles to go around, and the fewer people there are, the more roles they each have to fill. He and his colleagues applied this finding to a variety of settings including churches (Wicker, 1969) and most famously in Barker and Gump's (1964) study *Big School, Small School*, where the principle of "undermanning" was demonstrated. Undermanning theory proposes that small settings offer greater opportunities of participation and integration. Overmanned settings leave many individuals with few and possibly no roles to play, other than passive (spectator) or even negative roles. Wicker (1973) speculated that as the population of a community increases, more people are left out, and those who are given roles to play are selected, among other things, on the basis of competence. In undermanned settings, persons are recruited into roles mostly based on availability, and competence is less important. There are interesting practice and research

issues that are suggested by these findings that could be useful in the area of social integration.

6.1 DEVALUED ROLES

As mentioned above, SRV's emphasis on positively valued social roles grew out of the historical analysis of deviancy roles (Wolfensberger, 1969) and the conclusion that such dynamics are still, by and large, present and at work in modern society. "People who are devalued by their society get cast by their society into roles that are societally devalued. In other words, the person is given a role identity that confirms and justifies society's ascription of low value or worth to the person" (Wolfensberger, 1992, p. 10). Though most of the debate concerning roles has occurred in relation to its purported fundamentality to valorization, the existing evidence supporting devaluation thesis could be of importance. There are three component parts to the role devaluation thesis. First, roles can be life defining, and when such roles are negative they can have devastating consequences for individuals. Second, some roles, including negative ones, have been systematically ascribed to groups or classes of individuals. Finally, many group roles are perpetuated by relatively robust stereotypes that shape the attendant attitudes of role incumbents and others in the social environment.

6.1.1 LIFE DEFINING ROLES

Some roles are so important that they are life defining. Thomas and Wolfensberger (1994) provided compelling arguments for the pervasive impact of the client role, especially on devalued individuals. Though the client role is open to all, it is expressed in valued ways for valued individuals (e.g., being the client of the stockbroker), but much less so when one is poor and thus very dependent for a very long period of time on a variety of human services. Thomas and Wolfensberger's description of the career client role is in many ways reminiscent of Goffman's (1961) description of the career of mental patient. Moreover, Wolfensberger argues that since for devalued persons, the client role is pervasive—it is the role that fills the most time—and that other roles are secondary and few in number, the client role becomes particularly defining, offering the individual fewer opportunities for learning skills associated with other roles and for being perceived as being able to learn the required skills for such roles.

This argumentation is very similar to Eagly and Johnson's (1990) discussion on the apparent sex differences in the behavior of organizational leaders, which are possibly the "product of the differing structural positions of the sexes within organizations" (p. 234). Like Thomas and Wolfensberger's client role, the pervasive influence of gender roles was found throughout a series of secondary roles by Eagly and her colleagues especially in situations where the role demands were ambiguous and where the gender roles would be particularly important in informing the role occupant on how he or she should behave. These results were found in relation to helping behavior (Eagly & Crowley, 1986), leadership style (Eagly & Johnson, 1990), and aggression (Eagly & Steffen, 1986). The above supports the notion that, for instance, the client role is primary for individuals who have few other important roles that occupy as much time and are as salient to their self-concept. Thus, their client role can be life determining and will have a pervasive influence on the performance of other roles, especially in equivocal situations.

Of particular interest to Wolfensberger's hypothesis on the client role is Eagly and Crowley's (1986) demonstration of the differences between the helping behaviors of men and women. As in the case of clienthood, the role of helper is open to all. But there are important differences between the helping behaviors and helping roles of men and those of women.

The beliefs that people hold about the differences between men and women can be summarized in terms of two dimensions, the communal and the agentic, both of which define positive, personal attributes. Communal gender stereotypic belief primarily describes a concern with the welfare of other people and women are believed to manifest this concern more strongly than men. The agentic dimension of gender stereotypic belief about personal qualities describes primarily an assertive and controlled tendency and men are believed to manifest this tendency more strongly than women. Gender roles thus cluster around these perceived qualities and provide the role occupant with opportunities for learning role competencies (p. 23).

It should not be surprising that, by and large, men and women internalize societal gender roles much in the same way that Thomas and Wolfensberger describe a person internalizing the client role because he is systematically provided with opportunities for performing the behaviors related to this role and then in turn "becoming" this role. It is a cyclical feedback process that is commonly known as the "self-fulfilling prophecy" made famous by the studies of Rosenthal and Jacobson (1968) (a term first coined by R. K. Merton, in 1948). Eagly's own work and other studies show that "higher status people are perceived as considerably more agentic than lower status people" (1986, p. 23). Women who are seen as being more communal are provided with communal role opportunites and little occasion for demonstrating agentic skills. Thus, one finds that women are likely to be employed in positions that have relatively low status, little power, and limited opportunity for advancement. Eagly and Crowley also note that communal helping is related to subservience, hence its impact on social status. At least for women, the forms of helping are expressed as compliance and are thus unassertive. Assertive forms of help are in keeping with higher social status and are usually associated with the male gender role. Thus heroism, which is primarily agentic in nature, is especially associated to the male gender role, whereas the emotional support and informal counseling, which are nurturant and communal in nature, are mostly associated with the female gender role. It would not be surprising to find that valued persons express the client role in much more agentic ways than devalued persons, who would be more passive and submitting. Though one would probably be hard pressed to qualify this dimension as being communal, it is easy to see the commonalities between Wolfensberger's line of argumentation for the client roles of handicapped devalued persons and those presented by Eagly for female gender role.

6.1.2 ROLES THAT ARE SYSTEMATICALLY ASCRIBED TO GROUPS OR CLASSES OF INDIVIDUALS

Wolfensberger maintains that there are roles that are systematically given to certain groups or classes of persons. There are, in fact, two parts to this argument, the first being that there are groups of individuals who hold similar positions, roles, beliefs, and attitudes that make them into identifiable groups and that these characteristics stand alone and apart from other visible physical characteristics. Second, certain roles are particularly reserved for these groups. This is Wolfensberger's

(1992) latrine worker argument, where immigrant populations are given the down-and-dirty jobs that none of the higher status classes are willing to take on.

Related to the above, in reference to role theory and gender differences, Alice Eagly (1987) suggests that the value of role theory lies in its capacity to describe parsimoniously the predictors of differences between groups of people, in her research on sex differences.

According to this theory, the contemporaneous influences arising from adult social roles are more directly relevant to sex differences in adult social behavior than is prior socialization or biology. Social roles are regarded as the proximal predictors of adult sex differences, although these roles may be linked to other, more distal factors such as childhood socialization pressures and biological predispositions (p. 9).

Early on, the eminent sociologist Peter Berger in his discussion of sociology (1963) affirms that human behavior and beliefs are particularly predictable within classes or groupings. It is these predictable behaviors and beliefs which in part lead to the creation of stereotypes. Thus value systems, religious and political affiliations, and vocational occupations are primarily a function of class, and in a pluralistic society, class acts as the magnet around which all of these cluster. It is interesting to note that Berger (1996) also affirms that in an upwardly mobile society, as the class of an ethnic group changes, so does its cluster of value systems, religious and political affiliations, and vocational occupations, thus the great unwashed—the eastern European Catholic immigrants who were the latrine cleaners of early 20th-century America—are now among the best educated and most upwardly mobile of its citizens.

Because of their nationality, gender, class, or impairment, classes of individuals may be systematically attributed certain roles and be subject to certain stereotypes and expectations. Peabody (1985) in his review of *National Characteristics* shows that Americans at least have a great deal of consensus on the different stereotypes that inform their perception of different nationalities. Moreover, gender role differences are so important that even here one may find important differences between the stereotypes held concerning Iranian women as opposed to Iranian men.

People's images of women and men of other nations should be affected by the relative status of the sexes in these nations. Because of men's higher status, they are disproportionately the protagonists of the observed events that foreigners use to form nationality stereotypes. Therefore, men should be perceived as possessing the attributes ascribed to their nationalities. In contrast, women should tend not to be perceived in terms of nationality stereotypes because women less often enact major roles in the highly publicized actions of their nations (p. 452).

The same could be said of classes of individuals who are marked by some form of impairment. Are there more commonalities between our stereotypes of, say, Iranian and British mentally retarded persons than about the typical citizens of these countries? If so, this is possible evidence that impairment stereotypes are of greater salience than national stereotypes.

6.1.3 STEREOTYPES

It is observable differences between groups and classes that lead to the formation of stereotypes. Early on, Donald Campbell (1967) argues that national stereotypes reflect the structural features of societies, e.g. agrarian versus industrialized. Eagly and Kite (1987) suggest that "the social roles that are available within a particular society shape the behaviour of the people, and this behaviour provides the basic observations from which images of nationalities are derived" (p. 452). Though individual members of a given group might express these roles in a variety of idiosyncratic ways, other groups will hold quite simplistic stereotypes, especially from a distance when there is no real interaction. Thus, stereotypes can be more or less accurate depending on how much information one group holds on the other. As Campbell points out, "the more remote and less well-known the outgroup, the more purely projective the content of the stereotype and the less accurate it will be." Eagly and Kite (1987) thus found that Americans were apt to believe that Iranians were particularly aggressive, proud, hostile, arrogant, and religious, though they had very little knowledge upon which to base these beliefs except for the regular newscasts of newsworthy events around the American Embassy hostage-taking incident (around 1979). "The inhabitants of these disliked countries were perceived as relatively unfriendly and unkind" (p. 461). The important thing to note here is that stereotypes are primarily about two groups of individuals. The first group, the perceivers, hold the stereotypes to be true and these stereotypes are more or less accurate, depending on the amount of information available to the perceivers. The other group, the perceived, occupy roles and are involved in role performances that more or less accurately reflect the stereotypes held by the other group.

In 1987, Alice Eagly and Mary Kite studied the stereotypes of nationalities as applied to both men and women. At the outset they observed that

> social roles are important because they determine the behaviors of group members, and observation of these behaviors are the basic data from which people form their images of groups of people. . . Because racial groups in American society are differentiated on the basis of social class, with blacks more socio-economically disadvantaged than whites, people often interact across racial lines and roles that differ in power and privilege. As a consequence the content of beliefs about racial groups reflects the characteristic behaviors ascribed to differing social classes (p. 451).

Moreover, differences in racial stereotypes are rendered even more complex by the stereotypes one holds concerning men and women. "People in the domestic role are thought to behave considerably more communally and less agentically than people in the employee role" (p. 452).

In many cases the stereotypes are based on interaction at a distance rather than face-to-face interaction. Stereotypes at a distance do not change very much and are mostly influenced by newsworthy events, where what is reported is the public behavior of the leadership or high-profile people of a nation. These, of course, would mostly be men, having, by and large, higher status and influence in most nationalities. Thus the stereotypes of nationalities are more similar to the stereotypes of the men than of the women of these nationalities.

On the other hand, face-to-face interactions create situations where stereotypes are continuously under review with greater and more accurate information feeding the feedback system. Thus we can perceive certain immediate benefits of personal social integration that could have some beneficial impact on the stereotypes people have of handicapped individuals or handicapped groups.

Eagly also observed that the types of roles that are available for observation in a given nationality are a function of these countries' economies and social structures. Thus we can perceive differences between the roles available in industrial nations versus the roles that are available in countries whose economies are based on subsistence agriculture. Certainly these roles will have a dramatic impact on the national stereotypes as we perceive them.

Campbell (1967) suggested that stereotypes were apt to be particularly strong when there were obvious differences between the perceiver and perceived. If individuals live elsewhere, look different, express themselves in different languages, have different cultures, live in different economic conditions and thus hold different occupational roles, and so on. As Berger (1992) suggested, there are group differences that can be scientifically ascertained and are not beyond being noticed by the common man.

It has been amply demonstrated in the literature that people react quite systematically to different physical characteristics. Clare Burstall (1976) showed that teachers systematically attended more positively to the most attractive students. Not surprisingly, with all this positive attention, these children did quite well in school. More recently, Eagly, Ashmore, Makhijani, and Longo (1991) did a meta-analytic review of research on the physical attractiveness stereotype and found much to confirm it. By and large, people are apt to ascribe more favorable personality traits and more successful light outcomes to attractive targets, thus suggesting that "beautiful is good" (p. 109). "We observe that better looking people receive more favorable reactions from others" (p. 111). Stereotypes are thus expressed as implicit theories that one might hold of a class of persons, such as beautiful means good. We should not be surprised if this then leads to a self-fulfilling prophecy effect for social skills and social adjustments. Very simply, more opportunities are provided the person because beautiful people are then sought out and given much social reinforcement. And the beautiful are apt to live up to this stereotype up to a point in that they were found to have more social competence than their unattractive counterparts. All of the above enhances the psychological well-being and achievement of persons seen to be attractive (Umberson & Hughes, 1987).

Thus, it is difficult for people to deny what they see and to deny the group they are part of. The social roles people occupy form an integral part of how they are perceived and how they view themselves. For groups of impaired persons, where the stigmata of impairment is obvious and who have been historically segregated and congregated, stereotypes are apt to be particularly strong and long-lasting, particularly when unimpaired people have a lack of firsthand knowledge about this group of individuals and are limited to "at a distance" information garnered from the media or other sources. Stereotypes are apt to be particularly powerful on both sides of the fence. Stereotypes can be more or less accurate depending on the information one has at hand. But as stereotypes are found to be inaccurate, more accurate ones will form. It is interesting that stereotypes formed at a distance do not resist long to firsthand knowledge that comes from one-to-one interaction. At the very least the stereotype for such an individual is apt to change (see Eagly & Kite, 1987).

7 THE ROLE AND THE PERSON

Though Wolfensberger (1983) seemed early on to indicate that there were important differences between the concepts of person and roles, later writings (Wolfensberger, 1992; see chapter 5 of this book) suggest that these differences are either less important or immaterial to the issue of valorization. Both authors (Wolfensberger, 1983; 1992; see chapter 5 of this book) write of the valuing the person controversy, possibly in reference to Perrin & Nirje (1985) and Nirje (1992), who suggest that persons must be integrated in their "integrity" not just by the "manipulation" of behaviors and appearances. Recently, Martin Elks (1994) suggested that roles did not stand as the equivalent of the person and that SRV was in a sense more reductionistic than Normalization. Perrin and Nirje (1985) suggest that North American Normalization (circa 1972) deals with appearances and conformity whereas Thomas and Wolfensberger (chapter 5 this book) counter that since one never encounters role-less persons, the "person," so to speak, so often idealized is nevertheless an abstraction. As Wolfensberger and Thomas (1994) point out, much of the current discussion on who or what is a "person" occurs in the realms of philosophy and ethics, and deals with establishing exclusionary criteria, a problematic issue from an SRV perspective. Moreover, Wolfensberger (1992) proposes that "roles are so powerful that they largely define who we are" (p. 20). Do role theorists make the claims of equivalency between the person and his roles? Is role theory as encompassing as SRV would seem to require?

There are two vantage points that should be considered in reviewing this question: the person as viewed by others, and the person as experienced by himself.

7.1   THE PERSON, ROLES, AND PERCEIVER

Turner (1978) proposes that it is through roles that we get to know people. He goes on to suggest that an observer will, in some situations, "merge" the role and the person, in other words, observers will equate the person with the roles he plays, especially if there are really no other cues to knowing such a person. Perceptions of roles help us create the person; the setting he is in, the social positions he occupies, the behaviors that he exibits, the persons he interacts with: his role set. In this sense, Turner suggests that the personality of the person is the sum of his roles, that the personality of a person is in the eye of the beholder. "Role person merger" occurs when our concept of a person is tied to one or some of the roles this person plays. In such circumstances there is a complete identification between the person and role he or she plays. In a sense the person is a simplifying assumption. It can be understood as the sum of roles or the sum of identities. According to Turner, role person merger is behavioral rather than cognitive, in the sense that a person's self-conception may be at variance with the role person merger. Finally, he suggests that some roles become so important in one's life that the person plays this role even in settings that do not demand it, to the point that other people will view "a particular role as accurately revealing a person" (p. 6).

Some roles become very defining of the person, especially in situations where a person might have access to very few roles. Thus, that Wolfensberger's (1969) historical deviancy roles are life defining is at the very least plausible. As shown above, the client role (Wolfensberger & Thomas, 1994) can have a perverse influence in the lives of devalued individuals. From the perceiver's perspective, this role person merger is particularly important when dealing with groups of people with whom the perceiver has very little direct experience.

In this sense, roles stand alone and are known independently of the people to whom they are attributed to, as when we are told of a person we do not otherwise know, that he or she plays such and such a role, we are already knowledgeable of that person. This very simple knowledge creates expectations. We could thus speak of roles independently of the persons who occupy them in general terms that describe groups of individuals. It is not surprising that some roles are truly universal and in fact are observed in most cultures (Newcomb, Turner, & Converse, 1975; Biddle, 1979). Role language is a common way of describing that which is; of describing others (Turner, 1978) but also of describing and understanding ourselves (Thoits, 1983; Biddle, 1979).

Role person merger should not be understood simplistically as an artifact of perceptual bias where the observer's understanding of a person is limited to his or her knowledge of the role(s) a person plays. Some roles are so important that they are definitive of the person from setting to setting and time to time (Biddle, 1979; Eagly, 1987; Turner, 1978). If such roles are truly defining, then their impact should not be limited to observers, but also be intimately experienced by the perceived. For Turner, who proposes that roles lead to behavioral predictability allowing others to know and recognize an individual (1990), such observed mergers relate the identification of the individual with a role (1978), leading Turner to propose that roles are an integral and defining part of personality (1988).

7.2   PERSON, ROLES, AND IDENTITY

Researchers and theorists who study roles from the perspective of the perceived often refer to the concept as "role identity" or "identity" (Biddle, 1979; Deaux, 1993; Stryker, 1987; Thoits, 1983).

> Role identities are self-conceptions in terms of one's position in the social structure (e.g., "I am a father, husband, welder, union member, uncle . . ."). Specifically, role identities are viewed here as self-conceptions based on enduring, normative, reciprocal relationships with other people (Thoits, 1991, p. 103).

Kay Deaux (1993) suggests that there is so much overlap between the concepts of social identity (social role) and personal identity (role identity) that such distinctions are for all intents and purposes "arbitrary and misleading. . . Personal identity is defined, at least in part, by group memberships, and social categories are infused with personal meanings" (p. 5).

A number of theorists have suggested that there is an important concordance between the roles a person has and who that person is. Peggy Thoits (1992), a prolific role theorist and researcher, writes:

In essence, identities are answers to the question "who am I?" in terms of the positions or roles that one holds ("I am a mother, a teacher, an aunt, a tennis player . . ."). Because identities define "who I am" they should be sources of existential meaning and purpose in life (pp. 236-237).

When people respond to the open-ended question "who am I?", they commonly include role descriptors as self-descriptors (Thoits, 1991). Role identities tell us who we are and give us guidance in terms of how to behave, thus providing us with "existential security" (Thoits, 1983). Thus, Thoits, in her theoretical work, proposes that identity and self-conception are based on role positions, which come together in a hierarchical structure of salience.

Park and Burgess, in their *Introduction to Sociology*, defined the term "person" as "an individual's conception of role" (quoted in Znaniecky, 1965). Ralph Turner (1978) suggests that some roles become so deeply merged with the person that they, in fact, become the person at the very least for observers but also having a pervasive effect upon the subject's personality. This proposition has certainly been amply demonstrated by Alice Eagly's (1987) research into gender roles, which she states have a dramatic impact on stereotypes, attitudes, and hence on the learning opportunities afforded to the role incumbent. Some roles become very defining of the person, especially in situations where a person might have access to very few roles.

Goffman's (1961) field studies on total institution inmates describe in very great detail how certain settings and social situations could be severely limiting in that many role opportunities were systematically excluded from an inmate's life experience. Alice Eagly, in her research, suggests a different version of the same argument when she states that incumbency in a gender role will spill over in other situations and settings, such as the workplace (Eagly & Johnson, 1990). It is interesting that Eagly and her colleagues also found that as secondary roles took on more importance, the spillover effect of gender roles could be much diminished.

The concept of social roles can account for much knowledge concerning the person we observe and a person's self-concept (Morgan & Schwalbe, 1990). Role theory accounts for the person in comprehensive terms. It speaks of the person as object of perception, and just as importantly it accounts for the person as self-experienced in terms that have been useful in generating research and theory. A number of researchers, including Thoits, Menaghan, and Stryker, have attempted to link self-concept as understood by role-identity to well-being and other important "feeling" states that are at the heart of some of criticisms that have in the past been aimed at SRV and North American Normalization (see section 8 below).

The social role concept seems to offer SRV a more comprehensive and encompassing view of the person than the various Normalization formulations. Wolfensberger's (1972) earliest formulation proposed actions for the "behaviors, appearances and interpretations" of the person and was criticized for dealing only with the "appearances" of the handicapped person and not recognizing the person's "integrity" (Perrin & Nirje, 1985). Moreover, the social role concept has a rich track record of research and theorizing that lends itself well to the action implications of both Normalization and SRV.

7.3   ROLE AVIDITY

As we have seen, roles take up a lot of conceptual space when thinking of the person. On the one hand, others perceive a person in roles and oftentimes think of that person in terms of the role or roles the person occupies. On the other hand, a person's identity is intimately tied to his roles. Thoits (1983) points out that Zimbardo's prison experiment, alluded to above, also demonstrates that in the absence of valued roles, persons will willingly, and with high commitment and enthusiasm, take on devalued role identities because these also provide a person with existential security. Roles tell us and others who we are. This provides an important explanation as to why persons readily take up the deviancy roles that Wolfensberger (1969) describes. It helps explain why individuals become locked into roles even when they are unappealing or negative, such as the class bully.

Thus, we may describe this willingness and even need of roles as "role avidity." This construct operates in two ways. Roger Barker and his colleagues (Barker, 1968; Barker & Gump, 1964; Barker & Wright, 1954) have described how settings and setting programs compel individuals to take positions of responsibility. Wicker (1979) has called these pressures "habitat claims." Thoits (1983, 1991) has argued that individuals are unable to remain roleless. Roles are essential to identity, and individuals will engage in an avid accumulation of roles

even when they are already overburdened. Thus role avidity proposes that in a social setting, an individual will take up an available role even if it is devaluing, unless the person has other settings or situations to go to where better roles are available.

8   ARE THE GOOD THINGS IN LIFE CONTINGENT UPON VALUED ROLES?

It is the creation and attribution of valued roles for persons that will assure social integration and access to the good things in life (Wolfensberger, 1983). Wolfensberger and Thomas (1994), in their recent overview of Social Role Valorization, assert that one of the premises underlying SRV "is that people who feel socially valued roles are more apt to get the good things of life than those in devalued roles." Wolfensberger, Thomas and Caruso (1996) list 17 good things of life, which include home, family, friendship, work, respect, and good health.

Though few studies that were surveyed measured these specific examples of the good things in life, there are nonetheless a number of studies that show that certain key roles were associated with physical health, psychological well-being, achievement, and the effective survival of life transitions, and provided a general sense of social support and community embeddedness, and, finally, ensured a certain degree of protection in times of distress.

Peggy Thoits is particularly well known as a researcher who has shown the links between psychological well-being, differences in psychological distress, and role identities. Because identities define "who I am," they should be sources of existential meaning and purpose in life (Thoits, 1992)—what Thoits elsewhere calls "existential security" (Thoits, 1983). In her review of the literature, Thoits (1991) concludes "corroboratively, a number of studies, some longitudinal, show that the accumulation of role identities is generally beneficial for psychological well-being" (p. 105). In reference to the vast social support literature that now exists, Thoits concludes that the multiplication of role identities is at the same time the multiplication of social connections. Cohen and Wills (1985), in their review of the social support literature, showed that in general the greater the social network of individuals, the greater was their psychological well-being. All of this should be reminiscent of some of the arguments put forward by

Wolfensberger in support of personal social integration of handicapped individuals (Wolfensberger, 1992). It would thus seem that social integration and social support can be defined and operationalized in terms of role theory.

It is not surprising that research also shows that some roles are more important than others in assuring psychological well-being (Menaghan, 1989) and are more protective in times of psychological distress (Cohen & Wills, 1985). Moreover, recent research by Blair Wheaton (1990) suggests that prior role history has a major impact on the stressfulness of more recent life transitions, such as marital breakup, job loss, retirement, widowhood, and so forth.

In support of the position that some roles are more important than others, Lois Verbrugge (1983), in her research review, found that being employed, being married, and parenthood were all significantly related to good physical health. Verbrugge's own research tends to show that the possible effects of these roles are additive. Thoits's review of the literature shows a clear relationship between some roles and mortality, even when controlling for certain illnesses.

As Cohen and Wills (1985) have shown in their review of the literature, mortality from all causes was greater among persons with relatively low levels of social support. Cohen and Wills go on to show that it is a high level of social integration that ensures health and well-being, whereas certain key relationships improve a person's capacity to cope with stressful events. Since it is roles that provide the opportunities for social relationships (indeed the role construct subsumes relationship), the number of roles has a direct bearing upon the size of an individual's social network. It is, however, certain key roles that buffer against highly stressful events. Thus, the role identities of friend, spouse, family member, and even possibly coworker, provide one with the opportunity of calling upon others for assistance in times of difficulty. The existence of these very important role identities is contingent upon the opportunity to engage in these role behaviors and, of course, the expectation that one can contribute and benefit from them.

9 ROLES AND EXPECTANCIES

The expectancies construct, often expressed as the self-fulfilling prophecy, can stand on its own (Rosenthal & Jacobson, 1968) but it is particularly useful as a component part of role theory. It is fundamental to Wolfensberger's conceptualization of social roles (1983, 1992) and has been part of the teachings on Normalization since the beginning, in 1969 (see Sarason, 1969; Wolfensberger, 1969, 1972). It is also a key component of Alice Eagly's research on gender roles.

From the beginning, expectancy research has been frought with controversy surrounding its purported potency (Brophy, 1983; Jussim, 1990) and concerning research methodology (Thorndike, 1968). The Wolfensberger presentation on role expectancy (one of the seven themes of the introductory SRV workshop) is problematic because, taking its cue from the early self-fulfilling prophecy research of Rosenthal and his colleagues, it overemphasizes the potency of expectancy at the expense of other complementary social dynamics, leaving one with the impression of a simple circular mechanism that "causes" role conformity. For instance, research does not always distinguish between more or less accurate perceptual biases, which, of course, could have a determining impact on the self-fulfilling effect. "Although erroneous expectations may create self-fulfilling prophecies, the extent to which they have thus far been found to do so is usually limited" (Jussim, 1990, p. 13). The SRV treatment of expectancies is also problematic because it does not distinguish between expectations occurring in "naturalistic" situations from those that are contrived for intervention and research purposes and which are thought to be more powerful than the former.

Jussim's (1990) meta-analytic review of expectancy research in "naturalistic" situations shows that overall the expectancy construct accounts for 20% of variance. This is less than the early claims of Rosenthal and others but is nonetheless nothing to sneeze at. Moreover, contrived expectations set up for research or intervention purposes can sometimes explain over 70% of the variance in the performance change of persons. This certainly supports the strategy of consciously engineering milieux, activities, and interactions that communicate high expectations and elicit behavior that conforms with these expectations. Moreover, expectations are particularly powerful when they are realistic and thus based on accurate perceptual biases.

Crosby and Clayton (1990), Jones (1990), and Ditto and Hilton (1990), as well as Eagly (1987), suggest that expectancies are a powerful tool of intervention that has so far not been sufficiently exploited from a programmatic or even social policy perspective.

In conclusion, the current SRV teachings on expectancies need to be updated: Naturalistic expectancies are not as powerful as SRV would seem to suggest in the creation and maintenance of devalued roles and identities. But contrived expectancies used to combat devaluation can be very effective indeed.

10 THE USEFULNESS OF SOCIAL ROLES AS A COMPONENT OF OTHER APPROACHES AND THEORIES OF PSYCHOSOCIAL INTERVENTION

If SRV's use of social roles were completely original, then its validity and usefulness would be in question. The fact that other researchers, theoreticians, and practitioners have found the concept useful is not irrelevant to the present debate.

Certainly in the general population there is a recognition that something has been achieved when a person of an otherwise devalued group attains a role of importance. Much was made of the fact that the 1995 Miss America, Heather Whitestone, is hearing-impaired. More recently there was much controversy but also accolades for the black woman who became Miss Italy. There was also much controversy over a proposed statue of the late president Franklin D. Roosevelt, and whether his physical impairment (he was wheelchair-bound) should be made obvious. Press coverage of the 1996 presidential race in the USA often referred to the poor and humble beginnings of both candidates. For North America, at least, there is a sense in the popular culture that every role is open to anyone from any social group. The ideal of upward mobility is rooted in the notion of roles, and so-called affirmative action programs operationalize this as a tool of intervention.

Biddle, in 1979, suggested that role theory offers education, psychiatry, clinical and counseling psychology, social work, community development, and leadership training "a vocabulary and the promise of empirical power"(p. 12). It is not surprising that SRV and Normalization are not the only service strategies to adopt the role schema. The impairment, disability, and handicap model defines "handicapped": that which limits or prevents fulfillment of a role that is normal for that individual (cited in Saint Claire, 1989, p. 16). This might

be of particular relevance since Nirje (1993) has recently changed his terminology for mental retardation to bring it closer to the World Health Organization (WHO) definition. Researchers in the field of mental retardation, such as Saint Claire (1989), have found the role component of the WHO definition a useful tool for conceptualizing new ways of assisting mentally retarded persons. Therapeutic approaches, such as those of George Kelly (1955/1963) and Jacob Moreno (Moreno, 1990), have been mentioned above. Structured learning methods in mental health, such as those proposed by Goldstein (Goldstein, Sprafkin, Gershaw, & Klein, 1980), use role play and scripting as key components.

More recently, the noted researcher Kenneth Heller (1993) pointed to the maintenance of "useful social roles" as one of the best methods of prevention for elderly persons. Heller, in his review of the relevant literature, shows that many informal roles convey positive valuation on the incumbents and are dependent not only on competence, but also on social support. According to Heller, thinking of prevention or intervention in terms of social roles opens up "new possibilities," at least for elderly persons.

A number of feminist researchers and theorists have used role theory for the purpose of analyzing gender differences and discrimination. Alice Eagly (1995) splendidly reviews the breadth of this work and the controversies that surround it. Though Eagly and other feminist researchers confine themselves to the study of the situation of women, the possible transfer and application of their research findings and theoretical refinements to other fields is, to say the least, exciting.

Eagly and Mladinic (1989) found evidence that attitudes and stereotypes about women are in the process of changing positively. They suggest that more and more people are becoming conscious of the low valuation of women and are monitoring their overt responses to avoid appearing prejudiced toward women. "Such a tendency could create a 'bend over backwards' effect in subjects' responses, resulting in attitudes and stereotypes about women that are biased in a positive direction" (p. 554). The relatively low attitude-belief correlations found for the subjects might suggest a process of societal change in the making, where, with time, members of society integrate new attitudes about women. However, Eagly and Mladinic note that positive attitudes do not necessarily translate into power and social position. But it does seem to be the necessary starting point.

Crosby and Clayton's (1990) review of affirmative action programs points to the need to design such interventions with a careful regard to expectancy effects. It is clear that such programs use the concept of roles (in the case of affirmative action, it is vocational roles) and related constructs, such as expectancies, as useful interventions to enact social policy. Jussim (1990) and Oseyrman and Markus (1990) all document the value and usefulness of role expectancy related research in creating and testing new strategies for social change.

Thus, social role theory as it is conceived of in SRV is not only a powerful theoretical tool for analyzing social devaluation, but it is also a powerful tool for developing strong and adaptive intervention strategies for and with devalued individuals and groups.

11 CONCLUSION

The concept of social role has been associated with Normalization from the very beginning. SRV's espousal of a role-oriented formulation can be seen as the result of Normalization's not-so-surprising evolution over the past 25 years. The social role concept comes complete with a rich and well-articulated history of theoretical and research enterprise. This work, as well as the role concept's grounding in the day-to-day experiences of the nonacademic, should greatly enrich SRV's own theory-building project as well as provide new impetus and new direction to its ambitions as a theory of psychosocial intervention.

The latest SRV formulation, which integrates the role concept, is a clear improvement over previous formulations that, in the case of North American Normalization, were more focused on exterior (behavioral, appearance, and setting) changes of the person or, in the case of Scandinavian Normalization, were accompanied by imprecise or undefined terminology that left a great deal to interpretation. The role concept gets as close to the person as language and conceptual structures allow. It accounts for the inner life as well as providing a comprehensive understanding of the person as object of perception. It accounts for the person realistically and comprehensively within narrow and broad social contexts. Much work remains to be done to fully integrate into SRV all the richness that is role theory.

On the other hand, SRV provides role theory with practical and comprehensive usefulness (Lemay, 1996b; 1996c). It adds to role theory a broad intervention dimension that can be tied to ideals of social justice and that can be seen as a radical challenge to a society that discriminates on the basis of ability and social position. It would seem that this grafting of role theory to Social Role Valorization could bear much fruit.

REFERENCES

BANK-MIKKELSEN, N. E. (1969). A metropolitan area in Denmark: Copenhagen. In R. B. KUGEL & W. WOLFENSBERGER (Eds.), *Changing patterns in residential services for the mentally retarded* (pp. 227-254). Washington, DC: President's Committee on Mental Retardation.

BARKER, R. (1968). *Ecological psychology: Concepts and methods for studying the human environment of behavior*. Stanford: Stanford University Press.

BARKER, R., & GUMP, P. V. (1964). *Big school, small school: High school size and student behavior*. Stanford: Stanford University Press.

BARKER, R., & WRIGHT, H. (1954). *Midwest and its children: The psychological ecology of an American town*. Evanston, IL: Row Peterson and Co.

BERGER, P. (1963). *Invitation to sociology*. New York: Doubleday.

BERGER, P. (1992). *A far glory: The quest for faith in an age of credulity*. New York: Anchor Books.

BERGER, P. (1996). Two cheers for class. *First Things, 64*, 18-20.

BIDDLE, B. J. (1979). *Role theory: Expectations, identities and behaviors*. New York: Academic Press.

BIDDLE, B. J. (1986). Recent developments in role theory. *Annual Review of Sociology, 12*, 67-92.

BLATT, B., & KAPLAN, F. (1966). *Christmas in purgatory: A photographic essay on mental retardation*. Boston: Allyn & Bacon.

BROPHY, J. E. (1983). Research on the self-fulfilling prophecy and teacher expectations. *Journal of Educational Psychology, 75*(5), 631-661.

BRONFENBRENNER, U. (1979). *The ecology of human development*. Cambridge: Harvard University Press.

BURSTALL, C. (1976). The Matthew effect in the classroom. *Educational Research, 21*(1), 19-25.

CAMPBELL, D. T. (1967). Stereotypes and the perception of group differences. *American Psychologist, 22*(10), 817-829.

CHAPPELL, A. L. (1992). Towards a sociological critique of the Normalisation principle. *Disability, Handicap & Society 7*(1), 35-51.

COHEN, S., & WILLS, T. A. (1985). Social support, social integration and the buffering hypothesis. *Psychological Bulletin, 98*(2), 310-357.

CROSBY, F., & CLAYTON, S. (1990). Affirmative action and the issue of expectancies. *Journal of Social Issues, 46*(2), 61-80.

DEAUX, K. (1993). Reconstructing social identity. *Personality and Social Psychology Bulletin, 19*(1), 4-12.

DITTO, P. H., & HILTON, J. L. (1990). Expectancy processes in the health care interaction sequence. *Journal of Social Issues, 46*(2), 97-124.

DYBWAD, G. (1969). Action implications, USA today. In R. B. KUGEL & W. WOLFENSBERGER (Eds.), *Changing patterns in residential services for the mentally retarded* (pp. 383-428). Washington, DC: President's Committee on Mental Retardation.

EAGLY, A. (1987). *Sex differences in social behavior: A social-role interpretation*. Hillsdale: Lawrence Erlbaum Ass.

EAGLY, A. (1995). The science and politics of comparing women and men. *American Psychologist, 50*(3), 145-158.

EAGLY, A., ASHMORE, R. D., MAKHIJANI, M. G., & LONGO, L. C. (1991). What is beautiful is good, but....: A meta-analytic review of research on the physical attractiveness stereotype. *Psychological Bulletin, 110*(1), 109-128.

EAGLY, A., & CROWLEY, M. (1986). Gender and helping behavior: A meta-analytic review of the social psychological literature. *Psychological Bulletin, 100*(3), 283-308.

EAGLY, A., & JOHNSON, B. T. (1990). Gender and leadership style: A meta-analysis. *Psychological Bulletin, 108*(2), 233-256.

EAGLY, A., & KITE, M. (1987). Are stereotypes of nationalities applied to both women and men? *Journal of Personality and Social Psychology, 53*(3), 451-462.

EAGLY, A., & MLADINIC, A. (1989). Gender stereotypes and attitudes toward men and women. *Personality and Social Psychology Bulletin, 15*(4), 543-558.

EAGLY, A., & STEFFEN, V. (1986). Gender and aggressive behavior: A meta-analytic review of the social psychological literature. *Psychological Bulletin, 100*(3), 309-330.

ELKS, M. (1994). Valuing the person or valuing the role? Critique of social valorization theory. *Mental Retardation, 32*(4), 265-271.

GOFFMAN, E. (1961). *Asylums: Essays on the social situation of mental patients and other inmates*. New York: Doubleday.

GOLDSTEIN, A. P., SPRAFKIN, R. P., GERSHAW, N. J., & KLEIN, P. (1980). *Skillstreaming the adolescent: A structured learning approach to teaching prosocial skills*. Champaign, IL: Research Press Co.

HANEY, C. W., BANKS, C., & ZIMBARDO, P. (1973). Interpersonal dynamics in a simulated prison. *International Journal of Criminology and Penology, 1*, 69-97.

HELLER, H. W., SPOONER, F., ENRIGHT, B. E., HANEY, K., & SCHILIT, J. (1991). Classic articles: A reflection into the field of mental retardation. *Education and Training in Mental Retardation, 26*(2), 202-206.

HELLER, K. (1993). Prevention activities for older adults: Social structures and personal competencies that maintain useful social roles. *Journal of Counseling and Development, 72*, 124-130.

HILBERT, R. A. (1981). Toward an improved understanding of "role." *Theory and Society, 10*, 207-226.

JONES, R. (1990). Expectations and delay in seeking medical care. *Journal of Social Issues, 46*(2), 81-95.

JUSSIM, L. (1990). Social reality and social problems: The role of expectancies. *Journal of Social Issues, 46*(2), 9-34.

KELLY, G. (1955/1963). *A theory of personality: The psychology of personal constructs*. New York: Norton Library.

KUGEL, R. B., & WOLFENSBERGER, W. (Eds.). (1969). *Changing patterns in residential services for the mentally retarded*. Washington, DC: President's Committee on Mental Retardation.

LEMAY, R. (1994). Problems of discourse concerning roles. *The International Social Role Valorization Journal/La Revue Internationale de la Valorisation des Rôles Sociaux, 1*(1), 45-46.

LEMAY, R. (1996a). Throwing slippers and other role behaviors: Eliza Doolittle becomes a lady. *The International Social Role Valorization Journal/La Revue Internationale de la Valorisation des Rôles Sociaux, 2*(2), 38-40.

LEMAY, R. (1996b). Normalization and Social Role Valorization. In A. DELL ORTO & P. MARINELLI (Eds.), *The encyclopaedia of disability and rehabilitation*. New York: MacMillan.

LEMAY, R. (1996c). La Valorisation des Rôles Sociaux et le Principe de Normalisation: des lignes directrices pour la mise en oeuvre de contexts sociaux et de services humans pour les personnes à risque de dévalorisation sociale. *The International Social Role Valorization Journal/La Revue Internationale de la Valorisation des Rôles Sociaux, 2*(2), 15-21.

MCKNIGHT, J. (1995). *The careless society: Community and its counterfeits*. New York: Basic Books.

MEAD, G. H. (1934). *Mind, self and society*. Chicago: University of Chicago Press.

MENAGHAN, E. (1989). Role changes and psychological well-being: Variations in effects by gender and role repertoire. *Social Forces, 7*(3), p. 693.

MILGRAM, S. (1974). *Obedience to authority*. New York: Harper Colophon.

MORENO, Z. T. (1989, Fall). Psychodrama, role theory and the concept of the social atom. *JGPPS*, 178-187.

MORGAN, D., & SCHWALBE, M. (1990). Mind and self in society: Linking social structure and social cognition. *Social Psychology Quarterly, 53*(2), 148-164.

NEWCOMB, T., TURNER, R., & CONVERSE, P. (1975). *The study of human interaction*. London: Routledge and Kegan Paul.

NIRJE, B. (1969). The Normalization principle and its human management implications. In R. B. KUGEL & W. WOLFENSBERGER (Eds.), *Changing patterns in residential services for the mentally retarded* (pp. 179-196). Washington, DC: President's Committee on Mental Retardation.

NIRJE, B. (1992). *The Normalization principle papers*. Uppsala, Sweden: Centre for Handicap Research, Uppsala University.

NIRJE, B. (1993). The Normalization principle: 25 years later. In U. LEHTINEN & R. PIRTTIMAA (Eds.), *Arjessa tapahtuu. Comments on mental retardation and adult education*. Finland: The Institute for Educational Research, University of Jyväskylä.

OLSHANSKY, S. (1972). Changing vocational behavior through Normalization. In W. WOLFENSBERGER (Ed.), *The principle of Normalization in human services* (pp. 150-163). Toronto, ON: National Institute on Mental Retardation.

OSEYRMAN, D., & MARKUS, H. (1990). Possible selves in balance: Implications for delinquency. *Journal of Social Issues, 46*(2), 141-158.

PARSONS, T. (1951). *The social system*. New York: The Free Press of Glencoe.

PEABODY, D. (1985). *National characteristics*. New York: Cambridge University Press.

PERRIN, B., & NIRJE, B. (1985). Setting the record straight: A critique of some frequent misconceptions of the Normalization principle. *Australia and New Zealand Journal of Developmental Disabilities, 11*, 69-74.

RIGGINS, S. H. (1993). Life as a metaphor: Current issues in dramaturgical analysis. *Semiotica, 95*(1/2), 153-165.

ROCHEBLAVE-SPENLÉ, A.-M. (1962). *La notion du rôle en psychologie sociale*. Paris: Presses Universitaires de France.

ROSENTHAL, R., & JACOBSON, L. (1968). *Pygmalion in the classroom: Teacher expectation in the classroom*. New York: Holt, Rinehart, & Winston.

SAINT CLAIRE, L. (1989). A multidimensional model of mental retardation: Impairment, subnormal behavior, role failures and socially constructed retardation. *American Journal on Mental Retardation, 94*(1), 88-96.

SARASON, S. (1969). The creation of settings. In R. KUGEL AND W. WOLFENSBERGER (Eds.), *Changing* patterns in residential services for the mentally retarded (pp. 341-358). Washington, DC: President's Committee on Mental Retardation.

SARASON, S. (1981). *Psychology misdirected.* New York: The Free Press.

STRYKER, S. (1987). The vitalization of symbolic interactionism. *Social Psychology Quarterly, 50*(1), 83-94.

SZIVOS, S. (1992). The limits to integration. In H. BROWN & H. SMITH (Eds.), *Normalisation: A reader for the nineties.* London: Tavistock/Routledge.

THOITS, P. (1983, April). Multiple identities and psychological well-being: A reformulation and test of the social isolation hypothesis. *American Sociological Review, 48,* 174-187.

THOITS, P. (1986, April). Multiple identities: Examining gender and marital status differences in distress. *American Sociological Review, 51,* 259-272.

THOITS, P. (1991). On merging identity theory and stress research. *Social Psychology Quarterly, 54*(2), 101-112.

THOITS, P. (1992). Identity structures and psychological well-being: Gender and marital status comparisons. *Social Psychology Quarterly, 55*(3), 236-256.

THOMAS, E. J., & BIDDLE, B. J. (1966). *Role theory: Concepts and research.* New York: John Wiley & Sons.

THOMAS, S., & WOLFENSBERGER, W. (1982).The importance of social imagery in interpreting societally devalued people to the public. *Rehabilitation Literature, 43*(11-12), 356-358.

THOMAS, S., & WOLFENSBERGER, W. (1994). The importance of social imagery in interpreting societally devalued people to the public. *The International Social Role Valorization Journal/La Revue Internationale de la Valorisation des Rôles Sociaux, 1*(1), 35-37. (First appeared in 1982 in *Rehabilitation Literature, 43*(11-12), 356-358)

THORNDIKE, R. L. (1968). Review of *Pygmalion* in the classroom. *American Educational Research Journal , 5*(4), 708-711.

TURNER, R. H. (1978). The role and the person. *American Journal of Sociology, 84*(1), 1-23.

TURNER, R. H. (1988). Personality in society: Social psychology's contribution to sociology. *Social Psychology Quarterly, 51*(1), 1-10.

TURNER, R. H. (1990). Role change. *Annual Review of Sociology, 16,* 87-110.

UMBERSON, D., & HUGHES, M. (1987). The impact of physical attractiveness on achievement and psychological well-being. *Social Psychology Quarterly, 50*(3), 227-236.

VERBRUGGE, L. (1983, March). Multiple roles and physical health of women and men. *Journal of Health and Social Behavior, 24,* 16-30.

WHEATON, B. (1990, April). Life transitions, role histories, and mental health. *American Sociological Review, 55,* 209-203.

WICKER, A. (1969). Size of church membership and members' support of church behavior settings. *Journal of Personality and Social Psychology, 13,* 278-288.

WICKER, A. (1969). Cognitive complexity, school size and participation in school behavior settings: A test of the frequency of interaction hypothesis. *Journal of Educational Psychology, 60*(3), 200-203.

WICKER, A. (1973). Undermanning theory and research: implications for the study of psychological and behavioral effects of excess human population. *Representative Research in Social Psychology, 4,* 185-206.

WICKER, A. (1979). *An introduction to ecological psychology.* Monterey, CA: Brooks/Cole Pub. Co.

WOLFENSBERGER, W. (1969). The origin and nature of our institutional models. In R. B. KUGEL & W. WOLFENSBERGER (Eds.), *Changing patterns in residential services for the mentally retarded* (pp. 59-171). Washington, DC: President's Committee on Mental Retardation.

WOLFENSBERGER, W. (1970). The principle of Normalization and its implication for psychiatric services. *American Journal of Psychiatry, 127,* 291-297.

WOLFENSBERGER, W. (1972). *The principle of Normalization in human services.* Toronto, ON: National Institute on Mental Retardation.

WOLFENSBERGER, W. (1980). The definition of Normalization: Update, problems, disagreements, and misunderstandings. In R. J. FLYNN & K. E. NITSCH (Eds.), *Normalization, social integration, and community services* (pp. 71-115). Baltimore: University Park Press.

WOLFENSBERGER, W. (1983). Social Role Valorization: A proposed new term for the principle of Normalization. *Mental Retardation, 21*(6), 234-239.

WOLFENSBERGER, W. (1992). *A brief introduction to Social Role Valorization as a higher order concept for structuring human services* (Rev. ed.). Syracuse, NY: Syracuse University, Training Institute for Human Service Planning, Leadership and Change Agentry.

WOLFENSBERGER, W., & GLENN, L. (1975). *Program analysis of service systems (PASS): A method for the quantitative evaluation of human services (3rd ed.).* Two vols.: Handbook and Field Manual. Toronto, ON: National Institute on Mental Retardation.

WOLFENSBERGER, W., & THOMAS, S. (1983). *Program analysis of service systems' implementation of Normalization goals (PASSING): Normalization criteria and ratings manual.* Toronto, ON: Canadian Institute on Mental Retardation.

WOLFENSBERGER, W., & THOMAS, S. (1994). An analysis of the client role from a Social Role Valorization perspective. *The International Social Role Valorization Journal, 1*(1), 3-8.

WOLFENSBERGER, W., THOMAS, S., & CARUSO, G. (1996). Some of the universal "good things of life" which the implementation of Social Role Valorization can be expected to make more accessible to devalued people. *The International Social Role Valorization Journal/La Revue Internationale de la Valorisation des Rôles Sociaux, 3*(2), 12-14.

WOLFENSBERGER, W., & TULLMAN, S. (1982). A brief overview of the principle of Normalization. *Rehabilitatio Psychology, 27*(3), 131-145.

ZNANIECKY, F. (1965). *Social relations and social roles: The unfinished systematic sociology.* San Francisco, CA: Chandler Publishing.

11

Normalization and residential services: The Vermont studies[1]

SARA N. BURCHARD

Normalization has had an *immeasurable* impact on human services, education, and the social fabric of North America since its introduction 25 years ago. It has revolutionized thinking about service delivery across the entire spectrum of human services. Normalization has changed how we view people with needs, how we view their place in our society, and how we view the role of human services. Public policy has moved from a position of removing people with mental-health, educational, or social needs in order to "fix" or contain them, to one of viewing the role of public policy and services as bringing supports to them and their families (Smull & Bellamy, 1990) in order to assist them to participate in and benefit from the services and opportunities offered in their communities. Normalization has promoted our most recent civil-rights movement in the USA, culminating in the passage of the Americans With Disabilities Act of 1990. Normalization may prove a major factor in health-care reform as the USA attempts to find more useful and cost-effective ways of meeting the health, mental-health, and supportive-care needs of its citizens.

The Normalization philosophy of inclusion, participation, and treatment en venue has gained momentum, increasing in scope and affecting persons and services far beyond those persons who are called mentally retarded or developmentally disabled. The philosophy and its effects on services have spread to the "treatment" of children with severe emotional disturbance and persons affected by chronic mental illnesses, permanent brain injury, long-term health problems, aging, or terminal illnesses. The legal and social recognition that "separate is not equal," and certainly not better, and that educational or other services to people need not be segregated to be individualized, has come a very long way since Brown and the Board of Education in 1959. That people are happier, do better, receive more respect and individualization, and have a better quality of life if they remain out of congregate, institutionalized settings and "special places" is a message that has been heard by many in direct-service and policy positions. However, the reality has not automatically followed the recognition nor even the legislation.

The ideas, derived from Normalization philosophy, of bringing services to people in their homes, schools, and communities and keeping people at home in their families as much as possible, whether they be medically fragile, developmentally disabled, or otherwise in need of support, have had a far-reaching impact on service philosophy and service provision. However, the impact has not been even in its implementation and acceptance. There exist strong forces in professional practice and training that focus on "specialties," that locate the "disability" in the person, that treat or fix the person in isolation from his or her life and family. There are also financial constraints and political realities that have prevented the implementation of Normalization practices for many persons.

While service philosophies and service systems have changed due to Normalization philosophy, the issues of implementation remain. Are our services designed to enhance the inclusion of persons with disabilities in recreation, leisure, work, education, and other services in their communities, supporting them to gain and maintain respect, social supports and friendships, and autonomy and independence, and to have access to lifestyles of their choice, similar to those available to other community members? It was from efforts to examine questions such as these that the Vermont studies grew.

1 THE VERMONT RESEARCH STUDIES

The program of research in which my colleagues and I have been engaged over the past 15 years at the University of Vermont resulted directly from the impetus provided by Normalization for the development and "humanization" of community-based services for persons with mental retardation. This program of research has been inextricably interwoven with evaluating Normalization practices as the latter have been followed and applied in the State of Vermont. A national leader in promoting and implementing practices based upon Normalization principles, Vermont was recently identified as first in the USA in terms of its rate of inclusion (79.4%) of students with disabilities in regular educational activities (*Annual Report to Congress*, 1991). Vermont has also been among the most progressive states in terms of its financial support for community services (Braddock & Fujiura, 1991; Braddock, Hemp, Fujiura, Bachelder, & Mitchell, 1989). Vermont closed its only institutional center for persons with mental retardation during the winter of 1994-1995, guaranteeing that public dollars go to support small community-based services.

The research described in this chapter was undertaken in an effort to support and evaluate the community residential services in Vermont as they were developing. Because the Vermont service system was predicated on the implementation of Normalization principles (Nirje, 1970; Wolfensberger, 1972), an examination of how Normalization principles are actually applied has been an essential part of our research program. Unlike research undertaken to examine the question "Does Normalization work?" (Zigler, Hodapp, & Edison, 1990), our work has asked "How well has the state

been accomplishing its social-policy objectives?" In effect, we have been interested primarily in how well Normalization principles have been implemented and only secondarily in the ways in which Normalization implementation has expressed itself in client outcomes. The research began in 1979 with a request from the Mental Retardation Services branch of the Vermont State Department of Mental Health (DMH) to develop staff competencies for persons working in the delivery of the then-new community mental-retardation services. Our program of research has evolved over the past 15 years to include an empirical examination of issues central to themes of Normalization.

The State of Vermont launched its drive to transform the delivery of mental-retardation services from an institution-based to a community-based system in the mid-1970s. The goals of community services were from the beginning framed from the perspective of the principle of Normalization as articulated by Wolf Wolfensberger (1972). DMH and advocates brought Wolfensberger to Vermont on several occasions, sent key policy-makers and providers to PASS (Wolfensberger & Glenn, 1975) and Normalization workshops, and had PASS evaluations completed for several local services in order to give coherent direction to the development and implementation of the new service system.

2 STAFF AND MANAGER COMPETENCIES

2.1 FIELD-BASED COMPETENCY DEVELOPMENT

Against this backdrop, members of the Psychology Department at the University of Vermont were asked to develop staff competencies for the newly developing, small community homes (by state mandate, residences were to house no more than six persons), in order to provide local agencies with criteria for hiring and training staff. Although nationally many were developing competencies and training based on expert opinion and academic training programs (Fiorelli & Keating, 1979), a different procedure was employed in Vermont. A field-based methodology was selected to generate and identify essential staff and manager competencies by capitalizing on the information and experience of those most directly involved in the delivery of community services. A large pool of potential competencies was generated, based on the methods of job analysis (delineating of the tasks that staff members performed in the course of their work, how much time these tasks took, and how important they were), critical-incident reporting (describing incidents that made staff feel especially competent or successful in carrying out their jobs, as well as incidents in which they especially felt in need of greater skill), structured interviews with direct-care staff and managers about how to support individuals to achieve maximum independence and integration into community living, and a review of competencies derived from expert opinion. Individuals throughout the state directly involved in providing community services for persons with mental retardation participated in this process.

The final step in identifying critical competencies was to have a broad sample of state mental-retardation professionals, including academicians, administrators, paraprofessionals, and advocates, use a forced-choice procedure to sort the competency statements into categories ("absolute prerequisite," "desirable prerequisite," "needs to be acquired with training," and "not essential"). This resulted in the identification of a core of 21 essential competencies for staff and managers of community residences for persons with mental retardation (Thousand, Burchard, & Hasazi, 1986).

There were several instructive and surprising results from this field-based, bottom-up generation of competencies. First, despite our research bias toward identifying skills that could be readily operationalized, the final pool of items contained many statements that could only be characterized as attitudes rather than behavioral skills. Second, those items identified by the vast majority of respondents as absolutely essential for service providers were primarily attitudes rather than skill-based competencies. Third, the most absolutely prerequisite competencies were closely related to Normalization philosophy, namely, high regard and *respect* for the individuals being served, provision of age-appropriate activities, enhancing consumer status, individualization, and choice. And fourth, the (re)discovery was made, after content analysis, that the core absolutely prerequisite competencies included Carl Rogers's (1969) famous basic elements essential for developing a successful helping relationship. The resulting competency statements were organized under two general headings based upon content: a set of value-based, humanistic Normalization/Person Orientation Competencies, and a set of Teaching/ Technical Skill Competencies. The set of 21 core competencies are presented in Table 11.1. As can be seen on inspection, 18 of the 21 core competencies belong to the value-based Normalization/Person Orientation category.

While the more commonly used methods of competency generation, namely, expert opinion and job analysis, generated skill and knowledge-based competency statements, the open-ended, field-based methods of interview and critical-incident analysis generated competencies related to interpersonal interaction and values. These were subsequently identified by all levels of informants as the most crucial.

2.2   COMPETENCY-VALIDATION STUDIES

If the identified attitudes, skills, and knowledge were in fact critical competencies for service providers, then they should be reflected in improved services for consumers. Two studies were conducted to validate the relationship of staff competencies to service outcomes, a concurrent and a predictive validation study.

In order to determine whether the quality of service recipients' programs were related to their providers' competence in Normalization practices and values, interpersonal skills, and teaching and training, it was necessary to identify, define, and develop measures of outcomes that reflected program goals. Since the articulated policy upon which all state programs were founded was implementation of Normalization and the developmental model, it was essential to measure those aspects of the residential programs under study. If programs were implementing Normalization, developmental training, and support in an effective manner, this should be reflected in service recipients' greater personal independence, community participation, integration, well-being, and satisfaction. Table 11.2 shows the constructs that we undertook to measure and the instruments used to measure them. It also shows the methods used to examine the relationship between staff competence and program quality in the 14 small group residences that existed within the state at that time (Burchard, Pine, Gordon, Joffe, Widrick, & Goy, 1987).

TABLE 11.1

CORE COMPETENCIES FOR STAFF AND MANAGERS OF SMALL COMMUNITY RESIDENCES

Level I: Absolutely Prerequisite for All Positions (13 Competencies)

Normalization/Person Orientation Competencies

Creates Normalization
1. Creates a homelike atmosphere in residence.
2. Provides age-appropriate activities, expectations, interactions.
3. Provides appropriate role models for clients and community: Represents norms in values, dress, behavior.

Knowledge and understanding of persons with special needs
4. Assists clients in being interpreted as valuable persons:
    a) Encourages age-appropriate activities.
    b) Encourages clients' interest in their appearance.
    c) Assists clients in appearing more attractive.
    d) Assists clients in displaying appropriate social behavior.
5. Shows investment in client growth and development:
    a) Commitment to the developmental model.
    b) Commitment to clients' receiving the most appropriate programs and high-quality services.
    c) Commitment to clients' achieving the utmost in individual development.
    d) Commitment to individualized treatment of clients.
6. Shows positive attitude toward persons with retarded development:
    a) Views clients as interesting and valuable persons.
    b) Is comfortable with clients in home and public settings.
    c) Is tolerant, patient with clients.
    d) Displays good disposition around clients.
    e) Gives of personal time to clients.
7. Shows respect for individual clients:
    a) Gives positive and corrective feedback to clients.
    b) Shows interest in interacting with clients on a social, verbal, and physical level.
    c) Enjoys clients as individuals.
    d) Enjoys participation in leisure and recreational activities with clients.
    e) Shows ability to communicate and relate to residents.
8. Shows empathy for clients:
    a) Identifies what client has to deal with in everyday life.
    b) Identifies clients' needs, interests, and desires.
    c) Shows concern for clients' social and emotional well-being.

Works cooperatively with others
9. Works as a team member.
10. Takes directions from supervisor:
    a) Cooperates with supervisor.
    b) Reaches agreement with supervisor.
11. Shows sincere interest in job: Shows interest in staying at least 1 year.
12. Shows commitment to and ability of working cooperatively with others: Staff, professionals, service providers, parents.

Teaching/Technical Competencies

Designs, manages, conducts, and evaluates training programs

13.   Shows concern with client progress:
- a)   Demonstrates pride in program, service delivery.
- b)   Demonstrates interest in data collection and monitoring.
- c)   Demonstrates interest in providing the most appropriate programs possible for client.
- d)   Demonstrates concern for consistent and regular implementation of resident programs.

Level II: Desirably Prerequisite for All Positions (8 Competencies)

Normalization/Person Orientation Competencies

Knowledge and understanding of persons with special needs

1.   Recognizes importance of household tasks for resident training and maintaining an acceptable residence.

2.   Demonstrates general counselling skills with clients:
- a)   Listens to clients' concerns, problems.
- b)   Assists clients in identifying and expressing feelings.
- c)   Assists clients in resolving interpersonal conflicts.
- d)   Assists clients in identifying appropriate behavior for social situations.

Works cooperatively with others

3.   Tolerates heavy workload, long hours.

4.   Shows professional manner with public:
- a)   Displays social amenities, courtesies.
- b)   Speaks positively of residential facility, residents, own job.
- c)   Takes and responds to messages, requests.

5.   Works independently without supervision:
- a)   Initiates activity with or for benefit of residents.
- b)   Carries out routine without prompts.

6.   Shows respect for parents:
- a)   Talks with parents in lay terms.
- b)   Communicates personal interest in parents.
- c)   Listens to parents' concerns and point of view.
- d)   Is sensitive to parents' needs.

Teaching/Technical Competencies

Knowledge of teaching and behavior management principles

7.   Shows concern for using the most positive, least intrusive interventions.

Practical skills related to managing a residence

8.   Is consistent and positive in consequating residents' behavior.

At the time of this study, there were few existing ways of measuring program Normalization that could be employed within our limited means. The resources to provide PASS (Wolfensberger & Glenn, 1975) or PASSING (Wolfensberger & Thomas, 1983) evaluations of all 14 programs were not available. A review of the literature found few published studies that had incorporated measures of program Normalization other than PASS (Eyman, Demaine, & Lei, 1979) or a local adaptation of PASS (Hull & Thompson, 1980, 1981). Other available measures of environmental factors related to Normalization, such as block treatment, lack of individualization, personal choice, autonomy, and physical appearance, were designed to identify institutional practices (Pratt, Luszcz, & Brown, 1980). These measures were insensitive to differences among Vermont programs, which had all been developed on the same model. All

were small residences (six or fewer residents), located within residential neighborhoods, with day or work programs for residents and an emphasis on age-appropriate activities and appearances. Therefore, a structured interview was developed for residence staff that indirectly assessed the degree to which the program they directed incorporated important principles of Normalization: individualization, privacy, autonomy, responsibility, and age-appropriate activities, rhythms, and lifestyle (Burchard et al., 1987). Although this instrument did not cover every important aspect of effective Normalization implementation, it did incorporate elements thought to differentiate among the Vermont programs. Other elements, such as age-appropriate dress and the physical appearance of rooms, homes, and the neighborhood, were consciously addressed by all of the programs, which therefore differed little on these aspects.

TABLE 11.2

CONSTRUCTS AND MEASURES TO EVALUATE THE RELATIONSHIP OF MANAGER COMPETENCE TO PROGRAM GOALS

Constructs	Measures
Manager competency	
1. Technical skills	
a) Developmental programming	Written test
b) Behavior management	Supervisor ratings
2. Normalization orientation	
a) Interpersonal skills	Written test
b) Sensitivity to client needs	Supervisor ratings
c) Normalization implementation	
Program quality	
1. Program Normalization	Careprovider interview:
a) In-home Normalization	-Residence
	-Lifestyle
	-Normalization
b) Community integration	-Out-of-home activities
	Direct observation
2. Client satisfaction	Resident interview:
a) Program satisfaction	-Resident satisfaction
b) Personal well-being	-Personal well-being
c) Relatives' satisfaction	Rating scale
3. Independence Training	
a) IPPs	Program review ratings
b) DMH satisfaction	State reviewer satisfaction
c) Home observations	Direct observation

To provide additional measures of Normalization practices and to cross-validate the staff Normalization interview, three other kinds of measures were incorporated into the study. Observational measures of staff and resident behavior in the home were used to assess age-appropriate activities, responsibility, and independence. A structured interview with residents about their lifestyle, including self-perceived independence, autonomy, responsibility, community access, privacy, and interpersonal relationships within the residence, was used to evaluate resident satisfaction and Normalization issues (Burchard, Pine, & Gordon, 1990). The final method of evaluating program implementation of Normalization principles was a measure of recent community activities. This measure, based on an interview with staff, asked the number and type of out-of-home activities in which each resident had participated during the previous two weeks. Using a prompt sheet of activities, staff were asked whether residents had gone as a group, singly, or in small numbers, and where the activity had taken place. Scores for programs were based upon the number of activities that had taken place in integrated settings with additional points for nongroup (individualized) activities. Only activities that involved the opportunity for contact or participation with nondisabled peers were scored.

Measures of developmental-model implementation were based on an examination of participants' individual program plans (mandated by the state to reflect training and progress in daily and community-living skills) and ratings of program quality made by state reviewers evaluating the programs for quality-assurance purposes. Finally, personal adjustment was evaluated by means of a structured interview with service recipients, in which a simple forced-choice format was used to evaluate self-perceived well-being. This measure was adapted for use with individuals with mental retardation (Seltzer, 1980) from an interview used to evaluate the general psychological well-being of adults from the general population (Dupuy, 1978).

Group-home manager competence was evaluated in two ways: by means of supervisor ratings of the manager's performance on each of 53 competencies identified as essential for manager job performance in the previous study (Thousand et al., 1986), and by means of an objective written assessment given to the manager. The written task involved analyzing a setting in which clients received services, designing a program to meet the clients' needs, and then demonstrating knowledge and skill in defining objectives, creating and collecting data, and behavior management.

The competency-validation process involved 14 small group homes with 78 residents and 14 managers, the latter also serving as direct-care providers. The results showed that manager competencies were highly and logically related to measures of program quality (Burchard et al., 1987). Variations in managers' competencies translated into measurably different program outcomes for residents in terms of program Normalization, community integration, developmental programming, resident activities, and resident well-being.

Managers with greater competency in technical skills had programs with more data-based Individualized Program Plans (IPP) and received higher ratings from state reviewers, who analyzed managers' written records as an important part of their biannual evaluations. These managers' programs, however, had lower scores on program Normalization, based on data gathered during the structured interviews, and residents in their programs were observed to engage in less personal and home care. Across all participants, engaging in these age-appropriate adult activities was related to higher self-reported well-being and to being in a program with a higher Normalization score (structured-interview data). Residents with severely handicapping conditions who lived with technically competent managers were observed to engage in more independent and self-initiated behavior. Managers with higher scores on Normalization/person orientation competencies had residents who were more actively involved in accessing community activities in more individual ways, one aspect of Normalization implementation included in our Normalization measures. It should be noted that competence in Normalization/person orientation areas and competence in teaching and technical skills were not necessarily mutually exclusive. In fact, in the subsequent predictive validation study, these two sets of competencies were highly correlated, which was not due merely to resident level of disability.

As small community programs in Vermont were about to expand rapidly, there was an opportunity to examine competencies in a predictive manner. Local agencies throughout Vermont included competency-based assessment procedures provided by our research group along with their usual procedures in interviewing potential managers. The candidate-assessment procedures included the written evaluation described above, a structured interview with candidates, a competency rating scale given over the phone to a person serving as the candidate's reference, and a similar competency rating from the candidate's previous employer. The agencies also used whatever procedures they had in place for candidate selection and made their decisions based upon their own criteria and/or the exigencies of the moment. Approximately 10 months later, measures of manager competence and program quality were assessed in the same way as in the original study, except that no direct observations were made of resident activities in the homes.

Seventy-two persons applying to become managers were evaluated. Twenty-five managers were hired, of whom 18 subsequently participated in the follow-up evaluation. They were managers and co-managers of small community residences for two to six residents of all levels of disability.

The results of the predictive study replicated the findings from the concurrent validation study (Burchard, Pine, Widrick, & Creedon, 1985). Managers with higher scores on Normalization competencies (value-based person-orientation and interpersonal skills), regardless of the level of disability of their residents, had programs a year later in which residents were more actively accessing the community. These managers' programs also received higher program-Normalization scores on the Normalization interview. Managers with higher technical competencies upon hiring, on the other hand, had better data-based individual program plans and higher satisfaction ratings from state reviewers 10 months later. The concurrent and predictive relationships found between the live-in residence-managers' competencies and program outcomes are shown in Table 11.3.

TABLE 11.3

CONCURRENT AND PREDICTIVE CORRELATIONS (r) BETWEEN MANAGER COMPETENCE AND PROGRAM QUALITY IN SMALL COMMUNITY RESIDENCES

| Program outcomes | Manager competence | | | |
| | Normalization/person orientation | | Technical skills | |
	Concurrent	Predictive	Concurrent	Predictive
Program Normalization	—	0.62	-0.49[a]	—
Community integration	0.60	0.48[a]/0.72	—	—
IPPs	—	0.65	0.62	0.52/0.78
State reviewer satisfaction	—	—	0.60	0.57/0.61
Independent activities	—	—	0.30	—
Self/home activities	—	—	-0.50[b]	—
Resident well-being	—	—	-0.35	—

Note. The predictive correlations were based on data collected 10 months after the managers were hired. More than one correlation in a cell reflects use of several competency measures during candidate assessment. There were 14 small homes in the concurrent study and 16 in the predictive study.

[a]Directional hypothesis. [b]Self-care, cooking, and house-care activities were significantly related to program-Normalization scores ($r = 0.28$) and to well-being ($r = 0.42$).

2.3 RESIDENT SATISFACTION

In order to evaluate programs from the consumer's perspective, data from the concurrent and predictive studies for those individuals living in small group homes who had been able to participate in the resident-satisfaction interview were pooled. There were 57 such individuals living in 12 small community group homes staffed primarily with one or two resident managers. Those individuals living in homes with more frequent opportunities for community-integrating activities had higher total scores on residence satisfaction, another measure of Normalization and covering the issues of autonomy, individualization, privacy, community access, and responsibility. There were 34 group-home residents who were unequivocal about wanting or not wanting to continue living in their residence and who were able to support their preference with a positive or negative reason. Wanting to stay was associated with programs with greater activation (activities at home, r = 0.57), positive social relations with other residents in the home (r = 0.41), and positive relations with the manager (r = 0.44) (Burchard, Pine, & Gordon, 1984). Those individuals who wanted to stay in their current residence were those whose managers were evaluated as having greater competence (r = 0.57), both technical and Normalization-related, and whose programs provided greater opportunities for individualized participation in community-based activities (r = 0.64). A regression analysis showed that while residents' personal characteristics were unrelated to wanting to stay in their respective group homes, manager Normalization competence explained 42% of the variance in the desire to stay, to the exclusion of other variables (Burchard et al., 1990).

2.4 CONCLUSION

This series of studies made it very clear that staff and manager competencies, particularly sensitivity to resident needs and to Normalization issues, had important effects on program quality. Staff competence in Normalization values, attitudes, and practices was reflected in the promotion of Normalization goals and in clients' activities and satisfaction with their living situation. These studies also showed that community access and participation, important corollaries of Normalization, are valued by residents and contribute to their satisfaction with their living environment.

3 STUDIES OF COMMUNITY ADJUSTMENT AND INTEGRATION

As service reform gained momentum throughout the 1970s and 1980s, a wide array of community mental-retardation services grew up (Bruininks, Rotegard, Lakin, & Hill, 1987). Most service systems were based upon the philosophy of Normalization and the developmental model. Despite disagreements about definitions and applications of Normalization philosophy (Zigler et al., 1990; Wolfensberger, 1980), the goal of community services was and is to promote independent functioning and a normalized lifestyle: what, where, how, and with whom people with disabilities spend their time, including physical and social integration and opportunities to engage in meaningful work for meaningful wages, alongside and in the same manner as persons of similar age in the broader community.

A key question was (and still is) the extent to which the array of community living arrangements and programs met the goals of the new social policy. That is, to what extent did these services provide opportunities to live, work, and recreate, and to exercise choice, independence, and individuality in the same manner as and alongside same-aged peers? Had the community programs stemming from the impetus and ideas of Normalization philosophy possibly created new forms of isolation and segregation? To what extent had the barriers of exclusion and differentness actually been broken down? And to what extent were the recipients of the new community supports being served to their satisfaction?

Based upon the success of our earlier studies and the obvious desirability of examining issues of program quality from a perspective that includes the individuals served, we proposed to conduct a longitudinal study of community adjustment among adults with mental retardation in Vermont. The types of residential settings selected were prevalent options across the nation for persons with mental retardation: small group homes (GHs); semi-independent, supervised apartments (SAs); and natural families (FHs). These types of settings differed widely from one another in terms of organizational structure and amount of support afforded, providing considerable variability in aspects of community living that are important elements of Normalization. The degree of personal independence, autonomy, and choice thus promised to vary across types of setting, as did the kind, degree, intensity, and duration of social support and the availability of peers for social activities and contact. The inclusion of persons living with their natural families furnished a useful comparison group for evaluating the quality of life and other program outcomes of individuals living in residences provided by the service system. In addition, a longitudinal study of community adjustment would provide an opportunity to elaborate our measures of those elements of Normalization implementation that would be most apt to differ among residential settings and provide an opportunity to examine the relationship of Normalization constructs to positive outcomes from the resident's perspective. It would also be possible to examine which settings and characteristics of settings best promoted Normalization outcomes.

Community adjustment is a very complex, multidimensional construct and requires the inclusion of a broad range of variables if researchers are to evaluate "how well people are doing" in community programs supposedly designed to promote their meaningful participation in their communities (Emerson, 1985). Our study proposed to examine a broad range of personal, environmental, and psychosocial variables, over a 3-year period, among persons living in these three types of residences. Its purpose was to evaluate how well Vermont programs were meeting the goals of the service system, from the perspective of the persons served as well as from that of the service system.

Natural-family homes were added since they were and continue to be the most frequent "placement" for individuals with disabilities. When examining lifestyle Normalization and psychosocial variables such as adjustment, friendships, social-support networks, and continuity of relationships, this group constituted a reasonable comparison group.

3.1 PARTICIPANTS AND SETTING

Participants for the longitudinal study were recruited on a statewide basis from provider agencies and advocacy organizations. Persons between the ages of 23 and 55 who had lived in their current residence for at least 8 months and would be able to participate in a simple interview format were recruited. There were 157 such individuals identified throughout the state: 57 in 20 group homes, 47 in 35 supervised apartments, and 52 living with their families. Of these, 133 agreed to participate. The participants included almost the entire population of persons in group homes and supervised apartments in Vermont when the research began. There was no way of determining how many persons were living with their natural families. Instead, such persons were recruited in proportion to the number of persons residing in group homes and apartments in their respective regions. An examination of family characteristics showed that their educational status and financial situations were similar to that of the range of households in Vermont.

All agency-sponsored residential programs were under state mandate and review to provide services based upon the philosophy of Normalization and the developmental model (Wolfensberger, 1972). Persons living in agency-operated settings were required to have suitable out-of-residence daytime activities lasting at least 4 to 6 hours per day, to be in a "homelike" milieu housing no more than six persons with disabilities, and to have a written plan for receiving services and developing skills. Within each geographical region, supervised apartments and group homes were administered by the same agency, which, in many cases, was also responsible for providing residents' day, work-activity, or community-employment program. Persons living with their family members and receiving services (usually day or work programs) also received them from the agencies in question. Hence, the philosophy of service provision was similar across all areas of the state and types of residential settings. Group homes (GHs) served from four to six persons, providing 24-hour supervision and training with one or two staff persons. Supervised apartments (SAs) served one or two (in one case, three) persons, providing supervision and training as needed by one or two staff persons but with no on-site, live-in supervision. Family homes (FHs) were not regulated by the state, and careproviders did not necessarily subscribe to any particular philosophy of service nor did they routinely provide training (Burchard, Hasazi, Gordon, & Yoe, 1991).

3.2 MEASURES AND PROCEDURE

The model for examining community adjustment and integration is shown in Table 11.4. As predictor variables, the model includes personal characteristics (age, gender, level of disability, length of prior institutionalization, social integration and environmental characteristics (residence type, Normalization of the physical environment, careprovider competencies or attitudes). Criterion variables included Normalization-related outcomes (lifestyle Normalization, type and extent of work, physical integration, social integration, and independent performance of daily and community-living skills) and personal-adjustment outcomes (behavior adjustment, type and extent of

social-support network, satisfaction with residence, work, social support, and well-being). Information for the predictor and Normalization outcome variables was obtained by personal structured interview with careproviders and record reviews while all personal adjustment outcomes except behavior ratings were obtained by private interview with the participant. Measures were obtained three times, at approximately annual intervals.

Environmental Normalization was assessed with a 38-item rating sheet completed by researchers based upon personal observation of the residence and neighborhood to assess proximity to services and Normalization factors related to the physical location and exterior and interior appearance. *Careprovider competencies* were measured by means of supervisor ratings. Because parents had no supervisors to rate their competencies, a 29-item self-rating scale of *Normalization attitudes* was constructed to reflect their attitudes and practices toward promoting independent functioning, personal responsibility, community integration, and age-appropriate activities of their adult family member with disabilities.

TABLE 11.4

VARIABLES RELATED TO NORMALIZATION OF LIFESTYLE AND ADJUSTMENT OF PERSONS WITH MENTAL RETARDATION LIVING IN COMMUNITY SETTINGS

Predictors	Indicators
Personal characteristics	*Lifestyle-Normalization indicators*
Age Gender Level of disability Length of prior institutionalization Social integration	Performance of adaptive behavior Residence-lifestyle Normalization Community integration: *-Physical integration* *-Community employment*
Environmental characteristics	*Personal adjustment indicators*
Location Normalization of environment Environmental opportunity Careprovider competency Parent Normalization attitudes	Residence satisfaction Work satisfaction Social support networks Personal well-being Severity of problem behaviors

The Community Adjustment Scale (Seltzer & Seltzer, 1976), completed by caretakers, was used to assess *performance of independent behavior* (129 yes/no items) and *environmental opportunity* (45 yes/no items). *Lifestyle Normalization* was assessed with the 34-item structured careprovider interview tapping residents' age-appropriate activities, responsibilities, autonomy, and rhythms that had been used in our earlier studies (Burchard et al., 1990). Measures of integration were based upon the number, type, social context, and source of initiation (structured by staff versus self- or peer-initiated) of out-of-residence, nonwork activities in which the participant had engaged during the previous 2 weeks, as enumerated by the careprovider.

Physical integration was operationalized as the frequency of activities that took place in the community where contact with other community members was possible and probable. Social integration was operationalized as the frequency of community activities carried out in the company of a nondisabled peer. *Community employment* was defined as paid work done in a community-integrated setting 20 to 40 hours per week (Burchard et al., 1991).

Measures of the personal-adjustment criterion variables included a 10-item careprovider rating of the frequency and severity of problem behavior, a 22-item Residence-Satisfaction Interview used previously to evaluate the participant's view of the independence, autonomy, responsibility, activation, community access, and personal relations in his or her residence, and an 18-item Personal Well-Being scale (Burchard et al., 1990). *Work satisfaction* was assessed with a 6-item forced-choice scale. The constituents of participants' social networks were generated from an interview adapted from Weinberg (1984). The persons from whom study participants received instrumental, emotional, and social support were enumerated, and participants' satisfaction with the frequency of contact and support provided by each network member was evaluated (Burchard, Rosen, Gordon, Yoe, Hasazi, & Simoneau, 1992).

Personal characteristics thought to affect the criterion measures were used as covariates: age, gender, and level of cognitive challenge. Previous institutionalization had no relationship to the criterion variables. The study sought to determine the extent to which community programs were meeting the social-policy goals of Normalization and habilitation and to assess the lifestyle satisfaction and well-being of the service recipients, from their self-reports. Data were collected from participants and their careproviders by trained graduate and postgraduate research assistants in annual interviews over a 3-year period.

The variables providing information on how well and to what extent Normalization practices were being incorporated into services were *environmental Normalization*: location and internal and external appearance of the residence; *lifestyle Normalization*: individualization, autonomy, personal responsibilities, choice, age-appropriate activities, and daily and seasonal rhythms; *community work; physical and social integration*: the number, type, social context, and initiation of out-of-home nonwork activities; and *residence-lifestyle satisfaction*: personal report concerning Normalization of lifestyle and satisfaction. (For more detailed descriptions of the nature, reliability, and validity of the measures, see Burchard et al., 1990, 1991, 1992. The data were analyzed according to a variety of procedures, including ANOVAs, ANCOVAs, correlations, and regressions.)

3.3   RESULTS FROM THE FIRST YEAR

The initial status of the study participants (38 in FHs, 54 in GHs, and 41 in SAs) was examined with regard to their lifestyle Normalization and personal adjustment. There were no differences in any outcomes related to prior institutionalization. However, because there were proportionately more persons with moderate retardation living in group homes than with their families or in apartments, level of mental retardation was included as a covariate in all analyses to statistically control for differences in disability.

Comparisons of program quality across the three different settings (see Table 11.5) showed that group home residents (GHs) were most like family home residents (FHs) on the majority of lifestyle-Normalization indicators. Apartment residents (SAs) experienced greater independence, residence-lifestyle Normalization, and physical and social integration than did persons in the other settings (Burchard et al., 1991). Although it may seem odd that persons living in their own family's home received lower scores on residence Normalization than persons in agency-operated settings, it must be remembered that these were adults living with fathers, mothers, or relatives who assumed the primary adult roles within the home. So, in general, FH residents experienced less autonomy, choice, and independence and fewer age-appropriate activities than did those in the agency-run homes. It should also be noted that although persons in apartments experienced more social integration, on average, than did those in group homes, the rate of activities over a 2-week period outside the home with nondisabled peers (who were neither staff nor family members) was extremely low. For most persons, there were no such activities (Burchard et al., 1992), the average rate of which ranged between less than once a week (GHs) and three times a week (SAs). (See Tables 11.6 and 11.7).

TABLE 11.5

MEAN COMPARISONS OF RESIDENCE TYPES ON LIFESTYLE NORMALIZATION INDICATORS

Indicator	Family home ($n = 38$, Year 1)	Group home ($n = 54$, Year 1)	Supervised apartment ($n = 41$, Year 1)	F
Performance of adaptive behavior[d] (% items yes)	51[a] (20)	52[a] (18)	69[b] (15)	14.30***
Lifestyle Normalization[d]	72.5[a] (12.0)	80.0[b] (10.1)	87.4[c] (6.7)	22.60***
Physical integration (av. no./wk.)	6.9[a] (5.1)	7.3[a] (4.8)	12.4[b] (9.0)	8.30***
Social integration (av. no./wk.)	1.2 (2.4)	0.9[a] (1.6)	3.1[b] (4.1)	6.94**
Community employment	24% ($n = 9$)	19% ($n = 10$)	37% ($n = 15$)	3.85 (χ^2)

Note. Physical integration = average weekly activities in the community. Social integration = average weekly community activities with nonhandicapped companions. Careproviders could not report activities (because the latter were too numerous) for 10 persons in apartments. Standard deviations are in parentheses. Community employment = part-time or full-time employment for wages in a nonsegregated setting.

[abc] Superscripts denote significant differences between group means. [d]Performance, lifestyle-Normalization, and social-integration measures were correlated with level of retardation, respectively, $r = -.45$, $-.26$, and $-.30$.

*$p < .05$.   **$p < .01$.   ***$p < .001$.

While persons living in SAs were leading the most normalized lifestyles of the three groups, they were most like persons living in their own homes with their own families (FHs) on the self-reported personal-adjustment indicators (Table 11.6). They reported greater residence satisfaction and well-being and rated their residence higher than did persons living in GHs, although careprovider ratings of behavior adjustment did not differ between the two groups.

Based upon comparisons of self-reported social networks (Table 11.7), participants were similar across settings in viewing network members as primarily supportive (87% satisfied), in having few (and primarily no) reciprocal relationships, and in identifying only about one relationship in which they saw themselves as a helper vis-à-vis a network member. Group-home residents had the largest networks and the most peers in their networks, due to their group-living situation. Persons in family homes had the fewest peer-friends (an average of 2), fewer of them dated (24%), and they had the fewest number of staff members in their networks (an average of 1). The persons most frequently cited as a source of support by participants were kin of those in family homes, and staff and peers about equally by those living in agency-run settings (Burchard et al., 1992).

3.4   CONCLUSIONS

These results showed quite consistent and significant differences with regard to the social policy goals of independent functioning, Normalization of lifestyle, and community integration between the three settings. Individuals who lived in SAs experienced the greatest residence-lifestyle Normalization, community access and integration, and independent performance of skills. Although persons in FHs were no different with regard to ability, their independent skill performance was similar to that of those in GHs while their residence-lifestyle Normalization was even less. These differences remain after using covariance techniques to control for ability differences and are systematically residence related. The organizational structures of the three settings, amount of supervision, number of coresidents, and role and relationship of

supervising adult all contributed to the differential residence-related outcomes found here (Burchard et al., 1991).

There were also significant between-setting differences in social characteristics and personal adjustment. On the outcome measures of adjustment and satisfaction, family-home residents had the highest average scores. Here, however, persons in SAs were more similar to persons in FHs than to those in GHs. It appears that group-living settings involving multiple housemates not of one's own choosing and live-in staff (i.e., group homes) entail less autonomy, choice, community integration, and personal satisfaction, and no greater social support, than other kinds of settings.

4   PREDICTORS OF NORMALIZED LIFESTYLES

To identify factors, beyond organizational features of the three different types of settings, that might be related to greater attainment of the program goals of Normalization and independent functioning, regression analyses were conducted. To be conservative, variables known to have a potentially considerable influence on the criterion, such as level of intellectual challenge, were entered first as a block for purposes of statistical control (Seltzer, 1986). Then, in order to determine which of a set of logically related predictors accounted for a significant increment in the variance of the dependent variable, the set of variables in question was entered using a backward-regression procedure. This is an exploratory procedure that eliminates variables that have only a negligible influence on the criterion. For all subjects combined, and after personal competence had been entered (25% of the variance), *location, residence-lifestyle Normalization*, and *opportunity* (having environmental opportunities and the autonomy to choose to engage in the activities available) together explained an additional 44% of the variance in *independent functioning* (in which 69% was accounted for in all). These factors of *location, residence-lifestyle Normalization*, and *opportunity* are all elements of Normalization as articulated by Wolfensberger (1972).

TABLE 11.6

MEAN COMPARISONS OF THE THREE RESIDENTIAL PROGRAMS ON PERSONAL-ADJUSTMENT INDICATORS DURING THE FIRST YEAR

Indicator	Family home (n = 38)	Group home (n = 54)	Supervised apartment (n = 41)	F
Home rating (% positive items)	89.5[a] (22.2)	67.6[c] (39.0)	75.3[b] (35.4)	4.67**
Residence satisfaction (% positive items)	76.8[a] (12.2)	68.7[b] (14.2)	79.8[a] (12.9)	8.82***
Work satisfaction (% positive items)	86.8 (20.5)	84.3 (24.6)	83.8 (28.1)	0.16
Social support satisfaction (% supportive)	87 (20)	86 (17)	86 (14)	0.17
Personal well-being (% positive items)	84.3[a] (14.5)	72.7[b] (19.2)	82.4[a] (17.5)	5.97**
Behavior rating: Severity (0-15)	2.03[a] (3.0)	5.12[b] (3.8)	4.24[b] (3.6)	8.26**
No problem cited (%)	56	17.6	29.3	14.02*** (χ^2)

Note. The first five variables are self-reports, the last two are informant reports based on careprovider report. Standard deviations are in parentheses.

[abc]Superscripts denote significant differences between group means.

*$p < .05$. **$p < .01$. ***$p < .001$.

In a regression model predicting *residence-lifestyle Normalization* from environmental factors, level of disability and place of residence were entered as a block first. Only residence type was a significant predictor of residence-lifestyle Normalization, accounting for 31% of the variance. When additional environmental variables were entered (backward), a combination of *community employment*, *location*, and *opportunity* accounted for an additional 35% of the variance. Where a person lived, both organizationally (residence type) and physically (location, access), opportunities provided or permitted by supervisors and other influential individuals in the person's life, and the opportunity to work were thus crucial for predicting residence-lifestyle Normalization. Gender, level of disability (for participants among whom there were none with significant physical or profoundly handicapping conditions), and performance of adaptive behaviors, on the other hand, were not.

Opportunity was the most consistent predictor of residence-lifestyle Normalization. Physical integration could be predicted only for group homes, with community location, staff competence, and residential lifestyle Normalization accounting for 24% of the variance. Scores on *social integration* (activities outside the home in the company of at least one nondisabled friend) were so low for persons in GHs and FHs that there were no predictors. For persons in apartments, social integration was predicted by residence-lifestyle Normalization and a location accessible to downtown and community sites (Burchard et al., 1985).

TABLE 11.7

SOCIAL-SUPPORT NETWORK CHARACTERISTICS BY TYPE OF RESIDENTIAL SETTING FOR 133 ADULTS WITH MENTAL RETARDATION LIVING IN THE COMMUNITY

Network characteristic (averages)	Group home		Supervised apartment		Family home	
Number of people	10.85	>	8.4		8.4	*
Percent supportive	86		86		87	ns
Number of kin	1.19		1.12	<	4.10	*
Percent supportive	94		98	>	79	*
Number of staff	3.6	>	2.8	<	1.1	*
Percent supportive	91		87		91	ns
Number of peers	5.3	>	3.0	>	1.9	*
Percent supportive	79		82	<	95	*
Percent with no peers without disabilities	70		49		61	*
Number of reciprocal relations	0.89		0.83		0.83	ns
Number of helping relationships (resident as helper)	1.20		1.54		1.71	ns
Percent who date	59		65		24	*

Note. * Denotes a reliable difference between groups by statistical test; *ns* denotes no difference between groups (Burchard et al., 1992).

TABLE 11.8

SELF-REPORTED NUMBER OF WEEKLY ACTIVITIES, BY ACTIVITY DIMENSION AND GROUP

Activity dimension	Supervised apartment ($n = 27$)	Normative comparison ($n = 27$)	Probability
A. *Total activities*	9.67	8.87	*ns*
B. *Location:*			
Relative's home	0.33	0.30	*ns*
Community	9.22	8.33	*ns*
Nonintegrated	0.11	0.15	*ns*
C. *Purpose:*			
Functional	2.70	3.15	*ns*
Social	5.59	4.96	*ns*
Isolated leisure	1.37	0.67	*ns*
D. *Social milieu:*			
Alone	3.96	3.26	*ns*
With friends	4.11[a]	4.70	*ns*
With family	0.30	0.82	*ns*
With staff	1.30[b]	na	—

Note. Independent *t* tests were used to analyze group differences; *ns* denotes no difference between groups.
[a]Mean number of activities with handicapped peers = 3.70; mean number of activities with nonhandicapped peers = 0.41. [b]Approximately 13% of total activities were supervised by staff (Rosen & Burchard, 1990).

5 NORMATIVE COMPARISON

Although the inclusion of participants living with their families provided an interesting comparison group for the examination of integration, Normalization, and adjustment issues, a normative comparison group was lacking. Given that the purpose of Normalization is to include persons with disabilities in community life, reduce differences, increase personal value, and promote lifestyles similar to those of nondisabled peers, it seemed appropriate to examine the lives of such community peers. A priori, there is no clear baseline against which to say that rates of physical or social integration, the types of and satisfaction with social networks, and so forth are similar to or different from those of community persons. How often, for example, do most people frequent banks, go shopping, or engage in social activities with friends? Some may work to avoid shopping trips or visits with neighbors, cherishing their time at home alone and undisturbed. Few studies have examined these issues.

Julie Rosen (Rosen & Burchard, 1990) sought to answer some of these questions by examining the lifestyle, activities, and satisfaction of a normative group of adults and comparing them with a group of persons with disabilities who were living in supervised apartments. Because few adults normatively live in group-home kinds of settings (with the exception of college students and communes) and few adults live at home with their parents, Rosen chose to study a category of adults with disabilities for whom a normative comparison group could be constructed: persons living independently in the community, either alone or, if with another adult, without extensive supervision.

Establishing a reasonable comparison group was not easy, because the modal living situation for adults is to live with a spouse, children, or significant other. This was the clearest lifestyle difference found among the participants in the longitudinal study: They were single, and none were living with a significant other. Nevertheless, by soliciting participants from among human-service workers, a normative comparison group was constituted, composed of 27 single adults between the ages of 23 and 35 who had no live-in significant other or children. The 27 comparison-group members were matched on the variables of age, gender, and community size with 27 persons living in SAs.

The results of this comparison were quite enlightening (see Table 11.8). There were no differences in the rate or type of activities in which the two groups engaged over a 2-week period. The rate (9/week), location, purposes, and social milieux of the activities were similar. The only distinguishing characteristic lay in the friendships enjoyed by members of each group. For members of the group from SAs, three-fourths of their activities with friends were with individuals who also had disabilities. This was not the case for the normative comparison group. Also, some activities of the SA residents were done in the company of staff, whereas the normative sample had no comparable relationship in their networks.

An examination of social-support networks revealed differences in the number of persons named (size) and in the types of relationships with network members. The comparison group named twice as many persons in their network. The proportion of network members who were relatives was similar in the two groups (less than 20% kin). However, while the remaining 80% of

network members were friends for the comparison group, only 40% were friends for the individuals living in SAs. The remaining 40% of their network members were staff.

There were no between-group differences, however, in the level of perceived support (high in both groups) or in the desire to increase contact with specific network members: Members of each group, on the average, wanted to see about 40% of their network more often. They felt the frequency of contact with the other 60% was sufficient. Lifestyle satisfaction and personal well-being were also similar and high for the two groups.

This study showed that the rate of community access and social participation with friends, lifestyle satisfaction, well-being, and satisfaction with social support experienced by a group of young adults with mental retardation living in SAs were entirely similar to those of a comparison group of single young adults living in similar communities. The main difference found was that the "friends" of the individuals living in the SAs included staff (40%) and other individuals with disabilities (35%-40%). If social integration is defined as participating with nondisabled peer companions, then these results indicate that social integration was not being achieved, even by those individuals who were living most independently and with the greatest lifestyle Normalization in their communities. On the other hand, the self-reported satisfaction and well-being of this group were quite high and not different from those reported by the normative comparison group.

6 LONGITUDINAL ANALYSES

The participants in the longitudinal study were selected to be as similar as possible on major personal characteristics that could significantly affect the relationship of environmental factors to program and personal outcomes. Because it is seldom possible to assign persons randomly to lifestyles and settings (Butterfield, 1987), participant selection and statistical procedures were used to control for confounding due to any systematic differences in cognitive level or behavioral challenges that may have been associated with type of residential setting.

TABLE 11.9

INDIVIDUAL MOST OFTEN NAMED, BY RELATIONSHIP AND GROUP

Relationship	Supervised apartment ($n = 27$)	Normative comparison ($n = 27$)
Kin	1 (3.7%)	0
Staff	14 (51.9%)	0
Handicapped peer	10 (37.0%)	0
Nonhandicapped peer	1 (3.7%)	27 (100%)
Advocate	1 (3.7%)	0
Best friend	9 (33.3%)	19 (70.4%)*

*$p < .05$.

The purpose of the longitudinal study was to examine whether individuals living in community settings were moving over time toward greater personal adjustment and lifestyle Normalization, or, on the contrary, toward more isolation in their community programs (as some had predicted). We also sought to investigate whether the environmental factors continued to be related to program outcomes and personal adjustment, as they had been in the cross-sectional analyses during the first year (Gordon et al., 1992).

6.1   STABILITY AND CHANGE OVER THREE YEARS

Throughout the 3-year study, persons living in supervised apartments continued to experience lifestyles that were closer than those of other participants to the program goals of Normalization: autonomy and independence in daily community living, and working, recreating, and living alongside and in the same manner as their community peers. These differences were found after differences due to cognitive functioning had been removed statistically. There was also considerable stability in indicators over time. Only residence-lifestyle Normalization and social integration changed. The former increased consistently over time, whereas the latter increased slightly and then returned to approximately the baseline rate in the third year. There was no indication within any setting that individuals' lifestyle Normalization in the broad sense, including all of the variables, was deteriorating. If anything, it was stable or increasing (see Table 11.10). Examination of the personal adjustment and satisfaction of participants showed similar patterns (see Table 11.11). The adjustment and satisfaction of individuals within each of the settings remained fairly constant or else improved over time. Again, persons living in SAs were most similar to those living with their families on measures of adjustment and satisfaction and had more favorable scores on these dimensions than those living in GHs. There was more change over time on these variables than there was on Normalization indicators, and change was in a positive direction. Independent ratings of behavior adjustment showed that persons living with their families had the fewest identified problems and the GH residents the most. Over time, adjustment ratings improved in all settings, improving the most for persons in group homes. Residence satisfaction and personal well-being also increased over time. Work satisfaction was high, stable, and did not differ between settings.

TABLE 11.10

MEAN SCORES ON LIFESTYLE NORMALIZATION INDICATORS FOR 114 PERSONS IN THREE TYPES OF COMMUNITY RESIDENCES FOR 3 CONSECUTIVE YEARS

Indicator	Family home (n=34)	Group home (n=42)	Supervised apartment (n=38)	
Performance of adaptive behavior (%)				
Year 1	49	51	71	LMR***
Year 2	50	52	73	ResType***
Year 3[a]	(35)	(45)	(79)	Time***
Lifestyle Normalization				
Year 1	73%	79%	88%	LMR**
Year 2	79%	84%	88%	ResType***
Year 3	79%	85%	90%	Time***
Physical integration[b]				
Year 1	7.3	7.4	12.3	LMR*
Year 2	7.4	6.5	11.0	ResType**
Year 3	8.0	7.6	9.6	Time ns
Social integration[c]				
Year 1	1.3	0.7	2.8	LMR*
Year 2	2.2	0.8	3.7	ResType*
Year 3	1.6	0.7	1.7	Time*
Community employment[d]				
Year 1	26%	12%	39%	Yr 1***
Year 2	24%	12%	34%	Yr 2 ns
Year 3	21%	19%	47%	Yr 3*

Note. Results of 3 x 3 analysis of variance procedure across 3 years and three residence types, with level of mental retardation (LMR) used as a covariate to control for group differences on this variable. ns = no significant difference.
[a]Performance-of-adaptive-behavior measure was shortened in Year 3; scores were thus on a new scale and not directly comparable to scores in previous years. [b]Average number of weekly activities in the community. [c]Average number of weekly community activities with nonhandicapped peers. Careproviders could not report integration scores for 10 persons in supervised apartments because their activities were too numerous. [d]Community employment = paid work in nonsegregated settings on a part-time or full-time basis. These comparisons were made by chi-square analysis.
*p < .05. **p < .01. ***p < .001.

TABLE 11.11

MEAN SCORES ON SELF-REPORTED PERSONAL-SATISFACTION INDICATORS FOR 114 PERSONS IN THREE TYPES OF COMMUNITY RESIDENTIAL SETTINGS OVER 3 CONSECUTIVE YEARS

Indicator	Family home (n=34)	Group home (n=42)	Supervised apartment (n=38)	
Home rating (% positive ratings)				
Year 1	93	75	75	LMR ns
Year 2	94	72	78	ResType***
Year 3	93	71	81	Time ns
Residence satisfaction (% positive ratings)				
Year 1	77	69	81	LMR ns
Year 2	80	76	84	ResType***
Year 3	83	73	84	Time***
Work satisfaction (% positive ratings)				
Year 1	86	83	94	LMR ns
Year 2	92	84	90	Res ns
Year 3	92	86	94	Time ns
Personal well-being (% positive ratings)				
Year 1	85	74	83	LMR ns
Year 2	87	76	85	ResType*
Year 3	88	82	85	Time***
Behavior rating: Severity[a]				
Year 1	2.0[x]	5.8[z]	4.0[y]	ResType***
Year 2	2.7[x]	6.2[y]	2.5[x]	Time*
Year 3	1.5[x]	4.6[y]	3.2[y]	Res X Time*[b]

Note. Results of 3 x 3 analysis of variance procedures across 3 years and three residence types with level of mental retardation (LMR) used as a covariate to control for group differences on this variable. ns = no significant difference (Gordon et al., 1992).
[a]Range of rating of severity of maladaptive behaviors = 0-15. [b]Means with different superscripts (i.e., [x,y,z]) across residence types within each year are significantly different from one another, which creates the significant interaction.
*p < .05. **p < .01. ***p < .001.

Examination of environmental variables other than residence type, which in and of itself encompassed major organizational differences, showed some interesting patterns. Measures based upon Normalization principles operationalized the constructs of *physical setting* (condition, appearance, and setting of the residence); *location of the residence* (maximizing accessibility to community resources); *provision of environmental opportunity* (availability and "permission"); *training of residents* provided by staff; and *staff competencies* or, in the case of the family-home participants, *parent Normalization attitudes.* Scores on these measures are shown in Table 11.12.

Supervised apartments, again, tended to receive the most favorable scores, except on environmental Normalization. Ratings of the apartments as homelike, having age-appropriate furnishings, being in a residential neighborhood, and so on, although generally high, were lower on the average than those of the other types of setting. This discrepancy may have been due to the relatively greater autonomy of the apartment residents to select, buy for, and maintain their residence. The furnishings were less middle-class and more impoverished than those in the corresponding family and group homes. This was almost surely affected by their financial status as well. Supervised apartments were not publicly financed, unlike the GHs, and were sometimes located in downtown areas rather than in residential neighborhoods. For these reasons, SAs received lower ratings on environmental Normalization. However, they received higher scores on other aspects of Normalization, and their residents had the highest levels of personal satisfaction with their lifestyles and autonomy.

Measures of location favoring access to services and activities showed that SAs were the most favorably located and that their residents had the highest level of environmental opportunity (availability of resources and permission to use them). While persons in SAs began with almost equivalent training from staff, over time the training they received decreased significantly compared to that provided to persons living in group homes. At the same time, the ratings of staff competence of persons associated with SAs increased over time.

These findings are not in the least anomalous. They clearly indicate that from the perspective of both staff and residents, the most interpersonally intensive and most closely supervised and monitored living settings (GHs) were the least personally desirable living (and for staff, working) environments. Good and more experienced staff appeared to be rewarded by becoming SA supervisors rather than continuing as live-in or shift GH staff. It is also notable that although GH residents continued to receive training from staff throughout the 3-year period, this was not reflected in increases in independent functioning, greater community access, or increased social integration. It thus appears that the necessity and opportunity afforded by more independent living, with staff support as needed, provided a greater impetus to skill acquisition than did training.

Community integration is also affected by the constitution, continuity, and stability of an individual's social network and support. Social networks, assessed on the basis of participants' self-reports, showed surprising stability over the 3-year period. Constitution of networks (size and types of relationships reported) and degree of satisfaction remained stable over the 3-year period, with two exceptions. The number of nondisabled peer friends, although very few in number, did increase over the 3 years, except for individuals living in GH settings (see Table 11.13). In addition, the number of reciprocal relationships (again mostly none and averaging less than one) did increase slightly over the 3 years. Persons in FHs and SAs reported the largest number of nondisabled peers in their social networks (frequently none, one, or two), and persons in SAs and GHs reported the most friends (almost always other persons with disabilities) in their networks. Over 50% of the persons living in SAs and GHs reported having girl or boy friends, while relatively few of those living at home reported such relationships (Table 11.13). These results show that active inclusion in friendship networks was minimal, beyond family members, housemates, or staff.

Social integration was not a fact of life for persons with mental retardation in any of the settings, including family homes. Many providers and others have reported great instability of community living by virtue of changes in staff, housemates, and residences (Bradley & Allard, 1992). Although there were staff and coresident changes for participants, particularly for those in GHs, this was not reflected by decreases in adjustment or well-being over time. These discontinuities, examined within participants' social networks,

TABLE 11.12

MEAN COMPARISONS ON ENVIRONMENTAL FACTORS FOR 114 PERSONS LIVING IN THREE TYPES OF COMMUNITY RESIDENCES FOR 3 CONSECUTIVE YEARS

	Family home (n=34)	Group home (n=42)	Supervised apartment (n=38)	
Normalization of physical environment of residence[a]				
(n = 106; 32, 42, 32)				
Year 1	2.95	2.98	2.89	LMR *ns*
Year 2	2.94	2.99	2.80	ResType*
Year 3	2.92	2.94	2.91	Time *ns*
Availability of community services[b]				
(n = 111; 33, 42, 36)				
Year 1	11	14	18	LMR* (-)
Year 2	11	15	19	ResType***
Year 3	11	16	19	Time*
Environmental opportunity[c] (%)				
(n = 99; 28, 34, 37)				
Year 1	59	68	86	LMR** (-)
Year 2	61	72	86	ResType***
Year 3	(54)	(61)	(91)	Time (Yr 1,2) *ns*
Training provided[d]				
(n = 66; na = not applicable, 32, 34)				
Year 1	na	54[x]	56[x]	LMR *ns*
Year 2	na	46[x]	27[y]	ResType**
Year 3	na	37[x]	12[y]	Time***
				Res X Time***[e]
Staff competence ratings[f]				
(n = 46; na = not applicable, 25, 21)				
Year 1	na	3.5[x]	3.7[x]	LMR** (+)
Year 2	na	3.9[x]	4.4[y]	ResType***
Year 3	na	3.6[x]	4.3[y]	Time***
				Time X Res***[e]

Note. Results are based on a 3 x 3 analysis of variance with level of mental retardation (LMR) used as a covariate to control for group differences on this variable. *ns* = no significant difference.
[a] Ratings of the physical appearance of the home, 0 (low) to 3 (high). [b] The number out of 20 generic services within walking distance of the home. [c] Careprovider rating of availability of and access to performance-of-adaptive-behavior items. Abbreviation of the scale in Year 3 invalidates direct comparison with previous years. [d] Percent of failed performance items for which home training is provided. [e] Different superscripts (i.e., [x,y]) indicate significantly different means by year, which explains the Time by ResType interaction. [f] Ratings of 40 competency statements by direct supervisor on scale from 1 (low) to 5 (high).
*p < .05. **p < .01. ***p < .001.

TABLE 11.13

SELF-REPORTED MEAN COMPARISONS OF SOCIAL-SUPPORT NETWORK CHARACTERISTICS FOR 114 PERSONS LIVING IN THREE TYPES OF RESIDENCE SETTINGS FOR 3 CONSECUTIVE YEARS

	Family home (n=34)	Group home (n=45)	Supervised apartment (n=38)	
Number of people in network				
Year 1	8.2	10.7	8.6	LMR *ns*[a]
Year 2	8.6	11.3	8.8	ResType***
Year 3	8.6	10.3	9.1	Time *ns*
Percent supportive				
Year 1	86	88	86	LMR *ns*
Year 2	91	87	90	ResType *ns*
Year 3	88	90	93	Time *ns*
Number of kin in network				
Year 1	4.1	1.3	1.1	LMR *ns*
Year 2	4.1	1.5	1.2	ResType***
Year 3	4.2	0.9	1.2	Time *ns*
Percent kin supportive				
(n = 57; 31, 15[b], 12[b])[c]				
Year 1	78	97	100	LMR *ns*
Year 2	89	92	97	ResType*
Year 3	91	100	97	Time *ns*
Number of staff in network				
Year 1	1.1	3.6	2.9	LMR *ns*
Year 2	0.6	3.8	2.5	ResType***
Year 3	0.7	3.7	2.8	Time *ns*
Percent staff supportive				
(n = 79; 7[d], 39, 33)				
Year 1	96	92	90	LMR* (+)
Year 2	100	90	94	ResType *ns*
Year 3	93	96	94	Time *ns*
Number of nonhandicapped peers				
Year 1	0.9	0.4	1.1	LMR* (-)
Year 2	1.1	0.4	1.1	ResType*
Year 3	1.6	0.4	1.7	Time**
Percent nonhandicapped peers supportive				
(n= 20[e]; 6, 3, 11)				
Year 1	94	100	86	LMR *ns*
Year 2	94	100	82	ResType *ns*
Year 3	88	83	90	Time *ns*
Number of reciprocal relationships				
Year 1	0.9	0.7	0.7	LMR *ns*
Year 2	1.1	0.7	0.7	ResType(*)
Year 3	1.4	0.9	0.9	Time*

Number who date[f]

Year 1	8/34	24/42	25/37	ResType***
Year 2	9/33	20/42	21/38	ResType(*)
Year 3	8/34	22/41	19/37	ResType*

Note. ns = no significant difference

[a]These results are based upon a 3 x 3 analysis of variance of Time and Residence Type, with level of mental retardation (LMR) used as a covariate. [b]Few persons in group homes or apartments named kin in their social networks. [c]Numbers in parentheses indicate the number contributing to each score for each measure. [d]Only 7 persons in family homes named staff in their networks. [e]Only 20 persons named a nonhandicapped peer in their social network. [f]These data are based upon careprovider report.

(*)$p < .10$. *$p < .05$. **$p < .01$. ***$p < .001$.

TABLE 11.14

PERCENT OF NETWORK MEMBERS STABLE OVER EACH OF 3 YEARS

Network characteristics		Group home (n=30)	Supervised apartment (n=37)	Family home (n=33)
Total stable	M	38%	31%	44%
	SD	(20)	(18)	(22)
Kin network	M	28%	39%	59%
stable	SD	(39)	(43)	(26)
Staff network	M	24%	45%	12%
stable	SD	(24)	(33)	(29)
Friends (hc)	M	50%	31%	42%
stable	SD	(29)	(32)	(35)
Friends (nhc)	M	14%	2%	4%
stable	SD	(25)	(8)	(16)

Note. hc = handicapped; nhc = nonhandicapped.

showed considerable stability as well as instability. With regards to network constituents, 30%-45% were stable over 3 years (i.e., the individuals identified were the same). Networks were most stable for persons living with their families (see Table 11.14).

Staff were most stable for persons in SAs, and peers with disabilities were most stable for those living in GHs. The lack of true social integration with respect to establishing friendships with nondisabled peers was

again evident in these results. Such relationships were rarely reported and, even when they existed, were very unstable (see Tables 11.14 and 11.15; also, Burchard & Hutchins-Fuhr, 1990).

TABLE 11.15

PERCENT OF INDIVIDUALS WITH STABLE SOCIAL-NETWORK MEMBERS OVER EACH OF 3 YEARS

Network characteristics	Group home (n = 38)	Supervised apartment (n = 37)	Family home (n = 33)
Any network members	97%	90%	100%
Kin members	27%	30%	97%
Staff members	63%	76%	9%
Friends (hc)	87%	59%	45%
Friends (nhc)	5%	5%	6%

Note. hc = handicapped; nhc = nonhandicapped.

6.2   NORMALIZATION, SATISFACTION, AND WELL-BEING OVER THREE YEARS

An analysis was conducted to investigate how objective environmental predictors affected three subjective, self-reported variables: *personal satisfaction with living environment, satisfaction with work or day program,* and *personal well-being* (Carpenter & Burchard, in preparation). Family-home data were examined separately, as the attitudinal measures of careprovider practices obtained in this group were not comparable to the competency measures obtained in the other groups. Hierarchical regression analysis was used to examine the relationship, among the 70 persons living in SAs or GHs, of four environmental predictors (*type of residence, living-environment Normalization, frequency of family contact, and type of work, whether paid, community-integrated or segregated*) to the criterion variables *residence satisfaction* and *personal well-being.* For the 32 persons living with their families, the environmental predictors for residence satisfaction were Normalization of the living environment and parent Normalization attitudes. Several other Normalization predictors were excluded:

physical location and appearance were not related to any self-reported measures of personal adjustment, and staff-competency measures (although significantly related to satisfaction outcomes in concurrent correlational analyses) had been too inconsistently reported to avoid the loss of many subjects. To examine satisfaction with work, all participants were combined, with type of work used to predict work satisfaction. Because of the possibility that where a person lived was in part determined by personal characteristics, age, gender, behavioral problems during Year 1, and level of retardation were always entered first in the regressions. Because residence type was consistently related to many outcome measures, it was always entered next. Also, in the cross-time regressions, prior significant predictors were always entered before current-year predictors. These analyses were thus very conservative in assessing the contribution of factors such as residence-lifestyle Normalization, parent Normalization attitudes, and type of work on personal-adjustment outcomes.

Normalization factors were significant predictors of personal lifestyle satisfaction for persons living in GHs and SAs, even after the prior entry of all other predictors. For persons in FHs, Normalization measures were significant predictors of both residence-lifestyle satisfaction and personal well-being. Work satisfaction for all participants was consistently related to being engaged in paid, integrated, community work rather than segregated day or work programs, a highly important aspect of a normalized lifestyle.

6.2.1   RESULTS

There was only one personal characteristic that was consistently predictive of satisfaction measures, namely, behavioral adjustment, as rated by a careprovider. For persons in GHs and SAs, behavior ratings were significant concurrent predictors of residence satisfaction, well-being, and work satisfaction; for persons in FHs, of residence satisfaction and work satisfaction.

Normalization factors were also predictive of satisfaction and well-being. For persons in GHs and SAs, type of residence (SAs) was always predictive of

residence satisfaction (accounting for 8% of the variance). Beyond what behavioral adjustment and residence setting explained, however, an additional significant amount of variance was explained by living-environment Normalization (13%). The only environmental variable that consistently predicted personal well-being was the frequency of family contact.

For persons living with their families, an environmental factor that predicted residence-lifestyle satisfaction, in addition to behavior ratings (10%-11% of the variance), was parental Normalization attitudes (11%-26%). For these individuals, the only factor, personal or environmental, that predicted well-being was residence-lifestyle Normalization. This Normalization measure had consistent predictive relationships with perceived personal well-being (14%, 29%, 35% of the variance, in Years 1, 2, and 3, respectively). Work satisfaction was predicted by behavior adjustment and type of work, an aspect of Normalization of lifestyle (6%-13%).

6.2.2   CONCLUSION

Whether measured directly by the lifestyle Normalization interview, assessed by parent attitudes, or evaluated indirectly by organizational characteristics, including personal control and autonomy of the residence setting (residence type), Normalization was consistently related to the outcomes of self-reported satisfaction and adjustment. This underlines the importance of implementing Normalization principles for the well-being and personal satisfaction of adults with mental retardation. Beyond the inherent significance and credibility of Normalization principles, in light of fundamental considerations of equity, human and civil rights, personal respect and dignity, and personal protection by way of an enhanced image and reduced perception of differentness, these results also indicate that the promotion of normalized lifestyles is perceived as desirable by service recipients themselves. The importance of and justification for pursuing the values derived from Normalization philosophy thus find added validation from the recipients of the ideology in practice.

7 RESEARCH AND PUBLIC POLICY

What do the results of this series of studies tell us about Normalization philosophy, the success of implementation of Normalization ideas, and ways of better serving individuals in community living? First, we found that staff Normalization competence and lifestyle Normalization are important to consumers, providing more opportunities for exercising choice, having access to the community, initiating activities with friends, and experiencing individualization and independence in daily living. These differences were not simply a function of variations in cognitive, behavioral, or residential-setting factors. Lifestyle Normalization and integration opportunities were, in turn, related to greater self-reported satisfaction with the living environment and, for those persons living with their families, to enhanced well-being.

Second, these studies unequivocally show that living environments, such as supervised apartments, that provide greater opportunities, autonomy, and independence, fewer housemates, and less restrictive supervision and control, achieve a closer approximation than other types of settings to the ideals of Normalization philosophy and the goals of social policy. By extrapolation from research reported in the literature, they surely surpass in this regard the large congregate settings that still exist in many states. Individuals living in SAs also expressed higher satisfaction and well-being than those in more congregate and more highly supervised settings. Their personal adjustment (which behaviorally began as no different from that of the GH residents) was no different from that of persons who had lived with their families most or all of their lives.

What does this mean for social policy? Despite recent articles discounting the importance of the physical and structural (organizational) characteristics of living settings (Zigler et al., 1990), ours are not the only studies that clearly show that structural features such as size and organization, as well as careprovider philosophy and competence, have a very strong impact on the people living within them (Campbell & Bailey, 1984; Parker & Boles, 1990). Our research shows that individuals take on more responsibility, exercise more choice and independence, and express greater personal satisfaction when they live individually or with one or two friends in a supported (but not "managed") situation, like most other adults. One needs only to think of the experience of most adults with group living, even in the absence of adult supervision and control. They find it very difficult to live together with three to five other adults for any length of time in one "family." The least that can be said is that although such a choice is available to people, few exercise it for any length of time, and then usually only under the most extreme economic exigencies.

These results also suggest, by extrapolation, that foster care is not an ideal setting to promote lifestyle Normalization or, perhaps, personal satisfaction. Such homes do not have the interpersonal history that families do, so unless providers have extraordinary Normalization competence, foster homes will probably be characterized by caretaking rather than life-sharing.

Third, these results tell us that social integration, as envisioned by advocates and providers, is not a reality for adults with mental retardation, not even for those in supervised apartments or for those who have lived with their families in their home communities all of their lives. Few name as members of their social network any community peer friends, that is, persons who provide companionship, instrumental or emotional support, or friendship. At the same time, careproviders report that adults with retardation engage in very few (and mostly no) activities that include a community adult other than staff, kin, or other individuals with disabilities. While young people in supervised apartments lead lives that look no different from those of other single adults living in the community with regard to access, activation, and satisfaction, their networks are only half as large and contain few or no nondisabled peer friends, and half their friends are staff members. Although the most integrated and experiencing the most normalized lifestyles, these apartment residents are not achieving community acceptance and integration, in the sense of having developed informal support (Rosen & Burchard, 1990; Wolfensberger, 1992).

Another major aspect of social integration and support is notably absent from the lives of persons with mental retardation, setting them apart and potentially depriving them of critical social support and personal satisfaction: They are rarely married or living with a partner, or raising children, which is by far the modal circumstance for adults in our society.

Nevertheless, the participants themselves were generally highly satisfied with the social support they received and with their friendships, regardless of their setting. There were no differences between groups on these outcomes, and care was taken to avoid acquiescence in responding. Participants generally had peer friendships (with exceptions found mainly in family homes), often named a peer as a best friend, and relied on peers for some of their support, although most was obtained from formal support. This begs the question of choice, at least for those who were living in settings with more opportunities and more choice, with respect to developing friendships, which are usually based upon shared interests, shared activities, opportunities for contact, and reciprocity. It may be that the constitution of networks is a function of the latter determinants of friendship development, rather than reflecting a social-policy failure. Or it may be due to a lack of opportunity or a lack of skills in making friendships outside of the service system. It is clear, however, that investigating fruitful ways of developing and supporting friendships and informal supports is an important agenda item for social policy.

Another surprising finding was the stability of the social-support networks over a 3-year time span. Vermont communities undoubtedly have greater stability than large urban cities, and these individuals did not move during that time. Nevertheless, about half the persons named were the same individuals in many networks across the 3 years.

7.1   RESEARCH LIMITATIONS

There were significant limitations to this research. It was completed within one small state that had a clearly articulated policy based on Normalization and a mandate to serve persons in settings no larger than six residents. This constituted a fairly homogeneous system. Participants in the longitudinal study were selected to be able to respond to simple interviews, which excluded individuals with severe disabilities. However, considering the results of our earlier staff-competency validation studies, which did include individuals with severe disabilities and a broader range of settings, we are of the opinion that had the adjustment and integration of persons with greater individual differences and living in a wider range of circumstances (more congregate sites and foster homes) been studied longitudinally, the results would have been even more pronounced with respect to the importance of careprovider attitudes and competencies and the impact of environmental Normalization. This, I believe, underlines the power and importance of efforts to employ Normalization principles in supporting people in the community. Even with a fairly "model" homogenous system and, in the later studies, a fairly homogeneous group of participants, relatively small differences in Normalization experiences and staff Normalization competencies among programs still had an important effect, in terms of autonomy, the independent performance of activities, individualization, physical and social integration, and personal satisfaction with residence and lifestyle.

7.2   CONCLUSION

As Edgerton (1988) pointed out after following, for over 3 decades, persons with mental retardation living in the community, many individuals adapt successfully, from their own perspective, if given the opportunity and supports available to other community members. They may lead financially impoverished lives and have much smaller networks, compared to some standards, but they may not view their lives or support as impoverished. It seems important, for social policy, to provide living and working opportunities that afford as much individualization, choice, and personal control as possible and, for service systems, to have more respect and faith in individuals' abilities to make and exercise choices, including lifestyle-related ones. At the same time, it is imperative to investigate ways of helping people obtain the opportunities and skills to develop and maintain friendships and to access support systems, both formal and informal, as needed throughout their lives.

Finally, to quote Wolf Wolfensberger on the relationship of "research, empiricism, and the principle of Normalization" (1980): "How much 'research'. . . should be conducted to support Normalization implications for attractive environments; . . . access to services; age-appropriate and culturally valued forms of personal appearance, labeling, activities, . . . decor; individualisation . . . programming; avoidance of crowding; competent and image-enhancing staff; warmth of interaction . . ." (p. 126). These are basic human values that should need little validation. Although it does indeed provide support and validation for the importance of Normalization values, even more to the point, the research presented above shows that environments are very important in furthering the goals of social policy. It shows which kinds of environments are organizationally better designed to promote Normalization values and which types of service providers foster the opportunities that environments provide. These factors, environmental organization and structure and staff competencies, contributed to the attainment of Normalization-derived social-policy goals, beyond any effect due to individual differences. Where one lives, whom one lives with, and how one lives are important factors in assisting persons with disabilities toward a lifestyle we all treasure. Our studies also point again to the limitations of the service system in establishing social integration for persons they are serving. This research should also serve as a caveat concerning the types of living arrangements that could militate against the provision of the best opportunities for lifestyle Normalization, namely, congregate, nonconsensual, other-controlled environments. It also points to the continued need for determining how to assist persons toward individualized, self-chosen personal integration as well as personal independence.

We have come a long way in the last 25 years, since the introduction of Normalization values. Many places are still fighting the conditions that Normalization was introduced to combat. Even in places where living conditions have been established that maximize Normalization values and hence opportunities for people, changing financial conditions now threaten the progress made, as cheaper solutions are sought. And there is a continuing need to discover how to make true social integration into our communities a reality for more people.

REFERENCES

Annual report to Congress on implementation of individuals with disabilities act (1991). Washington, DC: U.S. Government Printing Office.

BRADLEY, V. J., & ALLARD, M. A. (1992). The dynamics of change in residential services for people with developmental disabilities. In J. W. JACOBSON, S. N. BURCHARD, & P. J. CARLING (Eds.), *Community living for people with developmental and psychiatric disabilities* (pp. 284-302). Baltimore: John Hopkins University Press.

BRADDOCK, D., & FUJIURA, G. (1991). Politics, public policy, and the development of community services in the United States. *American Journal of Mental Retardation, 95,* 369-387.

BRADDOCK, D., HEMP, R., FUJIURA, G., BACHELDER, L., & MITCHELL, D. (1989). *The third national study of public spending for mental retardation and developmental disabilities: Summary.* Chicago: University of Illinois, Institute for Study of Developmental Disabilities.

BRUININKS, R. H., ROTEGARD, L. L., LAKIN, K. C., & HILL, B. K. (1987). Epidemiology of mental retardation and trends in residential services in the United States. In S. LANDESMAN & P. VIETZE (Eds.), *Living environments and mental retardation* (pp. 17-42). Washington, DC: American Association of Mental Retardation.

BURCHARD, S. N., HASAZI, J. E., GORDON, L. R., & YOE, J. (1991). A comparison of lifestyle and adjustment in three community residential alternatives. *Research in Developmental Disabilities, 12,* 127-142.

BURCHARD, S. N., & HUTCHINS-FUHR, M. (1990, December 7). *Comparison of characteristics of social support and personal satisfaction over three years for adults living in the community.* Paper presented at the annual meeting of the Association for Persons with Severe Handicaps (TASH), Chicago.

BURCHARD, S. N., PINE, J., & GORDON, L. R. (1984, August 28). *Relationship of manager competence and program Normalization to client satisfaction in group homes.* Paper presented at the annual meeting of the American Psychological Association, Toronto.

BURCHARD, S. N., PINE, J., & GORDON, L. R. (1990). Manager competence, program Normalization and client satisfaction in group homes. *Education and Training in Mental Retardation, 25,* 277-285.

BURCHARD, S. N., PINE, J., GORDON, L. R., JOFFE, J. M., WIDRICK, G. C., & GOY, E. (1987). The relationship of manager competence to residential program quality in small community residences. In J. A. MULICK & R. ANTONAK (Eds.), *Transitions in mental retardation* (Vol. 2, pp. 47-69). Region X AAMD Monograph. Norwood, NJ: Ablex Press.

BURCHARD, S. N., PINE, J., WIDRICK, G. C., & CREEDON, S. (1985, December 5). *The relationship of entry-level competencies to job performance and program quality in small community residences.* Paper presented at the annual meeting of the Association for Persons with Severe Handicaps (TASH), Boston.

BURCHARD, S. N., ROSEN, J. W., GORDON, L. R., YOE, J., HASAZI, J. E., & SIMONEAU, D. (1992). Evaluation of social support and lifestyle satisfaction in community living arrangements for persons with mental retardation. In J. W. JACOBSON, S. N. BURCHARD, & P. J. CARLING (Eds.), *Community living for people with developmental and psychiatric disabilities (pp. 137-154).* Baltimore: John Hopkins Press.

BUTTERFIELD, E. C. (1987). Why and how to study the influence of living arrangements. In S. LANDESMAN & P. VIETZE (Eds.), *Living environments and mental retardation* (pp. 43-60). Washington, DC: American Association of Mental Retardation.

CAMPBELL, V. A. & BAILEY, C. J. (1984). Comparison of methods for classifying community residential settings for mentally retarded individuals. *American Journal of Mental Deficiency, 89,* 44-49.

CARPENTER, M., & BURCHARD, S. N. (in preparation). *Environmental predictors of residence satisfaction, psychological well-being, and work satisfaction of adults with mental retardation: A longitudinal study.* Burlington, VT: University of Vermont, Psychology Department.

DUPUY, H. J. (1978, October 17). *Self-representations of general psychological well-being of American adults.* Paper presented at the annual meeting of the American Public Health Association, Los Angeles.

EDGERTON, R. B. (1988). Aging in the community: A matter of choice. *American Journal of Mental Retardation, 92,* 331-335.

EMERSON, E. B. (1985). Evaluating the impact of deinstitutionalization on the lives of mentally retarded people. *American Journal of Mental Deficiency, 90,* 277-288.

EYMAN, R. K., DEMAINE, C. G., & LEI, T. (1979). Relationship between community environments and resident changes in adaptive behavior: A path model. *American Journal of Mental Deficiency, 83,* 330-338.

FIORELLI, J. S., & KEATING, D. J. (1979). Overview. In J. S. FIORELLI (Ed.), *A curriculum model for preservice training of alternative living arrangement direct service personnel.* Philadelphia: Temple University, Developmental Disabilities Center.

GORDON, L. R., BURCHARD, S. N., HASAZI, J. E., YOE, J. T., DIETZEL, L. C., & SIMONEAU, D. (1992). Stability and change in the life-style and adjustment of adults with mental retardation living in community residences. In J. W. JACOBSON, S. N. BURCHARD, & P. J. CARLING (Eds.), *Community living for people with developmental and psychiatric disabilities (pp. 167-182).* Baltimore: John Hopkins Press.

HULL, J. T., & THOMPSON, J. C. (1980). Predicting adaptive functioning of mentally retarded persons in community settings. *American Journal of Mental Deficiency, 85,* 253-261.

HULL, J. T., & THOMPSON, J. C. (1981). Factors contributing to Normalization in residential facilities for mentally retarded persons. *Mental Retardation, 19,* 69-73.

LANDESMAN, S., & BUTTERFIELD, E. C. (1987). Normalization and deinstitutionalization of mentally retarded individuals. *American Psychologist, 42,* 809-816.

NIRJE, B. (1970). Symposium on Normalization. The Normalization principle: Implications and comments. *Journal of Mental Subnormality, 16*(31), 62-70.

PARKER, R., & BOLES, S. (1990). Integration opportunities for residents with developmental disabilities: Differences among supported living sites and residents. *Education and Training for the Mentally Retarded, 25,* 76-82.

PRATT, M. W., LUSZCZ, M. A., & BROWN, M. E. (1980). Measuring dimensions of quality of care in small community residences. *American Journal of Mental Deficiency, 85,* 188-194.

ROGERS, C. R. (1969). The interpersonal relationship: The care of guidance. *Harvard Review, 39,* 475.

ROSEN, J., & BURCHARD, S. N. (1990). Community activities and social support networks of adults in semi-independent living: A social comparison. *Education and Training in Mental Retardation, 25,* 193-204.

SELTZER, G. B. (1980). *Residential satisfaction and community adjustment.* Paper presented at the annual meeting of the American Association of Mental Deficiency, San Francisco.

SELTZER, G. B., & SELTZER, M. M. (1976). *The community adjustment scale.* Cambridge, MA: Educational Projects, Inc.

SELTZER, M. M. (1983). Nonexperimental field research methods. In J. L. MATSON & J. A. MULICK, (Eds.), *Handbook of mental retardation* (pp. 557-570). New York: Pergamon.

SMULL, M. W., & BELLAMY, G. T. (1990). Community services for adults with disabilities: Policy challenges in the emerging support paradigm. In L. H. MEYER, C. A. PECK, & L.

BROWN, (Eds.), *Critical issues in the lives of people with severe disabilities* (pp. 527-536). Baltimore: Brookes.

THOUSAND, J., BURCHARD, S. N., & HASAZI, J. E. (1986). Field-based generation and social validation of manager and staff competencies for small community residences. *Applied Research in Mental Retardation, 7,* 263-283.

WEINBERG, R. B. (1984). *Development of self-report for reliably measuring the social support system.* Paper presented at the annual meeting of the American Psychological Association, Toronto.

WOLFENSBERGER, W. (1972). *The principle of Normalization in human services.* Toronto: National Institute on Mental Retardation.

WOLFENSBERGER, W. (1980). Research, empiricism, and the principle of Normalization. In R. J. FLYNN & K. E. NITSCH (Eds.), *Normalization, social integration, and community services* (pp. 117-129). Baltimore: University Park Press.

WOLFENSBERGER, W. (1992). *A brief introduction to Social Role Valorization as a high-order concept for structuring human services* (Rev. ed.). Syracuse, NY: Syracuse University, Training Institute for Human Service Planning.

WOLFENSBERGER, W., & GLENN, L. (1975). *Program analysis of service systems (PASS): A method for the quantitative evaluation of human services* (3rd ed.). Toronto, ON: National Institute on Mental Retardation.

WOLFENSBERGER, W., & THOMAS, S. (1983). *PASSING (Program analysis of service systems' implementation of Normalization goals): Normalization criteria and ratings manual* (2nd ed.). Downsview, ON: National Institute on Mental Retardation.

ZIGLER, E., HODAPP, R. M., & EDISON, M. R. (1990). From theory to practice in the care and education of mentally retarded individuals. *American Journal of Mental Retardation, 95,* 1-12.

NOTE

1. This research was supported in part by the Vermont State Department of Mental Health (DMH) and the National Institute of Disability and Rehabilitation, Research Grants Nos. 1-33-GH-40203 and 1-33-MH-50078. The author wishes to acknowledge the assistance of the participants, their families, state and local community mental retardation providers, and former DMH director Ronald Melzer, whose support, cooperation, and participation were essential. The author also wishes to acknowledge her many colleagues whose contributions to this research over the years were substantive and invaluable: Joseph Hasazi, Lawrence Gordon, Joan Pine, Jacqueline Thousand, James Yoe, Julie Rosen, Marc Carpenter, Gary Widrick, Justin Joffe, and Moira Hutchins-Fuhr.

12

Integration of persons with developmental or psychiatric disabilities: Conceptualization and measurement

ROBERT J. FLYNN AND TIM D. AUBRY

The integration of people with disabling conditions is a key corollary of Normalization and Social Role Valorization (SRV). Although often imprecisely defined, *integration* has been a central, even paradigmatic, objective of social policy in many countries for much of the last quarter-century. It also remains a topic of enduring relevance. Within the last few years, for example, the Association internationale de recherche scientifique en faveur des personnes handicapées mentales (AIRHM) has published the proceedings of a conference on social integration in mental retardation (Ionescu, Magerotte, Pilon, & Salbreux, 1993), and the Office des personnes handicapées du Québec (1994) has published the proceedings of another international conference on integration in virtually every disability subfield.

Integration has been an explicit goal of legislation in a number of countries, as the following examples illustrate. In the United States, the adoption in 1987 of the federal Developmental Disabilities Assistance and Bill of Rights Act Amendments of 1987 (Pub. L. No. 100-146) made integration, productivity, and independence core criteria for assessing service effectiveness. *Integration* was defined as follows in Pub. L. No. 100-146:

the use . . . of the same community resources . . . and participation in the same community activities in which nondisabled citizens participate, together with regular contact with nondisabled citizens, and the residence . . . in homes or in home-like settings

which are in proximity to community resources, together with regular contact with nondisabled citizens in their communities. (§ 102[8], cited in Davidson & Adams, 1989, p. 299)

Davidson and Adams (1989) affirmed that the concept of integration in Pub. L. No. 100-146 was inspired directly by the Normalization principle, particularly Wolfensberger's (1972) and Nirje's (1976) contributions.

In Quebec, integration began as a recognizable movement around 1975 (Bolduc, 1989), with the 1980s marked by an increasing application of the principles of Normalization, SRV, and integration. In 1984, the Office des personnes handicapées du Québec, a government body, advocated a global policy of impairment prevention and social integration with the publication of *À part . . . égale. L'intégration sociale des personnes handicapées: Un défi pour tous*. The overall objectives of this influential report were adopted by the Quebec government, and in 1988, a working group within the Quebec Ministry of Health and Social Services published a policy statement and action plan for services in mental retardation. As Bolduc (1989, p. 5) noted, this official document emphasized SRV, social integration, community participation, and the conversion of institutional resources into individualized, community-based services.

In Belgium, in 1995, the government of the French-speaking part of the country, La Wallonie, made integration a cornerstone of its policies concerning persons with disabilities (Haelewyck, 1995-1996). According to Haelewyck, however, although a range of physically integrated residential options exist in Europe, integration practices are not often widely applied.

In light of the centrality of the concept of integration for the past quarter-century, it is surprising that little systematic attention has been given to defining or measuring it clearly. As a result, there is little consensus on its exact meaning, essential components, or boundaries (Storey, 1989). The present chapter attempts to bring a measure of order and clarity to this rather confused situation by reviewing how integration has been conceptualized and measured in the literature of developmental and psychiatric disability and by suggesting how the concept might most usefully be defined and investigated.

The largest number of papers on integration that we located through PsycINFO, ERIC, and manual searches were related to mental retardation and developmental disabilities, no doubt because of the prominence of Normalization and SRV in this field. We found a smaller but still sizable number of references to the concept in the literature on psychiatric disability, but relatively few in that devoted to physical disability. We thus limited our review to the literature on mental retardation/developmental disabilities and psychiatric disabilities. To keep our task within manageable bounds, we reviewed a representative rather than exhaustive set of books and papers on the topic of integration. We also decided to focus mainly on the integration of adults into community living. Specialized topics (e.g., children's integration into schools, or adults' integration into employment, leisure, art, or religious institutions) are thus beyond the scope of the chapter.

In the first section, we survey the main ways in which integration has been conceptualized and measured in the literature of mental retardation and developmental disabilities. To anticipate our findings, physical and social integration have usually (but not always) been distinguished from each other, with physical integration seen as a precondition but not a guarantee of social integration. Social integration has most often been defined as referring to social interaction and relationships between human service clients and ordinary citizens, although at least one

definition also includes interactions among human service clients within its purview. In the second section, we review the ways in which integration has been conceptualized and measured in the literature of psychiatric disability. As well, findings on the community, facility, and individual-level correlates of integration are presented in this section. Finally, in the third and concluding section, we make some suggestions for conceptualizing, measuring, and conducting research on integration.

1 CONCEPTUALIZATION AND MEASUREMENT OF INTEGRATION IN THE LITERATURE ON MENTAL RETARDATION AND DEVELOPMENTAL DISABILITIES

Of the writers on integration encountered in our review of the developmental disabilities literature, Wolfensberger is the one who has taken the most pains to define the term clearly. His original and evolving conceptualization has served as a touchstone for other writers on integration and is thus an appropriate starting point for this review.

1.1 WOLFENSBERGER'S EVOLVING CONCEPTUALIZATION OF INTEGRATION AS PHYSICAL AND SOCIAL IN NATURE, AND AS PERSONAL SOCIAL INTEGRATION AND VALUED SOCIAL PARTICIPATION

1.1.1 WOLFENSBERGER'S NORMALIZATION-BASED DEFINITION OF PHYSICAL AND SOCIAL INTEGRATION

In *The Principle of Normalization in Human Services,* Wolfensberger (1972) formulated one of the first and what was to prove one of the most influential definitions of integration, which he saw as composed of two major elements, physical and social integration. Physical integration was conceptualized as a precondition of, but fundamentally less important than, social integration:

The two integrations: physical and social

   If integration is one of the major means for achieving and acknowledging societal acceptance, as well as for accomplishing adaptive behaviour change, then we must distinguish between and elaborate upon its dimensions and components. First of all, let us define integration as being the opposite of segregation; and the process of integration as consisting of those practices and measures which maximize a person's (potential) participation in the mainstream of his culture.

For a (deviant) person, integration is achieved when he lives in a culturally normative community setting in ordinary community housing, can move and communicate in ways typical for his age, and is able to utilize, in typical ways, typical community resources: developmental, social, recreational, and religious facilities; hospitals and clinics; the post office; stores and restaurants; job placements; and so on.

Ultimately, integration is only meaningful if it is social integration; *i.e.* if it involves social interaction and acceptance, and not merely physical presence. However, social integration can only be attained if certain preconditions exist, among these being physical integration, although physical integration by itself will not guarantee social integration . . .

Social integration takes place on the "person level" and involves the close interaction of (potentially) deviant individuals with those who are not so perceived. However, physical integration generally involves buildings or at least "settings," *i.e.* a physical setting which permits or facilitates social interaction. In the context of this discussion, the building will probably be one in or through which human services are mediated.

Physical integration (or segregation) of a service facility is determined by four factors to be discussed below: its location (in the sense of distance from resources and social groupings; its physical context to other facilities and settings; access to it; and its size, in the sense of number of (deviant) persons grouped together in or by the building. This fourth point is sometimes also referred to as dispersal . . .

Integration can be facilitated (or inhibited) not only by physical but also by social circumstances. A service could conceivably be optimally integrated physically, and yet suffer from extensive social segregation. For instance, despite optimal location, such factors as agency policy, service structures, and/or social circumstances might keep a deviant person out of the cultural mainstream, and segregated from normative and normalizing social intercourse. Thus, a person needs not only to be *in*

but also *of* the community. (Wolfensberger, 1972, pp. 47-48)

Wolfensberger and Glenn (1975, 1989) operationalized their Normalization-based conceptual definitions of physical and social integration in specific PASS 3 ratings. Data collected with PASS 3 in North America and Europe indicate that physical integration is typically much more satisfactory than social integration. For example, in a sample of 626 programs evaluated with PASS 3, located in the USA (57%), Canada (32%), and France (10%), and serving mainly (65%) persons with mental retardation, Flynn, Guirguis, Wolfensberger, and Cocks (in press) found that the mean level of attainment on two PASS subscales measuring physical integration, namely, *setting* (M = 73% of the maximum possible weighted score) and *accessibility* (M = 71%), was well above the 50% level that the authors of PASS consider "minimally acceptable" service quality. In contrast, an analysis of the same sample of programs carried out for the present chapter showed that the mean score on the single PASS 3 rating most directly assessing social integration, *Socially integrative social activities*, was much below the minimally acceptable level (M = 23% of the maximum possible weighted score).

1.1.2 WOLFENSBERGER AND THOMAS'S SRV-BASED DEFINITION OF PHYSICAL AND SOCIAL INTEGRATION

Subsequently, in PASSING, Wolfensberger and Thomas (1983, 1989) defined integration, both physical and social, in even more precise terms:

INTEGRATION: The open participation of people with other people in culturally normative amounts, settings, and activities. The term is used mostly to refer to the participation and inclusion of *devalued* people with non-devalued ones. Integration can range from zero to extensive, and can also be thought of as being both physical and social.

Physical integration consists of the physical presence of a (devalued) person or persons in ordinary settings, activities, and contexts, where non-devalued people are also present, but such physical integration does not necessarily mean that the devalued person or persons actually have interactive contact with the non-devalued citizens. For example, a group of handicapped children could be physically integrated into a typical school for ordinary youngsters, and although the children would share the same facility and perhaps even attend some of the same functions (such as school-wide assemblies and athletic events), the handicapped children might not have any genuine social contact with their fellow non-handicapped students.

On the other hand, *social integration* consists of participation by a (devalued) person or persons in social interactions and relationships with non-devalued citizens that are culturally normative both in quantity and quality, and that take place in normative activities and in valued, or at least normative, settings and contexts. Thus, social integration goes far beyond the mere physical presence of both devalued and non-devalued people in the same physical space. (Wolfensberger & Thomas, 1983, p. 18)

Wolfensberger and Thomas (1983, 1989) operationalized their conceptual definitions of physical and social integration in specific PASSING ratings. As with PASS 3, data collected with PASSING suggest that human service programs are much better at achieving reasonably satisfactory physical integration than social integration. For example, in a sample of 633 PASSING evaluations, conducted in the United States (54%), Canada (37%), Australia (6%), the UK (2%), and New Zealand (1%), and serving persons with developmental disabilities (39%), "mixed" disabling conditions (36%), psychiatric disabilities (10%), aging (7%), or physical disabilities (3%), Flynn, Guirguis, Wolfensberger, & Cocks (in press) found that the mean scores on two PASSING subscales assessing physical integration, setting ($M = 47\%$) and accessibility ($M = 55\%$), were at approximately the level (50% of the maximum possible weighted score) that the authors of PASSING view as constituting "minimally acceptable" service quality. In contrast, analyses of the same sample of programs conducted for the present chapter revealed that the mean scores on the two individual PASSING ratings that are the most direct measures of social integration, Image-Related Other Integrative Client Contacts & Personal Relationships ($M = 20\%$) and Competence-Related Other Integrative Client Contacts & Personal Relationships ($M = 9\%$), were much lower.

1.1.3 WOLFENSBERGER'S MOST RECENT DEFINITION OF ("REAL") INTEGRATION AS "PERSONAL SOCIAL INTEGRATION AND VALUED SOCIAL PARTICIPATION"

Recently, Wolfensberger (1998a) provided an updated version of his definition of integration. In presenting it as one of 10 major themes underlying SRV, and in contrasting it with the rejection, distantiation, and segregation that are often imposed on societally devalued people, Wolfensberger defined integration as follows:

From an SRV perspective, "integration" means "personal social integration and valued social participation." This in turn would require (a) *valued* participation, (b) with valued people (c) in valued activities that (d) take place in valued settings. Among the things this would imply is that as much as possible, devalued people would be enabled: to live in normative housing within the valued community, and with (not just near) valued people; to be educated with their non-devalued peers; to work in the same facilities as ordinary people; and to be involved in a positive fashion in worship, recreation, shopping, and all the other activities in which members of society engage.

If a person is already in devalued roles or is at risk of role degradation, then the more this person is observed in places frequented by valued people in society, in actual association with people in valued roles, and in activities that are valued (e.g., active or productive ones), the more role-valorization benefits are apt to accrue to that person, often first in the image domain, and sometimes also, and derivatively, in the competency domain. This is especially apt to be true if the valued people associate with that person without feeling coerced or resentful about it.

In order for personal valued social integration of a devalued person to be truly successful, a number of supports must be present and operational, including ideological and administrative supports, people who can competently transact the integration, positive imaging of the persons to be integrated, supports that will enable the person to remain in the community in the first place from childhood on, and a comprehensive continuum of service options for people in need throughout their lives, including sufficient fall-back options in case one level of integration is unsuccessful.

We emphasize most emphatically that what today is commonly called "inclusion" is also very often *not* social role-valorizing integration, because one or more of the four elements of such integration (a, b, c, or d above) is lacking. For instance, a person of devalued identity could be engaged with valued people in devalued activities (e.g., pornography) in devalued settings (e.g., a drug house), and the person's participation could be either valued or devalued. Even the placement of impaired children in regular school classes—commonly called "inclusion"—could lack the element of valued participation. In fact, it is often because the presence of a devalued person is coerced that this presence is neither desired nor valued. While this kind of "inclusion" certainly has some arguments in its favor, it would not meet the SRV criteria of integration, and one should not pretend otherwise. (pp. 123-124)

Finally, Wolfensberger (1998b) recently provided further clarification of his definition of ("real") integration as "personal social integration and valued social participation," in contrasting it with "mainstreaming" and especially with "inclusion":

The column editor [i.e., Wolfensberger] never used the term "mainstreaming" when it was popular, nor the term "inclusion" that replaced it almost overnight.

The term "mainstreaming" was popular from ca. 1970-1990. One author surveyed the literature, and found 40 different meanings of the term. It was used to mean everything from a person residing in an institution with 1000 other handicapped residents, to putting a mentally handicapped offender into a "generic" prison among other offenders, to dumping a person without supports leaving the person to sink or swim, all the way to what we mean by real integration. The term "inclusion" succeeded the term "mainstreaming" almost overnight about 1990 as a favorite craze term. Sometimes, the term "total inclusion" is even used. Inclusion is also a very imprecise construct. It *could* mean what we mean by real integration, but more often, it means that the devalued person is in the midst of devalued people—perhaps even with heavy-duty supports—but regardless whether the surrounding others are tolerant, supportive, and accepting or not. It is thus based more on a "right-to-be-there" concept than a "wanted-and-valued-in-participation" concept . . .

In our SRV teaching, "real" integration is "personal social integration and valued social participation" (PSI & VSP). It has been defined as "valued participation by a (devalued) person in a culturally normative quantity of contacts, interactions, relationships, and roles with ordinary and valued citizens, in valued (or at least normative) activities, and in valued (or at least ordinary) physical and social settings." For short, we sometimes call PSI and VSP "real integration."

Note that there could be valued participation in valued settings and valued activities, but that the elements of *societal* participation could be lacking. For instance, a wealthy recluse who engages in valued activities could do so with only a very restricted number of other valued people, and in very valued but self-segregated settings.

The key difference between our formulation of real integration and the currently popular inclusion ideology is this: we see *valued* participation as something than can only occur on a *voluntary* basis. After all, one cannot force people to value others, their presence, or their participation. In contrast, inclusion is based on a rights (primarily legal rights) notion that *prefers* valued presence, but will enforce an *involuntary* devalued presence and participation if voluntary valued participation is not forthcoming, or not forthcoming all at once. However, some people would also apply the term "inclusion" to participation of devalued persons with non-devalued ones in *de*valued activities in open society, in either valued *or* devalued settings, as long as these are not "segregated" ones. (pp. 58-59)

1.2 NIRJE'S SIXFOLD CONCEPTUALIZATION OF INTEGRATION: PHYSICAL, FUNCTIONAL, SOCIAL, PERSONAL, SOCIETAL, AND ORGANIZATIONAL

In 1980, Nirje added a new appendix, "On Integration," to his famous paper on Normalization. Therein, he defined integration as having six facets (Nirje, 1980, pp. 47-49). Three of Nirje's facets (i.e., physical, functional, and organizational integration) appear to correspond approximately to certain aspects of Wolfensberger's physical integration, and three (social, personal, and societal integration) to aspects of Wolfensberger's social integration. Also, Nirje leaves relatively implicit what is explicit (and indeed central) for Wolfensberger, namely, that social interactions and relationships, to be genuinely socially integrative of devalued persons, must involve nondevalued, ordinary citizens.

The following multiple definition of integration and its consequent facets or levels can be distinguished:

1. Physical integration enables a handicapped person to share the basic security needs that are drawn from physical settings and to experience the normal rhythms of the day, the week, the year, and of the life cycle. Physical integration means that homes should be located in residential areas, that classes be offered in regular school buildings, that work be available in industrial and business areas, and that leisure be found in ordinary leisure time environments, as much as possible.

2. Functional integration is an expansion of physical integration. A person, even if physically handicapped, should be able to function in and have access to necessary and ordinary segments of the environment, such as dining halls, restaurants, swimming pools, rest rooms, and transportation.

3. Social integration is the interpersonal or impersonal social relationships in neighborhoods, in schools, in work situations, and in the community at large. Manners, attitudes, respect, and esteem are mutually involved here. This interface is also affected by public attitudes of the media and by the public image of handicapped persons.

4. Personal integration is related to the developing and changing needs for personal interaction with significant persons. It includes the opportunities to have a satisfactory private life with meaningful relationships, for example, for the child: parents, siblings, relatives, and friends; and for the adult: relatives, friends, marriage partner, and children. . . .

5. Societal integration relates to the expressive functioning as a citizen regarding legal rights and the opportunities for growth, maturity, and self-attainment through respected expressions of self-determination. Thus, individual program and planning decisions should, as much as possible, belong to the handicapped person in the routine dealings with his own conditions of life, options, and future. Also, the same recognition given to any other social body should be given to handicapped people regarding their opportunities to express themselves as a group. . . .

6. Organizational integration. Those organizational forms and administrative structures that assist and support the furthering of the above

facets of integration of handicapped people are consequently more appropriate than other, more restrictive, forms and structures. In general, this is achieved by utilization of public generic agencies as much as possible. In situations where required specialization of services cannot be developed within regular services or when equivalent services cannot be developed within regular services or when equivalent services simply do not exist in the generic services area, the special services developed should be patterned after and aligned with general services as much as possible.

Nirje's distinctions among different forms of integration have had an impact on policy and research. In Quebec, for example, the Ministry of Health and Social Services (Groupe de travail, 1987, 1988) distinguished among physical, functional, and social integration in its policy directives. Also, Pedlar (1990) referred to Nirje's conceptualization in noting that the physical and functional integration of people with mental retardation in Sweden appeared to be much more extensive than their social integration.

1.3 STOREY'S FOURFOLD CONCEPTUALIZATION OF INTEGRATION, AS COMPOSED OF PHYSICAL INTEGRATION, SOCIAL INTEGRATION, RELATIONSHIPS (SOCIAL SUPPORT), AND SOCIAL NETWORKS

Storey's (1989) paper is one of the few that has attempted to synthesize writings on integration. According to Storey, integration—although a critical outcome for people with disabilities—has been an elusive term. Citing Mank and Buckley (1989), Storey stated that four different components of integration have often been considered: physical integration, social integration, relationships, and social networks. Each has been defined (albeit skeletally) as follows (with Wolfensberger's influence apparent in the definition of the first two elements):

Physical integration: "The necessary first step for other forms of integration . . . Without physical integration, there cannot be social integration, relationships, and social networks. But mere physical presence may not necessarily lead to other forms of integration" (Storey, 1989, p. 281).

Social integration: "Regular access to interactions with individuals without identified handicaps and regular use of normal community resources" (Will, 1984, p. 2; cited in Storey, 1989, p. 281). Thus, interactions are a necessary condition of social integration.

Relationships: "Social relationships are often defined in connection to social support and may be analyzed in terms of quantity, structure, and function" (House & Kahn, 1985; cited in Storey, 1989, p. 283). "Relationships depend on social interactions that are ongoing and usually involve reciprocal participation in activities" (Mank & Buckley, 1989, p. 320; cited in Storey, 1989, p. 283).

Social networks: "Social networks . . . generally refer to the people identified as socially important to a person" (Storey, 1989, p. 283).

Concerning the operational definition of integration, Storey listed a number of measures that have been used in the literature for each of the four components, both on the molecular level of discrete behaviors and on the molar level of global ratings. In the case of social integration, molecular measures have included social skills and discrete measures of social interaction. Storey noted that such measures can be criticized because there is little evidence that the behaviors assessed are related to successful lifestyle changes. He also asserted that little is currently known about relationships among measures of the four integration components.

Storey's summary schema usefully introduces the mainstream social science concepts of *social networks* and *social support* into the assessment and study of integration. Although absent (at least in their usual social-science meanings) from Wolfensberger's and Nirje's conceptualizations of integration, these two concepts provide essential tools for studying the structure of socially integrative relationships, the psychological functions that they fulfill for the individual, and the antecedents and consequences of integration. Thus, as we note in the third part of the present chapter, mainstream social science constructs such as these hold considerable potential for enriching Normalization and SRV theory and research. Fortunately, the two research groups whose work we examine next—Sara Burchard and her colleagues at the University of Vermont, and Stephen Newton and Robert Horner and their colleagues at the University of Oregon—have established numerous illuminating conceptual, empirical, practice, and policy links

between social networks and social support, on the one hand, and physical integration and social integration, on the other.

1.4 INTEGRATION IN THE RESIDENTIAL SERVICES RESEARCH OF SARA BURCHARD AND HER COLLEAGUES AT THE UNIVERSITY OF VERMONT

Over the last 15 years, Sara Burchard and her colleagues have carried out one of the most systematic programs of research related to Normalization and integration of which we are aware. (For a synthesis of their work, see Burchard's contribution [chapter 11] to the present volume.) Her group has examined the extent to which Normalization and integration principles—the basis of Vermont social policy in developmental disabilities during this period—have actually been implemented in community residential services for adults with mental retardation. Directly inspired by Wolfensberger's (1972) conceptualization of Normalization and integration, Burchard and her colleagues have investigated the antecedents and consequences of key issues related to the quality and effectiveness of community residential services for persons with mental retardation: staff and managers' Normalization-related and other competencies; residents' degree of lifestyle Normalization and physical and social integration; the size and composition of residents' social networks; and residents' degree of stress, social support, community adjustment, satisfaction with their living situation, and personal well-being. At the risk of some overlap with her chapter, we shall focus here on findings from the work of Burchard and her colleagues that are directly pertinent to the topic of integration.

1.4.1 RESEARCH ON COMMUNITY INTEGRATION

Burchard, Pine, Gordon, Joffe, Widrick, and Goy (1987) examined the relationship between the competencies of residence managers and the community integration and satisfaction of 78 adults with mental retardation who were living in 14 community residences. Thus, early in their research program, Burchard et al. (1987) used the more global term *community integration,* rather than the more specific terms of *physical integration* and *social integration* that they came to use later. *Community integration* was defined, conceptually, as the integration of clients into community activities, and operationally, as the number of individualized and integrating activities in which clients had participated during the last two weeks (see Burchard, Gordon, & Pine, 1990). Burchard et al. (1987) found that managers' competencies in Normalization were significantly, positively, and strongly related to residents' level of community integration ($r = .60$, $p < .05$). Subsequently, Burchard, Gordon, and Pine (1990) studied the relationship between the competence in Normalization principles of 12 group home managers and the level of community integration (defined as before) and satisfaction with their living situation of 57 adults with mental retardation residing in these homes. Burchard et al. (1990) found that the greater the manager's Normalization-related competence, the more integrated ($r = .64$, $p < .025$) and satisfied ($r = .51$, $p < .001$) were the residents. Also, the more integrated the residents, the more satisfied they were with their living situation ($r = .64$, $p < .001$).

As noted by Burchard in chapter 11 of the present volume, both her own and her group's data on residential staff and managers' competencies made it very clear that such competencies—especially an awareness of and responsiveness to resident needs, and an awareness of value-based Normalization issues—had an important positive impact on program quality. Specifically, these staff and manager competencies were associated with service goals more consistent with Normalization (the policy basis of Vermont's community services), with more frequent engagement by residents in individualized and integrated activities, and with greater satisfaction by residents with their living situation.

1.4.2   RESEARCH ON PHYSICAL AND SOCIAL INTEGRATION

In a new, 3-year longitudinal study, Burchard, Hasazi, Gordon, and Yoe (1991) followed 133 adults who had a borderline, mild, or moderate degree of mental retardation. Fifty-four were residents of group homes, 38 lived in supportive apartments, and 41 resided with their natural families. In this study, Burchard et al. (1991) replaced the global construct of *community integration* with the more precise concepts of *physical integration* and *social integration.* This decision was no doubt directly influenced by Wolfensberger's distinction between these two terms (Wolfensberger, 1972; Wolfensberger & Thomas, 1983). Burchard et al. (1991) operationally defined *physical integration* as the mean number of resident activities per week (over the last 2 weeks and as reported by staff members) that had taken place in the community or in other nonsegregated environments (i.e., outside of work or day-program settings). *Social integration,* on the other hand, was operationally defined as the mean number of these weekly activities that had occurred in the company of a nondisabled peer or companion.

Burchard et al. (1991) found that residents' level of mental retardation was significantly and inversely correlated ($r = -.30$) with their degree of social integration and that physical integration was much more common than social integration, in each type of residential setting. In the supportive apartments, the means for physical and social integration were, respectively, 12.4 versus 3.1 activities per week; in the group homes, 7.3 versus 0.9; in the natural families, 6.9 versus 1.2; and, for the sample as a whole, 8.76 versus 1.95. In light of these data, Burchard et al. (1991) concluded that a much higher level of physical integration than of social integration had been attained, in spite of residents' daily access to nonsegregated community settings. (This finding—a virtual constant in the community services literature, in various service fields and countries—is echoed in several chapters in the present volume. It is also highly supportive of the utility of Wolfensberger's [1972, 1998b; Wolfensberger & Glenn, 1975; Wolfensberger & Thomas, 1983] and others' [Burchard et al., 1991; Burchard, Rosen, Gordon, Hasazi, Yoe, & Dietzel, 1992; Gordon, Burchard, Hasazi, Yoe, Dietzel, & Simoneau, 1992; Newton, Olson, & Horner, 1995; Newton, Ard, Horner, & Toews, 1996; Storey, 1989] explicit conceptual and operational distinction between physical and social integration.)

In another study drawn from their 3-year longitudinal research, Burchard et al. (1992) measured residents' social networks by means of an adaptation of Weinberg's (1984) Social System Self-Assessment (SSSA). Administered in the form of an interview with each resident, the SSSA produced five scores: (a) social network size (i.e., the number of individuals named as persons providing support); (b) multiplexity (i.e., the resident's relationship to the persons named, such as relative, staff member, friend, service worker, or employer); (c) balance between stress and support (i.e., the proportion of network members perceived by the resident as a source of positive support rather than of stress); (d) satisfaction with contacts (i.e., the proportion of network members with whom the frequency of contact was perceived by the resident as sufficient); and (e) reciprocity (i.e., the number of relationships characterized by mutual initiation of contact and social support).

For the 133 residents as a group, the social network of the "typical" resident included a mean of 9.4 individuals (as calculated from Table 10.2 in Burchard et al., 1992, p. 143), of whom 2.0 were relatives, 2.6 residence staff members, 4.4 peers (3.6 with disabilities, 0.89 without disabilities), and 0.4 advocates or staff in generic or vocational services. On average, only 0.8 of the residents' relationships with these persons were reciprocal. Concerning residents' desired frequency of social contacts with members of their network (as calculated from Table 10.3 in Burchard et al., 1992, p. 145), 62% of the residents wanted more contact with relatives, 59% wanted more with nondisabled peers, 53% wanted more with staff members, and 47% wanted more with peers who had disabilities. For the sample as a whole, only the proportion of the entire network or of the peer network that was perceived as a source of positive support had a significant, positive correlation with residents' satisfaction with their living situation and feeling of personal well-being. This suggests that residents' *experience* of social interactions and social integration (i.e., of the supportiveness or not of the persons with whom they have social interactions and relationships)

is likely to be crucial for their satisfaction with their living situation and personal well-being. Burchard and her colleagues have illuminated this neglected topic—the subjective side of social interactions and social integration—very directly and clearly.

Rosen and Burchard (1990) compared the social networks and community activities of 27 adults with mild mental retardation (all were living in supportive apartments and drawn from the larger sample of 133 residents) and 27 adults without disabilities in Vermont. The members of the two groups were matched for marital status (all were single), sex, age, and size of community of residence. Rosen and Burchard found no significant differences between the groups with regard to their total number of community activities, activity settings (with family or relatives, in the community, or in an isolated place), activity objectives (functional, social, or solitary leisure), or the people interacted with (no one [alone], friends, family, or staff). Nor did the groups differ in terms of their perceived network support or satisfaction with the frequency of their social contacts. On the other hand, the groups were very different with respect to the characteristics of their friends: 90% of the friends of the persons with mental retardation were themselves mentally retarded; the nondisabled adults had social networks that were twice as large as those of the adults with mental retardation, with a greater proportion of friends (79% versus 48%); and the reciprocal relationships of the nondisabled adults were seven times more frequent than those of the adults with mental retardation. Also, 100% of the nondisabled adults named a nondisabled peer as the most important source of social support, compared to only 4% of the persons with mental retardation. In short, in spite of the successful physical integration observed among the 27 residents of supportive apartments, social integration was extremely limited.

Hasazi, Burchard, Gordon, Vecchione, and Rosen (1992) assessed, in the same sample of 133 adults with mental retardation, the influence of stress and objective and subjective social support on adjustment to community life. The measure of *objective social support,* based on interviews with individual residents, included four elements: the total number of individuals in the resident's social network, the number of peers with disabilities, the number of peers without disabilities, and the number of relatives. *Subjective*

279

social support (i.e., residents' satisfaction with support) was operationally defined as the proportion composed of individuals in the resident's social network who were perceived as sources of support. Hasazi et al. (1992) found that the residents who were the most socially integrated and satisfied with their social support were also most satisfied with their living situation. Furthermore, those whose social network included a greater number of nondisabled persons or relatives suffered less stress.

Gordon et al. (1992) studied the 114 individuals among the total sample of 133 (86%) who had remained in the same type of residence throughout the 3 years of the project. Controlling statistically for differences among the residents of the three different types of residential settings, Gordon et al. found that residents in supportive apartments showed the greatest degree of independence, lifestyle Normalization, and physical and social integration. Compared with the apartment residents, the group home residents had social networks that were smaller and contained a larger number of peers with disabilities. The group home residents were also less satisfied with their personal relationships with staff and coresidents and with their degree of independence. Those living with their natural families had a less normalized lifestyle than residents in the other two types of settings and participated less in independent activities in the community than those who lived in apartments. Overall, Gordon et al. found, over the 3 years of the study, that the residents in each type of setting were highly stable in terms of their physical and social integration, lifestyle, adjustment, and satisfaction. Moreover, Gordon et al. concluded that persons with mental retardation must be afforded greater opportunities for the exercise of control, choice, and independence and must also be helped to achieve a higher level of social integration.

1.4.4 CONCLUSION CONCERNING THE RESEARCH OF BURCHARD AND HER COLLEAGUES

Among the major strengths of the work by Burchard and her colleagues are its broad and up-to-date theoretical framework and its focus on current social policy concerns. Refreshingly, these researchers have shed new light on central Normalization and social integration issues by drawing upon several mainstream social science perspectives, including social network, social support, stress, and ecological theory. In producing strong empirical support for the usefulness of Normalization and integration principles in the structuring of community services, Burchard and her colleagues have also shown the way to more theoretically grounded and fruitful Normalization and SRV-related research. Their work also has many points of contact with that of the research group at the University of Oregon, whose research we look at next.

1.5 INTEGRATION IN THE SOCIAL-LIFE RESEARCH OF STEPHEN NEWTON, ROBERT HORNER, AND THEIR COLLEAGUES AT THE SPECIALIZED TRAINING PROGRAM, UNIVERSITY OF OREGON

1.5.1 CONCEPTUAL FRAMEWORK CENTERED ON UNDERSTANDING AND IMPROVING THE SOCIAL LIVES OF PERSONS WITH MENTAL RETARDATION

In a foundational paper, Newton, Horner, Ard, LeBaron, and Sappington (1994) described the conceptual model underlying their research. They noted that services have undergone a shift from an emphasis on health, safety, and skill development to a stress on the provision of "lifestyle support." As a result, there has been increased recognition of the importance of improving the social relationships of persons with disabilities, including their engagement in preferred daily activities and their realization of valued lifestyle outcomes, such as physical and social integration. Concomitantly, a shift in focus has also occurred, from the individual with a disability to his or her relationship with other community members.

Like Burchard and her colleagues, Newton and Horner and their colleagues employ a number of central social science concepts—social support, social interaction, social networks, and social relationship stability—that are highly relevant to the study of integration issues. *Social support*, first of all, "consists of verbal and/or nonverbal information or advice, tangible aid, or action that is proffered by social intimates or inferred by their presence and has beneficial emotional or behavioral effects on the recipient" (Gottlieb, 1983, p. 28; cited in Newton et al., 1994, p. 393). Social support has six functions through which it produces a generally beneficial impact on physical and mental health: material aid, behavioral assistance, intimate interaction, guidance, feedback, and positive social interaction (Barrera & Ainsley, 1983). Measures such as the 23 social support scales reviewed by Heitzmann and Kaplan (1988) can be used to measure social support, including the specific supportive behaviors received by a respondent, the functional properties of the support, or the respondent's perception of available social support or satisfaction with available support. According to Newton et al. (1994), the limited research that exists on social support among persons with mental retardation suggests that many rely on paid caregivers or other persons with disabilities as sources of support. (They also cite, however, Edgerton's [1988] long-term follow-up in 1985 of a group of persons with mental retardation who had left Pacific State Hospital in California many years earlier to live on their own. Interestingly, Edgerton's follow-up indicated that people's reliance on benefactors declined markedly over time, that most had personal relationships in which they received and gave assistance, and that four acted actually as benefactors for persons without mental retardation.)

Social interaction occurs when "two or more people jointly engage in an activity of daily life: making a purchase, having a conversation, eating dinner, playing basketball, celebrating a birthday, and so on" (Newton et al., 1994, p. 396). Measures of social interaction may assess the frequency, duration, type, or function of the interactions engaged in. According to Newton, Olson, and Horner (1995), *social interaction, social contact,* and *social integration* have often been used in the literature as synonyms, to refer to the engagement of an individual with mental retardation in an activity (e.g., attending a concert or going grocery shopping) with a nonimpaired community member. Research on community living programs indicates that such social integration (i.e., social contact between people with mental retardation and persons other than human service personnel or other program participants) is infrequent.

A *social network* "is simply a set of actors—individuals or other social entities—and their relationships with each other" (Koehly & Shivy, 1998, p. 3). Social network analysis is a methodology that uses indices of relatedness among individuals to produce representations of social structures and positions inherent in dyads or groups. The network indices may include the number of persons who provide the target individual with the type of relationship under study (*network size*); the social roles occupied by network members (*composition*); how often interactions take place between a target individual and other network members (*frequency*); the cohesiveness of a group of individuals (*density*); the ties between two particular members (*reciprocity*); the cohesiveness of a subgroup of members (*cliquing*); the degree to which a particular individual initiates interactions or relationships (*actor centrality*); the extent to which other network members initiate interactions with a given individual (*actor prestige*); and the degree to which certain individuals remain separate from network interactions (*isolates*). Software packages capable of assessing such indices and carrying our social network analyses include UCINET IV (Borgatti, Everett, & Freeman, 1992) and STRUCTURE (Burt, 1991). In mental retardation, social network analysis has concentrated mainly on network size, composition, and reciprocity. Individuals living in community settings have been found to have larger support networks than those living with their families. Also, individuals without disabilities have been found to have networks that are larger and marked by considerably greater reciprocity than those of persons with mental retardation (Newton et al., 1994).

Social relationship stability is "the stability, or maintenance, of social relationships" (Newton et al., 1994, p. 398). Despite the obvious importance of the topic, particularly for persons with mental retardation whose lives, in many cases, have been marked by a high degree of relationship discontinuity, there has been little research on the topic. In one of the few such studies, Newton, Olson, and Horner (1995) studied the social relationships between 11 adults who had mild to profound mental retardation and 14 unimpaired community members (i.e., who were neither family members, persons paid to provide services to the individual with mental retardation, or persons with mental retardation, and who had participated in one more activities with one or two of the persons with mental retardation at least once every three months during the last year). On average, the community members had known the individual with mental retardation for 6.5 years (range = 1-23 years), and had taken part in an activity with this person more than once a month during the preceding 12 months. Ten of the 14 community members were currently employed in the field of mental retardation (but did not work with the person with mental retardation in question), and two had previously worked in the field. In terms of the social support functions provided, the community members indicated that they usually provided emotional support to the person with mental retardation, often provided feedback, access to other people, information, and material aid, and "sometimes" provided help in making major life decisions. The community members felt that they were engaged in relatively reciprocal relationships with "friends" and even "best friends," receiving about as much emotional support as they gave and only a little less of the other types of support than they gave (Newton, Olson, & Horner, 1995).

1.5.2 PHYSICAL AND SOCIAL INTEGRATION AS VALUED OUTCOMES

Newton, Ard, Horner, and Toews (1996) conceptualized physical and social integration as valued outcomes that are indicators of the quality of life (QOL) of people with mental retardation. Efforts to enhance QOL occur within the context of Oregon's Residential Outcomes System (formerly known as the Valued Outcomes Information System) and are evaluated in terms of two broad kinds of indicators: satisfaction on the part of the person with mental retardation with his or her residential services, and the "valued outcomes" that he or she experiences. The valued outcomes that are tracked on a continuous basis are the following:

Physical integration refers to participation in community activities (as measured by the number of community activities experienced each week).

Social integration refers to being *of* the community, and not merely *in* the community, and is defined as occurring when a person with mental retardation participates in an activity with someone who is not paid to provide him or her with support (as measured by the number of activities experienced each week with people other than residential program staff or other program participants). (As Newton et al. [1996] note, this definition of social integration is not meant to denigrate the valuable relationships that people with

mental retardation have with staff. Rather, it is meant to ensure that relationships with staff members do not become substitutes for relationships with other community members.)

Functional independence refers to the number of activities a person engages in on his or her own each week, without staff support.

Relative independence refers to the person's increasing independence on task analysis steps associated with instructional activities specified on his or her Individualized Support Plan.

Frequency of activities refers to the pace of a person's life (i.e., number of "valued activities" experienced each week), tailored to personal preferences.

Variety of activities refers to the diversity of a person's life (i.e., the number of different activities experienced each week), as a reflection of the person's current and emerging interests.

Activity preference refers to activities that reflect a person's unique lifestyle preferences (number of preferred activities experienced each week).

As of June 1993, in more than 85% of Oregon's 313 twenty-four-hour residential programs, direct service staff had been trained in the use of the Residential Outcomes System and were using it with fidelity (Newton et al., 1996). Research indicates that the physical and social integration of people with mental retardation and the size of their social networks increased following implementation of the Residential Outcomes System (Newton & Horner, 1993, 1995; Newton et al., 1996).

1.5.3 EFFORTS TO INCREASE SOCIAL RELATIONSHIPS AND SOCIAL INTEGRATION

Newton, Horner, and their colleagues, at the Specialized Training Program at the University of Oregon, have not been content merely to observe and measure the social relationships and social integration of persons with mental retardation. They have also been proactive in trying to increase both. Their work has the considerable merit of showing how research can help to improve the lives of persons with disabilities.

In an initial paper in this vein, Kennedy, Horner, and Newton (1989) studied the patterns of social contact experienced by 23 adults with severe disabilities living in community settings in the state of Washington. The participants, who were aged 21 to 58 (M = 34 years) and had been assessed as severely disabled by mental health professionals, had a variety of intellectual and physical impairments. The researchers measured the participants' social contacts over a 30-month period. The average participant was found to engage in social contacts with 64 different people during the 30-month period, not counting people with whom they lived or people who were paid to provide support to them. During a typical 4-week period, participants engaged in 15 interactions with people other than those they lived with or who were paid to provide support. Thirty-two percent of the interactions were with family members, 13% with best friends, and 55% with friends and acquaintances.

Kennedy, Horner, and Newton (1990) next investigated the links between the social networks and activity patterns of 20 other persons classified as severely disabled. The latter were between 22 and 56 years of age (M = 39 years) and lived in community apartments or small homes. The average participant's social network was found to be composed of 15 persons, of whom 4 (29%) were family members, 6 (40%) were paid to provide support, 3 (20%) were coresidents or coworkers, and 2 (12%) were friends or neighbors. Participants engaged in an average of 456 activities per month, at home (89%) or in the community (11%). The larger the participant's social network, the more frequent were his or her monthly activities. The strongest positive correlations were found between the number of family members in the participant's social network and the frequency and variety of his or her activities.

Newton and Horner (1993) then turned to a more active study that attempted to improve the social relationships of three women with severe disabilities. The investigators evaluated an intervention consisting of a "social guide," that is, a staff person responsible for coordinating the implementation of "community network strategies" that were intended to increase the social networks and social integration of the three participants. These strategies included the following: altering the women's activity patterns, to increase the frequency of selected preferred activities, which, in turn, would lead to greater social integration; matching the women's activity interests (e.g., in fishing) with the activity interests (e.g., in fishing) of friends or neighbors; and teaching the women to engage in social-reciprocation activities, such as inviting a friend to dinner or sending a thank-you note. Newton and Horner found that the intervention was accompanied by increases in participants' social networks, rate of activities, and social integration. These gains were maintained at a 12-week follow-up.

Ouellette, Horner, and Newton (1994) further assessed the viability of altering activity patterns as a strategy for improving social networks and social integration. The participants were five adults with moderate to severe intellectual disabilities. They were between 20 and 39 years of age and lived with one or two live-in support staff and a maximum of two other persons with disabilities. Each participant and his or her support staff chose five preferred activities. The intervention, which lasted 6 months, attempted to increase the frequency of participants' target activities and thereby increase their social networks and social integration. In general, Ouellette et al. found that the intervention was associated with an increase in the variety of participants' community activities that involved social integration, with the primary change being the development of new friendships.

1.5.4 CONCLUSION ON THE RESEARCH PROGRAM OF NEWTON, HORNER, AND THEIR COLLEAGUES

The work of the Oregon group is very promising in its focus on testing practical ways of improving the social life of people with mental retardation. Their research has shown that activity patterns and social networks can indeed grow, thereby mediating increases in social integration. Overall, their work suggests that more emphasis be placed on the relationship between people's activities and other aspects of their social lives, as well as on their preferred modes of social participation. Also, like the research program of Burchard and her colleagues at the University of Vermont, that of Newton et al. (1994) demonstrates clearly that physical and social integration issues are very fruitfully approached from mainstream perspectives such as social network and social support theory.

1.6 RESEARCH ON INTEGRATION AS EMBEDDED WITHIN THE BROADER CONSTRUCT OF "COMMUNITY ADJUSTMENT"

In contrast to the work of Burchard, Newton and their colleagues, which was informed by a clear conceptualization of integration (stemming from Wolfensberger's [1972] distinction between physical and social integration), the studies in the present section do not seem to have been rooted in a clear conceptual definition of integration. This may be because integration was viewed as a component of a broader construct, *community adjustment,* which itself has been notoriously difficult to define with precision. In the absence of a clear conceptual definition of integration, the research in the present section strikes one as largely measurement-driven. Although employing sophisticated latent-variable factor-analytic techniques, these studies seem less helpful in understanding integration than those reviewed in the two preceding sections.

McGrew, Bruininks, Thurlow, and Lewis (1992) wished to establish improved measures of the construct, *community adjustment and integration.* With data from a sample of 239 young adults with mild, moderate, or severe mental retardation, McGrew, Bruininks, Thurlow, et al. (1992) used latent-variable factor analysis to identify four empirical integration dimensions: *integration into a social network* (as indexed by the number and variety of friends, with or without disabilities, staff members, etc.); *integration into recreational and leisure activities* (e.g., social or solitary, formal or informal, community or domestic activities); *integration into economic and community activities* (e.g., amount of monthly benefits, payment of income tax, possession of a bank account, amount of monthly salary, type of economic activity during the day, type of residence); and *support service requirements* (e.g., number of factors limiting social activities, number of support services received, etc.).

In the same sample of 239 young adults, McGrew, Bruininks, and Thurlow (1992) investigated the relationship between the four adjustment and community integration factors just mentioned and adaptive/maladaptive behavior (assessed with the Inventory for Client and Agency Planning; Bruininks, Hill, Weatherman, & Woodcock, 1986). Statistically significant canonical correlations were found between adaptive/maladaptive behavior and, respectively, integration into economic and community activities ($r_c = .74$), requirement for support services ($r_c = .47$), integration into social networks ($r_c = .38$), and integration into recreational and leisure activities ($r_c = .30$). Adaptive/maladaptive behavior thus appeared to be related to community adjustment and integration, especially to the two factors that entail independence within the community (i.e., integration into economic and community activities, and support service requirements). However, in the absence of a clear conceptual definition of community adjustment and integration, one wonders to what extent the items used to measure integration were conceptually and empirically distinct from those used to measure adaptive/maladaptive behavior.

Anderson, Lakin, Hill, and Chen (1992) studied social integration in a national sample of 370 older persons with mental retardation who were 63 years of age or over. Again, without providing a clear conceptual definition of social integration or clearly distinguishing it from physical integration, Anderson et al. measured the concept in terms of four major factors: integration into the home (as indexed by participation in household tasks); integration into recreational and leisure activities (in six different categories); integration into social relationships (with neighbors, friends, nondisabled persons, and family members); and use of community resources (supermarkets, stores, libraries, churches, banks, seniors' centers, public transportation). (The latter dimension would appear to be tapping physical rather than social aspects of integration.) A total social integration score was obtained by summing the scores for the four subscales (the intercorrelations of which ranged from 0.38 to 0.63).

Anderson et al. (1992) found that the personal variable most strongly related to social integration was the level of mental retardation, with persons with a lower level of disability better integrated on each of the four indicators. Overall, the degree of social integration of the elderly research participants was very low, in part because 52% were living in public residential institutions. Only 45% had met a neighbor, and a mere 14% had visited a neighbor's home. The residential settings of 28% were so isolated that interaction with neighbors was virtually impossible. Fifty-three percent never visited friends or had no friends;

when they did have friends, the latter usually lived in the same residential setting. Only 31% of the participants had regular social contact with nondisabled persons other than staff, and 51% had no contact with their families (half, in fact, had no family). The participants' use of community resources and participation in household tasks was also low. Participants in the study who lived in community settings (i.e., family-care or group homes) were physically and socially better integrated than those living in public or private institutions, even though 40% of those living in the community had no close friends and only 50% had regular contact with nondisabled persons other than staff.

Halpern, Nave, Close, and Nelson (1986) used confirmatory factor analysis procedures to validate a conceptual model of community adjustment and integration that consisted of four dimensions: *occupation* (operationalized in terms of three indicators: employment; disposable monthly income after housing cost; and integration with nondisabled persons, which was seen as occurring mainly in the workplace); *residential setting* (three indicators: residence comfort and cleanliness; quality of residential neighborhood; and access to community services and resources); *social support and security* (three indicators: social network and frequency of leisure activities; security with respect to minor abuse; and security with respect to major abuse); and *satisfaction* (three indicators: overall satisfaction with the three preceding dimensions; self-satisfaction or self-esteem; and satisfaction with residential program). Halpern et al. (1986) found that data from a sample of 257 mentally impaired adults were consistent with the conceptual model. They added that, in future, the integration of disabled persons with nondisabled persons may be expected to transcend the occupational realm and to encompass the three other aspects of community adjustment.

Using the foregoing model as a conceptual framework, Halpern (1989) reviewed some 30 studies conducted on the community adjustment of young disabled adults. He found that although occupational adjustment tended to be low, residential adjustment was more encouraging. Also, although in Halpern's opinion social interactions and social networks (made up largely of other young disabled persons) were rather weak, the level of personal satisfaction and self-esteem among the young disabled adults was relatively high.

This suggests that the links between social networks, social integration, and psychological well-being need careful investigation, along the lines indicated by the work of Burchard and her colleagues and that of Newton, Horner, and their research group.

1.7 SCHALOCK'S RESEARCH ON INTEGRATION ("SOCIAL INCLUSION") AS EMBEDDED WITHIN QUALITY OF LIFE

Schalock (1996, 1997) recently defined quality of life (QOL) as an overarching principle applicable to the betterment of both society and the lives of people with disabilities. In Schalock's approach, QOL is composed of eight core dimensions: emotional well-being, interpersonal relations, material well-being, personal development, physical well-being, self-determination, social inclusion, and rights. Within the domain of *social inclusion* (the term that Schalock now uses as a broad synonym for *integration*), QOL enhancement techniques include working with natural social support networks, promoting positive roles and lifestyles, stressing normalized and integrated environments, providing opportunities for community integration, and supporting volunteerism (Schalock, 1997). (For another discussion of QOL, see Heal's contribution to the present volume [chapter 9]. Heal sees QOL as more fundamental than and an alternative to Normalization and SRV.)

Schalock, Keith, Hoffman, and Karan (1989) originally proposed a 28-item Quality of Life Index that assesses three major dimensions: control of the environment, involvement in community activities, and social relations. Subsequently, Schalock and Keith (1993) developed a 40-item Quality of Life Questionnaire that assesses both objective and subjective indicators of satisfaction, competence/ productivity, empowerment/independence, and community integration/social belonging. In a sample of 715 persons with mental retardation, Schalock, Lemanowicz, Conroy, and Feinstein (1994) found that of 18 independent variables, five (which had beta coefficients of 0.10 or more in absolute size) were the most important predictors of the person's QOL Index score: adaptive behavior, challenging behavior, weekly earnings, home type (congregate versus community care), and the frequency of integrated activities, including social visits and community activities.

Campo, Sharpton, Thompson, and Sexton (1997) found that QOL Index scores of persons with severe or profound mental retardation were positively related to their having a large number of socially supportive human service staff, family, and friends in their social networks, a high degree of individualization in their home environment, and high levels of participation in home and community-integrated activities.

These research results appear broadly consistent with Schalock's conceptualization of integration as a domain within QOL, although it is not clear to what extent the "integrated activities" or "community activities" in question represent physical rather than social integration (as previously defined), or both. Also, these results appear to suffer from predictor-criterion overlap: Schalock et al. (1994) explicitly noted that such overlap was present in their study, and, from the description by Campo et al. (1997) of the variables in their study, one suspects that it was also present in their research.

1.8 INTEGRATION IN THE RESEARCH OF CAMIL BOUCHARD AND MARC DUMONT AT THE LABORATOIRE DE RECHERCHE EN ÉCOLOGIE HUMAINE ET SOCIALE (LAREHS), UNIVERSITÉ DU QUÉBEC À MONTRÉAL

In line with its longstanding commitment to Normalization, SRV, and integration, the province of Quebec funded a large-scale longitudinal study of social integration and quality of life among persons with mental retardation who were living in the community. A report summarizing the findings from this ambitious investigation was recently published (Bouchard & Dumont, 1996). The sample included approximately 500 adults residing in a range of publicly funded community residential options and 125 adults, 120 adolescents, and 64 children living with their natural families. Bouchard and Dumont thus conducted what is doubtless one of the largest studies of its type ever conducted in the French-speaking world. Besides analyzing the living situation of a sizable and roughly representative sample of persons with mental retardation in Quebec, the investigation also produced a number of instruments of good psychometric quality that will no doubt prove useful for other French-language researchers.

1.8.1 DEFINITION OF SOCIAL INTEGRATION

Operating from within an ecological and interactional perspective, Bouchard and Dumont (1996) defined one of their key terms and dependent variables, *social integration,* as follows:

> an observable and measurable state (or style) of an individual, resulting from the (more or less) autonomous exercise of (more or less) freely chosen activities that allow him or her to interact with other persons (impaired or not) in the community, in more or less specialized contexts in which nonimpaired and impaired persons may be found. (Bouchard & Dumont, 1996, p. 4; translated from the French by Robert Flynn)

This definition of social integration has the merit of being careful and explicit. It should be noted, however, that it is very different from the definitions reviewed earlier that explicitly limit the term *social integration* to activities and interactions between persons with impairments, such as mental retardation, and ordinary citizens (cf. Burchard et al., 1991, 1992; Gordon et al., 1992; Newton et al., 1995, 1996; Storey, 1989; Wolfensberger, 1972, 1998b; Wolfensberger & Glenn, 1975; Wolfensberger & Thomas, 1983).

Given their definition, it is not surprising that Bouchard and Dumont (p. 4) assert that it is possible to imagine a "socially integrated" person whose network of friends might be quite large but whose repetitive social activities would take place mainly in an institution, or a second "socially integrated" person who might carry out a wide variety of social activities but usually alone and in natural settings. For Bouchard and Dumont (1996, p. 4), these two persons would simply be exhibiting different styles of "social integration." On the other hand, the other authors just cited who make a clear distinction between physical and social integration, would no doubt refer to the first individual as largely "physically segregated" and, if his or her activities and social interactions also took place mainly with other institutional residents, as quite "socially segregated" as well. They would doubtless also consider the second individual to be mainly physically integrated but—depending on the frequency of his or her interactions with ordinary citizens—as tending to be either socially integrated or not.

In interpreting Bouchard and Dumont's (1996) findings, therefore, many of which are interesting and useful, it is imperative to keep in mind that by *social integration,* they mean essentially "engagement in freely chosen social activities and in the social interaction that may accompany such activities." In theory, their definition of social integration thus subsumes *both* social interactions between impaired human service clients and ordinary citizens (i.e., what some other writers have seen as the heart of social integration) *and* the physical presence of an impaired human service client in ordinary settings, without interactive contact with ordinary citizens (i.e., what other writers have considered to be physical integration). In practice, however, given that social interactions between impaired clients and ordinary citizens (except when the latter are family members) are empirically rare (as demonstrated by the research of Bouchard and Dumont, 1996; Burchard et al., 1991; etc.), Bouchard and Dumont's "social integration" basically reduces, empirically, to what the other authors cited have defined as "physical integration."

1.8.2   ANTECEDENTS AND CONSEQUENCES OF SOCIAL INTEGRATION

With respect to social integration as they defined it, Bouchard and Dumont (1996) found the following:

1. There were several distinct *styles* or *profiles* of integration, two exhibited by persons who are less autonomous and two by those who are more autonomous. Thus, people with mental retardation were not simply more or less integrated; they were also integrated in different ways. These integration styles were associated with a number of factors: people's degree of autonomy, their appearance, the presence of behavioral problems, the size and number of residential options, the quality of the neighborhood, the support offered by service administrators to direct-service workers, the efforts made to integrate people, and the years of experience of frontline workers.

2. The *level* of integration (as measured mainly in terms of weekly activities) was directly related to the person's basic activities, to efforts made by direct-service workers and parents, and, to a more modest degree, to the quality of the neighborhood where the person with mental retardation lives.

3. People's level of social integration was not directly linked to their level of psychological well-being. Thus, social integration should be pursued in and for itself, as a right of citizenship, rather than as a necessary and sufficient condition of people's psychological well-being.

4. There was a very strong relationship between the person's level of social integration (as measured largely by his or her weekly activities) and his or her level of adaptive-behavior skills. In fact, the predictive coefficient at both Time 1 and Time 2 was 0.93 (i.e., close to unity). (As we noted in relation to somewhat similar findings produced by McGrew, Bruininks, Thurlow, et al., 1992, however, one must ask to what extent the measurement of adaptive behavior and of engagement in weekly activities was truly independent. In principle, it would seem to be very difficult to assess adaptive behavior skills—which must be inferred from what a person typically does—in a way that is truly independent of his or her actual level of competence in carrying out weekly activities.)

5. Service workers' and parents' efforts to promote integration were directly related to the level of integration observed.

6. The person's level of adaptive-behavior skills was also the best predictor of his or her level of psychological well-being, with a predictive coefficient of 0.49 at both Time 1 and Time 2. (The same question about predictor-criterion independence can also be posed here.)

7. The existence of behavior problems was a strong negative influence on adults' integration and a source of frustration for service personnel and parents.

8. The person's level of adaptive skills was strongly related to the type of residence to which he or she was assigned and thus to the integration programs associated with the different types of setting.

9. The presence of an experienced service worker in the life of a person with mental retardation was positively related to the latter's psychological well-being.

10. The social networks of persons with mental retardation were very small, ranging from an average of 4 members for adults to 7 members for adolescents. Service workers and fellow residents made up a large proportion of these networks, especially for people living in large residential settings, and family members constituted a large part of the networks of people living with their families.

11. Romantic relationships were almost nonexistent.

12. The larger the residential setting, the fewer the number of integration activities and the more numerous the activities taking place within the residence.

13. Service workers' integration efforts were positively related to the friendliness of neighbors' attitudes toward the residents.

Overall, the research by Bouchard and Dumont adds a great deal of descriptive and explanatory detail to our knowledge of the community living situation of adults, adolescents, and children with mental retardation. It thus contains many helpful insights for parents, administrators, and direct service personnel.

1.9 INTEGRATION WITHIN BUELL AND MINNES'S ADAPTED ACCULTURATION PERSPECTIVE ON DEINSTITUTIONALIZATION

The last conceptualization that we shall review in this section was developed by Buell and Minnes (1994) of Queen's University (Kingston, Ontario). Buell and Minnes begin with an acculturation framework that, as used in crosscultural psychology (Berry, 1984), defines four basic ways in which smaller groups can interact within a larger, dominant culture. These four options result from answers to two key issues, namely, whether it is considered valuable for the smaller cultural group to maintain (1) its distinctive cultural identity and characteristics, and (2) its relationships with other groups. The first option, *integration,* results from an affirmative answer to both issues (i.e., the smaller group wishes to maintain both its cultural identity and characteristics and positive relations with the dominant culture). The second option, *assimilation,* is the result when the smaller group does not wish to maintain its distinctive cultural identity and characteristics but does want to have positive relations with the larger culture. The third option, *segregation* or *separation,* is the result when the smaller group wishes to maintain its cultural identity and characteristics but does not have positive relations with the larger culture, either because it has the power to separate itself from the dominant culture or, lacking such power, is segregated from (and presumably by) the larger culture. The fourth option, *marginalization,* is the result when the smaller group does not wish to maintain its distinctive identity and characteristics and does not have positive relations with the dominant culture.

In adapting this acculturation framework to developmental disabilities and specifically to deinstitutionalization and service-delivery efforts, Buell and Minnes (1994) define persons with developmental disabilities as the smaller cultural group. For them, the two key issues then become (1) Is it considered to be of value to recognize and support the unique characteristics of persons with developmental disabilities? and (2) Is it considered to be of value for persons with developmental disabilities to maintain relationships with other groups, including the wider society? In Buell and Minnes's adapted acculturation framework, the first option, *integration,* results from a service-delivery emphasis on supporting developmentally disabled persons' distinctive characteristics and on maintaining their relationships with other groups and the larger community. The second option, *assimilation,* results from a de-emphasis on developmentally disabled persons' distinctive characteristics while supporting their relations with the wider culture. The third option, *segregation,* results from an emphasis on supporting developmentally disabled persons' unique characteristics while preventing their ties with the wider society. The fourth option, *marginalization,* results from a de-emphasis on both developmentally disabled persons' unique characteristics and their relations with the broader culture.

According to Buell and Minnes (1994), the goal of Normalization (the term they use to refer to both Normalization and SRV) is assimilation, not integration:

> Here [i.e., for Normalization] the aim of service delivery is to develop "behaviours and characteristics as culturally normative as possible" [Wolfensberger, 1972, p. 28] ultimately indistinguishable from the general public, that is, a service delivery that transforms people from visible to invisible [Rhoades & Browning, 1982]. The adapted acculturation framework shows that service delivery based on Normalization principles is a resolution to Issue ONE that de-emphasizes the unique characteristics of persons with developmental disabilities. The answer is no to "whether the unique characteristics of persons with developmental disabilities are recognized and supported." This is explicitly stated in the definition of Normalization . . .

Service delivery based on Normalization would define a successful outcome as assimilation. (pp. 99-100)

In a review of deinstitutionalization outcome studies undertaken since 1972 (the year in which Wolfensberger's book on Normalization appeared), Buell and Minnes (1994) found that only 46% of the studies provided enough descriptive information to be coded as belonging to one of their four outcome categories. According to their Table 3 (p. 102), 26% of the studies were coded as exhibiting a *segregation* outcome, 17% an *integration* outcome, 2% an *assimilation* outcome, and 0% a *marginalization* outcome. Buell and Minnes interpreted their findings as contradicting Normalization because, empirically, integration and segregation were much more frequent outcomes of deinstitutionalization than assimilation.

We have included Buell and Minnes's (1994) conceptualization of integration because of its direct relevance to the primary objective of the present chapter, which is not the place for a detailed critique of their interpretation of Normalization/SRV or of their adapted acculturation framework. It must be pointed out, however, that Buell and Minnes's article suffers from a number of weaknesses and misconceptions, including the following:

1. Buell and Minnes do not take adequate account of the basic Normalization/SRV literature, including Wolfensberger's (1980) lengthy consideration of Normalization-related disagreements and misunderstandings, PASS (Wolfensberger & Glenn, 1975), and PASSING (Wolfensberger & Thomas, 1983). The Normalization/SRV literature argues that Normalization can be partial as well as full (Wolfensberger, 1980) and that, contrary to what Buell and Minnes (1994) assert, Normalization/SRV not only permits but often positively *requires* specialized supports to meet the needs of particular individuals (Wolfensberger, 1972, 1980; Wolfensberger & Glenn, 1975; Wolfensberger & Thomas, 1983). Earlier in the present chapter (pp. 266-267), for example, the need for supports was stated explicitly, in the third paragraph of the citation from Wolfensberger's (1998a) SRV monograph. This passage is consistent with his earlier writings on the topic.

2. Contrary to Buell and Minnes's argument, Normalization/SRV is concerned with individuals and individual outcomes, and not only with service delivery and service-delivery outcomes (Wolfensberger, 1980).

3. Normalization/SRV would almost certainly recognize as acceptable outcomes *both* integration and assimilation (even defined in the narrow service-delivery oriented and deinstitutionalization-related way preferred by Buell and Minnes), depending on the needs and characteristics of the people concerned. Thus, their interpretation of Normalization/SRV is inaccurate when they assert, in the citation given earlier (Buell & Minnes, 1994, p. 99), that the Normalization-derived "answer is no to 'whether the unique characteristics of persons with developmental disabilities are recognized and supported.' This is explicitly stated in the definition of Normalization."

4. The fact that Buell and Minnes's review of the deinstitutionalization literature found that segregation was a relatively frequent outcome would not surprise most people, least of all proponents of Normalization. This finding merely establishes that deinstitutionalization has often produced disappointing results, and can by no means be laid at the feet of Normalization/SRV. Wolfensberger (1980, p. 96) pointed out many years ago that "it is a constant struggle to secure even the most modest compliance with any of its [Normalization's] implications."

2 CONCEPTUALIZATION AND MEASUREMENT OF INTEGRATION IN THE LITERATURE ON PSYCHIATRIC DISABILITY

2.1 INTEGRATION WITHIN THE FIELD OF PSYCHIATRIC DISABILITIES

Deinstitutionalization and the development of community services supporting persons with psychiatric disabilities in the community has formed the cornerstone of mental health policy in many Western countries over the past 3 decades (Mechanic & Rochefort, 1990). As a result, a massive relocation of persons with psychiatric disabilities has taken place from institutions to community settings. A central objective of deinstitutionalization and associated community services has been the reintegration into the community of persons with persistent mental health problems (Segal & Aviram, 1978).

A review of the research literature on persons with psychiatric disabilities living in the community reveals a relatively small number of studies of integration into the community. Segal and Aviram (1978) conducted the first and most influential such study on this issue, investigating the "social integration" of persons with psychiatric disabilities who were living in sheltered-care facilities in California. Most subsequent studies on community integration of this population have relied heavily on Segal and Aviram's original definition of what they termed "external" social integration. Consequently, we have limited ourselves here to investigations that used their original definition or variations of it. Moreover, rather than attempting an exhaustive review, we have selected those published studies that we consider the most important investigations on the integration of persons with psychiatric disabilities. After examining conceptual and operational definitions of social integration, we present empirical findings on levels of integration attained by persons with psychiatric disabilities and key variables correlating with integration. We conclude with a discussion of the implications of the literature reviewed for practice and future research.

2.1.1 CONCEPTUAL AND OPERATIONAL DEFINITIONS OF SOCIAL INTEGRATION

Segal and Aviram's (1978) conceptual definition has been the one most widely used to describe the integration of persons with psychiatric disabilities in the community. According to them, five levels of involvement make up social integration: presence, access, participation, production, and consumption. *Presence* refers to the amount of time spent in the community. *Access* consists of the degree to which places, services, and social contacts are available to an individual. *Participation* is defined as the extent of involvement in activities with other people. *Production* refers to whether or not an individual participates in income-producing employment. Finally, *consumption* refers to the extent to which an individual manages his or her personal finances and purchases goods and services. Each level of involvement is seen as constituting a separate and sufficient condition that reflects integration into the community. A person's overall level of social integration is defined as the sum of his or her five levels of involvement.

Based on the location of involvement, Segal and Aviram (1978) distinguished between internal and external integration. *Internal integration* was defined as involvement occurring within sheltered-care facilities. The facility was considered the focus, and involvement was defined in relation to individuals, resources, or activities available within the facility. In contrast, *external integration* referred to involvement outside the facility, that is, in the community and shared with the general population. For purposes of the present chapter, we shall limit our attention to *external* integration, because only the latter is consistent with definitions of social integration in other areas of disability. As such, it subsumes access and use of community resources, as well as participation in activities with other members of the community.

Based on this conceptualization, Segal and Aviram (1978) developed a measure of external integration. Factor analyses of the responses of 393 residents of sheltered-care facilities for persons with psychiatric disabilities produced seven external-integration subscales: attending to oneself (e.g., involvement and time outside of the facility); access to community resources (e.g., library, community center, place of worship); access to basic or personal resources (e.g., meals, clothing, health care); access and participation with family members; access and participation with friends; social interaction through community groups (e.g., volunteer activities, social groups); and use of community facilities (e.g., visit to a park, attendance at an entertainment event). Scores on these subscales were summed to produce an overall external integration score.

Several subsequent studies developed briefer measures of "community" integration by selecting items from Segal and Aviram's (1978) external-integration scale that reflected behavioral involvement in leisure and work-related activities in the community (see, for example, Kruzich, 1985, or Nelson, Hall, Squire, and Walsh-Bowers, 1992).

2.1.2 EXTENT OF (EXTERNAL) SOCIAL INTEGRATION

Segal and Aviram's (1978) study provides the best estimate of the level of external social integration experienced by persons with psychiatric disabilities living in community sheltered-care facilities. In general, the picture that emerges from their research is one of varying degrees of social integration within this population, of whom the majority, however, describe themselves as having relatively low levels of involvement in the community. Specifically, Segal and Aviram identified a continuum of integration consisting of five levels, from low to high.

The first (least integrated) group was made up of individuals who had no independent access to community resources (e.g., stores or public transportation) or basic resources (e.g., laundry facilities or meals) and no contact with any community residents outside the facility. It was estimated that 12% of the sheltered-care population operated at this level. At the second level, individuals were able to access community resources and other basic resources; however, they had only minimal contact with family or friends, had no interaction with other community members, and never participated in activities or used recreational facilities in the community. The largest group of individuals (40%) from the postpsychiatric sheltered-care population were at this level. A group of similar size (38%) comprised the third level of the continuum. Besides being able to access resources in the community, they also reported having some contact with family and friends outside their facility. However, members of this group rarely used community facilities or interacted with other community members. Relatively few individuals (9%) were at the fourth level, which included those who sometimes used community facilities and interacted with community members. Finally, a very small group of individuals (1%) was at the highest level of integration, reporting easy access to resources in the community, frequent participation in community activities, and numerous contacts with family, friends, and other community residents.

It is difficult to determine the generalizability of Segal and Aviram's (1978) survey results to persons with psychiatric disabilities in other locales and the extent to which their findings may have changed over the past 20 years. A follow-up of Segal and Aviram's sample 10 years after the original survey showed a small decrease (5%) in participants' overall level of social integration, even after the researchers had corrected their data for the contribution that an increase in age had made to the reduction (Segal & Kotler, 1993).

In more recent research conducted in Ottawa, Ontario, Aubry and Myner (1996) compared the community integration of persons with psychiatric disabilities with that of their nondisabled neighbors. For their study, Aubry and Myner used a broadened definition of community integration that included physical presence in the community, corresponding to Segal and Aviram's (1978) definition of external integration, in addition to psychological and social aspects contributing to community integration. The researchers defined physical presence in the community as physical integration. Psychological aspects of community integration, referred to as psychological integration, involved the extent to which individuals perceived themselves as being similar to neighbors and felt part of the neighborhood. Social aspects of community integration, called social integration in the study, entailed the degree of social contact with neighbors.

A comparison of a group of 51 persons with psychiatric disabilities with a group of 51 nondisabled matched according to sex and location (i.e., living within one square block) on the different types of community integration found differences between the two groups emerging only in the area of social integration (Aubry & Myner, 1996). In particular, persons with psychiatric disabilities were found to have much less social contact with their neighbors.

An item-by-item examination of differences on the social integration measure showed differences emerging especially in relation to closer forms of contact (e.g., going on a social outing, being invited into a person's home) requiring spending more time with neighbors, with persons with psychiatric disabilities rarely engaging in these kinds of contacts (Aubry & Myner, 1996). The researchers concluded that their findings suggested that persons with psychiatric disabilities were achieving some community integration, at least in being present in and feeling part of the community, when compared to their neighbors. However, Aubry and Myner noted that they were lagging in the most important type of integration, namely having regular social interaction with nondisabled persons living in physical proximity.

Overall, research on the extent of external social integration suggests that the majority of persons with psychiatric disabilities have achieved only limited integration in the community and remain for the most part socially isolated from nondisabled persons. It is important to note that the majority of studies examining integration of this population have focused on those individuals with psychiatric disabilities who live in congregate housing programs. Recent service initiatives in North America have focused on supporting persons with psychiatric disabilities to live independently in regular housing with the assumption that it will facilitate greater integration (Carling, 1990; Ridgway & Zipple, 1990). No research to date has examined whether placing persons in these living contexts will indeed produce integration comparable to that of nondisabled community residents.

2.2 CORRELATES OF (EXTERNAL) SOCIAL INTEGRATION

Researchers have identified three types of correlates of the integration of persons with psychiatric disabilities in the community, namely, community, facility, and individual characteristics, representing different levels of analysis. Therefore, our review of findings on correlates will be organized according to these clusters of characteristics.

2.2.1 COMMUNITY CHARACTERISTICS

Studies examining community characteristics have focused on the population makeup of the geographical area in which an individual lives, the location of his or her residence in relation to community resources, and the response of community residents. Trute and Segal (1976) investigated census-tract characteristics that predicted external social integration among samples of persons with psychiatric disabilities living in sheltered-care facilities in California and Saskatchewan. Census-tract characteristics predictive of greater social integration among urban residents included a greater proportion of seniors (i.e., over 65 years old) and youth (i.e., between 15 and 24 years old), a greater proportion of households of six or more persons, a larger proportion of rented occupied dwellings, and a lower proportion of low-income families (i.e., less than $15,000) and middle-aged persons (i.e., 35 to 54 years old). Census-tract predictors of greater social

integration in rural areas included a higher proportion of rented dwellings and nonfamily members in households, a higher proportion of youth under 15, a lower proportion of individuals aged 15 to 24, and a lower proportion of married individuals.

Based on their findings, Trute and Segal (1976) identified geographic areas that facilitated higher external social integration for persons with psychiatric disabilities. In particular, they concluded that "supportive" communities were those that had moderate social organization, having neither high social cohesion nor severe social disorganization. Suburban areas with a high proportion of single family dwellings are typically socially cohesive, while communities with severe social disorganization are those with high levels of crime, delinquency, drug consumption, and suicide (e.g., inner-city ghettos and slum areas). Recent research suggests that a majority of persons with psychiatric disabilities live in less desirable, high-crime neighborhoods that would be characterized as socially disorganized (Newman, 1994).

Using Trute and Segal's (1976) California sample of sheltered-care residents, Segal, Baumohl, and Moyles (1980) developed a typology of neighborhoods to identify urban areas that are facilitative of sheltered-care residents' external social integration. Factor analyses of census-tract data related to the location of sheltered-care facilities produced five dimensions: degree of political conservatism based on voting patterns, family orientation (i.e., high rate of family- and owner-occupied homes), socioeconomic status, crime rates, and degree of nontraditional political activity (i.e., based on political affiliation and voting patterns in referendums). The neighborhoods found to be most conducive of the social integration of persons with psychiatric disabilities were liberal and nontraditional in political orientation and of mixed-income composition. Neighborhoods with conservative, working-class populations also appeared to facilitate social integration. In contrast, neighborhoods with conservative, middle-class populations appeared to impede social integration.

Segal et al. (1980) also examined neighborhood "restrictiveness" (i.e., the receptivity or lack thereof of community residents, as perceived by facility operators and sheltered-care residents). The results of these analyses were used to explain the different levels of social integration associated with different types of neighborhoods. In particular, an extreme negative reaction by community members appeared to present a significant barrier to sheltered-care residents' achieving social integration. In both liberal mixed-income and conservative working-class neighborhoods, on the other hand, a moderate amount of negative reaction by community residents was typically present and appeared to stimulate social integration by constructively pressuring facilities to provide good services.

The importance of neighbors' reactions was further highlighted in Segal and Aviram's (1978) findings. Of all the predictors at different levels examined in their study, a positive response of neighbors (i.e., being invited into neighbors' homes, having ongoing meaningful contact with neighbors) was found to be the most important in determining social integration. Conversely, the frequency of complaints to operators of sheltered-care facilities was negatively related to social integration. Similarly, Aubry and Myner (1996) found that more social interaction with neighbors by nondisabled residents in a neighborhood was associated with greater social contact with neighbors by persons with psychiatric disabilities living in the same neighborhood.

Other community characteristics reported by Segal and Aviram (1978) as impeding the external social integration of persons with psychiatric disabilities living in sheltered-care facilities included greater facility distance from community resources and rural facility location. Facilities that were more distant from community resources (e.g., parks, libraries, medical services, vocational rehabilitation) frequently developed their own programs and services, which encouraged the isolation of their residents from the rest of the community. The lower degree of social integration achieved by persons in rural facilities was explained in terms of a lesser degree of openness in rural communities toward facility residents. Also, rural facilities tended to house older individuals who were more chronically disabled than those residing in urban facilities.

Kruzich (1985) extended these findings on facility location by examining social integration among persons with psychiatric disabilities living in different-sized cities. She found individuals in cities of 10,000 to 100,000 inhabitants to be the most integrated, followed by those in small towns and rural areas (i.e., population less than 10,000). Individuals in cities over 100,000 proved to be the least integrated. These findings were interpreted as showing that midsized cities (10,000 to 100,000) had the right amount and kind of community resources to facilitate community participation, whereas in large cities greater distances to community resources and safety concerns impeded social integration.

In sum, the findings on the relationship between community characteristics and external social integration highlight the importance of ecological factors. Variables such as city size; neighborhood population mix; community residents' response to facilities, their occupants, and their neighbors; and distance to community resources appear to be important determinants of the social integration of persons with psychiatric disabilities. In fact, both Segal and Aviram (1978) and Kruzich (1985) found community characteristics to be more important predictors of social integration than facility or individual characteristics. Unfortunately, housing programs for persons with psychiatric disabilities have often been located in communities and neighborhoods with characteristics that are more likely to impede social integration (Goldstein, Brown, & Goodrich, 1989; Newman, 1994).

2.2.2 FACILITY CHARACTERISTICS

Segal and Aviram (1978) identified two facility variables as significant predictors of external social integration: the extent to which a facility has an ideal psychiatric environment and the degree to which facility residents are isolated from the community. Based on Moos's (1972) conceptualization of the social climate of community-oriented programs, an "ideal psychiatric environment" referred to a setting with high levels of resident involvement, staff and resident support, and spontaneity and autonomy, and which communicated clear expectations of residents, provided training opportunities in practical skills, and encouraged the expression of anger and open discussion of problems. Not surprisingly, more ideal psychiatric environments were found to produce greater external social integration of residents.

The other facility characteristic found by Segal and Aviram to be predictive of external social integration was the extent that facilities promoted contacts with family and neighbors. Overall, however, Segal and Aviram (1978) found facility characteristics to be less important predictors of integration than community or individual characteristics.

Kruzich (1985) found three facility characteristics to be predictive of external social integration, after controlling for age, psychosocial functioning, and involvement with others outside the residence: depersonalizing staff practices, availability of social skills training in facilities, and type of facility. Specifically, facilities with staff who recognized residents' individuality (e.g., by ensuring that residents had personal possessions or by celebrating their birthdays) and had more social-skills training tended to produce higher levels of social integration. In addition, residents living in congregate-care facilities reported higher levels of external social integration than those in intermediate-care or nursing facilities.

Nelson et al. (1992) compared the external social integration of persons living in different types of housing programs. Their results showed that individuals living in group homes or supported apartments (i.e., independent living with support tailored to needs) experienced greater external social integration than individuals living in board-and-care homes. Individuals in group homes and supported apartments also received more support from friends and professionals and reported more independent functioning than those living in board-and-care homes. Nelson and his colleagues suggested that their findings support the development of more supportive residential options for persons with psychiatric disabilities living in the community.

Given the wide variety of housing programs that have been developed (Trainor, Morrell-Bellai, Ballantyne, & Boydell, 1993), the contribution of facility characteristics to social integration of its residents is an important issue that has received surprisingly little research attention. Housing programs have been one of the major vehicles for integrating deinstitutionalized psychiatric patients into the community. Further research is needed on the program factors and residence characteristics that facilitate or impede integration in order to help improve existing housing programs and develop new housing models.

2.2.3   INDIVIDUAL CHARACTERISTICS

A number of individual characteristics have been found to be associated with external social integration. In particular, greater external social integration is related to a lower level of psychopathology; a higher level of psychosocial ability; possession of more spending money; being a voluntary resident in a housing facility; having greater control over one's finances; being of younger age; being more involved with others outside the facility, including neighbors; and exchanging more support with social-network members (Aubry & Myner, 1996; Kruzich, 1985; Nelson et al., 1992; Segal & Aviram, 1978).

Segal and Aviram (1978) identified having sufficient spending money, having control over one's finances, and being a voluntary resident as individual characteristics that a residential setting could alter in order to improve residents' external social integration. These findings suggest that residents in settings that promote autonomy tend to be more socially integrated in the community.

Nelson et al. (1992) investigated the relationship of different social-network transactions to different areas of community adaptation, including the community integration of persons with psychiatric disabilities. They found that receiving unsupportive transactions related to emotional and social issues from social network members and providing supportive transactions to network members were positively related to external social integration. These findings were interpreted as reflecting the fact that involvement in community activities exposes persons with psychiatric disabilities to both positive and negative aspects of social contact with others.

As previously mentioned, Segal and Kotler (1993) performed a 10-year follow-up of persons living in sheltered care facilities in California who had participated in Segal and Aviram's (1978) original study. On average, the participants showed a small decrease in external social integration over the 10-year period. The specific aspects of social integration showing the greatest decline included access to and participation with family (-31%), access to basic and personal resources (-30%), and taking care of one's own purchasing needs (-26%). The researchers concluded that the length of residency in sheltered-care facilities contributed to increased dependence inside the facility and decreased integration outside the facility.

Finally, Aubry and Myner (1996) found that greater physical presence in the community (i.e., consonant with Segal and Aviram's external social integration) for persons with psychiatric disabilities was related to having more contact with neighbors but not to their psychological integration (i.e., feeling part of the neighborhood) nor to their subjective quality of life (i.e., global life satisfaction). Not surprisingly, they also reported that greater contact with neighbors for persons with psychiatric disabilities was related to them having a higher level of psychological integration.

2.3 SUMMARY ON THE INTEGRATION OF PERSONS WITH PSYCHIATRIC DISABILITIES IN THE COMMUNITY

A number of conclusions can be drawn from our review of the literature on the external social integration of persons with psychiatric disabilities in the community. It would appear that after 30 years of deinstitutionalization, the integration of persons with psychiatric disabilities into the community remains an elusive goal. On the one hand, persons with psychiatric disabilities are present in the community to the extent of accessing and using resources on their own. On the other hand, only a small proportion appear to have regular interactions with family, friends, or other community residents.

Research suggests that environmental factors, in the form of community characteristics and facility characteristics, play an important role in facilitating or impeding integration. The importance of where persons with psychiatric disabilities live has probably been underestimated. The location of housing programs for this population often appears to have been based mainly on finding neighborhoods whose residents will not oppose having them in close proximity (Goldstein et al., 1989). Also, despite the empirical evidence of the importance of ecological factors, minimal attention appears to have been placed on designing residential programs that will promote community integration.

It is noteworthy that most of the research examining the integration of persons with psychiatric disabilities has been conducted on residents of specialized congregate-housing programs. In the wake of deinstitutionalization, such programs have served as the main mechanism for facilitating the community integration of persons with psychiatric disabilities in Canada and the United States (Cutler, 1986; Trainor et al., 1993). At the same time, opportunities for living in specialized housing programs are only available to a small percentage of persons with psychiatric disabilities in North America (Randolph, Ridgway, & Carling, 1991; Trainor et al., 1993).

Homelessness, single-room occupancy hotels, overnight shelters, and nursing homes make up the most prevalent living situations for this group (Mechanic & Rochefort, 1990). Although it has not been investigated empirically, the assumption is highly tenable that individuals in these settings experience much less integration into the community than those living in housing programs.

Strong criticisms have recently emerged of specialized congregate housing that purports to integrate persons with psychiatric disabilities (Carling, 1990, 1992; Ridgway & Zipple, 1990). Specifically, it has been argued that this housing approach may actually serve as a barrier to the assumption of normal roles in the community by segregating and stigmatizing persons with psychiatric disabilities (Ridgway & Zipple, 1990).

An alternative approach, involving independent living in normal housing with necessary supports, is currently being proposed. Much of the current focus in psychiatric rehabilitation in North America is related to developing effective community supports that will enable this kind of independent living (Blanch, Carling, & Ridgway, 1988).

A limitation of the definition of external social integration developed by Segal and Aviram (1978) and adopted by other researchers is that it defines integration in a relatively passive fashion, such that the term is limited to accessing and using resources and participating in activities in the community, with, at best, minimal involvement with nondisabled community members being seen as necessary (Sherman, Frenkel, & Newman, 1986). This early conceptualization of integration may reflect the original objectives of deinstitutionalization, which focused more on physically locating individuals in the community than on helping them build strong social relationships with other members of the community.

As in the case of the integration of people with other disabilities, a call for more active and equitable community participation in the areas of housing, work, and social interaction is being made by persons with psychiatric disabilities, their family members, and many support-providers working with them (Carling, 1990). In line with this evolution, some researchers have recently broadened the definition of social integration to include social network transactions (Parks & Pilisuk, 1984; Nelson et al., 1992) and social interactions with friends, neighbors, and relatives (Aubry & Myner, 1996; Sherman et al., 1986; Trute, 1986). Future research in this area would do well to follow their lead, using an expanded conceptualization of integration that includes active involvement with nondisabled community residents.

3 CONCLUSION

The foregoing review of the literature in developmental and psychiatric disability makes it clear that the concept of integration, which for the last quarter-century has been a key objective of service programs, government legislation, and social policy, has also begun to have an impact on and benefit from the scrutiny of empirical research. Indeed, a new emphasis on variables such as integration, lifestyle Normalization, social support, and personal satisfaction has begun to replace the often vague and conceptually barren construct of "adjustment to the community" that dominated much earlier research (Gordon et al., 1992). However, in order that research on integration realize its considerable potential, we believe that a number of steps need to be taken.

First, clear conceptual and operational definitions of integration are essential. The most insightful and informative research in the literature reviewed was based on such definitions. Moreover, of the various conceptualizations of integration reviewed, we see Wolfensberger's "personal social integration and valued social participation" as ultimately the richest and most useful. It will be recalled that Wolfensberger (1998b, p. 59) defined "real" integration as "valued participation by a (devalued) person in a culturally normative quantity of contacts, interactions, relationships, and roles with ordinary and valued citizens, in valued (or at least normative) activities, and in valued (or at least ordinary) physical and social settings." Even though research and common experience suggest that "real" integration, so defined, is relatively rare, the concept affords a high and worthy target at which service supports, practices, and policies may productively aim.

Second, other forms of integration (which are likely to be variants of physical integration) are also worth investigating, whether we refer to them as community presence, community integration, or participation in community activities. What is important is that such phenomena be clearly distinguished from personal social integration and valued social participation. In the same vein, we think it essential that physical integration and social integration continue to be clearly differentiated from one another, as research in a number of countries has consistently shown that the attainment of physical integration is typically much more satisfactory than the achievement of social integration.

Third, future theorizing and empirical research on integration should be more directly informed by and embedded in well-established social science theoretical frameworks, such as social network, social support, social role, or stress-coping theory. In making such links, researchers could profitably follow the lead of Lemay in his work on social roles (chapter 10 in this volume); Burchard and her colleagues' research on Normalization in residential services (summarized in chapter 11 in this volume); Newton and his colleagues' investigation of the social lives of persons with mental retardation; Bouchard and Dumont's research on community living among adults, adolescents, and children with mental retardation; and Nelson and his colleagues' research on the social networks and exchange of social support among persons with psychiatric disabilities. The conduct of the kind of research on integration that we have in mind would require a detailed knowledge of both Normalization and SRV as well as of mainstream social science sources, such as Cohen and Wills (1985), Hobfoll and Vaux (1993), and Veiel and Baumann (1992), to cite but a few examples.

Fourth, there is an urgent need for a multidimensional, psychometrically sound measure of integration on the individual level. The foregoing review indicates that no such measure currently exists.

Bouchard and Dumont's (1996) measures are based on a conceptualization of social integration that we believe (as we noted earlier) is too closely akin to "physical integration" or simply "social-activity-based social interactions" to fill the gap, and PASS (Wolfensberger & Glenn, 1975) and PASSING (Wolfensberger & Thomas, 1983) are pitched primarily at the program rather than the individual level. Wolfensberger's (1998b) conceptual definition of "real" integration, as "personal social integration and valued social participation," would be an appropriate starting point for the construction of such a measure.

Fifth, there is a need to further identify the individual and environmental antecedents of integration. Burchard and her colleagues and Bouchard and Dumont showed, for example, that the level of impairment and the level of adaptive behavior, respectively, influence the extent and style of integration. Similarly, the literature in both developmental and psychiatric disability indicated that different residential environments were associated with different levels of integration. Burchard et al. (1992), for example, observed that in supportive apartments (i.e., in the type of residential setting promoting the highest level of personal responsibility, independence, and control over one's own life), the highest levels of independent behavior, lifestyle Normalization, physical integration, and job insertion were to be found. They also found that apartment residents, like those who live with their natural families, were more socially integrated and more satisfied with their residential situation than those living in group homes.

Sixth, the research of Burchard and her colleagues, Halpern and his colleagues, and Bouchard and Dumont suggests that integration and psychological well-being may, under many conditions, be relatively independent phenomena. To the extent that integration constitutes an *objective* aspect and psychological well-being a *subjective* aspect of QOL, this finding of relative independence is not surprising. In fact, it is consistent with the weak relationship often found in the empirical literature between objective and subjective indicators of QOL. Embedding future integration research within a social network and social support framework, as we suggested earlier, would doubtless clarify the specific conditions under which integration and psychological well-being may be expected to be relatively independent or, on the contrary, related.

Finally, in light of the very limited amount of interaction reported in the literature between people with developmental or psychiatric disabilities and the general public (other than members of the people's families), more applied research along the lines of that of Newton, Horner, and their colleagues would certainly be desirable. The Oregon group appears to be virtually unique in its emphasis on devising and evaluating practical ways of improving the social relationships of people with mental retardation, including their relationships with ordinary citizens. Encouragingly, the Oregon research has shown that increases in activity patterns, social networks, and preferred modes of social participation are related to increases in social relationships and integration. Their work, like that of Burchard and her colleagues, of Bouchard and Dumont, and of Nelson and his colleagues, illustrates the promise of social network, social role, and social support theory as fundamental perspectives from which to approach integration issues and, more broadly, many Normalization and SRV questions.

REFERENCES

ANDERSON, D. J., LAKIN, K. C., HILL, B. K., & CHEN, T. H. (1992). Social integration of older persons with mental retardation in residential facilities. *American Journal on Mental Retardation, 96,* 488-501.

AUBRY, T., & MYNER, J. (1996). Community integration and quality of life: A comparison of persons with psychiatric disabilities in housing programs and community residents who are neighbors. *Canadian Journal of Community Mental Health, 15,* 5-20.

BARRERA, M., JR., & AINSLEY, S. L. (1983). The structure of social support: A conceptual and empirical analysis. *Journal of Community Psychology, 11,* 133-143.

BERRY, J. W. (1984). Cultural relations in plural society: Alternatives to segregation and their sociopsychological implications. In N. MILLER & M. B. BREWER (Eds.), *Groups in contact: The psychology of desegregation* (pp. 11-27). San Francisco: Academic.

BLANCH, A. K., CARLING, P. J., & RIDGWAY, P. (1988). Normal housing with specialized supports: A psychiatric rehabilitation approach to living in the community. *Rehabilitation Psychology, 33,* 47-55.

BOLDUC, M. (1989). *Lignes directrices d'une recherche évaluative portant sur la qualité de vie et l'intégration sociale des personnes présentant une déficience intellectuelle.* Québec, QC: Ministère de la Santé et des Services sociaux, Direction de l'évaluation, Service de l'évaluation, réadaptation et services de longue durée.

BORGATTI, S. P., EVERETT, M. G., & FREEMAN, L. C. (1992). UCINET IV (Version 1.64) [Computer software]. Columbia, SC: Analytic Technologies.

BOUCHARD, C., & DUMONT, M. (1996). *Où est Phil, comment se porte-t-il et pourquoi? Une étude sur l'intégration sociale et le bien-être des personnes présentant une déficience intellectuelle.* Québec, QC: Gouvernement du Québec, Ministère de la Santé et des Services sociaux, Direction générale de la planification et de l'évaluation.

BRUININKS, R., HILL, B., WEATHERMAN, R., & WOODCOCK, R. (1986). *Inventory for client and agency planning.* Allen, TX: DLM Teaching Resources.

BUELL, M. K., & MINNES, P. M. (1994). An acculturation perspective on deinstitutionalization and service delivery. *Journal on Developmental Disabilities, 3,* 94-107.

BURCHARD, S. N., GORDON, L. R., & PINE, J. (1990). Manager competence, program Normalization and client satisfaction in group homes. *Education and Training in Mental Retardation, 25,* 277-285.

BURCHARD, S. N., HASAZI, J. S., GORDON, L. R., & YOE, J. (1991). An examination of lifestyle and adjustment in three community residential alternatives. *Research in Developmental Disabilities, 12,* 127-142.

BURCHARD, S. N., PINE, J., GORDON, L. R., JOFFE, J. M., WIDRICK, G. C., & GOY, E. (1987). The relationship of manager competence to program quality in small community residences. In J. A. MULICK & R. F. ANTONAK (Eds.), *Issues in therapeutic intervention. Transitions in mental retardation* (Vol. 2). Norwood, NJ: Ablex.

BURCHARD, S. N., ROSEN, J. W., GORDON, L. R., HASAZI, J. S., YOE, J., & DIETZEL, L. C. (1992). A comparison of social support and satisfaction among adults with mental retardation living in three types of community residential alternatives. In J. W. JACOBSON, S. N. BURCHARD, & P. J. CARLING (Eds.), *Community living for people with developmental and psychiatric disabilities* (pp. 137-154). Baltimore: John Hopkins University Press.

BURT, R. S. (1991). STRUCTURE (Version 4.2) [Computer Software]. New York: Columbia University, Center for the Social Sciences.

CAMPO, S. F., SHARPTON, W. R., THOMPSON, B., & SEXTON, D. (1997). Correlates of the quality of life of adults with severe or profound mental retardation. *Mental Retardation, 35,* 329-337.

CARLING, P. (1990). Major mental illness, housing, and supports: The promise of community integration. *American Psychologist, 45,* 969-975.

CARLING, P. (1992). Homes or group homes: Future approaches to housing, support and integration for people with psychiatric disabilities. *Adult Residential Care Journal, 6,* 87-96.

COHEN, S., & WILLS, T. A. (1985). Stress, social support, and the buffering hypothesis. *Psychological Bulletin, 98,* 310-357.

CUTLER, D. L. (1986). Community residential options for the chronically mentally ill. *Community Mental Health Journal, 22,* 361-373.

DANSEREAU, J., DUTEAU, C., ELY, P., & FLYNN, R.J. (1990). *Évaluation des programmes résidentiels en santé mentale de l'Outaouais.* Hull, QC: Conseil régional de la Santé et des Services sociaux de l'Outaouais.

DAVIDSON, P. W., & ADAMS, E. (1989). Indicators of impact of services on persons with developmental disabilities: Issues concerning data-collection mandates in P. L. 100-146. *Mental Retardation, 27,* 297-304.

DEVELOPMENTAL DISABILITIES ASSISTANCE AND BILL OF RIGHTS ACT AMENDMENTS OF 1987. Pub. L. No. 100-147, §101, Stat. 840 (1987).

EDGERTON, R. B. (1988). Aging in the community: A matter of choice. *American Journal on Mental Retardation, 92,* 331-335.

ELLIS, J. W. (1990). Presidential address 1990—Mental retardation at the close of the 20th century: A new realism. *Mental Retardation, 28,* 263-267.

FELCE, D. (1995). Summing up: Safeguarding quality. In D. Pilling & G. Watson (Eds.), *Evaluating quality in services for disabled and older people* (pp. 213-216). London, UK & Bristol, PA: Jessica Kingsley Publishers.

FLYNN, R. J. (1993). Intégration et évaluation de programmes: Comparaisons internationales. In S. IONESCU, G. MAGEROTTE, W. PILON, & R. SALABREUX (Eds.), *L'intégration des personnes présentant une déficience intellectuelle* (pp. 5-15). Actes du IIIe Congrès de l'Association internationale de recherche scientifique en faveur des personnes handicapées mentales (AIRHM). Trois-Rivières, QC: Université du Québec à Trois-Rivières et AIRHM.

FLYNN, R. J. (1994). L'intégration sociale entre 1982 et 1992: Définitions conceptuelles et opérationnelles. In OFFICE DES PERSONNES HANDICAPÉES DU QUÉBEC (Ed.), *Élargir les horizons: Perspectives scientifiques sur l'intégration sociale* (pp. 515-525). Sainte-Foy, QC & Paris: Éditions Multimondes et Agence Ibis Press.

FLYNN, R. J., GUIRGUIS, M., WOLFENSBERGER, W., & COCKS, E. (in press). Cross-validated factor structures and factor-based subscales for PASS and PASSING. *Mental Retardation.*

FLYNN, R. J., LAPOINTE, N., WOLFENSBERGER, W., & THOMAS, S. (1991). Quality of institutional and community human service prograrns in Canada and the United States. *Journal of Psychiatry and Neuroscience, 16,* 146-153.

GOLDSTEIN, M. B., BROWN, C. H., & GOODRICH, E. J. (1989). Public preferences and site location of residential treatment facilities. *Journal of Community Psychology, 19,* 186-193.

GOTTLIEB, B. H. (1983). *Social support strategies: Guidelines for mental health practices.* Beverly Hills, CA: Sage.

GORDON, L. R., BURCHARD, S. N., HASAZI, J. E., YOE, J. T., DIETZEL, L. C., & SIMONEAU, D. (1992). Stability and change in the life-style and adjustment of adults with mental retardation living in community residences. In J. W. JACOBSON, S. N. BURCHARD, & P. J. CARLING (Eds.), *Community living for people with developmental and psychiatric disabilities* (pp. 167-182). Baltimore: John Hopkins University Press.

GROUPE DE TRAVAIL MINISTÉRIEL SUR L'EXAMEN DES PROGRAMMES. (1987). *L'intégration des personnes présentant une déficience intellectuelle, un impératif humain et social. Rapport préliminaire.* Québec, QC: Ministère de la Santé et des Services sociaux.

GROUPE DE TRAVAIL MINISTÉRIEL SUR L'EXAMEN DES PROGRAMMES. (1988). *L'intégration des personnes présentant une déficience intellectuelle, un impératif humain et social, orientations et guide d'action.* Québec, QC: Ministère de la Santé et des Services sociaux.

HAELEWYCK, M. C. (1995-1996). *Le réseau de*

soutien social et les activités des personnes adultes qui présentent un retard mental et vivent dans des conditions résidentielles contrastées. Unpublished doctoral dissertation, Faculté des Sciences Psycho-Pédagogiques, Université de Mons-Hainaut, Belgique.

HALPERN, A. S. (1989). A systematic approach to transition programming for adolescents and young adults with disabilities. *Australia and New Zealand Journal of Developmental Disabilities, 15,* 1-13.

HALPERN, A. S., NAVE, G., CLOSE, D. W., & NELSON, D. (1986). An empirical analysis of the dimensions of community adjustment for adults with mental retardation in semi-independent living programs. *Australia and New Zealand Journal of Developmental Disabilities, 12,* 147-157.

HASAZI, J. E., BURCHARD, S. N., GORDON, L. R., VECCHIONE, E., & ROSEN, J. W. (1992). Adjustment to community life: The role of stress and support variables. In J. W. JACOBSON, S. N. BURCHARD, & P. J. CARLING (Eds.), *Community living for people with developmental and psychiatric disabilities* (pp. 111-124). Baltimore: John Hopkins University Press.

HEAL, L. W. (1988). The ideological responses of society to its handicapped members. In L. W. HEAL, J. I. HANEY, & A. R. NOVAK AMADO (Eds.), *Integration of developmentally disabled individuals into the community* (2nd ed., pp. 59-67). Baltimore: Paul H. Brookes.

HEITZMANN, C. A., & KAPLAN, R. M. (1988). Assessment of methods for measuring social support. *Health Psychology, 7,* 75-109.

HOBFOLL, S. E., & VAUX, A. (1993). Social support: Social resources and social context. In L. GOLDBERGER & S. BREZNITZ (Eds.), *Handbook of stress: Theoretical and clinical aspects* (2nd ed., pp. 685-705). New York: Free Press.

HOUSE, J. S., & KAHN, R. L. (1985). Measures and concepts of social support. In S. COHEN & S. L. SYME (Eds.), *Social support and health* (pp. 83-108). Orlando, FL: Academic Press.

IONESCU, S., MAGEROTTE, G., PILON, W., & SALBREUX, R. (1993). *Intégration des personnes présentant une déficience intellectuelle.* Actes du IIIe Congrès de l'Association internationale de recherche scientifique en faveur des personnes handicapées mentales, Trois-Rivières, Québec, 23-25 août 1993. Trois-Rivières, QC: Université du Québec à Trois-Rivières et AIRHM.

JACOBSON, J. W., BURCHARD, S. N., & CARLING, P. J. (1992). Summary: Community living and community engagement. In J. W. JACOBSON, S. N. BURCHARD, & P. J. CARLING (Eds.), *Community living for people with developmental and psychiatric disabilities* (pp. 303-306). Baltimore: John Hopkins University Press.

KENNEDY, C. H., HORNER, R. H., & NEWTON, J. S. (1989). Social contacts of adults with severe disabilities living in the community: A descriptive analysis of relationship patterns. *Journal of the Association for Persons With Severe Handicaps, 14,* 190-196.

KENNEDY, C. H., HORNER, R. H., & NEWTON, J. S. (1990). The social networks and activity patterns of adults with severe disabilities: A correlational analysis. *Journal of the Association for Persons With Severe Handicaps, 15,* 86-90.

KOEHLY, L. M., & SHIVY, V. A. (1998). Social network analysis: A new methodology for counseling research. *Journal of Counseling Psychology, 45,* 3-17.

KOZLESKI, E. B., & SANDS, D. J. (1992). The yardstick of social validity: Evaluating quality of life as perceived by adults without disabilities. *Education and Training in Mental Retardation, 27,* 119-131.

KRUZICH, J. M. (1985). Community integration of the mentally ill in residential facilities. *American Journal of Community Psychology, 13,* 553-564.

LAKIN, K. C., & BRUININKS, R. H. (1985). Contemporary services for handicapped children and youth. In R. H. BRUININKS & K. C. LAKIN (Eds.), *Living and learning in the least restrictive environment* (pp. 3-22). Baltimore: Paul H. Brookes.

MANK, D. M., & BUCKLEY, J. (1989). Strategies for integrating employment environments. In W. KIERNAN & R. SCHALOCK (Eds.), *Economics, industry, and disability: A look ahead* (pp. 319-335). Baltimore: Paul H. Brookes.

MCGREW, K. S., BRUININKS, R. H., & THURLOW, M. L. (1992). Relationship between measures of adaptive functioning and community adjustment for adults with mental retardation. *Exceptional Children, 58,* 517-529.

MCGREW, K. S., BRUININKS, R. H., THURLOW, M. L., & LEWIS, D. (1992). Empirical analysis of multidimensional measures of community adjustment for young adults with mental retardation. *American Journal on Mental Retardation, 96,* 475-487.

MECHANIC, D., & ROCHEFORT, D. A. (1990). Deinstitutionalization: An appraisal of reform. *Annual Review of Sociology, 16,* 301-327.

MOOS, R. (1972). Assessment of the psychosocial environment of community-oriented psychiatric treatment programs. *Journal of Abnormal Psychology, 79,* 9-18.

NELSON, G., HALL, G. B., SQUIRE, D., & WALSH-BOWERS, R. T. (1992). Social network transactions of psychiatric patients. *Social Science and Medicine, 34,* 433-445.

NEWMAN, S. J. (1994). The housing and neighborhood conditions of persons with severe mental illness. *Hospital and Community Psychiatry, 45,* 338-345.

NEWTON, J. S., & HORNER, R. H. (1993). Using a social guide to improve social relationships of people with severe disabilities. *Journal of the Association for Persons With Severe Handicaps, 18,* 36-45.

NEWTON, J. S., & HORNER, R. H. (1995). Feedback to staff on resident lifestyle: A descriptive analysis. *Behavior Modification, 19,* 95-118.

NEWTON, J. S., HORNER, R. H., ARD, JR., W. W., LEBARON, N., & SAPPINGTON, G. (1994). A conceptual model for improving the social life of individuals with mental retardation. *Mental Retardation, 32,* 393-402.

NEWTON, J. S., OLSON, D., & HORNER, R. H. (1995). Factors contributing to the stability of social relationships between individuals with mental retardation and other community members. *Mental Retardation, 33,* 383-393.

NEWTON, J. S., ARD, JR., W. R., HORNER, R. H., & TOEWS, J. D. (1996). Focusing on values and lifestyle outcomes in an effort to improve the quality of residential services in Oregon. *Mental Retardation, 34,* 1-12.

NIRJE, B. (1969). The Normalization principle and its human management implications. In R. B. KUGEL & W. WOLFENSBERGER (Eds.), *Changing patterns in residential services for the mentally retarded.* Washington, DC: President's Committee on Mental Retardation.

NIRJE, B. (1976). The Normalization principle and its human management implications. In R. B. KUGEL & A. SHEARER (Eds.), *Changing patterns in residential services for the mentally retarded.* Washington, DC: President's Committee on Mental Retardation.

NIRJE, B. (1980). The Normalization principle. In R. J. FLYNN & K. E. NITSCH (Eds.), *Normalization, social integration and community services* (pp. 31-49). Baltimore: University Park Press.

OFFICE DES PERSONNES HANDICAPÉES DU QUÉBEC. (1984). *À part . . . égale. L'intégration sociale des personnes handicapées: Un défi pour tous.* Drummondville: Les Publications du Québec.

OFFICE DES PERSONNES HANDICAPÉES DU QUÉBEC. (1994). *Élargir les horizons: Perspectives scientifiques sur l'intégration sociale.* Sainte-Foy, QC & Paris: Éditions Multimondes et Agence Ibis Press.

OUELLETTE, L., HORNER, R. H., & NEWTON, J. S. (1994). Changing activity patterns to improve social networks: A descriptive analysis. *Behavioral Interventions, 9,* 55-66.

PARKS, S. H. & PILISUK, M. (1984). Personal support systems of former mental patients residing in board and care facilities. *Journal of Community Psychology, 12,* 230-244.

PEDLAR, A. (1990). Normalization and integration: A look at the Swedish experience. *Mental Retardation, 28,* 275-282.

PERREAULT, G. J. (1992). Une attitude de gagnant. *L'Intégration, 3*(4), 2.

PILLING, D. (1995). Do PASS and PASSING pass? A critique of PASS/ING. In D. PILLING & G. WATSON (Eds.), *Evaluating quality in services for disabled and older people* (pp. 50-60). London, UK & Bristol, PA: Jessica Kingsley Publishers.

RANDOLPH, F. L., RIDGWAY, P., & CARLING, P. J. (1991). Residential program for persons with severe mental illness: A nationwide survey of state-affiliated agencies. *Hospital and Community Psychiatry, 42,* 1111-1115.

RIDGWAY, P., & ZIPPLE, A. (1990). The paradigm shift in residential services: From the linear continuum to supported housing approaches. *Psychosocial Rehabilitation Journal, 13*, 11-31.

RHOADES, C., & BROWNING, P. (1982). Normalization of a deviant subculture: Implications of the movement to resocialize mildly retarded people. *Mid-American Review of Sociology, 7*(1), 139-170.

ROSEN, J. W., & BURCHARD, S. N. (1990). Community activities and social support networks: A social comparison of adults with and adults without mental retardation. *Education and Training in Mental Retardation, 25*, 193-204.

SCHALOCK, R. L. (1990a). Where do we go from here? In R. L. SCHALOCK (Ed.), *Quality of life: Perspectives and issues* (pp. 235-240). Washington, DC: American Association on Mental Retardation.

SCHALOCK, R. L. (1990b). Attempts to conceptualize and measure quality of life. In R. L. SCHALOCK (Ed.), *Quality of life: Perspectives and issues* (pp. 141-148). Washington, DC: American Association on Mental Retardation.

SCHALOCK, R. L. (1994). Quality of life, quality enhancement, and quality assurance: Implications for program planning and evaluation in the field of mental retardation and developmental disabilities. *Evaluation and Program Planning, 17*, 121-131.

SCHALOCK, R. L. (1996). Reconsidering the conceptualization and measurement of quality of life. In R. L. SCHALOCK (Ed.), *Quality of Life. Vol. I: Conceptualization and measurement* (pp. 123-139). Washington, DC: American Association on Mental Retardation.

SCHALOCK, R. L. (1997). Can the concept of quality of life make a difference? In R. L. SCHALOCK (Ed.), *Quality of Life. Vol. II: Application to persons with disabilities* (pp. 245-267). Washington, DC: American Association on Mental Retardation.

SCHALOCK, R.L., & KEITH, R. D. (1993). *Quality of life questionnaire.* Worthington, OH: IDS Publication Co.

SCHALOCK, R. L., KEITH, K. D., HOFFMAN, K., &

KARAN, O. C. (1989). Quality of life: Its measurement and use. *Mental Retardation, 27*, 25-31.

SCHALOCK, R. L., LEMANOWICZ, J. A., CONROY, J. W., & FEINSTEIN, C. S. (1994). A multivariate investigative study of the correlates of quality of life. *Journal on Developmental Disabilities, 3*, 59-73.

SEGAL, S. P., & AVIRAM, U. (1978). *The mentally ill in community-based sheltered care: A study of community care and social integration.* New York: John Wiley & Sons.

SEGAL, S. P., BAUMOHL, J., & MOYLES, E. W. (1980). Neighborhood types and community reaction to the mentally ill: A paradox of intensity. *Journal of Health and Social Behavior, 21*, 345-359.

SEGAL, S. P., & KOTLER, P. (1993). Sheltered care residence: Ten year personal outcomes. *American Journal of Orthopsychiatry, 63*, 80-91.

SHERMAN, S. R., FRENKEL, E. R., & NEWMAN, E. S. (1986). Community participation of mentally ill adults in foster family care. *Journal of Community Psychology, 14*, 120-133.

STOREY, K. (1989). A proposal for assessing integration. *Education and Training in Mental Retardation, 24*, 279-287.

TRAINOR, J., MORRELL-BELLAI, T. L., BALLANTYNE, R., & BOYDELL, K. M. (1993). Housing for people with mental illness: A comparison of models and an examination of the growth of alternative housing in Canada. *Canadian Journal of Psychiatry, 38*, 494-501.

TRUTE, B. (1986). Sheltered housing for the chronic psychiatric patient: The influence of operators of board and care facilities in community participation. *Canadian Journal of Community Mental Health, 5*, 31-38.

TRUTE, B., & SEGAL, S. (1976). Census tract predictors and the social integration of sheltered care residents. *Social Psychiatry, 13*, 153-161.

VEIEL, H. O. F., & BAUMANN, U. (Eds.). (1992). *The meaning and measurement of social support.* New York: Hemisphere.

WEINBERG, R. B. (1984, August). *Development of self-report for reliably measuring the social support system.* Paper presented at the Annual Convention of the American Psychological

Association, Toronto, Ontario.

WILL, M. (1984). *Supported employment for adults with severe disabilities: An OSERS program initiative.* Washington, DC: Office of Special Education and Rehabilitative Services.

WOLFENSBERGER, W. (1972). *The principle of Normalization in human services.* Toronto: National Institute on Mental Retardation.

WOLFENSBERGER, W. (1980). The definition of Normalization: Update, problems, disagreements and misunderstandings. In R. J. FLYNN & K. E. NITSCH (Eds.), *Normalization, social integration, and community services* (pp. 71-115). Baltimore: University Park Press.

WOLFENSBERGER, W. (1998a). *A brief introduction to Social Role Valorization: A high-order concept for addressing the plight of societally devalued people, and for structuring human services* (3rd ed., rev.). Syracuse, NY: Syracuse University, Training Institute for Human Service Planning, Leadership and Change Agentry.

WOLFENSBERGER, W. (1998b). "Mainstreaming" and "inclusion" versus real integration [Section of column, "Social Role Valorization news and reviews"]. *International Social Role Valorization Journal, 3*(1), 58-60.

WOLFENSBERGER, W., & GLENN, L. (1975). *Program analysis of service systems: A method for the quantitative evaluation of human services.* Vol. 1: *Handbook.* Vol 2: *Field manual* (3rd ed.). Toronto: National Institute on Mental Retardation.

WOLFENSBERGER, W., & GLENN, L. (1989). *Programme d'analyse des systèmes de services (PASS 3): Méthode d'évaluation quantitative des services humains* (version européenne). Agen, France: Comité Européen pour le Développement de l'Intégration Sociale.

WOLFENSBERGER, W., & THOMAS, S. (1983). *PASSING (Program Analysis of Service Systems' Implementation of Normalization Goals): Normalization criteria and ratings manual.* (2nd ed.) Toronto: National Institute on Mental Retardation.

WOLFENSBERGER, W., & THOMAS, S. (1989). *PASSING (Programme d'analyse des systèmes de services—Applications des buts de la valorisation des rôles sociaux): Manuel des critères et des mesures de la valorisation des rôles sociaux* (2nd. ed.) (M. Roberge, Trans.; J. Pelletier, Adapt.). Toronto: G. Allan Roeher Institute & Les Communications OPELL.

13

"It does my heart good": How employers perceive supported employees

JUDITH SANDYS

For most adults in our society, work provides not only economic resources, but also a wide range of noneconomic benefits, including status, self-esteem, a sense of belonging, and self-actualization. Those who do not work are stigmatized, kept poor, and, if considered unable to work (rather than merely unwilling), looked upon as objects of pity and charity (Anthony, 1977; Macarov, 1980; Ozawa, 1982; Rinehart, 1987; Stone, 1984). It is therefore not surprising that studies confirm that for most people, working is an important determinant of quality of life (Chestang, 1982; Michalos, 1986; O'Toole, 1974; Warr, 1987).

Historically, people with intellectual disabilities have been excluded from workforce participation. Perceived as dependent and in need of care, they have had to rely on the state for their resources. Because this group is seen as "deserving," they have typically been treated more generously than those perceived as able to work but not willing to. Nonetheless, exclusion from workforce participation has served to cut them off from both the economic and noneconomic benefits of work and to deny their status as full citizens (Murphy & Rogan, 1995; Oliver, 1990).

In recent years there has been an ever increasing emphasis on promoting opportunities for people with intellectual disabilities to work in regular settings within the community. One manifestation of this has been the development of the supported employment model. Traditionally, vocational rehabilitation programs sought to provide training (most often within

sheltered workshop settings) to individuals with regard to work skills and behaviors, and then to find jobs for those assessed as "job ready." Unlike this train-then-place approach, supported employment programs utilize a place-then-train framework—the individual is placed in a work situation consistent with their interests and talents, and training and support are provided at the work site in order to ensure the success of the work situation. The underlying assumption is that the nature and quality of support ensures "success," rather than "readiness" for employment. First developed in the United States in the mid-1970s, supported employment programs have expanded rapidly in that country and more recently in Canada (Annable, 1989; Mcloughlin, Garner & Callahan, 1987; Murphy & Rogan, 1995; Wehman, Kregel, Shafer, & West, 1989; Wehman & Moon, 1988; West, Revell, & Wehman, 1992; Revell, Wehman, Kregel, West, & Rayfield, 1994).

This article presents the findings of a study that explores the perspectives of employers of people with intellectual disabilities hired through the involvement of supported employment programs. Using in-depth qualitative interviews, 21 employers in 18 different employment settings were interviewed. The study explores how these employers explain and understand their involvement with the program, their perceptions of the individual they have hired, and their views on the issue of employment of people with intellectual disabilities in general.

1 THEORETICAL CONTEXT

An underlying premise of this article is that issues relating to workforce participation for people with intellectual disabilities can only be understood within a wider context that looks at work and disability as they relate to the welfare state in a capitalist society. Perceptions of what constitutes work and who is able to work, the meanings attached to work, and the strategies undertaken to encourage workforce participation (for those assumed to be able to work) are all shaped by the perceived needs of a capitalist economy and the values inherent therein. At the same time, within the welfare state there are ideals of humanitarianism, equality, and justice, a belief that the state has some responsibility to ensure a minimum level of well-being to all citizens, and in particular to those who are perceived as unable to provide for themselves. More than 3 decades ago, Wilensky and Lebeaux (1965) spoke of the ongoing "compromise between the values of economic individualism and free enterprise on the one hand, and security, equality and humanitarianism on the other" (pp. 138-139).

Within any society there is a configuration of dominant values to which most members of that society subscribe. These values comprise the "implicit or explicit conceptions of what individuals consider to be either ideal ends or desirable means of achieving these ends" (George & Wilding, 1985, p. 127). Invariably, there will be contradictions among values, forcing choices and compromises among them. The shared value base of a society affects not only the behavior of individuals within it, but also the way societal problems are defined and in the policies that are developed to deal with these (Deakin, 1987; Gilbert, 1983; Gilbert & Specht, 1986; Hindess, 1987).

All this is is highly consistent with Social Role Valorization (SRV) theory (Wolfensberger, 1983, 1985, 1992), which posits a relationship between the treatment accorded to people with disabilities and the extent to which they are valued or devalued within society. "Human perceptual processes," notes Wolfensberger (1992), "are by their very nature evaluative" (p. 2). Since we cannot avoid making evaluative judgments about what we perceive, all people are perceived positively or negatively by others. Hence, "devaluation is something that is done to another person by a perceiver; it is not something which is inherent in the person perceived" (p. 2). SRV theory contends that the process of being identified as different and negatively valued (stigmatized) will have a profound effect on the individual's identity and subsequent behavior. However, SRV/Normalization theory challenges the seeming inevitability of a deviant and devalued status and identity based on disability (or other source of stigma) and suggests that the negative impact of a particular negatively valued attribute may be offset if the person is perceived to fill positively valued roles in society. Just as negative roles confer devalued status, so positive ones confer valued status. Given the high value placed on work, those who are unable, or who are perceived as unable, to work as a result of a disability are likely to be devalued and treated accordingly. The goal of Social Role Valorization is to enable people with disabilities or other conditions that confer a devalued status to move from that status to one that is valued within society. Supported employment programs are seemingly highly consistent with Social Role Valorization theory in their attempt to enable people with disabilities to fulfill the valued role of worker. This study seeks to examine the manner in which the dominant and often contradictory values in our society are expressed in employer responses concerning people with intellectual disabilities. Further, it examines the extent to which the role of worker, a role that is highly valued within our society, affects the way people with intellectual disabilities are perceived by employers and explores the impact of supported employment practices on these perceptions.

It is important to note that this is not a study of the experiences of supported employees but one that focuses on employers of supported employees. Since Social Role Valorization theory emphasizes the impact of perception, and since employers play a pivotal role in determining whether an individual with an intellectual disability will gain access to their workplace, it is important to understand their perceptions if we are to develop policies and practices that promote more positive outcomes. As Oliver (1990) notes, "it is not disabled people who need to be examined but able-bodied society; it is not a case of educating disabled and non-disabled people for integration, but of fighting institutional disablism" (p. 112).

2 METHODS

This study used a qualitative design. "The phenomenological basis of the qualitative approach means that the researcher studies how informants make meaning out of their situations" (Biklen & Moseley, 1988, p. 155). In this instance, it is believed that the data generated through in-depth qualitative interviews of a small number of employers would generate more significant and useful information than, for example, would a survey type questionnaire to a much larger sample.

Participants were located primarily through contacts with organizations that operated supported employment programs in or near Toronto. For the purposes of this study, the term *employer* was operationalized to include those who had decision-making authority with regard to hiring, and those who were involved in the development and/or implementation of hiring policy. It included some employers who were not paying people a regular (i.e., minimum wage or better) salary and several who did not have ongoing supervisory responsibility for a specific supported employee. Since the goal of the study was to explore a wide range of employer perspectives, respondents were selected to provide as much diversity as possible, in terms of the characteristics of the employers, employment settings, and jobs.

Interviews were generally about 1½ hours in length. While an interview guide was used to ensure that key topics were covered with each employer, questions were informal and open-ended. As Patton (1980) notes, "the fundamental principle of qualitative interviewing is to provide a framework within which respondents can express their own understandings in their own terms." In all instances, employers were very eager to talk and to share their views, resulting in a great deal of rich and detailed data. Except in two instances (one where the tape recorder malfunctioned, the other where the person so chose) all interviews were audio-taped and later transcribed eliminating identifying information. Because the focus was explicitly on the experiences of the employers, there was no systematic observation of the supported employees nor were they interviewed. However, on a less formal basis there were often opportunities to observe supported employees at their jobs, to talk with them, and to observe interaction between employers and supported employees.

In the tradition of qualitative research, data analysis began almost at the outset of the study, after which data collection and analysis continued simultaneously (see, for example, Glaser & Strauss, 1967; Miles & Huberman, 1984; Taylor & Bogdan, 1984). Memos and field notes served to capture initial impressions, thoughts, and hunches (Bogdan & Biklen, 1982; Spradley, 1979). These were helpful in identifying emerging themes that were used to construct typologies or classification schemes as a basis for interpreting the data. The informal observational data enhanced the interpretation of the interview data, often providing behavioral confirmation of the themes expressed by the employers.

3 THE PEOPLE AND THE PLACES

Three of the interviews were with employers who were not directly involved with a supported employee on an ongoing basis. This included three women (in two interviews) from human resource departments of large corporations and one man from a setting where a person had been employed until shortly before the interview took place. The women, who ranged in age from late 20s to mid-30s, all had university degrees; the man, in his late 30s, had no university education.

The employers in direct contact with supported employees were quite diverse in terms of gender, age, and educational level. Of the 17 employees, 11 were men and 6 were women. They ranged in age from early 20s to over 60 and included those with university degrees, some university or community college education, high school, or less. Employment settings included small and large enterprises, service and manufacturing organizations, for-profit and nonprofit settings. Settings with supported employees included: catering service, hotel kitchen, hospital audiovisual department, bank, fast-food restaurant, factories, car dealership, municipal planning department, administrative offices, and a discount department store.

The employers involved in this study were employing a total of 16 people with intellectual disabilities hired through supported employment programs, including one setting where there were two people. Supported employees ranged in age from the early 20s to late 40s, with most being between 25 and 35. They had been employed for as little as 6 months and as long 4½ years, with between 1 and 2 years being most typical. Of the 16 supported employees, 8 were working full-time and 8 were working part-time. All those who worked part-time were paid minimum wage or above (up to $10.25 per hour). Of the eight who worked full-time, two were paid above minimum wage. The remaining six were paid amounts ranging from nothing (one person) to $60 per week.

4 FINDINGS

4.1 THE DECISION TO HIRE: BALANCING ALTRUISM AND PRODUCTIVITY

The process that culminated with the hiring of the person with an intellectual disability was sometimes initiated by the employer but more frequently by the supported employment program. Where employer-initiated, employers generally related this to reasons of self-interest, most often related to productivity concerns—labor shortages or the need for low-cost labor:

> The thought was a cost-saving measure for the dishwashing area. To be quite honest, that was the first thought.

> It's very hard to get help . . . We're a manufacturing concern and it's just very plain repetitive work. It's very competitive and we can't afford to pay gross premiums for our labor. So we started looking for alternate sources of employment.

> I think Fast Food would admit that starting this program [to hire people with disabilities] was not altogether out of altruistic motives, but that it was out of necessity. They had a labor crunch, really the worst labor crunch ever. They had to find alternate sources of employees. They found an untapped pool.

One employer indicated that his company had initiated contact with the supported employment program in order to fulfill employment equity requirements.

More common were the situations where the supported employment program approached an employer. In these instances employers gave various rationales to explain their decision to hire the individual. While in some instances the decision was clearly related to self-interest (the person was perceived to be able to do a particular job or task successfully, or would help to meet employment equity targets), more typically employers perceived their decision, at least in part, to be based on altruistic or humanitarian concerns. They interpreted the request from the supported employment program as a request to help. When asked if the organization would have hired the young woman whom they were employing even if she had only been able to do one very simple task, one employer commented:

> Yes, we probably would have. But you have to understand that the owners of this lab are very charitable people . . . they care very much.

Others related their decision to a desire to be fair, using words similar to these employers:

> Everybody should have a chance. These people want to work like everybody else. Why shouldn't they?

> You give everybody a chance.

> Everybody deserves a chance.

Nevertheless, altruistic/humanitarian motives tended to be constrained by productivity-related concerns. People had the "right" to work, but only if they were able to do the job.

> I think that they deserve just as much a chance.

> As it's the right job . . . I think that's the bottom line.

Employers generally felt that in order to be employed, people had to be able to do some productive work, although the amount that was considered acceptable varied considerably. As well, employers often felt that some medical conditions (e.g., severe seizures), the inability to comprehend and follow directions, and/or the presence of unacceptable behaviors such as extreme aggressiveness would preclude employment. They did not see everybody as being able to work.

4.2 DIFFERENCES AND CHALLENGES: DILEMMAS OF SUPPORT WITHIN THE WORKPLACE

Employers reported that the experience of employing a person with an intellectual disability differed in many respects from their usual experiences and often presented significant challenges.

The supported employees often took longer to learn the tasks required of them, thereby requiring more input from the employer and coworkers: "I find that if you give them half a chance, and you're patient with them—it's a matter of repetition, constant repetition, which at times can drive you pretty well around the bend."

In terms of behavior, the supported employees were often perceived to be very childlike:

[Referring to a woman in her late 20s:]

I realized that I had to treat her as someone who is much younger, like someone who is in the sixth or eighth grade, someone who needed to be told what to do and what was expected of her. But she has really progressed. Now I can treat her as a young woman of mid high school age . . .

Bob likes to be pampered. He likes it when you tell him what to do or scold him. He puts his head down and grins. You can tell that he likes it. You have to treat him like a 10-year-old child . . .

We have to treat Tom like he's a 10-year-old . . .

With all due respect, I find I relate to him more like a 5-year old . . .

She's like a kid.

Some supported employees were reported to exhibit behaviors that were menacing or disruptive, including "fake seizures," emotional outbursts, destruction of property when upset, strange mannerisms, and poor grooming and/or hygiene.

You really have to watch him when he gets a cold, because he starts taking cold medication and he flips out on cold medication. . . . You won't know what he's going to do. One day he locked himself in a car and wouldn't get out.

If he thinks he's made an error he will start doing a jerking motion with his head and his arms and will fling them open to a point where it's almost like a bird taking flight.

As a result, employers reported engaging in tasks they did not usually encounter with nondisabled employees.

Something else we did that we felt would help was for her to bring in a log book. We wrote down specific jobs she had to do each day . . . then at the end of the day I would write down what she did, whether she had a good day or a bad day.

He has a problem with body odour. . . . Sometimes people he works with will complain that it is so bad they can't stand to work with him. When that happens I have to talk with him. I tell him that he has to be clean, that people don't like it. . . . After that he will be fine for quite a while. But then it starts again.

Employers were not alone in their efforts to deal with the challenges presented by the supported employee. They had available to them the assistance of a staff person from the supported employment program (referred to here as the support worker). As is typical for such programs, the support worker was very involved when the supported employee first began working, and became less active as the person adjusted to the work and the workplace. Overall, employers felt very positively about the program staff, seeing them as competent and caring people. While there were occasional complaints about staff turnover, or about something a support worker did or did not do, these were very much the exception.

One role of the support worker was to assist in training the supported employee to do the required tasks. While for some employers this was very important, others felt that they could do any required training themselves. More important was assistance when problems arose with the person's behavior. If the person was late repeatedly or did not show up for work, if the person seemed upset or exhibited troublesome or inappropriate behavior, if the person's work performance worsened, if there were difficulties between the person and other employees—in these and other situations, the employer was expected to contact the supported employment program so that the reasons for the difficulties could be explored and remedial action developed. Where problems persisted, the support worker remained very much involved. Generally, employers felt that the support worker played a key role in the success of the placement.

Employers identified closely with the staff of the supported employment program and saw themselves working collaboratively with them. They saw themselves not simply hiring a particular individual, but being a part of a program designed to assist people with intellectual disabilities: "[It is satisfying] just participating in a program like this and dealing with the people."

4.3 EMPLOYER SATISFACTION: GAINING SATISFACTION THROUGH THE ACCOMPLISHMENTS OF SUPPORTED EMPLOYEES

For virtually all the employers interviewed in this study, the experience of employing a person with an intellectual disability through a supported employment program had proven to be a very positive experience. The supported employees were seen to be reliable and hardworking: "She's a very good employee. She's extremely reliable. . . . I feel confident in leaving her in the unit if I happen to be called out."

Employers spoke about the variety of tasks that their handicapped employees have been able to learn: "She spends a lot of her time assembling planning documents for us, punching them, putting them in numerical order and assembling them on a plastic ring. She does photocopying and she delivers newspapers within the department once a week. . . . [Also] lots of folding of maps and plans, and putting them in their proper slots."

Sometimes this contributed to the overall efficiency of the operation: "She has taken away some of the jobs that the technicians were doing to let them do more complicated things. And it's actually helped us, because it has to be done regardless."

However, even more important to these employers were the benefits that were seen to accrue to the supported employee. These employers reported that work was very important in their own lives. They described themselves as workaholics and indicated that they had worked hard to achieve success. The importance of work for them extended beyond the remuneration it generated. In discussing the benefits of working for the supported employees they again focused on the noneconomic benefits, only rarely mentioning financial benefits. (In fact, for a significant number of people the financial benefits were modest or nonexistent.)

They were impressed with the individual's motivation to work: "It's very inspiring to see a man with such limited mental ability trying so hard and succeeding and accomplishing things."

They talked about the person's development and improved well-being—skills they had acquired, ability to relate to people, maturity, self-esteem, sense of self worth, sense of belonging, and so forth:

She's certainly more sociable. . . . Now she looks at you in the face and talks to you directly. . . .

We've given her the chance to feel that she's doing a job and that she's a needed person. . . . And I think we've also done wonders for her self-confidence. . . .

It's inspiring. . . . It's incredible how much he has developed.

To have played a part in bringing about these benefits was clearly a source of satisfaction to these employers:

To know that we've provided an opportunity for these individuals to work and everything that goes with that. I'm not talking about the money so much as the self-esteem and the feeling of belonging much more than they would otherwise have.

I like working with Bob. I like working with slower people. It gives you a good feeling if you can teach them something, if they are out there working.

It does my heart good to see how much he has developed.

4.4 EMPLOYER RESPONSES TO EMPLOYMENT EQUITY/AFFIRMATIVE ACTION; CHOICE OR OBLIGATION?

While employers articulated a belief in the "right" of people with intellectual disabilities to work in the community, described the experience as positive, and felt that more employers should be encouraged to hire such individuals, there was little support for strengthened employment equity/affirmative action legislation that might require employers to hire people with disabilities.

In this regard, this group was not different from many other employers. An informal survey of 30 employers by a Toronto consulting firm reported in *The Globe and Mail* (Gibb-Clark, 1991) reiterated some of the common sources of opposition to any kind of quota system. The primary reason given by those employers was that to impose quotas would undermine the merit system that is at the very heart of our economy.

While the employers interviewed for this study did on occasion raise this objection, they tended more often to frame their response in very different terms. Rather than simply opposing such legislation because it might not be in their own best business interests, they maintained that it would not be in the interests of people with disabilities. They argue that forcing employers to hire people with disabilities would result in employers resenting their presence. Under these circumstances, they would not exhibit the same kind of care and concern for the well-being of the disabled employee:

> I don't think you can force it on employers. . . . It would be very difficult for an individual with a handicap to cope with a hostile situation.

> You would have a negative attitude on the part of the employer right off the bat.

Furthermore, if forced to hire, it was argued, employers would seek people with the most minimal handicaps and ignore those with more seriously handicapping conditions.

5 ANALYSIS AND DISCUSSION

Given the amount of effort involved for employers, why do they feel so positive about the experience? The most cynical perspective would suggest that the direct benefits to the employer, whether in terms of providing "cheap labor," contributing to the efficiency of the operation, or helping to meet employment equity targets, outweighed any inconvenience to the employer. Certainly these motivations played a significant part in some situations. However, they would seem insufficient to explain the overwhelmingly positive attitudes of the employers or the sometimes considerable energy they devoted to making the situation successful.

Rather, it would seem that employers who hire people with intellectual disabilities through supported employment programs may interpret what they are doing within an ethic of care. They define what they are doing primarily in terms of "helping" someone, and come to measure their own success by the extent to which the person appears to benefit from the situation. While they do not, by any means, abandon their productivity expectations entirely, these may be modified by other considerations. The interpretation of hiring a person with an intellectual handicap as a humanitarian act may be strengthened by the involvement of the supported employment program.

Employers often perceived the request from the supported employment program as a request to "help."

Interpreting the employment of people with intellectual disabilities within an ethic of care has a number of implications, both positive and negative. On the positive side, it seems to buy a higher level of tolerance for the person with the disability, increasing the range of challenges with which an employer is prepared to contend. Behaviors such as repeated lateness, absence, emotional outbursts, aggressiveness, and poor-quality work are responded to differently when the person is identified as having an intellectual disability and when the person has been placed in the job with the involvement of a supported employment program. While such behaviors would likely elicit a negative reaction—perhaps disciplinary action or even dismissal—in the case of a nonlabeled person, in the instance of a person with an intellectual disability hired through a supported employment program, these behaviors are interpreted as part of the person's "problem" and the employer assumes greater responsibility for trying to ameliorate them.

Because employers define their own success in terms of how well the person is perceived to be doing, there is an incentive for employers to invest their energy in eliciting positive outcomes. For these employers, work is something that is challenging and fulfilling; they work hard to ensure that it is so for the handicapped employee too. Helping the individual to expand the range of tasks they can do certainly contributes to the productivity or efficiency of the workplace. However, for these employers it is also a sign that they are being successful in terms of helping the individual to develop and grow. Some employers go to considerable lengths to enable the person to do different and more challenging tasks, even when there may be no direct or immediate benefits to that employer. In several instances employers arranged for the individual to work in a different department for part of the time, in order to provide new learning opportunities and challenges.

If this ethic of care has some positive outcomes, it also has some that are negative, in fact or potentially. At its worst, a mind-set in which the employer defines her/his role as providing a service that will contribute to the personal development of an individual may serve to obscure the fact that the person is performing work for which he or she should be appropriately remunerated. It may lead to situations where not paying the person according to the same standards as others is justified or legitimated by the perception that the employer is providing a service and that the person is benefitting in other ways. One finds situations where an individual's productivity was reported to be equal or similar to others doing the same job, but where the person was not receiving anything approaching the same rate of pay. Various rationales were offered for paying people less than minimum wage, including that pay was not important to the individual, that paying the person more might jeopardize his or her pension, or that paying a regular wage would create higher productivity expectation resulting in too much pressure on the person.

Employers in these situations rarely feel any sense that they are being exploitive. Indeed they take pride in the role they have played in contributing to the well-being of the individual and may even interpret not paying a regular wage as a necessary part of the helping process. The fact that they are realizing some economic or practical advantage is seen as fair exchange for the service that they are providing to the individual (e.g., promoting development) and to the larger society (e.g., taking care of the individual, reducing costs to government). An employer who is paying half of minimum wage explained: "The benefit is twofold. You are lowering the amount of money the government has to spend on taking care of people with intellectual handicaps and you are saving 50% of the wage."

Another (potentially) negative outcome of the ethic of care is to reinforce the perception of the person with an intellectual handicap as dependent, childlike, and in need of care. Employers reported many childlike behaviors. Assuming that these are accurately reported (and there is no reason to assume otherwise), it is also true that employers spoke to and about people as though they were much younger than their chronological age. To what extent does perceiving people as childlike elicit childish behavior, and vice versa? Wolfensberger and Thomas (1983) speak of the power of "role expectancies and role circularities" (p. 25). We know that the expectations we hold of people have a powerful influence in shaping the behaviors that are elicited, and that these in turn will

serve to reinforce our initial expectations. While it is impossible to determine the extent to which employer expectations influenced the way people were perceived and responded to, and the impact of this on their subsequent behavior, one can assume some interrelationship between these elements.

It is important to note that negative role expectancies surround people with disabilities throughout their lives. They are socialized into their role as dependent and childlike over many years and in many settings. The foregoing discussion is not meant to suggest that employers alone create or sustain these roles, nor that it is entirely within their power to change them or the behaviors they may have elicited. It is to suggest that the idea that enabling a person with a disability to work in the community can or will suddenly erase this history is unrealistic. Instead, the employers may get entangled in the web of role expectancies that has been woven around the person. While there were many positive benefits reported for the people with disabilities who were working for these employers, in a good many situations this did not affect the perception of them as dependent and childlike.

The involvement of the supported employment program was in many ways reassuring to the employers, offering support and assistance with difficulties that arose. It drew in the employer as part of the helping team that would, together, assist the person with the disability. It provided an opportunity for the employers to see themselves in the new role of helper or counselor. All this drew the employer into a situation where new rules applied, where success is measured not in productivity or dollars, but in terms of personal development, growth, and self-esteem. At the same time, the message of the supported employment program is that this is a person who is "different," who may act in unusual ways, who needs to be handled differently and with particular skill.

Employers may interpret what they are doing as a humanitarian or altruistic act, regardless of their initial motivation for hiring the person, and regardless of the extent to which there are material benefits accruing from the person's employment. Because hiring such an individual is seen as falling within the purview of altruism, employers are very resistant to any thoughts of legislation that might compel them to do so. While they may decry the prejudices, callousness, and insensitivity of other employers, or speak eloquently about the "right" to work of people with disabilities, ultimately hiring a person with an intellectual handicap is defined as an altruistic act that employers should be encouraged but cannot be compelled to do. They say, in effect: "I do it because I am a kind and generous person and I want to help. But don't try to force me to do it."

Essentially these employers were maintaining that efforts to legislate the employment of people with disabilities, including those with intellectual handicaps, would take the act of hiring such an individual out of the arena of altruism. To employ such a person would be a legal obligation, rather than an altruistic response. In such an event, many of the rewards that accrued to the employer, in terms of defining themselves (and being defined by others) as a good and caring person, would be at risk of being lost.

6 CONCLUSIONS AND IMPLICATIONS

This study deals with employers who have hired people with intellectual disabilities with the involvement of supported employment programs. Because no effort was made to select a representative sample, it is very possible that the employers who were located through contacts with supported employment programs represent those whom the agencies considered particularly successful. Generalizations from this population to any other must be made with extreme caution. One cannot assume that the responses on all issues are characteristic of all employers. The study does not answer the question as to why some employers hire people with intellectual handicaps and some do not. It does not answer the question as to why some placements "succeed" and some do not. Nevertheless, the study does help to identify some of the challenges inherent in efforts to promote valued roles for people with intellectual disabilities through workforce participation in the context of a society that places a high value on productivity at the same time as it seeks to promote equality and humanitarianism. It demonstrates the impact of the value base of welfare capitalism on the meanings that employers attach to their experiences with supported employees and on how such individuals are perceived.

There is growing evidence that supported employment programs have failed to meet their initial promise (Mank, 1994; Wehman & Kregel, 1995). While the number of people in supported employment programs has continued to increase, the number of people in segregated employment has increased even faster. Supported employment initiatives have had minimal impact on those with the most severe disabilities. Further, supported employment often means part-time employment, low wages, and continued social isolation. Despite this, supported employment programs represent a far more positive alternative than segregated, sheltered settings. Research on the outcomes of supported employment programs indicate that people take pride in having a "real job," experience increased self-esteem, learn new skills, and are perceived as more independent and more confident by those who know them. Generally, they express considerable satisfaction in working in the community despite any shortcomings they experience with their particular job (Inge, Banks, Wehman, Hill, & Shafer, 1988; Moseley, 1987, 1988; Pedlar, Lord, & Van Loon, 1989).

Social Role Valorization theory is rich and complex, stressing the interplay between societal values and the devaluation of specific individuals, groups, and classes of people. It recognizes that people invariably fill multiple roles, with each having an impact on how people are perceived and treated within society. Nevertheless, there is perhaps a tendency for service providers to think that finding one particular valued role for an individual will overcome the impact of other, devalued, roles. This study does support the relationship between valued roles and positive life experiences. While outcomes were not entirely positive, as evidenced by work that was most often part-time and poorly paid (or not paid), the role of worker did affect the way that employers perceived the supported employee. While the focus of the study was not on the experiences of the supported employees, the data that were available in this regard did suggest many positive outcomes. However, while the role of worker may have had a positive impact, it did not overcome or erase the impact of the other more characteristic and negative roles into which people with disabilities are so often cast.

There is a tendency in the supported employment literature to presume that if service providers can only figure out how to do it "right," supported employment will yield the desired outcomes. One dramatic manifestation of this is the growing emphasis on "natural supports" (Hagner, 1992; Nisbet & Hagner, 1988; Rogan, 1996; Test & Wood, 1996), where it is presumed that support provided by coworkers is more "natural" and effective than program-generated support. Certainly seeking new and better ways to deliver supported employment services is a worthy goal, and this study does suggest some issues that supported employment programs need to address. Greater sensitivity to the way people with disabilities are interpreted in the workplace, careful modeling of appropriate behavior, efforts to minimize the employer's care-giving role, and a more clearly defined expectation that pay will be forthcoming all might be expected to have some impact. In particular, proponents of "natural support" must ensure that these efforts do not further reinforce the perception of supported employees as dependent and childlike.

Nevertheless, it must be recognized that the very existence of these programs, located within the social service system and designed with the specific purpose of helping this population fit into the existing structure of the workforce, has within it certain inherent limitations. This reinforces the perception of people with intellectual disabilities as being in need of care and suggests that it is the people with disabilities who need to change, rather than the society in which they live. As long as the task of enabling people with intellectual disabilities to work in the community is seen primarily as the responsibility of the social service sector, the people served by these programs are at risk of being interpreted as needing and receiving care, even when they are working and contributing. As long as employers feel that they are doing the individual a favor by hiring him or her, people with intellectual disabilities remain vulnerable to exploitation. Enabling people with intellectual disabilities to be accorded their full rights as citizens demands that we develop policies that support their inclusion in the workplace not as a favor, but as a right.

REFERENCES

ANNABLE, G. (1989). *Supported employment in Canada 1988: Final report.* Winnipeg, MB: Canadian Council on Rehabilitation and Work.

ANTHONY, P. D. (1977). *The ideology of work.* London: Tavistock Publications.

BIKLEN, S. K., & MOSELEY, C. R. (1988). "Are you retarded?" "No, I'm Catholic": Qualitative methods in the study of people with severe handicaps. *Journal of the Association for Persons with Severe Handicaps, 13*(3), 155-162.

BOGDAN, R. C., & BIKLEN, S. K. (1982). *Qualitative research for education: An introduction to theory and methods.* Boston: Allyn and Bacon.

CHESTANG, L. W. (1982). Work, personal change and human development. In S. H. AKABAS & P. A. KURZMAN (Eds.), *Work, workers, and work organizations: A view from social work* (pp. 61-89). Englewood Cliffs, NJ: Prentice-Hall.

DEAKIN, N. (1987). *The politics of welfare.* London: Methuen.

GEORGE, V., & WILDING, P. (1985). *Ideology and social welfare.* London: Routledge & Kegan Paul.

GIBB-CLARK, M. (1991, May 16). Employment equity worries firms. *The Globe and Mail.*

GILBERT, N. (1983). *Capitalism and the welfare state: Dilemmas of social benevolence.* New Haven: Yale University Press.

GILBERT, N., & SPECHT, H. (1986). *Dimensions of social welfare policy* (2nd ed.). Englewood Cliffs, NJ: Prentice-Hall.

GLASER, B., & STRAUSS, A. L. (1967). *The discovery of grounded theory: Strategies for qualitative research.* Chicago: Aldine Press.

HAGNER, D. C. (1992). The social interactions and job supports of supported employees. In J. NISBET (Ed.), *Natural supports in school, at work and in the community for people with severe disabilities* (pp. 217-239). Baltimore: Paul H. Brookes.

HINDESS, B. (1987). *Freedom, equality, and the market: Arguments on social policy.* London: Tavistock Publications.

INGE, K. J., BANKS, P. D., WEHMAN, P., HILL, J. W., & SHAFER, M. S. (1988, June). Quality of life for individuals who are labelled mentally retarded: Evaluating competitive employment versus sheltered workshop employment. *Education and Training in Mental Retardation.*

MACAROV, D. (1980). *Work and welfare: The unholy alliance.* Beverly Hills, CA: Sage Publications.

MANK, D. (1994). The underachievement of supported employment. *Journal of Disability Policy Studies 5*(2), 1-23.

MCLOUGHLIN, C. S., GARNER, J. B., & CALLAHAN, M. (1987). *Getting employed, stating employed.* Baltimore: Paul H. Brookes.

MICHALOS, A. C. (1986). Job satisfaction, marital satisfaction, and the quality of life: A review and a preview. In F. M. ANDREWS (Ed.), *Research on the quality of life* (pp. 57-83). University of Michigan, Survey Research Center: Institute for Social Research.

MILES, M. B., & HUBERMAN, A. M. (1984). *Qualitative data analysis: A source book of new methods.* Beverly Hills: Sage Publications.

MOSELEY, C. R. (1987). *The job satisfaction of workers in supported employment.* Paper presented at the 1987 TASH Annual Conference.

MOSELEY, C. R. (1988). Job satisfaction research: Implications for supported employment. *Journal of the Association for Persons With Severe Handicaps, 13*(3), 211-219.

MURPHY, S. T., & ROGAN, P. M. (1995). *Closing the shop: Conversion from sheltered to integrated work.* Baltimore: Paul H. Brookes.

NISBET, J., & HAGNER, D. (1988). Natural supports in the workplace: A reexamination of supported employment. *Journal of the Association for Persons With Severe Handicaps, 13*, 260-267.

OLIVER, M. (1990). *The politics of disablement.* London: Macmillan.

O'TOOLE, J. (Ed.). (1974). *Work and the quality of life.* Cambridge: MIT Press.

O'TOOLE, J. (1974). Introduction. In J. O'TOOLE (Ed.), *Work and the quality of life* (pp. 1-23). Cambridge: MIT Press.

OZAWA, M. N. (1982). Work and social policy. In S. H. AKABAS & P. A. KURZMAN (Eds.), *Work, workers, and work organizations: A view from social work* (pp. 32-60). Englewood Cliffs, NJ: Prentice-Hall.

PATTON, M. G. (1980). *Qualitative evaluation methods.* Beverly Hills, CA: Sage Publications.

PEDLAR, A., LORD, J., & VAN LOON, M. (1989). *The process of supported employment and quality of life.* Kitchener: Centre for Research and Education in Human Services.

REVELL, W. G., WEHMAN, P., KREGEL, J., WEST, M., & RAYFIELD, R. (1994, December). Supported employment for persons with severe disabilities: Positive trends in wages, models and funding. *Education and Training in Mental Retardation and Developmental Disabilities,* 256-261.

RINEHART, J. W. (1987). *The tyranny of work* (2nd ed.). Toronto, ON: Harcourt Brace Jovanovich.

ROGAN, P. (1996). Natural supports in the workplace: No need for a trial. *Journal of the Association for Persons With Severe Handicaps, 21,* 178-180.

SPRADLEY, J. P. (1979). *The ethnographic interview.* New York: Holt, Rinehart, and Winston.

STONE, D. A. (1984). *The disabled state.* Philadelphia: Temple University Press.

TAYLOR, S. J., & BOGDAN, R. (1984). *Introduction to qualitative research methods: The search for meanings (*2nd ed.). New York: John Wiley & Sons.

TEST, D., & WOOD, W. (1996). Natural supports in the workplace: The jury is still out. *Journal of the Association for Persons With Severe Handicaps, 21,* 155-173.

WARR, P. (1987). *Work, unemployment and mental health.* Oxford: Clarendon Press.

WEHMAN, P., & KREGEL, J. (1995). At the crossroads: Supported employment ten years later. *Journal of the Association for Persons With Severe Handicaps, 20,* 286-299.

WEHMAN, P., KREGEL, J., SHAFER, M. S., & WEST, M. (1989). Supported employment implementation I: Characteristics and outcomes of persons being served. In P. WEHMAN, J. KREGEL, & M. S. SHAFER (Eds.), *Emerging trends in the National Supported Employment Initiative: A preliminary analysis of twenty-seven states* (pp. 46-74). Richmond: Virginia Commonwealth University, Rehabilitation Research and Training Center on Supported Employment.

WEHMAN, P., & MOON, M. S. (Eds.). (1988). *Vocational rehabilitation and supported employment.* Baltimore: Paul H. Brookes.

WEST, M., REVELL, W. G., & WEHMAN, P. (1992). Achievements and challenges I: A five-year report on consumer and system outcomes from the supported employment initiative. *Journal of the Association for Persons With Severe Handicaps, 17*(4), 227-235.

WILENSKY, H. L., & LEBEAUX, C. N. (1965). *Industrial society and social welfare.* New York: Russell Sage Foundation.

WOLFENSBERGER, W. (1983). Social Role Valorization: A proposed new term for the principle of Normalization. *Mental Retardation, 21*(6), 235-239.

WOLFENSBERGER, W. (1985). An overview of Social Role Valorization and some reflections on elderly mentally retarded persons. In M. JANICKI & H. WISNIEWSKI (Eds.), *Aging and developmental disabilities: Issues and approaches* (pp. 61-76). Baltimore: Paul H. Brookes.

WOLFENSBERGER, W. (1992). *A brief introduction to Social Rrole Valorization as a high order concept for structuring human services* (Rev. ed.). Syracuse, NY: Syracuse University, Training Institute for Human Service Planning, Leadership and Change Agentry.

WOLFENSBERGER, W., & THOMAS, S. (1983). *Program analysis of service system implementation of service system goals* (2nd ed.). Normalization criteria and rating manual. Toronto, ON: National Institute on Mental Retardation.

14

A comprehensive review of research conducted with the program evaluation instruments *PASS* and *PASSING*

ROBERT J. FLYNN

Given the international prominence of the principles of Normalization and Social Role Valorization (SRV) in service policy, planning, and practice over the last quarter-century, as attested in many chapters of the present volume, it is not surprising that the main program evaluation instruments that these theoretical approaches have inspired have also been influential. Program Analysis of Service Systems (PASS 3; Wolfensberger & Glenn, 1975, 1989) and Program Analysis of Service Systems' Implementation of Normalization Goals (PASSING; Wolfensberger & Thomas, 1983, 1989) are currently used in the United States, Canada, the United Kingdom, France, Spain, Switzerland, Australia, and New Zealand, in fields such as mental retardation, mental health, and aging, to assess the quality of residential, vocational, recreational, and other types of community services, in terms of their consistency with Normalization and SRV principles, respectively. PASS and PASSING sessions are also organized on a regular basis in several of the countries just mentioned to train evaluators and teach the specific service implications of Normalization and SRV theory (see Thomas, chapter 15, this volume).

The present chapter is intended to provide a virtually exhaustive review of studies carried out during 1971-1998 with the various editions of PASS (Wolfensberger & Glenn, 1969, 1973, 1975, 1989) and PASSING (Wolfensberger & Thomas, 1980, 1983, 1989). The primary purpose of the review is to bring the entire body of PASS and PASSING research to the attention of users of the instruments and of a wider audience of interested evaluators and researchers. The chapter covers every published or unpublished study that was based on a sizable number of PASS or PASSING evaluations and of which I was aware. The review excludes reports from routine PASS or PASSING evaluations of single programs or of a small number of services (hundreds of such reports exist).

A total of 48 studies are reviewed herein: 1 conducted with PASS 1 (Wolfensberger & Glenn, 1969), 3 with PASS 2 (Wolfensberger & Glenn, 1973), 20 with the regular (i.e., complete) version of PASS 3 (Wolfensberger & Glenn, 1975, 1989), 7 with short forms of PASS 3, 5 with adaptations of PASS 3, and 12 with the second edition of PASSING (Wolfensberger & Thomas, 1983, 1989). (No studies appear to have been carried out with the initial, experimental version of PASSING; Wolfensberger & Thomas, 1980.) The 48 studies have been grouped according to the instrument in question, and, within their respective groupings, they are discussed in chronological order of appearance. The review includes as many methodological details and substantive findings from each individual study as I thought necessary to enable readers to understand the study and assess its relevance to their own needs and interests. The chapter concludes with several critical comments and practical suggestions intended to encourage the publication of more high-quality PASS and PASSING research in the future.

Several search procedures were used to locate the 48 studies. Those appearing during 1971-1979 were covered in an earlier review (Flynn, 1980), the essence of which has been retained here in the interests of comprehensiveness. The great majority are from 1980-1998 and were located through computerized searches of the *Social Science Citation Index,* PsycINFO, and *Dissertation Abstracts International* databases, as well as through manual searches of relevant journals. Unpublished studies known to the author were also included.

1 STUDIES BASED ON PASS

1.1 STUDIES BASED ON PASS 1

Macy (1971) carried out the only PASS 1 study, based on the initial, unpublished version of the instrument (Wolfensberger & Glenn, 1969). PASS 1 was used in 1970 and 1971 to assess and allocate funding to new community mental retardation services in Nebraska. Macy found that total PASS scores correlated highly with movement by clients with mental retardation from a less advanced to a more advanced status (e.g., from training to independent employment).

1.2 STUDIES BASED ON PASS 2

Flynn (1975, 1977) and Flynn and Sha'ked (1977) conducted the only published studies that used PASS 2, the second edition of the instrument (Wolfensberger & Glenn, 1973). Flynn's (1975) monograph, a summary of which may be found in the PASS 3 *Handbook* (pp. 25-27), consisted of a statistical analysis of 102 PASS 2 program evaluations that had been carried out in the US and Canada during 1973-1974. The 102 programs were an accidental sample of PASS assessments, comprising an estimated one-third of all assessments made with PASS 2. The results suggested that average service quality (as indexed by a mean total PASS score of +229 on a scale ranging from -849 to +1,000) was only modestly above zero.

The latter was the point defined by the authors of PASS as constituting a "minimally acceptable" level of service quality.

A subsequent study (Flynn, 1977), based on an enlarged accidental sample of 151 PASS 2 evaluations, extended the findings of the earlier monograph. The internal consistency of PASS 2 was estimated to be 0.90 (coefficient α) in the sample of programs, 93% of which were community-based and 72% of which served persons with mental retardation. Average service quality (as indexed by a mean total PASS score of +276) was only modestly above the minimally acceptable level, and performance on those ratings tapping social integration was particularly weak. In fact, despite their primarily community-based nature, the 151 programs were found to be more socially segregative than integrative. Ratings concerned with service proximity and accessibility and with features of the service setting tended to be more satisfactory than those concerned with aspects of the service program. Finally, PASS 2 was found capable of discriminating between different types of programs. Specifically, community programs had a higher mean total PASS score than institutional programs ($p < .001$). Also, an inverse monotonic relationship emerged between program quality and the age category of the clients served (young children, school-aged children and adolescents, adults, and elderly): the older the clients, the lower the total PASS score ($p < .05$).

In the third PASS 2 study, Flynn and Sha'ked (1977) conducted a further analysis of the data from this sample of 151 programs. A primary objective of this study was to determine the major PASS correlates of the rating *Age-Appropriate Sex Behavior,* and to offer recommendations for improving the quality of sex-related agency services. The strongest correlates of normative sex behavior included an agency emphasis on physical and social integration, normative personal appearance, specialization (coherence) of the service model, and developmental growth.

1.3 STUDIES BASED ON PASS 3

Although PASS 3 (Wolfensberger & Glenn, 1975, 1989) has been largely superseded by PASSING in training and service-evaluation activities in the USA, Canada, Australia, and New Zealand, it is still used in the United Kingdom, France, and some other countries and has been the subject of more research than earlier versions of PASS or PASSING. PASS 3 is used by a team of external raters trained to evaluate a human service program on 50 different items or "ratings." Following detailed guidelines in the PASS *Field Manual* (Wolfensberger & Glenn, 1975), individual team members first rate the service independently. Then, in an often lengthy "conciliation" session, the team pools its information, resolves any discrepancies among individual members' ratings, and generates a single, team-conciliated set of ratings. Later, the team forwards a detailed written report containing its findings and recommendations. The total PASS score (the sum of the scores obtained on the 50 individual ratings) is an index of overall service quality. Seventy-three percent of the total score reflects Normalization-related ratings, with the other 27% covering administrative issues, broadly defined.

Berry, Andrews, and Elkins (1977) reported on their evaluation of 36 educational, vocational, and residential programs serving persons with moderate and severe mental retardation in the three Australian states of Queensland, Victoria, and New South Wales (Andrews and Berry, 1978, provide a brief published version of the original research report). The 36 programs constituted a nonrandomly selected quota sample. In each state, 12 programs (3 schools, 3 sheltered workshops, 3 residential programs, and 3 activity-therapy centers) were assessed. The major findings of Berry et al. (1977) were as follows. First, the mean total PASS score of +316 indicated that service quality in the 36 programs was somewhat higher than minimally acceptable. (Flynn [1980] suggested, however, that this mean score was considerably higher than that observed in similar North American services because of a possible upward bias in scoring, due to the inability of the Australian raters to attend the standardized PASS 3 training sessions that, at the time, were conducted only in North America.) Second, large differences emerged among different types of programs: Schools (serving younger clients) had the highest PASS scores, followed by sheltered workshops, residential programs, and activity-therapy centers. Third, several common weaknesses were apparent across all 36 programs, in the areas of administration, culture-appropriateness, accessibility, and geographical setting.

As part of a research program aimed at discovering which environmental variables promote growth in adaptive behavior in developmentally disabled persons, Eyman, Demaine, and Lei (1979) tested the predictive validity of six PASS 3 factors that Demaine, Silverstein, and Mayeda (1980; see below) had derived on a sample of 98 residences serving 245 persons with developmental disabilities. Eyman et al. related the residential facility factor scores to longitudinal measures of adaptive change obtained on the 245 residents, most of whom had remained in the same home during the 3-year study period. At least three annual ratings made by case workers using the Adaptive Behavior Scale (ABS; Nihira, Foster, Shellhaas, & Leland, 1974) were available for each resident. Three ABS factor scores were computed for each resident: personal self-sufficiency, community self-sufficiency, and personal-social responsibility. Average annual change on each of the three ABS factors was then calculated for each client over the 3-year period. In order to test whether differences in residential environments were related to differences in client developmental gains, Eyman et al. used a path-analysis framework in which the dependent variable in each of three separate analyses was the mean annual client change on each of the ABS factors, the exogenous (predetermined) variables were client age and IQ, and the intervening variables were the client's initial score on the respective ABS factor and the client's residence's scores on the six PASS 3 factors. The main findings of this validation study were as follows. Residents who were older (18 years and over), or who had mild or moderate retardation, showed greater developmental gains than did younger or more impaired residents. On the ABS dimension of personal self-sufficiency, residents who gained the most were older, had higher IQs, or lived in facilities with higher scores on the PASS 3 factors of environmental blending with the neighborhood, location and proximity of services, and comfort and appearance, and lower scores on ideology-related administration. Average annual gains in community self-sufficiency were greater in clients who had higher IQs or who lived in settings with higher scores on the PASS 3 factors of administrative policies, location and proximity, and comfort and appearance. Average annual gains in personal-social responsibility were positively related to older age, higher IQ, or residence in a facility with higher scores on location and proximity, and on comfort and appearance, but with lower scores on ideology-related administration. The first PASS 3 factor, application of Normalization principles, was not related to developmental gain on any of the ABS domains. (It should be noted that the labeling of the first PASS factor as "application of Normalization principles" is potentially misleading, because several other PASS factors—environmental blending of services with the neighborhood, location and proximity of service, and comfort and appearance of service setting—also assessed the application of Normalization principles and were related to developmental gains.) Finally, a moderately strong, statistically significant, canonical correlation of .456 ($p < .001$) was found between the six PASS 3 factors and the three ABS domain changes.

Demaine, Silverstein, and Mayeda (1980) examined the validity and utility of PASS 3 by assessing whether the instrument was able to fulfill one of its main purposes, namely, quantitatively evaluating the quality of human service programs. Demaine et al. factor-analyzed PASS scores gathered on 98 residential facilities serving developmentally disabled persons in California. Of the residential settings, 83% served 6 persons or fewer, 8% served 7 to 50, and 9% served more than 50. Slightly more than half of the settings were in suburban neighborhoods, with 40% in rural areas. Instead of being conducted by a team of trained raters, the PASS evaluations were conducted in a nonstandard way, by a single trained rater familiar with each facility who rated it from a PASS-structured written report. A pilot study, carried out to check on this nonstandard method, found that conventional PASS team evaluations, conducted on 5 of the 98 facilities, produced a statistically nonsignificant mean difference of only 40 points. The factor analysis by Demaine et al. yielded seven factors, six of which were interpretable: I: compliance with Normalization principles; II: administrative policies pertaining to Normalization principles; III: Issues of Normalization with regard to programming and physical setting; IV: issues related to the administration of services; V: physical location and availability of services; and VI: comfort and functional nature of the physical setting. Demaine et al. noted that Eyman et al. (1979) had already provided initial evidence of the validity of the

six PASS factors for predicting behavioral outcomes of developmentally disabled persons.

Flynn (1980) used a sample of 256 American and Canadian programs (58% in the field of mental retardation and 63% conducted during PASS training workshops) to compare service quality in five different types of programs: institutional residences and community-based residential, child development, educational, and vocational programs. The service quality indices used were the total PASS score and four subscales empirically derived through factor and item analyses. Internal consistency (Cronbach's α) was high in the case of the total PASS scale (0.91) and of the two longest subscales, Normalization-Program (19 items, $\alpha = 0.90$) and Normalization-Setting (12 items, $\alpha = 0.80$). It was lower but still adequate in the case of the two shorter subscales, Administration (8 items, $\alpha = 0.64$) and Proximity and Access (4 items, $\alpha = 0.67$). To facilitate comparisons among these different service quality indices, all weighted PASS scores were linearly transformed to a common metric, the percentage of the maximum possible score (cf. Flynn, 1980, p. 337). There are both similarities and differences in the composition of the six factors found by Demaine et al. (1980) and the four discovered by Flynn (1980). The differences may be due to differences in factor-analytic techniques, in the procedures used to carry out the PASS evaluations, or the size and composition of the respective samples (the greater homogeneity of the exclusively residential sample used by Demaine et al. may, for example, have produced somewhat lower inter-item correlations and the emergence of a somewhat larger number of factors).

Global service quality in the sample was only modest: The mean total PASS score represented only 47% of the total possible weighted score. The total PASS score did discriminate, however, among the various types of institutional and community programs in the sample: Community child-development services scored highest, institutional residences scored lowest, and Canadian services scored 5% higher than American programs. As noted by Heal and Fujiura (1984, pp. 215-216), multivariate profile analyses of the four subscale scores provided further evidence of the discriminant and thus construct validity of PASS as a measure of Normalization. For example, child development services (in which integration was relatively more likely than in the other types of programs) outscored the other types of services on Normalization-Program, community residential services scored highest on Normalization-Setting, and the four types of community programs scored higher than the institutional residences on Proximity and Access. The different PASS profiles characteristic of each type of service suggested priority targets for efforts aimed at improving service quality (Flynn, 1980, pp. 352-353): the service setting and administrative processes in the case of the child development programs; program content and administrative issues in the case of the community residences; all three areas in the case of the educational and vocational programs (including a much greater emphasis on integration); and replacement by community residential options in the case of the institutional residences. Flynn (1980) also pointed out that the four empirically derived PASS factors could be used to improve the coherence and quality of evaluation reports. A visual profile of the four subscale scores could be presented, with the presentation of results, analyses, and recommendations organized around the key dimensions of service quality assessed by the four PASS subscales.

In his doctoral research in public administration, Ross (1981) compared the three main accreditation instruments in use at the time in the field of disability: PASS 3, the standards of the Accreditation Council for Services for Mentally Retarded and Other Developmentally Disabled Persons (ACMRDD), and the standards of the Commission on Accreditation of Rehabilitation Facilities (CARF). Based on an analysis of the similarities and differences among these three approaches, Ross prepared a "consolidated" set of standards that incorporated what he saw as the most salient aspects of each; 32 were common to the three instruments, 11 unique. In a survey of administrators of community rehabilitation programs, Ross found that three of the common standards were strongly rejected: use of volunteers, the notion of "culture-appropriateness," and integration of disabled and nondisabled persons within the same program. The administrators appeared to prefer a pluralistic accreditation system adaptable to local circumstances rather than a single instrument or approach.

In her doctoral thesis in clinical psychology, Golden (1982) examined discrepancies between Normalization theory and actual practices in community residences serving persons with psychiatric disabilities. She hypothesized that community residences do not meet Normalization criteria and that the level of Normalization of the residence is associated with both the interpersonal environment within the home and with residents' social engagement outside the home. Golden assessed 8 community residences in Massachusetts by means of PASS and then compared residences with high and low PASS scores on two dependent variables: internal interactions (as measured by Bales's [1950] method) and the frequency of residents' social involvement. She found that the community residences were physically integrated into their communities but socially distant from ordinary citizens because of programmatic and administrative inadequacies. Moreover, the interpersonal process was found to be powerful in either fostering or undermining Normalization. Overall, the residences were task-oriented and hierarchical rather than socioemotionally and democratically oriented, with staff tending to elicit responses and residents expressing little disagreement.

Gallant's (1983) doctoral research in education investigated 3 elementary school programs for children labeled "trainable mentally retarded," aged 6 to 8, in Michigan and Ontario. The goal was to explore, in a qualitative fashion, differences between integrated and segregated settings. PASS assessments of the three programs showed that the total PASS score of the integrated program (+159) was higher than those of the two segregated programs (-310 and -572), although all three were weak, both programmatically (in the areas of model coherency, individualization, intensity of relevant programming, and developmental growth orientation) and administratively. The integrated program offered a more normalizing support system, greater accessibility, and a more appropriate size.

For her doctoral-dissertation research in social welfare, Perlik (1984) used the physical integration section of PASS (i.e., the six ratings of Local Proximity, Regional Proximity, Access, Physical Resources, Program-Neighborhood Harmony, and Congregation and Assimilation Potential) to assess the physical structure of 30 community residences in Massachusetts for people with mental retardation. Risk-taking by residents was found to be related to their level of adaptive behavior, the presence of other handicaps, the length of time they had been in the residence, and the tenure of the program manager.

In an invited paper delivered at a symposium on the costs and effects of deinstitutionalization, Flynn (1985) reported on an augmented sample of 519 PASS 3 evaluations that included the 256 reported in the 1980 chapter. Two-thirds of the assessments stemmed from PASS training workshops, 69% were of programs located in the United States (with the other 31% in Canada), 85% were segregated (i.e., served only persons with some potentially or actually devaluing condition), 81% were evaluations of community-based programs, 59% involved programs serving adults, 58% of the programs were operated by private, not-for-profit agencies, and 53% were in the field of mental retardation, with a further 10% in mental health, 5% in aging, and 4% in physical impairment. Factor analysis was again used to derive PASS subscales, with those emerging being very similar to those in Flynn (1980). The newly derived subscales were given the same names as before: Normalization-Program, 16 items (Cronbach's $\alpha = 0.90$); Normalization-Setting, 11 items ($\alpha = 0.79$); Administration, 9 items ($\alpha = 0.71$), and Proximity and Access, 4 items ($\alpha = 0.67$). The same kinds of programs were compared as in the earlier chapter (institutional residences and community-based child development, educational, vocational, and residential programs). As in the 1980 study, all four types of community programs were superior, in terms of overall service quality (as assessed by the total PASS score), to the institutional residences, with the child development services better than the other kinds of community programs. Also, on the four PASS subscales, the various types of services tended to have distinctive strengths and weaknesses: The child development programs were the strongest programmatically, while the community residences and child development services were the best in terms of Normalization of the setting. On the other hand, across all five kinds of programs, Proximity and Access was the single strongest dimension of service quality, with Administration tending to be uniformly weak.

Heal and Daniels (1986) investigated the costs and effects of three residential alternatives (natural homes, group homes, and landlord-supervised apartments) in northern Wisconsin. A total of 29 adults with developmental disabilities lived in the community residences. The total PASS 3 score was used to assess the level of Normalization achieved in the residences (2 group homes, 2 apartments, and 9 natural homes). The individual resident was the unit of analysis employed, and total PASS scores for residents were related to five other measures: client satisfaction, the individual resident's contribution in labor and money to his or her own residential service, society's contribution in labour and money to the resident's residential service; and Parts I and II of the AAMD Adaptive Behavior Scale (ABS; Nihira et al., 1974). Overall, Heal and Daniels found that with controls for scores on Parts I and II of the ABS and for the individual's contribution to his or her own residential service costs, individuals in apartments and especially in natural homes were exposed to more normalizing environments, were more satisfied, and required lower societal expenditures than those in group homes. Heal and Daniels also suggested that all three forms of community residences were more normalized and less costly than institutional placement would have been.

Webb, Wells, and Hornblow (1986) used PASS 3 to measure the level of Normalization of 3 hospital residential units, housing 24 to 38 intellectually handicapped persons, and 4 community residences, each with 6 to 10 residents. In this article, which was based on Webb's (1983) doctoral dissertation research, the behavior of 24 residents was measured before and after they moved from the hospital to the community residences. Webb et al. (1986) found some overlap between the scores in the two types of settings, although the community residences tended to have higher Normalization scores (approximately 50% to 80% of the maximum possible score) than the hospital units (approximately 33% to 52%). Second, whether in the hospital or in the community, units with higher Normalization (PASS) scores had younger and more intelligent residents who also behaved more adaptively and less maladaptively. Twenty-four residents changed living environments, with 19 moving to more normalized settings. Interestingly, during the year following the move, the adaptive behavior of the 19 residents who moved to a more normalized setting actually declined. This was due not to the increased Normalization level of the new home but rather to the fact that the adaptive behavior of those who had moved worsened and became similar to the average adaptive behavior of the other residents in their new home. The maladaptive behavior of those moving to a more normalized environment did not change, although that of comparison residents in one of the hospital units did improve significantly. Also, although the day-to-day behavior of residents who had moved changed very little, they talked less, were socially isolated more often, and were happy less frequently, after the move. Webb et al. concluded that the decline in adaptive behavior and in well-being following the move may have been due to the fact that intensive training programs existed in the hospital units but not in the community residences. They thus suggested that training programs are needed, beyond a mere move from one residential environment to another, to develop and maintain intellectually handicapped people's functioning, social competence, and happiness.

Picard's five-volume study (1988a, 1988b, 1988c, 1988d, 1988e) of adaptation and social integration among mentally retarded persons living in family-care homes ("familles d'accueil") is one of the most ambitious investigations to have been conducted with PASS 3 and certainly the most exhaustively reported. Funded by the Quebec Council on Social Research and the Regional Council for Health and Social Services in the Quebec City area, Picard's research assessed the effects of personal characteristics, the residential environment, and services received on residents' adaptation and social integration. Using a cross-sectional, correlational research design, Picard (1988a) studied 52 persons who had moved from institutional settings to one of 22 family-care homes in the Quebec City region. Nine percent of the homes were located in a downtown area, 50% were suburban, 22% were semi-urban, and 9% were rural. Picard (1988b) used Flynn's (1980) PASS subscales to evaluate the degree of Normalization of 21 of the family-care environments. A French version of the Adaptive Behavior Scale (Lessard, 1975) served as the measure of adaptive behavior. Social integration was assessed with a "Questionnaire d'intégration sociale" (QIS) constructed by Picard. Picard (1988b) assessed the reliability of PASS, both between and within teams. Two 2-person PASS rating teams assessed the same family-care home, and each team then evaluated a different set of 10 homes. One team rated the home evaluated in common about 4% higher than the other team (interteam agreement), while members of the same team differed by only 2% in their ratings of their respective set of 10 homes (intrateam agreement).

Substantively, Picard (1988b) found the average quality of the 21 family-care homes to be similar to the norms reported by Flynn (1985) for community residences. Picard also found a high degree of variability in the quality of the homes: The mean total PASS score (summing across 43 rather than 50 ratings) in his sample of 21 homes was 45% of the maximum possible weighted score (range = 28% to 78%). Picard discovered that the two strongest dimensions of quality were Normalization-Setting ($M = 62\%$, range = 36% to 95%) and Proximity and Access ($M = 61\%$, range = 5% to 92%), both related more to physical than to social integration. The two weakest aspects were Normalization-Program ($M = 41\%$, range = 10% to 91%) and Administration ($M =$ approximately 22%, according to Figure 2 in Picard, 1988b, p. 50, with the 21 homes getting the same score on Administration because they were all administered by a single agency).

Picard (1988e) also assessed the degree of association between the characteristics of the 52 residents and the 21 family home environments by assigning to each resident the PASS scores for his or her own home (a procedure that attenuates person-environment correlations). His findings were largely in conformity with hypotheses derivable from Normalization and Social Role Valorization theory. At the level of the individual resident, for example, higher PASS scores were significantly ($p < .05$) associated with living in a family-care home that had a smaller number of residents. This relationship was found on Normalization-Program, Normalization-Setting, and the total PASS score. Higher resident-level PASS scores were also associated with living in more specialized, intensive, and developmentally oriented residences (a relationship found on Normalization-Program, Proximity and Access, and the total PASS score) and in urban residences (found on Proximity and Access and the total PASS score).

As he had also hypothesized, Picard found that the PASS 3 scales were better predictors of social integration than of adaptive behavior. The PASS measures accounted for relatively little variance in the 11 measures of adaptive behavior used and none were among the best predictors of the individual resident's global level of adaptive behavior (cf. Picard, 1988e, Table 53, p. 175). There were, however, a few significant ($p < .05$) PASS/adaptive behavior correlations: Residents in homes scoring higher on

Normalization-Program had higher scores on socialization; those in homes scoring higher on Proximity and Access had fewer economic-activity and self-direction skills; and those in homes scoring higher on the total PASS scale were more competent in the use of numbers and time. In contrast, the PASS scales were systematically and strongly related to Picard's seven measures of social integration, with Normalization-Program emerging as the second best predictor of the resident's overall level of social integration (the best was the length of institutionalization; cf. Picard, 1988e, Table 60, p. 190). Other significant PASS/social integration correlations included: residents in homes scoring higher on Normalization-Program engaged more frequently in integrative activities, needed less assistance in participating in these activities, and had a higher overall level of social integration; those in homes scoring higher on Normalization-Setting had, unexpectedly, fewer diversified social contacts; those in homes scoring higher on Proximity and Access took part in more activities outside the home; and those in homes scoring higher on the total PASS scale had contacts with a more diverse range of persons, including ordinary citizens.

In a detailed research monograph, Borthwick-Duffy, Widaman, Little, and Eyman (1992) reported the findings from an ambitious 3-year longitudinal study of foster family care. The goal of the research was to identify characteristics of the individual and of the home environment that were likely to affect development and quality of life. The sample was composed of 333 persons with mental retardation who were 21 years of age or younger at the beginning of the study. They were drawn from a four-county region of Southern California served by a regional center that had a strong preference for community placements, especially family-care placements. The core analyses were based on a subsample of 148 persons who were assessed in Years 1, 2, and 3 and whose placements were stable throughout the 3 years of the study. The sample members resided in a total of 151 family care homes. The primary careprovider in each home furnished data on each resident, as did 95% of the natural parents.

In all, nine instruments were used to assess four targets: the person with mental retardation, the careprovider, the home, and the natural parents. Three instruments were employed to measure characteristics of the home. The first was PASS 3, with Flynn's (1980) four PASS factors being used: Normalization-Program, Normalization-Setting, Administration, and Proximity and Access. PASS was completed by project staff during the 1st year in which a given family care home took part in the research. It was completed only once because the researchers felt that the characteristics of the home were unlikely to change during the 3-year study period. The second environmental instrument was a modified version of Bradley and Caldwell's (1979) Home Observation for the Measurement of the Environment (HOME). The modified scale (Foster HOME, or FHOME) covered the same domains as the original instrument: provision of stimulation through equipment, toys, and experience; stimulation of mature behavior; provision of a stimulating physical and language environment; avoidance of restriction and punishment; pride, affection, and thoughtfulness; provision of masculine role models; independence of parental control; child-centered flexibility; and family integration. The FHOME was also administered only once, during the 1st year that a given home was in the study, because little variance was found across homes on most items. The third measure of the environment was the Home Quality Rating Scale (HQRS), designed by the project researchers. The HQRS was intended to measure the sense of love and attachment exhibited by the caretaker toward the person with mental retardation, the intrafamilial dynamics related to the target person, and family participation in care of the target person. The HQRS covered five domains: harmony of home and quality of parenting, concordance in support of child care, openness and awareness of the careprovider, quality of the residential environment or dwelling, and quality of the residential area or neighborhood. HQRS ratings were completed three times, during each year of the study.

As part of their larger study, Borthwick-Duffy et al. (1992) hypothesized and tested a quality-of-life model consisting of four major dimensions: the residential environment, interpersonal relations, community involvement, and stability (i.e., tenure in placement). The first dimension (residential environment), in turn, was composed of affective, cognitive, physical, and Normalization components. Flynn's (1980) Normalization-Program and Normalization-Setting

PASS 3 factors were used to measure the Normalization component. Confirmatory factor analysis (implemented with LISREL 7; Jöreskog & Sörbom, 1988) revealed that a single third-order factor, Environment, provided an adequate fit to the data, when estimated on all 333 sample members. This result was possible only because the affective, cognitive, physical, and Normalization-related aspects of environmental quality had a sufficiently high intercorrelation.

The quality of the residential environment was found to exert a positive influence on interpersonal relationships (within the foster care home and with the natural family and friends and neighbors), though not until the 3rd year. This suggested that some environmental characteristics may have a slow but important cumulative effect on the lives of residents. The Normalization component of the residential environment was found to be, in part, a product of the people—clients and caretakers—living in the home. Specifically, clients who were older or more severely retarded tended to live in homes that were less normalized. Also, careproviders who were older or who had more experience or training were found to provide less normalized environments, whereas caretakers with more formal education had homes that were more normalized. Borthwick-Duffy et al. (1992) speculated that older and more experienced caretakers may have acquired their basic routines and philosophy of care before the advent of Normalization, and that the recency of caretaker training may be more related to Normalization than is the amount of such training.

Mindel and Rosentraub (1992) evaluated the implementation and impact of an experimental program in Texas, Home and Community Services (HCS), in which persons with mental handicaps who qualified for Medicaid assistance moved from state institutions to community-based residences. The new program also maintained people in the community who were at risk of being institutionalized. It placed special emphasis on developing small, family-sized, normalized living environments for each individual served, with tailored treatment programs, individualized daily schedules, and client involvement in planning daily activities. During its 3 years of operation, the evaluation collected data on 72 persons who were in the HCS program for 3 years and on 214 persons who were in it for 2 years only. HCS participants who had lived in an institution prior to the program were matched with a comparison group of institutionalized persons on diagnosis, IQ, age, race, and length of institutionalization. HCS participants living in the community before joining the program were also matched with community residents on the same variables (except the last). Implementation of Normalization was assessed with seven (unspecified) rating areas from PASS and three ratings developed by Conroy and Feinstein (1985). Periodic checks on the interrater reliability of these measures produced coefficients in the 0.85-0.95 range. The impact of the new program was assessed in terms of adaptive behavior in four domains (communication, daily living skills, socialization, and motor skills) and of maladaptive behavior. The instrument used was the Vineland Adaptive Behavior Scales (VABS; Sparrow, Balla, & Cicchetti, 1984).

In assessing the *implementation* of the experimental program, Mindel and Rosentraub (1992) found that the Normalization scores of the living environments of the previously institutionalized HCS clients improved significantly ($p < .05$) from Year 1 to Year 2, before leveling off between Years 2 and 3. In contrast, no change in the living environments of the institutionalized comparison-group subjects took place over the 3-year period. Thus, compared with state institutions, the HCS program did succeed in creating more normalized living environments. No differences were found, however, between the Normalization scores of the living arrangements of HCS participants living in the community before joining the program and the scores of comparison-group members, nor did the scores of either group change over the 3-year study period. Hence, for participants coming from the community, HCS living arrangements were no more normalized than those of the community-based comparison subjects. Concerning the *impact* of the HCS program on adaptive and maladaptive behavior, the data suggested that the program was of greatest value for previously institutionalized persons with a diagnosis of severe or profound retardation, regular medical needs, and/or initially high levels of maladaptive behavior. Improvements were slight for other clients. Mindel and Rosentraub (1992) recommended that the U.S. government should expand innovative Medicaid-waiver options such as the HCS but also encourage more flexible approaches to the design of community living environments than were tried by the HCS program.

In Great Britain, Carson, Dowling, Luyombya, Senapti-Sharma, and Glynn (1992) compared two traditional in-patient psychiatric rehabilitation wards with the Tomswood Hill project, a new residential program based on Normalization principles. Designed to prepare "hard to place" hospital residents for eventual resettlement in the community, the new project consisted of a small-scale domestic setting on the hospital grounds. Its creators felt that the advantages of having the backup of experienced psychiatric hospital staff outweighed the "deviancy image juxtaposition" problems posed by close proximity to the hospital. The project manager attended a PASS course and then initiated a program of staff training designed to combine principles drawn from good psychiatric nursing care with the best ideas from Normalization theory (e.g., the use of ordinary housing, the provision of genuine choices, the sharing of information with participants, high-quality staff-resident interactions, respectful language, personalization of care, etc.). The researchers compared the Tomswood Hill project, serving 7 residents, with two in-patient rehabilitation wards, serving 31 and 12 residents, respectively. The evaluation instruments included PASS and measures of behavior, quality of life, staff attitudes to treatment, ward management, and resident satisfaction. Carson et al. found that residents in the Normalization project had a significantly higher level of quality of life, were exposed to the most individualized and resident-oriented ward-management practices, and were accompanied more frequently into the community by staff members. Staff in the Normalization project were more satisfied with their work. Carson et al. suggested that their study was important because it contributed to the scarce literature comparing innovative Normalization projects with more traditional psychiatric service options and also because it was one of the few studies within a psychiatric as opposed to a mental-retardation context to have examined the application of Normalization principles.

Flynn (1993) reported on the level of physical and social integration in an augmented sample of 626 PASS 3 evaluations in a paper given at an international conference devoted to the theme of integration. Evaluated between 1975 and 1987, the 626 programs were located mainly in the United States (57%) and Canada (32%), with another 10% in France. Sixty-five percent of the programs served persons with intellectual handicaps, 79% had been evaluated during PASS training workshops, and 58% served adults. Thirty-seven percent were community residences, 16% institutional residences, 15% work preparation or employment programs, and 9% child development programs. The same PASS factors and subscales as in Flynn (1985) were used. In the sample of 626 programs as a whole, overall service quality (as indexed by the total PASS score) was 43% of the maximum possible score, that is, somewhat below the "minimally acceptable" level of 50%. The mean for Proximity and Access was higher than for the other three subscales, with the mean for Normalization-Setting also higher than the means for Normalization-Program and Administration. Moreover, differences among the PASS subscales were considerably greater than were differences among the three countries for which there were enough programs in the sample to permit comparisons: the USA ($n = 350$), Canada ($n = 195$), and France ($n = 59$). Overall service quality fell between 46% of the maximum possible weighted score (Canada) and 40% (USA). In the case of all three countries, Proximity and Access was clearly the best dimension of service quality, followed by Normalization-Setting, Normalization-Program, and Administration. Finally, overall service quality (total PASS score) was highest in the subgroup of community child development programs ($n = 50$), followed by community residences ($n = 214$), community educational services ($n = 38$), community vocational programs ($n = 87$), and institutional residences ($n = 93$).

Williams (1995) provided an interesting report on the results of PASS 3 and PASSING evaluations in Great Britain. (A brief description of his PASSING-related findings may be found in the section of the present chapter devoted to PASSING research.) His chapter was part of a book (Pilling & Watson, 1995) devoted, in large part, to a mainly favorable critique of PASS and PASSING as evaluation tools. Williams presented data from 13 service evaluations that suggested that PASS 3 had an acceptable level of reliability. Concerning the validity of PASS 3, Williams presented data from 52 evaluations of British residential services. As expected, the instrument discriminated among the various types of residences: 5 hospital wards formed the lowest-scoring group (*Mdn* = 9% of the maximum possible score); a group of 7 ordinary houses managed by social service, voluntary, or private agencies scored considerably better (*Mdn* = 44%); and 3 life-sharing homes constituted the highest-scoring group (*Mdn* = 63%). Williams also noted that the average scores for large residences (more than 8 places) in Britain evaluated with PASS 3 (*n* = 37; *Mdn* = 20% of the maximum possible PASS score) were similar to those for institutional residences in North America assessed with PASSING (*n* = 23; *M* = 21%, as reported by Flynn et al., 1991). Similarly, the average scores for small residences (less than 8 places) in Britain assessed with PASS 3 (*n* = 27; *Mdn* = 40%) were similar to the average scores for community group residences in North America evaluated with PASSING (*n* = 79; *M* = 37%, again as reported by Flynn, LaPointe, Wolfensberger, & Thomas, 1991).

Williams (1995) gave an illustration of how PASS (or PASSING) can be used to compare service programs within a single agency, as well as groups of similar services with each other. He also noted that British data on services that have been evaluated with PASS or PASSING on several occasions suggest that little change takes place over time unless the service has undergone major structural change (e.g., a move from a single large building to smaller dispersed units). He also observed that, as in North America, many British day services (e.g., adult training centers) score poorly on PASS, due probably to a lack of model coherency. Williams's chapter also contains useful discussions of the key evaluation issues of improving services, identifying service users' major life needs, and reporting the results of an assessment to various stakeholder groups.

In another British study, Perry and Felce (1995) collected data on several measures of service quality (including PASS 3) in a sample of 14 community homes in Wales serving people with learning difficulties (i.e., developmental disabilities). All were small, staffed residences, ranging in size from 1 to 7 places. Each house was observed for 11 hours a day for 3 days over a 2-year period. PASS rating clusters were used to assess the following aspects of quality of life: quality of housing, social and community integration, social interactions, development, activity,

and autonomy and choice. Rank-order correlations (r_s) were computed to see to what extent different measures of quality within each category agreed with one another. The PASS physical-facility appearance subscore correlated consistently and significantly with the Characteristics of the Physical Environment (CPE) scale (Rotegard, Bruininks, & Hill, 1981), an index mainly of internal housing quality (range of rank-order correlations with the CPE scale = 0.41-0.64). Similarly, several PASS indicators of social and community integration were significantly and substantially correlated with the frequency of social contacts and community activities (range of r_s = 0.53-0.59). The PASS Interactions rating was significantly and negatively correlated (r_s = -0.65 and -0.49 in Years 1 and 2, respectively) with the social distance dimension of the Group Home Management Schedule (GHMS; Pratt, Luszcz, & Brown, 1980), a social-interaction measure. The PASS cluster of ratings known as "developmental growth orientation" was significantly correlated (r_s = 0.61 and 0.46 in Years 1 and 2, respectively) with the personal growth dimension of the Community Oriented Programs Environment Scale (COPES; Moos, 1974). The PASS ratings *Age-Appropriate Activities, Routines, and Rhythms* and *Culture-Appropriate Activities, Routines and Rhythms* were very strongly correlated (r_s = 0.73 and 0.78) with the Index of Participation in Domestic Life scores for Years 1 and 2, respectively (IPDL; Raynes, Sumpton, and Pettifer, 1989). Finally, the PASS ratings related to age-appropriate autonomy and rights and individualization were strongly negatively correlated (r_s = -0.59 and -0.64) with the scores for Years 1 and 2, respectively, of a GHMS autonomy/choice measure calculated by summing across the GHMS dimensions of depersonalization, block treatment, and rigidity of routine. Perry and Felce concluded that broad agreement existed among those measures (including PASS) assessing similar aspects of quality of life. They also recommended that process perspectives on quality of service and quality of life be complemented by data on outcomes.

Felce and Perry (1997) presented and discussed the strictly PASS-related data collected during their earlier study of service quality in 14 community residences in Wales (Perry & Felce, 1995). Three-member PASS teams, made up of experienced raters, visited each home for 2 days, and then arrived at a conciliated score on each PASS rating. Overall, average (mean) service quality was highest on the PASS rating clusters concerned with physical integration ($M = 67\%$ of the maximum possible score), quality of setting ($M = 45\%$), and social integration ($M = 42\%$). Average quality was relatively low, however, on the rating clusters concerned with age-appropriate interpretations and structures ($M = 32\%$), developmental growth orientation ($M = 18\%$), model coherency ($M = 11\%$), and administration ($M = 16\%$). The total PASS score was also fairly low ($M = 35\%$). Size of residence interacted with the ability level of the residents, such that smaller residences (1 to 3 residents) serving people with higher scores on part 1 of the Adaptive Behavior Scale (Nihira et al., 1974) were of higher quality than were larger residences (4 to 7 residents) serving less able persons. Overall, Felce and Perry (1997) found the 14 residences, as a group, to be reasonably homelike and to be located well enough to permit residents to have access to the surrounding community. However, the personnel working in them tended not to possess the organized means and competencies necessary to promote residents' development, and administrative practices were also weak. Felce and Perry (1997) concluded that as much attention must now be given to the technical proficiency and quality of community services as has previously been paid to their size, location, accessibility, and staffing. That is, service personnel must focus primarily on understanding people's needs, responding in relevant and intense ways to these needs, and helping people achieve greater self-direction, personal development, and social integration.

Flynn, Guirguis, Wolfensberger, and Cocks (in press) carried out the most definitive factor analysis to date of PASS 3, employing a large sample and cross-validation procedures. Their paper consisted of two separate factor-analytic studies: Study 1 concerned PASS (and will be discussed now), while Study 2 dealt with PASSING (and will be described later, in the section devoted to PASSING research). In Study 1, Flynn et al. were able to use a larger sample of PASS 3 evaluations ($N = 626$) than had been available in previous factor analyses of the instrument. The evaluations had been conducted in several countries, including Canada, the USA, France, and Switzerland, during the period 1975-1987. Seventy-nine percent of the evaluations had been carried out during PASS training workshops, and another 14% had been conducted during official evaluations. In all cases, the assessments had been conciliated under the direction of experienced team leaders. Flynn et al. first conducted an exploratory factor analysis (EFA) on a randomly chosen half of the sample ($n = 313$) in order to identify the number of factors in the instrument and the items that were especially good indicators of each factor (i.e., that had an absolute factor loading of at least 0.50). They followed this with a confirmatory factor analysis (CFA) that successfully cross-validated the model derived in the EFA. Four factors proved necessary and sufficient to represent the factor structure of PASS (see Table 14.1).

The first factor, Program, consisting of the *content* of a service program, included items tapping service processes consistent with the Normalization principle, such as age-appropriate possessions and culture-appropriate activities, routines and rhythms. The second factor, Setting, assessed the correspondence between the facility and neighborhood in which the program was located and the Normalization principle (e.g., the degree of "fit" between the facility and its function, and between the facility and the neighborhood). The third factor, Administration, assessed program management, evaluation, and self-renewal processes. The fourth factor, Accessibility, measured the proximity and accessibility of the program to client-users and their families and to pertinent physical resources. The subscales formed from each of these four factors were found to be homogeneous and, together, had a very strong multiple correlation with the total PASS score in the overall sample of 626 evaluations ($R = 0.97$, $p < .001$). Flynn et al. (in press) suggested that their results promised to enhance the practical usefulness of PASS as an evaluation instrument by providing factorially valid and sensitive measures that would facilitate comparisons among and within programs and enable PASS evaluators to organize their field assessments more coherently around the core service dimensions of program, setting, administration, and accessibility.

TABLE 14.1

FOUR CROSS-VALIDATED PASS 3 FACTORS—PROGRAM, SETTING, ADMINISTRATION, AND ACCESSIBILITY—AND THE ITEMS COMPOSING EACH (ADAPTED FROM FLYNN ET AL., IN PRESS)

Factor 1: Program (14 items)
14. Socially Integrative Social Activities
16. Age-Appropriate Personal Appearance
17. Age-Appropriate Activities, Routines, and Rhythms
18. Age-Appropriate Labels and Forms of Address
19. Age-Appropriate Autonomy and Rights
20. Age-Appropriate Possessions
21. Age-Appropriate Sex Behavior
23. Culture-Appropriate Personal Appearance
24. Culture-Appropriate Activities, Routines, and Rhythms
27. Model Coherency
29. Social Overprotection
30. Intensity of Relevant Programming
33. Individualization
34. Interactions

Factor 2: Setting (3 items)
8. Function Congruity Image
9. Building-Neighborhood Harmony
28. Physical Overprotection

Factor 3: Administration (5 items)
37. Consumer and Public Participation
38. Education of the Public
40. Ties to Academia
47. Planning Process
48. Program Evaluation and Renewal Mechanisms

Factor 4: Accessibility (3 items)
1. Local Proximity
3. Access
4. Physical Resources

1.4   STUDIES BASED ON SHORT FORMS OF PASS 3

Fiorelli (1978) derived a 15-item PASS short form by selecting items from PASS 2 and PASS 3 and used the instrument to examine the behavior of 4 adults with

mental retardation for 5 to 6 weeks before and for 5 to 6 weeks after they moved from institutional (less normalized) to community-apartment (more normalized) settings. Fiorelli (1978; summarized in Fiorelli & Thurman, 1979) used videotaped recording and a complex behavior-coding system to investigate whether, as Normalization theory would predict, client behavior would become more normalized following movement to a more normalized residential environment. Overall, Fiorelli (1978) found clients manifested many favorable behavioral changes during the initial 5 to 6 weeks of community living.

Flynn and Heal (1981) derived and validated an 18-item PASS 3 short form. While recognizing that the full instrument should be used when an evaluation is intended to guide official decision-making about a particular program, Flynn and Heal suggested that a short form of PASS might be useful for other purposes, such as carrying out "spot checks" on a program or group of services or conducting research studies in which a standardized measure of Normalization was needed but in which financial resources would not permit a large number of evaluations to be carried out with the PASS long form. The 18-item short form was derived as follows. The 50 PASS 3 items were first screened for their ability to make relatively subtle discriminations among four types of community residences (i.e., apartments and small, medium, and large group homes). Second, factor and item analyses were conducted on the 25 items that were found to discriminate, ultimately leaving 3 relatively independent PASS subscales: Normalization-Program (8 items, $\alpha = 0.85$), Normalization-Setting (6 items, $\alpha = 0.64$), and Administration (4 items, $\alpha = 0.62$). Using data collected by Heal with a 3-person team in another sample of 14 community residential programs, Flynn and Heal found that interrater reliability (intraclass correlations) was generally excellent, for both the long and the short form of PASS. For the complete, 50-item PASS 3 scale, interrater reliability was 0.70 for a single rater and 0.94 for the mean of seven raters. For the 18-item short form, the corresponding figures for Normalization-Program were 0.72 and 0.95, for Normalization-Setting, 0.34 and 0.78, and for Administration, 0.83 and 0.97. Flynn and Heal further studied interrater reliability with data collected by 2 two-person teams that had each assessed 4 institutional cottages with the

PASS 3 short form during the initial phase of the longitudinal Pennhurst evaluation (cf. Conroy, 1979). For Normalization-Program and Normalization-Setting, interrater reliability estimates were again high, ranging from 0.82 to 0.97 for single raters to 0.97 to 0.99 for 7-person teams. Very low intercottage variance on Administration produced interrater reliability coefficients that were zero or close to zero. Cross-validation of the PASS 3 short form on 7 independent samples produced multiple correlations between the short and long form that ranged from 0.89 to 0.98. Moreover, the convergent and discriminant validity of the first two subscales of the short form was good. Evidence was also produced that was supportive of the criterion-related validity of the long and short forms of PASS. Regression analyses carried out in a sample of 173 programs with complete data on all PASS and external criterion variables showed that services had significantly higher total PASS and Normalization-Program scores if they were located in Canada rather than in the USA, were community-rather than institution-based, served a smaller number of clients, and had a higher proportion of staff with college degrees. Programs had significantly higher Normalization-Setting scores if they were located in Canada, were integrated, and were residential in nature.

Conroy, Efthimiou, and Lemanowicz (1982) employed Flynn and Heal's (1981) PASS 3 short form in a longitudinal study that addressed the hypothesis that more normalized settings would facilitate more normative and independent client behavior. Conroy et al. compared changes in the adaptive behavior of a sample of 70 persons with mental retardation who remained at Pennhurst Center in Pennsylvania and 70 clients who left Pennhurst (77% had severe or profound retardation). The two groups were matched on gender, level of retardation, chronological age, years institutionalized, self-care ability, and IQ. All 140 subjects resided at Pennhurst at Time 1 (the initial assessment). A follow-up assessment took place 2 years later, when half, under the terms of a Federal court order, had moved to community living arrangements. The research design was a quasi-experimental, prepost, nonequivalent control group design. The goal was to identify specific demographic and environmental variables that might be associated with client growth. The adaptive behavior of the deinstitutionalized clients alone improved significantly, although neither group's maladaptive behavior changed significantly. The partial correlation between the total score on the PASS 3 short form and gains in adaptive behavior, controlling for the client's initial level of adaptive behavior, was -0.25 ($p = 0.05$), indicating that clients coming from institutional cottages that had lower PASS scores (i.e., lower levels of Normalization, individualization, and physical pleasantness) gained more after moving to community residential settings. The total PASS score was positively correlated with a measure of the physical quality of the institutional cottages derived from standards of the Accreditation Council for Services for Mentally Retarded and Other Developmentally Disabled Persons (ACMRDD), a finding that is supportive of the concurrent validity of the PASS short form. Overall, Conroy et al. found support for their basic Normalization hypothesis that relocation to more normalized settings would facilitate clients' adaptive functioning.

In their final report on the 5-year longitudinal Pennhurst study, Conroy and Bradley (1985) provided data on the complete set of PASS evaluations carried out both at Pennhurst (with two-person teams) and in the community (with one-person teams only, the latter a data-collection procedure that precluded the assessment of interrater reliability as well as the reliability and validity-related safeguard of conciliation between team members). Conroy and Bradley found that, for 157 study participants, the mean increase in PASS short form scores was 404 points, from -232 at Pennhurst in 1979 to +172 in the community in 1982. (The standard deviation of the increase in scores was not given, however, making interpretation of this gain difficult.) In later waves of measurement, carried out on 320 clients residing in the same community residence in both 1983 and 1984, the total score on the PASS 3 short form had a simple correlation of 0.31 ($p < .001$) with the 1983 level of adaptive behavior and a partial correlation of 0.12 ($p < .05$) with gain in adaptive behavior between 1983 and 1984 (cf. Conroy & Bradley, 1985, pp. 156-157). Thus, clients tended to make larger gains in community residences with higher Normalization scores.

Interestingly, Conroy and Bradley (1985) found that the PASS short form was useful (i.e., sensitive and dis-criminating) not only before but also after the focus of their research shifted from Pennhurst to the community. In contrast, the researchers had to abandon other environmental measures after the move to the community, either because of insensitivity to client growth (the case with the experimental ACMRDD standards) or because of "ceiling" effects (found with the Resident Management Survey, developed by King, Raynes, and Tizard, 1971, and with the Characteristics of the Treatment Environment, developed by Jackson, 1969).

On the other hand, Conroy and Bradley (1985, pp. 159ff) expressed dismay upon finding that their environmental measures, including the PASS 3 short form, were correlated with characteristics of the residents of the setting being evaluated, with residents having higher levels of adaptive behavior being found in higher-quality and more normalizing residential settings. In my opinion, however, it seems erroneous to expect environmental measures to be completely independent of resident attributes. The reason is simple: The greater the challenge presented by a particular client or group of clients (in relation to demanding goals such as the promotion and attainment of social integration, developmental growth, or positive social imagery), the more likely it is, empirically, that a program serving such clients will have difficulty in meeting the challenge and will therefore attain a lower score on PASS, PASSING, or other environmental measures. (Incidentally, in chapter 9 of the present volume, Heal presents data that I interpret as consistent with my position on this issue. The findings of Borthwick-Duffy et al., 1992, presented earlier in this chapter, are also consistent with my position.)

Conroy and Bradley (1985) also expressed concerns about year-to-year fluctuations in PASS short form scores, observed during their annual assessments of the same community living arrangements. This issue of potential score (i.e., trait) instability, in the absence of any real change in program quality, is obviously crucial and deserving of further research. It is thus doubly unfortunate that, contrary to standard PASS practice, Conroy and Bradley chose to use single raters rather than teams of raters (even 2-person teams) during the community phase of the Pennhurst study. This decision made it impossible for them to separate true-score variance (i.e., year-to year changes in service quality) from error variance (i.e., changes due to rater bias).

In his doctoral dissertation in special education, Korn (1987) studied the issue of the interteam reliability of PASS. He developed a standardized, videotape-based stimulus called SPIRA (Simulated PASS Inquiry-Related Assessment) based on 20 mainly administration-related PASS ratings. The rating performance of two 5-member PASS teams was compared, one team having received 5 days of training, the other 1 day only. No differences were found between the two formats. Korn recommended SPIRA as one means of enhancing PASS-related reliability research and training.

Conroy (1996) compared the quality of life experienced by people living in small intermediate care facilities for the mentally retarded (ICFs/MR) in Pennsylvania with that experienced by people residing in group homes in the same state. There were 51 people in each group, matched on adaptive behavior, challenging behavior, age, and gender. The typical ICF/MR had eight residents, versus three for the typical group home. Clients were assessed in 1992 on a battery of measures that had evolved from those used in the Pennhurst Longitudinal Study (Conroy & Bradley, 1985) and were compared on a total of 35 indicators of quality of life. One of these was a Normalization Index, which Conroy and his colleagues had created by selecting 10 of the 18 items contained in Flynn and Heal's (1981) 18-item PASS short form. According to Conroy (1996), Devlin (1989) found the Normalization Scale to have interrater reliability of 0.64 and test-retest reliability of 0.90. (Unfortunately, several important details are unclear from Conroy's [1996] article: whether the reliability coefficient of 0.64 was derived on the 18-item or the 10-item PASS short form, the type of reliability coefficient in question, or whether reliability here is that for a single rater or of the mean of several raters.)

Conroy's (1996) methodology and conclusions were criticized by Crinella, McCleary, and Swanson (1998). Besides publishing Conroy's (1998) reply to his critics, Taylor (1998), the editor of *Mental Retardation*, in which Conroy's article had been published, also asked the journal's statistical consultant, Heifetz (1998), to conduct an independent review of the papers by Conroy (1996) and Crinella et al. According to Heifetz's (1998) analysis of Conroy's findings, quality of life was superior for residents in community living arrangements (CLA) on 8 of 34 measures, including the 10-item Normalization Index ($p < .01$), which was thus shown to be capable of discriminating between the two types of residential settings. (It may be noted in passing that Heifetz found the quality of life of ICF/MR residents to be higher than that of CLA residents on only 1 of the 34 measures.)

Lemay (1997) conducted the most recent PASS short-form study, a rare longitudinal assessment of program change, over a 5-year period. Working as a 2-person team, Lemay and a colleague used Flynn and Heal's (1981) 18-item PASS 3 short form to evaluate, in 1996, the quality of 15 large community residences ("pavillons") in Quebec, each serving 10 to 14 residents with psychiatric disorders. The residences had originally been evaluated with the short form in 1991. Lemay found no significant change in the sample of 15 residential programs over the 5-year period on the Program subscale of the PASS 3 short form (1991 M = 43% versus 1996 M = 42%, ns), but a significant improvement on the other two subscales, Setting (1991 M = 36% versus 1996 M = 45%, $p < .05$) and Administration (1991 M = 39% versus 1996 M = 55%, $p < .001$). Despite these gains, service quality was still quite low. Lemay made a number of recommendations aimed at improving the residences, including a reduction in the number of residents to no more than 4 to 6 per setting, greater similarity among residents (along dimensions such as interests and age) to promote social interaction and a sense of community, increased personal space and individualization, implementation of a developmental model congruent with the needs and capacities of each resident, and increased involvement with ordinary citizens in each local community.

1.5   STUDIES BASED ON ADAPTATIONS OF PASS 3

These studies have been included in the present review for the sake of completeness and because of their overall relevance for PASS research. In the early 1980s, Hull and Thompson published several papers that were based on an adaptation of PASS 3 (Hull, Keats, & Thompson, 1984; Hull & Thompson, 1980, 1981a, 1981b). In their initial study, Hull and Thompson (1980) examined the degree to which individual, residential, and community characteristics were related to the adaptive functioning of 369 persons with mental retardation living in 144 community settings (board-and-care facilities and staffed residences) in Manitoba. Residents' median age was

36 (range, 18 to 73) and their median IQ was 54 (range, low 20s to above 90). Sixty-five percent of the residents had previously been institutionalized. Thirty aspects of environmental Normalization were assessed by means of a 172-item measure, itself based on 30 PASS 3 ratings. The median interrater reliability achieved on the new instrument (percentage of identical responses from two interviews) was 93%. Adaptive functioning was assessed with Marlett's (1977a, 1977b) Adaptive Functioning Index (AFI). In a series of stepwise regression analyses, based on cross-sectional data, several aspects of "environmental Normalization" were found to predict various dimensions of adaptive behavior. A higher score on the Personal Routines AFI subscale (assessing the extent to which the activities, routines, and rhythms in a residence are appropriate to adults in North American culture) was predicted by a residential environment that promoted socially integrating activities (i.e., nonsegregated vocational, educational, recreational, and social activities), was urban, had more adequate transportation facilities, and encouraged independence and age-appropriate activities among residents. A higher score on the Community Awareness AFI subscale (tapping skills such as transportation usage, budgeting, shopping, cooking, and leisure) was predicted by a residential environment that promoted residents' independence, was optimistic about residents' potential to live more independently, presented a positive external image, provided opportunities for freedom and initiative, and (unexpectedly) had a physical setting of somewhat poorer quality. A higher score on the Social Maturity AFI subscale (reflecting skills such as communication, consideration, getting and keeping friends, and solving problems) was predicted by a residential environment that promoted socially integrating activities, fostered appropriate interactions between staff and residents, promoted residents' socially appropriate appearance, and (unexpectedly) was characterized by less socially appropriate ways of addressing residents and a less adequate internal physical environment. Finally, a higher total AFI score was predicted by a residential setting that promoted socially integrative activities, fostered residents' independence and socially appropriate appearance, had more adequate transportation facilities, avoided social overprotection, featured more appropriate staff-resident interactions

and (unexpectedly) had a lower-quality physical setting and less adequate community resources. Overall, Hull and Thompson (1980) interpreted their findings as consistent with growing evidence that "environmental Normalization, in addition to being an ideology, is an effective technology for promoting more independent functioning by retarded persons" (pp. 260-261).

In a conceptually and methodologically parallel study, this time of 296 persons formerly institutionalized because of psychiatric disabilities and now living in 157 community board-and-care facilities in Manitoba, Hull and Thompson (1981a) investigated the extent to which individual, residential, and community characteristics were related to the residents' adaptive functioning. In homes with 1 to 2 residents, all residents were included in the study; in larger homes, data were collected on a maximum of 3 randomly selected residents. The median age of the residents was 57 (range, 19-81); 51% were female. Nearly all had previously been institutionalized, for a median length of time of 7.5 years (range = a few months to more than 20 years). Most (75%) had a diagnosis of "schizophrenia," while the others had diagnoses of "psychosis," "alcohol problems," or "neurotic behavior problems." Marlett's (1977a, 1977b) AFI was again used to assess adaptive behavior, and the 172-item adaptation of PASS used in the previous study served as the measure of environmental Normalization. In several stepwise regression analyses, based on cross-sectional data, various aspects of "environmental Normalization" were found to predict different dimensions of adaptive behavior. A higher score on the Personal Routines AFI subscale (see definition above) was predicted by a residential environment manifesting less social overprotection, more appropriate resident-staff interactions, a more adequate geographic location within its region, less verbal abusiveness, more opportunities for freedom and initiative, more adequate transportation facilities, a greater emphasis on activities promoting social integration, and more age-appropriate possessions and activities. A higher score on the Community Awareness AFI subscale was predicted by a residential setting characterized by less social overprotection, more appropriate resident-staff interactions, a more adequate location within its region, the conveying of a more positive image of residents, more appropriate resident appearance, more

opportunities for freedom and initiative, and more adequate community resources. A higher score on the Social Maturity AFI subscale was predicted by a residential environment manifesting less social overprotection, a more adequate regional location, more emphasis on socially integrative activities, more appropriate resident appearance, more opportunities for freedom and initiative, less verbal and physical abusiveness, and more appropriate social activities. Finally, a higher overall AFI score was predicted by a residential environment marked by less social overprotection, more appropriate resident-staff interactions, more activities promoting social integration, more appropriate personal appearance among residents, more adequate regional location, more opportunities for freedom and initiative, and less verbal abusiveness. In general, Hull and Thompson (1981a) found that environmental variables accounted for a much greater portion of the variance in adaptive behavior than did individual-level variables. They concluded, as before, that environmental Normalization appeared to be an effective technology, and not simply an ideology, in services to persons with psychiatric disabilities.

Hull and Thompson (1981b) used the same 172-item adaptation of PASS 3 and the same sample of 296 persons with psychiatric disabilities living in the community in Manitoba to study the determinants of the level of Normalization in a residence. A stepwise regression analysis found that environmental Normalization was predicted by a higher average level of resident adaptive behavior, a smaller number of residents, a higher average level of family income in the community, a smaller proportion of male residents, a shorter average length of previous institutionalization, an independent living residence rather than a board-and-care home, and a smaller number of disability groups in the residence. Overall, Hull and Thompson (1981b) suggested that the most normalizing residences tended to be smaller, to provide more opportunities for independence, to serve only one disability group (i.e., persons with psychiatric difficulties), and to be located in a middle-income community with higher-quality homes, more community resources, and more potentially integrating activities. Residence-level characteristics such as these were more important correlates of environmental Normalization than were client variables.

333

Combining their samples of persons with mental retardation (cf. Hull & Thompson, 1980) and psychiatric disabilities (cf. Hull & Thompson, 1981a), Hull et al. (1984) provided a descriptive overview of the adaptive behavior of 665 intellectually or psychiatrically disabled residents and of the environmental quality obtained in the 278 Manitoba community residences in which they were living. The authors' measures of adaptive behavior and environmental quality were, again, the AFI and the 172-item adaptation of PASS, respectively. Hull et al. found that the psychiatrically disabled residents had a significantly higher average level of overall adaptive behavior than the mentally retarded residents, although the difference was not large. In both types of residents, higher total adaptive behavior scores were associated with higher IQ, lower chronological age, longer institutionalization, higher average family income in the community where the disabled person's residence was located, and urban location of the residence. The mean environmental Normalization score for the 278 community residences was 63%, with little difference in quality between mental retardation and mental health residences. Independent living residences scored much higher, however, than board-and-care residences, foster homes, or staffed group homes. The "average" Manitoba community residential service was near the top end of the "minimally acceptable" range of service quality (as operationally defined by the adaptation of PASS), with 8% below minimally acceptable standards and 14% in the "very good" or "near-ideal" range. On the other hand, the mean scores on certain important ratings fell in the "less than minimally acceptable" range: residences tended to be concentrated in certain neighborhoods (which reduced their integrative potential), did not place sufficient emphasis on activities promoting social integration, and unduly restricted residents' freedoms. Across all of the community residences, the level of environmental Normalization in a home and the level of adaptive functioning of residents in that home were moderately and positively correlated ($r = 0.49$), both for psychiatrically disabled clients ($r = 0.54$) and for mentally retarded residents ($r = 0.41$). Hull et al. interpreted these findings as consistent with a reciprocal pattern of causality, in which more normalized environments promoted more adaptive behavior and more competent residents shaped their residential settings in the direction of greater Normalization.

Mulvey, Linney, and Rosenberg (1987) examined the relationship between organizational control and treatment-program Normalization in 30 community-based settings for juvenile offenders in six U.S. states. A modified version of PASS 3 was used to assess treatment programming. Based on Flynn and Heal's (1981) short form, 35 of the 50 PASS ratings were selected. The descriptors for these ratings were then rewritten to be more relevant to the adolescent population served. Two raters completed the modified PASS instrument independently, with interrater reliability of 0.92. Cluster analysis, based on the total PASS score and data from other measures, was used to group the settings into four clusters, from least institutionalized (most normalized) to most institutionalized (least normalized). Contrary to the researchers' main hypothesis, organizational control and program design were found to be unrelated. The most normalized facilities, however, which had the highest total PASS scores, also had the lowest use of medication, the lowest level of staff concern about assaults, and the most favorable attitude toward the rate of family involvement.

2 STUDIES BASED ON PASSING

PASSING (Wolfensberger & Thomas, 1983, 1989) assesses two major dimensions of Social Role Valorization, client social image-enhancement and client competence-enhancement, in four program areas: physical settings (especially the service facility and neighborhood in which the latter is located); service-structured groupings and relationships among people; service-structured activities and other time uses; and miscellaneous other issues. PASSING assesses only those aspects of service quality that reflect a program's adoption and implementation of Social Role Valorization. By omitting the administrative issues contained in PASS, the authors of PASSING hoped that a larger pool of people, including ordinary citizens and some service recipients, could learn to apply the tool than had proved possible with PASS (Wolfensberger, 1994). PASSING consists of 42 items or ratings, each composed of five levels, with Level 1 representing very poor service quality, Level 3 neutral quality, and Level 5 ideal quality. Trained evaluation-team members first rate a service program independently, on all 42 items. In a lengthy discussion session, the PASSING team then comes to a team-conciliated (consensual) rating of the quality of the program on each of the 42 items. The conciliated scores are then translated from levels into weighted scores. The total PASSING score, formed by adding the weighted scores of the 42 items, can range from a minimum of -1,000 (extremely poor service quality), through zero (minimally acceptable service quality), up to a maximum of +1,000 (ideal quality).

In her doctoral dissertation, Jacobs (1983) conducted an exploratory methodological study of PASSING. In an evaluation of 5 service programs (3 community residences for mentally retarded persons, an integrated day-care program for preschool-aged children, and a sheltered workshop for adults), she found that PASSING displayed high internal consistency and high interrater reliability. Team-conciliated scores were lower than those resulting from the simple averaging of individual raters' scores, with evidence suggesting that the team leader influenced team members during the conciliation process. Also, teams of 2 to 3 members produced scores that were almost as reliable as those from larger teams. Jacobs made suggestions for simplifying the method of determining the final total score as well as the team process used.

Lutfiyya, Moseley, Walker, Zollers, Lehr, Pugliese, Callahan, and Centra (1987) used PASSING to assess seven community residences serving people with mental retardation ("residents") in New York state. The settings included a home for 3 residents that was part of an intentional Christian community, l'Arche; a staffed apartment for three young men; a group home for 4 women; an intermediate care facility for the mentally retarded (ICF/MR) for 8 adolescents; and three "small residential units" (SRUs), one for 12 children, one for 12 adults, and one for 12 adults with "challenging behavior." The three SRUs were on the grounds of a large state institution located in a rural town. The PASSING assessment was intended to examine the quality of life of residents of the SRUs and to compare it to that of people in other residential settings.

Of the seven residences, the four that were rated the lowest on PASSING were the ICF/MR and the SRUs.

The ICF/MR also appeared to be of lower quality than the other three settings according to the evaluators' subjective impressions. Lutfiyya et al. (1987) acknowledged three limitations of their study: small sample size, a single approach to assessing quality, and a lack of control for possible differences among the residents of the different kinds of settings.

Dansereau, Duteau, Ely, and Flynn (1990) used the French version of PASSING (Wolfensberger & Thomas, 1989) to evaluate the quality of 38 community residences in western Quebec that served 172 persons with mainly psychiatric disabilities. The study also assessed residents' level of physical and social integration, by means of a newly constructed instrument (Ely & Flynn, 1989), and residents' subjective quality of life (QOL), by means of Lehman's (1988) QOL interview. Of the 172 residents, 72% had an official diagnosis of schizophrenia, paranoid schizophrenia, or major affective disorder, 14% had a diagnosis of mental retardation, 9% another or an unknown diagnosis, and 5% had no psychiatric diagnosis. The residents ranged in age from 18 to 92 (M = 47.3, SD = 13.2) and had been in this type of community residence for an average of 9.5 years (SD = 3.7, range = 24 days to 19.3 years). The 38 community residences included 29 family-care homes ("familles d'accueil"), 2 group residences and 2 apartments that were part of a formal psychiatric rehabilitation program, and 1 group residence and 4 apartments affiliated with a community mental health agency. Most of the PASSING evaluations were carried out by the same three-person team (occasionally, two-person and four-person teams were used). The PASSING teams conciliated their scores in all instances.

The total PASSING instrument had an internal consistency of 0.89. Four subscales were constructed by a factor analysis carried out on the sample of 213 programs investigated by Flynn et al. (1991; see below): SRV-Setting (14 ratings, Cronbach's α = 0.62), SRV-Program (15 ratings, α = 0.84), Beauty & Comfort (3 ratings, α = 0.75), and Accessibility (3 ratings, α = 0.86). The mean level of overall service quality in the 38 community residences, as indexed by the total PASSING score, was -156 (SD = 228), equal to 42% of the maximum possible weighted score. On the PASSING subscales, the mean level of service quality was best on SRV-Setting (52% of the maximum possible score) and Accessibility (51%), both reflecting aspects of physical integration. Service quality was noticeably weaker on the SRV-Program (M = 34%) and Beauty and Comfort (M = 42%) dimensions. The urban residences scored significantly higher than the rural residences on the total PASSING scale as well as on three of the four subscales (SRV-Setting, SRV-Program, and Accessibility).

Concerning residents' QOL, the 70 residents willing and able to take part in a lengthy QOL interview rated themselves and their personal life-situations on a 7-point scale of global life satisfaction (where 1 = "terrible", 7 = "delighted"). Their overall mean score (M = 3.92) was close to the midpoint of 4 ("more or less satisfied"). The respondents were most satisfied in the specific domains of education (M = 5.6), religion (M = 5.1), and physical security (M = 5.1), least satisfied in that of personal finances (M = 3.6), and at an intermediate level of satisfaction with respect to their living situation (M = 4.9), health (M = 4.8), social relations (M = 4.8), work (M = 4.7), leisure (M = 4.6), and relationship with their own family (M = 4.5). Regarding residents' physical and social integration, their most frequent daily activities were watching television and listening to the radio. Their activities showed little variety and were usually carried out alone or with another resident. The interviewees reported very little contact with ordinary citizens, including their own families.

Flynn et al. (1991) collaborated on a methodologically and substantively oriented analysis of a sample of 213 PASSING evaluations conducted in the United States (51%), Canada (45%), and the United Kingdom (4%), mainly during PASSING training workshops (96%). The programs served mainly mentally retarded persons (40%), clients with "mixed" (different) impairments (38%), or psychiatrically impaired persons (6%). Several findings were of primarily methodological interest. First, the similarity of Pearson and Spearman correlations among the total PASSING scale and Wolfensberger and Thomas's five rationally derived subscales indicated that PASSING data could be treated with interval-level, parametric procedures, with little fear of serious distortion. Second, internal consistency was high for the total scale (Cronbach's α = 0.89) and barely adequate to relatively high for the four subscales that were composed of more than one

rating: Intensity (6 items), 0.62; Integrativeness (9 items), 0.66; Image Projection (19 items), 0.80; and Felicity (7 items), 0.60. Third, intraclass correlations, computed on individual raters' preconciliation data, indicated that excellent levels of interrater reliability (near or above 0.90) were attainable for the mean computed across raters in teams of 5 to 9 members, and that for teams of this size even the reliability of a single rater was moderately high (in the 0.54-0.70 range). Fourth, the total PASSING scores established by the standard practice of conciliation were moderately to highly similar to, although lower than, the scores established simply by averaging the individual raters' preconciliation scores. Substantively, the mean level of service quality in the sample (-368, equal to 32% of the maximum possible weighted score) was found to be considerably lower than zero. A score of zero is equal to 50% of the maximum possible weighted score and considered by the authors of PASSING to be the "minimally acceptable" level of service quality. Service quality was especially weak in the clinically crucial domains of Program Relevance (12% of the maximum possible weighted score) and Intensity (26%). An analysis of variance showed that the mean for Canadian services (35% of the maximum possible weighted score) was significantly higher than that for U.S. services (30%), the mean for community group residences (37%) was significantly higher than those for vocational programs (28%) and institutional residences (11%), and there was no country-by-service-type interaction.

In his doctoral dissertation (supervised by the author of the present review), Ely (1991) examined the relationship between the quality of the community residences evaluated with PASSING by Dansereau et al. (1990) (as described earlier) and the quality of life (QOL) and social integration of 70 persons with psychiatric disabilities who were living in the residences at the time of the PASSING assessments. Ely found evidence of the predictive and construct validity of PASSING in examining its links with two types of social integration. *Strong* social integration was operationalized as the frequency of activities undertaken by a person with a psychiatric disability inside or outside the residence in the company of a socially valued person (i.e., a member of the resident's own family or an ordinary citizen, excluding human service personnel). *Weak* social integration, on the other hand, consisted of the frequency of the psychiatrically disabled person's activities outside the residence, regardless of his or her accompaniment by another person or the latter's valued or devalued identity. (A synonym for weak social integration, so defined, would thus be "physical presence in the community"). Among the 70 study participants, strong and weak social integration were significantly but only weakly related ($r = 0.28$, $p < .05$). Although neither type of social integration was significantly related to global measures of subjective QOL, strong social integration was significantly correlated with subjective QOL in the specific life-domain of satisfaction with family ($r = 0.29$, $p < .05$), and weak social integration was significantly related to subjective QOL in the specific life-domains of satisfaction with finances ($r = 0.23$, $p < .05$) and education ($r = 0.46$, $p < .05$).

Almost all of the PASSING scales (which were the same as those used in Dansereau et al., 1990; Pelletier, 1992; and Flynn, 1993) significantly predicted the level of weak social integration among the 70 persons with psychiatric disabilities, although not their level of strong social integration. The measure of weak social integration was correlated with the PASSING scales as follows: with the total PASSING scale, $r = 0.31$, $p < .01$; with SRV-Setting, $r = 0.27$, $p < .05$; with SRV-Program, $r = 0.26$, $p < .05$; with Beauty and Comfort, $r = 0.13$, ns; and with Accessibility, $r = 0.36$, $p < .01$. It should be noted, moreover, that these correlations were attenuated (lowered) somewhat by the fact that the same PASSING scores were necessarily assigned to all clients living in the same community residence, thereby reducing the variation among the PASSING scores. This reduced variation in the PASSING scores, in conjunction with residents' extremely limited average amount of strong social integration, doubtless contributed to the fact that no significant association was found between the PASSING scales and the measure of strong social integration. PASSING was significantly correlated, however, with residents' subjective QOL in the directly relevant life-domain of satisfaction with their living situation (despite the problem of attenuated correlations just mentioned). Specifically, the psychiatrically disabled person's satisfaction with his or her living situation was significantly related to the total PASSING score of his or her residence ($r = 0.28$, $p < .05$) and to its SRV-Setting score ($r = 0.30$, $p < .01$). Ely (1991)

discovered that the quality of the 29 family-care homes present in the larger sample of 38 community residences was powerfully predicted by two variables: urban versus rural location, and size. *Urban* family-care homes and family-care homes housing a *smaller* number of psychiatrically disabled residents were of significantly higher quality. Using the subsample of 29 family-care homes (15 of which were rural and 14 urban), Ely entered urban versus rural location, size (number of residents), and a location-by-size interaction term in successive steps of a hierarchical regression model. Urban-versus-rural location, by itself, accounted for 57% of the variance in the total PASSING score, 40% in the SRV-Setting score, and 34% in the SRV-Program score ($p < .001$ in each case). Size accounted for an additional 10% of the variance in the total PASSING score ($p < .01$), an additional 26% of the variance in the SRV-Setting score ($p < .001$), but no additional variance in the SRV-Program score. The location-by-size interaction term accounted for no additional variance in any of the analyses. Although these findings are generalizable only to similar samples, in which the rural residences are physically and socially more isolated and larger than the urban ones, they do point to the possibility, in such situations, of making major gains in service quality through careful attention to the two highly manipulable variables of residence location and size.

Pelletier (1992) reported on an evaluation of an entire regional service system in Quebec conducted by an eight-member team with the French-language version of PASSING (Wolfensberger & Thomas, 1989). The purposes of the evaluation were several: to assess the quality of services in the region in question; to inform the Quebec Ministry of Health and Social Services, regional planning bodies, and service agencies about the degree to which official provincial policies of Social Role Valorization and social integration had been implemented in services to persons with developmental disabilities; to pilot-test a feasible method for conducting regional evaluations of service quality and policy implementation that could be used in other regions in Quebec; and, ultimately, to improve the quality of services. Working in two-person teams over a 1-month period, the evaluators assessed a total of 39 programs (30 urban, 9 rural), selected through systematic and random sampling procedures to be approximately representative of programs in the region. The programs evaluated with PASSING served 282 persons (53% male, 47% female; 73% adults, 27% children and adolescents), who comprised 26% of the total of 1,099 persons with developmental disabilities served within the region during the previous year. The 39 programs included 2 for children and their families, 4 community-support programs for adults, 24 residential programs (11 family-care homes ["familles d'accueil"], 7 community group residences, 3 apartments, and 3 institutional units), and 9 vocational programs (5 sheltered employment programs, 2 community work-placement programs, and 2 work-preparation programs). The four PASSING factors presented in Dansereau et al. (1990) were used to organize and present the findings.

The mean PASSING scores obtained by the sample of 39 services, expressed as a percentage of the maximum possible weighted scores, were as follows: total PASSING score, 47% (*SD* = 19%), SRV-Setting, 57% (*SD* = 19%), SRV-Program, 37% (*SD* = 24%), Beauty and Comfort, 48% (*SD* = 27%), and Accessibility, 63% (*SD* = 24%). On each dimension, the mean level of service quality in the region emerged as somewhat higher than that found in a comparison sample of mainly North American services of the same type. Nevertheless, scores on the same two subscales, both related mainly to physical integration—Accessibility and SRV-Setting—were the highest in each sample. The discriminative power of PASSING was illustrated by the fact that the range of quality in the sample of 39 programs was found to be enormous, with total PASSING scores stretching from very high (82% of the maximum possible weighted score, in the case of a child and family service) to very low (17%, in the case of a residential program). Services to children and their families scored highest on the total PASSING score (*M* = 79%), followed by community-support services for adults (62%), residential services (45%), and vocational programs (38%). Among the different kinds of residential services, apartments (*M* = 55%) and family-care homes (52%) achieved the highest mean total PASSING scores, compared with 35% for the combined category of community group residences and institutional residences. Among the different types of vocational programs, the community work-placement programs (*M* = 54%) scored considerably better than the work-preparation (34%) and sheltered-work programs (32%).

Overall, Pelletier (1992) concluded that important gains in service quality had been made within the region during the preceding decade, particularly with regard to the physical integration of service settings and thus of persons with developmental disabilities themselves. Also, consumers had come to reside in and use formal and informal settings that tended to favor their personal development, enhance their social roles, and increasingly approximate culturally valued settings. Furthermore, 6 of the 39 programs assessed (15%) had total PASSING scores that surpassed 70% of the maximum possible weighted score and could thus be considered "excellent." These were spread across the child-family, adult community-support, residential, and vocational areas, and served 34% of the consumers encountered during the evaluation. Another 17 programs (43%), covering the four major categories and eight subtypes of services and serving 60% of the consumers met during the evaluation, surpassed the "minimally acceptable" level. Pelletier estimated that another 6 (15%) could be brought up to this level relatively quickly and easily and that 6 others (15%) could be brought up to this level over a longer period. On the other hand, 10 services (26%), serving 22% of the clients encountered, were judged to be poor. Of these, 5 appeared improvable over the shorter run and 3 over the longer run, but, in Pelletier's opinion, elimination of the remaining 2 merited serious consideration by regional decision makers.

Pelletier (1992) noted that SRV and social-integration principles had become firmly rooted within the regional system, in a variety of ways, both conceptually and procedurally, and were well understood and accepted by top service leaders and managers. On the other hand, many middle managers and direct-service workers appeared to have a relatively superficial grasp of SRV and social-integration concepts, and consumers were often not adequately involved in decisions affecting them. Pelletier formulated detailed observations concerning the strengths and weaknesses of each major service subsystem (child-family, adult community-support, residential, and vocational), identified the features characteristic of the high-quality services assessed, made suggestions relevant to the assembling of a high-quality PASSING evaluation team, and made recommendations to the regional governing body and service agencies and to the Quebec Ministry of Health and Social Services.

In an invited paper presented to an international conference on the integration of persons with mental retardation, Flynn (1993) compared the quality of different types of services in Canada and the USA, using an augmented sample of 406 PASSING evaluations. More than half (52%) of the programs assessed were located in Canada, 46% in the USA, and the other 2% in the UK. Seventy-seven percent of the evaluations had been made during PASSING training workshops, with the rest conducted during official assessments. Three-quarters of the programs served persons with mental retardation (who often also had other impairments), and 70% served adults. The same PASSING factors and subscales as in Dansereau et al. (1990) and Pelletier (1992) were used. For the entire 42-item instrument, internal consistency (Cronbach's α) was high (0.92). For the four PASSING subscales, the α coefficients were as follows: SRV-Setting, 0.82, SRV-Program, 0.89, Beauty and Comfort, 0.69, and Accessibility, 0.76.

The mean overall service quality (total PASSING score) in the sample of 406 programs was 34% of the maximum possible weighted score, considerably below the "minimally acceptable" level of 50%. Comparisons among the four PASSING subscales indicated that the mean level of service quality was higher on Accessibility (M = 57% of the maximum possible weighted score) than on the other three subscales, with the mean for SRV-Setting (43%) also higher than the means for SRV-Program (25%) and Beauty and Comfort (34%). The Canadian means on the total scale and four subscales were 8% to 11% higher than those for the American programs and, in both countries, Accessibility was the single best dimension of service quality, followed by SRV-Setting, Beauty and Comfort, and SRV-Program.

Pilon, Arsenault, and Gascon (1993), in the published version of a longer research report (Pilon, Arsenault, & Gascon, 1994), studied the impact of moving from an institutional setting to community-based family-care homes on social integration and quality of life. Pilon et al. (1993) followed for one year a sample of 36 adults who were mentally retarded, after they had left one of five institutional environments. The researchers also followed a control sample of 36 mentally handicapped "stayers" who remained in an institutional milieu during the year-long period and had been individually matched with the group of "movers" on the variables of physical health, deficits, maladaptive behavior, and overall developmental level. Using a quasi-experimental (pretest/post-test, nonequivalent control group) design, Pilon et al. studied the impact of leaving the institution on residents' social integration and quality of life. They were also interested in determining the contribution of selected individual variables (resident and staff characteristics) and environmental factors (residence social climate and level of implementation of Social Role Valorization) on any changes found. Social integration was measured by means of the Inventaire d'Intégration Sociale, a Quebec version of the Valued Outcomes Information System (VOIS; Newton et al., 1988). Quality of life was assessed with the Inventaire de Bien-Être, an instrument constructed by Pilon and his colleagues. The social climate of the institutional and community settings was evaluated with Quebec versions of Moos's Ward Atmosphere Scale (Moos & Hoots, 1968) and Community-Oriented Programs Environment Scale (Moos & Otto, 1972), and the level of residential SRV was assessed with PASSING.

Compared with their peers who remained in an institutional milieu, the "movers" experienced significant gains in quality of life and social integration, even though their social contacts were found to be limited largely to family-care or agency personnel and to other mentally handicapped residents. The social climate of the community settings was also found to be more favorable to social integration than was that of the institutions. Finally, on the four PASSING factors used by Dansereau et al. (1990) and Flynn (1993), Pilon et al. (1993) found that the 10 family-care homes that had been assessed with PASSING scored significantly higher than the three institutional settings evaluated with the tool. Specifically, on SRV-Setting, the family-care homes had a mean score of 69% of the maximum possible weighted score versus a mean of 7% for the institutions; on SRV-Program, the respective means were 37% versus 11%; on Beauty and Comfort, 68% versus 17%, and on Accessibility, 63% versus 23%. Interestingly, the weakest area for the family-care homes was clearly the same one found in the other PASSING studies reviewed, namely, SRV-Program. Pilon et al. also discovered that the image-related ratings on the SRV-Program scale appeared considerably more resistant to short-term improvement than the competence-related ratings.

Vandergriff and Chubon (1994), in an article based on the first author's doctoral thesis (Vandergriff, 1991), used PASSING to assess the quality of six types of residential environments: natural or family homes, supervised apartments, boarding homes, community training homes, community residences, and regional campus facilities. The purpose of the research was to test two hypotheses: that quality of life would covary with the type of residential setting, and that persons with a higher level of intellectual functioning would experience a higher quality of life. The investigators studied a total of 120 adults who were mentally retarded, 20 from each of the six types of setting, and 30 at each of four levels of intellectual functioning (i.e., mild, moderate, severe, and profound retardation). The four levels of retardation were subsequently collapsed into high-IQ and low-IQ groups. Quality of life was assessed with the Resident Choice Assessment Scale (RCAS; Durant, Kearney, & Mindell, 1987), and the Life Situation Study (LSS; Chubon, 1990). Behavioral competencies were assessed with Parts I and II of the AAMD Adaptive Behavior Scale (Nihira et al., 1974). Unfortunately, PASSING was completed by a single staff psychologist (rather than a team of raters) during visits to each of the residences where study participants lived. Analysis of variance (ANOVA) on the PASSING scores and *post hoc* tests showed that the six types of residences differed from one another, with the supervised apartments attaining the highest score, on average, followed, in order, by the community training homes, family homes, community residences, regional campus, and boarding homes. Moreover, the PASSING scores from the six types of setting were found to be very highly correlated both with the mean LSS score for each kind of setting ($r = 0.91$, $p < .01$) and with the mean RCAS score ($r = 0.98$, $p < .001$), but not with the mean ABS-I or ABS-II scores. Vandergriff and Chubon found support for both hypotheses: quality of life did covary with the type of setting, and persons of a higher level of intellectual functioning experienced a higher quality of life (as assessed by the LSS and RCAS) than those of a lower level of functioning.

Williams's (1995) report on PASS 3 and PASSING evaluations in Great Britain noted that the average (median) total PASSING score for large residences (more than 8 places) in Britain ($n = 31$; $Mdn = 16\%$) was similar to that for institutional residences in North America that had been assessed with PASSING ($n = 23$; $Mdn = 21\%$, as reported by Flynn et al., 1991). The average total PASSING score for small residences (less than 8 places) in Britain evaluated with PASSING ($n = 5$; $Mdn = 38\%$) was also similar to that observed in community group residences in North America that had been assessed with PASSING ($n = 79$; $Mdn = 37\%$, again as reported by Flynn et al., 1991).

Cocks (1998) reported on a Safeguards Project in Perth, western Australia, in which PASSING was used as one among several mechanisms for promoting good service quality. In 1954, an agency was founded by a group of parents of young children who had multiple and severe disabilities. The following year, the agency opened a hostel that eventually provided residential services for 36 young people, as an alternative to a large mental hospital. The children remained in the hostel until adulthood. Between 1987 and 1993, the agency relocated its clients from the hostel to community homes in suburban Perth. In 1993, at the end of the transition, a total of 41 clients were living in 13 community homes (three homes had 2 residents each, six homes had 3 each, three homes had 4 each, and one home had 5).

At the end of the transition period, in 1993, the agency established its Safeguards Project, to ensure an ongoing focus on the provision of high-quality services and the attainment of good outcomes. The project included internal and external evaluation components. The internal safeguarding process consisted of linking 43 "themes" (i.e., agency aspects or client outcomes) to specific actions that would safeguard each of the themes. The external evaluation consisted of a PASSING evaluation, together with the use of 15 administration-related PASS items and a "model-coherency analysis." The latter examined the extent to which the service model used by the agency was consistent with clients' needs. The total PASSING scores for each of the 13 community homes were converted to a percentage of the maximum possible weighted score (Cocks, 1998). The mean total PASSING score was 43% (range = 26%-71%), higher than the average of 32% attained in the 213 PASSING evaluations analyzed by Flynn et al. (1991). Also, service quality was found to be significantly better in the 2-person homes than in those for 3, 4, or 5 residents.

Flynn et al. (in press) produced the most definitive factor analysis of PASSING to date, employing a large sample and cross-validation procedures. In the second study contained in their paper (the first study from this same paper was discussed earlier, in the section devoted to PASS 3), Flynn et al. (in press) factor-analyzed a sample of 633 PASSING program evaluations. The purpose of their study was to derive, through exploratory and confirmatory factor analyses, a relatively definitive, cross-validated factor structure for PASSING. They also intended to construct factor-based subscales that would be useful for program evaluation purposes. The sample of 633 PASSING evaluations, conducted between 1983 and 1995, were all "team-conciliated" assessments (i.e., based on the consensus of a group of raters who used the instrument under the guidance of an experienced team leader). Eighty-three percent of the evaluations had been conducted during PASSING training workshops, while 14% had been carried out as official evaluations. Fifty-three percent had been carried out in the United States, 37% in Canada, 7% in Australia, and 1% each in the United Kingdom and France. Thirty-eight percent were assessments of community group residences, 23% of vocational services, 11% of institutional residential programs, and 7% of early-childhood or school-based education programs. Of the programs evaluated, 40% served persons with mental retardation, 10% clients with psychiatric difficulties, 7% people who were elderly; and 36% served persons with "mixed" (different) conditions.

Flynn et al. (in press) first carried out an exploratory factor analysis (EFA) on a randomly chosen half of the sample ($n = 316$), in order to establish the number of factors present in the 42 PASSING items and identify those items that would provide good indicators of the factors (Bentler & Wu, 1995). A confirmatory factor analysis (CFA) was then conducted on the other random half of the sample ($n = 317$) in order to cross-validate the EFA. Three cross-validated PASSING factors, Program, Setting, and Accessibility, emerged from these procedures (see Table 14.2). Factor 1 (Program) reflects the *content* of the service evaluated with PASSING. Its 15 items capture both image-related and competency-related aspects of the program,

consistent with the SRV conceptual underpinnings of PASSING. Factor 2 (Setting) measures the *physical location* in which the service is situated, including the building and its surrounding neighborhood. Factor 3 (Accessibility) assesses the degree to which the service setting provides *ready access* to clients and their families, to the wider public, and to a wide range of pertinent community resources, such as eating places, shops, libraries, post offices, and so forth. Three homogeneous PASSING subscales were formed from their new factors, and these subscales had a very strong multiple correlation ($R = 0.97$, $p < .001$) with the total PASSING score in the overall sample of 633 programs. Flynn et al. (in press) suggested that their findings could increase the utility of PASSING as an evaluation tool by providing factorially valid measures that would facilitate comparisons among and within programs and permit evaluators to organize their assessments more tightly around the core service dimensions of Program, Setting, and Accessibility.

3 CONCLUSION

I wish to conclude this review of PASS and PASSING research with several observations and suggestions that are intended to enhance future research, training, and evaluation practice with the instruments.

1. When assessed against the demanding criteria embodied in PASS and PASSING, the overall quality of many human service programs appears to be quite modest. For example, in the two large samples of evaluations carried out with PASS ($N = 626$) and PASSING ($N = 633$) that were analyzed by Flynn et al. (in press), the mean total PASS score was only 43% of the maximum possible weighted score, and the mean total PASSING score was only 32% of the maximum possible weighted score. (The difference between these means–43% versus 32%—is probably due more to inter-instrument than to intersample differences, although both influences may be at work.) These results are consistent with Felce and Perry's recent observation that community services personnel often appear to lack the organized means and competencies necessary to successfully promote the personal development and social integration of the people whom they serve. Felce and Perry (1997) deservedly insist that as much attention must now be paid to improving

the technical proficiency and quality of community services as has previously been devoted to the size, location, accessibility, and staffing of such services.

TABLE 14.2

THREE CROSS-VALIDATED PASSING FACTORS—PROGRAM, SETTING, AND ACCESSIBILITY—AND THE ITEMS COMPOSING EACH (ADAPTED FROM FLYNN ET AL., IN PRESS)

Factor 1: Program (15 items)

14. Image Projection of Intraservice Client Grouping—Social Value
16. Image-Related Other Integrative Client Contacts and Personal Relationships
18. Service Worker-Client Image Match
20. Image Projection of Program Activities and Activity Timing
21. Promotion of Client Autonomy and Rights
23. Image-Related Personal Possessions
24. Image Projection of Personal Labeling Practices
35. Competency-Related Intraservice Client Grouping—Composition
36. Competency-Related Other Integrative Client Contacts and Personal Relationships
37. Life-Enriching Interactions Among Clients, Service Personnel, and Others
38. Program Support for Client Individualization
39. Promotion of Client Sociosexual Identity
40. Program Address of Clients' Service Needs
41. Intensity of Activities and Efficiency of Time Use
42. Competency-Related Personal Possessions

Factor 2: Setting (8 items)

1. Setting-Neighborhood Harmony
2. Program-Neighborhood Harmony
5. External Setting Appearance Congruity With Culturally Valued Analogue
7. External Setting Age Image
9. Image Projection of Setting—Physical Proximity
10. Image Projection of Setting—History
12. Image Projection of Program-to-Program Juxtaposition
13. Service-Neighborhood Assimilation Potential

Factor 3: Accessibility (3 items)

28. Setting Accessibility—Clients and Families
29. Setting Accessibility—Public
30. Availability of Relevant Community Resources

Fortunately, excellent progress has recently been made in identifying and validating the personal competencies needed by human service personnel to promote people's development and integration (see Burchard chapter 11, this volume), and this knowledge deserves wide dissemination and application. In the crucial task of service quality improvement, PASS and PASSING can also be invaluable tools, because they focus attention directly on the priorities mentioned by Felce and Perry (1997): understanding people's needs, responding in relevant and intense ways to these needs, and helping people achieve greater personal development, self-direction, and social integration.

2. The relatively definitive factor analyses by Flynn et al. (in press) show that PASS and PASSING have similar factor structures. Specifically, each instrument includes Program, Setting, and Accessibility factors (PASS alone covers administrative issues and thus has a fourth factor, Administration). This factorial similarity is not surprising, given Wolfensberger's senior authorship of both instruments and his strong emphasis in each on the assessment of human-service "universals" (i.e., issues of fundamental importance to human service programs).

3. Relatedly, it is probably a common emphasis on basic service issues that accounts for a striking parallel between, on the one hand, the PASS and PASSING factors of Program, Setting, Accessibility and (in the case of PASS) Administration and, on the other hand, the core structural and functional service dimensions that ecologically oriented researchers (e.g., Felce, 1988; Landesman, 1988; Meador, Osborn, Owens, Smith, & Taylor, 1991) have identified as central in the evaluation of residential services. According to Meador et al. (1991), *structural* features of a residential program include the physical characteristics of the service facility (e.g., size, siting, convenience of location, adequacy of furnishings and utilities, etc.), as well as the socioeconomic status and population density of the neighborhood, the experience and training of staff, and so forth. The PASS and PASSING Setting and Accessibility subscales assess many of these structural aspects. *Functional* features, on the other hand, include the day-to-day operation of the program, such as the amount and quality of interactions between staff and residents, the types of activities in which residents engage, the network of relationships with individuals and agencies in the

community, the meeting of clients' needs, the opportunity for habilitation, the independence afforded clients, the administrative organization and resource-allocation pattern in the program, and so on. The PASS and PASSING Program and the PASS Administration subscale evaluate many of these functional features. Consistent with the findings of Meador et al., the PASS and PASSING research reviewed in this chapter suggests that services with similar structural features may have very different functional features. Specifically, the studies reviewed here indicate that the structural aspects of services (as measured by the Setting and Accessibility subscales of PASS and PASSING) are usually of considerably higher quality than their functional aspects (as measured by the Program and Administration subscales).

4. Users of PASS and PASSING who have employed earlier versions of the Program, Setting, Accessibility, and (in the case of PASS) Administration subscales to organize the various phases of an evaluation—data-gathering, team-conciliation, provision of verbal feedback, and report-writing—have often remarked that the use of these empirically derived subscales adds considerable coherence and unity to the evaluation process. In my opinion, incorporation of the relatively definitive versions of the subscales (Flynn et al., in press) into the organization and scoring of PASS and PASSING would improve both instruments and enhance training and field applications with each.

5. Pelletier's (1992) report is a good illustration of the potential of PASS and PASSING to serve as qualitative frameworks or "lenses," and not merely as quantitative tools, for assessing and improving large-scale regional service systems, as well as individual programs or agencies. Pelletier's report is also a particularly useful example of how the PASS or PASSING evaluator can help administrators and service personnel to identify *which* service features are particularly strong or weak, and *why*.

6. Ely (1991) found that the potentially manipulable variables of the urban versus rural location of residential services, and the number of people served in the typical residence, were powerful predictors of PASSING scores. This suggests that, at least in certain residential-service contexts, quality may be considerably enhanced by careful attention to the location and size of services. We may thus add a

nuance to our third point (above), namely, that while good quality on the structural dimensions of services in no way guarantees good performance on their functional aspects, structural features such as location and size may, in some situations, act as powerful facilitators or inhibitors of functional aspects such as the frequency and quality of social interactions, relationships, and integration. Attention to the interplay between the structural and functional features of services is thus likely, in any given situation, to be very important for service planning and evaluation.

7. It is clear from the studies reviewed that relatively high levels of interrater reliability and internal consistency are attainable with PASS and PASSING, and that postconciliation scores bear a moderate to strong relationship to (although they tend to be somewhat lower than) individual preconciliation ratings (cf. Flynn & Heal, 1981; Flynn et al., 1991; Jacobs, 1983). In this regard, it should be emphasized that single-rater evaluations (which are contrary to standard PASS and PASSING practice) are to be avoided, because interrater reliability cannot be calculated in such situations and the benefits of pooling information and conciliating ratings by two or more raters are lost.

8. The present review has uncovered a good deal of evidence that is supportive of the concurrent, predictive, discriminant, factorial, and construct validity of PASS and PASSING. The fact, for example, that both instruments consistently differentiate between community and institutional services, as well as between various types of community programs, is supportive of their discriminant validity. The finding that PASS (e.g., Picard, 1988e) and PASSING (e.g., Ely, 1991) predict specific aspects of social integration and quality of life is supportive of their predictive validity. The successful cross-validation of the factor structures of PASS and PASSING (Flynn et al., in press) provides good evidence of factorial validity. Despite these promising findings, however, PASS and PASSING researchers should, whenever possible, gather data on client outcomes, as advocated by Perry and Felce (1995), in order to clarify the conditions under which high service quality and responsive program environments are likely to foster desirable client outcomes.

9. Finally, although I was able to locate 48 studies

for this review, the publication of more systematic research on PASS and PASSING, in peer-reviewed journals, would be highly desirable. To date, PASS and PASSING have frequently been used to educate service personnel in a number of fields and countries about the specific implications of the principles of Normalization and Social Role Valorization (see Thomas chapter 15, this volume). They have also been used relatively frequently on the local level to assess and improve individual service programs or agencies (as noted in several chapters in the present volume). The present review suggests, however, that they have been used considerably less often as instruments in formal research or evaluation studies. While their relatively widespread use as training and evaluation tools in the "real world" is impressive and has played an important role in bringing about positive service changes in a number of countries (as attested by several chapters in Pilling & Watson, 1995, and in the present volume), PASS and PASSING (and the services they are used to evaluate) would no doubt benefit from more frequent use by researchers and evaluators who are oriented to the publication of their findings. Such contributions are likely to have a significant impact on the direction that service policies and practices take over the long term.

REFERENCES

ANDREWS, R. J., & BERRY, P. B. (1978). The evaluation of services for the handicapped promoting community living. *International Journal of Rehabilitation Research, 1,* 451-461.

BALES, R. F. (1950). *Interaction process analysis.* Cambridge, MA: Addison-Wesley.

BENTLER, P. M., & WU, E. J. C. (1995). *EQS for Windows user's guide.* Encino, CA: Multivariate Software.

BERRY, P. B., ANDREWS, R. J., & ELKINS, J. (1977). *An evaluative study of educational, vocational and residential programs for the moderately to severely mentally handicapped in three states.* St. Lucia, Queensland, Australia: University of Queensland, Fred & Eleanor Schonell Educational Research Centre.

BORTHWICK-DUFFY, S. A., WIDAMAN, K. F., LITTLE, T. D., & EYMAN, R. K. (1992). *Foster family care for persons with mental retardation* (AAMR Monograph No. 17). Washington, DC: American Association on Mental Retardation.

BRADLEY, R. H., & CALDWELL, B. M. (1979). Home observation for measurement of the environment: A revision of the preschool scale. *American Journal of Mental Deficiency, 84,* 235-244.

CARSON, J., DOWLING, F., LUYOMBYA, G., SENAPTI-SHARMA, M., & GLYNN, T. (1992). Normalisation . . . and now for something completely different. *Clinical Psychology Forum, 49,* 27-30.

CHUBON, R. A. (1990). *Manual for the life situation survey.* Columbia, SC: University of South Carolina, Rehabilitation Counseling Program.

COCKS, E. (1998). Evaluating the quality of residential services for people with disabilities using program analysis of service systems' implementation of Normalization goals (PASSING). *Asia & Pacific Journal on Disability, 1.*

CONROY, J. W. (1979). *Longitudinal study of the court-ordered deinstitutionalization of Pennhurst: Report on assessment of institutional environments.* Philadelphia: Temple University, Developmental Disabilities Center.

CONROY, J. W. (1996). The small ICF/MR program: Dimensions of quality and cost. *Mental Retardation, 34,* 13-26.

CONROY, J. W. (1998). Response to Crinella, McCleary, and Swanson. *Mental Retardation, 36,* 225-226.

CONROY, J. W., & BRADLEY, V. J. (1985). *The Pennhurst longitudinal study: A report of five years of research and analysis.* Philadelphia & Boston: Temple University, Developmental Disabilities Center & Human Service Research Institute.

CONROY, J., EFTHIMIOU, & LEMANOWICZ, J. (1982).

A matched comparison of the developmental growth of institutionalized and deinstitutionalized mentally retarded clients. *American Journal of Mental Deficiency, 86,* 581-587.

CONROY, J. W., & FEINSTEIN, C. S. (1985). Attitudes of the families of CARC v. Thorne class members. *Interim Report Number 2, Connecticut Applied Research Project.* Philadelphia: Conroy & Feinstein Associates.

CRINELLA, F. M., MCCLEARY, R., & SWANSON, J. M. (1998). How a regression artifact makes ICFs/MR look ineffective. *Mental Retardation, 36,* 219-225.

DANSEREAU. J., DUTEAU, C., ELY, P., & FLYNN, R. J. (1990). *Évaluation des programmes résidentiels en santé mentale dans l'Outaouais.* Hull, QC: Conseil régional de la Santé et des Services sociaux de l'Outaouais.

DEMAINE, G. C., SILVERSTEIN, A. B., & MAYEDA, T. (1980). Validation of PASS 3: A first step in service evaluation through environmental assessment. *Mental Retardation, 18,* 131-134.

DEVLIN, S. (1989). *Reliability assessment of the instruments used to monitor the Pennhurst plaintiff class members.* Philadelphia: Temple University, Developmental Disabilities Center.

DURANT, B., KEARNEY, C., & MINDELL, J. (1987). *Measuring choice in residential settings: The residential choice assessment scale (RCAS).* Paper presented at the annual meeting of the Association for the Advancement of Behavior Therapy, Boston.

ELY, P. W. (1991). *Quality of life and social integration of psychiatrically disabled citizens in community residences.* Unpublished doctoral dissertation, University of Ottawa.

ELY, P. W., & FLYNN, R. J. (1989). *The social integration scale/L'Échelle d'intégration sociale.* Unpublished manuscript, University of Ottawa, School of Psychology.

EYMAN, R. K., DEMAINE, G. C., & LEI, T. (1979). The relationship between foster care environments and resident changes in adaptive behavior: A path model. *American Journal of Mental Deficiency, 83,* 330-338.

FELCE, D. (1988). Behavioral and social climate in community group residences. In M. P. JANICKI,

M. W. KRAUSS, & M. M. SELTZER (Eds.), *Community residences for persons with developmental disabilities: Here to stay* (pp. 133-147). Baltimore: Paul H. Brookes.

FELCE, D., & PERRY, J. (1997). A PASS 3 evaluation of community residences in Wales. *Mental Retardation, 35,* 170-176.

FIORELLI, J. S. (1978). *A comparison of selected categories of behavior in more and less normalized living environments* (Evaluation and Research Technical Report 78-10). Philadelphia: Temple University, Developmental Disabilities Program.

FIORELLI, J. S., & THURMAN, S. K. (1979). Client behavior in more and less normalized residential settings. *Education and Training of the Mentally Retarded, 14,* 85-94.

FLYNN, R. J. (1975). *Assessing human service quality with PASS 2: An empirical analysis of 102 service program evaluations* (NIMR Monograph No. 5). Toronto, ON: National Institute on Mental Retardation.

FLYNN, R. J. (1977). Evaluating Normalization, social integration, and administrative effectiveness. *Psychosocial Rehabilitation Journal, 1*(3), 1-12.

FLYNN, R. J. (1980). Normalization, PASS, and service quality assessment: How normalizing are current human services? In R. J. FLYNN & K. E. NITSCH (Eds.), *Normalization, social integration, and community services* (pp. 323-357). Baltimore: University Park Press.

FLYNN, R. J. (1985). Assessing the effectiveness of deinstitutionalization: Substantive and methodological conclusions from the research literature. In *Deinstitutionalization: Costs and effects* (pp. 75-102). Ottawa: Canadian Council on Social Development.

FLYNN, R. J. (1993). Intégration et évaluation de programmes: Comparaisons internationales. In S. IONESCU, G. MAGEROTTE, W. PILON, & R. SALABREUX (Eds.), *L'intégration des personnes présentant une déficience intellectuelle* (pp. 5-15). Actes du IIIe Congrès de l'Association Internationale de Recherche scientifique en faveur des personnes Handicapées Mentales (AIRHM). Trois-Rivières, QC: Université du Québec à Trois-Rivières et AIRHM.

345

FLYNN, R. J., GUIRGUIS, M., WOLFENSBERGER, W., & COCKS, E. (in press). Cross-validated factor structures and factor-based subscales for PASS and PASSING. *Mental Retardation*.

FLYNN, R. J., & HEAL, L. W. (1981). A short form of PASS 3: A study of its structure, interrater reliability, and validity for assessing Normalization. *Evaluation Review, 5,* 357-376.

FLYNN, R. J., LAPOINTE, N., WOLFENSBERGER, W., & THOMAS, S. (1991). Quality of institutional and community human service programs in Canada and the United States. *Journal of Psychiatry and Neuroscience, 16,* 146-153.

FLYNN, R. J., & SHA'KED, A. (1977). Normative sex behavior and the person with a disability: Assessing the effectiveness of the rehabilitation agencies. *Journal of Rehabilitation, 43*(5), 34-38.

GALLANT, W. A. (1983). *Comparative study of integrated and non-integrated educational programs for children classified as trainable mentally retarded in Ontario using program analysis of service systems (PASS) as a tool of evaluation.* Unpublished doctoral dissertation, Wayne State University.

GOLDEN, S. J. (1982). *Normalization in mental health community residences.* Unpublished doctoral dissertation, University of Rhode Island.

HEAL, L. W., & DANIELS, B. S. (1986). A cost-effectiveness analysis of residential alternatives for selected developmentally disabled citizens of three northern Wisconsin counties. *Mental Retardation Systems, 3*(2), 35-49.

HEAL, L. W., & FUJIURA, G. T. (1984). Methodological considerations in research on residential alternatives for developmentally disabled persons. *International Review of Research in Mental Retardation, 12,* 205-244.

HEIFETZ, L. J. (1998). Break the data-bank with Monte Carlo? Statistical problems in the dispute between Conroy (1996) and Crinella, McCleary, and Swanson (1998). *Mental Retardation, 36,* 227-236.

HULL, J. T., KEATS, J. G., & THOMPSON, J. (1984). Community residential facilities for the mentally ill and mentally retarded: Environmental quality and adaptive functioning. *Canadian Journal of Community Mental Health, 3,* 5-14.

HULL, J. T., & THOMPSON, J. C. (1980). Predicting adaptive functioning of mentally retarded persons in community settings. *American Journal of Mental Deficiency, 85,* 253-261.

HULL, J. T., & THOMPSON, J. C. (1981a). Predicting adaptive functioning among mentally ill persons in community settings. *American Journal of Community Psychology, 9,* 247-268.

HULL, J. T., & THOMPSON, J. C. (1981b). Factors which contribute to Normalization in residential facilities for the mentally ill. *Community Mental Health Journal, 17,* 107-113.

JACKSON, J. (1969). Factors of the treatment environment. *Archives of General Psychiatry, 21,* 39-45.

JACOBS, N. J. (1983). *An exploratory study of "PASSING," a tool for the evaluation of Normalization of social services.* Unpublished doctoral dissertation, University of Wisconsin-Madison.

JÖRESKOG, K. G., & SÖRBOM, D. (1988). *LISREL 7: A guide to the program and applications.* Chicago: SPSS.

KING, R., RAYNES, N., & TIZARD, J. (1971). *Patterns of residential care: Sociological studies in institutions for handicapped children.* London: Routledge & Kegan Paul.

KORN, M. (1987). *Development of an instructional system for research and training on primarily administrative aspects of the program analysis of service systems.* Unpublished doctoral dissertation, Syracuse University.

LANDESMAN, S. (1988). Preventing "institutionalization" in the community. In M. P. JANICKI, M. W. KRAUSS, & M. M. SELTZER (Eds.), *Community residences for persons with developmental disabilities: Here to stay* (pp. 105-116). Baltimore: Paul H. Brookes.

LEHMAN, A. F. (1988). A quality of life interview for the chronically mentally ill. *Evaluation and Program Planning, 11,* 51-62.

LEMAY, R. A. (1997). *PASS 3–Lanaudière (1996): Projet d'évaluation des quinze pavillons en santé mentale (CHRLD).* Rapport soumis à la Régie régionale de la Santé et des Services sociaux de Lanaudière. Ottawa: Author.

LESSARD, J. C. (1975). *Échelle de comportement*

adaptif AAMD/ABS (Édition expérimentale). Cité universitaire, QC: Université Laval.

LUTFIYYA, Z. M., MOSELEY, C., WALKER, P., ZOLLERS, N., LEHR, S., PUGLIESE, J., CALLAHAN, M., & CENTRA, N. (1987). *A question of community: Quality of life and integration in "small residential units" and other residential settings.* Syracuse, NY: Syracuse University, Center on Human Policy.

MACY, B. (1971). *Analysis of 1970 and 1971 PASS scores.* Lincoln, NB: Nebraska Office of Mental Retardation.

MARLETT, N. J. (1977a). *Adaptive functioning index standardization manual.* Calgary, AB: Vocational and Rehabilitation Research Institute.

MARLETT, N. J. (1977b). *Adaptive functioning index rehabilitation programs manual.* Calgary, AB: Vocational and Rehabilitation Research Institute.

MEADOR, D. M., OSBORN, R. G., OWENS, M. H., SMITH, E. C., & TAYLOR, T. L. (1991). Evaluation of environmental support in group homes for persons with mental retardation. *Mental Retardation, 29,* 159-164.

MINDEL, C. H., & ROSENTRAUB, M. S. (1992). Normalization and community-based living: The implementation and impact of a Medicaid-waiver program. *New England Journal of Human Services, 12*(2), 15-23.

MOOS, R. (1974). *The social climate scales: An overview.* Palo Alto, CA: Consulting Psychologists Press.

MOOS, R., & HOOTS, P. (1968). The assessment of the social atmosphere of psychiatric wards. *Journal of Abnormal Psychology, 73,* 595-604.

MOOS, R., & OTTO, J. (1972). The Community-Oriented Program Environment Scale: A methodology for the facilitation and evaluation of social change. *Community Mental Health Journal, 8,* 28-37.

MULVEY, E. P., LINNEY, J. A., & ROSENBERG, M. S. (1987). Organizational control and treatment program design as dimensions of institutionalization in settings for juvenile offenders. *American Journal of Community Psychology, 15,* 321-335.

NEWTON, S., BELLAMY, G. T., BOLES, S. M., STONER, S., HORNER, R., LE BARON, N., MOSKOWITZ, D., ROMER, M., & SCHLESSINGER, D. (1988) *Valued Outcomes Information System (VOIS): Operational manual.* Eugene, OR: University of Oregon, Center on Human Development.

NIHIRA, K., FOSTER, R., SHELLHAAS, M., & LELAND, H. (1974). *AAMD Adaptive Behavior Scale, 1974 revision.* Washington, DC: American Association on Mental Deficiency.

PELLETIER, J. (1992). *Évaluation de la qualité des services du réseau de la déficience intellectuelle de la région 04 à l'aide de la méthode PASSING.* Gatineau, QC & Gloucester, ON: Les Communications OPELL.

PERLIK, S. E. (1984). *Risk taking in the lives of people in community residences who are mentally retarded.* Unpublished doctoral dissertation, Florence Heller Graduate School for Advanced Study in Social Welfare, Brandeis University.

PERRY, J., & FELCE, D. (1995). Objective assessments of quality of life: How much do they agree with each other? *Journal of Community and Applied Social Psychology, 5,* 1-19.

PICARD, D. (1988a). *La réinsertion sociale des personnes handicapées mentales en familles d'accueil. Tome 1: Caractéristiques personnelles des bénéficiaires.* Québec, QC: Centre de Services sociaux de Québec, Service de la Recherche.

PICARD, D. (1988b). *La réinsertion sociale des personnes handicapées mentales en familles d'accueil. Tome 2: Caractéristiques socio-démographiques et normalisantes des familles d'accueil.* Québec, QC: Centre de Services sociaux de Québec, Service de la Recherche.

PICARD, D. (1988c). *La réinsertion sociale des personnes handicapées mentales en familles d'accueil. Tome 3: Caractéristiques des services en milieux institutionnel et de réinsertion.* Québec, QC: Centre de Services Sociaux de Québec, Service de la Recherche.

PICARD, D. (1988d). *La réinsertion sociale des personnes handicapées mentales en familles d'accueil. Tome 4: Degré d'adaptation et d'intégration sociale des bénéficiaires.* Québec, QC: Centre de Services sociaux de Québec, Service de la Recherche.

347

PICARD, D. (1988e). *La réinsertion sociale des personnes handicapées mentales en familles d'accueil. Tome 5: Comparaison et mise en relation des différentes catégories de variables.* Québec, QC: Centre de Services sociaux de Québec, Service de la Recherche.

PILLING, D., & WATSON, G. (Eds.). (1995). *Evaluating quality in services for disabled and older people.* London, England & Bristol, PA: Jessica Kingsley Publishers.

PILON, W., ARSENAULT, R., & GASCON, H. (1993). Le passage de l'institution à la communauté et son impact sur la qualité de vie et l'intégration sociale de la personne présentant une déficience intellectuelle. In S. IONESCU, G. MAGEROTTE, W. PILON, & R. SALABREUX (Eds.), *L'intégration des personnes présentant une déficience intellectuelle* (pp. 255-266). Actes du IIIe Congrès de l'Association internationale de recherche scientifique en faveur des personnes handicapées mentales (AIRHM). Université du Québec à Trois-Rivières et AIRHM.

PILON, W., ARSENAULT, R., & GASCON, H. (1994). *Le passage de l'institution à la communauté et son impact sur la qualité de vie et l'intégration sociale de la personne présentant une déficience intellectuelle.* Québec, QC: Centre de recherche Université Laval Robert-Giffard.

PRATT, M. W., LUSCZC, M. A., & BROWN, M. E. (1980). Measuring the dimensions of the quality of care in small community residences. *American Journal of Mental Deficiency, 85,* 188-194.

RAYNES, N. V., SUMPTON, R. C., & PETTIFER, C. (1989). *The Index of Participation in Domestic Life.* Manchester: University Department of Social Policy and Social Work.

ROSS, E. C. (1981). *Accreditation and programs for persons with developmental disabilities: A search for compatibility and coordination.* Unpublished doctoral dissertation, George Washington University.

ROTEGARD, L. L., BRUININKS, R. H., & HILL, B. K. (1981). *Environmental characteristics of residential facilities for mentally retarded people.* Minneapolis, MN: Dept. of Psychoeducational Studies, University of Minnesota.

SPARROW, S. S., BALLA, D. A., & CICCHETTI, D. V. (1984). *Vineland Adaptive Behavior Scales: Interview edition, survey form manual.* Circle Pines, MN: American Guidance Service.

TAYLOR, S. J. (1998). Point, counterpoint, and a statistical reiew on community living research: The editor's perspective. *Mental Retardation, 36,* 217-218.

VANDERGRIFF, D. V. (1991). *The psychological and psychosocial impact of various residential treatment milieus on adults with mental retardation.* Unpublished doctoral dissertation, University of South Carolina.

VANDERGRIFF, D. V., & CHUBON, R. A. (1994). Quality of life experienced by persons with mental retardation in various residential settings. *Journal of Rehabilitation, 60*(4), 30-37.

WEBB, O. J. (1983). *The effects of different residential environments on the behavior of intellectually handicapped adults.* Unpublished doctoral dissertation, University of Otaggo (Christchurch, New Zealand).

WEBB, O. J., WELLS, J. E., & HORNBLOW, A. R. (1986). Institutions versus community placements: The effects of different residential environments on the behavior of intellectually handicapped adults. *New Zealand Medical Journal, 99,* 951-954.

WILLIAMS, P. (1995). The results from PASS and PASSING Evaluations. In D. PILLING & G. WATSON (Eds.), *Evaluating quality in services for disabled and older people* (pp. 61-77). London, England & Bristol, PA: Jessica Kingsley Publishers.

WOLFENSBERGER, W. (1994). *Overview of "PASSING": A Normalization/Social Role Valorization-based human service evaluation tool.* Syracuse, NY: Syracuse University, Training Institute for Human Service Planning, Leadership and Change Agentry.

WOLFENSBERGER, W., & GLENN, L. (1969). *Program analysis of service systems (PASS): A method for the quantitative evaluation of human services* (1st ed.). Omaha: Nebraska Psychiatric Institute.

WOLFENSBERGER, W., & GLENN, L. (1973). *Program analysis of service systems (PASS): A method for the quantitative evaluation of human services* (2nd ed.). Vol. 1: *Handbook.* Vol. 2: *Field manual.* Toronto, ON: National Institute on Mental Retardation.

WOLFENSBERGER, W., & GLENN, L. (1975). *Program analysis of service systems (PASS): A method for the quantitative evaluation of human services* (3rd ed.). Vol. 1: *Handbook.* Vol. 2: *Field manual.* Toronto, ON: National Institute on Mental Retardation.

WOLFENSBERGER, W., & GLENN, L. (1989). *Analyse de programmes pour les systèmes de services (PASS): Méthode d'évaluation quantitative des services humains. Manuel pratique* (Version européenne de 1989 traduite de la 3e édition anglophone de 1975). Genève: Comité Européen pour le Développement de L'Intégration Sociale (CEDIS).

WOLFENSBERGER, W., & THOMAS, S. (1980). *Program analysis of service systems' implementation of Normalization goals (PASSING)* (Experimental ed.). Syracuse, NY: Syracuse University, Training Institute for Human Service Planning, Leadership and Change Agentry.

WOLFENSBERGER, W., & THOMAS, S. (1983). *PASSING (Program analysis of service systems' implementation of Normalization goals): Normalization criteria and ratings manual* (2nd ed.). Toronto, ON: National Institute on Mental Retardation.

WOLFENSBERGER, W., & THOMAS, S. (1989). *PASSING (Programme d'analyse des systèmes de services—applications des buts de la Valorisation des Rôles Sociaux): Manuel des critères et des mesures de la Valorisation des Rôles Sociaux* (2ème ed.). (M. Roberge, Trans.; J. Pelletier, Adapt.). Toronto, ON: Institut G. Allan Roeher & Les Communications OPELL.

Part 5

Dissemination and Impact of Normalization and Social Role Valorization Through Training and Education

15

Historical background and evolution of Normalization-related and Social Role Valorization-related training

SUSAN THOMAS

1 INTRODUCTION

In this paper, I will be speaking primarily about the North American scene, both because (a) that is what I am most familiar with, and (b) historically, many people from other places came to North America to learn Normalization and/or Social Role Valorization (SRV), returned to their own homes, and there imitated or adapted what they had seen in North America. Thus, many training developments related to Normalization/SRV in other places have been based to a greater or lesser extent on those in North America.

The perspective that I will offer on the impact of Normalization and SRV training is based on three sources. One is my having worked for Professor Wolf Wolfensberger at Syracuse University since 1973 (he hired me about one month after he himself arrived in Syracuse), with only two hiatuses, one of 4 months in 1975 and one of 9 months in 1977-1978.

The second source of information is the archives kept at the Training Institute for Human Service Planning, Leadership and Change Agentry at Syracuse University, which Dr. Wolfensberger directs. This Training Institute is the body that was largely responsible for launching systematic training workshops in Normalization, and later SRV, in the United States, though it also conducted extensive training throughout Canada, and sporadically in England and Australia.

The third source of information is Dr. Wolfensberger's oral history and remembrances of "the way things were."

2 AN ORIENTATION TO LEVELS AND DIMENSIONS OF SOCIETAL CHANGE

Wolfensberger initially taught Normalization in a way that divided potential action implications into three or four levels of social organization, and two dimensions. This yielded six boxes, as shown in Table 15.1.

The levels were those of the person; the primary and intermediate social systems; and the societal systems. The person level referred to the specific person who was devalued or at risk of such devaluation. The primary social systems were a person's family, friends, and peer group. Intermediate social systems meant such things as school, neighborhood, service agency, and community. Though the primary and intermediate social systems were recognized as distinct, they were collapsed into one level on the chart, for ease of teaching and discourse. The societal systems level referred to larger social systems, such as the school system of an entire state or nation, the laws of the land, and the mores of a society.

The levels referred to the party or entity being acted upon, so to speak, rather than to the party doing the acting. Thus, the person level referred to a specific person to whom normalizing measures would be applied, not to specific individuals working to implement Normalization. After all, as an individual, one could work on any of the levels, even the societal one. The primary social systems referred to families or peer groups to whom normalizing measures would be applied, not to families who were pursuing Normalization for a family member. After all, such families might be acting on the secondary social systems level, such as trying to change a service agency, and so on.

In other words, there is a difference between taking action on a certain level, and an action being directed toward change in a certain level. It is the latter that the three levels in the chart tried to capture. In the long run, actions taken on any level could eventually impact on any of the other levels. For example, a state law could change the lives of many specific persons to whom it applies, changes in families and services could eventually result in changes in an entire system of service delivery, and action taken on the primary and intermediate social systems level might eventually affect societal level social systems. Of course, any action on any level is not guaranteed of results, which is one more reason why actions taken must not be equated with impacts.

The two dimensions were those of interaction and interpretation. First, Wolfensberger had spoken largely about what he called interaction, meaning what is done to and with people. Later in 1970, he added a second dimension, that of interpretation, which referred to how people were presented or interpreted to others.

TABLE 15.1

A SCHEMA OF THE EXPRESSION OF THE NORMALIZATION PRINCIPLE ON THREE LEVELS OF TWO DIMENSIONS OF ACTION

Level of action	Dimension of action	
	Interaction	*Interpretation*
Person	Eliciting, shaping, and maintaining normative skills and habits in persons by means of direct physical and social interaction with them	Presenting, managing, addressing, labeling, and interpreting individual persons in a manner emphasizing their similarities to, rather than differences from, others
Primary and intermediate social systems	Eliciting, shaping, and maintaining normative skills and habits in persons by working indirectly through their primary and intermediate social systems, such as family, classroom, school, work setting, service agency, and neighborhood	Shaping, presenting, and interpreting intermediate social systems surrounding a person or consisting of target persons so that these systems as well as the persons in them are perceived as culturally normative as possible
Societal systems	Eliciting, shaping, and maintaining normative behavior in persons by appropriate shaping of large societal social systems, and structures such as entire school systems, laws, and government	Shaping cultural values, attitudes, and stereotypes so as to elicit maximal feasible cultural acceptance of differences

The chart, as shown in Table 15.1, was included in the 1972 textbook *The Principle of Normalization in Human Services* (Wolfensberger, 1972, p. 32), and Wolfensberger's Normalization teaching continued to incorporate some version or other of this useful chart, mostly to show that a great many and very diverse actions were required in order to bring Normalization about, that these actions needed to take place at many different levels, and that Normalization had impacts on different levels of societal organization. The chart was also used to emphasize that how people were seen by others—i.e., their interpretation—was very important, just as important as direct habilitational and other clinical services. Impressing this latter fact very strongly on people was so necessary then because it was a novel idea—so much so that it was very hotly contested for much of the 1970s, and elements of it occasionally continue to be contested even now. For instance, as late as 1993, the Muscular Dystrophy Association in the US vehemently defended its annual fund-raising telethons that have characteristically been full of child and pity imagery.

But even prior to the 1972 *Normalization* text, Wolfensberger had already written about the need for normalizing action to take place on these three levels. In a Nebraska publication of February 1970 (Wolfensberger, 1970a, p. 4), he noted that "retarded persons should be presented and interpreted to others in such a way as to emphasize . . . their similarities to . . . others" (the first level), "retarded persons should receive services which make them less deviant" (the second level), and "the attitudes and values of society should be shaped so as to be more accepting and tolerant of...differentness" (the third level). Similarly, in a September 1970 article in the *American Journal of Psychiatry* (Wolfensberger, 1970b, p. 292), he said that "deviant persons should be helped to be able to become less deviant and nondeviant people to remain nondeviant" (first level), and that "the attitudes and values of society should be shaped to be more accepting and tolerant of . . . differentness" (third level). However, for this psychiatric audience, he also referred to the three levels of action as being "clinical, public interpretation, and societal change" (Wolfensberger, 1970b, p. 296), rather than those of person, primary and intermediate social systems, and society as a whole. And he noted that in the field of

mental disorder, a disproportionate amount of effort and address are directed at the clinical, or person, level, and not at the other two (p. 296).

In his first (rebuffed) attempt in 1970 to publish an article on Normalization for the field of mental retardation, he also included the 2 x 3 chart and asked colleagues for critique of this chart especially. As Normalization training evolved, and particularly as Normalization was reconceptualized into Social Role Valorization (SRV) (Wolfensberger, 1983, 1984, 1985, 1991a, 1992), the dimension of interpretation was gradually refined and eventually renamed—around 1982—"social image enhancement," that is, those things that primarily affected a party's image in the eyes of others. The interaction dimension was supplanted by a construct of personal competency enhancement, with social interaction implications being embedded in various components of the chart.

When the first monograph on SRV was published in 1991, and then in 1992 in a revised edition (Wolfensberger, 1991a, 1991b, 1991c, 1991d, 1992), it also contained the 2 x 3 chart, though by this time the chart had been revised to accord with how SRV was by then conceptualized and taught. This chart, as it appeared in the 2nd (1992) edition of the monograph, but with two minor revisions, is shown on Table 15.2.

It still had the three levels of person, primary and intermediate social systems, and larger social systems, with specific action implications "sorted" into six boxes, depending on which level and which dimension a particular implication best fit.

However, by the early 1990s, it had become evident that collapsing the primary and intermediate social systems into a single level may have been a mistake, because so many people had a tendency to focus on the intermediate systems—the schools, the vocational services, organized services in general—and overlook the many implications to *primary* social systems, such as family and friends. But because of inertia and competing demands on our time, the full separation of this second level into two distinct levels has not yet been accomplished in the publications on Normalization/SRV, though it is being worked into the teaching package on SRV that the Syracuse University Training Institute uses and has been making available to qualified SRV trainers. (This has been done since the 1994 conference and is included here as Table 15.3.)

TABLE 15.2

SOCIAL ROLE VALORIZATION ACTION IMPLICATIONS

	Primarily to enhance social images	Primarily to enhance personal competencies
Individual person	*Creating physical and social preconditions to the enhancement of social perceptions of individuals by others* *Age-appropriate and culturally valued: • Personal appearance and dress • Personal labels and forms of address • Personal possessions • Rights • Activities, including those perceived as risky *Promotion of challenging role expectations and valued social roles *Attachment of other valued personal symbolisms	*Creating physical and social preconditions to the enhancement of competencies of individuals* *Precise, relevant address of competency needs *Intensity of relevant service *Individualization of programming *Prevention/reversal of impairments *Provision of stable, secure, and ongoing relationships *Enablement of continuity with physical environments and objects *Teaching of self-mastery/self-discipline *Enrichment of experiential world *Extension of appropriate autonomy and rights *Teaching of appropriate sociosexual identity and expression *Imposition of adaptive, competency-promoting social roles
Individual's primary and intermediate social systems	*Creating physical and social preconditions to the enhancement of social images via aspects of social systems* *Age-appropriate and culturally valued: • Activities, schedules, and routines • Names of services, facilities, groupings, and activities *Image-enhancing facility locations and appearances *Positively imaged service workers *Image-enhancing groupings and juxtapositions with more valued/less devalued others	*Creating physical and social preconditions to the enhancement of competencies via aspects of social systems* *Service proximity to: • Clients and their families • Population centers and their resources *Ease of client and public access to/from service system *Competency-challenging and demanding facilities and programs *Dispersal rather than congregation of groupings and services *Competency-promoting groupings and juxtapositions with more advanced persons within social systems *Competent service workers and other people
Larger society of individual or group	*Creating physical and social preconditions to social image enhancement throughout society* *Education and positive attitude-shaping of public *Modeling of positive attitudes and interactions with devalued people *Rightful and generic funding of services	*Creating physical and social preconditions to competency enhancement throughout society* *Nondiscrimination laws *Accessible public settings *Adaptive service personnel training structures *Comprehensiveness and continuity within and across service systems *Adaptive and flexible funding patterns that provide incentives for more role-valorizing forms of services

TABLE 15.3

SOCIAL ROLE VALORIZATION ACTION IMPLICATIONS

	Primarily to enhance social images	**Primarily to enhance personal competencies**
Individual person	*Arranging physical and social conditions for a specific person so that they are likely to enhance positive perceptions of that individual by others* *Age-appropriate and culturally valued: • Personal appearance and dress • Personal labels and forms of address • Personal possessions • Rights • Activities, including those perceived as risky *Promotion of challenging role expectations and valued social roles *Attachment of other valued personal symbolisms	*Arranging physical and social conditions for a specific person so that they are likely to enhance the competencies of that individual* *Precise, relevant address of competency needs *Potency of relevant service *Individualization of programming *Prevention/reversal of impairments *Competency-challenging and demanding physical setting *Competency-challenging and demanding activities and rhythms *Provision of competency-enhancing possessions and material supports *Provision of stable, secure, and ongoing relationships *Enablement of continuity with physical environments and objects *Teaching of self-mastery/self-discipline *Enrichment of experiential world *Access to competency-related community resources *Extension of competency-enabling autonomy and rights *Inculcation of appropriate sociosexual identity and rights *Installing people into adaptive, competency-promoting social roles
Individual's primary social systems	*Arranging physical and social conditions in a primary social system so that they are likely to enhance positive perceptions of a person in and via this social system* *Age-appropriate and culturally valued: • Activities, schedules and routines • Names (if any) of groupings and activities *Image-enhancing setting location and appearance *Positively imaged other members of the social system *Image-enhancing groupings and juxtapositions with more valued/less devalued others in that social system	*Arranging physical and social conditions of a person's primary social system so that they are likely to enhance that person's competencies* *Competency-promoting groupings and juxtaposition with models, members, servers, and mentors in that social system

Intermediate/ secondary social systems	*Arranging physical and social conditions in secondary social systems so that they are likely to enhance positive perceptions—in and via those social systems—of people in them, and of others like them* *Age-appropriate and culturally valued: • Activities, schedules and routines • Names of services, facilities, groupings, and activities *Image-enhancing setting locations and appearances *Dispersal rather than congregation of groupings and services *Positively imaged servers *Image-enhancing groupings and juxtapositions with more valued/less devalued others *Combinations of service elements so as to be model coherent, and protect images even if the major need is in the competency domain	*Arranging physical and social conditions in secondary social systems so that they are likely to enhance the competencies of people in them* *Service proximity to population centers and community resources *Ease of access to/from service system settings for recipients, their families, and public *Competency-challenging and demanding settings and programs *Competency-promoting groupings and juxtapositions with more advanced persons within social systems *Competent servers and mentors in that system *Comprehensiveness and continuity of provision within and across services so as to allow movement according to competency level *Combinations of service elements so as to be model coherent, and protect competencies even if the major need is in the image domain
Larger society of individual, group, or class	*Arranging physical and social conditions throughout society so that they are likely to enhance positive perceptions of classes of people* *Education and positive attitude-shaping of the public *Positive media portrayal *Public modeling of positive attitudes and interaction with devalued people *Funding patterns that incentive image enhancement of (devalued) people, including by rightful and generic funding of services	*Arranging physical and social conditions throughout society so that they are likely to enhance the competencies of classes of people* *Laws against unjust/unjustified discrimination *Public settings that are physically accessible to impaired people *Adaptive training structures for service personnel *Funding patterns that incentive more competency-enhancing forms of services

Deborah Reidy (chapter 16) and I both believe that the mandate we received from the book editors to prepare our presentations on this topic was either derived from considerations of that original 2 x 3 chart, or at least reflects it, because we were given the charge to present on "the impact of . . . training . . . [on the] personal, service, and policy" levels, and respondents to this paper are supposed to address how training in Normalization and SRV has affected specific persons, services, and societal policy.

Thus, one can see that from very early on, it was recognized that normalizing actions needed to be taken, and changes needed to be made, on many levels of social organization. This deserves emphasizing because one of the criticisms or misunderstandings that have beset Normalization from the beginning (and that continue to occur with regard to SRV as well) is that it focuses *only* on changes expected from devalued people, something along the lines of, "Normalization or SRV wants to change devalued people but does not ask society to make any changes or accommodation for them." But another criticism has been that it focuses *only* on what services should do, or *only* on what society should do, which usually goes something like, "Normalization or SRV calls upon society to make all sorts of adaptations and accommodations but has no clinical implications to devalued people themselves." In other words, different critics have noted that Normalization/SRV does address one or another of the four levels and have concluded that it addresses *only* one such level.

Further, the charge has often been made that Normalization/SRV is concerned *only* with one of the two dimensions. This usually takes the form of, "Normalization/SRV is all about image, about 'dressing up' devalued people, but does nothing to enhance their behavioral competency." The opposite criticism is that "Normalization/SRV is concerned only with how devalued people need to change, thus putting all the onus on them."

These charges have always been baseless, because Normalization and SRV are concerned with *both* dimensions, and with *all* levels of social organization. But they will probably continue to be made, particularly since the vast majority of critiques of Normalization and SRV have come from parties who had neither acquainted themselves with the basic literature, nor been to any of the longer SRV training events of two to three days' duration.

Among other things, this tells us that, unlike with many other subject matters, most people—including those in academia—obviously have not learned Normalization or SRV well, or primarily, from the source literature on it. Instead, the bulk of Normalization/SRV competence—at least as concerns the breadth of its relevance and its depth of application—has come from an oral training culture, primarily in the form of short-term training workshops, as I will elaborate.

3 THE TRAINING CULTURE IN NORMALIZATION/SRV

From the very beginning of the Normalization movement, training of one sort or another was a major mechanism for disseminating Normalization ideas. For instance, Bank-Mikkelsen, Nirje, and Grunewald gave speeches and presentations to many groups during their visits to the US. Nirje especially used many slides, many of which were very dramatic in those days. Then Wolfensberger took up this practice of giving short talks on Normalization to different groups, as did others, mostly in connection with promoting what was then the new Nebraska state plan for community-based comprehensive service systems for mentally retarded people across that state.

But training was not the only mechanism for spreading Normalization ideas. Another was writing and publication, such as several chapters in the book *Changing Patterns in Residential Services for the Mentally Retarded* (Kugel & Wolfensberger, 1969), Wolfensberger's first refereed publication solely devoted to Normalization (Wolfensberger, 1970b); the *Normalization* book itself (Wolfensberger, 1972); numerous articles on it—both pro and con—in the professional literature; the 1980 Flynn and Nitsch book; the various editions of PASS (Wolfensberger & Glenn, 1969, 1973, 1975); then PASSING (Wolfensberger & Thomas, 1980, 1983, 1988); and the SRV monograph (Wolfensberger, 1991a, 1991b, 1991c, 1991d, 1992).

A third mechanism for dissemination of the ideas was study tours in which people would visit model services, even whole service systems, that were built on Normalization. Hopefully, the visitors would learn a lot about Normalization from this, and then return home and implement services there that incorporated these ideas, even if they did not exactly duplicate whatever they had seen. Remember that for a long time—throughout most of the 1970s—community services were still a very new, even radical idea in North America. Group homes were new and few in number. Many handicapped children were still excluded from schooling altogether, or were in segregated schools of low quality. Many adults had no day program at all, or only one of an arts-and-crafts/leisure nature, rather than work. And so on. So visiting services that incorporated Normalization principles was, on the one hand, necessary—otherwise some people might never see such services—and on the other hand very instructive, because these services were so different in many ways from the service scene with which people of that time would have been familiar.

Indeed for very many people, it was actually seeing services that had adopted Normalization that opened their eyes to what Normalization was and meant, how revolutionary it was, and that it could really "work." Even when people had heard about Normalization, or read about it, even if they had attended presentations and slide shows on it (such as were given frequently in the early 1970s), the radicality of what Normalization proposed often did not sink in unless and until they had visited an entire service system based on Normalization.

For instance, in the late 1960s and early 1970s particularly, a large number of people toured services in Denmark and Sweden, where Normalization was pioneered, and it was this seeing that made believers out of them. Many of these visitors included senior people and decision makers in human services.

Similarly, the Eastern Nebraska Community Office of Retardation (ENCOR) in the area around Omaha, Nebraska, was the first entire *system* in North America of comprehensive community services for retarded people that was based on Normalization. It became famous, and was also one of the first centers of concentrated and sustained Normalization teaching in North America. As a result, Nebraska generally, and the ENCOR system specifically, became as busy as a railroad station for several years, with people from all over the world coming to see what was being done.

At least within the Normalization conceptualization that was developed and promoted by Wolfensberger, there had also always been the recognition—from very early on—that in order for Normalization to be successfully implemented, there had to be good change agentry. That is, people had to know how to bring about change; what legislation to pursue; how to develop and implement service plans; how to coordinate services; how to change public attitudes for the better; and so on. Thus, at least within Wolfensberger's promotion of Normalization, training people in change agentry skills was always a major thrust and seen as necessary accompaniment to learning about Normalization and applying it. The two were seen to go hand in hand, with Normalization providing the ideology, and change agentry being the technical skills for putting it into practice, with the law providing the sometimes needed enablement or mandate. For example, in his training workshops on how to plan and implement comprehensive, community-based, and Normalization-based service systems, Wolfensberger taught that adaptive human service systems rested on "three legs" (see Figure 15.1), two of which—implementation and legislation—were in the nature of change agentry. It was largely in these workshops on planning and implementing comprehensive, Normalization-based service systems that the change agentry knowledge was conveyed. These workshops were 5 days long at first, and then expanded to 6.

Also, until PASSING came along in 1983, the training workshops on PASS (more about these later)

all included some coverage of change agentry, because only 70% of PASS dealt with Normalization, and the rest with other nonprogrammatic adaptive service practices.

FIGURE 15.1
ADAPTIVE HUMAN SERVICE SYSTEMS STAND ON THREE "LEGS"

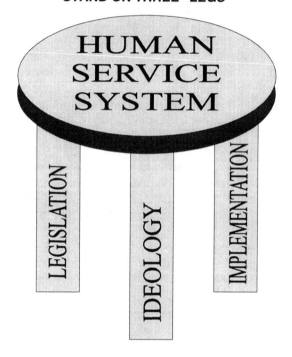

Further, the early Normalization leaders recognized that if there was a serious effort to implement Normalization, then there would also have to be numerous small service settings varying widely in type. In other words, services would be highly dispersed (rather than congregated), and specialized (rather than all-purpose or multipurpose). These two concepts of dispersal and specialization were repeatedly emphasized from the first in Normalization training. This had major implications to service system planning and implementation, in that dispersal and specialization of services meant that the service system and its management would be terribly *complex*. However, few people other than Wolfensberger recognized or emphasized this as he did in his training, and as can be documented by the overheads that were used in early such training into the late 1970s. (Unfortunately, not all the early teaching aids were kept as they underwent successive revision, and we only now realize what a loss this is because it is more difficult to document how the training evolved over time.) For instance, it was in the aforementioned training workshops on planning and implementing comprehensive service systems—developed by Wolfensberger starting in 1971 at what was then called the National Institute on Mental Retardation in Toronto—that the complexity of a normalizing service system was heavily stressed, and implications to service governance and coordination were worked out. Wolfensberger drafted most of that workshop material into manuscripts in hopes that it might eventually be published, though that never came about because there were so many other projects competing for his time.

4 THE MOST COMMON KINDS OF TRAINING IN NORMALIZATION/SRV

Training in Normalization, and later SRV, typically took four major forms.

4.1 SHORT PRESENTATIONS

The first consisted of presentations of 1 hour or so in length. As mentioned, first Bank-Mikkelsen, Nirje, and Grunewald, then Wolfensberger, and then others, gave such presentations widely at the start of the Normalization movement. For instance, in order to gain support from the citizenry for the then new Nebraska state plan for normalizing services for the mentally retarded, town meetings open to the public were held in 1969-1970 all over the state. At these meetings, the basic tenets of Normalization would be presented in such a way as to persuade and gain the support of the public (who would have to support legal changes and pay taxes for much of the new services) by capitalizing on the things the Nebraska public valued and was familiar with. For instance, conditions in institutions were shown to be offensive to ideals of human dignity. Group homes, apartments, and other community residential services were interpreted as offering to retarded people the same kinds of places to live that other people want to live in. Education and training were emphasized as reducing or preventing personal dependency. Work services were presented as

capitalizing on the "frontier spirit" of independence, pulling one's share, making a contribution, rather than just being "on the dole." Parents, professionals, and ordinary citizens were recruited and prepared to testify that they thought this was the right thing to do, and that they supported it and were willing to help pay for it. Because the purpose of these presentations was to recruit support for the state's shift from an institutional to a community service system, (a) they were given almost only in Nebraska, and (b) they focused as much on explaining the new state plan and persuading people to support it as they did on explaining Normalization. In other words, these early presentations were a mixture of Normalization orientation and change agentry. This campaign was so successful that the benefits, in terms of continued public support for community services in Nebraska, have continued to this day.

In other places, and to other groups as well, short speeches and presentations on Normalization were given. For instance, there might be a session on it at a cerebral palsy conference. There might be a keynote address on Normalization at an annual convention of parent associations. Someone might be invited to address a group of educators on Normalization. And so forth.

Once the new Nebraska state plan had been accepted and the services started up, then the newly hired workers in these newly established services were given 1- to 2-day orientation training in Normalization that had to be specially designed. This orientation training can be thought of as the transition to the second form of training, which will be covered next.

4.2 SHORT-TERM INTENSIVE WORKSHOPS

The second form of training, and the one that perhaps people are most familiar with, was the short-term intensive workshop that might last 2 to 5 full days (and sometimes nights as well), in which participants were taught the theory and implications of Normalization, usually via a combination of lectures, small group discussions, and practicum experiences. For instance, in the early PASS workshops that initially lasted 5 days, there would be 2 days of lecture on Normalization theory and its specific implications, lavishly illustrated with overhead transparencies and slides. For the next 2 days and nights, participants

361

would go out in small teams led by more experienced persons (called team leaders), and each team would practice-assess two existing services. Teams would gather information about these services through a combination of interviews, tours, and review of records, and then apply the PASS evaluation tool to each service, determining its performance on each of the ratings that make up the instrument. On the last day, the teams would reconvene into a large group, and participants would hear about the findings of all the other teams, trainers would draw lessons for the participants, and there might be additional lectures on advanced issues or the next steps.

For very many people, participating in a PASS training workshop was a consciousness-transforming experience. Often, participants went through the first practicum assessment fighting and resisting all the way but had a breakthrough during the second practicum and began to really understand, and often embrace, what Normalization implied. It was often the fact that their PASS training had been so world-changing for them that generated in many people their deep commitment to Normalization ideals and to seeing these implemented. However, I repeat that this type of PASS training workshop was just one of several training formats by which people learned about Normalization.

Initially, at least in North America, Normalization was taught in short presentations, as mentioned, and then within a 5-day PASS workshop, starting in June 1973. The first long (5-day) freestanding Normalization workshop that was not part of a PASS workshop was not offered until 1975, but from then on there were both separate Normalization workshops, as well as PASS workshops in which people could learn Normalization.

Also, soon after PASS training got going, advanced PASS workshops were developed and given, the first one in 1974. In these training events (which could only be attended by people who had successfully participated in an introductory PASS workshop), participants were taught more advanced and difficult issues, and applied PASS to more difficult and challenging types of services, such as a "soft" service, or one given in dispersed sites, or one that dealt with a new, unusual, or difficult need or clientele, such as a detentive service. These advanced events helped people gain greater competency with Normalization and PASS, identified problematic issues, helped to

refine what Normalization would mean for difficult service areas, and helped prepare participants to advance as Normalization teachers.

Another type of advanced training workshop begun in the early 1980s was that on the construct of *Model coherency*, which was based on a supremely important insight into how services should be structured and run. The construct was originally conceptualized as *Specialization*, and that is how it was written into the 1st (1969) and the 2nd (but first published) editions of PASS (Wolfensberger & Glenn, 1973). For the 3rd edition of PASS (Wolfensberger & Glenn, 1975), it was refined and renamed Model coherency. Workshops to teach people how to design model coherent services have ranged from one to two days in length, and sometimes these have been followed by practicum exercises of one to two days in the design of a specific kind of service for a specific type of people, or for people with a specific type of problem.

Then, with the publication of PASSING in 1983, PASSING training workshops began to be conducted, initially with basically the same format as PASS: lectures on the theory and principles, followed by practice assessments of real services by small teams, and then a plenary session of all participants for team reports and interpretations of the findings by senior trainers. In PASSING, various elements that make up Model coherency were included separately, such as coherent groupings of recipients, and appropriate match of servers to the type of service and the needs and identities of recipients. But in order to keep the PASSING instrument relatively simple, no single Model coherency rating was included in PASSING as it had been in PASS.

And, just as there were advanced PASS training workshops, so, too, an advanced PASSING training workshop was eventually devised and first held in January 1993, in which participants would assess more challenging types of services and would also tackle the construct of Model coherency. However, for the Advanced PASSING workshops, the concept of Model coherency was drastically revised from how it had been written for the 3rd edition of PASS, and a new freestanding rating of *Model coherency Impact* was written. So in advanced PASSING workshops, participants would apply to a more difficult type of service PASSING, plus the *Model coherency Impact* rating, plus the nonnormalization-related ratings of

PASS, that is, those that dealt with administrative and similar nonprogrammatic issues.

At first, introductory SRV teaching was embedded in the PASSING workshops, much as introductory Normalization had been taught as part of PASS workshops. However, starting in about the mid-1980s, introductory SRV began to be taught in separate workshops. Thus, a person would first go to a 2- or 3-day SRV training workshop, and then either immediately or later go to a 4½- or 5-day PASSING training workshop. This separation was done for two reasons.

1. When the two topics were taught back-to-back, participants had to attend a weeklong event, and not many people would be able to get away for an entire week of training at a time.

2. By separating the two events, many more people could and would come to SRV training, and learn SRV, than would be interested in attending PASSING. Thus, several SRV training events might be held, each of them attended by anywhere from 20 to 100 or more participants, and then a single PASSING training event would be held to which approximately 30 to 50 people might go who had earlier attended an SRV workshop. This made SRV training more frequent, and PASSING training less frequent but more efficient.

4.3 VARIATIONS ON "STANDARD" WORKSHOPS

In addition to what one might call the standard workshops, there were all sorts of Normalization training events that were designed and offered by many different parties, and included everything from lecture presentations ranging anywhere from an hour to a full day, to practicum workshops, to events that engaged participants in a lot of exercises of different types, to ones that focused on designing services consistent with Normalization for one single person, to ones that helped participants try to solve particularly intractable clinical problems. There have been events offered specifically to families, workers in particular disciplines, workers in specific agencies, handicapped people themselves, citizen advocates, clergy and religious, voluntary associations such as what were then called the Associations for the Mentally Retarded in Canada, and citizens in town-hall-type meetings. There have been trainings that looked specifically at Normalization in residential services, or at Normalization and education, or at Normalization and

work services. There were training workshops on Normalization and mental disorder, and on Normalization and aging.

In all these three types of training mentioned so far, participants tended to respond in one of two ways: Either with hostile rejection and defensiveness, or with enthusiastic embrace.

4.4 EMBEDDING NORMALIZATION INTO HUMAN SERVICE WORKERS' PREPARATION

Apart from various kinds of workshops, the fourth major form of training was the incorporation—either implicitly or explicitly—of Normalization into the curriculum of human service worker preparation programs, such as in colleges and universities. Sometimes, an entire course on Normalization or SRV would be taught. Sometimes, the ideas of Normalization or SRV would be incorporated in major ways into other courses. Some agencies and organizations developed their own Normalization and SRV training materials for ongoing in-service training for their own staff.

5 SOME DIFFERENCES BETWEEN NORMALIZATION TRAINING AND SRV TRAINING

As of this time, there has been less variation in how SRV training is offered than there has been in Normalization training. For one thing, as I will elaborate a bit later, SRV training has been provided mostly to human service workers, rather than to other groups of people, for reasons I will also explain later. Further, the SRV training culture has so far been more rigorous in requiring people to go through certain types and sequences of training and preparation before they are considered qualified to conduct SRV training. This has meant that there are fewer people actually doing SRV training, and therefore fewer variations on it.

Yet further, the emphasis so far in the development of the SRV material, and in teaching it in training events, has been on giving participants the coherent logic and integrity of the overarching theory and its assumptions. Once people have understood that, then they will be better able to themselves perceive and generate implications—perhaps implications that were not obvious when they received their training. The development of the SRV training materials is still moving in this direction. In contrast, the early days of Normalization training tended to emphasize the implications. In fact, specific implications that are today taken pretty much for granted were shocking—earthshaking—to people then, such as not locking people up, not segregating people unnecessarily, fostering a positive personal appearance for people, and even little things such as people being free to talk on the telephone when they wanted to, group homes for adults having a liquor cabinet, and so forth. Thus, in early Normalization training, a great deal of time was devoted to teaching—and fighting over—specific implications.

I believe that one of the impacts of the dissemination of Normalization ideas has been precisely that many of the implications that used to be so fiercely contested are now taken for granted by many people. In other words, the Normalization concepts have penetrated not only the human service culture, especially in mental retardation, but also the larger culture, so that they are much less controversial. For instance, the importance of age-appropriate appearance and routines, at least physical integration, and homelike residences is now largely accepted.

Further, the evolution of SRV theory—and of the SRV training package—have resulted in more time being spent during training events on explaining the overarching theory more fully. However, this has also meant that the specific implications have to be covered in less detail because there is not enough time to do more.

In a later section, I will return to other changes that have taken place over time in Normalization/SRV training.

6 SOME FACTS ON THE NUMBER AND "KINDS" OF PEOPLE TRAINED

The Training Institute for Human Service Planning, Leadership and Change Agentry at Syracuse University in Syracuse, New York, has tried to keep a record of all the people who have ever attended at least the longer events on Normalization, PASS, SRV, and/or PASSING that have been conducted either by the Training Institute itself, or by close associates who send to the Training Institute the lists of participants at

their events. By longer events, I mean standard Normalization workshops of 2 or more days, full-length PASS workshops of at least 5 days, 2- and 3-day or longer SRV workshops, full-length PASSING workshops, and Model coherency training. This does not count all the many shorter presentations—anywhere from 1 to 2 hours to a full day—that have been given on Normalization and SRV, nor the shorter presentations on PASS and PASSING that have been given by the Training Institute and its close associates, nor the variations on these that have been given by others, nor college-level courses in Normalization/SRV.

In addition, there are parties who conduct long events related to Normalization or SRV, but of whose events and participants the Training Institute has not kept a tally. This includes such training that has been conducted not only in the United States and Canada, but also in England, Australia, Ireland, New Zealand, France, Belgium, Switzerland, Spain, Norway, and Iceland, and possibly in other countries as well.

Thus, counting *only* those people on record at the Training Institute, and only the longer events, a conservative estimate is that probably several 10,000 people have participated in longer Normalization, SRV, and related training events, offered by the Institute and its associates. Of course, some people have attended several events (e.g., both SRV and PASSING).

A 1992 estimate (Williams, 1992) of the numbers of people who had by then participated just in PASS training in the United Kingdom was 4,000. By 1986, 27,000 copies of PASS and 45,000 of *The Principle of Normalization in Human Services* had been produced (Wolfensberger, 1986), and both books are still in print and still being sold. Note that none of these figures count those people who attended related training events conducted by the Training Institute that were not on Normalization or SRV, such as those on the "Liberation of Devalued People From Bondage and Dependency," nor the workshops mentioned earlier on planning and change agentry.

The vast majority of the people who have participated in these various kinds of training have been from the field of mental retardation, with much smaller representations from the fields of mental disorder and aging, and yet fewer altogether from other fields, such as physical impairment, poverty, homelessness, blindness, deafness, and corrections.

Currently, efforts are under way in some locales to make more significant inroads specifically into the domains of mental disorder and physical handicap. In Australia, many people in the field of aging have received SRV and PASSING training, in good part because some of the people who have given major support to the establishment of an SRV and PASSING training culture there work in services to the elderly in the Adelaide area. In New Zealand, the fledgling SRV training culture seems to be centered more on aging than in any locale other than South Australia.

Now while training could never be expected to bring about all the changes that would be required for the implementation of Normalization/SRV in families, in service systems, and in society as a whole, training—rather than public relations campaigns or other means—has been nonetheless the major mechanism for the dissemination of Normalization and SRV, and continues to be so. The only exception appears to have been the public relations and attitude-change campaign started circa 1968 in Nebraska, mentioned earlier, in connection with what was then the new Nebraska state plan for community services for the retarded.

7 SOME CHANGES THAT HAVE TAKEN PLACE IN THE TRAINING AND TRAINING CULTURE

Next, I will review a number of significant changes that have occurred since the early days of training that have been sketched.

7.1 THE "KINDS" OF PEOPLE RECEIVING TRAINING

Early on in the dissemination of Normalization, training was given very broadly to people at different levels of society, and in different positions to effect change—parents, legislators, service administrators, planners, direct service workers, advocates—rather than to specific groups. As mentioned, this broad-based dissemination was done not only in order to spread Normalization ideas, but also (at least in Nebraska) with the specific purpose of garnering support for the Nebraska state plan of normalizing services for the retarded, and for similar efforts elsewhere.

Later, as also mentioned, presentations on Normalization were specifically designed and offered to people in one type of position, or with a particular identity. For instance, legislators were targeted for training in certain locales, as were funders, service providers, and parents of handicapped people. Such people were consciously and actively recruited to attend both the "generic" and the specific kinds of presentations, and many of them did.

Because Normalization dissemination or training events were attended by people from all societal levels, but especially by those at the second (primary and intermediate systems) and third (social policy) level, Normalization ideas began to be incorporated into human services at several different levels as well. For instance, service administrators and direct service workers tried to shape their own programs to be more normalizing, but so, too, did service planners for entire states or provinces begin to incorporate Normalization principles into state and provincial plans. Some locales implemented large-scale deinstitutionalization programs and invested a great deal of money into initiating community services. On the federal level in the US, all the states were mandated in 1975 to provide an appropriate education for all handicapped children.

When, in 1970, Wolfensberger sat on the subcommittee of the Joint Commission on Accreditation of Hospitals (JCAH) that revised the standards for mental retardation institutions (which eventually became the standards for mental retardation residential services generally, which, in turn, eventually fed into the standards for mental retardation services generally), he was able to persuade his fellow subcommittee members to make Normalization the foundation for these standards. These standards were widely disseminated, adopted, and applied to services that wanted to receive accreditation. Thus in order to be accredited, services had to implement at least some of these measures. Further, the accreditors received training from the JCAH on how to apply the standards, which also constituted a form of dissemination of Normalization ideas.

Also, Pennsylvania adopted statewide regulations for its community residential services for the mentally retarded that were largely based on Normalization implications as embodied in the ratings of the PASS service evaluation instrument. This, too, meant that throughout the community residential service system in that entire state, Normalization ideas spread.

The early 1970s also saw the beginning of class-action lawsuits on behalf of handicapped people. Lawyers for the plaintiffs very quickly (sometimes almost overnight) oriented themselves to the literature on Normalization, and included Normalization ideas in the legal remedies they were pursuing, which would then be mandated if the lawsuit were won. Of course, there were other influences on these developments as well, but certainly Normalization training was one of them.

However, over time, a de facto change took place, at least in North America. First, the participants at the most common type of Normalization or SRV training —the short-term intensive training workshops—began to be almost only and entirely human service workers. Fewer and fewer family members attended. Hardly any lawmakers or people at a high policy-setting level attended anymore. (However, in recent years, there has been some resurgence of attendance by parents and advocates.) Thus, eventually (though not through any conscious policy decision, but as a result of a confluence of many dynamics, only some of which will be explained below), the bulk of the Normalization and SRV training has come de facto to be rendered to, and directed at, only one sector of the second of the three levels in the chart, that is, to people working in a paid capacity in the intermediate social systems: the paid, formal, organized human services of which so many devalued people are clients for a good part of their lives.

Obviously, other types of dissemination and training, and other forms thereof, and other ways of bringing about desired changes, are needed. (I will return to this shortly.) But the training of human service workers has simply become by far the predominant form of dissemination of Normalization and SRV.

A second change is that the service workers who attend training have increasingly become people who work at or close to the lowest direct service level. Administrators, board members, or others who would set policy for an agency have become less likely to attend. This is a contrast to the early 1970s, particularly, when there was a great eagerness by senior people to learn of new ideas and developments, and they would attend all sorts of workshops in order to acquire new ideas to introduce into their own services. However, since the late 1970s, senior leaders have become increasingly overwhelmed with administrative and bureaucratic demands, and rarely seem to attend seminal learning events. Furthermore, it appears that an increasing percentage among them have acquired an attitude that they know vastly more than in fact they do, and their reasoning seems to be that they would not have been able to attain senior positions if they had not known so much more than other people. In reality, the opposite may now be the case because junior people are vastly more likely to attend learning events than senior people and to be familiar with new or valid ideas. This, in turn, may have contributed to yet further reduced attendance by senior people who may feel threatened or demeaned by attending events with people other than their peers.

7.2 THE SPONSORSHIP OF THE TRAINING

Another remarkable change that has taken place has to do with the sponsorship of the training. In the beginning, Normalization training was largely sponsored by either human service agencies or by some kind of body that was not a direct service provider, but had a major high-level organizational identity. For instance, for a long time, the major sponsor of Normalization and related training in Canada was what was then called the National Institute on Mental Retardation (now the G. Allan Roeher Institute) in Toronto. Though not itself a provider of services to handicapped people, it was an arm of the voluntary parents' associations and was a major provider of support services *to* direct service providers throughout Canada. It had a publishing division, as well as a large library; it conducted all sorts of training; it developed position papers and lobbied government; and so on.

But over time, this, too, changed, particularly starting in the 1980s, so that Normalization (and later SRV) training began to be less and less sponsored by groups and organizations such as these, or by human service-providing agencies. For this there were several reasons.

1. Agencies had, or said they had, less money to support training, though this may be a doubtful claim.

2. Human services began more and more to be driven by a "craze" mentality that lusts and runs after one new craze idea or scheme after another. With great rapidity, new ideas, strategies, and techniques get introduced into the service field. Almost all get greeted with great hype and with expectations that each one—

and if not this one, then the next one—will be the long-awaited answer, perhaps even *the* definitive solution, to this or that human service problem. And then, as each one disappoints (and they all must, since there can be no definitive human solutions to the problems of suffering, division, devaluation, and hatred), people flock to the next craze that comes down the pike. Thus, even when something valid, legitimate, and useful (such as Normalization or SRV) makes an appearance in human services, it is simply not apt to hold the attention of a craze-crazy service field for long. (For an analysis of the craze culture in society, the sciences, and human service, see Wolfensberger, 1994.)

In contrast to what craze-crazy people yearn for, SRV is definitely not quick-and-easy to learn, and it is most certainly not quick or easy to implement. Further, if one takes SRV seriously, one never stops learning about what it can and cannot do, what its limitations are, how it applies in specific instances, and so forth. SRV does not offer tricks that change with the fashion and preferences of the times. Rather, it offers very high-level interrelated universals—about human nature, human perception, human interaction, attitude formation and change, and pedagogy. SRV also does not offer or promise any definitive solutions, neither to the problem of human devaluation generally, nor even to the problems that devaluation can inflict in just one life. It does offer valid strategies, that is, strategies that—*if they were implemented*—have a strong probability of being able to improve the plight of individual devalued persons, of specific groups, and of entire devalued classes, though possibly not until the future. All this has meant that Normalization especially and, to some extent, SRV are seen by many people as old hat, possibly even backward and retrograde, as compared to the new ideas that are always coming along, and that—in a craze mentality—must by definition be better or at least preferable.

3. Also, Normalization began to be seen as something that had become sufficiently known and understood, and that was now being done, so that more training or learning about it was no longer necessary or cost-efficient. For instance, people seemed to think that if they supported "mainstreaming," or, more recently, "inclusion"; if they used the latest language conventions, such as so-called "people first" language; if they knew about age-appropriateness, or endorsed "supported employment," then they knew all there was

to know about what Normalization had to offer—and maybe even more.

There are at least two ironies in these changes so far reviewed that took place in Normalization or SRV training. One is that in the late 1980s, a lot of people in human services, and especially in mental retardation, began to say that Normalization was now passé. By this they meant that it was no longer relevant, that Normalization had been "achieved" and that now it was time to move on to other things. But the ironic thing is that a lot of these people had never endorsed or promoted or practiced or implemented Normalization in the first place. So it was not that they had actually done it and were now ready to move on to other things; it was rather that they had *never* done it or liked it and were now ready and anxious—as they had always been—to move on (or even back) to other things.

A second irony is that to this day, the performance of services for devalued people on instruments such as PASSING that measure Normalization/SRV quality is normatively very poor: Rarely does a service even score in the positive range, and most are deeply in the negative range. This raises the interesting question that if Normalization is passé because it has been achieved, then why are so many services showing such abysmally poor Normalization quality? It also raises the question whether it is really possible for a service to be good according to currently popular, nonpassé criteria, but abysmal according to measures of Normalization/SRV quality.

7.3 THE EXPECTATIONS FOR THE TRAINING

Another big difference between the early days of Normalization training and the contemporary scene has to do with both the hopes and the opportunities for implementing what gets taught in such training. The early days of Normalization training were indeed heady: Sweeping change was in the air; for the first time, monies were becoming available, or available in significant amounts, for what were then the very new community services such as group homes; people's old stereotyped and limiting expectations for the retarded were being overthrown; the new mind-set was that anything was possible. Those who had embraced Normalization and worked in institutional services ran up against a great deal of hostility and opposition to making changes there, but those who worked in community services found much more receptivity. In fact, as mentioned, many new community services were founded with Normalization as a philosophical basis. While even in the best of services it was always a struggle to implement Normalization, still people found that it was possible to do many new things that were major victories—even paradigm shifts. For instance, many service settings got placed where they ought to be. Many service environments were greatly beautified and made comfortable. Many people moved out of abysmal institutions into pleasant community settings and even into independent living. The more obvious, grosser violations of age-appropriate and enhancing language and decor were often corrected. Children who had been denied an education were accepted into school. Handicapped people were challenged, and permitted, to become more competent and independent. Much innovative prosthetic technology became available, and was used to help profoundly and multiply handicapped people become more competent and active. And so on.

But over time, and *at least in North America,* this scene, and people's perception of it, has begun to change, and for several reasons. One is that now that some of the easier, more obvious obstacles to the full, valued participation of devalued people in society have been addressed, other, more difficult, more subtle obstacles are becoming apparent and refusing to yield. A useful analogy for this is the current talk of the "glass ceiling" in the world of work. It refers to the fact that groups who had previously been almost totally excluded from top management had begun to make great inroads but eventually ran up against seemingly invisible obstacles that still kept them from top positions. In the same way, people are finding that some of the implications of Normalization/SRV are indeed very difficult to obtain. For instance, while the physical presence and integration of devalued people into many sectors of society have been greatly furthered, the real valued social integration and participation of such people in society have turned out to be much more difficult to achieve.

Yet another major glass-ceiling-type obstacle to the implementation of Normalization/SRV is service workers' own devaluations of the people they serve, though much of this devaluation is unconscious. People do not want good things to happen to those whom they devalue, but instead want to see bad things

done to them. Where the devalued party is a service recipient, and where the devaluers are service workers, then the service workers will not give their wholehearted support to social-role-valorizing measures in that service and for its clients. They may give lip service, they may give grudging cooperation, they may do what is actually required of them—but they will not give genuine or glad or committed support. And in fact, they will often do things that sabotage or undercut social-role-valorizing measures. This, too, constitutes a serious obstacle to the implementation of SRV, at least within the service system.

A second reason—and a most critical one—that expectations of the training have changed is that people are now finding it very difficult to implement Normalization/SRV within the formal, organized service system, in part because there are larger societal dynamics that are antagonistic to Normalization/SRV, or for that matter, to any adaptive service measure. For this and other reasons, the workers within these services are actually less and less permitted to do what SRV would require.

Thus, while in the beginning, the major emphasis of the training itself, and of those who took it, was to change human services so that they were more normalizing for the people they served, more and more, people who attend the training now seem to be getting from it knowledge of Normalization/SRV that they can try to use in their own lives but that they will probably not be allowed to use much in any paid service engagements.

This particular development has also led to a shift of emphasis, at least in the formal training in SRV and related issues that is conducted by the Training Institute and its associates, though perhaps not in the training conducted by other parties. Namely, there is now a conscious emphasis in such SRV training on what people can do in their personal lives outside and apart from the formal service structures. In other words, there is more emphasis on what one can do as an ordinary citizen, a friend, a volunteer advocate, a parent, sibling, or other relative of a devalued person, rather than on what should be done to change entire systems, or on what agencies and service systems need to become. However, this does not mean that action only on the personal level is emphasized. As mentioned earlier, the levels refer to the parties being acted upon, rather than the parties doing the acting. Thus, even as a lone individual, acting on one's own and outside of any work role, one could still take action directed toward even the higher of the levels, such as those of the secondary social systems and even society as a whole.

Even though this change in the teaching so far has emphasized primarily what one can do as an individual working outside the organized service structures, it would also be possible for primary and even some secondary social systems to work outside the organized structures, and on any of the three societal levels. For instance, families, friends, and intentional voluntary communities could take action apart from the organized structures.

Also, at the same time as SRV began to be formulated, and to be widely taught, there has been an ascendancy of a major competing concept or even paradigm in human services, namely, one based on a radical individualism that revolves around power and self-determination, emphasizing the "empowering" of devalued people and the granting to them of the liberty to make whatever choices they wish—especially via rights legislation and judicial rulings—and the devil (which society is seen to be) take the hindmost. Many people have attempted to find congruences between this paradigm of power and SRV/Normalization, but this is only possible to the extent that the measures promoted by the power and empowerment ideology are congruent with the lawfulness of social science as expressed via SRV. After all, much of the empowerment model is ideology, not science, and much of it is inconsistent with empirical reality. However, what the differences are between the empowerment ideology and SRV goes beyond the scope of this paper. An analysis of them is in progress and, it is hoped, will eventually be published. Here, I only want to note that the rise of radical individualism, with its deluded obsession with power and formalisms, has become an ever increasing obstacle to the broader dissemination and adoption of SRV today.

8 THE QUESTION OF "TRAINING FOR THE GENERAL PUBLIC"

A number of people who try to promote and implement Normalization/SRV have struggled with the issue of how to get the message across to the wider public, the general citizenry. Since many people interested in this question had themselves learned

Normalization/SRV via training workshops, often their first effort was to devise or conduct some "training" for the general public. However, these efforts have usually fizzled, and for several good reasons.

1. Unless people are pressured or forced to come to an event, they will usually only attend something that interests them. For instance, the public will usually only attend such things as free lectures, public hearings, school board and town council meetings, and so on, if the topic is one in which they *already* have an interest, such as a school board decision that will affect their own taxes or their own children. Members of the general public who have little or no social contact with devalued people, or no personal commitments to such people, would therefore have very little motivation to attend training events having to do with such persons.

2. Even where members of the public have the motivation to attend such training offered to them, the nature of life in modernistic society today is such that people simply have less free time and leisure to attend public lectures, even ones that "sound interesting" to them and that they really want to attend. People seem to have many more demands on their time than they can handle. Even public figures whom one could expect to have an interest in such issues, such as local government leaders, may not have the leeway to go to learning and training events.

There have, of course, been efforts in the past to gain support from the general public for various measures that Normalization/SRV would imply or require. For instance, as mentioned, when the state of Nebraska was moving from an institutional to a community service system in the late 1960s, and all sorts of normalized community services—sometimes, the first of their kind in the entire US—were being implemented, there were public presentations all across the state. However, these did not really constitute Normalization *training* per se. Rather, they were presentations that explained and promoted normalizing services, and aimed at garnering public and political support for such, and for related issues: changes in the governance of services, new taxing and tax-use patterns and policies, and so forth.

It is interesting to note who attended these presentations and why they came. First of all, there was a significant number of human service workers, as well as pa-rents of handicapped people. But apart from these two groups, there were people who saw themselves as opinion leaders and decision makers in their community, such as clergy, people who held office in local government, and newspeople. Also in attendance were those who had an intense interest in political affairs generally, such as people who were deeply opposed to governmental or tax encroachment, and people who envisioned themselves as possibly running for office sometime in the future. It also has to be remembered that in that region of the US, politics and governance were and are very much a grassroots affair, so local interest in these types of things was higher than in other regions.

Thus, people who want to convey Normalization/SRV to the public need to ask themselves at least two crucial questions, namely: (a) Where and how does the public today get its new ideas? and (b) What elements of Normalization/SRV is it reasonable to expect the public to learn?

To me, the answer to the first question is very clear. Like it or not, and for better *or* worse, the public gets most of its information today from the visual media, and, more specifically, from television. Thus, today, many people probably have had their attitudes about people with Down's syndrome shaped more by the U.S. ABC television program *Life Goes On* (about a family whose son has Down's syndrome) than by anything else. Similarly, television films and news articles about physically handicapped people, elderly people, street people, and so-called autistic people, are probably one of the dominant influences on the knowledge, opinion, and attitudes of most people in society to these groups. In fact, even human service workers are deeply shaped by seeing films such as the 1988 *Rain Man*. I will return to this issue later.

One question all this raises is *why* one would want the general public to be knowledgeable about Normalization and SRV. What would be one's goals? Is it because one wants them to be more receptive to Normalization and SRV implications that impinge on their own lives? That can be accomplished without them ever hearing the terms Normalization or SRV.

Is it because one found learning about Normalization and SRV a life-changing experience for oneself, and one wants others to have the same experience? But unless ordinary people have some close personal engagement with a devalued party, such as a family member, or work in services to devalued people, they might not be very likely to find

Normalization or SRV even interesting, let alone life-changing.

Is it because one hopes that ordinary people in society, rather than organized services, will be doing much of the positive interacting with devalued people, and sometimes the managing of the lives of competency-impaired ones? That is a noble desire, but it does not seem to take account of the reality that, like it or not, the vast majority of devalued groups *will* continue to have extensive contact with organized human services; and their lives *will* be extensively managed by people in such services.

It therefore seems both a more rational and more realistic goal to aspire to help ordinary people be more supportive of Normalization/SRV *measures* than to try to "teach them Normalization or SRV." In other words, it is much more likely that one could teach the public significant conceptual "chunks" of Normalization or SRV thinking or implications, than that one could teach them the theory *qua* theory, or in its global form.

For instance, one could convey to people the importance of what today is commonly called "access," that is, that devalued people should have the opportunities to use community resources, and that there should not be physical or social obstacles to such use. One can teach the public the merit of devalued people living in the same kinds of places as other people live, going to school like other children, working like other adults, and generally following the same routines of life as do other people. Ordinary people can easily understand the importance of a decent income and that it is unfair for people to be locked away merely for who they are rather than for anything they have done. And so on. And these elements of Normalization/SRV can also be conveyed in language that the public would use. For instance, one would probably not talk to them about "culturally valued analogues," but one could certainly talk about devalued people being enabled to do things as much as possible the way ordinary people do them, and to have the same kinds of opportunities that ordinary people would like to have in their own lives. In fact, it was exactly this idiom that was used with the Nebraska population during the late 1960s for the state community services plan, and that won them over.

Thus, rather than formal "training" focused specifically on Normalization/SRV ideas in order to create a grassroots movement by and from the general public that, in turn, will demand services that are more normalizing or social-role-valorizing, it seems that the following three strategies are much more relevant for reaching and teaching the public.

1. One overarching strategy is to do those things which increase the positive identification of valued people with devalued ones; that is, which help valued people see devalued people as being very much like themselves. For instance, the more devalued people live in places just like those where valued people live; the more they go to school like valued people, and do in school the same things that valued students do; the more they work at the same types of jobs and in the same types of places and following the same schedules that valued people do; the more they dress the way valued people of the same age dress; and so on, the more valued people are likely to see in devalued people a reflection of themselves. And the more people see others as like themselves, the more positively they are apt to view these others, the more they will be willing to interact with these others, and the more good things of life they are likely to extend to them—and the more the negative values they hold toward them will shift to positive ones. After all, people generally want good things to happen to themselves, so they will usually want good things to happen to and for those whom they see as like themselves.

Among other things, this implies *aggressively* attending to the images of and about devalued people that are conveyed on all levels of society: personal, primary and intermediate social systems, and societal. For instance, the appearance of specific devalued persons should be as positive as possible. The names, location, and appearance of service settings for devalued people should be as positive as possible. And so on. Doing this plants positive images and associations about devalued people in the minds of the public, which predisposes them to be more accepting, receptive, and positive when it comes to asking for their support and cooperation.

2. A related overarching strategy is to create the occasions and conditions under which positive interactions of valued with devalued people can take place, and where positive expectations for devalued people will be conveyed.

Among other things, this means that integration of devalued people into society must be experienced by the valued sector as reasonably pleasant, so as not to repel or frighten ordinary people. One can see that this strategy conflicts with much of what is commonly taught and practiced by those parties who endorse a power-based approach to dealing with society's rejection of various devalued groups. Such parties typically promote that handicapped or other devalued people should be present where they want, the way they want, doing what they want, and the impact on valued people and society be damned. Often, this "inclusion" is promoted in a belligerent fashion, and by raw force of law, rather than by persuasive and socializing means. Yet if valued people do not experience the presence and participation of devalued people in society as pleasant and positive, then they will *not* have an accepting mental disposition toward such people. Moralizing about it, and passing laws about it, will do little to change their hearts; and *in the long run*, it can even lead to outcomes opposite to the desired ones. One should just ask oneself, if children in school walk away from an interaction with a devalued peer in bodily pain, crying, holding themselves where they have been punched, pinched, and gouged, just how is this supposed to lead to positive valuation of the devalued party by these children, their parents, and their teachers?

Relatedly, the public is not likely to be positively disposed and receptive to integrative strategies unless it is convinced that those who propose and implement such strategies have good common sense and are not going to do something that is foolish, or even hurtful, to either the valued or devalued parties. Again, we can contrast this recognition of the need to earn the public's trust with the stance of those who would include everyone in everything regardless of whether such people pose a danger to others, and regardless of what the public response might be.

Strategies 1 and 2 are closely interrelated and affect each other. The more valued people can be brought to positively identify with devalued ones, the more they will be receptive to the integration of devalued people in the valued life of society. And the more devalued people are *adaptively* integrated into valued social life, the more will valued people be able to identify with them.

3. The third major strategy for "capturing," so to speak, the public is to use the very avenues by which they are most apt to be shaped indirectly, namely, the

media. Thus, the interpretations of devalued people in national fund-raising appeals, in movies, and on television, and in the press should be as positive as is realistically and honestly possible. Devalued people should be included—in a natural, noncontrived and nonthreatening way—in the depiction of ordinary as well as valued life and its activities.

Actually, though much still remains to be done, in many respects much progress along the above lines has already been made in the media. There, we find a large number of positive interpretations of many types of devalued people, especially in contrast to how people—such as retarded ones—used to be shown in a very negative light in the media. Some presentations of handicapped people in the media include them continuously, as in a long-running television serial, while others are one-shot and sporadic. However, this of course does not mean that every such depiction in the media is positive, even if there are good intentions behind it. For instance, some show devalued people involved in valued activities with valued people in valued contexts, while others emphasize how different they are from other people, even in some cases when the presentation of these different people is a sympathetic one.

If one does all these things—facilitating identification of valued with devalued people, creating occasions for positive interactions with and expectations of devalued people, and making positive use of the media—then one is de facto engaged in changing attitudes. And such an attitude change campaign has to be (a) directed at all levels of society, rather than only one or a few; and (b) long-term in orientation, rather than aiming for a quick-and-easy fix, such as can sometimes be enforced by law and court rulings. The problem is that while many people talk a good deal about attitude change, few ever study how to do it right, and then apply the strategies known to be valid and effective. Further, few people are prepared to pay the costs of doing it right, which include (among other things) making a commitment to the long haul and accepting all sorts of short-term sacrifices for the sake of long-term gain. There are three reasons this seems to be so hard for most people. (a) Many of the benefits of specific attitude change measures —especially the systemic ones—are apt to come about slowly and over the very long run. (b) Most of the benefits will come about so indirectly—like bread cast

upon the waters—that they cannot be clearly attributed to a specific earlier action or actor. (c) Most people—especially these days—are incapable of investing themselves heavily and over the long run in an enterprise of which they may not live to see the result, and where they are not able to take credit for whatever result may be apparent in their lifetime.

However, we should note that positive attitude change can result even when there is no concerted attitude change effort. For instance, much of the address of people's image has to do with helping valued people identify positively with devalued ones. Similarly, Citizen Advocacy—in which individual volunteer advocates represent the interests of individual impaired protégés—helps to build positive interpersonal identification, and to improve attitudes (at least of the advocates), even though Citizen Advocacy is not an attitude change effort but a justice and protective one.

Of course, all this raises the question of just who will foster positive interactions and integration of devalued people with valued people in society? Who will assume responsibility and initiative for helping valued people identify with devalued ones? Who will attend to the image of societally devalued people? Obvious candidates are people among the workers in human services to them, their families and advocates, and the affected people themselves to the degree that they are capable of doing so—and not all of them are. But if such people are to do these things for and with devalued parties, then they need to learn what is important to do. Thus, somewhere along the line, there has to be SRV training in order to form leaders, value- and opinion-shapers, and so on, who can disperse and disseminate SRV ideas to those who cannot be expected to undergo training themselves. Accordingly, SRV training is still needed.

If one thinks about what I have proposed, one can see that the strategies that are most likely to be effective in recruiting broad public support for Normalization/SRV implications and ideas are some of the very implications *of* Normalization/SRV! For instance, the address of the negative image of devalued people and their adaptive integration into society are both implications of Normalization/SRV, as well as strategies to gain support for measures that are normalizing/social-role-valorizing.

Note, too, that these three measures of facilitating

positive interpersonal identification, facilitating positive interactions, and interpreting people positively in the media, can and should take place on all levels of society. For instance, there needs to be image enhancement of specific devalued people, of and in services to them, and of their interpretation in and by the law, the public media, and so on. Similarly, there needs to be adaptive integration into society of specific devalued persons. Services to them should be physically integrated into valued and resource-rich locales in the community, and there need to be systemic changes (such as in public housing policy) to facilitate at least some such integration. And so on.

These strategies are *not* apt to create sophistication among the general public about Normalization/SRV, or provide in-depth knowledge of these principles. In fact, even if a long-term attitude change strategy were successfully implemented, ordinary members of the public would be apt to be living out and supporting Normalization/SRV even while not knowing the meaning of the terms, while not being able to explain Model coherency, while not knowing the difference between age-appropriate and culture-appropriate, and so on. But it seems that it is more important that the general public be *doing* and *supporting* Normalization/SRV than conversant with the theory.

In the next chapter, Deborah Reidy will take up and further expand on the question of "training for the general public" and on how actions more concordant with Normalization/SRV might be fostered in them.

REFERENCES

FLYNN, R. J., & NITSCH, K. E. (EDS.). (1980). *Normalization, community services, and social integration.* Baltimore: University Park Press.

KUGEL, R. B., & WOLFENSBERGER, W. (1969). *Changing patterns in residential services for the mentally retarded.* Washington, DC: President's Committee on Mental Retardation.

WILLIAMS, P. (1992, November 20). An open letter to participants at the "SRV summit" at Cazenovia, NY, December 1992. (Available from author)

WOLFENSBERGER, W. (1970a, February). Ideology power. *The Nebraska Contributor, 1*(1), 1-6.

WOLFENSBERGER, W. (1970b). The principle of Normalization and its implications for psychiatric services. *American Journal of Psychiatry, 127,* 291-297.

WOLFENSBERGER, W. (1972). *The principle of Normalization in human services.* Toronto, ON: National Institute on Mental Retardation.

WOLFENSBERGER, W. (1983). Social role valorization: A proposed new term for the principle of Normalization. *Mental Retardation, 21*(6), 234-239.

WOLFENSBERGER, W. (1984). A reconceptualization of Normalization as social role valorization. *Mental Retardation* (Canada), *34*(7), 22-26.

WOLFENSBERGER, W. (1985). Social role valorization: A new insight, and a new term, for the principle of Normalization. *Australian Association for the Mentally Retarded Journal, 9*(1), 4-11.

WOLFENSBERGER, W. (1986). Die Entwicklung des Normalisierungsgedankens in den USA und in Kanada. In Bundesvereinigung Lebenshilfe (Ed.), *Normalisierung: Eine Chance für Menschen mit geistiger Behinderung* (pp. 45-62). Marburg/Lahn: Lebenshilfe. (Edited address, in Bericht des Ersten Europäischen Kongresses der Internationalen Liga von Vereinigungen für Menschen mit geistiger Behinderung. Hamburg, October 1985. Vol. 14, Grosse Schriftenreihe of Lebenshilfe)

WOLFENSBERGER, W. (1991a). *A brief introduction to Social Role Valorization as a high-order concept for structuring human services.* Syracuse, NY: Syracuse University, Training Institute for Human Service Planning, Leadership and Change Agentry.

WOLFENSBERGER, W. (1991b). *Die Bewertung der sozialen Rollen: Eine kurze Einführung zur Bewertung der sozialen Rollen als Grundbegriff beim Aufbau von Sozialdiensten.* (C. Agad & A. Bianchet, Trans.). Genf (Geneva), Schweiz (Switzerland): Éditions des Deux Continents.

WOLFENSBERGER, W. (1991c). *La valorisation des rôles sociaux: Introduction à un concept de référence pour l'organisation des services*. (A. Dupont, V. Keller-Revaz, J.-P. Nicoletti, & L. Vaney, Trans.). Geneva, Switzerland: Éditions des Deux Continents.

WOLFENSBERGER, W. (1991d). *La Valorizzazione del Ruolo Sociale: Una breve introduzione al concetto di valorizzazione del ruolo sociale inteso come concetto prioritario per la strutturazione dei servizi alle persone* (M. Costantino & A. Domina, Trans.). Geneva, Switzerland: Éditions des Deux Continents.

WOLFENSBERGER, W. (1992). *A brief introduction to Social Role Valorization as a high-order concept for structuring human services* (2nd ed., rev.). Syracuse, NY: Syracuse University, Training Institute for Human Service Planning, Leadership and Change Agentry.

WOLFENSBERGER, W. (1994). The "Facilitated Communication" craze as an instance of pathological science: The cold fusion of human services. In H. C. SHANE (Ed.), *Facilitated communication: The clinical and social phenomenon* (pp. 57-122). San Diego: Singular Press.

WOLFENSBERGER, W., & GLENN, L. (1969). *Program Analysis of Service Systems (PASS): A method for the quantitative evaluation of human services* (Limited mimeograph ed.). Omaha, NE: Nebraska Psychiatric Institute.

WOLFENSBERGER, W., & GLENN, L. (1973). *Program Analysis of Service Systems (PASS): A method for the quantitative evaluation of human services* (2nd rev. ed.). *Handbook. Field Manual*. Toronto, ON: National Institute on Mental Retardation.

WOLFENSBERGER, W., & GLENN, L. (1975). *Program Analysis of Service Systems (PASS): A method for the quantitative evaluation of human services* (3rd ed., rev.). *Handbook. Field Manual*. Toronto, ON: National Institute on Mental Retardation.

WOLFENSBERGER, W., & THOMAS, S. (1980). *Program Analysis of Service Systems' Implementation of Normalization Goals (PASSING)* (Experimental ed.). Syracuse, NY: Syracuse University, Training Institute for Human Service Planning, Leadership and Change Agentry.

WOLFENSBERGER, W., & THOMAS, S. (1983). *PASSING (Program Analysis of Service Systems' Implementation of Normalization Goals): Normalization criteria and ratings manual* (2nd ed.). Toronto, ON: National Institute on Mental Retardation.

WOLFENSBERGER, W., & THOMAS, S. (1988). *PASSING (Programme d'analyse des systèmes de services application des buts de la valorisation des rôles sociaux). Manuel des critères et des mesures de la valorisation des rôles sociaux* (2nd ed.). (M. Roberge, Trans.; J. Pelletier, Adap.). Toronto, ON: Institut G. Allan Roeher & Les Communications Opell.

374

16

Social integration: How can we get there from here? Reflections on Normalization, Social Role Valorization and community education

DEBORAH REIDY

1 BACKGROUND: DEINSTITUTIONALIZATION AND DASHED HOPES

My first formal exposure to Normalization theory occurred in 1980, when I went to a PASS workshop in Danvers, Massachusetts. At the time, I was founding director of a very small residential agency in western Massachusetts serving four young women with severe multiple disabilities, including mental retardation.

Around 1982, I became very interested in working with community members to positively affect their attitudes toward people with disabilities. In 1983, I began a project that was to be named Education for Community Initiatives (ECI). Initially a component of a Normalization-based values training project, the Safeguards Project, ECI later became an independent project whose purpose was to stimulate community members to take an interest in the situation of people with disabilities and to take actions that would positively affect their lives. During the project's 10-year history, we experimented with a number of means and methods to interest community members in the life experiences of people with disabilities (and, to a lesser extent, of devalued people in general) in order to encourage them to undertake constructive actions on their behalf. Some of our educational activities took the form of training events but most were experiential. For example, we developed a number of educational projects that brought together people with disabilities and other community members to collaboratively

address issues of mutual benefit. We also created several projects that assisted children and adults with disabilities to become active members of voluntary associations or recreational activities of their choosing, and then provided education and consultation to support their participation.

The early 1980s marked an active period of deinstitutionalization from the two state institutions serving people with mental illness and retardation in western Massachusetts, as well as a rich period of Normalization and other values-based training in our area. Many service workers active in the 1980s eagerly embraced the deinstitutionalization movement as the latest service reform. We operated on the assumption that the physical presence of people with disabilities[1] in communities would automatically lead to social integration, although, had we been asked, we probably would have denied this. Normalization training had taught us that, along with deinstitutionalization, certain service practices would facilitate social integration, practices such as small groupings, dispersed settings, nearness to generic resources, and attention to enhancing both the image and competency of the individuals served. However, most of our hopes, energy, and resources focused on the act of "springing" people with disabilities from institutions and physically establishing them in community settings.

Once people were living in the community, many of the anticipated social integration benefits failed to materialize. Although physically present in their new communities, people with disabilities typically continued to have relationships largely with their staff and with other devalued people. Community members tended to be tolerant of, but disinterested in, the presence of people with disabilities. While our efforts were fraught with shortcomings, these shortcomings did not fully account for the lack of progress in attaining broad community support for the presence and improved life conditions of people with disabilities. I have since concluded that we held unreasonably high expectations regarding the possible impact of the mere physical presence of people with disabilities within communities. As a consequence, we placed too much emphasis on deinstitutionalization as a single-path strategy. The next section will consider possible contributors to the unreasonable expectations of the deinstitutionalization effort.

2 SEARCHING FOR A CULPRIT

In retrospect, it is remarkable that we would assume community members might automatically go out of their way to welcome people who had been absent from society for years and years. Not only were people with disabilities absent, but their absence was accompanied by powerful negative messages about their lack of capacity or right to be part of ordinary community life. And even those individuals with disabilities who continued to live in their home communities struggled to be accepted.

As a consequence of the continued lack of acceptance of people with disabilities, I, and others of my generation, became disheartened and even disillusioned. Some of us even became angry with community members for their reluctance to welcome people, or we blamed services and service workers for this so-called "failure."

How might these overinflated expectations of the deinstitutionalization movement be accounted for? The following are several possible explanations:

1. As mentioned above, we assumed that the physical presence of people with disabilities within community life would automatically lead to social integration. Normalization and Social Role Valorization teach that physical presence creates *preconditions* for social integration. In addition, they teach that supports and services must actively work to deepen community integration and participation, assist in the development of valued roles, and so on. Wolfensberger had warned as early as 1972 that "physical integration by itself will not guarantee social integration" (p. 48). Despite this unambiguous assertion, many people who were trained in Normalization and Social Role Valorization became disappointed or disillusioned when social integration was not an inevitable result of physical presence. We had, most likely unconsciously, pinned our hopes on the possibility that hundreds of years of intentional separation of people with disabilities from their communities could be counteracted quickly, employing a relatively small array of positive actions. This view is consistent with many shortsighted approaches in our field (and, indeed, in our society) that promise easy answers to significant social problems, with relatively little investment of time or other resources. Another assumption underlying the emphasis on deinstitutionalization was the belief that fighting against a "bad thing" (e.g., institutionalization) would accomplish the same ends as working toward a "good thing" (e.g., social integration). In fact, we have seen in other social movements (e.g., school desegregation), that merely reversing or undoing a wrong will not inevitably create a positive condition. Bradley (1994) writes: "Wolfensberger's warning that physical integration was not sufficient to guarantee social integration has been heeded by planners and policy-makers only since the late 1980s. Instead of moving to accomplish physical and social integration simultaneously, the field has focused first on physical integration and is now learning Wolfensberger's lesson that integration is more than just the opposite of segregation" (p. 12).

2. Perhaps if we had oriented ourselves more to the vast body of knowledge available on community attitude change, we might have pinned fewer hopes on the impact of deinstitutionalization alone. Many of us acted as if well-intended actions alone would be sufficient, as long as they were carried out in a community setting. We had little sense of strategy. This certainly was my approach, and I have encountered many other enthusiastic service workers and advocates who, like myself, fumbled along in a random fashion, occasionally rediscovering time-tested

principles of community change. As mentioned, around 1982, I became very interested in the issue of community education and attitude change. During the 10 years of Education for Community Initiatives, I encountered numerous sources of information about community organizing and community education that had already been tested and refined. This information I literally stumbled upon and it is still unknown to the majority of people in our field, even those interested in community integration.

3. There is another reality that may have contributed to the emphasis on deinstitutionalization as a primary strategy. This was the fact that many of the change agents of the 1980s, including those who studied Normalization and Social Role Valorization, had a deep service orientation and very little experience or even interest in the larger community. Though we may have understood intellectually the need for broader social change in order to accomplish the goals of Normalization, we did not have the experience or the worldview to effect change in that arena. While earlier generations of service workers addressed the broader social change level (see, for example, Wolfensberger & Menolascino, 1970), our generation focused its efforts largely on service development and reform. Most of my peers had few community ties, belonged only to disability-related voluntary organizations, and some even held an elitist distaste for the pedestrian nature of everyday community life. It was only when we began to lose faith in the capacity of services to bring about positive life conditions for people with disabilities that we became intrigued by the potential of communities and of "everyday community life."

Today, services bear the brunt of our disillusionment. A theme underlies much of today's progressive thinking: Services themselves are solely responsible for the bad things happening to people with disabilities—if people would only be restored to their communities without the negative influence of services, then they would be accepted. This disenchantment with services often manifests itself as an idealization of community life and, in many cases, a categoric rejection of any positive role that might be played by formal supports and services.

Despite the current hope invested in the promise of "community living," there is little evidence that explicit community education is carried out on a widespread or systematic basis. For example, deinstitutionalization efforts unaccompanied by community education or positive social integration are the norm. Community education and social integration are seen as something to be tackled once the "real work" of getting people out of institutions or setting up programs is complete, even by those who profess to be proponents of social integration. Virtually no resources are committed to community education, although the unwelcoming attitudes of community members are often described as a major barrier to social integration.

To compound the problem, certain assumptions held by some of our field's conceptual leaders are problematic. For example, proponents of the latest ideas in service delivery (e.g., "supported living," "bridgebuilding," "circles of friends") often express unreasonably optimistic beliefs about the willingness and capacity of communities to welcome returning members with disabilities. The evidence to support these beliefs is found in the stories of a small number of individuals whose successes can usually be attributed to massive effort on the part of highly committed family or service workers, and seldom to the "kindness of strangers." I have somewhat facetiously termed this view the *prairie home companion* vision of supporting people with disabilities, because of its romanticized and generally unrealistic notions of community life.

Another problematic assumption is that individual successes will be sufficient, if enough accumulate, to produce significant societal attitude change. Alfie Kohn addressed this issue well when he described the "entrenched reluctance of Americans to consider structural explanations for problems." He wrote, "We are moved to help a hungry individual but oblivious to how broad social policies have created hunger on a massive scale." While working at the individual level can have many positive outcomes, there must also be those who address issues at the systemic and structural level. However, a bias toward individual action is currently evident in our field.

Perhaps the most troubling problem with the thinking of progressives in the field is the continued *service reform* emphasis. Even proponents of "supported living" pay almost exclusive attention to staff roles, organizational structures, and policy considerations, with little emphasis on potential roles of community members, a point to which I will return.

With 25 years of experience in Normalization, Social Role Valorization, and deinstitutionalization, the field is in a time of transition. We are clearly assessing the impact of our efforts to date and searching for clarity about where to go from here. Many of our assumptions about what would work to accomplish the goals we set in the 1970s and 1980s have proven to be wrong, and yet we have not fully taken stock of our experience and learned from it. Instead, we have tended to either transfer our unreasonable expectations to another arena, the community, or become disillusioned and cynical about the possibility of ever achieving our goals. If we are ever to bring about social integration for devalued people, we need to look clearly at what might constitute reasonable expectations of community members in realizing our goals on behalf of people with disabilities, and then develop strategies to involve community members. The remainder of this chapter will sketch some thoughts on these topics.

3 PARADIGM OF SUPPORT: A REFORM IN PARADIGM-SHIFT CLOTHING

Over the past 25 years, beliefs about what might constitute "success" in our work have evolved considerably. In 1976, when I began working in this field, most efforts focused on creating facsimiles of real life. Phrases such as "homelike environment" and "creating conditions that are, as much as possible, *like* those of typical people" were commonly used to describe our aspirations. The language has changed and so has the thinking. Now phrases like "helping people have a *real* home" or a "*real* job" are heard instead, reflecting the recent emphasis on helping people with disabilities to have ordinary, typical, valued lives—real lives in real communities.

Adopting this new vision means adopting goals that are more complex and more subtle than were the goals of the 1970s and 1980s. They include assisting devalued people to hold valued roles within their communities; supporting them to be fully integrated on a personal level, including having a wide range of relationships with unpaid, valued others; and enabling people to engage in meaningful, age-appropriate activities in integrated settings. For each of these goals to be realized requires that change agents pay attention

to systemic and structural considerations, not just to act at the individual level. More importantly, the realization of these new goals necessitates the willing participation of an additional set of actors—the "general public"—as well as those on whom we relied to build the existing service system. Along with this additional set of actors, different means, methods, and strategies are likely to be necessary to enlist their support and involvement.

Current discussions in the field of developmental disabilities have begun to focus on providing "community supports" rather than community services, sometimes called a "paradigm of support." This new orientation reflects an increased emphasis on social networks and informal community supports, through the identification of existing relationships and informal community connections for an individual with a disability, and the subsequent establishment of formal arrangements that build on and strengthen the existing informal supports.

Ashbaugh, Bradley, and Blaney (1994) compiled an extensive description of strategies for moving toward a paradigm of support that attempted to address virtually every aspect of adopting and implementing this approach. This recent emphasis on community membership and natural supports is consistent with earlier work of people such as McKnight and Wolfensberger. Yet it can be distinguished from their work in that it appears to derive more from a desire to restructure services—service reform—than from a profound lack of faith in any form of support other than the informal, a view that is reflected in both Wolfensberger's and McKnight's work. Wolfensberger (1983) writes, "in a world that is falling apart and where virtually every single social glue that can hold a society together is coming unstuck . . . the promotion of communality is another essential and basic priority. We need a communality by means of which people at risk of social rejection and devaluation are included and embedded in communal, supportive, primary and secondary social groups and networks" (p. 2). McKnight (1987) writes, "Those who seek to institute the community vision believe that beyond therapy and advocacy is the constellation of community associations. They see a society where those who were once labelled, exiled, treated, counseled, advised, and protected are, instead, incorporated in community where their contributions, capacities, gifts, and fallibilities will allow a network of relationships involving work, recreation, friendship, support, and the political power of being a citizen" (p. 57). While Wolfensberger's position emphasizes the impending collapse of most existing social structures, including human services, and McKnight critiques the damage done to community life by professional services, both advocate an emphasis on "extrastructural supports" or the "associational life" of a community as a primary response to the needs of devalued people.

The paradigm of support appears to hold more promise for creating positive conditions in the lives of people with disabilities than many traditional service arrangements: It acknowledges the need for most people with disabilities to have some mediating presence in the process of helping them to be integrated within their communities, yet strives to keep this presence in the background and focused on meeting the needs of people served. But amid the emerging thicket of detail about staff roles, organizational structures, and legal and policy considerations, there is a notable lack of attention to the roles, responsibilities, and strategies needed to enlist the willing support of community members in bringing about this new vision. This is troubling; I fear that the paradigm of support is merely an updated service reform, rather than a radical departure from our former ideas (a reform in paradigm-shift clothing, one might say). What will make this paradigm of support truly radical is its acknowledgment and attention to the *fundamental role* of communities and community members in achieving the vision we have set.

Once their fundamental role is acknowledged, we then need to determine what might be reasonable to expect from them—in a nonidealized fashion—and to identify how such involvement might be enlisted. The next section will address this question.

4 REASONABLE EXPECTATIONS OF COMMUNITY MEMBERS: WHAT ARE THEY? HOW MIGHT THEY BE MET?

I have given a great deal of thought to this question of expectations and would like to propose my list of "bottom-line" expectations reasonable to hold for individual community members and communities

regarding people who are devalued. Obviously, this list reflects my own evolving thinking about "what we can pin our hopes on" and thus where efforts might most fruitfully be invested.

1. That many human beings will make an effort to be decent to one another on an interpersonal basis. Kendrick (1994) writes:

> social acceptance, inclusion, and the accordance of personal worth do not primarily come through agencies. Rather these qualities of life require the will and commitment of ordinary people. When these qualities become the norm, then a commensurate change in social pattern will occur . . . people should be encouraged toward personal responsibility to one another within the range of appropriate personal obligation. (p. 367)

TABLE 16.1

PROPOSITIONS REGARDING "REASONABLE EXPECTATIONS" OF COMMUNITY MEMBERS AND COMMUNITIES

1. Many human beings will make an effort to be decent to one another on an interpersonal basis.
2. Voluntary institutions founded on explicit values and principles emphasizing a sense of community and service will make a special effort to treat people well and model this to others (e.g., religious, service, and fraternal organizations).
3. Social policy and the law will serve to *set limits* on the categoric rejection, mistreatment, exclusion, and discrimination of devalued people.

PROMISING EDUCATIONAL STRATEGIES TO ENCOURAGE THE FULFILLMENT OF THESE EXPECTATIONS

1. Work directly with community members to raise consciousness, encourage actions, and promote positive personal contact with devalued people, especially through work with *voluntary associations*.
2. Reach key decision makers, policy setters, the media, etc., with information relevant to their areas of interest and expertise.

---

2. That voluntary societal institutions founded on explicit values and principles emphasizing a sense of community and service, such as religious, service, and fraternal organizations, will make a special effort to treat people well and to model this to others.

3. That social policy and the law will serve to *set limits* on the categoric rejection, mistreatment, exclusion, and discrimination of devalued people, although their positive potential is fast diminishing.

If the above expectations were to be adopted, what might community members need to know or believe in order to fulfill them? One tempting answer within the present context might be that community members need to know Social Role Valorization (SRV) theory. After all, SRV contains within it virtually everything an advocate or supporter of devalued people might need to know about devaluation and potential responses. Yet, as Susan Thomas has stated: "it seems both a more rational and more realistic goal to aspire to help ordinary people be more supportive of Normalization/SRV *measures* than to try to teach them Normalization or SRV." (Chapter 15, p. 360.)

TABLE 16.2

FORMS OF COMMUNITY EDUCATION POTENTIALLY CONTRIBUTING TO ACTIONS CONSISTENT WITH SOCIAL ROLE VALORIZATION

1. Upbringing, e.g., religious, educational, family
2. Positively experienced personal contact with devalued people
3. Attitudes and values of key leaders, decision makers, and role models
4. Participation in voluntary associations
5. Social policy and law
6. Media, e.g., magazines, books, television, interactive video, movies.
7. Structures, processes, and conduct of people within human services

---

In fact, community members *already* learn many messages about devalued people—both positive and negative—through a number of cultural "media." These "media," which include such things as one's upbringing, personal contact with devalued people, the attitudes of key leaders, social policy and the law, and so forth, can be capitalized on to bring about positive attitude change. While a full explication of the ways these cultural "media" convey such messages is beyond the scope of this chapter, Table 16.2 provides examples of a number of major ways messages about devalued people are conveyed.

I would like to highlight two targets for focused attention in order to encourage and assist community members to meet the expectations outlined earlier. These areas do not receive sufficient attention in our field. They are:

1. To work at the interpersonal level, that is, directly with community members so that they may be more aware of the circumstances of devalued people and more receptive to acting on their behalf and welcoming them into community life. While it is feasible to work with individual community members, educational activities with members of voluntary associations can reach individual community members *as well as* influence community attitudes and values. The literature on voluntary associations describes a number of important functions they play in our society. One of the most important is the creation and maintenance of community values through the provision of a context for shaping and affirming these values. Another relevant function of voluntary associations is their importance in bringing about social integration in the generic sense (Smith, 1978). A third function of voluntary associations relevant to the goal of positive attitude change is their role in providing educational experiences for their members (e.g., League of Women Voters, Sunday School, etc.) (Smith, 1978). Working with members of community organizations also has the practical benefit of reaching more people at a time, and creating a context where members might be supported to further develop and maintain their newfound consciousness.

2. To work at the systems level, i.e., to reach key decision makers, policy setters, representatives of the media, and others who shape broad attitudes and actions—not necessarily with SRV training but with information relevant to their areas of interest and expertise. This might include imagery and positive roles taught to members of the media; the importance of integration taught to those who set public policy; the reality of conflict of interest, the effects of complexity,

and other systemic topics taught to policy makers, legislators, and so forth. "Education" is meant in a broad sense and might include advocacy, lobbying, and other actions that promote a specific agenda, as well as more traditional forms of education.

TABLE 16.3

FUNCTIONS OF VOLUNTARY ASSOCIATIONS THAT MAKE THEM CANDIDATES FOR COMMUNITY EDUCATION EFFORTS

1. Providing a context for shaping and affirming community values (Amis & Stern, 1974; Banton & Sills, 1968; Bellan, Madsen, et al., 1985; Berger & Neuhaus, 1977; Smith, 1978)
2. Bringing about social integration (Berger & Neuhaus, 1977; Milofsky, 1988; Smith, 1978)
3. Providing educational experiences (Smith, 1978)

---

5 PROMISING PEDAGOGIES FOR BRINGING THE SRV MESSAGE TO COMMUNITIES

Based on the writing of educators concerned with oppression and psychologists interested in empathy and prosocial behavior, three pedagogies appear to be especially effective in creating more positive attitudes regarding devalued people. They are:

1. Consciousness-raising, that is, the process of identifying and critiquing the ideologies controlling our beliefs and our lives. Evans (1987) writes, "Controlling ideology can be compared to the water in which fish swim: it is so much a part of our ordering environment that we do not even recognize its existence, to say nothing of its dominating power" (p. 268). SRV training is one powerful consciousness-raising experience that enables participants to examine our society's controlling ideologies, especially regarding devaluation. However, many other consciousness-raising tools also exist.

2. Action. Rather than listening to a lecture or reading a book, actually engaging in constructive action on behalf of devalued people can be educational. In fact, a number of writers assert that action is a *precursor* to change in values and behavior, not merely a consequence (Evans, 1987; Kennedy, 1987a; Kennedy, 1987b; Kohn, 1990; Staub, 1989).

TABLE 16.4

SOME MAJOR STRATEGIES FOR ARRANGING POSITIVELY EXPERIENCED INTEGRATIVE CONTACTS, INTERACTIONS, AND RELATIONSHIPS

1. Address characteristics and conditions of devalued persons that are apt to elicit rejection from others and therefore prevent/inhibit integration.
   a. Reduce anxiety and rejection-provoking personal characteristics of devalued persons, e.g., poor grooming, poor body hygiene, offensive/intrusive habits.
   b. Encourage, develop, and instill valued social habits.
   c. Disperse devalued people, and services to them, throughout community and neighborhood.
   d. Reduce/eliminate compensate for negative images attached to devalued persons/groups.
   e. Foster valued social roles for devalued people and present/interpret them to others in such roles.

2. Help potential integrators to identify with devalued persons.
   a. Find and emphasize backgrounds, interests, activities, and involvements that devalued persons and potential integrators share.
   b. Pair up devalued and valued persons in cooperative tasks at which the chances of success are relatively good, e.g., board/committee work, school projects, neighborhood cleanup.
   c. Request/elicit/structure satisfying direct personal helping involvements by valued persons with devalued ones, e.g., Citizen Advocacy.

3. Reward and reinforce any integrative gestures or acts by valued persons, e.g., private interpretations, praise, commendations, comments to significant others, public letters.

3. Positively experienced personal contact. Optimally, there would be positive experiences with more than one individual in order that stereotypes held about devalued people might begin to break down. As Kohn (1990) writes:

> Maximizing personal knowledge, minimizing distance and anonymity, are useful not just for humanizing in general but specifically for overcoming the obstacle of deindividuation. Assumptions about a particular group are shattered as one comes into contact with its members, one by one. At first the stereotypes persist and remain in uneasy coexistence with direct knowledge about an individual: He's one of the *good* X's. Eventually, as one comes to know too many counterexamples—and the chief reason prejudice endures is that this happens too rarely—the stereotypes tremble and collapse. (p. 145)

Crucial to the shattering of stereotypes is positive contact with people who serve as *counterexamples*. In fact, a negative experience can cause stereotyping or reinforce existing negative stereotypes. There are several conditions associated with personal contact that make it most likely to have a positive effect, some of which are taught in SRV training workshops in the module on "personal social integration and valued social participation." Table 16.4 describes some strategies suggested by SRV teaching which might assist in this.

Some ways of fostering positively experienced personal contact include assisting devalued people to become members of voluntary associations, promoting citizen advocacy relationships between members of community groups and devalued persons, or encouraging members of community groups to work collaboratively with members of advocacy groups of devalued persons toward a common goal.

Positively experienced personal contact alone may not be sufficient to bring about long-term attitude change. Zimbardo, Ebbesen, and Maslach (1977) write that such contact must be accompanied by other conditions in order to sustain a change in attitude about devalued people. This is one reason why working with community organizations to create a receptive climate for responding to devalued people is probably more effective than working only with individuals:

> A second approach used . . . has assumed that contact or physical proximity between members of the group in question, would make attitudes more favorable. . . . There is some equivocal evidence that as long as the contact continues, the prejudiced attitudes may weaken. However, once the person returns to a situation where the norms do not support tolerant attitudes, the newfound tolerance slips back into old prejudiced habits of thought, speech, and action. (p. 163)

An especially effective combination of educational approaches, whether they be with members of voluntary associations or others, is to create opportunities for constructive personal contact between a devalued person and others, and then to offer opportunities for consciousness-raising and other kinds of learning as follow-up. I have termed this combination of approaches "contextual learning," because it enables the learner to develop a connection to a devalued individual, then provides a context for understanding the situation of that individual including cultural and structural contributors to their devaluation.

In Normalization or SRV training with staff, one can usually assume that staff already have personal contact with people who are devalued. What they may be missing is a broader framework of understanding of such things as patterns of devaluation, the impact of unconsciousness on actions, and so forth that can be taught in an SRV course. However, community members who do not know devalued people personally may first need such contact as a way to engage or interest them. Personal contact can provide the motivation to learn more about the broader situation of devalued people. Then the additional information can be offered, using a variety of approaches. This additional information enables the learner to put that personal contact into a frame of reference—to see that many of the individual's experiences are common to a whole class or group. Without the personal contact, the learner has no immediate need to know or apply what is being learned. Without the broader learning, a person can be positively disposed toward an individual but not understand the larger patterns affecting his or her life.

Contextual learning is one important strategy for anyone interested in social change. There are a few models of this kind of education. The Highlander Center in New Market, Tennessee, is one example. The Plowshares Institute in Simsbury, Connecticut, is another. Both combine explicit education/training with intentional opportunities for personal contact.

TABLE 16.5

PROMISING PEDAGOGIES FOR BRINGING THE SRV MESSAGE TO COMMUNITIES

Consciousness-raising, i.e., the process of identifying and critiquing the ideologies influencing our beliefs and our lives.

Three dimensions:
* Personal
* Organizational
* Systemic

Action, i.e., constructive actions on behalf of devalued people.

Positively experienced personal contact

Effective combination of approaches

1. Opportunities for constructive personal contact with a devalued individual, combined with
2. Opportunities for consciousness-raising and broader education with links to the devalued individual.

"CONTEXTUAL LEARNING"

6 CONCLUSION

Since the late 1960s, our vision of what might be possible for people with disabilities has expanded considerably. Rather than working toward facsimiles of real life, the aim is for people with disabilities to have ordinary, typical, valued lives—real lives in real communities. The success of this new vision requires the willing participation of community members—"ordinary people." While it is probably unreasonable to expect that communities will, of their own accord, systematically rise to the challenge of integrating people with disabilities and provide them with the needed support, there are certain reasonable expectations of community members and communities. In order to prepare and support community members to fulfill these expectations, direct efforts at community education and attitude change need to be carried out. SRV training is not the most feasible approach to accomplish the desired outcomes with an audience of community members, but there are many possible strategies to teach about devaluation and SRV *measures*. Especially promising audiences include individual community members who might have contact with devalued people at the interpersonal level, and especially members of religious, service, and fraternal organizations. Contextual learning, that is, pedagogies that build on opportunities for constructive personal contact between devalued people and other community members, and that provide additional information and understanding regarding matters arising from such contact, are likely to be especially effective forms of education.

REFERENCES

ASHBAUGH, J. W., BRADLEY, V. J., & BLANEY, B. C. (1994). Implications for future practice and systems design. In V. J. BRADLEY, J. W. ASHBAUGH, & B. C. BLANEY (Eds.), *Creating individual supports for people with developmental disabilities* (pp. 491-508). Baltimore: Paul H. Brookes.

BRADLEY, V. J. (1994). Evolution of a new service paradigm. In V. J. BRADLEY, J. W. ASHBAUGH, & B. C. BLANEY (Eds.), *Creating individual supports for people with developmental disabilities* (pp. 3-10). Baltimore: Paul H. Brookes.

EVANS, R. A. (1987). Education for emancipation: Movement toward transformation. In A. EVANS, R. EVANS, & W. KENNEDY (Eds.), *Pedagogies for the non-poor.* (pp. 257-286). Maryknoll, NY: Orbis Books.

KENDRICK, M. (1994). Public and personal leadership challenges. In V. J. BRADLEY, J. W. ASHBAUGH, & B. C. BLANEY (Eds.), *Creating individual supports for people with developmental disabilities* (pp. 361-372). Baltimore: Paul H. Brookes.

KENNEDY, W. B. (1987a). The ideological captivity of the non-poor. In A. EVANS, R. EVANS, & W. KENNEDY (Eds.), *Pedagogies for the non-poor* (pp. 232-256). Maryknoll, NY: Orbis Books.

KENNEDY, W. B. (Ed.). (1987b). Conversations with Paolo Friere on pedagogies for the non-poor. In A. EVANS, R. EVANS, & W. KENNEDY (Eds.), *Pedagogies for the non-poor* (pp. 219-231). Maryknoll, NY: Orbis Books.

KOHN, A. (1990). *The brighter side of human nature: Altruism and empathy in everyday life.* New York: Basic Books.

MCKNIGHT, J. (1987). Regenerating community. *Social Policy, 17,* 54-58.

SMITH, D. H. (1978, November). The impact of the voluntary sector on society. *Boston College Magazine,* 4-9.

STAUB, E. (1989). Individual and societal (group) values in a motivational perspective and their role in benevolence and harmdoing. In N. EISENBERG, J. REYKOWSKI, & E. STAUB (Eds.), *Social and moral values: Individual and societal perspectives* (pp. 45-61). Hillsdale, NJ: Lawrence Erlbaum Associates.

WOLFENSBERGER, W. (1972). *The principle of Normalization in human services.* Toronto, ON: National Institute on Mental Retardation.

WOLFENSBERGER, W. (1983). A brief reflection on where we stand and where we are going in human services. *Institutions, Etc., 6*(3), 20-23.

WOLFENSBERGER, W. (1994). A personal interpretation of the mental retardation scene in light of the "signs of the times." *Mental Retardation, 32*(1), 19-33.

WOLFENSBERGER, W., & MENOLASCINO, F. J. (1970). Reflections on recent mental retardation developments in Nebraska. I: A new plan. *Mental Retardation, 8*(6), 20-27.

ZIMBARDO, P. G., EBBESEN, E. B., & MASLACH, C. (1977). *Influencing attitudes and changing behavior: An introduction to method, theory, and applications of social control and personal power* (2nd ed.). Reading, MA: Addison-Wesley.

NOTE

1. Throughout this part of the paper, both the terms *people with disabilities* and *devalued people* are used. When referring specifically to people with disabilities or to trends most relevant within the disability field, the former term is used.

17

Education in applying the principle of Normalization as a factor in the practical arts of improving services for people with disabilities

JOHN O'BRIEN

We should regard practice as the only means (other than accident) by which whatever is judged to be honourable . . . can be kept in concrete experienceable existence. [p. 26]

To praise thinking above action because there is so much ill considered action in the world is to help maintain the kind of world in which action occurs for narrow and transient purposes. To seek after ideas and to cling to them as means of conducting operations, as factors in practical arts, is to participate in creating a world in which the springs of thinking will be clear and ever flowing. [p. 111]

—John Dewey (1929/1988)

1 A DESIGN FOR LEARNING

In the development of better formal services for socially devalued people, the genius of the principle of Normalization[1] flows from the practical interaction of three components. Two of these components are ideas, arising from its definition, and one is educational, arising from a common (though by no means universal) teaching practice. The definition (a) sets a direction for learning-through-action that is clear and convincing, as well as indefinite and conditional; and (b) rests on a deep appreciation of the everyday workings of the powers of social devaluation. Some methods for teaching its application give learners the experience of stepping outside the certainties of everyday human service work into a role that can be the seedbed for a new understanding of the situation of people with disabilities.

This interaction of concept and experience outlines a powerful design for personal and organizational learning. The definition clearly and economically specifies what practitioners at every level of human service work should avoid and what they should create more of, without limiting or prescribing how to do so. This exemplifies the sociotechnical design principle of "minimum critical specification," which is vital to developing adaptive capacity in rapidly changing environments (Morgan & Ramirez, 1983). The educational experience of looking at services from the perspective of service recipients as socially devalued people invites learners to engage their feelings and beliefs in creating a new reading of (a) effects of existing practice; (b) alternative ways of acting toward socially devalued people and (c) better ways of organizing services for them (Morgan, 1986; Schön, 1983; Weick, 1993).

The principle of Normalization offers a clear direction for learning-through-action by specifying a commonsense standard for judgment: Services should use socially valued means to promote socially valued lives. Once people are awakened to this way of seeing, the pervasiveness of service practices that vary wildly from what is typical, much less what is socially valued[2], convinces some people that they should do better. From discovering how little most residences are like real homes, how little most day activities are like real jobs, how little special education resembles ordinary schooling, and how well these differences are obscured by everyday beliefs about people with disabilities, people working to apply the principle of Normalization often decide that exploration of one or another socially valued analogies to the form of service under consideration offers a way forward. They work to provide real homes, real jobs, and real schooling. In doing so, they repeatedly confront the protean forms of social devaluation.

2 "AS MUCH AS POSSIBLE"—THE MOTOR FOR LEARNING

Once practitioners learn, through action and continuing reflection, to move away from the most obvious expressions of devaluation, the indefiniteness of the principle of Normalization, indicated in the phrase "as much as possible," becomes salient in at least three ways. First, the multiple and interacting ways in which services influence the extent to which people lead valued lives become evident. For instance, apparently disconnected images unthinkingly imposed by a program form a pattern that reveals the common root of multiple devaluing practices in a negative and stereotyped perception of the role of people with disabilities and leads to a call for greater consciousness as essential to reform. These multiple influences are distinguished in the 34 Normalization-related PASS ratings (Wolfensberger & Glenn, 1978) or the 42 PASSING ratings (Wolfensberger & Thomas, 1983), and the different weights attached to each rating provide hints in making trade-offs among them.

Second, the myriad analogies of what is socially valued invite imaginative attention to what is fitting for individual people, given the resources potentially available to them as citizens; as members of particular cultures, religious groups, and families; and as inhabitants of a particular place. "Home" may be nothing like any particular group home, but the people housed there might draw on different resources to create a variety of very different real homes for themselves.

Third, realization grows that some important qualities of a valued life are not things that can be delivered by service programs. These virtues result only from shared, lifelong struggles for personal and community development, balance, and maturity. No practitioner, whether a disabled person or an assistant, ever finishes learning what it means to be a responsible citizen, or to be a friend, or to make good use of one's autonomy, or to develop and express one's gifts, or to bear well with suffering.

The principle of Normalization contains this indefiniteness with the conditional phrase, "as much as possible," which provides a motor for continuing learning through repeated cycles of action and reflection. This conditional phrase brings high aspiration firmly in contact with everyday life in a way that invites practitioners to acknowledge and actively engage multiple constraints in their pursuit of socially valued lives. "As much as possible" acknowledges limits arising from the level of overall resources available in a society and in a community; a person's disability, given access to assistive and instructional technology; a person's choice, given opportunity and assistance; and the human condition. These limits are framed as constraints to be actively engaged in the process of learning rather than used as excuses for inaction or shoddy work. Active engagement will change the limits in uncertain and unpredictable ways: A disabled person who experiences the expectations and rewards of filling a valued job role will face new developmental challenges with different resources than a person left to languish as a client in an activity center. Some challenges may be daunting and the person's resources may be insufficient, but the set of constraints is changed by seeking as valued a way as possible to offer the person occupation. Consciously engaging a system of constraints by taking incremental steps to modify them, and then reflecting carefully on the problems and possibilities posed by the resulting set of constraints, is fundamental to any good design process (Alexander, 1964).

"As much as possible" defines an expanding horizon. As action creates new problems and new possibilities, the sense of what is possible expands. So rapidly have some people with disabilities and their allies moved into new territories that dealing with the rate of change in relevant information becomes a problem in itself. It is demanding to find out about rapidly proliferating social inventions and challenging to discern what will lead people toward more valued lives. Neither the rush to embrace the latest fad nor the out-of-hand dismissal of new approaches as "crazes" are helpful in discovering the limits of what is possible, however useful these strategies may be to defend against overload. Both foolish optimism and hopeless pessimism serve the powers of social devaluation.

3 THE POWERS OF SOCIAL DEVALUATION

Those who apply the principle of Normalization do not find a smooth road that they can traverse from darkness into light just by working smart and hard. Their work is not like sculpting hard stone or building a highway in difficult terrain. The situations they struggle to change don't passively assume the shape of their meticulously implemented designs as a simple function of craft and persistence. The situations they

struggle to change fight back. There is even more to this intractability than the political difficulty of persuading or commanding people with diverse interests to cooperate, or the managerial problems of accounting for complex uncertainty. The social systems they must transform so that people with disabilities have decent living conditions are dynamically conservative (Schön, 1971): No sooner do they find ways to expand available valued roles than some other force comes into play to push disabled people out of them.

Much teaching about the principle of Normalization descriptively labels this systemic capacity to fight back social devaluation, and elucidates its dynamics: There are powerful and actively oppressive forces inherent in human social organization that assign disabled people to devalued roles and cast them out of ordinary society into settings that congregate, segregate, control, and further stigmatize them. Efforts to offer people valued social roles and good life conditions are themselves stamped by these forces, usually in ways that are not apparent to change agents until ironic or downright destructive consequences ensue.

FIGURE 17.1

COMPLEMENTARY PATHS TO SERVICE REFORM

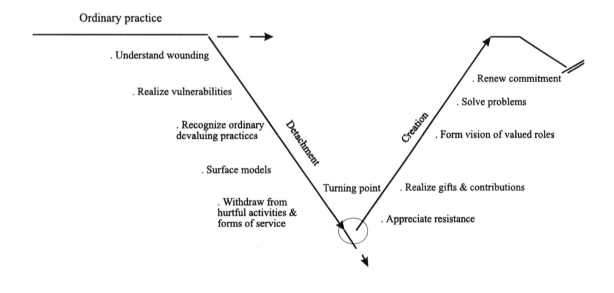

This descriptive approach to the workings of oppression helps to alert learners to the sorts of opposition they will contend with as they apply the principle of Normalization. However, beyond the tautology that devaluation is based on social perception of negatively valued difference, it fails to satisfy the deeper question of why social devaluation exists. As fundamentally important as one's answer to this deeper question is, part of the practical utility of the principle of Normalization comes from the fact that people with very different analyses and very different beliefs about why social devaluation occurs (and what its proper name is)[3] find common ground for agreement about how social devaluation works itself out and what might be done to constructively engage it.

4 COMPLEMENTARY PATHS TO REFORM

Learning to reform services by accepting the challenge of "as much as possible" while contending with the shifty forces of social devaluation does not follow a linear course. One idealized way to understand the kind of learning necessary is to see it as a journey that follows two complementary paths: a path of detachment, which clarifies what should be avoided, and a path of creation, which somewhat expands the extent of "as much as possible," at least in the life of a few people. The path of detachment begins with a break from the unconscious routine of ordinary practice and ends in a conscious choice to stop those aspects of ordinary practice that are harmful. The decision to withdraw from these practices brings a turning point that opens a path of creation. Following the path of creation ends in a new level of ordinary practice that embodies greater capacity to support new and more valued roles and experiences. This equilibrium leads in its turn to the opportunity for a further detachment from devaluing actions and service forms. At any point a learner can refuse the next step and go back to routine practice; indeed, most of the contingencies in the service environment will shape the learner toward unconscious routine.

FIGURE 17.2

MULTIPLE CREATIVE PATHS

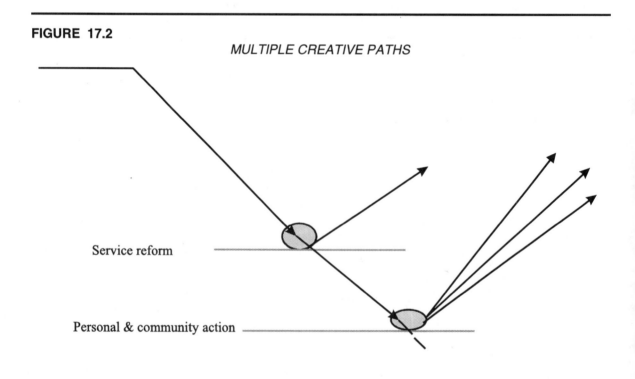

Service reform

Personal & community action

These two paths are only complementary if the traveler chooses to make them so. There are at least two ways of failing the test set by the principle of Normalization (symbolized by the dashed lines on figure 17.1): one can mindlessly continue ordinary practice ("We are already offering people 'as much as possible'"), or one can follow the path of detachment past the turning point and withdraw from the possibility of any creative action ("Nothing can work perfectly, so nothing is worth doing in this arena").

Of course, there are many creative paths that do not involve working to reform services. One's reading of the possibilities for formal service reform might lead to creative effort to build up informal services; or one might feel a call to deeper personal engagement in sharing life with devalued people (Zipperlen & O'Brien, 1994).

5 THE PATH OF DETACHMENT

The path of detachment leads through a deepening understanding of the many, systematically related ways in which disabled people are commonly wounded by socially typical beliefs and practices to a realization that devalued people are vulnerable in ways that call for vigorous and principled response. This teaching is commonly done in lectures about the wounds or common experiences of handicapped people. Then the learner comes to recognize at least some of the many specific ways that ordinary service practices reinforce negative beliefs and amplify devalued people's vulnerability. The team assessment of an actual service using the Normalization-related ratings in PASS, or using PASSING, teaches this in an unparalleled way. The learner then is in a position to bring to the surface some of the assumptions or models that generate devaluing effects as a consequence of their form and content. Usually these faults express and reinforce one or another of the common devaluing roles disabled people are cast into. Team analysis of what PASS calls the "model coherency" of a service can teach this in a thorough way. The path of detachment then leads the learner to a decision: Will he or she accept the discipline of withdrawing energy from activities and service forms now recognized as hurtful?

It is, of course, usually easy to advocate for stopping hurtful practice when one visits a program staffed by others whose flaws glare in the light of one's external assessment. It is harder when one is called on to notice and withdraw from harmful routines of one's own. Understandably, if regrettably, many find this shift from seeing others' devaluing practices to rooting out one's own very difficult. The fact that most efforts at Normalization-related education to date have lacked the organizational resources to provide extended support for transferring learning from intensive workshops to everyday practice helps to account for this. Many who can't walk the path of detachment in their own practice simply shake their heads at the strange and devaluing ways of foreigners ("Thank goodness we're nothing like the staff I assessed during the workshop"). A few people get stuck in the defensive role of refining their criticism of others rather than working for change in their own situations (perhaps by becoming PASS or PASSING groupies or, even worse, consultants).

6 THE TURNING POINT

The decision to withdraw from activities and service forms unmasked as hurtful brings the learner to another decision: whether to withdraw completely from the work of reforming services and to pursue a more communitarian or personalistic commitment to devalued people, or to look for a path of creation that has a good chance of leading toward reformed services. Identifying this decision is not to make a moral judgment in favor of service reform; it is only to say that moving away from service reform leads a person away from one of the central challenges of the principle of Normalization—which, as exhaustively defined by the written PASS and PASSING books, is almost completely about reforming service practice. There can be great merit in deciding not to step back into the service world and embracing some other commitment. And, given the craziness of service systems, following the path of detachment right out of the service world may sometimes be the most prudent course of action as well.

Some people do not seem to find a creative path. They may be daunted by the long-term action required to take even small creative steps. They may be paralyzed by an analysis so critical that it leaves no room for action. They may be so disappointed by greater awareness of the negative results of practices in which they had placed their faith that nothing seems worth doing. While people who do not make the turn from the way of detachment to one of the paths of creation may be able to minimize the harm they do, they have little chance of doing good.

7 THE PATH OF CREATION

Once chosen, the path of creation opens new ground because making things a bit better is seldom as simple as just reversing negative practice. Involuntary segregation oppresses people, but identifying integration as a goal only begins a process of understanding what it means and how to take steps toward its achievement. One of the most common sources of perversion of positive efforts comes from this kind of facile reversal, as, for instance, when the remedy for domination and deprivation of autonomy is unthinkingly defined as "choice" and more "choice."

It may be that the linear construction of PASS and PASSING ratings increases the potential for this error: on these scales, level 1 (the lowest level of quality) and level 5 (typically the highest level of quality) are presented as poles. But real reform usually takes far more than simply climbing from the bottom rung to the top rung of the ladder one is already on. Instead, one must step onto another ladder, which often rests against a different wall. For example, simpleminded commitment to self-determination or choice will be positively dangerous to intellectually disabled people unless it happens in the context of great effort at weaving a safety net of relationships in which the person recognizes others as a trustworthy source of guidance and authority.

So the climb up the path of creation begins with an expanded awareness of the identity of people with disabilities that complements rather than negates the reality of their wounds and vulnerabilities. On this path, disabled people are revealed as both wounded and capable of resistance; both vulnerable due to disability and capable of bringing important gifts. It is the potential for resistance and the gifts and capacities of particular disabled people, in a particular social context, that energizes and directs the path of creation.[4]

The learner begins by deepening appreciation for the ways some people with disabilities and some families with disabled members and some service workers have resisted the forces of devaluation, especially those expressed through the professional bureaucracies that have become typical in this generation. Then the path leads to a realization of the gifts and contributions disabled people can make to the life of the learner's own community. These gifts typically lie hidden under the devaluing certainties that define modern life (Wolfensberger, 1988).

Here a significant difference between the two paths comes into focus: It is possible to understand what not to do by contemplating the situation of devalued people as a class in society (i.e., abstractly or universally); but expanding the meaning of "as much as possible" in practice requires alliance with specific disabled people and knowledge of their identity in specific communities. It is, therefore, necessarily concrete and particular. A learner can draw on richer images of what is possible, and draw many valid lessons for change, by listening thoughtfully to stories of what others have achieved, but a learner can only create a new capacity to offer better life conditions in a particular community and in company with particular people.

The next step along the way of creation is the articulation of a vision or image of a desirable future in which people would have greater opportunities for membership, contribution, and more valued social roles. Such an image will provide direction, energy, and invitation for some other people to become allies in the effort to create a change. While this image guides service reform, it is clearly different from a plan for service change. It specifies what roles service workers will need to assist people in taking and playing, but not how they will organize themselves to do so.

Next, the path of creation leads to efforts to align, and often to increase, the personal, family, community, and service resources available to people in order to increase the chances that they will occupy the social roles that will make it possible for them to contribute and to experience the benefits of community membership. Here is where a service interested in becoming more relevant will find rich and challenging information for agency and system planning.

This alignment of personal, associational, and service resources is often very imperfect. Service funds may be so entangled in bureaucratic requirements that they are next to useless, or family members may deeply disagree with one another, or a disabled person may want something but be unwilling to sustain disciplined effort to achieve it. But, however imperfect, this alignment is the basis for problem solving.

As change unfolds and difficulties accumulate, there will be flurries of problem-solving activity. Service providers will need to attend to how they can provide adequate assistance at an efficient price and how they can participate in identifying the negative effects of the change and, as much as possible, safeguarding people from them.

As disabled people and their allies experience the benefits and the new problems arising from change, there will be many opportunities to renew and deepen commitment by joining in celebrating accomplishments and mourning losses and by supporting one another to carry on the work of constructive change.

The path of creation reaches the level ground of ordinary practice when people are established in new and valued roles and the assistance they require is available as part of everyday service activity. This

period of ordinary practice continues until another cycle of learning begins with a renewed awareness of the wounds and vulnerabilities that endure despite the previous round of reform.

8 CONCLUSION

Failure to appreciate either the power of social devaluation or the promise of working hard to continually expand what is possible blunts the principle of Normalization's effectiveness as a guide for the creation of better services, and feeds the widespread temptation to approach deep and enduring ethical issues with superficial and transient techniques. Only by forming and sustaining heart-to-heart alliances with devalued people can people concerned to improve services walk the complementary paths of detachment and creation toward a somewhat more just and inclusive community. The result will inevitably be far from utopian, but the journey will sober and delight those who make it.

REFERENCES

ALEXANDER, C. (1964). *Notes on a synthesis of form.* Cambridge. MA: Harvard University Press.

DEWEY, J. (1929/1988). *The quest for certainty.* Carbondale. IL: Southern Illinois University Press.

MORGAN, G. (1986). *Images of organization.* Newbury Park, CA: Sage.

MORGAN, G., & RAMIREZ, R. (1983). Action learning: A holographic metaphor for guiding social change. *Human Relations, 37*(1), 1-28.

O'BRIEN, J., & LOVETT, H. (1993). *Finding a way toward everyday lives: The contribution of person-centered planning.* Harrisburg, PA: Department of Public Welfare.

O'BRIEN, J., & LYLE O'BRIEN, C. (1990). What's worth working for? Perspective on human service leadership. In V. BRADLEY & H. BERSANI (Eds.), *Quality assurance for individuals with developmental disabilities: It's everybody's*

business. Baltimore: Paul H. Brookes Publishers.

SCHÖN, D. (1971). *Beyond the stable state.* New York: Random House.

SCHÖN, D. (1983). *The reflective practitioner.* New York: Norton.

WEICK, K. (1993). Organizational redesign as improvisation. In G. HUBER & W. GLICK, (Eds.), *Organizational change and redesign: Ideas and insights for improving performance.* New York: Oxford University Press.

WINK, W. (1993). *Engaging the powers.* Philadelphia: Fortress Press.

WOLFENSBERGER, W. (1978). The ideal service for socially devalued people. *Rehabilitation Literature, 39*(1), 15-17.

WOLFENSBERGER, W. (1988). Common assets of mentally retarded people that are commonly not acknowledged. *Mental Retardation, 26*(2), 63-70.

WOLFENSBERGER, W. (1994). A personal interpretation of the mental retardation scene in light of the "signs of the times." *Mental Retardation, 32*(1), 19-33.

WOLFENSBERGER, W., & GLENN, L. (1978). *Program analysis of service systems (PASS): A method for the quantitative evaluation of human services: Vol. 2. Field manual* (3rd ed.). Toronto, ON: National Institute on Mental Retardation.

WOLFENSBERGER, W., & THOMAS, S. (1983). *PASSING (Program analysis of service systems' implementation of Normalization goals):* *Normalization criteria and ratings manual* (2nd ed.). Toronto, ON: National Institute on Mental Retardation.

ZIPPERLEN, H., & O'BRIEN, J. (1994). *Cultivating thinking hearts: Letters from the lifesharing safeguards project.* Harrisburg, PA: Pennsylvania Developmental Disabilities Council.

NOTES

1. This chapter follows the definition of the principle of Normalization offered by Wolfensberger and Glenn (1978) and by Wolfensberger and Thomas (1983). The principle of Normalization has wide application to socially devalued people and many implications for informal services and social change efforts outside of formal services (see Thomas, chapter 15, this volume). However, this chapter focuses narrowly on its application in attempts to reform formal services, mostly by workers in services for people with mental retardation. Recent deliberations among people currently involved in SRV teaching distinguish several types of service, but here I mean the work done by someone employed by an agency whose mission is to assist people with disabilities. I recognize that many people currently associated with teaching about SRV/Normalization would not agree with my framing the principle in terms of philosophical pragmatism, indeed, some might think it misleading for me to do so, but this is the perspective that has framed my own service reform work.

2. For a painfully funny parody of these practices, see Wolfensberger (1978); the appallingly low scores that continue to be typical when services are evaluated against straightforward Normalization criteria testify to the unfortunate endurance of these practices (Flynn, chapter 14, this volume).

3. Wolfensberger himself has thought deeply on this question and its implications (see Wolfensberger [1994] for a very partial summary). Unfortunately, he has not published extensively on the implications of his moral analysis for SRV/Normalization, though he and his associates have taught a great deal about this in workshops presented by the Training Institute. Others have criticized the principle of Normalization on the grounds that its analysis of the political and material conditions of disabled people is shallow and naive (see, for example, Oliver, chapter 6, this volume). I have learned a great deal from Walter Wink's (1993) theological ethics, especially as he explicates the workings of what the New Testament calls the "powers and principalities."

4. It is possible, as above, to identify relatively widely used educational practices to guide people along the path of detachment. Fewer educational activities have been developed to guide people along the path of creation. Some beginning examples of these approaches include: Model Coherency workshops presented by Wolfensberger's Training Institute; a variety of approaches to person-centered planning (see O'Brien & Lovett [1993], for a review); and Framework for Accomplishment (see O'Brien & Lyle O'Brien [1990], for a conceptual outline of this process).

18

The impact of Normalization and Social Role Valorization in Scandinavia

KRISTJANA KRISTIANSEN

Examining the impact of one thing upon another is nearly always problematic, as most everything occurs in larger contexts. This is perhaps especially true in the area of societal change. Social phenomena are, of course, a reflection of the larger dynamics of their time and place, but also evolve in a complex interplay of mutual influence. A phenomenon such as Normalization develops parallel and often concurrent with related societal trends, making discernment of impact of one element or dimension difficult if not improbable to separate from another. An example would be the question of central authority devolving into structures of local control and provision. While much of this direction is consistent with and even partially shaped by the ideological and theoretical dimensions of Normalization and Social Role Valorization, decentralization has also been part of a larger societal trend with probably its own origins and momentum.

Furthermore, the notion of impact contains more than mere influence: It implies a force that arrives from somewhere else and strikes something. In the case of Normalization, the force did not have to travel very far to travel to Scandinavia, as its early ideas were developed and nurtured there. Normalization developed within the emerging Scandinavian welfare state ideology, and at least in part for this very reason it remains even more difficult to extricate the impact of Normalization (and more recently Social Role Valorization) out of this sociopolitical context.

Recognizing these limitations, some basic themes of impact can still be described. The themes or areas of impact that follow are presented to some extent in chronological order, but with some clear overlap, and conclude with a description of some of the actual resultant impacts. It is also important to point out that major differences exist among the three Scandinavian countries. This paper has a particular focus on Norway, both because it is the least known by others and most familiar to the author. More specific descriptions of impact also are to be found in chapter 20 concerning research from Norway and Sweden.

1 NORMALIZATION AS AN IDEOLOGICAL ENERGY SOURCE

It is not coincidental that the developing Scandinavian welfare states provided the cradle for the early ideas of Normalization. The rhetoric of Scandinavian welfare has consistently been infused with a passionate quest for fairness and justice, solidarity with the disadvantaged, and an equitable distribution of the good life. What is perhaps most noteworthy is how easy it has been in the last half-century for Scandinavian citizens to have at least superficial consensus on what is right and just.

The first ripple of impact that one could ascribe to Normalization is as an ideological energy source. Although Normalization was often no more than a word, it was used consistently in contexts describing something wrong that should and could be made right. This gave Normalization a symbolic power that created emotional energy and a potential force for change.

In the midst of other social movements of the 1960s, where groups such as racial minorities, women, and students were claiming oppression, questioning authority, demanding attention, and seeking liberation, Normalization created a more specific rallying point around the needs of disabled people. Normalization as a "battle-cry" was exemplified by Bank-Mikkelsen (1967), declaring the situation for retarded people as a part of the larger questions of class struggle and civil rights.

A central factor of Normalization as an ideology has included the recognition of all people as fellow human beings of equal worth. This "perceptual revolution" has continued to challenge and reshape both public images and professional notions of "who people are," their capabilities, and their needs. An understanding of who and what is human has been also essential in interpreting what had been happening as acceptable or not. Scandinavian society was not able to recognize injustice without identifying with the situation and experience of the victims. A recognition of fellow humanity suffering in inhumane conditions fueled a growing moral outrage, which was further enflamed by media coverage of scandalous conditions and treatment of huge congregations of people long hidden from public scrutiny. Such unveilings were important to engage the public will and a collective commitment to act.

2 NORMALIZATION AND SRV: MAGNET FOR ALLIANCES

Normalization provided a new perspective and rallying point for social critique, and did so in ways that both strengthened some existing alliances but also even more importantly provided a platform for the formation of new alliances. Parents, advocates, and other concerned citizens could join together with enlightened (or at least disgruntled?) service workers in a common cause, forming an important new basis for cooperation.

National organizations of parents and families of retarded people had been established in Denmark in 1952 (known as LEV) and in Sweden in 1956 (known as FUB), and were later often held together and strengthened by the glue of the Normalization ideology. Perhaps particularly because of the close working relationship with Niels Erik Bank-Mikkelsen in Denmark and Karl Grunewald and Bengt Nirje in Sweden, these parent organizations often articulated their demands under a "Normalization banner." Both organizations had strong influence on shaping legislation, reorganization of services, and particular aspects of service provision, including the right to receive treatment and education and other services previously denied, and also to participate in the decision-making process. The Norwegian association was not formed until 1967 but has since then been a major factor in shaping social reform directions and standards.

Networks involving people with impairments and that in varying degrees are controlled by themselves, are a trend to a large extent fostered by the Normalization movement. There are probably two reasons for this. First, elements such as liberation from service system control, and supports for greater autonomy and participation in decision making have been important parts of most formulations of Normalization, including specific ratings in PASS (Wolfensberger & Glenn, 1975a). Second, the leaders of the Normalization movement have been active initiators of these related alliances. Certainly Bengt Nirje's role as ombudsman in Sweden, and the 1970 Malmö conference, are two examples of an important milestone for movements such as People First, and other groups organized around the idea of self-determination. The work of Gunnar and Rosemary Dybwad and the International League also provided a common ground for the developing ideas of both Normalization and self-advocacy. Perhaps more important for the most vulnerable members of society are the citizen advocacy alliances inspired directly by the ideas and work of Wolf Wolfensberger (see Wolfensberger, 1972; 1992; and Wolfensberger & Zauha, 1973).

Normalization has continued to function as a magnet, attracting some and repelling others. It has aroused the curiosity of the curious, initially perhaps especially the interests of those critical of the status quo, and to a lesser extent those with alternative visions. Informal and formal networks have formed that perhaps otherwise would not have come together. Examples would be conferences, joint publication efforts, and study trips with Normalization as a key theme.

More recently, access to the international SRV network offers both contact to a training and research network, and an *identity* with a *mission*. This identity-and-mission also can be likened to a magnet, as it attracts some and repels others. In part because of its more definitive character, SRV can in this way serve as an invitation and a call to decision.

3 NORMALIZATION AS A GUIDE FOR SOCIOPOLITICAL REFORM

Progression from moral outrage toward societal change in Scandinavia has involved a great hope and faith in the collective state and its public reforms. Achieving an equitable standard of living for all citizens, including people who previously had been neglected or segregated, has often been interpreted as a question of clarifying legal entitlements, altering national resource allocations, and reorganizing public delivery structures. The expectation has been that the state can and should deliver what its citizens need, so that the extension of citizenship status has been seen as a key task in the Normalization process.

"Normalization" is frequently mentioned as a guiding principle in major legislative documents concerning social reform in all three Scandinavian countries. This became increasingly true in Norway, and is certainly less and less true in Denmark.

In 1959 the Danish parliament put into effect Act 192, which both described the rights for mentally retarded people and outlined a reorganization of the national service structures and content. (An English-language translation of the sections of this Act is available in Bank-Mikkelsen, 1969, pp. 245-254.) For its time in history, this law was remarkable in its comprehensiveness and underlying intentions of attention to the needs of a very neglected group. This legislation was extended 2 years later to also include people who were blind or deaf.

This document includes the following oft-quoted goal for this reform in its statement of objectives: "The Care-service for the mentally retarded should seek to create conditions for the mentally retarded as close to what is normal as is possible" (Danmark: lov nr. 192). Much of this Danish legislation was influenced and formulated by Bank-Mikkelsen in close collaboration with the parents organization and a few concerned professionals.

The phrase from this legislation has had a much greater international impact than it perhaps merits. It may not even have been noticed if it were not for the subsequent attention to Bank-Mikkelsen and attention to the content of the Act. Certainly one central influence was its attracting the attention of Sweden, and the resultant close collaboration with Karl Grunewald and Bengt Nirje. The phrase itself has been mistakenly called "the Bank-Mikkelsen definition of Normalization," although it is not a definition, does not include the word Normalization, and he is not the sole author of the phrasing. He later called this phrase "the basis of the theory later to be called Normalization" (1980, p. 56). This phrase is also often interpreted outside of its context (which was as a statement of the purpose and objectives of a reorganization of services), such that many have incorrectly argued that Bank-Mikkelsen's definition is a goal or ends-oriented one. (Further, this is often contrasted to Nirje's later work, which is described as means or process-oriented, a description and contrast that is equally hard to substantiate if one examines original sources.)

The 1959 Danish Act actually had a greater focus on establishing a right to treatment and service than on citizenship rights. This reflected what Bank-Mikkelsen later called "a new knowledge that mental retardation is a dynamic condition which can be influenced by treatment, education, and training," calling this also "a new objective for services" (1980, p. 55). The Act also created a new professional worker education and identity for "care assistants." Altogether this represented an early sign of what we would now describe as belief in the developmental assumption and possibly a step toward a commitment to competency enhancement.

A Norwegian government report *Service Development for the Disabled* from 1966 states in its sections on objectives and major guidelines that the disabled should have the "same standard of living, freedom of choice to plan one's life as others . . . to the degree that this is possible. . . Society must alter conditions so that people with disabilities receive the medical, pedagogical, and social assistance they need to fully develop their capacities. An important principle in this new way of thinking is Normalization.

This means that one should not draw unnecessary lines of separation between the disabled and others with regard to medical and social care, schooling, education, occupation, and general welfare" (St. Meld. 88: 66-67). In the history of Norwegian reform, this policy statement has later been referred to "as an important break with segregative care patterns" (St. Meld. 67: 86-87:4). In addition to being a statement of anti-discrimination, this clause has also provided the groundwork for what in SRV/PASS language we know as the "utilization and development of generic resources." It furthermore includes explicit recognition of people having capacities that can be developed, and that this requires modifications in their surroundings. This may be interpreted as positive assumptions about developmental potential, coupled with a view of disability that recognizes societal conditions as a contributing factor.

In July 1968, the Swedish *Law on Care for the Mentally Retarded* went into effect (SFS 1967:94). (An English-language summary of some sections is found in Nirje, 1969, pp. 188-195.) This law described in great detail both service entitlements for the mentally retarded, and clarified a more decentralized locus of responsibility and organization of care structures. It further stipulated that schooling and occupation shall occur, and that these activities shall occur outside the residence, in accordance with normative daily and weekly rhythms.

A 1977 Norwegian government committee report entitled *The Disabled in Society* contains the following statements: "Normalization of the situation for the disabled requires a Normalization of programs and services," and also calls for an "end to discriminating and segregative arrangements, to be replaced with supports based in local communities and having one's special needs met through the generic public system" (St. Meld. 23:77-78).

The Danish 1959 legislation was amended or modified in 1970, 1974, and 1979, and repealed in 1980. Present legislation in Denmark gives the mentally retarded the same rights as other citizens and grants them access to the generic social support system. More recent legislation in Sweden went into effect in July 1986 and contains clearer specifications of care, service, and supports. More responsibility is placed on other public sectors, such as education and health for people's more general needs. This law also more formally assures mentally retarded people the right to services, on a voluntary and not compulsory basis, and access to a court of law in case of denial, violation, or appeal. A new Swedish law for mentally retarded people came into effect in January 1994. This law mandated institutional closure, with plans to be completed by the end of 1994, and further stipulated "ten rights." Central elements are rights for a personal assistant, respite care, and a general increase in self-determination. (An English summary of this law is available in Malena Sjöberg [1994]).

Both Danish and Swedish legislation have been described inside and outside Scandinavia as "Bills of Rights" for the mentally retarded. Much of this thinking also provided the groundwork for the United Nations' Declaration of Rights for the Mentally Retarded, in 1971. Norway has never had a specific law clarifying rights or legal entitlements for a specific group. The Norwegian National Association for the Mentally Retarded (NFPU) has consistently argued that the Norwegian constitution and other national laws apply to all citizens. More recently the need to have certain rights clarified in specific laws is being discussed again.

It is also noteworthy that the word Normalization in early Norwegian public documents occurs in legislation regarding the entire disabled population (*funksjonshemmete*), not only the mentally retarded, and occurs consistently in recent years in official documents regarding national reforms in mental health and special education, as well as leading public documents regarding services for older people with impairments.

In both Norway and Sweden, it is common to find *Normalization* and *integration* formulated alongside each other as dual policy goals or guiding principles. This implies that integration is something else or in addition to what lies implicit or explicit in Normalization, and many confuse the two terms, use them interchangeably, or assign them a similar content. Similarly, there is a lack of consensus on whether Normalization is a goal in itself or a means toward an end (and if so, what end?). Both policy documents and leaders in the human service field have claimed that "Normalization is the goal, integration the means," while others state the exact opposite. More recently, people claim that "inclusion" is the means and "integration" is the goal, although Wolfensberger's formulations of "integration" have proposed it as a means.

Much of the Norwegian national policy occurring in juxtaposition with the word *Normalization* can be interpreted as a commitment to an "administrative Normalization," including both decentralization of provision responsibility to local levels and an evolution from special, segregated care toward a single public and generic system for all citizens. As recently as 1994, Norwegian government reports imply that Normalization is the same as deinstitutionalization and/or normalized housing.

The word *Normalization* has been present in Scandinavian public policy documents at many levels for a long time. But its use is sporadic, inconsistent, and perhaps even coincidental, often occurring isolated from any definition or explicit content.

One could argue that the use of the word at least implies some sort of good intentions, but the presence of the word in even the most binding legislation has had a questionable impact, beyond its power as an ideological symbol.

The expression *normaliseringsprincipp* ("Normalization principle") can actually be found in Swedish documents as early as 1949, in contexts discussing access to the workforce for a category of people considered able to work. That this word was only just "discovered" in these early documents says something about the impact of a phrase alone.

The very role of legislation in social change is at once partly culture-bound to its host society and yet also partly universal in its underlying assumptions and hopes. A Norwegian government report, *Care of the Mentally Retarded*, states: "Although there is considerable consensus that care provision is a public issue, one also recognizes that clarification of legal rights is not sufficient without political will and resources for implementation" (NOU 1973:25, p. 49). Recent research in Norway indicates a tremendous gap between official intentions and public rhetoric about Normalization and actual practice (Sandvin, 1993; Stangvik, 1993; Kristiansen, 1994; Ramsdal, 1994). Still, such government policy reports have an important role and function of bringing issues into the public arena for debate and discussion, often invited and enflamed by the media, and in this way have a wide impact on public sentiment and on discussions in the human service fields.

4 EXPORT OF IDEOLOGY

Visits to other European countries and North America by Bank-Mikkelsen, Grunewald and Nirje and their presentations at many international conferences in the 1960s provided well-known impacts on the work of all of us in the field of human services. The Scandinavian principle of Normalization has attracted a great deal of interest and attention, and many international visitors came to see it in action. The tremendous attention awarded to the ideas from around the world has also had some "rebound impact" within Scandinavia. What had at first seemed reasonable and logical and simple became more interesting for many because of the attention it received. And the visits themselves were often mutually rewarding.

The most powerful resultant export has been *ideological in nature* and *inspirational in function*. Essentially what was exported was a set of beliefs about what was right and some examples of "how to do it." Bengt Nirje's slide presentations of the late 1960s gave many people clear visual images of what was possible, especially perhaps with regard to alternative living arrangements. Wolf Wolfensberger has repeatedly credited this contact as the source of his original interest in the topic.

Much of what appears to be exported these days is rhetoric about "rights" and "citizenship," which have startling popularity in countries where citizenship and legal entitlements guarantee little if anything.

5 DEBATE: CONTENT AND IMPLICATIONS

Bengt Nirje's systemic statement of the Normalization principle in 1969 provided the world with eight descriptive components, which gave content to the phrase "normal life." Access to a more typical life *was seen as a human right*. Nirje's descriptions of typical life rhythms, patterns, and conditions and the similar ideas offered by Bank-Mikkelsen were seen as important in order to be able to identify what society should be providing, or, increasingly, what one should be entitled to.

Initially, there was little debate in Scandinavia: Normalization seemed politically reasonable, easy to understand and accept, and essentially a pragmatic question with regard to implementation. It entered the political arena at a time when resources were plentiful. At some point the questioning started, and it was initially primarily theoretical, conceptual, and practical in nature, rather than ideological. Who or what should be normalized? Who says what is normal and who wants to be that anyway? Would it work anywhere? Does it apply to everyone? How do we actually do it? Mounting opposition was often based on misconceptions according to anyone's definition and, at least on the surface, seldom of an ideological nature.

The first organized effort in Scandinavia to grapple with these issues was Project Mental Retardation at the University of Uppsala in Sweden. This group has continued to provide an academic and research base in Scandinavia, with Normalization, integration, and quality of life as central areas of concern. Their primary interest has been to operationalize Normalization and integration for empiric purposes, as part of an ongoing attempt to investigate and document living conditions and institutional reform for mentally retarded people.

One was, however, still left with the question of how things went wrong in the first place. Why had some groups in society been denied service and support and instead been segregated and stripped of their dignity and rights? What explanations does any society have for generations of bad treatment? Can we actually address the problem, if we do not understand the larger dynamics that caused the problem? Who might be in danger now, and why?

The search for relevant theory has led some to the work of Wolfensberger. Wolfensberger's work was originally introduced into the Scandinavian literature in 1971 and 1972 by Karl Grunewald (1971, 1972) with Swedish and Danish translations of *Origin and Nature of Our Institutional Models* (1969). Shortly after, the importance of social roles were discussed in two Norwegian government reports from 1973. The report *Care of the Mentally Retarded* contained a noteworthy summary of Rolf (sic) Wolfensberger's work included in the section on future guidelines:

> The provision of care is undergoing an intensive evolution, and as an introduction to describing future patterns of care it is useful to take a closer

look at the forces that underlie this process. One then discovers that societal attitudes toward the mentally retarded are determined to a very great extent by the role or roles the mentally retarded have had, and that changes in service forms have been a natural consequence of changes in role and associated attitudes. (NOU 1973:25, p. 48)

This is followed by a matrix showing role perceptions, associated societal reactions, and resultant care models.

The same year, a Norwegian government report, *Integration and the Aged*, focused very heavily on the importance of social roles, especially for older people who leave their roles as worker and breadwinner. This paper also stated that "the value assigned to the characteristic of age will affect older people's status and position" and that "age is increasingly viewed as a negative characteristic" (NOU 1973:60, p. 9). This report refers to the work of Rosow that three dimensions are important for social integration: "society's values, formal and informal group memberships, and social roles."

Although a number of Scandinavian writers have since attributed Wolfensberger with making major contributions to the theoretical dimensions of Normalization, there exist no further translations of his writings in any Scandinavian language. Particularly in the Swedish literature one finds a sweeping dismissal of the Wolfensberger formulations, although it is clear the authors have either not read or perhaps not understood the literature. The main thread of critique is that Wolfensberger has reduced Normalization to individual-fixing and does not address societal issues. This is often also considered to be "typically American," which has added to the general dismissal and disinterest.

6 IMPORT OF THEORY AND TRAINING TO NORWAY

By the late 1980s, Norway had several major societal reforms under way, with Normalization stated as the guiding principle. Some of the central political decisions were the 1988 law requiring closure of the centralized mental retardation facilities, a school reform replacing segregated special education with integration in local public schools for everyone, a decentralization of service provision in mental health and mental retardation to the local (*kommune*) level, and a "normalizing" of residential care for older persons and those in centralized rehabilitation facilities. All of this was happening with no consensus at any level about the content or implications of Normalization, yet with a great eagerness to "do" it and with a number of social reforms already in full swing.

Norwegian government reports from 1989 stressed the importance of "knowledge and competence in Normalization" (St. Meld. 47:89-90). Prior to this time no organized training or education in Normalization had been available in any Scandinavian country, outside of a few short seminars or speeches. In 1990 the Norwegian Ministry of Social and Health Services recognized this as an important priority and initiated a national training effort to be initially financed for 2 years. Although the most pressing need was in the field of mental retardation, where a comprehensive reform was under way, the Ministry emphasized that competency in Normalization was relevant for other "groups in society at risk of being socially excluded" and that "Wolf Wolfensberger's work is of special interest in this regard."

This attempt represented a significant set of assumptions and understandings: (a) that social exclusion is set in focus, (b) that Normalization has applicability beyond the mental retardation field, (c) that Wolfensberger's work was worthy of attention, and (d) that training should be a part of social reform.

Three "known experts in Normalization" were invited to lead this training effort, two of whom had studied Wolfensberger's work in North America. Training was organized as three similar but independent efforts, one of which was known as the Social Role Valorization Project. Nearly 1,000 people have attended 3-day workshops in the last 3 years (1992 to 1994), and many have attended follow-up events on specific topics. Follow-up events have included 39 persons who have attended PASS (Wolfensberger & Glenn, 1975a; 1975b) or PASSING (Wolfensberger & Thomas, 1983) in other countries, a few who have attended other Training Institute events in other countries, and many who have attended events by Michael Kendrick in Wales and Norway in 1992. A number of books and reports have also been published, representing an important contribution to the Norwegian literature.

Norway remains the only Scandinavian country to have instituted formalized training in Normalization/ SRV, including events via the international network. Historians and researchers can assist us in answering the question "So what?"

7 NORMALIZATION AND SRV: ACTUAL IMPACTS

7.1 INSTITUTIONAL REFORM

One of Normalization's first impacts on service provision in Scandinavia was actually an expansion and extension of the institutional care system, and in all areas of life: residential, education, occupation, leisure, treatment, and special services.

In fact, the 1959 Danish legislation had established an independent system for mental retardation services. The oft-quoted phrase "as normal as possible" included life inside as well as outside institutions. In the first 15 years of the Danish reform, the number of people served in institutions doubled (Bank-Mikkelsen, 1967).

Birger Perlt from Denmark has described three phases of institutional reform that are equally applicable to developments in Sweden and Norway (Perlt, 1990; Tøssebro, 1992):
- the struggle for institutions
- the struggle within institutions
- the struggle against institutions.

Expansion of the institutional system was partly a response to the demand for services for people who previously had received little or nothing, but it was also influenced by the idea of separate environments for different normative daily and weekly activities. The result was an increase in number of residential places, but also additional buildings and services on the institutional grounds that had other functions, such as occupational areas and leisure activity buildings. This was true both within the field of mental retardation and mental health.

Norwegian government policy was recommending expansion of the existing mental retardation system as late as 1974 (St. Meld. 88:74-75), although an improvement of living conditions was a clearer rationale. Normalization provided rough guidelines through this entire institution-improvement phase of reform. Living quarters were "normalized": made more homelike, especially with regard to sleeping, eating, and personal hygiene areas. There was a greater emphasis placed on schooling, occupation, treatment, and social/leisure activities. Policy statements indicated both a belief in the capacity to learn and develop, that people should receive the help they needed, and that this would require a variety of settings, routines, and expertise. There was an associated massive increase in resource expenditure and staff training.

When institutional conditions were identified as unacceptable, the first interpretation was that they were also fixable. It was yet another conceptual leap to critique the institutional mode of service as degrading, unnecessary, and probably harmful. The ideology of Normalization provided a frame of reference to assist in this awareness. Today all three Scandinavian countries have clear policies on deinstitutionalization and decentralization of service supports to local levels. As late as 1987, about one-third of the approximately 17,000 mentally retarded people in Norway still lived in institutions, and nearly half of these in the large centralized institutions. In 1988 the Norwegian parliament mandated closure of this system. Mental health reform has shown a similar pattern, although slower in evolution.

7.2   NEARLY NORMATIVE HOUSING

Today, living conditions and especially housing standards are greatly improved for mentally retarded people in Scandinavia, and for most other previously neglected groups as well. According to plan, by 1995 all Norwegians with mental retardation will have their own home. In reality, many will live in group homes with an internal atmosphere that ranges from homelike to institutionlike, with lives still dominated by "home care" professionalism.

One can predict that Denmark may continue to have more examples of what can be interpreted by others as small segregated, congregated care homes. A partial explanation is that there exists a cultural analogue of communal living in the general population. Additionally, Denmark has long been a more pluralistic society than Sweden or Norway, and one hears such comments as "It is normal to be different in

Denmark." There is also a recognized tendency to encourage and cultivate subcultures in Denmark, often coupled with rhetoric about the right to choose to be different. There are some specific trends we can document in Norway that are related to the Normalization training effort. Segregated care models for older people have been most challenged in Norway in localities where Normalization training has occurred. Second, housing for people with special needs has often been unnecessarily dominated by the health sectors and professions, in terms of administrative routines and staffing patterns and competencies.

7.3   SCHOOLS FOR ALL

Segregated "special" schools are closed or being closed in Scandinavia, as part of the Nordic campaign of "schools for all." Local education authorities have the responsibility of implementation and provision. In Norway, this reform is going under the banner of "Normalization and integration." Actual results in all three countries thus far would best be classified as physical and administrative integration. The National Research Council in Norway has been funding a number of projects around the restructuring of special education in accordance with these goals since 1994.

7.4   EMPLOYMENT

More people with disabilities now have real jobs in integrated workplaces than before, and certainly day activity in general has become more work-oriented and more age-appropriate in all Scandinavian countries. The Scandinavian countries show variation in their national commitment to including people with disabilities in the workforce, which to some extent reflects variations in national values. The 1994 Swedish law gave unemployed mentally retarded adults the right to "day activity." The right to work may be most valued in Norway, and certainly admittedly least so in Denmark, where unemployment is higher in the general population but also less likely to be defined as problematic.

The Norwegian Department of Employment initiated a national effort of supported employment initiatives 2 years ago, an important step toward removing responsibility for day occupation from the health and social care sectors. Norway began offering intensive staff training in supported employment in 1994, including introductory modules on SRV for those who did not previously have such training. Another example is a book edited by two persons from the Department of Employment entitled *Arbeid med bistand* ("Supported Work"), with an introductory chapter on "Normalization and SRV as the ideological and theoretical basis for supported employment." Supported employment in Norway is seen as a responsibility of the Department of Employment, not that of Health and Social Services. However, most people with mental retardation and other impairments in Scandinavia are still without real jobs, tending to have worklike occupation in sheltered or segregated settings, without a real wage.

7.5   LEISURE AND CULTURAL

More so than in other countries, the provision of and support for cultural, leisure, and sport activities for everyone is seen as a responsibility of the public sectors in Scandinavia. And certainly more individuals with disabilities are now participating both to a greater extent and in a greater amount in such activities. Some segregated activities are still directly provided and encouraged by public and voluntary sectors. Other localities encourage the use of generic resources and activities, but often structure attendance and participation in larger-than-normative groupings, or at non-normative times of the day or week. However, some localities consciously support more use of ordinary community activities, clubs, teams, and associations.

One inspiring example from the Ålesund community in western Norway has the following objective: "That each citizen will, through their own usual leisure and cultural interests and activities, come into contact with people with disabilities and experience them participating in valued activities and social roles" (Svisdahl, 1994).

7.6   INDIVIDUALIZED SUPPORTS

The availability of individualized supports for participation in a variety of activities and settings in home communities and in society has been a central articulated aim of Normalization in all three Scandinavian countries, with some progress. Families receive more help at home than previously, and the options are increasingly flexible. A personal assistance model for physically disabled people is another example and has been much influenced by the international independent living movement. Most personal support arrangements are purchased, including many that have social integration as a purpose where other supports could be encouraged.

7.7   AUTONOMY

Both individuals and organized collectivities of disabled people and other oppressed groups have a greater voice in Scandinavian society than before. This includes being involved in decision making about one's own life and also in larger societal processes. These voices are also teaching society about oppression by the telling of personal and collective histories. This is a voice that is both more competent, more encouraged, and more listened to and acted upon by others. There is some evidence of related competency enhancement, such as workshops to assist individuals in understanding the different political platforms and how to vote in an election.

7.8   IMAGES, POSITIVE ROLE PERCEPTIONS, AND LANGUAGE CHANGE

There is overwhelming evidence of conscious language change, in terms of labeling and interactions. As with other countries and languages, one also sees examples of politically correct language games and/or language change instead of real change. But the general trends are well intentioned and mostly positive.

Particularly through Normalization/SRV training and its associated literature, more people and organizations in Norway have become aware of the power and dynamics of imagery, with resultant (and conscious) removal of much deviancy imagery and several creative attempts at positive alternatives.

7.9   ADMINISTRATIVE NORMALIZATION

Normalization has had a clear role in defining sector responsibility for groups previously managed under a total institution model. Responsibility for education, employment, housing, transportation, and so forth are becoming slowly redefined as not appropriate to the realm of health and social services. In Norway, introduction of the construct of the culturally valued analogue has been helpful, both in clarifying the appropriateness of service function, and sector responsibility.

7.10 IDENTIFYING NEED FOR STAFF DEVELOPMENT AND WORKER COMPETENCY

Normalization and SRV raise fundamental questions of what people need and have unveiled the need for many new staff competencies in many new settings. This has major implications for existing professional educations, competencies in the present workforce, and the general competencies of the "average citizen." In Norway we have a project looking at how (if possible) to build in more SRV in undergraduate and graduate education in all fields of public service. A major challenge here is to maintain a fidelity to the needs of societally devalued groups rather than strengthen the interests of professions or organizations.

7.11 FRAMEWORKS FOR SERVICE QUALITY

Normalization and SRV have had some clear and other less direct but visible impacts on questions of service relevance and quality. A number of frameworks and checklists have been developed to analyze, describe, and measure degree of quality in relation to Normalization. Many of these have their roots in the PASS instrument. In Norway, the constructs of culturally valued analogue and culturally valued means have proved helpful for comparative analysis and in identifying clearer pictures of positive and constructive alternatives.

7.12 TYPE OF RESEARCH QUESTIONS

Normalization and SRV have provided new perspectives to formulate research questions and perhaps especially to identify and measure progress in the area of social reform. Variations reflect how the different countries formulate the central tenets of Normalization, and also reflect dominant signs of their times. This is discussed in greater detail in chapter 20 by this author together with Mårten Söder and Jan Tøssebro.

7.13 DEBATE

If Normalization and SRV have had no other impact in the world, it has created a much-needed, ongoing and heated debate. It may even be that the lack of clarity around the concept has had a healthy (albeit unintentional) impact by stimulating a greater interest and a closer examination of what lies explicit and implicit in the various formulations and their often subtle yet extensive implications and possible consequences. Debates have brought into the public arena many critical questions about human needs, priorities, definitions of handicap and disability, the importance and meaning of compensation, what it means to be dependent on services, and what it means or could mean to serve. Research in Norway following the three training projects has documented a tendency for persons with Normalization/SRV training to be more able to identify with the individual person who needs support, rather than with other interests or perspectives such as professional or personal (Kristiansen, 1994; Ramsdal, 1994).

7.14 CHALLENGES TODAY

In Norway, there is a clear interest *in learning about Normalization and SRV*, coupled with an understanding that it is more difficult and personally challenging than previously thought. This is in contrast to Denmark, where one rarely hears Normalization mentioned.

The most basic *misunderstandings* still flourish, and several are particularly hazardous in today's society. Some of the more dominant and dangerous misconceptions about what is central to both Normalization and SRV include the following:

- equivalent to dismantling the institutional system, perhaps including the abolishment of all formal services, and relying on "natural supports."
- receiving (only) the "same as others," and neglecting to identify and meet people's specific individual needs.
- that label-removal is sufficient, especially if replaced with the bestowing of "citizenship" labels.
- to be "accepted as one is" (usually coupled with decreased commitments to positive

developmental assumptions and competency enhancement) in societies that in reality are less and less tolerant and accepting.

- equivalent to self-determination and legal entitlements, and that this will be sufficient for achieving needed societal changes.

In addition to understanding and attempting to correctly address these misunderstandings and perversions, it is also important to understand the dynamics that allow them to persist. A major problem in Scandinavia remains the coupling of Normalization to people with mental retardation, or as broad as "disabilities," preventing many from seeing other emerging patterns of societal devaluation.

The Scandinavian *welfare state* has at least two intrinsic structural problems, which are problematic in relation to Normalization and most certainly to SRV. The first is the result of what began as good intentions of Scandinavian welfare to guarantee economic security for everyone and to protect workers and jobs. Social security benefits are now presenting a barrier for many people with disabilities in the argument for real wages. Equally serious are the unions who protect the interests and rights of service workers, even when the relevance of a service is called into question. Communities dependent on institutions for their livelihood experience a recycling of institutions, requiring that new inmate populations be available. Also typical is staff-transfer from the (rejected) institutional system into community care, justified in part as job protection. This happens in spite of documented institution-culture-transfer with the personnel. SRV has been helpful for many in raising consciousness about the function of much of the service empire in shaping and maintaining structural societal devaluation, which is occurring these days in harder-to-decipher forms.

The second issue in a welfare state is that of responsibility. In a society where everyone has learned that the collective state has always provided, one continues to expect this provision to be the government's responsibility. These expectations include those of service workers, average citizens, and persons and families who need help and support. When the collective public state decentralizes its service structures, the issue of responsibility is highlighted. Betterment of living conditions in the material realm may be technically possible for a society to engineer, but the Normalization of social relationships requires something more. SRV assists many to recognize the limits of dependence on the public sector to both commit itself to solutions and to be able to provide them, and that expecting public supports and services to function obscures personal obligation. SRV includes a clear invitation to be called to decision in solidarity and alliance with those who are disadvantaged and oppressed, and to be personally engaged in the task.

REFERENCES

BANK-MIKKELSEN, N. E. (1967). Legislative aspects of mental retardation. International League of Societies for the Mentally Handicapped conference. Stockholm.

BANK-MIKKELSEN, N. E. (1969). A metropolitan area in Denmark: Copenhagen. In R. B. KUGEL & W. WOLFENSBERGER (Eds.), Changing patterns in residential services for the mentally retarded (pp. 227-254). Washington, DC: President's Committee on Mental Retardation.

BANK-MIKKELSEN, N. E. (1980). Denmark. In R. FLYNN & K. NITSCH (Eds.), Normalization, social integration, and community services (pp. 51-70). Baltimore: University Park Press.

Danmark: lov nr. 192 af 5. juni 1959: Om forsorgen for åndssvage og andre særlig svagtbegavede. Copenhagen.

GRUNEWALD, K. (Ed.). (1971). Manniskohantering på totale vårdsinstitutionar: från dehumanisering til normalisering. Natur och kultur. Stockholm.

GRUNEWALD, K. (Ed.). (1972). Menneskemanipulering på totalinstitutioner: fra dehumanisering til normalisering. Thaning & Appel. København.

KRISTIANSEN, K. (1994). Normalisering og endringsarbeid: sluttrapport til Sosialdepartementet. THH. Trondheim.

NIRJE, B. (1969). The Normalization principle and its human management implications. In R. B. KUGEL & W. WOLFENSBERGER (Eds.), *Changing patterns in residential services for the mentally retarded* (pp. 179-195). Washington, DC: President's Committee on Mental Retardation.

NOU 1973:25. Omsorg for psykisk utviklingshemmede: målsetting og retningslinjer Sosialdepartementet. Oslo.

NOU 1973:60. Eldres integrasjon. Sosialdepartementet. Oslo.

PERLT, B. (1990). "Fra lighet til frihed". PU-bladet. nr. 4. 8-12.

RAMSDAL, H. (1994). Iverksetting av normalisering: evaluering av kommunalt opplæringsprogram om normalisering. Sosial- og helsedepartementet. Oslo.

SANDVIN, J.T. (1993) "Fra særomsorg til særlig omsorg" in Visnes, T. (Ed.) Fra særomsorg til særlig omsorg. Universitetsforlaget. Oslo. pp. 61-93.

SFS 1967:94. Lag angående omsorger om vissa psykiskt utvecklingsstörda. Stockholm.

SJÖBERG, M. (1994). New rights for persons with functional impairments. *New Sweden, 402*, Swedish Institute.

St. Meld. 88:66-67. Om utviklingen av omsorgen for funksjonshemmede. Sosialdepartementet. Oslo.

St. Meld. 23:77-78. Funksjonshemmede i samfunnet. Sosialdepartementet. Oslo.

St. Meld. 67:86-87. Ansvar for tiltak og tenester for psykiske utviklingshemma. Sosialdepartementet. Oslo.

St. Meld. 47:89-90. Om gjennomføring av reformen for mennesker med psykisk utviklingshemming. Sosialdepartementet. Oslo.

STANGVIK, G. (1993). En kommune for alle. AHL-forskning. Alta.

SVISDAHL, M. (1994). Notat om kultur og fritidsaktiviteter. Ålesund kommune.

TØSSEBRO, J. (1992). Institusjonsliv i velferdstaten:

Levekår under HVPU. Ad Notum Gyldendal. Oslo.

WOLFENSBERGER, W. (1969). The origin and nature of our institutional models. In R. B. KUGEL & W. WOLFENSBERGER (Eds.), *Changing patterns in residential services for the mentally retarded* (pp. 59-171). Washington, DC: President's Committee on Mental Retardation.

WOLFENSBERGER, W. (1972). *The principle of Normalization in human services.* Toronto, ON: National Institute on Mental Retardation.

WOLFENSBERGER, W. (1992). *A brief introduction to Social Role Valorization as a high-order concept for structuring human services* (2nd ed., rev.). Syracuse, NY: Syracuse University, Training Institute for Human Service Planning, Leadership and Change Agentry.

WOLFENSBERGER, W., & GLENN, L. (1975a, reprinted 1978). *Program analysis of service systems (PASS): A method for the quantitative evaluation of human services: Vol. 1. Handbook* (3rd ed.). Toronto, ON: National Institute on Mental Retardation.

WOLFENSBERGER, W., & GLENN, L. (1975b, reprinted 1978). *Program analysis of service systems (PASS): A method for the quantitative evaluation of human services: Vol. 2. Field manual* (3rd ed.). Toronto, ON: National Institute on Mental Retardation.

WOLFENSBERGER, W., & THOMAS, S. (1983). *PASSING (Program analysis of service systems' implementation of Normalization goals): Normalization criteria and ratings manual* (2nd ed.). Toronto, ON: National Institute on Mental Retardation.

WOLFENSBERGER, W., & ZAUHA, H. (Eds.). (1973). *Citizen advocacy and protective services for the impaired and handicapped.* Toronto, ON: National Institute on Mental Retardation.

NOTE

The author remains responsible for all translations to English from Danish, Swedish, and Norwegian, unless otherwise indicated.

19

The origin of the Normalization principle in Sweden and its impact on legislation today

ANNA HOLLANDER

1 INTRODUCTION

In Scandinavia we can trace the origin of the Normalization principle back to the middle of the 20th century with the development of services for developmentally disabled persons. A government committee appointed in 1943 to investigate ways of making available means of employment and self-support developed a sociopolitical idea that became the guiding principle for their work. The idea was termed "the Normalization principle."

Thus, in Scandinavia, the Normalization principle expresses the sociopolitical proposition that the handicapped person has the right to participation in the broader society. It became a starting point for the development of services for handicapped persons that took place in the 1950s (Eriksson, 1985). Today, we can easily follow the tracks of this sociopolitical policy in a series of Acts of Parliament that have contributed to the realization of the Normalization principle from 1954, 1967, 1986, and 1994.

The Normalization principle as a sociopolitical concept and its consequences have been the subject of debate over the last 40 years. I believe that the Scandinavian concept has at times been thoroughly misused, which has led to discussions very foreign to the original formulations and intentions.

I will with this paper describe the background of the Swedish welfare state as the basis of the Normalization principle and show how the principle is applied today in special legislation and welfare policy to promote equality and participation for the disabled.

2 THE BASIS OF THE SWEDISH WELFARE STATE AS THE ORIGIN OF THE NORMALIZATION PRINCIPLE

Contrary to a frequently stated view, Sweden did not shape its modern welfare system as a reaction to the economic crisis of the 1930s (Flora, 1986; Alestalo & Kuhnle, 1984). Since 1932, when the first minority social democratic government was formed, the dominant political parties became gradually favorable for state intervention and an increasing public responsibility in social policy, but there were large disagreements between and within parties on what should be done and how (Baldwin, 1990; Marklund, 1988; 1992).

After 1945 there was consensus among the major political parties concerning the major state welfare reforms with the industrial trade union movement actively forcing the issue (Olsson, 1990). The beliefs in social solidarity and equality values became the basis for the new social welfare programs (Baldwin, 1990). Although social democrats and trade unionists particularly concentrated on welfare for the working class and white-collar workers, the commitment to support people outside the workforce was also strong (Olsson, 1990). Under a comprehensive social welfare system, marginal groups such as persons who are disabled, persons who are elderly, and children would receive quality service and support as a *right* and as a part of the provision for the overall welfare of the society. The Normalization principle thus developed during a period when discussions were taking place throughout society concerning the implementation of welfare policy. The ambition to create a welfare state required that society develop social and health services that would enable all citizens, even persons otherwise disabled, to live a good life. The Normalization principle was and continues to be an application of a philosophy of rights where the full benefits of citizenship are conferred upon all persons.

This perspective shows that the Normalization principle is not an invention—a nice man's idea—but an ideology that came out of a broadly based social consensus that had broad public support. However, the dominant parts of the welfare reforms were work-oriented and based on income compensation to the working population rather than cash payments to persons who were marginal because of poverty, unemployment, or disability (Ginsburg, 1992). Cash compensation for persons who are unemployed and relief for persons who are poor has played a decreasing role in social spending, while the costs for income transfers and labor market policies have increased constantly since 1945 (Marklund, 1992). This system is now undergoing change, and it is difficult to predict the future. But public support for the welfare system is still very strong in Sweden, and it seems that it will be difficult to destroy.

3 THE REALIZATION OF THE NORMALIZATION PRINCIPLE

During the 1960s the Normalization principle became a concept that, up to present day, has greatly influenced and characterized the work within the organizations responsible for services to the developmentally disabled in Sweden. This principle gained prominence during the period that led to the development of the 1967 Act for Services to the Mentally Retarded (Eriksson, 1985). As Nirje and Perrin have already pointed out, the Scandinavian version of the Normalization principle is the logical

extension of the welfare state's relationship to persons who are disabled. This view also implied a repudiation of institutional life and institutional systems of services. This version of the Normalization principle thereby expressed a sociopolitical position that starts with the right to participation in society.

Nirje has described the sort of life that should be possible for persons who are developmentally disabled. Nirje also places emphasis on self-determination. Both Perrin and Nirje have shown that it is the idea of self-determination that differentiates the Scandinavian model of Normalization from Wolfensberger's. Accepting individuals as they are, acknowledging differences, and providing opportunities and resources for personal growth based on individual preference eliminates some of the serious consequences of third-party decision making. The concept of Normalization is complex and in some senses contradictory. Facilitating and realizing participation and equality for persons with functional impairments must, in the full sense of these terms, involve all of society, including those who have no personal experience of functional impairments. One might suggest that implementing Normalization is a critical stage in the process of deepening democracy.

The universal social security system as it developed created a specific role for individual social services such as social assistance and special services for persons who are handicapped. Intervention by the state in these areas is seen as a recognition of structural tensions in modern society that are not always conducive to meeting the needs of the individual, and not because of abnormality or charity. Social security has lessened the role of stigma in connection with extra services based on need. This model, not only in theory but also in practice, was able to minimize the numbers of persons who have had to claim individually means-tested or needs-tested services.

Today the process of reform is guided by the principles of self-determination, availability, participation, and continuity. These principles emanate from the thesis of universal human equality (SOU, 1992:52, p. 8). The Normalization principle has more or less been replaced by the principle of self-determination. However, it is only to a minor extent that the general aspects of self-determination and the other above principles have been the subject of deliberations and positive action.

From the point of view of individuals with special needs, the Swedish model contains both positive and negative aspects. As a result of the efficient coverage of social security and relatively generous benefits, most individuals can rely on receiving the basics for daily living. However, the monolithic character of the system gives individuals very few alternatives, especially in those parts of the service system that are focused on services for people with special needs. The focus today is therefore to strengthen opportunities for independence and free choice for persons with severe disabilities.

4 LEGISLATION FOR SUPPORT AND SERVICES FOR PERSONS WITH CERTAIN DISABILITIES

Sweden is very much a society governed by law. Legislation continues to be used to promote welfare. During the last 20 years, several changes have taken place in the ways that support services are delivered. The emphasis on self-determination gives persons with disabilities opportunities to participate in society. This partly depends on how service providers succeed in expressing the intentions of their self-determined clients. With the proliferation of legislation, from the perspective of the individuals who are disabled, it can be increasingly difficult to know about their legal rights (Hollander, 1993).

In order to improve the possibilities for persons with disabilities to enjoy the basic opportunities of social participation, new legal rights are defined in three new pieces of legislation: the Act on Supports and Services for Persons With Certain Disabilities (LSS); the Social Services Act (SOL), which places certain obligations on service providers; and the Health and Medical Services Act (HSL). These changes are designed to develop and guarantee general accessibility and coverage for every social sector, with regard to matters affecting persons who are disabled. The challenge will be to find a balance between individualized and generalized measures that reflect a holistic view and are appropriate to the needs of persons who are disabled.

As a logical result of the definition of disability being framed in terms of the relationship between a person and the environment, Sweden abolished certain specific pieces of legislation that proclaimed the special rights of persons with specific disabilities. Thus people with developmental disabilities and other people with severe disabilities should be treated the same as other citizens, even in the legal system. In accordance with efforts to integrate the various issues concerning the disabled, special sections have instead been inserted into other laws such as the Social Services Act, the Education Act, the Work Environment Act, and so on.

Today we still find exceptions to this general rule of not having specific legislation for special groups of people (Hollander, 1993). The Act on Special Services for Developmentally Disabled Persons was replaced in 1994 by the Special Act on Supports and Services for Persons With Certain Disabilities. The rationale for such special legislation is that people with severe disabilities need extra support and personal services because of their disabilities and because their living conditions are affected by their disabilities. In a special survey report, the Commission on Policies for the Disabled in Sweden showed that severely disabled persons were disadvantaged in many respects and had not been able to share, on the same terms as other members of the community, the growth of national prosperity. The new legislation proposes to give people with severe disabilities legal rights to extra services and supports to be able to live a normal life together with other people in society. The services covered by this new legislation are: counseling; other kinds of professional support; personal assistance; short stays away from home mainly as respite to relieve relatives otherwise responsible for care; daily activities (but not work) in day centers or other kinds of occupations; specially designed housing, leisure, recreation; and so on.

A number of people have used the law to demand as their right the support and services they require from public authorities. They have used the system of appeal, which is seen as a very important instrument for individuals to confront the power of public authorities.

The use of judicial review has also been successful. The courts are protecting the legal rights to services for persons with disabilities. However, the rule of law does not seem to hold the same importance for some public authorities where a number of county councils have refused to execute court decisions. The role of legislation is ambiguous as a means of creating welfare, equality, and self-determination for people with severe disabilities. Laws seem to cover up underlying disagreements as to what specific goals ought to be pursued. The interpretation of the law makes it obvious for many people who are disabled that the right to services is not always a question of self-determination. Often, it is a question of disability, gender, class, and power.

The main problem we face in Sweden and, I think, in most other countries in the world is that the interests of disabled people are not given priority in the development of society. We must not only question the interpretation of concepts such as "normal" and "Normalization," but also "rights" and "rights thinking." There is no doubt that in Sweden, the use of rights legislation has increased the access of disabled persons to the social services they need and that make their lives easier. But rights legislation has not meant more influence and participation in society. Moreover, disabled persons share this experience with other groups of citizens who do not have disabilities, such as women, children, refugees, and elderly persons. At the heart of this problem, we find questions of power, gender, and social relations between citizens. Thus, what must be done to change society in order to establish social justice for all? The values and normative structures in rights legislation can provide a vehicle for such change.

REFERENCES

ALESTALO, M., & KUHNLE, S. (1984). *The Scandinavian route*. Research Report No. 31. Helsinki: University of Helsinki.

BALDWIN, P. (1990). *The politics of social solidarity*. Cambridge UK: Cambridge University Press.

DALLEY, G. (1993). Social welfare ideologies and Normalisation: Links and conflicts. In H. BROWN & H. SMITH (Eds.), *Normalisation: A reader for the nineties*. London: Routledge.

ERIKSSON, K. (1985). *The principle of Normalization: History and experience in Scandinavian countries*. Uppsala, Sweden: Uppsala University, Centre for Handicap Research.

FLORA, P. (1986). *Growth to limits: The Western European welfare state since World War II, 1. Sweden, Norway, Finland, Denmark*. Berlin: de Gruyer.

GINSBURG, N. (1992). *Division of welfare*. London: Sage.

HOLLANDER, A. (1993). Rights to special services for people with developmental disabilities in Sweden. *Scandinavian Journal of Social Welfare, 2*, 63-68.

MARKLUND, S. (1988). Welfare state policies in the tripolar class model of Scandinavia. *Politics and Society, 16*, 469-485.

MARKLUND, S. (1992). The decomposition of social policy in Sweden. *Scandinavian Journal of Social Welfare, 1* (1), 2-11.

OLSSON, S. E. (1990). *Social policy and welfare state in Sweden*. Lund: Arkiv.

SOU 1992:52. *A society for all*. Final report of the 1989 Commission on Policies for the Disabled. Stockholm.

WEST, S. (1992). *Socio-political values and the principle of Normalization*. Final Paper. Atkinson College Social Work.

20

Social integration in a welfare state: Research from Norway and Sweden

KRISTJANA KRISTIANSEN, MÅRTEN SÖDER, AND JAN TØSSEBRO

1 INTRODUCTION

This chapter is concerned with research from Norway and Sweden about persons with developmental impairments and the services they receive. Most research has been related to national reform efforts, particularly in the field of mental retardation, and attempts to evaluate these reforms. Research has, however, not been limited to narrow evaluative questions, but also more fundamental ones about past and present aspirations and patterns, nature of social relations and welfare, and dilemmas in determining appropriate research paradigms, strategies, and criteria for measurement.

Patterns of human service in Norway and Sweden resemble past developments and current trends in many other European countries, as well as in North America. Large-scale, centralized institutions for people with mental retardation were built to a growing extent during the first 6 decades of this century, although at different times and different paces in the two countries. This was an era dominated by containment and control, categorization, centralization, and institutionalization, patterns already in place in countries such as France and England, as well as in the field of mental health in Scandinavia, where state asylums were established in the late 1800s. Initial reform efforts in the 1960s and 1970s were basically aimed at improving the institutional-based system, whereas current trends are in opposite directions: physical and social integration instead of segregation; supports for greater personal autonomy instead of control by others, individualized forms of support instead of categorical and congregative responses; supports in own community settings instead of in institutions; and a decentralization of responsibility and service provision to local levels.

Specific examples include the phasing out of segregated "special" schools to be replaced by supported education within the generic public school system, and the dismantling of long-stay residential institutions to be replaced by supports for participation in one's own community, including a home of one's own. Also similar to many other countries, these changes in Norway and Sweden have been most dramatic in the field of mental retardation, with mental health reforms initially evolving more slowly and quietly.

These changes have been accompanied by ideologically charged phrases such as normalization, integration, equality, participation, self-determination, solidarity, and "one society for all." As official social policy goals these phrases have been important symbolic slogans, more than clear guidelines for practical implementation. Mostly what one has witnessed thus far is a mixed-improvement movement. Living conditions for many individuals and groups previously neglected appear to be improving. More individuals are now participating in a greater variety of activities in their home communities, in roles such as homeowner, classmate, wage-earner, churchgoer, voter, club member. One is also increasingly aware that while physical and organizational integration have vastly improved, many individuals remain socially isolated and feel lonely, and that as improvement in living conditions occurs, new challenges and dilemmas are revealed. All of this requires that researchers continually ask new questions, both about the type of questions being asked and the ways that questions can and should be answered.

Normalization and integration have continued to be central social policy objectives in Norway and Sweden for more than 25 years. While lack of clarity and consensus as to the specific content of these ideas has been problematic from an implementation perspective, the same lack of clarity has encouraged debate and analysis, and has contributed to subsequent concept evolution. Social research (sociological, psychological, educational) in both Norway and Sweden has been greatly stimulated by reform effort aimed at these dual goals of normalization and integration. The intention of this chapter is to provide an overview of that research as well as to call attention to some features that are rather unique in an international perspective. One section of this chapter reviews two generations of research about integration, showing how research questions have changed: from a focus on the relation between physical and social integration to questions about the nature of social relationships and everyday life, as well as broader questions about ideologies, their development, and societal role and function. The next section presents some approaches and dilemmas concerning research surveys on living conditions, their relation to the Scandinavian welfare state ideology, as well as some dilemmas in using these surveys as measures. The final section highlights several aspects of the central dilemma: the tension between paternalism and individualism. One might even say that this dilemma is at the heart of debates about the welfare state in general, and in any case is a recurrent dilemma in social policy debates.

Both Norway and Sweden have long been described as model welfare states, and much of what is discussed in this chapter is presented within this context of the Nordic welfare state. If we understand the original meaning of "wel-fare" as "traveling well and safely through the journey of life," it becomes something we would wish for ourselves and those we care about. The term *welfare* has positive connotations in the Nordic countries, compared to its usage in other languages and cultures.

From a distance, Norway and Sweden may appear similar, but there are also many differences, some of which sometimes seem important and enduring. Some of these differences may become more apparent in the future, as Sweden joins the European Union and Norway does not. Although this chapter has as its central focus the

circumstances for people with mental retardation in these two countries, the issues and dilemmas raised are intended for a wider readership, both in the interests of other groups at risk of social exclusion and within other societal contexts.

2 FIRST GENERATION OF RESEARCH ON INTEGRATION: WHAT HAPPENS WHEN PEOPLE ARE INTEGRATED?

The integration of persons with mental retardation has been ambitious as a political goal and diffuse as a conceptual vision. Attempts to evaluate the extent to which integration has occurred, and to interpret its results, have reflected this lack of clarity.

In Sweden, two "generations of research" can be identified, the first of which refers to research examining and evaluating the first attempts at integration. Several such projects were started in Sweden in the early 1970s. Some of them studied integration in preschool and school. Others were focused on housing, looking at the results of moving persons from institutions into other types of sheltered accommodation such as group homes. Some "first generation" research is evident in Norway, although primarily in the field of education, encompassing studies about the effects of integrated schools, and primarily carried out by special educators.

The goal of integration contained two basic lines of argument: an ideological or political-ethical one, and an empirical or more instrumental one. Each of these two directions has different implications for research.

The goal of integration, for example, could be argued from an ideological standpoint: that integration in itself is "right" and "good." The institutional service model, in particular, was interpreted as a violation of basic values and rights. Segregation in institutions included control over where one lived, with whom, and under what circumstances. It was seen to violate basic values of freedom, choice, equality, and opportunity. In this perspective, the alternatives to institutions such as "integration" were interpreted as "good" because of accordance with these basic values. Whether to integrate or not is then a political question, or one of societal consensus, rather than a research question. The role of research is not to answer whether this is a right or wrong decision, but rather to describe and measure the progress of what is already concluded to be "right," to measure the degree to which social policy missions are being implemented.

The second line of argument represents a more strategical or instrumental view: One could also argue that integration is "good" because of its positive effects for the individual person, by promoting personal development. In the field of mental retardation, one asked questions reflecting these assumptions, such as whether a person's self-image improved, whether learning and general adaptive development occurred more rapidly in integrated contexts, and so on. In other words, research questions attempted to describe and analyze whether or not community integration had had positive or negative effects on the individual person's development. From this perspective, integration has to, so to speak, prove itself. Butterfield has called deinstitutionalization and integration "natural experiments" (1987), and the role of research is to answer the question whether life in community has positive or negative effects on different aspects of the individual. Living arrangements are thus seen as independent variables whose effects on the person with mental retardation could and should be scientifically assessed.

Both the ideological and the instrumental dimensions were present in the Scandinavian debate, although the distinction between them was not explicitly stated. From an international perspective, it is probably safe to say that the dominant argument in Scandinavia was ideological in nature: integration as "good in itself." This is also mirrored in the questions asked by early research. Its main focus was on how far the goals of social integration had been reached, not on its effects on personal development. In an international comparison, the absence of research on—most notably—adaptive behavior is striking.

The results of this first generation of evaluative research show one major pattern: Whether in preschool (Hill & Rabe, 1987), school (Söder, 1978; Dalen, 1977; Asmervik, 1976), or housing (Söder, 1970; Kebbon et al., 1981), results indicated that the goals of social integration had not been fulfilled. In analyzing this outcome, a distinction was often made between different forms or aspects of integration: physical, functional, social, and societal (Söder, 1970). Physical integration referred to the mere "physical mixing" of disabled with nondisabled persons. Functional integration referred to the extent to which disabled and nondisabled persons were using the same functions and resources in the environment. Social integration referred to social relationships and feelings of belonging with others, regardless of disability. Societal integration referred to the extent to which rights and living conditions were the same for disabled persons as compared to nondisabled persons. Most research indicated that the physical placement of persons with developmental disabilities was to varying degrees connected to functional integration. The dimensions of functional integration could perhaps also be called level of participation. It concerned, for example, the degree to which pupils in school were sharing the same facilities and participating in the same activities as nondisabled pupils, the degree to which persons living in group homes were using generic amenities and facilities in their society (using ordinary buses, shopping in stores, visiting cinemas and theaters). Although the degree of such functional integration, or participation, was shown to vary, it was sometimes concluded that the level was in any case greater than in institutions. At the time, this was not a trivial result, as deinstitutionalization was still a "hot" issue.

The degree of social integration was also shown to vary, although at the lower end of a scale; generally, different studies showed that social relations between the "integrated" person with disabled and nondisabled peers/neighbors were not very frequent or well developed. In some studies of housing integration, social isolation was pointed out as a major problem.

The interpretation and practical conclusions drawn from these findings varied. Some persons argued that physical integration was in itself positive, creating natural learning situations for social and adaptive behavior and, by supporting people with disabilities to be part of the life experience of others, could in the long run help change attitudes and prepare the grounds for social integration. Others maintained that integration was only meaningful to the extent that it meant being socially included, and that physical integration was interpreted only as a first step to that end. Or, as Gustavsson (1992) put it, physical integration meant making society accessible for disabled persons.

Quite another, perhaps more important, question was how the advantages and disadvantages in society should be dealt with (Gustavsson, 1992). One practical conclusion drawn from this perspective argued for greater consciousness among staff, to raise the ambition and conscious purpose from mere physical integration toward social integration, and some projects were developed where ways of working in group homes and schools were focused as a way of facilitating the accomplishment of that goal.

The first generation of research was thus focused on issues about social relations to nondisabled persons as the indicator of the extent to which the goals had been met. During the 1980s the scope of research interest broadened. One project led by Sonnander and Nilsson-Embro (1984) described and measured life circumstances for groups with impairments, using a number of "quality of life" indicators. As rated by the interviewers, persons with developmental disabilities scored below the mean on a 5-point scale, while populations categorized as nondisabled and those with physical disabilities received higher ratings. The study also showed that developmentally disabled persons had access to more activities than they made use of, and that their social networks were poorly developed and rarely of their own choosing. Interviewers also typically described those interviewed with developmental disabilities as having a negative self-image. Asked about their own satisfaction with different spheres of their lives, however, the majority of those interviewed expressed satisfaction. The only indicator with a positive correlation between assigned (by others) and self-reported ratings was in the area of leisure-time activities.

This project provided new insights and dilemmas, and created what could later be called a "bridge" over to a second (and ongoing) generation of research.

3 SECOND GENERATION OF INTEGRATION RESEARCH: BROADENING THE PERSPECTIVE

Present-day research studies and projects in Sweden more or less grew out of the results of the earlier first generation of research. Present studies in Norway are more the result of increased research allocations earmarked to evaluate the effects of recent reform efforts, including the comprehensive reorganization of mental retardation services.

Three types of research can be distinguished: research on social relations, research on everyday life experiences, and historical studies about development of ideologies and service practices. To a certain extent, each of these areas has its counterpart in international research. A fourth area of research in Norway and Sweden is the use of living conditions surveys as a method to evaluate reforms. This

tradition is—as far as we know—unique to Scandinavia, and will therefore be discussed in greater depth in section 4 of this chapter. It should also be noted that the following three-part classification is not intended to be comprehensive, but is rather an attempt to describe major patterns, which then excludes some important contributions. This would include Stangvik's important work in adaptation of the normalization principle (1987) to a local context, and his efforts to make this a practical tool (1994), and an ongoing related study by Kristiansen (1994).

3.1 SOCIAL RELATIONS

The first generation of research led to more basic questions about social relations. How did social relationships become established, especially between disabled persons and their nondisabled peers? What were the social experiences of all concerned? Attention was directed to environmental, interpersonal, and personal factors that invited and facilitated social integration. Gustavsson (1992) has attempted theoretically to identify conditions for the development of social integration, using the classical gemeinschaft and gesellschaft dichotomy (Tönnies, 1963), in order to specify the typical conditions of social relations in modern, urban societies. The conditions for social integration are dependent upon the fact that social relations are to an increasing extent a reflection of personal preference and choice. This "micro-social-pluralism" manifests itself as a growing individualism, where persons with less-valued traits tend to be rejected. Gustavsson argues this as a key to understanding why "integration reforms" have not been as successful as hoped for. They have been built on a rather nostalgic (naive?) view of a stable and tight social network—gemeinschaft—which has little basis in modern societies (Gustavsson, 1992).

This insight does not necessarily mean that integration is impossible, but only more unlikely and/or difficult to achieve. One example that illustrates this is an empirical study of social processes in a housing block in a midsized Swedish city. Nilsson (1993) carried out a longitudinal study on this housing block, which had been redesigned to facilitate social integration of older people, as well as those with physical and mental disabilities. Her results describe a waning enthusiasm after the first few years, coupled with small changes—less engagement in the common affairs by nondisabled tenants, greater numbers of disabled persons being placed there, more structured segregative leisure-time activities offered—all of which tended to accumulate to create what was recognized and described as patterns of segregation. By describing and making these changes visible, and a subject of discussion, the trend was reversed. Today the block is relatively well-functioning in terms of social integration. Nilsson points to three characteristics that have been important to create and maintain this state: conscious physical planning that creates natural informal meeting places, a well-composed range of leisure-time activities capable of integrating all tenants, and the presence of informal voluntary leadership who personally engage themselves in the everyday lives of people living there. With reference to the Tönnies dichotomy, Nilsson characterizes the social life in the block as "Gesellschaft with some distinct features of Gemeinschaft" (p. 158).

These examples illustrate the change in emphasis from evaluative questions about social relations and toward a deeper probing into the nature of social relations, and the nature of segregative as well as integrative societal processes.

3.2   STUDIES OF EVERYDAY LIFE

One criticism of the early integration studies has been that they centered too much on a particular kind of social relation: spontaneous, voluntary friendship relations between disabled and nondisabled persons. Often such freely given, mutually rewarding relationships were seen as the criterion for judging successful social integration, disregarding the fact that other forms of social relationships can be close and rewarding, as well as important facilitators of social integration (see, for example, Tøssebro, 1992a). There has been a tendency (albeit often implicit) that relationships with family, staff, or others with impairments are "not social integration." The question of what constitutes "good social integration" has come increasingly into the spotlight as physical integration of persons with severe impairments has progressed.

There has thus been a growing interest in studying the everyday life experiences of persons with disabilities. These studies are not as much focused on social relationships alone, but attempt to capture the total life experiences of persons before, during, and after the deinstitutionalization process, often using qualitative methods.

One example is a longitudinal ethnographic study of about 30 persons with severe mental retardation moving from an institution to group homes. Anchored in their own experiences, several themes have thus far been identified as critical, such as autonomy and the importance of communication (Jeppsson, 1989). A corresponding example from Norway is a project where 5 persons moving out of institutions are being followed. In addition to an ethnographic descriptive approach, anthropologist Sundet is attempting to identify the social meanings of what is being experienced, including the effect of different kinds of rationales as determinants on the lives of people outside the institution (Sundet, 1993). These studies disclose that personal choice and influence are seen to be severely limited in daily life. This pattern is confirmed by Jarhag's (1993) study of severely impaired people living in group homes, where programmatic routines leave very few margins for residents to make decisions according to their own preferences. Sundet has described much of this pattern as a "cultural lag": The routines that dominated institutional life are transferred when the organizational frame is changed (Sundet, 1993). Wuttudal's recent work expands this in her studies on support workers in residential services, and identifies how the content and cultural meaning of "home" is often "invaded" by the worker's style of intervention and organizational workplace culture (1994).

Söder, Barron, and Nilsson (1990) studied the life situations of 60 persons with different severe disabilities and identified the following obstacles to personal autonomy and influence: bureaucratic forms of organization, bureaucratic rules, professionalism, and stereotypes. It is worth noting that these obstacles are the same as the general characteristics of the welfare state, which are currently the target of neoliberal criticism. On one hand, if such criticisms are valid, they may be as much, if not more so, for persons with severe impairments who would be more likely to need and/or be dependent on public welfare services. But it also indicates that the interest in autonomy, influence, and self-determination is in alignment with the more general criticism of the welfare state. This could also be interpreted as an extension of "new individualism" into the disability field, as part of a more universal shift away from collectivism and societally defined norms for decency and toward a faith in the individual's personal freedom of choice and subjective satisfaction.

Compared to other countries, the use of the "quality of life" concept to capture the everyday life situation has been very minimal and attempts to construct standardized measures for quality of life nearly nonexistent, with the exception of the aforementioned study. One reason is the trust in standard-of-living surveys to cover the essential areas, and to do so in ways that are more objective (than subjective) and collective (rather than individualistic). Additionally, the "quality of life" concept has been criticized because of its linkage with discussions on right to treatment, euthanasia, and abortion, as well as in the field of health economics, where concepts such as "quality adjusted remaining lifetime" are used to determine the presumed benefit of services (Söder, 1991; Kirkebæk, 1991; Kristiansen, 1993).

3.3 DISCURSIVE ANALYSIS OF IDEOLOGY

A third category of the current generation of integration research are attempts to examine ideologies in broader historical and societal contexts. Of special interest are studies seeking to understand the roots of idea systems, such as normalization and integration, in relation to the emergence of the welfare state. One explicit underlying assumption is that one can better understand society, particularly modernization and the development of the welfare state, by identifying the patterns of experience for marginalized groups. Ericsson (1992) has argued that some basic idea of normalization (including use of the term itself) is present in public documents from the 1940s, used by a committee investigating the future direction of labor market training for physically impaired persons. This is one of many signs that normalization has developed continually alongside the Scandinavian welfare ideology, with heightened interest after World War II. Sandvin (1994) has recently begun to study the developments of social policy in terms of phases of differentiation (specialization, categorical segregation) and de-differentiation. De-differentiation and decentralization are tempting trends today in an era when bureaucratic structures are seen as top-heavy and expensive. This is further fueled by the strong belief by some in local social networks, and the hope that generic systems can and will develop the capacity to deal with all kinds of unique "special" problems.

In an attempt to explain past and current ideological shifts, Söder has hypothesized a basic ambivalence in value structures (1992). He describes historical shifts as resulting from a mismatch between ideologies that have evolved from concrete problems, which then become incompatible and unable to resolve the new problems created. When, for example, normalization and integration are formulated as responses to the problem of segregation, they become obsolete constructs in relation to the problems many people with disabilities face today, who have been described (albeit erroneously) as "integrated" and in "normalized" settings.

Discursive historical analysis has grown out of the previously mentioned interest in understanding current thought and practice in a broader sociohistorical perspective. Such research questions may seem quite removed from the original evaluative questions concerning degree and type of integration. But they can also be seen as a natural and more in-depth continuation of the questions and results of "first generation" research in the field, as part of a search to understand why and how integration became an issue in the first place.

3.4 NEW REALITY, NEW RESEARCH QUESTIONS

There are several reasons for the shift of emphasis between what have above been referred to as first- and second-generation research, three of which deserve to be mentioned in this context.

First, many would argue that integration has become a relatively noncontroversial issue in Sweden and Norway. The pressure on researchers to evaluate certain conditions in order to legitimate the need for comprehensive reform is no longer as strong as it was in the early 1970s. Debates "for or against" integration are fewer, replaced by questions and challenges about practical strategies and consequences.

Second, earlier-held expectations by some that physical integration would more or less lead to social integration began to wane with increasing attempts to integrate people with more complex and severe disabilities. Instead, comparatively more interest has been given to questions about which forms of social relationships are possible and desirable for severely disabled persons, and also looking more broadly at total life experience.

Third, in the first generation of research in Sweden, researchers were often contracted directly by national boards or a county council, often disconnected from research and academic communities. Today in Sweden and Norway, there is more conscious effort to foster disability research within centers of academia. This may account for the breadth and depth of the questions being asked, and also may contribute to a greater sensitivity to the "fashion" effects of respective disciplines, since some research developments can be understood as reflecting larger trends within such fields as sociology, anthropology, and psychology.

4 LIVING CONDITIONS AND THE WELFARE STATE

The theme of living conditions has always had a central place in discussions of the welfare state in Scandinavia, both as a main objective of governmental programs and also as a focus for research efforts. This has long been true for the population in general, and more recently also for people with disabilities. When the welfare state is seen to have a role in ensuring better living conditions for certain disadvantaged groups, a number of ideological questions begin to appear. This section is an attempt to highlight and discuss some of these questions and dilemmas, in relation to current research approaches. Questions such as collective responsibility and/or individual choice also lie at the heart of today's most heated debates in human services and critiques of normalization, and thus deserve this lengthier discussion.

4.1   USE OF SURVEYS

Scandinavian research has a long-established tradition of using standardized surveys to monitor the major areas of living conditions, such as housing, occupation, earnings, health, leisure and recreation, social network, and property ownership. In addition to documenting patterns of change in general, a central purpose of these surveys has been to identify and monitor patterns of difference and inequality among populations and groups. These surveys have been providing input into the sociopolitical agenda for over 20 years and are institutionalized in Norway and Sweden as ongoing public sector activities at the national level. Since the 1970s, these surveys have been carried out on samples of the general nondisabled population.

Until recently, however, the use of living conditions surveys to reveal patterns of inadequacy and inequality has been rare within disability research and unheard of in the field of mental retardation. Currently a number of larger-scale, nationally financed evaluations using a living conditions survey approach are under way in both Norway and Sweden, including inter-Nordic comparison (Tøssebro, 1988, 1992a; Kebbon , 1992; Tideman, 1992; Åkerström, 1993).

4.2   BETTER OR GOOD ENOUGH?

The current studies are basically evaluative in nature and purpose, intended to measure current reform efforts and impacts. The first question asked is fairly straightforward: Are living conditions for people with mental retardation improving? This research question suggests use of a pre- and post-test design, comparing living conditions "before" and "after" implementation of a reform. The question of "improvement," however, is somewhat anemic today, since living conditions for mentally retarded people have been gradually improving in Norway and Sweden for the past 25 years, and the new wave of reforms is intended to be something more (or different) than a mere continuation of an existing trajectory.

In Norway, for example, the service system was to be changed because it was judged to be not good enough according to sociopolitical standards. According to a major public committee report, living conditions for people with mental retardation were described as "humanly, socially, and culturally unacceptable" (NOU, 1985, p. 12). This critique demands that researchers ask a different question: not Are living conditions improving?, but rather How much improvement is "good enough" to be deemed acceptable? In order to discern or discuss this, it is necessary to have data for comparison, as in, What is life like for other people of the same age in this locality? The use of the living conditions surveys appears to easily meet this need for comparative data.

4.3   COMPARATIVE STUDIES: WHY NOW?

There is reason to ask why such comparative studies appear now, and also possibly why only in Scandinavia. One simple explanation is that the tradition of living conditions surveys already exists and is well-established as a public sector function. Second, since one of the major explicitly stated objectives in the present reforms is to improve living conditions, the use of such surveys to assess change is a logical choice of approach, especially given the existence of the method.

At a less obvious level, certain ideas embodied in the Scandinavian welfare state are important in this discussion. In one sense, the welfare state is a package of programs enabling and supporting the basic welfare of its citizenry. But there is another, larger (and somewhat more elusive) idea incorporated in the numerous changes in public sector tasks and responsibilities in many Western countries after World War II. British sociopolitical scientist Marshall called this the emergence of "social citizenship" (1950), whereas recent studies about welfare states frequently use the concept of "decency" (Mohan, 1988; Esping-Andersen, 1990; Bryson, 1992; Mishra, 1990). The underlying belief is that everyone is entitled to decent living conditions, not because of one's labor-market value, but because of one's citizenship status. In addition, the decency principle contains a public dimension: the notion of public responsibility that living conditions for all citizens should pass as decent according to collectively agreed upon (but not necessarily explicit) standards.

Further, there is consensus in Scandinavia that general living conditions measures are considered to somehow be indicators of "the good life." As in other societies, however, one does hear arguments against this such as "different people value different things" or that "the good life is a personal, subjective experience." Scandinavian sociology provides three counterarguments, each one of which anchors the objective measures in factors important enough to cut through individual/subjective variation, at least in terms of influencing social policy. Briefly, these three strategies are:

1. The *consensus-based* perspective (Johanssen, 1970), which suggests that while agreement on the good life may be difficult or impossible, most people in a society could probably agree to a reasonable degree what constitutes poor or unacceptable conditions, and that such consensus is sufficient for constructing central elements in social policy.

2. The second strategy has its foundation in *resources/exchange* theory, which argues that some measures of living conditions, such as earnings, wealth, social resources, and employment, are not ends in themselves, but rather are resources to obtain or achieve what one wants. With reference to social policy, the resources one can mobilize to fulfill one's choices are more important than the personal tastes involved in actual preferences (NOU, 1976).

3. The *needs-based* and Maslow-inspired strategy, which argues that certain broad dimensions of welfare are anchored in basic human needs (Allhardt, 1975, 1976).

The point is not whether these strategies are right or not, but rather that all of them (most explicitly the consensus perspective) give great attention to social political relevance. None of the three strategies would define a dissatisfied millionaire worse off (or more eligible for public support) than a poor, homeless, undernourished person who was reporting contentment. The conceptual labyrinth of "the good life" is simplified by a political focus. The issue is not to illuminate or unravel the philosophical complexities of defining the good life, but rather to understand the public duty and responsibility with regard to access to, and distribution of, the good life.

4.4 COMPARATIVE STUDIES: WHY NOT BEFORE?

Given the fact that the use of living conditions surveys in Norway and Sweden have as part of their purpose to uncover social differences as a step in the government's addressing such inequality, the more interesting and surprising question is not why this approach is appearing now, but rather why the use of living conditions surveys has not been used before for this greatly disadvantaged group of the population.

How can it be that while the decency principle was evolving during the 1950s and 1960s in Scandinavia, and was said to encompass all citizens, as late as 1971 half of the mentally retarded people in long-stay residential services were still sharing rooms, frequently with more than three persons who were often total strangers (NOU, 1973)? Most conceptual discussions and related research on the welfare state, whether national or comparative in scope, focus primarily on the large economic transfer schemes. It is illustrative to note the differences between political debates on retirement benefits and disability pensions on one hand, and services for people with learning impairments on the other. In both cases, the demand has been for increased public expenditure, but in the case of services for people with mental retardation, the ambition was typically translated initially into the more modest purposes of increasing the number of beds, and prior to the 1960s, discussions about "quality" were nearly nonexistent.

Media-enflamed scandals during the 1960s resulted in changing public opinion and shifts in social policy. In a certain sense, the welfare state was aroused. There were gradual changes for the better with regard to living conditions, but certainly not quantum leaps. In particular, the demarcation between common decency standards and institution-based living conditions continued to be clear. One explanation is that living conditions in an institutional setting have different (unspoken yet "known") criteria than for others in other settings in society.

In the 1980s, there were clear differences between official guidelines for institutional standards in Norway and what was otherwise deemed acceptable for others in society. An example is the institution-based objective that "by 1988 three-quarters of the residents should have their own room of at least eight square meters." Yet according to standards set for generic housing by the Bureau of Statistics, a space of $8m^2$ would be considered overcrowding, and the Norwegian National Housing Bank would reject any loan application from an ordinary citizen on this point alone, as it is in violation of decent housing standards.

The comprehensive reform that has started in Norway as of 1990 has a political rhetoric that may recharge the arguments for common decency standards. Norwegian public committee reports (NOU, 1985) explicitly couple the concept of normalization with acceptable living standards and specifically mention the life domain areas traditionally catalogued in living conditions surveys in their service evaluations. The current reform in Norway has "normalization and improvement of living conditions" as its official purpose (Parliamentary bill Ot.prp.48 [1987-1988]), and in the Parliamentary debate, shortcomings were listed in the areas of employment, income, education, participation in leisure and cultural activities, and so on (statement by member of Parliament, K. Helland). The gap between the publicly sanctioned mandates and actual practice may remain wide. But the political recoupling of welfare state standards to conditions for people with mental retardation both makes it easier to advocate for such normative standards, and makes it reasonable for the fields of research to evaluate current and future changes as an extension of the welfare

state to include all citizens, assessing living situations according to cultural norms and "decency criteria." An essential aspect is the altered public perception of people with mental retardation as fellow citizens, flowing in part from the reconceptualization of mental retardation as a social issue rather than a medical one.

4.5 A MIXED LIVING CONDITIONS APPROACH

It may appear from the foregoing discussion that living conditions surveys and decency are closely connected, but this is only partially true. A description and comparison of important life domains is likely to increase the capability to be able to detect and monitor major inequalities and unacceptable conditions, at least when it comes to those variables regularly measured in these surveys. In discussions of living conditions for the general population, many factors are taken for granted and go unmentioned and thus unmeasured in the surveys. Yet many of these factors are factors not necessarily granted to people with mental retardation, and/or are factors that may have great significance in their lives and thus deserve to be considered in the evaluative process, in addition to what the normative surveys will reveal.

For example, living conditions also have meaning: A home is more than a house, and a house is more than a place to stay. In an ethological perspective, one's home is the core private territory, marking off an area where one's privacy is expected to be respected and protected, and where entrance by others is usually invited or at least permitted. This is something so taken for granted that most of us do not consciously think about it, except on occasion of violation. If territoriality is no longer violated (as was previously the common practice in most residential institutions in Norway [Tøssebro, 1992b]), then housing has changed its meaning in a way that is probably important to identify in our quest for decency criteria. Similarly, from a semiotic perspective, housing tells a tacit story, sending out a set of signals to the world about its inhabitants. The large institutions are hugely visible monuments, symbols of societal exclusion and devaluation, sometimes with a dash of danger and mystery. Having a key to one's own front door and an ordinary street address are symbols and images of a new status for many individuals, examples that indicate symbolic elements of "home" that are important to describe and document in a societal reform.

A related challenge is that "decent/good enough living conditions" would also include having one's individual needs for support and development addressed. Receiving *only* what others receive may not be appropriate or adequate for an individual with extra needs, which may require something more or different than only what is "normative."

We would thus suggest that a general living conditions approach is fundamentally sound as a method disability research, but the approach will require a few modifications, a few extra or highlighted variables, that are of special importance to many or most people with disabilities who have historically been politically and socially excluded as a class of people.

5 EPILOGUE: THE PATERNALISTIC DILEMMA

It should be obvious from the previous sections that social research in the field of disability in Norway and Sweden is rather diverse and pluralistic in its approaches. Quantitative approaches, including use of living conditions surveys, have revealed inadequacies in terms of culturally defined expectations and decency norms. From qualitative studies one gets in-depth glimpses into the experiences of everyday life, which help us better identify with people's lives, and also may be helpful in our attempts to understand the societal processes that create or maintain deviations from the societal norms of decency.

Each of these perspectives, however, has an explicit or implicit normative dimension to it. The way we describe, interpret, and understand what is real will have implications for how we will act to maintain or change that reality. The tension between a quantitative/objective approach on the one hand and a qualitative/subjective approach on the other hand arises when one begins drawing normative conclusions. The rationale behind use of living standards surveys grew out of a "social-engineering logic," such that the purpose of the surveys was to provide input for rational decision making, to ameliorate "bad" living conditions and inequalities. This quest for decency—although ideally based on a democratic political process—can also be expressed as something to be implemented in the interests of disadvantaged citizens, *whether they want it or not*. In

contrast to this "paternalistic" approach, a more subjective and individualistic approach is implicit in many of the more qualitative everyday life studies. More specifically, the descriptions in these studies of the powerlessness and subordination of mentally retarded persons calls for more sensitivity in listening and thinking about issues of power and autonomy. Growing struggles for increased self-determination and self-advocacy groups demanding "control over our lives" sharpen the immediacy of this debate.

This paternalistic dilemma is at the root of present more general discussions about the nature and future of the welfare state. It is thus larger than only a question concerning people with disabilities. To put it simply, one can accuse the paternalistic approach of being a well-meaning but oppressive tendency of the state to interfere with what individual citizens say they want or what they can do with their lives. This argument is central to the neoliberal critique of the welfare state, where individual "freedom of choice" is considered a more important aim than politically and collectively determined standards. The subjective/individualistic component is also at the core of many popular conceptualizations of "quality of life," with claims such as "quality of life has no meaning apart from the experience of individuals" (Taylor & Bogdan, 1990, p. 28). Such sentiments cannot be solved by arguing that certain objective conditions lead to subjective experiences, since studies show no strong relationship between objective and subjective measures (Campbell, Converse, & Rodgers, 1976; Veenhoven, 1984).

In this final section we hope to articulate and discuss this paternalistic dilemma in relation to the research approaches previously discussed. What intensifies this discussion as a dilemma is when individuals or groups choose, or are willing to accept or approve of, conditions that are what others in society would consider unacceptable, indecent, or inadequate when compared to others of the same age in the same society. Since present day "modernistic" thinking tends to favor the individualistic/subjective perspective over collective/objective "paternalism," we will look most closely at certain problems with the individualistic perspective. We have focused our attention on two central problem types: the use of subjective reports and the issue of respect for individual freedom and preference.

5.1   THE FIRST PROBLEM TYPE: USING SUBJECTIVE REPORTS

The question here is whether it is possible (and/or desirable) to let a person's own subjective experience be the (only) guide in research, evaluation, and service development. A number of typical questions exist to document or measure "life satisfaction" or "situation contentment" factors. What is important is to examine whether there are experiences or processes involved in shaping or influencing the construction of reported well-being that may affect how we should interpret what is reported. What follows is an attempt to identify and describe three categories of such processes.

1. *Restricted perspectives.* Reported satisfaction is usually the result of a comparison between a situation and a frame of reference. We compare our situation with persons, roles, or alternatives we know about and that we could somehow imagine ourselves in and identify with, and we do this often almost unconsciously. All frames of reference are constructed within some kind of restricted perspective, and the boundaries of such frames are dependent on a number of factors, such as what one has experienced (and not). Many people with disabilities, especially those who have lived many years in institutional settings, have a resultant frame of reference so dominated by experience deprivation that what one then may report to "want" or "like" is very likely to be very limited. One may in fact expect a correlation between degree of deprivation (exclusion from ordinary, valued conditions) and what one says one wants or deems acceptable.

This is often reinforced by the frames of reference and expectations of others, both relatives and staff, who may have low expectations or limited alternative role visions for the person they know of as disabled. The standard for comparison then becomes (usually not stated, but implied) "good enough for people such as him." Another form of restricted perspective is that of retrospective improvement. If conditions are "better than before," then the frame of reference for judgment and evaluation is affected by what might in fact be great forward leaps, yet which could still be significantly below average according to societal norms. This can be illustrated by a mother (interviewed in Norway in 1989 prior to her son's moving out of an institution),who said:

The first years were terrible . . . 30 on a ward. But today is different, only 6 on a ward, and he has his own room . . . There is even a swimming pool. Sad they're closing it down now, when they are all having such a good time.

Would she have been as content if her nondisabled 35-year-old son shared a house with 6 others but at least had his own room? What is her frame of reference for judging the situation as "good enough"?

2. *Contextual adaptation.* Human beings are known to be very adaptive, both psychologically and physically, in part perhaps as a means of self-preservation. This also applies to our subjective well-being. People with incapacitating medical problems still report satisfaction with life in the same way as others do, except when they have recently experienced deterioration (Eriksen, Næss, & Thorsen, 1989). One man who had lived homeless in London for several years said, "I got so used to life on the streets that I often didn't notice anymore that I was hungry and cold and smelled badly until after I had come in somewhere and had a meal and a bath." It seems that the initial response to any change in conditions is to become more (or less) satisfied, but the longer-term response is to adapt—to change—one's frame of reference. Such an interpretation is in keeping with conclusions from Inglehart's studies on values (1977) and the quality of life studies by Campbell, Converse, & Rodgers, (1976). Others have indirectly substantiated this claim by adding that longer-term satisfaction (or disappointment) is better termed a personality characteristic rather than a response to life conditions. In any case, if it is true that a person (or group) will with time adjust to very different situations to the point of no longer noticing, including conditions initially experienced by themselves as hurtful or degrading or unpleasant, then certain reports must be interpreted from a different frame of reference than only the reporting person's own perspective.

3. *Identity defense.* It appears to be natural to defend who and what we are, and especially the identities and roles we know we have. Some months ago on Norwegian television was a program interviewing adolescents with cancer. All of the participants were at the time without symptoms, but many had uncertain prognoses. Many expressed shock, anxiety, and practical problems, but also presented an attitude one could summarize as "I would not have

been deprived of this experience." In addition to possibly more existential explanations, a partial explanation relative to our discussion is that we all tend to defend our identity, even if (when) that means defending or reporting satisfaction with situations such as a medical setback or very unsatisfactory conditions.

When combined with adaptation processes, one could predict that in the extreme, some persons may be willing to accept very poor conditions, perhaps even expressing not only satisfaction but gratitude. People have been known to "choose" degrading and unsatisfactory conditions, not only because they are known and familiar, but worse, because one has accepted that one does not deserve more or better. At this extreme point, one can talk about internalization of societal devaluation.

5.2   THE SECOND PROBLEM TYPE: RESPECT FOR INDIVIDUAL FREEDOM AND PREFERENCE

Self-determination can be seen as an end in itself, or it can also be regarded primarily as a means. Some interpret self-determination as the right to direct one's own action to fulfill one's own preferences. Since the subject is the only person with firsthand knowledge of these preferences, then self-determination is a presupposition for fulfillment. But the right to direct one's own action does not necessarily concur with the ability to fulfill one's preferences. Apart from the obvious that not everything we may want will come true no matter what we do (no matter who we are), other prerequisites may also in any case be necessary, such as existence of alternatives, knowledge of alternatives, and supported access to them, and the ability to predict likely consequences of choosing one option or route over another. If such presuppositions are invalid, less externally imposed control would automatically lead to more active control, but not necessarily to more fulfillment of one's own preferences, in fact, but rather to more mistakes. Would we call this self-determination? In the example of one young Norwegian man with mental retardation living for the first time in his own home, both he and

staff were pleased with his new environment, his privacy, and his self-determination. Staff were less proud when they realized that even if he knew how to buy meat or fish for dinner every day, he did not know how to use the stove. Surely it was not his self-determination or preference to choose to eat it raw, as he had for many weeks (Jenssen, 1992). In such instances, arguments for self-determination as end-in-itself or as means-only will lead us in opposite directions.

No one doubts that greater personal autonomy, self-determination, and having more choice and control over one's life is important. But it is then also essential to remember that most of us have also received support and assistance in learning how to make choices, what to consider, and have some sort of way that we have learned to weigh alternatives and possible consequences. Persons who have been controlled by others up through adult life, and been excluded from ordinary life experiences, often simply do not know how to make decisions. In any case, in situations where self-determination is the dominant aim, and without supports for learning how to make decisions, we end up with examples such as "he wants to sit in the corner and rock all day," or someone who "decided" to go outside for a walk in the snow wearing only underwear, or someone who destroys their health and teeth by "choosing" to spend all their pocket money on sweets.

Both of the above problem types refer to important conflicting considerations and possible pitfalls. On the one hand, one can argue that individual satisfaction is a better tool of social control than for social policy, since persons living in poor or unacceptable living conditions will tend to adapt or "feel content," and others may report that "he is content with his lot," altogether serving to powerfully sanction and maintain the poor conditions. A fierce focus on self-determination can further legitimate staff withdrawal, less public expenditure, and can turn out to be not "dignity of risk," but rather outright neglect. On the other hand, we ourselves would not use any of the arguments described in the above two problem types to tolerate having our own opinions or self-determination ignored in our own lives. Why then, it is argued, should it be less offensive to ignore the wishes or opinions of a person who, for example, has mental retardation?

This dilemma is very real and as such cannot be easily resolved. As social scientists, however, our task is to be mindful of the possible pitfalls and risks, especially for the most vulnerable groups in our societies. And in everyday life this dilemma needs to be balanced. Such balancing is subject to negotiations and change, and with current trends favoring individualism and more pluralism, the individual may end up being more autonomous but less powerful. Autonomy is gained but at what cost and for whom?

REFERENCES

ÅKERSTRÖM, B. (1993). *Kartlegging av levnadsvilkor för utvecklingsstörda i Jämtlands län 1991.* Uppsala: Centrum för handikappforskning.

ALLHARDT, E. (1975). *Att ha, att Älska, att Vara.* Lund: Argos forlag.

ALLHARDT, E. (1976). Dimensions of welfare in a comparative Scandinavian study. *Acta Sociologica, 19,* 227-239.

ASMERVIK, S. (1976). *Eleven i dina hænder. Hur samspelet mellan lærare och "problemelev" kan förbättras.* Lund: Prisma.

BRYSON, L. (1992). *Welfare and the state.* London: MacMillan.

BUTTERFIELD, E.C. (1987). Why and how to study the influence of living arrangements. In S. LANDESMAN, & P. VIETZE (Eds.). *Living environments and mental retardation.* Washington, DC: AAMR.

CAMPBELL, A., CONVERSE, P.E., & RODGERS, W.L. (1976). *The quality of American life.* New York: Russell Sage Foundation.

DALEN, M. (1977). *Integrering av funksjonshemmete i skolen.* Oslo: Universitetsforlaget.

ERICSSON, K. (1992). Boliger for mennesker med psykisk utviklingshemming: konsekvenser av et medborgerperspektiv. In J. T. SANDVIN (Ed.), *Mot Normalt: samfunnsideologier i forandring* (pp. 125-146). Oslo: Kommuneforlaget.

ERIKSEN, J., NÆSS,S., & THORSEN,V. (1989). Jeg må jo egentlig være fornøyd. *INAS-rapport, 89,* 12. Oslo.

ESPING-ANDERSEN, G. (1990). *The three worlds of welfare capitalism.* Cambridge: Polity Press.

GUSTAVSSON, A. (1992). Livet i "integrasjonssamfunnet": en analyse av nærhetens sosiale betydning. In J. T. SANDVIN (Ed.). *Mot Normalt: samfunnsideologier i forandring.* (pp. 203-243). Oslo: Kommuneforlaget.

HILL, A., & RABE, T. (1987). *Psykist utvecklingsstörda barn i kommunal förskola: integrering belyst ur ett socialpsykologiskt perspektiv.* Göteborg Studies in Educational Sciences, 61. Gothenburg: Acta Universitatis Gothuburgensis.

INGLEHART, R. (1977). *The silent revolution: Changing values and political styles among western publics.* Princeton, NJ: Princeton University Press.

JARHAG, S. (1993). *Inflytande i vardagslivet: nästudie av tre utvecklingsstörda personers inflytande i sitt vardagsliv.* Hälsohögskolan FOU rapport 1993, 1. Jönköping.

JENSSEN, K. (1992). *Hjemlig omsorg i offentlig regi.* Oslo: Universitetsforlaget.

JEPPSSON, K. (1989). *Gäst i verkligheten: uppföljning av livsvillkoren för utvecklingsstörda som flyttar ut från vårdhem.* Socialförvaltningen. Örebro läns landsting. Rapport no. 3. Örebro.

JOHANSSEN, (1970). *Om levnadsnivåundersökningen.* Stockholm: Almenne förlaget.

KEBBON, L., GRANAT, K., ERICSSON, K., LÖRLIUS, J., NILSSON, A. C., & SONNANDER-JEBERCU, K. (1981). *Evaluering av öppna omsorgsformer.* Delegationen för Social Forskning. Rapport 1981, 2. Uppsala.

KEBBON, L. (1992). *KOMUT-prosjektet: Utvärding av kommunalisering av omsorger för utvecklingsstörda.* Uppsala: Centrum for handikappforskning..

KIRKEBÆK, B. (1991). Design of menneskekvalitet. *Social Kritikk—Tidskrift for social analyse og debat, 16.* Copenhagen.

KRISTIANSEN, K. (1993). *Normalisering og*

verdsetjing av sosial rolle. Oslo: Kommuneforlaget.

KRISTIANSEN, K. (1994). *Normalisering og endringsarbeid.* Trondheim: Trondheim Helsefaghøgskole/Sosialdepartementet.

LARSON, S.A. & LAKIN, K.C. (1991). Parent attitudes about residential placement before and after deinstitutionalization: A research synthesis. *Journal of the Association for Persons With Severe Handicaps, 16,* 25-38.

MARSHALL, T. H. (1950). *Citizenship and social class.* Cambridge: Cambridge University Press.

MISHRA, R. (1990). *The welfare state in capitalist society.* New York: Harvester Wheatsheaf.

MOHAN, B. (1988). *The logic of social welfare.* Hemel-Hempstead: Harvester.

NILSSON, G. (1993). *Boendeintegrering som process: ett kvarter och dess människor.* Tema hälso- och sjukvården i samhallet. Linköping: Universitet i Linköping.

NOU 1973:25. *Omsorg for pyskisk utviklingshemmete: målsetting og retningslinjer.* Oslo: Sosialdepartementet.

NOU 1976:28. *Levekårsundersøkelsen —sluttrapport.* Oslo: Sosialdepartementet.

NOU 1985:34. *Levekår for psykisk utviklingshemmede.* Oslo: Sosialdepartementet.

Ot. prp. 48 (1987-1988) Oslo.

SANDVIN, J. T. (1994). Reform or dissembling? Towards community services in Norway. *Care in Place, 1*(1), 43-52.

SÖDER, M., BARRON, K., & NILSSON, J. (1990). *Inflytande fr människor med omfattande funktionshinder.* SOU nr. 90:19. Stockholm: Allmänna förlaget.

SÖDER, M. (1970). *Bostadsintegrering av utvecklingsstörda..* Uppsala: Stiftelsen ALA. Rapport nr. 93.

SÖDER, M. (1978). *Tränings-och grundsærskolans fysiska och funktionelle integrering.* Uppsala: Sociologiska Institutionen. Uppsala Universitet.

SÖDER, M. (1991). Livskvalitet og handicap. *Social Kritikk: Tidskrift for social analyse og debat, 16.* Copenhagen.

SÖDER, M. (1992). Normalisering og integrering: omsorgsideologier i et samfunn i endring. In J.

T. SANDVIN, (Ed.). *Mot Normalt: Omsorgsideologier i forandring* (pp. 41-66). Oslo: Kommuneforlaget.

SONNANDER, K., & NILSSON-EMBRO, A. C. (1984). *Utvecklingsstördas livskvalitet.* Uppsala: Projekt Mental Retardation.

STANGVIK, G. (1987). *Livskvalitet for funksjonshemmete, bind I.* Oslo: Universitetsforlaget.

STANGVIK, G. (1994). *Funksjonshemmete inn i lokalsamfunnet.* Oslo: Universitetsforlaget.

SUNDET, M. (1993). The cultural lag. In J. T. SANDVIN & FROSTAD-FASTING (Eds.). *Intellectual disability research: Nordic contributions.* Nordlandsforskning rapport nr. 93:16. Bodø.

TAYLOR, S. & BOGDAN, R. (1990). Quality of life and the individual's perspective. In R. SCHALOCK (Ed.). Quality of life (pp. 27-40). Washington DC: American Association for Mental Retardation (AAMR).

TIDEMAN, M. (1992). *Når kommunen blivit hovudman.* Uppsala: Centrum för handikappforskning.

TÖNNIES, F. (1963). *Community and society.* New York: Harper & Row. (English translation from German edition of 1912)

TØSSEBRO, J. (1988). *Velferd for psykisk utviklingshemmete.* Trondheim: Trondheim Helsefaghøgskole.

TØSSEBRO, J. (1992a). *Institusjonsliv i velferdstaten: Levekår under HVPU.* Oslo: Ad Notum Gyldendal.

TØSSEBRO, J. (1992b). Hvorfor så negative? Pårørendes syn på institusjonsavvikling. In J. T. SANDVIN (Ed.). *Mot Normalt: Omsorgsideologier i forandring (pp.* 91-124). Oslo: Kommuneforlaget.

TØSSEBRO, J. (1993). Gode levesteder for psykisk utviklingshemmete: en paternalists dilemma. In B. GJÆRUM (Ed.), *Kunnskap og ettertanke* (pp.123-140). Oslo: Universitetsforlaget.

VEENHOVEN, R. (1984). *Conditions of happiness.* Reidel: Dortrecht.

WUTTUDAL, K. (1994). *Tjenesteyting i boliger til psykisk utviklingshemmete.* Trondheim: Allforsk.

21

The impact of Normalization and Social Role Valorization in the English-speaking world

MICHAEL KENDRICK

The method used in this section to evaluate the impact of Social Role Valorization (SRV) in selected English-speaking countries is to examine whether issues explicitly addressed by the theory have changed in directions consistent with it. Any such changes might conceivably be unrelated to the influence of SRV. In the case of those described herein, however, most important figures in the field would probably acknowledge that SRV had a significant, even if not an exclusive, impact. It is also plausible that "SRV-consonant effects" have been (at least partly) due to SRV only in conjunction with other important factors, with SRV acting as a catalyst. This is consistent with Wolfensberger's (1991a) description of SRV as a tool for utilizing and enhancing adaptive positive values and traditions in a particular culture.

Part of the problem in identifying the specific impact of SRV and Normalization in many English-speaking countries is that many other similar-appearing and often allied social movements have simultaneously been at work; a list of these would include deinstitutionalization, independent living, community living, civil and human rights, inclusion, community services, least restrictive alternative legalisms, human rights, empowerment, and so on. These movements or ideas have often shared varying degrees of similarity with SRV as to their goals, premises, and constituencies, yet they are not at all identical to SRV. In some cases these movements were themselves partly a spin-off from classical SRV formulations.

An advantage with the Wolfensberger SRV formulation is that it is composed of a well-delineated set of ideas cast in a "definitive" version. The SRV theory has been clearly enunciated by Wolfensberger as was the earlier Normalization formulation that he modified into a blend of the work of Nirje, Bank-Mikkelsen, and other now obscure Scandinavians who preceded them. This property of being a distinctly defined body of ideas is not at all shared by these other more fragmentary idea systems that tend to be considerably more opaque as to what their parameters and messages are. Yet taken together, these allied movements often pursued a strikingly similar agenda for social change. Some of the more noteworthy of these common agendas included a rejection of the second-class status of disabled persons; a negative view of institutionalization as a form of service; equality of disabled persons in treatment, rights, and citizenship; the challenging of negative images and stereotypes; and so forth.

It may be impossible to fathom the precise contribution of each of these social movement fragments and their theories on the broader societies of the industrialized English-speaking world since they were so often a united phenomenon. Nonetheless, one can certainly claim in the case of SRV that these societies have tended to move in many of the directions called for by SRV theory. It may well be that social forces are at work in addition to SRV that have produced these "SRV desiderata effects." For instance, while the SRV theory only partially borrows from or resonates with the American civil rights movement and the "baby boom" protest movements of the 1960s, these, nevertheless, created a backdrop of rising expectations in which a then radical critique of an obscure human service field (e.g., disability) could find a welcome response. Rather rapidly, this theory of Normalization/SRV became a benchmark reference for the field's mainstream even though its propositions were originally massively at variance with actual practice.

There is no question that, at the very least, Normalization and then SRV have served as major reference points for the field of developmental disabilities since their rapid adoption worldwide, beginning in the 1960s. This status is not shared by any rival theory. The SRV ideas have also impacted other fields such as mental health, aging, and child welfare, but its effect in these areas has been much less noticeable. Equally, the status of SRV in these fields is far more marginal even to the point where most leaders in these fields have only cursory familiarity with it. As a consequence, the ideas contained in SRV have not been taken as far and their eventual impact has been far more restrained.

The SRV consonant effects in the developmental disabilities area are most noticeable in the realm of formal service, but they also have percolated into public and private life so much that one may now perceive a broadening cultural impact. As much as Normalization/SRV had as its initial major focus the realm of services, its resultant cultural impact has deeply marked our civil and personal lives. What follows is a summary of only some of the more obvious areas where an SRV consonant effect has taken place.

1 EFFECT ON SOCIAL CONSCIOUSNESS AND PUBLIC PERCEPTIONS

Prior to the broad diffusion of Normalization and Social Role Valorization, the state of disabled persons, especially those who were institutionalized, was abject. The arrival of Normalization on the scene brought about a remarkable challenge both to the misery of the institutions and to the much more hidden marginalization of disabled persons within community

life. A great deal of this challenge was in the form of the radical Normalization-based proposition that persons who were cast down and rejected as socially devalued persons could actually thrive and prosper under a regime of being treated as most citizens would prefer to be treated. This proposition has shifted many of the perspectives and beliefs that have oppressed persons with disabilities.

1.1   THE CULTURALLY VALUED ANALOGUE

The culturally valued analogue is a deceptively simple proposition of Wolfensberger's principle of Normalization that was carried on into SRV. The socially embedded alienation of devalued persons from society rested heavily on the premise that such persons are not like other people and therefore need not be treated like others. This in turn legitimized the routine accord of less than acceptable treatment to socially devalued persons. This notion (and unconscious habit) was directly challenged by the assertion that many such persons would thrive if one treated them as other more valued persons were treated. From matters as small as dressing and appearing like others to matters as large as entitlements to public education, the lines demarcating the socially valued from the outcasts have been shifted noticeably in favor of moving many of the latter from social deviance to a kind of personal and social participation in community. The idea of helping such persons lead "ordinary lives" was a prospect that had seemed heretofore unthinkable. All of this has had an immense impact because it has gradually established the necessary positive awareness and understanding of socially devalued persons that would permit them to experience community life in a pattern closer to that which their fellow citizens took for granted. Even though the vast majority of these persons had always lived in "the community," their social roles have changed substantially in favor of being more positively valued.

1.2   DEFINITION OF HUMANNESS

When people are oppressed, it is often due to an idea that is hostile to their humanity. This idea is the ordering mechanism of reality that results in their continued suffering. Over the last decades we have observed perhaps the most striking shift in consciousness as people have moved away from seeing socially devalued persons as being less than human. The Normalization/SRV challenge was rather straightforwardly portrayed as rendering to devalued persons the opportunity to be supported to live as others do. A significant property of such a change has been the enrichment of what it has meant to be human (like others) that had been previously denied to people. Instead of being treated as subhuman and, consequently, deprived of the riches of ordinary life, the reverse has become manifest—the extension to devalued persons of the wealth of enjoyment and opportunities available to most citizens, including the recognition that their needs, wants, and full identity were essentially the same as their fellow human beings.

1.3 RISING EXPECTATIONS OF DEVELOPMENTAL POTENTIAL

When people are discarded and accorded low value it is not uncommon for there to be indifference to what people actually are and what they could be. In order for this potential to be perceived and pursued, there must be a decisive shift in perception. One of the chief demands of the Normalization/SRV ethic has been its emphasis on the developmental model. This, in turn, has invariably led to a challenge of the low sense of possibility accorded to those who are outcast and devalued. This has invariably meant an increase in the possibilities for growth and development and the breaking of perversely low perceptions of what was realistically possible.

1.4 DESTIGMATIZING CHALLENGES TO NEGATIVE ROLE STEREOTYPING (I.E., SOCIAL-IMAGE TRANSFORMATION)

It has now become obvious that persons with disabilities (and many other groups) have been bound up and afflicted by widely held negative public images of who they were. Often these were unconsciously internalized by both the perceiver and the perceived. With the advent of Normalization/SRV has come an intense awareness of the hidden dynamics of deviancy image juxtapositions and the broader interplay between

negative social images and the conduct of social devaluation. In fact, for many of those exposed to intense Normalization or SRV training, the phenomenon of deviancy imaging revealed and concretized what had been sensed but never quite systematically articulated. More broadly, even among those not acquainted with formal training or writings, we have witnessed several decades of declining negativity to many disabled persons in almost all dimensions of their lives. While such a process is understandably incomplete, it is startling to see how many negative stereotypes have been challenged and how many positive ones have found their way into public consciousness. One of the most remarkable of these is the gradual lessening of the fear many persons have had of those persons called mentally retarded.

1.5 THE ACQUISITION AND GRANTING OF VALUED SOCIAL ROLES AND ROLE PERCEPTIONS

If one considers the narrow range of positive social roles that were in the past available and the often harsh existences that disabled people have historically led, one could conclude that established social conditions were their enemy. In contrast, the variety, value, and richness of roles they can now routinely enjoy is quite astonishing. Persons with disabilities seem to be everywhere these days, doing all sorts of unexpected things in every walk of life and in all manner of life settings, including school, work, family life, holidays, leisure, athletics, art, literature, and so on. While these social changes are by no means pervasive, the expansion of available—and attributed or acquired—valued social roles for disabled persons has taken place in a major and noticeable way.

2 EFFECTS ON SERVICES AND SERVICE-DELIVERY CULTURES

The original Normalization formulations in Scandinavia were rather more broadly focused on everyday life and culture. With the Wolfensberger formulations, it still maintained much of these cultural emphases but added a much stronger, explicit, and highly targeted critique of conventional service practices. This became most manifest in the PASS and PASSING tools, which were specifically devoted to the application of Normalization to services. Many of the changes suggested by application of these tools have now become commonplace. What follows is a sampling of service practices that arose out of Normalization/SRV training, evaluations, and writings.

2.1 THE RISE OF AN UNPRECEDENTED QUANTITY AND VARIETY OF FORMAL COMMUNITY SERVICES TO SUPPORT COMMUNITY LIVING

The last quarter-century has seen the rise of a wide variety of publicly supported services, particularly in the area of disability, where there has been an unsurpassed expansion of such services. Conceivably, this growth could have proceeded along the lines of congregate and institutional services, as has been the case in other fields such as aging. An important part of Normalization/SRV thinking has been that community living and valued social participation are only possible with the right enabling supports. Virtually all of the essential community services upon which disabled persons depend for community living have arisen in the last quarter-century and have evolved in accord with broad SRV formulations. While not all community services have proven to be relevant or of high quality, their existence nonetheless is integral to the ability of disabled persons to function within society. It is also worthwhile to note that these services have often been so pioneering in nature that the endless numbers of severely impaired persons now living near-typical lives in communities would have been inconceivable a quarter-century ago. A large part of this technical and professional ground breaking would not have been attempted were it not for the embrace of SRV-concordant strategies and goals.

2.2 DEINSTITUTIONALIZATION

Probably the single most dramatic impact of Normalization/SRV has been the gradual abandonment of public residential institutions as the centerpiece of service delivery. While this phenomenon is by no means equivalent in every case or country, it does seem fair to say that the general direction taken has been

unequivocally away from large institutions. Initially this meant the creation of smaller "midi" and "mini" institutions, but, increasingly, even these are coming to be seen as undesirable. The ways in which deinstitutionalization has been carried out have varied from the exemplary to the negligent, yet the principle that persons shouldn't be institutionalized has itself now become an embedded ethic of the field. Literally billions of public dollars have been diverted from institutions to newly created community services. Unfortunately, the institutional system continues to prosper in other fields as can be seen in the growth of nursing homes and other similar congregate settings.

2.3 SUPPORT FOR PERSONS TO LIVE IN NORMATIVE HOUSING

One of the major teachings of Normalization/SRV that was considered radical at one time was that persons with impairing conditions could and should live in ordinary homes in ordinary neighborhoods. As extreme as that may have seemed when first proposed, it has now come to be the normative ethic for both adult and children's service delivery. In terms of the overall budget of publicly funded community services, up to 80% of such expenditures are now devoted to some form of community housing. It should also be noted that there currently no longer exists any group or class of individuals remaining in residential institutions that does not have similar persons simultaneously being served somewhere in community housing options. This is a remarkable fulfillment of the initial claim of Normalization/SRV, that is, provided the appropriate supports are available, it is possible for virtually all persons to live in normative community settings.

2.4 INTEGRATED EDUCATION

A quarter-century ago it was routine for persons with disabilities to be denied access to public education, or if they did get education it was most probably offered in segregated settings. Today this overall pattern does not hold. Though not as dramatic or as wholesale as the adult deinstitutionalization, it is still possible to perceive a similar establishment of an antisegregation ethic in this area. Moreover, the field

428

has seen a growth in the technical proficiency of integrated educational supports with the result that schools now include students whose impairments or conduct would have made education—let alone integration—unfeasible a generation ago. Also noteworthy has been the expansion of generic educational opportunities for adults with disabilities. These have happened not only in the formal adult education realm, but also in informal and vocational adult education opportunities.

2.5   WORK, EMPLOYMENT, AND TRAINING

While it has always been true that disabled persons have been part of the workforce—often in unnoticed and invisible ways and occasionally in highly stereotypic roles—the conditions faced a quarter-century ago were those of a massive service commitment to segregated vocational programs. The balance in this pattern has been unmistakably shifted in favor of a greater emphasis on decreasing the dominance of segregated employment and training in favor of work in integrated employment settings. This movement gained particularly dramatic momentum in the 1980s and has meant a gradual erosion of the mainstay of segregated vocational programming—the sheltered workshop. Even those whose degree of impairment diminishes the likelihood of their being competitively employed might nonetheless find themselves working subcompetitively in open settings. However, notwithstanding this (recent) trend, supported employment is still not available to large segments of persons in sheltered workshops.

2.6   INTEGRATED LEISURE AND SUPPORTED COMMUNITY PARTICIPATION

While leisure may not have attracted the same dramatic interest as have the questions of work and homes, it also has been a context within which the formerly segregated and outcast have gradually been absorbed into the broader patterns of recreation and leisure of our communities. Further, a wide variety of formerly segregated and categoric recreation programs have given way to experiments with integrated programs. Even those areas of segregated recreation that have expanded during this period (e.g., Special

Olympics) are increasingly under fire to give way or adapt to the social integration ethic. It is now not uncommon or even remarkable to witness persons with disabilities participating in all forms of integrated recreation and leisure opportunities. Further, these numbers now include persons whose impairments are quite visible and consequential and who require considerable support to participate.

2.7   USE OF GENERIC SERVICES AND RESOURCES

The Normalization/SRV theory has from its inception argued for the proposition that socially devalued persons would benefit from the safeguarded use of generic services and resources. A quarter-century ago it was not uncommon, particularly for institutionalized persons, to receive the bulk of their professional medical, dental, nursing, education, psychological, and other services from nongeneric sources. Even persons living in the community tended to use nongeneric services (e.g., "special" education, etc.). These conditions no longer apply in the sense that while there is still the use of nongeneric services, this is decreasing in favor of the use of more generic ones. Nonetheless, there are still many areas where this trend has been very modest, though positive, such as dental services, transportation, and so on.

2.8   GROWTH OF PROTECTIVE LEGISLATION SERVICES AND OTHER FORMAL SAFEGUARDS

One measure of the worth and value of persons may be whether any efforts are made by their society to assure that they will be treated well. In this sense, persons with disabilities have come from a situation where few intentional protective services and safeguards existed to one where there are now numerous such safeguards. These have been consciously put in place, sustained through time, and had noticeable impact. Such measures include the public declaration of rights, human rights commissions, a variety of laws and regulations, protective service workers, oversight and monitoring mechanisms, advocacy arrangements, litigation, guardianship, quality assurance/enhancement systems, independent investigation, citizen review boards, self-advocacy, and so forth. While these measures often relate rather narrowly to specific matters of vulnerability or mistreatment, they are collectively strong evidence of a commitment to assure to persons with disabilities greatly enhanced social roles and protected life conditions approaching, if not surpassing, the protections available to ordinary citizens. When such an array systematically masses itself, it is at least prima facie indicative of an institutionalized resolve to stop the mistreatment and neglect of the persons affected.

2.9 THE ROLE OF PERSONS WITH DISABILITIES WITHIN THEIR FAMILIES

The family, even in its present state of debilitation, is a major social institution. This generation has seen the return to their families of countless individuals who had formerly been excluded from everyday family life via the residential institutions. While it was still common a generation ago for such persons to inhabit institutions in their childhood years, this practice has been massively reduced—particularly in public institutions. Further, the vast majority of families are now maintaining their disabled children within the family home and within the family lifestyle. Persons with disabilities are now commonly involved alongside everyone else in meals, chores, outings, visits, vacation, family gatherings, shopping, and so on. It is still typical to see such persons continuing their family ties, even as adults living separately from families. While such patterns had been common for many people long before SRV, the SRV influence has nonetheless been to intensify such integration even where the person's impairments pose substantial hardships and sacrifice. It is also notable that there has been a growth in family support services for the purpose of keeping families together.

3 INSTRUCTIVE AMBIGUITIES IN THE POSSIBLE IMPACT OF SRV

The preceding brief overview might be thought of as social or cultural changes that have arisen in a direct linear sense from the logic of SRV. One could simplistically see these effects as mechanistically related to the theory. For instance, if the theory called for a given effect (e.g., integration), and one then subsequently sees a push emerge toward integration, then one could reasonably surmise that the theory has been faithfully adopted by the adherents and its predicted effects would materialize in due course. In the many ways already outlined, this has occurred. Yet there is much more to the impact of SRV than has been intended. What follows are some further phenomena that have coexisted with an "SRV positive" impact yet show that SRV has not been adopted in the simple linear sense already mentioned.

3.1 ADOPTION OF SELECTIVE ELEMENTS OF SOCIAL ROLE VALORIZATION

It would seem that most people would concur with the prima facie evidence of a lessening of the social exclusion and perceived deviancy of people who are disabled. This, however, is an overall effect that is not necessarily upheld in particulars or even in major subportions of the aggregate. A good example of this can been seen in special education, where it has become more common for students with disabilities to be able to attend local schools along with their age peers. Nonetheless, it is also common that these students have remained largely socially isolated, poorly taught and supported, segregated, stigmatized, neglected, and so forth. As such, a good amount of what SRV calls for has been de facto rejected even though some important elements of SRV have simultaneously been adopted in the very same example. For instance, some students may be well integrated, the majority may share common travel arrangements to school, some developmental education is going on, some good personal relationships between disabled and typical students are present, and so on.

The lessons from these "mixed" impact situations may be many but certainly one of them needs to be that SRV's impact is not likely to be coherent, systematic, and unified in practice. It matters not that many of the people involved are unaware, uninterested in, and largely unable to be particularly rigorous and systematic in their use of SRV theory. Such persons do not exist in this instance to become exemplars of either SRV logic or practice and would be quite content to utilize it only inasmuch as it has some pragmatic value. Thus, even though they are resolutely engaged in an exercise that will advance some SRV aims, their commitment to and clarity about SRV may be highly ambivalent and/or confused. As a consequence, it might be preferable to describe SRV as only partially generating SRV consonant impacts especially within social contexts that only subscribe to fragments of SRV.

This preceding observation nonetheless creates a particular conceptual difficulty as to both the immediate and long-term impact of SRV. If the persons involved in adopting SRV are not even conscious or knowledgeable that they are operating in accordance with SRV theory, is it realistic to see this phenomenon as an SRV consonant impact? This is a particularly acute issue since Wolfensberger has often stressed the importance of consciousness of SRV principles as an anchor of a viable SRV strategy. This problem becomes particularly important over the long term where the systematic holding to SRV goals would require the thoughtful adoption and pursuit of SRV rationales. Certainly, not only are SRV consonant impacts not necessarily reflective of systematic SRV adoption but they may actually only contain minimal SRV compliance.

3.2 PERVERSE, CONFUSED, OR INCORRECT USES OF SRV

Much as in the prior instance, there are many circumstances in which SRV is not wholeheartedly and genuinely adopted. Many deinstitutionalizations conform to this standard of SRV usage in that in many important ways, the life of the person may now be validly social role valorized. Nonetheless, the eventual impact of SRV may be negative. A good example of this can be seen in sheltered workshop deinstitutionalizations where the transfer of such persons to so-called community-based employment amounts to a form of mini-institutionalization, for example, where enclaves are equated with normative employment. In many cases, this is done using SRV language, aims, and legitimacy simply because SRV is the current coin of the realm. Predictably, the use and effects of SRV in such cases will be cynical and perverse. However, even if such action were simply based on confusion or errors about what SRV actually means, the effect on the people served would not be particularly different. Motivation and intent, even if positive, cannot overcome the limitations of incoherent

service thinking and models. Well-intentioned people (of which there are always legions) have taken initiatives that are not consistent with SRV theory yet may be equated with it in their own minds. These ill-advised uses can create many regrettable results that could otherwise be avoided. These have included the use of nursing homes as a "generic" service, the "dumping" of persons from institutions in too-rapid deinstitutionalizations, the nondiversion of persons from criminal proceedings in the interest of "natural consequences," the alienation of a family's interests in the course of assuring normative independence, the promotion of self-indulgence and promiscuity in the name of freedom, the creation of mini-institutions instead of more authentic homes, and so on.

3.3 WEAK, MEDIOCRE, NONRIGOROUS USES OF SRV

The level of difficulty involved in trying to simultaneously maximize the many aspects of SRV theory has created a predictable continuum of impacts that range from "easy SRV" to "very challenging SRV." For instance, it is relatively easy these days to foster community group membership of pleasant persons with minor disabilities. It might be quite another matter to arrange such situations where the individual may be behaviorally aggressive or inappropriate, unable to communicate, in need of extensive physical assistance, or multiply disabled. If, in addition, the community group was hostile to begin with, soured because of prior failed integrations, or otherwise politicized, the challenge level would go up. Consequently, there may be few incentives to undertake difficult SRV tasks in relation to easier ones. Similarly, some SRV defenses of devalued persons will be of even greater challenge because siding with the oppressed person may sometimes bring the supporter into moral, political, and legal conflict with the authorities or even one's friends.

3.4 CONTROVERSY, ACCEPTANCE AND RECOGNITION OF SRV

One of the notable impacts of SRV has been its ability to create SRV controversies. Wherever SRV has been taught, promoted, or implemented, it seems to have been to some degree divisive. One element of this has been undoubtedly the relative merits of the training and adherents. Nonetheless, the ideas themselves seem to have been inherently challenging (in whole or in part) quite apart from the occasionally provocative nature (or not) of those who have championed SRV. It is noteworthy that the vast number of these controversies seems eventually to have resulted in the SRV viewpoint prevailing. Such an eventual outcome can obscure the processes at work leading to such effects. One of these is the dialectic between controversy and acceptance engendered by SRV proponents to further their aims. In many ways, the impact of SRV has been one of challenging social standards or habits as they relate to socially devalued persons. Since everyone devalues others to some degree, there are no shortages of SRV shortcomings to point out, deny, or otherwise struggle with. Even where SRV proposals have achieved some measure of acceptance, it is noteworthy that SRV itself may not be appropriately recognized as having been a factor in achieving this result. In fact, one of the by-products of many of these controversies seems to have been a desire to achieve SRV consonant effects with as little reference to SRV as possible. Identification with SRV seems to marginalize its adherents, vis-à-vis the mainstream, even though SRV has impacted the mainstream rather substantially. SRV seems to improve society's treatment of socially devalued persons, yet the process of SRV adoption is very costly to SRV proponents.

A good example of this is the controversy generated worldwide as to whether people could live (normatively) outside of institutional settings. Those who proposed such a notion were initially considered extremists while those who allowed that "there will always be a need for an institution" were seen as more moderate and reasonable. In time, the advocates for SRV were "proven right" in the sense that their theoretical claim was supported by the facts of implementation. Today such a claim would have a greater prima facie validity and would not seem unreasonable because common practice has caught up with this particular element of SRV. It is interesting that in other reasonably similar fields (e.g., mental health, aging, rehabilitation, etc.), such a claim would still be controversial. The point not to miss is that SRV seems to have been effective but at some cost to those who embrace it—particularly at early stages.

A second observation is that SRV seems to have been most seminal at points where it undertakes to correct certain elements of social devaluation that have yet to obtain a "counter status quo consensus" in favor of their change. For instance, SRV adherents were in the early ranks of the antisheltered workshop efforts and later in the "natural supports" reactions to segregationist forms of supported employment. As these social critiques obtained a following, SRV faded from recognition. A similar pattern can be noted in the education "inclusion" movement, the recent relationships/community building genre, the integrated leisure movement, the "supportive living" movement, and so forth.

3.5   COEXISTENT COUNTER-SRV TRENDS

While SRV seems to have made substantial progress in influencing society concerning disabled persons, it would be notably incomplete to let matters rest there. It is crucially important to note trends that either suggest that SRV may be at its outer limits in terms of impact and that there are recent phenomena that are logically contradictory to SRV theory. These trends are numerous. Some of the more obvious are the so-called "community living" situations that are nothing more than mini-institutions; the widespread preference of many expectant parents to forego having a disabled child when advised in advance via amniocentesis; the continued normativeness of segregated leisure and recreation; the deep resistance to integration in schools; the extensive private institutionalization of disabled persons in nursing homes; the automatic use of "do not resuscitate" orders for disabled persons in generic health care settings; the above-average reported abuse of disabled persons; the continued stigmatization of disabled persons; the routine social rejection and social isolation; "job ghettoization" of disabled persons in quasi-integrated settings; and the inability of SRV to impact other fields.

In one sense these are not new "countertrends" so much as the continued expression of a social devaluation that is now only partially under siege from SRV consonant influences. Still, they represent ample evidence that while SRV goals have obtained considerable social influence, that influence has only partially held in check the social devaluation inherent in people and the social order. Thus it remains an open question whether the currently strong SRV influence will eventually collapse or strengthen beyond this generation. As a consequence of this ambiguity it is useful to see impact at a point in time. If valuations of people and groups can have a renaissance, it is equally true that devaluations can regain ground, for example, the return to institutional "snake pits" after the moral treatment era, neo-Nazism, antisemitism, ethnic hatred, and so on.

A further interesting dimension beyond the previous question of point-in-time balances of social value is the question of whether ground gained during periods of upward social valuations constitute a preventive safeguard or bulwark against future social devaluations. For instance, people who have never worked in "old style" residential institutions nonetheless often create institution-like conditions in community settings—almost a neocustodialization. This would seem to suggest that the deeper lessons of SRV are not well appreciated or understood even though the setting itself may have come into existence because of indirect SRV influences. It may seem unthinkable to some that "old" social devaluations will reappear in "new" contexts. Nonetheless, one might wonder how or even if SRV will have some influence on unanticipated "retro" social devaluations.

3.6   SCOPE AND FOCUS OF SRV INFLUENCE

SRV has been largely influential in the developmental disabilities field and in particular in what North Americans call the mental retardation field. Not surprisingly, its origins are in this field, and its major exponents are from it as well. Even though Wolfensberger has crafted SRV to be recognizable as a more universal theory, it has not to this point had the hoped-for broader impact. It has had less direct impact on the physical disability movement, which sees itself as more organized around the "independence" theme. In mental health its impact has been present, but it has gained greatest acceptance among community mental health advocates, especially those that de-emphasize professional and medical authority and those that favor noninstitutional supports. For instance, many aspects

of SRV have had considerable popularity in the United Kingdom with dissident nurses, psychologists, and rights-oriented "consumer" advocates. In Canada many of the most progressive community service advocates in mental health have drawn heavily from Normalization and to a much lesser extent from SRV.

In the aging field, it has had its greatest adherence in Australia with typically sporadic interest appearing elsewhere at the margins of the field. It has not managed to find a substantial presence in the addictions, corrections, psychotherapeutic, medical, psychological, or social work fields or professions and is virtually unheard of outside of special education in the broader education field. It has no substantial citizen movement adherents outside of the developmental disability field, and even there it is often portrayed as the theory of a prior generation of activists, that is, it is said to be passé. Its academic prominence follows similar patterns to its pattern of adoption in the service fields.

None of this per se excludes SRV's claim to a more universal applicability, but it does point out the very important difference between the theoretical uses and constituency for SRV and the actual historical impact. It is also noteworthy that the uses and prominence of SRV in the aging field in Australia (and most recently New Zealand) is comparatively recent (i.e., 1980s and early 1990s). Also, even in areas where a form of standardized Normalization was widely taught in the 1970s (e.g., Canada, eastern USA, and the United Kingdom), it has not necessarily followed that SRV teaching enjoyed a broad level of popularity. Alternately, SRV has found new audiences not involved in earlier Normalization teaching eras (e.g., SRV in the midwest of the USA in the 1990s, and SRV in Australia in the 1980s). Curiously, even though many have declared both Normalization and SRV to be passé, the level of SRV training currently under way in English dwarfs by a large margin even the most intensive levels obtained in the 1970s or 1980s.

Another related phenomenon is the proliferation of "soft-focus" SRV training and writings evident today, particularly in the developmental disability sector. While much of this teaching and writing does not mention SRV, its content relies heavily on what might be considered "classical" SRV thinking and theorizing. In fact, to the naive, "soft-focus" SRV teachings are considered equivalent to "hard-core" SRV. Again, in this instance much of the easier content of SRV is adopted even as formal allegiance and alliance with SRV is jettisoned. The two are interrelated phenomena in the sense that the appetite for "soft-focus" SRV is substantially related to a rejection of "hard-core" SRV teaching, that is, a preference for a "softer" packaging of the SRV message.

Conceivably, SRV could be "rediscovered" at any point and applied to other areas either theoretically or practically. Equally, it may simply fade from view as its current generation of adherents passes away. Yet these are much too simple prognostications for ideas that are now largely in the public domain. A plentitude of other possibilities could, in fact, occur were there people with an interest. The "whys" of impact remain obscure even though the effects of SRV can be described with a certain amount of generality. Since social devaluation is so intrinsic to human experience, it remains a quite reasonable path of inquiry to try to ascertain whether SRV truly impacts on society as per its theoretical claims.

Wolfensberger has often said in recent years that SRV is a social scientific theory that itself is dependent on positive ideology and morality in order to address social devaluation. In other words, SRV could not have achieved much alone were it not for adherents who made value choices in favor of devalued persons and then used SRV to pursue goals based on these positive values choices. While SRV does not prescribe such choices, it does seem to have had the impact of encouraging people to deal with values issues, that is, it seems to have had a "values engagement" impact. This "values engagement" phenomenon seems to be characterized by at least some people identifying values as core matters in terms of how people are to be treated. In fact, the actual values that given people might specifically endorse may vary widely, yet all of these people would typically highlight "values in general" as important. It is noteworthy to add that though Wolfensberger has claimed that SRV cannot and does not answer values questions—it is a social/scientific theory not a value system—nonetheless, this distinction is commonly lost on most adherents who feel to the contrary that by embracing SRV—or one of its many "look-alikes"—they have indeed embraced a guiding philosophy or value system for services.

4 SRV TRAINING LITERATURE

The major literature on SRV (as distinct from Normalization) is almost entirely Wolfensberger's except perhaps in the UK. The SRV term and formulation are only briefly summarized by Wolfensberger in the major professional literature. Very recently, Wolfensberger (1991a, 1991b, 1991c, 1991d, 1992) has published an expanded monograph in English, French, Italian, and German. Increasingly, the SRV terminology seems to be finding usage, but it is still largely a rarity. In many ways, the Normalization term and conceptualization remain far more dominantly present in the professional literature of the fields where they have had some penetration. It may be too early (only a decade) to conclude very much about the eventual fate of SRV, but it nonetheless seems (to this point in time) to have been comparatively a smaller ripple than was Normalization.

The Normalization literature is much more abundant in the 1980s and 1990s than in the 1970s. The literature on Normalization does not share a common definition of what is meant by the term. In many cases, Normalization seems to have meant whatever the author needed it to mean. The Wolfensberger formulation has massively overshadowed the earlier Scandinavian formulations as the most widely cited authoritative or definitive version.

A notable variation on this general pattern is in the case of the United Kingdom. In 1981, Alan Tyne adapted a Normalization monograph by John O'Brien (O'Brien & Tyne, 1981) that was in itself a paraphrase of the Wolfensberger definition of Normalization. This formulation was widely disseminated in the UK and has gained some prominence as essentially a functional equivalent of the (earlier) Wolfensberger material even though it is, in essence, a derivation. Nonetheless, it is referenced in more recent UK literature as being definitive for purposes of establishing what is meant by Normalization. This instance is emblematic of the general problem of the popular impact of something called "Normalization," where the precise meaning of the term is not necessarily shared. The "Normalization" literature is in fact substantially concerned with establishing arguments either in favor or against Normalization—whatever it may mean to the writers. This literature is notably abundant in the United

Kingdom and Australia and only marginally present in New Zealand and Canada. The USA has produced some academic literature but little popular writings on the subject.

The chief dissemination of the bulk of Normalization/SRV literature has been done by the various training groups who have had a specific commitment to Normalization/SRV training. Perhaps the most substantial of these in the 1970s had been the National Institute on Mental Retardation in Canada (now the G. Allan Roeher Institute). This body had self-consciously abandoned such a mission in the early 1980s but had, up until that point, been a major worldwide influence as well as a significant publisher of Normalization-derived materials. Also remarkable was its pioneering attempt to install a systematic national Normalization training system. This system remained in place until the early 1980s but gradually declined into a handful of poorly networked provincial and local groups carrying on SRV training.

Nonetheless, throughout North America there eventually grew a wide variety of specifically focused Normalization/SRV training efforts. These were quite varied and included both state and more local variants, stretching from Georgia to New Brunswick and British Columbia, and Washington to Indiana and Southern Ontario. None were national—with the exception of the Training Institute, established by Wolfensberger at Syracuse University—though they were all very effectively networked.

In the UK, the Campaign for Mental Handicap Education and Research Association (CMHERA) has operated a nonstop Normalization/SRV training system nationally since the 1980s, and a variety of smaller, more local affiliates have appeared during this period. CMHERA has also served as the major source of Normalization literature for the country. On occasion, CMHERA has facilitated trainings in Ireland.

In Australia there has been a number of state-based Normalization/SRV training efforts since 1980. These, in effect, merged formally as a systematic national effort only recently, though the trend toward this had begun by the late 1980s. New Zealand had no designated training groups until recently but had some relatively consistent efforts to disseminate the ideas during the 1980s.

Only a few articles have been written about these training efforts but it is estimated by this writer that tens of thousands of persons have received some form of in-depth Normalization/SRV/PASS/PASSING training. These training events have been much more the primary means by which SRV has been disseminated and adopted. While there are increasingly large differences between standardized and nonstandardized trainings that have worried many of those involved, this has not, thus far, created separate schools of SRV thought. A single body to coordinate SRV training and development exists for Canada and the USA, and a similar structure has been formed in Australia. Various attempts have been made to craft a similar body under CHMERA in the UK. No unifying international body yet exists to further SRV work, training, and materials, nor has one been attempted. Nonetheless, Wolfensberger's Training Institute has served as a locus for such contacts as have a number of other individuals.

As a final note, it is remarkable that despite the general evidence of SRV influence and adoption there remains considerable skepticism even among SRV's strongest allies that the theory has had anything but a marginal impact. Embedded in this is a widespread feeling that SRV's influence is much too weak given the massiveness of social devaluation. In some locations such as the UK, parts of Canada, and so on, there exists considerable pessimism even about the future of SRV, that is, that its best days are behind it. Naturally, this view is offsct by a sense in Wolfensberger and others that the theory will continue to evolve and impact things long after this generation of adherents passes from the scene.

REFERENCES

O'BRIEN, J., & TYNE, A. (1981). *The principle of Normalization: A foundation for effective services.* London: Campaign for Mentally Handicapped People and Community and Mental Handicap Educational and Research Association.

WOLFENSBERGER, W. (1991a). *A brief introduction to Social Role Valorization as a high-order concept for structuring human services.* Syracuse, NY: Syracuse University, Training Institute for Human Service Planning, Leadership and Change Agentry.

WOLFENSBERGER, W. (1991b). *La valorisation des roles sociaux: Introduction à un concept de référence pour l'organisation des services* (A. Dupont, V. Keller-Revaz, J. P. Nicoletti, & L. Vaney, Trans.). Geneva, Switzerland: Éditions des Deux Continents.

WOLFENSBERGER, W. (1991c). *La valorizzazione del ruolo sociale: Una breve introduzione al concetto di valorizzazione del ruolo sociale inteso come concetto prioritario per la strutturazione dei servizi alle persone* (M. Costantino & A. Domina, Trans.). Geneva, Switzerland: Éditions des Deux Continents.

WOLFENSBERGER, W. (1991d). *Die Berwertuna der sozialen Rollen: fine kurze Einfuhruna zur Bewertuna der sozialen Rollen als Grundbeariff beim Aufbau von Sozialdiensten* (C. Agad & A. Bianchet, Trans.). Geneva, Switzerland: Éditions des Deux Continents.

WOLFENSBERGER, W. (1992). *A brief introduction to Social Role Valorization as a high-order concept for structuring human services* (2nd ed., rev.). Syracuse, NY: Syracuse University, Training Institute for Human Service Planning, Leadership and Change Agentry.

22

The impact of Normalization and Social Role Valorization in Canada

ANDRÉ BLANCHET

This country is vast with 10 provinces and 3 territories having jurisdiction over the organization of social and health services. Over the last 20 years, I have had occasion to visit each of these provinces and to meet many people who have handicaps, their families and advocates, and professionals and administrators. All have influenced the various levels of support that exist in each of these regions. It has a lot more than symbolic significance that the 1994 conference that reviewed Normalization and SRV was held in Canada—and moreover in Ottawa, which is, in a sense, the very boundary between the French and English cultures—where the Scandinavian idea of Normalization has had the greatest impact.

When, at the beginning of the 1970s, Wolfensberger came to teach and lead a team at the National Institute for Mental Retardation and a few months later Nirje came to work for the Ontario government, we had the privilege to live through an exhilarating period of new and exciting ideas and favorable sociopolitical conditions that nourished the hopes and actions of families and young professional dissidents.

Let me list the elements that I think were the most important.

1. A vision and a practice of consumer participation, which was at the heart of the work of G. Allan Roeher, the then director of the Canadian Association for Mental Retardation (CAMR). Allan, like many of the reformers of that era, came from the province of Saskatchewan, where governments, with the participation of agricultural cooperatives, were the first in Canada to establish in 1944 a hospitalization insurance program and then in 1960 a health insurance regime. It was also in Saskatchewan, in 1964, that we witnessed the first closing of an institution—Weyburn—in good measure because of the leadership of its medical superintendent, Hugh Lefave. Also, again before all other provinces, Saskatchewan was the first to decentralize its social services. It was not surprising, therefore, that the CAMR wanted to establish a network of integrated community services, COMSERV, where families, in collaboration with local administrations, would establish the required services and supports to allow persons with handicaps to live their lives in the community. I can still see Wolfensberger explaining to us, with many overheads, the necessity of a central point of responsibility and the interdependent relationships or "chaining" between different levels of responsibility.

2. A relatively sophisticated parent association movement was beginning to understand that the role of parents was not so much in the delivery of services, but more in the area of advocacy for better living conditions for their sons and daughters. In Quebec, for example, between the short period of 1970 and 1976, local parent associations withdrew from the administration of services, which then became managed by public corporations under a new law on social services. There were many associations in the country that had already attained the third stage, as described by Wolfensberger (1973), that of advocacy and political representation.

3. A number of young professional dissidents, many of whom were present at the 1994 Ottawa

437

Conference, who were drawn and in certain cases fascinated by the possibilities of change that were doable with the application of Normalization. They came in great numbers from all parts of the country, to seminars and workshops of the National Institute on Mental Retardation (the former name of the G. Allan Roeher Institute) to learn all those important things that the university had not taught them. Many returned to their corners of the country, convinced that one had to work with families to change the system that was then in place. They became members, oftentimes informally, in the "brotherhood" of change agents.

On a more global scale, there was this Canadian sociopolitical reality and historical tradition based more heavily on social justice than in the United States that usually defines Canada as between the social democracies of Europe, particularly Scandinavia, and the American culture. This social justice tradition permitted then and still today to define an identity typically Canadian quite different from that of the United States despite the powerful attraction of American culture. Though social policies for persons with handicaps were almost nonexistent at that time, this context was sympathetic to the development of policies aimed at integration, like those described by Jacques Pelletier (chapter 25 in this volume), or the inclusion of the rights of persons with handicaps within the Canadian Charter of Rights and Freedoms and this without having recourse to the courts, as was the case in the United States.

The question that we must ask, a quarter-century later, is the following: Have all these hopes borne fruit and, more analytically, what developments in Canada today are, to repeat Michael Kendrick's expression, consonant with Normalization or Social Role Valorization?

Let us review as precisely as possible, taking into consideration the variations between provinces, the situation of persons with intellectual handicaps in Canada.

1. Institutionalization and congregate life milieux. Despite the closing here and there of institutions—one in Newfoundland, another for children in New Brunswick, one in Saskatchewan, another in British Columbia—we can estimate that there are still close to 10,000 people who reside in such institutions. Moreover, and this to me is what is most alarming, few

people will have the possibility to live where they or their families will have chosen. Many live in group homes, which, in certain provinces, exceed in size that which is the recognized and acceptable cultural norm for residences in industrialized countries. The number of children in pediatric hospitals and especially in chronic care hospitals (pediatric extended care) remains high. For example, in British Columbia, which has looked at this problem very closely, we estimate that there are still 60 children and young adults who are in these extended care centers. The transfer of mentally handicapped adults from institutions to nursing homes has been broadly practiced, particularly in Ontario.

2. School integration. Despite many efforts and some successes in each of the provinces where, by and large, school policy has been coherent with school integration, a great deal remains to be done. We estimate in British Columbia that 40 of the 75 school boards of the province have managed to integrate children, though this reality is quite fragile and risks changing according to priorities and available funding in the school boards. Other provinces, such as Quebec, despite individual successes, continue to maintain a sector of special schools and classes that continue to grow.

3. Employment and significant work. Despite the fact that sheltered workshops are slowly disappearing and that employment support initiatives are to be found everywhere in the country, we estimate that over 80% of persons who are intellectually handicapped are without employment or without significant day activity.

4. Poverty. More than 90% of adults with intellectual handicaps live from income support programs. The available allocation represents a monthly amount that is 70% under the poverty line according to standards established by the Canadian Council on Poverty.

5. Law. Despite the Charter of Rights voted in Quebec and in Canada in 1977 and 1982, respectively, few decisions of the superior courts of this country have had a national impact. We will come back to this point.

6. Solitude and social isolation. Here, again, despite some famous initiatives (like the Joshua Committee), many persons live in great isolation with

few ties to their family, friends, or advocates, and this is especially true for those who have left institutions and group homes and who almost tragically form a kind of sacrificed generation.

Despite this dark tableau, which testifies to inherent tendencies of discrimination that are more or less conscious in our societies, it is quite important to nonetheless highlight those initiatives related to Normalization and SRV that continue to show promise.

1. The development of advocacy is, to me, the strong point.

(a) Inspired by Judith Snow and Marsha Forest in Ontario, support networks exist around the country. The Maps process, developed by Snow and Forest, is used in school areas, communities, and families, particularly when such groups need to refocus their strength when faced with difficult situations. Of course, these groups exhaust themselves. They have to start their operations all over again because of conflicts of interest, and this has sometimes resulted in disillusionment and even personal tragedies. However, they have also assisted in breaking the isolation of many persons, offered the necessary supports, and in general been much more consistent than citizen advocacy groups because they have been more sustained.

(b) Very individualized services have emerged, for instance, the microboards organization inspired by the work of David Wetherow in Manitoba. Again, there are enormous risks of converting family and friendly relations into administrative relations. However, the experience in British Columbia—where over the last 2 years, more than 30 of these microboards have been established, sustaining in community persons whose needs are very complex—is worthy of more research and analysis and should create much interest.

2. The emergence of welcoming committees, as influenced by the work of John McKnight (1995). From Newfoundland to British Columbia, and passing by the Italian community of Montreal, in small villages and in the neighborhoods of great cities, there exists in an embryonic form the intention of welcoming home persons who are returning after a long life in institutions.

3. The emergence of associations and of groups of young families created most often around the fight for school integration. Particularly in Ontario, but now in all provinces, these groups work apart from traditional parent associations and have the advantage of not being burdened by the responsibility of delivering services. They are also very clear in what they want for their children: no segregation, no group homes, no special classes, and life in the community like for other families. The Family Focus Conference in British Columbia, which is the annual event where these young families meet, now brings together more than twice the number of participants than the traditional annual conference of the provincial association for community integration.

4. The continued rapid growth of People First and the creation, in 1991, of a national People First movement giving them their own voice, nationally and provincially. Their message is clear: to leave behind the oppression of which they have been and continue to be the victims. People First of Canada also wants to play a role on the international scene. One of the great moments of my life was participating in 1993 at the International People First Congress held in Toronto, where 1,300 delegates from 32 countries worked and exchanged for a week. There exists within this movement a potential for change that is difficult to evaluate for the moment.

5. In the field of legislation, despite the existence of very few national laws, I wish to underline the Supreme Court's judgment concerning Eve, which has made illegal the nontherapeutic sterilization without consent of persons in Canada. There was also the Stephen Dawson ruling in British Columbia, which, despite a very difficult application, has made illegal the withholding of medical treatment because of physical and mental handicap. Also, because of the action of the National Parent Association, every person in this country, especially those living in institutions, has the right to vote and the right to receive the information necessary to exercise this right.

Whether these developments are directly or indirectly related to Normalization or to SRV is a question that is to me quite academic. What I find important is to underline that Normalization and SRV and all of the intense activity that was generated around these theories, particularly in the 1970s in Canada, created a favorable terrain for the emergence of these initiatives. One has only to consider the supports available for persons with mental handicaps and compare them to the services in mental health and services to elderly persons to realize that despite all of the lacunae, they compare very favorably. These other fields also benefited from the same sociopolitical environment and yet have not done as well, possibly because they remained aloof of such ideas.

In closing, I would like to speak very briefly about a question that on its own should be the object of a conference: The ethical dimension of Normalization and SRV. Fundamentally, these ideas have proclaimed the right to equality and the respect of the choices of individuals of a same community by the valuing of the social roles of those members who are at risk. And more than that, it allows the establishment between the members of one and the same community conditions that promote relationships between people. In this sense Normalization and SRV are very close to the thought of that Canadian who has greatly influenced the lives of tens of thousands of persons in this country. Jean Vanier said: "Life in the community is a great adventure. My hope is that many persons will be able to live this adventure which is in the end one of interior liberation—the liberty of loving and of being loved." There is much of this in what was discussed at the Ottawa conference.

REFERENCES

BLANCHET, A. (1990). *Retour dans la communauté des personnes polyhandicapées: L'expérience de la Colombie-Britannique au Canada*. Geneva, Switzerland: Éditions des Deux Continents.

ENDICOTT, O. (1990). *The right of persons with intellectual handicaps to receive medical treatment*. Discussion Paper. Canadian Association for Community Living.

G. ALLAN ROEHER INSTITUTE. (1988). *Le revenu précaire: Le système de pensions d'invalidité au Canada*. Toronto, ON: Author.

G. ALLAN ROEHER INSTITUTE. (1990). *Poor places: Disability-related residential and support services*. Toronto, ON: Author.

GOVERNMENT OF CANADA. (1982). *Canadian Charter of Rights and Freedoms. Section 15* Part 1. Constitution Act. Ottawa.

LAMARCHE, C. (1991). *La criée novatrice: Pour repenser l'intégration au seuil de l'an 2000*. Conference. Montreal, Canada.

McKNIGHT, J. (1995). *The careless society: Community and its counterfeits*. New York: Basic Books.

MINISTÈRE DES AFFAIRES SOCIALES. (1977). *Livre blanc: Proposition de politique à l'égard des personnes handicapées*. Gouvernement du Québec.

PAPPERT, A. (1983). *The Stephen Dawson case and the media: A report*. Toronto, ON: National Institute on Mental Retardation.

VANIER, J. (1979). *Community and growth*. Toronto, ON: Griffin House.

VELA HOUSING SOCIETY. (1994). *Microboards' guiding principles and functions*. Vancouver.

WOLFENSBERGER, W. (1972). *Normalization: The principle of Normalization in human services*. Toronto, ON: National Institute on Mental Retardation.

WOLFENSBERGER, W. (1973). *The third stage in the evolution of voluntary associations for the mentally retarded*. Toronto, ON: International League of Societies for the Mentally Handicapped, & National Institute on Mental Retardation.

WOLFENSBERGER, W. (1992). *A brief introduction to Social Role Valorization as a higher order concept for structuring human services* (Rev. ed.). Syracuse, NY: Syracuse University, Training Institute for Human Service Planning, Leadership and Change Agentry.

WOLFENSBERGER, W., & GLENN, L. (1975, reprinted 1978). *Program analysis of service systems (PASS): A method for the quantitative evaluation of service systems: Vol. 1. Handbook. Vol. 2. Field Manual* (3rd ed.). Toronto, ON: National Institute on Mental Retardation.

23

The impact of Normalization and Social Role Valorization in the United Kingdom

TONY WAINWRIGHT

1 INTRODUCTION

This chapter discusses the contributions from Kristjana Kristiansen (chapter 18), Michael Kendrick (chapter 21), and Jacques Pelletier (chapter 25) from the viewpoint of a clinical psychologist from the United Kingdom. Before approaching the main topics that they raise, I would like to set the U.K. scene and give some personal background that I bring to this critique.

I have worked in human services for the past 15 years and for most of that time, Normalization has been something of a guiding framework for me. I have worked in community settings and in large institutions. I now work at St. Lawrence's Psychiatric Hospital in Cornwall, which still has over 200 people living there. This hospital started its career in the 12th century, when it served people with leprosy. It is located on what was historically a good begging route and while begging for alms may be thought of as belonging to history, it is alive and well in the UK as it is in most other parts of the world. Leprosy, too, is still a major disabling illness and this should provide a reflective context for any positive statements we can make about service improvements or optimism in the UK and elsewhere.

These three papers broadly agree that there have been some improvements in the lives of people with disabilities in the countries they have surveyed, and many of these developments are also to be found in the UK. I would have liked to have devoted more space to the many achievements of the U.K. scene, but my purpose is to specifically discuss selected issues raised by these three papers.

In particular, I will not be discussing the extensive training program of PASS and PASSING, which Alan Tyne and Paul Williams have led throughout the 1980s through the auspices of the Campaign for Mental Handicap Education and Research Association (CMHERA), nor with this and other organizations that are continuing training and consultation in this area. The impact of this training initiative should not be underestimated, as a very large number of influential workers in human services have been exposed to Normalization and SRV through its agency. I will also not discuss the very considerable movement toward more normalized settings such as the development of ordinary housing as a service form. Finally, I will not be covering any of the issues that center on the advocacy movement.

2 THE U.K. CONTEXT

Some major milestones in the development of the "ordinary life" ideas and the introduction of Normalization and SRV into the UK are shown in Table 23.1, and the context in which Normalization has been operating in the UK is presented in Table 23.2. I will set out four main points here.

TABLE 23.1

SOME MILESTONES IN THE INTRODUCTION OF NORMALIZATION AND SRV INTO THE UK

1957	"Brooklands" (see J. Tizard, 1960) moving young people from hospital into "ordinary housing"
1958	Establishment of adult training centers
1963	Architecture for the disabled is the hot topic
1964	Wolf Wolfensberger working with Jack Tizard et al.
1965	Wessex 25 place hostels developed
1971	Campaign for Mental Handicap (CMH) established
1975	Visits from/to Danish and Swedish services
1976	Visits to ENCOR/COMSERV
1978	CMHERA established
1979	First Normalization and PASS workshops held in UK
1979	Ordinary life initiatives at King's Fund begin
1979	Jay Report on "Mental Handicap Nurse Training" published
1980	Supported house in Skelmersdale opens
1981	NIMROD opens/Andover experiment begins
1982	First PASS workshop held in Dublin
1983	All Wales Strategy for mental handicaps services published
1983	CMHERA participates in first PASSING in US
1984	First PASSING workshop in UK
1985	Speak Out starts
1987	First Moral Coherency workshop held in UK
1988	First Sanctity of Life workshop held in UK
1989	Campaign for Mental Handicap becomes Values Into Action
1989	First SRV workshop in Belfast
1990	NIMROD evaluated using PASS

Raynes, Pratt, & Roses, 1979; Malin, 1987). This was an established, extensive, and robust knowledge base. Furthermore, international exchanges took place between U.K. workers and our colleagues from the Scandinavian countries. The reason for making this point is that it sometimes seemed that when Normalization or SRV were being presented, the world started thinking about the need for services to change to reflect new ideas in, say, 1972, when the Normalization book was published (Wolfensberger, 1972). This was not the case.

TABLE 23.2

THE U.K. CONTEXT

Strong clinical/community traditions

- mental hospital decline both mental health (since 1948) and learning difficulties (since 1970) although varied in different parts of the UK
- radical right-wing government since 1979 with powerful ideology
- commercialization of welfare
- managerialism purchasers and providers of care
- consumerism—user power
- cash crisis—recession
- value for money-targeting of resources-rationing
- health divide widening (see Phillimore, Beattie, & Townsend, 1994).

Firstly, Normalization did not arrive in the UK into a theoretical or practice vacuum. As Wolfensberger has noted in chapter 3, his work with Jack Tizard and Neil O'Connor at the Maudsley Hospital in London in the early 1960s was very influential in his thinking. Tizard and O'Connor continued with their work throughout the 1960s and 1970s in collaboration with such people as the Clarkes, Albert Kushlick and, more recently, David Felse and Norma Raynes (see, for example, Tizard, Sinclair, & Clarke, 1975; Kushlick, 1975;

The second contextual point is that the rundown of the large asylums began in England quite early. Indeed, 1948 saw peak occupancy just before the establishment of the National Health Service and the new welfare state. The novel availability of benefits outside institutions, together with the optimism of the therapeutic community movement, led to a sharp decline in numbers, and deinstitutionalization literature began to accumulate in both the mental health and learning disability fields. By the mid-1960s it had become government policy to close the old asylums, with speeches by ministers arguing that the dreadful conditions had to end. While we know this is a complex story, taking a different route in England from either Wales, Scotland, or Northern Ireland (and the learning disability population in fact grew during the two postwar decades) the rhetoric of community care was well under way. Indeed, some community services had already developed, and this led to the formation of a separate community mental health ideology with a different history to that of SRV.

A third pivotal issue is the political and ideological context of Mrs. Margaret Thatcher's first administration, around which Normalization had to grow. As noted in Table 23.2, the notion of individual responsibility was central to this ideology, and the oft-quoted statement that there is no such thing as society highlight the difficulties SRV as a manifestly competing set of ideas would have. I have noted in Table 23.2 some positive and negative consequences of the Thatcher agenda.

The final contextual issue has been the strong evidence from census and other data, and particularly from the work of Peter Townsend (see, for example, Phillimore, Beattie, & Townsend, 1994), that the poor have gotten poorer and sicker and the rich richer and healthier over the last decade or so. As devalued people are, almost by definition, overrepresented in or, some would say, coextensive with the poor, the service improvements that we have undoubtedly seen are perhaps more marginal than we sometimes like to believe. It is noteworthy that the Health of the Nation initiatives do not mention poverty as a cause of ill health (see HMSO, 1990).

3 COMMENTS ON THE CHAPTERS

3.1 COMMENTS ON CHAPTER 18 BY KRISTJANA KRISTIANSEN

Running through this chapter is a theme concerning the significance of high-level social policy and law concerning disabled groups and the influence Normalization has had on these. So, an important system issue is the legislative framework surrounding the entitlements, rights, and protection afforded to disabled people. As she sketched in her paper, there

are a range of laws in this area. This is also covered more briefly in the other two chapters. While it is emphasized that the presence of such laws does not guarantee their effectiveness, their absence and the intensity of opposition—particularly ideologically powerful opposition—to such laws may be seen as an indication of the low legal standing of disabled people.

What is the situation in the UK as far as the policy reforms and legislation are concerned, and how far has Normalization influenced them? While I am not a legal expert, my own reading of the situation is that there is virtually no legal framework protecting the rights of disabled people. One contemporary event in the UK highlights this situation, where a private member's bill in the House of Commons providing rights for disabled people (which has cross-party support) has just been blocked by a government minister "talking it out." It has been explicitly stated that the government is opposed to such a law as it would cost money and decrease the UK's international competitiveness. The Disability Movement won't let things go, however, and the European Court of Justice may make some interesting rulings in the near future. Liberty, the Human Rights organization in the UK, has also recently published a report (Liberty, 1994) framing the experience of disabled people in terms of the abuse of human rights and is submitting its report to the United Nations. While Normalization per se has not been a strong force in this area, it has played a part.

The only aspect of recent legislation that provides a specific role for consumers is the Community Care Act 1990, but this supports only weak involvement and more often is honored in the breach than in its observance.

One other device considered rather eccentric by many has been the Citizen's Charter. This did not emerge from pressure from below, but from the Prime Minister's efforts to make "public services more accountable." There is some debate over whether it is completely ineffective and simply gives the right to complain or is revolutionizing the way public services view their responsibilities to their "customers." Both might be true!

Two brief further pointers to the future can be seen. In one recent court case, children have been granted the right to sue education authorities if their educational needs are not met. The second point is that ordinary citizens now have a statutory right to see their own health records. We are getting less secretive, but it is slow progress.

Some 15 years ago, however, things were different. The Jay Report on "Mental Handicap Nurse Training" had just been published (HMSO, 1979), with a chapter on a model service written by Derek Thomas (currently director of the National Development Team for Learning Disability Services). Still an excellent statement of the principles of the rights of people with learning difficulties, it was informed by visits to services such as ENCOR, which had been established using the Normalization principle. This report, together with the work of Alan Tyne and others on the "Ordinary Life" working group organized by the Kings Fund, led directly to the one national policy document firmly influenced by Normalization, namely, the All Wales Strategy (AWS). This document does not mention Normalization specifically, and is mentioned elsewhere in this volume as an example of Normalization being influential but too controversial to acknowledge explicitly. The AWS has been remarkable in driving services for people with learning disabilities in Wales toward patterns we would recognize as advocated by Normalization.

One example of this is in Clwydd, North Wales, where Grahame Harper has been able to develop comprehensive services for different client groups covering both Health and Social Services. He reports this to have been possible through the following mechanisms: the AWS; Normalization/SRV; frameworks for accomplishments that John O'Brien has developed; John McKnight's work on community building and competence; personal commitment by many people locally; and, finally, having the management clout to make things happen. These are all necessary for a successful enterprise.

In summary, despite the efforts of many groups, social policy legislation has not extensively incorporated Normalization ideas.

The next point concerns the notion of "alliances" developed in Dr. Kristiansen's paper and how SRV attracts and repels support: the U.K. situation is summarized in Table 23.3.

The picture is of rather weak alliances between SRV and other major organizations and ideologies in the field. As noted in Table 23.3, with some notable exceptions, there are no major organizations that have adopted Normalization. This may reflect the overconcentration in SRV circles on learning disabilities, and this has perhaps not been helpful to either SRV as a set of ideas, or the groups of people who may have benefited from their application.

TABLE 23.3

SUMMARY OF THE U.K. SITUATION

1. SRV as a guide for social policy reform and protective legislation?

- Virtually no legislative framework for disability rights
- The Jay Report and the All Wales Strategy for learning difficulties services strongly influenced by SRV
- Rather weak consumer-led planning as part of the Community Care Act 1990
- Citizenship ideas through the Citizen's Charter having some weak impact

2. SRV as a magnet for alliances?

- Few if any major voluntary organizations have Normalization/SRV as their mission
- Few if any service-user organizations or disability organizations have adopted Normalization or SRV
- Strong local alliances built particularly in North West Region of England and in Wales
- Links with political parties or other political organizations marginal if any

---

The voluntary sector has had a rather ambivalent relationship with these ideas. Among organizations for children, Barnardos (North West) and the Children's Society (see Williams & Race, 1988) have had strong connections with SRV, and their impact on the wider service field has not been insignificant.

The training department of MIND, our major mental health campaigning organization, was developing Normalization as a central plank of its work but eventually rejected it.

In the learning disability field, MENCAP—a U.K. charity for persons with learning disabilities and their families—has had a very mixed view of Normalization and SRV, and on the whole has been rejecting it in fundamental ways, although more recently it has adopted policies that reflect an awareness of the importance of image issues, particularly in its advertising.

Services for older people have been notable for the lack of influence by SRV.

As already noted by Michael Oliver (chapter 6), the disability movement in the UK is not closely allied with SRV either theoretically or practically (see also Oliver, 1990). The criticisms of SRV from this perspective are found in a number of chapters (see, for example, Oliver and Perrin in this volume, chapters 6 and 8, respectively) and they underline the task faced if common ground is to be found.

3.2 COMMENTS ON CHAPTER 25 BY JACQUES PELLETIER

TABLE 23.4

POSSIBLE REASONS FOR IMAGE PROBLEMS OF SRV

- Association with death-making teaching
- Conservative service system
- The way we have done our training
- Its perceived cultural identity is alien (either Scandinavian or North American)
- Complexity leading to misunderstandings
- Lack of clarity about the status of the SRV "movement"

One particularly pertinent section in this chapter concerns how SRV itself is imaged, and the author makes the case that it is seen as radical rather than commonsensible. While this agrees with my own experience, it is also seen, as noted elsewhere in this volume, as being paternalistic, controlling, and judgmental. Considerations of how this imagery is dealt with and why it has developed are important issues for us in the UK, as SRV has not been a widely popular viewpoint over the past few years. This is connected with the lack of alliances mentioned above,

but also there is a strongly held view that it is taught in too dogmatic a way, which leads to converts rather than flexible thinkers. There are some possible themes that may bear on this, which are outlined in Table 23.4.

3.3 COMMENTS ON CHAPTER 21 BY MICHAEL KENDRICK

The question "Are things going well or badly?" arises from the notion of "SRV consonant effects."

Two areas are illustrative of the U.K. situation. First, there is a mixed picture concerning public perception of disabled people. For those with mainly physical disabilities, there has been some remarkable progress. People with physical disabilities are routinely positively imaged in athletics (as "disabled athletes") and disabled people have radio and television programs presented by disabled people. However, there is often very devaluing press coverage of disabled people.

An example in the *Boston Evening News* (Grahame, 1994) has the headline "Caring for children who never grow up." The first paragraph reads: "Mums and dads cry at weddings when their offspring fly the nest. Some parents cry much oftener because they know their children will always be fledglings with broken wings."

This article/ad describes a new facility for adults with learning disabilities. We have a long way to go in getting the message across that devaluing imagery is damaging.

Second, I am also less than convinced that, taking the disability world as a whole, things are improving. One indication is in the field of services for older people. My own hospital, for example, has sold its 100-year-old Radial Building to a nursing-home-providing company that may develop a large nursing home on-site. Another is a recent decision by the U.K. government to change its criteria concerning allocation of NHS continuing care facilities, which may be the beginning of further exclusion of older people from services to which they should be entitled. It is in the elderly field that the scandals are likely to be seen, although children's services seem to be running them a pretty close second.

4 CLOSING REMARKS

Finally, it is clear that there are many areas where SRV has had a substantial impact on improving the lives of handicapped people. However, it is largely a first world ideology (but see Billimoria, 1993, for a discussion of the application of Normalization to India) and can be seen as generally reflecting the concerns of these countries. As the world becomes a smaller, more interdependent place, the wider political and ideological context must not be neglected or SRV will become an interesting set of old ideas but not relevant to the real world of the 21st century.

REFERENCES

BILLIMORIA, R. B. (1993). *Principle and practice of Normalization: Experiences from Sweden and application to India.* Uppsala University, Uppsala: Centre for Handicap Research.

GRAHAME, A. (1994, April 6). Caring for children who never grow up. *Boston Evening News.*

HER BRITANNIC MAJESTY'S STATIONERY OFFICE (HMSO). (1979). *The Jay Report.* Report of the Committee of Enquiry Into Mental Handicap Nursing and Care. London: Author.

HER BRITANNIC MAJESTY'S STATIONERY OFFICE (HMSO). (1990). *Health of the nation* (5 volumes). London: Author.

KUSHLICK, A. (1975). Epidemiology and evaluation of community services for the mentally handicapped. In M. J. BEGAB & S. A. RICHARDSON (Eds.), *The mentally retarded and society: A social science perspective* (pp. 325-343). Baltimore: University Park Press.

LIBERTY. (1994). *Access denied. Occasional report.* Liberty (formerly National Council for Civil Liberties).

MALIN, N. (Ed.). (1987). *Reassessing community care.* London: Croom Helm.

OLIVER, M. (1990). *The politics of disablement: Critical texts on social work and the welfare state.* Macmillan.

PHILLIMORE, P., BEATTIE, A., AND TOWNSEND, A. N. D. (1994). Widening inequality of health in Northern England, 1981-91. *British Medical Journal, 308,* 1125-1128.

RAYNES, N., PRATT, M., & ROSES, S. (1979). *Organisational structure and the care of the mentally retarded.* London: Croom Helm.

TIZARD, J. (1960, April 2). Residential care of mentally handicapped children. *British Medical Journal,* 1041-1046.

TIZARD, J., SINCLAIR, L., & CLARKE. (1975). *Varieties of residential experience.* London: Routledge and Kegan Paul.

WILLIAMS, P., & RACE, D. (1988). *Normalization and the Children's Society.* CMHERA.

WOLFENSBERGER, W. (1972). *The principle of Normalization in human services.* Toronto, ON: National Institute on Mental Retardation.

Normalization and Social Role Valorization in Australia and New Zealand

PETER MILLIER

1 HISTORY

Normalization and Social Role Valorization have had a comparatively short history in Australia and New Zealand. There has not been a culture of PASS such as that which influenced policy, practice, and research in North America and the United Kingdom in the 1960s and 1970s. PASS was used sporadically for research and evaluation in Australia in the 1970s by researchers at the Schonell Institute in Queensland and by some workers in the Commonwealth Rehabilitation Service (part of the Commonwealth Government Disability Services). It was not underpinned by any systematic or sustained presentation of (then) Normalization theory or training in the conduct of PASS such as had occurred in the US and Canada and, as a consequence, both the content and process of PASS events were probably incompletely understood and articulated. There were a number of evaluation instruments that derived from PASS, such as Community Health Evaluation of Service Systems (CHESS), which were quite widely used in Australia in the mid-1970s, and the "Blue Book," which was developed by the then New Zealand Institute of Mental Retardation and published in 1980. The Blue Book focused on standards for residential services. CHESS did not acknowledge its indebtedness to PASS but the Blue Book did, one of the authors of the latter publication having been involved in PASS workshops in Canada during the 1970s. In turn, the Blue Book influenced the development of an interagency standards document in

Western Australia and subsequent intellectual disability service evaluation instruments now used by the Standards and Monitoring Service (SAMS) in New Zealand.

Until 1980 most of the attempts to use PASS or instruments derived from PASS were based on an emerging sense of the need for measures of service accountability and quality, but were not embedded in a broader strategy to change or develop the pattern of services for people with intellectual disabilities. However, there was a mood and a movement for change that was influenced by several factors. First, there had been a number of young, enthusiastic, and, in some instances, dissident professionals recruited into intellectual disability services during the 1970s. These workers challenged prevailing views about how best to provide services for people with intellectual disabilities and, in particular, the dominance of the medical profession. Second, there was a tradition in both countries of inviting progressive leaders in the field to visit. Thus, people such as Jack Tizard, Gunnar and Rosemary Dybwad, Albert Kushlick and the Clarkes had visited, lectured, met with key professionals, policy makers, and parents throughout Australia and New Zealand and communicated their ideas. Third, most of the key players had read and clearly been influenced by *The President's Committee on Mental Retardation* (Kugel & Wolfensberger, 1969) and *The Principle of Normalization in Human Services* (Wolfensberger, 1972). A number of people from Australia and New Zealand were also aware of

ENCOR in Nebraska and COMSERV in Canada. Indeed quite a few visited Nebraska and Ontario and some stayed on to work there.

The visit by Wolfensberger in 1980 was pivotal in the development of Normalization and SRV in Australia. For the first time, people were exposed to a full presentation of (then) Normalization theory by Wolfensberger and Lyn Breedlove, and a significant number also attended the first PASSING workshop in Adelaide. At that stage, the PASSING manual was still in draft form. During his visit Wolfensberger also conducted a workshop on Planning Comprehensive Service Systems, and a group of people who attended took copious notes, which were circulated, read, and extensively discussed. These, together with the COMSERV monographs, became the basis for much service planning and development in a number of Australian states as well as influencing and informing *New Directions*, the report of the Handicapped Programs Review, which was established by the Commonwealth government in 1983 and published in 1985.

2 IMPACT

Normalization and SRV have had a considerable impact on legislation, policy, and practice in the areas of disability (particularly intellectual disability) and aged care, but the impact or influence has not always been obvious or given due recognition. It is not surprising that the principles underpinning Normalization and SRV (if not the theory) should find a certain resonance in Australia and New Zealand. There is a tradition of social democracy in both countries that inspired the original settlement ideals of justice and egalitarianism, although clearly this tradition did not necessarily extend to the original inhabitants. Both countries vied to be the first to give women the right to vote, and there is an equally long tradition of social welfare measures to provide a safety net for people who are unable to provide for or care for themselves. Thus, many people have found it easy to equate Normalization and SRV with (or to recast them in the language of) social justice, participation, and equity or, more colloquially, as a "fair go," which may in part account for some of the misunderstandings and misconceptions about the theory.

3 IMPACT ON DISABILITY LEGISLATION, POLICY, AND PRACTICE

It would be a mistake to assume that the impact of Normalization and SRV, or subsequent developments in legislation, policy, and practice in Australia and New Zealand (or even among Australian states and territories), have been the same everywhere. To a large extent, responses in various places are a reflection of the different histories of responding to the needs of people with an intellectual disability. For instance, the New Zealand Intellectually Handicapped Children's Society (IHC), the national voluntary association for people with intellectual disabilities, has been involved extensively in service provision, whereas in Australia, the National Council on Intellectual Disabilities (formerly AAMR) has not. However, many of its affiliated local and state voluntary associations do run services. Western Australia was arguably ahead of most Australian states in moving away from medical domination of services, and also away from large institutions toward smaller (albeit still quite large) hostels situated in local communities. In some states the government and voluntary sector worked together very closely, as did state and commonwealth funding agencies. In other places there was considerable tension and competition between the sectors, or state and commonwealth bureaucrats and workers did not talk to each other except through their respective ministers. New Zealand has only one government so it has largely avoided the problems of lack of coordination and overlap of responsibilities that have tended to occur in Australia.

In many respects, however, the scene was depressingly similar and familiar. There were many large institutions, mostly old and government-run, reflecting the history of the domination of those services by the mental health system. There had been some purpose-built institutions built in Australia during the 1960s for people with intellectual disabilities, but their newness did not mitigate the institutional thinking of the mental hospitals from whence most of those services had transferred. In New Zealand, the state institutions were known as "psychopedic hospitals," or "training schools," clearly reflecting the origins of the thinking and practices of the people who planned and ran them.

The period from 1976 to 1986 was one of great excitement and turbulence. There were many reports to governments concerning the need to reform and restructure services for people with disabilities. In Australia, the most influential of these were *The Law and Persons With Handicaps—Volumes 1 & 2* (Government Printer, 1979, 1981) prepared in South Australia by the Committee on the Rights of Persons With Handicaps, which was chaired by Sir Charles Bright, a retired Supreme Court Judge, and *New Directions* (Australian Government Publishing Service, 1985), the report of the Handicapped Programs Review, which had been established by the then Commonwealth Minister for Community Services, Senator Don Grimes. There were a number of reports to the various state governments including, among others, the McCoy Report (1981) in South Australia, the Beecham Report (1982) in Western Australia, and the Richmond Report (1983) in New South Wales, all of which charted new directions for disability services (and, in the case of Richmond, psychiatric services as well) in their respective states.

Normalization and SRV were clearly a major influence, either explicitly or implicitly, in all of these reports. Some reports used Nirje's definition of Normalization but Wolfensberger's concepts. Others mentioned Wolfensberger more specifically in relation to the need to develop Citizen Advocacy and other safeguards. Still others did not mention Normalization but made frequent reference to terms such as *least restrictive alternative, the developmental model, moral and legal rights, participation,* and *equity.* A number of the people involved in the various reviews and reports discovered that it was not strategic to use the language of Normalization/SRV, or to mention Wolfensberger, so they used other words to describe the principle or the concepts being discussed. One of the people closely involved with the Handicapped Programs Review said that there was a suspicion of jargon and things American. Participants in the review agreed for the most part with the principles underpinning Normalization and SRV but not the language.

It was hardly surprising then, that *New Directions* and the Disability Services Act (1986), should be imbued with the language of rights and equity although it is worth noting that the Objectives of the Act contain specific reference to the use of culturally valued means, meeting individual needs, promotion of image

and competency enhancement, physical and social integration, autonomy and rights and advocacy, which are all Normalization/SRV concepts, or derive from the theory.

Notwithstanding the impact of Normalization and SRV on disability policy and legislation in Australia, their impact on practice has been much more oblique. There appear to be some close parallels with the North American and Scandinavian experiences as described by Michael Kendrick and Kristjana Kristiansen in their papers. For example, implementation efforts have been impeded by confusion about Normalization/SRV, not just in the definition and exposition of the Nirje and Wolfensberger formulations, but more especially by the lack of a systematic, coherent articulation of Normalization/SRV in legislation, policy, and practice. Normalization, SRV, and social integration have been seen as synonymous with deinstitutionalization or, for political reasons, have been a hidden or covert aspect of policy and practice, often concealed under the banner of rights and social justice.

On the other hand, Normalization and SRV appear to have made a much greater impact at the local and personal level. Thus, certain services or agencies, usually discrete and small, together with some parent, consumer, and advocacy groups, have embraced, not just the rhetoric, but also the reality of what it means to support a person with an intellectual disability, to advocate on his or her behalf, or to provide services to a group of people using Normalization/SRV principles. For the most part, the people involved are part of the SRV network in Australia.

In New Zealand, the link between Normalization/SRV and disability legislation, policy, and practice, while acknowledged, has also been covert. The IHC, which today provides services for 3,000 people throughout New Zealand, was apparently well ahead of its government counterpart in developing a philosophy and standards for services in the late 1970s, of which the Blue Book formed an important part. There has also been a tradition in IHC of involving families and people with intellectual disabilities in decisions about service provision and evaluation, and this tradition has been continued in the evaluation sphere by the now independent Standards and Monitoring Service. However, there seems to have been less willingness among key leaders in services in New Zealand to acknowledge the extent to which

Normalization and SRV have influenced policy and practice. As has been the case in Australia, there is a strong aversion to the jargon, if not the concepts, and perhaps in the case of New Zealand, there has been an even stronger resistance than in Australia to the perception of a hegemony of ideas and language emanating from North America.

In both Australia and New Zealand, Normalization and SRV are taught as part of basic and postbasic courses in colleges of education and universities with varying degrees of understanding and competence. Generally speaking, the more closely the people teaching these courses are linked to the SRV network, the better are the course content and processes. In some instances people who are teaching courses seem to have had very little exposure to SRV and PASSING, nor do they appear to have much contact with people with intellectual disabilities in their personal or professional lives.

4 IMPACT ON AGED CARE LEGISLATION, POLICY, AND PRACTICE

Normalization and SRV have also had a significant impact on developments in aged care in Australia. Between 1980 and 1989 there were four reports and reviews conducted by, or on behalf of, the Commonwealth Department of Community Services (the Department has since changed its name several times), which have led to substantial changes in aged care policies and practices. The McLeay Report (Australian Government Publishing Service, 1982) focused on the high cost of nursing home care and the way funds were distributed in favor of institutional care. This led to changes in aged care residential programs to ensure more equitable distribution of funds to home and extended care support and to nursing homes and hostels. The Giles Report (Australian Government, 1984) and The Rees Review (Australian Government, 1986) focused on the goals of nursing home care and the provision of appropriate and quality care. Although cost was clearly a consideration, standards of care were also addressed by both Giles and Rees and, among other things, led directly to the development of standards for nursing homes and a process for evaluating nursing home care. Ronalds

(1989a, 1989b) investigated and made recommendations regarding the rights of residents in nursing homes and hostels. As important as these reviews and reports were to developments in aged care, probably of more importance was the environment in which they were conducted. At that time there were a number of key people within the Commonwealth Department of Community Services, including the state director in Adelaide, who, together with leaders in several aged care services in South Australia and Victoria, had attended Wolfensberger's 1980 workshops. Subsequently they formed a group, together with some people working in the disability field, that initially concentrated on learning more about Normalization/SRV and PASSING through a series of small-scale evaluations, informal discussions, and some introductory events for people with whom they worked. This in turn led to the development of embryonic Normalization/SRV groups in Adelaide, Melbourne, and Sydney but, more importantly, it helped develop a small core of people who were able to influence changes in policy, practice, and legislation throughout the 1980s. A strategic alliance was forged that has influenced many subsequent developments. Initially, many of the efforts at reform using Normalization/SRV principles and concepts were focused on improvements in the environments and conditions in nursing homes and hostels, but since the late 1980s there has been much more focus on programs to support and assist elderly people in their own homes and neighborhoods. As in disability, there was much enthusiasm and many mistakes. Some agencies have fallen away but others have continued to develop policies and practices that have Normalization/SRV as their basis. One agency in South Australia has been working at this for the past 14 years and is clearly regarded as a leader in the field of aged care by many, although the agency is also regarded as a "slightly eccentric relative" by some agencies and workers.

There are many parallels between developments in aged care and disability, but there are some differences. There has tended to be less involvement or commitment by service recipients and their advocates in aged care than in disability. On the other hand, reform in disability may be more difficult given its longer history and whole-of-life implications than in aged care. While more people in disability seem to have an understanding of, and commitment to, reforms based on Normalization/SRV, few have full agency or organizational support. While both disability and aged care are beset with increasing formalization and managerialism, some people in the Australian SRV network believe that there may be more lasting reform in aged care than in disability.

5 SRV NETWORK IN AUSTRALIA AND NEW ZEALAND

There is a network of SRV training and interest groups throughout Australia and, more recently, in New Zealand. There have been several phases in the development of these groups. Initially, the focus tended to be on meeting informally to learn more about the theory and its implications; then, gradually, to establish larger groups, many of which have been sponsored or supported by agencies for the purpose of conducting training workshops and sponsoring visits by people from overseas. Most of the groups, whether formally or informally constituted, have moved away from agency auspice to individual membership, although it would be foolish to pretend that these groups would be able to function as well as they have without the support of agency benefactors. The various groups have been assisted in their development through regular visits by people in the North American network especially, including Michael Kendrick, who has been most influential, Bruce Uditsky, Judith Sandys, A. J. Hildebrand, Zana Lutfiyya, and Darcy Elks. Wolfensberger and Susan Thomas have visited Australia twice recently (in 1989 and 1992), during which they have conducted many of the events offered regularly in North America by the Training Institute.

A significant number of people from the Australian network have also visited North America to study services and service developments, to attend various workshops and training events conducted by the Training Institute and its associates, and to spend time with various people in the North American network. Two people have spent extended periods at the Training Institute to develop their SRV training leadership skills and now act as senior trainers at SRV and PASSING workshops throughout Australia and New Zealand.

A national SRV group (ASG) was established in Australia in 1993. It is composed of individual members who either are working as independent SRV trainers or are working to achieve this status; also people who promote and develop SRV training. The goals of ASG are: (a) to develop an Australian SRV training culture with the development of SRV as a central function; (b) to safeguard and enhance the quality of SRV training and development in Australia; and (c) to provide a forum for problem-solving issues related to the implementation of SRV principles. Among a series of strategic objectives for ASG, the development of SRV trainers, together with the identification promotion and development of potential leaders, are undoubtedly the most important.

Strategic alliances and affiliations have been formed with consumer, parent, and advocacy groups, both nationally and in various Australian states. These alliances have been reinforced by consumer, parent, and advocate participation in Wolfensberger's workshops in Adelaide in 1992, as well as participation and involvement by various members of ASG in workshops and training events conducted by Zana Lutfiyya and A. J. Hildebrand at the National Citizen Advocacy Conference in Sydney in 1993, and in early 1994 in a series of workshops for parents conducted throughout Australia by Darcy Elks on behalf of the National Parent Information Project.

Another development that looks potentially fruitful has been the link with training courses at universities around Australia and New Zealand. Several members of the ASG are involved in teaching and/or administering courses in special education and disability studies, and they are meeting together to develop and coordinate strategies for teaching and conducting research projects related to SRV and PASSING.

Bengt Nirje and John O'Brien have both visited Australia (indeed, John has been a regular visitor over a number of years) to conduct various workshops, seminars, and consultancies. These have been conducted mainly on behalf of the National Council on Intellectual Disabilities (NCID) or affiliated agencies in the various states. While these events have been arguably impactful and indeed have contributed significantly to agency thinking and practices, they have not been linked for the most part to the SRV network or to the goal of SRV leadership development.

6 CRITIQUE, ANALYSIS, AND RESEARCH

Undoubtedly, one of the weakest points in the development of Normalization/SRV in Australia and New Zealand has been the lack of informed critique, analysis, and research. Most of the Normalization/SRV critique in the literature in both disability and aging (e.g., Shaddock & Zilber, 1991; Branson & Miller,1992; Stern, 1992, 1993; Graycar, Dorsch, & Mykyta, 1986; Fopp, 1990) has been of a very low level and characterized by many misconceptions and misunderstandings. Indeed, some critics (Branson & Miller, 1992) do not even provide references to suggest that they have read the basic Normalization/SRV texts. Others (Shaddock & Zilber, 1991) who do mention some of the readings do not seem to understand the profound differences between Wolfensberger's and Nirje's formulations of Normalization/SRV or much about the politics of change agentry. They make a statement toward the end of their so-called critique that "the Handicapped Programs Review did not need to mention Normalisation to justify its *New Directions*" whereas, in fact, as mentioned in this paper, Normalization and SRV were widely discussed during the review and many Normalization/SRV themes were included in the Objects of the Disability Services Act (1986), but a strategic decision was taken not to mention Normalization/SRV or Wolfensberger. There have been responses to some of the critiques (e.g., Kendrick, 1992; Wolfensberger, 1994; Wolfensberger & Thomas, 1994) that address many of the incorrect assumptions and misconceptions raised by Stern (1992), Shaddock and Zilber (1991) and Branson and Miller (1992), respectively. These, in turn, raise strategic questions that the Australasian SRV network needs to consider. For instance, should we be responding to critics in this way or should we become preemptive and create a climate of informed critique about some of the real issues, especially about the implementation of SRV in services and around individuals, or about the limits and limitations of services in areas such as relationships, autonomy, and rights, or indeed about the limits and limitations of SRV as a response to devaluation and wounding.

It is gratifying to see some research and writing beginning to emerge in the aged care area, and research is about to commence to analyze the results of PASSING evaluations in Australia and New Zealand, as has been done by Flynn, Lapointe, Wolfensberger, & Thomas (1991) in Canada and the United States.

7 SUMMARY AND CONCLUSIONS

Normalization/SRV in Australasia is young and vital but still fragile. The network in Australia has, for the most part, committed itself to SRV theory as propounded by Wolfensberger, which has been a surprise to some and a disappointment to others. The development of Normalization and SRV in the disability arena in Australia have in many respects mirrored developments in North America and Scandinavia. We have repeated many of the mistakes, but there have been some fruitful developments. The development of SRV in aged care policy and practice is unique. There has been a lot of mutual exchange between Australia and North America that has been beneficial. We have appreciated the need to form strategic alliances with consumer, parent, and advocacy groups. In Australia, in particular, we have been committed to working collaboratively and are strong as a group—there are no SRV hotshots. A major issue for us is not poor ideology but, rather, poor understanding, poor practice, and poor strategy. Normalization and SRV have had an impact, but the jury is still out.

REFERENCES

AUSTRALIAN GOVERNMENT PUBLISHING SERVICE. (1982). *In home or at home: Accommodation and home care for the aged*. Report from the House of Representatives Standing Committee on Expenditure. (The McLeay Report)

AUSTRALIAN GOVERNMENT PUBLISHING SERVICE. (1984). *Private nursing homes in Australia: Their conduct, administration and ownership*. Senate Select Committee on Private Hospitals and Nursing Homes. (The Giles Report)

AUSTRALIAN GOVERNMENT PUBLISHING SERVICE. (1985). *New Directions: Report of the Handicapped Programs Review*.

AUSTRALIAN GOVERNMENT PUBLISHING SERVICE. (1986). *Nursing homes and hostels review*. Steering Committee Review of Nursing Homes and Hostels. (The Rees Review)

BRANSON, J., & MILLER, D. (1992). Normalisation, community care and the politics of difference. *Australian Disability Review, 4*, 17-28.

FLYNN, R. J., LAPOINTE, N., WOLFENSBERGER, W., & THOMAS, S. (1991). Quality of institutional and community human service programs in Canada and the United States. *Journal of Psychiatry and Neuroscience*, 146-153.

FOPP, R. (1990). Normalization: Some critical observations. *Australian Journal on Ageing, 9*, 15-19.

GOVERNMENT PRINTER. (1981). *The law and persons with handicaps, Volumes 1 & 2*. South Australia. (The Bright Report)

GOVERNMENT PRINTER (1982). *The future delivery of services for people with intellectual disability in Western Australia*. Western Australia. (The Beecham Report)

GOVERNMENT PRINTER, NSW. (1983). *Inquiry into health services for the psychiatrically ill and developmentally disabled*. (The Richmond Report)

GRAYCAR, A., DORSCH, M., & MYKYTA, L. (1986). Challenging the new orthodoxy. *Australian Society*, 25-27.

KENDRICK, M. (1992). Additional thoughts on "rationality" and the service system. *Australian Disability Review, 4*(1), 1-16.

KUGEL, R. B., & WOLFENSBERGER, W. (Eds.). (1969). *Changing patterns in residential services for the mentally retarded*. Washington, DC: President's Committee on Mental Retardation.

RONALDS, C. (1989a). *I'm still an individual*. Canberra: Department of Community Services and Health.

RONALDS, C. (1989b). Residents' rights in nursing homes and hostels: Final report. Canberra: Australian Government Publishing Service.

SAHC. (1981). *A new pattern of services for intellectually handicapped people in South Australia*. (The McCoy Report)

SHADDOCK, A. J., & ZILBER, D. (1991). Current service ideologies and responses to challenging behaviour: Social Role Valorization or vaporization? *Australian and New Zealand Journal of Developmental Disabilities, 17*, 169-175.

STERN, W. (1992). A plea for rationality. *Australian Disability Review, 4*, 3-10.

STERN, W. (1993, December). Good intentions are not enough. *ACROD Newsletter*, 24-28.

WOLFENSBERGER, W. (1972). *The principle of Normalization in human services*. Toronto, ON: National Institute on Mental Retardation.

WOLFENSBERGER, W. (1994). Review of Shaddock & Zilber's current service ideologies. *The International Social Role Valorization Journal, 1*(1), 49-50.

WOLFENSBERGER, W., & THOMAS, S. (1994). A critique of a critique of Normalisation. *Australian Disability Review, 1*, 15-19.

25

The impact of Normalization and Social Role Valorization in francophone countries and communities from the late 1960s to the 1990s

1 OVERVIEW

Normalization and Social Role Valorization have had varying types and degrees of impacts in francophone countries and communities around the world as an ideology, as a framework for the evaluation and organization of human services, and as an instrument for social change. Where Normalization/SRV impacted, it was a major influence in the way we perceive persons with disabilities and human service users, and the way services and supports are organized.

Although we celebrate 25 years of the formulation of the principle of Normalization, Normalization and its SRV reformulation are still relatively new to many francophone communities. Normalization and SRV have essentially impacted Quebec as a jurisdiction in specific human services, while having localized impacts on specific services in other countries, and no impact at all in others.

The most visible impact of Normalization and SRV have been on service delivery systems in Quebec and francophone Canada, especially in the area of services for developmentally disabled persons. Essentially, these service systems gradually evolved from a segregated institutional model to a community integrated model. Such a change constitutes a positive development in and of itself but with intrinsic

drawbacks and limitations, as we will later explore. These developments mirror those in the US and the rest of Canada. The scope of such service system evolution was essentially local but touched a broader group of service users in francophone Europe; however, there has not been a major shift from institutional services to community based services in francophone Europe, where, to begin with, institutions tend to be smaller and physically closer to communities.

Normalization and SRV were very late in being made available in French: although much was said about Normalization/SRV through the years, and although much was done in the name of Normalization/SRV or Normalization/SRV interpretations, relatively few individuals had ever read a comprehensive text about Normalization/SRV in French until PASSING (Wolfensberger & Thomas, 1988) was published in French in 1988 and Le principe de la valorisation des rôles sociaux (Wolfensberger, 1991) was published in 1991. This situation was made worse by the use of unauthorized and poor translations and interpretations that were used to promote (or discredit) Normalization/SRV. So not only was English Normalization/SRV material unavailable in French, misinterpretations of Normalization/SRV or related works such as PASS (Wolfensberger and Glenn, 1975) were disseminated and used.

As in anglophone communities, Normalization and SRV were initially transmitted through two evaluation tools based on Normalization (PASS) or Social Role Valorization (PASSING). Most of the individuals who participated in these early PASS sessions were professionals and civil servants, many of them working in the field of developmental disabilities. They had allies in the parents' movement, but often these allies were from the Toronto-based National Institute on Mental Retardation (NIMR). Francophone allies in the parents' movement took longer to come on board, as most parents were suspicious at the outset about Normalization/SRV, although they tended to support potential changes to a service system they considered of poor quality. Finally Normalization and SRV came on the scene at a time when the service system was ripe for change and at a time when financial resources were plentiful. There were three consequences to these factors: (a) initial comprehension of Normalization and SRV were coloured by an evaluative perspective and by PASS-PASSING teaching methods; (b) Normalization and SRV were initially promoted and used by civil servants and agency managers with tacit support from the parents' movement; and (c) political and economic circumstances enabled the initial promoters of Normalization/SRV to have a substantial impact on policy development and on service systems for developmentally disabled persons.

Such was the case in Quebec in the 1970s, a situation not unlike other communities elsewhere in North America. When Normalization and SRV were introduced in francophone Europe, the initial reaction in some circles was similar to what happened in North America, but it never materialized as a systematic movement, although Normalization/SRV promotion benefited from more sustained efforts; as well, written material and quality teaching in French became available relatively early on.

To fully understand the scope and complexities of the impact Normalization and SRV have had in francophone communities, one must analyze it from cultural, historical, and systemic perspectives.

2 SOME HISTORICAL PERSPECTIVES

The influence of Normalization/SRV on public policy development and service system changes in francophone countries and communities is linked to historical factors.

Normalization/SRV thinking has been part of the picture in Canada and Quebec since the late 1960s when it was introduced through the Canadian Association for the Mentally Retarded (now called the Canadian Association for Community Living [CACL]) and its technical arm, the National Institute on Mental Retardation (now called the G. Allan Roeher Institute) and their related networks. In Quebec, the Association du Québec pour les déficients mentaux (now the Association du Québec pour l'intégration sociale [AQIS]) and its technical arm, the Institut Canadien Français pour la déficience mentale, later named the Institut québécois pour la déficience mentale (IQDM), were the main organizations that promoted Normalization/SRV. As in the rest of Canada, Normalization/SRV activism was based on an alliance between a parent/consumer movement and individuals in government and service agencies involved with persons with developmental disabilities. Since Normalization and SRV were available only in English, only a few Québécois were initially exposed comprehensively to the ideology. Although Normalization and SRV made their way in government policy and service systems for developmentally disabled persons, they would remain for many years concepts shared basically by an elite composed of some civil servants and service managers in the field of developmental disabilities; its impact was therefore concentrated on one group of service users. Most of these initial leaders and promoters of Normalization/SRV were humanists and idealists with a vision to improve the lives of service users, but they faced a service system that was very strong and did not want to change. To produce change they sometimes had to act decisively and in controversial fashion, which made them look like radicals and helped image Normalization/SRV as dogmatic, or "pie-in-the-sky." This phenomenon could explain why things eventually "got done," over a long period, sometimes in policy, sometimes in services, but never in a concerted and systems-wide way, at least not until the late 1980s. It also explains why to this day Normalization and SRV still have a reputation of being very radical rather than an ideology based on common sense and basic Judeo-Christian values.

As it now stands in Canada and in Quebec, Normalization- and SRV-inspired values, such as social integration, are universally accepted as the philosophical base for the organization of human services, particularly in the field of disabilities. Normalization and SRV are part of policy, regulations, and everyday operation of human services. If there is a problem today it is that Normalization and SRV are taken for granted. The parents' and consumer movements in North American francophone communities, and specifically in Quebec, now embrace Normalization/SRV and are usually in a good position to create change, as they have generally transformed themselves from service providers to advocacy organizations.

Normalization and SRV were introduced in francophone Europe—France, Switzerland, and Belgium—via Canada and Quebec in the early and mid-1980s. An organization called CEDIS (Comité Européen pour le développement de l'intégration sociale), an offshoot of initial PASS training sessions in Normandy and South Western France, was formed and continues today its involvement in Normalization/SRV dissemination, mostly through training sessions and service evaluations. Normalization and SRV have a reputation in francophone Europe as being "American" ideologies, based on American values and culture, although the origins of Normalization are European and SRV is very close to francophone European values. While Normalization and SRV have had less impact in Europe than in North America because they are still relatively new, their influence ranges beyond the field of developmental disabilities. As well, although Normalization and SRV were introduced through PASS training sessions, SRV and PASSING are increasingly being taught and written about; as well, a number of Europeans (through CEDIS or privately) have taken the Normalization/SRV leadership from the initial group of Canadians involved and have developed teaching capabilities that outweigh in quantity and quality what is generally available in North American francophone communities. One important aspect of the current situation is the fact that Normalization and SRV in francophone Europe do not have a consumer base, nor do they enjoy the formal support of consumer or parents' associations (such as CACL's equivalents) or that of high-ranking civil servants, as was the case in North America. As well, the International League of Societies for Persons With Mental Handicaps, based in Brussells and with a certain influence in some francophone circles, has not promoted the Wolfensberger-inspired formulations of Normalization and SRV. As a result, Normalization/SRV leadership in Europe is mostly concentrated on a small number of individual service managers, university professors, and human service professionals, all of whom tend to have local influence. In recent years, however, CEDIS has been able to link up with European Community agencies, where the concepts of Social Role Valorization and social integration are gaining acceptance.

Normalization and SRV have yet to be introduced to other countries where French culture is still a factor, notably the former colonies of France and Belgium in the African continent. The one notable exception is the French Department of La Réunion, in the Indian Ocean, and its neighboring country, Mauritius Island, where for a few years in the mid- to late 1980s PASS and Normalization/SRV were introduced and had some impact within service systems and associations.

3 CULTURAL PERSPECTIVES OF NORMALIZATION AND SRV IN FRANCOPHONE COUNTRIES

3.1 HOW NORMALIZATION AND SRV WERE TRANSMITTED

Historically, one must bear in mind that Wolf Wolfensberger's (1972) *The Principle of Normalization in Human Services* was never made available in French. As well, related works such as PASS were only available in francophone Europe in the late 1980s in its approved version. In fact, the Wolfensberger Normalization/SRV Monograph (*La valorisation des rôles sociaux*) was printed in French and made available only in 1991: This was really the first ever systematic summary of Normalization/SRV available in French. For the past 25 years, Normalization and SRV have basically been transmitted through word of mouth in francophone communities. In other words, although Normalization and SRV have had some influence, and although for many years many people have claimed to be knowledgeable about them, it is only recently that they have been available in written form, as well as through competent training sessions.

3.2 COMMUNITIES WHERE NORMALIZATION AND SRV HAVE MADE A DIFFERENCE

Normalization and SRV have varying degrees of impact in some countries and/or communities but not in all. North American communities, specifically Quebec and Acadian communities in New Brunswick, as well as some French Canadian communities in Ontario, were more or less influenced by Normalization/SRV. Of those communities, Quebec was where the impact of Normalization/SRV was and still is felt the most. In fact, Quebec is the francophone community throughout the world where Normalization and SRV have impacted the most on its legislation, public policy and service systems. Not surprisingly, most initial francophone Normalization/SRV supporters and leaders came from Quebec, and it is through that community that other francophone communities in Europe were originally exposed to Normalization/SRV.

Normalization and SRV have had some impact in European countries such as France and its territories, as well as Belgium and some Swiss Cantons. However, in those countries, Normalization and SRV were either episodically influential, within specific communities and agencies, and involving a small group of persons, or were merely one of many social influences that served to modify certain aspects of the service system picture.

Normalization and SRV have not had any impact in North or Continental African countries where French is spoken, as in the former colonies of France or Belgium.

3.2.1 QUEBEC

On the policy level, Normalization first appeared in the influential 1977 Livre Blanc (Ministère des Affaires Sociales, 1977)—Policy Statement White Book—regarding the government's policy proposals for handicapped individuals. This was the Quebec government's first attempt at a comprehensive social policy statement with a view to promote the social integration of handicapped persons. Supporters of Normalization/SRV were very influential in this work. In 1989 the Office for the Handicapped (Office des personnes handicapées, 1989) produced a policy document reproducing the 1977 framework and

framing the community and comprehensive service system concept. Again, this policy statement and framework was very much influenced by Normalization and SRV and by some of their promoters. In 1987 and 1988, the government produced a policy document (Ministère de la Santé et des Services Sociaux, 1988) and related strategies for the systematic transformation of institutions for developmentally disabled persons into community-based services. The next few years saw the beginning of a massive deinstitutionalization effort inspired by these documents. As with initial policy papers, these were greatly influenced by individuals and organizations linked to the consumer organizations supporting SRV and social integration. These policy orientations in the field of developmental disabilities were consolidated further by the government's policy on families (Secrétariat à la famille, 1992) and its welfare policy (Ministère de la Santé et des Services Sociaux, 1992).

All of these policy developments were instrumental in consolidating what was to be the greatest impact of Normalization/SRV in Quebec: the massive deinstitutionalization process and community-based service development in the field of developmental disabilities.

This process of massive deinstitutionalization was part of a larger process in North America that originated in the late 1960s in the US in large part as a product of class action advocacy for the benefit of persons with developmental disabilities based on constitutional grounds; as a result of advances in pharmacology and psychiatry that permitted large numbers of patients to be discharged from psychiatric hospitals; and for economic considerations. The process in Canada, as far as developmentally handicapped persons were concerned, was slower in developing and did not start systematically until the 1980s: this is due in part to the fact that the process was not triggered by constitutional rights or fueled by court procedures, but by a gradual social policy paradigm shift with regard to persons with developmental disabilities. Such changes were essentially brought about through long-term efforts of advocacy organizations. As far as the field of psychiatry and mental health is concerned, the Canadian process mirrors that of the US, which basically amounted to political and administrative policy decisions to reduce hospital beds and release patients in community settings, but without much in terms of community support systems and without clear strategies to develop them.

A basic feature of deinstitutionalization processes in North America is the development of community-based alternatives to replace institutional models for persons with disabilities. This is also true in Quebec and francophone Canada, although in Quebec the deinstitutionalization process has been one of transformation of institutional resources and bureaucracies into community-based service systems and bureaucracies. Those efforts have produced massive developments of community-based services that have enhanced the potential of service systems to provide persons with developmental disabilities an improved quality of life. There are, however, some important shortcomings to this strategy. One is that institutions are still an important (and expensive) part of the service delivery system, leaving most communities with a double system: an institutional system that uses up a large portion of public funds to serve a small group of individuals, and a community-based system that has yet to receive proper funding to fulfill its claim that *all* persons with disabilities can and should live and be supported in the community. Another is the fact that while large institutions are closing, the institutional culture is being systematically reproduced in the community; as a result, natural support systems such as families and personal networks are being replaced by professional services.

3.2.2   OTHER CANADIAN COMMUNITIES

In other Canadian francophone communities, Normalization and SRV have essentially the same impact as in Quebec with the exception that SRV in its English format was somewhat more accessible to French Canadians and Acadians, who tend to be more bilingual than francophone Québécois.

3.2.3   FRANCE

The impact of Normalization/SRV in France is essentially a product of the individual efforts of a cadre of human service managers and consultants. Contrary to North America, these Normalization/SRV promoters hail from a larger variety of human services, namely social services, mental health, and rehabilitation, with a larger service user base, namely young persons, senior citizens, (ex)psychiatric patients, as well as disabled individuals. While larger in scope as far as service domains are concerned, Normalization/SRV influence in France is not nationwide but tends to be regional. As well, the impact is often less visible than in North America since institutions (the focus of advocacy and change agentry in North America) and services tend to be smaller to begin with. This in turn makes it more of a challenge to change service patterns, especially since these patterns are quite a bit older than those in North America and tend to "look better" or at least "not as bad" as the larger North American institutions. Nevertheless, Normalization and SRV have had important impacts in northern France (Dunkerque area), in Lower Normandy, in the Charente regions, and in the Lot and Garonne region in southwestern France. One interesting influence has been in the field of child protection services in southwestern France, as well as services for drug abusers; other influences in service systems are especially evident in vocational services for developmentally disabled adults. The biggest differences in Normalization/SRV impacts between North America and Europe are that European service systems have longer traditions, tend to sustain smaller agencies, and take more time to change than their North America counterparts. As a North American Francophone who works in this continent as well as in Europe, I would tend to caution my North American colleagues: Because we change so easily and massively does not mean our services are better than those of the Franco-Europeans; and though some of our services seem to look better, many of them are nonetheless of poorer quality than those services in Europe that have tended to change very slowly. In fact, I believe, recent developments in Quebec, where huge service organizations have been put in place, are jeopardizing much of what has been done in the past 25 years, whereas services in francophone Europe, because they have remained organized within reasonable dimensions (i.e., where service managers know the names of their service users and interact with them), tend to continue to improve, albeit slowly. Normalization and SRV have also had an impact on evaluation techniques and program development. Recent works by Joing (1993) and Dupont (1989) in the field of evaluation, and by Pelletier, Dupont, and Tessier (1994) in the field of programming, make extensive use of contemporary Normalization/SRV literature.

Normalization/SRV influence in Switzerland is similar to that in France, but on a smaller scale. Geneva is probably the one canton where it has had the most impact with services in mental health and in developmental disabilities. Although small in scope, this influence has nonetheless been very important with some psychiatric community services and within the sphere of influence enjoyed by the Geneva Association for Intellectually Handicapped Persons and their friends. Some community-based services in the field of mental health in Geneva rank with the best of their kind in Europe or the rest of the world and are openly promoting Normalization/SRV values as the basis for their organization. The field of child protection is also very much influenced by Normalization/SRV in Geneva, a recent but significant trend. Finally, the University of Geneva (department of special education) has for the past years used and developed contemporary Normalization/SRV literature in its courses to undergraduate students and supports to community groups.

3.2.5   BELGIUM

In Belgium, Normalization and SRV have had a very important impact through the Département d'orthopédagogie at the university of Mons-Hainault. This university department has trained a number of frontline professionals with Normalization/SRV as a foundation who in turn have played an important role in the slow but steady evolution toward the social integration of developmentally disabled persons. As well, the department has been influential in recent government policy development. It is interesting to note that Mons is the only example of sustained and effective Normalization/SRV leadership and influence within francophone communities that emanates from an academic setting: other universities and colleges

offer credit courses featuring Normalization/SRV, but none go as far as Mons. Only Syracuse University's Training Institute would compare in Anglo-Saxon communities, although the latter is strictly concerned with SRV and SRV-related work, while Mons uses Normalization/SRV as a values system within its general curriculum. This being said, as with the Training Institute at Syracuse University, Normalization/SRV activism and promotion in Mons are based on the dedication of a few individuals who are promoting SRV values in their work without any support, and indeed most often, against official academic and administrative policies of the universities they work in.

3.3   THE LEGACY OF NORMALIZATION AND SRV IN FRANCOPHONE COMMUNITIES

3.3.1   SOCIAL POLICY

Many industrialized countries where disabled persons had been massively institutionalized, segregated, and congregated over the last 50 to 100 years have in the past 25 years developed some forms of social policies aimed at promoting their social integration. Such policies usually were successful in reducing the number of persons living in inadequate institutional settings (deinstitutionalization) and/or increasing the development of community-based resources; at least such is the case in North America and its francophone communities, notably Quebec. In these jurisdictions, social integration of disabled individuals has become the official norm, the accepted policy. In Quebec, as in other Canadian provinces and communities, Normalization/SRV had an important impact on the development and implementation of so-called "progressive" social policies for disabled persons and, specifically, on persons with developmental disabilities. In other fields, Normalization/SRV had an indirect and secondary impact, serving as support to develop and implement social policies that were part of an international trend toward social integration, but not as a leading force. Such is also the case in francophone Europe, where social integration of devalued persons is the present trend and fashion, at least in theory, without Normalization and SRV as major contributors. In other francophone countries, disabled persons have not been institutionalized as massively, so there has been no need for policies promoting social integration. On the contrary, there seems to be an increasing pressure to develop segregated institutions in some of these countries.

3.3.2 A TRANSFORMED SERVICE SYSTEM

In North American francophone communities, the evolution from asylums to smaller community-based services is directly related to Normalization/SRV thinking. This is the most important and visible legacy of Normalization/SRV.

Related to this development is the fact that disabled persons are more visible in communities than 25 years ago and have begun taking a more prominent place as citizens. However, visibility does not mean social integration. While more people are physically integrated, it would seem that for most, personal social integration remains the unfulfilled promise of Normalization/SRV. A simple review of jobs and salaries for disabled persons will show for instance that while disabled persons benefit from the economy in terms of care and services, they have yet to participate as contributors to the economy. In Europe, small institutions continue to be the norm, as they have been for many generations, although the actual physical integration of persons is increasing.

Perhaps the most frustrating systemic development traced to Normalization/SRV-inspired reforms, at least in North America, and most notably in Quebec, has been the emergence of massive, public service bureaucracies and service management organizations that have replaced the old order of institutions and community services. This trend is especially evident in the field of developmental disabilities, where the bureaucracies and literal "empires" have replaced smaller community services as well as natural family-based supports. These new organizations have enormous powers, can easily intrude in people's personal lives (and systematically do), and, by replacing natural supports by service systems, will ultimately destroy many of the positive effects of the past 25 years. Some would say that this process is very much under way.

Related to the above, the human service industry is constantly growing, to the point now where instead of integrating and supporting communities and families, they replace them. The amount of money being spent in service organizations is mind-boggling, but the actual services received by disabled persons and their families, as well as their level of quality, has not grown as much and as fast.

Finally, large institutions have often been replaced by settings that look nice, that seem to offer good supports and services, but that often end up becoming smaller (institutional) versions of the ones they replaced.

This being said, disabled persons generally enjoy significantly better living conditions than they did 25 years ago, and although Normalization/SRV cannot take all of the credit, we can say that they played a most important and key role in promoting change in the quality of life conditions for disabled persons and their families.

3.3.3 A NAIVE BELIEF IN SERVICE SYSTEMS

Again related to the service system legacy of Normalization/SRV, the transformation of service systems have led us to believe, here in North America at least, that a system could be invented that would assure lives of quality in the community for socially devalued persons. Such an artificial support system does not yet exist, nor will it ever, but we persist in developing or searching for one, at the same time destroying the only natural system that can support the social integration of persons: their families and personal networks.

It is perhaps time to return to the essence of Normalization/SRV: using them as a guide, as a value base, but not trying to change the world through social engineering in order to make it "Normalization/SRV perfect."

3.3.4 COMMENTS ON A NEW VOCABULARY

Normalization and SRV were influential in raising our level of consciousness regarding labels that stigmatize people. Words used to describe conditions and persons who live with them have positively evolved. This being said, this trend has recently developed a tendency toward correctness whereby some words are not to be used. Some will bend over backward to use words that are so neutral and "nonstigmatizing" that they simply do not mean anything and might well prove to be detrimental to disabled persons as they tend to trivialize or minimize conditions that require important personal supports. Nevertheless, Normalization and SRV have left us with many new words, some of which have become part of everyday vocabulary in human services: Normalization remains the most prominent, as well as the most misunderstood and misused. In French the word *Normalisation* was never easy to accept, understand, or use, perhaps because we never got a chance to read about it in French. *Valorisation des rôles sociaux*, on the other hand, has become accepted and less prone to misinterpretations, again perhaps because we now have a few written texts and because

some teaching has been available. It is a pleasure for us Francophones to see that Anglo-Saxons now have to grope with Social Role Valorization instead of the former Normalization.

4 CONCLUSION

There can be no doubt that Normalization and SRV have had a profound impact in human services throughout the Western world, including its francophone communities. It is an ideology that permeates social policy and service systems. It is likely that this impact will continue and perhaps even amplify over the next decades in francophone communities, particularly in European communities.

REFERENCES

DUPONT, A. (1989). *L'évaluation dans le travail social*. Geneva, Switzerland: Éditions I.E.S.

JOING, J.-L. (1993). *L'audit de la qualité dans les établissements médico-sociaux*. Toulouse, France: Éditions PRIVAT.

MINISTÈRE DE LA SANTÉ ET DES SERVICES SOCIAUX. (1988). *L'intégration des personnes présentant une déficience intellectuelle: Un impératif humain et social* (Document de consultation). Gouvernement du Québec.

MINISTÈRE DE LA SANTÉ ET DES SERVICES SOCIAUX. (1992). *La politique de la santé et du bien-être*. Gouvernement du Québec.

MINISTÈRE DES AFFAIRES SOCIALES. (1977). *Livre Blanc. Proposition de politique à l'égard des personnes handicapées*. Gouvernement du Québec.

OFFICE DES PERSONNES HANDICAPÉES DU QUÉBEC (OPHQ). (1989). *À part. . . égale. L'intégration des personnes handicapées: Un défi pour tous*. Gouvernement du Québec.

PELLETIER, J., DUPONT, A., & TESSIER, C. (1994). *Le plan de services individualisés*. Geneva, Switzerland: Éditions des Deux Continents.

SECRÉTARIAT À LA FAMILLE. (1992). *Familles en tête. 2e plan d'action en matière de politique familiale, 1992-1994*. Gouvernement du Québec.

WOLFENSBERGER, W. (1972). *The principle of Normalization in human services*. Toronto, ON: National Institute on Mental Retardation.

WOLFENSBERGER, W. (1991). *La valorisation des rôles sociaux: Introduction à un concept de référence pour l'organisation des services* (A. Dupont, V. Keller-Revaz, J. P. Nicoletti, & L. Vaney, Trans.). Geneva, Switzerland: Éditions des Deux Continents.

WOLFENSBERGER, W., & GLENN, L. (1975, reprinted 1978). *Program analysis of service systems (PASS) : A method for the quantitative evaluation of service systems. Vol. 1 Handbook. Vol. 2 Field Manual* (3rd ed.). Toronto, ON: National Institute on Mental Retardation.

WOLFENSBERGER, W., & THOMAS, S. (1983). *PASSING (Program analysis of service systems' implementation of Normalization goals): Normalization criteria and ratings manual* (2nd ed.). Toronto, ON: National Institute on Mental Retardation.

WOLFENSBERGER, W., & THOMAS, S. (1988). *PASSING (Programme d'analyse des sytèmes de services application des buts de la valorisation des rôles sociaux): Manuel des critères et des mesures de la valorisation des rôles sociaux* (2e éd.). (M. Roberge, Trans.; J. Pelletier, Adap.). Gloucester, ON: Communications OPELL.

26

The impact of Social Role Valorization[1] on government policy in Quebec

ANDRÉ DIONNE

1 FOREWORD

In this brief commentary, I will attempt to describe SRV's influence by the application of its corollaries in the organization of services. This approach will only peripherally call into play the factors that come out of SRV-related evaluation instruments such as PASS (Wolfensberger & Glenn, 1975) or PASSING (Wolfensberger & Thomas, 1988). Using PASS or PASSING would undoubtedly have quickly led us to a dead end. Large systems including social service systems are often limited by all sorts of constraints that are often of an economic nature.

One notes, however, that SRV (Wolfensberger, 1972, 1983, 1991) has brought about a new form of discourse that is now part of the service tradition at least in the field of mental retardation. I would like to have said that this was the case for the whole of social services. However, one must conclude that it is the field of mental retardation that has most been influenced by this school of thought. One need only remember that its origins are to be found in services to mentally retarded persons in Nebraska and then at the National Institute on Mental Retardation in Toronto.

I will be examining SRV in the context of the development of government policy. In Quebec, the current organization of social and health services dates back to 1970, when following the publication of the recommendations of a commission of inquiry on income security, health, and social services (Gouvernement du Québec, 1971), the government proceeded with the development of a network of services, which had been, up until then, but a rosary of health and social service institutions spread out across Quebec's vast geography.

It was, for Quebec, the last of the great reforms that had started during the 1960s. To quote sociologist Fernand Dumont (1971), we were "rested and refreshed like no other people of the Western world, and haunted by the dreams accumulated through a long night, we started many projects in a house quickly cleaned. It was the extraordinary morning of the quiet revolution." After reforms in education, electricity, the Quebec pension system, and the Quebec Deposit and Investment Fund, Quebec endeavored to put into place a safety net of social solidarity.

A decentralized system was created where the province of Quebec was divided into social and health services regions according to the principles of regional self-sufficiency, accessibility to service, universality, gratuity, continuity, personalization, and service quality.

The challenging of existing services and of the forms of service provisions came principally from parent associations for the mentally retarded. From the beginning of the 1950s, the association's movement put the emphasis on the development of a social service system that would be integrated into the community.

The first manifestation of that ideology related to SRV can be found in the Bédard Commission Report on Psychiatric Services (Gouvernement du Québec, 1962). The principal conclusions of this commission proposed an end to the construction of asylums on the periphery of population centers; the introduction of mental health services in general hospitals; and, finally, the removal of mentally retarded persons from asylums and the creation of a network of life training centers, which was the name given to residential rehabilitation centers for mentally retarded persons. Improving service quality, then, consisted of opening schools for the children of the institutional network of the Ministry of Family and Welfare by the Ministry of Education of Quebec. The first mention of organizational criteria that might have at least a superficial relationship to SRV emerged from the 2nd volume of a report from the Ministry of Family and Welfare presented to the Royal Commission of Enquiry on Education in March 1962 (Gouvernement du Québec, 1963-1966). In this document, the emphasis was placed on the smallness of residential services, established as "life units" (unités de vie) within the institution, and the specialization of services through individualized teaching, but no mention is made of the separation of functions. This report mentions that the structuring of life conditions similar to those found in a family will facilitate the development of children within an institutional milieu.

FIGURE 26.1

RESIDENTIAL PLACEMENTS IN REHABILITATION CENTERS

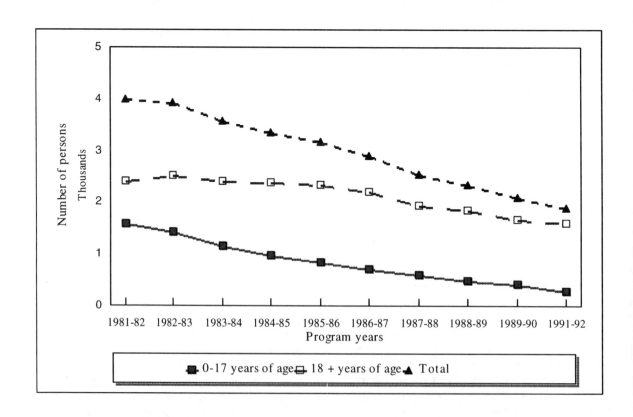

Finally, it is at the beginning of the 1970s that a text mentions Normalization without, however, providing any kind of definition of what it might mean. All that is mentioned are some of its corollaries related to physical, social, and school integration. This document, *Preliminary Reflections Prior to the Writing of a Program Guide (Réflexion préalable à la confection de mémoire de programme)* (Bouffard & Perron, 1972), was requested by the government's Treasury Board and eventually led to the *Program Guide: Children Services (Mémoire des programmes—Les services à l'enfance)* (Gouvernement du Québec, 1973) in which group homes and developmental day centers are identified as service development priorities. This text also discusses social integration of clients, although the text anticipates that a certain number of severely mentally retarded individuals will have to remain within institutions.

The 1970s were marked by many contradictory actions. While the discourse concerned itself with social integration, institutions continued to be built; the last three institutions were inaugurated in 1975. At the same time, the utilization of institutional placement continued to increase dramatically, reaching 4,000 persons—children and adults—in 1981 in the mental retardation sector. This does not include an approximately equal number of persons, principally adults, who were placed within the psychiatric hospital network.

Starting in 1982-1983, the number of persons with mental retardation placed in institutions diminished significantly. This trend maintained itself until 1992, the last year for which we have data (see Figure 26.1).

We will return later to review these data, but for the moment let us review SRV's impact on the social service system through legislation.

2 LEGISLATION

In the mid-1980s the government created a commission of inquiry to review the funding of social and health services. The Rochon Commission (Gouvernement du Québec, 1988), named after its chairman, Dr. Jean Rochon, brought about an updating of the organization of services. The law that came out of the commission's work (Gouvernement du Québec, 1993) states in section 1 that the "system has the goal of maintaining and improving the physical, mental and social capacity of persons, to act on their environments and help accomplish the roles that they wish to assume." Moreover, in paragraph 5, it goes on to state that the social service system aims "to further the rehabilitation of persons and their social integration." The legislation also emphasizes that the realization of its objectives requires that it "make accessible services in a continuous fashion in order to respond to the needs of individuals, families and groups" (section 2.4) and proposes "that the reason of being of services are the persons who require them" (section 3.1). The legislation, which was last amended in December 1993, also provides service users the right to be heard when they have grievances (section 29).

Prior to these major amendments by the Rochon Commission, there were in Quebec some 67 corporations that provided services in the mental retardation sector within each region. The 1993 reform reduced the number to 31.

During the review process, certain hypotheses were advanced that would have led to the grouping of residential services for elderly persons with community services and rehabilitation services for mentally retarded clients. This would have led to an unfortunate juxtaposition of clients. These notions were set aside, and organizations are now structured around the common characteristics of their client groups.

Over and above these grouping considerations, legislators gave mental retardation rehabilitation centers (section 310) responsibility for recruiting and organizing family-type resources (foster homes). Until recently, foster families had been the exclusive responsibility of community social service centers, where many different devalued client groups were served, such as young offenders, psychiatric patients, and persons requiring marriage counseling, and so forth. This new organization of services will further the continuity and specialization of services as well as provide foster families with the necessary supports. Foster families for adults go under the heading of *Résidence d'accueil* (or *receiving homes*) for the placement of adults or elderly persons.

I would not want to leave this section on Quebec legislation related to SRV without mentioning the joint efforts of the Human Rights Commission and the Office for Handicapped Persons of Quebec, who have published recommendations that emphasize the rights of clients to obtain an integrated education of quality and without discrimination. *The Access of Children Identified as Mentally Retarded Within the Regular School System (L'accès des enfants identifiés comme présentant une déficience intellectuelle au cadre ordinaire d'enseignement)* (OPHQ, 1991) was adopted by the Human Rights Commission on June 19, 1991, and by the Office for Handicapped Persons of Quebec on August 23, 1991. This document notes that a school board that decides to segregate children who are mentally retarded into special classes would then be in contravention to the Education Act and the Charter of Rights and Freedoms of Persons: The grouping of students who are mentally retarded into special classes constitutes discrimination; the use of mental retardation categories to register students in special classes constitutes a discrimination based on a handicap, unless one can demonstrate that students thus categorized are unable to be integrated in regular classes (p. 14). Consequently, it was recommended that the Education Act be amended by adding a disposition that would lead to adapted educative services for handicapped students and who are at risk of having some difficulties in adapting or learning and that these services and measures be available within the regular classroom.

FIGURE 26.2

EDUCATIONAL ASSISTANCE AT HOME

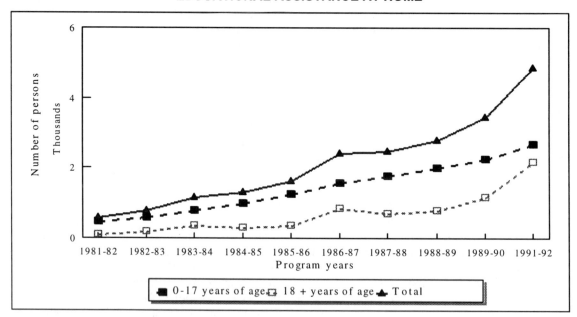

3 THE 1988 MINISTERIAL DECLARATION ON SOCIAL INTEGRATION

The translating of Social Role Valorization into services was affirmed in a 1988 orientation and action guide (Ministère de la Santé et des Services Sociaux, 1988) entitled *L'intégration des personnes présentant une déficience intellectuelle* (*The Integration of Persons With Mental Retardation*). This important government policy document states that "Social Role Valorization of handicapped persons must constitute the basic orientation of our policies and actions" (p. 14) and proposes a strategy aimed at gradually restricting the number of persons who are admitted to institutions because of mental retardation. More precisely, institutions were asked to restrict admissions and promote social integration of mentally retarded persons, whether or not they had other associated deficiencies or handicaps.

The minister's declaration required the following actions:

- starting in 1989, the residential needs of children had to be met by services integrated into the community;
- before 1989, the elimination of admissions to long-term care in hospitals or institutions for mentally retarded persons;
- before 1991, requests for residential services for adults had to be directed to community-integrated services;
- the social reintegration of 50% of the persons currently in institutions over the next 5 years.

A review of the data in Figure 26.1 shows that in 1992, 53% of mentally retarded persons had left institutions. We also see that starting in 1982-1983, the population of institutionalized clients decreases continuously throughout the decade. From 1981-1982 to 1991-1992, the number of persons 18 years of age and less decreased from 1,575 to 277. However, from 1988-1989 to 1991-1992 the number of institutionalized persons decreased by only 215, which represents a proportion of 15% of the total number of persons institutionalized within the mental retardation network. Thus, the publication of the orientation guide on integration (in 1988) does not seem to have had a dramatic impact on the integration of persons. Rather, it seems to have confirmed already well-established service trends.

Moreover, these data seem to demonstrate a certain priority accorded to the youngest institutionalized residents.

FIGURE 26.3

EDUCATIONAL ASSISTANCE IN DAY-CARE CENTERS

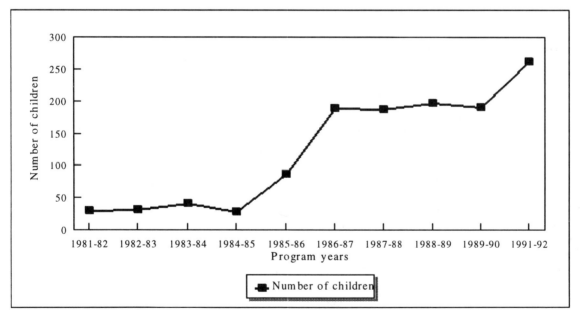

FIGURE 26.4

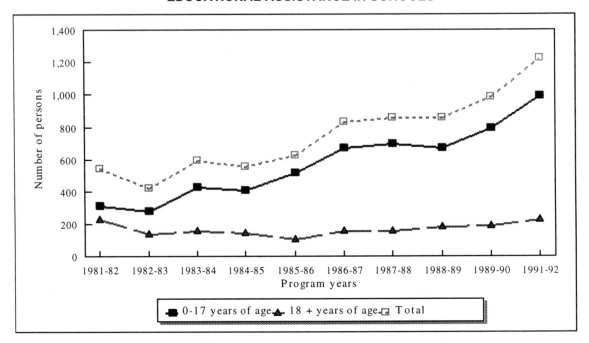

EDUCATIONAL ASSISTANCE IN SCHOOLS

4 EDUCATION PROGRAMS

As the residential institutions were emptying, there seems to have been a concomittant increase in the development of educational services, which facilitated integration with socially valued peers. Thus home support (Figure 26.2) showed a regular increase while educational assistance in regular day care (Figure 26.3) increased in a spectacular fashion from 1983-1984. This trend echoes the development of support programs within schools (Figure 26.4). Consequently, the number of places in rehabilitative day programs for persons 17 years of age or less diminished dramatically (Figure 26.5).

At the same time Figure 26.5 shows that the number of places for adults within institutional day centers increased, revealing the difficulty that the professional service system continues to have in serving an increasing number of adults. These difficulties could increase over the next few years because the Ministry of Education has decided to apply age restrictions in the Quebec Education Act thus excluding adults 21 years of age and over from schools. Consequently, the efforts to integrate within the work environment will have to be multiplied notably through some forms of companionship and placements within typical work situations.

5 RESIDENTIAL SERVICES

Group homes were the 1970s residential formula to physically integrate clients. At the same time, foster families were increasingly used for youth and children, which explains the decrease in the number of group home places for those under 18 years of age. Moreover, the development of family residential resources for adults throughout the 1980s led to a proportional decrease in the number of clients within group homes.

FIGURE 26.5

DAY PROGRAMS

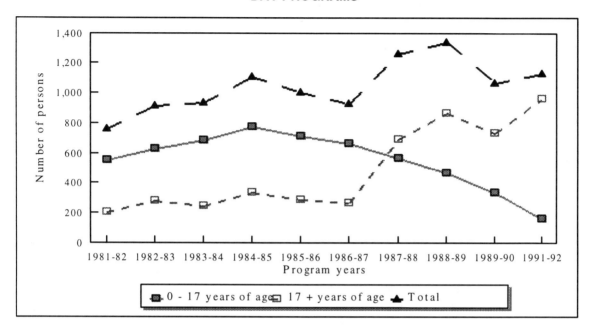

6 SERVICE QUALITY AS MEASURED BY PASSING

The above 1988 declaration placed much emphasis on the improvement of services to persons and their families. The evaluation of service quality was proposed as the best method for verifying the extent to which the services offered were of quality and conformed to the values, orientations, and practices highlighted by the minister in his declaration. The Ministry of Health and Social Services identified the Mauricie-Bois-Franc region as a demonstration region and hired Jacques Pelletier (1992) as head of an evaluation project that used PASSING as its primary evaluation tool.

Out of 39 service settings evaluated, 6, or 15%, of the sample reached or surpassed 70% of the maximum possible score on the PASSING scale. These results are very positive especially when compared to the PASSING results for services in North America,

which are significantly lower. Given the extent and the diversity of the sample, these results are particularly remarkable and suggestive of a network of services that attempts to implement SRV and to improve the life conditions of handicapped persons. These 6 services served 97 clients—not including family members—or 34% of the persons directly served by the services that composed the total sample.

Moreover, 17 of the 39 services that were evaluated surpassed the minimal quality requirements as set out in PASSING. These 17 services served 148 clients. Thus, 43% of services evaluated serving 60% of the clients within the sample achieved or surpassed the acceptable level of quality as measured by PASSING. One should thus commend the commitment of the persons working within these services.

This experiment showed a very effective way of evaluating service quality. Analogous evaluations should in the future be organized in other service regions.

7 CONCLUSION

The key to service quality in Quebec is the adoption of a model based on the growth and development of persons and the attribution of valued social roles, such as that of being the owner of one's own residence.

As was highlighted by the Human Rights Commission and the Office of Handicapped Persons, the dissemination of service strategies, such as those that come from SRV, requires removal of the barriers between regular and specialized professional education and training. This could imply the review of teaching and training programs for social service professions at college and university levels.

Moreover, a research and training center should be established at a university in order to assist in the development of strategies for the improvement of service quality through the use of Social Role Valorization.

REFERENCES

BOUFFARD, D., & PERRON, M. (1972). *Réflexion préalable à la confection de mémoire de programme: Les services à l'enfance inadaptée.* Québec: Ministère des Affaires Sociales.

DUMONT, F. (1971). *La Vigile du Québec.* Montréal: Les Éditions HURTUBISE HMH.

GOUVERNEMENT DU QUÉBEC (1962) *Rapport de la Commission d'étude des hôpitaux psychiatriques au Ministère de la Santé de la Province de Québec.*

GOUVERNEMENT DU QUÉBEC (1963-1966). *Commission royale d'enquête sur l'enseignement dans la province de Québec.*

GOUVERNEMENT DU QUÉBEC (1971). *Rapport de la commission d'enquète sur la santé et les services sociaux. Partie 4 Vol. IV.*

GOUVERNEMENT DU QUÉBEC (1993). *Loi sur les services de santé et les services sociaux,* L. R. Q., Chap. S - 4.2.

GOUVERNEMENT DU QUÉBEC (1973). *Les Services à l'enfance: mémoire de programmes.* Québec: Ministère des affaires sociales.

GOUVERNEMENT DU QUÉBEC (1988). *Rapport de la Commission d'enquête sur les services de santé et les services sociaux.*

MINISTÈRE DE LA SANTÉ ET DES SERVICES SOCIAUX DU QUÉBEC (1988). *L'intégration des personnes présentant une déficience intellectuelle: Un impératif humain et social* (Document de consultation). Gouvernement du Québec.

MINISTÈRE DE LA SANTÉ ET DES SERVICES SOCIAUX DU QUÉBEC (1992). *La politique de la santé et du bien-être.* Québec: Gouvernement du Québec.

MINISTÈRE DES AFFAIRES SOCIALES. (1977). *Livre Blanc. Proposition de politique à l'égard des personnes handicapées.* Gouvernement du Québec.

OFFICE DES PERSONNES HANDICAPÉES DU QUÉBEC (OPHQ). (1991). *L'accès des enfants identifiés comme présentant une déficience intellectuelle au cadre ordinaire d'enseignement.* Gouvernement du Québec.

PELLETIER, J. (1992). *Évaluation de la qualité des services du réseau de la déficience intellectuelle de la région 04 à l'aide de la méthode PASSING.* Gloucester, ON: Communications OPELL.

WOLFENSBERGER, W. (1972). *The principle of Normalization in human services.* Toronto, ON: National Institute on Mental Retardation.

WOLFENSBERGER, W. (1983). Social Role Valorization: A proposed new term for the principle of Normalization. *Mental Retardation, 21*(6), 234-239.

WOLFENSBERGER, W. (1991). *La valorisation des rôles sociaux: Introduction à un concept de référence pour l'organisation des services* (A. Dupont, V. Keller-Revaz, J. P. Nicoletti, & L. Vaney, Trans.). Geneva, Switzerland: Éditions des Deux Continents.

WOLFENSBERGER, W., & GLENN, L. (1975, reprinted 1978). *Program analysis of service systems (PASS): A method for the quantitative evaluation of service systems. Vol. 1 Handbook.*

Vol. 2 Field Manual (3rd ed.). Toronto, ON: National Institute on Mental Retardation.

WOLFENSBERGER, W., & THOMAS, S. (1988). *PASSING (Programme d'analyse des systèmes de services application des buts de la valorisation des rôles sociaux): Manuel des critères et des mesures de la valorisation des rôles sociaux* (2e éd.). (M. Roberge, Trans.; J. Pelletier, Adap.). Gloucester, ON: Communications OPELL.

NOTE

1. Social Role Valorization (Wolfensberger, 1991), as it is referred to in this article, includes its predecessor, the principle of Normalization, especially as it was formulated by Wolf Wolfensberger (1972).

Part 7

Personal Impact of
Normalization
and Social Role Valorization

27

The impact of Normalization and Social Role Valorization on my life

PETER PARK, WITH BETH FRENCH

In 1960, about 10 years before the philosophy of Normalization was developed, I moved to Oxford Regional Centre. I was 21 years old. I had lived at home with my family until then, going to high school, having regular friends, getting into regular trouble, learning how to drive, and all those typical things. My parents and some friends were advised by the doctors that my epilepsy would be better controlled in the institution, so there I went.

What hit me first, and what I remember most, was the regimentation. It was a lot worse than what I imagined the army would be like. There were about 7,000 people existing there at that time, in 1960. I can't say living, we existed. At the time, we were called inmates. We spent all our time on wards or in "cottages." The only activity was listening to the radio that the staff controlled. They picked the station and the volume. They thought we should listen to childish programs. I slept in a room with 14 other people I certainly wasn't related to. I hadn't even met them before. We did everything there. We ate, slept, drifted around all day, according to a mysterious schedule developed by someone I never knew or saw. You weren't considered part of it.

I had 18 inches of space between my bed and the wall. That was my space. You couldn't decorate your patch of wall because you never knew from one day to the next if you were going to be moved. I had two sets of institutional clothes. You had to use their dentist, their doctors, I didn't even have the right to pick my own barber.

I found the empty time unbearable. In those early years there was absolutely nothing to do. You couldn't go outside unless you were escorted by the staff. You couldn't even read. My father would bring me books from the library so that they would not take them away. You never had a chance to read the newspaper and find out what was going on in the world. You were already isolated enough, but that kind of thing made you feel even more cut off.

I went to ceramics for the first 3 years just so I would have something to do with my hands. After that, I luckily managed to get a "job" in the storage department, where all the supplies for the institution were handled. I knew someone who was quitting, and I asked him to tell the boss that I would be interested—no pay, of course—but at least I was busy from 9 to 5 each day.

I spent a lot of time on the punishment ward, especially at first, because I hadn't learned their rules yet. Most of the time I was in the time-out cell, no clothes, bare walls, and occasionally I was just on the ward. Mind you, the door was always locked. I figure I spent about 9 of the 18 years there. You were always heavily drugged on "D" ward. One major misdemeanor was looking at members of the opposite sex. I was often sent there for that and other misdeeds like getting angry or refusing to take medication. I wouldn't take some medication that they tried to give me because I didn't know the reason for it and I was afraid of the side effects. We knew we were being used as human guinea pigs.

By 1972 or 1973, we were called residents. They started talking to me about getting out. It was just talk, though. They did set up a life skills program, and eventually I was moved to a room that I shared with another resident. We could hang pictures on the walls and rearrange the furniture. Around 1977, they also started paying me $3.50 a week for my work in the stores. Looking back, I know that was the readiness training model. I didn't really care, because the only thing that kept me going was the thought of getting out. I always kept that ray of hope in my mind.

The "moving out" that I had longed for just happened one day in 1978. At noon someone told me there was an opening in a group home in Ingersol and I was going there at 1:30 that day. I wasn't asked, and my parents were not even told. In fact, my parents were not told until I called them 3 years later. I had lost contact with them. I wondered why they hadn't called me. When we finally talked, Mom said she was sorry I was out because she thought I was better cared for in the institution, and that she did not have to worry about me there. I told her I was the one having to live with the life in that place and I was glad to be out. That conversation was really hard. My brother and sister had known about the move, but they had kept this from my mother. That was also hard, but the hardest thing was that my dad had died and no one had even told me that he was sick.

There were 10 people in the group home, and during the day I was bused back to the institution to work. I didn't like living there. I realized that to have the life I had dreamed about for all those years, I would have to advocate for myself. I got moved to a different group home in another town, and within a short while I was in my own apartment in the Supported Independent Living Program. I had gone right through the continuum. That process took 22 years of my life.

The most ironic thing about that experience was that the problem of uncontrolled seizures, the reason for the move to the institution in the first place, was only resolved after I left when I found a good doctor on my own. So much for that helping system.

In about 1980, I attended a PASS course. The course really made me stop and think. My attending it caused a major incident. I was working in the sheltered workshop. The director called me up on the floor in front of other people and said: "Pete, you had no right to take that course. Who paid for it? It is for my staff only. Whose time did you use?" My response was: "It was my time, my holidays, I paid for it. The reason I took it was that I was curious to know what the staff were taught. As well, I was an interested self-advocate, and we all have the right to associate with whomever we please and further, as of today, I am walking out of this workshop for good." I quit the workshop that very day. The association director raised the roof. Imagine someone like me attending such a radical course. After 20 years of institutionalization, I still didn't control my own life. Maybe he was afraid I would uncover the truth about the system. Of course, I didn't need to take a course to learn that the so-called "helping system" hurts.

Since then, I have learned more about Normalization and Social Role Valorization. I know that this helped me to realize that *I* was not the problem. It made me question the way I had been treated. It also made me realize I had to respect myself.

I think Normalization and SRV have played roles in helping people like me to lead better lives. People now try to help people who have been labeled to live a more normal life in the community. We now have more diverse communities where people with different abilities can learn from each other. I imagine that without Normalization, I might still be in the institution. It was due to this theory that they thought about deinstitutionalization.

My story is still evolving, but now I choose the direction. I live in a different kind of institution—marriage. My wife, Terry, and I are building a life together, and we think about the future because I have put the past where it belongs—behind me. I carry out a lot of different roles that I am proud of. I am a husband, the Director of Information and Resources for People First of Canada, a co-op member, a board member, a colleague, a neighbor, and friend.

Often I am a teacher, helping people realize that throughout all these experiences, good and bad, I have been Peter Park, a man who just wants to do a decent day's work and go home at night to the place where I have chosen to live and to the people I choose to live with.

28

The personal impact of Normalization-related and Social Role Valorization-related training

JOE OSBURN

I have been asked to respond to Susan Thomas (chapter 15) and Deborah Reidy (chapter 15) who have written about the impact of Normalization-related and Social Role Valorization-related training as vehicles of personal, service, and policy change, and to do so particularly from the personal perspective. I take this charge to mean that I should concern myself with the effects of Normalization/SRV *training* on its recipients, including, of course, myself. (The impact of training on individuals should also be distinguished from the impact of Normalization/SRV *actions* on individuals, which, as Susan Thomas points out in her paper, is one of the four levels to which such actions are directed.) However, I would like to note at the outset that I claim no special expertise on this subject. By now, I would estimate that several tens of thousands of people throughout the (Western) world have undergone Normalization/SRV training. I am sure that that experience has had some sort of personal impact on each of them, which they could certainly relate as well as, or better than, I could my own. So the thoughts that I will now offer about the personal significance of Normalization/SRV training are based on my own experiences with this training over the past 20 years, as well as those of many other people whom I witnessed having been changed by Normalization/SRV training.

In order to describe the impact of Normalization/SRV training on me personally, I would like to first describe what I was like before Normalization/SRV training. Thirty years ago I was on the liberal fringes of, but still quite caught up in, the culture of human service professionalism and political activism. I think I really believed that right thinking by right politicians and the right service managers would result in the right actions on behalf of poor and oppressed people. I felt I was a part of a great struggle between good and evil, the forces of liberation and oppression, and that in that struggle it was important to be aligned with the poor and the oppressed. I saw many wrongs that needed to be righted, and I thought that human services, done right, could accomplish much good.

However, I also saw that human services were often *not* done right, that, in fact, they often made life much harder for the poor and the oppressed, that they did not need to be that way, and that they could and should be made better. This is why I liked the then emerging idea of accountability. I thought services should be held responsible for being good to, and doing good for, the people who needed their help. Acting on this belief seemed to naturally lead me further and further away from direct service and into human service supervision and management, where I really thought I would have sufficient scope of influence and responsibility to help services become better.

The first human service job I held where I felt I could actually do something about accountability was more than 20 years ago, and it quickly taught me that services were not all that eager to change, nor did the term *accountability* mean the same thing to me as it did to most of the human service administrators, boards, founders, and politicians on whom I tried it out. Most of them talked about accountability but saw no real need for change in their own pet services since these were already models of service quality. This is when I first heard the religious dictum "If it ain't broke, don't fix it!" Far from being deterred by these obstacles, I was spurred to learn more about how to help services change. It was hard going at first, and when I eventually did begin to gain a foothold, it led to one of the major turning points of my life.

What happened was that in 1973 a friend, Rex Kerr, and I got "promoted" to a human service job for which neither of us was trained or experienced, nor could we turn to anyone around us who knew any more about it than we did. Our new job title was "Planning Associate," and we were to plan and evaluate certain categories of human services in an eight-county urban region in Indiana.

The whole idea of evaluation was just beginning to emerge on the human service scene at about that time, primarily as an accountability mechanism following the huge increases in public funds that were allocated to human services in the 1960s and 1970s, such as during the so-called "War on Poverty" in the US. There was hardly anything written on the subject of service evaluation. There were virtually no formal courses on the topic anywhere in the undergraduate, graduate, or postgraduate realms of academia. There were no professional workshops or training events. There were no objectified broadly accepted standards of program or overall service quality. There were no recognized formal instruments for program or service evaluation. There was no language to describe a good service or, for that matter, a bad service. As Dr. Wolfensberger used to point out during PASS training events, "People often assumed that services were good simply because they existed." What little credible information did exist on the topic of evaluation tended to be particularistic to specific types of service models or clinical interventions. Even most of this was oriented to individualized assessments of persons.

But in spite of this void, we both took our new job seriously, and tried hard on our own to educate ourselves about how to do it. We spent a lot of time looking in libraries, talking with people, and so on, but had very little success finding anything that was helpful. We were about to give up looking and had decided to try to make up our own service evaluation instrument when providence struck.

We had been interviewing the director of a large mental retardation service agency with the hope of incorporating his ideas into the evaluation instrument we planned to develop. He said he really did not have any ideas and did not know of anything written on the subject. But, as we were leaving his office, a thought crossed his mind. He may have once gotten something in the mail, he said, that might pertain to our concerns, but he was not sure because he had not really looked at whatever it was. Still, we were welcome to it if he could find it. He shuffled through the papers on his desk, then the drawers, the file cabinets, and finally his bookshelf, but couldn't find what he was looking for. On our way out, I happened to notice and pointed out to him a large manila envelope that had fallen down on the floor behind his bookshelf. He looked and said that just might be the piece of mail he had in mind, so we helped him move the bookshelf and, sure enough, it was. He handed the envelope to Rex, who happened to be standing nearest, but Rex handed it on to me because he had several other articles to review that night. Lives turn on such little moments! I took it home, and later that night I opened it up. It was a little orange, magazine-sized book that turned out to be *PASS 2*, the first published edition of PASS. I started to read it.

I identify that as my "moment of first impact." From the very first moment I started to read *PASS*, I was hooked. I couldn't put it down. I read it from cover to cover in one sitting. It was the best thing I had ever read—not just on service evaluation, but on human services, period. I read it again the next morning. It just all made perfect sense to me. It rang true. It was powerful. It was lucidly written, not mushy like so much other writing in the field. It stood in such contrast because it took a stance on what should and shouldn't be—on what was good and desirable, and what was bad and hurtful. I was impressed (actually stunned) not only by its intellectual and technical quality, but even more by its moral rigor and its "realness." It did not try to be "value-free." It did not aspire to moral neutrality. It was very radical and quite revolutionary in this regard.

Well, I have to tell you, I loved PASS. It changed me indelibly, instantaneously, as people do get changed when the scales are removed from their eyes. And all this was just from reading the book. I had not even met Dr. Wolfensberger yet! You can imagine the impact on me when, just a few weeks later, in early 1974, I went to the first PASS workshop that was being held in Syracuse, New York, and *guess who* was my team leader there! The man himself! I've never been the same since. In fact, I really cannot make a distinction between the impact on me of Normalization/SRV training, and the personal and intellectual influence of Dr. Wolfensberger. That was the starting point for me in terms of what has since become my life's work and identity.

From that beginning, I wanted to learn as much as I could about all of this, and so basically started going to every training event that Dr. Wolfensberger and the Training Institute offered. After the first couple of these, the agency I was working for stopped paying my way, especially when it dawned on them that I was actually serious about evaluating services rather than merely endorsing them, and that what I was learning in these workshops threatened the established order they had been duly hired to preserve. After the third workshop, I had to take unpaid leave and vacation time and also pay my own way to all the many other training events I attended. Of course, it was all worth it, and usually Dr. Wolfensberger waived the fee anyway.

After a while, Dr. Wolfensberger invited me to make a presentation at a workshop, then to team-lead at a PASS workshop for the first time, and then again, and again, and so on. In 1975, he came to Indianapolis to conduct a PASS workshop, which was a major event for us. I was a "floater" over several teams at that workshop; and so it went. In 1977, I went to work for Dr. Wolfensberger at the Training Institute in Syracuse. That is when my education *really* began! (If ever there was anyone who personified intensity, high demands, and positive expectations for others, it is Dr. Wolfensberger.) There, I was blessed with many wonderful opportunities, especially getting to know and work closely with some extremely talented people who have had a deep and lasting influence on my life. Besides Dr. Wolfensberger, these included Susan Thomas, Guy Caruso, Darcy (Miller) Elks, Lynn Breedlove, and Steve Tullman, when we all worked together at the Training Institute.

Something that had almost as much impact on me as reading *PASS* and attending all those early training events was hearing for the very first time Dr. Wolfensberger's presentation of the most common "wounds" of societally devalued people. It was clearly the most eloquent statement about the life experiences of devalued people that I had ever heard. To me, it had all the power of stark indisputable truth. I was deeply moved. I felt as if I had just been given some *key illumination* of my feelings about what happens to poor and handicapped people. It was for me an astounding insight. It strengthened my commitment and helped provide a sense of real priority and even urgency in my work. After hearing that presentation, I came to believe that one of the most important things I could do for wounded people was to help others to see and understand their wounds and how they were struck. It gave me a way to clarify my own thinking about why I thought it was important to try to help devalued people. After all, what could be more important than to try to address these awful things that happen to them?

The first time Dr. Wolfensberger presented his formulation of the "wounds," there were (I think) only six. However, even more important to me than the specific number and types of wounds themselves was the fact that I had just been given an entirely new, existential *way of thinking* about the lives of devalued people. That insight penetrated deeply and was so powerful that it caused my own eyes (and those of many others) to be opened to a whole new level of consciousness, not just about devalued people, but even about humanity itself and life in general. It also enabled the realization of all sorts of other wounds. And so, almost each of the early presentations of the common wounds discovered still more wounds that had to be added to the presentation because our understanding had been so deepened. Soon there were nine wounds, then 12, then 16. And now, we talk about 21 common negative life experiences of devalued people. Like Normalization/SRV, the wounds insight was unequivocal in taking the side of the devalued person. It was a tremendous insight that I believe could only have been achieved within the context of an unshakable belief in the inherent dignity and infinite worth of all people. This whole perspective on the lives of devalued people was (and is) for me part of the essential wisdom for human service, without which—no matter how much else is known or done—a service or server will be totally misdirected with regard to the realities of life for devalued people, do no good, and probably much harm.

The personal impact of this whole pattern of experiences related to Normalization/SRV went beyond just my work. It deeply affected how I lived, mainly by returning me to a renewed conviction about my earlier service ideals and especially my Catholic religious heritage and basic Christian beliefs. It caused and helped me to reaffirm and rethink my outlook on many things. It gave me direction and also an anchor in something real. It opened the door to a better understanding of many other realities, that is, human nature, the fallenness of the world and all of its creatures, the imperial nature of all worldly structures—including of human services—the need for both direct voluntary personal engagement with devalued people and for communality with them and with like-minded people, and much more.

In addition to the profound initial impact of Normalization/SRV training, I have also been deeply affected by my long involvement with it. Earlier, I mentioned that I have been involved in Normalization/SRV training for over 20 years. For example, the book *The Principle of Normalization in Human Services* was published in 1972, and I first learned about it in 1973. The socialpolitical atmosphere that existed at that time, when Normalization and PASS were first being introduced, was much different than that of today in terms of the number and vehemency of its antagonists. Many hostile and resistant elements came to the training and fought it tooth and nail. They did not like what they were seeing and hearing, mainly, I think, because Normalization/PASS meant they would have to stop doing what they were doing as well as making a good living at it. Change was in the wind. They felt threatened by Normalization/PASS and wanted to stop it. Normalization/PASS espoused fundamental changes that stood in sharp contrast to the prevailing service thinking, service structures, practices, and attitudes of the day. I remember Dr. Wolfensberger used to show an overhead that was a picture of a wall with the handwritten words "Mene, mene, Tekel, upharsin!" (Dan. 5:25), presumably to help certain participants know that the handwriting was already on the wall. This revolutionary stature of Normalization certainly added to the impact it had on me 20 years ago, which undoubtedly is different that its impact on those encountering Normalization/SRV for the first time today, when there is much wider assent to Normalization/SRV ideas and many obvious advances in service practices, even though vast shortcomings still persist and the expressions are often far more subtle.

Nevertheless, I think there is a general consistency in the way people talk about how Normalization/SRV training has affected them. One thing that seems almost universally true about such training is that it *does* have an impact on the persons who receive it.

Relatedly, the impact of Normalization/SRV training on individuals is usually significant: Hardly anyone feels neutral about it. The extent of the impact, and responses to it, may vary from person to person, but it always seems to be definite and long-lasting. This point is worth noting: The fact that Normalization/SRV training does indeed have an impact on its recipients clearly distinguishes it from all sorts of other human service-related training experiences that are so ephemeral they leave no real mark.

Further, I know many people like myself whose life course has been largely shaped by their Normalization/SRV training. In other words, such training was the essential determinant of their lifetime Normalization/SRV-consistent service involvements. The longer the connection is sustained over time, the more powerful the initial impact is likely to have been; and, conversely, the longer a person stays involved with activities related to Normalization/SRV, the deeper and more pervasive its influence is likely to be on that person.

Finally, I believe that, in general, the overall impact of Normalization/SRV training on those who have received it has been positive, and, indeed, very much so. This is not to deny that many individuals have also been very discomfited and even downright disturbed by it. However, I know many people who at first hated Normalization/SRV but have since come around to being among its staunchest defenders and promoters. I do not know anyone who has actually been harmed by Normalization/SRV training itself, although I do know some who have been distressed and even eventually turned off by how their concerns about Normalization/SRV training, and particularly its implementation, have or have not been responded to. I also know many people who have been distressed by the implications of Normalization/SRV for their own personal vested interests. Furthermore, I know of many people, including myself, who have been brought to some degree of frustration or hurt as a result of their efforts to *act* on their Normalization/SRV beliefs. Such frustrations and hurts are inevitable. And finally, I realize that there are shortcomings in Normalization/SRV training, and in Normalization/SRV trainers, again including myself, in spite of ongoing efforts to address them, and that such shortcomings certainly color people's perception of their Normalization/SRV training experiences.

In preparation for this paper, several of my friends in Indiana (Mike Morton, Deb McCarty, and Sherry Kurtz) met with me and talked about the impact of Normalization/SRV training on them. The act of sharing our personal experience of this training was very helpful and strongly illustrated how much we had in common with many other people in this regard. I would like to conclude with a list of reflections that these friends and others have shared with me about the impact Normalization/SRV training has had on them. No doubt some of you will find some of your own experiences expressed in these statements as well.

- "There was power in the logic and internal coherency of Normalization."
- "The ideas clicked for me."
- "They were useful and practical. They were overarching. They were intellectually profound, accurate, and truthful."
- "I could not help but see things differently, especially the things being done to devalued people. It made real what was really happening in people's lives."
- "These were ideas and values I wanted to and could incorporate with my personal life."
- "Normalization provided something to aspire to."
- "It gave a clear sense of how important it is to share these beliefs and ideas with others. It enables me to be useful to others."
- "I had seen and worked in places that did not seem in touch with the people they served. Normalization training gave me words and ideas to explain these things."
- "I had a sense of the scales falling off my eyes. It gave definition to things I felt."
- "The first time I went to SRV/PASSING training, I had a sense of seeing life in perspective, a brief sense of total clarity."
- "It permanently changed the way I looked at society."
- "I've given up the belief that things are always going to get better. There is a certain freedom in giving up such false hopes."
- "It increased my own personal sense of accountability—complacency is not okay anymore."

481

29

The impact of Normalization and Social Role Valorization on a state-level practitioner from the USA

DAVID B. SCHWARTZ

I am not a scholar of Normalization or Social Role Valorization (SRV). Nor am I a trainer with knowledge of the enormous variation in awareness of Normalization or SRV in the various states of the United States. I can speak only as a practitioner, and a practitioner in one particular place, the State of Pennsylvania. Yet since a microcosm often can tell us about the macrocosm, I hope that what I have to say may be relevant to the issues that we are considering here.

Many of us seem to share a concern with people whom we term, in our nomenclature, "devalued." In our concern, we are not solely focused on the individual, but upon the subtle interrelationships between the individual and what one might term "health and well-being of the society."

What are the subtle laws governing the situation of the poor and vulnerable? How might their lives be improved through what might be called, in its original sense, "social work"?

For many of us, Normalization and, later, SRV appeared as a lens illuminating the incredible ordered complexity of social processes. For me, setting into practice without this lens would have been akin to setting into medical practice without a microscope. With this microscope, I set off 10 years ago to a new state—Pennsylvania—a place in which I knew no one.

Many of us here have embarked upon similar journeys.

I might say as an aside that I also took with me certain realistic expectations about the work of social change from study with Wolf Wolfensberger, which might be most succinctly summarized in a quote by Oscar Wilde that I have kept on a card over my desk for all these years, which notes "No good deed goes unpunished." This turned out to be true.

When I arrived in Pennsylvania, an incident took place that engraved itself upon my attention and memory. A group of parents of adult children with a rare form of mental retardation asked to meet with key local and state officials about starting a group home. When the parents met with all of us, they said "we really usually want a group home of about 40 people, but we know that you like things smaller in Pennsylvania, so we're willing to have one for only 16." All of the state and county bureaucrats shook their heads. "If you want to have one for three people," they responded, "you can have one right away. If you want one for four people, it will take a bit longer."

I was astonished. After all, I had come across the border from New York State, where at that time the conversation would be exactly reversed. Parents would want places that tended to be smaller, and state officials would tell them how large they had to be in order to be "cost effective" and to qualify for funding.

But here all of the representatives of the bureaucracy not only *knew* that "small was beautiful," but they could tell you *why*.

I searched around for a reason why my new state should be so different. Finding the cause didn't take long at all—almost anyone could tell me why. In the early 1970s a fellow named Mel Knowlton came to Pennsylvania after working with Dr. Wolfensberger and set up the state community services system. He erected all of these community living arrangements based entirely upon Normalization training, mainly PASS. There were at that time no regulations—Mel used only training.

The effects of this effort were twofold. In the first place, an understanding of some of the key tenets of Normalization had "percolated," to use Michael Kendrick's phrase, into the understanding of significant portions of the society in general. This is what I had observed at the meeting. In the second place, this training effort had precipitated the existence of key leaders with common conviction and ideology. In Kristjana Kristiansen's phrase, Normalization had served as a "magnet for alliances." The immediate effect was that I found that I was not alone after all—that there were throughout the state a number of other people who were the products of a similar education. From this base, a core group formed. This group of us attempted to generate a "second stage" of social activism based upon Normalization and SRV.

In this second stage we didn't need to worry about persuading people that community living was better than institutions, or that small group homes were better than large ones. These convictions were already firmly established. Instead, we had the opportunity to pursue further ramifications of what was by then Social Role Valorization. Instead of being concerned about group homes, we pursued policies and funding to promote citizen-owned homes for adults, and real adoptive homes instead of foster care for children. We promoted real jobs through supported employment and similar options rather than sheltered workshops. We pursued real education. And, among other things, we funded and promoted citizen advocacy and a number of other citizen advocacy-inspired approaches to personal relationships and mutuality. Finally, we created a training institute that was funded for 8 years for about $1 million to serve as a philosophical "spark plug" for the entire effort. After 8 years, the increasing

understanding behind actions such as these culminated in a vision statement for the Developmental Disabilities Planning Council that explicitly included SRV language: "We envision a Commonwealth in which all citizens have valued roles, are appreciated for their contributions, and are linked together in mutuality and interdependence."

Others can judge how coherent the council's actions have been with this statement.

What have been the effects of this second stage of Normalization- and SRV-inspired work? There have been, I believe, four: First, ideas that were divisive when introduced are now generally accepted and have perhaps "percolated deeper" into social consciousness. For instance, an originally somewhat bitterly disputed policy to reduce the importance of sheltered workshops in favor of supported work has now become a more acknowledged policy. Council efforts to promote recognition of informal safeguards such as relationships as opposed to formal regulations and laws have also seemed to enter general conversations and actions to some degree.

Second, a new generation of leaders has emerged. This is important because a number of us felt a responsibility to pass on the opportunities that we had to another generation of people, and this seems to some degree to have happened.

Third, we seem to be witnessing a kind of metamorphosis in the inspiring philosophy. This effect was quite unexpected to me. Any explicit interest in Normalization and SRV seems to have faded, being succeeded by a driving interest in personal relationships and associational life.

Fourth, this has been accompanied by the fading of support for SRV training that once existed. I find it very curious to see this taking place at the same time that social activism and passionate action seem undiminished and perhaps even increasing.

I can only speculate on what this apparent fading of SRV from discussions might mean. Various possibilities have been proposed, if indeed history shows this to be a true phenomenon at all.

The first is a point that is frequently raised and that has to do with the question of training method, or what might be termed the "hidden curriculum" of Normalization and SRV training. The question seems to be increasingly raised whether curricularization is synonymous with effective learning. An earlier comment from the floor here criticizing the lack of diversity of instructors may relate to this point; this caused us considerable difficulty with our constituency in Pennsylvania.

Second, there is a certain tendency, common in social movements, to fundamentalism at the extreme, perhaps leading to what Jacques Pelletier noted as dogmatism, or elitism, and to promoting a misconceived "social engineering" approach to social improvement.

Finally, there are those who ask whether a social philosophy must be systematic in order to be vigorous, truthful, and useful.

I mentioned metamorphosis. Is it possible that the first two stages of Normalization and SRV in Pennsylvania are currently turning into a third stage that differs in significant ways from the two stages preceding it? Is it possible that a change occurs once the limits of social services as a basis for action are touched? Might this have to do with rediscovering hospitable traditions in culture, upon which theories of Normalization and SRV are predicated, as mentioned by Michael Kendrick in citing Wolfensberger?

Philosophies, like microscopes, are tools. Having brought us this far, how far will this philosophy yet take us? Might it emerge, like a yogic mantra, as something that becomes transformed through intense concentration and repetition? Intense study of any subject can lead to surprising changes in the student.

Perhaps Pennsylvania, and other states in the United States, may usefully serve as settings in which whatever path this may lead can be observed. Part of the Jeffersonian ideal of American government, after all, had to do with the importance of diversity, of states as social laboratories. For anyone working in such a social laboratory, it is well known that the work required can often be isolating and lonely. Further evolution in guiding philosophy may also be divisive in itself. Yet, in all of this, there is something that sustains us. In the words of the great Goethe: "To know that there are people with whom we are in accord, and who are living along with us, even in silence, makes this lonely planet into a peopled garden."

Our presence together at this gathering seems to me a moving reminder of this fact.

Part 8

The Future

30

Concluding reflections and a look ahead into the future for Normalization and Social Role Valorization

WOLF WOLFENSBERGER

1 INTRODUCTION

In my opening chapter (chapter 3), I spoke about the past, which is much safer than speaking about the future, especially when one owns one of the most extensive historical archives in private possession in one's field. It is much riskier to boast about owning the archives of the future.

It would be nice to deliver what people call an upbeat note at the end of this conference, but I have long put realism above feel-good-ism, and I see the future as a very mixed bag for Normalization and Social Role Valorization (SRV), and as rather gloomy for society as a whole and hence also for human services. Also, the future does not care if you like it or not! You don't need to boo or applaud it; you get it whether you like it or not.

In my concluding remarks, I have departed considerably from the notes I had originally prepared. The reason is that in light of the radical individual rights position so often presented at this conference, I felt an urgent need to warn participants of where this ideology would lead.

2 LIKELY PROBLEMS IN THE FUTURE OF NORMALIZATION AND SOCIAL ROLE VALORIZATION

In the future, Normalization and SRV are apt to encounter both some old problems as well as some newer ones, both to be selectively sketched below.

2.1 THE PERSISTENCE OF CERTAIN EARLIER PROBLEMS

In my first chapter, I mentioned some of the common kinds of responses to Normalization from the late 1960s into the early 1980s. A more extensive documentation of early objections, misunderstandings, or misinterpretations had been presented in 1980 (Wolfensberger, 1980). One thing that we can anticipate in the future is that certain earlier problems will continue to persist, such as the following:

- People thinking that they know Normalization or SRV when they do not.
- People failing to distinguish between different formulations.

- Researchers coming up with well-intended simplified "operational definitions" that yield equivocal results and interpretations.
- People outright inventing their own formulations, thereby sowing confusion and chaos. Of course, the sowing of confusion and chaos is always a bad sign as to what the moral forces at work are.

A problem long with us, though not much highlighted so far, is the amazing fact that academia has hardly been able to deal with Normalization/SRV. With extremely few exceptions, the academic and research culture (prior to this conference) has dealt with Normalization/SRV at a superficial, low, or simpleminded level. Academic critics have often not even read the core documents of the theory—something they would not get away with in regard to any other topic. Many academic publications that deal with Normalization/SRV issues, if they even reference its literature at all, do so in the most superficial fashion and/or to the less relevant publications; and sometimes, Normalization or its elements are even attributed to authors of secondary sources. Yet Normalization—at least as I have formulated it—and SRV even more so, are very high-level, multidimensional, and subtle schemas of great parsimony and elegance that should be a pleasure and a challenge for scholars to tackle. That they have done so poorly at it gives one little room for optimism.

2.2 NEW, AND PRIMARILY IDEOLOGICAL, OBJECTIONS TO NORMALIZATION AND SRV

By roughly the mid-1980s, some relatively new objections to SRV became prominent, which grew out of four ideological positions, usually with intimate connections to a misleadingly labeled "postmodernist" ideology and to the so-called political correctness (PC) culture, both of which we must unfortunately expect to be around for quite a while.

2.2.1 RACIAL-CONFLICT IDEOLOGY OBJECTIONS

One set of objections revolved around issues of racial-conflict ideology, and to what degree Normalization and SRV would be liberating of oppressed racial minorities, or be yet another oppression in disguise. Such issues had occasionally emerged before, but they acquired more steam as time went by. So far, these issues have proven to be next-to-impossible to deal with, for at least two reasons. (a) They often were simply not advanced within a context of rationality. Some of the things that injected and maintained irrationality into the debate included deep personal woundedness, fear, and paranoia—based, of course, in good part on historical realities, habits of casting everything into a conflict model, and, increasingly, an unforgiving counterracism. (b) These issues often proved to be moving targets, with arguments getting rapidly switched as one tried to tackle them. Since these debates have often been oral, the sparsity of a written exchange contributed to a frustrating lack of closure on relevant points, be it in agreement *or* disagreement.

2.2.2 FEMINISM OBJECTIONS

A second area of critique came from sectors of feminism. It was also often not amenable to debate—rational or otherwise. What also makes debates difficult is that feminism itself is split into so many different "schools," which is not quite the same as the "moving target" phenomenon.

2.2.3 OBJECTIONS REVOLVING AROUND DENIAL OF HUMAN DIFFERENCES AND IMPAIRMENTS, AND/OR THEIR IMPLICATIONS

A third type of critique has something to do with various kinds of denials of either the significance—or at least the consequences—of human differences and the way these are viewed, and of human universals in dealing with differences.

One expression of this has been the elevation ("celebration") of human diversity to a religion—a willful maximization of diversities or multiculturalism in society.

A second expression is intertwined with a denial of the very existence of human impairments, or their implications and consequences. For instance, there has been an irrational pretense that there is no such thing as mental competency impairment unless one is "brain-dead." This denial of reality has also been fed by excesses of social constructivism that would tell us that there is no such thing as unintelligent people, and hence, mental retardation. This kind of thinking has, of course, emerged in all sorts of other derivative manifestations, such as the "facilitated communication" craze that virtually denies mental impairment and about which I will have more to say later. (See Biklen and Duchan [1994] for the constructivist position, and Shane [1994] for a critique of "facilitated communication.")

Another version of this problem has been the interpretation that people are merely "differently abled," or "temporarily able-bodied." Valid as this may be in a certain sense, it is almost always accompanied by failure to deal with real human limitations in a realistic fashion and to accept that strategies of image enhancement and/or competency enhancement may have a legitimate contribution to make.

The extreme of this position is the one that in so many words conveys that "handicapped is beautiful," and which objects to anyone trying to do anything to ameliorate a human impairment. This position has proven to be unamenable to rational discussion. In some circles, there even seems to prevail outright hatred of nonhandicapped people. One extreme example has been a certain sector of militant deaf people who would—if they could—forbid any kind of surgical efforts to improve the hearing of hearing-impaired persons, or at least of persons whose hearing has been impaired since early age.

Probably because of their denial of the existence or significance of human impairments, or the fact that virtually by definition, an impairment involves subtraction from a normative and more natural form or function, many objectors to Normalization/SRV who are bodily or mentally impaired have had great difficulty dealing with the situation of people who are societally devalued for reasons *other than* impairment, or even in perceiving that it is social devaluation of negatively valued characteristics generally, rather than of human impairment specifically, that is the more basic source of the bad things that are done to impaired persons.

2.2.4 RADICAL RIGHTS ORIENTATION OBJECTIONS

A fourth domain of critique has come out of the modernistic orientation to individual rights, self-determination, and self-advocacy. This is ironic because these were extensively concordant with Normalization in its early days but then began to work increasingly at cross-purposes, at least with the Wolfensberger formulation of Normalization and SRV, and have become major competitors of the latter.

One criticism—or misunderstanding—of my formulation of Normalization from early days (and of SRV later on) has been that they offer, or even impose, a single monolithic response to a particular situation. This is a mistaken notion for at least three reasons.

First, Normalization and SRV usually afford many valued action options with regard to any one particular issue, not just a single alternative. For instance, there is usually not just one culturally valued analogue for addressing a specific need, but many.

Second, recognition of a person's desires has always been one of the elements of my Normalization and SRV formulations, though admittedly not the only one. For instance, already in the 1972 text on *The Principle of Normalization in Human Services,* I pointed out that

> The Normalization principle can be viewed as being neutral as to whether a specific deviant person or group *should* be normalized. That decision must be based on criteria and values which exist independent of the Normalization principle. Here it is useful to recall that our society considers it appropriate that normalizing measures be *offered* in some circumstances, and *imposed* in others. (Wolfensberger, 1972, p. 28)

All along, I have been more up-front in pointing out that even the most libertarian society will not allow everything, and that devalued people cannot expect to have "choices" of liberties that are not even granted to *valued* people. But it is interesting that, hardly anyone ever seems to respond to my systematic analysis of how one might resolve situations where a conflict may arise between a person's desires on the one hand and Normalization desiderata or societal mandates on the other, an early version of which I wrote (Wolfensberger, 1980) in the book by Flynn and Nitsch (1980).

More recently, I have achieved even greater clarity that the SRV formulation is merely a heuristic tool of social science and should be considered outside the domain of "religion" (Wolfensberger, 1992c, and in more elaborate form after the Ottawa conference in

Wolfensberger, 1995). SRV can tell us what is likely to happen *if* we do this instead of that, and what we must do *if* we want to increase the likelihood that a person or class is valued in the eyes of very imperfect other people who will never be made perfect by laws, force, guns, threats, or economic policies. Yet yesterday, I thought I heard it said by a speaker that Caesar's law is not dependent on all sorts of things, and is something freestanding—again, I guess, some kind of god. What people with such arguments will need is a healthy dose of "if this, then that" therapy (an allusion to the titles of the two above-cited articles).

2.3 A PARTIAL RESPONSE TO SOME NEWER OBJECTIONS

It is difficult in this context to present a sufficient response to the many newer objections that have been raised against my formulations of Normalization and SRV. However, I will give a partial reply to at least a few.

2.3.1 A BRIEF ELUCIDATION OF CERTAIN SHORTCOMINGS OF THE RADICAL RIGHTS POSITION

In this context, I will only mention five shortcomings—actually, absurdities—of the radical rights orientation.

2.3.1.1 *The arrogation of absolute lordship over one's life*

There is an attitude of arrogation of absolute lordship over one's life. In other words, each person is his/her own god and master, and should never be under anyone else's authority. A related argument is that no one has the right to judge for anyone else what should be done. Accordingly, in this view, human services or advocacy only exist to give (or do for) a person what that person wants, not to seek any (other) goal of rehabilitation, social policy, or individual or social betterment. Thus, in this view, the only legitimacy of Normalization/SRV is in whatever emphasis they give to autonomy and rights, and anything else that Normalization and SRV promote would only be valid and good if it was what (devalued) people themselves said they wanted.

2.3.1.2 *Radical separation of the individual from the common good, and a blindness about the antagonism between comitus polity and individualism/"diversity"*

The radical rights position is so totally focused on individualism—and on individualism in the here-and-now—that all considerations of implications to the larger good, to community and society, and to posterity are swept aside. Combined with the radical self-ownership concept, *each* person becomes an individual unconnected "solo rights bearer."

Relatedly, the radical rights people are utterly illogical about the fact that there is no way in which there can be the diversity that they want to "celebrate," including radical self-determination, and at the same time exist a society that is characterized by *comitas* and *polis,* i.e., that has a reasonably friendly, civilized atmosphere and an at least workable functional political structure. Instead, what there will be is what we *are* getting this very minute: social and societal collapse and then chaos. No highly diverse society can function well, if at all. This is one of the big reasons that almost every time a society becomes more heterogeneous—usually by imperial expansions and conquests—it eventually either converges upon a shared identity, or it falls apart again into more homogeneous components that share a strong bond, such as language, ethnic identity, or religion. One does not have to like it, but that is the way things are and will be.

Even more absurd is the notion that *any* society can have comity with polity if *everyone* in it claims unlimited rights and is unwilling to surrender their rights for the larger good.

In this modernistic age, the very ideas of liberty and freedom are not conceived in the same way as they have been historically—at least in Western thought. Historically, liberty has been seen as intimately tied to responsibility and obligations, and as only able to be exercised by people of strong moral fiber, with good self-discipline, self-control, and the capacity for self-sacrifice. Thus, liberty was largely seen as the freedom to choose the good. However, the modern interpretation of liberty is that it consists of emancipation from any hardship or inconvenience, from religious and church dictates, from human nature, from any secular laws that a person thinks are unreasonable or burdensome, from a community's standards of morality and public order, from any restraints or restrictions on sex, from the needs and demands of one's spouse and children, from any reasonable requests from others and even from the laws of nature, as in the expectation that one should be free from any negative consequences of one's actions, especially ones that take a long time to come to fruition.

In light of these considerations, one thing that was particularly striking in the presentations and discussions by the Scandinavians (other than Kristiansen) and by Perrin is that I cannot recall that there was any mention of the obligations of the people to whom Normalization or rights would be extended.

When, on top of everything, a radical individualism and a solo rights bearer attitude is promoted in a societal context in which cultural values and habits supportive of the larger good are collapsing, then such a rights orientation will, in the long run and in a very complex fashion, actually contribute to a rise in social incompetence. Even if it should come to pass that social incompetence becomes less devalued, or even gets "celebrated"—as has, in fact, been happening—it will eventually lead to a decline in societal welfare. After all, a society in which incompetence is normative, and is even valued, will become a miserable, materially impoverished, and dysfunctional society—a bit like the foolish city of Abdera in ancient Greek folklore, with its equivalents of Schilda in German folklore, Seldwyla in Swiss literature, and Chelm in Yiddish lore.

In fact, I am hereby not only warning, but *promising,* that those who continue to sow the seeds of a false, deceptive, radical individualism will reap the whirlwind of destruction. And to Bengt Nirje and the Scandinavians I add that there can be no "welfare state" based only and/or primarily on individual rights, in defiance of the realities of what is needed for collective long-term welfare.

2.3.1.3 A naive reliance on Caesar's law

What is the source of legal rights? Legal rights are granted by other humans, and that via Caesarean arrangements. This is why those who put their (highest) hopes in legal rights look to the state—i.e., to Caesar—as the guarantor of the entitlements of the solo rights bearers. In other words, they are putting

their trust in princes, which is always foolish. Historically, legal rights come and go with the political realities of the moment, and even with the economic situation of the moment. Most societies of the world have never even had a strong, formal, and enduring individual rights basis, and the material wealth currently possessed by the West that has enabled an expansion of individual rights is a very short eyeblink in history that has already begun to pass. On the other hand, even under the most desperate societal conditions, and where legal rights are nonexistent, there are still many things one can do to role-valorize people at risk of being devalued. Nor should we forget that the law may be very much present—but also very disadvantageous to people with weaknesses, afflictions, or of devalued identity, and with little prospect that such laws will change unless things are done *first* that will change societal attitudes.

A common corollary of a reliance on law and Caesar's might is a categoric objection to strategies that would win over hearts and minds, and instead, a reliance on the force behind the law.

2.3.1.4 Decommunitization via radical individual rights is murderous of vulnerable people

I have a second warning related to the first one; namely, there will *always* be people who are not capable of competent self-determination and/or who have characteristics or habits not easily tolerated by other people. If they do not have alliances with persons who have greater competence or standing in society or if they systematically reject all such alliances and all forms of "for-speakership," guardianship, protectorships, and so forth (even very competent and caring ones), then things *will* go very ill with them. In fact, there *will* be genocide of some of these weaker parties. Again I warn that questions of what one likes to feel about this are irrelevant; this is the way it *is*, as a matter of fact.

2.3.1.5 Alienation of the radical rights position from the realities of human nature

Actually, it is not only the radical rights lobby that can no longer acknowledge the realities of human nature; it is the culture of modernism behind this position that breeds reality-alienated people, as I will explain later. It is particularly appalling that human services are full of people who are supposed to help others, but who—from ignorance or denial—are alienated from the most basic realities of human nature. How can one help human beings if one functions on the basis of false premises about human nature? I call this normative contemporary mentality "normative insanity." This is also one of the normative incompetencies of modernistic people I alluded to earlier, and one of many things that put the human service systems into a failure mode.

Some of the realities about human nature relevant to the debate at issue here are that social and societal devaluation is a universal, despite the cultural differences in their targets or expressions; that all social systems have a limit to their capacity to assimilate dissimilar people; and that for many strategies of winning hearts and minds, the use of force is no substitute, i.e., one cannot bludgeon humans into liking others, being good to them, and wanting them around. Again, one may not like these facts, but denial will not get rid of them.

Any and all forms of *polis* are extremely deficient—even the best. Those that take account of human nature are therefore bad enough. But those built on fantasies about human nature are usually even worse!

In this connection, it is also ironic that the modernists demand that handicapped (or societally devalued) people are accepted the way they are—but do not accept all other people the way *they* are!

2.3.2 CONCLUSION TO THE RESPONSE TO NEWER OBJECTIONS

Of course, all of the above objections combine in various ways, which should not surprise us considering that their roots are largely in the values and culture of modernism, about which more later.

For instance, consider that formerly Normalization was often rejected with arguments such as that institutions are not really so bad or could be made better; segregation is good for both segregators and segregatees; impaired people should be given happiness rather than developmental demands; aged people are not devalued in society; and so on. Today's arguments—and probably tomorrow's too—are very

likely to have something to do with assertions that in order to be (better) accepted by other people, nobody should be expected to need to do anything, or have anything done to them. Again, this argument seems to boil down to a radical self-determination and entitlement ideology, coupled with a reality-segmenting mind-set, as if what such critics demand could ever possibly happen in any society.

The radical rights position does not merely have shortcomings, it is an outright abomination. It is not only a religion, but an idolatry, namely, one that would make humanity a conglomerate of godlets, each person being a god over his/her own self. Someone has described this situation as one in which there are billions of gods—and each one a very "jealous god" at that.

That so many people have become too mind-darkened to see these things is one of the reasons for pessimism. However, if one goes over Nirje's writings of the late 1960s and the 1970s, one will not find that his position was a radical rights one, such as we have heard stated by some people at this conference, and such as Perrin has projected back into history in an act of historic revisionism that is a hallmark of the constructivism and political correctness culture of modernism. One simple reason that Nirje's early formulation was not based on a radical rights position is that this position did not really become prominent in the larger culture until the 1980s. If the radical rights position is really Nirje's today, then it needs to be distinguished as a new and different formulation of his earlier Normalization concept. Indeed, he really should not even call it Normalization at all, but simply what it is: an assertion of radical individual autonomy, in disregard of overall societal and long-term welfare. The use of the term *Normalization* would merely be confusing things.

3 QUESTIONS COMMONLY RAISED ABOUT THE FUTURE OF NORMALIZATION AND SRV

Also relevant to the future are two questions that are often asked these days. One is whether Normalization and SRV are—as some people put it—passé. After all, "Beyond Normalization" has become a very popular title for conferences and publications, usually by people who have never embraced Normalization in the first place. For instance, only days after our own conference, there will be a world conference under the theme "Beyond Normalization" in Iceland, and a few weeks after that, a course is to be held in Copenhagen entitled "From Normalization to Inclusion." The second question commonly asked is whether Normalization is still implementable even if it is not passé. Both questions are addressed below.

3.1   ARE NORMALIZATION AND SRV OUTMODED OR PASSÉ?

As to the question of whether Normalization and SRV are passé, I have three observations and/or predictions to make.

1. In my own mind, Nirje's 1969 formulation, and its various minor later revisions, is passé in the sense that it has been subsumed by my later and broader formulations, as stated by a series of publications starting in 1970 (Wolfensberger, 1970a, 1970b, 1971a, 1971b, 1972, 1983, 1991a, 1992a; Wolfensberger & Glenn, 1973a, 1973b, 1975a, 1975b; Wolfensberger & Thomas, 1983; Wolfensberger & Tullman, 1982). A large proportion of prescriptions that derive from Nirje's traditional formulation (as distinguished from Perrin's) would also derive from Wolfensberger's, except that the Wolfensberger formulation would derive yet additional ones and is vastly more powerful in offering resolutions of conflicts between competing or incompatible prescriptions.

2. However, for years to come we can expect that there will be people in various parts of the world who will prefer Nirje's formulation and for at least four reasons: (a) For reasons of cultural pride or related factors. It is possible that in parts of Scandinavia, the formulations of Nirje, and/or very similar ones, will be widely preferred for at least some time. (b) For the very reason that it is simpler. After all, once one memorizes and applies the eight major implications that have not changed since 1969, one pretty much knows the Nirje system. In contrast, SRV is vastly more complicated to learn and practice. (c) Because it is *not* Wolfensberger's. People who like Normalization, but dislike anything associated with my name, often take refuge in Nirje's Normalization. (d) Nirje's traditional formulation, being focused on

conditions of human impairment rather than on the superordinate and more relevant reality of social devaluation, permits many people to avoid the controversies that have attended the broader Wolfensberger formulation. For instance, Nirje's formulation deals almost entirely with what I used to call (see Yates' chapter 4, in this volume) the "interaction" dimension and much less with what I used to call the "interpretation" dimension of Normalization. This makes it much easier for people to say that they are implementing Normalization because they will not have to tackle difficult—and often still controversial and unpopular—issues of imagery. Also, it is the broader Wolfensberger formulations that have drawn ire (often misdirected) from political correctness circles, feminists, racial minority members, and groups that celebrate unorthodox sex habits. Apparently, even some people who agree with SRV intellectually have retreated from at least some of its broad formulations because they did not want to deal with the wrenching controversies that attend it. In contrast, how many people would argue against access to a normal rhythm of the day, the week, or the year, a decent economic status, and so forth?

3. My third observation is that many ideas and practices spawned in Normalization/SRV have become conventional wisdom and will continue to be applied very widely, even though they are rarely applied in conjunction with a systematic high-order theory of which they were initially derivatives. We have to understand that a higher mental scheme such as a theory or even a religion can permeate what people do and say without ever being explicated. In that sense, several major elements of Normalization theory now permeate not only praxis in large sectors of human service, but also in larger society. At the same time, one cannot say that Normalization theory is the only reason this has happened, since to each such practice, more than one idea or societal force may have contributed. I believe that we can now point to the following such ideas and practices in the larger culture and human services broadly:

a. The importance of integration in general. However, Flynn's (1993) finding that 626 services assessed with PASS and 406 assessed with PASSING scored best on the ratings for access to clients and families shows that these Normalization desiderata related to integration have been the ones taken more to heart by formal human services since 1969 than those related to actual person integration. Social, rather than merely physical, integration is one of the elements where the gap between understanding and acceptance of Normalization/SRV on the one hand, and implementation thereof on the other, is much wider in formal services than outside of them.

b. The importance of language in interpreting people.

c. The issue of age-appropriateness. One now finds the term being used not only in the professional literature, but also in the popular one, though it is hardly ever credited to its source, e.g., in the 1973 version of PASS (Wolfensberger & Glenn, 1973a,b).

d. The according of all sorts of personal rights to all sorts of devalued people.

e. The need for, and relevance of, schooling for just about all children.

f. The importance of making facilities and sites accessible to people in wheelchairs.

g. That families who have handicapped members should receive help.

h. That vastly less can be expected of residential institutions than people used to think when they saw institutions as "the answer."

Further, in specific service areas or fields (such as those of developmental impairment), a number of Normalization-derived ideas have become common wisdom:

a. The importance of issues of grouping size, and that smaller is usually better.

b. The importance of not congregating devalued people together.

c. The importance of personal appearance of devalued people.

d. That residences for devalued people should at least be homelike.

Another way of putting this is that many parties and movements these days that reject Normalization and SRV are coasting heavily on the impact that they produced, or to which they contributed and will continue to do so. To many such people, Normalization and SRV are passé, but as mentioned, they rarely considered them *actuel* in the first place, even as they were strongly shaped by them.

However, such people also commonly misapply ideas from Normalization/SRV, as we have already amply seen. For instance, Normalization theory played a large role in raising people's consciousness of the importance of language use, especially about impaired people. But soon, certain idioms and grammars were adopted that are used almost exclusively in reference to devalued people but not in ordinary discourse, as exemplified by so-called "people first" language. Another example is that even people who are not legal-rights or self-determination radicals may mindlessly apply self-determination constructs to people who are altogether incapable of self-determination, or who are capable of vastly less adaptive self-determination than they are expected or interpreted to exercise. Sometimes this is done under popular phrases or schemes such as "supported employment" or "supported living." Another example is the way the construct of integration was first degraded into "mainstreaming," and after that craze was worn out, into its current successor, "inclusion." Things like these are commonly seen and interpreted as being "beyond Normalization." But it continues to be obvious that as these people treat Normalization/SRV as passé, they are laying themselves wide open to much error. For instance, one of the ironies here is that services claimed to be of a postnormalization or post-SRV nature often score very low on the PASSING instrument that measures the quality of services in reference to Normalization/SRV criteria, and for that matter, on many other instruments as well. Also, if everyone is so beyond Normalization, why are their services normatively model-incoherent, as assessment after assessment has shown?

In this connection, it may also be instructive to recall the elements of Normalization and SRV that are the least understood, accepted, or implemented: the inevitability of social devaluation, to the degree this is a social science issue; the unconsciousness and hidden systemicness of many devaluing practices and patterns; the conservatism corollary; several image issues, especially outside the language domain; many grouping issues and implications; the need for culturally valued/least devalued forms of protection, to the degree that this is an empirical issue; the fact that devalued people and their advocates need to "court" rather than brow-beat valued society; model coherency; and the boundaries of Normalization/SRV and issues that straddle the boundaries.

3.2 ARE NORMALIZATION AND SRV (STILL) IMPLEMENTABLE?

The second question was whether Normalization and SRV will be implementable even if they are not passé. This issue has been a recurring topic of discussion in the North American Social Role Valorization Development, Training and Safeguarding Council, which consists mostly of SRV trainers and other people with a long record of Normalization and SRV leadership (see Thomas [1994] for a lengthier description of the council).

This issue needs to be examined in relation to the direction in which North American society overall is going, and even beyond this, the direction of Western civilization, the developed world, and to some degree the world order overall.

3.2.1 THE IMPENDING COLLAPSE OF WESTERN CIVILIZATION AND ITS RELEVANCE TO THE IMPLEMENTATION OF NORMALIZATION AND SOCIAL ROLE VALORIZATION

As I have spelled out in many presentations and publications, and most recently in a February 1994 article in *Mental Retardation* (Wolfensberger, 1994a), I am convinced that all three—North America, Western societies, and the world—are "going to hell in a wheelbarrow." What is happening in the former Soviet Union, Yugoslavia, the Middle East, Somalia, the Sudan, Rwanda, Burundi, South Africa, other African countries, and Haiti, will be recapitulated in many other places. Even Italy is falling apart. In some parts of the world, health collapses are occurring, as exemplified by Russia and equatorial Africa. Even where it does not come to large-scale internal warfare, there will be a collapse of polity and order such as we are already seeing in the former Soviet Union, Haiti, Italy, and U.S. cities such as East St. Louis, MO, Camden, NJ, and so on (see Wolfensberger & Thomas [1995] on the latter two). Both the forerunners and the consequences of such big collapses include the increasing dysfunctionality of all sorts of social institutions, including formal ones, such as human service organizations, and less formal ones, such as families that are collapsing all over the world, even in underdeveloped countries and "traditional" societies ("More Mothers," 1995).

One of the things blinding people to the collapsing world order is that in different places, the collapse is taking different forms, at least initially. People do not see the connection between the collapse in rich versus poor countries, African versus Western countries, Italian versus U.S. versions, and so forth. Yet poverty and/or chaos are the common outcomes, with warfare (internal or external) and/or high mortality (for all reasons) being frequent concomitants.

In order to understand what I see as the collapse of civilization and society, one has to understand what I also see as the new "religion" of our society, and indeed of all societies in the Western world. In other contexts, I elaborate on this value system at great length; here, I can only give the briefest summary.

This new religion, which I call "modernism," consists of five major elements:

1. Materialism, which takes the form not only of obsession with possessions, goods, and consumption, but also (and more importantly), the form of obsession with objects, material processes, and technology; and (most importantly) a de-spiritualized worldview that denies the existence, or at least relevance, of any god or gods.

2. Individualism, which is an idolatry of the *individual* human (rather than of a human collectivity, as in certain other value systems), attended by self-maximization regardless of cost to anyone else, as already mentioned earlier, and an uncoupling of the individual from the larger social context.

3. Sensualism, which has been elevated to a high value in this religion. This means that comfort, convenience, pleasure, sex, "thrills," "highs," and a preoccupation with the body and its youthfulness are exalted. Indeed, they are considered things to which people are "entitled."

4. Externalism, which I define as the decline of inner substance and the inner life among so many people, and instead, a turning to—and indeed a reliance on—external supports of all sorts, be it other people, guru figures, cults, crazes, the media (especially TV), drugs (legal, illegal, and medical), and so on.

5. "Here-and-now-ism," that is, a focus on the moment, an ignorance of the past, and even a denial of its relevance, and a total lack of concern about the future, or at least a totally unrealistic approach to the future, including a denial of the fact that what people do now will profoundly shape the future.

As many of you have heard me speak before—perhaps *ad nauseam*—my point is that these are the values and habits of modernistic society, that they are being embraced worldwide, and, most relevant to our point, that they are inherently *in*capable of sustaining polity with comity. In the aforementioned 1994 article in *Mental Retardation,* I inventorized which major U.S. societal institutions were in which stage of collapse. (Table 30.1 is an updated version of that inventory.) In the US, chaos is mostly the result of a collapse of values and of competencies, and the rise of new values incompatible with *polis* and *comitas.* There is hardly a single social institution or structure in U.S. society that is *not* in collapse—with the ominous exception of the military!

TABLE 30.1

SELECTED LISTING: SOCIAL/CULTURAL/HUMAN SERVICE INSTITUTIONS, STRUCTURES, AND "GLUES" THAT ARE IN VARIOUS STAGES OF DYSFUNCTIONALITY OR COLLAPSE

A. In an advanced state of collapse	*B. In an extensive state of collapse*	*C. On a downhill slope or entering a state of collapse*
*Traditional family & home life *Competent reproduction, & child-rearing *Many religious institutions & structures *Many traditional legal & cultural norms regarding human life, sexuality, & morality *Traditional medical ethics *Cities, city government, & city life *Nuclear energy *Private security forces *General public education (elementary & secondary) *Child welfare & foster care *Criminal justice, prisons, & corrections *Much of "mental health," particularly its residential forms *Much of mental talk treatment *Medical care to the indigent *Nursing homes for the mentally retarded	*Financial institutions: banks, insurance, credit systems *The political system *Elements of the judicial system *Hospital medicine *Public police forces *Personal safety/security *Functionality of federal & state governments *Large sections of infrastructures (roads, bridges, sanitation) *Rural towns *Roles & relationships of generations to each other *Elements of higher education *Language, & thus the traditional role of, & capacity for, communication *Labor unionism *Public assistance/welfare *Visiting/home health services *General nursing homes *Much of the community residential system, not subsumed in other categories	*Drinking water: supply & quality *Certain agricultural sectors *The jury system *The postal service *Private pension funds *Professional accounting ethic *Elements of office/clinic medicine *Sheltered or "supported" work *Ambulance & rescue services *Higher (postsecondary) education

Aside from the fact that the ascendancy of destructive values is making it less and less possible to implement Normalization and SRV, the same outcome is also derived from the fact that the economies of developed nations have become more and more "postprimary production" ones. This means that their economies are utterly dependent on the creation and maintenance of large classes of (their own) needy and dependent people in order to sustain the livelihood and materialistic lifestyle of the classes of more privileged people. This reality has been extensively analyzed since 1977 by John McKnight at Northwestern University in Chicago (e.g., see the recent compendium of his earlier papers in McKnight, 1995), and by myself in my teaching and writing (e.g., Vater, Scheuing, & Wolfensberger, 1994; Wolfensberger, 1989, 1992b, 1994a). Even if I were wrong about any number of my interpretations, the current postprimary production economy realities could, by themselves alone, totally destroy the overall beneficence of a societal service system.

At any rate, for whatever reason, the fact is that it is simply no longer as possible as it once was to accomplish anything positive within formal human services, or, for that matter, on any structural level. In some contexts, it has become almost *im*possible. This has also meant that within structural contexts, such as human service agencies, SRV is only minimally implementable, and the portions that are implementable are largely nullified by the many awful things that get done at the same time. Even Normalization/SRV features that once were relatively easy to implement (e.g., greater life-sharing between service clients and paid staff) have become extensively disabled. Since my views on these matters have been published, and reprints are available, I will not go into further detail here.

In the good old days, it was mostly myself saying these things, but now even some of the media columnists are shouting it from the rooftops (e.g., Pike, 1994). No matter how real this collapse is, there have been and will be widespread denials of it, and of its calamitous consequences. But then, I am reminded of the fact that 2 weeks before Germany surrendered in World War II, in 1945, there were still millions of Germans who fully expected to win the war. The very day in 1975 before Saigon fell and the U.S. embassy was evacuated by helicopters, the U.S. ambassador cabled Washington that the American presence in Saigon could be expected to endure at least another year (Church, 1995).

As I have been saying for years, one of the reasons that so many people fail to see that formal services are already bankrupt in terms of their overall impact is that tidbits of occasional benefits to selected individuals keep dribbling out of it, and people are so dazzled by these tokens that they can no longer see the service atrocities and form a valid overall judgment. This source of error in judging a reality is very similar to the many others in making decisions and the judging of probabilities that Tversky and Kahneman (1974) began to inventorize in the 1970s under the title, "judgment under uncertainty," which started a new subfield of inquiry into such phenomena.

In the aforementioned SRV Council, there is much agreement on the verbal-intellectual level (though less on other levels, I suspect) that not much good can be expected from formal services. This would, of course, include, but not be limited to, SRV implementation. There is also extensive but not full agreement among council members on the extent and definitiveness of the societal collapse, and therefore on what can still be expected from societal structures, or even from most members of society. Outside of the SRV Council, and in the circles of Normalization/SRV opponents, there is even less agreement with my assertion that the direction in which society is headed is a very bad one indeed. In fact, some people see what I have interpreted as decadence to be progress, and they see even better (i.e., more decadent) things ahead.

However, in the SRV Council, there *is* total agreement that there is much that anyone can do in their personal lives outside of formal structures. But, of course, to the extent that community (including the family) is collapsing within society, even the good that can be done in the informal domain will be a drop in the bucket as compared to the need, which will get bigger as societal collapse progresses. And in a collapsing society, there are simply not enough people to role-valorize all the people who need it, nor will there be enough good things available to convey even to those in valued roles, as mentioned in the presentation by Susan Thomas (chapter 15, in this volume). The material goods of the world will probably end up extremely disproportionately in the hands of those with greatest material power, as we have recently seen in Somalia; nor will there be much—if anything—in the way of legal rights. But even the people who end up with the material wealth will experience severely dysfunctional lives.

None of this is a sound rationale for calling for material empowerment of all devalued classes as an overarching "solution" or even strategy. I am saying this because a prominent source of critique of Normalization/SRV in recent years have been proponents of a certain kind of materialistic philosophy, which seems to me to be old Marxism put into new clothes because these proponents have been discombobulated and are ashamed to profess Marxism in the face of its sudden collapse around the world. These parties might assert that if my dire prediction were true, it would be merely one more reason to pursue a policy of material empowerment of the devalued classes. I want to pre-empt this kind of argument right away: Except in ideological fantasyland, there will be no army divisions, no air forces, and no navies of retarded people, of senile people, of blind and deaf people, of people in wheelchairs, and so on. When polity and comity collapse, these classes will *not* be the ones who end up in possession or command of the wealth, the communications system, the armies, the cannons, the planes, the ships, the ammunition, or the food depots. Instead, these people will be in the same situation in which they have always been throughout history, and their only securities will be in whatever deep relationship commitments have been made to them by others, and especially by people who *do* have competencies and/or resources, including those who are willing to share their last slice of bread with them.

3.2.2 THE DEGRADATION OF THE MENTAL FUNCTIONING OF MODERNISTIC PEOPLE

However, even if we assume for the moment that civilization does not collapse and that human service structures still have more functionality than dysfunctionality, the prevailing cultural values are nonetheless inimical to many features of Wolfensberger's formulations of Normalization and SRV. Among the many bad things that the values and habits of modernism do to people, four are of special

relevance to my point. (a) They engender a mind-set that segments reality and that cannot relate elements of reality to each other. (b) They create a mentality of entitlement. (c) People look to technology and medicine as a source of miraculous achievements that deliver the means for satisfying one's entitlements. (d) People expect results and the satisfaction of their entitlements in a here-and-now-istic fashion, and nothing less will do.

As I have elaborated at greater length elsewhere (in workshops, and in Wolfensberger, 1991b, 1994b), all this contributes to a craze mentality both in the larger society, the sciences, and in human services. This mentality is now vastly more prevalent than it was in the early 1970s, as pointed out by Susan Thomas and Deborah Reidy in their chapters in this book on the impact of Normalization/SRV training. Now, anything that does not have the lustre of novelty does not appeal to the vast majority of human service workers, and to some extent others as well.

There are at least two good reasons why a craze mentality in relation to the address of human problems is profoundly inimical to Normalization and SRV.

1. SRV and at least the two major traditional formulations of Normalization apply very high-level interrelated universals, i.e., laws of human functioning that transcend culture and are timeless. But crazes are extremely cut off (segmented) from such considerations and deploy the most superficial, isolated end-point tactics. For example, people are cracking left and right because of the larger cultural realities, and what do human service people give them? Things like what I call "hand-before-eyes-shaking therapy" (legitimized by the fancy term "eye movement desensitization and reprocessing"), "massage at a distance" (legitimized by the incongruous term "therapeutic touch"), and similar crazy, perverse, or merely ineffective things.

2. SRV and the above two kinds of Normalization yield action strategies that, by the very nature of their being strategies, require patient long-term application, often of a difficult nature, with eventual benefits often not being traceable back to any specific action. But anything established that has universal and enduring validity gets viewed as "old," outdated, and uninteresting, and long-term delay of gratification is also not tolerable to modernistic people. So they turn to the crazes that tickle their ears by promising quick

and easy results. When a new craze comes along, people drop everything else—often including things that they have done all their lives and that "worked"—and jump on it. Obviously, these crazes are counterproductive to Normalization/SRV, or at the very least, extremely displacing thereof.

The so-called "facilitated communication" (FC) craze of the early 1990s, mentioned earlier, is a very good example of these points, and a heavy warning. History may soon tell us that it was the most crazish craze that ever hit services and relationships concerned with retarded, so-called autistic, and, to some extent, cerebrally palsied people. It swept through these fields like a flu epidemic. That this should happen in the autism culture is not surprising because it has always been an irrational craze territory. That it should hit cerebral palsy hard is also understandable, because the people there have always been wondering about "locked-up minds." But as limited as the embrace of Normalization/SRV has been in mental retardation, it has been more extensive there than in any other field. Therefore, the fact that people in this field jumped so precipitously and uncritically on the FC craze tells us that they (a) were deeply frustrated and dissatisfied with what they had been doing, and (b) were overripe to believe in quick-and-easy miracles. Even some people with extensive background in Normalization/SRV, and other solid training, cracked and fell to FC. Maybe one thing we can read from this is that people are saying that they have taken Normalization/SRV as far as they are going to, or have been allowed to, and they consider the payoff of this limited implementation very unsatisfactory and frustrating. This is even worse news for SRV than for Normalization, because SRV asks far more. This tells us that the as yet vastly unrealized potential of SRV is not likely to be pursued and realized by many people, or taken very far. Instead, we can expect craze-craziness to continue, though in forms different from, and usually less dramatic than, FC, because FC has been one of the most extreme human service crazes in those fields where it found its greatest acceptance.

The balancing good news is that SRV grounding also preserved a great many people from falling to the FC craze, but that does not mean that they are not also very frustrated, and vulnerable to falling for some other exciting new thing that is thrown before them.

3.2.3 THE LOW LIKELIHOOD THAT NORMALIZATION/SRV WILL PENETRATE, OR OVERCOME, "SHRINKERY"

I also see little reason to be optimistic that what I deliberately called the "shrink field" will embrace Normalization/SRV. One very straightforward reason is that such an acceptance would deprive an immensely powerful sector of human service workers of most of their power, economic advantage, and prestige. To a large extent, the field of mental retardation got away from the long-enduring stranglehold of the shrink people, and they will not let the same thing happen to the field of mental disorder.

3.2.4 THE POSSIBILITY OF A RETURN TO CONCEPTUAL CHAOS

All the foregoing also raises the distinct possibility that there will be a reversion to the futile or chaotic conceptual situation that existed prior to the early 1970s that I sketched in my earlier chapter, and that largely still prevails in the mental field, with many low-level, and a few high-level, crazes attracting large followerships concurrently and successively. Admittedly, concepts such as absolute individual self-determination (which is one of the postnormalization concepts widely promoted) are not low-level, but they are three other things: (a) totally destructive; (b) totally irrational; and (c) in many ways, devoid of consciousness of context, in that we live in a world in which individual options of a positive nature are rapidly being taken away, while the realm of so-called "choice" consists increasingly of immoral things of greater number. For instance, we may soon be able to watch TV with mostly vacuous or outright morally decadent content on 500 channels. That is the kind of "choice" that modernism promotes and celebrates!

3.2.5 THE ABSENCE OF A PROMINENT PERSON OR BODY TO PROMOTE, PRESERVE, AND ELABORATE NORMALIZATION/SRV

One major source of pessimism for the future is that there is no one single outstanding personage or strongly established entity or institution that has made the preservation, elaboration, or application of Normalization/SRV a major focus of its efforts. There are entire institutes with vast funding devoted to all sorts of crazes, or to possibly valid but low-level ideas, schemes, techniques, or technologies, but none to Normalization/SRV. There are professors and entire university departments that have and share a major theoretical focus—in some cases that of "inclusion"—but not one on Normalization/SRV, though it is of a higher order and subsumes other things that many people *have* taken up as their cause. For a while, what used to be called the National Institute on Mental Retardation (later the G. Allan Roeher Institute, and now the Roeher Institute) in Canada was a major institutional base for Normalization publishing, training, and promotion, but it has abandoned this role in favor of both certain cultural values that I referred to earlier, as well as the craze culture of human services.

3.2.6 A SMALL HOPEFUL NOTE

In contrast to the above point, one of the most positive developments in the last few years has been the establishment of largely informal bodies devoted to the promotion and safeguarding of SRV and its dissemination. Of greatest promise has been the establishment and evolution of the aforementioned North American SRV Council. Its discussions have been tremendously helpful to all of its members, and through them to many other people. We have all been able to clarify many of our thoughts about SRV, and several members, including me, have been stimulated by it to expand and refine SRV theory, and to write on various topics related to it. Stimulated by the council, the new bilingual *International SRV Journal* was launched in 1994. Also, it would have been difficult to hold this conference without the council, or to hold it at the same level of quality. However, most of all, I see the SRV Council as one of the major safeguards on SRV work for some years to come.

Also, one modestly reassuring thought is one that recent SRV teaching by members of the SRV Council has increasingly emphasized, namely, that even where the structures fail, those with SRV knowledge will have many things to fall back on in their human relations that they might otherwise not have known; but ultimately, how one comports oneself in dire circumstances will be more determined by one's religion, one's character, and one's personality. But many of us have been strengthened in all three of these through our engagement with Normalization and SRV, and our efforts to teach and promote them.

4 CONCLUSION

In conclusion, let us remember what Chou En-lai said when he was asked in 1989 what he thought of the French revolution of 1789. After a long pause, he said, "It is too soon to tell." I must admit that I feel much more confident in predicting all sorts of things, including the collapse of viable polity in the world, than in predicting the future of Normalization and SRV.

REFERENCES

BIKLEN, D., & DUCHAN, J. F. (1994). "I am intelligent": The social construction of mental retardation. *Journal of the Association for Persons With Severe Handicaps, 19*(3), 173-184.

CHURCH, G. J. (1995, April 24). Saigon: The final 10 days. *Time,* 25-35.

FLYNN, R. J. (1993). Intégration et évaluation de programmes: Comparaisons internationales. In S. IONESCU, G. MAGEROTTE, W. PILON, & R. SALABREUX (Eds.), *L'intégration des personnes présentant une déficience intellectuelle* (pp. 5-15). Actes du IIIe Congrès de l'Association Internationale de Recherche scientifique en faveur des personnes Handicapées Mentales (AIRHM). Trois-Rivières: Université du Québec à Trois-Rivières et AIRHM.

FLYNN, R. J., & NITSCH, K. E. (Eds.). (1980). *Normalization, social integration, and community services.* Baltimore: University Park Press.

MCKNIGHT, J. (1995). *The careless society: Community and its counterfeits.* New York: Basic Books.

More mothers are breadwinners and caregivers, world-wide study says. (1995, May 31). *Syracuse Herald Journal,* A1.

PIKE, O. (1994, April 17). Bloody chaos is winning out over order around the world. *Syracuse*

Herald American, C11.

SHANE, H. C. (Ed.). (1994). *Facilitated communication: The clinical and social phenomenon.* San Diego: Singular Publishing Group.

THOMAS, S. (1994). A brief history of the SRV Development, Training, and Safeguarding Council. *SRV/VRS: The International Social Role Valorization Journal/La Revue Internationale de la Valorisation des Rôles Sociaux, 1*(2), 15-18.

TVERSKY, A., & KAHNEMAN, D. (1974). Judgment under uncertainty: Heuristics and biases. *Science, 185,* 1124-1131.

VATER, A., SCHEUING, H-W., & WOLFENSBERGER, W. (1994). *"Euthanasie": Damals und heute.* Mosbach I. O.,Germany: Johannes-Anstalten. (Fachtagung auf dem Schwarzacher Hof der Johannes-Anstalten Mosbach, 13 June 1994).

WOLFENSBERGER, W. (1970a). Ideology power. *Nebraska Contributor, 1*(1), 1-6.

WOLFENSBERGER, W. (1970b). The principle of Normalization and its implications for psychiatric services. *American Journal of Psychiatry, 127,* 291-297.

WOLFENSBERGER, W. (1971a). Will there always be an institution? I: The impact of epidemiological trends. *Mental Retardation, 9*(5), 14-20.

WOLFENSBERGER, W. (1971b). Will there always be an institution? II: The impact of new service models: Residential alternatives to institutions. *Mental Retardation, 9*(6), 31-38.

WOLFENSBERGER, W. (1972). *The principle of Normalization in human services.* Toronto, ON: National Institute on Mental Retardation.

WOLFENSBERGER, W. (1980). The definition of Normalization: Update, problems, disagreements, and misunderstandings. In R. J. Flynn & K. E. Nitsch (Eds.), *Normalization, social integration, and community services* (pp. 71-115). Baltimore: University Park Press.

WOLFENSBERGER, W. (1983). Social Role Valorization: A proposed new term for the principle of Normalization. *Mental Retardation, 21*(6), 234-239.

WOLFENSBERGER, W. (1989). Human service policies: The rhetoric versus the reality. In L. BARTON (Ed.), *Disability and dependency* (pp.

23-41). London: Falmer Press. (Disability, Handicap and Life Chances Series)

WOLFENSBERGER, W. (1991a). *A brief introduction to Social Role Valorization as a high-order concept for structuring human services.* Syracuse, NY: Syracuse University, Training Institute for Human Service Planning, Leadership and Change Agentry.

WOLFENSBERGER, W. (Ed.) (1991b). Crazeology (whole issue). *TIPS (Training Institute Publication Series), 11*(2 & 3).

WOLFENSBERGER, W. (1992a). *A brief introduction to Social Role Valorization as a high-order concept for structuring human services* (Rev. ed.). Syracuse, NY: Syracuse University, Training Institute for Human Service Planning, Leadership and Change Agentry.

WOLFENSBERGER, W. (Ed.). (1992b). Post-primary production economy (whole issue). *TIPS (Training Institute Publication Series), 12*(2, 3).

WOLFENSBERGER, W. (l992c, April). The "if this, then that" formulation in SRV-related decision-making. *CMHERA (Community & Mental Handicap Educational & Research Association) Newsletter, 1,* 4-7. (New Series)

WOLFENSBERGER, W. (1994a). A personal interpretation of the mental retardation scene in light of the "signs of the times." *Mental Retardation, 32*(1), 19-33.

WOLFENSBERGER, W. (1994b). The "facilitated communication" craze as an instance of pathological science: The cold fusion of human services. In H. C. SHANE (Ed.), *Facilitated communication: The clinical and social phenomenon* (pp. 57-122). San Diego: Singular Publishing Group.

WOLFENSBERGER, W. (1995). An "if this, then that" formulation of decisions related to Social Role Valorization as a better way of interpreting it to people. *Mental Retardation, 33*(3), 163-169.

WOLFENSBERGER, W., & GLENN, L. (1973a). *PASS (Program analysis of service systems): A method for the quantitative evaluation of human services. Vol 1. Handbook* (2nd ed.). Toronto, ON: National Institute on Mental Retardation.

WOLFENSBERGER, W., & GLENN, L. (1973b). *PASS (Program analysis of service systems): A method for the quantitative evaluation of human services. Vol. 2. Field manual* (2nd ed.). Toronto, ON: National Institute on Mental Retardation.

WOLFENSBERGER, W., & GLENN, L. (1975a). *PASS (Program analysis of service systems): A method for the quantitative evaluation of human services. Vol. 1. Handbook* (3rd ed.). Toronto, ON: National Institute on Mental Retardation. (Reprinted 1978)

WOLFENSBERGER, W., & GLENN, L. (1975b). *PASS (Program analysis of service systems): A method for the quantitative evaluation of human services. Vol. 2. Field manual* (3rd ed.). Toronto, ON: National Institute on Mental Retardation. (Reprinted with corrections, 1978)

WOLFENSBERGER, W., & THOMAS, S. (1983). *PASSING (Program analysis of service systems' implementation of Normalization goals): Normalization criteria and ratings manual* (2nd ed.). Toronto, ON: National Institute on Mental Retardation.

WOLFENSBERGER, W., & THOMAS, S. (1995). Reply to Newnes's "A commentary on 'Obstacles in the professional human service culture to implementation of Social Role Valorization and community integration of clients.'" *Care in Place, 2*(1), 56-62.

WOLFENSBERGER, W., & TULLMAN, S. (1982). A brief outline of the principle of Normalization. *Rehabilitation Psychology, 27*(3), 131-145.

Part 9

Appendix

A comprehensive bibliography on Normalization, Social Role Valorization, *PASS*, and *PASSING*, 1969-1999

CAROLE ST-DENIS AND ROBERT J. FLYNN

This comprehensive bibliography includes approximately 800 items. We created it as a working tool for the reader interested in the extensive literature on Normalization, Social Role Valorization, PASS, and PASSING. The bibliography covers the literature in English and French for a 30-year period, beginning in 1969, the year of publication of Kugel and Wolfensberger's classic monograph, *Changing Patterns in Residential Services for the Mentally Retarded*, in which Nirje's celebrated article on Normalization appeared, and ending in early 1999, when work on the present volume was completed. The bibliography is as complete as we could make it, and incorporates the 241 items from Nitsch, Armour, and Flynn's earlier bibliography on Normalization and PASS (see Flynn and Nitsch's [1980] volume, pp. 395-409). This updated and greatly expanded bibliography is more than three times as long as the earlier one. Each item is identified as pertaining primarily to Normalization (N), Social Role Valorization (SRV), PASS (PS), PASSING (PG), or some combination thereof.

To be included, an item had to make more than a fleeting reference to or have more than a peripheral relationship with one or more of the following terms: *Normalization, Social Role Valorization, Program Analysis of Service Systems (PASS),* and *Program Analysis of Service Systems' Implementation of Normalization Goals (PASSING)*. We limited our systematic search of the literature to references published in English or French, although we did include a few items coming to our attention that were in languages other than English or French. In deciding to include an item, we made no judgment about its quality or importance.

We thank Paul Jenkins, Kristjana Kristiansen, Jo Massarelli, Susan Thomas, Tony Wainwright, and Wolf Wolfensberger for their contributions to the bibliography. We would also appreciate being made aware of any omissions.

COMPREHENSIVE BIBLIOGRAPHY

AANES, D., & HAAGENSON, L. (1978). Normalization: Attention to a conceptual disaster. *Mental Retardation, 16*, 55-56. (N)

ABESON, A., BURGDORF, R. L., CASEY, P. J., KUNZ, J. W., & MCNEIL, W. (1974). Access to opportunity. In N. HOBBS (Ed.), *Issues in the classification of children: A sourcebook on categories, labels, and their consequences (Vol. 2)*. San Francisco: Jossey-Bass. (N)

ALASZEWSKI, A., & ONG, B. N. (1990). *Normalisation in practice: Residential care for children with a profound mental handicap*. London: Routledge. (N)

AMERICAN ALLIANCE FOR HEALTH, PHYSICAL EDUCATION AND RECREATION. (1977). *Integrating persons with handicapping conditions into regular physical education programs: A bibliography and literature analysis* (Rev. ed.). Washington, DC: Author. (N)

AMUNDSON, R., DYER, L., HENDERSON, W., & RATHBONE-MCCUAN, E. (1991). Vacation therapy: A community Normalization experience for persons with long-term mental illness. *Psychosocial Rehabilitation Journal, 14*(3), 81-91. (N)

ANDERSON, R. M., GREER, J. G., & DIETRICH, W. L. (1976). Overview and perspectives. In R. M. ANDERSON, & J. G. GREER (Eds.), *Educating the severely and profoundly retarded.* Baltimore: University Park Press. (N)

ANDERTON, J. M., ELFERT, H., & LAI, M. (1989). Behavior-modification and Normalization in conflict. *Sociology of Health & Illness, 11,* 253-278. (N)

ANDREWS, R. J., & BERRY, P. B. (1978). The evaluation of services for the handicapped promoting community living. *International Journal of Rehabilitation Research, 1,* 451-461. (PS)

ANGERS, M. (1992). "Created" communities and "natural" community. Special issue: The clubhouse model. *Psychosocial Rehabilitation Journal, 16,* 117-123. (N)

ANONYMOUS. (1975). PASS. *Currents, 2*(3), 5-8. (PS)

ANONYMOUS. (1982). Normalization or exclusion: The chances to find jobs and persons leaving special schools. *Mid-American Review of Sociology, 7,* 139-170. (N)

ANONYMOUS. (1983). Give Normalisation a chance. *Mental Retardation, 21,* 76. (N)

ANONYMOUS. (1994). Association to promote the principles of Social Role Valorisation. *Training & Evaluation for Change Newsletter, 21.* Kent Town, SA. (SRV)

ANONYMOUS. (1994). Review of the conference, "25 years of Normalization, Social Role Valorization, and social integration: A retrospective and prospective view." *International Social Role Valorization Journal, 1*(2), 39-42. (N, SRV)

ANSTEY, T. J., & GASKIN, M. (1985). Service providers' understanding of the concept of Normalization. *Australia and New Zealand Journal of Developmental Disabilities, 11,* 91-95. (N)

ASHMAN, A. F., & SUTTIE, J. (1995). Changing existing services for older people with an intellectual disability. *Australia & New Zealand Journal of Developmental Disabilities, 20,* 189-204. (N)

ASSOCIATION FOR ADVOCACY FOR CHANGE THROUGH TRAINING. *Changing lives, changing communities.* Carlton South, Victoria, Australia: Author. (N, SRV)

BAILEY, D., & MCWILLIAM, R. (1990). Normalizing early intervention. *Topics in Early Childhood Special Education, 10*(2), 33-47. (N)

BAKER, B. L., SELTZER, G. B., & SELTZER, M. M. (1977). *As close as possible: Community residences for retarded adults.* Boston: Little, Brown and Company. (N)

BAKER, F. M., BAKER, R. J., & MCDANIEL, R. S. (1975). Denormalizing practices in rehabilitation facilities. *Rehabilitation Literature, 36*(4), 112-115, 119. (N)

BALDWIN, S. (1985). Models of service delivery: An assessment of some applications and implications for people who are mentally retarded. *Mental Retardation, 23*(1), 6-12. (N)

BALDWIN, S. (1985). Sheep in wolf's clothing: Impact of Normalisation teaching on human services and service providers. *International Journal of Rehabilitation Research, 8*(2), 131-142. (N)

BALDWIN, S. (1989). Applied behaviour analysis and Normalisation: New carts for old horses? A commentary. *Behavioural Psychotherapy, 17,* 305-308. (N)

BALDWIN, S. (1989). Applied behaviour analysis and Normalization: Reason, rhetoric and rationality. *Behavioural Psychotherapy, 17,* 314-315. (N)

BALDWIN, S., & HATTERSLEY, J. (1991). *Mental handicap: Social science perspectives.* London: Tavistock/Routledge. (N)

BALDWIN, S., & STOWERS, C. (1987, Spring). Normalisation and elderly persons: In whose best interests? *American Archives of Rehabilitation Therapy,* 34-42. (N)

BANK-MIKKELSEN, N. E. (1969). A metropolitan area in Denmark: Copenhagen. In R. KUGEL & W. WOLFENSBERGER (Eds.), *Changing patterns in residential services for the mentally retarded.* Washington, D.C.: President's Committee on Mental Retardation. (N)

BANK-MIKKELSEN, N. E. (1976). Denmark. In R. KUGEL & A. SHEARER (Eds.), *Changing patterns in residential services for the mentally retarded* (Rev. ed.). (DHEW No. [OHD] 76-21015.) Washington, DC: President's Committee on Mental Retardation. (N)

BANK-MIKKELSEN, N. E. (1977). Right to normal living conditions. *Enlightenment* (Pennsylvania Association for Retarded Citizens), *1*(3), 4-8. (N)

BANK-MIKKELSEN, N. E. (1978). Misconceptions of the principle of Normalization. In *FLASH on the service for the mentally retarded, III.* Publication No. 44. Copenhagen: The Personnel Training School. (N)

BANK-MIKKELSEN, N. E. (1980). Denmark. In R. J. FLYNN & K. E. NITSCH (Eds.), *Normalization, social integration, and community services* (pp. 51-70). Baltimore: University Park Press. (N)

BANO, A., CROSSKILL, D., PATEL, R., RASHMAN, L., & SHAH, R. (1993). Dark shadows on a white wall: A black perspective on Wolfensberger's theory of Normalisation. In A. BANO, D. CROSSKILL, R. PATEL, L. RASHMAN, & R. SHAH, *Improving practice with people with learning disabilities.* London: Central Council for Education and Training in Social Work. (N)

BARNETT, B. H. (1979). Communitization and the measured message of normal behavior. In R. L. YORK & E. EDGAR (Eds.), *Teaching the severely handicapped* (Vol. IV). Seattle, WA: American Association for the Education of the Severely and Profoundly Handicapped. (N)

BARNEY, W. D. (1977). "Normalisation": What does it mean and how does it work? *Intellectual Handicap Review* (New Zealand), *16*(4), 17-25. (N)

BAROFF, G. S. (1974). *Mental retardation: Nature, cause, and management.* Washington, DC: Hemisphere Publishing Co. (N)

BASS, M. S. (1978). Surgical contraception: A key to Normalization and prevention. *Mental Retardation, 16*(6), 399-404. (N)

BATES, P., & PANCSOFAR, E. (1983). Project EARN (Employment and Rehabilitation = Normalization): A competitive employment training program for severely disabled youth in the public schools. *British Journal of Mental Subnormality, 29*(57, Pt. 2), 97-103. (N)

BAYES, K. A. (1969). *British architect's view on Normalization.* London: Design Research Unit. (Mimeographed) (N)

BAYLEY, M. (1991). Normalisation or "Social Role Valorization": An adequate philosophy? In S. BALDWIN & J. HATTERSLEY (Eds.), *Mental handicap: Social science perspectives.* London: Tavistock/Routledge. (N, SRV)

BECKEY, D. M. (1982). Normalization's theoretical status and future residential models. *Australia and New Zealand Journal of Developmental Disabilities, 8*(2), 97-104. (N)

BECKMAN-BRINDLEY, S., & TAVORMINA, J. B. (1978). Normalization: A new look. *Education and Training of the Mentally Retarded, 13*(1), 66-68. (N)

BELLAMY, G. T., NEWTON, J. S., LEBARON, N. M., & HORNER, R. H. (1990). Quality of life and lifestyle outcome: A challenge for residential programs. In R. L. SCHALOCK & M. J. BEGAB (Eds.), *Quality of life: Perspectives and issues* (pp. 127-137). Washington, DC: American Association on Mental Retardation. (N)

BERCOVICI, S. M. (1983). *Barriers to Normalization.* Baltimore: University Park Press. (N)

BERNSTEIN, G. S., & KARAN, O. C. (1979). Obstacles to vocational Normalization for the developmentally disabled. *Rehabilitation Literature, 40*(3), 66-71. (N)

BERRY, P. B., ANDREWS, R. J., & ELKINS, J. (1977). *An evaluative study of educational, vocational and residential programs for the moderately to severely mentally handicapped in three states.* St. Lucia, Queensland, Australia: University of Queensland, Fred and Eleanor Schonell Educational Research Centre. (PS)

BIKLEN, D. (1979). The case for deinstitutionalization. *Social Policy, 10*(1), 48-54. (N)

BIKLEN, D., & DYBWAD, G. (1979). A perspective on the social and cultural history of severely and profoundly retarded persons. In S. G. SELLARS (Ed.), *Strategies for increasing career education and opportunities for severely mentally retarded perons.* College Park: University of Maryland, Department of Industrial Education, Center of Rehabilitation & Manpower Services. (N)

BILLIMORIA, R. B. (1993). *Principle and practice of Normalization: Experiences from Sweden and application to India.* Uppsala: Uppsala University, Centre for Handicap Research. (N)

BISSONNIER, H. (1977). Current developments in the field of mental retardation: A tentative assessment and critical study. *International Child Welfare Review, 32.* (N)

BJAANES, A. T., & BUTLER, E. W. (1974). Environmental variation in community care facilities for mentally retarded persons. *American Journal of Mental Deficiency, 78*(4), 429-439. (N)

BLAKE, R. (1986). Normalisation and boarding homes: An examination of paradoxes. *Social Work in Health Care, 11*(2), 75-86. (N)

BLANCHET, A. (1999). The impact of Normalization and Social Role Valorization in Canada. In R. J. FLYNN & R. A. LEMAY (Eds.), *A quarter-century of Normalization and Social Role Valorization: Evolution and impact.* Ottawa, ON: University of Ottawa Press. (N, SRV)

BLANEY, B. C. (1992). Commentary. In S. MOSS (Ed.), *Aging and developmental disabilities: Perspectves from nine countries* (pp. 93-96). International Exchange of Experts and Information in Rehabilitation (IEEIR) Monograph No. 52. Durham, NH: University of New Hampshire, Institute on Disability. (N, SRV)

BLANEY, B. C. (1994). Adulthood or oldness: In search of a vision. In V. J. BRADLEY, J. W. ASHBAUGH, & B. C. BLANEY (Eds.), *Creating individual supports for people with developmental disabilities: A mandate for change at many levels* (pp. 141-151). Baltimore: Paul H. Brookes. (SRV)

BLATT, B. (1987). The community imperative and human values. In R. F. ANTONAK & J. A. MULICK (Eds.), *The community imperative revisited. Transitions in mental retardation, Vol. 3* (pp. 237-246). Norwood, NJ: Ablex Publishing Corp. (N)

BLOOM, B. (1974). *"Normalization" and educational policies.* Toronto, ON: National Institute on Mental Retardation. (Paper prepared for the Saskatchewan Association for the Mentally Retarded) (N)

BLUNDEN, R. (1988). Mental Handicap: The feasibility of Normalisation—An introduction. In E. KARAS (Ed.), *Current Issues in Clinical Psychology.* New York & London: Plenum Press. (N)

BONDE, B. (1982). Normaliseringsprincippet [Danish]. *Skolepsykologi, 19*(2), 99-128. (N)

BOOTH, M. C. (1989). *Normalization in non-profit small group homes for mentally retarded adults.* Unpublished doctoral dissertation, University of California, Los Angeles. (N)

BORTHWICK-DUFFY, S. A. (1989). Quality of life: The residential environment. In W. E. KIERNAN & R. L. SCHALOCK (Eds.), *Economics, industry, and disability: A look ahead* (pp. 351-363). Baltimore: Paul H. Brookes. (N)

BOSCHEN, K. A., & KRANE, N. (1992). A history of independent living in Canada. *Canadian Journal of Rehabilitation, 6*(2), 79-88. (N)

BOUCHARD, C., & DUMONT, M. (1996). *Où est Phil, comment se porte-t-il et pourquoi? Une étude sur l'intégration social et le bien-être des personnes présentant une déficience intellectuelle.* Québec, QC: Gouvernement du Québec, Ministère de la Santé et des Services sociaux, Direction générale de la planification et de l'évaluation. (N)

BOUCHERAT, A. (1987). Normalisation in mental handicap: Acceptance without question? *Bulletin of the Royal College of Psychiatrists, 11,* 423-425. (N)

BOUTET, M., HURTEAU, M., LACHAPPELLE, R., & LALONDE, M. (1993). La mise en marche de l'approche communautaire dans le cadre de l'intégration sociale des personnes présentant une déficience intellectuelle: Projet-pilote. In S. IONESCU, G. MAGEROTTE, W. PILON, & R. SALBREUX (Eds.), *L'intégration des personnes présentant une déficience intellectuelle* (pp. 295-297). Actes du IIIe congrès de l'Association Internationale de Recherche scientifique en faveur des personnes Handicapées Mentales. Trois-Rivières, QC: Université du Québec à Trois-Rivières et AIRHM. (SRV)

BOWD, A. D. (1988). *To provide a home environment: Normalization of residential services for developmentally handicapped persons in the Lakehead Region.* Thunder Bay, ON: Lakehead Association for Community Living. (N)

BOWD, A. D. (1989). Client satisfaction and Normalization of residential services for persons with developmental handicaps. *Canadian Journal of Community Mental Health, 8*(1), 63-73. (N)

BOYD, W., & HARTNETT, F. (1975). Normalization and its implications for recreation services. *Journal of Leisurability, 2*(1), 22-27. (N)

BRADLEY, V. J. (1978). *Deinstitutionalization of developmentally disabled persons: A conceptual analysis and guide.* Baltimore: University Park Press. (N)

BRADLEY, V. J. (1994). Evolution of a new service paradigm. In V. J. BRADLEY, J. W. ASHBAUGH, & B. C. BLANEY (Eds.), *Creating individual supports for people with developmental disabilities: A mandate for change at many levels* (pp. 11-32). Baltimore: Paul H. Brookes. (N)

BRADY, M. P., & CUNNINGHAM, J. (1985). Living and learning in segregated environments: An ethnography of Normalization outcomes. *Education and Training of the Mentally Retarded, 20,* 241-252. (N)

BRANDON, A., & BRANDON, D. (1987). Do you really understand Normalization? *Community Living, 1*(1) (N).

BRANDON, D. (1991). Implications of Normalisation work for professional skills. In S. RAMON (Ed.), *Beyond community care: . and integration work.* London: MacMillan Education Ltd. (N)

BRANDON, D. (1991). *Increasing value: The implications of the principle of Normalization for mental illness services.* Manchester, England: Salford University College. (N)

BRANDON, D., & BRANDON, A. (1988). *Putting people first: A handbook on the practical application of ordinary living principles.* London: Good Impressions. (N)

BRANSON, J., & MILLER, D. B. (1991). Normalisation and the socio-cultural construction of "disabilities": Towards an understanding of schooling, discipline and the integration programme. In M. LOVEGROVE & R. LEWIS (Eds.), *Classroom discipline.* Melbourne: Longman Cheshire. (N)

BRANSON, J., & MILLER, D. (1992). Normalisation, community care and the politics of difference. *Australian Disability Review, 4,* 17-28. (N)

BRATT, A., & JOHNSTON, R. (1989). "Changes in life style for young adults with profound handicaps": Reply. *Mental Handicap Research, 2,* 107-108. (PG)

BRECHIN, A., & SWAIN, J. (1988). Professional/client relationships: Creating a "working alliance" with people with learning difficulties. *Disability, Handicap and Society, 3,* 213-226. (N)

BRICKEY, M. (1974). Normalization and behavior modification in the workshop. *Journal of Rehabilitation, 40*(6), 15-16, 44-46. (N)

BRITON, J. (1970). Normalisation: What of and what for. *Australian Journal of Mental Retardation, 5,* 224-229. (N)

BRITON, J. (1977). Behavior modification, Normalization and person-orientedness. *Australian Journal of Mental Retardation, 4*(8), 4-12. (N)

BRONSTON, W. G. (1976). Concepts and theory of Normalization. In R. KOCH & J. C. DOBSON (Eds.), *The mentally retarded child and his family: A multidisciplinary handbook* (Rev. ed.). New York: Brunner/Mazel. (N)

BROWDER, D. M. (1991). *Assessment of individuals with severe disabilities: An applied behavior approach to life skills assessment* (2nd ed.). Baltimore: Paul H. Brookes. (N)

BROWN, H. (1992). What price theory if you cannot afford the busfare: Normalisation and leisure services for people with learning disabilities. *Health and Social Care in the Community, 2,* 153-159. (N)

BROWN, H. (1994). An ordinary sexual life? A review of the Normalisation principle as it applies to the sexual options of people with learning disabilities. *Disability & Society, 9*(2), 123-144. (N)

BROWN, H., & ALCOE, J. (1987). Lifestyles: An approach to training staff in Normalisation principles. *Social Work Education, 6*(3), 21-22. (N)

BROWN, H., & SMITH, H. (1989). Whose "ordinary life" is it anyway: A feminist critique of the Normalisation principle. *Disability, Handicap and Society, 4,* 105-118. (N)

BROWN, H., & SMITH, H. (1992). Assertion, not assimilation: A feminist perspective on the Normalisation principle. In H. BROWN & H. SMITH (Eds.), *Normalisation: A reader for the nineties* (pp. 149-171). London & New York: Tavistock/Routledge. (N)

BROWN, H., & SMITH, H. (1992). Introduction. In H. BROWN & H. SMITH (Eds.), *Normalisation: A reader for the nineties* (pp. xiv-xxii). London & New York: Routledge. (N)

BROWN, H., & SMITH, H. (Eds.). (1992). *Normalisation: A reader for the nineties.* London & New York: Routledge. (N)

BROWN, H., & SMITH, H. (1992). Postscript. In H. BROWN & H. SMITH (Eds.), *Normalisation: A reader for the nineties* (pp. 172-177). London & New York: Routledge. (N)

BROWN, J. L. (1973). Can we describe how we normalize the life style of the deviant child? *Involvement, 6*(1), 1-7. (N)

BROWN, L., THOMAS, M. D., ALLEN, D. G., & GILCHRIST, L. D. (1994). Mental health reform: Client and family member perspectives. *Education and Program Planning, 17,* 81-92. (N)

BROWN, R. L. (1987). Rehabilitation in Australia: A look at someone else's backyard. *Australia and New Zealand Journal of Developmental Disabilities, 13*(3), 127-132. (N)

BRUININKS, R. H. (1990). There is more than a zip code to changes in services. *American Journal on Mental Retardation, 95,* 13-15. (N)

BUELL, M. K. (1996, May). Deinstitutionalization of persons with developmenal disabilities: Normalization and service delivery re-evaluated. *Dissertation Abstracts International, 56*(11-B), 6459. (N)

BUELL, M. K., & MINNES, P. M. (1994). An acculturation perspective on deinstitutionalization and service delivery. *Journal on Developmental Disabilities, 3,* 94-107. (N)

BUNTINX, W. (n.d.). Dutch translation of PASS 3. Utrecht: Bishop Bekkers Institute. (Mimeographed) (PS)

BUNTINX, W. (1979). [Reflections on the measurement of the quality of service delivery.] *Ruit, 18.* (In Dutch) (PS)

BURCHARD, S. N. (1999). Normalization and residential services: The Vermont studies. In R. J. FLYNN & R. A. LEMAY (Eds.), *A quarter-century of Normalization and Social Role Valorization: Evolution and impact.* Ottawa, ON: University of Ottawa Press. (N)

BURCHARD, S. N., GORDON, L. R., & PINE, J. (1990). Manager competence, program Normalization and client satisfaction in group homes. *Education and Training in Mental Retardation, 25,* 277-285. (N)

BURCHARD, S. N., HASAZI, J. S., GORDON, L. R., & YOE, J. (1991). An examination of lifestyle and adjustment in three community residential alternatives. *Research in Developmental Disabilities, 12,* 127-142. (N)

BURCHARD, S. N., PINE, J., & GORDON, L. R. (1990). Manager competence, program Normalization and client satisfaction in group homes. *Education and Training in Mental Retardation, 25,* 277-285. (N)

BURCHARD, S. N., PINE, J., GORDON, L. R., JOFFE, J. M., WIDRICK, G. C., & GOY, E. (1987). The relationship of manager competence to program quality in small community residences. In J. A. MULICK & R. F. ANTONAK (Eds.), *Issues in therapeutic intervention. Transitions in mental retardation, Vol. 2* (pp. 47-69). Norwood, NJ: Ablex. (N)

BURCHARD, S. N., ROSEN, J. W., GORDON, L. R., HASAZI, J. S., YOE, J., & DIETZEL, L. C. (1992). A comparison of social support and satisfaction among adults with mental retardation living in three types of community residential alternatives. In J. W. JACOBSON, S. N. BURCHARD, & P. J. CARLING (Eds.), *Community living for people with developmental and psychiatric disabilities* (pp. 137-154). Baltimore: The John Hopkins University Press. (N)

BURCHARD, S. N., & THOUSAND, J. (1988). Staff and manager competencies. In M. P. JANICKI, M. W. KRAUSS, & M. M. SELTZER (Eds.), *Community residences for persons with developmental disabilities: Here to stay.* Baltimore: Paul H. Brookes. (N)

BURISH, T. G. (1979). A small community model for developing normalizing alternatives to institutionalization. *Mental Retardation, 17*(2), 90-92. (N)

BURKHARD, J. S., & GOLDMAN, R. (1982). The right to be retarded. *Milieu Therapy, 2*(1), 38-44. (N)

BURNS, J., & ROBERTS, T. (1988, Autumn). A feminist perspective on the Normalization principle. *Psychology of Women Newsletter* (British Psychological Society), 12-17. (N)

BUTLER, E. W., & BJAANES, A. T. (1977). A typology of community care facilities and differential Normalization outcomes. In P. MITTLER (Ed.), *Research to practice in mental retardation: Care and intervention* (Vol. 1). Baltimore: University Park Press. (N)

BUTLER, E. W., BJAANES, A. T., & HOFACRE, S. (1975). *The Normalization process and the utilization of community agencies, services and programs by community care facilities.* Unpublished manuscript, University of California, Riverside. (N)

BUTTERFIELD, E. C., & GOW, L. (1987). Civil rights and social answers to the question, "How evil are Normalisation, deinstitutionalisation and mainstreaming?" In E. A. BARTNIK, G. M. LEWIS, & P. A. O'CONNOR (Eds.), *Technology, resources and consumer outcomes: Proceedings of the 23rd national conference of the Australian Society for the Study of Intellectual Disability.* Perth, Western Australia: P. E. Publications. (N)

CALLAHAN, M. (1985). Barriers to Normalization: The restrictive management of retarded persons. *Schizophrenia Bulletin, 11,* 230-254. (N)

CAMPAIGN FOR PEOPLE WITH MENTAL HANDICAPS (CMH). (1981). *The principle of Normalisation: A foundation for effective services.* London: CMH. (N)

CANDAPPA, M., & BURGESS, R. G. (1989). "I'm not handicapped—I'm different": "Normalisation", hospital-care, and mental handicap. In L. BARTON (Ed.), *Disability and dependency* (pp. 69-83). London: Falmer Press. (N)

CARSON, J. DOWLING, F., GLYNN, T., & OLIVER, N. (1994). The role of Normalization in psychiatric rehabilitation: An empirical investigation. *Care in Place, 1,* 231-243. (N)

CARSON, J., DOWLING, F., LUYOMBYA, G., SENAPTI-SHARMA, M., & GLYNN, T. (1982). Normalisation . . . and now for something completely different. *Clinical Psychology Forum, 49,* 27-30. (N, PS)

CARSON, J., DOWLING, F., LUYOMBA, G., SENAPATTI-SHARMA, M., & GLYNN T. (1993). The influence of Normalisation on psychiatric services. In M. P. J. WELLER & M. MUIJEN (Eds). (1993). *Dimensions of community mental health care.* London: W. B. Saunders/Balliere Tindall. (N)

CARSON, J., MCALPIN, B., GLYNN, T., & SHAW, E. (1989). *The role of Normalisation in the community care of the mentally ill.* Unpublished paper, Claybury Hospital. (N)

CARSON, S. (1992). Normalisation, needs and schools. *Educational Psychology in Practice, 7,* 216-222. (N)

CARUSO, G. (1996). Review of B. GOLFUS & D. E. SIMPSON's "When Billy broke his head . . . and other tales of wonder." *International Social Role Valorization Journal, 2*(2), 42-43. (SRV)

CHAPPELL, A. L. (1992). Towards a sociological critique of the Normalization principle. *Disability, Handicap and Society, 7*(1), 35-51. (N)

CHAPPELL, A. L. (1994). A question of friendship: Community care and the relationships of people with learning difficulties. *Disability and Society, 9,* 419-434. (N)

CHICOINE, F. (1979). Quelques réflexions sur la Normalisation. *Déficience Mentale/Mental Retardation, 29*(3), 49-51. (N)

CLARK, H. B., ET AL. (1983). Environmental and architectural planning for community-based, residential treatment facilities. *Journal of Rehabilitation Administration, 7*(1), 28-33. (N)

CLELAND, C. C., & SLUYTER, G. V. (1973). The heterobedfast ward: A model for translating "Normalization" into practice. *Mental Retardation, 11*(1), 44-46. (N)

CLIFFORD, L. X. (1984). A reaction to "Social Role Valorization." *Mental Retardation, 22,*147. (SRV)

CLIFFORD, P. (1987, April). Why I haven't joined the Normies: Some doubts about Normalisation. *South East Thames Rehabilitation Interest Group Newsletter.* (N)

CNAAN, R. A., ET AL. (1988). Psychosocial rehabilitation: Toward a definition. *Psychosocial Rehabilitation Journal, 11*, 61-77. (N)

COCKS, E. (1985). *Roadblocks to appropriate services for persons with an intellectual disability in Australia.* Paper presented at the 1994 conference of the Australian Group for the Scientific Study of Mental Deficiency, Melbourne, Australia. (N)

COCKS, E. (1998). Evaluating the quality of residential services for people with disabilities using program analysis of service systems' implementation of Normalization goals (PASSING). *Asia & Pacific Journal on Disability, 1.* (SRV, PG)

COHEN, C. (1978). An eclectic approach to counseling the retarded. *Journal of Applied Rehabilitation Counseling, 9*(2), 17-20. (N)

COHEN, E. S. (1988). The elderly mystique: Constraints on the autonomy of the elderly with disabilities. *Gerontologist,* 24-31. (N)

COHEN, S. (1977). Normalization and the right to a better life. In S. COHEN, *Special people: A brighter future for everyone with physical, mental, and emotional disabilities.* Englewood Cliffs, NJ: Prentice-Hall. (N)

CONDELUCI, A., & GRETZ-LASKY, S. (1987). Social Role Valorization: A model for community re-entry. *Journal of Head Trauma Rehabilitation, 2,* 49-56. (SRV)

CONGDON, D. M. (1974). Croak of incompetence: Exhibitionism. *Mental Retardation, 12.* (N)

CONROY, J. W. (1996). The small ICF/MR program: Dimensions of quality and cost. *Mental Retardation, 34,* 13-26. (N, PS)

CONROY, J. W., & BRADLEY, V. J. (1985). *The Pennhurst longitudinal study: A report of five years of research and analysis.* Philadelphia: Temple University Developmental Disabilities Centre. Boston: Human Service Research Institute. (PS)

CONROY, J. W., EFTHIMIOU, & LEMANOWICZ, J. (1982). A matched comparison of the developmental growth of deinstitutionalized mentally retarded clients. *American Journal of Mental Deficiency, 86,* 581-587. (PS)

CONWAY, A. (1976). Normalization: A beginning without an end. *Education and Training of the Mentally Retarded, 11*(4), 341-345. (See also McDowell, F. [1977]. [Editor's] Correction. *Education and Training of the Mentally Retarded, 12*[2], 73.) (N)

COUCHMAN, W., GRAY, B., & KENNY, B. (1987). Three steps to Normalisation. *Senior Nurse, 6*(3), 11-2. (N)

CRAWFORD, D. (1974). Some practical implications of the concept of Normalisation. *Australian Children Limited, 4*(12), 362-367. (N)

CRAWFORD, D. (1976). *Normalization and integration: The community.* Working paper prepared for the Symposium on Normalization and Integration—Improving the Quality of Life sponsored by the National Association for Retarded Citizens for the International League of Societies for the Mentally Handicapped, August 17-20, Airlie, VA. (N)

CROUSE, E. C., PATE, B., & LEFKOVITZ, P. M. (1983). A survey of partial hospitalization programs in the state of Indiana. *International Journal of Partial Hospitalization, 2*(1), 43-55. (N)

CULLEN, C. (1991). Experimentation and planning in community care. *Disability, Handicap & Society, 6*(2), 115-128. (N, SRV)

CURTIS, C. K. (1984). Consumer assessment of services. *Remedial and Special Education, 5*(4), 45-46. (N)

DALLEY, G. (1992). Social welfare ideologies and Normalisation: Links and conflicts. In H. BROWN & H. SMITH (Eds.), *Normalisation: A reader for the nineties* (pp. 100-111). London & New York: Tavistock/Routledge. (N)

DANIELS, J. Y. (1974). On words (Letter to the Editor). *Mental Retardation, 12*(1), 52. (N)

DANSEREAU, J., DUTEAU, C., ELY, P., & FLYNN, R. J. (1990). *Évaluation des programmes résidentiels en santé mentale dans l'Outaouais.* Hull, QC: Conseil régional de la santé et des services sociaux de l'Outaouais. (PG)

DARLING, R. B. (1987). The economic and psychosocial consequences of disability: Family-society relationships. *Marriage & Family Review, 11,* 45-61. (N)

DATTILO, J. (1991). Mental retardation. In D. R. AUSTIN & M. E. CRAWFORD (Eds.), *Therapeutic recreation: An introduction* (pp. 163-188). Englewood Cliffs, NJ: Prentice-Hall. (N)

DAY, P. R. (1987). Mind the gap: Normalisation theory and practice. *Practice, 1*(2), 105-115. (N)

DEMAINE, G. C., WILSON, S., SILVERSTEIN, A., & MAYEDA, T. (1978, May). *Facility ratings based on a tested organizational nomenclature and a validated PASS 3.* Paper presented at the 102nd annual meeting of the American Association on Mental Deficiency, Denver. (PS)

DEMAINE, G. C., SILVERSTEIN, A. B., & MAYEDA, T. (1980). Validation of PASS 3: A first step in service evaluation through environmental assessment. *Mental Retardation, 18,* 131-134. (PS)

DERN, T, A. (1983). Obstacles to the implementation of the Normalization principle in human services: A response. *Mental Retardation, 21,* 77. (N)

DESILVA, R. M., & FAFLAK, P. (1976). From institution to community—A new process? *Mental Retardation, 14*(6), 25-28. (N)

DIONNE, A. (1999). The impact of Social Role Valorization on government policy in Quebec. In R. J. FLYNN & R. A. LEMAY (Eds.), *A quarter-century of Normalization and Social Role Valorization: Evolution and impact.* Ottawa, ON: University of Ottawa Press. (N, SRV)

DIONNE, C., LANGEVIN, J., & ROCQUE, S. (1993). Changement de paradigme en éducation. In S. IONESCU, G. MAGEROTTE, W. PILON, & R. SALBREUX (Eds.), *L'intégration des personnes présentant une déficience intellectuelle* (pp. 159-165). Actes du IIIe congrès de l'Association Internationale de Recherche scientifique en faveur des personnes Handicapées Mentales. Trois-Rivières, QC: Université du Québec à Trois-Rivières et AIRHM. (N, SRV)

DUCUIO, R. F. (1978). *The measurement of normalizing characteristics of residential environments for moderately retarded adults.* Unpublished doctoral dissertation, Columbia University. (N)

DUPONT, A. (1989). *L'évaluation dans le travail social.* Geneva, Switzerland: Éditions I.E.S. (SRV, PG)

DUPONT, A. (Ed.). (1990). *Psychiatrie et integration communautaire.* Genève: Deux Continents. (SRV)

DUPONT, A. (1993). The European services: Denmark. European Association for Mental Health in Mental Retardation Symposium: The mental health of Europeans with learning disabilities (1992, Veldhoven, Netherlands). *Journal of Intellectual Disability Research, 37*(Suppl. 1), 37-39. (N)

DUPONT, A. (1994). Valorisation des rôles sociaux et santé mentale: Le rôle de travailleur productif dans l'entreprise sociale. *Revue internationale de la valorisation des rôles sociaux, 1*(1), 19-28. (SRV)

DURAND, J., & NEUFELDT, A. H. (1975). *Comprehensive vocational service systems* (NIMR Monograph No. 4). Toronto, ON: National Institute on Mental Retardation. (N)

DURAND, J., & NEUFELDT, A. H. (1980). Comprehensive vocational services. In R. J. FLYNN & K. E. NITSCH (Eds.), *Normalization, social integration and community services* (pp. 283-298). Baltimore: University Park Press. (N)

DYBWAD, G. (1969). Action implications, U.S.A. today. In R. KUGEL & W. WOLFENSBERGER (Eds.), *Changing patterns in residential services for the mentally retarded.* Washington, DC: President's Committee on Mental Retardation. (N)

DYBWAD, G. (1973). Is Normalization a feasible principle of rehabilitation? In United Cerebral Palsy of New York City (Ed.), *Models of service for the multihandicapped adult.* New York: United Cerebral Palsy of New York City, Inc. (N)

DYBWAD, G. (1976). Normalization and integration—Shifting empires. In *FLASH on the service for the mentally retarded, III.* Publication No. 44. Copenhagen: The Personnel Training School, 1978. Published version of a working paper prepared for the Symposium on Normalization and Integration—Improving the Quality of Life sponsored by the National Association for Retarded Citizens for the International League of Societies for the Mentally Handicapped, August 17-20, Airlie, VA. (N)

DYBWAD, G. (1980). Avoiding misconceptions of mainstreaming, the least restrictive environment, and Normalization. *Exceptional Children, 47*(2), 85-88. (N)

DYBWAD, G. (1982). Normalization and its impact on social and public policy. In G. FOSS & R. E. NELSON (Eds.), *Advancing your citizenship: Normalization re-examined.* Proceedings of a National Conference on Normalization and Contemporary Practice in Mental Retardation. Eugene, OR: University of Oregon, Rehabilitation Research and Training Center in Mental Retardation. (N)

DYBWAD, G., & DYBWAD, R. (1977). Current problems in severe mental handicap. *International Journal of Child Welfare, 32,* 62-86. (N)

EAYRS, C.B., & ELLIS, N. (1990). Charity advertising: For or against people with mental handicap? *British Journal of Social Psychology, 29,* 349-66. (N, SRV)

EDGERTON, R. B., & BERCOVICI, S. (1976). The cloak of competence: Years later. *American Journal of Mental Deficiency, 80*(5), 485-497. (N)

EDGERTON, R. B., EYMAN, R. K., & SILVERSTEIN, A. B. (1974). Mental retardation system. In N. HOBBS (Ed.), *Issues in the classification of children: A sourcebook on categories, labels, and their consequences* (Vol. 2). San Francisco: Jossey-Bass. (N)

EDITORIAL. (1978). *British Journal of Mental Subnormality, 24*(1), 1-3. (N)

EISENRING, J. J. (1979, August). *Evaluation procedures of Normalisation.* Paper presented at the 5th International Congress of the International Association for the Scientific Study of Mental Deficiency, Jerusalem, Israel. (N)

ELKINS, J. (1985). Evaluating special education programs in Australia: A partnership between government and voluntary organizations. *Studies in Educational Evaluation, 11,* 43-53. (PS)

ELKS, M. A. (1994). Valuing the person or valuing the role? Critique of Social Role Valorization theory. *Mental Retardation, 32,* 265-271. (N, SRV)

ELKS, M. A. (1995). Reflections of a PASSING team leader. *CMHERA Newsletter, 16,* 6-10. (N, SRV, PG)

ELKS, M. A., & West, R. (1982). Attitudes to mildly retarded people and community living. *Australia and New Zealand Journal of Developmental Disabilities, 8,* 33-41. (N)

ELLIS, J. W. (1990). Presidential address 1990: Mental retardation at the close of the 20th century: A new realism. *Mental Retardation, 28*(5), 263-267. (N)

ELY, P. W. (1991). *Quality of life and social integration of psychiatrically disabled citizens in community residences.* Unpublished doctoral dissertation, School of Psychology, University of Ottawa, Canada. (PG)

EMERSON, E. (1990, December). Consciousness raising, science and Normalisation. *Clinical Psychology Forum, 30 ,* 36-40. (N)

EMERSON, E. (1992). What is Normalisation? In H. BROWN & H. SMITH (Eds.), *Normalisation: A reader for the nineties* (pp. 1-18). London & New York: Tavistock/Routledge. (N)

EMERSON, E., & McGILL, P. (1989). Normalization and applied behaviour analysis: Rapprochement or intellectual imperialism? *Behavioural Psychotherapy, 17,* 309-313. (N)

EMERSON, E., & McGILL, P. (1989). Normalisation and applied behaviour analysis: Values and technology in services for people with learning difficulties. *Behavioural Psychotherapy, 17,* 101-117. (N)

ENGELSMAN, E. L. (1989). *Drugs: A case for Normalization.* Paper presented at a conference of the Victorian Drug Rehabilitation & Research Fund, Melbourne, Australia, November 10-12. (N)

ENGLEHARDT, K. F. (1978). Principles of Normalization. In J. CURRY & K. PEPPE (Eds.), *Mental retardation: Nursing approaches to care.* St. Louis, MO: C. V. Mosby. (N)

EPSTEIN, H. R. (1982). Means, ends, and the principle of Normalization: A closer look. *Education and Training of the Mentally Retarded, 17,* 153-156. (N)

ERICSSON, K. (1985). *The origin and consequences of the Normalization principle.* Paper presented at the IASSMD Congress, New Delhi. Uppsala, Sweden: Mental Retardation Project. (Monograph) (N)

ERICSSON, K. (1986). Der Normalisierungsgedanke: Entstehung und Erfahrungen in skandinavischen Ländern. In Bundesvereinigung Lebenshilfe (Ed.), *Normalisierung: Eine Chance für Menschen mit geistiger Behinderung* (pp. 33-44). Marburg Lahn: Lebenshilfe. (N)

ERICSSON, K. (1987). Normalization: History and experiences in Scandinavian countries. *Superind. Digest,* 6(4), 124-130. (N)

ERICSSON, K., ERICSSON, P., GRANAT, K., & GRANAT, S. (1975). Integrated living: Towards a normal way of life. *REAP, 1*(1-2), 21-35. (N)

EVANGELISTA, N., ET AL. (1985, August). *From institution to community residence: Assessing environments for retarded people.* Paper presented at the annual meeting of the American Psychiatric Association, Toronto, ON. (ERIC Document Reproduction Service No. ED 259 521) (PS)

EVANS, D. P. (1980). *The dust of our turning: The implementation of the Normalization principle in American society.* Unpublished doctoral dissertation, University of Colorado at Boulder. (N)

EYMAN, R. K., DEMAINE, G. C., & LEI, T.-Z. (1979). Relationship between community environments and resident changes in adaptive behavior: A path model. *American Journal of Mental Deficiency, 83*(4), 330-338. (PS)

FALTA, P., & CAYOUETTE, G. (1977). Social change through integrated housing. *Rehabilitation Digest, 8*(4), 4-6. (N)

FELCE, D. (1995). Chairman's introduction—PASS and PASSING in the context of their time. In D. PILLING & G. WATSON (Eds.), *Evaluating quality in services for disabled and older people* (pp. 13-24). London: Jessica Kingsley. (PS, PG)

FELCE, D. (1995). Exploring quality of life and its relationship to PASS: Looking for agreement. In D. PILLING & G. WATSON (Eds.), *Evaluating quality in services for disabled and older people* (pp. 114-125). London: Jessica Kingsley. (PS)

FELCE, D. (1995). Summing up--Safeguarding quality. In D. PILLING & G. WATSON (Eds.), *Evaluating quality in services for disabled and older people* (pp. 213-216). London: Jessica Kingsley. (PG, PS)

FELCE, D., & PERRY, J. (1997). A PASS 3 evaluation of community residences in Wales. *Mental Retardation, 35,* 170-176. (PS)

FERAGUS, J. (1984). L'évaluation de l'action sociale: La valorization du handicapé. *Revue Française des Affaires Sociales,* (1), 103-129. (N, PS)

FERLEGER, D. (1978). The failure of institutions for the retarded: Pennhurst, a "monumental example of unconstitutionality." *Health Law Project Library Bulletin, 3*(3), 1-11. (N)

FERLEGER, D. (1978). The future of institutions for retarded citizens: The promise of the *Pennhurst* case. In *Mental retardation and the law: A report on status of current court cases.* Washington, DC: President's Committee on Mental Retardation. (N)

FERLEGER, D., & BOYD, P. A. (1979). Anti-institutionalization: The promise of the *Pennhurst* case. *Stanford Law Review, 31*(4), 717-752. (N)

FERNS, P. (1992). Promoting race equality through Normalisation. In H. BROWN & H. SMITH (Eds.), *Normalisation: A reader for the nineties* (pp. 134-148). London & New York: Tavistock/Routledge. (N)

FERRARA, D. M. (1979). Attitudes of parents of mentally retarded children toward Normalization activities. *American Journal of Mental Deficiency, 84*(2), 145-151. (N)

FIORELLI, J. S. (1978). *A comparison of selected categories of behavior in more and less normalized living environments* (Evaluation and Research Technical Report 77-10). Philadelphia: Temple University, Developmental Disabilities Program/University Affiliated Facility. (PS)

FIORELLI, J. S., & THURMAN, S. K. (1979). Client behavior in more and less normalized residential settings. *Education and Training of the Mentally Retarded, 14*(2), 85-94. (PS)

FISHER, E. B. (1976). New ideas from old countries: Implementing the concept of Normalization in Scandanavia. *A VISCO, 7*(2), 1-8. (N)

FLAKER, V. (1994). On the values of Normalization. *Care in Place, 1*(3), 225-230. (N, SRV)

FLYNN, A. G., & WEISS, S. K. (1977). *ANDI: A Normalization and development instrument* (2nd ed.). Sacramento, CA: California State Department of Health. (N)

FLYNN, R. J. (1975). *Assessing human service quality with PASS 2: An empirical analysis of 102 service program evaluations* (NIMR Monograph No. 5). Toronto, ON: National Institute on Mental Retardation. (PS)

FLYNN, R. J. (1977). Evaluating Normalization, social integration, and administrative effectiveness. *Psychosocial Rehabilitation Journal, 1*(3), 1-12. (PS)

FLYNN, R. J. (1980). Normalization, PASS, and service quality assessment: How normalizing are current human services? In R. J. FLYNN & K. E. NITSCH (Eds.), *Normalization, social integration, and community services* (pp. 323-357). Baltimore: University Park Press. (PS)

FLYNN, R. J. (1981). Normalization, social integration, and sex behavior: A service approach and evaluation method for improving rehabilitation programs. In A. SHA'KED (Ed.), *Human sexuality in rehabilitation medicine* (pp. 37-66). Baltimore: Williams & Wilkins. (N, PS)

FLYNN, R. J. (1985). Assessing the effectiveness of deinstitutionalization: Substantive and methodological conclusions from the research literature. *Deinstitutionalization: Costs and effects* (pp. 75-102). Ottawa, ON: Canadian Council on Social Development. (PS)

FLYNN, R. J. (1985). L'évaluation des programmes de désinstitutionnalisation: Conclusions sur le fond et sur la méthodologie tirées de la littérature. Dans *La désinstitutionnalisation: Coûts et incidences* (pp. 77-104). Ottawa, ON: Conseil canadien de développement social. (PS)

FLYNN, R. J. (1993). *Intégration et évaluation de programmes: Comparaisons internationales.* In S. IONESCU, G. MAGEROTTE, W. PILON, & R. SALBREUX (Eds.), *L'intégration des personnes présentant une déficience intellectuelle* (pp. 5-15). Actes du IIIe congrès de l'Association Internationale de Recherche scientifique en faveur des personnes Handicapées Mentales. Trois-Rivières, QC: Université du Québec à Trois-Rivières et AIRHM. (PS, PG)

FLYNN, R. J. (1994). De la Normalisation à la valorisation des rôles sociaux: Évolution et impact entre 1982 et 1992. In Office des personnes handicapées du Québec (Ed.), *Élargir les horizons: Perspectives scientifiques sur l'intégration sociale* (pp. 73-78). Sainte-Foy, QC, & Paris, France: Éditions Multimondes et Agence Ibis Press. (N, SRV)

FLYNN, R. J. (1994). L'intégration sociale entre 1982 et 1992: Définitions conceptuelles et opérationnelles. In Office des personnes handicapées du Québec (Ed.), *Élargir les horizons: Perspectives scientifiques sur l'intégration sociale* (pp. 515-525). Sainte-Foy, Québec, & Paris, France: Éditions Multimondes et Agence Ibis Press. (N, SRV)

FLYNN, R. J. (1999). A comprehensive review of research conducted with the program evaluation instruments PASS and PASSING. In R. J. FLYNN & R. A. LEMAY (Eds.), *A quarter-century of Normalization and Social Role Valorization: Evolution and impact.* Ottawa, ON: University of Ottawa Press. (PS, PG)

FLYNN, R. J., & AUBRY, T. D. (1999). Integration of persons with developmental or psychiatric disabilities: Conceptualization and measurement. In R. J. FLYNN & R. A. LEMAY (Eds.), *A quarter-century of Normalization and Social Role Valorization: Evolution and impact.* Ottawa, ON: University of Ottawa Press. (N, SRV, PS, PG)

FLYNN, R. J., DANSEREAU, J., DUTEAU, C., & ELY, P. (1990, June). *Evaluation of service quality in community residences for psychiatrically disabled adults.* Paper (poster) presented at the annual meeting of the Canadian Psychological Association, Ottawa, ON. (PG)

FLYNN, R. J., & GRANEY, B. (1979). *A formative evaluation of the Southern Alberta Comprehensive Community Services Experimental and Demonstration Project.* Toronto, ON: National Institute on Mental Retardation. (N)

FLYNN, R. J., GUIRGUIS, M., WOLFENSBERGER, W., & COCKS, E. (in press). Cross-validated factor structures and factor-based subscales for PASS and PASSING. *Mental Retardation.* (PS, PG)

FLYNN, R. J., & HEAL, L. W. (1981). A short form of PASS 3: A study of its structure, interrater reliability, and validity for assessing Normalization. *Evaluation Review, 5,* 357-376. (PS)

FLYNN, R. J., LAPOINTE, N., WOLFENSBERGER, W., & THOMAS, S. (1991). Quality of institutional and community human service programs in Canada and the United States. *Journal of Psychiatry and Neuroscience, 16*(3), 146-153. (PG)

FLYNN, R. J., & LEMAY, R. A. (Eds.). (1999). *A quarter-century of Normalization and Social Role Valorization: Evolution and impact.* Ottawa, ON: University of Ottawa Press. (N, SRV, PS, PG)

FLYNN, R. J., & LEMAY, R. A. (1999). Normalization and Social Role Valorization at a quarter century: Evolution, impact and renewal. In R. J. FLYNN & R. A. LEMAY (Eds.), *A quarter-century of Normalization and Social Role Valorization: Evolution and impact.* Ottawa, ON: University of Ottawa Press. (N, SRV)

FLYNN, R. J., & NITSCH, K. E. (1980). Normalization: Accomplishments to date and future priorities. In R. J. FLYNN & K. E. NITSCH (Eds.), *Normalization, social integration, and community services* (pp. 363-393). Baltimore: University Park Press. (N)

FLYNN, R. J., & NITSCH, K. E. (Eds.). (1980). *Normalization, social integration, and community services.* Baltimore: University Park Press. (N, PS)

FLYNN, R. J., & SHA'KED, A. (1977). Normative sex behavior and the person with a disability: Assessing the effectiveness of the rehabilitation agencies. *Journal of Rehabilitation, 43*(5), 34-38. (N, PS)

FOSS, G., & NELSON, R. E. (Eds.). (1982). *Advancing your citizenship: Normalization re-examined.* Proceedings of a National Conference on Normalization and Contemporary Practice in Mental Retardation. Eugene, OR: University of Oregon, Rehabilitation Research and Training Center in Mental Retardation. (N)

FOXX, R. M. (1985). Social skills training: The current status of the field. *Australia and New Zealand Journal of Developmental Disabilities, 11*, 237-243. (N)

FRAM, J. (1974). The right to be retarded—normally. *Mental Retardation, 12*, 32-33. (N)

FRASER, J. G. (Ed.). (1977). *Normalizing environments for the developmentally disabled: Symposium proceedings.* Columbia, SC: University of South Carolina and South Carolina Department of Mental Retardation. (N)

FREEMAN, S., LE BOURDAIS, I., OTIS, R., & TARDIF, J. (1982). Les services offerts aux déficients mentaux: Du passé au présent. *Apprentissage et Socialisation, 5*, 231-240. (N)

FRITZ, M., WOLFENSBERGER, W., & KNOWLTON, M. (1971). *An apartment living plan to promote integration and Normalization of mentally retarded adults.* Toronto, ON: Canadian Association for the Mentally Retarded (National Institute on Mental Retardation). (N)

GALLANT, W. A. (1983). *Comparative study of integrated and non-integrated educational programs for children classified as trainable mentally retarded in Ontario using Program Analysis of Service Systems (PASS) as a tool of evaluation.* Unpublished doctoral dissertation, Wayne State University, Detroit. (PS)

GALLOWAY, C., & CHANDLER, P. (1980). The marriage of special and generic early education services. In R. J. FLYNN & K. E. NITSCH (Eds.), *Normalization, social integration, and community services* (pp. 187-213). Baltimore: University Park Press. (N)

GANGES, A. G. (1970). Architecture. In J. WORTIS (Ed.), *Mental retardation: An annual review* (Vol. II). New York: Grune & Stratton. (N)

GANNON, P. (1986). Research with moderately, severely, profoundly retarded and autistic individuals (1975 to 1983): An evaluation of ecological validity. *Australia and New Zealand Journal of Developmental Disabilities, 12*, 33-51. (N)

GARDNER, J. F., & CHAPMAN, M. S. (1993). *Developing staff competencies for supporting people with developmental disabilities: An orientation handbook* (2nd ed.). Baltimore: Paul H. Brookes. (N)

GILBERT, T. (1993). Learning disability nursing: From Normalization to materialism—Towards a new paradigm. *Journal of Advanced Nursing, 18*, 1604-1609. (N)

GILBERT, T., TODD, M., & JACKSON, N. (1998). People with learning disabilities who also have mental health problems: Practice issues and directions for learning disability nursing. *Journal of Advanced Nursing, 27*, 1151-1157. (N)

GILDEMEISTER, R. (1991). Normalization of eroded daily life: Methodizing everyday life in institutional contexts. In G. ALBRECHT, H. U. OTTO, S. KARSTEDT-HENKE, & K. BOLLERT (Eds.), *Social prevention and the social sciences: Theoretical controversies, research problems, and evaluation strategies* (pp. 183-197). Berlin, Germany: Walter de Gruyter. (N)

GLEASON, J. J. (1989). *Special education in context: An ethnographic study of persons with developmental disabilities.* Cambridge, England: Cambridge University Press. (N)

GLEESON, B. J. Disability studies: A historical materialist view. *Disability & Society, 12,* 179-202. (N, SRV)

GLENNERSTER, H., & KORMAN, N. (1990). Normalisation is not easy. *Community Care, 3/5,* 25-27. (N)

GOLDEN, S. J. (1982). *Normalization in mental health community residences.* Unpublished doctoral dissertation, University of Rhode Island. (N, PS)

GOLDMAN, F. (1978). Environmental barriers to sociosexual integration: The insider's perspectives. *Rehabilitation Literature, 39*(6-7), 185-189. (N)

GOODFELLOW, R. A. (1974). *Group homes: One alternative.* Syracuse, NY: Human Policy Press. (N)

GORDON, L. R., BURCHARD, S. N., HASAZI, J. E., YOE, J. T., DIETZEL, L. C., & SIMONEAU, D. (1992). Stability and change in the life-style and adjustment of adults with mental retardation living in community residences. In J. W. JACOBSON, S. N. BURCHARD, & P. J. CARLING (Eds.), *Community living for people with developmental and psychiatric disabilities* (pp. 167-182). Baltimore: The Johns Hopkins University Press. (N)

GORMAN, V. (1984). Facts and fallacies of Normalisation. *Nursing Mirror, 158,* 18. (N)

GRAVES, P. (1978). Early intervention: A personal view. *Australian Journal of Mental Retardation, 5*(3), 85-87. (N)

GREEN, A. M. (1976). Some factors relating to the effectiveness of improved physical environment and normalising training programmes in hospitals for the mentally retarded, *REAP, 2*(3), 176-192. (N)

GREENSPAN, S., & CERRETO, M. (1989). Normalization, deinstitutionalization, and the limits of research: Comment on Landesman and Butterfield. *American Psychologist, 44,* 448-449. (N)

GREINER, G. M., & LINSTRA, R. F. (1994). Social Role Valorization: A collision of religion, "scientific theory," and government's legitimate role to train employees. *Journal of Church and State, 36,* 821-831. (SRV)

GRIFFITHS, M., & SCHIMMER, C. (1987). *Normalisation and individual programme planning: A practical model of staff development.* London: Royal Society for Mentally Handicapped Children and Adults. (N)

GRUNEWALD, K. (1971). Manniskohantering pa totala vardinstitutioner: Fran dehumanisering till normalisering. Stockholm: Natur och Kultur, pp. 19-35. (Swedish language translation of NIRJE, B. [1969]. The Normalization principle and its human management implications. In R. KUGEL & W. WOLFENSBERGER [Eds.], *Changing patterns in residential services for the mentally retarded.* Washington, DC: President's Committee on Mental Retardation.) (N)

GRUNEWALD, K. (1972). Menneskemanipulering pa total institutioner: Fra dehumanisering til normalisering (pp. 26-46). Copenhagen: Thaning & Appels. (Danish language translation of NIRJE, B. [1969]. The Normalization principle and its human management implications. In R. KUGEL & W. WOLFENSBERGER [Eds.], *Changing patterns in residential services for the mentally retarded.* Washington, DC: President's Committee on Mental Retardation.) (N)

GRUNEWALD, K. (1974). *The concept of Normalization.* Paper presented at the 10th Graduate Teaching Symposium, Cognition-Affect and Developmental Disorders`. Rochester, N.Y.: Monroe Developmental Center. (N)

GRUNEWALD, K. (1975). Sweden: Services and developments. In J. WORTIS (Ed.), *Mental retardation and developmental disabilities: An annual review* (Vol. 7). New York: Brunner/ Mazel. (N)

GRUNEWALD, K. (1976). Sweden. In R. KUGEL, & A. SHEARER (Eds.), *Changing patterns in residential services for the mentally retarded* (Rev. ed.). (DHEW No. [OHD] 76-21015). Washington, DC: President's Committee on Mental Retardation. (N)

GRUNEWALD, K. (1977). Community living for mentally retarded adults in Sweden. *Current Sweden, 159,* 1-10. (N)

GRUNEWALD, K. (1986, April). The intellectually handicapped in Sweden: New legislation in a bid for Normalization. *Current Sweden, 345,* 1-10. (N)

GRUNEWALD, K. (1986). *Normalization and integration of persons with mental retardation in Sweden today.* Stockholm, Sweden: National Board of Health and Welfare. (N)

GUNZBURG, H. C. (1970). The hospital as a normalising training environment. *British Journal of Mental Subnormality, 16,* 71-83. (N)

GUNZBURG, H. C. (1973). The hospital as a normalising training environment. In H. C. GUNZBURG (Ed.), *Advances in the care of the mentally handicapped.* London: Bailliere Tindall. (N)

GUNZBURG, H. C. (1973). The physical environment of the mentally handicapped VIII: "39 Steps" leading towards normalized living practices in living units for the mentally handicapped. *British Journal of Mental Subnormality, 19,* 91-99. (N)

GUNZBURG, H. C. (1982). Book review of "Normalization, social integration, and community services" by R. J. FLYNN & K. E. NITSCH (Eds.). *British Journal of Mental Subnormality, 28*(Pt. 2), 100-102. (N)

GUNZBURG, H. C. (1988). Editorial. *British Journal of Mental Subnormality, 34*(67, Pt. 2), 73-74, 142. (N)

HAMALIAN, C. S., & LUDWIG, A. J. (1976). Practicum in Normalization and advocacy: A neglected component in teacher training. *Education and Training of the Mentally Retarded, 11*(2), 172-175. (N)

HARPER, D. J. (1994). Evaluating a training package for staff working with people with learning disabilities prior to hospital closure. *British Journal of Developmental Disabilities, 40*(78, Pt 1), 45-53. (N, SRV)

HASAZI, J. E., BURCHARD, S. N., GORDON, L. R., VECCHIONE, E., & ROSEN, J. W. (1992). Adjustment to community life: The role of stress and support variables. In J. W. JACOBSON, S. N. BURCHARD, & P. J. CARLING (Eds.), *Community living for people with developmental and psychiatric disabilities* (pp. 111-124). Baltimore: The Johns Hopkins University Press. (N)

HATTERSLEY, J. (1991). The future of Normalisation. In S. BALDWIN & J. HATTERSLEY (Eds.), *Mental handicap: Social science perspectives.* London: Tavistock/Routledge. (N)

HAWORTH, A. P. (1988). *Social policy development in relation to Normalization and integration of developmentally handicapped adults.* Unpublished doctoral dissertation, University of Waterloo, ON. (N)

HAYES, S. (1991). Pilot prison programs. *Australia and New Zealand Journal of Developmental Disabilities, 17,* 209-216. (N)

HEAL, L. W. (1990). Bold relief or bold re-leaf? *American Journal on Mental Retardation, 95,* 17-19. (N)

HEAL, L. W. (1999). Are Normalization and Social Role Valorization limited by competence? In R. J. FLYNN & R. A. LEMAY (Eds.), *A quarter-century of Normalization and Social Role Valorization: Evolution and impact.* Ottawa, ON: University of Ottawa Press. (N, SRV)

HEAL, L. W., & DANIELS, B. S. (1986). A cost-effectiveness analysis of residential alternatives for selected developmentally disabled citizens of three northern Wisconsin counties. *Mental Retardation Systems, 3*(2), 35-49. (PS)

HEAL, L. W., & FUJIURA, G. T. (1984). Methodological considerations in research on residential alternatives for developmentally disabled persons. *International Review of Research in Mental Retardation, 12,* 205-244. (PS)

HEAL, L. W., SIGELMAN, C. K., & SWITZKY, H. N. (1978). Research on community residential alternatives for the mentally retarded. In N. ELLIS (Ed.), *International review of research in mental retardation* (Vol. 9). New York: Academic Press. (N)

HEAL, L. W., SIGELMAN, C. K., & SWITZKY, H. N. (1980). Research on community residential alternatives for the mentally retarded. In R. J. FLYNN & K. E. NITSCH (Eds.), *Normalization, social integration, and community services* (pp. 215-258). Baltimore: University Park Press. (N)

HEGARTY, J. R. (1977). Review of "Program Analysis of Service Systems (PASS 3)" by W. WOLFENSBERGER AND L. GLENN and of "Assessing human service quality with PASS 2" by R. J. FLYNN. *Journal of Mental Deficiency Research, 21*(3), 235-236. (PS)

HELD, K. R. (1993). Ethical aspects of sexuality of persons with mental retardation. In M. NAGLER (Ed.), *Perspectives on disability* (2nd ed., pp. 255-259). Palo Alto, CA: Health Markets Research. (N)

HELLER, H. W., SPOONER, F., ENRIGHT, B. E., HANEY, K., & SCHILIT, J. (1991). Classic articles: A reflection into the field of mental retardation. *Education & Training in Mental Retardation, 26*(2), 202-206. (N, SRV)

HENDRIX, E. (1981). The fallacies in the concept of Normalization. *Mental Retardation, 19*(6), 295-296. (N)

HERSH, A., CARLSON, R. W., & LOSSINO, D. A. (1977). Normalized interaction with families of the mentally retarded—To introduce attitude and behavior change in students in a professional discipline. *Mental Retardation, 15*(1), 32-33. (N)

HETHERINGTON, R. W., SUTTILL, J., HOLMLUND, C., & FREY, D. D. (1979). Evaluation of a regional resource center for multiply handicapped retarded children. *American Journal of Mental Deficiency, 83,* 367-379. (N)

HOGAN, M. F. (1980). Normalization and communitization. Implementation of a regional community-integrated service system. In R. J. FLYNN & K. E. NITSCH (Eds.), *Normalization, social integration, and community services* (pp. 299-312). Baltimore: University Park Press. (N)

HOGAN, M. F., & MacEACHERON, A. E. (1980). *Plan evaluation guide.* Toronto, ON: National Institute on Mental Retardation. (N)

HOGG, J. (1997). Intellectual disability and ageing: Ecological perspectives from recent research. *Journal of Intellectual Disability Research, 41*(Pt. 2), 136-143. (N)

HOLLANDER, A. (1999). The origin of the Normalization principle in Sweden and its impact on legislation today. In R. J. FLYNN & R. A. LEMAY (Eds.), *A quarter-century of Normalization and Social Role Valorization: Evolution and impact.* Ottawa, ON: University of Ottawa Press. (N)

HOLMES, D. L. (1990). Community-based services for children and adults with autism: The Eden family of programs. Special issue on residential services. *Journal of Autism and Developmental Disorders, 20,* 339-351. (N)

HOREJSI, C. R. (1979). Applications of the Normalization principle in the human services: Implications for social work education. *Journal of Education for Social Work, 15*(1), 44-50. (N)

HORNER, R. D., HOLVOET, J., & RINNE, T. (1976). *Programming for Normalization* (Personnel training program for teachers of the severely handicapped, The Kansas Neurological Institute.) Lawrence, KS: University of Kansas, Department of Special Education, Professional Training Development Unit. (N)

HUDSON, B. (1988). Do people with a mental handicap have rights? *Disability, Handicap, and Society, 3,* 227-237. (N)

HULL, J. T. (1980). Environmental Normalization: A factor analysis. *Psychosocial Rehabilitation Journal, 4*(1), 20-26. (N, PS)

HULL, J. T., KEATS, J. G., & THOMPSON, J. C. (1984). Community residential facilities for the mentally ill and mentally retarded: Environmental quality and adaptive functioning. *Canadian Journal of Community Mental Health, 3,* 5-14. (N, PS)

HULL, J. T., & THOMPSON, J. C. (1980). Environmental Normalization in residential services: Towards a shortened version. *Psychosocial Rehabilitation Journal, 4*(3), 23-28. (N, PS)

HULL, J. T., & THOMPSON, J. C. (1980). Predicting adaptive functioning of mentally retarded persons in community settings. *American Journal of Mental Deficiency, 85,* 253-261. (N, PS)

HULL, J. T., & THOMPSON, J. C. (1981). Factors contributing to Normalization in residential facilities for mentally retarded persons. *Mental Retardation, 19,* 69-73. (N, PS)

HULL, J. T., & THOMPSON, J. C. (1981). Factors which contribute to Normalization in residential facilities for the mentally ill. *Community Mental Health Journal, 17*(2), 107-113. (N, PS)

HULL, J. T., & THOMPSON, J. C. (1981). Predicting adaptive functioning among mentally ill persons in community settings. *American Journal of Community Psychology, 9,* 247-268. (N, PS)

HUMM-DELGADO, D. (1977). *Community living for mentally retarded persons: Community residences for adults in Massachusetts.* Unpublished doctoral dissertation, Brandeis University, Florence Heller School of Advanced Study in Social Welfare. (PS)

HUMM-DELGADO, D. (1978, May). *Community living for mentally retarded persons: Community residences for adults in Massachusetts.* Paper presented at the 102nd annual meeting of the American Association on Mental Deficiency, Denver, Colorado. (PS)

HURTEAU, M., & BOUTET, M. (Eds.). (1993). *Vers une intégration dans la communauté. Projet-pilote d'intervention auprès des personnes présentant une déficience intellectuelle. Cahier no. 1, Fondements théoriques.* Trois-Rivières, QC: Fondation le Parrainnage. (SRV)

HUTCHINSON, M. L., & LORD, J. C. (1975). Recreation integration—Disabled in community programs. *Recreation Canada, 33*(3). (N)

HUTCHISON, P., & MCGILL, J. (1992). *Leisure, integration and community.* Concord, ON: Leisurability Publications Inc. (SRV)

INSTITUT NATIONAL POUR LA DÉFICIENCE MENTALE. (1975). *Services résidentiels: La communauté et le choix d'un domicile pour personnes handicapées.* Downsview (Toronto), ON: Author. (N)

INSTITUT NATIONAL POUR LA DÉFICIENCE MENTALE. (1977). Chapitre 3: Normalization. In *Le manuel d'orientation sur la déficience mentale, Partie 1* (Rev. Ed.). Toronto, ON: Auteur. (N)

IONESCU, S. (1993). De l'intégration comme ideologie, comme pratique et comme objet d'étude. In S. IONESCU, G. MAGEROTTE, W. PILON, & R. SALBREUX (Eds.), *L'intégration des personnes présentant une déficience intellectuelle* (pp. 35-41). Actes du IIIe congrès de l'Association Internationale de Recherche scientifique en faveur des personnes Handicapées Mentales. Trois-Rivières, QC: Université du Québec à Trois-Rivières et AIRHM. (N)

ISAACSON, R. L., & VAN HARTESVELDT, C. (1978). The biological basis of an ethic for mental retardation. In N. R. ELLIS (Ed.), *International review of research in mental retardation* (Vol. 9). New York: Academic Press. (N)

JACKSON, R. (1983). Mental retardation and criminal justice: Some issues and problems. *British Journal of Mental Subnormality, 29*(56), 7-12. (N)

JACKSON, R. (1989). The road to enlightenment. *Social Work Today, 21*, 24. (N)

JACKSON, R. (1994). The Normalisation principle: Back to basics? *British Journal of Developmental Disabilities, 40*(79, 2), 175-179. (N)

JACOBS, N. J. (1983). An exploratory study of "PASSING," a tool for the evaluation of Normalization of social services. Unpublished doctoral dissertation, University of Wisconsin-Madison. (PG)

JACOBSEN, J. W. (1989). Behavior modification and Normalization in conflict? *Mental Retardation, 27*, 179-180. (N)

JACOBSON, J. W., & REGULA, C. R. (1988). Program evaluation in community residential settings. In M. P. JANICKI, M. WYNGAARDEN KRAUSS, & M. MAILICK SELTZER (Eds.), *Community residences for persons with developmental disabilities: Here to stay.* Baltimore: Paul H. Brookes. (PS)

JANICKI, M. P. (1981). Personal growth and community residence environments: A review. In H. C. HAYWOOD & J. R. NEWBROUGH, *Living environments for developmentally retarded persons.* Baltimore: University Park Press. (PS)

JENSEN, C. C., WATSON, L. S., DEWULF, M. J., JOHNSON, S. P, ET AL. (1992). Normalization of mealtimes for persons with developmental disabilities: Implementation by professional and direct-care staff. *Behavioral Residential Treatment, 7*, 355-371. (N)

JOING, J.-L. (1993). *L'audit de la qualité dans les établissements médico-sociaux.* Toulouse, France: Éditions PRIVAT. (SRV, PG)

JONES, M. (1986). An examination of the lifestyle of residents of a group home. *Australia and New Zealand Journal of Developmental Disabilities, 12*, 133-137. (N)

JONES, R., & WITHERS, J. (1991). Normalisation and clinical psychology: From infatuation to scepticism. *Clinical Psychology Forum, 35*(9), 18-20. (N)

JOYCE, P., & CORRIGAN, P. (1986). Work is the key to promote Normalisation. *Social Work Today, 15*(12), 12-13. (N)

KAMINER, R. K., & JEDRYSEK, E. (1987). Risk in the lives of children and adolescents who are mentally retarded: Implications for families and professionals. In R. F. ANTONAK & J. A. MULICK (Eds.), *The community imperative revisited. Transitions in mental retardation, Vol. 3* (pp. 72-88). Norwood, NJ: Ablex Publishing Corp. (N)

KAZDIN, A. E., & MATSON, J. L. (1981). Social validation in mental retardation. *Applied Research in Mental Retardation, 2,* 39-53. (N)

KEARLY, P. (1988). Historical and philosophical issues in Normalization of handicapped individuals. *Child & Youth Services, 10*(2), 3-33. (N)

KEBBON, L. (1982). Normalization in Sweden-quality and limitations: Model of analysis. Six papers presented at the IASSMD Congress, Toronto. Uppsala, Sweden: University of Uppsala, Mental Retardation Project. (N)

KEBBON, L. (1986, November). *Normalization, integration and the quality of life: The ideal and the reality.* Paper presented at the conference on Mental Handicap and Community Care: The Challenge of Implementation in Sweden and Britain, University of Kent at Canterbury. (N)

KEBBON, L. (1987). Le principe de la Normalisation. In S. IONESCU (Ed.), *L'intervention en déficience mentale. Volume 1. Problèmes généraux. Méthodes médicales et psychologiques.* Bruxelles: Mardaga. (N)

KEBBON, L. (1993). The European services: Sweden. *Journal of Intellectual Disability Research, 37*(Suppl. 1), 62-65. (N)

KEBBON, L. (1997). Nordic contributions to disability policies. *Journal of Intellectual Disability Research, 41* (Pt. 2), 120-125. (N)

KEBBON, L., HJÄRPE, J., & SONNANDER, K. (1982). *Research findings on the evaluation of the Normalization principle.* Paper presented at the IASSMD Conference, Toronto, ON. (N)

KEITH, K. D. (1979). Behavior analysis and the principle of Normalization. *AAESPH Review* (American Association for the Education of the Severely/Profoundly Handicapped), *4*(2), 148-151. (N)

KENDRICK, M. (1994). Some reasons why Social Role Valorization is important. *International Social Role Valorization Journal, 1*(1), 14-18. (SRV)

KENDRICK, M. (1999). The impact of Normalization and Social Role Valorization in the English-speaking world. In R. J. FLYNN & R. A. LEMAY (Eds.), *A quarter-century of Normalization and Social Role Valorization: Evolution and impact.* Ottawa, ON: University of Ottawa Press. (N, SRV)

KIERNAN, W. E. (1979). Habilitation: A dynamic system. In G. T. BELLAMY, G. O'CONNOR, & O. C. KARAN (Eds.), *Vocational rehabilitation of severely handicapped persons: Contemporary service strategies.* Baltimore: University Park Press. (N)

KINKAIDE, P. S. (1975). Normalization and the handicapped. *Mental Retardation Bulletin, 3*(1), 128-132. (N)

KINKAIDE, P. S. (1978). Normalization and the handicapped. In A. F. ASHMAN & J. P. DAS (Eds.), *Mental retardation: Facts and issues.* Edmonton: University of Alberta, Centre for the Study of Mental Retardation. (N)

KISANJI, J. (1995). Interface between culture and disability in the Tanzanian context: Part II. *International Journal of Disability, Development & Education, 42,* 109-124. (N)

KLEIN, T., GILMAN, E., & ZIGLER, E. (1993). Special Olympics: An evaluation by professionals and parents. *Mental Retardation, 31,* 15-23. (N)

KNIGHT, R. C., ZIMRING, C. M., & KENT, M. J. (1977). Normalization as a social-physical system. In M. J. BEDNAR (Ed.), *Barrier-free environments.* Stroudsburg, PA: Dowden, Hutchinson & Ross. (N)

KNIGHT, R. C., ZIMRING, C. M., WEITZER, W. H., & WHEELER, H. C. (Eds.). (1977). *Social development and normalized institutional settings: A preliminary research report.* Amherst: University of Massachusetts, Environment and Behavior Research Center. (N)

KNOWLTON, M., CHESLER, K. L., & OLSON, D. (1975). *PASS narrative recommendation implementation manual.* Harrisburg, PA: Pennsylvania Department of Public Welfare, Office of Mental Retardation. (PS)

KOKASKA, C. (1974). Normalization: Implications for teachers of the retarded. *Mental Retardation, 12*(4), 49-51. (N)

KÖNIG, A. (1992). "Normalisierung" konkret—Wolfensbergers Verfahren PASSING. In *Qualitätsbeurteilung und-entwicklung von Wohneinrichtungen für Menschen mit geistiger Behinderung* (pp. 37-84). Marburg/Lahn, Deutschland: Lebenshilfe. (PG)

KORN, M. (1987). *Development of an instructional system for research and training on primarily administrative aspects of the Program Analysis of Service Systems.* Unpublished doctoral dissertation, Syracuse University. (PS)

KOZLOFF, M. A., HELM, D. T., & CUTLER, B. C. (1987). Parent training: Working to increase Normalization and prevent institutionalization. In J. A. MULICK & R. F. ANTONAK (Eds.), *Transitions in mental retardation, Vol. 2.* Norwood, NJ: Ablex Publishing Corporation. (N)

KRISTIANSEN, K. (1991). Normalization: From debate to action paradigm? In *Sharing a vision of the future: Nordic contributions.* Uppsala, Sweden. (N)

KRISTIANSEN, K. (1994). *Normalisering of verdsetjing av sosial rolle* (Norwegian). Oslo: Kommuneforlaget. (N, SRV)

KRISTIANSEN, K. (1999). The impact of Normalization and Social Role Valorization in Scandinavia. In R. J. FLYNN & R. A. LEMAY (Eds.), *A quarter-century of Normalization and Social Role Valorization: Evolution and impact.* Ottawa, ON: University of Ottawa Press. (N, SRV)

KRISTIANSEN, K., SÖDER, M., & TØSSEBRO, J. (1999). Social integration in a welfare state: Research from Norway and Sweden. In R. J. FLYNN & R. A. LEMAY (Eds.), *A quarter-century of Normalization and Social Role Valorization: Evolution and impact.* Ottawa, ON: University of Ottawa Press. (N)

KRISTIANSEN, K., & TYNE, A. (1985). *Using PASS in organisational change.* Unpublished document, David Solomons House. (PS)

KRULIK, T. (1980). Successful "Normalization" tactics of parents of chronically ill children. *Journal of Advanced Nursing, 5,* 573-578. (N)

KURTZ, R. A. (1975). Advocacy for the mentally retarded: The development of a new social role. In M. J. BEGAB & S. A. RICHARDSON (Eds.), *The mentally retarded and society: A social science perspective.* Baltimore: University Park Press. (N)

KURTZ, R. A. (1977). *Social aspects of mental retardation.* Lexington, MA.: Lexington Books. (N)

LAKIN, K. C., & BRUININKS, R. H. (1985). Social integration of developmentally disabled persons. In K. C. LAKIN & R. H. BRUININKS (Eds.), *Strategies for achieving community integration of developmentally disabled citizens.* Baltimore: Paul H. Brookes. (N)

LAMB, H. R. (1979). Staff burnout in work with long-term patients. *Hospital and Community Psychiatry, 30,* 396-398. (N)

LANDESMAN, S., & BUTTERFIELD, E. C. (1987). Normalization and deinstitutionalization of mentally retarded individuals: Controversy and facts. *American Psychologist, 42,* 809-816. (N)

LANDESMAN, S., & BUTTERFIELD, E. C. (1989). Cooperation and knowledge are essential to achieve goals of Normalization. *American Psychologist, 44,* 449. (N)

LASKI, F. (1978). Right to services in the community: Implications of the Pennhurst case. *Health Law Project Library Bulletin, 3*(5), 1-9. (N)

LASKI, F. (1979). Legal strategies to secure entitlement to services for severely handicapped persons. In G. T. BELLAMY, G. O'CONNOR, & O. C. KARAN (Eds.), *Vocational rehabilitation of severely handicapped persons: Contemporary service strategies.* Baltimore: University Park Press. (N)

LEHR, D. H., & NOONAN, M. J. (1989). Issues in the education of students with complex health care needs. In F. BROWN & D. H. LEHR (Eds.), *Persons with profound disabilities: Issues and practices* (pp. 139-160). Baltimore, MD: Paul H. Brookes. (N)

LEMAY, R. A. (1994, June). *Are we beyond Normalization? Social Role Valorization as a comprehensive strategy for achieving a "Society for All."* Invited paper presented to the International Conference, "Beyond Normalization: Towards a Society for All," sponsored by the United Nations, Reykjavik, Iceland. (N, SRV)

LEMAY, R. A. (1994). Ed Roberts, and the World Institute on Disabilities. *International Social Role Valorization Journal, 1*(2), 45-46. (SRV)

LEMAY, R. A. (1994). Problems of discourse concerning roles. *International Social Role Valorization Journal 1*(1), 45-46. (SRV)

LEMAY, R. A. (1994). A Reikjavik journal. *International Social Role Valorization Journal, 1*(2), 39-44. (N, SRV)

LEMAY, R. A. (1994). A review of the "Standard Rules on the Equalization of Opportunities for Persons With Disabilities," 1994. United Nations Department for Policy Coordination and Sustainable Development. *International Social Role Valorization Journal 1*(2), 47-51. (SRV)

LEMAY, R. A. (1995). Normalization and Social Role Valorization. In A. E. DELL'ORTO & R. P. MARINELLI (Eds.), *Encyclopedia of disability and rehabilitation* (pp. 515-521). New York: Simon & Schuster Macmillan. (N, SRV)

LEMAY, R. A. (1996). "Get clothes to support your intentions." *International Social Role Valorization Journal 2*(1), 26. (SRV)

LEMAY, R. A. (1996). La Valorisation des rôles sociaux et le principe de Normalisation: Des lignes directrices pour la mise en oeuvre de contextes sociaux et de services humains pour les personnes à risque de dévalorisation sociale. *Revue Internationale de la Valorisation des Rôles Sociaux, 2*(2), 15-21. (N, SRV)

LEMAY, R. A. (1996). Throwing slippers and other role behaviors: Eliza Doolittle becomes a lady. *International Social Role Valorization Journal, 2*(2), 38-40. (SRV)

LEMAY, R. A. (1997). *PASS 3–Lanaudière (1996): Projet d'évaluation des quinze pavillons en santé mentale (CHRLD).* Rapport soumis à la Régie régionale de la santé et des services sociaux de Lanaudière. Ottawa, ON: Author. (PS)

LEMAY, R. A. (1998). Review of R. WIESS & K. KASMAUSKI'S (1997) "Aging: New answers to old questions." *International Social Role Valorization Journal, 3*(1), 50-51. (SRV)

LEMAY, R. A. (1999). Roles, identities, and expectancies: Positive contributions to Normalization and Social Role Valorization. In R. J. FLYNN & R. A. LEMAY (Eds.), *A quarter-century of Normalization and Social Role Valorization: Evolution and impact.* Ottawa, ON: University of Ottawa Press. (N, SRV)

LENSINK, B. (1974). One service system at work. In C. CHERINGTON & G. DYBWAD (Eds.), *New neighbors: The retarded citizen in quest of a home.* Washington, DC: President's Committee on Mental Retardation. (N)

LENSINK, B. (1976). ENCOR, Nebraska. In R. KUGEL & A. SHEARER (Eds.), *Changing patterns in residential services for the mentally retarded* (Rev. ed.). (DHEW No. [OHD] 76-21015). Washington, DC: President's Committee on Mental Retardation. (N)

LEPPAN, S. (1975). Program Analysis of Service Systems (PASS): A method for the quantitative evaluation of human services. *New Horizon, 9*(4), 27-29. (PS)

LIEBERMAN, L. M. (1987). Is the learning disabled adult really necessary? *Journal of Learning Disabilities, 20*(1). (N)

LIMBRICK, D. (1983). *Results of the quantitative assessment of human service quality using PASSING on a group of independent living units run by Aged Cottage Homes Inc.* Lady Grenfell Price Grove, Australia. (PG)

LINDLEY, R., & WAINWRIGHT, T. (1992). Normalisation training: Conversion or commitment? In H. BROWN & H. SMITH (Eds.), *Normalisation: A reader for the nineties* (pp. 19-34). London & New York: Tavistock/Routledge. (N)

LINN, B. J., & BOWERS, L. A. (1978). The historical fallacies behind legal prohibitions of marriages involving mentally retarded persons—The eternal child grows up. *Gonzaga Law Review, 13*(3), 625-690. (N)

LIPPMAN, L. (1977). "Normalization" and related concepts: Words and ambiguities. *Child Welfare, 56*(5), 301-310. (N)

MACKAY, D. N., MACKEY, T., McDONALD, G., & GOLLOGLY, J. (1988). Normalization: The impossible dream? *British Journal of Mental Subnormality, 34*(67, Pt. 2), 75-77. (N)

MACLEAN, M. J., & BONAR, R. (1983). The Normalization principle and the institutionalized elderly. *Canada's Mental Health, 31*(2), 16-18. (N)

MACY, B. (1971). *Analysis of 1970 and 1971 PASS scores.* Lincoln, NE: Nebraska Office of Mental Retardation. (PS)

MADLE, R. A. (1978). Alternative residential placements. In J. T. NEISWORTH & R. M. SMITH (Eds.), *Retardation: Issues, assessment, and intervention.* New York: McGraw-Hill. (N)

MALIN, N. A. (1981). Services for the mentally handicapped in Denmark. *Child Care, Health and Development, 7*, 31-39. (N)

MALONEY, M. P., & WARD, M. P. (1979). Chapter 2: History of mental retardation and intelligence; Chapter 10: Treatment provisions for the mentally retarded. In M. P. MALONEY & M. P. WARD, *Mental retardation and modern society.* New York: Oxford University Press. (N)

MARLETT, N. J. (1976). Normalization. In J. P. DAS & D. BAINE (Eds.), *Mental retardation for special educators.* Springfield, IL: Charles C. THOMAS. (N)

MARTIN, G. L. (1976). The future for the severely and profoundly retarded: Institutionalization, Normalization, Kin Kare. In D. GIBSON & R. I. BROWN (Eds.), *Managing the severely retarded.* Springfield, IL: Charles C THOMAS. (N)

MASON, B. G., & MENOLASCINO, F. J. (1979). The right to treatment for mentally retarded citizens: An evolving legal and scientific interface. *Creighton Law Review, 10*(1), 124-169. (N)

MATSON, J. L., SADOWSKI, C., MATESE, M., & BENAVIDEZ, D. (1993). Empirical study of mental health professionals' knowledge and attitudes towards the concept of age appropriateness. *Mental Retardation, 31*, 340-345. (N)

MATTHEWS, P. R. (1977). Recreation and the Normalization of the mentally retarded. *Therapeutic Recreation Journal, 11*(3), 112-114. (N)

MAY, A. E. (1985). Steps towards Normalization: A revision of "39 Steps." *British Journal of Mental Subnormality, 31*(61, Pt. 2), 108-113. (N)

MAY, D. C. (1988). Plastic surgery for children with Down syndrome: Normalization or extremism? *Mental Retardation, 26*, 17-9. (N)

MAYS, M. (1977, Winter). Normalization: Concept or misconception? *Developmental Disabilities Now.* (N)

McCORD, W. (1982). The outcome of Normalization: Strengthened bonds between handicapped persons and their communities. *Education and Training of the Mentally Retarded, 18*, 153-157. (N)

McCORD, W. (1983). From theory to reality: Obstacles to the implementation of the Normalisation principle in human services. *Mental Retardation, 20*(6), 248. (N)

McCORD, W. T., & MARSHALL, W. (1987). Missing the mark: Normalization as technology. In D. B. SCHWARTZ, J. McKNIGHT, & M. KENDRICK (Eds.), *A story that I heard: A compendium of stories, essays, and poetry about people with disabilities and American life* (pp. 71-85). Harrisburg, PA: Pennsylvania Developmental Disabilities Planning Council. (N)

McCORMACK, B., RAFFERTY, M. & LYNCH, C. (1990). *Mental handicap. Values to practice: A practical course in Normalisation for front line staff—Tutor's manual.* Dublin, Ireland: Open Road and St. Michael's House Training. (N)

McDANIEL, C. O. (1987). Is Normalization the answer for mentally retarded offenders? *Corrections Today, 49*, 184-187. (N)

MCGILL, P., & CUMMINGS, R. (1990). An analysis of the representation of people with mental handicaps in a British newspaper. *Mental Handicap Research, 3*(1), 60-69. (N)

MCGILL, P., & EMERSON, E. (1992). Normalisation and applied behaviour analysis: Values and technology in human services. In H. SMITH & H. BROWN (Eds.), *Normalisation: A reader for the nineties* (pp. 60-83). London & New York: Tavistock/Routledge. (N)

MCINTOSH-WILSON, E. (1978). Standards and accreditation procedures related to the protection and advocacy systems. In C. D. RUDE & L. D. BAUCOM (Eds.), *Implementing protection and advocacy systems: Proceedings of a national developmental disabilities conference.* Lubbock, TX: Research & Training Center in Mental Retardation. (N)

MCKENNA, P. (1989, April). *Evaluation of the Normalization principle in a progressive democracy: What can we learn from Sweden.* Paper presented at Young Adult Institute, 10th Annual Conference, New York. (N)

MECREDY-WILLIAMS, B. (1979). Marriage law and the mentally retarded. *Canadian Journal of Family Law, 2*(1), 63-80. (N)

MENOLASCINO, F. J. (1974). The role of parent associations in obtaining and monitoring normalized services for the mentally retarded. In F. J. MENOLASCINO & P. H. PEARSON (Eds.), *Beyond the limits: Innovations in services for the severely and profoundly retarded.* Seattle, WA: Special Child Publications. (N)

MENOLASCINO, F. J. (1977). *Challenges in mental retardation: Progressive ideology and services.* New York: Human Sciences Press. (N)

MENOLASCINO, F. J., & EATON, L. F. (1980). Future trends in mental retardation. *Child Psychiatry and Human Development, 10*(3), 156-168. (N)

MESIBOV, G. B. (1976). Alternatives to the principle of Normalization. *Mental Retardation, 14*(S), 30-32. (N)

MESIBOV, G. B. (1976). (Respondents—J. P. Chapman, D. G. Hansen, B. Pieper, R. C. Sullivan, R. M. Smucker, & A. P. Scheiner). Implications of the Normalization principle for psychotic children. *Journal of Autism and Childhood Schizophrenia, 6*(4), 360-378. (N)

MESIBOV, G. B. (1990). Normalization and its relevance today. *Journal of Autism and Developmental Disorders, 20*(3), 379-390. (N)

MESIBOV, G. (1992). Response to Thompson and McEvoy. *Journal of Autism and Developmental Disorders, 22,* 672-673. (N)

MEYER, J. (1986). The religious education of persons with mental retardation. *Religious Education, 81,* 134-139. (N)

MEYERS, R. (1978). *Like normal people.* New York: McGraw-Hill. (N)

MIDGLEY, G. (1995). Evaluation and change in service systems for people with disabilities. In D. PILLING & G. WATSON (Eds.), *Evaluating quality in services for disabled and older people* (pp. 33-49). London: Jessica Kingsley. (PS, PG)

MILES, M. (1984). *Some questions about the Normalization principle in the Asian context.* Peshawar, Pakistan: Mental Health Center. (N)

MILLER, M. B. (1974). Review of the Normalization principle in human services by WOLF WOLFENSBERGER. *American Journal of Mental Deficiency, 78*(4), 505-506. (N)

MILLIER, P. (1999). Normalization and Social Role Valorization in Australia and New Zealand. In R. J. FLYNN & R. A. LEMAY (Eds.), *A quarter-century of Normalization and Social Role Valorization: Evolution and impact.* Ottawa, ON: University of Ottawa Press. (N, SRV)

MINDEL, C. H., & ROSENTRAUB, M. S. (1992). Normalization and community-based living: The implementation and impact of a Medicaid-waiver program. *New England Journal of Human Services, 12*(2), 15-23. (PS)

MIRON, G., & KATODA, H. (1991). Education for persons with handicaps in Japan, the USA and Sweden. *Scandinavian Journal of Educational Research, 35*(3), 163-178. (N)

MITRA, S. B. (1979). Habilitation programming for severely retarded adolescents and adults—Experiment in Normalization. *International Journal of Rehabilitation Research, 2*(1), 95-97. (N)

MITTLER, P. (1987). Le concept de Normalisation comme principe de la théorie et de la pratique éducationnelles. *Bulletin de Psychologie, 40,* 741-745. (N)

MITTLER, P. (1988). The concept of Normalisation as a principle of educational theory and practice. *International Journal of Rehabilitation Research, 11,* 261-268. (N)

MOISE, L. E. (1978). Comment: Slogans are not enough. *The Exceptional Parent, 8*(2), 49-50. (N)

MOLONY, H., & TAPLIN, J. (1988). Deinstitutionalization of people with developmental disability. *Australia and New Zealand Journal of Developmental Disabilities, 14*(2), 109-122. (N)

MOONILAL, J., BOUDEVIN, Y., & KADISH, M. (1978). *The effect of Normalization on the self-concept of mentally retarded adults.* Unpublished master's essay, San Diego State University. (N)

MOSS, S. (Ed.). (1992). *Aging and developmental disabilities: Perspectives from nine countries.* Durham, NH: University of New Hampshire, Institute on Disability. (N, SRV)

MULICK, J. A., & KEDESDY, J. H. (1988). Self-injurious behavior, its treatment and Normalization. *Mental Retardation, 26,* 223-229. (N)

MULLER, N. D. (1984). The law: A point of view. *Australia and New Zealand Journal of Developmental Disabilities, 10,* 179-181. (N)

MULVEY, E. P., LINNEY, J. A., & ROSENBERG, M. S. (1987). Organizational control and treatment program design as dimensions of institutionalization in settings for juvenile offenders. *American Journal of Community Psychology, 15,* 321-335. (PS)

MURPHY, A., & CROCKER, A. C. (1987). Impact of handicapping conditions on the child and family. In H. M. WALLACE, R. F. BIEHL, A. C. OGLESBY, & L. T. TAFT (Eds.), *Handicapped children and youth: A comprehensive community and clinical approach* (pp. 26-41). New York: Human Sciences Press. (N)

MURPHY, S. T., & NISBET, J. (1987). Disabled adolescents in the community. In P. KNOBLOCK (Ed.), *Understanding exceptional children and youth* (pp. 392-422). Boston: Little, Brown & Co. (N)

NALIS, H. (1990). *Normalisierung und integration in einem wiener modell fur gemeinwesenintegriertes wohnen geistig behinderter erwachsener.* Unpublished doctoral dissertation, Universitaet fur Bildungwissenschaften Klagenfurt (Austria). (N)

NATIONAL INSTITUTE ON MENTAL RETARDATION. (1973). *Curriculum guides for Level I and Level II. National Manpower Model.* Toronto, ON: Author. (N)

NATIONAL INSTITUTE ON MENTAL RETARDATION. (1977). Chapter 3: Normalization. In *Orientation manual on mental retardation, Part I* (Rev. ed.). Toronto, ON: Author. (N)

NATIONAL INSTITUTE ON MENTAL RETARDATION. (1978). *Program analysis training (PAT): An experimental approach based on Program Analysis of Service Systems.* Toronto, ON: Author. (N, PS)

NATIONAL INSTITUTE ON MENTAL RETARDATION. (1978). *Residential services: Community housing options for handicapped people* (Rev. ed.). Toronto, ON: Author. (N)

NATIONAL INSTITUTE ON MENTAL RETARDATION. (1979). *Report of an evaluation-consultation team on the progress of the Quebec North Shore ComServ Project.* Toronto, ON: Author. (N)

NEISWORTH, J. T., & MADLE, R. A. (1975). Normalized day care: A philosophy and approach to integrating exceptional and normal children. *Child Care Quarterly, 4*(3), 163-171. (N)

NEISWORTH, J. T., & SMITH, R. M. (Eds.). (1978). *Retardation: Issues, assessment, and intervention.* New York: McGraw-Hill. (N)

NELSON, R. (1978). Creating community acceptance for handicapped people. Springfield, IL: Charles C. THOMAS. (N)

NEMETH, S. (1979). [A short report of a try-out of PASS 3.] *Ruit, 17.* (In Dutch) (PS)

NEUFELDT, A. H. (1973). Normalization and the human services (Review of Normalization: The principle of Normalization in human services by W. WOLFENSBERGER). *Canada's Mental Health, 21*(6), 19-22. (N)

NEWNES, C. (1994). A commentary on "Obstacles in the professional human service culture to implementation of Social Role Valorization and community integration of clients." *Care in Place, 1*(1), 57-64. (SRV)

NICOLETTI, J. P. (1994). L'évaluation et ses enjeux dans le développement de la valorisation des rôles sociaux: De l'évaluation implicite à l'évaluation explicite pour une expertise au service de tous. *Revue Internationale de la Valorisation des Rôles Sociaux, 1*(1), 29-34. (SRV)

NIHIRA, L., & NIHIRA, K. (1975). Normalized behavior in community placement. *Mental Retardation, 13*(2), 9-13. (N)

NIRJE, B. (1969). The Normalization principle and its human management implications. In R. KUGEL & W. WOLFENSBERGER (Eds.), *Changing patterns in residential services for the mentally retarded.* Washington, DC: President's Committee on Mental Retardation. (N)

NIRJE, B. (1969/1994). Le principe de Normalisation et des implications dans le maniement du comportement humain. *Revue Internationale de la Valorisation des Rôles Sociaux, 1*(2), 24-29. (N)

NIRJE, B. (1970). The Normalization principle: Implications and comments. *British Journal of Mental Subnormality, 16*(2), 31, 62-70. (N)

NIRJE, B. (1971). Toward independence: The Normalization principle in Sweden. *Déficience Mentale/Mental Retardation, 21,* 2-7. (N)

NIRJE, B. (1972). The right to self-determination. In W. WOLFENSBERGER, *The principle of Normalization in human services.* Toronto, ON: National Institute on Mental Retardation. (N)

NIRJE, B. (1973). The Normalization principle—Implications and comments. In H. C. GUNZBERG (Ed.), *Advances in the care of the mentally handicapped.* London: Bailliere, Tyndall, Cox. (N)

NIRJE, B. (1976). The Normalization principle. In R. KUGEL & A. SHEARER (Eds.), *Changing patterns in residential services for the mentally retarded* (Rev. ed.). (DHEW No. [OHD] 76-21015). Washington, DC: President's Committee on Mental Retardation. (N)

NIRJE, B. (1980). The Normalization principle. In R. J. FLYNN & K. E. NITSCH (Eds.), *Normalization, social integration, and community services* (pp. 31-49). Baltimore: University Park Press. (N)

NIRJE, B. (1985). The basis and logic of the Normalization principle. *Australia and New Zealand Journal of Developmental Disabilities, 11,* 65-68. (N)

NIRJE, B. (1991). Niels Erik Bank-Mikkelsen in memoriam. *Australia and New Zealand Journal of Developmental Disabilities, 17*(2), 265-267. (N)

NIRJE, B. (1992). Bank-Mikkelsen: Founder of Normalization principle. *News & Notes* (American Association on Mental Retardation), *5*(2), 4. (N)

NIRJE, B. (1992). *The Normalization principle papers.* Uppsala, Sweden: Uppsala University, Centre for Handicap Research. (N)

NIRJE, B. (1993). The Normalization principle: 25 years later. In U. LEHTINEN & R. PIRTTIMAA (Eds.), *Arjessa tapahtuu. Comments on mental retardation and adult education.* Finland: University of Jyväskylä, The Institute for Educational Research. (N)

NIRJE, B. (1994). Le principe de Normalisation et ses implications dans le maniement du comportement humain. *Revue Internationale de la Valorisation des Rôles Sociaux, 1*(2), 24-29. (N)

NIRJE, B. (1999). How I came to formulate the Normalization principle. In R. J. FLYNN & R. A. LEMAY (Eds.), *A quarter-century of Normalization and Social Role Valorization: Evolution and impact.* Ottawa, ON: University of Ottawa Press. (N)

NITSCH, K. E., ARMOUR, A., & FLYNN, R. J. (1980). A Normalization bibliography. In R. J. FLYNN & K. E. NITSCH (Eds.), *Normalization, social integration, and community services* (pp. 395-409). Baltimore: University Park Press. (N)

NOVAK, A. R., HEAL, L. W., PILEWSKI, M. E., & LAIDLAW, T. J. (1980, May). *Independent apartment settings for developmentally disabled adults: Dimensions of successful placement.* Paper presented at annual meeting of the American Association on Mental Retardation, San Francisco. (PS)

O'BRIEN, J. (1980). *The principle of Normalization.* Atlanta, GA: Georgia Advocacy Office. (N)

O'BRIEN, J. (1980). The principle of Normalization: A foundation for effective services. In J. GARDNER, L. LONG, R. NICHOLS, & D. IAGULLI (Eds.), *Program issues in developmental disabilities: A resource manual for surveyors and reviewers.* Baltimore: Paul H. Brookes. (N)

O'BRIEN, J. (1985). *Normalization training through PASS 3: Team leader manual.* Decatur, GA: Responsive Systems Associates. (PS)

O'BRIEN, J. (1994). Nobody outruns the trickster: A brief note on the meaning of the word "valorization." *International Social Role Valorization Journal, 1*(2), 34-35. (SRV)

O'BRIEN, J. (1995). Comment on SRV. *CMHERA Newsletter, 16,* 4-5. (SRV)

O'BRIEN, J. (1999). Education in applying the principle of Normalization as a factor in the practical arts of improving services for people with disabilities. In R. J. FLYNN & R. A. LEMAY (Eds.), *A quarter-century of Normalization and Social Role Valorization: Evolution and impact.* Ottawa, ON: University of Ottawa Press. (N)

O'BRIEN, J., & LYLE, C. (1986). *Framework for accomplishment.* Decatur, GA: Responsive Systems Associates. N)

O'BRIEN, J., & POOLE, C. (1978). *Planning spaces: A manual for human service facilities development.* Atlanta, GA: Georgia Association for Retarded Citizens. (N)

O'BRIEN, J., & POOLE, C. (1981). *Applying the principle of Normalization in the comprehensive evaluation process.* Atlanta, GA: Responsive Systems Associates. (N)

O'BRIEN, J., & TYNE, A. (1981). *The philosophy and practice of Normalisation.* London: Campaign for the Mentally Handicapped. (N)

O'BRIEN, J., & TYNE, A. (1981). *The principle of Normalisation: A foundation for effective services.* London: Campaign for Mentally Handicapped People. (N)

O'CONNOR, G. (1976). *Home is a good place: A national perspective of community residential facilities for developmentally disabled persons* (AAMD Monograph No. 2). Washington, DC: American Association on Mental Deficiency. (N)

O'HAGAN, M. (1995). Finding our way home: Segregation, Normalisation and the struggle for self-determination. *Community Mental Health in New Zealand, 9,* 12-17. (N)

OLIVER, M. J. (1999). Capitalism, disability, and ideology: A materialist critique of the Normalization principle. In R. J. FLYNN & R. A. LEMAY (Eds.), *A quarter-century of Normalization and Social Role Valorization: Evolution and impact.* Ottawa, ON: University of Ottawa Press. (N)

OLSHANSKY, S. (1966). Passing: Road to Normalization for ex-mental patients. *Mental Hygiene, 50,* 86-88. (N)

OLSHANSKY, S. (1972). Changing vocational behavior through Normalization. In W. WOLFENSBERGER, *The principle of Normalization in human services.* Toronto, ON: National Institute on Mental Retardation. (N)

OLSHANSKY, S. (1974). Mental retardation: Another view. *Journal of Applied Rehabilitation Counseling, 5,* 131-137. (N)

OLSON, R. S. (1985). Normalization, a concept in analysis: Revaluation of a devalued person. *Rehabilitation Nursing, 10*(6), 22-23. (N)

OSBURN, J. (1996). What makes a good PASSING team leader? *International Social Role Valorization Journal, 2*(1), 27-28. (PG)

OSBURN, J. (1998). An overview of Social Role Valorization theory. *International Social Role Valorization Journal, 3*(1), 7-12. (SRV)

OSBURN, J. (1999). The personal impact of Normalization-related and Social Role Valorization-related training. In R. J. FLYNN & R. A. LEMAY (Eds.), *A quarter-century of Normalization and Social Role Valorization: Evolution and impact.* Ottawa, ON: University of Ottawa Press. (N, SRV, PS)

OWEN, M. S., & SYMONS, F. J. (1993). Normalization, habilitation, and personal choice for persons with developmental disabilities. *Developmental Disabilities Bulletin, 21*(2), 13-20. (N)

PAGE, A. C. (1991). Teaching developmentally disabled people self-regulation in sexual behaviour. *Australia and New Zealand Journal of Developmental Disabilities, 17,* 81-88. (N)

PAPPAS, V., & REILLY, M. (1978). *Are the Joneses with you?* A simulation designed to address Normalization and other issues related to community based housing for the developmentally disabled. Bloomington, IN: Indiana University, Developmental Training Center. (N)

PARK, P., WITH FRENCH, B. (1999). The impact of Normalization and Social Role Valorization on my life. In R. J. FLYNN & R. A. LEMAY (Eds.), *A quarter-century of Normalization and Social Role Valorization: Evolution and impact.* Ottawa, ON: University of Ottawa Press.

PARNICKY, J. J. (1974). Retardation, Normalization and evaluation. In W. C. SZE & J. HOPPS (Eds.), *Evaluation and accountability in human service programs.* Cambridge, MA: Schenkman. (N)

PARNICKY, J. J., & AGIN, D. (1975). *Pathways towards independence: A Normalization training program for moderately retarded adults.* Columbus, OH: Ohio State University, Nisonger Center. (N)

PEAT, MARWICK, MITCHELL, & CO. (1976). *The financial requirements of normalized residential services and facilities for persons with developmental disabilities.* Springfield, IL: Governor's Advisory Council on Developmental Disabilities. (N)

PEDLAR, A. (1990). Normalization and integration: A look at the Swedish experience. *Mental Retardation, 28*(5), 275-282. (N)

PELLETIER, J. (1990). Le plan de service individualisé (PSI): Outil d'intégration et de Valorisation des Rôles Sociaux de la personne qui risque ou subit la dévalorisation. In A. Dupont, (Ed.). (1990). *Psychiatrie et integration communautaire.* Genève: Deux Continents. (SRV)

PELLETIER, J. (1990). *Évaluation de la qualité des services, de la gestion et de la structure organisationnelle du Centre Nor-Val à l'aide des méthodes PASS et PASSING et autres méthodes d'analyse.* Victoriaville, QC: Le Centre Nor-Val. (PS, PG)

PELLETIER, J. (1992). *Évaluation de la qualité des services du réseau de la déficience intellectuelle de la région 04 à l'aide de la méthode PASSING.* Gatineau, QC, & Gloucester, ON: Les Communications OPELL. (PG)

PELLETIER, J. (1993). *L'intégration sociale et la valorisation des rôles sociaux: Le défi de la qualité dans les réseaux contemporains de services.* Communication présentée lors du IIIe Congrès de l'Association internationale de recherche scientifique en faveur des personnes handicapées mentales, à l'Université du Québec à Trois-Rivières, Québec, Canada. (SRV, PG)

PELLETIER, J. (1999). The impact of Normalization and Social Role Valorization in francophone countries and communities from the late 1960s to the 1990s. In R. J. FLYNN & R. A. LEMAY (Eds.), *A quarter-century of Normalization and Social Role Valorization: Evolution and impact.* Ottawa, ON: University of Ottawa Press. (N, SRV)

PELLETIER, J., DUPONT, A., & TESSIER, C. (1994). *Le plan de services individualisés.* Geneva, Switzerland: Éditions des Deux Continents. (SRV)

PENNEY, R. K. (1988). Compatibility of early intervention programmes with Normalisation. *Bulletin of the Australian Psychological Society, 10*(1), 28-30. (N)

PERLIK, S. E. (1984). *Risk taking in the lives of people in community residences who are mentally retarded.* Unpublished doctoral dissertation, Florence Heller Graduate School for Advanced Study in Social Welfare, Brandeis University. (PS)

PERRIN, B. (1999). The original "Scandinavian" Normalization principle and its continuing relevance for the 1990s. In R. J. FLYNN & R. A. LEMAY (Eds.), *A quarter-century of Normalization and Social Role Valorization: Evolution and impact.* Ottawa, ON: University of Ottawa Press. (N)

PERRIN, B., & NIRJE, B. (1985). Setting the record straight: A critique of some frequent misconceptions of the Normalization principle. *Australia & New Zealand Journal of Developmental Disabilities, 11*, 69-74. (N)

PERRIN, B., & NIRJE, B. (1989). Setting the record straight: A critique of some frequent misconceptions of the Normalization principle. In A. BRECHIN & J. WALMSLEY (Eds.), *Making connections.* London: Hodder & Stoughton. (N)

PERRY, J., & FELCE, D. (1995). Objective assessments of quality of life: How much do they agree with each other? *Journal of Community and Applied Social Psychology, 5*, 1-19. (PS)

PERSKE, R. (1972). The dignity of risk. In W. WOLFENSBERGER, *The principle of Normalization in human services*. Toronto, ON: National Institute on Mental Retardation. (N)

PERSKE, R. (1972). The dignity of risk and the mentally retarded. *Mental Retardation, 10*(1), 24-27. (N)

PERSKE, R. (1973). *New directions for parents of persons who are retarded*. Nashville, TN: Abingdon Press. (N)

PERSKE, R. (Ed.). (1977). *Improving the quality of life: A symposium on Normalization and integration*. Arlington, TX: National Association for Retarded Citizens. (N)

PERSKE, R., & MARQUISS, J. (1973). Learning to live in an apartment: Retarded adults from institutions and dedicated citizens. *Mental Retardation, 11*(5), 18-19. (N)

PHILLIPS, M. J. (1985). "Try harder": The experience of disability and the dilemma of Normalization. *Social Science Journal, 22*(4), 5-57. (N)

PICARD, D. (1988). *La réinsertion sociale des personnes handicapées mentales en familles d'accueil. Tome 1: Caractéristiques personnelles des bénéficiaires*. Québec, QC: Centre de Services Sociaux de Québec, Service de la recherche. (PS)

PICARD, D. (1988). *La réinsertion sociale des personnes handicapées mentales en familles d'accueil. Tome 2: Caractéristiques socio-démographiques normalisantes des familles d'accueil*. Québec, QC: Centre de Services Sociaux de Québec, Service de la recherche. (PS)

PICARD, D. (1988). *La réinsertion sociale des personnes handicapées mentales en familles d'accueil. Tome 3: Caractéristiques des services en milieux institutionnel et de réinsertion*. Québec, QC: Centre de Services Sociaux de Québec, Service de la recherche. (PS)

PICARD, D. (1988). *La réinsertion sociale des personnes handicapées mentales en familles d'accueil. Tome 4: Degré d'adaptation et d'intégration sociale des bénéficiaires*. Québec, QC: Centre de Services Sociaux de Québec, Service de la recherche. (PS)

PICARD, D. (1988). *La réinsertion sociale des personnes handicapées mentales en familles d'accueil. Tome 5: Comparaison et mise en relation des différentes catégories de variables*. Québec, QC: Centre de Services Sociaux de Québec, Service de la recherche. (PS)

PIERCE, T. B., LUCKASSON, R., & SMITH, D. D. (1990). Surveying unstructured time of adults with mental retardation living in two community settings: A search for Normalization. *Exceptionality, 1*, 123-134. (N)

PILLING, D. (1995). Do PASS and PASSING pass? A critique of PASS/ING. In D. PILLING & G. WATSON (Eds.), *Evaluating quality in services for disabled and older people* (pp. 50-60). London: Jessica Kingsley. (N, PS, PG)

PILLING, D. (1995). Introduction. In D. PILLING & G. WATSON (Eds.), *Evaluating quality in services for disabled and older people* (pp. 1-9). London: Jessica Kingsley. (N, SRV, PS, PG)

PILLING, S. (1995). QUARTZ, PASSING and user involvement: Meeting points and departure points. In D. PILLING & G. WATSON (Eds.), *Evaluating quality in services for disabled and older people* (pp. 135-147). London: Jessica Kingsley. (PG)

PILLING, D., & MIDGLEY, G. (1995). PASS/ING and ACF in action: Similarities and differences in evaluating services. In D. PILLING & G. WATSON (Eds.), *Evaluating quality in services for disabled and older people* (pp. 84-105). London: Jessica Kingsley. (PS, PG)

PILLING, D., & WATSON, G. (Eds.). (1995). *Evaluating quality in services for disabled and older people* (pp. 84-105). London: Jessica Kingsley. (PS, PG)

PILON, W., ARSENAULT, R., & GASCON, H. (1993). Le passage de l'institution à la communauté et son impact sur la qualité de vie et l'intégration sociale de la personne présentant une déficience intellectuelle. In S. IONESCU, G. MAGEROTTE, W. PILON, & R. SALBREUX (Eds.), *L'intégration des personnes présentant une déficience intellectuelle* (pp. 255-266). Actes du IIIe congrès de l'Association Internationale de Recherche scientifique en faveur des personnes Handicapées Mentales. Trois-Rivières, QC: Université du Québec à Trois-Rivières et AIRHM. (PG)

PITTOCK, F., & POTTS, M. (1988). Neighbourhood attitudes to people with a mental handicap: A comparative study. *British Journal of Mental Subnormality, 34,* 35-46. (N)

POMERANTZ, D. J., & MARHOLIN, D. (1977). Vocational habilitation: A time for change. In E. SONTAG, J. SMITH, & N. CERTO (Eds.), *Educational programming for the severely and profoundly handicapped.* Reston, VA: Council for Exceptional Children, Division on Mental Retardation. (N)

POWER, P. W., & MARINELLI, R. P. (1974). Normalization and the sheltered workshop: A review and proposals for change. *Rehabilitation Literature, 35*(3), 66-72, 78. (N)

POWERS, L. (1977). Science and art in mainstream education: Toward the Normalization of the handicapped child. *Amicus, 2*(4), 37-41. (N)

PROVENCAL, G., & EVANS, D. (1977, Summer). *Normalization: Means or ends?* Paper presented at the Mental Health Symposium, Boyne Mountain, Michigan. (N)

RACE, D. G. (1981, December). Normalisation in an abnormal city: Problems of applying Western concepts to Hong Kong. *Proceedings of the 6th Asian Conference on Mental Retardation.* (N)

RACE, D. G. (1987). Normalisation: Theory and practice. In N. MALIN (Ed.), *Reassessing community care* (pp. 62-79). Beckanham, UK: Croom Helm. (N)

RACE, D. G. (in press). *Social Role Valorization and the English experience.* London: Wilding & Birch.

RAMON, S. (1988). Skills for Normalisation work. *Practice, 2,* 2. (N)

RAMON, S. (1988). Towards Normalisation: Polarisation and change. In S. RAMON & M. GIANNICHEDDA (Eds.), *Psychiatry in transition: The British and Italian experiences.* London: Pluto Press. (N)

RAMON, S. (Ed.). (1991). *Beyond community care: Normalisation and integration work.* London: MacMillan Education Ltd. (N)

RAPLEY, M. (1990). Is Normalisation a scientific theory? *Clinical Psychology Forum, 29,* 16-20. (N)

RAPLEY, M., & BALDWIN, S. (1995). Normalisation: Metatheory or metaphysics? A conceptual critique. *Australia & New Zealand Journal of Developmental Disabilities, 20,* 141-157. (N)

RAVEN, M. (1988). Application of Orem's self-care model to nursing practice in developmental disability. *Australian Journal of Advanced Nursing, 6*(2) 16-23. (N)

RAY, J. S. (1976). The family training center: An experiment in Normalization. In R. M. ANDERSON & J. G. GREER (Eds.), *Educating the severely and profoundly retarded.* Baltimore: University Park Press. (N)

REID, A. H. (1989). Psychiatry and mental handicap: A historical perspective. *Journal of Mental Deficiency Research, 33,* 363-368. (N)

REIDY, D. (1996). Practices of mental health programs considered stigmatizing by consumers/survivors: Consistency with Social Role Valorization. *International Social Role Valorizaton Journal, 2*(1), 4-11. (SRV)

REIDY, D. (1999). Social integration: How do we get there from here? Reflections on Normalization, Social Role Valorization, and community education. In R. J. FLYNN & R. A. LEMAY (Eds.), *A quarter-century of Normalization and Social Role Valorization: Evolution and impact.* Ottawa, ON: University of Ottawa Press. (N, SRV)

REIZENSTEIN, J. E., & MCBRIDE, W. A. (1977). Normalizing social-environment for mentally retarded adults. *Journal of Architectural Research, 6,* 10-23. (N)

RENSHAW, J. (1995). Quality measurement in the All-Wales strategy. In D. PILLING & G. WATSON (Eds.), *Evaluating quality in services for disabled and older people* (pp. 127-133). London: Jessica Kingsley. (PG)

RETISH, P., HOY, M., & BOAZ, B. (1978). Systems Unlimited—Normalization exemplified. *Mental Retardation, 16*(4), 313-316. (N)

RHOADES, C. (1975). *A sociological challenge to Normalization as applied to community alternative residential facilities.* (Working Paper No. 86). Eugene: University of Oregon, Rehabilitation Research and Training Center in Mental Retardation. (N)

RHOADES, C. M. (1981). *A sociological look at the impact of Normalization: Implications of the movement to community integrated mildly retarded adults.* Unpublished doctoral dissertation, University of Oregon. (N)

RHOADES, C., & BROWNING, P. (1977). Normalization at what price? *Mental Retardation, 15*(2), 24. (N)

RHOADES, C., & BROWNING, P. (1982). Normalization of a deviant subculture: Implications of the movement to re-socialize mildly retarded people. *Mid-American Review of Sociology, 7*(1), 139-170. (N)

ROBINSON, T. (1989). Normalisation: the whole answer? In A. BRECHIN & J. SWAIN (Eds.), *Making connections: Reflecting on the lives and experiences of people with learning difficulties.* London: Hodder & Stoughton. (N)

ROCHE, V. (1987). Normalization theory and service delivery: Conflict or compatibility? IN E. A. BARTNIK, G. M. LEWIS, & P. A. O'CONNOR (Eds.), *Technology, resources and consumer outcomes: Proceedings of the 23rd national conference of the Australian Society for the Study of Intellectual Disability.* Perth, Western Australia: P.E. Publications. (N)

RODEN, D. W. (1974). "Who's norm or whose norm?" *Australian Children Limited, 4*(12), 367-372. (N)

RODGERS, C. (1987). Maternal support for the Down's syndrome stereotype: The effect of direct experience of the condition. *Journal of Mental Deficiency Research, 31,* 271-278. (N)

RODRIGUEZ, R. (1980). *Toward independent living: Normalization, a process and a goal.* Albany, NY: Bureau of Staff Development & Training, New York State Office of Mental Retardation & Developmental Disabilities. (N)

ROEHER, A., FLYNN, R. J., HARTNETT, F., & HARSHMAN, F. (1974). Assessing the national recreation study. *Journal of Leisurability, 1*(4), 34-41. (N)

ROGOFF, M. L. (1989). The mentally retarded/mentally ill. In A. LAZARE (Ed.), *Outpatient psychiatry: Diagnosis and treatment* (2nd ed., pp. 550-568). Baltimore, MD: Williams & Wilkins. (N)

ROMNEY, D. M., BROWN R. I., & FRY, P. S. (1994). Improving the quality of life: Prescriptions for change. *Social Indicators Research, 33,* 237-272. (N)

RONNING, J. A. (1982). Perspektiver pa utvikling av livsvilkar for psykisk utviklingshemmete [Norwegian]. *Tidsskrift for Norsk Psykologforening, 19,* 488-500. (N)

ROOS, P. (1970). Normalization, de-humanization, and conditioning—Conflict or harmony? *Mental Retardation, 8*(4), 12-14. (N)

ROOS, P. (1972). Reconciling behavior modification procedures with the Normalization principle. In W. WOLFENSBERGER, *The principle of Normalization in human services.* Toronto, ON: National Institute on Mental Retardation. (N)

ROOS, P. (1976). Normalization, de-humanization, and conditioning—Conflict or harmony? In R. M. ANDERSON & J. G. GREER (Eds.), *Educating the severely and profoundly retarded.* Baltimore: University Park Press. (N)

ROOS, S. (1978). The future of residential services for the mentally retarded in the United States: A Delphi study. *Mental Retardation, 16*(5), 355-356. (N)

ROOS, P., & McCANN, B. M. (1977). Major trends in mental retardation. *International Journal of Mental Health, 6*(1), 3-20. (N)

ROOS, P., Patterson, E. G., & McCANN, B. M. (1979). *Expanding the developmental model.* Unpublished manuscript, National Association for Retarded Citizens, East Arlington, Texas. (N)

ROSE-ACKERMAN, S. (1982). Mental retardation and society: The ethics and politics of Normalisation. *Ethics, 93,* 81-101. (N)

ROSEN, J. W., & BURCHARD, S. N. (1990). Community activities and social support networks: A social comparison of adults with and adults without mental retardation. *Education and Training in Mental Retardation, 25,* 193-204. (N)

ROSEN, M., CLARK, G. R., & KIVITZ, M. S. (1977). Beyond Normalization. In M. ROSEN, G. R. CLARK, & M. S. KIVITZ, *Habilitation of the handicapped.* Baltimore: University Park Press. (N)

ROSEN, M., & KIVITZ, M. S. (1973). Beyond Normalization: Psychological adjustment. *British Journal of Mental Subnormality, 19,* 64-70. (N)

ROSMAN, M. D., & BERKMAN, I. P. (1986). Application of the Normalization principle to support groups for parents with children in residential treatment. *Residential Group Care and Treatment, 3*(3), 53-63. (N)

Ross, E. C. (1981). *Accreditation and programs for persons with developmental disabilities: A search for compatibility and coordination.* Unpublished doctoral dissertation, George Washington University. (PS)

Rotatori, A. F., Banbury, M., & Sisterhen, D. (1986). Overview of counseling exceptional students. In A. F. Rotatori, P. J. Gerber, F. W. Litton, & R. A. Fox (Eds.), *Counseling exceptional students* (pp. 21-38). New York: Human Sciences Press. (N)

Roth, G. (1975). Normalization. *DD Advocate, 2*(4), 1-2. (N)

Rovins, G. (1990). Exploring the environmental effectiveness of Normalization principles for older persons with developmental disabilities. *Adult Residential Care Journal, 4*(1), 37-49. (N)

Rowitz, L. (1987). The American mental retardation service system. *Journal of Mental Deficiency Research, 31,* 337-347. (N)

Rumelhart, M. A. (1983). The Normalization of social interaction: When shared assumptions cannot be assumed. *Qualitative Sociology, 6,* 149-162. (N)

Rutherford Turnbull, H., III. (1988). Ideological, political, and legal principles in the community-living movement. In M. P. Janicki, M. Wyngaarden Krauss, & M. Mailick Seltzer (Eds.), *Community residences for persons with developmental disabilities: Here to stay.* Baltimore: Paul H. Brookes. (N)

Ryan, J. (1989). The concept of Normalization as a principle of practice. *Curriculum Inquiry, 19,* 379-403. (N)

Ryan, R. (1987). Treating disability: A critique of Normalization. In E. A. Bartnik, G. M. Lewis, & P. A. O'Connor (Eds.), *Technology, resources and consumer outcomes: Proceedings of the 23rd national conference of the Australian Society for the Study of Intellectual Disability.* Perth, Western Australia: P.E. Publications. (N)

Saleh, L. (1976). *Normalization and integration: Begin at the beginning.* Working paper prepared for the Symposium on Normalization and Integration—Improving the Quality of Life sponsored by the National Association for Retarded Citizens for the International League of Societies for the Mentally Handicapped, August 17-20, Airlie, VA. (N)

Sandler, A. G., Thurman, S. K., Meddock, T. D., & DuCette, J. P. (1985). Effects of environmental modification on the behavior of persons with severe handicaps. *Journal of the Association for Persons With Severe Handicaps, 10,* 157-163. (N)

Sandys, J. (1999). "It does my heart good": How employers perceive supported employees. In R. J. Flynn & R. A. Lemay (Eds.), *A quarter-century of Normalization and Social Role Valorization: Evolution and impact.* Ottawa, ON: University of Ottawa Press. (SRV)

Scheerenberger, R. C., & Felsenthal, D. (1977). Community settings for M R persons: Satisfaction and activities. *Mental Retardation, 15*(4), 3-7. (N)

Schopler, E. (1989). Excesses of the Normalization concept. *American Psychologist, 44,* 447-448. (N)

Schultz, R. (1994). *Review of the impact of the involvement of Aged Cottage Homes with Social Role Valorisation since 1980.* Aged Cottage Homes Inc., South Australia. (SRV, PG)

Schuster, J. W. (1990). Sheltered workshops: Financial and philosophical liabilities. *Mental Retardation, 28,* 233-239 (N)

Schwartz, C. (1977). Normalization and idealism. *Mental Retardation, 15*(6), 38-39. (N)

Schwartz, D. (1999). The impact of Normalization and Social Role Valorization on a state-level practitioner from the USA. In R. J. Flynn & R. A. Lemay (Eds.), *A quarter-century of Normalization and Social Role Valorization: Evolution and impact.* Ottawa, ON: University of Ottawa Press. (N, SRV)

Sellin, D. F. (1979). *Mental retardation: Nature, needs, and advocacy.* Boston: Allyn and Bacon. (N)

Shaddock, A. J., & Zilber, D. T. (1991). Current service ideologies and responses to challenging behaviour: Social Role Valorization or vaporization? *Australia and New Zealand Journal of Developmental Disabilities, 17,* 169-175. (SRV)

Shearer, A. (1972, October). *Normalisation?* (Campaign for the Mentally Handicapped Discussion Paper No. 3.) Paper presented at the 5th International Congress on Mental Retardation of the International League of Societies for the Mentally Handicapped, Montreal. (N)

SHEERIN, F. (1998). Parents with learning disabilities: A review of the literature. *Journal of Advanced Nursing, 28*, 126-133. (N)

SHEPPARD, R. (1991). Sex therapy and people with learning difficulties. *Sexual and Marital Therapy, 6*, 307-316. (N)

SHERRILL, C. (1980). Posture training as a means of Normalization. *Mental Retardation, 18*(3), 135-138. (N)

SILVER, E. J., LUBIN, R.A., & SILVERMAN, W. P. (1984). Serving profoundly mentally retarded persons: Staff attitudes and job satisfaction. *American Journal of Mental Deficiency, 89*, 297-301. (N)

SIMEONSSON, R. J., GRUNEWALD, K., & SCHEINER, A. (1976). Piaget and Normalization: Developmental humanism. *REAP, 2*(4), 229-242. (N)

SIMEONSSON, R. J., GRUNEWALD, K., & SCHEINER, A. (1978). Normalization and Piagetian theory. In R. WEIZMANN, R. BROWN, P. J. LEVINSON, & P. A. TAYLOR (Eds.), *Piagetian theory and its implications for the helping professions. Vol. I: Emphasis—Social work and psychological services* (Proceedings of the 7th Inter-disciplinary Conference, Children's Hospital of Los Angeles). Los Angeles: University of Southern California. (N)

SINHA, C. (1986). Psychology, education and the ghost of Kaspar Hauser. *Disability, Handicap and Society, 1*, 245-259. (N)

SINSON, J. C. (1993). *Group homes and community integration of developmentally disabled people: Micro-institutionalisation?* London: Jessica Kingsley. (N)

SINSON, J. C. (1994). Normalization and community integration of adults with severe mental handicap relocated to group homes. *Journal of Developmental and Physical Disabilities, 6*, 255-270. (N)

SKARNULIS, E. R. (1976). *Normalization and integration: The environment and the right to risk.* Working paper prepared for the Symposium on Normalization and Integration--Improving the Quality of Life sponsored by the National Association for Retarded Citizens for the International League of Societies for the Mentally Handicapped, August 17-20, Airlie, VA. (N)

SKARNULIS, E. (1979). Support not supplant, the natural home: Serving handicapped children and adults. In S. MAYBANKS & M. BRYCE (Eds.), *Home-based services for children and families: Policy, practice and research.* Springfield, IL: Charles C. THOMAS. (N)

SLUYTER, G. V. (1994). Creating a vision for mental health services: A survey of states. *Administration and Policy in Mental Health, 21*, 247-250. (N)

SMITH, F. R. (1982). Hendrix on Normalization concept. Response. *Mental Retardation, 20*(6), 271. (N)

SMITH, H., & BROWN, H. (1992). Defending community care: Can Normalization do the job? *British Journal of Social Work, 22*(6), 685-693. (N)

SMITH, H., & BROWN, H. (1992). Inside-out: A psychodynamic approach to Normalisation. In H. BROWN & H. SMITH (Eds.), *Normalisation: A reader for the nineties* (pp. 84-99). London & New York: Tavistock/Routledge. (N)

SMOKOSKI, F. J. (1971). The mentally retarded ARE different. *Mental Retardation, 9*, 52-53. (N)

SOEFFING, M. Y. (1974). Normalization of services for the mentally retarded--A conversation with Dr. Wolf Wolfensberger. *Education and Training of the Mentally Retarded, 9*, 202-208. (N)

SOLUM, E., & STANGVIK, G. (1993). *Livskvalitet for funksjonshemmede: Vol. 2. Et hjelpemiddel for planlegging og utvikling av tiltak og tjenester* (3rd ed.). (Norwegian). Oslo, Norway: Universitetsforlaget. (N)

SONNANDER, K. (1990). *Normalization and quality of life.* Paper presented at Young Adult Institute Congress, New York. (N).

SPECIAL DESIGN TEAM ON NORMALIZATION (State of California, Health and Welfare Agency). (1978). Module 1: Normalization. In *Way to go.* Baltimore: University Park Press. (N)

SPINAK, J. (1975). Normalization and recreation for the disabled. *Journal of Leisurability, 2*(2), 31-35. (N)

SRV DEVELOPMENT, TRAINING AND SAFEGUARDING COUNCIL (1994). Statements of definition, identity, and functioning. *International Social Role Valorization Journal, 1*(1), 53-55. (SRV)

STANGVIK, G. (1987). *Livskvalitet for funksjonshemmede: Normaliseringsprinsippet som grunnlag for forbedring av livskvalitet.* (Norwegian). Oslo, Norway: Universitetsforlaget. (N)

ST-DENIS, C., & FLYNN, R. J. (1999). A comprehensive bibliography on Normalization, Social Role Valorization, PASS, and PASSING, 1969-1999. In R. J. FLYNN & R. A. LEMAY (Eds.), *A quarter-century of Normalization and Social Role Valorization: Evolution and impact.* Ottawa, ON: University of Ottawa Press. (N, SRV, PS, PG)

STEER, M. (1986). Human services in the 80's. *Journal of Community Services, 6.* (N)

STERNER, R. (1978). A note on some common misconceptions about Normalization and integration. In *FLASH on the service for the mentally retarded, III.* Publication No. 44. Copenhagen: The Personnel Training School. (N)

STIRLING, E. (1996). Social Role Valorization: Making a difference to the lives of older people? In R. T. WOODS (Ed.), *Handbook of the clinical psychology of ageing* (pp. 389-422). Chichester, England: Wiley. (SRV)

SWEEDLER, D. (1978). Massachusetts isn't Denmark. In *FLASH on the service for the mentally retarded, III.* Publication No. 44. Copenhagen: The Personnel Training School. (N)

SZIVOS, S. (1991). Consciousness-raising: An attempt to redress the more repressive aspects of Normalisation, but not its more positive ones. *Clinical Psychology Forum, 29,* 29-31. (N)

SZIVOS, S. (1992). The limits to integration? In H. BROWN & H. SMITH (Eds.), *Normalisation: A reader for the nineties* (pp. 112-133). London & New York: Tavistock/Routledge. (N)

SZIVOS, S. E., & Griffiths, E. (1990). Consciousness raising and social identity theory: A challenge to Normalisation. *Clinical Psychology Forum, 28,* 11-15. (N)

SZIVOS, S. E., & Griffiths, E. (1991). Group processes involved in coming to terms with a mentally retarded identity. *Mental Retardation, 29,* 333-341. (N)

SZIVOS, S. E., & Travers, E. (1988). Consciousness raising among mentally handicapped people: A critique of the implications of Normalization. *Human Relations, 41*(9), 641-653. (N)

TASK FORCE ON STANDARDS, ONTARIO ASSOCIATION OF CHILDREN'S MENTAL HEALTH CENTRES (n.d.). *Applying programme standards for children's mental health centres in Ontario.* Toronto, ON: Author. (N)

TENNANT, L., HATTERSLEY, J., & CULLEN, C. (1978). Some comments on the punishment relationship and its relevance to Normalization for developmentally retarded people. *Mental Retardation, 16*(1), 42-44. (N)

THOMAE, I. (1976). *Normalization and integration: Special services for special needs.* Working paper for the Symposium on Normalization and Integration-Improving the Quality of Life sponsored by the National Association for Retarded Citizens for the International League of Societies for the Mentally Handicapped, August 17-20, Airlie, VA. (N)

THOMAS, D. (1988). Putting Normalization into practice. In E. KARAS (Ed.), *Current issues in clinical psychology.* New York & London: Plenum Press. (N)

THOMAS, S. (1994). A brief history of the SRV Development, Training, and Safeguarding Council. *International Social Role Valorization Journal, 1*(2), 15-18. (SRV)

THOMAS, S. (1994). Review of FEIN'S "Analyzing psychotherapy: A social role interpretation." *International Social Role Valorization Journal, 1*(1), 52. (SRV)

THOMAS, S. (1994). Review of "I'm not handicapped—I'm different." *International Social Role Valorization Journal, 1*(2), 56. (N)

THOMAS, S. (1994). Some thoughts about Social Role Valorization evoked by events commemorating the 50th anniversary of D-day. *International Social Role Valorization Journal, 1*(2), 38-39. (SRV)

THOMAS, S. (1996). Recent news vignettes on the power of valued social roles. *International Social Role Valorization Journal, 2*(1), 29. (SRV)

THOMAS, S. (1996). A review and some reflections on some early writings on social roles. *International Social Role Valorization Journal, 2*(1), 30-35. (SRV)

THOMAS, S. (1996). Review of J. MCGILL'S "Developing leisure identities: A pilot project of Bramton Caledon Community Living and the Ontario Ministry of Citizenship, Culture and Recreation." *International Social Role Valorization Journal, 2*(2), 43-44. (SRV)

THOMAS, S. (1996). Some further thoughts on SRV prompted by recent news items. *International Social Role Valorization Journal, 2*(2), 40. (SRV)

THOMAS, S. (1999). Historical background and evolution of Normalization-related and Social Role Valorization-related training. In R. J. FLYNN & R. A. LEMAY (Eds.), *A quarter-century of Normalization and Social Role Valorization: Evolution and impact.* Ottawa, ON: University of Ottawa Press. (N, SRV, PS, PG)

THOMAS, S., & WOLFENSBERGER, W. (n.d.). *Let's "sell" handicapped people instead of selling them out.* Unpublished manuscript, Syracuse University, Training Institute for Human Service Planning, Leadership, and Change Agentry. (N)

THOMAS, S., & WOLFENSBERGER, W. (1982). The importance of social imagery in interpreting societally devalued people to the public. *Rehabilitation Literature, 43,* 356-358. (N)

THOMAS, S., & WOLFENSBERGER, W. (1994). L'importance de l'imagerie sociale dans l'interprétation des personnes socialement dévalorisées aux yeux du public. *Revue internationale de la valorisation des rôles sociaux, 1*(1), 35-37. (N)

THOMAS, S., & WOLFENSBERGER, W. (1999). An overview of Social Role Valorization. In R. J. FLYNN & R. A. LEMAY (Eds.), *A quarter-century of Normalization and Social Role Valorization: Evolution and impact.* Ottawa, ON: University of Ottawa Press. (SRV)

THOMPSON, J. R., & McEvoy, M. A. (1992). Normalization: Still relevant today. *Journal of Autism and Developmental Disorders, 22,* 666-672. (N)

THOMPSON, T., & Carey, A. (1980). Structured Normalization: Intellectual and adaptive behaviour changes in a residential setting. *Mental Retardation, 18,* 193-197. (N)

THOMPSON, T., Robinson, J., Graff, M., & Ingenmey, R. (1990). Home-like architectural features of residential environments. *American Journal on Mental Retardation, 95*(3), 328-341. (N)

THORN, B. E. (1978). *Normalization and recreation service delivery systems.* Unpublished doctoral dissertation, Pennsylvania State University. (N)

THORNTON, C. (1996). A focus group inquiry into the percpetions of primary health care teams and the provision of health care for adults with a learning disability living in the community. *Journal of Advanced Nursing, 3,* 1168-1176. (N)

THOUSAND, J. S., BURCHARD, S. N., & HASAZI, J. E. (1986). Field-based generation and social validation of managers and staff competencies for small community residences. *Applied Research in Mental Retardation, 7,* 263-283. (N)

THRONE, J. M. (1975). Normalization through the Normalization principle: Right ends, wrong means. *Mental Retardation, 13*(5), 23-25. (N)

THURMAN, S. K., & FIORELLI, J. S. (1979). Perspectives on Normalization. *Journal of Special Education, 13*(3), 339-346. (N)

THURMAN, K. K., & GABLE, R. A. (1976). Mental retardation services: Social traps and social fences. *Mental Retardation, 14*(5), 16-18. (N)

TINSLEY, D. J., O'CONNOR, G., & HALPERN, A. S. (1973). *The identification of problem areas in the establishment and maintenance of community residential facilities for the developmentally disabled* (Working Paper No. 64). Eugene, OR: University of Oregon, Rehabilitation Research and Training Center in Mental Retardation. (N)

TRAINOR, J., & BOYDELL, K. (1986). The politics of Normalisation. *Canada's Mental Health, 34*(1), 19-24. (N)

TRUDEL, G., & DESJARDINS, G. (1990). L'attitude du personnel face à la sexualité des personnes séjournant en institution psychiatrique. *Science et Comportement, 20*(3-4), 194-210. (N)

TSE, J. W. (1991). Directions in the field of mental retardation in the 1990s: An Asian perspective. *International Social Work, 34,* 339-352. (N)

TURNER, J. C. (1977). Comprehensive community support systems and adults with seriously disabling mental health problems: Definitions, components and guiding principles. *Psychosocial Rehabilitation Journal, 1*(3), 39-47. (N)

TYERMAN, C., & SPENCER, C. (1980). Normalised physical environment for the mentally handicapped, and its effect on patterns of activity, social relations and self-help skills. *British Journal of Mental Subnormality, 50,* 47-54. (N)

TYNE, A. (1981). Impact of the Normalisation principle on services for the mentally handicapped in the United Kingdom. *Research Highlights, 2,* 23-34. (N)

TYNE, A. (1987). Keeping up to the PASS mark: Evaluation of community services. *Community Living, 1*(4), 8-9. (PS)

TYNE, A. (1989). Normalisation: The next steps. *Community Living, 3,* 7-8. (N)

TYNE, A. (1992). Normalisation: From theory to practice. In H. BROWN & H. SMITH (Eds.), *Normalisation: A reader for the nineties* (pp. 35-46). London & New York: Tavistock/Routledge. (N)

TYNE, A. (1995). Framework for accomplishment. In D. PILLING & G. WATSON (Eds.), *Evaluating quality in services for disabled and older people* (pp. 180-190). London: Jessica Kingsley. (N, SRV, PS, PG)

TYNE, A. (1995). What have we been learning from PASS and PASSING in workshops and real evaluations? In D. PILLING & G. WATSON (Eds.), *Evaluating quality in services for disabled and older people* (pp. 25-32). London: Jessica Kingsley. (PS, PG)

VACC, N., & CLIFFORD, K. F. (1995). Individuals with a physical disability. In N. A. VACC & S. B. DEVANEY (Eds.), *Experiencing and counseling multicultural and diverse populations* (3rd ed., pp. 251-271). Muncie, IN: Accelerated Development. (N)

VANDERGRIFF, D. V. (1991). *The psychological and psychosocial impact of various residential treatment milieus on adults with mental retardation.* Unpublished doctoral dissertation, University of South Carolina. (PG)

VANDERGRIFF, D. V., & CHUBON, R. A. (1994). Quality of life experienced by persons with mental retardation in various residential settings. *Journal of Rehabilitation, 60*(4), 30-37. (PG)

VANEY, L. (1990). Désinstitutionalisation, Valorisation des Rôles Sociaux et moyens d'évaluation. In A. Dupont, (Ed.). (1990). *Psychiatrie et integration communautaire.* Genève: Deux Continents. (SRV)

VANEY, L. (1990). L'intégration et ses niveaux: Un moyen favorisant la valorisation des rôles sociaux. *CEDIS Info* (Comité Européen pour le Développement de l'Intégration Sociale), *1,* 3-10. (SRV)

VARELA, R. (1988). Self-determination and Normalization among adolescents: The family as a crucible of values. In *Self-determination. Transition Summary, 5.* Washington, DC: National Information Center for Handicapped Children and Youth. (N)

VINK, R. (1979). PASS: Een manier om zwakzinnigenzorg inhoudelijk te beoordelen. *Klik, 8*(3), 4-6. [PASS: A way for evaluating care delivery] (PS)

VITELLO, S. J. (1974). Cautions on the road to Normalization. *Mental Retardation, 12*(5), 39-40. (N)

WAHLSTROM, V., & STERNER, R. (1978). Normalizing and integrating the whole family. In *FLASH on the service for the mentally retarded III.* Publication No. 44. Copenhagen: The Personnel Training School. (N)

WAINWRIGHT, T. (1986). Normalisation: A valuable set of ideas. *SPRING Newsletter, 6,* 28-33. (N)

WAINWRIGHT, T. (1998). Review of F. DAVIS' (1975) "Deviance Disavowal" and T. Kitwood and K. Bredin's (1992) "Person to person." *International Social Role Valorization Journal, 3*(1), 47-50. (SRV)

WAINWRIGHT, T. (1999). The impact of Normalization and Social Role Valorization in the United Kingdom. In R. J. FLYNN & R. A. LEMAY (Eds.), *A quarter-century of Normalization and Social Role Valorization: Evolution and impact.* Ottawa, ON: University of Ottawa Press. (N, SRV)

WALMSLEY, J. (1992). Point of view. Opening doors: A role for open learning in developing valued social roles. *British Journal of Mental Subnormality, 38*(75, Pt. 2), 135-142. (SRV)

WALTON, W. T., ROSENQVIST, J., & SANDLING, I. (1989). A comparative study of special education contrasting Denmark, Sweden, and the United States of America. *Educational and Psychological Interactions, 99.* (N)

WARREN, F. (1987, November). Social Role Valorization: An enabling principle. *News & Notes: A Quarterly Newsletter of the American Association on Mental Retardation, 2.* (SRV)

WEBB, O. J. (1983). *The effects of different residential environments on the behaviour of intellectually handicapped adults.* Unpublished doctoral dissertation, University of Otaggo, Christchurch, New Zealand. (PS)

WEBB, O. J., WELLS, J. E., & HORNBLOW, A. R. (1986). Institutions versus community placements: The effects of different residential environments on the behaviour of intellectually handicapped adults. *New Zealand Medical Journal, 99,* 951-954. (PS)

WEBBER, G. (1995). Gentle teaching, human occupation and Social Role Valorisation. *British Journal of Occupational Therapy, 8,* 261-263. (SRV)

WEDEKING, R., FRANK, H., & THIMM, W. (1980). Normalization and rehabilitation as objects of socio-political measures concerning the mentally retarded in Denmark and the Federal Republic of Germany: An intercultural comparative study. *International Journal of Rehabilitation Research, 3*(3), 327-338. (N)

WESLEY CENTRAL MISSION (1991). *Changing lives, changing communities: An introduction to Social Role Valorisation.* Melbourne, Australia: Wesley Central Mission. (SRV)

WESSMAN, L. (1970). *Normalization and integration.* Stockholm: National Swedish Board of Education. (N)

WHITEHEAD, S. (1992). The social origins of Normalisation. In H. BROWN & H. SMITH (Eds.), *Normalisation: A reader for the nineties* (pp. 47-59). London & New York: Tavistock/Routledge. (N)

WHITMAN, C. (1991). *Heading toward normal: Deinstitutionalization for the mentally retarded client.* Unpublished doctoral dissertation, Union Institute. (N)

WILHITE, B., HAMILTON, K., & REILLY, L. (1988). Recreational travel and the elderly: Marketing strategies with a Normalization perspective. *Activities, Adaptation and Aging, 12*(1), 59-72. (N)

WILLER, B., & CORRIGAN, J. D. (1994). Whatever it takes: A model for community-based services. *Brain Injury, 8,* 647-659. (SRV)

WILLER, B., GOLDBERG, B., INTAGLIATA, J., & KRAUS, S. (1980). Current concepts in mental retardation. *American Family Physician, 22*(4), 139-143. (N)

WILLIAMS, P. (1987). *Data on the performance of service groups on PASS.* London: Community and Mental Handicap Educational and Research Association. (PS)

WILLIAMS, P. (1988). The nature and foundations of the concept of Normalisation. In E. KARAS (Ed.), *Current issues in clinical psychology, II.* New York: Plenum Press. (N)

WILLIAMS, P. (1989). Changes in life style for young adults with profound handicaps. *Mental Handicap Research, 2,* 105-106. (PG)

WILLIAMS, P. (1991). "From theory to practice in the care and education of mentally retarded individuals": Reaction. *American Journal on Mental Retardation, 96,* 224-225. (N)

WILLIAMS, P. (1995). The PASS and PASSING evaluation instruments. In D. PILLING & G. WATSON (Eds.), *Evaluating quality in services for disabled and older people.* London: Jessica Kingsley. (PS, PG)

WILLIAMS, P. (1995). Residential and day services. In N. MALIN (Ed.), *Services for people with learning disabilities.* London: Routledge. (PG, PS)

WILLIAMS, P. (1995). The results from PASS and PASSING evaluations. In D. PILLING & G. WATSON (Eds.), *Evaluating quality in services for disabled and older people* (pp. 61-77). London: Jessica Kingsley. (PS, PG)

WILLIAMS, P. (1998). New PASS subscores. *International Social Role Valorizaton Journal, 3*(1), 13-16. (PS)

WILLIAMS, P., & RACE, D. (1988). *Normalisation and the Children's Society.* London: Community and Mental Handicap Educational and Research Association. (N)

WILSON, C., & BARTAK, L. (1997). Staff understanding of Normalisation and Social Role Valorisation: Anstey and Gaskin (1985) revisited. *Journal of Intellectual & Developmental Disability, 22,* 213-219. (N, SRV)

WILSON, K. B. (1995) Assisted living as a model of care delivery. In L. M. GAMROTH, J. SEMRADEK, & E. M. TORNQUIST (Eds.), *Enhancing autonomy in long-term care: Concepts and strategies.* New York: Springer. (N)

WINTON, P. (1990). Promoting a normalizing approach to families: Integrating theory with practice. *Topics in Early Childhood Special Education, 10*(2), 90-103. (N)

WOLFE, P. S. (1993). Increased access to community resources. In P. WEHMAN (Ed.), *The ADA mandate for social change* (pp. 241-253). Baltimore: Paul H. Brookes. (N)

WOLFENSBERGER, W. (n.d.). *The limits of Normalization.* Unpublished manuscript, Syracuse University, Training Institute for Human Service Planning, Leadership, and Change Agentry. (N)

WOLFENSBERGER, W. (1970). The principle of Normalization and its implications to psychiatric services. *American Journal of Psychiatry, 127*(3), 291-297. (N)

WOLFENSBERGER, W. (1972). *The principle of Normalization in human services.* Toronto: National Institute on Mental Retardation. (N)

WOLFENSBERGER, W. (1975). The principle of Normalization as it applies to services for the severely handicapped. In H. MALLIK, S. USPEH, & J. MULLER (Eds.), *Comprehensive vocational rehabilitation for severely disabled persons.* Washington, DC: George Washington University, School of Medicine, Job Development Laboratory. (N)

WOLFENSBERGER, W. (1975). Values in the field of mental health as they bear on policies of research and inhibit adaptive human-service strategies. In J. C. SCHOOLAR & C. M. GAITZ (Eds.), *Research and the psychiatric patient.* New York: Brunner/Mazel. (N)

WOLFENSBERGER, W. (1976). A brief overview of PASS and FUNDET: Purposes, uses, structure, content, and meaning. *Rehabilitation Psychology News, 4*(1), 9-13. (PS)

WOLFENSBERGER, W. (1977). A brief overview of the principle of Normalization. In S. A. GRAND (Ed.), *Severe disability and rehabilitation counselor training.* Albany, NY: State University of New York at Albany (for the National Council on Rehabilitation Education). (N)

WOLFENSBERGER, W. (1977). The Normalization principle and some major implications to architectural-environment design. In M. J. BEDNAR (Ed.), *Barrier-free environments.* Stroundsburgh, PA: Dowden, Hutchinson & Ross. (N)

WOLFENSBERGER, W. (1977). Normalizing activation for the profoundly retarded and/or multiply handicapped. In B. BLATT, D. Biklen & R. BOGDAN, *An alternative textbook in special education: People, schools and other institutions.* Denver: Love Publishing Co. (N)

WOLFENSBERGER, W. (1977). The principle of Normalization. In B. BLATT, D. BIKLEN, & R. BOGDAN, *An alternative textbook in special education: People, schools and other institutions.* Denver: Love Publishing Co. (N)

WOLFENSBERGER, W. (1978). The ideal human service for a societally devalued group. *Rehabilitation Literature, 39*(1), 15-17. (N)

WOLFENSBERGER, W. (1978). The Normalization principle and some major implications to architectural-environment design. Atlanta, GA: Georgia Association for Retarded Citizens. (N)

WOLFENSBERGER, W. (1979). An attempt toward a theology of social integration of devalued/handicapped people. *Information Service* (Publication of the Religion Division of the American Association on Mental Deficiency), *8*(1), 12-26. (N)

WOLFENSBERGER, W. (1979). The case against the use of the term "disability." *Rehabilitation Literature, 40*(10). (N)

WOLFENSBERGER, W. (1980). A brief overview of the principle of Normalization. In R. J. FLYNN & K. E. NITSCH (Eds.), *Normalization, social integration, and community services* (pp. 7-30). Baltimore: University Park Press. (N)

WOLFENSBERGER, W. (1980). The definition of Normalization: Update, problems, disagreements, and misunderstandings. In R. J. FLYNN & K. NITSCH (Eds.), *Normalization, social integration, and community services* (pp. 71-115). Baltimore: University Park Press. (N)

WOLFENSBERGER, W. (1980). Research, empiricism, and the principle of Normalization. In R. J. FLYNN & K. E. NITSCH (Eds.), *Normalization, social integration, and community services* (pp. 117-129). Baltimore: University Park Press. (N)

WOLFENSBERGER, W. (1982). *The principle of Normalization in human services* [Japanese; S. Shimizu & Y. Nakazono, Trans.]. Tokyo: Gakuen-Sha/Tuttle-Mori Agency. (N)

WOLFENSBERGER, W. (1983). A brief reflection on where we stand and where we are going in human services. *Institutions, Etc., 6*(3), 20-23. (SRV)

WOLFENSBERGER, W. (1983). *Guidelines for evaluators during a PASS, PASSING, or similar assessment of human service quality.* Toronto, ON: National Institute on Mental Retardation. (PS, PG)

WOLFENSBERGER, W. (1983). *Normalization-based guidance, education and supports for families of handicapped people.* Toronto, ON: National Institute on Mental Retardation & Georgia Advocacy Office. (N)

WOLFENSBERGER, W. (1983). Précis du principe de "Normalisation" et quelques implications pour les personnes âgées. *Gérontologie et Société* (cahiers de la Fondation nationale de Gérontologie), Numéro spécial, 59-62. (N)

WOLFENSBERGER, W. (1983). Social Role Valorization: A proposed new term for the principle of Normalization. *Mental Retardation, 21*(6), 234-239. (N, SRV)

WOLFENSBERGER, W. (1984). Further reactions to Social Role Valorization: Rejoinder. *Mental Retardation, 22,* 255-256. (SRV)

WOLFENSBERGER, W. (1984). A reconceptualization of Normalization as Social Role Valorization. *Canadian Journal on Mental Retardation, 34*(2), 22-26. (N, SRV)

WOLFENSBERGER, W. (1985). An overview of Social Role Valorization and some reflections on elderly retarded persons (pp. 61-76). In M. P. JANICKI & H. M. WISNIEWSKI (Eds.), *Aging and developmental disabilities.* Baltimore: Paul H. Brookes. (SRV)

WOLFENSBERGER, W. (1985). Social Role Valorization: A new insight, and a new term, for Normalization. *Australian Association for the Mentally Retarded Journal, 9*(1), 4-11. (N, SRV)

WOLFENSBERGER, W. (1986). Die Entwicklung des Normalisierungsgedankens in den USA und in Kanada. In BUNDESVEREINIGUNG LEBENSHILFE (Ed.), *Normalisierung: Eine Chance für Menschen mit geistiger Behinderung* (pp. 45-62). Marburg/Lahn: Lebenshilfe. (N)

WOLFENSBERGER, W. (1987). Values in the funding of social services. *American Journal of Mental Deficiency, 92,* 141-143. (SRV)

WOLFENSBERGER, W. (1989). Human service policy: The rethoric versus the reality. In L. BARTON (Ed.), *Disability and dependency* (pp. 23-41). London: Falmer Press. (SRV)

WOLFENSBERGER, W. (1989). *The new genocide of handicapped and afflicted people.* Syracuse, NY: Syracuse University, Training Institute for Human Service Planning, Leadership and Change Agentry. (SRV)

WOLFENSBERGER, W. (1989). Self-injurious behavior, behavioristic responses, and Social Role Valorization: A reply to Mulick and Kedesdy. *Mental Retardation, 27,* 181-184. (SRV)

WOLFENSBERGER, W. (1991). *A brief introduction to Social Role Valorization as a high-order concept for structuring human services.* Syracuse, NY: Syracuse University, Training Institute for Human Service Planning, Leadership & Change Agentry. (SRV)

WOLFENSBERGER, W. (1991). *Die Bewertung der sozialen Rollen: Eine kurze Einführung zur Bewertung der sozialen Rollen als Grundbegriff beim Aufbau von Sozialdiensten* (C. Agad & A. Bianchet, Trans.). Geneva, Switzerland: Éditions des Deux Continents. (SRV)

WOLFENSBERGER, W. (1991). *La valorisation des rôles sociaux: Introduction à un concept de référence pour l'organisation des services* (A. Dupont, V. Keller-Revaz, J. P. Nicoletti, & L. Vaney, Trans.). Geneva, Switzerland: Éditions des Deux Continents. (SRV)

WOLFENSBERGER, W. (1991). *La Valorizzazione Del Ruolo Sociale: Una breve introduzione al concetto di valorizzazione del ruolo sociale inteso come concetto prioritario per la strutturazione dei servizi alle persone* (M. Costantino & A. Domina, Trans.). Geneva, Switzerland: Éditions des Deux Continents. (SRV)

WOLFENSBERGER, W. (1991). Reflections on a lifetime in human services and mental retardation. *Mental Retardation, 29*(1), 1-15. (SRV)

WOLFENSBERGER, W. (1991). *Some thoughts on the relationship of Christianity and Social Role Valorization.* Unpublished paper written for discussion at a life-sharing retreat. (SRV)

WOLFENSBERGER, W. (1992). *A brief introduction to Social Role Valorization as a high-order concept for structuring human services.* (2nd ed., rev.). Syracuse, NY: Syracuse University, Training Institute for Human Service Planning, Leadership and Change Agentry. (SRV)

WOLFENSBERGER, W. (1992). Deinstitutionalization policy: How it is made, by whom and why. *Clinical Psychology Forum, 39*, 7-11. (SRV)

WOLFENSBERGER, W. (1992). *A guideline on protecting the health and lives of patients in hospitals, especially if the patient is a member of a societally devalued class.* Syracuse, NY: Syracuse University, Training Institute on Human Service Planning, and Change Agentry. (SRV)

WOLFENSBERGER, W. (1992). The "if this, then that" formulation in SRV decision-making. *Voice of Social Role Valorisation in Britain (CMHERA), 1*, 4-7. (SRV)

WOLFENSBERGER, W. (1992). Response to Eric Emerson. *Voice of Social Role Valorisation in Britain (CMHERA), 3*, 3-6. (SRV)

WOLFENSBERGER, W. (1992). Review of E. EMERSON'S (1992) "What is Normalisation?" Chapter in H. BROWN & H. SMITH (Eds.), *Normalisation: A reader for the 1990s* (pp. 1-18). London & New York: Routledge. *CMHERA Newsletter* (Britain), *3*, 3-6. (N)

WOLFENSBERGER, W. (1994). *Overview of "PASSING": A Normalization/Social Role Valorization-based human service evaluation tool.* Syracuse, NY: Syracuse University, Training Institute for Human Service Planning, Leadership and Change Agentry. (N, SRV, PG)

WOLFENSBERGER, W. (1994). Qu'est-ce que l'intégration grise, est-ce bon ou mauvais? *Revue Internationale de la Valorisation des Rôles Sociaux, 1*(2), 36. (SRV)

WOLFENSBERGER, W. (1994). Review of "Normalisation: Theory and practice." *International Social Role Valorization Journal, 1*(2), 55. (N)

WOLFENSBERGER, W. (1994). Review of "Putting people first." *International Social Role Valorization Journal, 1*(2), 55. (N)

WOLFENSBERGER, W. (1994). Review of SHADDOCK & ZILBER'S "Current service ideologies." *International Social Role Valorization Journal, 1*(1), 49-50. (SRV)

WOLFENSBERGER, W. (1994). Social Role Valorization news and reviews/Annotations et nouvelles: La VRS en bref. *International Social Role Valorization Journal, 1*(2), 57-66. (SRV)

WOLFENSBERGER, W. (1994). What is grey integration, and is it good or bad? *International Social Role Valorization Journal, 1*(2), 35-36. (SRV)

WOLFENSBERGER, W. (1995). *A brief introduction to Social Role Valorization: A high-order concept for addressing the plight of societally devalued people, and for structuring human services* [revised translation of W. WOLFENSBERGER. (1992). *A brief introduction to Social Role Valorization as a high-order concept for structuring human services* (2nd ed.). Syracuse, NY: Syracuse University, Training Institute for Human Service Planning, Leadership and Change Agentry] (Y. Tomiyasu, Trans.). Tokyo, Japan: K. K. Gakuensha. (SRV)

WOLFENSBERGER, W. (1995). An "if this, then that" formulation of decisions relating to Social Role Valorization as a better way of interpreting it to people. *Mental Retardation, 33*, 163-169. (SRV)

WOLFENSBERGER, W. (1995). Of "Normalization," lifestyles, the Special Olympics, deinstitutionalization, mainstreaming, integration, and cabbages and kings. *Mental Retardation, 33*, 128-131. (N)

WOLFENSBERGER, W. (1996). Recherche, empirisme et le principe de Normalisation. *Revue internationale de la valorisation des rôles sociaux, 2*(2), 22-28. (N)

WOLFENSBERGER, W. (1996). Reply to John O'Brien's "Nobody outruns the trickster: A brief note on the meaning of the word 'Valorization.'" *International Social Role Valorization Journal, 2*(1), 16-20. (SRV)

WOLFENSBERGER, W. (1996). Review of "Normalization and deinstitutionalization of mentally retarded individuals: Controversy and facts." *International Social Role Valorization Journal, 2*(1), 38-39. (N, SRV)

WOLFENSBERGER, W. (1996). Social Role Valorization news and reviews/Annotations et nouvelles: La VRS en bref. *International Social Role Valorization Journal, 2*(1), 42-51. (SRV)

WOLFENSBERGER, W. (1994). Social Role Valorization news and reviews/Annotations et nouvelles: La VRS en bref. *International Social Role Valorization Journal, 2*(2), 45-58. (SRV)

WOLFENSBERGER, W. (1998). *A brief introduction to Social Role Valorization: A high-order concept for addressing the plight of societally devalued people, and for structuring human services.* (3rd ed., rev.) Syracuse, NY: Syracuse University, Training Institute for Human Service Planning, Leadership and Change Agentry. (SRV)

WOLFENSBERGER, W. (1998). Social Role Valorization news and reviews/Annotations et nouvelles: La VRS en bref. *International Social Role Valorization Journal, 3*(1), 54-70. (SRV)

WOLFENSBERGER, W. (1999). A contribution to the history of Normalization, with primary emphasis on the establishment of Normalization in North America between 1967-1975. In R. J. FLYNN & R. A. LEMAY (Eds.), *A quarter-century of Normalization and Social Role Valorization: Evolution and impact.* Ottawa, ON: University of Ottawa Press. (N)

WOLFENSBERGER, W. (1999). Concluding reflections and a look ahead into the future for Normalization and Social Role Valorization In R. J. FLYNN & R. A. LEMAY (Eds.), *A quarter-century of Normalization and Social Role Valorization: Evolution and impact.* Ottawa, ON: University of Ottawa Press. (N, SRV)

WOLFENSBERGER, W. (1999). Response to Professor Michael Oliver. In R. J. FLYNN & R. A. LEMAY (Eds.), *A quarter-century of Normalization and Social Role Valorization: Evolution and impact.* Ottawa, ON: University of Ottawa Press. (N)

WOLFENSBERGER, W., & GLENN, L. (1973). *Program analysis of service systems (PASS): A method for the quantitative evaluation of human services (2nd ed.). Vol. I: Handbook. Vol. II: Field manual.* Toronto, ON: National Institute on Mental Retardation. (PS)

WOLFENSBERGER, W., & GLENN, L. (1975). *Program analysis of service systems: A method for the quantitative evaluation of human services (3rd ed.). Vol. I: Handbook. Vol. II: Field manual.* Toronto, ON: National Institute on Mental Retardation. (PS)

WOLFENSBERGER, W., & GLENN, L. (1989). *Analyse de programmes pour les systèmes de services (PASS): Méthode d'évaluation quantitative des services humains. Manuel pratique* (Version européenne de 1989 traduite de la 3e édition anglophone de 1975). Geneva, Switzerland: Comité Européen pour le Développement de l'Intégration Sociale (CEDIS). (PS)

WOLFENSBERGER, W., & THOMAS, S. (1980). *Program Analysis of Service Systems' Implementation of Normalization Goals (PASSING)* (Experimental ed.). Syracuse, NY: Syracuse University, Training Institute for Human Service Planning, Leadership and Change Agentry. (PG)

WOLFENSBERGER, W., & THOMAS, S. (1981). The principle of Normalization in human services: A brief overview. In *Research Highlights, No. 2.* Aberdeen, Scotland: University of Aberdeen, Department of Social Work. (N)

WOLFENSBERGER, W., & THOMAS, S. (1983). *PASSING (Program Analysis of Service Systems' Implementation of Normalization Goals): Normalization criteria and ratings manual* (2nd ed.). Downsview, ON: National Institute on Mental Retardation. (PG)

WOLFENSBERGER, W., & THOMAS, S. (1989). *PASSING (Programme d'analyse des systèmes de services: Applications des buts de la valorisation des rôles sociaux): Manuel des critères et des mesures de la valorisation des rôles sociaux* (2e éd.). (M. Roberge, Trans.; J. PELLETIER, Adapt.). Toronto, ON: Institut G. Allan Roeher & Les Communications OPELL. (PG)

WOLFENSBERGER, W., & THOMAS, S. (1994). An analysis of the client role from a Social Role Valorization perspective. *International Social Role Valorization Journal, 1*(1), 3-8. (SRV)

WOLFENSBERGER, W., & THOMAS, S. (1994). Constraints and cautions in formulating recommendations to a service, especially in the context of an external PASS or PASSING evaluation. *International Social Role Valorization Journal, 1*(2), 3-6. (PS, PG)

WOLFENSBERGER, W., & THOMAS, S. (1994). A critique of a critique of Normalization. *Australian Disability Review, 1,* 15-19. (N)

WOLFENSBERGER, W., & THOMAS, S. (1994). Obstacles in the professional human service culture to implementation of Social Role Valorization and community integration of clients. *Care in Place, 1*(1), 53-56. (SRV)

WOLFENSBERGER, W., & THOMAS, S. (1995). Reply to Newnes's "A commentary on 'Obstacles in the professional human service culture to implementation of Social Role Valorization and community integration of clients.'" *Care in Place, 2*(1), 56-62. (SRV)

WOLFENSBERGER, W., & THOMAS, S. (1996). The problem of trying to incorporate a model coherency analysis into a PASSING assessment. *International Social Role Valorization Journal, 2*(1), 12-15. (PS, PG)

WOLFENSBERGER, W., & THOMAS, S. (1998). Review of A. L. CHAPPELL'S (1992) "Towards a sociological critique of the Normalisation principle." *International Social Role Valorization Journal, 3*(1), 37-47. (N)

WOLFENSBERGER, W., THOMAS, S., & Caruso, G. (1996). Some of the universal "good things of life" which the implementation of Social Role Valorization can be expected to make more accessible to devalued people. *International Social Role Valorization Journal, 2*(2), 12-21. (SRV)

WOLFENSBERGER, W., THOMAS, S., & Caruso, G. (1997). Some of the universal "good things in life" which the implementation of Social Role Valorization can be expected to make more accessible to devalued people. *International Social Role Valorization Journal, 2*(2), 12-14. (SRV)

WOLFENSBERGER, W., & TULLMAN, S. (1982). A brief outline of the principle of Normalization. *Rehabilitation Psychology, 27*(3), 131-145. (N)

WOMERSLEY, R. (1993, June). *SRV leadership and the moral imperative: Can there be one without the other?* Presentation to the Australian SRV Group, Melbourne, Australia. (SRV)

XEROMERITOU, A. (1993). The European services: Greece. *Journal of Intellectual Disability Research, 37*(Suppl. 1), 49-52. (N)

YATES, J. (1994). John McKnight and the fallible community. *International Social Role Valorization Journal, 1*(2), 30-34. (N, PS)

YATES, J. (1999). The North American formulation of the principle of Normalization. In R. J. FLYNN & R. A. LEMAY (Eds.), *A quarter-century of Normalization and Social Role Valorization: Evolution and impact.* Ottawa, ON: University of Ottawa Press. (N)

YORK-MOORE, M. (1973). Normalization: Common sense plus understanding. *APEX, 1*(1), 16-18. (N)

ZIEGLER, H. (1989). *Changing lives, changing communities.* Melbourne, Australia: Wesley Central Mission. (SRV)

ZIGLER, E., Hodapp, R. M., & Edison, M. R. (1990). From theory to practice in the care and education of mentally retarded individuals. *American Journal on Mental Retardation, 95,* 1-12. (N)

ZIGLER, E., Hodapp, R. M., & Edison, M. R. (1990). Themes in the debate about Normalization: Rejoinder. *American Journal on Mental Retardation, 95*(1), 30-31. (N)

ZIGLER, E., & Muenchow, S. (1979). Mainstreaming: The proof is in the implementation. *American Psychologist, 34*(10), 993-996. (N)

ZIGLER, E., & Muenchow, S. (1980). Mainstreaming: The proof is in the implementation. *Annual Progress in Child Psychiatry and Child Development*, 574-579. (N)

ZIPPERLIN, H. R. (1975). Normalization. In J. WORTIS (Ed.), *Mental retardation and developmental disabilities: An annual review* (Vol. 7). New York: Brunner/Mazel. (N)

ZNEIMER, E. (1977). Slogans are not enough. *The Exceptional Parent, 7*(4), 46-48. (N)

Part 10

Indexes

Author index

Subject index